Index to Inspiration,

A Thesaurus of Subjects for Speakers and Writers

FWF Useful Reference Series No. 103

OTHER FAXON TITLES BY NORMA OLIN IRELAND

INDEX TO FAIRY TALES, 1949–1972, INCLUDING FOLKLORE, LEGENDS AND MYTHS IN COLLECTIONS

INDEX TO FULL LENGTH PLAYS, 1944 to 1964

AN INDEX TO MONOLOGS AND DIALOGS

AN INDEX TO MONOLOGS AND DIALOGS, SUPPLEMENT

INDEX TO SCIENTISTS OF THE WORLD FROM ANCIENT TO MODERN TIMES: BIOGRAPHIES AND PORTRAITS

AN INDEX TO SKITS AND STUNTS

INDEX TO WOMEN OF THE WORLD FROM ANCIENT TO MODERN TIMES: BIOGRAPHIES AND PORTRAITS

THE PAMPHLET FILE IN SCHOOL, COLLEGE, AND PUBLIC LIBRARIES

THE PICTURE FILE IN SCHOOL, COLLEGE, AND PUBLIC LIBRARIES

Index to Inspiration,

A Thesaurus of Subjects for Speakers and Writers

Compiled by

Norma Olin Ireland

F. W. FAXON COMPANY, INC./WESTWOOD, MASSACHUSETTS

ISBN 0-87305-103-3
Library of Congress Catalog Card Number 75-35464

MANUFACTURED IN THE UNITED STATES OF AMERICA

DEDICATION

To Tom and Myrt Clark of Pasadena, California, who have inspired me in so many ways: *comfort* and *kindness* in my grief after the passing of my husband, Dave; true and unfailing *friendship* for some twenty-five and more years; *generosity* in gifts of books and beautiful things; and lastly, their wonderful example of a *sense of humor* and *youthfulness* in their "golden years."

PREFACE

In this work, "Inspiration" is used in the broad sense of the term and means not only religious inspiration, but creative inspiration as well. The *Index* includes references to inspire speakers and writers on all manner of subjects, both early and modern, serious and humorous, with some emphasis on current problems of the day, especially on topics of moral significance.

Scope

We have analyzed 220 books, both large and small volumes, as found in representative libraries. In order to extend the *Index's* usefulness, we have also indexed many "self-help" books commonly found in the home. Some may question the inclusion of a few humorous books, but we feel that humor can well be used to convey messages or emphasize certain points. The same applies to epigrams, proverbs, and short quotations. Since most books of quotations are indexed by key-word, first line, or author, this *subject index* will fulfill the need for ready reference to quotations on particular subjects. The large, standard quotation books are not included, but only some special collections which are especially suitable for our purpose.

We have not striven for uniformity of length in the topics indexed, because of the variety of users' needs. (See *How to Use This Index* on page ix.) Age of books was not a criterion for selection, either, although we have tried to include as many recent books as possible along with books still active in libraries. The percentage of books indexed, according to date of publication, is as follows:

1970–1975	— 19%
1960's	— 40%
1950's	— 23%
1940's	— 13%
1930's and earlier	— 5%

We feel the age of a book is no factor, except for book-availability, because most collections include classic material as well as modern. Books such as *Peace of Mind* and *Human Destiny* will be referred to for decades, and Hubbard's *Scrap Book* will always be a standard. Today's moral and national problems can well be discussed in the light of history.

Arrangement

We have arranged this index alphabetically, word-by-word, in one alphabet. Inclusive pagination is provided, except in cases where the great number of references in one book has made listing the index-page more desirable. Easy-to-remember symbols are used to refer to books indexed, according to the Key starting on page 1. Since some of the books indexed have two sections, one paginated and one listing quotations by numbers, we have used either page or numerical references in indexing, and sometimes both, depending on the system used in a particular book.

Subject-Headings

Over 4,300 headings have been used in this *Index,* not counting subheadings or cross-references. We have determined our own subject headings, while considering the headings used in the most important collections. The establishment of this large number of subjects was no small task, as you can imagine.

The subjects fall into two classes, roughly speaking: categories (or attributes), and concrete subjects. The singular form of the subject is usually used for categories, the plural for concrete subjects, although there are some exceptions. There are very few proper names included (none of persons living, to our knowledge), and "folklore" names are very incidental.

The forms of subject-headings are adapted to the particular subjects. We have used two words joined by *and* (compound headings) in some cases when the entry refers to closely related material which is not easily separated to make it easier for the user. Adjectival and inverted headings were found to be most applicable for these inspirational subjects.

We have employed many cross–references because the headings used in the indexes of the compilations covered were never uniform. Obviously, we did not want to use both *Bravery* and *Courage,* for instance, but in some cases we have used very similar subjects when a check of the dictionary revealed some slight line of demarcation. Users get weary of too many cross-references and thus we have tried to "hold them down" to a percentage favored by indexers. We have included *see also* references which will enable the user to fully check the various gradations of his subject. Words with the prefix *Self-* were especially difficult because of the many shades of meaning involved.

For the convenience of the *Index's* users, we also have tried to follow the choice of subject-headings as given in the books indexed, and this has sometimes led to the duplication of related subjects (e.g., *Freedom*

and *Liberty*). The existence of such related headings is reflected in the use of *see also* references not only from general to specific subjects, but also back and forth from subjects of equal or similar importance.

How to Use This Index

In using this *Index,* it is recommended that you first choose the general theme on which you wish to speak or write, e.g. *Maturity.* First of all, check the books indexed under that general subject, then decide on the related topics you wish to emphasize, such as *Self-knowledge, Marriage,* etc., then the concrete ideas which will relate to the type of audience you will reach. Lastly, in checking your books, watch for titles of quotation-books or humorous ones, to spark up your article or address. Think of certain favorite writers, and then refer to their books: e.g., what would Bishop Sheen say on that subject?

Remember, please, in looking up references on pages given, that there has been some use of synonyms in assigning subjects. Obviously, we could not include all synonyms as cross-references, so if you don't find a quotation or article on that subject, look for its synonym and play "Password"!

Most "Inspirational" Books

In perusing the 220 books included, we have noted certain titles of inspirational value which impressed us most. We have long been a collector of beautiful and inspirational quotations, poetry, essays, etc., and thus have judged these books by this yardstick: "How many passages in this volume are especially noteworthy?" Here are the authors and/or books which we considered most inspirational:

Adams, J. Donald. *The new treasure chest.*

Barrows, Marjorie. *One thousand beautiful things.*

Bartlett, Robert M. *Discovery—a guidebook for living.*

Braude, Jacob M. *Speaker's encyclopedia of stories, quotations and anecdotes.*

Evans, Richard L. (*All* of his books.)

Henry, Lewis C. *5000 quotations for all occasions.*

Howell, Clinton T. *Lines to live by.*

Kohn, Harold E. (*All* of his books.)

Lair, Jess. *"I ain't much, baby—but I'm all I've got."*

Lindbergh, Anne Morrow. (*All* of her books.)

Morris, Audrey Stone. *One thousand inspirational things.*

Peterson, Wilferd A. (*All* of his books.)
Watson, Lillian Eichler. *Light from many lamps.*
White, Stewart Edward. *The job of living.*

The *Bible* would of course be included in this list, and references to inspirational passages in it will be found in many books of quotations.

Acknowledgments

We wish to thank Mrs. Dorothy T. Norton, assistant in the Fallbrook branch of the San Diego County Library, who so willingly secured interlibrary loans for us; and again, Mrs. Geraldine Bauer, Librarian of the same library, for her help in securing books "over and above the call of duty," as well as staff members of the various California libraries which made books available for our use.

This book also gives us an opportunity to personally remember and acknowledge the "inspiration" given us by members of our family, friends and co-workers, in so many different ways. Some of these have passed on, but their memory is very fresh—in their influence on our life and work. Using the terminology of the *Index,* here is our list of personal inspiration:

David E. Ireland (my late husband): Love, Marriage, Goodness, Sense of humor, Courage, Music, Love of animals

Carl Leroy Olin (my father): Kindness, Nature, Love of animals, Cheerfulness, Country life

Jessie Latimer Olin (my mother): Books and reading, Education, Morality, Music, Art

Lucretia Olin Rowe (my oldest sister): Service to humanity, Kindness, Religion, Courage

Halcyon Olin Harper (my sister): Art—drawing and painting

Mrs. Katherine Saal (my first-grade teacher): Appreciation, Understanding, Scholarship

Dr. O. E. Olin (professor, minister, friend): Philosophy, Religion, Ethics

Dean Albert I. Spanton (professor, minister, friend): Scholarship, Literature, Letter writing

Miss Catherine Henry (librarian): Books and reading, Public service, Librarianship

Miss Marion Ewing (librarian): Books and reading, Librarianship, Appreciation

Dr. Louis Shores (librarian-author, editor): Authorship, Encouragement, Librarianship

General Charles Farnsworth (Army general, neighbor, friend): Community service, Youth in old age, Enthusiasm; Neighborliness

Dr. Harry Benjamin (physician): Love of humanity, Hope, Understanding

Miss Jessie Hunsberger (friend): Friendship (over 60 years), Music

Mrs. Marguerite Zepp Chapin (friend): Friendship (over 60 years), Travel

Mrs. Kathleen Hostetler Hilliard (friend): Friendship (over 60 years), Courage

F. W. Faxon Company (publishers of my books since 1935, 40 years ago): Trust, Encouragement

Conclusion

My husband's thoughts on *inspiration,* written to a friend, were these: "I feel that a person who has had a great influence on your life *does* live on, for years and years, possibly centuries: the work he has done, the *inspiration* he has given others who in turn passed it on—and undoubtedly it will carry on through many generations. It does seem a shame to lose him . . . but I am inclined to think that the good things that a man does are passed on in the way of inspiration to younger people, and that we should let *that* be the monument upon which to pass our opinion."

LIST OF COLLECTIONS ANALYZED

IN THIS WORK

AND

KEY TO SYMBOLS USED

ADAMS — NEW
Adams, J. Donald. *The new treasure chest. An anthology of reflective prose.* New York, E. P. Dutton & Co., Inc., 1953. 440p.

ALBERT — STOP
Albert, Dora. *Stop feeling tired and start living.* Englewood Cliffs, N.J., Prentice-Hall, Inc., 1959. 212p.

ALEXANDER'S TREASURE.
A. L. Alexander's treasurehouse of inspirational poetry and prose. Garden City, N. Y., Doubleday & Co., 1966. 365p.

APPLEGARTH — HEIR.
Applegarth, Margaret T., ed. *Heirlooms.* New York, Harper & Row, 1967. 319p.

ASIMOV — TREASURY
Asimov, Isaac. *Treasury of humor.* Boston, Houghton Mifflin, 1971. 431p.

AUDEN — CERTAIN
Auden, W. H. *A certain world. A commonplace book.* New York, The Viking Press, 1970. 438p.

BACH — MAKE
Bach, Marcus. *Make it an adventure.* Englewood Cliffs, N. J., Prentice-Hall, Inc., 1962. 207p.

BAILLIE — DIARY
Baillie, John. *A diary of readings. Being an anthology of pages suited to engage serious thought one for every day of the year gathered from the wisdom of many centuries.* New York, Charles Scribner's Sons, 1955. 385p.

BARKER — TREAT
Barker, Raymond Charles. *Treat yourself to life.* New York, Dodd, Mead & Co., 1954, 1957. 152p.

BARROWS — 1000
Barrows, Marjorie. *One thousand beautiful things.* New York, Hawthorn Books, Spencer Press, 1967. 456p.

BARTLETT — DISCOVERY
Bartlett, Robert M. *Discovery — a guidebook for living.* New York, Association Press, 1941. 160p.

BENNETT — HOW
Bennett, Arnold. *How to live on twenty-four hours a day.* New York, Doubleday & Co., Inc., 1910. 103p.

BLANTON — FAITH. *See also* PEALE — FAITH
Blanton, Smiley and Norman Vincent Peale. *Faith is the answer.* New York, Abingdon-Cokesbury Press, 1940. 223p.

BOAS — HISTORY
Boas, George. *The history of ideas.* New York, Charles Scribner's Sons, 1969. 238p. paper.

BOOK PROVERBS
Book of proverbs and epigrams. New York, Ottenheimer Publishers, n.d. 143p.

BOTKIN — ANECDOTES
Botkin, B. A., ed. *A treasury of American anecdotes.* New York, Bonanza Books, 1947. 321p.

BOTKIN — TREASURY
Botkin, B. A., ed. *A treasury of American folklore. Stories, ballads, and traditions of the people.* New York, Crown Publishers, 1944. 932p.

BRADSHAW — HOME.
Bradshaw, Gene. *Homespun ideas for real living.* New York, Pageant Press, Inc., 1960. 132p.

BRAUDE — SOURCE
Braude, Jacob M. *Braude's source book for speakers and writers.* Englewood Cliffs, N. J., Prentice-Hall, Inc., 1968. 351p.

BRAUDE — SPEAKER'S
Braude, Jacob M. *Speaker's encyclopedia of humor. Stories, quotes, definitions for every situation.* Englewood Cliffs, N. J., Prentice-Hall, Inc., 1961. 387p.

BRAUDE — STORIES
Braude, Jacob M. *Speaker's encyclopedia of stories, quotations and anecdotes.* Englewood Cliffs, N. J., Prentice-Hall, Inc., 1959. 476p.

CARRUTHERS — SPARKS
Carruthers, Thomas N. *Sparks of fire, and other thoughts about things that matter.* New York, Morehouse-Gorham Co., 1953. 166p.

CASSELBERRY — HOW
Casselberry, William S. *How to work miracles in your life. The golden secret of successful living.* West Nyack, N.Y., Parker Publishing Co., Inc., 1964. 206p.

CERF — LAUGH
Cerf, Bennett. *Laugh day. A new treasury of over 1000 humorous stories and anecdotes.* Garden City, N. Y., Doubleday & Co., Inc., 1965. 496p.

CLARK — WINDOWS
Clark, Glenn. *Windows of heaven.* New York, Harper, 1954. 188p.

COPELAND — 10,000
Copeland, Lewis and Faye Copeland, eds. *10,000 jokes, toasts and stories.* Garden City, N. Y., Halcyon House, 1940. 1020p.

COPELAND — WORLD'S
Copeland, Lewis, ed. *World's great speeches.* Garden City, N. Y., Garden City Publishing Co., 1942. 748p.

COWAN — WIT
Cowan, Lore and Maurice Cowan. *The wit of women.* Nashville, Aurora Publishers, Inc., 1970. 171p.

CURTIS — DAILY
Curtis, Donald. *Daily power for joyful living.* Englewood Cliffs, N. J., Prentice-Hall, Inc., 1963. 242p.

CURTIS — GOLDEN
Curtis, Donald. *The golden bridge: Science of Mind in daily living.* West Nyack, N. Y., Parker Publishing Co., Inc., 1969. 211p.

CURTIS — HUMAN
Curtis, Donald. *Human problems and how to solve them.* Englewood Cliffs, N. J., Prentice-Hall, Inc., 1962. 212p.

CURTIS — NEW
Curtis, Donald. *New age understanding.* Unity Village, Mo., Unity Books, 1973. 143p.

CURTIS — PRACTICAL
Curtis, Charles P., Jr. and Ferris Greenslet. *The practical cogitator, or the thinker's anthology.* Boston, Houghton Mifflin, 1945. 577p.

DALY — PERSONALITY
Daly, Sheila John. *Personality plus!* Rev. ed. New York, Dodd, Mead & Co., 1964. 163p.

DAY — MEDITATIONS
Day, Dorothy. *Meditations.* New York, Newman Press, 1970. 81p.

DETHERAGE — SUNRISE
Detherage, Mary. *Sunrise to sunset.* Nashville, Tenn., Abingdon Press, 1966. 208p.

DIRKSEN — QUOT.
Dirksen, Everett McKinley and Herbert V. Prochnow. *Quotation finder.* New York, Harper & Row, Publishers, 1971. 279p.

DROKE — CHRISTIAN
Droke, Maxwell and the Editors of *Quote.* *The Christian leader's golden treasury.* Indianapolis, Ind., Droke House, 1955. 620p.

DU NOÜY — HUMAN
du Noüy, Lecomte. *Human destiny.* New York, Longmans, Green & Co., 1947. 289p.

DU NOÜY — ROAD
du Noüy, Lecomte. *The road to reason.* Ed. and trans. by Mary Lecomte du Noüy. New York, Longmans, Green & Co., 1949. 254p.

EDWARDS — USEFUL
Edwards, Tryon. *Useful quotations. A cyclopedia of quotations, prose and poetical.* New York, Grosset & Dunlap, 1933. 734p.

EMMONS — MATURE
Emmons, Helen B. *The mature heart.* New York, Abingdon-Cokesbury Press, 1953. 160p.

ESTEVE — EXPERIENCE
Esteve, Sirio. *The experience.* New York, Random House, 1974. 160p.

EVANS — FAITH
Evans, Richard L. *Faith, peace, and purpose.* Cleveland, World Publishing Co., 1966. 242p.

EVANS — QUOTE
Evans, Richard L. *Richard Evans' quote book.* Salt Lake City, Utah, Publishers Press, 1971. 256p.

EVANS — THIS
Evans, Richard L. *This day . . . and always.* 10th ed. New York, Harper & Brothers, 1942. 200p.

EVANS — THOUGHTS I
Evans, Richard L. *Thoughts for one hundred days. Selected from Thoughts for the day and The spoken word as heard on radio.* Salt Lake City, Utah, Publishers Press, 1971. 222p.

EVANS — THOUGHTS II (OPEN DOOR)
Evans, Richard L. *. . . an open door . . . Vol. II: Thoughts for 100 days. Selected from Thoughts for the day and The spoken word as heard on radio.* Salt Lake City, Utah, Publishers Press, 1971. 210p.

EVANS — THOUGHTS III (OPEN ROAD)
Evans, Richard L. *. . . an open road . . . Vol. III: Thoughts for 100 days. Selected from Thoughts for the day and The spoken word as heard on radio and television.* Salt Lake City, Utah, Publishers Press, 1971. 212p.

EVANS — THOUGHTS IV
Evans, Richard L. *Thoughts for one hundred days, Vol. IV. Selected from Thoughts for the day and The spoken word as heard on radio and television.* Salt Lake City, Utah, Publishers Press, 1971. 224p.

EVANS — UNTO
Evans, Richard L. *Unto the hills.* New York, Harper & Brothers, 1940. 163p.

FELLEMAN — POEMS
Felleman, Hazel. *Poems that live forever.* Garden City, N. Y., Doubleday & Co., Inc., 1965. 454p.

FLESCH — UNUSUAL
Flesch, Rudolf. *The book of unusual quotations.* New York, Harper & Row, Publishers, 1957. 338p.

FLINT — GRAHAM
Flint, Cort R. *The quotable Billy Graham.* Anderson, S. C., Droke House/Hallux, 1966. 158p.

FOGG — 1000
Fogg, Walter. *One thousand sayings of history. Presented as pictures in prose.* New York, Grosset & Dunlap, 1929; rpt. Gryphon Books, 1971. 919p.

FORBES — THOUGHTS
The Forbes scrapbook of thoughts on the business of life. New York, Forbes, Inc., 1950. 574p.

FOX — MAKE
Fox, Emmet. *Make your life worth while.* New York, Harper & Brothers, 1946. 239p.

FRANCIS — FOR
Francis, Connie. *For every young heart.* Englewood Cliffs, N. J., Prentice-Hall, Inc., 1962. 191p.

FRANKE — BUCKLEY
Franke, David, comp. *Quotations from Chairman Bill. The best of William F. Buckley, Jr.* New York, Pocket Books, 1966. 326p. paper.

FRIDY — MEDITAT.
Fridy, Wallace. *Meditations for adults.* New York, Abingdon Press, 1965. 143p.

FULLER — EPIGRAMS
Fuller, Edmund, ed. *Thesaurus of epigrams.* Garden City, N. Y., Garden City Publishing Co., 1943, 1948. 378p.

FULLER — THESAURUS
Fuller, Edmund, ed. *Thesaurus of anecdotes.* New York, Crown Publishers, 1942. 489p.

FUN FARE
Fun Fare. A treasury of Reader's Digest *wit and humor.* Pleasantville, N. Y., The Reader's Digest Association, Inc., 1949. 316p.

GARLAND — SUBJECT
Garland, George Frederick. *Subject guide to Bible stories.* New York, Greenwood Publishing Corp., 1969. 365p.

GEORGE — BOOK
George, Daniel, ed. *A book of anecdotes.* New York, The Citadel Press, 1958. 445p.

GINIGER — COMPACT
Giniger, Kenneth Seeman. *The compact treasury of inspiration.* New York, Pocket Books, Inc., 1955. 288p. paper.

GINOTT — BETWEEN
Ginott, Haim G. *Between parent and teenager.* New York, Macmillan Co., 1969. 256p.

GOLD — LETTERS
Gold, Don. *Letters to Tracy from Don Gold.* New York, D. McKay Co., 1972. 142p.

GOUDGE — COMFORT
Goudge, Elizabeth. *A book of comfort, an anthology.* New York, Coward-McCann, Inc., 1964. 384p.

GRIZER — WIT
Grizer, Leon, comp. & ed. *Wit and wisdom in business. A collection of great thoughts by great minds.* New York, Exposition Press, 1972. 509p.

GUIDEPOSTS. *See also* BLANTON; PEALE; UNLIMITED POWER

GUIDEPOSTS — FAITH
The Guideposts *treasury of faith.* Carmel, N. Y., *Guideposts Magazine,* Guideposts Associates, Inc., 1970. 496p.

HADFIELD — DELIGHTS
Hadfield, John, comp. *A book of delights.* London, Hulton Press, 1956. 256p.

HADFIELD — LOVE
Hadfield, John, comp. *A book of love.* London, Edward Hulton, 1958. 256p.

HALVERSON — PERSPECTIVE
Halverson, Richard C. *Perspective. Devotional selections for business men.* Los Angeles, Cowman Publications, Inc., 1957. 120p.

HARNSBERGER — MARK
Harnsberger, Caroline Thomas, ed. *Mark Twain at your fingertips.* New York, Beechhurst Press, Inc., A. Cloud, Inc., 1948. 559p.

HARRAL — FEATURE
Harral, Stewart. *The feature writer's handbook. With a treasury of 2,000 tested ideas for newspapers, radio, and television.* Norman, Okla., University of Oklahoma Press, 1958. 335p.

HENRY — 5000
Henry, Lewis C., ed. *5000 quotations for all occasions.* Philadelphia, The Blakiston Co., 1945. 346p.

HILL — THINK
Hill, Napoleon. *Think and grow rich.* New York, Hawthorn Books, Inc., W. Clement Stone, Publisher, 1937, 1967. 293p.

HOBE — TAPESTRIES
Hobe, Phyllis, ed. *Tapestries of life.* Philadelphia, A. J. Holman Co.; rpt. J. B. Lippincott Co., 1974. 255p.

HOFFER — REFLECT.
Hoffer, Eric. *Reflections on the human condition.* New York, Harper & Row, 1972. 97p.

HOLMAN — PSYCH.
Holman, Charles T. *Psychology and religion for everyday living.* New York, Macmillan Co., 1949. 178p.

HOLMES — DESIGN
Holmes, Ernest and Willis H. Kinnear. *A new design for living.* Los Angeles, Science of Mind Publications, 1959, 1967. 236p. paper.

HOLMES — I'VE
Holmes, Marjorie. *I've got to talk to somebody, God.* Garden City, N. Y., Doubleday & Co., Inc., 1968, 1969. 121p.

HOOKER — INDEX
Hooker, Zebulon Vance, II. *An index of ideas for writers and speakers.* Salem, Va., Roanoke College, The Author, 1965. 304p. paper.

HOVEY — TREASURY
Hovey, E. Paul. *The treasury of inspirational anecdotes, quotations and illustrations.* Westwood, N. J., Fleming H. Revell Co., 1959. 316p.

HOW TO LIVE
How to live with life. Introduction by Arthur Gordon. Pleasantville, N. Y., Reader's Digest Association, 1965. 576p.

HOWELL — BETTER
Howell, Clinton T. *Better than gold.* Nashville, Tenn., Thomas Nelson, Inc., 1970, 1973. 200p.

HOWELL — LINES
Howell, Clinton T., comp. & ed. *Lines to live by. Better than gold. The inspiration anthology.* The Author, 1968. 175p.

HUBBARD — SCRAP
Hubbard, Elbert. *Elbert Hubbard's scrap book containing the inspired and inspiring selections, gathered during a life time of discriminating reading for his own use.* New York, William H. Wise Co., Roycroft Distributors, 1923. 228p.

HULME — LIVING
Hulme, William E. *Living with myself.* Englewood Cliffs, N. J., Prentice-Hall, Inc., 1964. 158p.

HUMES — INSTANT
Humes, James C. *Instant eloquence. A lazy man's guide to public speaking.* New York, Harper & Row, 1973. 247p.

HUNTER — GEMS
Hunter, Milton R., comp. *Gems of thought.* Salt Lake City, Utah, Bookcraft, 1949, 1970. 120p.

HUXLEY — YOU
Huxley, Laura Archera. *You are not the target.* New York, Farrar, Straus & Co., 1963. 289p.

IDEAS
Ideas. A volume of ideas, notions and emotions, clear or confused, which have moved the minds of men. New York, Hawthorn Books, Inc., n.d. 470p.

IRION — YES
Irion, M. *Yes, world; a mosaic of meditation.* New York, Richard W. Baron Publishing Co., 1970. 146p.

JACKSON — COPING
Jackson, Edgar Newman. *Coping with the crises in your life.* New York, Hawthorn Books, 1974. 218p.

JOHNSON — BEDSIDE
Johnson, Helen and Horace Johnson. *The bedside treasury of inspiration.* Englewood Cliffs, N. J., Prentice-Hall, Inc., 1956. 368p.

JONES — IF
Jones, Jim. *If you can count to five.* Long Beach, Calif., Whitehorn Publishing Co., 1957. 218p.

KAHN — LESSONS
Kahn, Robert I. *Lessons for life.* Garden City, N. Y., Doubleday & Co., 1963. 240p.

KAUFFMAN — FOR
Kauffman, Donald T. *For instance. Current insights, anecdotes, quotations, questions for teachers, ministers, speakers and discussion leaders.* Garden City, N. Y., Doubleday & Co., Inc., 1970. 263p.

KELLER — OPEN
Keller, Helen. *The open door.* Garden City, N. Y., Doubleday & Co., 1902, 1957. 140p.

KELLER — YOU
Keller, James. *You can change the world! The Christopher approach.* New York, Longmans, Green & Co., 1948. 387p.

KENNEDY — FRESH
Kennedy, Gerald. *Fresh every morning.* New York, Harper & Row, Publishers, 1966. 194p.

KENNEDY — READER'S
Kennedy, Gerald, comp. *A reader's notebook.* New York, Harper & Brothers, 1953. 340p.

KEYS HAPPINESS
Keys to happiness. A Reader's Digest *guide to successful living.* Pleasantville, N. Y., Reader's Digest Association, 1955. 575p.

KIN — DICTIONARY
Kin, David, ed. *Dictionary of American proverbs.* New York, Philosophical Library, 1955. 286p.

KNIGHT'S ILLUS.
Knight, Walter B. *Knight's illustrations for today.* Chicago, Moody Press, 1970. 359p.

KNIGHT'S TREAS.
Knight, Walter B. *Knight's treasury of illustrations.* Grand Rapids, Mich., William B. Eerdmans Publishing Co., 1963. 451p.

KOHN — ADVENTURES
Kohn, Harold E. *Adventures in insight.* Grand Rapids, Mich., William B. Eerdmans Publishing Co., 1967. 159p.

KOHN — BEST
Kohn, Harold E. *Best wishes — for common days and special days.* Grand Rapids, Mich., William B. Eerdmans Publishing Co., 1969. 171p.

KOHN — PATHWAYS
Kohn, Harold E. *Pathways to understanding. Outdoor adventures in meditation.* Grand Rapids, Mich., William B. Eerdmans Publishing Co., 1958. 196p.

KOHN — THOUGHTS
Kohn, Harold E. *Thoughts afield. Meditations through the seasons.* Grand Rapids, Mich., William B. Eerdmans Publishing Co., 1959. 171p.

KOHN — THROUGH
Kohn, Harold E. *Through the valley, Nature's clues to victorious living.* Grand Rapids, Mich., William B. Eerdmans Publishing Co., 1957. 172p.

KOHN — TOUCH
Kohn, Harold E. *A touch of greatness.* Grand Rapids, Mich., William B. Eerdmans Publishing Co., 1965. 205p.

KOPPLIN — SOMETHING
Kopplin, Dorothea S. *Something to live by.* Garden City, N. Y., Doubleday & Co., Inc., 1945. 204p.

KRISHNAMURTI — THINK
Krishnamurti, Jiddu. *Think on these things.* Ed. by D. Rajàgopal. New York, Harper, 1964. 224p.

KRISHNAMURTI — URGENCY
Krishnamurti, Jiddu. *The urgency of change.* Ed. by Mary Lutyens. New York, Harper & Row, Publishers, 1970. 154p.

KRONENBERGER — ANIMAL
Kronenberger, Louis. *Animal, vegetable, mineral. A commonplace book.* New York, The Viking Press, 1972. 335p.

LAIR — BABY
Lair, Jess. *"I ain't much, baby — but I'm all I've got."* Greenwich, Conn., Fawcett Publications, Inc., 1969, 1972. 253p. paper.

LANGDON — TEACH.
Langdon, Grace and Irving W. Langdon. *Teaching moral and spiritual values. A parent's guide to developing character.* New York, The John Day Co., 1962. 124p.

LIDDLE — THOUGHT I, II, III
Liddle, Verle A. and Theron C. Liddle. *A thought for today* (Includes I, II, III). Salt Lake City, Utah, Liddle Enterprises, 1963, 1972. 200p.

LIDDLE — THOUGHT IV
Liddle, Verle A. and Theron C. Liddle. *A thought for today.* Vol. IV. Salt Lake City, Utah, Liddle Enterprises, 1966. 48p. paper.

LIDDLE — THOUGHT V
Liddle, Verle A. and Theron C. Liddle. *A thought for today.* Vol. V. Salt Lake City, Utah, Liddle Enterprises, 1967. 48p. paper.

LIEBMAN — HOPE
Liebman, Joshua Loth. *Hope for man. An optimistic philosophy and guide to self-fulfillment.* New York, Simon & Schuster, 1966. 250p.

LIEBMAN — PEACE
Liebman, Joshua Loth. *Peace of mind.* New York, Simon & Schuster, 1946. 203p.

LINDBERGH — GIFT
Lindbergh, Anne Morrow. *Gift from the sea.* New York, Pantheon, 1955. 128p.

LINDBERGH — UNICORN
Lindbergh, Anne Morrow. *The unicorn, and other poems.* New York, Pantheon, 1956. 86p.

LINDEMAN — EMERSON
Lindeman, Eduard C., ed. *Basic selections from Emerson: essays, poems and apothegms.* New York, New American Library, Mentor Books, 1954. 215p. paper.

LIST — LIVING
List, Jacob Samuel. *Living one day at a time.* New York, Philosophical Library, 1962. 96p.

LOCKRIDGE — WORLD'S
Lockridge, Norman, ed. *World's wit and wisdom.* New York, Dorene Publishing Co., 1936, 1945. 585p.

LUPTON. *See* SPEAKER'S DESK

LYTLE — LEAVES
Lytle, Clyde Francis, ed. *Leaves of gold. An anthology of prayers, memorable phrases, inspirational verse and prose.* Williamsport, Pa., The Coslett Publishing Co., 1963. 200p.

McCRACKEN — WHAT
McCracken, Robert J. *What is sin? What is virtue?* New York, Harper & Row, Publishers, 1966. 94p.

McDONAGH — INVIT.
McDonagh, Enda. *Invitation and response. Essays in Christian moral theology.* New York, Sheed and Ward, 1972. 206p.

MALTZ — CREATIVE
Maltz, Maxwell. *Creative living for today.* New York, Trident Press, 1967. 225p.

MANCHEE — SECRET
Manchee, Fred. *The secret of being a somebody.* New York, Thomas Nelson & Sons, 1960. 245p.

MANDEL — STORIES
Mandel, Morris. *Stories for speakers.* New York, Jonathan David, 1964. 294p.

MANDELBAUM — CHOOSE
Mandelbaum, Bernard. *Choose life.* New York, Random House, 1968. 295p.

MAUROIS — ART
Maurois, André. *The art of living.* Trans. from the French by James Whitall. New York, Harper & Brothers, 1940. 323p.

MAXWELL — COURAGE
Maxwell, Arthur S. *Courage for the crisis. Strength for today, hope for tomorrow.* Mountain View, Calif., Pacific Press Publishing Association, 1962. 258p.

MENNINGER — BLUE.
Menninger, William C. *Blueprint for teen-age living.* New York, Sterling Publishing Co., Inc., 1958. 221p.

MILLER — HARVEST
Miller, Ernest R. *Harvest of gold.* Norwalk, Conn., The C. R. Gibson Co., 1973. 87p.

MODERN ELOQUENCE (14)
Thorndike, Ashley H., ed. *Modern eloquence. A library of the world's best spoken thought. Vol. XIV. Anecdotes and epigrams.* Rev. by Adam Ward. New York, P. F. Collier & Son Corp., 1941. 440p.

MONTAPERT — DISTILLED
Montapert, Alfred Armand. *Distilled wisdom.* Englewood Cliffs, N. J., Prentice-Hall, Inc., 1964, 1965. 355p.

MORE WORDS
More than words. Junior high school resource book. Greenwich, Conn., The Seabury Press, 1955. 179p.

MORRIS — 1000
Morris, Audrey Stone. *One thousand inspirational things.* New York, Hawthorn Books, Spencer Press, 1968. 435p.

MYERS — THUNDER
Myers, T. Cecil. *Thunder on the mountain.* New York, Abingdon Press, 1965. 176p.

NEW JOY
The new joy of words. Selections of literature expressing beauty, history, humor, inspiration or wisdom. Chicago, J. G. Ferguson Publishing Co., 1961. 256p.

NEW TOPICAL
The new topical text book. Rev. & enl. ed. London, Oliphants Ltd., 1948, 1958. 319p.

NICHOLS — NEW
Nichols, William, ed. *A new treasury of Words to live by.* New York, Simon & Schuster, 1947, 1959. 242p.

NICHOLS — THIRD
Nichols, William, ed. *The third book of Words to live by.* New York, Simon & Schuster, 1955, 1962. 256p.

NIZER — THINKING
Nizer, Louis. *Thinking on your feet.* New York, Pyramid Books, 1963. 239p. paper.

PATTERNS FOR LIVING
Campbell, Oscar James, Justine Van Gundy, and Caroline Shrodes, eds. *Patterns for living.* Alternate ed., Part I. New York, The Macmillan Co., 1947. 878p.

PEALE — COURAGE
Peale, Norman Vincent, ed. *Norman Vincent Peale's treasury of courage and confidence.* New York, Family Library, 1970, 1974. 256p. paper.

PEALE — FAITH. *See also* BLANTON — FAITH
Peale, Norman Vincent, and Smiley Blanton. *Faith is the answer.* Rev. & enl. ed. Carmel, N. Y., Guideposts Associates, Inc., 1955. 280p.

PEALE — GUIDE
Peale, Norman Vincent. *A guide to confident living.* New York, Prentice-Hall, Inc., 1948. 248p.

PEALE — GUIDEPOSTS
Peale, Norman Vincent. *The* Guideposts *anthology.* New York, Prentice-Hall, Inc., 1953. 333p.

PEALE — SIN
Peale, Norman Vincent. *Sin, sex and self-control.* Garden City, N.Y., Doubleday & Co., Inc., 1965. 207p.

PEALE — STAY
Peale, Norman Vincent. *Stay alive all your life.* Carmel, N. Y., Guideposts Associates, Inc., 1957. 300p.

PETERSON — ART
Peterson, Wilferd A. *The Art of living, day by day. 365 thoughts, ideas, ideals, experiences, adventures, inspirations, to enrich your life.* New York, Simon & Schuster, 1972. 411p.

PETERSON — NEW
Peterson, Wilferd A. *The new book of the Art of living. A new series of twenty-seven essays.* New York, Simon & Schuster, 1962, 1963. 61p.

PETERSON — TWENTY
Peterson, Wilferd A. *Twenty-three essays on the Art of living, including 17 essays individually published in the pages of* This Week *magazine.* New York, Simon & Schuster, 1960, 1961. 53p.

PETTY — PROMISES
Petty, Jo, comp. *Promises and premises.* Norwalk, Conn., C. R. Gibson Co., 1962. 86p.

PETTY — WINGS
Petty, Jo, comp. *Wings of silver.* Norwalk, Conn., C. R. Gibson Co., 1967. 89p.

PHILLIPS — CHOICE
Phillips, Dorothy Berkley, ed. *The choice is always ours. An anthology on the religious way. Chosen from psychological, religious, philosophical, poetical and biographical sources.* Co-edited by Elizabeth Boyden Howes and Lucille M. Nixon. New York, Harper & Row, Publishers, 1948, 1960. 430p.

PORTER — HALO
Porter, Jean Kelleher. *Halo for a housewife.* New York, Bruce Publishing Co., 1962. 136p.

PRICE — NO
Price, Eugenia. *No pat answers.* Grand Rapids, Mich. Zondervan Publishing House, 1972. 145p.

PRICE — WIDER
Price, Eugenia. *The wider place . . . where God offers freedom from anything that limits our growth.* Grand Rapids, Mich., Zondervan Publishing House, 1966. 250p.

PROCHNOW — PUBLIC
Prochnow, Herbert V., and Herbert V. Prochnow, Jr. *The public speaker's treasure chest. A compendium of source material to make your speech sparkle.* Rev. and enl. ed. New York, Harper & Row, Publishers, 1942, 1964. 516p.

PROCHNOW — SPEAKER'S
Prochnow, Herbert V. *The speaker's treasury of stories for all occasions.* New York, Prentice-Hall, Inc., 1953. 344p.

PROCHNOW — SUCCESS.
Prochnow, Herbert V., and Herbert V. Prochnow, Jr. *The successful toastmaster. A treasure chest of introductions, epigrams, humor, and quotations.* New York, Harper & Row, Publishers, 1966. 502p.

PULLAR - STRECKER — PROVERBS
Pullar-Strecker, H. *Proverbs for pleasure. Uncommon sayings collected, arranged and annotated.* New York, Philosophical Library, 1955. 202p.

RAU — ACT
Rau, Neil. *Act your way to successful living.* Englewood Cliffs, N. J., Prentice-Hall, Inc., 1966. 150p.

READER'S DIGEST. *See* FUN FARE; HOW TO LIVE; KEYS HAPPINESS

READER'S — GETTING
Getting the most out of life. An anthology from The Reader's Digest. Pleasantville, N. Y., The Reader's Digest Association, 1946. 250p.

READER'S — 20TH
The Reader's Digest *twentieth anniversary anthology.* Pleasantville, N. Y., The Reader's Digest Association, 1941. 123p.

REDHEAD — LIVING
Redhead, John A. *Living all your life.* New York, Abingdon Press, 1961. 142p.

ROGERS — TIME
Rogers, Dale Evans. *Time out, ladies!* Westwood, N. J., Fleming H. Revell Co., 1966. 118p.

SAFIAN — INSULTS
Safian, Louis A., comp. *2000 insults for all occasions.* New York, Citadel Press, Castle Books, 1965. 224p.

SAFIAN — MORE
Safian, Louis A., comp. *2000 more insults.* New York, Citadel Press, Castle Books, 1967. 192p.

SAGENDORPH — OLD
Sagendorph, Robb, ed. *The old* Farmer's Almanac *sampler.* New York, Ives Washburn, Inc., 1957. 306p.

SATURDAY — ADVENT.
Saturday Evening Post. Adventures of the mind, from The Saturday Evening Post. Ed. by Richard Thruelsen and John Kobler. New York, Alfred A. Knopf, 1960. 285p.

SCHERMERHORN — 1500
Schermerhorn, James. *1500 anecdotes and stories — for after dinner speaking.* New York, A. L. Burt, 1928. 397p.

SEABURG — GREAT
Seaburg, Carl, ed. *Great occasions. Readings for the celebration of birth, coming-of-age, marriage, and death.* Boston, Beacon Press, 1968. 462p.

SELDES — GREAT
Seldes, George. *The great quotations.* New York, Pocket Books, 1960. 1086p. paper.

SHEBAN — WISDOM
Sheban, Joseph, ed. *The wisdom of Gibran: aphorisms and maxims.* New York, Philosophical Library, 1966. n.p.

SHEEN — CONTENT.
Sheen, Fulton J. *Fulton J. Sheen's guide to contentment.* New York, Simon & Schuster, 1967. 186p.

SHEEN — LIFT
Sheen, Fulton J. *Lift up your heart.* Garden City, N. Y., Garden City Books, 1950, 1952. 213p.

SHEEN — THOUGHTS
Sheen, Fulton J. *Thoughts for daily living.* Garden City, N. Y., Garden City Books, 1951, 1956. 190p.

SHEEN — WAY
Sheen, Fulton J. *Way to happiness.* Garden City, N. Y., Garden City Books, 1949, 1954. 192p.

SHERMAN — YOUR
Sherman, Harold. *Your key to happiness.* Greenwich, Conn., Fawcett Publications, Inc., 1954. 158p.

SIMPSON — CONTEMP.
Simpson, James B., comp. *Contemporary quotations.* New York, Galahad Books, 1964. 500p.

SIMPSON — '54
Simpson, James Beasley. *Best quotes of '54, '55, '56.* New York, Thomas Y. Crowell Co., 1957. 374p.

SPEAKER'S DESK
Lupton, Martha, ed. *The speaker's desk book.* New York, Grosset & Dunlap, 1937. 695p.

STRAIT — SPEAKER'S
Strait, C. Neil, comp. *The speaker's book of inspiration. A treasury of contemporary religious & inspirational thought.* Atlanta, Ga., Droke House/Hallux, 1972. 197p.

STREIKER — WHO
Streiker, Lowell D., ed. *Who am I? Second thoughts on man, his loves, his gods.* New York, Sheed & Ward, 1970. 216p.

SUTER — PRAYERS
Suter, John Wallace. *Prayers for a new world.* New York, Charles Scribner's Sons, 1964. 244p.

TANKSLEY — FRIEND
Tanksley, Perry. *Friend gift.* Old Tappan, N. J., Fleming H. Revell Co., 1972. 80p.

TAYLOR — WITH
Taylor, Richard. *With heart and mind.* New York, St. Martin's Press, 1973. 147p.

THURMAN — MOOD
Thurman, Howard. *The mood of Christmas.* New York, Harper & Row, Publishers, 1973. 127p.

UNLIMITED POWER
The unlimited power of prayer. A new Guideposts *anthology . . .* Carmel, N. Y., Guideposts Associates, Inc., *Guideposts Magazine,* 1968. 294p.

VOGUE — ARTS
Vogue. The arts of living. New York, Simon & Schuster, 1954. 178p.

VOSS — QUOTATIONS
Voss, Carl Hermann, comp. *Quotations of courage and vision.* New York, Association Press, 1972. 270p.

WALLIS — TREASURE
Wallis, Charles L. *The treasure chest. A heritage album containing 1064 familiar and inspirational quotations, poems, sentiments, and prayers from great minds of 2500 years.* New York, Harper & Row Publishers, 1965. 248p.

WALLIS — WORDS
Wallis, Charles L. *Words of life. A religious and inspirational album containing 1100 quotations from the minds and hearts of writers of twenty centuries and illustrated by scenes of the Holy Land.* New York, Harper & Row, Publishers, 1966. 248p.

WALTERS — HOW
Walters, Barbara. *How to talk with practically anybody about practically everything.* Garden City, N. Y., Doubleday & Co., Inc., 1970. 195p.

WATSON — LIGHT
Watson, Lillian Eichler. *Light from many lamps.* New York, Simon & Schuster, 1951. 325p.

WEBB — EDGE
Webb, Lance. *On the edge of the absurd.* New York, Abingdon Press, 1965. 158p.

WEISFELD — PULPIT
Weisfeld, Israel H. *The pulpit treasury of wit and humor.* New York, Prentice-Hall, Inc., 1950. 182p.

WELK — GUIDE.
Welk, Lawrence. *Guidelines for successful living.* Minneapolis, Minn., T. S. Denison & Co., Inc., 1968. 176p.

WHEELIS — MORALIST
Wheelis, Allen. *The moralist.* New York, Basic Books, Inc., 1973. 170p.

WHITE — JOB
White, Stewart Edward. *The job of living.* New York, E. P. Dutton & Co., Inc., 1948. 196p.

WHITE — LIFE
White, Ellen G. *Life at its best.* Mountain View, Calif., Pacific Press Publishing Association, 1964. 314p. paper.

WILCOX — HEART
Wilcox, Ella Wheeler. *The heart of the New Thought.* Chicago, A. C. McClurg & Co., 1926. 92p.

WOODS — BUSINESS.
Woods, Ralph L., ed. *The businessman's book of quotations.* New York, McGraw-Hill Book Co., Inc., 1951. 303p.

WOODS — CONTENT.
Woods, Ralph L., comp. & ed. *A treasury of contentment. Inspirational selections in which man affirms life's worth and celebrates its rewards.* New York, Trident Press, 1969. 381p.

WOODS — INSPIR.
Woods, Ralph L., ed. *A treasury of inspiration.* New York, Thomas Y. Crowell Co., 1951. 498p.

WOODS — RELIGIOUS
Woods, Ralph L., comp. & ed. *The world treasury of religious quotations.* New York, Hawthorn Books, Inc., 1966. 1106p.

WOODS — WELLSPRINGS
Woods, Ralph L., ed. *Wellsprings of wisdom. Fascinating stories and parables that guide and inspire.* Norwalk, Conn., The C. R. Gibson Co., 1969. 82p.

WORDS CHANGE
Words to change lives. A kaleidoscopic view of contemporary religious expression. New York, Association Press, 1957. 128p. paper.

WORDS — INSPIR.
Words of inspiration. Writings from the past to brighten the present and give promise for the future. Chicago, J. G. Ferguson Publishing Co., 1963. 224p.

ZOBELL — SPEAKER'S
Zobell, Albert L., Jr., comp. *Speaker's scrapbook.* Salt Lake City, Utah, Bookcraft, Inc., 1970. 160p.

INDEX TO INSPIRATION

A

ABANDONMENT
See also **Self-sacrifice**
Woods — *Religious* p.1

ABASEMENT. *See* **Self-criticism; Shame**

ABDUCTION
Lockridge — *World's* #2345
Unlimited Power — p.28-32

ABILITY
See also **Efficiency; Genius; Leaders and leadership; Talent**
Braude — *Source* #1-3, 262-264
Braude — *Stories* p.13-14
Detherage — *Sunrise* p.41, 65, 175-177
Dirksen — *Quot.* #339, 509, 862, 998, 1178-1180
Edwards — *Useful* p.1
Forbes — *Thoughts* p.28, 57, 113, 147, 153, 169, 238, 264, 267, 318-319, 336, 358, 399, 408, 510
Garland — *Subject* p.3
Grizer — *Wit* p.15-16
Henry — *5000* p.1
Hovey — *Treasury* #1-6, 19-20, 118, 298, 301, 331, 355, 937, 1567, 1733, 1857
Kin — *Dictionary* p.3, 69
Liddle — *Thought* (I, II, III) p.34, 91, 116, 140, 145, 162
Lockridge — *World's* #162, 165, 257, 693, 1528
Lytle — *Leaves* p.182, 185
Montapert — *Distilled* p.1-2, 51
Prochnow — *Public* #9, 675, 1687, 2749-2751, 3920
Prochnow — *Speaker's* p.12
Prochnow — *Success.* #1257, 1507
Reader's — *Getting* p.113-116

ABNORMALITY
See also **Crime and criminals; Handicapped;** etc.
Adams — *New* p.16
Braude — *Source* #4

ABODES. *See* **Home; Houses**

ABOLITION
Botkin — *Anecdotes* p.147
Seldes — *Great* p.1

ABORTION
McDonagh — *Invit.* p.133-167
Seldes — *Great* p.1
Woods — *Religious* p.1-2

ABROAD. *See* **Travel**

ABSENCE
See also **Farewells; Loneliness**
Braude — *Source* #5
Braude — *Speaker's* #1-3
Braude — *Stories* p.14
Dirksen — *Quot.* #1181, 1838
Edwards — *Useful* p.1-2
Flesch — *Unusual* p.1
Forbes — *Thoughts* p.45
Henry — *5000* p.1
Kin — *Dictionary* p.3
Lockridge — *World's* #2316
Liddle — *Thought* (I, II, III) p.143
Lytle — *Leaves* p.95
Prochnow — *Public* #90, 1986, 2706, 3921-3922
Schermerhorn — *1500* p.1

ABSENT-MINDEDNESS
See also **Daydreaming**
Asimov — *Treasury* #135, 136
Botkin — *Treasury* p.464-465
Braude — *Speaker's* #1-4
Copeland — *10,000* p.384-387
Dirksen — *Quot.* #14
Evans — *Thoughts III (Open Road)* p.135-137
Flesch — *Unusual* p.1
Fuller — *Thesaurus* #81-90
Fun Fare p.299-300, 310
Grizer — *Wit* p.17
Humes — *Instant* p.20-21
Kohn — *Best* p.100-103
Prochnow — *Public* #318, 1877
Prochnow — *Speaker's* p.12-13
Schermerhorn — *1500* p.1-2

Speaker's Desk #236, 580, 665, 805, 899, 920, 936, 1013, 1074
Weisfeld — *Pulpit* p.133

ABSOLUTE
Braude — *Source* #6
Du Noüy — *Human* p.46, 130-133, 225
Hoffer — *Reflect.* p.9
Ideas p.1-3
Keller — *Open* p.62-63
Phillips — *Choice* p.181
Woods — *Religious* p.2-3

ABSOLUTION. *See* **Atonement; Forgiveness**

ABSTINENCE
See also **Asceticism; Moderation; Self-denial; Sobriety; Temperance**
Baillie — *Diary* #177
Book Proverbs p.53, 106-107
Edwards — *Useful* p.2
Evans — *Thoughts IV* p.114-115
Flesch — *Unusual* p.1
Forbes — *Thoughts* p.244, 393, 457
Garland — *Subject* p.3-4
Kin — *Dictionary* p.3
Lockridge — *World's* #3600, 5621
Schermerhorn — *1500* p.2
Woods — *Religious* p.3, 191

ABSTRACT
See also **Ideas and ideology**
Applegarth — *Heir.* p.260
Curtis — *Practical* p.49, 51-53, 56-57
Flesch — *Unusual* p.1-2

ABSURDITY
See also **Fools and foolishness; Nonsense;** etc.
Edwards — *Useful* p.2
Flesch — *Unusual* p.2
Forbes — *Thoughts* p.242, 244, 362, 435
Kin — *Dictionary* p.4
Lytle — *Leaves* p.76
Prochnow — *Public* #273

ABUNDANCE
See also **Possessions; Wealth**
Dirksen — *Quot.* #510, 1500-1501
Evans — *This* p.63-64
Forbes — *Thoughts* p.129, 162, 215, 219, 294, 321, 425, 468, 507
Garland — *Subject* p.4, 233-234
Holmes — *Design* p.111, 135-140, 223-224
Kin — *Dictionary* p.4
Kohn — *Best* p.41-43
Kohn — *Through* p.137-139
Prochnow — *Public* #2638, 3923

ABUSE. *See* **Cruelty;** etc.

ACADEMIC FREEDOM
Dirksen — *Quot.* #432
Franke — *Buckley* p.1
Woods — *Religious* p.3

ACADEMIC LIFE. *See* **Universities and colleges**

ACCENTS
Asimov — *Treasury* #10, 309
Botkin — *Anecdotes* p.38
Botkin — *Treasury* p.272
Edwards — *Useful* p.3
Lockridge — *World's* #3694
Speaker's Desk #74, 206
Weisfeld — *Pulpit* p.31, 76
, *French*
Asimov — *Treasury* #569
, *German*
Asimov — *Treasury* #430
, *Irish*
Copeland — *10,000* p.975-981
, *Italian*
Asimov — *Treasury* #429
, *Jewish*
Asimov — *Treasury* #310-313
, *Negro*
Copeland — *10,000* p.968-975
, *Scottish*
Asimov — *Treasury* #411
, *Western*
Copeland — *10,000* p.959-967

ACCEPTANCE
See also **Agreement; Self-acceptance**
Evans — *Unto* p.118
Flesch — *Unusual* p.2, 322
Fun Fare p.290
Giniger — *Compact* p.203
Ginott — *Between* p.31-33
Guideposts — *Faith* p.218-222
Holmes — *Design* p.68-70, 101-102, 182, 205, 208, 214-215
Holmes — *I've* p.6
How to Live p.512
Jones — *If* p.23, 322
Kahn — *Lessons* p.119-133
Kohn — *Pathways* p.55-58
Lair — *Baby* p.19-20, 164, 228-229
Lytle — *Leaves* p.107
Menninger — *Blue* p.37-38
Montapert — *Distilled* p.2
More Words p.2-4
Phillips — *Choice* p.55, 77, 141, 189

Prochnow — *Public* #1842-1843, 2691
Prochnow — *Success.* #823
Sheen — *Content.* p.121-140
Speaker's Desk #292, 321, 647, 1033
Tanksley — *Friend* p.47
Unlimited Power p.216-220, 244-246
Vogue — *Arts* p.147-153
Wallis — *Words* p.51
Woods — *Content.* p.53, 267, 304-305, 307, 309-312, 315, 352
Woods — *Religious* p.3

ACCIDENT
See also **Chance; Fate; Fortune; Luck; Misfortune;** types of accidents
Alexander's Treasure. p.142-143
Edwards — *Useful* p.3
Evans — *Thoughts III (Open Road)* p.35, 45, 57, 100, 160, 186, 207, 211
Evans — *Thoughts IV* p.114, 118, 168
Flesch — *Unusual* p.2
Forbes — *Thoughts* p.68, 123, 334, 381, 480
Fuller — *Thesaurus* #1736
Grizer — *Wit* p.18
Guideposts — *Faith* p.42-46, 277-281
Harnsberger — *Mark* p.1-2
Harral — *Feature* p.71
Henry — *5000* p.1
Keys Happiness p.271-273, 298-300, 454-456, 521-522
Kin — *Dictionary* p.4
Myers — *Thunder* p.101
Prochnow — *Public* #366, 493, 537, 645, 974, 1055, 1249, 1477
Prochnow — *Speaker's* p.13
Prochnow — *Success.* #945, 1064
Reader's — *20th* p.65-70
Seaburg — *Great* p.176, 242, 247, 288-289, 291, 360, 362
Sherman — *Your* p.63-67
Speaker's Desk #177, 698, 930, 1133, 1165
Woods — *Religious* p.3

ACCLAMATION. *See* **Praise**

ACCOMPLISHMENT. *See* **Achievement; Deeds**

ACCORD. *See* **Agreement; Peace**

ACCOUNTING
Flesch — *Unusual* p.2-3
Forbes — *Thoughts* p.336
Prochnow — *Public* #4301

ACCURACY
See also **Truth**
Edwards — *Useful* p.3
Flesch — *Unusual* p.3
Forbes — *Thoughts* p.186, 195, 200, 205
Fuller — *Thesaurus* #91-92
Grizer — *Wit* p.20
Mandel — *Stories* p.1

ACCUSATION
See also **Blame; Self-blame**
Dirksen — *Quot.* #1182
Grizer — *Wit* p.20
Kin — *Dictionary* p.5
Lockridge — *World's* #5091
Lytle — *Leaves* p.27
Nizer — *Thinking* p.109
Speaker's Desk #200

ACHIEVEMENT
See also **Deeds; Fame; Fulfillment; Glory; Honor**
Braude — *Source* #7-8, 11-15
Braude — *Stories* p.14-16
Curtis — *Daily* p.197
Detherage — *Sunrise* p.41, 49, 190
Dirksen — *Quot.* #168-169, 750, 781, 1103, 1183-1184, 1626, 2390
Edwards — *Useful* p.140
Evans — *Quote* p.41-51
Evans — *Thoughts III (Open Road)* p.196
Evans — *Unto* p.93
Flesch — *Unusual* p.3, 15, 65, 67
Forbes — *Thoughts See* index p.541
Garland — *Subject* p.4-5
Grizer — *Wit* p.18-21
Hadfield — *Delights* p.72-127, 200-216
Harnsberger — *Mark* p.2
Hobe — *Tapestries* p.13-15
Hoffer — *Reflect.* p.85, 89-90
Hovey — *Treasury* #7-22, 25, 71, 768, 811, 1001, 1046, 1211-1212, 1362, 1412, 1440, 1550
How to Live p.308-313
Hubbard — *Scrap* p.104
Jones — *If* p.25-26
Kennedy — *Reader's* #1-2
Kin — *Dictionary* p.4-5, 72
Kohn — *Pathways* p.177-180
Liddle — *Thought IV* p.7-13, 24, 44-45
Liddle — *Thought V* p.11, 16, 19, 26, 36, 38, 44, 46
Lytle — *Leaves* p.9-11, 54, 68, 135, 179
Maltz — *Creative* p.29-30
Miller — *Harvest* p.55-58

Montapert — *Distilled* p.2-4, 112-115
Nichols — *Third* p.42-65, 93-94
Nizer — *Thinking* p.75, 114, 140
Peale — *Stay* p.247-263
Peterson — *Twenty* p.46-47
Phillips — *Choice* p.42, 100
Prochnow — *Public* #186, 259, 2753-2764, 2979-2983
Prochnow — *Speaker's* p.14
Prochnow — *Success.* #170, 263, 1208, 1559, 1688-1689
Redhead — *Living* p.107-115
Taylor — *With* p.144-145
Voss — *Quotations* p.11-13
Wallis — *Treasure* p.1-4, 8, 207, 211
Watson — *Light* p.133-159
Woods — *Content.* p.22, 26, 70
Woods — *Inspir.* p.50-83
Woods — *Religious* p.3-4
Zobell — *Speaker's* p.9-11

ACORNS
Esteve — *Experience* p.51
Kin — *Dictionary* p.5

ACOUSTICS. *See* **Sound**

ACQUAINTANCE
See also **Associates; Companionship; Friends and friendship**
Edwards — *Useful* p.3
Flesch — *Unusual* p.3
Forbes — *Thoughts* p.88, 329, 393
Henry — *5000* p.1-2
Lockridge — *World's* #4793
Prochnow — *Public* #3925
Prochnow — *Success.* #1508
Schermerhorn — *1500* p.4-5

ACQUIESCENCE. *See* **Acceptance; Agreement**

ACQUISITION
See also **Money; Possessions; Property; Wealth**
Edwards — *Useful* p.3, 212
Flesch — *Unusual* p.102
Forbes — *Thoughts* p.115, 138, 229, 258, 290, 310, 333, 355, 404, 433, 441, 460, 469, 493, 501
Garland — *Subject* p.117
Harnsberger — *Mark* p.2
Kin — *Dictionary* p.5
Lytle — *Leaves* p.149
Montapert — *Distilled* p.166-167, 169-170
Prochnow — *Success.* #1793
White — *Job* p.178-181, 185-186

ACROBATS. *See* **Athletics; Gymnastics**

ACRONYMS
Auden — *Certain* p.4-5

ACROPOLIS
Curtis — *Practical* p.431

ACTING. *See* **Actors and actresses**

ACTION
See also **Adventure; Deeds;** etc.
Applegarth — *Heir.* p.43, 206-207
Baillie — *Diary* #150
Braude — *Source* #18-28
Braude — *Stories* p.16
Curtis — *Daily* p.152-153
Curtis — *Practical* p.69, 71
Detherage — Sunrise p.63-68
Dirksen — *Quot.* #222, 752, 1839, 2344
Edwards — *Useful* p.3-5
Evans — *This* p.29-30, 43-44
Flesch — *Unusual* p.3-4
Flint — *Graham* p.9
Forbes — *Thoughts* See index p.539
Fox — *Make* p.208
Fuller — *Epigrams* p.11-12
Grizer — *Wit* p.21-24
Henry — *5000* p.2-3
Hoffer — *Reflect.* p.39
Holmes — *Design* p.42, 46
Hovey — *Treasury* p.22-24; *See* index p.293
Hulme — *Living* p.140-142
Humes — *Instant* p.9, #42-45, 50-56, 1268-1270, 1276-1277
Kauffman — *For* p.189-191
Keller — *Open* p.68
Kennedy — *Reader's* #3-8
Kin — *Dictionary* p.5-6
Krishnamurti — *Think* p.155
Liddle — *Thought I, II, III See* index p.195
Liddle — *Thought IV* p.15, 19, 33, 36, 38-39, 41, 46
Liddle — *Thought V* p.16, 23, 36
Lockridge — *World's* #164, 1083, 1412, 3254, 4008, 4311, 5271, 5849
Lytle — *Leaves* p.5-9, 24, 186
Mandel — *Stories* p.1-2
Montapert — *Distilled* p.5-6
Peale — *Guideposts* p.27-53
Peterson — *Art* p.264
Peterson — *New* p.58-59
Phillips — *Choice* See index p.424
Prochnow — *Public* #2765-2766, 3926-3927
Prochnow — *Success.* #1509-1512
Seldes — *Great* p.2-4
Sheban — *Wisdom* no p.
Speaker's Desk p.1-3

Wallis — *Treasure* p.5-8, 112, 212
Wallis — *Words* p.26, 160
Wheelis — *Moralist* p.11, 18, 27-28, 98, 116, 148
Woods — *Content.* p.31, 35, 37, 53, 55-56, 70, 203, 231, 284
Woods — *Inspir.* p.188-222
Woods — *Religious* p.4-6
Words — *Inspir.* p.207

ACTIVITY
See also **Work**
Albert — *Stop* p.11-12, 19-20, 46-50, 60, 95-96, 110-111, 203
Applegarth — *Heir.* p.304
Casselberry — *How* p.171-176
Curtis — *Practical* p.57
Flesch — *Unusual* p.4
Forbes — *Thoughts* p.103, 143, 146, 156, 337, 426, 461, 497
Garland — *Subject* p.5-6
Keys Happiness p.157
Phillips — *Choice* p.317
Prochnow — *Public* #1954
Unlimited Power p.180-183
Woods — *Religious* p.6
Zobell — *Speaker's* p.11-12

ACTORS AND ACTRESSES
See also **Hollywood, Calif.; Television; Theater**
Asimov — *Treasury* #22
Cerf — *Laugh* p.43-49
Copeland — *10,000* p.581-584
Cowan — *Wit* p.143-167
Dirksen — *Quot.* #118, 147, 253, 255
Edwards — *Useful* p.5
Fogg — *1000* #95
Fuller — *Epigrams* p.12-13
Fuller — *Thesaurus* #1406-1431
George — *Book* p.6, 13, 53, 161, 174
Grizer — *Wit* p.24-25
Harral — *Feature* p.285-286
Henry — *5000* p.2
How to Live p.286-291
Lockridge — *World's* #887-898, 984, 1071
Nichols — *New* p.80-81
Nichols — *Third* p.197-198
Nizer — *Thinking* p.26, 32, 78, 93, 100
Peale — *Guideposts* p.217-220
Prochnow — *Public* #699, 1356, 1882
Prochnow — *Speaker's* p.15
Prochnow — *Success.* #957, 1169, 1513
Schermerhorn — *1500* p.5-6
Seldes — *Great* p.4
Woods — *Religious* p.6

ADAM AND EVE
See also **Garden of Eden**
Asimov — *Treasury* #377, 471, 475
Botkin — *Anecdotes* p.190-191
Cowan — *Wit* p.9-69
Flesch — *Unusual* p.4
Harnsberger — *Mark* p.2-3, 106
Henry — *5000* p.3
Kin — *Dictionary* p.6
Lockridge — *World's* #5801
Prochnow — *Public* #1611
Weisfeld — *Pulpit* p.66
Woods — *Religious* p.7

ADAPTATION. *See* **Adjustment**

ADDAMS HOUSE
Botkin — *Anecdotes* p.106

ADEQUATENESS. *See* **Satisfaction**

ADJECTIVES
Flesch — *Unusual* p.4
Humes — *Instant* p.15-16

ADJUSTMENT
Braude — *Source* #29
Du Noüy — *Human* p.81, 83-84, 86-94, 122-123, 138-139, 142, 166, 170-171, 204, 218, 235
Flesch — *Unusual* p.4
Forbes — *Thoughts* p.472, 487
Fox — *Make* p.152
Kin — *Dictionary* p.6
Lindeman — *Emerson* p.190-191
Lytle — *Leaves* p.140
Maltz — *Creative* p.203-204
Mandel — *Stories* p.2-3
Montapert — *Distilled* p.6
Nichols — *New* p.65-66
Prochnow — *Public* #77, 2116
Prochnow — *Success.* #1514-1515
Speaker's Desk #1048
Wheelis — *Moralist* p.8

ADMINISTRATION *See* **Business; Government**

ADMIRALS
Botkin — *Anecdotes* p.188

ADMIRATION
See also **Affection; Esteem; Praise**
Applegarth — *Heir.* p.253
Dirksen — *Quot.* #325, 754, 2016
Edwards — *Useful* p.6
Flesch — *Unusual* p.4
Forbes — *Thoughts* p.141, 400
Fuller — *Epigrams* p.13-14
Grizer — *Wit* p.25
Henry — *5000* p.3-4

Kin — *Dictionary* p.6
Lockridge — *World's* #305, 691, 2302, 2376, 3070, 3473, 3890
Montapert — *Distilled* p.6-7
Prochnow — *Public* #263, 2767-2768
Prochnow — *Success.* #1454, 1479, 1516-1517
Wallis — *Words* p.79

ADMONITION. *See* **Advice**

ADOLESCENCE
See also **Children; Teenagers; Youth**
Adams — *New* p.340
Braude — *Stories* p.16-17
Ginott — *Between* p.25-26, 28-29
Hoffer — *Reflect.* p.36-37
How to Live p.139-162
Jackson — *Coping* p.105-112
Kennedy — *Reader's* #9
Keys Happiness p.518-520
Liebman — *Hope* p.195-211
Prochnow — *Public* #1612
Sheban — *Wisdom* no p.
Woods — *Religious* p.7

ADOPTION
Flesch — *Unusual* p.4
Flint — *Graham* p.9
Fuller — *Thesaurus* #981
Keys Happiness p.469
Lytle — *Leaves* p.85
New Topical p.5-6
Schermerhorn — *1500* p.6
Unlimited Power p.264-267
, Ceremony of
Seaburg — *Great* p.411-412

ADORATION. *See* **Worship**

ADRENALINE
Lair — *Baby* p.181

ADSORPTION
Du Noüy — *Road* p.131-132

ADULATION. *See* **Flattery; Praise**

ADULTERY
Flint — *Graham* p.9, 91
Kin — *Dictionary* p.6
Lockridge — *World's* #5123, 5187, 5209
More Words p.4-5
Myers — *Thunder* p.107-118
Prochnow — *Public* #2466
Woods — *Religious* p.8-9

ADULTS
See also names of adults, e.g. **Parents; Women**
Braude — *Source* #31
Harral — *Feature* p.71
Keys Happiness p.425-426
Menninger — *Blue.* p.57-58, 192-196
Seaburg — *Great* p.51-85

ADVANCEMENT
See also **Growth; Progress**
Curtis — *Practical* p.490
Forbes — *Thoughts* p.7, 46, 122, 155, 481
Garland — *Subject* p.6-7
Grizer — *Wit* p.25
Kin — *Dictionary* p.6

ADVANTAGE
Dirksen — *Quot.* #755
Flesch — *Unusual* p.5
Forbes — *Thoughts* p.25, 147
Lockridge — *World's* #4249, 5153
Montapert — *Distilled* p.7
Prochnow — *Public* #1419, 3928
Prochnow — *Success.* #798

ADVENT
See also **Christmas**
Fridy — *Meditat.* p.133-136
More Words p.5-6, 56-59
Strait — *Speaker's* p.167-168
Suter — *Prayers* #380

ADVENTURE
See also **Action; Discovery; Travel**
Applegarth — *Heir.* p.31, 97
Bach — *Make* p.3-59, 63-129, 133-206
Barrows — *1000 See* index p.445
Bartlett — *Discovery* p.8-9, 13-14
Clark — *Windows* p.66
Edwards — *Useful* p.725
Flesch — *Unusual* p.5
Forbes — *Thoughts* p.148, 261, 341, 350, 457, 474
Henry — *5000* p.54
Hovey — *Treasury* #14, 27, 41, 45, 75, 88, 106, 147, 380, 679, 986
Humes — *Instant* #57-59
Kennedy — *Reader's* #10-13
Lockridge — *World's* #12
Lytle — *Leaves* p.38
Montapert — *Distilled* p.7-8
New Joy p.185
Peterson — *Twenty* p.24-25
Prochnow — *Public* #2283, 2293
Sheen — *Content.* p.121-124
Vogue — *Arts p.119-128*
Wallis — *Treasure* p.24, 70, 84, 207
Wallis — *Words* p.4, 38, 76, 106, 132, 152, 154, 159

Woods — *Content.* p.67, 70-72, 77
Woods — *Inspir.* p.1-49

ADVERSITY
See also types of adversity, e.g. **Disaster; Failure; Grief; Illness; Poverty; Trouble;** etc.
Braude — *Source* #32-35
Braude — *Stories* p.19
Detherage — *Sunrise* p.59, 61, 157
Dirksen — *Quot.* #756-758, 1105, 1840-1841, 1985, 2135-2136
Droke — *Christian* p.7-8
Edwards — *Useful* p.6-8, 681
Evans — *Quote* p.53-66
Evans — *This* p.44
Evans — *Thoughts I* p.69, 81, 89, 121-122, 178
Evans — *Thoughts III (Open Road)* p.35-41
Evans — *Unto* p.113, 119
Flesch — *Unusual* p.5
Forbes — *Thoughts* p.7, 61, 98, 165, 345, 401, 406, 410, 459
Garland — *Subject* p.7-8
Grizer — *Wit* p.25-26
Harnsberger — *Mark* p.3
Henry — *5000* p.4
Hobe — *Tapestries* p.217
Hovey — *Treasury* #406, 855, 1161
How to Live p.351-382
Hubbard — *Scrap* p.45, 95, 112, 174, 191
Keller — *Open* p.30
Keys Happiness p.107-108
Kin — *Dictionary* p.6-7, 268
Liddle — *Thought I, II, III* p.135
Lockridge — *World's* #3764, 4028
Lytle — *Leaves* p.5, 13, 57
Mandel — *Stories* p.3
Montapert — *Distilled* p.8-9
Phillips — *Choice* p. 145, 235
Prochnow — *Public* #1424, 1989, 2546, 2769-2778, 3929-3931
Prochnow — *Success.* #1191, 1518-1520
Speaker's Desk p.3-4
Tanksley — *Friend* p.28
Voss — *Quotations* p.13-16
Wallis — *Treasure* p.124, 226, 228
Woods — *Content.* p.112, 315
Woods — *Inspir.* p.346-377
Woods — *Religious* p.9

ADVERTISING
See also **Billboards; Publicity; Slogans;** etc.
Botkin — *Anecdotes* p.63
Braude — *Source* #36-42
Braude — *Speaker's* #5-10
Braude — *Stories* p.17-18
Cerf — *Laugh* p.377-382
Edwards — *Useful* p.8
Flesch — *Unusual* p.5
Forbes — *Thoughts* p.104, 173, 221, 330, 389, 399, 478, 499, 519
Fuller — *Epigrams* p.14
Fuller — *Thesaurus* #2101-2108
Fun Fare p.37, 42, 94, 118, 241
George — *Book* p.8, 210, 387
Grizer — *Wit* p.26-30
Harral — *Feature* p.71-73
Henry — *5000* p.4
Hovey — *Treasury* p.24-26; #33-41, 109, 294, 381, 1146, 1471, 1488, 1502, 1648, 1668
Hubbard — *Scrap* p.54
Ideas p.403-404
Kauffman — *For* p.217
Kennedy — *Reader's* #14
Keys Happiness p.303
Kin — *Dictionary* p.7
Lair — *Baby* p.101-103
Mandel — *Stories* p.3
Modern Eloquence (14) p.277-278
Montapert — *Distilled* p.9
Peale — *Guideposts* p.147-150
Prochnow — *Public* #68, 427, 597, 1045, 1267, 1507, 1525, 1828, 4271
Prochnow — *Speaker's* p.15
Prochnow — *Success.* #970, 988, 1521-1523
Schermerhorn — *1500* p.6-9
Seldes — *Great* p.4-7
Simpson — *Contemp.* p.86-91
Woods — *Business.* p.1
Woods — *Religious* p.9

ADVICE
See also **Counseling; Guidance**
Book Proverbs p.131
Braude — *Source* #43-54
Braude — *Speaker's* #11-13
Braude — *Stories* p.19-20
Dirksen — *Quot.* #138, 265, 294, 368, 511, 1627, 1842-1844, 2277
Edwards — *Useful* p.8-9
Evans — *Faith* p.53
Evans — *Quote* p.187-194
Evans — *Thoughts II (Open Door)* p.47, 156-159
Evans — *Unto* p.77-112
Flesch — *Unusual* p.5-6
Forbes — *Thoughts* p.200, 203, 244, 248, 294, 329, 345, 391, 399, 401, 457, 511
Fuller — *Epigrams* p.14-16
Garland — *Subject* p.8
Grizer — *Wit* p.30-32
Harnsberger — *Mark* p.3-4
Henry — *5000* p.4-5
Hovey — *Treasury* #453
Howell — *Better* p.9-16

Hubbard — *Scrap* p.100
Keys Happiness p.505-506
Kin — *Dictionary* p.7
Liddle — *Thought IV* p.14
Lockridge — *World's* #3422, 5868; *See* index p.571
Lytle — *Leaves* p.69
Modern Eloquence (14) p.279
Montapert — *Distilled* p.9-10
Prochnow — *Public See* index p.485; #2448
Prochnow — *Speaker's* p.15-16
Prochnow — *Success.* #374, 416, 487, 500-501, 886, 911, 1413, 1493, 1524
Sheban — *Wisdom* no p.
Simpson — *Contemp.* p.249-258
Speaker's Desk #18, 629, 699, 745, 764, 879-880, 884, 912, 1089, 1099, 1137. *See also* index p.4-7, 297
White — *Job* p.97-98

ADVOCATES
Ginott — *Between* p.63-64
Kin — *Dictionary* p.7

AERONAUTICS. *See* **Aviation**

AESTHETICS
Ideas p.5-7
Lockridge — *World's* #5584

AFFABILIITY. *See* **Agreement; Cheerfulness**

AFFAIRS. *See* **Business**

AFFECTATION. *See* **Hypocrisy; Insincerity; Pretension**

AFFECTION
See also **Admiration; Esteem; Friends and friendship; Heart; Love; Tenderness**
Baillie — *Diary* #277, 279
Curtis — *Practical* p.537-539
Dirksen — *Quot.* #166
Edwards — *Useful* p.10-11
Evans — *Unto* p.12
Flesch — *Unusual* p.7, 152
Forbes — *Thoughts* p.136, 240, 276, 360
Garland — *Subject* p.8
Harnsberger — *Mark* p.4-5, 241
Henry — *5000* p.157
Hobe — *Tapestries* p.119, 130
Hubbard — *Scrap* p.227
Kin — *Dictionary* p.7, 149
Lockridge — *World's* #2317, 2827, 4173, 5170
Montapert — *Distilled* p.10, 241
New Topical p.6
Nichols — *Third* p.68-87
Peterson — *Art* p.352
Phillips — *Choice* p.203, 206
Prochnow — *Public* #853, 3937
Prochnow — *Success.* #1986-1987
Sheban — *Wisdom* no p.
Unlimited Power p.146-147
Wallis — *Treasure* p.169-170
Woods — *Religious* p.10

AFFINITY. *See* **Relationships**

AFFIRMATION
See also **Agreement**
Curtis — *Daily* p.229-242
Flesch — *Unusual* p.7
Fox — *Make* p.130
Holmes — *Design* p.30, 39, 59, 186, 214-215, 218-220
Maltz — *Creative* p.196-197
Montapert — *Distilled* p.10-11
Phillips — *Choice* p.214
Woods — *Religious* p.10

AFFLICTION
See also **Disease; Handicapped; Illness; Pain**
Dirksen — *Quot.* #759, 1185-1193, 1268, 1403-1404, 1597, 1937, 2324
Edwards — *Useful* p.11-13
Evans — *Unto* p.50, 119
Forbes — *Thoughts* p.35, 98, 165, 272
Fuller — *Thesaurus* #701-707
Garland — *Subject* p.9
Henry — *5000* p.5
Hobe — *Tapestries* p.217
Hubbard — *Scrap* p.171
Keller — *Open* p.129
Kin — *Dictionary* p.8
Lockridge — *World's* #2824
Lytle — *Leaves* p.13
Montapert — *Distilled* p.11
New Topical p.6-8
Phillips — *Choice* p.137-138, 144
Prochnow — *Public* #2487, 2496
Prochnow — *Success.* #1525
Voss — *Quotations* p.16-18
Wallis — *Words* p.179
White — *Life* p.276-279
Woods — *Religious* p.10

AFFLUENCE. *See* **Wealth**

AFFRONT. *See* **Insult**

AFRICA
See also **Negroes**
Cerf — *Laugh* p.447-449
Flint — *Graham* p.9-10
Franke — *Buckley* p.2-3

Guideposts — *Faith* p.180-184
Hovey — *Treasury* #169, 335, 554-555, 740, 931, 1069, 1278, 1327
Prochnow — *Success.* #184, 841
Simpson — *Contemp.* p.149
Unlimited Power p.268-272

"AFTER-DINNER" STORIES
Schermerhorn — *1500* p.9-12

AFTERLIFE. *See* **Eternity; Immortality**

AFTERNOON
Auden — *Certain* p.99-100

AGE
See also **Antiquity; Experience; Middle-age; Old age; Ruin; Time**
Adams — *New* p.15, 22, 248
Alexander's Treasure. p.167, 217, 307
Auden — *Certain* p.5-12
Braude — *Source* p.55-76
Braude — *Speaker's* #14-21
Braude — *Stories* p.21-24
Curtis — *Daily* p.214-220
Detherage — *Sunrise* p.157-158, 180, 184-185
Dirksen — *Quot.* #39, 226, 335, 337, 760-763, 899, 1020, 1194-1199, 1845-1888, 2049, 2325, 2330
Droke — *Christian* p.9-12
Edwards — *Useful* p.13-15, 725
Evans — *Quote* p.29-40, 62, 105, 110
Felleman — *Poems* p.245-268
Flesch — *Unusual* p.7
Forbes — *Thoughts* p.232, 373, 444
Fuller — *Epigrams* p.16-19, 329
Fuller — *Thesaurus* #671-678
Garland — *Subject* p.10
Grizer — *Wit* p.33-34
Hadfield — *Love* p.221
Harnsberger — *Mark* p.5-6
Henry — *5000* p.5-6
Hobe — *Tapestries* p.187, 218
Holmes — *I've* p.7-8
Howell — *Better* p.17-20
Humes — *Instant* #60-62
Jackson — *Coping* p.144-151
Kin — *Dictionary* p.8
Liddle — *Thought I, II, III* p. 19, 38, 48, 60, 75, 88, 102, 105, 115
Liddle — *Thought V* p. 13, 27-29
Lockridge — *World's* See index p.571
Lytle — *Leaves* p.5, 18
Maltz — *Creative* p.180-182
Mandel — *Stories* p.3-6
Modern Eloquence (14) p.280-281
Montapert — *Distilled* p.11-12
Peterson — *Art* p.26
Prochnow — *Public* See index p.485
Prochnow — *Speaker's* p.16-19
Prochnow — *Success.* p.2090, 2102-2103; See index p.485
Reader's — *20th* p.16
Seldes — *Great* p.7
Sheban — *Wisdom* no p.
Strait — *Speaker's* p.13-14
Suter — *Prayers* #431-442
Voss — *Quotations* p.18-21
Wallis — *Treasure* p.9-14
Woods — *Content.* p.321-325
Woods — *Religious* p.11
Zobell — *Speaker's* p.12-13

AGGRAVATION. *See* **Anger; Frustration**
Albert — *Stop* p.144-145, 154-155
Garland — *Subject* p.10
Liebman — *Peace* p.91-98
Maltz — *Creative* p.88-89
Menninger — *Blue.* p.55
Patterns for Living p.511-518
Prochnow — *Public* #2428
Seldes — *Great* p.7-8
White — *Job* p.68-69
Woods — *Religious* p.11

AGITATION
See also **Argument; Radicals and radicalism; Reform; Violence**
Edwards — *Useful* p.15-16
Kennedy — *Reader's* #15
Lockridge — *World's* #2795, 3874
Maltz — *Creative* p.130
Seldes — *Great* p.8

AGNOSTICISM
See also **Atheism; Unbelief and unbelievers**
Curtis — *Practical* p.505-507
Du Noüy — *Human* p.189
Edwards — *Useful* p.16
Flesch — *Unusual* p.7
Guideposts — *Faith* p.29-30
Liebman — *Peace* p.153-157
Seldes — *Great* p.8-10
Tanksley — *Friend* p.52
Woods — *Religious* p.11-12

AGREEABILITY. *See* **Cheerfulness**

AGREEMENT
See also **Cooperation**
Braude — *Source* #9-10, 16-17
Braude — *Stories* p.397-398
Clark — *Windows* p.60
Dirksen — *Quot.* #15
Evans — *This* p.128, 133-134
Flesch — *Unusual* p.7-8
Forbes — *Thoughts* p.43, 101, 196, 321, 373, 437, 470

Fox — *Make* p.145
Garland — *Subject* p.10
Grizer — *Wit* p.34-35
Kin — *Dictionary* p.8-9, 52, 54, 262, 277
Montapert — *Distilled* p.12-13
Prochnow — *Public* #156, 243, 912, 2311
Prochnow — *Success.* #362, 1067, 1530
Woods — *Religious* p.13

AGRICULTURE
See also **Country life; Earth; Farmers and farming; Nature;** etc.
Braude — *Source* #615-616
Braude — *Stories* p.147
Dirksen — *Quot.* #13, 1148
Edwards — *Useful* p.16-17, 728
Flesch — *Unusual* p.87
Forbes — *Thoughts* p.238, 250
Garland — *Subject* p.10-11
Harnsberger — *Mark* p.118-119
Harral — *Feature* p.73, 151-153
Henry — *5000* p.6, 87
Hooker — *Index* p.224-231
Hubbard — *Scrap* p. 21, 34, 39, 148
Lockridge — *World's* #3794, 3874
Lytle — *Leaves* p.49
New Topical p.8-9
Prochnow — *Public* #14, 230, 612, 799, 822, 1033, 1688, 3070-3071
Prochnow — *Speaker's* p.19-20, 123-127
Prochnow — *Success.* #1531-1532
Sagendorph — *Old* p.166-178
Woods — *Business.* p.1-2
Woods — *Content.* p.93, 97, 102, 106, 113, 116, 350
Woods — *Religious* p.13

AIMS. *See* **Ambition; Aspiration; Desire; Goals; Ideals and idealism; Purpose**

AIR
Woods — *Content.* p.200

AIR CONDITIONING
Harral — *Feature* p.73
Prochnow — *Public* #840
Prochnow — *Success.* #621, 1131, 1209

AIRPLANES. *See* **Aviation**

AIRSHIPS, PREDICTIONS OF
Fogg — *1000* #775, 1096

ALABAMA
Botkin — *Anecdotes* p.20, 79, 122, 192, 294, 300
Botkin — *Treasury* p.231, 434, 673, 682, 904

ALACRITY. *See* **Haste; Punctuality**

ALADDIN'S LAMP
Wallis — *Treasure* p.18

ALAMO, THE
Fogg — *1000* #680

ALARM. *See* **Fear**

ALASKA
Braude — *Source* #1691-1693

ALCHEMY
See also **Gold; Philosopher's Stone**
Edwards — *Useful* p.17

"ALCOHOLICS ANONYMOUS"
Bach — *Make* p.16-17
Curtis — *Human* p.151-153
How to Live p.357-362
Keys Happiness p.100-102
Lair — *Baby* p.13-14
Nichols — *New* p.224-225

ALCOHOLISM
Albert — *Stop* p.69, 187, 195
Alexander's Treasure. p.31
Asimov — *Treasury* #130, 132, 150, 165, 176, 301, 410, 593
Botkin — *Anecdotes* p.8, 13, 77, 82, 138, 196
Braude — *Speaker's* p.22-23, #389-400
Braude — *Stories* p.25-27; #506-509
Cerf — *Laugh* p.165-170
Copeland — *10,000* p.123-133
Curtis — *Human* p.151-153, 161-162
Daly — *Personality* p.111-115
Droke — *Christian* p.137-146
Edwards — *Useful* p.144-145
Flesch — *Unusual* p.8, 68
Flint — *Graham* p.10-11
Forbes — *Thoughts* p.339, 461, 472
Fuller — *Epigrams* p.93-96
Fuller — *Thesaurus* #36-55
Ginott — *Between* p.183-190
Grizer — *Wit* p.129-130
Guideposts — *Faith* p.69-73, 139-142
Hadfield — *Delights* p.65-66
Harnsberger — *Mark* p.92
Henry — *5000* p.68

Hovey — *Treasury* #327, 560, 671, 1668, 1693
How to Live p.357-362
Hunter — *Gems* p.5-6
Johnson — *Bedside* p.8-10
Kauffman — *For* p.17-18, 85-86
Kennedy — *Reader's* #281
Keys Happiness p.381-384
Kin — *Dictionary* p.26, 74, 133
Knight's Illus. p.10-15
Lair — *Baby* p.225-226
Lockridge — *World's* #1968, 1975, 2675-2676, 2683, 2688, 2698-2702, 2704, 2708-2709, 4967, 5634
Menninger — *Blue.* p.147-167
Modern Eloquence (14) p.151-157
Montapert — *Distilled* p.116-117
New Topical p.73
Peterson — *Art* p.393
Prochnow — *Public* #463, 892, 950, 956, 1469, 2365, 2538
Sagendorph — *Old* p.81-88
Schermerhorn — *1500* p.207-208
Seldes — *Great* p.296-298
Sheban — *Wisdom* no p.
Speaker's Desk See index p.299 (Drinking, Drunkards)
Unlimited Power p.135-138, 197-200
Walters — *How* p.88-89
Weisfeld — *Pulpit* p.4-5, 18, 28, 97
White — *Life* p.106-110
Woods — *Content.* p.128, 172, 177, 180
Woods — *Religious* p.13-14, 255

ALERTNESS
Braude — *Source* #77-79
Huxley — *You See* index p.283
Reader's — *Getting* p.18
Speaker's Desk #55

ALFALFA
Kohn — *Best* p.46

ALGAE
Du Noüy — *Human* p.58-60

"ALICE IN WONDERLAND"
Woods — *Wellsprings* p.64-66

ALGEBRA
Auden — *Certain* p.13
Prochnow — *Public* #177

ALIBIS. *See* **Excuses**

ALIENATION. *See* **Estrangement**

ALIMONY
Braude — *Source* #81-82
Harral — *Feature* p.73-74
Prochnow — *Public* #1614

ALIVENESS. *See* **Life and living; Vivacity**

ALL SAINTS' DAY
Lindbergh — *Unicorn* p.30-31

ALLAH
Woods — *Religious* p.14

ALLEGATIONS. *See* **Accusations**

ALLEGIANCE. *See* **Loyalty; Patriotism**

ALLEGORY. *See* **Mythology**

ALLERGY
Peale — *Guideposts* p.71-75
Prochnow — *Success.* #608

ALLIANCES. *See* **Treaties**

ALLIES. *See* **Friends and friendship**

ALLIGATORS
Asimov — *Treasury* #268
Prochnow — *Success.* #1101

ALLOWANCES
Prochnow — *Success.* #1221

ALMA MATER. *See* **Universities and colleges**

ALMANACS
Botkin — *Anecdotes* p.xxiii-xxiv, 134
Sagendorph — *Old* p.3-12
Words — *Inspir.* p.99-107

ALMIGHTY. *See* **God**

ALMS. *See* **Charity**

ALONENESS. *See* **Loneliness; Solitude**

ALOOFNESS. *See* **Reserve; Snobs and snobbery**

ALPHA
Prochnow — *Public* #2281, 2748

ALPHABETS. *See* **Language; Words**

ALPS
Auden — *Certain* p.15-16

ALTARS
Applegarth — *Heir.* p.142, 230
New Topical p.10-11
Wallis — *Treasure* p.209

ALTERNATIVE. *See* **Choice**

ALTRUISM. *See* **Benevolence; Charity; Generosity; Good;** etc.

ALUMNI. *See* **Universities and colleges, Alumni of**

AMALEKITES
New Topical p.11-12

AMATEURS. *See* **Beginners and beginnings**

AMAZEMENT. *See* **Surprise**

AMAZONS
Prochnow — *Public* #2284

AMBASSADORS
Asimov — *Treasury* #153
Edwards — *Useful* p.18
George — *Book* p.14-15, 72, 114
Kin — *Dictionary* p.9
Lockridge — *World's* #3750

AMBIDEXTROUSNESS
Prochnow — *Public* #847

AMBIGUITY. *See* **Obscurity**

AMBITION
See also **Aspiration; Enterprise; Goals; Purpose;** etc.
Book Proverbs p.114
Braude — *Source* #84-88
Braude — *Stories* p.28-29
Curtis — *Human* p.11
Dirksen — *Quot.* #513, 765-767, 1200-1205, 1851-1852, 2350
Edwards — *Useful* p.18-19
Evans — *Unto* p.57, 110, 128
Flesch — *Unusual* p.9
Flint — *Graham* p.11
Fogg — *1000 See* index p.877
Forbes — *Thoughts* p.38, 53, 94, 130, 142, 209, 260, 266, 346, 376, 389-390, 435, 443, 468, 496, 518
Fuller — *Thesaurus* #96-97
Garland — *Subject* p.13
Grizer — *Wit* p.36-37
Harral — *Feature* p.74
Henry — *5000* p.6-7
Hovey — *Treasury* p.27-28; #51-57, 530, 1704
Hubbard — *Scrap* p.23, 25, 27, 70, 112
Kennedy — *Reader's* #16
Kin — *Dictionary* p.9
Krishnamurti — *Think* p.14-15, 51-57, 138-139, 153-154
Liddle — *Thought I, II, III* p.67, 110
Lockridge — *World's See* index p.571
Lytle — *Leaves* p.188
Mandel — *Stories* p.7-8
Menninger — *Blue.* p.99-100
Modern Eloquence (14) p.282
Montapert — *Distilled* p.14-15
Morris — *1000 See* index p.427
New Topical p.12
Nichols — *New* p.12-13
Phillips — *Choice* p.90
Prochnow — *Public* #405, 1041, 1839, 1956, 1972, 1991, 2794-2798, 3943-3948
Prochnow — *Speaker's* p.20-21
Prochnow — *Success.* #1534-1538
Seldes — *Great* p.12-13
Sheban — *Wisdom* no p.
Speaker's Desk p.7-8, #513, 619, 964, 1079
Voss — *Quotations* p.21-23
Wallis — *Treasure* p.4
Woods — *Business.* p.2
Woods — *Content.* p.22, 35, 41, 43, 92, 113, 115-116
Woods — *Inspir.* p.50-83
Woods — *Religious* p.15-16
Woods — *Wellsprings* p.62-63
Words — *Inspir.* p.116

AMBIVALENCE
Asimov — *Treasury* #529

AMBROSIA
Prochnow — *Public* #2286

AMBULANCES
Harral — *Feature* p.74

"AMEN"
More Words p.7
Wallis — *Treasure* p.204

AMERICA
See also **Democracy; Government; Republic; United States**
Applegarth — *Heir.* p.58, 225
Barrows — *1000 See* index p.438
Braude — *Stories* p.29-31
Cerf — *Laugh* p.452-458
Copeland — *10,000* p.1-38
Droke — *Christian* p.13-20
Edwards — *Useful* p.19, 725
Evans — *Unto* p.55
Flesch — *Unusual* p.9
Flint — *Graham* p.11-12
Forbes — *Thoughts* p.51, 123, 134, 141, 177, 221, 230, 425; *See also* index p.540
Fuller — *Epigrams* p.20, 330

Grizer — *Wit* p.37-42
Harnsberger — *Mark* p.7-8
Henry — *5000* p.7-8
Hill — *Think* p.153
Hoffer — *Reflect.* p.34
Hovey — *Treasury* p.28-31; *See also* index p.293
Hubbard — *Scrap* p.96
Humes — *Instant* #63-81
Kauffman — *For* p.20-21
Kennedy — *Reader's* #17-25
Kin — *Dictionary* p.10
Liddle — *Thought I, II, III* p.22, 51, 65, 81, 87, 127, 130-131, 147, 189-190, 193
Liddle — *Thought IV* p.31, 46
Liddle — *Thought V* p.19, 21, 28, 30, 42, 45
Lindbergh — *Gift* p.26
Lockridge — *World's* #968, 989, 994, 2801, 4152, 4154, 4758
Montapert — *Distilled* p.15-16
New Joy p.70-74, 210-211
Nichols — *Third* p.249-250
Peterson — *Art* p.167, 326
Peterson — *New* p.10-11
Prochnow — *Public* #1881, 1918, 2799-2801, 4365
Prochnow — *Success.* #231, 763, 885
Seldes — *Great* p.13-19
Simpson — *Contemp.* p.91-103
Voss — *Quotations* p.23-25
Wallis — *Treasure* p.173, 176-178, 198
Wallis — *Words* p.93, 106, 222
Watson — *Light* p.287-318
Woods — *Business.* p.3-5
Woods — *Religious* p.16-17
Words — *Inspir.* p.139

, *Abundance in*
Kauffman — *For* p.23-24
Nichols — *Third* p.84-85
, *Discovery of*
Schermerhorn — *1500* p.113-114
, *Founding of*
Kohn — *Best* p.155-157
Myers — *Thunder* p.43-44
, *Future of*
Adams — *New* p.30
Bartlett — *Discovery* p.148-150
Dirksen — *Quot.* #520, 524
Forbes — *Thoughts* p.287
Hunter — *Gems* p.6-7
Kauffman — *For* p.18-19, 22-23
Nichols — *Third* p.225-251
Words — *Inspir.* p.131
, *Heritage of*
Words — *Inspir.* p.183-184, 195-196
, *Love for*
Keller — *Open* p.46
, *Power of*
Kauffman — *For* p.21
, *Prayer for*
Kohn — *Best* p.157-159
, *Presidents' quotations on*
New Joy p.70-74
, *Priorities of*
Kauffman — *For* p.21-22
, *Spiritual strength of*
Flint — *Graham* p.140
, *Way of life in*
Dirksen — *Quot.* #516, 526-527

AMERICAN CREED
Dirksen — *Quot.* #534

AMERICAN LEGION
Harral — *Feature* p.74
Seldes — *Great* p.28-29

AMERICAN REVOLUTION. *See* **United States — History — Revolution**

AMERICANS AND AMERICANISM
See also **Patriotism**
Asimov — *Treasury* #406
Braude — *Source* #89-95
Braude — *Speaker's* #24-25
Copeland — *1000* p.181-185
Dirksen — *Quot.* #34, 332, 358, 531-534, 567, 569, 573-574, 669, 768, 973, 1136, 1140, 2346
Flesch — *Unusual* p.9
Flint — *Graham* p.12
Forbes — *Thoughts See* index p.540
Franke — *Buckley* p.8
Grizer — *Wit* p.42-43
Hubbard — *Scrap* p.227
Keys Happiness p.25-30
Kin — *Dictionary* p.10
Kronenberger — *Animal* p.5-15
Lockridge — *World's* #3781, 5015, 5018
Modern Eloquence (14) p.283-285
New Joy p.96
Nichols — *Third* p.237-238
Prochnow — *Public* #1012, 1075, 1288, 1561, 1619, 4351, 4381
Prochnow — *Success.* #304
Seldes — *Great* p.19-28
Sheban — *Wisdom* no p.
Speaker's Desk #297, 337, 339, 398, 691, 725, 836, 971
Woods — *Business.* p.5-6
Woods — *Religious* p.17
Words — *Inspir.* p.70-71, 130

AMIABILITY. *See* **Cheerfulness**

AMINO ACIDS
Du Noüy — *Road* p.127-128

AMMONITES, THE
New Topical p.12-13

AMNESIA
Asimov — *Treasury* #42

AMOEBAS
Taylor — *With* p.123-133

AMORITES, THE
New Topical p.13

AMPHIBIANS
Du Noüy — *Human* p.73-77
Prochnow — *Public* #861

AMPLIFYING
Humes — *Instant* p.6-7, 13-14
Prochnow — *Public* #1347

AMUSEMENTS
See also **Hobbies; Pleasure; Recreation**; types of amusements
Braude — *Source* #96-97
Dirksen — *Quot.* #774, 1853
Edwards — *Useful* p.19-20, 139
Flesch — *Unusual* p.9-10
Forbes — *Thoughts* p.103, 312, 431
Harral — *Feature* p.74
Henry — *5000* p.8
Hubbard — *Scrap* p.31, 190
Lockridge — *World's* #2659, 5650, 5666
New Topical p.13
Prochnow — *Public* #542, 3949
Prochnow — *Success.* #1539
Woods — *Religious* p.17-18

ANACHRONISMS
Speaker's Desk #903

ANAGRAMS
Auden — *Certain* p.16-18

ANAKIM, THE
New Topical p.13-14

ANALOGY
See also **Comparison**
Edwards — *Useful* p.20-21
Flesch — *Unusual* p.10
Lytle — *Leaves* p.5, 22
Nizer — *Thinking* p.63

ANALYSIS
See also **Reason and reasoning; Self-analysis**
Curtis — *Practical* p.57, 209-210
Du Noüy — *Human* p.18-19, 22
Du Noüy — *Road* p.35, 41, 47-48, 55, 68, 95, 147
Flesch — *Unusual* p.10
Forbes — *Thoughts* p.180, 213, 461-462
Fox — *Make* p.140
Garland — *Subject* p.13
Lockridge — *World's* #3429

ANARCHY
See also **Radicals and radicalism; Revolution; Violence**
Curtis — *Practical* p.546
Edwards — *Useful* p.21, 725
Forbes — *Thoughts* p.285, 374
Henry — *5000* p.8
Humes — *Instant* #82-89
Ideas p.9-11
Lockridge — *World's* #4560
Seldes — *Great* p.29-32
Woods — *Religious* p.18

ANATOMY
Curtis — *Practical* p.54
Flesch — *Unusual* p.10
Prochnow — *Success.* #1294

ANCESTRY
See also **Genealogy; Heredity; Parents and parenthood**
Applegarth — *Heir.* p.108-111
Braude — *Source* #98-101
Braude — *Speaker's* #26-28
Dirksen — *Quot.* #775, 951, 1000, 1132, 2352
Edwards — *Useful* p.21-22
Flesch — *Unusual* p.10
Fogg — *1000* #184, 202
Forbes — *Thoughts* p.19, 349, 377, 383, 516
Fuller — *Epigrams* p.20-22
Harnsberger — *Mark* p.8
Henry — *5000* p.8-9
Hubbard — *Scrap* p.21, 165
Ideas p.11-13
Kin — *Dictionary* p.10
Liddle — *Thought I, II, III* p.88, 114, 118, 136, 157
Lockridge — *World's* #2747, 3226
Prochnow — *Public* #60, 540, 784, 1016, 2802, 4337
Prochnow — *Speaker's* p.21
Prochnow — *Success.* #786, 1540-1542
Schermerhorn — *1500* p.15
Seldes — *Great* p.33-34
Sheban — *Wisdom* no p.
Wallis — *Words* p.42

ANDERSEN, HANS CHRISTIAN
Unlimited Power p.277-280

ANCHORS
Prochnow — *Public* #642
Words Change p.30-33

ANCIENTS, THE
Adams — *New* p.103
Flesch — *Unusual* p.10
Lockridge — *World's* #3235
Prochnow — *Public* #1992

ANECDOTES
See also **Biography; Stories and story-telling**; under names of individuals and subjects
Botkin — *Treasury* p.176-177, 406-488
Edwards — *Useful* p.22-23
Flesch — *Unusual* p.10
Kronenberger — *Animal* p.17-23
Modern Eloquence (14) p.133-150, 239-269
Sagendorph — *Old* p.207-242

ANESTHESIA
Auden — *Certain* p.18-21
Harral — *Feature* p.74
Prochnow — *Public* #831

ANGELS
See also **Cherubim; Heaven**
Auden — *Certain* p.22
Botkin — *Anecdotes* p.192
Edwards — *Useful* p.23
Flesch — *Unusual* p.10
Garland — *Subject* p.14
Goudge — *Comfort* p.314-322
Harnsberger — *Mark* p.8
Hobe — *Tapestries* p.70
Kin — *Dictionary* p.10
Liddle — *Thought I, II, III* p.143
Lindbergh — *Unicorn* p.23-24
Lockridge — *World's* #3671, 5731
More Words p.7-8
New Topical p.14
Prochnow — *Public* #860
Prochnow — *Speaker's* p.22
Prochnow — *Success.* #924
Seldes — *Great* p.34
Sheen — *Content.* p.180-182
Taylor — *With* p.98
Woods — *Religious* p.18, 416-417

ANGELUS
New Joy p.61

ANGER
See also **Annoyances; Frustration; Quarrels; Resentment; Temper**
Albert — *Stop* p.82-88, 90-96, 101-102, 155-156, 198-199
Alexander's Treasure. p.42
Book Proverbs p.53, 80
Braude — *Source* #102-112
Braude — *Stories* p.32
Curtis — *Practical* p.114
Dirksen — *Quot.* #202, 838, 1206-1210, 1854-1855
Droke — *Christian* p.21-24
Edwards — *Useful* p.23-24, 520
Evans — *Faith* p.77
Evans — *Quote* p.153-162
Evans — *Thoughts I* p.56-57, 70-72, 87, 101-104, 141
Evans — *Thoughts II (Open Door)* p.27-28
Evans — *Thoughts III (Open Road)* p.29-30, 36, 66, 91-92, 99-100
Evans — *Thoughts IV* p.107-108
Flesch — *Unusual* p.10-11
Flint — *Graham* p.12-13
Forbes — *Thoughts* p.11, 25, 38, 75, 85-86, 158, 164, 168, 191, 199, 370, 383, 398, 477
Fox — *Make* p.59
Fuller — *Epigrams* p.22
Garland — *Subject* p.14, 153
Ginott — *Between* p.91-110
Grizer — *Wit* p.43-44
Harnsberger — *Mark* p.9
Henry — *5000* p.9
Hobe — *Tapestries* p.202
Holmes — *I've* p.58
Hovey — *Treasury* #31-32, 74-78
How to Live p.391-395, 478
Hubbard — *Scrap* p.78, 82, 164, 205
Huxley — *You See* index p.287
Johnson — *Bedside* p.76, 299
Kennedy — *Reader's* #26-31
Kin — *Dictionary* p.10-11, 102, 283
Krishnamurti — *Think* p.61, 90-91
Lair — *Baby* p.141, 172-173
Liddle — *Thought I, II, III* p.13-14 39, 66, 85, 89, 94, 137, 155
Liddle — *Thought IV* p.5, 16, 24-25, 36
Liebman — *Peace* p.91-98
Lockridge — *World's* #3077, 3345, 5798
Lytle — *Leaves* p.24, 121-122, 178
McCracken — *What* p.22-27
Mandel — *Stories* p.8-9
Montapert — *Distilled* p.16-17
New Topical p.14-15
Prochnow — *Public* #778, 2368, 2528, 2532, 2607, 2724, 3950-3954
Prochnow — *Speaker's* p.22
Prochnow — *Success.* #987, 1543
Seldes — *Great* p.34, 500
Speaker's Desk #451, 464
Woods — *Religious* p.18-19, 357

ANGLICAN CHURCH
Flesch — *Unusual* p.11

ANGUISH. *See* **Pain; Suffering**

ANIMAL "CRACKERS"
Fun Fare p.56, 71, 105, 237-238, 280

ANIMALS
Adams — *New* p.167, 286
Applegarth — *Heir.* p.19-25
Barrows — *1000* p.58, 112-113, 191, 287, 320, 339
Cerf — *Laugh* p.83-100
Dirksen — *Quot.* #2-3, 160, 1858, 1932-1933, 1977-1978, 2153, 2155-2156, 2245-2246
Du Noüy — *Human See* index p.279
Esteve — Experience p.47-48, 54, 56
Flesch — *Unusual* p.11
George — *Book See* index p.443
Goudge — Comfort p.71-83
Hadfield — *Delights* p.125-127
Harnsberger — *Mark* p.9
Harral — *Feature* p.75
Henry — *5000* p.9-10
Kennedy — *Reader's* #32-35
Kin — *Dictionary* p.11, 22
Kohn — *Pathways* p.85-86
Lockridge — *World's* #3178, 3412, 4385, 5251
New Topical p.26-27
Nichols — *Third* p.117-118
Prochnow — *Public* #151, 325, 646, 2577
Prochnow — *Speaker's* p.22-23
Prochnow — *Success.* #562, 592, 975, 1500
Seldes — *Great* p.35, 70-71
Speaker's Desk #90, 211, 216, 449, 505, 606, 658, 773, 1124, 1183
Wallis — *Treasure* p.163
Woods — *Religious* p.19

, *Comparisons with*
Botkin — *Treasury* p.273, 275
Webb — *Edge* p.36-38, 42

, *Conduct of*
Wheelis — *Moralist* p.10-11

, *Cruelty to*
Hubbard — *Scrap* p.20

, *Extinct species*
Kohn — *Through* p.271-273

, *Farm*
Sagendorph — *Old* p.142-150

, *Mythical*
Botkin — *Treasury* p.360, 557, 638-650

, *Names of*
Auden — *Certain* p.271-273
Kronenberger — *Animal* p.132-133

, *Sympathy with*
Adams — *New* p.220

, *Wild*
Kohn — *Pathways* p.85-86
Peterson — *Art* p.155

ANIMISM
Curtis — *Practical* p.47
Woods — *Religious* p.19

ANIMOSITY. *See* **Antagonism; Hatred; Opposition**

ANNIVERSARIES
Asimov — *Treasury* #557
Emmons — *Mature* p.145
Mandel — *Stories* p.8
Prochnow — *Public* #148, 870
Wallis — *Treasure* p.169

, *Golden*
Peterson — *Art* p.203

ANNOUNCEMENTS
Prochnow — *Public* #1020, 1047, 1067

ANNOYANCES
See also **Frustration**
Garland — *Subject* p.161
Kahn — *Lessons* p.143-144
Kin — *Dictionary* p.11
Nichols — *Third* p.45-46
Prochnow — *Public* #2291
Prochnow — *Success.* #1075
Speaker's Desk #293, 582
Wallis — *Treasure* p.225

ANNUITIES
Lockridge — *World's* #1775

ANOINTING
See also **Baptism**
New Topical p.15-16

ANONYMITY
Braude — *Speaker's* #29-30
Lockridge — *World's* #5538
Prochnow — *Public* #729
Woods — *Religious* p.19

ANSWERS
Flesch — *Unusual* p.11
Fun Fare p.6-7, 57, 101, 132, 136, 189, 228-229, 261, 265, 288, 294
Kin — *Dictionary* p.11
Montapert — *Distilled* p.17
Prochnow — *Public* #134, 445, 631, 1433, 1842, 2528
Weisfeld — *Pulpit* p.1-18

ANTAGONISM
See also **Hatred; Opposition**
Braude — *Source* #32, 113
Forbes — *Thoughts* p.107, 135, 246, 501
Grizer — *Wit* p.45
Hovey — *Treasury* #79-84, p.32-33
Unlimited Power p.146-147

ANTARCTICA
Nichols — *Third* p.53-54
Woods — *Content.* p.244

ANTELOPES
Applegarth — *Heir.* p.24

ANTHROPODS (insects)
Du Noüy — *Human* p.58, 67, 72, 74, 77-79, 97, 126, 155-158, 168

ANTHROPOLOGY
Curtis — *Practical* p.69
Hooker — *Index* p.179-186
Patterns for Living p.501-511

ANTHROPOMORPHISM
Sheban — *Wisdom* no p.
Woods — *Religious* p.19-20

ANTI-CHANCE
See also **God**
Du Noüy — *Human* p.38, 189-190, 202, 225, 247
Du Noüy — *Road* p.111n, 113, 126, 130, 139, 156, 183, 195, 221

ANTICHRIST
See also **"God is dead" movement**
New Topical p.26-27
Seldes — *Great* p.35-36
Woods — *Religious* p. 20

ANTICIPATION
See also **Expectation; Foresight and hindsight; Hope**
Book Proverbs p.109
Edwards — *Useful* p.24-25
Evans — *Unto* p.40
Grizer — *Wit* p.45
Montapert — *Distilled* p.17-18
Nizer — *Thinking* p.23, 28, 41, 142, 176, 197
Prochnow — *Public* #2803-2804
Pullar-Strecker — *Proverbs* #5
Wallis — *Words* p.97, 214

ANTICLIMAX
Asimov — *Treasury* #1-48

ANTI-INTELLECTUALISM
Franke — *Buckley* p.9
Woods — *Religious* p.21

ANTIQUES
Braude — *Source* #114-115
Braude — *Speaker's* #31-32
Braude — *Stories* p.32
Grizer — *Wit* p.45
Prochnow — *Public* #1304, 1506, 1620
Prochnow — *Success.* #1300
Schermerhorn — *1500* p.15

ANTIQUITY
See also **Age; Archaeology; History; Monuments; Mythology; Past; Ruin; Time; Tradition**
Applegarth — *Heir.* p.109
Curtis — *Practical* p.483
Dirksen — *Quot.* #1857
Edwards — *Useful* p.25
Flesch — *Unusual* p.11
George — *Book* p.18, 305
Hubbard — *Scrap* p.218
Ideas p.14-16
Kin — *Dictionary* p.11-12
Lockridge — *World's* #1775, 1987, 4530

ANTISEMITISM
Asimov — *Treasury* #313-314, 320-321, 357-358
Grizer — *Wit* p.46
Ideas p.16-17
Mandel — *Stories* p.10
Seldes — *Great* p.36-37
Woods — *Religious* p.21-22

ANTS
Applegarth — *Heir.* p.21
Botkin — *Anecdotes* p.94
Forbes — *Thoughts* p.384
Harnsberger — *Mark* p.9-12
Kin — *Dictionary* p.12
Prochnow — *Public* #624, 2518, 2559

ANVILS
Kin — *Dictionary* p.12

ANXIETY
See also **Care; Fear; Uncertainty; Worry**
Albert — *Stop* p.104-105, 115
Baillie — *Diary* #93
Blanton — *Faith* p.64-86
Dirksen — *Quot.* #1211-1214
Edwards — *Useful* p.25-26, 202
Evans — *Thoughts II (Open Door)* p.15
Flesch — *Unusual* p.11
Flint — *Graham* p.13
Forbes — *Thoughts* p.146, 162, 207, 240, 309, 400, 437, 459, 474
Garland — *Subject* p.15-16
Ginott — *Between* p.24-27, 169, 179-186, 236-237

Hulme — *Living* p.55-58, 65-68
Ideas p.13-14
Kin — *Dictionary* p.12, 73
Kohn — *Through* p.101-104
Lockridge — *World's* #5520
Mandel — *Stories* p.13
Menninger — *Blue.* p.24-32
Montapert — *Distilled* p.18-19
Peale — *Faith* p.55-79
Phillips — *Choice* p.107, 141
Prochnow — *Public* #285
Seldes — *Great* p.37
Tanksley — *Friend* p.14
Woods — *Religious* p.22

APARTHEID
Woods — *Religious* p.22-23

APARTMENTS
Schermerhorn — *1500* p.15-17

APATHY. *See* **Indifference**

APES
See also **Monkeys**
Applegarth — *Heir.* p.23
Dirksen — *Quot.* #1858
Kin — *Dictionary* p.12
Seldes — *Great* p.38-39

APHORISMS. *See* **Epigrams; Proverbs**

APOLLO
Prochnow — *Public* #2303, 2363
Schermerhorn — *1500* p.17

APOLOGUES
Botkin — *Anecdotes* p.xxv

APOLOGY
See also **Excuses; Humility; Regret; Self-defense**
Adams — *New* p.193
Braude — *Source* #116-117
Braude — *Stories* p.33
Dirksen — *Quot.* #1629
Edwards — *Useful* p.26
Evans — *Thoughts IV* p.49-50
Flesch — *Unusual* p.12
Grizer — *Wit* p.46
Henry — *5000* p.10
Prochnow — *Public* #2287
Prochnow — *Success.* #792
Schermerhorn — *1500* p.17-18
Wallis — *Treasure* p.114

APOSTATES
New Topical p.16

APOSTLES
Applegarth — *Heir.* p.249
More Words p.8-10
New Topical p.16-17
Woods — *Religious* p.23

APOSTLES' CREED
Woods — *Religious* p.23

APOTHEGMS. *See* **Epigrams; Epitaphs; Proverbs; Quotations**

APOTHEOSIS
Lytle — *Leaves* p.86

APPALACHIANS
Botkin — *Treasury* p.319, 326-327, 555

APPAREL. *See* **Clothes**

APPARITIONS
See also **Ghosts**
Lockridge — *World's* #80

APPEAL
Lytle — *Leaves* p.155

APPEARANCE
See also **Cleanliness; Clothes; Face; Neatness**; etc.
Book Proverbs p.79
Dirksen — *Quot.* #214, 1859
Edwards — *Useful* p.27, 350
Evans — *This* p.29-30, 104
Evans — *Thoughts IV* p.128-129
Evans — *Unto* p.90
Flesch — *Unusual* p.12
Forbes — *Thoughts* p.25, 196, 493
Fox — *Make* p.115
Grizer — *Wit* p.46-47
Henry — *5000* p.10
Holmes — *Design* p.103-104
Kennedy — *Reader's* #36
Kin — *Dictionary* p.12-13, 151, 228
Kohn — *Adventures* p.59-63
Kohn — *Touch* p.32-36
Liddle — *Thought I, II, III* p.105, 119, 187
Lockridge — *World's See* index p.571
Lytle — *Leaves* p.40, 112
Mandel — *Stories* p.12-13
Montapert — *Distilled* p.20
Prochnow — *Public* #504, 576, 863, 894, 2184, 2682, 3955-3957
Prochnow — *Speaker's* p.24
Prochnow — *Success.* #1544
Sheban — *Wisdom* no p.
Taylor — *With* p.140-143

APPETITE
See also **Desire; Diet; Eating; Food; Self-control; Temperance**

Dirksen — *Quot.* #1860, 2193-2194
Edwards — *Useful* p.27
Evans — *This* p.63
Evans — *Thoughts IV* p.113, 164
Forbes — *Thoughts* p.88, 146, 166, 387, 459
Henry — *5000* p.10
Kin — *Dictionary* p.13
Prochnow — *Public* #2805
Prochnow — *Speaker's* p.24
Prochnow — *Success.* #1544

"APPETIZERS"
Speaker's Desk #68

APPLAUSE
See also **Compliments; Flattery; Praise**
Dirksen — *Quot.* #1861
Edwards — *Useful* p.27-28
Forbes — *Thoughts* p.172, 258, 375
Henry — *5000* p.11
Hovey — *Treasury* #16, 1201
Kin — *Dictionary* p.13
Liddle — *Thought I, II, III* p.45, 151
Lockridge — *World's* #3196
Prochnow — *Public* #2806
Prochnow — *Success.* #1546
Speaker's Desk #49

APPLE TREES
Applegarth — *Heir.* p.22, 282-283, 289

APPLES
See also **Cider**
Applegarth — *Heir.* p.284
Asimov — *Treasury* #100
Botkin — *Anecdotes* p.225
Hobe — *Tapestries* p.18
Hubbard — *Scrap* p.92
Kin — *Dictionary* p.13
Prochnow — *Public* #20, 390, 611
Prochnow — *Speaker's* p.24
, *Golden*
Alexander's Treasure. p.47

APPLESEED, JOHNNY
Applegarth — *Heir.* p.289
Botkin — *Anecdotes* p.145, 225
Botkin — *Treasury* p.256, 261-270

APPLICATIONS
Forbes — *Thoughts* p.164, 173, 192, 316, 439
How to Live p.319-324
Montapert — *Distilled* p.20-21
Prochnow — *Public* #614, 805
Schermerhorn — *1500* p.18-19
Walters — *How* p.136-140

APPOINTMENTS
Montapert — *Distilled* p.21

APPRAISAL. *See* **Analysis**

APPRECIATION
See also **Admiration; Esteem; Gratitude; Self-esteem; Taste**
Auden — *Certain* p.211-214
Braude — *Source* #121-124
Braude — *Speaker's* #33-35
Edwards — *Useful* p.28, 111, 134
Emmons — *Mature* p.100
Evans — *This* p.145
Evans — *Thoughts I* p.15, 184-185, 219
Garland — *Subject* p.17
Grizer — *Wit* p.47
Hobe — *Tapestries* p.24-26
Hovey — *Treasury* #85-87, p.33
How to Live p.67
Kennedy — *Reader's* #37-39
Kin — *Dictionary* p.13
Kohn — *Best* p.77-82
Liddle — *Thought I, II, III* See index p.195
Liddle — *Thought IV* p.25, 40, 43-45
Lytle — *Leaves* p.5, 31, 42
Mandel — *Stories* p.10-12
Montapert — *Distilled* p.21
Peterson — *Art* p.185
Prochnow — *Public* #2807-2808
Prochnow — *Success.* #870, 1175
Speaker's Desk #130, 158, 651, 1024
Wallis — *Treasure* p.3
Welk — *Guide.* p.144-146
White — *Job* p.125, 127-130, 139-140, 144-145

APPREHENSION. *See* **Fear; Worry**

APPROBATION. *See* **Applause; Approval; Praise; Self-praise**

APPROPRIATENESS. *See* **Suitability**

APPROVAL
See also **Applause, Praise**
Evans — *Unto* p.7
Forbes — *Thoughts* p.12, 22
Ginott — *Between* p.31-33
Harnsberger — *Mark* p.12
Mandel — *Stories* p.10

APRIL
Hubbard — *Scrap* p.171
Kin — *Dictionary* p.14
New Joy p.229

APRIL FOOLS' DAY
Botkin — *Treasury* p.359
Weisfeld — *Pulpit* p.34

APTITUDE. *See* **Ability; Intelligence**

APTNESS. *See* **Suitability**

ARABIANS
Asimov — *Treasury* #372, 485, 587-588
Curtis — *Practical* p.223-228
Kohn — *Touch* p.144-145
Woods — *Wellsprings* p.32

ARABIC APOTHEGMS
Dirksen — *Quot.* #975

ARBOR DAY
Harral — *Feature* p.76

ARBORVITAE
Auden — *Certain* p.25-26

ARCADIA (paradise)
Ideas p.17-20

ARCHAEOLOGY
Dirksen — *Quot.* #359

ARCHBISHOPS
Weisfeld — *Pulpit* p.12, 30-31, 32, 40, 115-116
Woods — *Religious* p.24

ARCHERS
Prochnow — *Public* #1692

ARCHES
Kin — *Dictionary* p.13

ARCHETYPE
Seldes — *Great* p.39

ARCHITECTS AND ARCHITECTURE
See also **Builders and building; Houses**
Auden — *Certain* p.28-30
Braude — *Source* #125
Edwards — *Useful* p.28-29
Fogg — *1000* #337, 1073
Fuller — *Epigrams* p.23
Fuller — *Thesaurus* #1301-1302
George — *Book* p.1, 151
Harral — *Feature* p.76
Henry — *5000* p.11
Hooker — *Index* p.254-260
Hovey — *Treasury* #478, 480, 527, 985, 1008, 1246, 1595, 1831
Humes — *Instant* #97-102
Kennedy — *Reader's* #40-44
Lytle — *Leaves* p.29, 35
Montapert — *Distilled* p.22
Prochnow — *Public* #623, 3958, 4307
Prochnow — *Speaker's* p.24-25
Prochnow — *Success.* #1547-1548
Sheen — *Thoughts* p.49-51
Simpson — *Contemp.* p.445-450
Woods — *Religious* p.24

ARCTIC
See also **Antarctica**
Peale — *Guideposts* p.221-224
Reader's *20th* p.18-24

ARDOR. *See* **Enthusiasm**

ARGENTINA
Hovey — *Treasury* #941
Simpson — *Contemp.* p.123

ARGONAUTS
Prochnow — *Public* #2293

ARGUMENT
See also **Agitation; Controversy; Quarrels; Reason and reasoning**
Albert — *Stop* p.93-94
Book Proverbs p.112
Braude — *Source* #126-133
Dirksen — *Quot.* p.187, 776, 999, 1290-1292, 1818, 1862-1864
Edwards — *Useful* p.29, 97, 99, 725
Flesch — *Unusual* p.12, 48
Forbes — *Thoughts* p.169, 330, 333, 339, 356, 415-416, 450
Garland — *Subject* p.17-18
Grizer — *Wit* p.47-48
Guideposts — *Faith* p.167-171
Harnsberger — *Mark* p.12
Henry — *5000* p.11-12
Holmes — *Design* p.80-81
Hubbard — *Scrap* p.94
Johnson — *Bedside* p.126-127
Kin — *Dictionary* p.14
Krishnamurti — *Think* p.114
Liddle — *Thought I, II, III* p.52, 61, 66, 72, 145
Liddle — *Thought V* p.23, 45
Lockridge — *World's* #689, 906, 1677-1678, 2031, 4342-4343
Montapert — *Distilled* p.22-23
Prochnow — *Public* #523, 691, 1108, 1215, 1894, 1944, 2415, 2809, 3959-3961, 4364
Prochnow — *Speaker's* p.25-26
Prochnow — *Success.* #359, 902, 1549, 1644
Reader's — *Getting* p.54
Seldes — *Great* p.39
Sheban — *Wisdom* no p.
Wallis — *Words* p.67

ARISTOCRACY
See also **Gentility; Nobility;** etc.
Adams — *New* p.77
Asimov — *Treasury* #452-456
Curtis — *Practical* p.379-382
Dirksen — *Quot.* #536
Edwards — *Useful* p.29-30
Hubbard — *Scrap* p.60
Kennedy — *Reader's* #45
Kin — *Dictionary* p.14
Lockridge — *World's* #1691
Seldes — *Great* p.39-43

ARISTOTLE
Flesch — *Unusual* p.12
Lockridge — *World's* #3581
Woods — *Religious* p.24

ARITHMETIC. *See* **Mathematics**

ARIZONA
Botkin — *Anecdotes* p.105, 107
Botkin — *Treasury* p.64, 69, 131n, 183, 280, 319-321, 337-338, 365, 560

ARK OF THE COVENANT
Harnsberger — *Mark* p.12
New Topical p.17
Prochnow — *Public* #2296

ARKANSAS
Botkin — *Anecdotes* p.16, 22, 24, 34, 68, 83, 100, 102, 226, 273
Botkin — *Treasury See* index p.132, 146, 926

ARKANSAS RIVER
Botkin — *Anecdotes* p.68
Botkin — *Treasury* p.47, 557

ARMAGEDDON
Prochnow — *Public* #2297

ARMAMENTS
Evans — *Unto* p.14
Kin — *Dictionary* p.14
New Topical p.19-20
Seldes — *Great* p.43-45
Woods — *Religious* p.24-25

ARMED FORCES
Asimov — *Treasury* #26, 30, 32, 164, 271-272, 297, 369, 639-640
Braude — *Speaker's* #4-12, 44-79
Edwards — *Useful* p.30
Fuller — *Epigrams* p.331
Fuller — *Thesaurus* p.428-441
Harral — *Feature* p.76-77
Kin — *Dictionary* p.15
Lockridge — *World's* #3218
New Topical p.17-18
Prochnow — *Public See* index p.486
Prochnow — *Speaker's* p.26
Prochnow — *Success.* #852, 887, 907, 919, 1060
Schermerhorn — *1500* p.19-22
Seldes — *Great* p.45-46
Simpson — *Contemp.* p.64-69
Simpson — *'54* p.1, 103, 256
Weisfeld — *Pulpit* p.104-109

ARMISTICE
See also **Veterans Day**
Fuller — *Thesaurus* #2396-2397
Harral — *Feature* p.77
Seldes — *Great* p.45

ARMORIES
See also **Armaments**
Harral — *Feature* p.77

ARROGANCE
See also **Boasting; Boldness; Snobbery**
Book Proverbs p.57
Braude — *Source* #136-137
Curtis — *Practical* p.374-376
Edwards — *Useful* p.30, 51
Flint — *Graham* p.14
Forbes — *Thoughts* p.182, 244
Hobe — *Tapestries* p.182, 198, 226
Kin — *Dictionary* p.15, 133
Kohn — *Best* p.51
Lockridge — *World's* #1257
Prochnow — *Public* #4303

ARROWS
New Topical p.20
Wallis — *Treasure* p.101

ART AND ARTISTS
See also **Painters and painting; Sculpture and sculptors;** related subjects
Applegarth — *Heir.* p.27-31, 94
Asimov — *Treasury* #139, 315
Barrows — *1000 See* index p.439
Bennett — *How* p.76-82
Braude — *Source* #138-145
Braude — *Speaker's* #80-93
Cerf — *Laugh* p.241-244
Copeland — *10,000* p.38-42
Curtis — *Practical* p.432, 434, 441-442
Dirksen — *Quot.* #118, 603, 777-778, 1059, 1137, 2319
Edwards — *Useful* p.30-31, 725
Flesch — *Unusual* p.13-14
Fogg — *1000 See* index p.878
Forbes — *Thoughts* p.105; *See* index p.540
Fuller — *Epigrams* p.23-25

Fuller — *Thesaurus* p.220-229
Garland — *Subject* p.18-19
George — *Book See* index p.443
Ginott — *Between* p.52-53
Gold — *Letters* p.17-26
Grizer — *Wit* p.48-49
Hadfield — *Delights* p.203
Harral — *Feature* p.77-78
Henry — *5000* p.12
Hobe — *Tapestries* p.95
Hovey — *Treasury* #494, 914, 1116, 1153, 1579, 1597, 1659
How to Live p.164-168
Howell — *Better* p.21-24
Hubbard — *Scrap* p.19, 24, 30, 38, 41, 44, 72, 89, 120, 153, 176
Humes — *Instant* #103-127
Ideas p.20-21
Johnson — *Bedside* p.11, 23, 45, 47, 76, 136, 250, 313
Kennedy — *Reader's* #46-49
Keys Happiness p.457-461
Kin — *Dictionary* p.15
Lockridge — *World's* #4066, 5546-5547, 5726; *See* index p.571-572
Mandel — *Stories* p.13-14
Modern Eloquence (14) p.286-287
Montapert — *Distilled* p.23-24
Nizer — *Thinking* p.72-73, 98, 100-101, 178
Patterns for Living p.297-468
Peale — *Guideposts* p.118-121
Phillips — *Choice See* index p.424
Prochnow — *Public* p.28, #704, 1868, 1880, 1994, 2349, 2810-2811, 3962-3964, 4275
Prochnow — *Speaker's* p.27
Prochnow — *Success.* #747, 751, 781, 790, 909, 1157, 1345, 1503, 1550-1554
Schermerhorn — *1500* p.22-24
Seldes — *Great* p.46-57
Sheban — *Wisdom* no p.
Simpson — *Contemp.* p.339-467
Simpson — *'54* p.3, 106, 262
Speaker's Desk #33
Wallis — *Treasure* p.29
Wallis — *Words* p.71, 105, 154
White — *Job* p.113, 117-122, 123-125, 127, 129, 131, 136-137
Woods — *Content.* p.260-262
Woods — *Religious* p.25-27, 30-31

, *Abstract*
Saturday — *Advent.* p.252-262
, *Academic*
Ideas p.3-5
, and *Christianity*
Woods — *Religious* p.27-28
, and *government*
Franke — *Buckley* p.9-10
, *and life*
Saturday — *Advent.* p.148-160
, *and morality*
Woods — *Religious* p.28
, *and nature*
Woods — *Religious* p.28
, *and religion*
Baillie — *Diary* #271
Woods — *Religious* p.28-30
, *and science*
Flesch — *Unusual* p.13
, *and theology*
Woods — *Religious* p.30
, *Beauty in*
Curtis — *Daily* p.151-152
Krishnamurti — *Urgency* p.89-92
, *Definition of*
Flesch — *Unusual* p.12-13
, *Inconsistency of*
Nizer — *Thinking* p.101
, *Indifference of*
Curtis — *Practical* p.432
, *in industry*
Ideas p.21-22, 39
, *Mediocrity of*
Nizer — *Thinking* p.73
, *Modern*
Ideas p.252-253
, *Nationalism in*
Adams — *New* p.249-250
, *Prehistoric*
Adams — *New* p.353

ARTICHOKES
Flesch — *Unusual* p.14

ARTIFICIAL INSEMINATION
Woods — *Religious* p.30

ARTIFICIALITY
Flesch — *Unusual* p.14

ARTIFICE. *See* **Deception**

ARYANS
Seldes — *Great* p.57

ASCETICISM
See also **Self-denial**
Book Proverbs p.125
Curtis — *Practical* p.353
Edwards — *Useful* p.32
Flesch — *Unusual* p.14
Ideas p.39-41
White — *Job* p.27-32, 174-175
Woods — *Religious* p.31-32

ASH WEDNESDAY
Curtis — *Practical* p.513

ASHER, TRIBE OF
New Topical p.21

ASHES
Lytle — *Leaves* p.21

ASIA
See also names of countries
Franke — *Buckley* p.10
Hovey — *Treasury* #335, 1069, 1327
Prochnow — *Success.* #222, 248

ASKING. *See* **Questions**

ASP (or adder)
New Topical p.21

ASPHYXIATION
Forbes — *Thoughts* p.163, 337

ASPIRATION
See also **Ambition; Desire; Ideals and idealism; Purpose**
Alexander's Treasure. p.162
Book Proverbs p.114
Detherage — *Sunrise* p.31-38, 104, 128
Dirksen — *Quot.* p.1215-1217, 2350
Edwards — *Useful* p.32
Flesch — *Unusual* p.15
Forbes — *Thoughts* p.219, 237, 250, 341, 377, 409, 487
Giniger — *Compact* p.37-90
Hovey — *Treasury* p.33-34, #88-89, 355, 482, 978
Howell — *Better* p.25-28
Hubbard — *Scrap* p.62
Kin — *Dictionary* p.15
Lockridge — *World's* #5075
Lytle — *Leaves* p.5, 35, 41
Montapert — *Distilled* p.24-25
Prochnow — *Public* #3965-3967
Voss — *Quotations* p.25-27
Wallis — *Treasure* p.15-20, 84
Wallis — *Words* p.122, 142, 167
White — *Job* p.118-119
Woods — *Inspir.* p.188-222
Woods — *Religious* p.32-33

ASPIRIN
Prochnow — *Public* #928

ASSASSINATION
Alexander's Treasure. p.168-174
Asimov — *Treasury* #283
Dirksen — *Quot.* #34
Franke — *Buckley* p.11, 145-146
Kin — *Dictionary* p.16
Seldes — *Great* p.57

ASSEMBLY. *See* **Meetings**

ASSENT. *See* **Agreement**

ASSERTIONS. *See* **Statements**

ASSES
Kin — *Dictionary* p.16
Lockridge — *World's* #4069
New Topical p.21-22

ASSETS
See also **Possessions; Wealth**
Forbes — *Thoughts* p.16, 147, 396, 406, 423
Grizer — *Wit* p.49
Harnsberger — *Mark* p.13-14
Montapert — *Distilled* p.25

ASSIMILATION
Dirksen — *Quot.* #836
Lockridge — *World's* #4881
Schermerhorn — *1500* p.24
Woods — *Religious* p.33

ASSISTANCE. *See* **Help**

ASSOCIATES
See also **Acquaintance; Business; Companionship; Society**
Edwards — *Useful* p.33
Henry — *5000* p.13
Kin — *Dictionary* p.16
Liddle — *Thought I, II, III* p.12, 32, 40, 44-45, 98, 106, 125, 170, 190
Montapert — *Distilled* p.25-26
Prochnow — *Success.* #1555
Seldes — *Great* p.57-59

ASSOCIATION
Edwards — *Useful* p.33-34
Evans — *This* p.5-6
Evans — *Unto* p.70
Forbes — *Thoughts* p.99, 237, 239, 275, 304, 351, 418
Grizer — *Wit* p.49
Kin — *Dictionary* p.16-17
Mandel — *Stories* p.14
Prochnow — *Success.* #202

ASSOCIATIONS. *See* **Organizations**

ASSUMPTION
Prochnow — *Public* #2316
Speaker's Desk See index p.297

ASSURANCE
See also **Confidence; Self-confidence**
Baillie — *Diary* #98
Detherage — *Sunrise* p.125-130, 155, 193
Flint — *Graham* p.14
Forbes — *Thoughts* p.161, 179

Garland — *Subject* p.19-20
Halverson — *Perspective* p.63
Holmes — *Design* p.63
Knight's Illus. p.15-17
Knight's Treas. p.1-5
Kohn — *Pathways* p.73-77
Mandel — *Stories* p.15
New Topical p.22

ASSYRIA
New Topical p.22-23

ASTONISHMENT. *See* **Surprise; Wonder**

ASTROLOGY
Curtis — *Practical* p.220
Flesch — *Unusual* p.15
George — *Book* p.24, 291
Humes — *Instant* p.53-54
Kauffman — *For* p.26-28
Woods — *Religious* p.33-34

ASTRONAUTS
Asimov — *Treasury* #267
Dirksen — *Quot.* #55
Guideposts — *Faith* p.110-115, 271-276, 444-447
Prochnow — *Public* #1173
Prochnow — *Success.* #573
Unlimited Power p.121-126
, *Prayer for*
Words — *Inspir. See* Preface

ASTRONOMY
See also **Stars; Sun;** etc.
Asimov — *Treasury* #79
Bartlett — *Discovery* p.51-54, 96
Curtis — *Practical* p.221, 245
Du Noüy — *Human* p.13-14, 32n, 198
Edwards — *Useful* p.34
Fogg — *1000* #125, 134
Harral — *Feature* p.78
Hobe — *Tapestries* p.92
Hooker — *Index* p.144-151
Prochnow — *Public* #270
Schermerhorn — *1500* p.24
Woods — *Religious* p.34

ASTUTENESS. *See* **Appreciation**

ASYLUMS. *See* **Mental hospitals**

ATHANASIAN CREED (subject)
Woods — *Religious* p.34

ATHEISM
See also **Agnosticism; "God is dead" movement; Unbelief**
Asimov — *Treasury* #492, 494-495
Bach — *Make* p.151-152
Baillie — *Diary* #159
Book Proverbs p.121
Braude — *Source* #151-155
Dirksen — *Quot.* #328, 779-780, 1686, 1696, 1865
Droke — *Christian* p.24-26
Du Noüy — *Human* p.40, 132, 189
Du Noüy — *Road* p.19-20
Edwards — *Useful* p.34-35
Flesch — *Unusual* p.15
Flint — *Graham* p.14
Forbes — *Thoughts* p.7, 488
Fuller — *Epigrams* p.25-26
Fuller — *Thesaurus* #1651-1659
Henry — *5000* p.13
Hovey — *Treasury* #147
Ideas p.41-43
Johnson — *Bedside* p.213
Kennedy — *Reader's* #50-52
Kin — *Dictionary* p.17
Knight's Illus. p.17-21
Knight's Treas. p.5-9
Kohn — *Through* p.53-57
Liddle — *Thought I, II, III* p.122, 134
Liddle — *Thought V* p.7, 33
Lockridge — *World's* #1707, 2912, 4611, 5231
Nizer — *Thinking* p.126
Peale — *Courage* p.216-217
Phillips — *Choice* p.399
Prochnow — *Public* #192, 3968-3969
Prochnow — *Success.* #1556-1558
Seldes — *Great* p.59-62, 509-510
Sheen — *Content.* p.163-167
Voss — *Quotations* p.28-30
Webb — *Edge* p.83-86
Weisfeld — *Pulpit* p.12, 60
Woods — *Religious* p.34-39, 394-395, 484-485, 493

ATHENS
Asimov — *Treasury* #126, 199
Curtis — *Practical* p.291-292, 376
Flesch — *Unusual* p.15

ATHLETES
Hovey — *Treasury* #16, 469, 1308, 1310, 1506, 1612, 1698
Prochnow — *Public* #1165
Prochnow — *Success.* #1003
, *in politics*
Franke — *Buckley* p.11
, *Olympic champion*
Peale — *Guideposts* p.169-173

ATHLETICS
See also **Exercise; Gymnastics; Recreation; Sports;** types of athletics
Humes — *Instant* #1265-1267

Prochnow — *Speaker's* p.28
Speaker's Desk #60, 75, 110

ATLANTIS
Ideas p.43-44

ATMOSPHERE
See also **Air**
Forbes — *Thoughts* p.372, 501
Rau — *Act* p.65-73

ATOMIC AGE
Braude — *Source* #156
Droke — *Christian* p.26-31
Flint — *Graham* p.14
Forbes — *Thoughts* p.83, 166
Grizer — *Wit* p.50

ATOMIC BOMB
Asimov — *Treasury* #471-472
Dirksen — *Quot.* #117, 571
Du Noüy — *Human* p.200, 205
Forbes — *Thoughts* p.41
Woods — *Religious* p.39-40

ATOMS
See also **Nuclear power and warfare**
Du Noüy — *Human* p.16, 18-19, 21-22, 28, 33, 41, 46, 56-59, 85
Du Noüy — *Road See* index p.241
Flesch — *Unusual* p.15
Forbes — *Thoughts* p.279, 312
Holmes — *Design* p.4, 7-8, 10-12, 54, 61, 89, 100
Hovey — *Treasury* p.34-36; #14, 90-96, 857, 973, 1290, 1449, 1596, 1700, 1731, 1792
Kennedy — *Reader's* #53-54
Seldes — *Great* p.62-64

ATONEMENT
See also **Repentance**
Evans — *This* p.82-83
Flint — *Graham* p.14-15
Garland — *Subject* p.20-21
Hovey — *Treasury* #717
More Words p.11-12
New Topical p.23-24
Phillips — *Choice* p.364
Seldes — *Great* p.1-2
Woods — *Religious* p.40

ATROCITIES. *See* **Cruelty; War**

ATROPHY
Kohn — *Pathways* p.86
Mandel — *Stories* p.15

ATTAINMENT. *See* **Achievement; Acquisition**

ATTEMPT. *See* **Effort**

ATTENDANCE. *See* **Presence**

ATTENTION
See also **Awareness; Consideration; Diligence; Observation; Vigilance**
Curtis — *Human* p.12-13
Edwards — *Useful* p.35
Evans — *Thoughts III (Open Road)* p.135-137
Flesch — *Unusual* p.15
Forbes — *Thoughts* p.354, 496
How to Live p.35
Kohn — *Adventures* p.14-17
Kohn — *Touch* p.61-64
Krishnamurti — *Think* p.148-149
Mandel — *Stories* p.15-16
Modern Eloquence (14) p.288
Montapert — *Distilled* p.26
Prochnow — *Public* #527, 761, 1994
Prochnow — *Success.* #839
Rau — *Act* p.18-27
Speaker's Desk #170, 854
White — *Job* p.107-108, 140

ATTICS
Prochnow — *Success.* #696

ATTIRE. *See* **Clothes**

ATTITUDE
See also **Action; Opinion; Position**
Albert — *Stop* p.28-33
Curtis — *Daily* p.186-191
Curtis — *Golden* p.144-145
Curtis — *Human* p.21-22, 30, 190-192, 199
Emmons — *Mature* p.27
Evans — *Faith* p.49, 51, 77-78, 106, 131, 173
Evans — *Quote* p.153-162
Evans — *This* p.103-104
Evans — *Thoughts I* p.58, 144
Evans — *Thoughts III (Open Road)* p.21, 55-61, 78, 95, 105, 141, 158, 199
Evans — *Thoughts IV* p.14-15, 23, 27, 77
Forbes — *Thoughts* p.55, 143
Grizer — *Wit* p.51
Holmes — *Design* p.198-199, 204
How to Live p.280-302
Lockridge — *World's* #1067
Lytle — *Leaves* p.185
Manchee — *Secret* p.128-131
Mandel — *Stories* p.16
Montapert — *Distilled* p. 26-27
Peterson — *Art* p.293
Phillips — *Choice* p.17, 81, 173, 263

Prochnow — *Public* #4312
Prochnow — *Success.* #609
Zobell — *Speaker's* p.14-15

ATTORNEYS. *See* **Lawyers**

ATTRACTION. *See* **Charm; Personality**

AUCTIONS
Braude — *Stories* p.34
Flesch — *Unusual* p.16
Fun Fare p.172-173
Harral — *Feature* p.79
Kin — *Dictionary* p.17
Prochnow — *Success.* #1560

AUDACITY. *See* **Boldness**

AUDIENCE
Braude — *Speaker's* #94-96
Fuller — *Thesaurus* #1436-1441
Harnsberger — *Mark* p.14-15
Hovey — *Treasury* #16, 75, 102-103, 484, 580
Nizer — *Thinking* p.20, 22, 24, 29, 34, 57, 70, 76, 80, 100, 113, 145
Prochnow — *Public* #8, 601, 668, 785, 1442
Speaker's Desk #55, 300, 1001, 1007, 1019
Welk — *Guide.* p.137-140

AUGUSTINE, SAINT
Baillie — *Diary* #129, 191
Phillips — *Choice* p.41, 186, 305, 385
Woods — *Religious* p.40

AUNTS
Nichols — *Third* p.23-25

AUSTERITY. *See* **Gravity**

AUSTRALIA
Kronenberger — *Animal* p.89-90

AUSTRIA
Lockridge — *World's* #4110
Simpson — *Contemp.* p.123

AUTHENTICITY
See also **Truth**
Book Proverbs p.107
Ginott — *Between* p.59, 73
Prochnow — *Public* #2401
Wheelis — *Moralist* p.39-41

AUTHORITY
See also **Discipline; Executives; Government; Power;** etc.
Adams — *New* p.347
Baillie — *Diary* #92
Dirksen — *Quot.* #776
Edwards — *Useful* p.35
Evans — *Unto* p.143
Fogg — *1000* #384
Forbes — *Thoughts* p.25, 36, 71, 124, 150, 374
Ginott — *Between* p.87-88
Henry — *5000* p.13
Kin — *Dictionary* p.17
Lockridge — *World's* #929, 1419, 1728, 3759, 3801, 3872, 3895, 4146, 5856
More Words p.12-13
Prochnow — *Public* #2386
Prochnow — *Success.* #1561
Seldes — *Great* p.64-67
Sheban — *Wisdom* no p.
Welk — *Guide.* p.67-69
Wheelis — *Moralist* p.70-72, 96
Woods — *Religious* p.41-42

AUTHORS
See also **Books and reading; Writing and writers;** types of authors, e.g. **Poets**
Alexander's Treasure p.297
Auden — *Certain* p.371-373
Cerf — *Laugh* p.275-286
Curtis — *Practical* p.393, 481
Dirksen — *Quot.* p.329, 1138, 2311
Flesch — *Unusual* p.16
Fuller — *Thesaurus* #1166-1219
Fun Fare p. 16, 99, 140, 283
George — *Book* p.443
Harnsberger — *Mark* p.15
Harral — *Feature* p.79
Kin — *Dictionary* p.17
Lockridge — *World's See* index p.572
Lytle — *Leaves* p.51, 160
Montapert — *Distilled* p.27-28
Nichols — *New* p.199-202
Prochnow — *Public* #72, 125, 414, 726, 890, 4392
Prochnow — *Speaker's* p.31
Schermerhorn — *1500* p.26-27
Simpson — *Contemp.* p.339-377
Simpson — *'54* p.6, 109, 264
Walters — *How* p.16
Woods — *Religious* p.41

AUTOBIOGRAPHY
Flesch — *Unusual* p.16
Lockridge — *World's* #5024
Wallis — *Words* p.154

AUTOCRACY. *See* **Dictatorship**

AUTOGRAPHS
Braude — *Stories* p.34
Harral — *Feature* p.79
Prochnow — *Public* #721, 738

Prochnow — *Speaker's* p.32
Walters — *How* p.175-176

AUTOMATION
See also **Machines and machinery**
Braude — *Sources* #168-174
Grizer — *Wit* p.51-52
Harral — *Feature* p.79
Kauffman — *For* p.30-31
Montapert — *Distilled* p.28
Prochnow — *Public* #1606
Prochnow — *Success.* #208
Seldes — *Great* p.67

AUTOMOBILES
See also **Drivers and driving**; etc.
Bartlett — *Discovery* p.20-21
Botkin — *Anecdotes* p.31, 33, 48, 90, 103, 112
Braude — *Source* #175-176
Braude — *Speaker's* #103-105
Braude — *Stories* p.35
Copeland — *10,000* p.77-91
Evans — *Unto* p.114
Forbes — *Thoughts* p.414, 502
Fuller — *Epigrams* p.26
Fuller — *Thesaurus* #1811
Grizer — *Wit* p.52-53
Harral — *Feature* p.80-81
Prochnow — *Public See* index p.487; #362
Prochnow — *Speaker's* p.32-33
Prochnow — *Success. See* index p.486
Schermerhorn p.27-29
, *Accidents with*
Lockridge — *World's* p.2743
Reader's — *20th* p.65-70
Unlimited Power p.24-27, 38-42, 144-147
, *Dealers for*
Manchee — *Secret* p.199
, *Factories for*
Botkin — *Treasury* p.540-542
, *Prediction of*
Fogg — *1000* #775

AUTOSUGGESTION
Albert — *Stop* p.73-74, 202-203
Hill — *Think* p.72-81
Montapert — *Distilled* p.28-29
Phillips — *Choice* p.159

AUTUMN
Alexander's Treasure. p.39, 74, 93
Auden — *Certain* p.339-341
Dirksen — *Quot.* #86, 88
Edwards — *Useful* p.36-37
Goudge — *Comfort* p.47-52
Hadfield — *Love* p.181-217
Henry — *5000* p.14
Hobe — *Tapestries* p.56-58
Hubbard — *Scrap* p.193
Kohn — *Adventures* p.129-132
Kohn — *Best* p.12-23
Kohn — *Thoughts* p.99-127
Lindbergh — *Unicorn* p.40-41
New Joy p.106
Patterns for Living p.12-14
Peterson — *Art* p.315
Prochnow — *Public* #1990, 1995
Prochnow — *Speaker's* p.121
Prochnow — *Success.* #247, 390, 1360, 1564
Sagendorph — *Old* p.32-35
Wallis — *Treasure* p.12, 184
Wallis — *Words* p.172
Woods — *Content.* p.64, 165, 216-217

"AVANT-GARDE"
Hoffer — *Reflect.* p.62-63
Ideas p.44-46

AVARICE
See also **Greed; Misers; Money;** etc.
Dirksen — *Quot.* #449, 1866
Edwards — *Useful* p.37
Flesch — *Unusual* p.16
Flint — *Graham* p.15
Fogg — *1000* #23, 76, 84, 472, 505, 682, 825
Forbes — *Thoughts* p.36, 38, 244, 340
Henry — *5000* p.14
Kin — *Dictionary* p.17
Lockridge — *World's* #518-519, 2002-2006, 3462, 4192
Lytle — *Leaves* p.25
McCracken — *What* p.34-38
Prochnow — *Public* #1985
Seldes — *Great* p.67-68
Woods — *Religious* p.42

AVENGING. *See* **Revenge**

AVERAGE
Evans — *This* p.22-23
Evans — *Thoughts III (Open Road)* p.159
Flesch — *Universal* p.16
Forbes — *Thoughts* p.74, 122, 235, 290, 306, 380, 426, 435, 496, 510
Hovey — *Treasury* p.37; #104-107
Lytle — *Leaves* p.74
Prochnow — *Speaker's* p.35

AVIATION
Asimov — *Treasury* #131
Bartlett — *Discovery* p.9-10
Botkin — *Anecdotes* p.80, 273
Cerf — *Laugh* p.439-441
Edwards — *Useful* p.37
Flesch — *Unusual* p.91

Fogg — *1000* #636, 775, 1000, 1061, 1096
Franke — *Buckley* p.3-4
Fun Fare p.14-15, 120-122
Hadfield — *Delights* p.116
Harral — *Feature* p.81-83
Henry — *5000* p.14-15
Keys Happiness p.476
Peale — *Guideposts* p.133-141
Peterson — *Art* p.235
Prochnow — *Public* #600, 2351
Prochnow — *Speaker's* p.20
Prochnow — *Success.* #165, 442, 743, 965, 1045, 1565-1566
Schermerhorn — *1500* p.29-31
Seldes — *Great* p.68
Webb — *Edge* p.45-46

, *Accidents in*
Guideposts — *Faith* p.306-309
Unlimited Power p.10-14
, *Pilots in*
Halverson — *Perspective* p.96

AVOCATIONS
See also **Amusements; Hobbies**
Forbes — *Thoughts* p.108, 388
Wallis — *Words* p.228

AVOIDANCE
Pullar-Strecker — *Proverbs* #5-7
White — *Job* p.31, 57, 68, 72-73, 109-111

AWAKENING
Ginott — *Between* p.57-58, 70-71
Hadfield — *Delights* p.13-32
Irion — *Yes* p.98-100
Nichols — *New* p.165-166, 231-232
Prochnow — *Public* #589
Tanksley — *Friend* p.79
Wallis — *Words* p.62, 224

AWARENESS
See also **Appreciation; Empathy;** etc.
Emmons — *Mature* p.9-17
Flesch — *Unusual* p.42
Flint — *Graham* p.15
Hobe — *Tapestries* p.141
How to Live p.164-173
Huxley — *You See* index p.283
Jones — *If* p.45-54
Kennedy — *Reader's* #55-57
Kohn — *Pathways* p.45-48
Kohn — *Touch* p.75-78
Krishnamurti — *Think* p.178-180
Krishnamurti — *Urgency* p.1-5
Montapert — *Distilled* p.29
Peterson — *Art* p.142
Peterson — *Twenty* p.18-19
Phillips — *Choice* p.6, 40, 100, 135, 276, 314
Wallis — *Treasure* p.21-26, 144
Wallis — *Words* p.154
Welk — *Guide.* p.167-168
Wheelis — *Moralist* p.11, 36, 42-43, 81, 83, 98, 109, 127-132
White — *Job* p.78-82, 109, 117, 161-164

AWE. *See* **Reverence; Wonder**

AWKWARDNESS
See also **Bashfulness**
Edwards — *Useful* p.37-38
Kin — *Dictionary* p.18
Prochnow — *Public* #973

AXES
Botkin — *Anecdotes* p.179, 280
Harnsberger — *Mark* p.16
Kin — *Dictionary* p.18
Lockridge — *World's* #5220
Prochnow — *Public* #2593
Woods — *Wellsprings* p.59-60

AXIOMS. *See* **Epigrams; Proverbs; Quotations**

B

BABBLERS. *See* **Bores and boredom; Gossip**

BABIES
See also **Birth**
Alexander's Treasure. p.98
Cerf — *Laugh* p.337-339
Copeland — *10,000* p.283-288
Dirksen — *Quot.* #1866
Edwards — *Useful* p.38, 288
Flesch — *Unusual* p.16
Fuller — *Epigrams* p.331
Fuller — *Thesaurus* #956-962
Fun Fare p.116-118, 298-299
Hadfield — *Delights* p.24-27
Hadfield — *Love* p.18, 24
Harnsberger — *Mark* p.17-18
Harral — *Feature* p.83-84
Henry — *5000* p.15, 133
Hobe — *Tapestries* p.167
Kin — *Dictionary* p.19
Prochnow — *Public* #183-184, 212, 217, 465, 643, 804, 972, 1064, 2434, 2812

Prochnow — *Speaker's* p.35-36
Prochnow — *Success.* #892, 1567
Schermerhorn — *1500* p.32, 34
Seaburg — *Great* p.178, 192-193, 195, 201, 210, 212, 242, 272, 277, 328, 341, 396
Wallis — *Treasure* p.51, 53, 56
Wallis — *Words* p.25, 113

, *Deformed*
Unlimited Power p.148-152

BABYLON
Curtis — *Practical* p.220
New Topical p.24-25

BABYSITTING
Prochnow — *Public* #23
Prochnow — *Success.* #711, 933, 1134

BACCALAUREATE
Dirksen — *Quot.* #238
Nizer — *Thinking* p.198-204
Prochnow — *Success.* #58, 261

BACCHUS
Kin — *Dictionary* p.19

BACHELORS
Braude — *Speaker's* #13-16, 106-108
Braude — *Stories* p.35-36
Copeland — *10,000* p.281-282
Edwards — *Useful* p.38
Fuller — *Epigrams* p.331-332
Harral — *Feature* p.84
Henry — *5000* p.15
Kin — *Dictionary* p.19
Lockridge — *World's* #874, 5171
Prochnow — *Public* #213, 450, 454, 747, 763, 1622
Prochnow — *Speaker's* p.36
Prochnow — *Success.* #1568-1569
Woods — *Content.* p.159
Woods — *Religious* p.43

"BACKSLIDING"
Dirksen — *Quot.* #1218-1219
Flesch — *Unusual* p.16
New Topical p.25

BACKWOODSMEN
Botkin — *Treasury* p.2-3, 51-52, 272-273, 321-323, 358-361, 429-434, 491

BACON
Kin — *Dictionary* p.19

BACTERIAL WARFARE
Kauffman — *For* p.36

BAGELS
Dirksen — *Quot.* #229

BAGPIPES
Asimov — *Treasury* #412
Schermerhorn — *1500* p.35

BAGS
Kin — *Dictionary* p.20

BAIT
Kin — *Dictionary* p.20

BAKERS
Botkin — *Anecdotes* p.260
Manchee — *Secret* p.199-200

BALANCE
See also **Moderation; Self-control**
Clark — *Windows* p.106, 178
Curtis — *Human* p.51-66
Evans — *Faith* p.27, 32-34, 109, 163-164
Evans — *Thoughts II (Open Door)* p.57-58, 176
Evans — *Thoughts IV* p.54-55, 75, 80, 159
Evans — *Unto* p.64, 84
Flesch — *Unusual* p.17
Forbes — *Thoughts* p.501
Halverson — *Perspective* p.107
Kin — *Dictionary* p.20
Kohn — *Thoughts* p.67-71
Mandel — *Stories* p.16-17
Montapert — *Distilled* p.29-30
Prochnow — *Public* #106
Wilcox — *Heart* p.91-92

BALDNESS
Braude — *Speaker's* #109-111
Braude — *Stories* p.36
Kin — *Dictionary* p.20
Lockridge — *World's* #5069, 5682
Prochnow — *Public* #2074
Prochnow — *Success.* #991, 1093
Schermerhorn — *1500* p.35-36
Weisfeld — *Pulpit* p.38

BALLADS
See also **Songs**
Botkin — *Treasury* p.818-843
Edwards — *Useful* p.38

BALLET
Nizer — *Thinking* p.74

BALLOONS
Fogg — *1000* #636
Hadfield — *Delights* p.115
Harral — *Feature* p.84

"BAMBOOZLERS"
Safian — *More* p.11-16

BANDS
Auden — *Certain* p.27-28
Harral — *Feature* p.84
Schermerhorn — *1500* p.36-37

BANJO
Kin — *Dictionary* p.20

BANKERS AND BANKING
Botkin — *Anecdotes* p.87, 168
Braude — *Source* #177-178
Braude — *Speaker's* #112-119
Braude — *Stories* p.36
Copeland — *10,000* p.441-443
Curtis — *Practical* #331-332
Flesch — *Unusual* p.17
Fuller — *Thesaurus* #2151-2158
Harral — *Feature* p.84-86
Henry — *5000* p.16
Lockridge — *World's* #3763
Manchee — *Secret* p.200-201
Prochnow — *Public* #237, 548, 707, 846, 947, 1835
Prochnow — *Speaker's* p.36-37
Prochnow — *Success.* #195, 580, 840
Schermerhorn — *1500* p.37-39
Seldes — *Great* p.68-69
Unlimited Power p.135-138
Woods — *Business.* p.6-7
Woods — *Wellsprings* p.54-55

BANKRUPTCY
Baillie — *Diary* #352
Evans — *Unto* p.19
Forbes — *Thoughts* p.197-395
Fuller — *Thesaurus* #2196-2198
Grizer — *Wit* p.53
Prochnow — *Public* #262, 1753
Prochnow — *Speaker's* p.37-38

BANQUETS. *See* **Dinners**

BAPTISM
Day — *Meditations* p.10-11
Hovey — *Treasury* p.37; #108-109, 311, 484, 557, 809, 1328
Lockridge — *World's* #5169
More Words p.14-15
New Topical p.25-26
Schermerhorn — *1500* p.39
Woods — *Religious* p.43-44

BAPTISTS
Botkin — *Anecdotes* p.24, 121, 124
Botkin — *Treasury* p.424-425, 427
Guideposts — *Faith* p.51-52
Simpson — *Contemp.* p.212-213
Speaker's Desk #282
Weisfeld — *Pulpit* p.130, 132, 144

BAR MITZVAH
Asimov — *Treasury* #374, 384

BARABBAS
Wallis — *Words* p.57

BARBARIANS
Curtis — *Practical* p.140

BARBARISM
Curtis — *Practical* p.144
Forbes — *Thoughts* p.83, 341
Woods — *Religious* p.44

BARBERS
Asimov — *Treasury* #189
Botkin — *Anecdotes* p.49, 84, 130
Braude — *Speaker's* #120-123
Braude — *Stories* p.36
Copeland — *10,000* p.74-77
George — *Book* p.104, 350
Harnsberger — *Mark* p.18-19
Harral — *Feature* p.86
Kin — *Dictionary* p.21
Manchee — *Secret* p.201-202
Prochnow — *Public* #185, 317, 546, 560, 655, 780, 1224, 1418
Prochnow — *Speaker's* p.38
Schermerhorn — *1500* p.40
Speaker's Desk #28, 280, 739
Words — *Inspir.* p.187-188

BARGAINS
See also **Economy; Thrift; Trade**
Asimov — *Treasury* #390
Braude — *Stories* p.36
Edwards — *Useful* p.38-39
Evans — *This* p.134-135
Flesch — *Unusual* p.17
Fuller — *Thesaurus* #2076-2082
Grizer — *Wit* p.53-54
Henry — *5000* p.16
Kin — *Dictionary* p.21
Lockridge — *World's* #3122, 5109, 5577
Montapert — *Distilled* p.30
Prochnow — *Public* #315, 896, 1623
Prochnow — *Speaker's* p.39
Speaker's Desk See index p.297

BARKING. *See* **Dogs, Barking of**

BARNS
Applegarth — *Heir.* p.30, 199

BARNUM, P.T.
Botkin — *Treasury* p.280, 358, 360-361

BARRELS
Kin — *Dictionary* p.21

BARRENNESS
Sheban — *Wisdom* no p.

BARRIERS
Hulme — *Living* p.119-132
Lockbridge — *World's* #3676
Wallis — *Words* p.13

BARS
See also **Cocktails and cocktail parties**
Asimov — *Treasury* #9, 48, 50-52, 584
Botkin — *Anecdotes* p.xxviii, 28, 187, 237-238, 240
New Joy p.230
Prochnow — *Public* #481

BARTER. *See* **Trade**

BASALT
Auden — *Certain* p.210-211

BASEBALL AND BASEBALL PLAYERS
Botkin — *Anecdotes* p.155, 267
Cerf — *Laugh* p.121-128
Clark — *Windows* p.118-119
Copeland — *10,000* p.622-623
Flesch — *Unusual* p.17
Fuller — *Thesaurus* #1821-1824
Guideposts — *Faith* p.38-41, 233-238
Harral — *Feature* p.86
New Joy p.131-133
Nichols — *Third* p.183-184
Peale — *Guideposts* p.113-117
Peterson — *Art* p.276
Prochnow — *Public* #567, 617, 637, 1578, 1831, 2263
Prochnow — *Speaker's* p.39
Prochnow — *Success.* #151, 157, 542, 1026, 1086, 1164
Schermerhorn — *1500* p.41-42
Speaker's Desk #791, 1183
Unlimited Power p.88-92
Weisfeld — *Pulpit* p.147
, *Negro*
Guideposts — *Faith* p.77-80

BASENESS. *See* **Depravity**

BASHFULNESS
See also **Blushing; Self-consciousness**
Edwards — *Useful* p.39, 132
Flesch — *Unusual* p.17
Prochnow — *Public* #1959

BASKETBALL PLAYERS
Unlimited Power p.261-263

BATHS AND BATHROOMS
See also **Cleanliness**
Auden — *Certain* p.31
Braude — *Stories* p.37
Flesch — *Unusual* p.17, 299
Guideposts — *Faith* p.337-340
Harnsberger — *Mark* p.19
Kin — *Dictionary* p.21
Lockridge — *World's* #4243
Prochnow — *Public* #153, 433, 498, 530, 555, 640
Prochnow — *Success.* #1176
Schermerhorn — *1500* p.42-43
Woods — *Content.* p.40

BATON TWIRLERS
Harral — *Feature* p.87

BATS
George — *Book* p.360

BATTLES
See also **War**
Dirksen — *Quot.* #258, 539, 782, 1583
Flesch — *Unusual* p.17-18
Fogg — *1000 See* index p.878-879
Forbes — *Thoughts* p.204, 304-305, 313, 324, 365, 446
Fuller — *Thesaurus* #2371-2385
Kin — *Dictionary* p.21
Lytle — *Leaves* p.89
Montapert — *Distilled* p.30-31
Prochnow — *Public* #2494
Prochnow — *Success.* #1570
Seldes — *Great* p.69-70
Woods — *Religious* p.44
, *Slogans of*
Fogg — *1000 See* index p.878

BAYONETS
Seldes — *Great* p.70

BAYS (lakes)
Kohn — *Adventures* p.55-56

BAZAARS
Harral — *Feature* p.87

BEACHES
Asimov — *Treasury* #278
Lindbergh — *Gift* p.13-17, 123-128
Woods — *Content.* p.61, 85, 204

BEADS
Peale — *Courage* p.148-152

BEAN, ROY
Botkin — *Treasury* p.131-132, 134-150

BEANS
Botkin — *Anecdotes* p.19, 233
Prochnow — *Public* #905

BEARDS
Braude — *Source* #179
Dirksen — *Quot.* #1868
Edwards — *Useful* p.39
Kin — *Dictionary* p.22
Prochnow — *Public* #113

BEARS
Applegarth — *Heir.* p.25
Asimov — *Treasury* #276
Botkin — *Anecdotes* p.34, 55
Botkin — *Treasury* p.24-26, 144, 175, 181, 446-447, 623, 656, 659
Kin — *Dictionary* p.22
New Topical p.26
Prochnow — *Public* #80, 722, 3970
Speaker's Desk #216, 635, 685

BEASTS. *See* **Animals**

"BEAT" GENERATION
Prochnow — *Success.* #728

BEATINGS (whippings)
Kin — *Dictionary* p.22

BEATITUDES
See also **Benediction; Blessings**
Garland — *Subject* p.23-24
Guideposts — *Faith* p.425-427
Hobe — *Tapestries* p.177
Johnson — *Bedside* p.3, 207-208
Prochnow — *Public* #2595-2603

"BEATNIKS." *See* **"HIPPIES"**

BEAUTY
See also **Nature;** etc.
Adams — *New* p.129, 154, 214
Alexander's Treasure. p.41, 49, 53, 57, 83, 175, 194, 206, 247, 261, 344
Applegarth — *Heir.* p.27, 87, 189-190, 255
Auden — *Certain* p.31-33
Baillie — *Diary* #152
Bartlett — *Discovery* p.48-49
Braude — *Source* #180-183
Braude — *Speaker's* #124-129
Braude — *Stories* p.37
Cowan — *Wit* p.134-142
Curtis — *Daily* p.145-158
Curtis — *Practical* p.45-47, 417-443
Detherage — *Sunrise* p.80, 155, 183
Dirksen — *Quot.* #341, 783, 1220-1221, 2387
Edwards — *Useful* p.39-41, 725
Emmons — *Mature* p.10, 58-60, 78, 92
Evans — *Quote* p.177-186
Flesch — *Unusual* p.18-19, 225
Forbes — *Thoughts* p.25, 148, 157, 174, 184, 191, 216, 249, 311, 314, 321, 341, 403-404, 467, 471, 514
Francis — *For* p.102-112
Fuller — *Epigrams* p.26-29, 332
Fuller — *Thesaurus* #661-669
Garland — *Subject* p.24
Hadfield — *Love* p.213
Harnsberger — *Mark* p.19-22
Henry — *5000* p.16
Hobe — *Tapestries* p.25, 62-63
Hubbard — *Scrap* p.15, 38, 56, 59, 92, 123, 187
Hovey — *Treasury* p.37; *See* index p.293
Huxley — *You See* index p.283
Johnson — *Bedside* p.14, 20, 63, 132, 160, 197, 249, 257, 334
Kahn — *Lessons* p.77-83
Keller — *Open* p.22, 73-74
Kin — *Dictionary* p.22, 115
Kohn — *Best* p.77-78
Kohn — *Thoughts* p.43-47, 50-61, 64
Krishnamurti — *Think* p.49-50, 71-77
Krishnamurti — *Urgency* p.89-92
Lair — *Baby* p.27-28
Liddle — *Thought I, II, III See* index p.195
Liddle — *Thought IV* p.22-23, 37
Liddle — *Thought V* p.12, 19
Lindbergh — *Gift* p.114-115
List — *Living* p.59-65
Lockridge — *World's See* index p.572
Lytle — *Leaves* p.5, 24, 40, 79
Mandel — *Stories* p.17
Menninger — *Blue.* p.92
Miller — *Harvest* p.9-16
Modern Eloquence (14) p.289
Montapert — *Distilled* p.32-33
Morris — *1000 See* index p.427
Nichols — *New* p.147-148
Peale — *Courage* p.127-128
Peale — *Guideposts* p.299-302
Peterson — *Art* p.169, 365, 393
Phillips — *Choice* p.48, 224, 247, 289, 294
Prochnow — *Public See* index p.487; #2119, 2278, 2303
Prochnow — *Speaker's* p.40
Prochnow — *Success.* #1571, 2184
Reader's — *Getting* p.6, 74-77
Seldes — *Great* p.71-72
Sheban — *Wisdom* no p.
Sheen — *Content.* p.57-59
Speaker's Desk p.8-11
Tanksley — *Friend* p.53
Voss — *Quotations* p.30-32

Wallis — *Treasure* p.14, 18, 25, 27-32, 156, 215
Wallis — *Words* p.13, 86, 91-92, 131, 137, 143, 159, 171, 173, 176, 186
Webb — *Edge* p.70-71
White — *Job* p.86, 128-129, 141-145
White — *Life* p.246-247
Woods — *Content.* p.48, 235, 237
Woods — *Inspir.* p.44, 223-240
Woods — *Religious* p.45-48
Zobell — *Speaker's* p.15-16

BEAUTY SHOP MANAGERS
Manchee — *Secret* p.202-203

BEDS AND BEDROOMS
See also **Sleep**
Applegarth — *Heir.* p.39, 130
Edwards — *Useful* p.41
Flesch — *Unusual* p.19
Fuller — *Epigrams* p.29-30
Hadfield — *Delights* p.232
Henry — *5000* p.17
Hobe — *Tapestries* p.54
Holmes — *I've* p.26
How to Live p.73-77
Irion — *Yes* p.126-127
New Topical p.27-28
Peale — *Courage* p.93
Prochnow — *Public* #464
Prochnow — *Success.* #994

BEECHER, HENRY WARD
Weisfeld — *Pulpit* p.19-21, 23-24, 38, 165

BEER
Kin — *Dictionary* p.23

BEES
See also **Honey**
Adams — *New* p.145
Applegarth — *Heir.* p.21-22, 197, 199, 255
Botkin — *Treasury* p.205, 557, 594, 598
Clark — *Windows* p.162-163
Curtis — *Practical* p.279
Flesch — *Unusual* p.19
Forbes — *Thoughts* p.35, 511
Fuller — *Epigrams* p.30
Goudge — *Comfort* p.348-351
Henry — *5000* p.17
Hobe — *Tapestries* p.91
Kin — *Dictionary* p.22-23
New Joy p.218
Prochnow — *Public* #232

BEETHOVEN, LUDWIG VAN
Hubbard — *Scrap* p.71
Wallis — *Words* p.180

BEGGARS AND BEGGING
See also **Poverty**
Braude — *Speaker's* #130-133
Flesch — *Unusual* p.19
Forbes — *Thoughts* p.164, 240, 409
Fuller — *Epigrams* p.30-31
Fuller — *Thesaurus* #2216-2219
Harnsberger — *Mark* p.22-23
Henry — *5000* p.17
Kin — *Dictionary* p.23
Montapert — *Distilled* p.33
Prochnow — *Public* #139, 659, 2314
Woods — *Religious* p.48
Woods — *Wellsprings* p.54-55

BEGINNERS AND BEGINNINGS
See also **Birth; Creation;** etc.
Alexander's Treasure. p.116-117
Bartlett — *Discovery* p.112-113
Braude — *Source* #184
Clark — *Windows* p.14-15
Dirksen — *Quot.* #245, 784
Du Noüy — *Road* p.49, 140, 145, 152, 175, 188-189
Edwards — *Useful* p.41
Emmons — *Mature* p.83, 143
Evans — *Faith* p.8, 10, 21, 51-52, 95-100, 115-116, 209-214
Evans — *Thoughts I* p.35, 82, 91, 93, 138-139, 184-185, 207
Evans — *Thoughts II (Open Door)* p.74-76, 97-98, 147-148
Evans — *Thoughts IV* p.86, 89, 113, 197-198
Flesch — *Unusual* p.8-9, 273
Forbes — *Thoughts* p.328, 455, 481
Goudge — *Comfort* p.21-22
Hadfield — *Delights* p.204
Henry — *5000* p.17
Hobe — *Tapestries* p.118
Hovey — *Treasury* #1163, 1182, 1452, 1521
Humes — *Instant* p.42, #128-136
Huxley — *You See* index p.283
Kin — *Dictionary* p.23-24, 243
Kohn — *Adventures* p.89-92
Liddle — *Thought I, II, III* p.40, 43, 76, 125-126, 134, 153, 156, 188, 192
Lytle — *Leaves* p.136, 176
Montapert — *Distilled* p.33-34
Nichols — *Third* p.36-37
Peterson — *Art* p.21
Prochnow — *Public* #1625, 3974-3975
Prochnow — *Success.* #214, 318, 1347
Wallis — *Words* p.212, 214

BEHAVIOR
See also **Conduct; Deeds; Etiquette; Habits;** etc.
Baillie — *Diary* #265
Boas — *History* p.78-80
Braude — *Source* #185-188
Braude — *Speaker's* #134-140
Braude — *Stories* p.37-38
Casselberry — *How* p.57-86
Dirksen — *Quot.* p.245, 784
Edwards — *Useful* p.41-42
Flint — *Graham* p.16
Forbes — *Thoughts* p.337-338
Fuller — *Thesaurus* p.1-15
Ginott — *Between* p.104-106, 149-150, 212
Grizer — *Wit* p.54
Harnsberger — *Mark* p.23
Hovey — *Treasury* #628
Hubbard — *Scrap* p.98, 143
Kin — *Dictionary* p.24
Lair — *Baby* p.79-83
Liddle — *Thought I, II, III* p.36, 40, 147
Lytle — *Leaves* p.130
Mandel — *Stories* p.18
Montapert — *Distilled* p.34
Nizer — *Thinking* p.19
Prochnow — *Public* #231
Prochnow — *Speaker's* p.40
Wheelis — *Moralist* p.27, 29, 43, 46-48, 95, 99, 116-117
Woods — *Religious* p.48-49
Words — *Change* p.14-17

BEHAVIORISM
Auden — *Certain* p.33-34
Seldes — *Great* p.72

BEING. *See* **Life and living**

BELGIUM
Simpson — *Contemp.* p.123

BELIEF
See also **Confidence; Faith; Opinion; Religion; Trust; Understanding;** etc.
Adams — *New* p.48
Auden — *Certain* p.34-35
Baillie — *Diary* #206
Braude — *Source* #189
Carruthers — *Sparks* p.73-91
Dirksen — *Quot.* #750, 762, 1869-1870, 2312
Edwards — *Useful* p.42, 107-108
Evans — *This* p.79-81
Evans — *Unto* p.16, 41-42, 44-45, 52, 85-87, 97, 122
Flesch — *Unusual* p.19-21
Flint — *Graham* p.16
Forbes — *Thoughts* See index p.541
Fuller — *Epigrams* p.31-32
Fuller — *Thesaurus* p.282-291
Garland — *Subject* p.24-25
Grizer — *Wit* p.55-56
Halverson — *Perspective* p.84
Harral — *Feature* p.87
Henry — *5000* p.17-18, 51
Hobe — *Tapestries* p.45-55
Hovey — *Treasury* p.38-40; *See* index p.293
Hubbard — *Scrap* p.168, 215
Keller — *Open* p.53, 138-140
Kennedy — *Reader's* #58-64
Kin — *Dictionary* p.24
Krishnamurti — *Urgency* p.98-101
Kronenberger — *Animal* p.5-7
Liddle — *Thought I, II, III* p.79, 93, 105, 120, 126, 155, 172
Lockridge — *World's* #3107, 3726, 4300
Lytle — *Leaves* p.64, 93
Maltz — *Creative* p.82-86, 95
Mandel — *Stories* p.18-19
Montapert — *Distilled* p.34-35
More Words p.15-16
Nichols — *New* p.163-164
Nizer — *Thinking* p.53, 116
Peale — *Courage* p.76-78
Peterson — *New* p.56-57
Prochnow — *Public* #163, 260, 1855, 1951, 2661-2662, 3976-3978, 4412
Prochnow — *Success.* #1572-1573, 1653
Seldes — *Great* p.72-77
Sheban — *Wisdom* no p.
Voss — *Quotations* p.33-36
Wallis — *Treasure* p.32, 76, 93, 162, 209
Wallis — *Words* p.1-4
Woods — *Content.* p.227, 233, 273, 278, 282-283
Woods — *Religious* p.49-55
, *Effect of conduct on*
Sheen — *Life* p.105-115
, *False*
Maltz — *Creative* p.82-86
, *Freedom of*
Bach — *Make* p.45-46
, *Joy in*
Hulme — *Living* p.133-145
, *Power in*
Peale — *Stay* p.1-22
, *Properties of*
Curtis — *Practical* p.31-32

BELLBOYS
Asimov — *Treasury* #416, 598

BELLS
Henry — *5000* p.18
Hobe — *Tapestries* p.172
Kin — *Dictionary* p.24

Maxwell — *Courage* p.252-258
Prochnow — *Public* #2332
Schermerhorn — *1500* p.68-69
Wallis — *Treasure* p.41
Woods — *Religious* p.55

BELLY
Flesch — *Unusual* p.21
Kin — *Dictionary* p.24
Lockridge — *World's* #4550

BELONGING
Detherage — *Sunrise* p.25-28
Evans — *Faith* p.221
Evans — *Thoughts III (Open Road)* p.16
Holmes — *Design* p.55
More Words p.16-17
Prochnow — *Success.* #1440

BELONGINGS. *See* **Clothes; Possessions;** etc.

BENEDICTINES
Phillips — *Choice* p.302, 368-369

BENEDICTION
Dirksen — *Quot.* #1223-1229
Hobe — *Tapestries* p.17
Petty — *Promises* p.86
Suter — *Prayers* #475-503
Wallis — *Treasure* p.59, 193

BENEFICENCE. *See* **Benevolence; Charity;** etc.

BENEFITS (personal)
Forbes — *Thoughts* p.117, 357, 412, 464, 495, 503
Kin — *Dictionary* p.25
Lockridge — *World's* #15
Prochnow — *Public* #3979-3980

BENEVOLENCE
See also **Charity; Gifts and giving; Generosity; Good; Kindness**
Book Proverbs p.128
Droke — *Christian* p.32
Edwards — *Useful* p.42-44, 335-336, 697
Evans — *Unto* p.30, 113
Flesch — *Unusual* p.21
Fogg — *1000* #785
Forbes — *Thoughts* p.114, 160, 197, 254, 371, 467
Garland — *Subject* p.26
Henry — *5000* p.152
Johnson — *Bedside* p.280
Lockridge — *World's* #274, 931, 2527, 3922
Lytle — *Leaves* p.129-130
New Topical p.150-151
Prochnow — *Success.* #1574
Woods — *Religious* p.542

BENJAMIN, TRIBE OF
New Topical p.28

BENZINE
Botkin — *Anecdotes* p.248

BEQUESTS. *See* **Gifts and giving; Wills**

BEREAVEMENT. *See* **Death; Grief;** etc.

BERLIN
Asimov — *Treasury* #457

BEST
See also **Excellence; Perfection;** etc.
Book Proverbs p.94-98
Dirksen — *Quot.* #115-116, 1633
Edwards — *Useful* p.44
Flesch — *Unusual* p.21
Hovey — *Treasury* p.40; #2, 129-132, 708, 1454
Kin — *Dictionary* p.25
Kohn — *Through* p.73-74
Lytle — *Leaves* p.11, 62, 116
Montapert — *Distilled* p.35-36
Peterson — *Art* p.320
Price — *Wider* p.241-250
Prochnow — *Success.* #1575
Redhead — *Living* p.17-25
Tanksley — *Friend* p.76

BETHLEHEM
Applegarth — *Heir.* p.21
Fridy — *Meditat.* p.132, 137
Kohn — *Best* p.87-90
Wallis — *Words* p.37-38, 55, 57

BETRAYAL
See also **Traitors**
Garland — *Subject* p.26
Holmes — *I've* p.104-105
Kin — *Dictionary* p.25, 73
Seldes — *Great* p.77-78

BETTERMENT
See also **Best; Improvement; Progress**
Flesch — *Unusual* p.21
Forbes — *Thoughts* p.327, 406
Hovey — *Treasury* #21, 36, 41, 341, 940, 1051
Kin — *Dictionary* p.25-26
Lytle — *Leaves* p.144, 146
Sheen — *Life* p.20-30

BETTING. *See* **Gamblers and gambling**

BEVERAGES. *See* **Drinks**

BHAGAVAD-GITA
Prochnow — *Success.* #1572, 2246

BIAS. *See* **Opinion; Prejudice**

BIBLE
See also **Christianity; God; Gospel; Jesus Christ; New Testament; Old Testament; Religion; Theology and theologians;** etc.
Applegarth — *Heir.* p.230, 233-238, 241, 292
Asimov — *Treasury* #294, 449, 464
Botkin — *Anecdotes* p.123-124, 132, 192, 240
Braude — *Source* #194-206
Braude — *Speaker's* #141-143
Braude — *Stories* p.39-40
Detherage — *Sunrise* p.99, 171
Droke — *Christian* p.32-37
Edwards — *Useful* p.44-48
Emmons — *Mature* p.48-51
Flesch — *Unusual* p.21-22
Flint — *Graham* p.16-18
Forbes — *Thoughts* p.12, 35, 204, 266, 308
Fox — *Make* p.81-82, 110, 128, 133-134, 218
Fuller — *Thesaurus* #1581-1586
Garland — *Subject* p.26-27
Halverson — *Perspective* p.120
Harnsberger — *Mark* p.23-25
Harral — *Feature* p.87
Henry — *5000* p.18
Hobe — *Tapestries* p.49, 52-53, 210
Hovey — *Treasury* p.40-46; *See* index p.293, 303
Howell — *Better* p.29-32
Hubbard — *Scrap* p.92, 227
Johnson — *Bedside* p.22, 40, 82, 143-144, 208, 356
Kennedy — *Fresh* p.164-166
Kennedy — *Reader's* #65-74
Kin — *Dictionary* p.26
Knight's Illus. p.22-29
Knight's Treas. p.9-20
Liddle — *Thought I, II, III* p.102, 107, 111, 162, 185, 190
Liddle — *Thought IV* p.21
Lytle — *Leaves* p.5, opp. 40, 44, 192
Mandel — *Stories* p.19-20
Montapert — *Distilled* p.36-37
Peale — *Courage* p.115-120, 218
Phillips — *Choice See* index p.424
Prochnow — *Public* #370, 1899, 1951, 2815, 2817
Prochnow — *Speaker's* p.40
Prochnow — *Success.* #1183, 1371, 1419, 1576-1578
Rogers — *Time* p.107-112
Seldes — *Great* p.78-81
Strait — *Speaker's* p.20-21
Suter — *Prayers* #148-155
Voss — *Quotations* p.36-38
Wallis — *Treasure* p.33-38
Wallis — *Words* p.5-10, 45, 223
Weisfeld — *Pulpit* p.134-143
White — *Life* p.55, 267-274
Woods — *Religious* p.55-68, 73
Zobell — *Speaker's* p.17-19

, and civilization
Woods — *Religious* p.73-74
, and doctrine
Woods — *Religious* p.74-75
, and history
Woods — *Religious* p.75-76
, and morality
Woods — *Religious* p.76
, and prayer
Woods — *Religious* p.76-77
, and youth
Kauffman — *For* p.32
, as literature
Woods — *Religious* p.77-78
, Illustrations for
Peale — *Guideposts* p.118-121
, Inspiration of
Woods — *Religious* p.68-70
, Interpretation of
Woods — *Religious* p.70-73
, Key words in
Fox — *Make* p.58-73
, Psalms of
Kauffman — *For* p.31-32
, Reading of (including reasons)
Carruthers — *Sparks* p.43-45
Evans — *Unto* p.48
Redhead — *Living* p.125-133
, Telefinalism and
Du Noüy — *Human* p.112-119, 239-240
, Translators and translations of
Carruthers — *Sparks* p.45-47
Guideposts — *Faith* p.254-258
Unlimited Power p.75-78, 112-117

BICYCLES
Harral — *Feature* p.87-88

BIGAMISTS
Prochnow — *Public* #755

BIGNESS. *See* **Importance**

BIGOTRY
See also **Discrimination; Intolerance; Prejudice**
Asimov — *Treasury* #359, 366, 380, 393, 418, 423-424, 431, 435, 438-439, 445, 464, 466
Bartlett — *Discovery* p.77-79
Braude — *Source* #207
Dirksen — *Quot.* p.1232-1233
Edwards — *Useful* p.49
Flesch — *Unusual* p.22
Forbes — *Thoughts* p.323, 363, 378
Fuller — *Thesaurus* #1626-1629
Hubbard — *Scrap* p.33
Humes — *Instant* #1196-1197
Lockridge — *World's* #1730
Prochnow — *Public* #131, 905
Prochnow — *Speaker's* p.40
Prochnow — *Success.* #1016
Seldes — *Great* p.82-83
Woods — *Religious* p.78

BILL OF RIGHTS
Curtis — *Practical* p.298-299
Grizer — *Wit* p.56
Seldes — *Great* p.83-84

BILLBOARDS
Harral — *Feature* p.242
Schermerhorn — *1500* p.47-48

BILLIARDS
Fuller — *Thesaurus* #1826-1827
Harnsberger — *Mark* p.25-26

BILLS. *See* **Debt**

"BILLY THE KID"
Botkin — *Treasury* p.69-71, 93-107, 503

BIOGRAPHY
See also **Anecdotes; Autobiography;** names of individuals
Dirksen — *Quot.* #787, 1634
Edwards — *Useful* p.49-50
Flesch — *Unusual* p.22
Harnsberger — *Mark* p.26
Henry — *5000* p.19
Peterson — *Art* p.356
Phillips — *Choice* p.191
Prochnow — *Public* #2818-2819, 3981-3982, 4310
Prochnow — *Success.* #1579-1580

BIOLOGY AND BIOLOGISTS
Curtis — *Practical* p.207-210
Du Noüy — *Road* p.50, 56-57, 145, 189, 231
Hooker — *Index* p.179-186
Lockridge — *World's* #3116, 4184
, and religion
Fogg — *1000* #550
, Future of
Reader's — *20th* p.45-47

BIRDS
Applegarth — *Heir.* p.33-37
Asimov — *Treasury* #157
Auden — *Certain* p.35-37
Botkin — *Treasury* p.638-644, 646
Curtis — *Practical* p.207
Du Noüy — *Human* p.6-7, 72
Flesch — *Unusual* p.22
Forbes — *Thoughts* p.140, 191, 387
Fun Fare p.258-259
George — *Book* p.97, 119, 128, 134, 199, 204, 385, 408
Goudge — *Comfort* p.60-66
Harnsberger — *Mark* p.26-28
Harral — *Feature* p.88-89
Henry — *5000* p.19
Hobe — *Tapestries* p.26, 52, 60, 161
Johnson — *Bedside* p.43-45, 107
Kin — *Dictionary* p.26
Krishnamurti — *Think* p.163-164
Lockridge — *World's* #2753
New Topical p.28-29
Prochnow — *Public* #564
Sagendorph — *Old* p.135-141
Wallis — *Words* p.18, 88, 168, 171, 228
Woods — *Content.* p.199, 204, 265
, and the sea
Adams — *New* p.354
, Determination of
Kohn — *Through* p.81
, Extinct species
Kohn — *Through* p.19
, Flight of
Lindbergh — *Unicorn* p.70-71
, Freedom of
Kohn — *Pathways* p.67-71
, Group names
Kronenberger — *Animal* p. 132-133
, Migration of
Bartlett — *Discovery* p.103-105
, Mythical
Botkin — *Treasury* p.638-643, 646-647
, Singing of
Irion — *Yes* p.109-112
Kohn — *Pathways* p.153-154
, Walking of
Kohn — *Pathways* p.25-26

BIRTH
See also **Babies; Life**
Asimov — *Treasury* #108
Braude — *Speaker's* #198-202
Day — *Meditations* p.9-10

Dirksen — *Quot.* #788, 994
Edwards — *Useful* p.50
Esteve — *Experience* p.20-21
Evans — *Quote* p.97-110
Flesch — *Unusual* p.26
Flint — *Graham* p.18
Fuller — *Thesaurus* #1011-1015
Henry — *5000* p.19-20
Hovey — *Treasury* p.47; #161-163
Hubbard — *Scrap* p.54
Kin — *Dictionary* p.26-27
Lockridge — *World's* #1984, 2500, 2542, 3143, 3226, 4036, 5176, 5645
Prochnow — *Public* #1509, 1547, 3983-3985
Prochnow — *Success.* #1491
Seaburg — *Great* p.1-49
Seldes — *Great* p.84
Speaker's Desk #1104
Wallis — *Words* p.36
Woods — *Content.* p.143
Woods — *Religious* p.78
, *Rate of*
Boas — *History* p.82-84
Dirksen — *Quot.* #690
, *Sex ratio of*
Du Noüy — *Road* p.61-62, 100, 104

BIRTH CONTROL
Braude — *Source* #209
Flint — *Graham* p.18-19
Liddle — *Thought I, II, III* p.50
Prochnow — *Public* #1852
Seldes — *Great* p.84-85
Woods — *Religious* p.78-81

BIRTHDAYS
Alexander's Treasure. p.8
Applegarth — *Heir.* p.63,169
Asimov — *Treasury* #63
Braude — *Source* #208
Dirksen — *Quot.* #303
Fuller — *Thesaurus* #1011-1015
Harnsberger — *Mark* p.28-30
Henry — *5000* p.20-21
Hobe — *Tapestries* p.54, 125
Kohn — *Best* p.161-165
Kohn — *Through* p.51
Lockridge — *World's* #2097
Lytle — *Leaves* p.19
Prochnow — *Public* #231, 242, 610
Prochnow — *Speaker's* p.41
Prochnow — *Success.* #1033, 1445
Speaker's Desk #37, 885
Wallis — *Treasure* p.12

"BIRTHDAZE"
Safian — *Insults* p.14-17
Safian — *More* p.17-19

BIRTHSTONES
New Joy p.231

BISHOPS
See also **Archbishops**
Auden — *Certain* p.38
Flesch — *Unusual* p.22
Fuller — *Thesaurus* #1491-1498
Kin — *Dictionary* p.27
More Words p.17-18
Schermerhorn — *1500* p.49
Weisfeld — *Pulpit* p.2-3, 14-15, 20, 26, 32-34, 36, 43, 45, 114-116, 133, 148, 157
Woods — *Religious* p.81-83

BITES AND BITING
Kin — *Dictionary* p.27

BITTERNESS
See also **Unhappiness**
Evans — *Unto* p.116
Forbes — *Thought* p.380, 415
Kin — *Dictionary* p.27
Liddle — *Thought I, II, III* p.30, 133
Woods — *Religious* p.83

BIZARRE
Botkin — *Anecdotes* p.204

BLACK (color)
Kin — *Dictionary* p.27
Prochnow — *Public* #1962

BLACK GNATS
Botkin — *Treasury* p.607

BLACK PLAGUE
Nizer — *Thinking* p.190

BLACKS (race). *See* **Negroes**

BLACKSMITHS
Guideposts — *Faith* p.250-253
Harral — *Feature* p.89

BLAME
See also **Excuses; Self-blame**
Braude — *Source* #210
Braude — *Speaker's* #144-148
Dirksen — *Quot.* #1040
Hovey — *Treasury* p.47-48; #164-168, 324, 682, 1266, 1467, 1641
Kin — *Dictionary* p.27, 61
Lockridge — *World's* p.374
Mandel — *Stories* p.20
Nichols — *New* p.31-32
Prochnow — *Public* #794, 898, 3986
Sheen — *Thoughts* p.168-170
Weinfeld — *Pulpit* p.55

BLESSED SACRAMENT. *See* **Sacrament**

BLESSEDNESS
See also **Saints and sainthood**
Baillie — *Diary* #236, 329
Dirksen — *Quot.* #789-790, 1234-1246, 1635
Edwards — *Usefulness* p.50-51
New Topical p.30
Phillips — *Choice* p.144
Prochnow — *Public* #2499
Wallis — *Words* p.52, 66, 149
Woods — *Religious* p.83-84

BLESSINGS
See also **Benediction; Prayer; Thankfulness; Thanksgiving**
Alexander's Treasure. p.328
Applegarth — *Heir.* p.48
Braude — *Source* #211
Emmons — *Mature* p.52-53
Evans — *Thoughts I* p.113-114, 119, 151
Evans — *Thoughts IV* p.147
Flesch — *Unusual* p.22
Forbes — *Thoughts* p.54, 294, 311, 350, 442
Fuller — *Epigrams* p.332-333
Garland — *Subject* p.27-28
Henry — *5000* p.21
Hobe — *Tapestries* p.16-17
Hovey — *Treasury* p.48; #62, 169-170, 483, 1024, 1032, 1193, 1269, 1497, 1686, 1777
Johnson — *Bedside* p.189-208
Kin — *Dictionary* p.28
Kohn — *Best* p.82-84
Liddle — *Thought I, II, III* p.170
Mandel — *Stories* p.21
Montapert — *Distilled* p.37
Peale — *Guideposts* p.209-212
Tanksley — *Friend* p.74
Voss — *Quotations* p.38-40
Wallis — *Treasure* p.131, 158, 215-216, 228
Welk — *Guide.* p.70-72
Woods — *Religious* p.84
Words — *Inspir.* p.54
Zobell — *Speaker's* p.19-20
, Prayer for
Unlimited Power p.243

BLIGHT
Lindeman — *Emerson* p.140-142

BLIND
Applegarth — *Heir.* p.96
Asimov — *Treasury* #240
Bartlett — *Discovery* p.118-119
Braude — *Stories* p.40-41
Dirksen — *Quot.* #82
Flesch — *Unusual* p.22
Forbes — *Thoughts* p.252, 270, 308, 361, 471, 487, 493, 495, 505
Garland — *Subject* p.28
Goudge — *Comfort* p.241
Guideposts — *Faith* p.34-37
Hadfield — *Love* p.87
Harral — *Feature* p.89
Henry — *5000* p.21
Hobe — *Tapestries* p.16, 108
Johnson — *Bedside* p.197
Keller — *Open* p.63-64, 82, 91, 96, 105-106, 115-116, 119-120, 128
Kin — *Dictionary* p.28
Lockridge — *World's* #4315, 4414
Mandel — *Stories* p.21-22
Peale — *Guideposts* p.190-193
Peterson — *Art* p.153
Prochnow — *Public* #2641, 2650, 3987
Reader's — *Getting* p.6, 165-169
Seldes — *Great* p.85
Unlimited Power p.127-130
Wallis — *Treasure* p.25-26
, Healing of
Guideposts — *Faith* p.363
, Spiritual
New Topical p.30
Woods — *Wellsprings* p.19

BLISS. *See* **Ecstasy; Happiness**

BLIZZARDS. *See* **Snow and snowstorms**

BLONDES
Kin — *Dictionary* p.28
Prochnow — *Public* #454
Seldes — *Great* p.85-86

BLOOD
Casselberry — *How* p.115-116, 121-122, 144-147
Du Noüy — *Humor* p.58-59
Forbes — *Thoughts* p.111, 416, 449, 466, 484
Henry — *5000* p.21
Kin — *Dictionary* p.28-29
Lockridge — *World's* #4847
New Topical p.30-31
Prochnow — *Public* #602, 1069, 1279, 2455
Seldes — *Great* p.86-88
Woods — *Religious* p.84-85
, and iron
Seldes — *Great* p.89
, and money
Curtis — *Practical* p.317-318
, and treasure
Seldes — *Great* p.89

, *Transfusion of*
Prochnow — *Public* #602

BLOOD POISONING
Guideposts — *Faith* p.228-232

BLOTTERS
Harral — *Feature* p.89
Prochnow — *Public* #1629

BLOWS
Kin — *Dictionary* p.29
, *Mental. See Trouble*

BLUEPRINTS
Asimov — *Treasury* #446
, *Mental. See Plans and planning*

"BLUESTOCKINGS"
Lockridge — *World's* #3702

BLUFFING
Prochnow — *Speaker's* p.41
Speaker's Desk #142, 176, 907, 1131

BLUNDERS. *See* **Mistakes**

BLUSHING
Edwards — *Useful* p.51
Flesch — *Unusual* p.22
Fuller — *Epigrams* p.32-33
Harnsberger — *Mark* p.30
Kin — *Dictionary* p.29
Lockridge — *World's* #5797
Menninger — *Blue.* p.29
Woods — *Religious* p.85

BOARDING HOUSES
Copeland — *10,000* p.72-74
Schermerhorn — *1500* p.49-50

BOASTING
See also **Conceit; Self-praise; Vanity**
Asimov — *Treasury* #382
Botkin — *Anecdotes* p.16
Botkin — *Treasury* p.2-52, 272-273, 276-317, 492, 555
Braude — *Stories* p.42
Dirksen — *Quot.* #1247-1248
Edwards — *Useful* p.51-52
Forbes — *Thoughts* p.438, 447, 481
Fuller — *Thesaurus* #101-103
Grizer — *Wit* p.59
Kin — *Dictionary* p.29, 32
Liddle — *Thought I, II, III* p.39, 150
Liddle — *Thought IV* p.24
Liddle — *Thought V* p.4, 19-20, 39
Lockridge — *World's* #1672, 3222, 3255, 3533, 4010, 4964, 5201
Mandel — *Stories* p.22
Montapert — *Distilled* p.37-38
Prochnow — *Public* #268, 293, 540, 1148, 1214, 1395, 1423, 1535, 2539, 2550, 2554
Prochnow — *Speaker's* p.41-44
Woods — *Religious* p.1029

BOATS
See also **Ships**
Applegarth — *Heir.* p.108
Fuller — *Thesaurus* #1816
Harnsberger — *Mark* p.30-31
Hobe — *Tapestries* p.54, 91
Kin — *Dictionary* p.29
Prochnow — *Public* #60, 491
Prochnow — *Speaker's* p.44
Prochnow — *Success.* #379
Woods — *Content.* p.125, 170, 196
, *Pilots of*
Botkin — *Anecdotes* p.70
Harnsberger — *Mark* p.357

BOBSLEDS
Prochnow — *Success.* #855

BODY
See also **Health; Illness; Mortals;** etc.
Adams — *New* p.105, 310
Albert — *Stop* p.12-17
Applegarth — *Heir.* p.163, 165, 168
Casselberry — *How See* index p.200
Curtis — *Daily* p.69-77, 80-82
Curtis — *Human* p.81, 84, 153, 163-165
Curtis — *Practical* p.25
Dirksen — *Quot.* #1249
Edwards — *Useful* p.52
Flesch — *Unusual* p.22
Flint — *Graham* p.19
Forbes — *Thoughts* p.10, 14, 194, 414, 433, 445, 501
Francis — *For* p.90-101
Fuller — *Epigrams* p.33
Henry — *5000* p.21-22
Holmes — *Design* p.9, 16-17, 42-43, 46-47, 74, 155-157
Holmes — *I've* p.61
Kohn — *Adventures* p.21-23
Kohn — *Touch* p.127-129
Lockridge — *World's* #45, 202, 513, 1685, 2380, 3633, 3817, 4401, 5068, 5276
Lytle — *Leaves* p.94
Mandelbaum — *Choose* p.30
Montapert — *Distilled* p.38-39

Phillips — *Choice* p.279-280
Pullar-Strecker — *Proverbs* #237-246
Sheban — *Wisdom* p.2
Woods — *Religious* p.85-86
, *and soul*
Adams — *New* p.225
Curtis — *Daily* p.70-71, 78-80
Flesch — *Unusual* p.23
Prochnow — *Success.* #1581
Woods — *Religious* p.86-88
, *Cellular structure of*
Du Noüy — *Human* p.158, 203-204
, *Chemical composition of*
Kohn — *Pathways* p.80

BOHEMIANISM
Flesch — *Unusual* p.23
Ideas p.51-52

BOLDNESS
See also **Confidence; Courage; Heroes and heroism; Rashness**
Albert — *Stop* p.102
Book Proverbs p.74
Edwards — *Useful* p.52
Flesch — *Unusual* p.23
Fogg — *1000 See* index p.880
Forbes — *Thoughts* p.217, 314, 325, 337, 460
Guideposts — *Faith* p.105-109
Henry — *5000* p.13
Kin — *Dictionary* p.30
Kronenberger — *Animal* p.26-27
New Topical p.31
Nichols — *New* p.96-97
Prochnow — *Public* #1860, 3988-3990
Prochnow — *Speaker's* p.44
Seldes — *Great* p.89-90
Speaker's Desk #59, 164, 426

BOLL WEEVILS
Botkin — *Treasury* p.354, 607, 916

BOLSHEVISM. *See* **Communism**

BONANZA
Prochnow — *Public* #2324

BONDAGE. *See* **Slaves and slavery**

"BONERS"
Botkin — *Treasury* p.485
Copeland — *10,000* p.842-847
Fuller — *Thesaurus* #106-119
Fun Fare p.3, 89, 187, 204, 212, 231, 240, 303
How to Live p.432-434

BONES
Kin — *Dictionary* p.30
Prochnow — *Public* #771

BONUSES
Harral — *Feature* p.89-90

BOOK REVIEWING
Flesch — *Unusual* p.23
Prochnow — *Success.* #1582

BOOKMARKS
Nichols — *Third* p.201-202

BOOKS AND READING
See also **Bible; Education; Knowledge; Literature; Study;** names of types of books, e.g. **Poetry**
Albert — *Stop* p.48
Alexander's Treasure. p.157
Applegarth — *Heir.* p.39-41, 154, 230
Baillie — *Diary* #1
Book Proverbs p.98
Braude — *Source* #212-218, 1423-1434
Braude — *Speaker's* #149-150, 1168
Braude — *Stories* p.41, 325
Cerf — *Laugh* p.286-293
Curtis — *Practical* p.3, 7, 66-67, 481-485
Detherage — *Sunrise* p.175-176
Dirksen — *Quot.* #225, 281, 538, 791-792, 1050, 1786, 1871, 2060
Droke — *Christian* p.37-42
Edwards — *Useful* p.52-56, 725, 522-527
Evans — *Quite* p.67-79
Evans — *Thoughts I* p.32-33
Evans — *Thoughts II (Open Door)* p.66, 191-197
Evans — *Unto* p.79
Flesch — *Unusual* p.23-25, 233-235
Fogg — *1000* #33, 154, 372, 432, 455, 664
Forbes — *Thoughts See* index p.541, 564
Fuller — *Epigrams* p.33-35
Fuller — *Thesaurus* #1221-1224
Fun Fare p.16, 99, 140-142, 283
Grizer — *Wit* p.57-59, 380
Guideposts — *Faith* p.209
Hadfield — *Delights* p.112
Harnsfield — *Mark* p.31-32
Harral — *Feature* p.90-91, 265-267
Henry — *5000* p.22-23, 233
Hobe — *Tapestries* p.113
Hovey — *Treasury* p.48-54; *See* index p.294-300
Howell — *Better* p.33-36
Howell — *Lines* p.103-105
Hubbard — *Scrap* p.8, 17, 20, 27, 37, 62, 72, 81, 120, 161, 171, 179, 221, 225

Johnson — *Bedside* p.313-314
Kahn — *Lessons* p.72-76
Kauffman — *For* p.34
Kennedy — *Reader's* #76-84, 910-915
Kin — *Dictionary* p.30, 210
Krishnamurti — *Think* p.30
Liddle — *Thought I, II, III* p.16, 25, 41, 56, 77, 82, 102, 124, 127, 174, 178
Liddle — *Thought IV* p.17, 21, 29, 36
Lockridge — *World's* #3095, 3145, 4170, 4846; *See also* index p.572
Lytle — *Leaves* p.25, 46-47, 106, 151, 158, 161, 192
Mandel — *Stories* p.23
Modern Eloquence (14) p.290-291
Montapert — *Distilled* p.39-41, 288-289
Morris — *1000 See* index p.427-428
New Joy p.17, 100, 105, 209, 250
New Topical p.31-32
Nichols — *Third* p.51-52, 178
Nizer — *Thinking* p.223-227
Patterns for Living p.302-315
Peale — *Courage* p.9
Peterson — *Art* p.139, 271, 356
Peterson — *Twenty* p.40-41
Phillips — *Choice* p.190, 201, 255
Prochnow — *Public* #403, 418, 1031, 3598-3606, 4199-4200, 4372; *See also* index p.488
Prochnow — *Speaker's* p.45
Prochnow — *Success.* #651, 2212-2215; *See also* index p.486
Reader's — *Getting* p.92-95
Sagendorph — *Old* p.178-187
Seldes — *Great* p.91-93
Sheen — *Thoughts* p.131-133
Simpson — *Contemp.* p.378-382
Voss — *Quotations* p.41-42
Wallis — *Words* p.8-10, 106, 142-143, 145-146
Woods — *Content.* p.210, 253-255
Woods — *Religious* p.88-89, 814
, *Art of*
Adams — *New* p.200
, *Burning of*
Seldes — *Great* p.93-94
, *Great*
Adams — *New* p.309
, *Marking of*
Peterson — *Art* p.197
, *Prohibited*
Woods — *Religious* p.89
, *Purpose of*
Adams — *New* p.198
, *Reading aloud*
How to Live p.341-343
Peterson — *Art* p.250
, *Required*
Lockridge — *World's* #820, 2476
, *Serious*
Bennett — *How* p.90-96
, *Titles of*
Flesch — *Unusual* p.291
, *Unwritten*
Peterson — *Art* p.253

BOOKSTORES AND BOOKSELLING
George — *Book* p.292, 317, 337
Schermerhorn — *1500* p.51-52

"BOOKWORMS"
Prochnow — *Public* #855

"BOOMERS"
Botkin — *Treasury* p.276

BOONE, DANIEL
Botkin — *Treasury* p.6, 276, 279

BOOSTING. *See* **Encouragement; Praise**

"BOOZERS"
Safian — *Insults* p.18-23
Safian — *More* p.20-25

BORES AND BOREDOM
See also **Indifference**
Albert — *Stop* p.36-51
Asimov — *Treasury* #222
Auden — *Certain* p.43-44
Bennett — *How* p.82-89
Braude — *Source* #219
Braude — *Speaker's* #151-153
Braude — *Stories* p.41-42
Dirksen — *Quot.* #275, 301
Edwards — *Useful* p.57, 162-163
Evans — *Faith* p.27, 37, 150
Evans — *Thoughts III (Open Road)* p.15, 55, 57, 59, 116, 131, 199
Evans — *Thoughts IV* p.15-16
Flesch — *Unusual* p.25-26, 285
Flint — *Graham* p.12, 19
Forbes — *Thoughts* p.103, 388
Fuller — *Epigrams* p.35-36
Henry — *5000* p.23
How to Live p.216-219
Huxley — *You See* index p.283-284
Kauffman — *For* p.35
Keller — *Open* p.114
Kennedy — *Reader's* #85-86
Kin — *Dictionary* p.30, 129
Liddle — *Thought IV* p.24-28
Lockridge — *World's* #175, 975, 1115, 2397, 2505, 2804, 4613
Montapert — *Distilled* p.41
Nichols — *New* p.191-192
Nizer — *Thinking* p.20

Peterson — *Art* p.212
Prochnow — *Public* #1496, 1568, 2370, 2823-2824
Prochnow — *Speaker's* p.46
Prochnow — *Success.* #709, 1320, 2419
Reader's — *Getting* p.213-214
Safian — *Insults* p.24-26
Schermerhorn — *1500* p.52-53
Seldes — *Great* p.95
Speaker's Desk #63, 84, 114, 250, 257
Walters — *How* p.85-88
Webb — *Edge* p.43-44
Woods — *Religious* p.89

BORROWERS AND BORROWING
See also **Credit; Debt and debtors**
Braude — *Source* #220-221
Braude — *Speaker's* #154-157
Dirksen — *Quot.* #274, 298, 793, 1251, 1872-1873
Edwards — *Useful* p.57
Fuller — *Epigrams* p.36
Fuller — *Thesaurus* #121-126
Henry — *5000* p.23
Hoffer — *Reflect.* p.56-57
Kin — *Dictionary* p.30-31
Lockridge — *World's* #2398, 3258, 4073
Mandel — *Stories* p.24
Montapert — *Distilled* p.41-42
Prochnow — *Public* #427, 872, 1847, 2542, 2610, 3995-3996
Schermerhorn — *1500* p.53
Speaker's Desk #62, 70, 115, 180, 263, 310, 748, 1113
Wallis — *Treasure* p.100

BOSSES. *See* **Executives; Leaders and leadership**

BOSTON, MASSACHUSETTS
Asimov — *Treasury* #21, 419, 450-452, 610
Botkin — *Anecdotes* p.7-9, 15-19, 43, 208, 278
Curtis — *Practical* p.443
Dirksen — *Quot.* #122, 256
Fun Fare p.52-53
Henry — *5000* p.23
Lockridge — *World's* #3752
Schermerhorn — *1500* p.54
Sheban — *Wisdom* no p.

BOSWELL, JAMES
Adams — *New* p.31

BOTANY
See also **Flowers; Plants;** etc.
Hooker — *Index* p.187-193
Lytle — *Leaves* p.86

BOTTLENECK
Halverson — *Perspective* p.41

BOTTLES
New Topical p.32

BOTTOM
Kin — *Dictionary* p.31

BOUNDARIES
Kin — *Dictionary* p.31
Kohn — *Pathways* p.87-90
Lockridge — *World's* #2085
Vogue — *Arts* p.140-145

BOUNTY
Harnsberger — *Mark* p.32
Sheban — *Wisdom* no p.

BOURGEOISIE
See also **Middle Class**
Curtis — *Practical* p.280-288, 316
Ideas p.53-54
Prochnow — *Public* #2445
Seldes — *Great* p.95-97
Woods — *Business.* p.7

BOWLING
Prochnow — *Success.* #935, 1141

BOWS
Kin — *Dictionary* p.32
New Topical p.32

BOXES
Taylor — *With* p.62-65

BOXING
Botkin — *Anecdotes* p.80
Cerf — *Laugh* p.128-130
Copeland — *10,000* p.623-625
New Joy p.178-179
Patterns for Living p.26-29
Prochnow — *Public* #350

"BOY FRIENDS"
Francis — *For* p.132-142

BOY SCOUTS OF AMERICA
Harral — *Feature* p.92-93, 283
Nichols — *Third* p.36-37
Nizer — *Thinking* p.139
Prochnow — *Success.* #145
Wallis — *Treasure* p.125
, *Leaders of*
Peterson — *Art* p.387

BOYLE'S LAW
Du Noüy — *Road* p.66-67

BOYS
See also **Brothers; Sons**
Alexander's Treasure. p.112, 115, 156

Applegarth — *Heir.* p.57
Braude — *Stories* p.421-422
Flesch — *Unusual* p.26
Forbes — *Thoughts* p.170, 293, 297, 420, 462
Harnsberger — *Mark* p.32
Henry — *5000* p.24
Hobe — *Tapestries* p.51, 73, 178-182, 202
Hovey — *Treasury* p.54-55; *See* index p.294
Hubbard — *Scrap* p.24
Keys Happiness p.332, 518-520, 548-549
Kin — *Dictionary* p.32
Lytle — *Leaves* p.88, 90
Prochnow — *Public* #81, 93, 294, 304, 408, 421, 490, 531, 1021, 2361
Prochnow — *Speaker's* p.46-47
Prochnow — *Success.* #864, 882, 891-892, 897, 958, 986, 1062, 1102, 1213
Rogers — *Time* p.51-53
Schermerhorn — *1500* p.55-56
Seldes — *Great* p.92
Wallis — *Treasure* p.51-52, 56, 125, 133
Wallis — *Words* p.41, 44, 92-93, 143
Words — *Inspir.* p.48, 52
, Definition of
Braude — *Stories* p.422-423
, Heart of
Peterson — *Art* p.237
, Homeless
Peale — *Guideposts* p.174-178

BRACELETS
Nichols — *Third* p.101-102

BRAGGING. *See* **Boasting; Conceit**

BRAHMA AND BRAHMANS
Hubbard — *Scrap* p.146
Woods — *Religious* p.90-91

BRAIN
See also **Intellectuals; Intelligence; Knowledge; Mind; Thought; Wisdom**
Casselberry — *How* p.64-65, 77-78
Dirksen — *Quot.* #174, 288
Du Noüy — *Human See* index p.280
Evans — *Thoughts III (Open Road)* p.76-77
Flesch — *Unusual* p.26
Forbes — *Thoughts* p.260, 313, 380, 483, 501
Fox — *Make* p.85
Grizer — *Wit* p.59-60
Harnsberger — *Mark* p.33
Harral — *Feature* p.93
Hill — *Think* p.236-245
Holmes — *Design* p.16-17, 52-53
Hovey — *Treasury* p.55, #242-244
Johnson — *Bedside* p.280-281, 283
Kin — *Dictionary* p.32
Mandel — *Stories* p.24
Modern Eloquence (14) p.292
Montapert — *Distilled* p.42
Prochnow — *Public* #228, 1475, 2387
Prochnow — *Speaker's* p.47
Prochnow — *Success.* #474, 1589
Sheen — *Thoughts* p.185-187

"BRAINWASHING"
Peterson — *Art* p.144

BRANCHES (boughs)
Kin — *Dictionary* p.31-32

BRANDS
Harral — *Feature* p.93

BRANDY
Flesch — *Unusual* p.26
Kin — *Dictionary* p.32

BRASS
New Topical p.32-33

"BRASS TACKS"
Grizer — *Wit* p.60

BRAVERY. *See* **Courage**

BRAZIL
Simpson — *Contemp.* p.124

BREAD
Adams — *New* p.156
Applegarth — *Heir.* p.183, 259
Dirksen — *Quot.* #1636
Evans — *Unto* p.15, 32, 40, 50, 84
Henry — *5000* p.24-25
Kin — *Dictionary* p.33
New Topical p.33
Peale — *Guideposts* p.71-75
Prochnow — *Public* #2622, 2568, 2594, 3997-3998
Seldes — *Great* p.98-99
Wallis — *Treasure* p.24, 31, 184
Wallis — *Words* p.13, 208
Woods — *Religious* p.91

BREAKFASTS
Flesch — *Unusual* p.26
Hadfield — *Delights* p.60
Keys Happiness p.176-178

Prochnow — *Public* #479, 634, 965
Prochnow — *Success.* #986

"BREAKS" (pauses)
Peterson — *Art* p.151

BREASTPLATE
New Topical p.34

BREATHING
Bradshaw — *Home.* p.23-30
Kin — *Dictionary* p.33
Reader's — *Getting* p.15-18
Wilcox — *Heart* p.82-84

BREEDING
Edwards — *Useful* p.222-223
Flesch — *Unusual* p.308-309
Harnsberger — *Mark* p.33
Kin — *Dictionary* p.33, 275
Montapert — *Distilled* p.43
Prochnow — *Success.* #1222, 2446

BREVITY
See also **Short cuts; Simplicity**
Asimov — *Treasury* #196
Braude — *Source* #223-225
Braude — *Stories* p.42
Detherage — *Sunrise* p.55-56, 113
Dirksen — *Quot.* #794, 1874
Edwards — *Useful* p.57-58
Flesch — *Unusual* p.27
Flint — *Graham* p.19
Fuller — *Epigrams* p.37
Fuller — *Thesaurus* #131-134
Grizer — *Wit* p.60-61
Henry — *5000* p.25
Kennedy — *Reader's* #88-90
Kin — *Dictionary* p.33
Liddle — *Thought I, II, III* p.39, 61, 68, 161, 183
Lockridge — *World's* #5548
Lytle — *Leaves* p.156, 161, 164
Mandel — *Stories* p.24-25
Montapert — *Distilled* p.43-44
New Joy p.166
Nizer — *Thinking* p.22
Prochnow — *Public* #2825-2826
Prochnow — *Speaker's* p.48
Prochnow — *Success.* #1590-1592
Speaker's Desk p.11-12; #30, 49, 88, 177, 348, 411, 516, 584, 734, 789, 955, 1028, 1115

BRIBERY
Braude — *Source* #226
Edwards — *Useful* p.58
Fogg — *1000 See* index p.414
Henry — *5000* p.25
Hubbard — *Scrap* p.58
Johnson — *Bedside* p.95
Kin — *Dictionary* p.33-34
Lockridge — *World's* #5856
Prochnow — *Public* #1016, 2345, 2827
Seldes — *Great* p.99
Speaker's Desk #458, 1075
Woods — *Religious* p.91

BRICKLAYERS
Asimov — *Treasury* #415
Botkin — *Treasury* p.531-532
Prochnow — *Public* #322

BRIDEGROOMS
See also **Husbands; Weddings**
Braude — *Speaker's* #17-28, 158-160
Prochnow — *Public* #171, 983, 301
Schermerhorn — *1500* p.57
Wallis — *Words* p.157

BRIDES
See also **Weddings; Wives**
Asimov — *Treasury* #300
Braude — *Speaker's* #17-28, 158-160
Fun Fare p.162-163
Keys Happiness p.551
Kin — *Dictionary* p.34
Prochnow — *Public* #301, 525, 657, 673, 838, 854, 856, 1271, 1825, 2062
Prochnow — *Speaker's* p.49
Prochnow — *Success.* #367, 961
Schermerhorn — *1500* p.56
Wallis — *Words* p.157

BRIDGE (game)
Asimov — *Treasury* #264, 351
Copeland — *10,000* p.610-612
Prochnow — *Public* #924, 1632

BRIDGES
See also names of bridges
Evans — *Thoughts II (Open Door)* p.19, 28
Flesch — *Unusual* p.26-27
Forbes — *Thoughts* p.143, 441, 492
Fox — *Make* p.139
Kin — *Dictionary* p.34
Kopplin — *Something* Preface
Lytle — *Leaves* p.121
, *Divine spirit as*
Nichols — *Third* p.157-158
, *Golden*
Curtis — *Daily* p.1-11, 19, 26, 34, 42, 48, 55, 61, 68, 76-77, 84-85, 92, 98, 106, 112, 118, 125-126, 133, 138, 145, 158, 165, 172, 178, 185, 197, 204, 220, 227-228
Curtis — *New* p.141-143

BRINKMANSHIP
Dirksen — *Quot.* #1637

BROAD-MINDEDNESS
See also **Frankness; Tolerance**
Braude — *Source* #1195
Dirksen — *Quot.* #188
Edwards — *Useful* p.725, 731
Evans — *Faith* p.137-141, 147
Evans — *Unto* p.32
Flesch — *Unusual* p.196
Grizer — *Wit* p.324
Kauffman — *For* p.152-154
Kennedy — *Reader's* #736-737
Keys Happiness p.252-254
Kohn — *Best* p.93-95
Kohn — *Through* p.129-131
Montapert — *Distilled* p.266
Nichols — *Third* p.99-100
Prochnow — *Public* #1212, 1499, 3480-3483
Prochnow — *Speaker's* p.33-35
Woods — *Religious* p.703

BROADWAY. *See* **New York City, Broadway**

BROKERS
Prochnow — *Public* #758

BROOKLYN BRIDGE
Botkin — *Treasury* p.595

BROOKS
New Topical p.34
Prochnow — *Public* #1981
Wallis — *Words* p.198

BROOMS
Kin — *Dictionary* p.34

BROTHERHOOD
See also **Equality; Fellowship; Humanity; Tolerance;** etc.
Alexander's Treasure. p.62
Applegarth — *Heir.* p.78, 172, 247, 251, 275
Baillie — *Diary* #103
Braude — *Source* #227-231
Braude — *Speaker's* #161-164
Braude — *Stories* p.42-43
Clark — *Windows* p.108
Day — *Meditations* p.48-49
Dirksen — *Quot.* #7, 795, 1252-1254, 2338
Droke — *Christian* p.42-45
Edwards — *Useful* p.58-59
Emmons — *Mature* p.106
Evans — *This* p.33-34
Evans — *Thoughts IV* p.203
Evans — *Unto* p.16, 98, 142
Flint — *Graham* p.20
Forbes — *Thoughts* p.23, 30, 71, 155, 181, 242, 421, 481, 487
Garland — *Subject* p.30-31
Giniger — *Compact* p.268-272
Grizer — *Wit* p.61
Harnsberger — *Mark* p.34
Henry — *5000* p.25
Hovey — *Treasury* p.55-59; *See* index p.294, 304
Hobe — *Tapestries* p.85-88, 171
How to Live p.566-567
Howell — *Better* p.37-40
Hubbard — *Scrap* p.17, 19, 24, 30, 32, 34-35, 39, 78
Humes — *Instant* #137-145
Kauffman — *For* p.35-37
Kennedy's — *Reader's* #91-99
Kopplin — *Something* p.179-190
Lytle — *Leaves* p.124, 127-129
Mandel — *Stories* p.25-27
Miller — *Harvest* p.35-42
Morris — *1000* **See** index p.431-432
New Joy p.43
New Topical p.156-157
Peale — *Guideposts* p.269-282
Phillips — *Choice* p.312
Prochnow — *Public* #4316
Prochnow — *Success.* #1420
Seldes — *Great* p.99-101
Sheban — *Wisdom* no p.
Sheen — *Content.* p.152-154
Voss — *Quotations* p.42-45
Wallis — *Treasure* p.39-42, 79, 177, 207
Wallis — *Words* p.11-14, 236
Woods — *Inspir.* p.166-187
Woods — *Religious* p.92-95, 570-571
Woods — *Wellsprings* p.45-46
Words Change p.128
Zobell — *Speaker's* p.24-28

BROTHERS
Alexander's Treasure. p.15
Dirksen — *Quot.* #1875
Forbes — *Thoughts* p.180, 192, 200, 492, 501
Kin — *Dictionary* p.34
Menninger — *Blue.* p.60
New Joy p.88-89
Prochnow — *Public* #20, 238, 465, 2657
Prochnow — *Success.* #976, 980, 1142, 1178, 1397, 1403
Wallis — *Words* p.27, 233
Weisfeld — *Pulpit* p.7

BROTHERS-IN-LAW
Asimov — *Treasury* p.624
Flesch — *Unusual* p.27

BROWNIAN MOVEMENT
Du Noüy — *Road* p.69, 86, 96, 118, 139, 197

BROWNIES
Applegarth — *Heir.* p.59

"BRUSH-OFFS"
Fun Fare p.136, 189-191

BRUTALITY. *See* **Cruelty**

BUDDHA AND BUDDHISM
Flint — *Graham* p.20
Kauffman — *For* p.54-55
Phillips — *Choice* p.159, 189, 277, 302
Woods — *Religious* p.95-96

BUDGETS
Braude — *Source* #232-233
Harral — *Feature* p.94
Prochnow — *Public* #47, 106, 471, 662, 1041, 1142
Prochnow — *Success.* #123, 355, 448, 498, 529
Reader's — *Getting* p.11-14
, *Governmental*
Dirksen — *Quot.* #13, 97, 2380

"BUFFALO BILL"
Botkin — *Treasury* p.68, 132, 150

BUFFALOES
Botkin — *Treasury* p.565, 584

"BUGBEARS." *See* **Problems; Trouble**

BUGS. *See* **Insects;** names of insects

BUILDERS AND BUILDING
See also **Architects and architecture; Houses**
Edwards — *Useful* p.59, 725
Flesch — *Unusual* p.27
Grizer — *Wit* p.61
Guideposts — *Faith* p.350-353
Hadfield — *Delights* p.216
Harral — *Feature* p.94
Henry — *5000* p.25
Hooker — *Index* p.247-253
Kin — *Dictionary* p.35
Lytle — *Leaves* p.35, 59, 132, 136, 171, 182
Manchee — *Secret* p.203-204
Mandel — *Stories* p.27
Montapert — *Distilled* p.44
Prochnow — *Public* #623, 2627, 3999-4000
Sheban — *Wisdom* no p.
Unlimited Power p.184-187
Wallis — *Treasure* p.87
Wallis — *Words* p.44, 46

BULBS (plants)
Flesch — *Unusual* p.299

BULGARIAN PROVERBS
Kronenberger — *Animal* p.35-36

BULLDOGS
Botkin — *Anecdotes* p.272
Flesch — *Unusual* p.27

BULLETS
Kin — *Dictionary* p.35
Prochnow — *Success.* #887
Seldes — *Great* p.102

BULLIES
Botkin — *Treasury* p.51, 411
Dirksen — *Quot.* #301
Kin — *Dictionary* p.35

BULLS AND BULLFIGHTING
Asimov — *Treasury* #239
Botkin — *Anecdotes* p.236, 247
Fuller — *Thesaurus* #1831

"BUMS." *See* **Tramps**

BUNYAN, PAUL
Botkin — *Anecdotes* p.90
Botkin — *Treasury See* index p.927

BURDENS
See also **Problems; Trouble; Worry;** etc.
Baillie — *Diary* #53
Braude — *Source* #234-236
Carruthers — *Sparks* p.165-166
Dirksen — *Quot.* #796
Emmons — *Mature* p.70, 75, 80
Evans — *Faith* p.3-10, 18, 223-224
Evans — *This* p.31-32
Evans — *Thoughts III (Open Road)* p.35-36, 41, 111, 186
Evans — *Unto* p.116, 119
Forbes — *Thoughts* p.96, 101, 195, 503
Garland — *Subject* p.31-32
Kennedy — *Reader's* #100
Keys Happiness p.337-340
Kin — *Dictionary* p.35
Lytle — *Leaves* p.13, 17, 154
Mandel — *Stories* p.28
Montapert — *Distilled* p.44-45
Price — *Wider* p.107-117
Prochnow — *Public* #1871, 2505, 4001-4003
Wallis — *Treasure* p.66, 123, 126, 238

Woods — *Religious* p.96
Words — *Inspir.* p.213-214

BUREAUCRACY
Braude — *Source* #237
Harral — *Feature* p.154
Humes — *Instant* #146-159
Prochnow — *Success.* #598
Seldes — *Great* p.102
Woods — *Business.* p.7-8
Woods — *Religious* p.96

BURGLARS AND BURGLARY
Dirksen — *Quot.* #2192
Fuller — *Thesaurus* #2581-2590
Harral — *Feature* p.94-95
Kin — *Dictionary* p.243
Krishnamurti — *Think* p.200-201
Menninger — *Blue.* p.122-123
More Words p.156-157
Myers — *Thunder* p.123-133
Prochnow — *Public* #181, 432, 447, 494, 500, 627, 2467, 2614
Prochnow — *Speaker's* p.49, 294
Prochnow — *Success.* #1199
Schermerhorn — *1500* p.59
Speaker's Desk #56, 142, 167, 346, 374, 512, 532, 640, 818, 880, 921, 959

BURIAL
See also **Cemeteries; Death; Graves**
Kin — *Dictionary* p.35
New Topical p.34-35
Prochnow — *Public* #2630
Woods — *Religious* p.96

BURR, AARON
New Joy p.152-153

BUSES AND BUS DRIVERS
Botkin — *Anecdotes* p.263
Copeland — *10,000* p.91-94
Guideposts — *Faith* p.323-325
Harral — *Feature* p.105
Kin — *Dictionary* p.35
Peale — *Guideposts* p.126-129
Prochnow — *Public* #246, 478, 1634
Prochnow — *Speaker's* p.49
Prochnow — *Success.* #582, 964, 990
, *School*
Woods — *Religious* p.96-97

"BUSHWACKERS"
Botkin — *Treasury* p. 71, 80

BUSINESS
See also **Advertising; Buying; Commerce; Executives; Industry; Salesmen and salesmanship; Trade**
Braude — *Source* #238-259
Braude — *Speaker's* #165-174
Braude — *Stories* p.43-47
Cerf — *Laugh* p.382-393
Copeland — *10,000* p.411-457
Curtis — *Golden* p.153-163
Dirksen — *Quot.* #34, 300, 567, 797, 1139, 1175, 1255, 1397, 1909-1910, 2305, 2386, 2388
Droke — *Christian* p.45-46
Edwards — *Useful* p.59-60, 725-726
Flesch — *Unusual* p.6, 27-28
Forbes — *Thoughts See* index p.542
Fuller — *Epigrams* p.37-39, 333
Fun Fare p.40, 62-63, 124-126, 216-219
Garland — *Subject* p.32-33
Grizer — *Wit* p.61-69
Harral — *Feature* p.95-105
Henry — *5000* p.26
Hooker — *Index* p.240-246
Hubbard — *Scrap* p.30, 61
Humes — *Instant* #160-175
Kennedy — *Reader's* #100-104
Kin — *Dictionary* p.36
Lockridge — *World's* #934, 2692, 3307, 3312, 3332, 3789, 4725
Modern Eloquence (14) p.195-212, 293-294
Montapert — *Distilled* p.45-46
New Joy p.173
Prochnow — *Public* #245, 757, 1351, 1635, 2828-2831
Prochnow — *Speaker's* p.49-53
Prochnow — *Success. See* index p.487
Pullar-Strecker — *Proverbs* #218-236
Schermerhorn p.59-61
Seldes — *Great* p.102-107
Simpson — *Contemp.* p.70-81
Simpson '54 p. 17, 121, 274
Speaker's Desk p.12-15; #105, 108, 186, 439, 483, 592, 968, 1174
Woods — *Business.* p.8-11
Woods — *Religious* p.97
Woods — *Wellsprings* p.52-53
, *Advice in*
Montapert — *Distilled* p.46-47
, *Agreement in*
Reader's — *Getting* p.95
, *and "Bunnies"*
Kauffman — *For* p.37-39
, *and ethics*
Kauffman — *For* p.39-41
, *and industry*
Copeland — *World's* p.410-413, 434-436, 438-442, 451-453, 688-689, 706-707
, *and possessions*
Fuller — *Thesaurus* p.364-409

, *Big*
Forbes — *Thoughts* p.40-41, 43, 218
Seldes — *Great* p.81-82
, *Conduct in*
Evans — *Unto* p.90
, *Failure of*
Asimov — *Treasury* #341-342
, *Fulfillment in*
Welk — *Guide.* p.46-48
, *Groups of*
Humes — *Instant* #25-26, 1198-1200
, *Home*
Peale — *Guideposts* p.190-198
, *Methods of*
Book Proverbs p.89
Hooker — *Index* p.240-246
Nizer — *Thinking* p.125
, *Rothschild's rules of*
Words — *Inspir.* p.90
, *Size of*
Woods — *Business.* p.13-16
, *Small*
Grizer — *Wit* p.430
Woods — *Business.* p.229-231
, *Success in*
Montapert — *Distilled* p.48-49
Words — *Inspir.* p.83
, *Time for*
Carruthers — *Sparks* p.31-32

BUSINESSMEN
Book Proverbs p.141
Forbes — *Thoughts See* index p.542
Fuller — *Thesaurus* #2236-2237
Grizer — *Wit* p.69-70
Keller — *You* p.262-278
Montapert — *Distilled* p.47-48
Nizer — *Thinking* p.125
Prochnow — *Public* #1757, 4004-4006
Prochnow — *Success.* #1124
Woods — *Business.* p.11-13

BUSYBODIES. *See* **Gossip**

BUSYNESS
Alexander's Treasure. p.154
Flesch — *Unusual* p.28
Forbes — *Thoughts* p.100-101, 251
Guideposts — *Faith* p.152-156
Hadfield — *Delights* p.76
Hobe — *Tapestries* p.115
Hovey — *Treasury* p.59-60; #267-270
How to Live p.205-208
Kin — *Dictionary* p.36, 179
Kohn — *Best* p.60-61
Lair — *Baby* p.230
Mandel — *Stories* p.28
Peale — *Guideposts* p.111-112
Prochnow — *Public* #2067
Prochnow — *Speaker's* p.53

BUTCHART GARDENS
Peterson — *Art* p.251

BUTCHERS
Botkin — *Anecdotes* p.200
Copeland — *10,000* p.423-426
Manchee — *Secret* p.204
Prochnow — *Public* #745, 1029

BUTLERS
Kin — *Dictionary* p.36

BUTTERFLIES
Applegarth — *Heir.* p.21, 197
Forbes — *Thoughts* p.298, 353
Goudge — *Comfort* p.67-69
Hobe — *Tapestries* p.18, 96, 192
Irion — *Yes* p.60-61, 126-127

BUTTONS
Flesch — *Unusual* p.28
Prochnow — *Public* #164, 670

BUYING
See also **Salesmen and salesmanship**
Flesch — *Unusual* p.28-29
Fuller — *Thesaurus* p.364-378
Grizer — *Wit* p.70-71
Kin — *Dictionary* p.36
Montapert — *Distilled* p.49
Prochnow — *Public* #608
Prochnow — *Success.* #1597
Pullar-Strecker — *Proverbs* #196-199

BUZZARDS
Botkin — *Treasury* p.672

BYRON, GEORGE GORDON, LORD
Flesch — *Unusual* p.29

BYSTANDERS
Dirksen — *Quot.* #284
Kin — *Dictionary* p.37

C

CAB DRIVERS. *See* **Taxis and taxi drivers**

CABBAGES
Kin — *Dictionary* p.38

CABINET MEMBERS
Fuller — *Thesaurus* #1951-1953

CABINET SHOPS
Harral — *Feature* p.105

CABLES
Fogg — *1000* #694

CADDIES
Harral — *Feature* p.105
Prochnow — *Public* #314, 460, 961
Schermerhorn — *1500* p.62

CAESAR, GAIUS JULIUS
Kin — *Dictionary* p.38
Seldes — *Great* p.107
Wallis — *Words* p.28
, and Christ
Baillie — *Diary* #35

CAFETERIAS
Lytle — *Leaves* p.136

CAGES
Kin — *Dictionary* p.38

CAIN
Evans — *This* p.33-34
Flint — *Graham* p.20
Harnsberger — *Mark* p.36

CAJUNS
Botkin — *Anecdotes* p.50

CAKES
Prochnow — *Public* #343, 438, 714

CALAMITY. *See* **Adversity; Disaster;** names of calamities

CALCULATION. *See* **Cunning**

CALCULATORS
Dirksen — *Quot.* #1642

CALCULUS
Du Noüy — *Road See* index p.242

CALENDARS
Curtis — *Practical* p.89-90
Evans — *Unto* p.11, 19
Keys Happiness p.285-288
Prochnow — *Public* #647

CALIFORNIA
Botkin — *Anecdotes* p.17, 87, 133, 148, 198-199, 263
Botkin — *Treasury* p.281, 323-324; *See* index p.927
Harnsberger — *Mark* p.36-37
Prochnow — *Public* #112, 1826
Speaker's Desk #86, 714
Weisfeld — *Pulpit* p.6

CALLING
Dirksen — *Quot.* #1256-1257
Kin — *Dictionary* p.38
Prochnow — *Public* #964, 2647
Woods — *Religious* p.97-98

CALLOUSNESS. *See* **Neglect; Unconcern**

CALMNESS
See also **Peace**
Alexander's Treasure. p.306
Book Proverbs p.110
Braude — *Source* #260-261
Edwards — *Useful* p.166
Evans — *Thoughts IV* p.107-108, 167
Flesch — *Unusual* p.29
Forbes — *Thoughts* p.84, 406, 512
Liddle — *Thought I, II, III* p.68, 124, 135
Lytle — *Leaves* p.123
Montapert — *Distilled* p.50
Nichols — *Third* p.107-124
Peale — *Guide* p.64-79
Peterson — *Art* p.40
Prochnow — *Public* #2082
Wallis — *Treasure* p.193
Watson — *Light* p.31-71

CALUMNY. *See* **Scandal; Slander**

CALVARY
Flint — *Graham* p.20-21
Hovey — *Treasury* #713, 716, 718, 732, 811
Maxwell — *Courage* p.142-151
More Words p.19-20
Wallis — *Words* p.25, 30, 55-58, 65
Woods — *Religious* p.98

CALVES
Kin — *Dictionary* p.38
New Topical p.36
, of Jeroboam
New Topical p.37

CALVINISM
Applegarth — *Heir.* p.69
Auden — *Certain* p.44-46
Edwards — *Useful* p.61-62
Hovey — *Treasury* p.60; #271-274
Seldes — *Great* p.108-109

CAMELS
Applegarth — *Heir.* p.20-21
Flesch — *Unusual* p.29
Kin — *Dictionary* p.39
Lytle — *Leaves* p.154

New Topical p.37
Prochnow — *Public* #2645
Woods — *Wellsprings* p.32

CAMOUFLAGE
Braude — *Stories* p.48
Mandel — *Stories* p.28-29

CAMPAIGNING. *See* **Elections; Politics and politicians**

CAMPBELLITES
Botkin — *Treasury* p.422

CAMPS AND CAMPING
Cerf — *Laugh* p.357-358
Fuller — *Thesaurus* #2451
Peale — *Guideposts* p.199-202
Prochnow — *Speaker's* p.54
Woods — *Content.* p.80, 355

CANAAN AND CANAANITES
Lytle — *Leaves* p.66
New Topical p.37-38

CANADA AND CANADIANS
Botkin — *Treasury* p.176, 224
Kronenberger — *Animal* p.90-91
New Joy p.150-151
Simpson — *Contemp.* p.124-125

CANADIAN MOUNTED POLICE
Peale — *Guideposts* p.221-224

CANCER
, *Prayer for recovery from*
Guideposts — *Faith* p.223-227, 462-466
Unlimited Power p.2-4, 108-111, 131-134, 138

CANDIDATES. *See* **Elections**

CANDLES
Kin — *Dictionary* p.39
Wallis — *Treasure* p.123
Wallis — *Words* p.118, 127
, *Lighting service*
Curtis — *New* p.124-126

CANDLESTICKS
New Topical p.38

CANDOR. *See* **Frankness; Truth**

CANDY
Harral — *Feature* p.106

CANNIBALS
Applegarth — *Heir.* p.111
Weisfeld — *Pulpit* p.125-126

CANOEING
Irion — *Yes* p.121-123
Kohn — *Pathways* p.121-122
Peterson — *Art* p.291
Prochnow — *Public* #1638

CANON LAW
Seldes — *Great* p.109

"CAN'T." *See* **Inability; Refusal**

CANTALOUPES
Prochnow — *Success.* #619

CANTERBURY, ARCHBISHOP OF
Dirksen — *Quot.* #535

CANTICLES. *See* **Hymns**

CAPABILITY. *See* **Ability; Capacity**

CAPACITY
See also **Ability**
Book Proverbs p.124
Braude — *Source* #265-266
Braude — *Stories* p.48
Forbes — *Thoughts* p.40, 401, 460, 491, 498, 510, 520
Garland — *Subject* p.34
Grizer — *Wit* p.72
Harnsberger — *Mark* p.38
Lockridge — *World's* #1850, 1981
Montapert — *Distilled* p.51
White — *Job* p.116, 183-184
Woods — *Religious* p.98

CAPE COD, MASSACHUSETTS
Botkin — *Anecdotes* p.74, 116, 210
Botkin — *Treasury* p.185, 192-199, 378, 631-636, 713

CAPITAL
See also **Labor; Money**
Braude — *Source* #267, 269-270
Curtis — *Practical* p.280-288, 327
Flesch — *Unusual* p.29
Forbes — *Thoughts* p.43, 85, 165, 174, 213, 216, 221, 300, 313, 328, 351, 394-395, 406, 421
Henry — *5000* p.27-28
Hill — *Think* p.149-153
Hubbard — *Scrap* p.27, 50, 175
Lockridge — *World's* #2757, 2759
Prochnow — *Public* #593
Prochnow — *Success.* #1291, 1598
Seldes — *Great* p.122-125
Woods — *Business.* p.16-19

CAPITAL GAINS
Woods — *Business.* p.20

CAPITAL PUNISHMENT
Edwards — *Useful* p.726
Franke — *Buckley* p.20-21
Ideas p.55-57
Myers — *Thunder* p.100
Woods — *Religious* p.98-99

CAPITALISM
Braude — *Source* #268
Curtis — *Practical* p.315-317
Dirksen — *Quot.* #2343, 2371
Flesch — *Unusual* p.29
Forbes — *Thoughts* p.36, 41, 98, 114, 122, 149, 153, 177, 224, 409, 475
Grizer — *Wit* p.72-73
Ideas p.57-58
Kauffman — *For* p.41-42
Prochnow — *Speaker's* p.54
Prochnow — *Success.* #1315
Seldes — *Great* p.111-122
Woods — *Business.* p.20-23
Woods — *Religious* p.99-100

CAPTAINS
Fox — *Make* p.32
Kin — *Dictionary* p.39

CAPTIVITY
Evans — *Unto* p.56, 58
Kin — *Dictionary* p.39
Price — *Wider* p.85-93

CARDS, PLAYING
See also **Bridge (game); Gamblers and gambling**
Braude — *Speaker's* #175-184
Edwards — *Useful* p.62-63
Flesch — *Unusual* p.30
Fuller — *Thesaurus* #1836-1840
Lockridge — *World's* #3435
New Joy p.48-49, 184, 187
Weisfeld — *Pulpit* p.44, 65, 111, 155
, *Folklore of*
New Joy p.48-49
, *Tables for*
Flesch — *Unusual* p.30

CARE
See also **Anxiety; Attention; Caution; Concern; Empathy; Protection; Prudence; Understanding**
Edwards — *Useful* p.63
Garland — *Subject* p.35
Henry — *5000* p.28
Johnson — *Bedside* p.23, 255, 282
Kauffman — *For* p.42-43
Kin — *Dictionary* p.40
Lockridge — *World's* #390, 5652
Mandel — *Stories* p.29-30
New Topical p.38, 114
Nichols — *Third* p.206-207
Prochnow — *Public* #1055, 1477, 1639, 2832
Prochnow — *Success.* #1599
Speaker's Desk #47, 394, 420-421, 567, 627, 671, 686, 717, 767, 846, 990
Webb — *Edge* p.66-73

CAREERS
See also **Education; Occupations; Professions**
Braude — *Source* #271-272, p.98-104, 153-159
Evans — *Thoughts IV* p.63-70
Johnson — *Bedside* p.214
List — *Living* p.29-33
Speaker's Desk #196, 483

CARELESSNESS
See also **Rashness**
Applegarth — *Heir.* p.19
Braude — *Source* #273-275
Dirksen — *Quot.* #1879
Evans — *Thoughts III (Open Road)* p.181, 195, 200
Fuller — *Thesaurus* #136
Grizer — *Wit* p.73
Henry — *5000* p.28
Hubbard — *Scrap* p.63
Kin — *Dictionary* p.40
Kohn — *Touch* p.23-26
Nizer — *Thinking* p.106
Prochnow — *Public* #1030
Speaker's Desk #167, 359

CARES. *See* **Trouble; Worry; etc.**

CARICATURE AND CARTOON
Asimov — *Treasury* #262-267; 470-472
Edwards — *Useful* p.63
Flesch — *Unusual* p.30
Fun Fare p.44, 71, 183, 260
Guideposts — *Faith* p.209
Weisfeld — *Pulpit* p.25

CARNEGIE HALL
Asimov — *Treasury* #352

CARNIVALS
See also **Fairs**
Harral — *Feature* p.106

CARPENTERS
Harral — *Feature* p.106
Kin — *Dictionary* p.40
Lytle — *Leaves* p.181
Prochnow — *Public* #1617
Prochnow — *Speaker's* p.55
Wallis — *Words* p.30, 37

CARS. *See* **Automobiles; Drivers and driving**

CARTS
Kin — *Dictionary* p.40

CARVER, GEORGE WASHINGTON
Applegarth — *Heir.* p.145
Holman — *Psych.* p.17, 25-27

CASH. *See* **Money; Wealth**

CASHIERS
Prochnow — *Public* #825

CASKS
Kin — *Dictionary* p.41

CASSOCKS
Lockridge — *World's* #2371

CASTE
Evans — *Unto* p.9
Harnsberger — *Mark* p.38

CASTLES
Applegarth — *Heir.* p.124
Kin — *Dictionary* p.41
Lytle — *Leaves* p.39
Prochnow — *Public* #44
Seldes — *Great* p.125
Wallis — *Treasure* p.18, 135, 137, 200

"CASTLES IN THE AIR." *See* **Aspiration; Daydreaming; Imagination; Wishes**

CASTOR OIL
Botkin — *Anecdotes* p.231

CASUALNESS. *See* **Informality**

CATACOMBS
Woods — *Religious* p.100

CATALOGS
Harral — *Feature* p.106

"CATCHES" (colloquies)
Botkin — *Anecdotes* p.256
Botkin — *Treasury* p.768-803

"CATCHING UP"
Evans — *Thoughts I* p.36-37

CATERPILLARS
Hobe — *Tapestries* p.192
Prochnow — *Success.* #723

CATFISH
Botkin — *Treasury* p.185

CATHARSIS
Ideas p.58-59
Phillips — *Choice* p.173, 253-254

CATHEDRALS
See also names of cathedrals
Applegarth — *Heir.* p.61, 217-218, 222, 283
Curtis — *Practical* p.508
Lockridge — *World's* #3012, 3980
Peterson — *Art* p.384
Wallis — *Treasure* p.59
Wallis — *Words* p.44, 239
Woods — *Religious* p.100

CATHERINE, SAINT
Phillips — *Choice* p.51

CATHOLICISM
Asimov — *Treasury* #479, 494
Day — *Meditations* p.7-8
Franke — *Buckley* p.23-25
Guideposts — *Faith* p.134-138
Kennedy — *Reader's* #105-109
More Words p.21-24
Seldes — *Great* p.125-132
Simpson — *Contemp.* p.216-226
Speakers' Desk #133, 674
Woods — *Religious* p.101-102, 869

, and non-Catholics
Woods — *Religious* p.100-101

, Doctrine of
Day — *Meditations* p.67

, Education of
Woods — *Religious* p.264-265

, Layman leadership of
Day — *Meditations* p.68

, New
Kauffman — *For* p.69

, Periodicals
Day — *Meditations* p.13

CATS
Alexander's Treasure. p.198-199
Applegarth — *Heir.* p.20, 25
Asimov — *Treasury* #56, 148
Auden — *Certain* p.53-57
Botkin — *Treasury* p.695, 711-712
Cerf — *Laugh* p.83-88
Dirksen — *Quot.* #2168
Flesch — *Unusual* p.30
Fuller — *Epigrams* p.39
Goudge — *Comfort* p.77-78, 358
Harnsberger — *Mark* p.38-39
Henry — *5000* p.28-29
Kin — *Dictionary* p.41
Lockridge — *World's* #5138
Prochnow — *Public* #1010, 1032, 2319

, and kittens
Henry — *5000* p.141
Hobe — *Tapestries* p.194

CAUSE (AND EFFECT)
See also **Consequences**
Baillie — *Diary* #286
Braude — *Source* #276-277
Braude — *Speaker's* #187-195
Braude — *Stories* p.48-49
Curtis — *Practical* p.235-236
Dirksen — *Quot.* #457, 799, 1168, 1880-1881
Du Noüy — *Human* p.7-9
Du Noüy — *Road* p.28, 41-42, 71-72, 74
Evans — *Faith* p.71
Evans — *Thoughts II (Open Door)* p.32, 75, 100
Evans — *Unto* p.125
Flesch — *Unusual* p.30
Forbes — *Thoughts* p.48, 139, 159, 232, 367, 371, 379, 392, 471
Grizer — *Wit* p.73
Henry — *5000* p.29
Hobe — *Tapestries* p.193
Holmes — *Design* p.4-5, 13-14, 22-23, 32, 60-63, 91
Kin — *Dictionary* p.42
Lytle — *Leaves* p.186
Montapert — *Distilled* p.52
Prochnow — *Public* #828
Seldes — *Great* p.132-134
Wallis — *Treasure* p.47
Woods — *Religious* p.102-103

"CAUSES." *See* **Charity; Politics and politicians**

CAUTION
See also **Consideration; Discretion; Prudence; Vigilance**
Braude — *Source* #278-281
Braude — *Stories* p.49
Edwards — *Useful* p.64
Forbes — *Thoughts* p.186, 314, 334, 400, 410, 514
Fuller — *Epigrams* p.39-40
Grizer — *Wit* p.73-74
Henry — *5000* p.29
How to Live p.292-295
Kin — *Dictionary* p.42-43
Liddle — *Thought V* p.46
Lytle — *Leaves* p.177
Montapert — *Distilled* p.52-53
Prochnow — *Public* #311, 322, 1020, 1189, 1415, 2833-2834
Prochnow — *Speaker's* p.55
Prochnow — *Success.* #1600-1601
Wallis — *Words* p.82
Woods — *Religious* p.103

CAVE-INS
Guideposts — *Faith* p.296-300

CAVE MEN
Asimov — *Treasury* #515, 528

CAVES
Curtis — *Practical* p.15
New Topical p.38

CAVIAR
Prochnow — *Public* #2334

CEDAR, THE
New Topical p.38-39

CELEBRATIONS
See also **Dinners; etc.**
Garland — *Subject* p.265
Harral — *Feature* p.106-107
Lytle — *Leaves* p.53, 100
Prochnow — *Public* #682

CELEBRITIES
See also **Biography; Fame; Heroes and heroism;** names of celebrities
Flesch — *Unusual* p.30
Fun Fare p.235-236
Harral — *Feature* p.107
Liddle — *Thought I, II, III* p.8
Lockridge — *World's* #1086, 3812
Prochnow — *Success.* #1602
Walters — *How* p.1-21
, Humor of
Copeland — *10,000* p.532-565
, Religious
Weisfeld — *Pulpit* p.19-40

CELIBACY
See also **Chastity**
Book Proverbs p.20
Flesch — *Unusual* p.30
Johnson — *Bedside* p.299
Lockridge — *World's* #5558
Seldes — *Great* p.134
Woods — *Religious* p.103-105

CELLS
Bartlett — *Discovery* p.94-95
Casselberry — *How* p.109-139
Du Noüy — *Human* p.37, 58, 70-71, 158, 203-204
Du Noüy — *Road See* index p.242
White — *Job* p.164-167

CEMETERIES
See also **Burial; Dead; Epitaphs; Graves**
Dirksen — *Quot.* #1882
Flesch — *Unusual* p.30
Harral — *Feature* p.107
Kin — *Dictionary* p43.
Kohn — *Adventures* p.49-54

Lockridge — *World's* #4965
Prochnow — *Public* #609, 858, 2405, 4009

CENSERS
New Topical p.39
, *Golden*
Hobe — *Tapestries* p.46

CENSORSHIP
See also **Books and reading, Burning of; Freedom, of speech; Freedom, of the press**
Curtis — *Practical* p.375
Edwards — *Useful* p.726
Evans — *This* p.98-99
Flint — *Graham* p.21
Fuller — *Epigrams* p.40
Fuller — *Thesaurus* #2351-2355
Harral — *Feature* p.107
Henry — *5000* p.30
Seldes — *Great* p.134-136
Woods — *Religious* p.105-106

CENSURE
See also **Criticism**
Book Proverbs p.105, 124
Braude — *Stories* p.49-50
Dirksen — *Quot.* #344, 1259-1260, 1422
Edwards — *Useful* p.64-65, 546-547
Flesch — *Unusual* p.30
Fogg — *1000 See* index p.896
Forbes — *Thoughts* p.124, 128, 160, 170, 172, 244, 337, 383, 404, 418
Liddle — *Thought V* p.13, 33, 36, 44
Lockridge — *World's* #480, 2061
New Topical p.219-220
Speaker's Desk #9, 284, 761, 999
Woods — *Religious* p.106

CENTER
Flesch — *Unusual* p.30-31
Kin — *Dictionary* p.161
Phillips — *Choice* p.43, 71, 83, 166, 173, 328
Wallis — *Words* p.123
Woods — *Religious* p.628-629

CENTIPEDES
Botkin — *Treasury* p.283, 291, 315
Fox — *Make* p. 35
Schermerhorn — *1500* p.67

CEREBRAL PALSY
Unlimited Power p.247-250

CEREMONY
Braude — *Source* #1213-1214
Curtis — *Practical* p.85
Edwards — *Useful* p.65, 443-444
Flesch — *Unusual* p.31
Humes — *Instant* p.46-51
Kin — *Dictionary* p.43
Lockridge — *World's* #3259, 4669
Phillips — *Choice* p.119, 279, 282, 294-295
Woods — *Religious* p.711, 867-868

CERTAINTY
See also **Assurance; Conviction; Facts; Thought, "Positive Thinking"; Truth**
Braude — *Source* #282
Curtis — *Practical* p.37, 39-40
Dirksen — *Quot.* #5, 156, 1764
Edwards — *Useful* p.478
Evans — *Thoughts III (Open Road)* p.206
Flesch — *Unusual* p.31, 218, 281-282
Forbes — *Thoughts* p.25, 47, 182, 191, 244, 289, 358, 395, 414, 439, 468
Garland — *Subject* p.36
Grizer — *Wit* p.74
Kin — *Dictionary* p.43, 194, 247
Liddle — *Thought I, II, III* p.164
Lockridge — *World's* #3766
Nichols — *New* p.61-62
Nichols — *Third* p.49-50
Prochnow — *Public* #2522
Prochnow — *Success.* #757
Wallis — *Treasure* p.65, 210
Wallis — *Words* p.217
Wheelis — *Moralist* p.8-10, 11-12, 144
Woods — *Religious* p.106, 746-747

CHAFF
Applegarth — *Heir.* p.99
Kin — *Dictionary* p.43

CHAGRIN. *See* **Anger**

CHAIN
Forbes — *Thoughts* p.54, 130, 161, 448, 463
Kin — *Dictionary* p.43
Sheban — *Wisdom* no p.
, *Links in golden*
Maxwell — *Courage* p.102-110

"CHAIN OF BEING," GREAT
Ideas p.183-184

CHAIN REACTION
Braude — *Source* #283-286

CHAIRMEN
See also **Speeches and speakers**
Braude — *Stories* p.50-51
Nizer — *Thinking* p.111-112
Prochnow — *Public* #73

CHAIRS
Flesch — *Unusual* p.31
Prochnow — *Success* #1603

CHALLENGE
Applegarth — *Heir.* p.96
Detherage — *Sunrise* p.36, 41
Dirksen — *Quot.* #53, 116, 2375
Fox — *Make* p.44
Garland — *Subject* p.37
Hobe — *Tapestries* p.183-184
Hovey — *Treasury #29, 81, 88,* 678, 1014, 1039
Howell — *Better* p.41-46
Howell — *Lines* p.43-50
Humes — *Instant* #176-184, 1201-1202
Keys Happiness p.465
Lair — *Baby* p.111-112
Nichols — *Third* p. 135-136
New Joy p.53
Peale — *Courage* p.26-27
Peterson — *Art* p.277
Prochnow — *Public* #312, 444, 843, 896
Prochnow — *Success.* #236, 288, 290, 293, 297
Streiker — *Who* p.119-146
Wallis — *Treasure* p.70
Woods — *Religious* p.106

CHAMBER OF COMMERCE
Harral — *Feature* p.107-108

CHAMPAGNE
Lockridge — *World's* #2544, 2668

CHAMPIONS
Guideposts — *Faith* p.207-209

CHANCE
See also **Fate; Gamblers and gambling; Luck; Opportunity;** etc.
Braude — *Source* #287
Dirksen — *Quot.* #17, 188-189, 541
Du Noüy — *Road* p.33, 42, 52-53, 67, 69, 83, 87, 104, 126, 140-144, 147, 154, 179, 183
Edwards — *Useful* p.65-66
Evans — *This* p.86-87
Evans — *Thoughts III (Open Road)* p.159, 169, 188
Evans — *Thoughts IV* p.168, 184-185, 198
Evans — *Unto* p.49
Flesch — *Unusual* p.31-32
Forbes — *Thoughts* p.68, 102, 249, 255, 355, 429
Fuller — *Epigrams* p.40-41
Grizer — *Wit* p.74-75
Henry — *5000* p.30
Hovey — *Treasury* p.60-61; #275-276
Kin — *Dictionary* p.44
Lockridge — *World's* #59, 639, 2010, 2047, 3852
Lytle — *Leaves* p.13, 53, 120
Montapert — *Distilled* p.53
Nichols — *New* p.82-83
Peterson — *Art* p.317
Prochnow — *Public* #767, 1480, 2566
Prochnow — *Success.* #1604
Seldes — *Great* p.136
Woods — *Content.* p.44
Woods — *Religious* p.106-107

, Laws of
Du Noüy — *Human* p. 9, 22-37, 41, 204, 224, 247

, Second
Carruthers — *Sparks* p.95-96

, Taking a
Evans — *Faith* p.102
Evans — *Thoughts II (Open Door)* p.65
Kohn — *Through* p.141-143

CHANGE
See also **Fickleness; Improvement; Progress; Reform and reformers; Transformation; Variety**
Adams — *New* p.176
Alexander's Treasure. p.79
Applegarth — *Heir.* p.278
Braude — *Source* #288-293
Curtis — *Practical* p.235, 376-377
Dirksen — *Quot.* #542, 800-802, 1835-1836
Edwards — *Useful* p.66-67
Emmons — *Mature* p.154
Evans — *This* p.176-176
Evans — *Thoughts I* p.81, 122, 193, 195-196, 217
Evans — *Thoughts II (Open Door)* p.15, 27, 123-124, 174-175
Evans — *Thoughts III (Open Road)* p.16-17, 30, 37-38, 46, 66, 192, 195, 210
Evans — *Thoughts IV* p.133, 168
Evans — *Unto* p.63-64, 75, 81, 113, 117, 140
Flesch — *Unusual* p.32-33

Forbes — *Thoughts* p.29, 105, 150, 159, 329, 349, 397, 426, 442, 460, 486, 489, 491
Fuller — *Epigrams* p.41
Garland — *Subject* p.37-38
Grizer — *Wit* p.75-76
Harnsberger — *Mark* p.39-40
Henry — *5000* p.30-31
Hoffer — *Reflect.* p.72-73
Holmes — *Design* p.22, 25-26, 31-32, 50-59, 121
Hovey — *Treasury* p.61; *See* index p.294
How To Live p.280-283
Humes — *Instant* p.30-31; #185-191
Hunter — *Gems* p.8-10
Kauffman — *For* p.43-44
Keller — *Open* p.80, 130
Kin — *Dictionary* p.44
Kohn — *Through* p.41-42
Krishnamurti — *Think* p.155-156
Lair — *Baby* p.21, 23, 71-77, 213
Lockridge — *World's* #2012, 2352, 2870, 4458, 5299
Lytle — *Leaves* p.53, 170
Mandel — *Stories* p.30-31
Montapert — *Distilled* p.53-54
Peterson — *Art* p.242, 256, 370
Phillips — *Choice* p.141
Prochnow — *Public* #16, 393, 1022, 2302, 2835
Prochnow — *Speaker's* p.55
Prochnow — *Success.* #272, 276-277, 821, 883, 1353, 1605-1606
Seldes — *Great* p.136-141
Wallis — *Treasure* p.226
Woods — *Business.* p.23-24
Woods — *Religious* p.107

, Adapting to
Menninger — *Blue.* p.20-24
, from God
Unlimited Power p.48-100
, Power to face
Kohn — *Through* p.63-66
, Teenager
Ginott — *Between* p.213-241

CHAOS. *See* **Ruin**

CHAPLAINS
Asimov — *Treasury* #509
Guideposts — *Faith* p.435-439
Weisfeld — *Pulpit* p.104-109, 173-174

, Prison
Weisfeld — *Pulpit* p.121-122, 124, 127

CHARACTER
See also names of individual traits, e.g. **Honesty, Integrity,** etc.

Adams — *New* p.204
Applegarth — *Heir.* p.43-49
Bach — *Make* p.123-125
Book Proverbs p.114
Braude — *Source* #295-308
Braude — *Speaker's* #196-197
Braude — *Stories* p.52-53
Curtis — *Human* p.137-138
Detherage — *Sunrise* p.65, 134, 139-140
Dirksen — *Quot.* #4, 152, 316, 387, 803-806, 1577, 1887-1889, 2278, 2327
Droke — *Christian* p.46-53
Edwards — *Useful* p.66-69
Evans — *Faith* p.26, 32, 43-46, 51, 65-68, 71, 81, 96, 107-109, 122, 129-130, 157-176, 181-182
Evans — *Quote* p.205-214
Evans — *This* p.44, 67, 157-158
Evans — *Thoughts I* p.11-12, 26-27, 60, 65, 68-69, 78, 90-91, 93, 97-98, 101, 144, 160, 167, 184-185, 189, 208-209
Evans — *Thoughts II (Open Door)* p.21, 46, 48, 54, 60, 89-90, 129-130, 134, 169-170, 174, 199
Evans — *Thoughts III (Open Road) See* index no p.
Evans — *Thoughts IV* p.69, 101, 103-104, 110, 116-117, 126-127, 130, 133, 155, 157, 195
Evans — *Unto* p.7, 13, 62, 89-90
Flesch — *Unusual* p.33
Forbes — *Thoughts See* index p.543
Fuller — *Epigrams* p.41-45, 333
Fuller — *Thesaurus* p.1-147
Garland — *Subject* p.38-39
Ginott — *Between* p.81, 90, 243
Grizer — *Wit* p.76-79
Halverson — *Perspective* p.66
Harnsberger — *Mark* p.40
Henry — *5000* p.31-32
Hobe — *Tapestries* p.40-42
Hovey — *Treasury* p.62-63; *See* index p.294
Howell — *Better* p.47-50
Howell — *Lines* p.97-102
Hubbard — *Scrap* p.107, 224-225
Johnson — *Bedside* p.21, 109-110, 214, 320-321
Kennedy — *Reader's* #110-114
Keys Happiness p.153-157
Kin — *Dictionary* p.44-45
Kohn — *Best* p.109-111
Krishnamurti — *Think* p.208-209
Liddle — *Thought I, II, III See* index p.195
Liddle — *Thought IV* p.8, 18, 35, 44

Liddle — *Thought V* p.18, 22, 24, 30
Lindeman — *Emerson* p.38-52
Lockridge — *World's See* index p.572
Lytle — *Leaves* p.43, 98, 131, 187
Mandel — *Stories* p.31-32
Modern Eloquence (14) p.295-296
Montapert — *Distilled* p.54-56
Morris — *1000* p.432-433
New Joy p.54
Nichols — *Third* p.133-134
Nizer — *Thinking* p.88
Phillips — *Choice* p.69
Prochnow — *Public* #976, 1151, 1874, 2052, 2836-2856, 4010-4012
Prochnow — *Speaker's* p.56-57
Prochnow — *Success.* #876
Seldes — *Great* p.141
Sheen — *Content.* p.61-63
Sheen — *Lift* p.63-72, 92-103
Sheen — *Thoughts* p.69-102
Speaker's Desk p.15-16
Strait — *Speaker's* p.22-23
Voss — *Quotations* p.45-48
Wallis — *Treasure* p.43-48, 130
Wallis — *Words* p.110, 124, 145, 179
Watson — *Light* p.161-183
Woods — *Religious* p.107-108
Zobell — *Speaker's* p.28-31

"CHARACTERS"
Botkin — *Anecdotes* p.74

CHARACTERS IN FICTION
Kronenberger — *Animal* p.36-39

CHARIOTS
New Topical p.40

CHARITY
See also **Benevolence; Generosity; Help; Philanthropy and philanthropists**
Applegate — *Heir.* p.77, 177, 250
Asimov — *Treasury* #346
Baillie — *Diary* #9, 49, 293
Braude — *Source* #309-311
Braude — *Stories* p.53-61
Dirksen — *Quot.* #188-189, 807-808, 1261-1265
Droke — *Christian* p.54-56
Edwards — *Useful* p.69-71, 727
Evans — *Unto* p.16, 95
Flesch — *Unusual* p.8, 33-34
Forbes — *Thoughts* p.14, 31, 89, 192, 275, 294, 322, 396-397, 437, 455, 468, 487, 497
Fuller — *Epigrams* p.45-46
Garland — *Subject* p.39
Grizer — *Wit* p.79
Guideposts — *Faith* p.162-166, 334-336
Henry — *5000* p.32-33
How To Live p.23-26
Hubbard — *Scrap* p.179
Humes — *Instant* p.1232-1233
Hunter — *Gems* p.10-11
Ideas p.61-63
Johnson — *Bedside* p.2, 5, 190, 248
Kahn — *Lessons* p.218-224
Kin — *Dictionary* p.9, 45, 72
Liddle — *Thought I, II, III* p.116, 139
Liddle — *Thought IV* p.10
Lockridge — *World's* #1149, 1277, 2014, 2413, 2423, 2528
Lytle — *Leaves* opp. p.72, 131
Maltz — *Creative* p.76
Mandel — *Stories* p.33-35
Montapert — *Distilled* p.56
New Joy p.47
New Topical p.40
Porter — *Halo* p.24-43
Prochnow — *Public* #2709, 2712-2714, 2716, 2857-2858, 4013-4015
Prochnow — *Speaker's* p.57
Prochnow — *Success.* #1165, 1607-1610
Sagendorph — *Old* p.46-48
Seldes — *Great* p.141-142
Sheban — *Wisdom* no p.
Speaker's Desk p.16-17
Wallis — *Words* p.49
Woods — *Business.* p.64
Woods — *Religious* p.15, 108-111
Zobell — *Speaker's* p.31-35
, and penance
McDonagh — *Invit.* p.79-95
, Dinners for
Nizer — *Thinking* p.187, 196
, Drives for
Harral — *Feature* p.140
, Formula for addresses on
Nizer — *Thinking* p.188
, Primacy of
McDonagh — *Invit.* p.59-78
, True
Phillips — *Choice* p.362

CHARLEMAGNE, CHARLES THE GREAT
Wallis — *Words* p.28

CHARM
See also **Beauty; Personality**
Alexander's Treasure. p.11
Braude — *Stories* p.61
Edwards — *Useful* p.726

Evans — *Unto* p.85
Flesch — *Unusual* p.34
Forbes — *Thoughts* p.330, 509
Holmes — *Design* p.79-81
Hovey — *Treasury* p.64; #288, 298-305, 1036
Lockridge — *World's* #835, 844, 882, 1021, 1770, 1976, 2378, 2509, 5076
Lytle — *Leaves* p.43
Prochnow — *Public* #64
Walters — *How* p.112-119

CHARTRES CATHEDRAL
Applegarth — *Heir.* p.223

CHARTS
Lytle — *Leaves* p.48, 94
Prochnow — *Success.* #1056

CHASTITY
See also **Innocence; Purity; Virtues**
Edwards — *Useful* p.71
Evans — *Faith* p.67, 153
Evans — *Thoughts I* p.27
Evans — *Thoughts III (Open Road)* p.81
Evans — *Thoughts IV* p.125, 134, 136-137
Flesch — *Unusual* p.34
Fuller — *Epigrams* p.46
Garland — *Subject* p.39
Hunter — *Gems* p.11-13
Johnson — *Bedside* p.231
Kin — *Dictionary* p.45, 270
Lockridge — *World's* #4195, 5654
Lytle — *Leaves* p.106
New Topical p.40-41
Reader's — *20th* p.75-84
Seldes — *Great* p.950
Sheban — *Wisdom* no p.
Woods — *Religious* p.111-112, 1034-1035
Zobell — *Speaker's* p.35-36
, Defined
Phillips — *Choice* p.349

CHATTER. *See* **Gossip; Talk**

"CHATTERBOXES"
Safian — *Insults* p.27-30
Safian — *More* p.26-29

CHAUFFEURS
Harral — *Feature* p.108
Prochnow — *Public* #114, 767

CHEAPNESS
See also **Economy; Thrift**
Flesch — *Unusual* p.34
Forbes — *Thoughts* p.146, 419
Hovey — *Treasury* p.64; #306-308, 861, 1618, 1624
Kin — *Dictionary* p.45
Prochnow — *Public* #1002, 1641
Prochnow — *Success.* #691, 1006

CHEATING
See also **Dishonesty**
Detherage — *Sunrise* p.111, 140
Dirksen — *Quot.* #229, 1892
Flesch — *Unusual* p.34
Flint — *Graham* p.21
Fuller — *Epigrams* p.46-47
Harnsberger — *Mark* p.41
Hovey — *Treasury* p.65; #309-310, 1313
Kin — *Dictionary* p.45
Lair — *Baby* p.136
Menninger — *Blue.* p.122-124, 127, 132-134
Prochnow — *Public* #283, 528, 2335
Prochnow — *Success.* #906
Woods — *Religious* p.112
Woods — *Wellsprings* p.34

CHECKROOMS
Harral — *Feature* p.108

CHECKS AND CHECKBOOKS
Flesch — *Unusual* p.25
Grizer — *Wit* p.79
Keys Happiness p.532
Prochnow — *Public* #63, 707, 846

CHEERFULNESS
See also **Happiness; Vivacity**
Adams — *New* p.28
Applegarth — *Heir.* p.181
Book Proverbs p.68
Braude — *Source* #312-313
Braude — *Stories* p.61
Dirksen — *Quot.* #1269-1270, 2331
Edwards — *Useful* p.19, 72-73, 102-103, 223-224
Flesch — *Unusual* p.8, 35, 107
Forbes — *Thoughts See* index p.543
Fuller — *Thesaurus* #141-143
Grizer — *Wit* p.79-80
Guideposts — *Faith* p.323-325
Harnsberger — *Mark* p.41
Henry — *5000* p.33-34
Hobe — *Tapestries* p.33, 79, 227
Hubbard — *Scrap* p.29-30, 68, 88
Johnson — *Bedside* p.15, 18, 63, 200, 206
Keys Happiness p.498

Liddle — *Thought I, II, III* p.6, 30, 52, 60, 95, 104, 106, 111, 128, 180
Liddle — *Thought IV* p.3, 8, 40, 42
Liddle — *Thought V* p.43
Lockridge — *World's* #251, 287, 347, 1409, 2410, 3228, 5846
Lytle — *Leaves* p.81, 84, 133
Montapert — *Distilled* p.56-57
Prochnow — *Public* #203, 1109, 1384, 1583, 2636
Prochnow — *Success.* #1805
Sheen — *Content.* p.175-177
Speaker's Desk #333, 643, 647, 676, 861, 1109
Voss — *Quotations* p.48-49
Wallis — *Treasure* p.156-158, 167
Wallis — *Words* p.15-20, 35, 137
Woods — *Religious* p.113

CHEERLEADERS
Prochnow — *Public* #902

CHEESE
Flesch — *Unusual* p.35
Kin — *Dictionary* p.46
Prochnow — *Public* #341, 1543
Prochnow — *Success.* #446

CHEFS. *See* **Cooks and cookery**

CHEMICAL TECHNOLOGY
Hooker — *Index* p.159-170

CHEMISTRY
Curtis — *Practical* p.72
Hooker — *Index* p.159-170
Lytle — *Leaves* p.95
Prochnow — *Public* #118
Prochnow — *Speaker's* p.57-58

CHERRY TREES
Applegarth — *Heir.* p.288
Hobe — *Tapestries* p.60
Wallis — *Treasure* p.31

CHERUBIM
New Topical p.41

CHESS
Asimov — *Treasury* #48, 120-121
Prochnow — *Public* #730

CHESTER CATHEDRAL
Applegarth — *Heir.* p.61

CHESTERFIELD, 4TH EARL OF
Flesch — *Unusual* p.35

CHESTNUTS
Asimov — *Treasury* #94

CHICAGO, ILLINOIS
Botkin — *Anecdotes* p.18, 21, 29, 42, 239
Botkin — *Treasury* p.124-280
Harnsberger — *Mark* p.41-42
Patterns For Living p.12-26

CHICAGO WORLD'S FAIR, 1893
Botkin — *Anecdotes* p.78

CHICKADEES
Kohn — *Pathways* p.137-139

CHICKENS
Applegarth — *Heir.* p.20
Asimov — *Treasury* #76, 96-97, 204
Botkin — *Anecdotes* p.184
Kin — *Dictionary* p.119
Prochnow — *Public* #102, 319, 510, 628, 745, 931, 1239
Seldes — *Great* p.142
Speaker's Desk #740, 1024, 1089
Weisfeld — *Pulpit* p.8

CHIGGERS
Botkin — *Treasury* p.607

CHILD LABOR
Nizer — *Thinking* p.211

CHILDBIRTH. *See* **Birth**

CHILDHOOD
See also **Infancy; Children**
Applegarth — *Heir.* p.51-59, 79, 230, 249, 298
Auden — *Certain* p.62-73
Detherage — *Sunrise* p.20, 23, 186
Dirksen — *Quot.* #809-812
Evans — *Unto* p.146
Flesch — *Unusual* p.35
George — *Book See* index p.443
Goudge — *Comfort* p.89-110
Hadfield — *Love* p.22
Harral — *Feature* p.108
Henry — *5000* p.34-35
Hobe — *Tapestries* p.178, 182
Johnson — *Bedside* p.247
Keller — *Open* p.47
Keys Happiness p.552-555
Lockridge — *World's* #3697
Modern Eloquence (14) p.101-110
Nichols — *New* p.189-213
Nichols — *Third* p.166-167
Peale — *Courage* p.183-187
Prochnow — *Public* #1999, 2715
Prochnow — *Success.* #1325, 1611-1613
Sheban — *Wisdom* no p.

Taylor — *With* p.77-78
, Crises of
Jackson — *Coping* p.88-104
, Happiness of
Liebman — *Hope* p.182-195
, Health of
Adams — *New* p.241
, Pressures of
How To Live p.133-138

CHILDLESSNESS
Holmes — *I've* p.18-22
Unlimited Power p.264-267

CHILDREN
See also **Adolescence; Babies; Childhood; Daughters; Sons; Youth;** etc.
Alexander's Treasure. p.14, 25, 107-110, 156, 204, 296, 321, 334
Bartlett — *Discovery* p.8
Book Proverbs p.44
Braude — *Source* #314-315
Carruthers — *Sparks* p.123-124
Cerf — *Laugh* p.340-357
Copeland — *10,000* p.288-331
Detherage — *Sunrise* p.20, 27-28
Dirksen — *Quot. See* index p.260
Droke — *Christian* p.56-69
Du Noüy — *Human* p.207-222
Edwards — *Useful* p.73-76
Emmons — *Mature* p.107-110
Evans — *This* p.111-113
Evans — *Thoughts II (Open Door)* p.22, 31-32, 36-37, 46, 94-95, 98, 113, 116, 128, 158, 163-164
Evans — *Thoughts III (Open Road) See* index no p.
Evans — *Thoughts IV See* index no p.
Evans — *Unto* p.106-109
Flesch — *Unusual* p.35-36
Flint — *Graham* p.21-23, 41
Forbes — *Thoughts See* index p.543
Fuller — *Epigrams* p.47-48
Fuller — *Thesaurus* #951-977
Fun Fare p.21, 74-75, 119, 206-207, 224-226, 298
Garland — *Subject* p.40
Grizer — *Wit* p.80-81
Guideposts — *Faith* p.157-161
Harnsberger — *Mark* p.42-43
Harral — *Feature* p.108-111
Hobe — *Tapestries* p.70, 135, 155, 167, 179
Holmes — *I've* p.71-86
Hovey — *Treasury* p.65-67; *See* index p.294
How To Live p.104-138
Hubbard — *Scrap* p.26, 42, 54, 64, 67, 177, 227
Huxley — *You See* index p.284
Johnson — *Bedside* p.119, 298-301, 304
Kahn — *Lessons* p.192-198
Keys Happiness p.152, 157, 223-226, 248-251, 385-388, 399-402, 446-448
Kin — *Dictionary* p.46
Knight's Illus. p.32-40
Knight's Treas. p.24-30
Liddle — *Thought I, II, III See* index p.195
Liddle — *Thought IV* p.4, 19, 30, 32, 37
Liddle — *Thought V* p.20, 22, 27, 31, 34, 40
Lockridge — *World's See* index p.573
Mandel — *Stories* p.35-39
Mandelbaum — *Choose* p.64-68
Modern Eloquence (14) p.297 298
Montapert — Distilled p.57-58
New Joy p.228
New Topical p.41-42
Peterson — *Art* p.270, 350
Prochnow — *Public See* index p.490
Prochnow — *Speaker's* p.58-60
Prochnow — *Success. See* index p.487; #1134, 1361
Reader's — *Getting* p.226-228
Rogers — *Time* p.35-42
Seaburg — *Great* p.165, 169, 175, 177, 180, 190, 192, 194-196, 198, 209-210, 212, 215, 272, 281, 290
Seldes — *Great* p.142-145
Sheen — *Thoughts* p.74-77, 87-89
Sheen — *Way* p.85-91
Speaker's Desk See index p.297
Tanksley — *Friend* p.38
Wallis — *Treasure* p.24, 49-56, 87, 90, 108, 129, 131-133, 167, 181
Wallis — *Words* p.13, 92-94, 109, 112-113, 127, 163-164
Walters — *How* p.66-68
Weisfeld — *Pulpit* p.65-75
Woods — *Control* p.147, 150-153, 156-157
Woods — *Religious* p.113-114
Words — *Inspir.* p.53
Zobell — *Speaker's* p.36-38
, Care of
Braude — *Stories* p.61-64
Harral — *Feature* p.108
, Contribution through
Carruthers — *Sparks* p.17-18
, Creative lives for
Maltz — *Creative* p.47-50
, Crippled. See **Handicapped**

, Crossness to
Holmes — *I've* p.13-22
, Discipline of
Braude — *Source* #316-317
, Eyes of
Adams — *New* p.253
, Future of
Baillie — *Diary* #175
Humes — *Instant* p.49-50; #1228-1231
, Good
New Topical p.42
, Guidance of
Braude — *Source* #318-319
, Learning of
See also **Education**
Kauffman — *For* p.44-45
, Likeness to
See also **Innocence**
Garland — *Subject* p.40
, Living with
See also **Family; Home**
Vogue — *Arts* p.163-168
, of God
Clark — *Windows* p.88
, Power of
How To Live p.115-118
, Reflection of
Day — *Meditations* p.15
, Retarded
Guideposts — *Faith* p.341-343
Harral — *Feature* p.217
Keys Happiness p.179-187
Peale — *Guideposts* p.239-242
Seaburg — *Great* p.226, 242, 277
Unlimited Power p.104-107
, Training of
Braude — *Source* #320-327
Holman — *Psych.* p.1-13
Ideas p.378-379
, Understanding of
White — *Life* p.33-41
, Unexpected
Holmes — *I've* p.18
, Viewpoint of
Clark — *Windows* p.140
, Wanted
Holmes — *I've* p.16-17
, Wicked
New Topical p.42-43
, Wondering of
Nichols — *Third* p.115-116

CHILDREN'S LITERATURE
Adams — *New* p.242
Auden — *Certain* p.291-292
Peterson — *Art* p.363
White — *Life* p.58-66

CHILE, CHURCH IN
Kauffman — *For* p.94-95

CHIMNEYS
Kin — *Dictionary* p.46
Taylor — *With* p.146-147

CHINA
Hovey — *Treasury* #243, 1278, 1459
Peale — *Guideposts* p.318-320
, Communist
Simpson — *Contemp.* p.125-126

CHINESE
Asimov — *Treasury* #434
Copeland — *10,000* p.758-761
Flesch — *Unusual* p.36-37
Schermerhorn — *1500* p.69-70
Speaker's Desk #480, 560, 764, 1029

CHINESE PROVERBS
Dirksen — *Quot.* #1843, 1853, 1875, 1975, 2032, 2155, 2247

CHIPS
Kin — *Dictionary* p.46

CHIROPODISTS
Harral — *Feature* p.111
Prochnow — *Public* #399, 1642

CHISELERS AND CHISELING. *See* **Swindlers**

CHITLINS
Botkin — *Treasury* p.425

CHIVALRY
Braude — *Stories* p.64
Dirksen — *Quot.* #1642
Edwards — *Useful* p.76
Evans — *Unto* p.89
Hubbard — *Scrap* p.99
Ideas p.63-65
Johnson — *Bedside* p.49-58
Lytle — *Leaves* p.128

CHOCOLATE
Gold — *Letters* p.115-116

CHOICE
See also **Decision; Freedom; Resolution; Will; Wishes**
Baillie — *Diary* #147
Book Proverbs p.116
Braude — *Source* #328-329
Braude — *Speaker's* #1071-1072, 1347-1348
Braude — *Stories* p.64-65
Curtis — *Practical* p.40
Detherage — *Sunrise* p.89
Dirksen — *Quot.* #816, 1140, 1900-1901

Edwards — *Useful* p.76-77
Evans — *Faith* p.121-122, 134, 159-160, 164-165
Evans — *This* p.42-43
Evans — *Thoughts I* p.61, 77-80, 154, 161
Evans — *Thoughts III (Open Road)* p.75, 81, 103-107, 109, 191-192, 201
Evans — *Thoughts IV* p.13, 17-18, 84, 88, 129, 145, 157, 199
Evans — *Unto* p.65, 68
Forbes — *Thoughts* p.307, 362, 485
Henry — *5000* p.35
Holmes — *Design* p.31, 76-77
Hovey — *Treasury* #706, 1066, 1171, 1313, 1760
Keller — *Open* p.48
Kin — *Dictionary* p.46-47, 198
Knight's Illus. p.40-42
Knight's Treas. p.30-34
Lindbergh — *Gift* p.119-120
Lockridge — *World's* #702, 2284, 4616
Lytle — *Leaves* p.9, 81, 179
Mandel — *Stories* p.39
Montapert — *Distilled* p.58-59
Peterson — *Art* p.369
Phillips — *Choice* p.24, 39
Prochnow — *Public* #123, 126, 2410, 2479, 2684-2865
Wallis — *Treasure* p.20, 48, 158-159
Wallis — *Words* p.72, 91
Wheelis — *Moralist* p.11, 36, 116, 127-128, 135
White — *Job* p.65-66, 107
Woods — *Religious* p.114

CHOIRS AND CHOIRBOYS
Auden — *Certain* p.73-74
Harral — *Feature* p.111
Schermerhorn — *1500* p.71
Unlimited Power p.164-168

"CHOSEN PEOPLE"
Woods — *Religious* p.114-115

CHRIST. *See* **Jesus Christ**

"CHRIST OF THE ANDES"
Fogg — *1000* #565

CHRISTENINGS
Prochnow —*Public* #333, 424, 615
Weisfeld — *Pulpit* p.10

CHRISTIAN SCIENCE
Asimov — *Treasury* #497
Schermerhorn — *1500* p.72
Seldes — *Great* p.158
Woods — *Religious* p.119-120

CHRISTIANITY
See also **Belief; Bible; Brotherhood; Christians; Church; Creeds; Cross; Faith; Gospel; Religion; Sects; Worship;** names of various denominations and religions
Applegarth — *Heir.* p.29, 44, 69, 218, 237
Baillie — *Diary* #57, 212
Bartlett — *Discovery* p.151
Book Proverbs p.132
Braude — *Source* #330-334
Carruthers — *Sparks* p.56-58, 78-80
Curtis — *Practical* p.24
Dirksen — *Quot.* #186, 237, 816, 2277
Droke — *Christian* p.70-74
Du Noüy — *Human* p.51, 170, 172-175, 178, 215-216, 228, 237-242, 251, 257, 264, 268-269
Edwards — *Useful* p.79-81, 726
Evans — *Unto* p.123
Flesch — *Unusual* p.37-38
Flint — *Graham* p.25-26
Forbes — *Thoughts See* index p.543
Fuller — *Epigrams* p.48-49
Halverson — *Perspective* p.95
Harnsberger — *Mark* p.43-44
Henry — *5000* p.37
Hobe — *Tapestries* p.50
Hovey — *Treasury* p.73-76; *See also* index p.294
Hulme — *Living* p.72-82
Johnson — *Bedside* p.13, 20, 57, 87-89, 109, 164, 187, 191, 235-236, 251, 317-319
Kennedy — *Reader's* #115-126
Keys Happiness p.103-106, 528-532
Liddle — *Thought I, II, III* p.49
Liddle — *Thought IV* p.8, 21, 42
Liddle — *Thought V* p.5, 10, 22, 28
Lockridge — *World's* #2353, 2915, 5183, 5704
McDonagh — *Invit.* p.1-21
Montapert — *Distilled* p.61-62
Nizer — *Thinking* p.125
Phillips — *Choice* p.26-27, 30, 33, 54, 91, 95, 119
Prochnow — *Success.* #1369, 1375, 1617
Seldes — *Great* p.145-158
Sheen — *Thoughts* p.180-182
Voss — *Quotations* p.49-51
Wallis — *Treasure* p.156, 177, 210-212

Wallis — *Words* p.4, 8, 27, 29, 45, 124, 213
Wheelis — *Moralist* p.51, 110-111, 136, 139, 148, 154
Woods — *Religious* p.119-127
, Accomplishments of
Kauffman — *For* p.52-53
, and redemption
Kauffman — *For* p.49-50
, Applied
Kauffman — *For* p.26, 40-41
, Around the world
Kauffman — *For* p.50-52
, Beginning
Fridy — *Meditat.* p.112
, Criticism of
Woods — *Religious* p.127-129
, Development of
Curtis — *Practical* p.222-223
, Everyday
Kauffman — *For* p.92-93
, Personal
Kauffman — *For* p.48-49
, Reason for
Flint — *Graham* p.115

CHRISTIANS
See also **Catacombs; Saints and sainthood;** etc.
Applegarth — *Heir.* p.27, 68, 71, 89, 94, 116, 245, 265, 301, 306
Baillie — *Diary* #159, 249, 320
Carruthers — *Sparks* p.26-27, 68-72
Edwards — *Useful* p.77-78
Emmons — *Mature* p.27
Flesch — *Unusual* p.37
Flint — *Graham* p.25, 27-28
Forbes — *Thoughts* p.3, 30, 37, 71, 179, 291, 294, 297, 324, 339-400, 473, 486, 500
Garland — *Subject* p.43
Guideposts — *Faith* p.161
Halverson — *Perspective* p.36, 87-88
Henry — *5000* p.36-38
Hobe — *Tapestries* p.87
Hovey — *Treasury See* index p.294
Montapert — *Distilled* p.60-61
More Words p.25-26
Phillips — *Choice* p.125, 321, 359, 412
Prochnow — *Public* #2101
Prochnow — *Success.* #1239, 1388, 1409, 1418
Redhead — *Living* p.79-86
Wallis — *Treasure* p.152, 158
Wallis — *Words* p.42, 213
Words — *Religious* p.115-119, 129-131
, Courage and devotion of
Fogg — *1000 See* index p.881
, Definition of
Kauffman — *For* p.49
, Duty of
Words Change p.52-53
, Ethics of
McDonagh — *Invit.* p.38-58
, Example and influence of
Knight's Illus. p.42-44
Knight's Treas. p.34-39
, Faith of
Fogg — *1000 See* index p.881
, Fellowship groups of
Unlimited Power p.201-205
, Life of
Carruthers — *Sparks* p.121-136
Day — *Meditations* p.32-33
Flint — *Graham* p.26-27
Kauffman — *For* p.47-48
Kennedy — *Reader's* #127-134
McDonagh — *Invit.* p.96-108
Menninger — *Blue.* p.84
Strait — *Speaker's* p.26-32
Tanksley — *Friend* p.29
, Marriage of
McDonagh — *Invit.* p.109-132
, Motive of
Baillie — *Diary* #327
, Persecution of
Nizer — *Thinking* p.128
, Rules for
Flint — *Graham* p.122
, Sharing by
Words Change p.56-59
, Society of
Woods — *Religious* p.120
, Thoughts of
Baillie — *Diary* #280
, Year of
Applegarth — *Heir.* p.65

CHRISTMAS
See also **Advent; Jesus Christ, Birth of**
Applegarth — *Heir.* p.24, 55, 74
Asimov — *Treasury* #229
Auden — *Certain* p.74-77
Barrows — *1000* p.92, 194, 342, 363, 414, 420, 422-423
Botkin — *Anecdotes* p.41
Braude — *Source* #335-337
Braude — *Speaker's* #203-206
Carruthers — *Sparks* p.84-86
Cerf — *Laugh* p.209-213
Curtis — *New* p.115-126
Dirksen — *Quot.* #99, 817-820
Droke — *Christian* p.74-85
Emmons — *Mature* p.158

Evans — *Faith* p.219-222
Evans — *Quite* p.233-240
Evans — *Thoughts II (Open Door)* p.119-120
Evans — *Thoughts IV* p.159-160
Evans — *Unto* p.11, 16-17
Flint — *Graham* p.28-29
Fridy — *Meditat.* p.132, 134, 137
Fuller — *Epigrams* p.334
Fun Fare p.148-150
Garland — *Subject* p.43
Goudge — *Comfort* p.177-178, 181-183
Guideposts — *Faith* p.42-46, 185-187, 341-343, 434
Halverson — *Perspective* p.98
Harral — *Feature* p.111-116
Hobe — *Tapestries* p.143-148
Hovey — *Treasury* p.76-87; #90, 334, 347, 383-434, 601, 666, 1056, 1115, 1118, 1193
Hubbard — *Scrap* p.79
Irion — *Yes* p.31-33
Kauffman — *For* p.206-207
Keller — *Open* p.84
Kennedy — *Reader's* #135-137
Knight's Illus. p.44-46
Knight's Treas. p.39-44
Kohn — *Best* p.87-103
Kohn — *Pathways* p.154
Kohn — *Thoughts* p.168-171
Kohn — *Through* p.51
Liddle — *Thought I, II, III* p.55, 90, 130, 158
Liddle — *Thought V* p.12, 17, 38, 40
Lytle — *Leaves* p.87, 124
New Joy p.223
Peale — *Courage* p.148-152, 190-194
Peterson — *Art* p.395, 397-406
Peterson — *New* p.14-15
Prochnow — *Public* #1147, 1511
Prochnow — *Speaker's* p.61
Prochnow — *Success.* #797, 1434, 1618-1620
Schermerhorn — *1500* p.72-73
Seldes — *Great* p.158
Sheen — *Thoughts* p.153-155
Strait — *Speaker's* p.168
Suter — *Prayers* #381-393
Tanksley — *Friend* p.23
Wallis — *Treasure* p.125, 169
Wallis — *Words* p.31-38, 66
Woods — *Content.* p.55
Woods — *Religious* p.131
Words — *Inspir.* p.80-81
Zobell — *Speaker's* p.38-41

, Early American (1861)
Nichols — *Third* p.251

, Greeting of
Thurman — *Mood* p.17-28

, History of
Thurman — *Mood* p.5-12

, Meditations for
Thurman — *Mood* p.29-108

, Mercenary
Fogg — *1000* #660

, Prayer for
Kauffman — *For* p.158-160
Kohn — *Best* p.91-93, 98-99

, Sermon for
Goudge — *Comfort* p.170-171

CHRISTOPHER, SAINT
Lindbergh — *Unicorn* p.45-47

"CHRISTOPHERS" (movement)
Keller — *You* p.v-xiii, 302, 331
Keys Happiness p.418-421

CHURCH
See also **Altars; Christianity; Clergymen; Congregation; God; Religion; Worship;** names of religions
Applegarth — *Heir.* p.52-53, 118, 214, 217-225, 264, 277
Baillie — *Diary* #90, 166, 334
Braude — *Source* #338-342
Clark — *Windows* p.138
Curtis — *Practical* p.128, 384
Dirksen — *Quot.* #821, 1281-1282, 1902-1903
Droke — *Christian* p.85-96
Du Noüy — *Human* p.ii, 118, 132, 140, 172-175, 179, 184, 215, 238, 240-241
Edwards — *Useful* p.82, 726
Emmons — *Mature* p.20-25
Evans — *Unto* p.32
Flesch — *Unusual* p.38
Flint — *Graham* p.11, 21, 23, 29-31
Forbes — *Thoughts See* index p.543
Fridy — *Meditat.* p.30, 50, 75-76, 83, 85, 107, 114-115
Fuller — *Epigrams* p.49-50
Fuller — *Thesaurus* #1526-1528
Fun Fare p.75-76, 303
Garland — *Subject* p.43-44
Harnsberg — *Mark* p.45
Harral — *Feature* p.116-121
Henry — *5000* p.38
Hobe — *Tapestries* p.178, 208-210
Hovey — *Treasury* p.87-108; *See also* index p. 294
How To Live p.538-541
Howell — *Better* p.51-54
Howell — *Lines* p.123-132
Hubbard — *Scrap* p.172, 197, 218
Kennedy — *Reader's* #138-152

Keys Happiness p.56-59
Kin — *Dictionary* p.47
Knight's Illus. p.47-54
Knight's Treas. p.44-55
Lindbergh — *Gift* p.53-54
Lytle — *Leaves* p.28, 62, 120, 132
Mandel — *Stories* p.40
Montapert — *Distilled* p.62
More Words p.27-29
New Topical p.45-46
Patterns For Living p.634-639
Peale — *Courage* p.38-40
Phillips — *Choice* p.29, 196, 306-307, 388
Prochnow — *Public* #4, 274, 425, 607, 620, 906, 936, 1473, 1643, 4023
Prochnow — *Speaker's* p.61-63
Prochnow — *Success.* #896, 1212, 1216, 1287, 1292, 1621
Rogers — *Time* p.95-99
Schermerhorn — *1500* p.73-75
Seldes — *Great* p.158-166
Sheban — *Wisdom* no p.
Strait — *Speaker's* p.33-43
Suter — *Prayers* #94-130
Voss — *Quotations* p.51-53
Wallis — *Treasure* p.57-62, 173, 184, 194
Wallis — *Words* p.39-46, 105, 109
Weisfeld — *Pulpit* p.49-64
Woods — *Content.* p.186, 271, 280, 295
Woods — *Religious* p.135-136
Words Change p.94-113
Zobell — *Speaker's* p.41-43

, Action of
Myers — *Thunder* p.18-20
, Agreement in
Kauffman — *For* p.53-54
, and churchmen
George — *Book See* index p.443
, and state
Seldes — *Great* p.166-169
Woods — *Religious* p.145-151
, Appeal of
Kauffman — *For* p.54-55
, Attendance in (including reasons for)
Braude — *Source* #345-357
Braude — *Speaker's* #207-223
Carruthers — *Sparks* p.54-56
Holman — *Psych.* p.71-72
Kohn — *Touch* p.79-85
, Authority of
Kauffman — *For* p.28-30
Woods — *Religious* p.136-137
, Behavior in
Baillie — *Diary* #165

, Bells of
Applegarth — *Heir.* p.190
, Changing
Irion — *Yes* p.24-27
, Choirs of. See **Choirs and choirboys**
, City
Words Change p.110-113
, Clergymen of. See *Clergymen*
, Collections in
Braude — *Source* #358-360
Braude — *Speaker's* #224-225
Fuller — *Thesaurus* #1561-1569
Weisfeld — *Pulpit* p.87-88, 110-114, 149
, Criticism of
Guideposts — *Faith* p.344-349
Woods — *Religious* p.131-132
, Definitions of
Woods — *Religious* p.133-135
, Discipline of
New Topical p.69
, Excellency of
New Topical p.82-83
, Failure of
Myers — *Thunder* p.16-18, 44-45
, Financing of
Kauffman — *For* p.94-95
, Goals of
Kauffman — *For* p.55-56, 59
, Groups in
Humes — *Instant* #30-31, 1203, 1204
, History of
Kennedy — *Fresh* p.32-34
, Hospitality of
Kauffman — *For* p.56-57
, Italian
Keys Happiness p.103-106
, Laymen of
Words Change p.126
, Love of
Words Change p.94-97
, Members as "ministers"
Kauffman — *For* p.59-60
, Membership in
Woods — *Religious* p.137-138
, Men in
Asimov — *Treasury* #113
Fuller — *Thesaurus* p.259-271
, Nature of
Woods — *Religious* p.138-142
, Necessity of
Baillie — *Diary* #275

, *of Israel*
New Topical p.46
, *on a hill*
Bach — *Make* p.31, 32
, *Organization in*
Flint — *Graham* p.101
, *Politics in*
Flint — *Graham* p.105-106
, *Popularity of*
Flint — *Graham* p.106
, *Prayer for*
Clark — *Windows* p.158
, *Reason for*
Carruthers — *Sparks* p.37-38
, *Services of*
Fuller — *Thesaurus* p.271-281
Mandel — *Stories* p.233
, *Standards of*
Kauffman — *For* p.56
, *Titles and names of*
New Topical p.271-272
, *Unity in*
Kauffman — *For* p.221
, *Visible*
Taylor — *With* p.80-81
, *Vitality of*
Woods — *Progress* p.142-143
, *Welfare of*
Zobell — *Speaker's* p.43-44
, *Women in*
Irion — *Yes* p.92-97
, *Work of*
Woods — *Religious* p.143-145
, *Workers of*
Carruthers — *Sparks* p.24-25
, *Year*
More Words p.29

CHURCHILL, WINSTON
Simpson — *'54* p.21, 130, 277

CHURCHYARDS. *See* **Cemeteries**

CICADAS. *See* **Locusts**

CICERO, MARCUS TULLIUS
Flesch — *Unusual* p.38
Lockridge — *World's* #3586

CIDER
Woods — *Content.* p.183-184

CIGARETTES
Flesch — *Unusual* p.38
Hunter — *Gems* p.14-20
Kauffman — *For* p.60-61
Knight's Illus. p.54-57
Knight's Treas. p.55-57

CIGARMAKERS
Kin — *Dictionary* p.47

CIGARS
Flesch — *Unusual* p.38
Lockridge — *World's* #2693-2694, 2705
Seldes — *Great* p.169

CIRCLES
Kin — *Dictionary* p.47
New Joy p.220
Peterson — *Art* p.173
Prochnow — *Success.* #1017
Wallis — *Words* p.87

CIRCUMLOCUTION
Flesch — *Unusual* p.38
Reader's — *Getting* p.199

CIRCUMSPECTION. *See* **Care; Prudence**

CIRCUMSTANCES
See also **Accident; Opportunity; Position;** etc.
Baillie — *Diary* #270
Bartlett — *Discovery* p.15-16
Book Proverbs p.130
Dirksen — *Quot.* #822-823, 888, 1045, 1681, 2208
Edwards — *Useful* p.82-83, 170
Flesch — *Unusual* p.38, 79
Forbes — *Thoughts See* index p.543
Grizer — *Wit* p.81-82
Harnsberger — *Mark* p.46
Henry — *5000* p.38-39, 79
Hovey — *Treasury* p.108; #252, 295, 528-536, 629, 660, 904, 1486, 1516
Keys Happiness p.217
Kin — *Dictionary* p.47-48
Kohn — *Pathways* p.131-133
Kohn — *Touch* p.180-181
Liddle — *Thought I, II, III* p.7, 12, 36, 61, 92, 111, 143
List — *Living* p.13-16
Lockridge — *World's* #60, 3864
Montapert — *Distilled* p.62-63, 136
New Joy p.59
Prochnow — *Public* #1627, 4345
Prochnow — *Speaker's* p.63
Prochnow — *Success.* #1622
Seldes — *Great* p.170
Woods — *Religious* p.151-152, 292

CIRCUS
See also **Animals; Clowns**
Asimov — *Treasury* #22
Cerf — *Laugh* p.49-56

Copeland — *10,000* p.581-584
Dirksen — *Quot.* #133
Harral — *Feature* p.121
Prochnow — *Public* #240, 328
Prochnow — *Speaker's* p.63
Woods — *Content.* p.84

CISTERNS
Maxwell — *Courage* p.9-14

CITADELS. *See* **Forts**

CITIES
See also **Civic affairs; Civic clubs; Suburbia; Towns**
Adams — *New* p.321
Alexander's Treasure. p.182
Copeland — *World's* p.663-675, 695-702
Dirksen — *Quot.* #34, 199, 545, 825, 1904-1905, 2384
Edwards — *Useful* p.83
Flesch — *Unusual* p.38-39
Fuller — *Epigrams* p.50
Harral — *Feature* p.227
Henry — *5000* p.39
Hobe — *Tapestries* p.115
Humes — *Instant* #206-225
Kauffman — *For* p.61-62
Kin — *Dictionary* p.48
Kronenberger — *Animal* p.39-40
Lockridge — *World's* #2082, 3165, 3167
New Topical p.47-48
Prochnow — *Public* #482, 1008, 2605, 4024-4025
Prochnow — *Success.* #1624
Schermerhorn — *1500* p.77-78
Sheban — *Wisdom* no p.
Strait — *Speaker's* p.44-45
Wallis — *Words* p.185
Woods — *Content.* p.78
Woods — *Religious* p.152
, and time
Adams — *New* p.337
, Dwellers in
Speaker's Desk #606, 747, 943
, Government of
Harral — *Feature* p.122
, Improvement of
Humes — *Instant* #1210-1212
, Laugh-provoking
Asimov — *Treasury* #202
, Life in
Prochnow — *Speaker's* p.64
, Meditation in
Irion — *Yes* p.85-88
, Modern
Auden — *Certain* p.77-80
, of God
Woods — *Religious* p.152
, of refuge
New Topical p.48
, Two (religious)
Woods — *Religious* p.152

CITIZENS
Flesch — *Unusual* p.38
Forbes — *Thoughts See* index p.543
Henry — *5000* p.39
Hovey — *Treasury* p.108-111; *See* index p.294
Montapert — *Distilled* p.63
Prochnow — *Success.* #1623
Wallis — *Words* p.110
Woods — *Religious* p.152

CITIZENSHIP
Dirksen — *Quot.* #387, 528, 619-620, 666, 709-712, 824, 1141, 2367
Droke — *Christian* p.96-97
Forbes — *Thoughts* p.5, 21, 235, 253, 259, 267, 275
Harnsberger — *Mark* p.46-47
Humes — *Instant* #192-205
Prochnow — *Success.* #1242
Sheban — *Wisdom* no p.
Wallis — *Treasure* p.176
Woods — *Business.* p.24-26
Woods — *Religious* p.152
Words — *Inspir.* p.141

CITIZENSHIP DAY
Harral — *Feature* p.122

CIVIC AFFAIRS
Dirksen — *Quot.* #2367, 2384
Harral — *Feature* p.122-123
Humes — *Instant* #226-228

CIVIC CLUBS
Harral — *Feature* p.123

CIVIL DEFENSE
Harral — *Feature* p.123

CIVIL LIBERTY. *See* **Civil rights; Freedom**

CIVIL RIGHTS
See also **Freedom; Races of man, relations of; Rights of man; Women, rights of**; etc.
Asimov — *Treasury* #85
Braude — *Source* #363-364
Dirksen — *Quot.* #7-8, 18, 81, 104, 547-552, 671, 1734, 2346
Flint — *Graham* p.31-32
Franke — *Buckley* p.29-31
Seldes — *Great* p.173-175
, for aged
Maltz — *Creative* p.183-184

CIVILITY. *See* **Courtesy; Etiquette**

CIVILIZATION
See also **Mankind; Progress;** etc.
Applegarth — *Heir.* p.44, 293
Bartlett — *Discovery* p.1-2, 5
Braude — *Source* #361-362
Braude — *Stories* p.65
Curtis — *Practical* p.19-20, 143-144, 148-156, 228, 547-548
Dirksen — *Quot.* #546, 826-830, 1794, 2375
Droke — *Christian* p.98-103
Du Noüy — *Human* p.124, 137-139, 142-154, 160-161, 173, 255-256
Du Noüy — *Road* p.195, 226, 240
Edwards — *Useful* p.84-85, 726
Flesch — *Unusual* p.39-40
Forbes — *Thoughts* See index p.543
Fuller — *Epigrams* p.50-51
Grizer — *Wit* p.82-83
Harnsberger — *Mark* p.47
Henry — *5000* p.39-40
Hovey — *Treasury* p.111; *See* index p.294
Humes — *Instant* #229-234
Johnson — *Bedside* p.45, 47
Keller — *Open* p.75
Kennedy — *Reader's* #153-163
Kohn — *Best* p.44-45
Liddle — *Thought I, II, III* p.65, 92, 105, 115, 149
Lockridge — *World's* #3632, 3640, 4216, 4496, 4984, 5757
Lytle — *Leaves* p.113
Montapert — *Distilled* p.63-64
Nichols — *Third* p.113-114, 145-146
Nizer — *Thinking* p.127-128, 209
Prochnow — *Public* #1593, 2867-2875, 4281
Prochnow — *Speaker's* p.64-65
Prochnow — *Success.* #322, 449, 467, 1172, 1470, 1625-1626
Seldes — *Great* p.170-172
Sheban — *Wisdom* no p.
Speaker's Desk #48
Wheelis — *Moralist* p.58, 79
Woods — *Business.* p.27
Woods — *Religious* p.152-154
, and books
Kauffman — *For* p.34
, and Christianity
Kauffman — *For* p.62-63
Woods — *Religious* p.154-155
, and religion
Woods — *Religious* p.155-156
, and slavery
Hubbard — *Scrap* p.48
, debt of
Phillips — *Choice* p.363

CLAIMS
Curtis — *Practical* p.395-397
Lockridge — *World's* #1523
Wallis — *Words* p.13

CLAMS
Harnsberger — *Mark* p.48-50

CLARITY. *See* **Clearness**

CLASSES (social)
See also **Bourgeoisie;** etc.
Dirksen — *Quot.* #503, 611, 645, 1743
Flesch — *Unusual* p.40
Forbes — *Thoughts* p.17, 27, 86, 146, 397, 469
Lindeman — *Emerson* p.183
Prochnow — *Public* #495
Seldes — *Great* p.175-183
Woods — *Business.* p.27, 156

CLASSICS AND CLASSICISM
Curtis — *Practical* p.431, 442-443
Flesch — *Unusual* p.40-41
Harnsberger — *Mark* p.50
Ideas p.65-68

CLASSIFICATION
See also **Organization**
Flesch — *Unusual* p.41
Lytle — *Leaves* p.84
Prochnow — *Success.* #1627

"CLASSROOM CLASSICS"
Fun Fare p.12, 114, 242-243

CLAUSTROPHOBIA
Prochnow — *Public* #622

CLAY
Applegarth — *Heir.* p.266
Kin — *Dictionary* p.48
Prochnow — *Public* #2584
Wallis — *Treasure* p.149

CLEANING
Guideposts — *Faith* p.337-340
Harral — *Feature* p.123

CLEANLINESS
See also **Purity**
Edwards — *Useful* p.85
Evans — *Thoughts III (Open Road)* p.75-86, 108, 208
Evans — *Thoughts IV* p.14-15, 19, 46, 96, 121, 124-125, 128-129, 136-137, 149, 205

Forbes — *Thoughts* p.392, 450
Fuller — *Epigrams* p.51
Henry — *5000* p.40
Holmes — *I've* p.36-37
Hovey — *Treasury* p.111-112, #555-558
Kennedy — *Reader's* #164
Kin — *Dictionary* p.48
Menninger — *Blue.* p.208, 218
Prochnow — *Public* #408, 433, 520, 704, 1940
Speaker's Desk #134, 138, 140, 316, 325, 425, 476, 486, 494, 847, 1121

CLEARNESS
Flesch — *Unusual* p.41-42
Kin — *Dictionary* p.48
Lockridge — *World's* #1745, 4017
Prochnow — *Public* #2000
Prochnow — *Success.* #1628-1629

CLEMENCY. *See* **Mercy; Pardon**

CLEMENS, SAMUEL L. (MARK TWAIN)
Botkin — *Anecdotes* p.204, 215
Harnsberger — *Mark See* index p.537-558
Peterson — *Art* p.225
Wallis — *Words* p.93
Weisfeld — *Pulpit* p.22-23

CLEOPATRA
Asimov — *Treasury* #43
Flesch — *Unusual* p.42
Lockridge — *World's* #5575

CLERGYMEN
See also **Chaplains; Evangelism and evangelists**
Applegarth — *Heir.* p.154, 220
Asimov — *Treasury* #259-260, 488, 490, 504, 589-590, 601
Botkin — *Anecdotes* p.xxv, 62, 111-132, 163, 192-193, 219, 224, 235
Botkin — *Treasury* p.411, 415-416, 422
Braude — *Source* #365-366, 1347-1350
Braude — *Speaker's* #1059-1065
Braude — *Stories* p.303
Carruthers — *Sparks* p.59-60
Copeland — *10,000* p.501-518
Day — *Meditations* p.66-69
Dirksen — *Quot.* #1458-1459
Droke — *Christian* p.419-425
Edwards — *Useful* p.393, 490-492
Flesch — *Unusual* p.42, 174, 203, 223-224
Flint — *Graham* p.109-110
Fogg — *1000* #65, 93, 95, 279, 309, 351, 571
Fuller — *Epigrams* p.240-242
Fuller — *Thesaurus* #1461-1477
Garland — *Subject* p.194, 223, 239-240
Guideposts — *Faith* p.85-89, 415, 435-439
Harnsberger — *Mark* p.50-51, 369-370
Harral — *Feature* p.218-220
Henry — *5000* p.40, 216-217
Hobe — *Tapestries* p.208
Hovey — *Treasury* p.258; #499, 888, 1628-1630; *See also* index p.299
Hubbard — *Scrap* p.52- 54
Kauffman — *For* p.57-60, 92
Kennedy — *Reader's* #671-682, 823-836
Kin — *Dictionary* p.197
Knight's Illus. p.243-251
Knight's Treas. p.277-292
Lockridge — *World's* #1973, 2618, 3744, 3900, 5698
Lytle — *Leaves* p.26, 45, 47, 129
Mandel — *Stories* p.209-210
Modern Eloquence (14) p.1-19
More Words p.110-111
New Topical p.166-167
Nizer — *Thinking* p.126-127
Peale — *Guideposts* p.245-250
Prochnow — *Public* #25, 150, 175, 564, 573, 735, 843, 955
Prochnow — *Speaker's* p.213-214, 239-240
Prochnow — *Success.* #1359, 2176
Schermerhorn — *1500* p.103-104, 246-249
Seldes — *Great* p.183-185, 300
Sheban — *Wisdom* no p.
Speaker's Desk p.203-205; *See* index p.298
Suter — *Prayers* #131-140
Wallis — *Words* p.42
Walters — *How* p.52-54
Weisfeld — *Pulpit* p.49-64, 91-103
Woods — *Content.* p.49
Woods — *Religious* p.156-159, 632-633, 717-718, 766-772
Words — *Inspir.* p.58
, Baptist
Weisfeld — *Pulpit* p.130, 132
, Criticism of
Woods — *Religious* p.158-159
, Episcopal
Weisfeld — *Pulpit* p.124-125
, Methodist
Weisfeld — *Pulpit* p.159
, Negro
Weisfeld — *Pulpit* p.61, 64, 76-77, 79-80, 117

, Presbyterian
Weisfeld — *Pulpit* p.9
, Scottish
Weisfeld — *Pulpit* p.166
, Titles and names
New Topical p.272-273
, Wives of
Unlimited Power p.180-183

CLERKS
Manchee — *Secret* p.205

CLEVELAND, GROVER
Harnsberger — *Mark* p.51-52

CLEVERNESS
See also **Ability; Genius; Talent**
Dirksen — *Quot.* #170
Flesch — *Unusual* p.42
Forbes — *Thoughts* p.107, 159, 213, 219, 242, 325, 406, 458, 473
Fuller — *Epigrams* p.52
Fuller — *Thesaurus* #526-541
Grizer — *Wit* p.83
Henry — *5000* p.40
Kin — *Dictionary* p.48-49, 233
Lockridge — *World's* #659, 664, 852, 1628, 2570, 3484, 4182, 4259, 4496, 5012
Manchee — *Secret* p.196-237
Montapert — *Distilled* p.64
Prochnow — *Public* #1955, 2245, 2288, 4026-4028
Prochnow — *Success.* #698, 1630
Speaker's Desk See index p.304

CLICHÉS
Flesch — *Unusual* p.42
Ginott — *Between* p.41-42, 67
Prochnow — *Public* #2246
Rau — *Act* p.116-125
Seldes — *Great* p.185

CLIMATE. *See* **Weather**

CLIMBERS AND CLIMBING
See also **Mountain-climbing**
Auden — *Certain* p.81-85
Dirksen — *Quot.* #1906-1907
Kin — *Dictionary* p.49
Montapert — *Distilled* p.64-65
Peterson — *Art* p.376
Wallis — *Treasure* p.18, 20

CLIPPINGS
Peterson — *Art* p.154

CLOCKS AND WATCHES
Applegarth — *Heir.* p.61-69
Forbes — *Thoughts* p.255, 273, 331, 468
Harnsberger — *Mark* p.52-54, 507-508
Harral — *Feature* p.123, 300-301
Keys Happiness p.285-288
Kin — *Dictionary* p.49
Peterson — *Art* p.19, 128
Prochnow — *Public* #178, 439, 519, 532, 535, 810-811, 1952, 2236, 2294
Prochnow — *Speaker's* p.65
Wallis — *Treasure* p.227
Wood — *Wellsprings* p.13
, Alarm
Flesch — *Unusual* p.8
Schermerhorn — *1500* p.13
, Molecular
Holmes — *Design* p.7-8

"CLOSED SHOP"
Ideas p.68-69
Seldes — *Great* p.185
Woods — *Business.* p.27-28

CLOSENESS
Kin — *Dictionary* p.172
Lytle — *Leaves* p.107
Prochnow — *Public* #2219

CLOTHES
See also types of clothing, e.g. **Hats**
Applegarth — *Heir.* p.49, 219
Book Proverbs p.76
Braude — *Source* #118-120, 157-161
Braude — *Speaker's* #1571-1581
Braude — *Stories* p.124-125
Edwards — *Useful* p.142-144
Evans — *Unto* p.11
Flesch — *Unusual* p.42
Forbes — *Thoughts* p.141, 386, 400
Fuller — *Epigrams* p.52-53
Fuller — *Thesaurus* #716-726
George — *Book See* index p.443
Grizer — *Wit* p.83-84
Harnsberger — *Mark* p.54-57, 91-92
Harral — *Feature* p.123-125, 241, 320
Henry — *5000* p.41, 67
Kin — *Dictionary* p.49, 74
Lockridge — *World's* #2712, 2717, 5044
Menninger — *Blue.* p.200, 215-217, 221
Montapert — *Distilled* p.65
New Topical p.99-100
Prochnow — *Public* #16, 70, 566, 606, 783, 1030, 1136, 1220, 1887, 1943, 2735, 2876-2877, 4060-4062, 4382
Prochnow — *Speaker's* p.66
Prochnow — *Success.* #953, 968
Walters — *How* p.121-124

White — *Life* p.96-102
, *Girls'*
Daly — *Personality* p.124-127
, *Men's*
Harral — *Feature* p.217
Kin — *Dictionary* p.259
Prochnow — *Public* #132
Prochnow — *Success.* #115
, *Old*
Wilcox — *Heart* p.11-13
, *Shopping for*
Fun Fare p.48-51
, *Teenager*
Ginott — *Between* p.23, 31-32, 34, 105-106, 238-239
, *Women's*
Rogers — *Time* p.79-84

"CLOUD OF GLORY"
Lair — *Baby* p.167
New Topical p.49

CLOUDS
Auden — *Certain* p.399-400
Baillie — *Diary* #115
Curtis — *Practical* p.199
Evans — *Useful* p.85
Goudge — *Comfort* p.29-30
Kin — *Dictionary* p.49
New Topical p.48-49
Wallis — *Treasure* p.118

CLOVER
Applegarth — *Heir.* p.100

CLOWNS
Kin — *Dictionary* p.50

CLUBS
See also names and types of clubs
Braude — *Speaker's* #226-228
Harral — *Feature* p.125

CLUMSINESS. *See* **Awkwardness**

COACHMEN
Botkin — *Anecdotes* p.193

COAL MINES AND MINING
Botkin — *Treasury* p.630, 864-873
Guideposts — *Faith* p.282-286
Hubbard — *Scrap* p.25
Kin — *Dictionary* p.50
Prochnow — *Public* #15
Seldes — *Great* p.185

COARSENESS
Lockridge — *World's* #132

COATS
Prochnow — *Public* #722, 978

COBBLERS. *See* **Shoemakers**

COCKSURENESS. *See* **Certainty**

COCKTAILS AND COCKTAIL PARTIES
See also **Bars**
Asimov — *Treasury* #584
Flesch — *Unusual* p.43
Fun Fare p.156-157, 307-308
Prochnow — *Success.* #562

CODES
Evans — *This* p.55-56
Hovey — *Treasury* p.113; #559-566, 638

CODFISH
Botkin — *Anecdotes* p.89, 206

COERCION. *See* **Force; Influence**

COEXISTENCE
Braude — *Source* #367
Franke — *Buckley* p.32-34
Ginott — *Between* p.19-20, 216-221, 226-237

COFFEE
Flesch — *Unusual* p.43
Harnsberger — *Mark* p.57-58
Harral — *Feature* p.125
Prochnow — *Public* #589
Prochnow — *Speaker's* p.66
Prochnow — *Success.* #918
, *Breaks for*
Braude — *Source* #368-369
Holmes — *I've* p.45-46

"COGITO ERGO SUM" (I think, therefore I exist)
Seldes — *Great* p.185-186

COINCIDENCE
See also **Accident; Chance**
Flesch — *Unusual* p.43
Prochnow — *Success.* #872
Speaker's Desk #29, 94, 547, 797, 835, 905

COINS. *See* **Numismatics**

"COKAYGNE, LAND OF"
Ideas p.69-70, 87

COLD (weather)
Harnsberger — *Mark* p.58-59
Kin — *Dictionary* p.50
Prochnow — *Public* #176, 180, 1015, 1921

COLD WAR
Franke — *Buckley* p.35
Ideas p.87-88

Seldes — *Great* p.186
Woods — *Religious* p.161

COLERIDGE, SAMUEL TAYLOR
Adams — *New* p.32

COLLATERAL
Prochnow — *Public* #383

COLLECT. *See* **Prayer**

COLLECTIONS
Flesch — *Unusual* p.43
Fuller — *Thesaurus* #2176-2179
Grizer — *Wit* p.84-85
Harral — *Feature* p.126
Kohn — *Pathways* p.15-18
Prochnow — *Public* #1011, 1035 1644
Prochnow — *Success.* #873

COLLECTIVE BARGAINING
Woods — *Business.* p.29-31

COLLECTIVISM
Curtis — *Practical* p.323-324
Franke — *Buckley* p.35-36
Ideas p.88-90
Seldes — *Great* p.187
Woods — *Business.* p.31-32
Woods — *Religious* p.161

COLLECTORS AND COLLECTING. *See* **Collections**

COLLEGE EDUCATION
Nichols — *New* p.18-19

COLLEGE HUMOR
Copeland — *10,000* p.373-409
Fun Fare p.114-115

COLLEGE STUDENTS
Cerf — *Laugh* p.358-365
Fuller — *Thesaurus* #1041
Manchee — *Secret* p.206-207
Peterson — *Art* p.301
, Religion of
Guideposts — *Faith* p.175-179

COLLEGES. *See* **Universities and colleges**

COLLISION
Prochnow — *Public* #267, 577, 1166

COLONIZATION
Dirksen — *Quot.* #554
Franke — *Buckley* p.38-39
Seldes — *Great* p.188
Woods — *Religious* p.161

COLOR
Applegarth — *Heir.* p.198
Flesch — *Unusual* p.43
Harnsberger — *Mark* p.59-60
Henry — *5000* p.41
Holmes — *I've* p.31-32
Kin — *Dictionary* p.50
Lockridge — *World's* #4900, 5050
Peterson — *Art* p.80
Prochnow — *Public* #980, 1062
, Spectrum of
White — *Job* p.78-82

"COLOR BAR" (races)
Ideas p.91-92

COLORADO
Botkin — *Anecdotes* p.35, 174-175, 230
Botkin — *Treasury* p.63, 225, 324, 377, 566, 612, 714
Woods — *Content.* p.80

COLUMBA, SAINT
Baillie — *Diary* #231

COLUMBUS, CHRISTOPHER
Harnsberger — *Mark* p.60-61
Liddle — *Thought I, II, III* p.177
Wallis — *Words* p.106, 124

COLUMNISTS
Harral — *Feature* p.127
Nizer — *Thinking* p.30, 82-83
Seldes — *Great* p.188

COMBAT. *See* **War**

COMBINATION
Woods — *Business.* p.32-33

COMBS
Kin — *Dictionary* p.50

"COMEBACKS"
Peale — *Guideposts* p.3-23

COMEDY AND COMEDIANS
See also **Clowns; Humor;** etc.
Asimov — *Treasury* #30, 39, 44, 171, 309
Dirksen — *Quot.* #323
Flesch — *Unusual* p.43
Guideposts — *Faith* p.134-138
Harnsberger — *Mark* p.61-62
Lockridge — *World's* #3889
Mandelbaum — *Choose* p.17
Nizer — *Thinking* p.77
Peale — *Guideposts* p.231-235
Seldes — *Great* p.188

COMFORT
See also **Consolation; Encouragement; Sympathy**
Applegarth — *Heir.* p.49
Detherage — *Sunrise* p.90, 128, 134, 140, 153, 189
Dirksen — *Quot.* #1211, 1281-1282, 1908
Emmons — *Mature* p.139-140
Evans — *Unto* p.62, 83, 121
Evans — *Useful* p.85-86
Flesch — *Unusual* p.43
Forbes — *Thoughts* p.4, 110, 146, 163, 199, 309, 378, 386, 469
Garland — *Subject* p.45-46
Goudge — *Comfort* p.238-289
Harnsberger — *Mark* p.62
Hobe — *Tapestries* p.35, 130, 145, 197, 219-235
Hovey — *Treasury* p.113; *See also* index p.294
Howell — *Lines* p.73-78
Hubbard — *Scrap* p.70
Kin — *Dictionary* p.51
Prochnow — *Public* #679, 2179, 2495
Seldes — *Great* p.188
Speaker's Desk #31, 36, 324, 446, 515, 537, 590, 876
Woods — *Religious* p.161
Words — *Inspir.* p.93

COMMAND AND COMMANDERS
See also **Armed forces; Authority; Executives**; etc.
Dirksen — *Quot.* #2099
Edwards — *Useful* p.86
Flesch — *Unusual* p.43
Forbes — *Thoughts* p.4, 17, 351. 365
Kin — *Dictionary* p.51
Montapert — *Distilled* p.66
Prochnow — *Public* #83, 996, 2628

COMMANDMENTS, TEN
Asimov — *Treasury* #487
Boas — *History* p.76
Braude — *Source* #1686
Evans — *Faith* p.12, 49, 80, 106, 114-115, 129, 154, 182
Evans — *Quote* p.81-96
Evans — *This* p.9
Evans — *Thoughts* p.37-38, 91, 156, 212
Evans — *Thoughts II (Open Door)* p.26, 89, 99-100, 117, 130, 175, 189
Evans — *Thoughts III (Open Road) See* index no p.
Evans — *Unto* p.29, 48-49, 52, 97, 123
Flesch — *Unusual* p.286
Flint — *Graham* p.32
Forbes — *Thoughts* p.64, 392, 477
Garland — *Subject* p.46-47
Grizer — *Wit* p.460
Hobe — *Tapestries* p.135
Hovey — *Treasury* #522, 645, 1078, 1136, 1163, 1425, 1555, 1583, 1689
Johnson — *Bedside* p.3
Lytle — *Leaves* p.47
Mandel — *Stories* p.248
Myers — *Thunder* p.11-175
New Topical p.49
Prochnow — *Public* #1592, 1942, 2296, 2460-2469
Seldes — *Great* p.906
Welk — *Guide.* p.73-74
Woods — *Religious* p.162
, and courtrooms
Kauffman — *For* p.63-64
, Greatest
Guideposts — *Faith* p.403-**407**
, Modern
Webb — *Edge* p.111-112
, Ten (individually)
First
Myers — *Thunder* p.24-37
Second
Myers — *Thunder* p.38-50
Third
Myers — *Thunder* p.51-64
Fourth
Myers — *Thunder* p.65-78
Fifth
Myers — *Thunder* p.79-93
Sixth
Myers — *Thunder* p.94-106
Seventh
Myers — *Thunder* p.107-118
Eighth
Myers — *Thunder* p.119-133
Ninth
Myers — *Thunder* p.134-147
Tenth
Myers — *Thunder* p.148-163

COMMENCEMENT
Asimov — *Treasury* #270
Dirksen — *Quot.* #92
Evans — *This* p.16-17
Evans — *Thoughts I* p.159-160
Evans — *Thoughts III (Open Road)* p.146-149, 158-159
Evans — *Thoughts IV* p.63-70
Forbes — *Thoughts* p.432
Hovey — *Treasury* #576-578; *See also* p.114, Index p.303
Peterson — *Art* p.185
Prochnow — *Public* #816, 1355, 2447
Prochnow — *Success.* #171, 233, 244

Schermerhorn — *1500* p.86
Tanksley — *Friend* p.54

COMMENDATION. *See* **Praise**

COMMERCE
See also **Business; Trade;** *etc.*
Dirksen — *Quot.* #1909-1910
Edwards — *Useful* p.86
Forbes — *Thoughts* p.139, 221, 401, 465, 514
Henry — *5000* p.41
Hooker — *Index* p.125-133
New Topical p.49-50
Prochnow — *Public* #4029-4030
Prochnow — *Success.* #1631-1632
Seldes — *Great* p.188-189

COMMERCIALISM
Evans — *Unto* p.11
Hubbard — *Scrap* p.169, 202

COMMITMENT
Auden — *Certain* p.86-87
Evans — *Thoughts I* p.60-61, 82, 92-93, 185
Flint — *Graham* p.9, 16, 32-33, 35
Hobe — *Tapestries* p.139
Hovey — *Treasury* p.114-115; #336, 579-583, 1462, 1587, 1619, 1624, 1740, 1778
Humes — *Instant* #235-238
Kauffman — *For* p.64
Kennedy — *Fresh* p.92-95
Phillips — *Choice* p.19, 158, 310, 372
Seaburg — *Great* p.272, 324, 333, 335, 340, 349, 355, 357, 380, 384, 389, 406
Woods — *Religious* p.162

COMMITTEES
Braude — *Source* #374
Braude — *Stories* p.69
Edwards — *Useful* p.726
Flesch — *Unusual* p.43
Liddle — *Thought I, II, III* p.103
Prochnow — *Public* #4322
Prochnow — *Success.* #631, 741, 1355, 1453, 1633
Woods — *Business.* p.33

COMMON LAW
Curtis — *Practical* p.393-394
Seldes — *Great* p.190

COMMON MAN
See also **Man** (Mankind)
Grizer — *Wit* p.85
Ideas p.59-61
Seldes — *Great* p.190-192
Woods — *Religious* p.162

COMMON SENSE
See also **Intelligence; Sense**
Braude — *Speaker's* #237
Dirksen — *Quot.* #831
Du Noüy — *Human* p.5-7, 182-183
Edwards — *Useful* p.86-87
Evans — *Unto* p.72
Flesch — *Unusual* p.43-44
Fogg — *1000* #350
Forbes — *Thoughts* p.5, 25, 78, 107, 147, 206, 289, 311, 331, 334, 342, 426, 433, 435, 465, 501
Fuller — *Thesaurus* #1156-1157
Grizer — *Wit* p.86, 217
Halverson — *Perspective* p.39
Henry — *5000* p.42
Johnson — *Bedside* p.77
Kauffman — *For* p.17
Keys Happiness p.307-309
Kin — *Dictionary* p.51, 230
Liddle — *Thought I, II, III* p.44, 54, 87, 146
Lockridge — *World's* #1512, 3220, 3388
Montapert — *Distilled* p.67
Prochnow — *Public* #1154, 1950, 2878-2879
Prochnow — *Success.* #1634
Seldes — *Great* p.192
Speaker's Desk p.17-19; #286-287, 365, 695, 709, 816
Wilcox — *Heart* p.36-39

COMMONPLACE
Flesch — *Unusual* p.44, 198
Hovey — *Treasury* p.115-116; #584-588
Kin — *Dictionary* p.51
Lytle — *Leaves* p.109
Mandel — *Stories* p.40
Seldes — *Great* p.192
Wallis — *Treasure* p.25, 237
Wallis — *Words* p.35, 88, 211, 239
Woods — *Content.* p.91, 93, 111

COMMONWEALTH
Seldes — *Great* p.192-194

COMMUNES
Kauffman — *For* p.64-66
Seldes — *Great* p.194

COMMUNICATION
See also **Children; Discussion; Letters and letter writing; Media; Parents and parenthood;** types of communication
Dirksen — *Quot.* p.732, 2318
Evans — *Thoughts III (Open Road)* p.16-17, 30, 48
Evans — *Thoughts IV* p.36
Evans — *Unto* p.57

Garland — *Subject* p.48
Harral — *Feature* p.127
Hovey — *Treasury* p.116; #589-590, 1036, 1121
Humes — *Instant* #239-243
Kennedy — *Reader's* #169
Lindbergh — *Gift* p.102-103
Lockridge — *World's* #5261
Mandel — *Stories* p.40-41
Seldes — *Great* p.194-195
Sheen — *Thoughts* p.129-141
Simpson — *Contemp.* p.339-467
Wallis — *Words* p.75, 88
Wheelis — *Moralist* p.82, 151-152
Woods — *Wellsprings* p.76

, Creative
Humes — *Instant* p.32-34

, Mass
Seldes — *Great* p.647

, Particulars in
Humes — *Instant* p.32-34

, Personal
Humes — *Instant* p.32-34, 44

, Plausible
Humes — *Instant* p.32-34

, Teenager
Ginott — *Between* p.35, 55, 73, 107-108

, vs. Secrecy
Kauffman — *For* p.215-216

COMMUNION
Applegarth — *Heir.* p.66, 307-308
Baillie — *Diary* #97
Clark — *Windows* p.166
Day — *Meditations* p.15-16
Emmons — *Mature* p.24-25
Fridy — *Meditat.* p.127
Garland — *Subject* p.48
Hobe — *Tapestries* p.109
Hovey — *Treasury* p.116-121; #258, 450, 470, 497, 591-604, 1038
Knight's Treas. p.206-208
Lockridge — *World's* #5169
Lytle — *Leaves* p.106
Maxwell — *Courage* p.166-174
More Words p.81-84
New Topical p.50
Strait — *Speaker's* p.46
Suter — *Prayers* #156-172
Wallis — *Words* p.167
Woods — *Religious* p.162-164
Woods — *Wellsprings* p.50-51

COMMUNISM
Braude — *Source* #375-377
Braude — *Speaker's* #238-245
Braude — *Stories* p.69, 169-170
Curtis — *Practical* p.344-345
Dirksen — *Quot.* #537, 556, 833, 1644-1647, 2368, 2371
Droke — *Christian* p.103-110
Edwards — *Useful* p.87
Flesch — *Unusual* p.44
Flint — *Graham* p.33-34, 81, 129
Forbes — *Thoughts* p.13, 36, 224, 391, 444, 475
Franke — *Buckley* p.41-43
Grizer — *Wit* p.86-90
Harnsberger — *Mark* p.62
Henry — *5000* p.42
Hoffer — *Reflect.* p.44-45
Hovey — *Treasury* p.121-123; #374, 454, 605-611, 926, 972, 1039, 1263, 1278, 1327
Hunter — *Gems* p.20-22
Ideas p.92-94
Kennedy — *Reader's* #170-180
Knight's Illus. p.59-62
Knight's Treas. p.61-65
Myers — *Thunder* p.97
Prochnow — *Public* #1210, 2880-2881, 4352
Prochnow — *Success.* #186, 213, 260, 289, 947, 1635-1636
Seldes — *Great* p.90, 195-202
Woods — *Business.* p.33-38
Woods — *Change* p.76-79
Woods — *Religious* p.164-166

, and Christianity
Keller — *You* p.39-40
Woods — *Religious* p.166-167
Words Change p.127-128

, Corruption in
Guideposts — *Faith* p.59-64

, Counteracting
Peale — *Guideposts* p.46-50

, Manifesto
Curtis — *Practical* p.280-288

, Morality of
Woods — *Religious* p.167-168

COMMUNITY
See also **Cities**; etc.
Harral — *Feature* p.128
Hovey — *Treasury* p.123-124; *See also* index p.295
Humes — *Instant* #244
Lockridge — *World's* #5118
Mandel — *Stories* p.41-42
Phillips — *Choice* p.381, 383, 389, 390
Wallis — *Words* p.43, 236
Wheelis — *Moralist* p.27, 70-71, 82-83, 85-92, 101-102, 129-132
Woods — *Religious* p.168-169

, and individual
Krishnamurti — *Urgency* p.138-139

, Chests of
Harral — *Feature* p.127

, Ethics of
McDonagh — *Invit.* p.38-58

, *Service of*
Humes — *Instant* #1263-1264
Menninger — *Blue.* p.35
, *Work of*
Day — *Meditations* p.60-64

COMMUTERS
Cerf — *Laugh* p.143-146
Prochnow — *Public* #1650
Prochnow — *Speaker's* p.70

COMPANIONSHIP
See also **Associates; Friends and friendship**
Alexander's Treasure. p.274-275
Applegarth — *Heir.* p.41, 48-49
Book Proverbs p.132
Braude — *Source* #378
Braude — *Speaker's* #29-30
Braude — *Stories* p.70
Dirksen — *Quot.* #200, 1791, 1849, 1911-1913, 1286-1287
Edwards — *Useful* p.87-88
Emmons — *Mature* p.29-31, 87
Evans — *Thoughts III (Open Road)* p.26, 65, 109, 117
Evans — *Unto* p.64
Flesch — *Unusual* p.44
Forbes — *Thoughts* p.116, 304, 330, 332, 354, 392, 404-405, 461
Henry — *5000* p.42
Hobe — *Tapestries* p.36
Holmes — *I've* p.32-33
Kin — *Dictionary* p.51-52
Krishnamurti — *Think* p.89-90
Lockridge — *World's* #2798, 3450, 3640, 5077
Lytle — *Leaves* p.79
Montapert — *Distilled* p.67-68
New Joy p.148
Peterson — *Art* p.44
Prochnow — *Public* #1979
Prochnow — *Success.* #1061
Reader's — *20th* p.11-13
Wallis — *Treasure* p.75, 99, 169
Wallis — *Words* p.20, 76, 81

COMPARISON
See also **Analogy; Contrast**
Edwards — *Useful* p.88
Evans — *This* p.145
Evans — *Thoughts II (Open Door)* p.117-118, 166-169
Flesch — *Unusual* p.44
Henry — *5000* p.43
Holmes — *I've* p.64
Kin — *Dictionary* p.52
Lockridge — *World's* #696
Lytle — *Leaves* p.28, 80
Prochnow — *Public* #736, 772

COMPASS
Applegarth — *Heir.* p.277
Prochnow — *Public* #211

COMPASSION
See also **Mercy; Pity; Sympathy**
Applegarth — *Heir.* p.204, 241
Dirksen — *Quot.* #6
Evans — *Thoughts IV* p.106-107, 167, 206-207
Flesch — *Unusual* p.44-45
Flint — *Graham* p.34, 130
Forbes — *Thoughts* p.105
Fridy — *Meditat.* p.59
Garland — *Subject* p.49
Hoffer — *Reflect.* p.24-25
Hovey — *Treasury* p.124; #616-620
Humes — *Instant* #245-248
Irion — *Yes* p.9
Johnson — *Bedside* p.2
Kauffman — *For* p.66
Lockridge — *World's* #495, 3785, 5764
Mandel — *Stories* p.42-43
Mandelbaum — *Choose* p.37-41
New Topical p.51
Phillips — *Choice* p.231
Prochnow — *Speaker's* p.69
Voss — *Quotations* p.53-56
Woods — *Religious* p.170-171
, *Teenager*
Ginott — *Between* p.57, 243

COMPENSATION
See also **Advantage; Benefits (Personal); Profit; Reward; Satisfaction**
Braude — *Source* #379-381
Braude — *Stories* p.70
Edwards — *Useful* p.88-89, 530
Evans — *Faith* p.92
Evans — *Thoughts I* p.108, 110, 119
Evans — *Thoughts II (Open Door)* p.99, 209
Evans — *Thoughts III (Open Road)* p.50, 158-159
Evans — *Thoughts IV* p.94, 109, 147
Evans — *Unto* p.117, 135
Flesch — *Unusual* p.45
Forbes — *Thoughts* p.99, 422, 442
Harnsberger — *Mark* p.62
Henry — *5000* p.43
Lindeman —*Emerson* p.73-88, 145-146
Lytle — *Leaves* p.31, 103, 150
Prochnow — *Public* #141, 366
White — *Job* p.51, 96, 103, 109
Woods — *Content.* p.44, 112
Woods — *Religious* p.821

COMPETENCE. *See* **Ability; Efficiency**

COMPETITION
See also **Rivalry**
Braude — *Source* #382-384
Braude — *Speaker's* #246-248
Braude — *Stories* p.70
Curtis — *Human* p.11
Curtis — *Practical* p.319-320, 325
Dirksen — *Quot.* #700, 1914-1915
Flesch — *Unusual* p.45
Forbes — *Thoughts* p.17, 145, 148, 205, 375, 423, 469, 490, 494, 508, 518
Fuller — *Epigrams* p.53-54
Fuller — *Thesaurus* #2116
Garland — *Subject* p.49
Grizer — *Wit* p.90-92
Holmes — *Design* p.150-151
Hubbard — *Scrap* p.227
Kin — *Dictionary* p.52
Kohn — *Thoughts* p.82-86
Mandel — *Stories* p.43
Modern Eloquence (14) p.299
Montapert — *Distilled* p.68-69
Nichols — *New* p.74-75
Phillips — *Choice* p.114
Prochnow — *Public* #1009, 1420, 2358, 4359
Prochnow — *Speaker's* p.70
Seldes — *Great* p.202-203
Welk — *Guide.* p.103-105
Woods — *Business.* p.38-43
Woods — *Religious* p.171

COMPLACENCY
See also **Assurance; Contentment; Righteousness; Satisfaction**
Braude — *Source* #385-386
Edwards — *Useful* p.89
Evans — *Faith* p.7-8, 143, 151-152, 213
Forbes — *Thoughts* p.160, 173, 300
Mandel — *Stories* p.43
Nizer — *Thinking* p.104, 173
Prochnow — *Success.* #802, 1231, 1318
Woods — *Religious* p.171, 940
, Prayer for
Unlimited Power p.83

COMPLAINING
See also **Discontent**
Asimov — *Treasury* #31
Book Proverbs p.105
Braude — *Source* #387-388
Dirksen — *Quot.* #175, 626
Edwards — *Useful* p.89, 237, 275, 726
Evans — *Thoughts III (Open Road)* p.110
Evans — *Unto* p.38
Flesch — *Unusual* p.45
Forbes — *Thoughts* p.387, 403, 468, 471, 476
Franke — *Buckley* p.43
Fuller — *Epigrams* p.54
Grizer — *Wit* p.92-93
Harnsberger — *Mark* p.62-63
Harral — *Feature* p.244
Henry — *5000* p.43
Hobe — *Tapestries* p.72
Hovey — *Treasury* p.124; #621-622
How To Live p.474-478
Huxley — *You* p.286
Johnson — *Bedside* p.277
Keys Happiness p.137-138
Kin — *Dictionary* p.52, 112
Kohn — *Touch* p.65-69
Lockridge — *World's* #2015, 3087
Lytle — *Leaves* p.16, 116
Maltz — *Creative* p.52
Mandel — *Stories* p.44
Montapert — *Distilled* p.69-70, 185
Prochnow — *Public* #1567, 2229
Prochnow — *Speaker's* p.70, 176-177
Prochnow — *Success.* #1008, 1637
Speaker's Desk #105, 425, 861, 982, 1015, 1176
Woods — *Religious* p.171

COMPLETENESS
Flesch — *Unusual* p.8, 45
Keys Happiness p.505-506
Wallis — *Treasure* p.163
Wallis — *Words* p.61

COMPLEXES
Curtis — *Practical* p.504

COMPLEXION. *See* **Skin**

COMPLEXITY
See also **Difficulties**
Braude — *Stories* p.70
Evans — *Unto* p.48
Flesch — *Unusual* p.45
Prochnow — *Public* #669, 1911
Sheen — *Comment.* p.71-73

COMPLIANCE. *See* **Agreement**

COMPLIMENTS
See also **Flattery; Praise**
Braude — *Stories* p.71-72
Edwards — *Useful* p.89
Flesch — *Unusual* p.45
Harnsberger — *Mark* p.63-64
Henry — *5000* p.43-44
Holmes — *I've* p.62

How To Live p.18-22
Keys Happiness p.41-44, 336, 340
Lockridge — *World's* #2017, 3719
Prochnow — *Public* #1931, 1953
Prochnow — *Speaker's* p.71
Speaker's Desk #40, 81, 752, 922, 959, 970, 988, 1003, 1018, 1067

COMPOSERS
Adams — *New* p.63
Fuller — *Thesaurus* #1311-1326
Prochnow — *Success.* #1502

COMPOSURE
See also **Calmness; Self-control**
Asimov — *Treasury* #420, 423
Nizer — *Thinking* p.95

COMPREHENSION. *See* **Understanding**

COMPROMISE
See also **Complacency; Expediency**
Applegarth — *Heir.* p.166
Braude — *Source* #389-391
Braude — *Speaker's* #249-251
Braude — *Stories* p.33, 72
Dirksen — *Quot.* #76, 361, 744, 834, 1034
Edwards — *Useful* p.89-90, 129-130
Evans — *Faith* p.98, 131, 139, 153
Evans — *This* p.63, 68-71
Evans — *Thoughts I* p.11, 27, 59, 61-62
Evans — *Thoughts II (Open Door)* p.146, 188-189
Evans — *Thoughts III (Open Road)* p.46, 105
Evans — *Thoughts IV* p.29, 137, 206
Evans — *Unto* p.82, 85-86
Flesch — *Unusual* p.45
Flint — *Graham* p.34-35
Forbes — *Thoughts* p.131, 137, 512
Fuller — *Epigrams* p.54-55
Garland — *Subject* p.50
Henry — *5000* p.44
Hubbard — *Scrap* p.66
Humes — *Instant* #249-257
Kennedy — *Reader's* #181
Kin — *Dictionary* p.52
Liddle — *Thought I, II, III* p.7, 41
Montapert — *Distilled* p.70
Phillips — *Choice* p.15
Prochnow — *Success.* #241, 1210
Seldes — *Great* p.203-206
Speaker's Desk p.19; #189, 678
Woods — *Religious* p.23

COMPULSION
See also **Force**
Dirksen — *Quot.* #1916
Evans — *Unto* p.69
Seldes — *Great* p.206
Sheen — *Content.* p.11-21

COMPUTERS
Asimov — *Treasury* #138, 247, 468
Grizer — *Wit* p.93
Prochnow — *Public* #1225
Prochnow — *Success.* #1047, 1298, 1314, 1365

CONCEALMENT
See also **Conspiracy; Secrecy**
Edwards — *Useful* p.90
Hovey — *Treasury* p.124-125; #623-625
Kin — *Dictionary* p.52
Prochnow — *Success.* p.1316
Sheban — *Wisdom* no p.

CONCEIT
See also **Boasting; Egoism and egotists; Self-praise**
Asimov — *Treasury* #205, 227-228
Book Proverbs p.126
Braude — *Source* #392-393
Braude — *Speaker's* #252-256
Braude — *Stories* p.72
Dirksen — *Quot.* #213, 221, 223, 295, 1917
Edwards — *Useful* p.90, 726
Evans — *This* p.31
Flesch — *Unusual* p.45
Forbes — *Thoughts* p.49, 211, 301, 421, 472
Fuller — *Epigrams* p.55-56
Grizer — *Wit* p.93-94
Harnsberger — *Mark* p.64
Henry — *5000* p.44
Holmes — *Design* p.87
How To Live p.274
Kin — *Dictionary* p.53
Liddle — *Thought I, II, III* p.71-72, 106-107, 110, 116, 133, 137, 145, 186
Liddle — *Thought V* p.27, 39
Lockridge — *World's* #665, 4825, 5504
Mandel — *Stories* p.45
Nizer — *Thinking* p.65
Prochnow — *Public* See index p.490-491
Prochnow — *Speaker's* p.71-72
Prochnow — *Success.* p.898, 908, 1162, 1168
Safian — *Insults* p.9-13
Woods — *Religious* p.171-172

CONCENTRATION
See also **Attention**
Asimov — *Treasury* #594
Curtis — *Human* p.13
Evans — *Thoughts III (Open Road)* p.135-137
Forbes — *Thoughts* p.182, 184, 197, 380, 423, 510
Grizer — *Wit* p.94
How To Live p.187-189, 441-443
Maltz — *Creative* p.191-193
Montapert — *Distilled* p.70-71
Nizer — *Thinking* p.113-114
Peterson — *Art* p.307
Phillips — *Choice* p.200, 241
Sherman — *Your* p.39-42
Vogue — *Arts* p.3-11
Wilcox — *Heart* p.74-75

CONCENTRATION CAMPS
Auden — *Certain* p.46-51

CONCERN
See also **Care; Empathy; Sympathy; Understanding**
Adams — *New* p.283, 392
Flint — *Graham* p.34
Hovey — *Treasury* p.125-126; #626-629
Ideas p.94-96
Kauffman — *For* p.66-69
Kohn — *Touch* p.148-151
Tanksley — *Friend* p.30

CONCERTS. *See* **Music**

CONCESSION. *See* **Compromise**

CONCISENESS. *See* **Brevity**

CONCLUSION
See also **Completeness; Ends and endings**
Flesch — *Unusual* p.45
Mandel — *Stories* p.46
Prochnow — *Public* #821, 1513
Prochnow — *Speaker's* p.72
Prochnow — *Success.* #278
Speaker's Desk #79, 81
Words — *Inspir.* p.51

CONCORD, MASSACHUSETTS
Lindeman — *Emerson* p.142

CONCORD. *See* **Agreement; Unity**

CONCRETE WORK
Kohn — *Touch* p.202

CONCRETENESS
Curtis — *Practical* p.51, 54, 56, 263

CONCUBINAGE
Lockridge — *World's* #4536

CONDEMNATION
See also **Criticism**
Flesch — *Unusual* p.45
Garland — *Subject* p.50-51
Kin — *Dictionary* p.53
Lockridge — *World's* #22, 4589
New Topical p.51
Speaker's Desk #465
Woods — *Religious* p.172

CONDESCENSION. *See* **Snobs and snobbery**

CONDITIONING
Krishnamurti — *Urgency* p.112-118

CONDITIONS
See also **Circumstances**
Flesch — *Unusual* p.46
Fox — *Make* p.55
Kin — *Dictionary* p.53
Kohn — *Pathways* p.107-110

CONDOLENCE. *See* **Sympathy**

CONDUCT
See also **Behavior; Ethics; Morality and morals**
Baillie — *Diary* #232
Braude — *Stories* p.72
Curtis — *Practical* p.77
Detherage — *Sunrise* p.44, 53, 66, 68
Edwards — *Useful* p.90-91
Evans — *Thoughts IV* p.99
Evans — *Unto* p.89, 131
Forbes — *Thoughts* p.8, 241, 394, 420
Harnsberger — *Mark* p.65
Henry — *5000* p.44
Hobe — *Tapestries* p.33
Hubbard — *Scrap* p.182, 211
Johnson — *Bedside* p.2-4, 11, 20, 63, 95, 125, 130, 171, 200, 206, 312, 318-320, 322, 340-341, 356
Kennedy — *Reader's* #182-186
Kin — *Dictionary* p.53
Kohn — *Touch* p.114-118
Liddle — *Thought IV* p.5, 12, 16
Lockridge — *World's* #383, 521, 1696, 2428, 2467, 3394, 4281, 4634, 4641
Montapert — *Distilled* p.71-72
Pullar-Strecker — *Proverbs* #103-166
Seldes — *Great* p.206
Wallis — *Treasure* p.111
Woods — *Religious* p.172
Zobell — *Speaker's* p.45
, and ethics
Wheelis — *Moralist* p.34-35
, Christian
New Topical p.51-52

, *Code of*
Prochnow — *Public* #1915
, *Effect on belief*
Sheen — *Lift* p.105-115
, *Teenager*
Ginott — *Between* p.34-35

CONDUCTIVITY
Du Noüy — *Road* p.66
Fuller — *Thesaurus* #1331-1339
Prochnow — *Public* #247, 570

CONFEDERATE MEMORIAL DAY
Harral — *Feature* p.128

CONFERENCES
See also **Committees**
Braude — *Stories* p.73
Dirksen — *Quot.* #131, 1648
Prochnow — *Success.* #677

CONFESSION
See also **Guilt; Sin; Truth**
Applegarth — *Heir.* p.49, 207
Book Proverbs p.121
Braude — *Stories* p.73
Dirksen — *Quot.* #85, 1918-1919
Edwards — *Useful* p.91
Flesch — *Unusual* p.46
Flint — *Graham* p.34
Henry — *5000* p.44
Kauffman — *For* p.69
Kin — *Dictionary* p.53
Knight's Illus. p.64
Knight's Treas. p.65-69
Liebman — *Peace* p.29-34
Lockridge — *World's See* index p.573
Lytle — *Leaves* p.73, 190
Mandel — *Stories* p.46
Montapert — *Distilled* p.72
New Topical p.52
Phillips — *Choice* p.253, 269
Prochnow — *Public* #1125
Schermerhorn — *1500* p.91-92
Seldes — *Great* p.206-207
Weisfeld — *Pulpit* p.1, 99
Woods — *Religious* p.172-175

CONFIDENCE
See also **Boldness; Courage; Faith; Overconfidence; Self-confidence; Trust**
Alexander's Treasure. p.251
Baillie — *Diary* #6
Braude — *Speaker's* #257-260
Braude — *Stories* p.73-74
Curtis — *Human* p.13, 15, 39, 150-166, 170-172
Detherage — *Sunrise* p.37, 47, 90, 127-129, 171
Dirksen — *Quot.* #1649-1650, 2042, 2051, 2359
Edwards — *Useful* p.91-92
Emmons — *Mature* p.82
Evans — *Faith* p.5-6, 128, 130
Evans — *This* p.189-190
Evans — *Thoughts* p.21-27, 137, 200
Evans — *Thoughts II (Open Door)* p.129-130, 169, 186-187
Evans — *Thoughts III (Open Road)* p.16-19, 48, 138
Evans — *Thoughts IV* p.67, 199, 207
Evans — *Unto* p.27, 34-35, 145
Forbes — *Thoughts See* index p.544
Garland — *Subject* p.51
Grizer — *Wit* p.94-96
Guideposts — *Faith* p.100-104, 202-204
Henry — *5000* p.45
Hobe — *Tapestries* p.225
Holmes — *Design* p.63
Hubbard — *Scrap* p.56, 97
Johnson — *Bedside* p.187
Kennedy — *Reader's* #187-190
Kin — *Dictionary* p.53-54
Lockridge — *World's* #445, 501, 2294, 2384, 2541, 2744, 3931
Lytle — *Leaves* p.152
Maltz — *Creative* p.110-123
Mandel — *Stories* p.46-47
Montapert — *Distilled* p.72-73
Nichols — *New* p.106-107
Prochnow — *Public* #1541, 4411
Prochnow — *Speaker's* p.72-73
Prochnow — *Success.* #960, 1201, 1345, 1391
Speaker's Desk p.19-20; #20, 222
Unlimited Power p.65-69
Wallis — *Treasure* p.63-66, 129
Watson — *Light* p.133-159
Weisfeld — *Pulpit* p.19
Woods — *Business.* p.45
Woods — *Religious* p.175
Woods — *Wellsprings* p.12

CONFIRMATION
Lytle — *Leaves* p.51
More Words p.33-34
Woods— *Religious* p.175-176

CONFLICT
See also **Argument; Battles; Opposition; Quarrels; Struggle; War**
Albert — *Stop* p.100-102
Edwards — *Useful* p.183
Evans — *Unto* p.84, 123
Flint — *Graham* p.35
Forbes — *Thoughts* p.145, 199, 243, 262, 421, 482
Holmes — *Design* p.132-133, 150-151
Hovey — *Treasury* p.126; #5, 83, 630-631, 1291

Kauffman — *For* p.70
Kohn — *Adventures* p.39-42
Krishnamurti — *Urgency* p.34-37
Prochnow — *Public* #2297
Rau — *Act* p.98-108
Seldes — *Great* p.207
Wheelis — *Moralist* p.31, 131-132
White — *Job* p.61-64
Woods — *Religious* p.176
, as modern evil
Phillips — *Choice* p.163
, of national opinion
Sheen — *Thoughts* p.21-23
, Roots of
Adams — *New* p.254
, Types of
White — *Job* p.68-71

CONFORMITY
See also **Codes; Customs; Standards**
Alexander's Treasure. p.190-191
Braude — *Source* #394-397
Evans — *Faith* p.147-148
Flint — *Graham* p.35
Grizer — *Wit* p.96
Hovey — *Treasury* p.126; #317, 632-638
Humes — *Instant* #258-263
Kauffman — *For* p.70-71
Kohn — *Touch* p.46-50
Krishnamurti — *Think* p.78-85
Menninger — *Blue.* p.64-65
Myers — *Thunder* p.33, 45-46
Price — *Wider* p.133-139
Saturday — *Advent.* p.263-274
Seldes — *Great* p.207-211
Woods — *Religious* p.176-177

CONFUCIUS
Curtis — *Practical* p.85
New Joy p.148
Prochnow — *Success.* #1628, 2068, 2091, 2290, 2367, 2410

CONFUSION
Braude — *Stories* p.74
Dirksen — *Quot.* #59, 1141
Evans — *This* p.123-124, 154-155
Forbes — *Thoughts* p.192, 274, 405, 466, 485
Kennedy — *Reader's* #191
Prochnow — *Public* #1442, 1533, 2050, 2400

CONGRATULATIONS
See also **Compliments; Praise**
Prochnow — *Public* #621

CONGREGATION
Hadfield — *Delights* p.222
Mandel — *Stories* p.47
Prochnow — *Public* #470, 1035
Wallis — *Words* p.127
Woods — *Religious* p.177

CONGREGATIONALISM
Woods — *Religious* p.177-178

CONGRESSMEN
See also **U.S.-Congress**
Botkin — *Anecdotes* p.137, 161-164, 166, 234
Dirksen — *Quot. See* index p.261
Harnsberger — *Mark* p.65-66
Nizer — *Thinking* p.68-69
Prochnow — *Success.* #469, 771
Weisfeld — *Pulpit* p.134-135

CONJUNCTIVES
Nizer — *Thinking* p.25

CONNECTICUT
Botkin — *Anecdotes* p.76, 138
Botkin — *Treasury* p.771-772, 781, 813

CONQUERORS AND CONQUEST
See also **War**
Applegarth — *Heir.* p.104
Dirksen — *Quot.* #558, 589, 836-837, 1920-1921
Flesch — *Unusual* p.46
Henry — *5000* p.45
Kin — *Dictionary* p.54
Lytle — *Leaves* p.96, 113
Montapert — *Distilled* p.73-74
Prochnow — *Public* #2892-2893
Prochnow — *Success.* #1639
Seldes — *Great* p.213
Woods — *Religious* p.178

CONSCIENCE
See also **Conviction; Honor; Integrity; Peace, of mind; Principles; Right; Soul; Virtues**
Albert — *Stop* p.134-135, 137-140
Auden — *Certain* p.87-88
Baillie — *Diary* #201, 289
Bartlett — *Discovery* p.12-13
Blanton — *Faith* p.87-109
Book Proverbs p.39
Braude — *Source* #398-400
Braude — *Stories* p.74-75
Carruthers — *Sparks* p.50-51
Dirksen — *Quot.* #168, 173, 443, 838, 842, 1289, 1922-1925
Droke — *Christian* p.110-113
Du Noüy — *Human* p.46, 109, 114, 151, 153, 187, 197, 270-271, 273
Edwards — *Useful* p.92-95
Evans — *Faith* p.9, 68, 74, 78, 87, 101-102, 117-118, 125, 132, 204
Evans — *Quote* p.205-214
Evans —*This* p.43-44, 144

Evans — *Thoughts I* p.15, 58, 68, 124, 197
Evans — *Thoughts II (Open Door)* p.65-66, 68, 100, 143, 184
Evans — *Thoughts III (Open Road)* p.38, 47, 49-51, 81, 108, 129-130, 170, 172
Evans — *Thoughts IV* p.14, 65, 76, 91-100, 103, 106, 145, 164, 204-205
Evans — *Unto* p.4-5, 7, 15, 32, 39, 59-60, 68, 84-85, 127, 131
Flesch — *Unusual* p.46-47
Flint — *Graham* p.35, 63-64, 87-88
Fogg — *1000* #408
Forbes — *Thoughts See* index p.544
Fuller — *Epigrams* p.57
Fuller — *Thesaurus* #146-147
Garland — *Subject* p.53
Grizer — *Wit* p.96
Harnsberger — *Mark* p.66-68
Henry — *5000* p.45-46
Hobe — *Tapestries* p.42
Holman — *Psych.* p.137-145
Hovey — *Treasury* p.126-127; #93, 247, 437, 639-642, 674, 678, 931, 990, 1039-1040, 1201, 1349, 1857
Hulme — *Living* p.59-71
Kennedy — *Reader's* #192-197
Kin — *Dictionary* p.54
Knight's Illus. p.64-66
Knight's Treas. p.69-71
Liddle — *Thought I, II, III* p.7, 132, 159, 164, 185
Liddle — *Thought V* p.17
Liebman — *Peace* p.23-37
Lockridge — *World's* #1259, 1546, 3424, 4078, 4547, 5068
Lytle — *Leaves* p.29, 185
Mandel — *Stories* p.47-49
Menninger — *Blue.* p.30-32
Montapert — *Distilled* p.74
More Words p.36-37
New Topical p.52-63
Peale — *Faith* p.81-107
Peterson — *Art* p.74
Phillips — *Choice* p.39, 46
Prochnow — *Public* #47, 143, 1651, 2108, 2117, 2894-2899, 4034
Prochnow — *Speaker's* p.73
Seldes — *Great* p.214-217
Sheban — *Wisdom* no p.
Speaker's Desk p.21-22
Voss — *Quotations* p.56-58
Wallis — *Treasure* p.74
Wallis — *Words* p.122
Webb — *Edge* p.103-110
Woods — *Wellsprings* p.46-47
Words — *Change* p.40-41
Zobell — *Speaker's* p.121-122
, and convictions
Strait — *Speaker's* p.47-49
, and law
Woods — *Religious* p.184
, and state
Woods — *Religious* p.178-185

CONSCIENTIOUS OBJECTORS
Ideas p.96-98
Woods — *Religious* p.185-186

CONSCIENTIOUSNESS
Prochnow — *Public* #568
Speaker's Desk #1024, 1154

CONSCIOUSNESS
See also **Awareness; Self-consciousness**
Clark — *Windows* p.82
Curtis — *Golden* p.37-39
Curtis — *Practical* p.101, 243-244
Du Noüy — *Road* p.33, 39, 52, 58, 69-70, 76, 107, 112, 145, 151, 189, 191, 237n
Flesch — *Unusual* p.47
Forbes — *Thoughts* p.115, 130, 307, 331
Fox — *Make* p.190
Garland — *Subject* p.53
Holmes — *Design* p.14, 24-25, 31-33, 44-45, 47
Ideas p.383-385
Keller — *Open* p.29
Peterson — *Art* p.295
Phillips — *Choice* p.5, 94, 98, 102, 104, 117, 119, 166, 237, 262, 390
Prochnow — *Public* #1430
Taylor — *With* p.116-118
Wheelis — *Moralist* p.151-152
White — *Job* p.62, 77-82, 106-107, 164-167
Woods — *Religious* p.186-187

CONSCRIPTION.*See* **Draft, Military**

CONSECRATION
See also **God, Will of**
Braude — *Source* #401
Fox — *Make* p.205
Garland — *Subject* p.53-54
Knight's Illus. p.67-70
Knight's Treas. p.72-77
Wallis — *Words* p.62

CONSENT. *See* **Agreement**

CONSEQUENCES. *See* **Results**

CONSERVATION
See also types, e.g. **Energy**
Dirksen — *Quot.* #1655
Harral — *Feature* p.129

Hovey — *Treasury* p.127-129; #86, 100, 643-649, 1415, 1500-1503, 1515
Sagendorph — *Old* p.112
Schermerhorn — *1500* p.90
Woods — *Business.* p.45

CONSERVATISM
See also **Caution; Discretion; Moderation**
Braude — *Stories* p.75
Curtis — *Practical* p.104, 330, 377
Dirksen — *Quot.* #362, 560-561, 1656-1657
Edwards — *Useful* p.95
Flesch — *Unusual* p.47
Fogg — *1000* #1007
Franke — *Buckley* p.44-47
Fuller — *Epigrams* p.57-58
Henry — *5000* p.46
Humes — *Instant* #264-275
Kennedy — *Reader's* #199
Prochnow — *Public* #1546, 2900
Prochnow — *Speaker's* p.73-74
Prochnow — *Success.* #1640
Seldes — *Great* p.217-222
Speaker's Desk p.22-23
Vogue — *Arts* p.65-70
Woods — *Business.* p.45-46
Woods — *Religious* p.187

CONSIDERATION
See also **Attention; Reflection; Study; Thought**
Baillie — *Diary* #87
Book Proverbs p.116
Dirksen — *Quot.* #313
Edwards — *Useful* p.95
Forbes — *Thoughts* p.81, 101, 166, 326, 355, 360, 392-393, 462
Grizer — *Wit* p.97
Johnson — *Bedside* p.152
Kin — *Dictionary* p.55, 67
Lockridge — *World's* #1545
Lytle — *Leaves* p.73, 131
Mandel — *Stories* p.49-50
Prochnow — *Success.* #534

CONSISTENCY
See also **Constancy**
Book Proverbs p.107
Braude — *Stories* p.76
Curtis — *Practical* p.443
Dirksen — *Quot.* #363, 1926
Edwards — *Useful* p.95
Evans — *Faith* p.149-150, 159, 168, 216, 225
Evans — *Thoughts I* p.69, 90-91
Evans — *Thoughts II (Open Door)* p.129-130, 198
Evans — *Thoughts III (Open Road)* p.107-108, 119, 141
Evans — *Thoughts IV* p.116, 205
Evans — *Unto* p.95
Flesch — *Unusual* p.48
Forbes — *Thoughts* p.26, 195
Garland — *Subject* p.54
Henry — *5000* p.46-47
Holmes — *Design* p.131-132
Hubbard — *Scrap* p.52
Kin — *Dictionary* p.55
Liddle — *Thought IV* p.4
Prochnow — *Success.* #1641
Seldes — *Great* p.222
Woods — *Religious* p.187-188

CONSOLATION
See also **Comfort; Encouragement; Sympathy**
Baillie — *Diary* #52, 217
Barrows — *1000 See* index p.438
Braude — *Stories* p.76
Edwards — *Useful* p.95-96
Evans — *Thoughts III (Open Road)* p.35
Garland — *Subject* p.54-55
Howell — *Lines* p.73-78
Kin — *Dictionary* p.55
Lockridge — *World's* #400, 2880, 4685
Lytle — *Leaves* p.51
Speaker's Desk #333, 537, 651, 676, 775, 799, 935, 943, 970, 982, 1070
Wallis — *Treasure* p.144
Woods — *Religious* p.188

CONSPICUOUSNESS
Kin — *Dictionary* p.55
Prochnow — *Public* #597

CONSPIRACY
See also **Secrecy; Treachery; Treason**
Edwards — *Useful* p.96
Evans — *Unto* p.47
Franke — *Buckley* p.47-49
Garland — *Subject* p.55
Lockridge — *World's* #3899
Prochnow — *Public* #897
Seldes — *Great* p.222

CONSTANCY
See also **Devotion; Faith; Loyalty**
Baillie — *Diary* #100
Edwards — *Useful* p.96, 198
Evans — *Unto* p.75
Flesch — *Unusual* p.47
Flint — *Graham* p.71-72
Fogg — *1000 See* index p.886
Forbes — *Thoughts* p.437, 468, 494
Fuller — *Epigrams* p.119-120
Kin — *Dictionary* p.45, 93
Lockridge — *World's* #21, 179-180, 259, 1229, 1495, 1739, 3933

Montapert — *Distilled* p.154
Wallis — *Treasure* p.219
Woods — *Religious* p.188

CONSTITUTION—U.S.
Dirksen — *Quot.* #6
Evans — *Faith* p.180, 189, 191
Evans — *Unto* p.59
Flesch — *Unusual* p.47
Fogg — *1000* #540, 714
Forbes — *Thoughts* p.23-24, 30, 105, 266
Franke — *Buckley* p.49
Henry — *5000* p.47
Hovey — *Treasury* p.129; #68, 70, 583, 650-656, 1046, 1666, 1699
Humes — *Instant* #276-279, 1206-1207
Hunter — *Gems* p.22-23
Kennedy — *Reader's* #200-201
Seldes — *Great* p.222-229
Sheen — *Thoughts* p.165-167
Woods — *Business.* p.46-47
Woods — *Religious* p.188
, Birth of
Curtis — *Practical* p.383-385

CONSTRUCTION. *See* **Builders and building**

CONSULTATION
Flesch — *Unusual* p.47
Prochnow — *Success.* #1022, 1642

CONSUMPTION
Kin — *Dictionary* p.55
Woods — *Business.* p.47-48

CONTEMPLATION
See also **Meditation; Thought**
Curtis — *New* p.66-68
Edwards — *Useful* p.96
Emmons — *Mature* p.30
Felleman — *Poems* p.291-317
Forbes — *Thoughts* p.518
Phillips — *Choice* p.162, 176-177, 180, 232
Wallis — *Treasure* p.212
Wallis — *Words* p.61
Woods — *Content.* p.238
Woods — *Religious* p.188-190

CONTEMPT. *See* **Arrogance; Insult; Ridicule**

CONTENTION. *See* **Argument; Conflict**

CONTENTMENT
See also **Happiness; Peace, of mind; Satisfaction**
Alexander's Treasure. p.45, 116, 307
Book Proverbs p.68
Braude — *Source* #402-405
Braude — *Speaker's* #261
Braude — *Stories* p.76-77
Curtis — *Practical* p.107
Dirksen — *Quot.* #366, 1293
Edwards — *Useful* p.97-99, 726
Emmons — *Mature* p.94
Evans — *Thoughts IV* p.74-75, 87
Flesch — *Unusual* p.48
Forbes — *Thoughts* p.115, 151, 210, 233, 413
Fuller — *Epigrams* p.58-59
Garland — *Subject* p.55-56
Giniger — *Compact* p.186-188
Grizer — *Wit* p.97-98
Henry — *5000* p.47-48
Hobe — *Tapestries* p.72, 74, 226
Hovey — *Treasury* p.130; #662-667
Howell — *Better* p.55-58
Hubbard — *Scrap* p.17, 101, 167
Johnson — *Bedside* p.62, 189, 195, 206, 244
Kin — *Dictionary* p.55-56
Kohn — *Through* p.25-28
Liddle — *Thought I, II, III* p.7, 111-112, 159
Liddle — *Thought IV* p.7, 9, 14, 23, 31, 35
Liddle — *Thought V* p.35, 40
Lockridge — *World's* #524
Lytle — *Leaves* p.84
Mandel — *Stories* p.50-53
Montapert — *Distilled* p.74-75
New Joy p.241-242
New Topical p.53
Peale — *Courage* p.198-199
Peterson — *Art* p.331
Prochnow — *Public* #628, 1102, 1354, 2666, 2730, 2901-2904, 4035-4036
Prochnow — *Success.* #1313, 1643
Sheban — *Wisdom* no p.
Sheen — *Way* p.14-16
Speaker's Desk p.23-25
Wallis — *Treasure* p.94, 162, 233
Wallis — *Words* p.47-52, 137
Watson — *Light* p.230-231, 259-277
Woods — *Inspir.* p.317-345
Woods — *Religious* p.190-191

CONTESTS
Fuller — *Thesaurus* #1881-1883
Harral — *Feature* p.129
Prochnow — *Success.* #309
, World's oldest
Evans — *This* p.101-102

CONTINUITY
Du Noüy — *Human* p.17-20, 38, 114
Du Noüy — *Road* p.30-34, 55-57, 75, 173-174, 190
Lytle — *Leaves* p.138

CONTORTIONISTS
Braude — *Stories* p.78
Prochnow — *Public* #330, 639

CONTRACT
Garland — *Subject* p.56-57
Prochnow — *Public* #774, 993, 4340
Seldes — *Great* p.229
, Law of
Curtis — *Practical* p.400

CONTRADICTION. *See* **Argument; Conflict; Opposition**

CONTRAST
See also **Comparison**
Book Proverbs p.13
Evans — *This* p.145
Halverson — *Perspective* p.100
Lytle — *Leaves* p.178
Nizer — *Thinking* p.142

CONTRIBUTIONS. *See* **Gifts and giving**

CONTRITION. *See* **Repentance**

CONTROL
See also **Power; Self-control**
Braude — *Stories* p.78
Garland — *Subject* p.57
Kohn — *Touch* p.179-182
Maxwell — *Courage* p.27-34
Prochnow — *Public* #1259
Woods — *Business.* p.48-50
, and knowledge
Wheelis — *Moralist* p.116
, Freedom from
Holmes — *Design* p.52-53

CONTROVERSY
See also **Argument; Conflict; Opposition**
Curtis — *Practical* p.293
Dirksen — *Quot.* #367
Edwards — *Useful* p.99-100
Flesch — *Unusual* p.48
Harral — *Feature* p.129
Henry — *5000* p.48, 197
Prochnow — *Public* #2636
Seldes — *Great* p.229, 708
Woods — *Religious* p.191-192

CONUNDRUMS
Botkin — *Treasury* p.484
Copeland — *10,000* p.869-880

CONVALESCENCE
Baillie — *Diary* #188
, Homes of
Guideposts — *Faith* p.405-406

CONVENIENCE
See also **Expediency**
Evans — *Thoughts II (Open Door)* p.144-145
Evans — *Unto* p.82-83
Prochnow — *Speaker's* p.75
Speaker's Desk #419, 655

CONVENTION
See also **Customs; Etiquette; Expediency**
Asimov — *Treasury* #619
Evans — *Unto* p.27
Harral — *Feature* p.129-130
Lockridge — *World's* #1252
Nizer — *Thinking* p.191
Seldes — *Great* p.230
, Delegates for
Prochnow — *Public* #1659

CONVENTIONS (meetings)
See also **Conferences**
Evans — *Thoughts IV* p.144
Prochnow — *Speaker's* p.75

CONVENTS
Flesch — *Unusual* p.48-49

CONVERSATION
See also **Communication; Speeches and speakers; Talk**
Adams — *New* p.29
Alexander's Treasure. p.274-275
Applegarth — *Heir.* p.71-75, 203
Braude — *Source* #406-409
Braude — *Stories* p.78
Curtis — *Practical* p.485
Daly — *Personality* p.7-12
Dirksen — *Quot.* #215, 246, 1066, 2245
Edwards — *Useful* p.100-102, 726
Evans — *Unto* p.62
Flesch — *Unusual* p.49-50
Flint — *Graham* p.36
Forbes — *Thoughts See* index p.544
Fuller — *Epigrams* p.59-60
Grizer — *Wit* p.98
Harnsberger — *Mark* p.68
Henry — *5000* p.48
Hobe — *Tapestries* p.34, 39, 120
How To Live p.417-420
Hubbard — *Scrap* p.56, 196, 214
Johnson — *Bedside* p.4, 11-13, 19-20, 127, 198-199, 309
Keys Happiness p.361-364
Kin — *Dictionary* p.56

Liddle — *Thought I, II, III* p.13, 77, 91, 112, 117, 125, 153, 167
Liddle — *Thought IV* p.3
Lockridge — *World's* #857, 2021, 2534-2538, 3020, 3189, 3379, 3485, 4199, 4271
Manchee — *Secret* p.30-33
Mandel — *Stories* p.54
Menninger — *Blue.* p.173-198
Modern Eloquence (14) p.300
Montapert — *Distilled* p.75-77
Prochnow — *Public* #185, 1100, 2125, 2905-2911
Prochnow — *Speaker's* p.75-77
Prochnow — *Success.* #1645-1646
Wallis — *Words* p.85
Woods — *Content.* p.122, 187
Woods — *Religious* p.192, 241-242
, Meaningful
Kohn — *Thoughts* p.100-101
, Starters for
Walters — *How* p.189-195
, with children
Keys Happiness p.248-251

CONVERSION
See also **Christianity; Religion; Salvation**; etc.
Asimov — *Treasury* #480
Baillie — *Diary* #38, 136, 142
Carruthers — *Sparks* p.161-162
Dirksen — *Quot.* #1294-1296
Edwards — *Useful* p.102
Flesch — *Unusual* p.50
Flint — *Graham* p.36
Fridy — *Meditat.* p.47
Fuller — *Thesaurus* #1621-1625
Garland — *Subject* p.57-58
Halverson — *Perspective* p.89
Hovey — *Treasury* p.130-132; #668-673, 841, 927
Kennedy — *Reader's* #202-205
Knight's Illus. p.71-73
Knight's Treas. p.77-79
Lockridge — *World's* #4974
Menninger — *Blue.* p.29
New Topical p.53
Phillips — *Choice* p.40
Redhead — *Living* p.70-78
Seldes — *Great* p.230
Unlimited Power p.61-64
Woods — *Religious* p.192-193
Words Change p.44-47

CONVICTION
See also **Belief; Conscience; Faith; Principles**
Alexander's Treasure. p.82
Braude — *Stories* p.79
Curtis — *Golden* p.144
Curtis — *Human* p.64-65, 69, 197
Curtis — *Practical* p.6
Dirksen — *Quot.* #842
Emmons — *Mature* p.84
Evans — *Unto* p.32, 83-84
Flesch — *Unusual* p.50
Forbes — *Thoughts* p.7, 60, 70, 100, 147, 204, 245, 463, 495
Fuller — *Epigrams* p.60-61
Garland — *Subject* p.58
Harnsberger — *Mark* p.69
Hobe — *Tapestries* p.40, 42
Holmes — *Design* p.188
Hovey — *Treasury* #120, 291, 515, 685, 709, 764, 1147, 1165, 1781
Kennedy — *Reader's* #206-207
Kin — *Dictionary* p.56
Kohn — *Touch* p.114-118
Liddle — *Thought I, II, III* p.12, 120
Liddle — *Thought IV* p.12, 26
Lockridge — *World's* #3543
Lytle — *Leaves* p.72, 168
Montapert — *Distilled* p.77
Nizer — *Thinking* p.169
Prochnow — *Public* #1459, 1652
Seldes — *Great* p.230-231
Wallis — *Treasure* p.111, 152
Wallis — *Words* p.132, 173
Woods — *Religious* p.194

CONVICTS. *See* **Prisoners**

CONVINCING
See also **Argument**
Grizer — *Wit* p.99
Harnsberger — *Mark* p.69
Kin — *Dictionary* p.56
Reader's — *Getting* p.54

CONVIVIALITY. *See* **Cheerfulness; Companionship**

COOKS AND COOKERY
See also **Diet; Dinners; Eating;** etc.
Auden — *Certain* p.59-61
Botkin — *Anecdotes* p.35
Braude — *Speaker's* #262-263
Edwards — *Useful* p.726
Flesch — *Unusual* p.50
Fuller — *Epigrams* p.61-62
Henry — *5000* p.48
Kin — *Dictionary* p.56
Lockridge — *World's* #939, 4011
Prochnow — *Public* #450, 657, 673, 815, 854, 899, 918, 4413
Prochnow — *Speaker's* p.77-78
Reader's — *20th* p.74
Speaker's Desk #42, 172, 476, 480

COOLIDGE, CALVIN
Fun Fare p.59-60
Schermerhorn — *1500* p.91

Weisfeld — *Pulpit* p.87

COOPERATION
See also **Agreement; Efficiency; Organization**
Braude — *Speaker's* #264-267
Braude — *Stories* p.79-80
Emmonds — *Mature* p.42, 111, 113
Forbes — *Thoughts See* index p.544
Garland — *Subject* p.58-59
Grizer — *Wit* p.99-100
Harvey — *Treasury* p.132; #5, 674-675
Holmes — *Design* p.131, 149, 151-152
Hubbard — *Scrap* p.20, 32, 78, 165, 211
Humes — *Instant* #1274-1275
Kennedy — *Reader's* #208-211
Kin — *Dictionary* p.56
Knight's Illus. p.73-74
Knight's Treas. p.79-80
Kohn — *Pathways* p.27-31
Krishnamurti — *Think* p.107-116
Lockridge — *World's* #3006
Lytle — *Leaves* p.121-122
Mandel — *Stories* p.54-56
Modern Eloquence (14) p.301
Montavert — *Distilled* p.77-78
Peterson — *Art* p.101
Prochnow — *Public* #1653
Seldes — *Great* p.231-232
Wheelis — *Moralist* p.75-84
Woods — *Business.* p.50-51
Woods — *Content.* p.30
Woods — *Religious* p.194
Woods — *Wellsprings* p.71-72

COORDINATION. *See* **Correlation; Harmony**

COPERNICUS, NICOLAUS
Wallis — *Words* p.124

COPYRIGHT
Harnsberger — *Mark* p.69

COQUETRY
Edwards — *Useful* p.102
Fuller — *Epigrams* p.62-63
Lockridge — *World's* #110, 252, 342, 359, 397, 401, 718, 1723, 4676

CORN
Botkin — *Treasury* p.172-173, 416, 557, 599-602, 605, 628
Kin — *Dictionary* p.56
Prochnow — *Public* #771

CORNERS
Kin — *Dictionary* p.56

CORNERSTONES
Hobe — *Tapestries* p.72
Wallis — *Words* p.3

CORNISH
Schermerhorn — *1500* p.92-93

CORPORATIONS
See also **Business; Capitalism; Industry**
Flesch — *Unusual* p.50-51
Harral — *Feature* p.130
Seldes — *Great* p.232-234
Wheelis — *Moralist* p.119
Woods — *Business.* p.52-53

CORRECTION
See also **Discipline; Punishment**
Book Proverbs p.124
Kin — *Dictionary* p.57
Prochnow — *Public* #864, 2426, 2517

CORRELATION
Clark — *Windows* p.156
Curtis — *Human* p.80-97

CORRESPONDENCE. *See* **Letters and letter writing**

CORROBORATION. *See* **Evidence**

CORRUPTION
See also **Bribery; Conspiracy; Dishonesty; Fraud; Treachery**
Braude — *Source* #410-411
Dirksen — *Quot.* #414, 567, 766, 980, 1109, 1146, 1350, 1732
Edwards — *Useful* p.103
Evans — *Unto* p.14, 55, 120
Flesch — *Unusual* p.51
Franke — *Buckley* p.49-50
Garland — *Subject* p.60
Henry — *5000* p.49
Hubbard — *Scrap* p.225
Kin — *Dictionary* p.57
Lockridge — *World's* #2667
Prochnow — *Public* #2217, 2614
Seldes — *Great* p.234-235
Woods — *Religious* p.194

COSMETICS
Prochnow — *Public* #2028
Woods — *Religious* p.194-195

COSMOPOLITANISM
Dirksen — *Quot.* #252
Lockridge — *World's* #5686
Prochnow — *Public* #1967

COSMOS
See also **Universe**
, Medieval
Auden — *Certain* p.88-89

, *Purpose of*
Irion — *Yes* p.34-38
, *Suicide of*
Sheen — *Thoughts* p.177-179

COSSACKS
Asimov — *Treasury* #320-321

COST
See also **Bargains; Expense; Extravagance**
Edwards — *Useful* p.726
Evans — *Thoughts III (Open Road)* p.77
Grizer — *Wit* p.101
Kin — *Dictionary* p.57
Prochnow — *Public* #591, 4320
Woods — *Business.* p.53

COST OF LIVING
Braude — *Speaker's* #828-829
Dirksen — *Quot.* #1660
Flesch — *Unusual* p.51
Grizer — *Wit* p.101-102
Prochnow — *Public* #1268
Prochnow — *Success.* #1647

COSTUME. *See* **Clothes**

COTTON
Botkin — *Anecdotes* p.193
Harral — *Feature* p.130

COTTON MILLS
Peale — *Guideposts* p.41-45

COUÉISM
Seldes — *Great* p.235

COUGARS
Botkin — *Treasury* p.622-623

COUNSELIING
See also **Advice; Guidance; Lawyers; Psychiatry and psychiatrists**
Book Proverbs p.131
Clark — *Windows* p.80
Dirksen — *Quot.* #368, 1297
Edwards — *Useful* p.103
Evans — *Faith* p.5-6, 53-54, 58, 116, 148
Evans — *Thoughts I* p.24-27, 34-35, 89, 104, 156, 199-202
Evans — *Thoughts II (Open Door)* p.37, 47, 94-95, 99, 156-159
Evans — *Thoughts III (Open Road)* p.18-19, 22, 48-49, 129, 141, 155, 158, 167
Evans — *Thoughts IV* p.15, 26, 36-37, 144
Forbes — *Thoughts* p.124, 165, 182, 203, 234, 248, 275, 294, 367, 476
Jackson — *Coping* p.168-175
Kin — *Dictionary* p.57
Montapert — *Distilled* p.78-79
More Words p.109-110
Porter — *Halo* p.110-118
Prochnow — *Public* #2503
Sheban — *Wisdom* no p.
Sheen — *Content.* p.108-110

COUNTERFEITING
Evans — *Unto* p.87
Lockridge — *World's* #5021
Prochnow — *Public* #480
Prochnow — *Success.* #593

COUNTER-REFORMATION
Curtis — *Practical* p.142

COUNTING RHYMES
Auden — *Certain* p.291
Botkin — *Treasury* p.769, 787
Kronenberger — *Animal* p.40-44

COUNTRY (state)
See also **Nationalism; Nations; Patriotism;** names of countries
Applegarth — *Heir.* p.129
Dirksen — *Quot.* #525, 564-565, 2286, 2307, 2316
Flesch — *Unusual* p.88
Forbes — *Thoughts* p.353, 369, 385, 392, 408, 415, 489, 496, 514
Harnsberger — *Mark* p.69-70
Ideas p.255-257
Keller — *Open* p.46

"COUNTRY BUMPKINS"
Fun Fare p.10, 57-59, 177, 214
Speaker's Desk See index p.298

COUNTRY CLUBS
Asimov — *Treasury* #358-359

COUNTRY LIFE
See also **Agriculture; Farmers and farming; Nature**
Botkin — *Treasury* p.408, 429
Copeland — *10,000* p.140-171
Curtis — *Daily* p.56-61
Dirksen — *Quot.* #88, 1148, 1927
Edwards — *Useful* p.104
Evans — *Thoughts IV* p.149-150
Flesch — *Unusual* p.51
Guideposts — *Faith* p.360-363
Henry — *5000* p.49
Hobe — *Tapestries* p.21, 114
Hovey — *Treasury* #86, 100, 643-649, 1415, 1500-1503, 1515
Hubbard — *Scrap* p.83, 210, 222, 225

Lockridge — *World's* #418
Montapert — *Distilled* p.79
Patterns For Living p.33-38
Prochnow — *Public* #482, 1387, 4362
Prochnow — *Success.* #521, 627, 705, 742, 1357
Sheban — *Wisdom* no p.
White — *Life* p.161-166
Woods — *Religious* p.195

COUNTRY STORES
Botkin — *Anecdotes* p.2-3

"COUP D'ETAT"
Prochnow — *Public* #2360

COURAGE
See also **Boldness; Confidence; Endurance**
Alexander's Treasure. p.18, 45, 114, 189, 225
Book Proverbs p.74
Braude — *Source* #222, 412-419
Braude — *Stories* p.80-83
Day — *Meditations* p.73
Detherage — *Sunrise* p.33, 127
Dirksen — *Quot.* #53, 55, 451, 539, 623, 863, 886, 1298-1299, 1928-1931, 1934, 2347
Droke — *Christian* p.113-118
Edwards — *Useful* p.57, 104-105. 673-674, 726
Emmons — *Mature* p.61-72
Evans — *Faith* p.3-4, 22, 114, 152
Evans — *Quote* p.153-162
Evans — *Thoughts I* p.12-14, 120-122, 128, 189
Evans — *Thoughts II (Open Door)* p.22, 60, 73-74, 88-90, 96-97, 124
Evans — *Thoughts III (Open Road)* p.35-39, 51, 86, 108, 121, 130, 139-140, 186, 200
Evans — *Thoughts IV* p.103-104
Evans — *Unto* p.21, 52
Flesch — *Unusual* p.26, 51, 214
Flint — *Graham* p.36-37
Forbes — *Thoughts* p.40, 149, 520; *See also* index p.545
Fuller — *Epigrams* p.63-64
Fuller — *Thesaurus* #151-153
Garland — *Subject* p.60-61
Giniger — *Compact* p.1-27
Grizer — *Wit* p.102-103
Guideposts — *Faith* p.287-290
Harnsberger — *Mark* p.33, 70
Harvey — *Treasury* p.132-134; *See also* index p.295
Henry — *5000* p.24, 49, 293
Hobe — *Tapestries* p.45, 211-213
Hovey — *Treasury* #28, 52, 1018, 1230, 1607
Howell — *Better* p. 59-62
Howell — *Lines* p.58-59
Hubbard — *Scrap* p.189
Hulme — *Living* p.150-155
Humes — *Instant* #280-290, p.42
Johnson — *Bedside* p.43, 84-108
Kahn — *Lessons* p.134-140
Kennedy — *Reader's* #212-220
Keys Happiness p.498, 504, 520-522
Kin — *Dictionary* p.32-33, 57-58
Knight's Illus. p.74-79
Knight's Treas. p.80-85
Krishnamurti — *Think* p.215-216
Langdon — *Teach.* p.35-45
Liddle — *Thought I, II, III See* index p.156, 196
Liddle — *Thought IV* p.4, 8, 12-15, 20, 26, 38, 42
Liddle — *Thought V* p.3-4, 18, 23, 26, 32, 35
Liebman — *Hope* p.134-141
Lockridge — *World's See* index p.573; #223-226, 1426, 1449, 1457, 2896, 3374, 3811, 5863, 5893
Lytle — *Leaves* p.5, 52-55, 194
McCracken — *What* p.71-76
Maltz — *Creative* p.76-77, 157-158
Mandel — *Stories* p.57
Mandelbaum — *Choose* p.202-206
Miller — *Harvest* p.49-54
Modern Eloquence (14) p.302
Montapert — *Distilled* p.42-43, 79-80, 90-91
Nichols — *New* p.93-95, 98-99
Nichols — *Third* p.53-56
Patterns For Living p.768-773
Peale — *Courage* p.94-112
Peterson — *Art* p.112, 329
Phillips — *Choice* p.86
Prochnow — *Public* #250, 654, 782, 1654, 2913-2922, 4037-4039
Prochnow — *Speaker's* p.47-48, 78-79
Prochnow — *Success.* #302, 770, 1196-1197, 1240, 1385, 1648
Reader's — *Getting* p.145-149
Seldes — *Great* p.97-98
Sheban — *Wisdom* no p.
Speaker's Desk #7, 426, 522, 906, 962, 1099
Strait — *Speaker's* p.50
Vogue — *Arts* p.103-109
Voss — *Quotations* p.58-60
Wallis — *Treasure* p.67-70, 84, 156, 158, 194, 212, 226, 231
Wallis — *Words* p.65, 68, 182
Watson — *Light* p.73-131

Woods — *Content.* p.45, 277, 280, 285, 293, 312, 358
Woods — *Inspir.* p.1-49
Woods — *Religious* p.91, 195, 1029
Words Change p.30-31
Words — *Inspir.* p.153-154
, from good habits
Maxwell — *Courage* p.155-206
, from great certainties
Maxwell — *Courage* p.209-258
, Pioneering
Peale — *Guideposts* p.321-325
, to live
Webb — *Edge* p.115-136

COURSERS
Sheban — *Wisdom* no p.

COURTESY
See also **Etiquette**
Alexander's Treasure. p.277
Applegarth — *Heir.* p.77-81
Asimov — *Treasury* #354
Bach — *Make* p.74-85
Baillie — *Diary* #203
Bartlett — *Discovery* p.121-122
Braude — *Source* #420-424
Braude — *Speaker's* #1030-1031
Braude — *Stories* p.83, 292
Dirksen — *Quot.* #340, 1661
Edwards — *Useful* p.83-84, 105, 473-475
Evans — *Faith* p.73, 167-168
Evans — *Thoughts I* p.183-186
Evans — *Thoughts III (Open Road)* p.27, 69-72, 78, 95, 99, 136
Evans — *Thoughts IV* p.37, 116-117, 205
Evans — *Unto* p.89
Flesch — *Unusual* p.51-52, 216
Forbes — *Thoughts* p.107, 112, 348, 398, 433, 502, 545
Fuller — *Thesaurus* #416-420
Goudge — *Comfort* p.210
Grizer — *Wit* p.103-104
Harnsberger — *Mark* p.362
Henry — *5000* p.49-50
Hobe — *Thesaurus* p.198
How To Live p.69-70, 410-412
Hubbard — *Scrap* p.26
Johnson — *Bedside* p.2, 4
Kennedy — *Reader's* #221-222
Kin — *Dictionary* p.48, 58, 193
Liddle — *Thought I, II, III* p.64, 185
Liddle — *Thought IV* p.11, 34, 44
Lockridge — *World's* #102, 271, 1985, 2561, 2721, 4193
Lytle — *Leaves* p.122, 125
Mandel — *Stories* p.58
Mandelbaum — *Choose* p.33
Modern Eloquence (14) p.303-304
Montapert — *Distilled* p.80-81
Prochnow — *Public* #242, 833, 845, 945, 982, 1058, 1207, 1263, 1413, 3535-3536
Prochnow — *Speaker's* p.79-80, 231
Prochnow — *Success.* #427, 510, 1422
Sheen — *Content.* p.145-147
Sheen — *Thoughts* p.49-51
Speaker's Desk p.25-26; *See* index p.298
Wallis — *Treasure* p.124, 133
Words — *Inspir.* p.167-168

COURTIERS
Edwards — *Useful* p.105-106
Fuller — *Epigrams* p.64-66, 334
Lockridge — *World's* #4692

COURTHOUSES
Harral — *Feature* p.131

COURTS
See also **Law; Lawyers; Supreme Court**; etc.
Botkin — *Anecdotes* p.10, 232, 246, 249
Fuller — *Thesaurus* p.441-451
Fun Fare p.110-111
Harral — *Feature* p.131
Kin — *Dictionary* p.58
Lockridge — *World's* #2552-2553, 2564, 2572, 3310, 3350, 4406
New Topical p.54-55
Schermerhorn — *1500* p.96-97
Seldes — *Great* p.239-240
, and commandments
Kauffman — *For* p.63-64
, Juvenile
Braude — *Stories* p.93-94
, "of last resort"
Peale — *Guideposts* p.329-333
, Opinions of
Simpson — *Contemp.* p.56-58
, Sentences
Copeland — *World's* p.8-11, 214-219, 298-299, 372-374
, Trials of
Braude — *Stories* p.93-94

COURTSHIP
See also **Love; Romance;** etc.
Book Proverbs p.20
Copeland — *10,000* p.197-226, 990-992
Edwards — *Useful* p.106
Fuller — *Epigrams* p.66-68

Fuller — *Thesaurus* #851-855
George — *Book* p.79, 119, 154, 237, 240, 312, 370, 413
Henry — *5000* p.312-313
Kahn — *Lessons* p.171-173
Kin — *Dictionary* p.281
Speaker's Desk #111, 296, 309, 335, 528, 559, 715, 745, 816, 972, 976, 1093
Woods — *Religious* p.196

COVENANT
Fox — *Make* p.128
Garland — *Subject* p.61
McDonagh — *Invit.* p.97-98
More Words p.37-39
New Topical p.55-56
Prochnow — *Public* #2582

COVETOUSNESS
See also **Avarice; Greed;** etc.
Dirksen — *Quot.* #291, 1344, 1866
Edwards — *Useful* p.106-107
Evans — *This* p.169-170
Evans — *Unto* p.49, 101, 104
Fox — *Make* p.30
Garland — *Subject* p.61
Harnsberger — *Mark* p.71
Hunter — *Gems* p.23-24
Kin — *Dictionary* p.58-59
Knight's Illus. p.79-81
Knight's Treas. p.85-88
Lockridge — *World's* #644, 1260
Montapert — *Distilled* p.81-82
More Words p.41-42
Myers — *Thunder* p.148-163
New Topical p.56
Prochnow — *Public* #2369, 2469
Woods — *Religious* p.196

COWARDICE
See also **Fear; Panic**
Applegarth — *Heir.* p.296
Day — *Meditations* p.19
Dirksen — *Quot.* #1924, 1934
Edwards — *Useful* p.107
Flesch — *Unusual* p.52
Forbes — *Thoughts* p.229, 319, 400, 425, 436
Fuller — *Epigrams* p.68
Fuller — *Thesaurus* #156-160
Harnsberger — *Mark* p.71-72
Henry — *5000* p.50
Hobe — *Tapestries* p.211
Kin — *Dictionary* p.59
Liddle — *Thought IV* p.20
Liddle — *Thought V* p.26
Liebman — *Peace* p.23-37
Lockridge — *World's* #394, 3255, 3847, 3931, 3983, 5733
Montapert — *Distilled* p.82
Prochnow — *Public* #937
Seldes — *Great* p.240
Wallis — *Treasure* p.70
Woods — *Religious* p.196

COWBOY SONGS
Kronenberger — *Animal* p.44-47

COWBOYS
Asimov — *Treasury* #163
Botkin — *Anecdotes* p.14, 85, 227
Botkin — *Treasury* p.97, 150, 175, 180, 192, 293, 367, 376, 379-383, 396, 566, 851
Fun Fare p.38-40
Prochnow — *Success.* #1084
Words — *Inspir.* p.56

COWS
See also **Calves**
Applegarth — *Heir.* p.24
Botkin — *Anecdotes* p.235
Botkin — *Treasury* p.385, 396, 451, 455, 569, 594, 596
Dirksen — *Quot.* #2-3, 1932-1933
Henry — *5000* p.50
Kin — *Dictionary* p.59
Prochnow — *Public* #226, 233, 320, 518, 822, 881, 886
Prochnow — *Speaker's* p.80-81
Prochnow — *Success.* #438, 479, 1061
Schermerhorn — *1500* p.97-98

COYOTES
Botkin — *Anecdotes* p.105
Botkin — *Treasury* p.181

"CRABS"
Safian — *Insults* p.38-42

"CRACKER BARREL" WIT
Botkin — *Anecdotes* p.2, 38, 90, 134, 256

"CRACKERS," GEORGIA
Botkin — *Anecdotes* p.10, 101

CRACKS
Flesch — *Unusual* p.52

"CRACKS AND SLAMS"
Botkin — *Anecdotes* p.16

CRADLES
Hobe — *Tapestries* p.112
Kin — *Dictionary* p.59
Prochnow — *Success.* #713

CRAFTS AND CRAFTSMEN
Applegarth — *Heir.* p.143
Day — *Meditations* p.33-34
Hadfield — *Delights* p.213
Harral — *Feature* p.131

Hooker — *Index* p.265-270
Hubbard — *Scrap* p.30, 62
Wallis — *Words* p.27

"CRAMMING." *See* **Examinations; Study**

CRANES
Hobe — *Tapestries* p.98

"CRANKS"
Safian — *More* p.30-33

CRAWDADS
Botkin — *Anecdotes* p.101
Botkin — *Treasury* p.580, 896

"CREAM PUFFS"
Safian — *Insults* p.43-45
Safian — *More* p.34-36

CREATION
Auden — *Certain* p.407-408
Botkin — *Anecdotes* p.189-190
Curtis — *Golden* p.32-33
Dirksen — *Quot.* #55, 87, 163, 199, 843, 1300-1301, 1460
Evans — *Unto* p.32
Fogg — *1000* #482
Forbes — *Thoughts* p.198, 248, 266, 297, 320, 342, 467, 470, 495, 514
Garland — *Subject* p.61-62
Guideposts — *Faith* p.444-447
Henry — *5000* p.50-51
Holmes — *Design* p.60-61, 124
Ideas p.99-100
Johnson — *Bedside* p.44-45, 49, 58, 134, 212-213
Kahn — *Lessons* p.81-83
Kohn — *Adventures* p.145-148
Lockridge — *World's* #744, 774, 4619
McDonagh — *Invit.* p.111-113
Mandel — *Stories* p.58
More Words p.42-43
New Topical p.56-57
Phillips — *Choice* p.28, 278
Prochnow — *Success.* #1652
Seldes — *Great* p.240-241
Taylor — *With* p.82-83
Wallis — *Words* p.138
White — *Job* p.113, 115, 118-123, 129-130, 135-139, 141
White — *Life* p.248-250
Woods — *Content.* p.57, 100
Woods — *Religious* p.197-201, 1025-1026
, Aim of
Adams — *New* p.116
, Comfort of
Goudge — *Comfort* p.21-83
, Continuous
Holmes — *Design* p.91-92
, Nature of
Holmes — *Design* p.15-16
, Value of
Albert — *Stop* p.50

CREATIVITY
See also **Invention; Originality**
Braude — *Stories* p.83
Clark — *Windows* p.86
Curtis — *Golden* p.76-90, 97
Dirksen — *Quot.* #171
Esteve — *Experience* p.103-109
Flesch — *Unusual* p.52
Harral — *Feature* p.132
Hoffer — *Reflect.* p.4
Holmes — *Design* p.1, 15-16, 18-21, 24-27, 46-47, 50, 76-77, 89-97, 181, 184-185, 205
How To Live p.199-224
Johnson — *Bedside* p.189
Keys Happiness p.385-388
Maltz — *Creative* p.1-9, 62-80, 110-123, 177-220
Mandelbaum — *Choose* p.220-223
Montapert — *Distilled* p.82-83
Peale — *Stay* p.45-64
Peterson — *Art* p.126, 343
Phillips — *Choice See* index p.425
Prochnow — *Public* #2449, 2923, 2925
Seldes — *Great* p.240-241
Sherman — *Your* p.43-57
Wallis — *Treasure* p.164
Welk — *Guide.* p.49-51
Woods — *Religious* p.201

CREATOR. *See* **God**

CREDIBILITY. *See* **Belief; Truth**

CREDIT
See also **Creditors; Debt; Trust**
Braude — *Source* #425
Braude — *Speaker's* #268-269
Braude — *Stories* p.83-87
Edwards — *Useful* p.107
Flesch — *Unusual* p.52
Forbes — *Thoughts* p.139, 230, 245, 264, 324, 408, 416, 442, 489
Fuller — *Epigrams* p.69
Fuller — *Thesaurus* #2166-2167
Grizer — *Wit* p.104-105
Harral — *Feature* p.132
Henry — *5000* p.51
Kin — *Dictionary* p.59
Lockridge — *World's* #891, 4007, 4030, 4195
Montapert — *Distilled* p.83
Prochnow — *Public* #368, 380, 989, 1891
Prochnow — *Speaker's* p.81
Seldes — *Great* p.241

Woods — *Business.* p.53-54
Speaker's Desk #130, 158, 651, 1024

CREDIT CARDS
Grizer — *Wit* p.105
Prochnow — *Success.* #410, 1226

CREDITORS
See also **Credit; Debt and debtors**
Dirksen — *Quot.* #1872
Edwards — *Useful* p.107
Grizer — *Wit* p.106
Henry — *5000* p.51
Liddle — *Thought I, II, III* p.72
Lockridge — *World's* #5226
New Topical p.57
Prochnow — *Public* #538, 1522
Pullar-Strecker — *Proverbs* #200-204

CREDOS. *See* **Creeds; Philosophy, of life**

CREDULITY. *See* **Belief; Truth**

CREEDS
See also **Belief; Denominations; Doctrine**
Alexander's Treasure. p.138, 199
Applegarth — *Heir.* p.78, 143, 247
Book Proverbs p.127
Braude — *Source* #426-428
Braude — *Stories* p.87-89
Carruthers — *Sparks* p.33-34
Edwards — *Useful* p.108-109
Flesch — *Unusual* p.52
Fogg — *1000* #149, 348, 492, 785, 851, 980, 1034, 1118
Garland — *Subject* p.62
Grizer — *Wit* p.106-107
Guideposts — *Faith* p.262-263
Harvey — *Treasury* p.134-136; #695-700, 769, 1011, 1654, 1712
Hobe — *Tapestries* p.46
Hubbard — *Scrap* p.128
Hunter — *Gems* p.1-2
Keller — *Open* p.32
Kin — *Dictionary* p.60
Lytle — *Leaves* p.38, 68
Montapert — *Distilled* p.84
More Words p.43-44
Seldes — *Great* p.241-242
Sheban — *Wisdom* no p.
Wallis — *Treasure* p.7, 32, 71-76, 133, 178, 207
Wallis — *Words* p.3, 14, 28, 82, 141
Wilcox — *Heart* p.8-10, 33-35, 82-84
Woods — *Religious* p.202-203
Words — *Inspir.* p.112-114, 133

CREEK INDIANS
Botkin — *Anecdotes* p.181

CRICKET (game)
George — *Book* p.33, 235

CRIME AND CRIMINALS
See also **Capital punishment; Corruption; Courts; Guilt; Justice; Juvenile delinquency; Law; Prisoners; Punishment;** types of crime and criminals
Braude — *Speaker's* #271-275
Droke — *Christian* p.119-121
Edwards — *Useful* p.109, 726
Evans — *Unto* p.27
Flesch — *Unusual* p.53
Flint — *Graham* p.10, 37
Fogg — *1000* #911, 1091, 1101, 1108
Franke — *Buckley* p.50-51
Fuller — *Epigrams* p.69-70
Fuller — *Thesaurus* p.459-464
Fun Fare p.191-193
Garland — *Subject* p.62
Grizer — *Wit* p.107-108
Guideposts — *Faith* p.55-58, 85-89
Harral — *Feature* p.132-134
Harvey — *Treasury* p.136; #71, 673, 701-702, 716, 795, 1263, 1507
Henry — *5000* p. 51-52
Hubbard — *Scrap* p.68, 111
Kauffman — *For* p.73-77
Kennedy — *Reader's* #889
Kin — *Dictionary* p.60
Knight's Treas. p.88-91
Liddle — *Thought I, II, III* p.89
Lockridge — *World's* #191-192, 925, 974, 1289, 2585, 3104, 3651, 4246
Montapert — *Distilled* p.85-86
Nizer — *Thinking* p.56, 119, 133, 211-213
Peale — *Guideposts* p.157-160
Prochnow — *Public* #29, 1046, 1602, 2406, 2926-2930, 4403
Prochnow — *Success.* #331, 583, 1384, 1654
Seldes — *Great* p.243-245
Sheban — *Wisdom* no p.
Simpson — *'54* p.24, 137, 278
Speaker's Desk #245, 768, 918, 1114, 1176
Unlimited Power p.56-60
Woods — *Religious* p.203-204

CRIMINOLOGY
Simpson — *Contemp.* p.58-63

CRIPPLES. *See* **Handicapped**

CRISES
Forbes — *Thoughts* p.4, 42, 60, 79, 370, 400, 442, 488, 516
Harvey — *Treasury* p.136-137; #703-706
Henry — *5000* p.52
Holmes — *I've* p.10-11
Humes — *Instant* p.38; #291-294
Keller — *Open* p.60
Kohn — *Best* p.109-111
Montapert — *Distilled* p.86
Phillips — *Choice* p.67, 95, 108
Tanksley — *Friend* p.26
Woods — *Religious* p.204
Words — *Change* p.10-37
, Aftermath management
Jackson — *Coping* p.193-200
, and growth
Hulme — *Living* p.88-91
, Anticipating
Jackson — *Coping* p.184-192
, Anatomy of
Jackson — *Coping* p.40-47
, Anthropology of
Jackson — *Coping* p.56-63
, Facing
Jackson — *Coping* p.3-11
, Management of
Jackson — *Coping* p.20-31
, National
Dirksen — *Quot.* #566
, Nature of
Jackson — *Coping* p.12-19
, Physiology of
Jackson — *Coping* p.48-55
, Psychology of
Jackson — *Coping* p.72-79
, Sociology of
Jackson — *Coping* p.64-71
, Therapy for
Jackson — *Coping* p.160-167
, Understanding of
Jackson — *Coping* p.32-39

CRITICISM
See also **Censure; Faults; Self-criticism**
Book Proverbs p.73
Botkin — *Anecdotes* p.54
Braude — *Source* #429-442, 623-624
Braude — *Speaker's* #276-281
Braude — *Stories* p.96
Curtis — *Practical* p.295, 363
Dirksen — *Quot.* #19, 173, 329, 559, 884, 1663, 1935-1936
Edwards — *Useful* p.109-111, 726
Evans — *Faith* p.14-16, 48, 77
Evans — *This* p.38-39
Evans — *Thoughts I* p.21, 71-72, 163, 186, 189, 198-200
Evans — *Thoughts III (Open Road)* p.58
Evans — *Unto* p.38
Flesch — *Unusual* p.53
Flint — *Graham* p.37
Fogg — *1000* #45, 103, 109, 158, 167, 196, 203, 398, 469, 472, 509, 581, 627, 754, 986
Forbes — *Thoughts* p.92-93, 95, 105, 244, 248, 381, 404, 445, 456, 470
Franke — *Buckley* p.52
Fuller — *Epigrams* p.71-72
Fuller — *Thesaurus* #1096-1105
Garland — *Subject* p.63
Ginott — *Between* p.49-50, 75-90
Grizer — *Wit* p.108-109
Harnsberger — *Mark* p.72-74
Henry — *5000* p.52
Hill — *Think* p.266-269
Hovey — *Treasury* p.137-138; #52, 168, 500, 525, 707-710, 1045, 1587
How To Live p.259-263
Hubbard — *Scrap* p.30, 89, 200, 226
Kauffman — *For* p.78-79
Kennedy — *Reader's* #223-232
Kin — *Dictionary* p.60, 91, 211, 214, 226
Knight's Treas. p.91-93
Liddle — *Thought I, II, III* p.6, 21, 30, 56, 101, 117, 130, 188
Lockridge — *World's* #4261; *See* index p.573
Lytle — *Leaves* p.74
Mandel — *Stories* p.58-60
Menninger — *Blue.* p.39, 67
Modern Eloquence (14) p.305-306
Montapert — *Distilled* p.86-87
New Topical p.222-223
Peale — *Courage* p.23
Peterson — *Art* p.355
Prochnow — *Public* #316, 352, 607, 890, 975, 994, 1146, 1177, 1669, 2007-2008, 2376, 2931-2937
Prochnow — *Speaker's* p.81-82
Prochnow — *Success.* #373, 620, 779, 1304, 1330, 1448, 1655-1657
Sheen — *Thoughts* p.117-118
Speaker's Desk p.26-28
Wallis — *Treasure* p.77-80
Woods — *Religious* p.204, 436-437
Zobell — *Speaker's* p.46-48

CROCKETT, DAVY
Botkin — *Treasury See* index p.928

CROCKETT ALMANACS
Botkin — *Treasury* p.273, 276, 321

CROCODILES
See also **Alligators**
Asimov — *Treasury* #268

CROOKEDNESS. *See* **Crime and criminals; Dishonesty; Fraud;** etc.

CROPS
See also **Grain**
Harral — *Feature* p.134
Prochnow — *Public* #138, 799
Sagendorph — *Old* p.127-135
Woods — *Wellsprings* p.30-31

CROSS
See also **Jesus Christ, Crucifixion of**
Applegarth — *Heir.* p.121, 247, 283
Carruthers — *Sparks* p.165-166
Clark — *Windows* p.164
Dirksen — *Quot.* #1935
Edwards — *Useful* p.111
Flesch — *Unusual* p.53
Flint — *Graham* p.37
Forbes — *Thoughts* p.310, 372
Fridy — *Meditat.* p.92, 94, 129
Garland — *Subject* p.63
Goudge — *Comfort* p.183-192
Harvey — *Treasury* p.138-141; *See* index p.295
Hobe — *Tapestries* p.227
Kennedy — *Fresh* p.49
Kin — *Dictionary* p.60-61
Knight's Illus. p.82-88
Knight's Treas. p.93-102
Kohn — *Best* p.124-127
Lytle — *Leaves* p.15, 126
Montapert — *Distilled* p.87
Phillips — *Choice* p.141, 342
Seldes — *Great* p.245
Strait — *Speaker's* p.51-54
Suter — *Prayers* #404-415
Tanksley — *Friend* p.49
Wallis — *Treasure* p.65
Wallis — *Words* p.30, 53-58, 98, 204
Woods — *Religious* p.204-208
, Bearers of the
Baillie — *Diary* #190
, Courage from the
Maxwell — *Courage* p.91-151
, Greek
Peterson — *Art* p.150
, Message of
Hulme — *Living* p.98-99
, of gold
Dirksen — *Quot.* #645
Fogg — *1000* #77
, Personal
List — *Living* p.94-95
, Stations of the
Guideposts — *Faith* p.374-379

CROSSBREEDING
Seldes — *Great* p.245-246

CROSS-EXAMINATION
Prochnow — *Public* #594

CROWD
See also **Mob**
Dirksen — *Quot.* #144, 369, 2298
Evans — *Faith* p.131
Evans — *This* p.21-34
Evans — *Thoughts III (Open Road)* p.121
Evans — *Thoughts IV* p.30
Evans — *Unto* p.77, 85
Flesch — *Unusual* p.54
Kin — *Dictionary* p.61
Kohn — *Pathways* p.151
Seldes — *Great* p.246
, as a god
Myers — *Thunder* p.33
, Contagion of
Curtis — *Practical* p.114

CROWN
Fogg — *1000 See* index p.882
Garland — *Subject* p.63-64
Hobe — *Tapestries* p.227
Kin — *Dictionary* p.61
Lockridge — *World's* #3809, 4851
Prochnow — *Public* #789

CROWS
Hobe — *Tapestries* p.184
Kin — *Dictionary* p.61

CRUCIFIXION. *See* **Calvary; Cross; Jesus Christ, Crucifixion of**

CRUELTY
See also **Persecution; Punishment;** etc.
Book Proverbs p.57
Edwards — *Useful* p.2-3, 111
Evans — *Thoughts III (Open Road)* p.98-99
Evans — *Unto* p.120
Flesch — *Unusual* p.54
Forbes — *Thoughts* p.158, 208
Harnsberger — *Mark* p.34-35
Henry — *5000* p.53
Hubbard — *Scrap* p.75
Kauffman — *For* p.122-123
Kin — *Dictionary* p.4, 94
Kohn — *Through* p.56
Lockridge — *World's* #532, 1998, 3720, 4761
Prochnow — *Public* #2152, 2752
Prochnow — *Success.* #973

Seldes — *Great* p.101, 246
Wallis — *Treasure* p.233
Wheelis — *Moralist* p.3-7
Woods — *Religious* p.75, 208

CRUSADES AND CRUSADERS
Curtis — *Practical* p.133
Dirksen — *Quot.* #845
Fogg — *1000* #502, 547, 776, 876, 885, 898
Johnson — *Bedside* p.87
Woods — *Religious* p.208

CRYING. *See* **Tears**

CRYSTALS
Du Noüy — *Road* p.88, 135-136

CUBA
Asimov — *Treasury* #181
Franke — *Buckley* p.22-23, 52-53, 147-148

"CUBAN CRISIS"
Guideposts — *Faith* p.428-434

CUCKOOS
Auden — *Certain* p.89-91

CUCUMBERS
Asimov — *Treasury* #101
Botkin — *Treasury* p.598, 600

"CUES"
Manchee — *Secret* p.85-88

CULTIVATION. *See* **Appreciation; Culture; Friends and friendship;** etc.

CULTS
White — *Job* p.179-181
Woods — *Religious* p.208

CULTURE
See also **Civilization**
Auden — *Certain* p.92
Braude — *Stories* p.97
Flesch — *Unusual* p.54
Flint — *Graham* p.38
Forbes — *Thoughts* See index p.545
Grizer — *Wit* p.109
Henry — *5000* p.53
Humes — *Instant* #295-297
Ideas p.100-102
Lockridge — *World's* #2755, 4124, 5544
Mandel — *Stories* p.61
Montapert — *Distilled* p.87-88
Phillips — *Choice* p.66, 114, 116, 121-122
Prochnow — *Public* #4285
Prochnow — *Success.* #1088
Seldes — *Great* p.246-248
, American
Krishnamurti — *Think* p.82-84
, and chemistry
Woods — *Religious* p.208-209
, and religion
Woods — *Religious* p.209-210
, Indian, East
Krishnamurti — *Think* p.82-84

CUNNING
See also **Cleverness; Deception**
Edwards — *Useful* p.111-112
Evans — *Thoughts II (Open Door)* p.88
Kin — *Dictionary* p.61
Lockridge — *World's* #419, 432, 655, 2571, 2719, 3767, 4177
Montapert — *Distilled* p.88
Prochnow — *Public* #2010, 2313

CURE
See also **Healing; Medicine; Self-cure**
Dirksen — *Quot.* #1938
Evans — *Unto* p.46, 52
Grizer — *Wit* p.109
Kin — *Dictionary* p.61
Lockridge — *World's* #328
Lytle — *Leaves* p.186
Montapert — *Distilled* p. 88-89

CURFEW
Menninger — *Blue.* p.181

CURIE, MADAME MARIE
Reader's — *20th* p.107-123

"CURIO-HUNTING"
Lockridge — *World's* #2615

CURIOSITY
See also **Questions; Wonder**
Applegarth — *Heir.* p.230
Braude — *Source* #443-444
Braude — *Speaker's* #282-284
Braude — *Stories* p.97
Curtis — *Practical* p.108, 220, 533-535
Dirksen — *Quot.* #370, 846
Edwards — *Useful* p.112-113, 295
Flesch — *Unusual* p.54
Flint — *Graham* p.38
Forbes — *Thoughts* p.35, 132, 166, 315, 373, 387, 422
Fuller — *Epigrams* p.72
Fuller — *Thesaurus* #161
Grizer — *Wit* p.109
Henry — *5000* p.53, 134

Kennedy — *Reader's* #233-234
Kin — *Dictionary* p.62
Kohn — *Adventures* p.35-37
Liddle — *Thought I, II, III* p.154, 186
Liddle — *Thought IV* p.42
Lockridge — *World's* #176, 2900, 5074
Prochnow — *Public* #695, 739, 866, 979, 2938
Prochnow — *Speaker's* p.82, 173
Prochnow — *Success.* #116, 1658-1659
Seldes — *Great* p.248
Speaker's Desk #131, 146, 265, 616, 652, 800, 829, 899, 981, 1025, 1057, 1111, 1164
Vogue — *Arts* p.25-31
Wallis — *Treasure* p.24
Wallis — *Words* p.144
Woods — *Religious* p.210

CURSES. *See* **Profanity**

"CURTAIN LINES"
Auden — *Certain* p.92-93

CUSTODIANS
Harral — *Feature* p.134-135

CUSTOMERS
Grizer — *Wit* p.110-112
Harral — *Feature* p.135
Kin — *Dictionary* p.62
Montapert — *Distilled* p.89-90

CUSTOMS
See also **Etiquette; Habits; Tradition**
Braude — *Source* #445-450
Braude — *Stories* p.98-100, 303
Curtis — *Practical* p.148-156
Edwards — *Useful* p.113-114, 492
Evans — *Unto* p.18, 64
Forbes — *Thoughts* p.192, 269, 324, 391, 402, 408, 504
Harnsberger — *Mark* p.74
Harral — *Feature* p.135
Henry — *5000* p.53
Hooker — *Index* p.134-143
Kin — *Dictionary* p.62, 197
Lockridge — *World's* #1142, 1494, 1702, 2043, 3188, 3468, 3820, 5116
Montapert — *Distilled* p.89
Seldes — *Great* p.248-250, 758
Wheelis — *Moralist* p.67
Woods — *Religious* p.210

CUTTING
Flesch — *Unusual* p.54

CYBERNETICS
Seldes — *Great* p.250

CYCLONES
Botkin — *Treasury* p.183, 512-520, 594, 611-612

CYGNETS
Auden — *Certain* p.93-94

CYMBALISTS
Asimov — *Treasury* #118

CYNICS AND CYNICISM
Adams — *New* p.387
Braude — *Source* #451
Carruthers — *Sparks* p.133-135
Dirksen — *Quot.* #248, 847
Edwards — *Useful* p.114
Evans — *Faith* p.67, 222
Evans — *Thoughts II (Open Door)* p.89, 123
Evans — *Thoughts III (Open Road)* p.65, 101, 116
Evans — *Unto* p.44
Flesch — *Unusual* p.54-55
Fogg — *1000 See* index p.882
Forbes — *Thoughts* p.15, 60, 139, 225, 269, 286, 517
Fuller — *Epigrams* p.72-73
Fuller — *Thesaurus* #166-170
Grizer — *Wit* p.112
Henry — *5000* p.54
Hubbard — *Scrap* p.83
Kennedy — *Fresh* p.85-87
Kin — *Dictionary* p.62
Kohn — *Touch* p.64
Liddle — *Thought I, II, III* p.93
Lockridge — *World's* #4912
Lytle — *Leaves* p.56
New Joy p.19
Prochnow — *Public* #1145, 1372, 1983
Prochnow — *Success.* #368, 1660-1661
Woods — *Religious* p.210

D

DAFFODILS
Hobe — *Tapestries* p.31
Unlimited Power p.273-276

DAILY LIVING. *See* **Life, and living, Daily routine of**

DAINTINESS. *See* **Cleanliness; Delicacy; Fastidiousness**

DAISIES
Hubbard — *Scrap* p.100
Wallis — *Treasure* p.155

DALLAS, TEXAS
Asimov — *Treasury* #59-60

DAMAGE. *See* **Destruction**

DAMS
Fun Fare p.23-26
Kin — *Dictionary* p.63

DAN, THE TRIBE OF
New Topical p.57-58

DANCERS AND DANCING
See also **Ballet**
Braude — *Speaker's* #285-290
Braude — *Stories* p.100
Daly — *Personality* p.31-34
Edwards — *Useful* p.114-115
Flesch — *Unusual* p.55
Flint — *Graham* p.38
Fuller — *Thesaurus* #1371, 1841
George — *Book* p.79, 258, 314, 339
Hadfield — *Love* p.106, 109, 112-115
Harral — *Feature* p.135-136
Henry — *5000* p.54
Holmes — *I've* p.117-118
Irion — *Yes* p.28-30
Kin — *Dictionary* p.63
Kronenberger — *Animal* p.56-57
Lindbergh — *Gift* p.104-106
Lockridge — *World's* #3773, 4370
Menninger — *Blue.* p.181-183, 185-187
Phillips — *Choice* p.267, 281-283
Prochnow — *Public* #399-640
Prochnow — *Success.* #508, 1662
Schermerhorn — *1500* p.100
Woods — *Content.* p.127, 147, 180-181, 183, 186, 262

DANDELIONS
Applegarth — *Heir.* p.195
Speaker's Desk #39

DANDYISM
Edwards — *Useful* p.115
Woods — *Religious* p.211

DANGER
See also **Courage; Fear;** etc.
Dirksen — *Quot.* #1939-1940
Edwards — *Useful* p.115
Flesch — *Unusual* p.55
Fox — *Make* p.136
Fuller — *Epigrams* p.73
Garland — *Subject* p.64-65
Henry — *5000* p.54
Hovey — *Treasury* p.143; *See also* index p.295
Kennedy — *Reader's* #235
Kin — *Dictionary* p.63-64, 135
Liddle — *Thought I, II, III* p.113, 142, 185
Liddle — *Thought IV* p.12, 32
Lockridge — *World's* #1547, 4497, 4754
Lytle — *Leaves* p.90
Montapert — *Distilled* p.90
Prochnow — *Public* #107, 781, 1407, 2322, 4040-4041
Prochnow — *Success.* #378
Seldes — *Great* p.250-251
Speaker's Desk #209
Woods — *Religious* p.211

DANISH PROVERBS
Dirksen — *Quot.* #1868, 1879, 1908, 1946, 1977, 2054

DANTE
Adams — *New* p.33-34

DARING. *See* **Adventure; Courage;** etc.

DARK AGES
Auden — *Certain* p.94-96
Flesch — *Unusual* p.55
Phillips — *Choice* p.384
Prochnow — *Public* #2367
Woods — *Religious* p.212

DARKNESS
See also **Night**
Evans — *This* p.161-176
Evans — *Thoughts III (Open Road)* p.38-39, 43, 191
Evans — *Unto* p.39
Flesch — *Unusual* p.55
Flint — *Graham* p.38
Forbes — *Thoughts* p.209, 356, 483
Garland — *Subject* p.65
Harnsberger — *Mark* p.75
Henry — *5000* p.54
Hovey — *Treasury* #343, 391, 963, 1244, 1294, 1397, 1416, 1418, 1421-1422, 1744
Keller — *Open* p.12-13, 97, 136
Kin — *Dictionary* p.64
Kohn — *Pathways* p.143-145
Lockridge — *World's* #2914, 4520
New Topical p.58
Nichols — *Third* p.33
Peale — *Courage* p.70-71

Phillips — *Choice* p.43, 75, 199, 269
Prochnow — *Public* #2011, 2680
Sheban — *Wisdom* no p.
Wallis — *Words* p.24, 33, 102, 118
Woods — *Content.* p.52
Woods — *Religious* p.212
, at noon
Nichols — *New* p.59-60
, Comfort in
Goudge — *Comfort* p.268-277
, Life's
Kohn — *Adventures* p.71-74
, Treasures of
Carruthers — *Sparks* p.75-77
, Voice in
Maxwell — *Courage* p.64-74

DARWINISM
Boas — *History* p.96-109
Woods — *Religious* p.212

DATA. *See* **Facts**

DATES AND DATING
Asimov — *Treasury* #1, 29, 296
Francis — *For* p.76-89
Kennedy — *Fresh* p.157-159
Menninger — *Blue.* p.175-187, 199-204
, Blind
Menninger — *Blue.* p.202
, Teenager
Daly — *Personality* p.18-30, 34-39, 46-56
Ginott — *Between* p.141-142, 162-163

DAUGHTERS
Alexander's Treasure. p.249
Edwards — *Useful* p.115
Garland — *Subject* p.65
Goudge — *Comfort* p.107-108
Grizer — *Wit* p.113
Henry — *5000* p.54-55
Hobe — *Tapestries* p.179
Holmes — *I've* p.75-76
Irion — *Yes* p.53-56
Kin — *Dictionary* p.64
Liddle — *Thought I, II, III* p.67, 74
Liebman — *Hope* p.160-181
Manchee — *Secret* p.236-237
New Joy p.152-153
Prochnow — *Public* #65, 76, 409, 483, 753
Reader's — *Getting* p.81-84
Woods — *Religious* p.212

DAVID (Biblical)
Asimov — *Treasury* #365

DAWN
See also **Day; Morning; Sunrise**
Applegarth — *Heir.* p.68
Auden — *Certain* p.96-98
Detherage — *Sunrise* p.15
Felleman — *Poems* p.395-406
Forbes — *Thoughts* p.186, 483, 516
Hadfield — *Delights* p.22
Lytle — *Leaves* p.41
New Joy p.39
Prochnow — *Public* #2035, 4407
Wallis — *Treasure* p.220
Woods — *Content.* p.23, 34, 57, 198-199, 266
Woods — *Religious* p.212

DAY
See also **Dawn; Light; Morning; Sunrise**
Applegarth — *Heir.* p.62-63, 66, 69, 81, 91
Dirksen — *Quot.* #1212, 1941-1945, 1993, 2301, 2309
Edwards — *Useful* p.115
Evans — *Unto* p.11, 22, 143
Flesch — *Unusual* p.55
Forbes — *Thoughts* p.186, 194, 237, 315, 376, 397, 516
Fuller — *Epigrams* p.73-74
Garland — *Subject* p.65
Henry — *5000* p.55
Hobe — *Tapestries* p.173, 193
Hovey — *Treasury* #16, 33, 78
Kin — *Dictionary* p.64
Lindeman — *Emerson* p.119-132
Lockridge — *World's* #3093
Lytle — *Leaves* p.170, 174
Montapert — *Distilled* p.91-92
New Topical p.58-59
Peterson — *Art* p.200, 316
Prochnow — *Public* #2702, 4042
Prochnow — *Success.* #1663-1664
Wallis — *Treasure* p.157, 168. 188, 219-222
Woods — *Content.* p.23, 30, 38, 46-48, 196, 198, 200, 219, 311, 314
Woods — *Religious* p.212-213, 1053
, Inventory of
Peterson — *Art* p.219
, Prayer for
Peterson — *Art* p.59
, Times of
Auden — *Certain* p.96-101

DAYDREAMING
Detherage — *Sunrise* p.21-24
Edwards — *Useful* p.63-64
Flesch — *Unusual* p.55-56
Fox — *Make* p.97
Guideposts — *Faith* p.3-27
Hadfield — *Delights* p.191

Kennedy — *Fresh* p.140-142
Liddle — *Thought I, II, III* p.173, 193
Mandel — *Stories* p.61
New Joy p.63

"DAYTOP PROGRAM"
Ginott — *Between* p.205-208

DE QUINCEY, THOMAS
Adams — *New* p.34

DEACONS
More Words p.46-47

DEAD
See also **Burial; Cemeteries; Death; Graves; Monuments**
Baillie — *Diary* #252
Dirksen — *Quot.* p.333, 360
Evans — *This* p.192-194
Flesch — *Unusual* p.56
Fogg — *1000* #706
Forbes — *Thoughts* p.117, 408, 448, 473
Keller — *Open* p.23, 57-59
New Topical p.59
Prochnow — *Public* #934, 2012
Speaker's Desk See index p.298
Woods — *Religious* p.213

DEAF
See also **Hearing**
Asimov — *Treasury* #237
Forbes — *Thoughts* p.493, 516
Garland — *Subject* p.66
Hill — *Think* p.41-47
Keller — *Open* p.105-106, 115-116, 119-120
Kin — *Dictionary* p.64
Prochnow — *Public* #1224, 1657
Prochnow — *Success.* #1133, 1297
Speaker's Desk #67, 403, 599, 812
Weisfeld — *Pulpit* p.46-47

DEATH
See also **Dead; Grief; Immortality; Resurrection;** etc.
Alexander's Treasure. p.50, 136-137, 251, 322
Applegarth — *Heir.* p.157
Asimov — *Treasury* #2, 5, 40-41, 109, 308, 317, 364, 394, 402, 532, 540-541, 544
Auden — *Certain* p.102-103
Baillie — *Diary* #25, 36, 66, 88, 126, 263
Barrows — *1000 See* index p.438
Braude — *Source* #452-458
Braude — *Stories* p.100
Clark — *Windows* p.144
Curtis — *Practical* p.496
Detherage — *Sunrise* p.191-197
Dirksen — *Quot.* #459, 1014; *See also* index p.262
Droke — *Christian* p.121-124
Du Noüy — *Human* p.62, 105-106
Du Noüy — *Road* p.53, 119, 133, 138
Edwards — *Useful* p.115-119, 409, 726
Emmons — *Mature* p.131-138
Esteve — *Experience* p.19-23
Evans — *Faith* p.193-206
Evans — *Quite* p.111-124
Evans — *This* p.156-157, 191-192
Evans — *Thoughts I* p.43-44, 49-51, 111-112, 120-122
Evans — *Thoughts II (Open Door)* p.101, 105-106, 210
Evans — *Thoughts III (Open Road)* p.35, 180, 191, 205-210
Evans — *Thoughts IV* p.118, 154-155, 158, 176-178
Evans — *Unto* p.4, 13, 120-121, 139-141, 145
Felleman — *Poems* p.271-287
Flesch — *Unusual* p.56, 69-70
Flint — *Graham* p.38-40
Fogg — *1000 See* index p.883
Forbes — *Thoughts See* index p.545
Fuller — *Epigrams* p.74-77
Fuller — *Thesaurus See* index p.306-312
Garland — *Subject* p.66
George — *Book See* index p.443
Giniger — *Compact* p.275
Gold — *Letters* p.119-124
Goudge — *Comfort* p.252-267
Hadfield — *Delights* p.242
Hadfield — *Love* p.229-230, 232
Harnsberger — *Mark* p.75-76
Harral — *Feature* p.136
Henry — *5000* p.55-57, 181
Hobe — *Tapestries* p.154, 156-158, 161, 163, 197
Holmes — *I've* p.109-112
Hovey — *Treasury See* index p. 295; p.143-147
How To Live p.510-562
Howell — *Better* p.63-66
Hubbard — *Scrap* p.15, 17, 43, 49, 76-77, 80, 97, 101, 108, 118
Irion — *Yes* p.16-17
Johnson — *Bedside* p.23-24, 193, 195-196, 247, 285, 338-356
Kahn — *Lessons* p.227-240
Keller — *Open* p.57-59, 80
Kennedy — *Fresh* p.154-155
Kennedy — *Reader's* #236-246
Keys Happiness p.271-273
Kin — *Dictionary* p.64-65, 168
Knight's Illus. p.88-96
Knight's Treas. p.102-105

Kohn — *Best* p.22-23, 132-136
Kohn — *Pathways* p.191-192
Kronenberger — *Animal* p.74
Lair — Baby p.125-131, 199-202, 228
Liddle — *Thought I, II, III* p.43, 78-79, 95, 109, 118, 125, 152, 181
Liebman — *Peace* p.105-133
Lindbergh — *Unicorn* p.21-47
Lockridge — *World's See* index p.574
Lytle — *Leaves* p.24-25, 77, 92-93, 95, 97, 108, 134, 192
Mandel — *Stories* p.61-63
Modern Eloquence (14) p.307-309
Montapert — *Distilled* p.92-93, 104-105
More Words p.47-48
New Joy p.226, 256
Nizer — *Thinking* p.128
Peale — *Courage* p.218-249
Peterson — *Art* p.386
Phillips — *Choice* p.12, 235
Price — *No* p.79-86
Prochnow — *Public* #2581, 2703, 2718, 2727, 3431; *See also* index p.492
Prochnow — *Speaker's* p.83-88
Prochnow — *Success.* #459, 1281, 1346
Reader's — *Getting* p.116
Seaburg — *Great* p.159-409
Seldes — *Great* p.251-255
Sheban — *Wisdom* no p.
Speaker's Desk p.28-31
Strait — *Speaker's* p.55-56
Suter — *Prayers* #459-462
Tanksley — *Friend* p.34, 70, 72
Voss — *Quotations* p.60-65
Wallis — *Treasure* p. 141-146
Wallis — *Words* p.36, 66, 99, 101, 154
Watson — *Light* p.104-119
Webb — *Edge* p.137-154
White — *Job* p.152-153
Woods — *Content.* p.280, 285-286, 290, 294, 324, 327, 337-338
Woods — *Inspir.* p.458-489
Woods — *Religious* p.213-221
Zobell — *Speaker's* p.48-50, 107-108

, and immortality
Howell — *Lines* p.157-165

, and resurrection
Kauffman — *For* p.80-82

, Anticipation of
See also **Death, Fear of**
Peale — *Guideposts* p.260-262

, Causes of (1809)
Kronenberger — *Animal* p.58

, Child's
Guideposts — *Faith* p.42-46, 467-471
Irion — *Yes* p.13-15
Kahn — *Lesson* p.161-164

, Definition of
Guideposts — *Faith* p.493-494
Kohn — *Through* p.89-92

, Egyptian thought of
Adams — *New* p.295

, Eternal
New Topical p.59-60

, Fear of
Baillie — *Diary* #169, 322
Guideposts — *Faith* p.492-493
Hill — *Think* p.276-278
Krishnamurti — *Think* p.128-129
Sheban — *Wisdom* no p.
Sherman — *Your* p.99-103
Woods — *Religious* p.221-222

, Hiding of
Lair — *Baby* p.129-130

, Ideas of
Adams — *New* p.356

, Inevitability of
Guideposts — *Faith* p.492-493

, Love stronger than
Sheen — *Thoughts* p.162-164

, Natural
New Topical p.60

, of soldier-son
Guideposts — *Faith* p.457-461

, Peacefulness of
Guideposts — *Faith* p.493

, Prayer of
Guideposts — *Faith* p.486

, Prediction of
Reader's — *Getting* p.204

, Preparation for
Guideposts — *Faith* p.254-258

, Prophetic essay on
Guideposts — *Faith* p.467-468

, Reason for
Kohn — *Through* p.93

, Return from
Guideposts — *Faith* p.451-456

, Spiritual
New Topical p.61

, Struggle with
Unlimited Power p.118-120

, "There is no . . ." (song)
Guideposts — *Faith* p.472-476

, Thoughts at
Baillie — *Diary* #202

, *Understanding of*
Guideposts — *Faith* p. 483-486
, *Wartime*
See also **Death, of soldier-son**
Adams — *New* p.228-230
Ideas p.137-139
, *Words at. See* **Words, Dying**

DEBATE
See also **Argument**
Braude — *Source* #459-460
Dirksen — *Quot.* #1818
Prochnow — *Public* #250, 2548

DEBT AND DEBTORS
See also **Credit; National debt**
Applegarth — *Heir.* p.116
Book Proverbs p.9
Braude — *Source* #461-463
Braude — *Speaker's* #291-301
Braude — *Stories* p.100-101
Dirksen — *Quot.* #42, 372, 1958
Edwards — *Useful* p.119-120
Emmons — *Mature* p.53-54, 157
Evans — *Faith* p.75-76, 168
Evans — *Quote* p.223-232
Evans — *Thoughts I* p.60, 92, 166
Evans — *Thoughts II (Open Door)* p.166-167
Evans — *Thoughts III (Open Road)* p.118, 211
Evans — *Thoughts IV* p.71-74, 78, 89, 193
Flesch — *Unusual* p.56
Forbes — *Thoughts* p.295, 373, 386, 393, 418, 421
Fuller — *Epigrams* p.77-79
Fuller — *Thesaurus* #2171-2174
Garland — *Subject* p.66
Grizer — *Wit* p.113
Harral — *Feature* p.136
Henry — *5000* p.57
Hubbard — *Scrap* p.104
Hunter — *Gems* p.24-25
Kennedy — *Fresh* p.12-21
Kin — *Dictionary* p.65
Liddle — *Thought I, II, III* p.163
Lockridge — *World's* #1185, 2027, 2042, 3001, 4180, 4850, 4953
Lytle — *Leaves* p.33, 55
Mandel — *Stories* p.63-64
Montapert — *Distilled* p.93
Prochnow — *Public* #396, 538, 571, 575, 666, 687, 806, 999, 1138, 1402, 1696, 1718, 1982, 2701, 2959, 4049
Prochnow — *Speaker's* p.88-89
Prochnow — *Success.* #472, 1425
Pullar-Strecker — *Proverbs* #200-204
Schermerhorn — *1500* p.104-105
Seldes — *Great* p.255
Speaker's Desk p.31-34; #70, 135, 189, 310, 474, 781, 808
Woods — *Business.* p.54
Words — *Inspir.* p.194

DECAY
Forbes — *Thoughts* p.105, 243, 365
Ideas p.102-104
Kin — *Dictionary* p.66
Lockridge — *World's* #4332
Woods — *Religious* p.222

DECEIT. *See* **Deception; Hypocrisy**

DECEMBER
Kohn — *Thoughts* p.167-169

DECENCY
See also **Morality and morals; Refinement;** etc.
Edwards — *Useful* p.120
Evans — *Unto* p.27
Fuller — *Epigrams* p.79
Harnsberger — *Mark* p.76
Henry — *5000* p.58
Lockridge — *World's* #2374, 2621, 5785

DECEPTION
See also **Betrayal; Hypocrisy; Self-deception; Treason**
Braude — *Stories* p.101
Dirksen — *Quot.* #1959-1960
Edwards — *Useful* p.31-32, 120
Esteve — *Experience* p.25-27
Evans — *This* p.4-5
Evans — *Unto* p.89, 91
Flesch — *Unusual* p.56
Flint — *Graham* p.40
Forbes — *Thoughts* p.128, 185
Fuller — *Epigrams* p.80
Garland — *Subject* p.66-67
Grizer — *Wit* p.114
Henry — *5000* p.58
Holman — *Psych.* p.50-51
Kennedy — *Reader's* #247-248
Kin — *Dictionary* p.66
Lockridge — *World's* #118, 120-121, 130, 184, 300, 360, 1063, 1527, 1700, 1704, 1713, 2052, 2539
Montapert — *Distilled* p.94
New Topical p.61-62
Prochnow — *Public* #2051, 2725, 2960-2964, 4050-4051
Prochnow — *Speaker's* p.89-90
Seldes — *Great* p.255-256
Speaker's Desk #330, 365, 418, 425, 783, 974

DECIMAL SYSTEM
Curtis — *Practical* p.220

DECISION
See also **Choice; Judgment**
Albert — *Stop* p.34, 120-122
Baillie — *Diary* #69
Braude — *Source* #464-471
Braude — *Stories* p.101
Casselberry — *How* p.5-56
Curtis — *Human* p.56-58, 62-64
Dirksen — *Quot.* #502, 855, 1961-1962, 2382
Edwards — *Useful* p.120-121
Evans — *Faith* p.12, 22, 54, 88, 97, 115, 121, 124, 139, 145, 155, 171
Evans — *Quote* p.53-66
Evans — *This* p.60-61
Evans — *Thoughts I* p.77-79, 117-118, 127-128, 133, 159-162, 165-166, 188-189
Evans — *Thoughts II (Open Door) See* index, no p.
Evans — *Thoughts III (Open Road) See* index, no p.
Evans — *Thoughts IV* p.13, 67, 79, 205
Flesch — *Unusual* p.56-57
Flint — *Graham* p.40
Forbes — *Thoughts See* index p.546
Fuller — *Epigrams* p.80-81
Fun Fare p.10-11
Garland — *Subject* p.67
Grizer — *Wit* p.114-115
Henry — *5000* p.58
Hill — *Think* p.156-169
Hobe — *Tapestries* p.50
Hovey — *Treasury* p.147-148; #7, 453, 755-756, 841, 906, 962, 1525, 1561, 1761
Kennedy — *Fresh* p.89-98
Kennedy — *Reader's* #249-252
Kin — *Dictionary* p.66
List — *Living* p.29-33
Lockridge — *World's* #3400
Lytle — *Leaves* p.12
Mandel — *Stories* p.64-65
Modern Eloquence (14) p.310
Montapert — *Distilled* p.94-95
New Topical p.62
Nichols — *Third* p.57-58
Peale — *Guideposts* p.133-136, 151-154
Prochnow — *Public* #446, 681, 1865, 2362, 2965–2966
Prochnow — *Success.* #801, 823, 826, 1665
Sheen — *Content.* p.63-65
Sherman — *Your* p.120-129
Speaker's Desk p.34
Tanksley — *Friend* p.60
Wallis — *Treasure* p.212
White — *Job* p.95-97, 186
Woods — *Religious* p.222-223

DECLARATION OF INDEPENDENCE
Botkin — *Anecdotes* p.137
Flint — *Graham* p.11
Hovey — *Treasury* #1058, 1069
Prochnow — *Success.* #739
Seldes — *Great* p.256-257
Woods — *Religious* p.223
Words — *Inspir.* p.137
, First draft of
New Joy p.210
, Religion in
Keller — *You* p.29-31
, Signing of
Fogg — *1000* #92, 231

DECORATION. *See* **Ornament**

DECORUM. *See* **Behavior; Decency**

DEDICATION
See also **Diligence; Perseverance**
Detherage — *Sunrise* p.33, 37, 87, 163
Franke — *Buckley* p.55
Garland — *Subject* p.67-68
Lytle — *Leaves* p.60
Mandel — *Stories* p.65
New Topical p.62-63
Peale — *Courage* p.125
Phillips — *Choice* p.84
Prochnow — *Success.* #235
Voss — *Quotations* p.65-66
, Valor from
Maxwell — *Courage* p.198-206

DEDICATIONS
See also **Anniversaries**
Copeland — *World's* p.330-331, 341-342, 431-433, 613-615, 618-619, 636-639
Fun Fare p.99-100
Humes — *Instant* p.49-50

DEDUCTION. *See* **Logic**

DEEDS
See also **Action; Good; Work**
Applegarth — *Heir.* p.108, 157, 212, 243, 279
Book Proverbs p.104
Dirksen — *Quot.* #458, 1616-1617, 1963-1965
Edwards — *Useful* p.121
Forbes — *Thoughts* p.130, 165, 287, 369, 386, 403, 466, 480, 484, 514; *See also* index p.546
Fuller — *Epigrams* p.81-82
Harnsberger — *Mark* p.76
Henry — *5000* p.58-59
Hobe — *Tapestries* p.14-15

Hovey — *Treasury* p.148; #757-758
Kin — *Dictionary* p.66
Kohn — *Touch* p.42-45, 57-60
Liddle — *Thought I, II, III* p.25, 94, 112, 114, 121, 146, 155
Liddle — *Thought IV* p.26, 28, 38, 46
Liddle — *Thought V* p.18, 23, 26
Lytle — *Leaves* p.23, 25, 176, 183
Mandel — *Stories* p.65-66
Montapert — *Distilled* p.4-5, 95-96
New Joy p.22-23, 25
Phillips — *Choice* p.175, 202, 318
Prochnow — *Public* #2967
Tanksley — *Friend* p.22
Wallis — *Treasure* p.8, 47
Woods — *Religious* p.6-7, 223-224

DEEPNESS. *See* **Depth**

DEER
Applegarth — *Heir.* p.20
Botkin — *Anecdotes* p.93
Botkin — *Treasury* p.33, 454, 585, 587, 604

DEFEAT
See also **Discouragement; Failure**
Asimov — *Treasury* #181
Bartlett — *Discovery* p.116-117
Braude — *Source* #472-474
Dirksen — *Quot.* #254, 1113, 1643, 1928, 2224, 2326
Edwards — *Useful* p.121-122
Emmons — *Mature* p.61
Flint — *Graham* p.40
Forbes — *Thoughts* p.167, 182, 272, 298, 430, 440, 467
Fuller — *Epigrams* p.82-83
Garland — *Subject* p.68
Henry — *5000* p.59
Hill — *Think* p.116-118
Holmes — *I've* p.63
Johnson — *Bedside* p.234
Keller — *Open* p.111
Kennedy — *Reader's* #253-254
Keys Happiness p.53-55
Knight's Illus. p.97-98
Liddle — *Thought I, II, III* p.124
Lockridge — *World's* #741, 3875
Montapert — *Distilled* p.96-97
Peale — *Courage* p.38
Phillips — *Choice* p.144
Prochnow — *Public* #1153, 1658, 2200, 2968
Prochnow — *Success.* #832, 1667
Seldes — *Great* p.257
Speaker's Desk p.34-35
Woods — *Religious* p.224

DEFECTS
See also **Faults**
Dirksen — *Quot.* #1390-1391, 1966
Edwards — *Useful* p.279-280
Evans — *Thoughts I* p.93-94, 163-164, 187, 199-200, 212
Evans — *Thoughts IV* p.157, 199, 206-207
Flesch — *Unusual* p.57
Lockridge — *World's* #4317
Lytle — *Leaves* p.76
Mandel — *Stories* p.142

DEFENSE
See also **Civil defense; Self-defense**
Dirksen — *Quot.* #176
Flesch — *Unusual* p.57
Fogg — *1000 See* index p.883
Harral — *Feature* p.136
Hulme — *Living* p.22-34
Kin — *Dictionary* p.66
Montapert — *Distilled* p.97-98
Prochnow — *Speaker's* p.91
Prochnow — *Success.* #1465
Seldes — *Great* p.257
Woods — *Business.* p.54-55
, American
Copeland — *World's See* index p.736-737
, and peace
Kauffman — *For* p.82-83
, Court
Copeland — *World's* p.74-77, 79-83, 112-117, 151-153, 413-416

"DEFENSE MECHANISM"
Menninger — *Blue.* p.27

DEFERENCE. *See* **Courtesy; Respect**

DEFICIENCY
Dirksen — *Quot.* #97
Keller — *Open* p.54
Kin — *Dictionary* p.279
Prochnow — *Success.* #335, 1501
Woods — *Business.* p.55-57

DEFILEMENT
New Topical p.63

DEFINITIONS
Braude — *Speaker's* #261-305
Cerf — *Laugh* p.225-229
Edwards — *Useful* p.122
Flesch — *Unusual* p.57
Fox — *Make* p.41-43
Fun Fare p.131, 279
Lytle — *Leaves* p.5, 43, 56, 103

Prochnow — *Public* #267, 365, 420, 514, 685, 984
Prochnow — *Speaker's* p.92
Simpson — *'54* p.25, 139, 279
Speaker's Desk See index p.298

DEFLATION
Phillips — *Choice* p.166

DEFORMITY. *See* **Handicapped**

DEGREES
Lytle — *Leaves* p.153

DEHUMANIZATION
Kauffman — *For* p.83-84
Woods — *Religious* p.224-225

DEISM. *See* **God, Belief in**

DEITY. *See* **God**

DEJECTION. *See* **Unhappiness**

DELAWARE
Botkin — *Anecdotes* p.153

DELAY
See also **Inaction; Procrastination; Time**
Baillie — *Diary* #58
Braude — *Speaker's* #1429-1431
Braude — *Stories* p.102
Dirksen — *Quot.* #1856, 1967, 2342
Edwards — *Useful* p.122-123
Evans — *Faith* p.91-94
Evans — *Thoughts II (Open Door)* p.59
Evans — *Thoughts III (Open Road)* p.145
Evans — *Thoughts IV* p.195, 197
Flesch — *Unusual* p.302
Fuller — *Epigrams* p.83
Grizer — *Wit* p.115
Henry — *5000* p.59
Hubbard — *Scrap* p.52
Kin — *Dictionary* p.67
Modern Eloquence (14) p.311
Montapert — *Distilled* p.98
Prochnow — *Public* #121, 2182
Prochnow — *Success.* #1125

DELETION
Braude — *Stories* p.102

DELIBERATION. *See* **Consideration; Thought**

DELICACY
See also **Cleanliness; Fastidiousness; Refinement; Sensibility; Tact; Taste**
Edwards — *Useful* p.123
Flesch — *Unusual* p.57
Lockridge — *World's* #131, 651
Prochnow — *Public* #2013, 2142

DELICATESSENS
Asimov — *Treasury* #386
Prochnow — *Public* #324, 1660

DELIGHT. *See* **Enjoyment; Joy**

DELINQUENCY
See also **Crime and criminals; Juvenile delinquency**
Garland — *Subject* p.70
Mandel — *Stories* #67
, Causes of
Braude — *Stories* p.90

DELIVERANCE
Woods — *Religious* p.225

DELIVERY
Mandel — *Stories* p.67

DELPHIC ORACLE
Asimov — *Treasury* #143

DELUGE. *See* **Flood**

DELUSION
See also **Deception; Mistakes; Self-deception; Superstition**
Braude — *Source* #475-476
Edwards — *Useful* p.123-124
George — *Book* p.28, 85, 88, 152, 155, 166, 191, 276, 374, 399
Mandel — *Stories* p.67-68

DEMAGOGUES
See also **Dictatorship**
Dirksen — *Quot.* #376
Henry — *5000* p.60
Hubbard — *Scrap* p.196
Kin — *Dictionary* p.67
Nizer — *Thinking* p.139
Prochnow — *Speaker's* p.92-93
Seldes — *Great* p.258-260
Woods — *Business.* p.56-58

DEMAND AND SUPPLY. *See* **Supply and demand**

DEMOCRACY
See also **Equality; Freedom; Republic;** etc.
Adams — *New* p.97
Bartlett — *Discovery* p.83-84
Boas — *History* p.37-39
Braude — *Source* #477-480
Braude — *Stories* p.102-104
Curtis — *Practical* p.317, 321-323, 353-354

Detherage — *Sunrise* p.93-95, 105, 162
Dirksen — *Quot.* #373-379, 464, 594. 664, 1763, 2370
Droke — *Christian* p.125-132
Edwards — *Useful* p.124, 726-727
Flesch — *Unusual* p.57-58
Fogg — *1000* #113, 516
Forbes — *Thoughts See* index p.546
Franke — *Buckley* p.58
Fuller — *Epigrams* p.83-84
Garland — *Subject* p.71
Grizer — *Wit* p.115-118
Harnsberger — *Mark* p.77
Henry — *5000* p.59-60
Hovey — *Treasury* p.148-149; *See also* index p.295
Hubbard — *Scrap* p.121, 179-180
Kennedy — *Reader's* #255-261
Keys Happiness p.340-344
Lindeman — *Emerson* p.199-200
Lockridge — *World's* #3881, 3901, 4735
Menninger — *Blue.* p.110-111, 113
Montapert — *Distilled* p.98-99
Nichols — *Third* p.247-248
Nizer — *Thinking* p.44, 90, 103, 115, 139
Peale — *Guideposts* p.305-309
Peterson — *Art* p.157
Prochnow — *Public* #4052-4053, 4289, 4293-4294, 4402
Prochnow — *Speaker's* p.93
Prochnow — *Success.* #213, 284, 1668-1669
Seldes — *Great* p.260-277
Speaker's Desk p.35-37
Voss — *Quotations* p.66-68
Wallis — *Treasure* p.88, 174-175, 178
Wallis — *Words* p.13, 76, 146, 236
Woods — *Business.* p.58-60
Woods — *Religious* p.225-228
Words — *Inspir.* p.187-188

DEMOCRATS
Botkin — *Anecdotes* p.61
Dirksen — *Quot.* #1666
Hovey — *Treasury* #278, 551, 1057
Prochnow — *Public* #418
Prochnow — *Success.* #192
Seldes — *Great* p.277-278

DEMONS
See also **Devil**
Woods — *Religious* p.228-229

DEMONSTRATIONS
Fox — *Make* p.132, 153-154, 163, 189
Kauffman — *For* p.180
Speaker's Desk #157

DENATIONALIZATION
Du Noüy — *Human* p.219-222

DENIAL
See also **Self-denial**
Flesch — *Unusual* p.58
Garland — *Subject* p.72
Hovey — *Treasury* p.149; #769-770
White — *Job* p.27-28, 33

DENOMINATIONS
See also **Creeds;** names of denominations
Hobe — *Tapestries* p.107
Hubbard — *Scrap* p.202
Prochnow — *Public* #1585
Schermerhorn — *1500* p.107-109
Wallis — *Words* p.44, 46
Woods — *Religious* p.229

DENTISTS
Asimov — *Treasury* #10, 127
Braude — *Speaker's* #304-305
Cerf — *Laugh* p.244-245
Copeland — *10,000* p.499-501
Flesch — *Unusual* p.58
Fuller — *Thesaurus* #1696-1697
Fun Fare p.106-109
George — *Book* p.86, 116, 301
Harnsberger — *Mark* p.77-78
Harral — *Feature* p.136-137
Manchee — *Secret* p.207
Prochnow — *Public* #376, 416, 435, 572, 727, 1661, 1670
Prochnow — *Speaker's* p.93
Prochnow — *Success.* #348
Schermerhorn — *1500* p.109
Speaker's Desk #190
, Fear of
Maltz — *Creative* p.15-16

DENUNCIATION
Kronenberger — *Animal* p.58-60

DENVER, COLORADO
Botkin — *Anecdotes* p.230, 252

DEPARTMENT STORES
Botkin — *Anecdotes* p.41
Fun Fare p.40

DEPARTURES. *See* **Farewells**

DEPENDABILITY
See also **Self-reliance**
Evans — *Thoughts II (Open Door)* p.130
Evans — *Thoughts III (Open Road)* p.125-126

Forbes — *Thoughts* p.107, 178, 392, 433, 467-468
Garland — *Subject* p.266
Mandel — *Stories* p.217
Menninger — *Blue.* p.38
Montapert — *Distilled* p.99
Prochnow — *Speaker's* p.259

DEPENDENCE
See also **Poverty; Weakness**
Book Proverbs p.115
Edwards — *Useful* p.124-125
Evans — *Thoughts III (Open Road)* p.175
Henry — *5000* p.60
Hobe — *Tapestries* p.85
Kin — *Dictionary* p.67
Krishnamurti — *Think* p.27-28
Krishnamurti — *Urgency* p.93-97
Lytle — *Leaves* p.70, 121
Mandelbaum — *Choose* p.121-125
More Words p.48-49
Prochnow — *Success.* #1670
, Teenage
Ginott — *Between* p.37-38

DEPORTMENT. *See* **Behavior**

DEPRAVITY
See also **Cruelty; Evil; Sin; Wickedness**
Edwards — *Useful* p.39, 125, 681-683
Flint — *Graham* p.41
Forbes — *Thoughts* p.455, 517
Lockridge — *World's* #2655
Lytle — *Leaves* p.80, 112

DEPRECIATION
See also **Values**
Evans — *Unto* p.37
Woods — *Business.* p.60-61

DEPRESSANTS
Menninger — *Blue.* p.153-155

DEPRESSION
See also **Adversity; Discouragement; Doubt;** etc.
Botkin — *Anecdotes* p.117, 279
Dirksen — *Quot.* #13, 118
Edwards — *Useful* p.727
Evans — *Thoughts I* p.57, 79, 139, 187
Evans — *Thoughts III (Open Road)* p.35-41
Flesch — *Unusual* p.27
Forbes — *Thoughts* p.48, 171, 409, 451, 466, 468, 491, 520
Garland — *Subject* p.72-73
Grizer — *Wit* p.118
Holmes — *Psych.* p.90-94
Huxley — *You See* index p.284
Lockridge — *World's* #447
New Joy p.204
Peale — *Stay* p.193-211
Prochnow — *Public* #857, 1518, 1571, 1662, 2370
Schermerhorn — *1500* p.110
Sheen — *Content.* p.76-78
Woods — *Business.* p.61-63
, Business
Peale — *Guideposts* p.15-19
Prochnow — *Public* #857, 1518

DEPRIVATION. *See* **Poverty**

DEPTH
Halverson — *Perspective* p.118
Kohn — *Best* p.37-40
Lockridge — *World's* #4954
Phillips — *Choice* p.106, 153, 249
Prochnow — *Public* #1450, 2501

DERISION. *See* **Ridicule**

DERMATOLOGISTS
Asimov — *Treasury* #124

DESCARTES, RENÉ
Lockridge — *World's* #1668-1669, 2606

DESCRIPTION
Dirksen — *Quot.* #572, 1667-1668
Flesch — *Unusual* p.58
Lockridge — *World's* #1995
Prochnow — *Public* #1006
Prochnow — *Speaker's* p.94
Prochnow — *Success.* #1671

DESERT
Garland — *Subject* p.73
Lockridge — *World's* #3813
New Topical p.66-67
Prochnow — *Public* #344, 2005
Prochnow — *Success.* #462

DESERTION. *See* **Abandonment**

DESIGN
Garland — *Subject* p.73
Lockridge — *World's* #164
Woods — *Religious* p.229-230

DESIRE
See also **Ambition; Aspiration; Covetousness; Goals; Love; Wishes**
Applegarth — *Heir.* p.255
Edwards — *Useful* p.125-127, 282
Evans — *Unto* p.61, 90, 103, 119, 123
Flesch — *Unusual* p.58-59

Forbes — *Thoughts See* index p.546
Fox — *Make* p.77
Fuller — *Epigrams* p.84-85
Giniger — *Compact* p.76-83
Henry — *5000* p.61
Hovey — *Treasury* p.149-150; #27, 34, 248, 317, 555, 771-776, 1751
Johnson — *Bedside* p.234-255, 310
Kennedy — *Reader's* #262-266
Kin — *Dictionary* p.68
Krishnamurti — *Think* p.26-27, 120-121
Liddle — *Thought I, II, III* p.135
Lockridge — *World's* #464, 3451, 5718
Montapert — *Distilled* p.99-100
Prochnow — *Public* #2491, 2969-2970
Prochnow — *Success.* #1672
Seldes — *Great* p.278-279
Speaker's Desk p.37-38; #513, 1148
Wallis — *Treasure* p.137, 226
Woods — *Religious* p.230-232, 543

, for riches
Hill — *Think* p.32-49

, Lack of
Krishnamurti — *Think* p.216-217

"DESK-POUNDING"
Dirksen — *Quot.* #69

DESOLATION. *See* **Loneliness; Misery**

DESPAIR
See also **Depression; Disappointment; Grief; Loneliness; Misery**
Albert — *Stop* p.159-160
Braude — *Stories* p.104
Curtis — *Practical* p.114
Dirksen — *Quot.* #856-857, 1305
Edwards — *Useful* p.127-128
Evans — *Unto* p.116
Flesch — *Unusual* p.59
Flint — *Graham* p.42-48
Fogg — *1000* #820
Forbes — *Thoughts* p.107, 173, 180, 195, 307, 315, 344, 363, 372, 385, 436, 473, 479, 483, 495
Fuller — *Epigrams* p.85-86
Henry — *5000* p.61
Johnson — *Bedside* p.113, 196
Kohn — *Adventures* p.74-75
Liddle — *Thought I, II, III* p.78, 170
Liddle — *Thought IV* p.13, 17
Lockridge — *World's* #1643
Lytle — *Leaves* p.23
Mandel — *Stories* p.68
Montapert — *Distilled* p.100-101
New Topical p.67
Prochnow — *Public* #1984, 2249, 2393
Sheban — *Wisdom* no p.
Sheen — *Thoughts* p.145-147
Speaker's Desk p.38-39
Wallis — *Treasure* p.226
Watson — *Light* p.147-152
Woods — *Religious* p.232-234
Words — *Inspir.* p.161-162

, and boredom
Kauffman — *For* p.35

, Conquered by faith
Webb — *Edge* p.125-129

, Modern
Adams — *New* p.413

DESPERATION
Braude — *Source* #481
Dirksen — *Quot.* #320, 446
Flesch — *Unusual* p.59
Kin — *Dictionary* p.68
Montapert — *Distilled* p.101
Prochnow — *Public* #1417
Prochnow — *Success.* #1673

DESPONDENCY. *See* **Depression; Despair; Unhappiness**

DESPOTISM
See also **Demagogues; Dictatorship; Tyrants and tyranny**
Edwards — *Useful* p.128
Evans — *Unto* p.33, 57, 124
Fogg — *1000* #744, 748, 975, 1053
Forbes — *Thoughts* p.99, 387, 408, 428
Henry — *5000* p.61
Lockridge — *World's* #1145-1146, 2727, 3647, 3721, 4662, 4665
Seldes — *Great* p.279-280
Sheban — *Wisdom* no p.
Wheelis — *Moralist* p.60
Words — *Inspir.* p.140

DESSERTS
Lockridge — *World's* #1434, 2496
Prochnow — *Speaker's* p.94

DESTINY
See also **Fate; Fortune; God; Luck**
Braude — *Stories* p.104
Curtis — *Practical* p.216
Dirksen — *Quot.* #858-860, 1968, 2338
Edwards — *Useful* p.128-129
Flesch — *Unusual* p.59

Fogg — *1000* #503
Forbes — *Thoughts* p.8, 54, 116, 162, 241, 278, 332, 372, 382, 475, 503
Fox — *Make* p.230-231
Grizer — *Wit* p.118-119
Guideposts — *Faith* p.36
Henry — *5000* p.61-62
Hobe — *Tapestries* p.85
How To Live p.563-572
Hubbard — *Scrap* p.8, 109, 185
Kin — *Dictionary* p.68
Kohn — *Thoughts* p.156-159
Krishnamurti — *Think* p.98-99
Liddle — *Thought I, II, III* p.23, 149
Lockridge — *World's* #884
Lytle — *Leaves* p.61
Mandel — *Stories* p.75
Montapert — *Distilled* p.102
New Joy p.42
Nichols — *New* p.14-15
Peterson — *Art* p.262
Phillips — *Choice* p.29, 80
Prochnow — *Public* #863, 4054-4055
Prochnow — *Success.* #1674
Seldes — *Great* p.280, 642
Sheban — *Wisdom* no p.
Voss — *Quotations* p.68-69
Wallis — *Treasure* p.19, 48, 145, 175, 233
Wallis — *Words* p.88, 153, 212, 224
Welk — *Guide.* p.24-25
Wilcox — *Heart* p.76-78
Woods — *Religious* p.234
Woods — *Wellsprings* p.77-82

, American
Dirksen — *Quot.* #530, 573-574, 773, 2349

, Eternal
Sheen — *Content.* p.117-119

, History of
Liebman — *Hope* p.48-71

DESTITUTION. *See* **Poverty**

DESTRUCTION
Curtis — *Practical* p.76, 534-535
Evans — *This* p.133
Forbes — *Thoughts* p.8, 41, 405, 422
Kahn — *Lessons* p.81-83
Kin — *Dictionary* p.63, 68
Prochnow — *Public* #477, 2624
Prochnow — *Speaker's* p.83
Seldes — *Great* p.280-283
Sheban — *Wisdom* no p.
Woods — *Religious* p.19

, Evaluation of
Wheelis — *Moralist* p.100-101

, Forces of
Adams — *New* p.64

DETAILS
Flesch — *Unusual* p.59
Grizer — *Wit* p.119
Lockridge — *World's* #918, 3661
Prochnow — *Public* #310, 596, 1878
Prochnow — *Success.* #888, 959
Watson — *Light* p.231-238

DETECTIVES
Fuller — *Thesaurus* #2556-2557

DETERIORATION
See also **Decay**
Evans — *Unto* p.83
Prochnow — *Success.* #347

DETERMINATION
See also **Decision; Will**
Book Proverbs p.74
Braude — *Speaker's* #306-307
Braude — *Stories* p.104-105
Dirksen — *Quot.* #1669
Fogg — *1000 See* index p.883
Forbes — *Thoughts See* index p.546
Grizer — *Wit* p.119-120
Guideposts — *Faith* p.202-204
Halverson — *Perspective* p.61
Kin — *Dictionary* p.68
Liddle — *Thought I, II, III* p.74, 80, 84, 102, 116-117, 119, 125, 132, 136, 146, 153
Lytle — *Leaves* p.49, 136
Manchee — *Secret* p.141-145
Mandel — *Stories* p.68-69
Montapert — *Distilled* p.103-104
Prochnow — *Public* #2215, 2971-2977
Prochnow — *Speaker's* p.94-95
Wallis — *Treasure* p.81-84

DETERMINISM
Curtis — *Practical* p.244-247
Du Noüy — *Human* p.47-48, 139, 178, 181-182, 247
Du Noüy — *Road* p.28, 105, 143-145, 157, 168-178, 182, 186
Flesch — *Unusual* p.59
Ideas p.106-108
Woods — *Religious* p.235-237

DETRACTION. *See* **Criticism; Slander; Withdrawal;** etc.

DEVELOPMENT
See also **Growth; Progress**
Forbes — *Thoughts* p.44, 156, 408, 505, 515
Garland — *Subject* p.74
Montapert — *Distilled* p.104

Phillips — *Choice* p.118, 133, 292-293, 320
White — *Job* p.41-42, 46, 56, 62, 67-68, 103, 116, 179-181, 187

DEVIATION. *See* **Change; Compromise; Instability**

DEVIL
See also **Evil; Hell;** etc.
Baillie — *Diary* #15, 185
Book Proverbs p.121
Botkin — *Anecdotes* p.127, 190, 192
Droke — *Christian* p.484-485
Edwards — *Useful* p.130
Evans — *Faith* p.13, 122, 125
Flesch — *Unusual* p.59-60
Flint — *Graham* p.40-41, 60, 125-126, 145
Forbes — *Thoughts* p.49, 313, 419, 458, 500
Fuller — *Epigrams* p.86
Garland — *Subject* p.74-75, 283
Halverson — *Perspective* p.79
Harnsberger — *Mark* p.423-424
Henry — *5000* p.62
Hobe — *Tapestries* p.28
Hoffer — *Reflect.* p.11-14
Hubbard — *Scrap* p.44
Hunter — *Gems* p.96-97
Ideas p.108-110
Kennedy — *Reader's* #267-269
Kin — *Dictionary* p.69
Knight's Illus. p.98-99
Knight's Treas. p.105-107
Lockridge — *World's* #2649, 4416
Modern Eloquence (14) p.312
More Words p.50
New Topical p.67-68
Prochnow — *Public* #457, 2578, 2642
Seldes — *Great* p.283-284
Sheban — *Wisdom* no p.
Woods — *Religious* p.237-241, 884

DEVOTION
See also **Love; Prayer; Worship**
Applegarth — *Heir.* p.296, 301
Edwards — *Useful* p.130
Forbes — *Thoughts* p.10, 118, 361, 404
Fuller — *Thesaurus* #171-173
Garland — *Subject* p.75
Hobe — *Tapestries* p.16, 106
Hovey — *Treasury* #64, 270, 513, 550
Kin — *Dictionary* p.69
Lockridge — *World's* #2415
Mandel — *Stories* p.69-70
Phillips — *Choice* p.38, 83-84, 164, 190, 229, 239, 393-416
Prochnow — *Public* #379
Tanksley — *Friend* p.42
Wallis — *Treasure* p.131-132
Wallis — *Words* p.46, 59-62
Woods — *Religious* p.240-241

DEVOUTNESS. *See* **Piety; Prayer; Religion**

DEW
Edwards — *Useful* p.130-131
Hadfield — *Delights* p.19
Henry — *5000* p.62

DEXTERITY. *See* **Ability**

DHARMA (Buddhist truth)
Woods — *Religious* p.241

DIAGNOSIS
Braude — *Speaker's* #308-310
Flesch — *Unusual* p.60
Prochnow — *Public* #487-969, 1063

DIALECT. *See* **Accents**

DIALECTICS AND MATERIALISM
Flint — *Graham* p.100
Ideas p.110-111
Kin — *Dictionary* p.69
Seldes — *Great* p.284

DIALOGUE. *See* **Conversation**

DIAMONDS
Asimov — *Treasury* #211, 369
Dirksen — *Quot.* #224
Kin — *Dictionary* p.69
Prochnow — *Public* #155

DIARIES
Auden — *Certain* p.108
Francis — *For* p.26-40
Keys Happiness p.408-411
Peterson — *Art* p.22

DICE
Edwards — *Useful* p.131
New Joy p.196
, Probabilities in
Du Noüy — *Human* p.30-31

DICKENS, CHARLES
Flesch — *Unusual* p.60

DICTATORSHIP
See also **Despotism; Tyrants and tyranny**
Braude — *Stories* p.105-106
Edwards — *Useful* p.727
Forbes — *Thoughts* p.46, 59, 83-84, 98, 118, 156, 314, 372, 505, 512, 517

Fuller — *Epigrams* p.86-87
Fuller — *Thesaurus* #2001-2011
Henry — *5000* p.62
Menninger — *Blue.* p.108-109
Nizer — *Thinking* p.103, 128, 134, 190
Prochnow — *Success.* #483
Seldes — *Great* p.284-286, 912
Woods — *Business.* p.63-64
Woods — *Religious* p.242, 994-995

DICTIONARIES
Flesch — *Unusual* p.60
Harnsberger — *Mark* p.79
Harral — *Feature* p.137
Prochnow — *Success.* #1675

DIET
See also **Cooks and cookery; Eating; Overweight; Vegetarianism**
Casselberry — *How* p.129-131, 147-158
Dirksen — *Quot.* #127, 266
Edwards — *Useful* p.131
Flesch — *Unusual* p.60
Garland — *Subject* p.76
Grizer — *Wit* p.120
Hadfield — *Delights* p.67
Harnsberger — *Mark* p.79
Hovey — *Treasury* p.150; #74, 314, 571, 777–779, 1862
Keys Happiness p.350, 392-396, 438-448, 517
Kin — *Dictionary* p.69
Kohn — *Thoughts* p.156-159
Lockridge — *World's* #1440, 5876
Mandel — *Stories* p.70
Montapert — *Distilled* p.105
Peale — *Guideposts* p.71-75
Prochnow — *Public* #253, 539, 619, 779, 1203, 1218, 1465
Prochnow — *Speaker's* p.95
Prochnow — *Success.* #435, 1139
Schermerhorn — *1500* p.112
White — *Life* p.92-95
, Laws of
Asimov — *Treasury* #329, 331-332, 476, 478

DIFFERENCE
See also **Disagreement; Individuals and individuality**
Braude — *Source* #482-489
Dirksen — *Quot.* #263, 1969
Edwards — *Useful* p.131
Evans — *This* p.5
Evans — *Unto* p.82, 85, 125, 143
Flesch — *Unusual* p.60
Forbes — *Thoughts* p.76, 99, 102, 152, 184, 261, 377, 437, 448, 508
Grizer — *Wit* p.120-121
How To Live p.284-285
Kin — *Dictionary* p.69
Krishnamurti — *Think* p.164
Lockridge — *World's* #138, 1265
Mandelbaum — *Choose* p.53-98
Menninger — *Blue.* p.50-61, 89-97
Montapert — *Distilled* p.105-106
Prochnow — *Public* #329, 419, 482, 553, 587, 638, 817, 847, 935, 1029, 1458, 1895
Prochnow — *Success.* #512, 1301, 1310, 1676-1677
Wallis — *Treasure* p.163, 174, 231
Wallis — *Words* p.81

DIFFICULTIES
See also **Adversity; Failure; Problems; Trouble; Worry**
Baillie — *Diary* #168
Dirksen — *Quot.* #381
Edwards — *Useful* p.131-132
Evans — *Faith* p.3-4, 7, 17, 21, 170
Evans — *Unto* p.119
Flesch — *Unusual* p.60-61
Forbes — *Thoughts See* index p.546
Fox — *Make* p.207
Fuller — *Epigrams* p.87-88
Garland — *Subject* p.76
Grizer — *Wit* p.121
Henry — *5000* p.62-63
Hovey — *Treasury* p.151; #294, 780-784
How To Live p.453-457
Lytle — *Leaves* p.14, 22, 44, 56
Mandel — *Stories* p.70-71
Modern Eloquence (14) p.313-314
Montapert — *Distilled* p.106-107
New Joy p.129
Prochnow — *Public* #95, 599, 2337, 2675
Prochnow — *Success.* #1678
Redhead — *Living* p.26-33
Speaker's Desk p.39-40;#106
Wallis — *Treasure* p.83, 184
Walters — *How* p.75-97
, Help in
Kohn — *Through* p.79-84
, Power over
Peale — *Stay* p.86-104

DIFFIDENCE. *See* **Bashfulness**

DIGESTION
See also **Indigestion**
Flesch — *Unusual* p.61

Huxley — *You See* index p.284
Kin — *Dictionary* p.70
Prochnow — *Success.* #1679

DIGNITY
See also **Honor; Pride; Self-respect;** etc.
Applegarth — *Heir.* p.178
Braude — *Source* #490-491
Day — *Meditations* p.17
Dirksen — *Quot.* #440, 815, 992, 1002, 2256, 2384
Edwards — *Useful* p.132-133
Evans — *Thoughts III (Open Road)* p.26, 77-81
Forbes — *Thoughts* p.28, 43, 114, 121, 377, 414, 440, 447, 504
Fuller — *Epigrams* p.88
Grizer — *Wit* p.122
Harnsberger — *Mark* p.79-80
Henry — *5000* p.63
Liddle — *Thought I, II, III* p.11
Liddle — *Thought IV* p.44
Liddle — *Thought V* p.21, 28
Lockridge — *World's* #2655, 2884, 3624, 3728, 3770
Prochnow — *Public* #1226, 2019, 4387
Prochnow — *Success.* #1430
Seldes — *Great* p.286-287
Woods — *Religious* p.242

DILEMMAS. *See* **Problems;** etc.

DILIGENCE
See also **Effort; Perseverance; Work**
Applegarth — *Heir.* p.296
Book Proverbs p.129
Dirksen — *Quot.* #1397
Edwards — *Useful* p.133
Evans — *Unto* p.12
Forbes — *Thoughts* p.338, 424, 437
Fuller — *Thesaurus* #176-177
Hobe — *Tapestries* p.15
Johnson — *Bedside* p.128
Liddle — *Thought I, II, III* p.98-99, 102, 154
Lockridge — *World's* #93
Montapert — *Distilled* p.107
New Topical p.69
Prochnow — *Public* #2543

DIN. *See* **Noise**

DINNERS
Dirksen — *Quot.* #343
Edwards — *Useful* p.133
Flesch — *Unusual* p.61-62
Fuller — *Thesaurus* #751-753
Fun Fare p.65-66, 291-292
Grizer — *Wit* p.53
Hadfield — *Delights* p.62
Harnsberger — *Mark* p.18
Kin — *Dictionary* p.247
Lockridge — *World's* #2099, 2703, 2706-2707, 2711, 2714-2715, 2724, 4909
Modern Eloquence (14) p.315
Nizer — *Thinking* p.19-21, 110-111
Prochnow — *Public* #17, 309, 324, 394, 398, 697
Prochnow — *Speaker's* p.96
Woods — *Content.* p.123, 185, 189

DINOSAURS
Du Noüy — *Human* p.66, 68, 75-76, 91, 170-171

DIPLOMAS
Prochnow — *Public* #1404

DIPLOMATS AND DIPLOMACY
Braude — *Stories* p.106
Dirksen — *Quot.* #60, 181, 233, 348, 1971-1972
Fogg — *1000* #423, 453, 603, 695, 853, 873, 928, 932, 1015, 1036, 1051
Franke — *Buckley* p.59
Fuller — *Epigrams* p.88
Fuller — *Thesaurus* #2021-2027
Grizer — *Wit* p.122-123
Henry — *5000* p.63
Lockridge — *World's* #3779
Mandel — *Stories* p.71
Prochnow — *Public* #216, 375, 502, 797, 1664-1665, 1892
Prochnow — *Speaker's* p.96
Prochnow — *Success.* #172, 346, 349, 616, 1152, 1286, 1680-1681
Pullar-Strecker — *Proverbs* #222-228
Schermerhorn —*1500* p.112-113
Seldes — *Great* p.287
Speaker's Desk #79, 95, 145, 163, 433, 440, 514, 592, 617, 872, 914, 954, 1071
Walters — *How* p.51-52

DIRECTION
See also **Purpose**
Braude — *Stories* p.106-107
Evans — *Quote* p.53-66
Evans — *Thoughts IV* p.188-190, 193-194
Forbes — *Thoughts* p.49, 279, 495
Halverson — *Perspective* p.93
Holmes — *Design* p.57-59, 214-215
Mandel — *Stories* p.71-72
Prochnow — *Public* #693
Speaker's Desk #2, 15, 695, 871
Wallis — *Treasure* p.231

, *Sense of*
Kohn — *Through* p.67-71
Maltz — *Creative* p.76

DIRECTNESS
Lytle — *Leaves* p.159

DIRECTORIES
Harral — *Feature* p.137-138

DIRT
Edwards — *Useful* p.133
Harnsberger — *Mark* p.81-82
Hubbard — *Scrap* p.39
Kin — *Dictionary* p.70
Lockridge — *World's* #3552, 4630
Prochnow — *Public* #265

DISABILITY. *See* **Handicapped**

DISAGREEMENT
See also **Argument; Quarrels;** etc.
Boas — *History* p.46-50
Braude — *Stories* p.107
Evans — *Thoughts I* p.47, 210
Evans — *Thoughts II (Open Door)* p.14
Evans — *Thoughts IV* p.87, 203
Evans — *Unto* p.85
Flesch — *Unusual* p.62
Forbes — *Thoughts* p.222, 373, 396
Garland — *Subject* p.78
Johnson — *Bedside* p.119
Prochnow — *Public* #1470
White — *Job* p.52, 70-71, 103, 110-111, 144-145
Woods — *Religious* p.243

DISAPPEARANCE
Prochnow — *Public* #2223-2224, 2260

DISAPPOINTMENT
See also **Defeat; Discouragement; Dissatisfaction; Failure; Unhappiness**
Bartlett — *Discovery* p.144
Braude — *Speaker's* #314
Braude — *Stories* p.107-108
Edwards — *Useful* p.133-134
Evans — *Faith* p.3-4, 18, 115, 170-201
Evans — *Thoughts II (Open Door) See* index no p.
Evans — *Thoughts III (Open Road) See* index no p.
Evans — *Thoughts IV* p.81-90, 106, 185
Evans — *Unto* p.105, 119
Forbes — *Thoughts* p.253, 364, 427, 476
Fuller — *Epigrams* p.89
Grizer — *Wit* p.123
Harnsberger — *Mark* p.82
Henry — *5000* p.63
Holmes — *I've* p.104-105
Knight's Illus. p.99-100
Montapert — *Distilled* p.107-108
Price — *No* p.15-30
Prochnow — *Public* #2096
Prochnow — *Speaker's* p.96-97
Reader's — *20th* p.49-50
Redhead — *Living* p.53-60
Speaker's Desk p.40; #248, 265, 442, 885
Tanksley — *Friend* p.18
Woods — *Religious* p.243

DISAPPROVAL. *See* **Criticism**

DISARMAMENT
Franke — *Buckley* p.59-60
Ideas p.112-113
Seldes — *Great* p.287-288

DISASTER
See also types of disasters, e.g. **Earthquakes**
Dirksen — *Quot.* #1163, 1747
Edwards — *Useful* p.60
Evans — *Unto* p.35, 121
Forbes — *Thoughts* p.57, 165, 274, 285
Henry — *5000* p.27
Kin — *Dictionary* p.38
Kohn — *Adventures* p.136
Lockridge — *World's* #2588
Prochnow — *Success.* #966
Walters — *How* p.99-109
Woods — *Religious* p.100
Words Change p.10-37

DISBELIEF. *See* **Doubt**

DISCERNMENT. *See* **Appreciation; Discrimination; Taste**

DISCIPLES
Flint — *Graham* p.41
Hovey — *Treasury* p.151; #350, 381, 497, 628, 785-789, 814, 820, 823, 1002, 1255, 1321, 1381
More Words p.51-52

DISCIPLINE
See also **Punishment; Self-control**
Braude — *Source* #492-493
Braude — *Stories* p.108
Detherage — *Sunrise* p.35, 38, 57-62, 90, 114
Dirksen — *Quot.* #1266-1268

Edwards — *Useful* p.134, 727
Emmons — *Mature* p.95
Evans — *Faith* p.50, 53-56, 64, 77
Evans — *Thoughts III (Open Road)* p.28, 50, 69, 106, 150, 168, 177, 186, 202
Evans — *Thoughts IV* p.144
Evans — *Unto* p.118, 132
Flesch — *Unusual* p.62
Flint — *Graham* p.41-42
Forbes — *Thoughts* p.163, 292, 312, 317, 340, 450
Garland — *Subject* p.78
Harral — *Feature* p.138
Hovey — *Treasury* p.152; #69, 220, 310, 326, 532, 611, 668, 790-795, 814, 843, 860, 1362, 1598, 1620, 1709, 1770
Hubbard — *Scrap* p.23, 222
Johnson — *Bedside* p.90, 109, 299-300
Kauffman — *For* p.84-85
Kennedy — *Fresh* p.159-162
Kennedy — *Reader's* #270-272
Keys Happiness p.399-402
Kin — *Dictionary* p.70
Krishnamurti — *Think* p.75-76, 104
Krishnamurti — *Urgency* p.60-63
Lair — *Baby* p.167-168
Liddle — *Thought IV* p.4
Lockridge — *World's* #4415
Lytle — *Leaves* p.11
Montapert — *Distilled* p.108-109
More Words p.52-53
Nichols — *New* p.116-118
Peale — *Guideposts* p.57-60
Phillips — *Choice* p.302
Prochnow — *Public* #1849
Seldes — *Great* p.288-289
Wallis — *Words* p.26, 222-223
Woods — *Religious* p.243
Words — *Inspir.* p.191

DISCOMFORT
White — *Job* p.83-84

DISCONTENT
See also **Complaining; Depression; Worry;** etc.
Alexander's Treasure. p.151
Baillie — *Diary* #83
Braude — *Stories* p.118
Dirksen — *Quot.* #575, 1306
Edwards — *Useful* p.134-135, 207
Evans — *Unto* p.14, 16, 37, 93, 103
Flesch — *Unusual* p.62
Forbes — *Thoughts* p.287, 347, 383, 419, 437, 464, 506
Guideposts — *Faith* p.47-50
Henry — *5000* p.63
Hubbard — *Scrap* p.78
Huxley — *You See* index p.284
Johnson — *Bedside* p.318
Kin — *Dictionary* p.70
Liddle — *Thought I, II, III* p.68, 80
Liddle — *Thought IV* p.23
Lockridge — *World's* #3090
Lytle — *Leaves* p.20, 36, 123, 135
Mandel — *Stories* p.72-74
Modern Eloquence (14) p.316
Montapert — *Distilled* p.109
Prochnow — *Public* #2978, 4291
Prochnow — *Success.* #1682-1683
Seldes — *Great* p.289
Speaker's Desk #447, 625, 765, 982, 1005, 1176
Vogue — *Arts* p.93-101
Woods — *Content.* p.302
Woods — *Religious* p.245
Woods — *Wellsprings* p.28-29
, *Creative*
Krishnamurti — *Think* p.38-44
, *Teenage*
Ginott — *Between* p.28-31

DISCORD. *See* **Argument; Disagreement; Quarrels**

DISCOURAGEMENT
See also **Defeat; Depression; Unhappiness**
Braude — *Source* #494-496
Braude — *Speaker's* #315-316
Braude — *Stories* p.108-109
Carruthers — *Sparks* p.82-84
Dirksen — *Quot.* #861
Evans — *Faith* p.14, 21-22, 39
Evans — *Quite* p.141-152
Evans — *Thoughts I* p.112, 120-124, 127-132, 139
Evans — *Thoughts III (Open Road)* p.35-41, 57, 59, 119, 145, 177, 180
Evans — *Thoughts IV* p.56, 81-90, 107, 169, 184, 199, 206
Flesch — *Unusual* p.62
Flint — *Graham* p.42
Forbes — *Thoughts* p.93, 110, 393, 409, 437, 446
Garland — *Subject* p.78-79
How To Live p.568-572
Keller — *Open* p.37
Knight's Illus. p.100-101
Kohn — *Best* p.112-113
Lockridge — *World's* #3384
Lytle — *Leaves* p.54, 116
Mandel — *Stories* p.72-73
Montapert — *Distilled* p.109-110
Peterson — *Art* p.84
Prochnow — *Public* #76
Speaker's Desk See index p.298

DISCOURTESY. *See* **Arrogance; Insult; Rudeness**

DISCOVERY
See also **Explorers and exploration; Innovation; Inventors and invention; Originality; Self-discovery**
Braude — *Stories* p.109
Curtis — *Practical* p.219-220
Detherage — *Sunrise* p.17-20
Edwards — *Useful* p.135
Evans — *Unto* p.114, 142
Flesch — *Unusual* p.90
Fogg — *1000* #144, 204-205, 264, 362, 608, 628, 739
Garland — *Subject* p.79
Harnsberger — *Mark* p.82-83
Hobe — *Tapestries* p.18
Kin — *Dictionary* p.94
Lockridge — *World's* #1530, 4043
Lytle — *Leaves* p.107, 180
Prochnow — *Public* #966, 1864, 2385
Prochnow — *Success.* #951
Speaker's Desk #119,1134
Vogue — *Arts* p.33-38
Wallis — *Treasure* p.24, 65
Wallis — *Words* p.142, 234

DISCRETION
See also **Care; Caution; Common sense; Judgment; Prudence**
Book Proverbs p.100
Braude — *Stories* p.109
Dirksen — *Quot.* #862-863, 2185
Edwards — *Useful* p.135
Flesch — *Unusual* p.62
Forbes — *Thoughts* p.144, 169
Fuller — *Epigrams* p.89-90
Fuller — *Thesaurus* #181-182
Henry — *5000* p.64
Hubbard — *Scrap* p.225
Johnson — *Bedside* p.12
Kin — *Dictionary* p.70
Lockridge — *World's* #1464, 1759, 2399, 5900
Lytle — *Leaves* p.177
Mandel — *Stories* p.73
Montapert — *Distilled* p.110
Prochnow — *Public* #654, 1666
Prochnow — *Success.* #1030
Speaker's Desk #224, 516, 521, 527, 539, 627, 905

DISCRIMINATION
See also **Appreciation; Intolerance; Taste**
Braude — *Stories* p.109-117
Evans — *This* p.5-6
Forbes — *Thoughts* p.244
Garland — *Subject* p.79-80
Peale — *Guideposts* p.269-273
Woods — *Religious* p.244

DISCUSSION
See also **Argument; Conversation; Talk**
Edwards — *Useful* p.135-136
Evans — *Thoughts II (Open Door)* p.21-25, 31-34, 38-39, 43-44, 158, 169-170, 183-188
Flesch — *Unusual* p.62
Forbes — *Thoughts* p.152, 161, 214, 427, 437
Kin — *Dictionary* p.70
Liddle — *Thought I, II, III* p.112, 133, 157
Lockridge — *World's* #4347
Montapert — *Distilled* p.110-111
Seldes — *Great* p.289-290

DISEASE
See also **Illness; Medicine;** etc.
Edwards — *Useful* p.136
Flesch — *Unusual* p.62
Fuller — *Thesaurus* #1721
Garland — *Subject* p.80
Henry — *5000* p.64
Holmes — *Design* p.101, 143, 158
Kin — *Dictionary* p.70-71
Lockridge — *World's* #2092
Menninger — *Blue.* p.157
New Topical p.69-70
Prochnow — *Public* #1180, 1621, 4286
Seldes — *Great* p.290
White — *Life* p.1, 87-89, 136-138

DISGRACE
See also **Defeat; Shame;** etc.
Asimov — *Treasury* #126
Dirksen — *Quot.* #864
Edwards — *Useful* p.136-137, 288
Garland — *Subject* p.80
Henry — *5000* p.64
Kin — *Dictionary* p.131
Seldes — *Great* p.508

DISGUISE
See also **Concealment; Hypocrisy**
Edwards — *Useful* p.137
Kin — *Dictionary* p.71
Lytle — *Leaves* p.97

DISHWASHING
Holmes — *I've* p.28-29
Prochnow — *Public* #918

DISHONESTY
See also **Corruption; Falsehood;** types of dishonesty
Alexander's Treasure. p.101-102
Braude — *Source* #497-498
Dirksen — *Quot.* #2317
Edwards — *Useful* p.137

Evans — *Unto* p.28, 35, 52, 72, 116
Flesch — *Unusual* p.63
Flint — *Graham* p.43
Garland — *Subject* p.80-81
Kahn — *Lessons* p.203-208
Kin — *Dictionary* p.60, 71, 88-89
Knight's Illus. p.156-159
Kohn — *Adventures* p.24
Krishnamurti — *Think* p.96-97
Menninger — *Blue.* p.135-137, 139-140
More Words p.61-63
Prochnow — *Public* #1602, 1655, 2625
Seldes — *Great* p.343-345
Woods — *Religious* p.204, 244, 324

DISHONOR. *See* **Disgrace**

DISILLUSIONMENT
See also **Cynics and cynicism; Disappointment**
Carruthers — *Sparks* p.133-135
Edwards — *Useful* p.727
Evans — *Faith* p.45, 222
Price — *No* p.31-40
Speaker's Desk #80, 113, 195-196, 480, 487, 512, 518, 777, 979

DISINTERESTEDNESS. *See* **Unconcern**

DISLIKE
Dirksen — *Quot.* #164
Flesch — *Unusual* p.63
Keys Happiness p.93-96

DISLOYALTY. *See* **Treachery; Treason**

DISOBEDIENCE
See also **Obstinacy; Rebellion; Self-will**
Edwards — *Useful* p.137
Evans — *This* p.143-144
Evans — *Unto* p.68
Flint — *Graham* p.43
Garland — *Subject* p.81
Knight's Illus. p.214-219
New Topical p.70
Seldes — *Great* p.290-291
Woods — *Religious* p.244

DISORDER
See also **Confusion**
Du Noüy — *Road* p.37, 67-68, 74, 83, 86, 106-107, 147
Evans — *This* p.39-40
Flesch — *Unusual* p.63
Prochnow — *Public* #2014, 2400
Woods — *Religious* p.244

DISPLAY
Flesch — *Unusual* p.63

DISPOSITION
See also **Character; Faults;** etc.
Applegarth — *Heir.* p.49
Curtis — *Human* p.136-142, 199
Edwards — *Useful* p.138
Harnsberger — *Mark* p.83
Kin — *Dictionary* p.71
Liddle — *Thought I, II, III* p.6
Montapert — *Distilled* p.111-112
Wallis — *Words* p.20

DISPUTE
See also **Argument; Controversy; Disagreement**
Book Proverbs p.112
Dirksen — *Quot.* #375, 382-383, 515, 1679
Flesch — *Unusual* p.63
Grizer — *Wit* p.124
Hoffer — *Reflect.* p.29-46
Kin — *Dictionary* p.71
Mandel — *Stories* p.73
Prochnow — *Public* #2292, 4055
Prochnow — *Success.* #1684-1685
Seldes — *Great* p.291-293
Voss — *Quotations* p.70-71
Woods — *Religious* p.244-245

DISSATISFACTION. *See* **Discontent**

DISSIPATION
See also **Excess; Indulgence;** types of dissipation
Edwards — *Useful* p.138
Evans — *Thoughts IV* p.165
Woods — *Religious* p.245

DISSYMMETRY
Du Noüy — *Human* p.22, 31, 33-34, 41-42, 87, 191
Du Noüy — *Road* p.113, 123-126, 126n, 128-133

DISTANCE
See also **Absence; Reserve**
Alexander's Treasure. p.124-125
Edwards — *Useful* p.138-139
Flesch — *Unusual* p.63
Kin — *Dictionary* p.71, 90
Lockridge — *World's* #5676
Prochnow — *Public* #631
Prochnow — *Success.* #1063, 1181
Speaker's Desk #584

DISTINCTION
See also **Fame; Greatness; Honor;** etc.
Edwards — *Useful* p.139, 158

Flesch — *Unusual* p.63
Prochnow — *Speaker's* p.97

DISTRACTION. *See* **Interruption**

DISTRESS. *See* **Affliction; Misery; Unhappiness;** etc.

DISTRUST. *See* **Doubt; Suspicion; Unbelief and unbelievers**

DISTURBANCE. *See* **Interruption; Noise;** etc.

DISUNITY. *See* **Division**

DIVERS AND DIVING
Botkin — *Treasury* p.552
Prochnow — *Success.* #995

DIVERSION. *See* **Amusements; Hobbies; Pleasure; Recreation;** types of diversion

DIVERSITY. *See* **Variety**

DIVIDENDS
Wilcox — *Heart* p.49-52

DIVINE LOVE. *See* **God, Love of**

DIVINITY. *See* **God**

DIVISION
Dirksen — *Quot.* #1973
Flint — *Graham* p.43
New Topical p.70-71
Phillips — *Choice* p.163
Sheban — *Wisdom* no p.
Woods — *Religious* p.246-247

DIVORCE
See also **Alimony; Marriage**
Braude — *Speaker's* #317-322
Copeland — *10,000* p.279-281
Droke — *Christian* p.132-136
Evans — *Faith* p.38, 47-48
Evans — *Thoughts I* p.92, 218
Evans — *Thoughts III (Open Road)* p.28-29
Evans — *Thoughts IV* p.44, 47-48
Flesch — *Unusual* p.64
Flint — *Graham* p.43-44, 91-92
Fuller — *Thesaurus* #906-911
Garland — *Subject* p.82
Harral — *Feature* p.138
How To Live p.363-366
Kahn — *Lessons* p.179-180, 183-184
Keys Happiness p.541-544
Liddle — *Thought I, II, III* p.166
Mandel — *Stories* p.74
New Topical p.71
Prochnow — *Public* #508, 1530
Prochnow — *Success.* #634
Schermerhorn — *1500* p.115-116
Speaker's Desk #613, 783, 1127
Woods — *Religious* p.247-248
, and war
Hunter — *Gems* p.114-115
, Evils of
Hunter — *Gems* p.27-28
, Rite of
Seaburg — *Great* p.413-416

DIXIE
Botkin — *Treasury* p.278, 287

DOCILITY. *See* **Humility; Meekness; Obedience; Resignation**

DOCTORS. *See* **Physicians**

DOCTRINE
See also **Belief; Creeds; Denominations**
Baillie — *Diary* #336
Dirksen — *Quot.* #384
Edwards — *Useful* p.139-140
Evans — *Unto* p.18, 52
Flesch — *Unusual* p.64-65
Harnsberger — *Mark* p.84
Henry — *5000* p.65
Lockridge — *World's* #3753
Prochnow — *Public* #2723
Prochnow — *Success.* #1686
Seldes — *Great* p.294-295
Wallis — *Words* p.29
Woods — *Religious* p.249-252
, and nations
Sheen — *Content.* p.163-186
, as symbolic truth
Phillips — *Choice* p.196
, Assimilation of
Baillie — *Diary* #62
, False
New Topical p.71
, in logic and science
Curtis — *Practical* p.23-26
, of the Gospel
New Topical p.71

DODGERS
Lockridge — *World's* #2775

DOG FENNEL
Botkin — *Treasury* p.269

DOGIES
Botkin — *Treasury* p.569, 853

DOGMA. *See* **Doctrine**

DOGMATISM
See also **Bigotry; Fanaticism**
Edwards — *Useful* p.140

Evans — *This* p.93-94
Kennedy — *Reader's* #274-277
Lockridge — *World's* #3743
Woods — *Religious* p.252-253

DOGS
Alexander's Treasure. p.14, 115, 161, 186-187, 293
Applegarth — *Heir.* p.19
Asimov — *Treasury* p.46, 48-49, 56, 425, 499, 609
Auden — *Certain* p.107-118
Botkin — *Anecdotes* p.61, 80, 90, 92, 255, 272
Botkin — *Treasury* p.495, 522, 533, 667, 670, 755
Cerf — *Laugh* p.83-88
Dirksen — *Quot.* #160, 1977-1978, 2047
Flesch — *Unusual* p.64
Fogg — *1000* #106, 448, 936, 943
Fuller — *Epigrams* p.92
Fun Fare p.56, 280-282
Goudge — *Comfort* p.76-77, 99-100, 357-358
Harnsberger — *Mark* p.85-90
Harral — *Feature* p.138-139
Henry — *5000* p.65-66
Kin — *Dictionary* p.62, 72
Lockridge — *World's* #4419
New Topical p.72
Prochnow — *Public* #180, 191, 335, 402, 490, 751, 784, 1513, 2565, 2745, 4373
Prochnow — *Speaker's* p.100-101
Prochnow — *Success.* #714, 816, 891, 1049, 1089, 1118, 1136, 1687
Schermerhorn — *1500* p.121-122
Speaker's Desk #24, 41, 70, 165, 227, 231, 588, 639, 645, 773, 868, 1014, 1115, 1126
Woods — *Wellsprings* p.36
, and husbands
Flint — *Graham* p.44
, and puppies
Hobe — *Tapestries* p.134, 194
Kin — *Dictionary* p.204
, barking of
Flesch — *Unusual* p.17
Kin — *Dictionary* p.21
, Shaggy
Cerf — *Laugh* p.39-42
, Talking
Botkin — *Anecdotes* p.255

DOGWOOD
Lindbergh — *Unicorn* p.38-39

DOING. *See* **Achievement; Deeds; Work**

"DO-IT-YOURSELF" TREND
Braude — *Source* #499
Braude — *Speaker's* #367-368
Harral — *Feature* p.139
Keys Happiness p.317-321
Prochnow — *Public* #46

DOLE. *See* **Charity**

DOLLARS
Flesch — *Unusual* p.66-67
Grizer — *Wit* p.126-127
Prochnow — *Public* #1222
Prochnow — *Success.* #1690
Woods — *Business.* p.64-65

DOMESTICITY. *See* **Family**

DON JUAN
Ideas p.117-118, 135

DON QUIXOTE
Ideas p.135-136

DONATIONS. *See* **Charity**

DONKEYS
Applegarth — *Heir.* p.20, 23
Botkin — *Anecdotes* p.90, 107
Goudge — *Comfort* p.72
Kin — *Dictionary* p.72
Prochnow — *Public* #369, 1107
Prochnow — *Success.* #946
Schermerhorn — *1500* p.124-125

"DO-NOTHINGISM"
Flesch — *Unusual* p.66
Knight's Illus. p.102-103
Safian — *More* p.37-40

DONS
Auden — *Certain* p.118-122

DOOLITTLE, JAMES
Peale — *Guideposts* p.133-136

DOOM. *See* **Destiny; Fate**

DOORS
Evans — *Thoughts II (Open Door)* *See* index, no p.
Fridy — *Meditat.* p.73
Hobe — *Tapestries* p.67, 86, 123
Hovey — *Treasury* p.152-154; *See also* index p.295
Irion — *Yes* p.57-60
Kin — *Dictionary* p.73
Lytle — *Leaves* p.115
Peale — *Courage* p.57
Peterson — *Art* p.297
Wallis — *Words* p.36, 38, 46, 75, 118, 197, 199
Woods — *Wellsprings* p.74-75

, *Closed*
Adams — *New* p.100
Baillie — *Diary* #51
, *Names on*
Irion — *Yes* p.80-82

DOPE. *See* **Drugs**

DOSTOEVSKI, FYODOR
Applegarth — *Heir.* p.240

"DOUBLE MEANING"
Auden — *Certain* p.122-123
Braude — *Stories* p.123-124
Speaker's Desk See index p.298

DOUBT
See also **Unbelief and unbelievers**
Applegarth — *Heir.* p.288
Baillie — *Diary* #168, 206, 341
Braude — *Source* #500-501
Curtis — *Practical* p.37
Edwards — *Useful* p.60, 140-142, 727
Evans — *Unto* p.16, 38, 41-43
Flesch — *Unusual* p.67
Flint — *Graham* p.44
Fogg — *1000* #811
Forbes — *Thoughts See* index p.547
Fuller — *Epigrams* p.92-93
Garland — *Subject* p.83
Grizer — *Wit* p.127-128
Halverson — *Perspective* p.30, 76
Harnsberger — *Mark* p.90-91
Henry — *5000* p.66
Hobe — *Tapestries* p.46, 53
Hovey — *Treasury* p.154; #3, 117-118, 803-809, 975, 1126, 1751
Hubbard — *Scrap* p.140
Keller — *Open* p.52
Kennedy — *Fresh* p.124-126
Kennedy — *Reader's* #278-279
Kin — *Dictionary* p.73
Liddle — *Thought I, II, III* p.24, 35, 49, 79, 118, 177, 179
Lytle — *Leaves* p.26, 71
Montapert — *Distilled* p.115-116
Price — *No* p.109-121
Prochnow — *Public* #341, 2984, 4059
Prochnow — *Speaker's* p.102
Prochnow — *Success.* #336, 393, 1505, 1691, 1693
Seldes — *Great* p.288, 295-296
Sheen — *Content.* p.97-99
Speaker's Desk #221, 382, 749, 829, 1067
Tanksley — *Friend* p.15
Voss — *Quotations* p.73-74
Wallis — *Treasure* p.26, 91, 94
Wallis — *Words* p.4, 55, 71-72
Woods — *Religious* p.253-254
Words — *Inspir.* p.48-51
, *Creative use of*
Kohn — *Adventures* p.68-70
, *Resolution of*
Baillie — *Diary* #113

DOUGHNUTS
Prochnow — *Public* #660

DOVES
Henry — *5000* p.66
New Joy p.36
New Topical p.72
Prochnow — *Public* #2502

DRAFT, MILITARY
See also **Conscientious objectors**
Botkin — *Anecdotes* p.14
Fogg — *1000* #228
Kennedy — *Reader's* #198
Franke — *Buckley* p.63-65
Woods — *Religious* p.187

DRAGONS
New Topical p.72

DRAGOONS
Prochnow — *Public* #2372

DRAMA
Fogg — *1000* #615
Fuller — *Thesaurus* #1386-1388
Harnsberger — *Mark* p.358-359
Harral — *Feature* p.139, 252
Henry — *5000* p.67
Hubbard — *Scrap* p.26
Lockridge — *World's* #926-927, 1126, 1831
Lytle — *Leaves* p.162
Nizer — *Thinking* p.100
Prochnow — *Public* #91
Prochnow — *Success.* #904, 927

DREAD. *See* **Anxiety; Fear**

DREAMS AND DREAMING
See also **Aspiration; Daydreaming; Imagination; Wishes**
Albert — *Stop* p.143-144
Alexander's Treasure. p.58, 177, 201, 228
Applegarth — *Heir.* p.94, 127, 136-137, 224
Auden — *Certain* p.123-129
Botkin — *Anecdotes* p.58
Botkin — *Treasury* p.452
Braude — *Source* #502-505
Braude — *Stories* p.124
Clark — *Windows* p.98
Curtis — *Daily* p.161-163
Curtis — *Practical* p.26
Dirksen — *Quot.* #750, 1981
Edwards — *Useful* p.142, 727

Evans — *This* p.85
Evans — *Unto* p.22
Flesch — *Unusual* p.68
Forbes — *Thoughts* p.100, 108, 327, 513; *See also* index p.547
Garland — *Subject* p.84
George — *Book* p.3, 63-65, 114, 141, 155, 170, 212, 391, 398
Grizer — *Wit* p.128-129
Hadfield — *Delights* p.184-199
Harnsberger — *Mark* p.91
Harral — *Feature* p.139-140
Henry — *5000* p.67
Hill — *Think* p.38-39
Hobe — *Tapestries* p.173
Hovey — *Treasury* #17, 422, 482, 610, 907, 958, 1162, 1289, 1823, 1828, 1836
Hubbard — *Scrap* p.131, 181
Johnson — *Bedside* p.22, 137-140, 144, 245
Kin — *Dictionary* p.73
Krishnamurti — *Urgency* p.102-107
Lockridge — *World's* #2363, 3357, 4234, 5738, 5781
Lytle — *Leaves* p.12, 36, 38-39, 177
Mandel — *Stories* p.75
Montapert — *Distilled* p.116
New Topical p.72-73
Peterson — *Art* p.221
Phillips — *Choice See* index p.425
Prochnow — *Public* #221, 1560, 2590, 2690
Prochnow — *Success.* #396, 1204, 1694
Sheen — *Content.* p.81-83, 85-86
Unlimited Power p.256-294
Wallis — *Treasure* p.3, 8, 14, 17-19, 144, 178, 234
Wallis — *Words* p.118, 121-122, 143
Woods — *Content.* p.27, 153, 160, 225, 242, 244
Woods — *Religious* p.254-255
Woods — *Wellsprings* p.77-82

, Actual
Keller — *Open* p.49

. American
Dirksen — *Quot.* #524

, as beginnings
Peterson — *Art* p.371

, Foretelling of
Peale — *Guideposts* p.91-92

, Science's debt to
Curtis — *Practical* p.84

"DRESSED AND UNDRESSED"
Safian — *Insults* p.46-50
Safian — *More* p.41-44

DRIFTING
Sheen — *Thoughts* p.18-20

DRIFTWOOD
Kohn — *Touch* p.198-199

DRILL
Fuller — *Thesaurus* #2461-2462
Prochnow — *Public* #973

DRINKING. *See* **Alcoholism**

DRINKS
See also **Toasts;** names of drinks
Braude — *Speaker's* #35-55
Harral — *Feature* p.87
Simpson — *Contemp.* p.456-459

DRIVERS AND DRIVING
See also **Automobiles; Chauffeurs; Safety; Traffic**
Applegarth — *Heir.* p.278
Braude — *Stories* p.379-392
Cerf — *Laugh* p.146-154
Ginott — *Between* p.179-183, 235
Grizer — *Wit* p.130-132
Guideposts — *Faith* p.94, 133
Harral — *Feature* p.140-141
Keys Happiness p.294-300
Kin — *Dictionary* p.74
Peterson — *Art* p.259
Prochnow — *Public* p.162, 167, 173, 193, 207, 361, 474, 625, 1058, 1124, 1309, 1473, 1528, 1781
Prochnow — *Success.* #392, 434, 455, 912, 962, 1006, 1053, 1138, 1171
Speaker's Desk See index p.303
Woods — *Content.* p.169

, and drinking
Kauffman — *For* p.85-86

, Backseat
Prochnow — *Public* #493

, Education of
Harral — *Feature* p.140
How To Live p.155-159

, License for
Grizer — *Wit* p.130

, Women
Prochnow — *Public* #338, 461, 577, 1076

"DROPOUTS"
Evans — *Faith* p.159
Evans — *Thoughts III (Open Road)* p.21, 119, 139, 146, 176, 178
Evans — *Thoughts IV* p.166
Ginott — *Between* p.221-222
Prochnow — *Success.* #1285

DROUGHT
Garland — *Subject* p.84
Kohn — *Thoughts* p.74-75

DROWNING
Kin — *Dictionary* p.74
Prochnow — *Public* #954

DROWSINESS. *See* **Sleep**

DRUDGERY
See also **Work**
Flesch — *Unusual* p.68
Forbes — *Thoughts* p.273, 277, 342
Kennedy — *Reader's* #280
Keys Happiness p.466-469
Wallis — *Treasure* p.237

DRUGS
See also **Medicine**
Albert — *Stop* p.9-10, 97-99
Baillie — *Diary* #172
Evans — *Thoughts III (Open Road)* p.76-77
Evans — *Unto* p.114
Franke — *Buckley* p.65-66
Gold — *Letters* p.103-106
Kauffman — *For* p.86-88
Kin — *Dictionary* p.74
Lair — *Baby* p.161
Menninger — *Blue.* p.168-172
Saturday — *Advent.* p.81-94
White — *Life* p.103-111
, and television
Kauffman — *For* p.87-88
, New
Wheelis — *Moralist* p.104, 151
, Teenage use of
Ginott — *Between* p.190-207
, Wonder
Harral — *Feature* p.328

DRUGSTORES AND DRUGGISTS
Braude — *Stories* p.125-126
Copeland — *10,000* p.421-423
Harral — *Feature* p.141
Manchee — *Secret* p.208-209

DRUMS
Prochnow — *Public* #79, 422

DRUNKENNESS. *See* **Alcoholism**

DRY CLEANING
Prochnow — *Public* #389

DUALISM
See also **Personality, Dual**
Du Noüy — *Human* p.108-109
White — *Job* p.160-161

DUBLIN, IRELAND
Lockridge — *World's* #5169

DUCKS
Botkin — *Anecdotes* p.97
Dirksen — *Quot.* #203
Goudge — *Comfort* p.364-366
Prochnow — *Public* #945, 2374

DUELS AND DUELING
Asimov — *Treasury* #302, 454
Edwards — *Useful* p.145
Fogg — *1000* #204, 826
Fuller — *Thesaurus* #801-803
George — *Book* p.101, 303, 373
Harnsberger — *Mark* p.93-94

DULLNESS. *See* **Bores and boredom; Monotony**

"DUMBBELLS"
Safian — *Insults* p.51-62
Safian — *More* p.45-57

DUPLICITY. *See* **Hypocrisy**

DURABILITY
Kin — *Dictionary* p.75
Mandel — *Stories* p.75-76

DUSK. *See* **Twilight**

DUST
See also **Dirt; Earth**
Botkin — *Treasury* p.296, 312, 319
Kin — *Dictionary* p.75

DUTCH
Botkin — *Treasury* p.740
Kin — *Dictionary* p.75
Schermerhorn — *1500* p.128-129

DUTCH PROVERBS
Dirksen — *Quot.* #2021, 2063, 2071

"DUTCH TREAT"
Prochnow — *Public* #1671

DUTY
See also **Obligations; Principles; Responsibility; Right; Trust**
Applegarth — *Heir.* p.84, 88, 209
Book Proverbs p.129
Curtis — *Practical* p.400
Day — *Meditations* p.32
Dirksen — *Quot.* #8, 481, 576-577, 711, 933, 1307-1308, 1670, 2355
Droke — *Christian* p.147-149
Edwards — *Useful* p.145-148, 727

Evans — *Faith* p.3, 12, 34, 40, 44, 76, 148, 166, 168, 202, 215
Evans — *Quote* p.41-51
Evans — *Thoughts I* p.92-93, 123-124
Evans — *Thoughts III (Open Road)* p.16, 39, 41, 56-57, 59, 108, 116-117, 145, 180
Evans — *Thoughts IV* p.103-104, 106, 116-117
Flesch — *Unusual* p.68-69
Fogg — *1000* #276, 278, 459, 494, 820, 1026
Forbes — *Thoughts* See index p.547
Fuller — *Epigrams* p.96
Garland — *Subject* p.85
Grizer — *Wit* p.132
Halverson — *Perspective* p.10, 31
Harnsberger — *Mark* p.94
Henry — *5000* p.68-69
Hubbard — *Scrap* p.19, 70, 88, 157
Johnson — *Bedside* p.83
Kennedy — *Reader's* #282-285
Keys Happiness p.505-506
Kin — *Dictionary* p.75
Liddle — *Thought I, II, III See* index p.196
Liddle — *Thought IV* p.11, 28, 32
Liddle — *Thought V* p.46
Lockridge — *World's* #1405, 2262, 2284, 3084, 3382, 3398, 5842
Lytle — *Leaves* p.53, 116, 169, 173
Mandel — *Stories* p.76
Mandelbaum — *Choose* p.105-130
Modern Eloquence (14) p.317-318
Montapert — *Distilled* p.117-118
Morris — *1000 See* index p.428
Peale — *Courage* p.27
Phillips — *Choice* p.246, 357
Prochnow — *Public* #2985-2990, 4063
Prochnow — *Speaker's* p.102
Prochnow — *Success.* #1343, 1696-1697
Seldes — *Great* p.298
Speaker's Desk p.41-42; #190, 681
Wallis — *Treasure* p.20, 31, 74
Wallis — *Words* p.17, 86
White — *Job* p.32-37
Woods — *Religious* p.255-258

DWELLINGS. *See* **Home; Houses**

DYING. *See* **Death**

DYING WORDS. *See* **Words, Dying**

DYNAMICS
Curtis — *Practical* p.245
Fox — *Make* p.14-16
Maltz — *Creative* p.38-50
Seldes — *Great* p.298
Woods — *Business.* p.65-66

DYNAMITE
Fox — *Make* p.51

E

EAGERNESS. *See* **Zeal**

EAGLES
Applegarth — *Heir.* p.37
Botkin — *Treasury* p.604
Dirksen — *Quot.* #1982
Kin — *Dictionary* p.76
New Topical p.73-74
Wallis — *Treasure* p.19
, American
Botkin — *Treasury* p.276-277, 284

EARLHAM COLLEGE
Botkin — *Anecdotes* p.272

EARLINESS
Dirksen — *Quot.* #1983
Harral — *Feature* p.141
Kin — *Dictionary* p.76
Liddle — *Thought I, II, III* p.11, 86
Prochnow — *Public* #4064
, in rising
See also **Awakening; Time**
Book Proverbs p.65
Dirksen — *Quot.* #870
Edwards — *Useful* p.148
Flesch — *Unusual* p.70
Harnsberger — *Mark* p.95
Henry — *5000* p.69
Montapert — *Distilled* p.118-119
New Topical p.74

EARNESTNESS
See also **Enthusiasm; Sincerity**
Dirksen — *Quot.* #871
Edwards — *Useful* p.148-149
Garland — *Subject* p.86
Grizer — *Wit* p.132-133
Henry — *5000* p.69
Montapert — *Distilled* p.119

Prochnow — *Public* #2991-2992
Speaker's Desk p.42-43

EARNINGS. *See* **Wages**

EARP, WYATT
Botkin — *Treasury* p.68

EARS
Flesch — *Unusual* p.70
Kin — *Dictionary* p.76
New Topical p.74
Prochnow — *Public* #590, 615, 1733, 2660, 2704

EARTH
See also **Agriculture; Country life; Farmers and farming; Nature; World**
Bartlett — *Discovery* p.16-17
Dirksen — *Quot.* #386, 593
Du Noüy — *Human* p.32n, 34, 55-57
Edwards — *Useful* p.149
Esteve — *Experience* p.145-149
Evans — *This* p.46-47, 184-185
Evans — *Thoughts IV* p.184-186, 198-199
Flesch — *Unusual* p.70
Garland — *Subject* p.86
Harral — *Feature* p.202
Henry — *5000* p.146
Hobe — *Tapestries* p.24
Hooker — *Index* p.171-178
Hubbard — *Scrap* p.89, 199
Ideas p.46-47
Keys Happiness p.527
Kin — *Dictionary* p.76
Lockridge — *World's See* index p.574; #2999
New Joy p.243
New Topical p.74-75
Nichols — *New* p.149-150
Peterson — *Art* p.209
Prochnow — *Public* #1325, 2473, 2561, 2665
Prochnow — *Speaker's* p.181
Seldes — *Great* p.298-299, 558-561
Sheban — *Wisdom* no p.
Taylor — *With* p.44-45
Woods — *Business.* p.130-131

EARTHQUAKES
Harnsberger — *Mark* p.95-96
New Topical p.75
, Alaskan
Guideposts — *Faith* p.301-305
Unlimited Power p.15-19
, Californian
Day — *Meditations* p.6-7

EARTHWORMS. *See* **Worms**

EASE
See also **Laziness; Leisure**
Flesch — *Unusual* p.70-71, 154
Flint — *Graham* p.45
Forbes — *Thoughts* p.4, 290, 378-379, 415, 417, 471
Kin — *Dictionary* p.76-77
Krishnamurti — *Think* p.194-201
Montapert — *Distilled* p.119-120
Peterson — *New* p.18-19
Prochnow — *Public* #2175, 2671
Prochnow — *Success.* #654, 1241, 1700
Reader's — *Getting* p.219-221
Woods — *Religious* p.258

EAST
Kin — *Dictionary* p.77
Sheban — *Wisdom* no p.
Woods — *Religious* p.258

EASTER
Immortality; Jesus Christ, Resurrection of
Auden — *Certain* p.131-134
Braude — *Source* #510
Curtis — *New* p.127-137
Dirksen — *Quot.* #106
Droke — *Christian* p.149-156
Emmons — *Mature* p.155
Evans — *Faith* p.193-206
Evans — *Thoughts I* p.49-51
Evans — *Thoughts II (Open Door)* p.108-110
Evans — *Unto* p.11-12
Flint — *Graham* p.44-45
Fridy — *Meditat.* p.97, 102
Garland — *Subject* p.86-87
Goudge — *Comfort* p.195-196
Harral — *Feature* p.142
Henry — *5000* p. 69-70
Hobe — *Tapestries* p.151-153
Hovey — *Treasury* p.154-158; #347, 484, 721, 797, 810-825; *See also* index p.303
Kohn — *Best* p.128-140
Liddle — *Thought I, II, III* p.10, 77, 161
Liddle — *Thought V* p.28
More Words p.54-55
Prochnow — *Success.* #257, 1402
Suter — *Prayers* #416-421
Wallis — *Words* p.63-68, 98-99
Webb — *Edge* p.137, 153
Woods — *Religious* p.258-259
, Prayer for
Kohn — *Best* p.130-131

EATING
See also **Diet; Dinners;** etc.
Auden — *Certain* p.134-142
Bradshaw — *Home* p.39-47
Edwards — *Useful* p.149

Flesch — *Unusual* p.35, 71
Fuller — *Epigrams* p.97-99
Fuller — *Thesaurus* #6-23
Fun Fare p.65, 156, 238-239, 307
Grizer — *Wit* p.133
Harral — *Feature* p.142
Henry — *5000* p.70-71
Keys Happiness p.321
Kin — *Dictionary* p.77-78
Mandel — *Stories* p.77
Montapert — *Distilled* p.120
Prochnow — *Public* See index p.493
Prochnow — *Success.* #1147, 1179, 1701-1702
Speaker's Desk #480, 790, 794, 881, 949, 1015

EAVESDROPPING. *See* **Listeners and listening**

ECCENTRICITY
See also **Individuals and individuality**
Dirksen — *Quot.* #171
Edwards — *Useful* p.150
Fuller — *Thesaurus* #196-209
George — *Book* p.47, 148, 175, 251, 356, 384, 394, 423
Keys Happiness p.218-222
Kronenberger — *Animal* p.60-65
Lockridge — *World's* #1512, 4591, 5116
Seldes — *Great* p.299-300

ECCLESIASTICS. *See* **Clergymen**

ECHOES
Auden — *Certain* p.143
Edwards — *Useful* p.150
Hadfield — *Delights* p.51
Harnsberger — *Mack* p.96
Lockridge — *World's* #4358
Mandel — *Stories* p.77
Peale — *Guideposts* p.209-212

ECLECTICISM
Lockridge — *World's* #5595

ECLIPSES
Auden — *Certain* p.144-146

ECOLOGY
See also **Earth; Environment;** etc.
Dirksen — *Quot.* #1163

ECONOMIC FREEDOM
Dirksen — *Quot.* #2365
Franke — *Buckley* p.67-68

ECONOMICS
Dirksen — *Quot.* See index p.262
Flesch — *Unusual* p.71
Forbes — *Thoughts* p.122-123, 202, 366, 369, 391, 488, 501, 504, 507
Franke — *Buckley* p.69
Grizer — *Wit* p.133-134
Hooker — *Index* p.65-76
Hovey — *Treasury* p.158; #826-827
Kennedy — *Reader's* #286
Prochnow — *Public* #291, 351, 1186
Prochnow — *Speaker's* p.103
Prochnow — *Success.* #255, 259
Seldes — *Great* p.300-303
Sheen — *Content.* p.167-169
Woods — *Wellsprings* p.28

, and Christianity
Woods — *Religious* p.259
, Control of
Woods — *Religious* p.259
, Equality of
Dirksen — *Quot.* #376
, Fears of
Liebman — *Peace* p.98-102

ECONOMISTS
Dirksen — *Quot.* #58, 143, 271, 1642
Edwards — *Useful* p.727
Liddle — *Thought I, II, III* p.124
Prochnow — *Public* #1673-1676
Prochnow — *Speaker's* p.103

ECONOMY
See also **Thrift**
Book Proverbs p.12
Dirksen — *Quot.* #873, 1671
Edwards — *Useful* p.150-151, 727
Flesch — *Unusual* p.71
Forbes — *Thoughts* p.56, 200, 245, 295, 310, 362, 396, 437, 439-440, 448, 454, 460
Fuller — *Epigrams* p.99-100
Fuller — *Thesaurus* #211-231
George — *Book* p.104, 367-368, 381, 397
Grizer — *Wit* p.134-135
Henry — *5000* p.71
Kin — *Dictionary* p.78
Lindeman — *Emerson* p.201
Lockridge — *World's* #3017, 4735
Montapert — *Distilled* p.120-121
Prochnow — *Public* #1003, 1328, 2993-2997, 4065-4066
Prochnow — *Success.* #168, 611
Speaker's Desk p.43-46; *See also* index p.299
Woods — *Business.* p.38, 66, 147-149

ECSTASY
See also **Happiness; Joy**
Adams — *New* p.381
Applegarth — *Heir.* p.29
Emmons — *Mature* p.43
Esteve — *Experience* p.71-75
Harnsberger — *Mark* p.96
Henry — *5000* p.21
Kin — *Dictionary* p.28
Woods — *Religious* p.84, 259-260

ECUMENISM
See also **Unity**
Asimov — *Treasury* #466
Flint — *Graham* p.45
Strait — *Speaker's* p.57
Woods — *Religious* p.260-262

EDEN, GARDEN OF. *See* **Garden of Eden**

EDGE
Kin — *Dictionary* p.78

EDISON, THOMAS
Kohn — *Touch* p.142
Nichols — *Third* p.187-188
Peterson — *Art* p.323

EDITORIALS
Grizer — *Wit* p.135

EDITORS
Copeland — *10,000* p.53-56
New Joy p.187
Schermerhorn — *1500* p.131-133
Seldes — *Great* p.303-304

EDOMITES, THE
New Topical p.76

EDUCATION
See also **Books and reading; Improvement; Knowledge; Learning; Schools; Self-improvement; Study; Teachers; Universities and colleges**
Adams — *New* p.27
Albert — *Stop* p.49
Alexander's Treasure. p.226
Applegarth — *Heir.* p.40, 227-228
Asimov — *Treasury* #455-456
Book Proverbs p.124
Braude — *Source* #511-528
Braude — *Speaker's* #401-406
Braude — *Stories* p.126-133
Curtis — *Daily* p.119-126
Detherage — *Sunrise* p.41-44, 178
Dirksen — *Quot. See* index p.262
Droke — *Christian* p.156-171
Du Noüy — *Human* p.xii, 207-222, 229-231, 244, 267-268, 270-271
Edwards — *Useful* p.151-156, 727
Evans — *Faith* p.76, 133, 157-176, 181
Evans — *Quote* p.67-79
Evans — *This* p.114-115
Evans — *Thoughts III (Open Road)* p.59-60, 181
Evans — *Thoughts IV* p.61-70, 109
Evans — *Unto* p.89, 106-107
Flesch — *Unusual* p.71-73, 293
Flint — *Graham* p.45-46
Fogg — *1000* #39, 44, 326, 354, 356, 420, 569, 700
Forbes — *Thoughts See* index p.17, 151, 170, 200, 311, 496, 547
Franke — *Buckley* p.69-72
Fuller — *Epigrams* p.339
Gold — *Letters* p.57-66
Grizer — *Wit* p.135-141
Harnsberger — *Mark* p.97-98, 477-478
Harral — *Feature* p.142-145
Henry — *5000* p.71-72
Hobe — *Tapestries* p.42, 178
Hoffer — *Reflect.* p.22
Hooker — *Index* p.110-124
Hovey — *Treasury* p.158-164; *See also* index p.295
Hubbard — *Scrap* p.43, 68, 73, 128, 211, 214
Humes — *Instant* #1219-1221
Johnson — *Bedside* p.77, 110
Keller — *You* p.60-82
Kennedy — *Reader's* #287-294
Keys Happiness p.25-30
Kin — *Dictionary* p.78
Liddle — *Thought I, II, III* p.5, 11, 89, 116, 144, 146-147, 149, 174
Liddle — *Thought IV* p.4, 6-7, 11, 22
Liddle — *Thought V* p.19, 29, 31
Lindeman — *Emerson* p.172-173
Lockridge — *World's See* index p.574; #5803
Lytle — *Leaves* p.5, 58
Mandel — *Stories* p.77-79, 255
Modern Eloquence (14) p.319-320
Montapert — *Distilled* p.121-124
Myers — *Thunder* p.32
New Joy p.16, 50
New Topical p.75
Nizer — *Thinking* p.79, 168, 203
Phillips — *Choice* p.111, 272-273
Prochnow — *Public See* index p.494
Prochnow — *Speaker's* p.104-110
Prochnow — *Success. See* index p.490
Sagendorph — *Old* p.156-166

Seldes — *Great* p.304-309
Simpson — *Contemp.* p.157-176
Simpson —*'54* p.31, 144, 287
Speaker's Desk p.46-51; *See* index p.299
Strait — *Speaker's* p.58-59
Voss — *Quotations* p.74-77
Wallis — *Treasure* p.35-36, 45, 85-90, 132-133, 231
Wallis — *Words* p.141-146, 233
Woods — *Business.* p.66
Woods — *Religious* p.262-264
Woods — *Wellsprings* p.34-35
Words — *Inspir.* p.146-147

, Aim of
Hubbard — *Scrap* p.145
Krishnamurti — *Think* p.7-15

, and democracy
Hubbard — *Scrap* p.21

, and ignorance
Hubbard — *Scrap* p.61

, and religion
Woods — *Religious* p.270-274

, Classical
Auden — *Certain* p.146-147

, Dangers of
Hubbard — *Scrap* p.55

, Definitions of
Flesch — *Unusual* p.72

, Home
Reader's — *Getting* p.150-153
White — *Life* p.49-57

, in thought formation
Curtis — *Practical* p.63-64

, "Instant answers to"
Kauffman — *For* p.88-89

, Liberal
Dirksen — *Quot.* #314, 388
Hubbard — *Scrap* p.90

, Meaning of
Hubbard — *Scrap* p.17

, Parents' rights in
Woods — *Religious* p.265-266

, Parochial
Woods — *Religious* p.266-267

, Progressive
Woods — *Religious* p.267

, Secularized
Woods — *Religious* p.268-269

, State
Woods — *Religious* p.269-270

, True
Adams — *New* p.94

, Value of
Nichols — *Third* p.243-244

EELS
Kin — *Dictionary* p.78

EFFECT. *See* **Cause (and effect)**

EFFECTIVENESS. *See* **Efficiency**

EFFICIENCY
See also **Ability; Diligence; Method; Standardization**
Braude — *Source* #1705
Braude — *Stories* p.133-134
Edwards — *Useful* p.727
Evans — *Thoughts IV* p.17, 65, 68-69, 86, 199
Evans — *Unto* p.3, 58
Flesch — *Unusual* p.73
Forbes — *Thoughts* p.111, 200, 387, 413, 449, 494, 518
Fuller — *Thesaurus* #2266-2270
Grizer — *Wit* p.141
Halverson — *Perspective* p.104
Henry — *5000* p.72
Kin — *Dictionary* p.78-79, 254
Lytle — *Leaves* p.169
Modern Eloquence (14) p.321-322
Montapert — *Distilled* p.124
Nizer — *Thinking* p.106
Peale — *Guide* p.147-165
Peterson — *Twenty* p.32-33
Phillips — *Choice* p.322
Prochnow — *Public* #136
Prochnow — *Speaker's* p.111
Prochnow — *Success.* #862, 1709
Schermerhorn — *1500* p.134
Speaker's Desk #240, 792, 1114
Wallis — *Treasure* p.4
Welk — *Guide.* p.90-92
Wheelis — *Moralist* p.10, 71-72
Woods — *Business.* p.67

"EFFICIENCY EXPERTS"
Copeland — *10,000* p.421
Prochnow — *Public* #316, 1022
Woods — *Business.* p.67

EFFORT
See also **Action; Diligence; Energy; Enterprise; Work**
Albert — *Stop* p.205
Braude — *Source* #529-532
Braude — *Speaker's* #407-410
Braude — *Stories* p.134
Du Noüy — *Human* p.178-179, 243-245
Edwards — *Useful* p.156
Evans — *Unto* p.32, 84
Forbes — *Thoughts* p.5, 130, 193, 198, 379, 403, 474
Garland — *Subject* p.88
Grizer — *Wit* p.141-142
Hovey — *Treasury* #9, 16, 20, 36, 97-99, 879-882; p.164-165
Kin — *Dictionary* p.79, 267-268
Kohn — *Thoughts* p.49-51

Liddle — *Thought V* p.14, 40
Lockridge — *World's* #1582
Mandel — *Stories* p.79-81
Montapert — *Distilled* p.125
New Joy p.93
Peterson — *Art* p.306
Prochnow — *Public* #177
Prochnow — *Success.* #578
Wallis — *Treasure* p.81, 83

EGGS
Botkin — *Anecdotes* p.56
Flesch — *Unusual* p.73
Fuller — *Epigrams* p.100
Harnsberger — *Mark* p.98
Kin — *Dictionary* p.79
Prochnow — *Public* #280, 285, 343, 649, 812, 941, 2065, 2090, 2195
Prochnow — *Success.* #1710
, Hatching of
Clark — *Windows* p.94-95

EGO
See also **Individuals and individuality; Self**
Dirksen — *Quot.* p.880
Esteve — *Experience* p.12-15, 41-51
Flesch — *Unusual* p.73
Forbes — *Thoughts* p.28, 392
Garland — *Subject* p.88-89
Phillips — *Choice See* index p.425
Prochnow — *Public* #1093, 1183
Sheen — *Lift* p.1-103
Woods — *Religious* p.274
, and moral law
Sheen — *Way* p.28-30
, Indestructible
Taylor — *With* p.136-138

EGOISM AND EGOTISTS
See also **Boasting; Conceit; Self-praise**
Braude — *Stories* p.134-135
Curtis — *Practical* p.106, 503
Dirksen — *Quot.* #281, 874, 1065, 1988-1989
Edwards — *Useful* p.156
Flesch — *Unusual* p.73-74
Forbes — *Thoughts* p.56, 130, 209, 492
Grizer — *Wit* p.143
Henry — *5000* p.72
Johnson — *Bedside* p.12, 19, 77, 162, 197
Kin — *Dictionary* p.79
Liddle — *Thought I, II, III* p.186
Lockridge — *World's* #2277, 2392, 5482
Mandel — *Stories* p.81
Phillips — *Choice See* index p.425
Prochnow — *Public* #1678-1679, 4069-4070
Prochnow — *Success.* #716, 1324, 1407, 1711
Safian — *More* p.62-66
Seldes — *Great* p.309-310
Sheen — *Thoughts* p.27-29
Sheen — *Way* p.20-22
Taylor — *With* p.18-22
Woods — *Religious* p.274

"EGO-TWISTS"
Fun Fare p.158-159

EGYPT AND EGYPTIANS
Asimov — *Treasury* #338
Botkin — *Anecdotes* p.132
Hovey — *Treasury* #902, 1075, 1150, 1752, 1849
New Topical p.76-78
Simpson — *Contemp.* p.126-127
, Scientific beginnings of
Curtis — *Practical* p.220-221
, Tablets of
Peterson — *Art* p.29

EIGHTY (years)
Flesch — *Unusual* p.74

EINSTEIN THEORY
Du Noüy — *Road* p.34, 70, 121, 167-169, 181, 193

ELATION. *See* **Joy**

"ELDORADO"
New Joy p.58

ELECTIONS
See also **Government; Politics and politicians; Votes and voting**
Dirksen — *Quot.* #22, 24-25, 51, 74, 110, 304, 582, 687, 1639, 1674-1676, 1826-1827
Flesch — *Unusual* p.29
Fuller — *Thesaurus* #1911-1921
Grizer — *Wit* p.71
Harral — *Feature* p.106, 145
Liddle — *Thought I, II, III* p.5, 25, 48, 92
Mandel — *Stories* p.81
New Topical p.78
Prochnow — *Public* #28, 35, 271, 1382, 1680
Prochnow — *Success.* #204, 571, 875, 1020
Schermerhorn — *1500* p.63-65
Seldes — *Great* p.310
Woods — *Religious* p.274-275

ELECTRICIANS
Manchee — *Secret* p.209-210
Prochnow — *Public* #1681

ELECTRICITY
Asimov — *Treasury* #255
Harral — *Feature* p.145-146
Hubbard — *Scrap* p.57
Prochnow — *Public* #850
Prochnow — *Speaker's* p.111
Prochnow — *Success.* #1054, 1284
Schermerhorn — *1500* p.134-135
Seldes — *Great* p.310

ELECTROMAGNETISM
Du Noüy — *Road* p.244

ELECTRONS
Du Noüy — *Human* p.11, 18-22, 46, 135-136, 188
Du Noüy — *Road* *See* index p.244

ELEGANCE
See also **Beauty**
Edwards — *Useful* p.156-157

ELEGIES
Auden — *Certain* p.147-149
Lytle — *Leaves* p.189

ELEMENTS
Du Noüy — *Road* p.48, 50-52, 83, 86, 103
Ideas p.148-150

ELEPHANTS
Applegarth — *Heir.* p.20
Asimov — *Treasury* p.57-60, 390, 406, 558
Botkin — *Anecdotes* p.270
Kin — *Dictionary* p.79
Prochnow — *Public* #59, 381, 430, 468, 701, 920, 1218, 1453, 1535, 1682
Prochnow — *Success.* #879, 1028, 1170
Schermerhorn — *1500* p.136
, and men
Adams — *New* p.195

ELEVATORS
Fun Fare p.197-198
Harnsberger — *Mark* p.98
Harral — *Feature* p.146
Prochnow — *Public* #1004
Prochnow — *Speaker's* p.111

"ELIXIR OF LIFE"
See also **Philosopher's stone**
Forbes — *Thoughts* p.66, 101, 484
Ideas p.139-140

ELOQUENCE
See also **Orators and oratory**
Botkin — *Treasury* p.272, 321, 435
Dirksen — *Quot.* #185, 871, 1990-1992, 2106
Edwards — *Useful* p.157-158
Evans — *Unto* p.8, 78
Flesch — *Unusual* p.74
Forbes — *Thoughts* p.133, 143, 465, 477
Garland — *Subject* p.90
Grizer — *Wit* p.143
Henry — *5000* p.72-73
Hubbard — *Scrap* p.87
Johnson — *Bedside* p.25
Kin — *Dictionary* p.79
Lindeman — *Emerson* p.203
Lockridge — *World's* #261-262, 1721, 2483, 2882, 3063
Lytle — *Leaves* p.26, 158, 161
Modern Eloquence (14) p.323-325
Montapert — *Distilled* p.125-126
Nizer — *Thinking* p.26, 29, 129
Prochnow — *Public* #3007-3008, 4071-4072
Prochnow — *Success.* #1712-1714
Speaker's Desk p.51-54
Woods — *Religious* p.275

ELUSIVENESS
Prochnow — *Public* #2231

ELYSIUM. *See* **Paradise**

EMANCIPATION. *See* **Freedom**

EMBALMING
New Topical p.78

EMBARRASSMENT
See also **Bashfulness**
Braude — *Speaker's* #411-412
Braude — *Stories* p.135
Evans — *Thoughts III (Open Road)* p.87, 97
Evans — *Thoughts IV* p.126
Flesch — *Unusual* p.74
Fun Fare p.27-29, 65, 212, 240, 303
Harnsberger — *Mark* p.98-99
Lockridge — *World's* #4544
Manchee — *Secret* p.23-25
Prochnow — *Public* #385
Prochnow — *Success.* #364
Speaker's Desk See index p.299

"EMBER DAYS"
More Words p.55-56

EMBEZZLEMENT
Prochnow — *Speaker's* p.111

EMERGENCE THEORY
Du Noüy — *Road* p.151-152, 155

EMERGENCY
Manchee — *Secret* p.26-30
Prochnow — *Public* #800
Prochnow — *Success.* #1365
, *Preparation for*
Kohn — *Through* p.125-127

EMERSON, RALPH WALDO
Flesch — *Unusual* p.74
Lindeman — *Emerson* p.151-215
Peterson — *Art* p.231

EMIGRATION
See also **Immigrants and emigrants**
Lockridge — *World's* #4270
Seldes — *Great* p.312

EMINENCE. *See* **Distinction; Fame; Greatness; Heroes and heroism**

EMISSION THEORY
Du Noüy — *Road* p.31-32

EMOTION
See also **Excitement; Sensibility;** types of emotion, e.g. **Anger**
Adams — *New* p.126
Albert — *Stop* p.82-83, 87, 105, 107, 152-154, 156-160, 164-168, 198
Alexander's Treasure. p.147-148
Edwards — *Useful* p.158, 196-197, 727
Flesch — *Unusual* p.74, 89
Forbes — *Thoughts* p.103, 119, 147, 154, 200, 232, 236, 240, 242, 273, 347, 405, 448, 452, 492
Fox — *Make* p.26
Garland — *Subject* p.90-91
Grizer — *Wit* p.143-144
Halverson — *Perspective* p.4
Harnsberger — *Mark* p.122
Holmes — *Design* p.73-74, 107, 213-214
Hovey — *Treasury* p.165, 182-185; #883-886, 1032-1039, 1646
Huxley — *You See* index p.284; *See* appendix p.279-282
Johnson — *Bedside* p.45, 90, 278
Jones — *If* p.133-139
Kennedy — *Reader's* #295
Kin — *Dictionary* p.93
Kohn — *Touch* p.16-17
Krishnamurti — *Think* p.82
Liddle — *Thought I, II, III* p.15, 162
Liebman — *Peace* p.195-199
Lockridge — *World's* #1491, 1554, 1832, 1849, 2532, 2925
Lytle — *Leaves* p.170
Mandelbaum — *Choose* p.16
Montapert — *Distilled* p.126, 153-154
Nizer — *Thinking* p.129
Peterson — *Art* p.406
Phillips — *Choice* p.42, 73, 233, 252
Prochnow — *Public* #2037, 4338
Prochnow — *Success.* #1464, 1486
Rau — *Act* p.44-54
Sheen — *Thoughts* p.64-66
Woods — *Religious* p.276, 332
, *and faith*
Baillie — *Diary* #340
, *Cycles of*
Reader's — *Getting* p.117-121
, *Hidden*
Menninger — *Blue.* p.62-67
, *in child training*
Holman — *Psych.* p.4-7
, *Negative*
Hill — *Think* p.232
Maltz — *Creative* p.81-95, 133-134
, *Parents' response to*
Ginott — *Between* p.65-66
, *Positive*
Hill — *Think* p.230-232
, *Scars of*
Maltz — *Creative* p.137-150

"EMOTIONS ANONYMOUS"
Lair — *Baby* p.13-14, 23

EMPATHY
See also **Sensitivity; Understanding**
Mandel — *Stories* p.82-83
Peterson — *Art* p.353
Peterson — *New* p.26-27
Wheelis — *Moralist* p.11, 128-132
, *for teenagers*
Ginott — *Between* p.73

EMPIRE
See also **Nations; States;** etc.
Dirksen — *Quot.* #583, 622, 2368
Edwards — *Useful* p.158
Flesch — *Unusual* p.74
Kennedy — *Reader's* #296
Saturday — *Advent.* p.121-134

EMPIRE STATE BUILDING
Botkin — *Anecdotes* p.263

EMPIRICISM
Taylor — *With* p.12-16

EMPLOYEES
See also **Employment; Labor; Work;** etc.
Braude — *Source* #533-539
Edwards — *Useful* p.727-728
Evans — *Thoughts II (Open Door)* p.85-88
Forbes — *Thoughts* p.51, 125, 176, 236, 285, 306, 408, 411, 469
Harral — *Feature* p.146
Keys Happiness p.153-157
Prochnow — *Public* #48, 62, 1915
Prochnow — *Speakers'* p.112
Woods — *Religious* p.276-277

EMPLOYERS
See also **Business; Employment; Executives; Industry; Leaders and leadership; Personnel**
Asimov — *Treasure* #3
Braude — *Speaker's* #413-460
Braude — *Stories* p.135-136
Evans — *Thoughts II (Open Door)* p.85-88
Forbes — *Thoughts* p.159, 176, 285, 408, 411, 561
Grizer — *Wit* p.144-145
Prochnow — *Speaker's* p.112
Wallis — *Words* p.229
Woods — *Business.* p.67-69

EMPLOYMENT
See also **Business; Employees; Employers; Industry; Labor; Work;** etc.
Baillie — *Diary* #13
Braude — *Source* #540-542
Braude — *Speaker's* #461-465
Dirksen — *Quot.* #1677, 2346
Edwards — *Useful* p.158-159
Flesch — *Unusual* p.74
Forbes — *Thoughts* p.49, 336, 361, 413, 458, 485
Fuller — *Thesaurus* p.392-403
Harral — *Feature* p.146-148
Montapert — *Distilled* p.126-127
Speaker's Desk #276, 314, 322, 383, 482, 551
Woods — *Business.* p.69-70
Woods — *Religious* p.277

EMPTINESS
See also **Bores and boredom; Loneliness**
Edwards — *Useful* p.159
Evans — *Thoughts III (Open Road)* p.181
Prochnow — *Public* #2228
Kin — *Dictionary* p.80
Lytle — *Leaves* p.132
Maltz — *Creative* p.90-91
Myers — *Thunder* p.28-29
Prochnow — *Speaker's* p.113

EMULATION. *See* **Imitation; Rivalry**

ENCHANTMENT
See also **Wonder**
Alexander's Treasure. p.124-125
Auden — *Certain* p.149-150
Kin — *Dictionary* p.80
Wallis — *Words* p.138

ENCLOSURES
Auden — *Certain* p.150-155

ENCORES
Prochnow — *Speaker's* p.113
Prochnow — *Success.* #897

"ENCOUNTERS, BRIEF"
Fun Fare p.4-5, 243

ENCOURAGEMENT
See also **Comfort; Guidance; Hope; Praise; Sympathy**
Braude — *Stories* p.136
Edwards — *Useful* p.159
Evans — *Faith* p.14-16, 21, 39-40, 126, 221
Evans — *Thoughts III (Open Road)* p.36
Evans — *Thoughts IV* p.206
Forbes — *Thoughts* p.277, 456
Garland — *Subject* p.91
Grizer — *Wit* p.145-146
Hovey — *Treasury* p.165; #168, 887-888
Kin — *Dictionary* p.80
Knight's Illus. p.100-101
Knight's Treas. p.108-110
Kopplin — *Something* p.23-56
Montapert — *Distilled* p.127
Prochnow — *Speaker's* p.113
Prochnow — *Success.* #294
Sheen — *Thoughts* p.148-149
Speaker's Desk #64, 257, 432, 528, 590, 775, 842
Woods — *Religious* p.277, 305

ENCYCLICALS
Day — *Meditations* p.27-28
Woods — *Religious* p.277

ENCYCLOPEDIAS
Prochnow — *Public* #1038

ENDEAVOR
See also **Effort**
Dirksen — *Quot.* #576
Evans — *Unto* p.95
Hubbard — *Scrap* p.142
Nichols — *Third* p.231-232
Wallis — *Words* p.123

ENDOCRINE GLANDS
Du Noüy — *Humor* p.108, 113, 155, 177-178

ENDS AND ENDINGS
See also **Death; Goals;** etc.
Dirksen — *Quot.* #1993
Edwards — *Useful* p.159
Evans — *This* p.173-174
Evans — *Thoughts I* p.165-166
Evans — *Thoughts II (Open Door)* p.149, 152
Evans — *Thoughts IV* p.86
Evans — *Unto* p.55
Flesch — *Unusual* p.90, 200
Hovey — *Treasury* p.183-184; #1042-1045
Kin — *Dictionary* p.143
Prochnow — *Public* #1424, 1549, 2447, 2646, 2659
Speaker's Desk See index p.301; #8, 28, 57, 80, 296, 329, 359, 447, 879, 965
Woods — *Religious* p.277
, Happy
Cerf — *Laugh* p.213-216
, Means of
Kin — *Dictionary* p.80
Seldes — *Great* p.312-314
, of the world
Ideas p.233-234
Woods — *Religious* p.277-278
, Surprise
Fun Fare p.255

ENDURANCE
See also **Courage; Strength**
Book Proverbs p.68, 113
Curtis — *Practical* p.116-117
Dirksen — *Quot.* #254
Edwards — *Useful* p.159-160, 205
Evans — *Thoughts I* p.69, 91-92, 109
Evans — *Thoughts III (Open Road)* p.35-41, 51, 111, 150, 179, 200
Evans — *Thoughts IV* p.70, 86, 88
Flesch — *Unusual* p.75, 231
Fogg — *1000 See* index p.886
Forbes — *Thoughts* p.33, 153, 377-378, 486, 520
Fuller — *Thesaurus* #216
Garland — *Subject* p.91-92
Henry — *5000* p.73
Kin — *Dictionary* p.80
Kohn — *Pathways* p.135-136, 143-145
Liddle — *Thought I, II, III* p.7, 151
Lockridge — *World's* #20, 411, 2403, 3565, 3695
Lytle — *Leaves* p.52, 56, 138
Montapert — *Distilled* p.127-128, 160
New Joy p.28, 219
Nichols — *Third* p.201-202, 222
Peterson — *Art* p.311
Porter — *Halo* p.69-77
Prochnow — *Success.* #2204
Watson — *Light* p.79-84
Woods — *Content.* p.45, 105
Woods — *Religious* p.339
Words — *Inspir.* p.209-210

ENEMIES
See also **Conflict; Hatred; Opposition; Rivalry**
Book Proverbs p.80
Braude — *Source* #543-552
Braude — *Speaker's* #56-60
Dirksen — *Quot.* #299, 875-877, 1309-1310, 1356, 1678, 1994, 2328
Droke — *Christian* p.171
Edwards — *Useful* p.160-161
Evans — *This* p.65
Flesch — *Unusual* p.75-77
Fogg — *1000* #148, 578, 913
Forbes — *Thoughts* p.38, 140, 199, 223, 244, 340, 344, 373, 411, 413, 467, 497, 510
Fox — *Make* p.67, 93-94
Fuller — *Epigrams* p.100-101
Garland — *Subject* p.7, 92
Grizer — *Wit* p.146
Harnsberger — *Mark* p.99
Henry — *5000* p.73
Hovey — *Treasury* p.111-113; #52, 468, 889-890, 996, 1009, 1032, 1124, 1263, 1455, 1788
How To Live p.413-416
Kennedy — *Reader's* #297
Keys Happiness p.461
Kin — *Dictionary* p.80-81, 97
Knight's Illus. p.104-106
Knight's Treas. p.111-113
Liddle — *Thought I, II, III* p.10, 13, 17, 21, 28, 96, 163, 169, 193
Lockridge — *World's* #883, 1013, 2280, 3883, 3924, 4386
Lytle — *Leaves* p.127-128
Manchee — *Secret* p.124-136
Mandelbaum — *Choose* p.78-80
Montapert — *Distilled* p.128
New Topical p.79
Prochnow — *Public* #903, 2364, 2547, 2611, 3009-3014, 4073-4075
Prochnow — *Success.* #944, 1424, 1715
Seldes — *Great* p.314-315
Unlimited Power p.146
Woods — *Content.* p.182
Woods — *Religious* p.278
Words — *Inspir.* p.177-178

ENERGY
See also **Effort; Strength;** types of energy
Albert — *Stop See* index p.210

Bartlett — *Discovery* p.35-36
Book Proverbs p.7
Braude — *Stories* p.137
Curtis — *Practical* p.116, 130-132
Du Noüy — *Road* p.31, 42, 52-53, 65, 70, 86, 97, 148, 229
Edwards — *Useful* p.16
Flesch — *Unusual* p.75
Forbes — *Thoughts* p.2, 80, 133, 187, 243, 341, 350, 353, 383, 479, 487, 504, 510
Garland — *Subject* p.92-93
Harnsberger — *Mark* p.99-100
Holmes — *Design* p.11-12, 25, 80, 89, 102, 197
Hovey — *Treasury* p.166; #51-52, 891-893
How To Live p.234-237
Hubbard — *Scrap* p.72
Huxley — *You See* index p.284-285
Keys Happiness p.162
Kin — *Dictionary* p.270
Lockridge — *World's* #4245, 4323, 5717
Modern Eloquence (14) p.326
Montapert — *Distilled* p.128-129
Peale — *Faith* p.27-54
Peale — *Stay* p.121-136
Peterson — *Art* p.177
Seldes — *Great* p.315-316
Sheen — *Thoughts* p.55-56
Woods — *Religious* p.278-279, 705

, and meditation
Krishnamurti — *Urgency* p.140-146

, Conservation of
Woods — *Religious* p.187

, Prayer as form of
Peale — *Guide* p.94-114

, Slump in
Unlimited Power p.153-156

ENGAGEMENTS
See also **Courtship**
Fuller — *Thesaurus* #856-857
Lockridge — *World's* #833
Prochnow — *Public* #1569

ENGINEERING AND ENGINEERS
Curtis — *Practical* p.331-333
George — *Book* p.27, 164
Harral — *Feature* p.148
Hooker — *Index* p.215-223
Krishnamurti — *Think* p.115-116
Prochnow — *Public* #918

ENGLAND
Cerf — *Laugh* p.415-423
Fuller — *Epigrams* p.101
Harnsberger — *Mark* p.100-103
Henry — *5000* p.73-75
Lockridge — *World's* #5159, 5490
New Joy p.126
Prochnow — *Success.* #1716-1718
Seldes — *Great* p.316-319

, and America
Flesch — *Unusual* p.75
Hubbard — *Scrap* p.187

, House of Lords in
Dirksen — *Quot.* #1711-1712

ENGLISH LANGUAGE
Dirksen — *Quot.* #543, 879, 1679
Flesch — *Unusual* p.75-76
Fun Fare p.304-307
Prochnow — *Public* #137, 443, 561, 680, 693, 751, 887, 1065, 1524, 1588, 1648, 4276, 4290
Prochnow — *Speaker's* p.113-114
Prochnow — *Success.* #1143, 1186, 1719

ENGLISHMEN
Asimov — *Treasury* #16, 405-406, 420-423, 536
Botkin — *Anecdotes* p.140, 195, 265
Edwards — *Useful* p.728
Flesch — *Unusual* p.76
Hovey — *Treasury See* index p.295
Kin — *Dictionary* p.81
Lockridge — *World's* #1980, 3151-3152, 3190, 3627, 3699, 4072, 5198, 5732, 5766
Schermerhorn — *1500* p.138-141
Speaker's Desk See index p.299

ENJOYMENT
See also **Amusements; Happiness; Joy; Pleasure**
Adams — *New* p.66
Applegarth — *Heir.* p.86, 148
Baillie — *Diary* #204
Dirksen — *Quot.* #880
Edwards — *Useful* p.161-162
Evans — *Unto* p.50
Flesch — *Unusual* p.76-77
Forbes — *Thoughts* p.16, 69, 103, 109, 143, 146, 163, 167, 253, 258, 441, 495
How To Live p.110-114
Hulme — *Living* p.142-145
Keller — *Open* p.131
Keys Happiness p.16-20, 537-540
Kin — *Dictionary* p.81
Lockridge — *World's* #3505, 3707, 4477, 4878, 5203
Montapert — *Distilled* p.129-130
Patterns For Living p.705-712

Prochnow — *Success.* #1720-1721
Wallis — *Words* p.19, 50, 52
Watson — *Light* p.23-30
Woods — *Religious* p.279
Words — *Inspir.* p.163-166
, *Limits of*
Hubbard — *Scrap* p.58

ENLIGHTENMENT
See also **Education; Knowledge; Science;** etc.
Hubbard — *Scrap* p.25
Lytle — *Leaves* p.44
Seldes — *Great* p.319
Woods — *Religious* p.279
, *Men of*
Dirksen — *Quot.* #387

ENMITY. *See* **Enemies**

ENOUGH. *See* **Sufficiency**

ENTERPRISE
See also **Effort; Energy; Free enterprise**
Braude — *Stories* p.137
Edwards — *Useful* p.163
Flesch — *Unusual* p.77
Forbes — *Thoughts* p.38, 45, 55, 98, 238, 261, 366, 447, 496
Halverson — *Perspective* p.26
Mandel — *Stories* p.83
Woods — *Religious* p.279

ENTERTAINERS
See also **Actors and actresses; Comedy and comedians;** etc.
Lockridge — *World's* #4653
Safian — *Insults* p.63-66
Safian — *More* p.58-61

ENTERTAINMENT
See also **Amusements; Recreation;** types of entertainment
Adams — *New* p.13
Asimov — *Treasury* #343, 345, 367
Braude — *Stories* p.137
Copeland — *10,000* p.567-622
Flesch — *Unusual* p.77
Johnson — *Bedside* p.308
New Topical p.79-80
Sagendorph — *Old* p.187-198

ENTHUSIASM
See also **Sincerity; Zeal**
Albert — *Stop* p.37-38, 41-42
Applegarth — *Heir.* p.93-97
Braude — *Stories* p.137
Detherage — *Sunrise* p.87
Dirksen — *Quot.* #881-882, 1680, 2329
Edwards — *Useful* p.163-164
Emmons — *Mature* p.93
Evans — *Thoughts III (Open Road)* p.127
Flesch — *Unusual* p.77
Flint — *Graham* p.47
Fogg — *1000* #795
Forbes — *Thoughts See* index p.548
Giniger — *Compact* p.28-36
Grizer — *Wit* p.147-148
Henry — *5000* p.75-76
Hovey — *Treasury* p.166; #894-901, 996, 1047, 1217, 1803
How To Live p.301
Hubbard — *Scrap* p.60
Ideas p.140-141
Johnson — *Bedside* p.11
Kennedy — *Reader's* #298-301
Kin — *Dictionary* p.81
Liddle — *Thought I, II, III* p.104
Liddle — *Thought IV* p.20, 23, 39
Lockridge — *World's* #3260, 4308
Lytle — *Leaves* p.22, 56, 185
Maltz — *Creative* p.66-68
Manchee — *Secret* p.152-154
Mandel — *Stories* p.83
Modern Eloquence (14) p.327-328
Montapert — *Distilled* p.130-131
New Joy p.64
Nichols — *New* p.104-105
Nichols — *Third* p.76-77
Peale — *Courage* p.112-129
Peale — *Stay* p.23-44
Prochnow — *Public* #3015-3017
Prochnow — *Speaker's* p.114
Prochnow — *Success.* #81
Seldes — *Great* p.319
Sheen — *Content.* p.73-76
Speaker's Desk p.54-56; #114, 851
Wallis — *Treasure* p.13
Wallis — *Words* p.138
Welk — *Guide.* p.154-155
Woods — *Religious* p.280

ENTROPY
Curtis — *Practical* p.238
Du Noüy — *Road See* index p.245

ENUNCIATION
Nizer — *Thinking* p.129

ENVELOPES
Lytle — *Leaves* p.186

ENVIRONMENT
See also **Circumstances; Opportunity;** types of environment
Curtis — *Practical* p.150-156
Edwards — *Useful* p.728

Evans — *Faith* p.121-122, 153, 213
Evans — *This* p.115
Evans — *Thoughts II (Open Door)* p.126-127
Evans — *Thoughts IV* p.96, 124-125
Grizer — *Wit* p.148
Holman — *Psych.* p.19-22
Hovey — *Treasury* p.166-167; #902-905
Keller — *Open* p.44
Kin — *Dictionary* p.81
Krishnamurti — *Think* p.68-69
Lair — *Baby* p.115
Lytle — *Leaves* p.54
Mandel — *Stories* p.83-85
Montapert — *Distilled* p.131-132
Sheen — *Thoughts* p.43-56
Woods — *Religious* p.279

, and heredity
Fogg — *1000* #145

, Beauty in
Curtis — *Daily* p.154-155

, for child training
Holman — *Psych.* p.9-10

, Reactions to
Holmes — *Design* p.107

, Spiritual
Kohn — *Through* p.109-111

, Technology and
Dirksen — *Quot.* #1664

ENVY
See also **Covetousness; Discontent; Jealousy; Rivalry**
Baillie — *Diary* #47
Book Proverbs p.57, 80
Braude — *Source* #553-558
Braude — *Stories* p.137-138
Dirksen — *Quot.* #1995
Edwards — *Useful* p.164-165
Evans — *This* p.169-170
Evans — *Unto* p.34
Flesch — *Unusual* p.77-78
Flint — *Graham* p.47
Forbes — *Thoughts* p.38, 146, 186, 287, 332, 422, 499, 504
Garland — *Subject* p.93
Grizer — *Wit* p.149
Harnsberger — *Mark* p.104
Henry — *5000* p.76
Hubbard — *Scrap* p.69, 145
Johnson — *Bedside* p.191, 195, 198, 206, 247, 252
Kin — *Dictionary* p.81-82
Knight's Illus. p.107
Liddle — *Thought I, II, III* p.19, 41, 145, 150
Liddle — *Thought V* p.37
Lockridge — *World's* See index p.575
Lytle — *Leaves* p.130
McCracken — *What* p.17-21
Manchee — *Secret* p.127-128
Mandel — *Stories* p.85
Montapert — *Distilled* p.132
New Topical p.80
Nichols — *New* p.74-75
Prochnow — *Public* #2469, 4076
Seldes — *Great* p.319
Woods — *Religious* p.280
Words — *Inspir.* p.171-172

EPHOD, THE
New Topical p.80-81

EPHRAIM, TRIBE OF
New Topical p.81

EPICURES
Flesch — *Unusual* p.78
Prochnow — *Public* #616

EPIDEMICS
Flesch — *Unusual* p.78

EPIGRAMS
See also **Proverbs;** under various subjects
Flesch — *Unusual* p.78
Fogg — *1000* See index p.884
Fuller — *Epigrams* p.v-viii, 101-102
Lockridge — *World's* #4223
Modern Eloquence (14) p.271-439
Nizer — *Thinking* p.54, 80
Peterson — *Art* p.378
Prochnow — *Success.* #304-727

EPILEPSY
Guideposts — *Faith* p.195-197

EPISTLES. *See* **Letters and letter-writing; New Testament**

EPITAPHS
Applegarth — *Heir.* p.19, 167, 198, 246, 292-293
Copeland — *10,000* p.805-816
Dirksen — *Quot.* #584
Edwards — *Useful* p.165
Flesch — *Unusual* p.78
Fogg — *1000* See index p.884-885
Fuller — *Epigrams* p.102-108
George — *Book* p.109, 137
Halverson — *Perspective* p.37
Henry — *5000* p.76-77
Keys Happiness p.312
Lockridge — *World's* #2035
Lytle — *Leaves* p.94, 129-130
Prochnow — *Public* #485, 1914, 1922
Prochnow — *Speaker's* p.114-115
Prochnow — *Success.* #1723
Schermerhorn — *1500* p.141-144

Seldes — *Great* p.320
, *Self–composed*
Fun Fare p.26

EQUALITY
See also **Democracy; Equity; Justice; Races of man, Relations of; Women, Rights of**
Adams — *New* p.49
Braude — *Source* #559-561
Braude — *Stories* p.138
Dirksen — *Quot.* #7-8, 34, 43, 391, 883-886, 2175
Edwards — *Useful* p.165-166, 334-335
Evans — *Thoughts I* p.149-150
Flesch — *Unusual* p.78-79
Fogg — *1000* #328
Forbes — *Thoughts* p.102, 114, 170, 197, 324, 406, 451, 501
Fuller — *Thesaurus* #2046
Garland — *Subject* p.93-94
Grizer — *Wit* p.149-150
Henry — *5000* p.77-78
Hovey — *Treasury* p.167; #250, 906-910
Kennedy — *Reader's* #302-303
Kin — *Dictionary* p.82
Lockridge — *World's* #1618, 1727, 2002, 4274
Lytle — *Leaves* p.67
Mandel — *Stories* p.86
Montapert — *Distilled* p.132-133
Prochnow — *Public* #3018-3019, 4077
Prochnow — *Success.* #1187, 1724-1728
Seldes — *Great* p.320-324
Sheban — *Wisdom* no p.
Voss — *Quotations* p.77-80
Woods — *Business.* p.73-75
Woods — *Religious* p.280-282
, *and freedom*
Krishnamurti — *Think* p.93-99
, *Economic*
Dirksen — *Quot.* #376
, *Human*
Adams — *New* p.390
, *of the sexes*
Ideas p.142-143
, *Prayer for*
Unlimited Power p.200

EQUANIMITY. *See* **Calmness; Peace; Self-control**

EQUATION
See also **Equality**
Flesch — *Unusual* p.79

EQUATOR
Flesch — *Unusual* p.79
Harnsberger — *Mark* p.105

EQUILIBRIUM
Du Noüy — *Human* p.86, 88-90, 120, 137-138
White — *Job* p.57-58

EQUIPMENT
Kin — *Dictionary* p.82
Lytle — *Leaves* p.150

EQUITY
See also **Equality; Fairness; Justice; Law**
Edwards — *Useful* p.166
Kin — *Dictionary* p.82
Seldes — *Great* p.324-325
Woods — *Business.* p.75

EQUIVOCATION. *See* **Evasion**

ERECTNESS
Prochnow — *Public* #2250

EROS AND EROTICISM
Seldes — *Great* p.325
Woods — *Religious* p.282

ERROR. *See* **Falsehood; Mistakes; Wrong**

ERUDITION. *See* **Knowledge; Learning**

ERUPTIONS
Auden — *Certain* p.155-162

ESCAPE
Alexander's Treasure. p.178-180
Clark — *Windows* p.84
Evans — *This* p.14-15, 37-51
Evans — *Unto* p.80
Flesch — *Unusual* p.79
Garland — *Subject* p.95
Hobe — *Tapestries* p.211
Hulme — *Living* p.22-34
Prochnow — *Public* #2489
Woods — *Religious* p.283
, *Caused by despondency*
Flint — *Graham* p.48
, *Necessity of*
Kohn — *Through* p.121-123

ESCAPISM
Halverson — *Perspective* p.78
Kennedy — *Reader's* #305-307
Menninger — *Blue.* p.162-164
Sheen — *Light* p.9-19

ESKIMOS
Auden — *Certain* p.162-165

ESSAYS AND ESSAYISTS
Lockridge — *World's* #4995
Prochnow — *Public* #624

ESSENCE
Lytle — *Leaves* p.105

ESSENTIALS
See also **Necessity**
Kauffman — *For* p.89-91
Montapert — *Distilled* p.134
, Life's basic
Kohn — *Pathways* p.81-83
, World's basic
Kohn — *Pathways* p.79-83

ESTEEM
See also **Admiration; Appreciation; Respect; Self-esteem**
Braude — *Stories* p.138
Edwards — *Useful* p.168-169
Forbes — *Thoughts* p.224, 272
Lockridge — *World's* #306, 1498-1500, 2028, 2930, 3225
Maltz — *Creative* p.77
Prochnow — *Public* #47, 1873
, Men's
Adams — *New* p.6

ESTIMATION. *See* **Appreciation; Criticism; Judgment; Opinion**

ESTRANGEMENT
See also **Enemies; Indifference;** etc.
Taylor — *With* p.27-30
Woods — *Religious* p.283

"ETCETERATION"
Curtis — *Practical* p.160-163

ETERNITY
See also **Immortality; Time**
Applegarth — *Heir.* p.62, 69, 100, 147, 261, 308
Baillie — *Diary* #77, 138
Braude — *Source* #562-565
Braude — *Stories* p.139
Curtis — *Daily* p.221-228
Curtis — *New* p.134-135
Dirksen — *Quot.* #393, 1311, 1944, 1996
Edwards — *Useful* p.169-170
Emmons — *Mature* p.131-138
Evans — *Thoughts II (Open Door)* p.58, 79, 105, 107-110, 207, 209-210
Evans — *Thoughts III (Open Road)* p.21, 32, 148, 157, 198-199, 202-208
Evans — *Unto* p.4, 145
Flint — *Graham* p.49
Forbes — *Thoughts* p.246, 286, 388, 405, 415, 433, 461
Garland — *Subject* p.95-96
Giniger — *Compact* p.273-282
Harnsberger — *Mark* p.105-106
Henry — *5000* p.78
Hobe — *Tapestries* p.11, 154-165
Hovey — *Treasury* p.168; #523, 796, 914-915, 1481
Hunter — *Gems* p.28-29
Kahn — *Lessons* p.227-240
Kauffman — *For* p.91
Keller — *Open* p.113
Kennedy — *Reader's* #308-310
Kohn — *Adventures* p.154-158
Liddle — *Thought I, II, III* p.118
Liddle — *Thought IV* p.21, 38
Lockridge — *World's* #2895, 5707
Lytle — *Leaves* p.41
Maxwell — *Courage* p.57-63
Montapert — *Distilled* p.135
Nichols — *New* p.176-177
Peterson — *Art* p.386
Phillips — *Choice* p.61, 136
Prochnow — *Public* #4080
Sheban — *Wisdom* no p.
Taylor — *With* p.23-26
Wallis — *Treasure* p.24, 95, 143, 221
Wallis — *Words* p.67, 100, 128
Wilcox — *Heart* p.26-27
Woods — *Religious* p.283-285
, Today's
Guideposts — *Faith* p.462-466

ETHICS
See also **Morality**
Asimov — *Treasury* #362
Book Proverbs p.122
Curtis — *Practical* p.73, 103-104
Dirksen — *Quot.* #168-169
Droke — *Christian* p.171-172
Flesch — *Unusual* p.79
Flint — *Graham* p.48
Forbes — *Thoughts* p.137, 207, 315, 359, 367, 370, 495, 499
Garland — *Subject* p.96
Hooker — *Index* p.27-36
Liddle — *Thought I, II, III* p.93, 98
Lockridge — *World's* #2907, 5000, 5585
Montapert — *Distilled* p.135-136
Seldes — *Great* p.327-328
Woods — *Religious* p.285-287
, and business
Kauffman — *For* p.39-41
, and fear
Sheen — *Way* p.136-138
, and ministry
Kauffman — *For* p.92
, Sovereignty of
Lindeman — *Emerson* p.89-103

ETHNOLOGY
See also **Races of man**
Curtis — *Practical* p.69

ETIQUETTE
See also **Behavior; Breeding; Conduct; Courtesy; Custom**
Applegarth — *Heir.* p.80, 218
Braude — *Sources* #566-567, 1083
Braude — *Speaker's* #466-469
Braude — *Stories* p.288
Detherage — *Sunrise* p.62, 66, 104
Dirksen — *Quot.* #259-260, 1661, 2278, 2327
Edwards — *Useful* p.170, 368-373
Evans — *Faith* p.73-74, 163-164
Evans — *Quote* p.163-175
Evans — *Thoughts I* p.66-68, 93
Evans — *Thoughts III (Open Road)* p.68-69, 71
Evans — *Thoughts IV* p.116-117, 159
Flesch — *Unusual* p.79, 163
Forbes — *Thoughts* p.50, 72, 103, 168, 239, 408, 413, 472, 514
Franke — *Buckley* p.81
Fuller — *Thesaurus* p.1-147
George — *Book* p.221, 307, 322
Grizer — *Wit* p.298
Harral — *Feature* p.212
Henry — *5000* p.169
Hobe — *Tapestries* p.175
How To Live p.410-434
Kin — *Dictionary* p.156
Liddle — *Thought I, II, III* p.38, 42, 65, 99, 126, 147
Liddle — *Thought IV* p.4
Liddle — *Thought V* p.12, 29, 36, 43
Lockridge — *World's* #1429, 3016, 3820, 5857
Mandel — *Stories* p.174
Montapert — *Distilled* p.249-250
Prochnow — *Public* #186, 676, 845, 1113, 1251, 4157, 4382
Prochnow — *Speaker's* p.116, 201-202
Prochnow — *Success.* #993, 1222, 2022-2023
Speaker's Desk p.140, 142; #134, 848
, Male
Daly — *Personality* p.39-43
, Table
Baillie — *Diary* #210
Daly — *Personality* p.143-146

EUCHARIST
Applegarth — *Heir.* p.16, 220
Wallis — *Treasure* p.134
Woods — *Religious* p.287-291

EUGENICS
See also **Heredity**
Edwards — *Useful* p.728
Ideas p.143-145
Seldes — *Great* p.328

EULOGY
See also **Praise**
Dirksen — *Quot.* #4
Fogg — *1000 See* index p.885
Humes — *Instant* p.48-50; #1240-1243
Weisfeld — *Pulpit* p.182

EUPHRATES, THE
New Topical p.81

EUROPE
See also names of countries
Cerf — *Laugh* p.443-447
Hovey — *Treasury* #335, 554, 1327, 1459, 1595, 1600
Lockridge — *World's* #3886, 4152
Seldes — *Great* p.328-329
Woods — *Religious* p.291

EUTHANASIA
How To Live p.378
Woods — *Religious* p.291

EVALUATION. *See* **Judgment**

EVANESCENCE
Lytle — *Leaves* p.108

EVANGELISM AND EVANGELISTS
See also **Revivals**
Flint — *Graham* p.48-49
Fuller — *Thesaurus* #1511-1516
Garland — *Subject* p.96
Guideposts — *Faith* p.47-50, 129-133
Halverson — *Perspective* p.70
Harral — *Feature* p.148
Hovey — *Treasury* p.168-170; #341, 527, 916-930
Schermerhorn — *1500* p.145
Strait — *Speaker's* p.60-61
Weisfeld — *Pulpit* p.17, 24, 36-37, 64, 80-81
Woods — *Religious* p.291-292

EVASION
See also **Concealment; Secrecy**
Dirksen — *Quot.* #152
Edwards — *Useful* p.166-167, 170
Reader's — *Getting* p.84
Reader's — *20th* p.16
Speaker's Desk #13, 703, 975, 1038, 1106

EVE. *See* **Adam and Eve**

EVENING
See also **Night; Sunset; Twilight**
Alexander's Treasure. p.86
Auden — *Certain* p.100-101
Detherage — *Sunrise* p.135
Edwards — *Useful* p.170
Henry — *5000* p.78-79
Hobe — *Tapestries* p.59, 112-113
New Topical p.81-82
Prochnow — *Public* #2017
Prochnow — *Success.* #370, 1729
Tanksley — *Friend* p.50

EVENTS
See also **Circumstances**
Flesch — *Unusual* p.113
Hovey — *Treasury* p.203; #99, 451, 1189-1191, 1206, 1424
Kin — *Dictionary* p.115
Montapert — *Distilled* p.187-188
Prochnow — *Success.* #1836

EVERLASTING LIFE. *See* **Eternity; Immortality**

EVERYONE
Kin — *Dictionary* p.83
Lytle — *Leaves* p.112

EVERYTHING
Kin — *Dictionary* p.83

EVIDENCE
See also **Facts; Law**
Edwards — *Useful* p.170-171
Flesch — *Unusual* p.80, 256-257
Fuller — *Thesaurus* #2521-2523
Grizer — *Wit* p.151
Harnsberger — *Mark* p.106
Henry — *5000* p.79
Hubbard — *Scrap* p.57
Hunter — *Gems* p.105-107
Kin — *Dictionary* p.83
Lockridge — *World's* #5808
Lytle — *Leaves* p.67-68
Prochnow — *Public* #2739
Prochnow — *Speaker's* p.117
Seldes — *Great* p.329
Speaker's Desk #162-163, 204, 206, 212, 350, 356, 422, 609, 860, 1171

EVIL
See also **Crime and criminals; Sin; Wickedness;** types of evil
Applegarth — *Heir.* p.48, 246
Botkin — *Treasury* p.50-51, 67-130, 175, 180-181. 359, 370
Dirksen — *Quot.* #394-395, 889, 1146, 1212, 1590, 1596, 1997, 2289
Droke — *Christian* p.230-231
Du Noüy — *Human* p.130-131, 133, 225, 236
Edwards — *Useful* p.171-173
Evans — *This* p.163-164, 166-167
Evans — *Thoughts III (Open Road)* p.81, 86-87, 105, 201
Evans — *Thoughts IV* p.127-128, 167, 199
Evans — *Unto* p.34, 36, 60, 68, 71, 84, 102
Flesch — *Unusual* p.16-17, 80
Forbes — *Thoughts See* index p.548
Fox — *Make* p.165-166
Fuller — *Epigrams* p.109
Garland — *Subject* p.97-98
Grizer — *Wit* p.151
Henry — *5000* p.79-80
Hobe — *Tapestries* p.153
Hoffer — *Reflect.* p.17-18
Holman — *Psych.* p.51-54
Holmes — *Design* p.98, 100-101, 112
Hovey — *Treasury* p.170-171; *See* index p.295
Hubbard — *Scrap* p.36
Johnson — *Bedside* p.63, 77, 91, 212
Keller — *Open* p.26-27
Kennedy — *Fresh* p.55-56
Kin — *Dictionary* p.20, 83
Liddle — *Thought I, II, III* p.7, 10, 29, 53, 61, 68, 156, 168, 184
Liddle — *Thought IV* p.31
Lindeman — *Emerson* p.192
Lockridge — *World's See* index p.575
Mandel — *Stories* p.86
Maxwell — *Courage* p.225-230
Montapert — *Distilled* p.136-137
Phillips — *Choice See* index p.425
Prochnow — *Public See* index p.494
Prochnow — *Speaker's* p.117
Prochnow — *Success.* #1730
Seldes — *Great* p.329-330
Sheen — *Way* p.112-114
Voss — *Quotations* p.80-82
Wallis — *Treasure* p.111
Wheelis — *Moralist See* index p.163
White — *Job* p.104, 141, 143-145
Woods — *Religious* p.292-300

EVOLUTION
Bartlett — *Discovery* p.145-147
Braude — *Source* #568-569
Braude — *Stories* p.139
Du Noüy — *Road See* index p.245

Evans — *Thoughts III (Open Road)* p.188-189
Fogg — *1000* #802, 811
Forbes — *Thoughts* p.8, 95, 313
Garland — *Subject* p.98-99
Henry — *5000* p.80
Hubbard — *Scrap* p.34, 169, 201
Keys Happiness p.412-417
Lytle — *Leaves* p.94
Prochnow — *Public* #405, 648, 803, 1394, 1917
Seldes — *Great* p.331
White — *Job* p.62, 64-65, 77, 138
Woods — *Religious* p.300-303
, Biological
Du Noüy — *Human See* index p.282
, Inorganic
Du Noüy — *Human* p.41-42, 45-46
, Moral
Du Noüy — *Human See* index p.282

EVONA, SAINT
Botkin — *Anecdotes* p.186-187

EXACTNESS
See also **Accuracy; Perfection**
Kin — *Dictionary* p.83
Prochnow — *Public* #2253
Prochnow — *Success.* #1731

EXAGGERATION
See also **Falsehood; Liars; Tall tales**
Botkin — *Anecdotes* p.90
Braude — *Stories* p.139
Edwards — *Useful* p.173
Flesch — *Unusual* p.80
Fuller — *Thesaurus* #221-226
Harnsberger — *Mark* p.107-109
Kin — *Dictionary* p.83
Liddle — *Thought I, II, III* p.127, 137
Lockridge — *World's* #4167
Mandel — *Stories* p.86-87
Prochnow — *Speaker's* p.117
Speaker's Desk See index p.299; #626

EXALTATION
Garland — *Subject* p.99
Prochnow — *Public* #2649
Speaker's Desk #97

EXAMINATIONS
Braude — *Source* p.570-571
Forbes — *Thoughts* p.66, 162, 172, 205, 389, 485
Hubbard — *Scrap* p.181
Krishnamurti — *Think* p.77
Lockridge — *World's* #878
Lytle — *Leaves* p.158
Prochnow — *Public* #104, 428, 592, 661, 680, 1049
Prochnow — *Success.* #1046
Speaker's Desk #51, 60, 66, 88, 101, 536, 1010

EXAMPLE
See also **Influence**
Applegarth — *Heir.* p.228
Baillie — *Diary* #297
Book Proverbs p.107
Braude — *Source* #572-573
Braude — *Stories* p.139-140
Dirksen — *Quot.* #1312, 1999
Edwards — *Useful* p.173-175
Evans — *Faith* p.49-52, 146, 173-174
Evans — *Quote* p.187-194
Evans — *Thoughts I* p.109, 198
Evans — *Thoughts II (Open Door)* p.26, 47
Evans — *Thoughts III (Open Road)* p.21, 121, 141, 152, 187
Evans — *Thoughts IV* p.116, 137, 157, 197
Flesch — *Unusual* p.80
Forbes — *Thoughts* p.66, 193, 203, 236, 408, 489
Fuller — *Epigrams* p.109-110
Fun Fare p.91
Harnsberger — *Mark* p.109
Henry — *5000* p.80
Hobe — *Tapestries* p.18, 107
Hovey — *Treasury* p.171; #938-941
Humes — *Instant* p.5-6, 13, 15, 304-305
Kin — *Dictionary* p.84
Knight's Illus. p.42-44
Liddle — *Thought V* p.37
Lockridge — *World's* #241
Lytle — *Leaves* p.61, 130
Mandel — *Stories* p.87
Mandelbaum — *Choose* p.273-283
Montapert — *Distilled* p.137
Prochnow — *Public* #94, 406, 775, 879, 905, 1684, 3028-3035, 4083-4085
Prochnow — *Speaker's* p.117-118
Prochnow — *Success.* #1262, 1278
Voss — *Quotations* p.82-83
Wallis — *Treasure* p.131, 149, 176, 202
Wallis — *Words* p.26
Woods — *Religious* p.303

EXCELLENCE
See also **Best; Greatness; Merit; Perfection**
Edwards — *Useful* p.175

Forbes — *Thoughts* p.173, 191, 343, 364, 384
Garland — *Subject* p.100
Henry — *5000* p.80
Humes — *Instant* #306-315
Mandelbaum — *Choose* p.224-228
Montapert — *Distilled* p.137-138
Prochnow — *Success.* #1732
Woods — *Religious* p.303-304

EXCELSIOR
Edwards — *Useful* p.174-176

EXCEPTION
Kin — *Dictionary* p.84
Lockridge — *World's* #4006

EXCESS
See also **Extremes; Intemperance;** types of excess
Braude — *Stories* p.140
Edwards — *Useful* p.176-177
Evans — *Faith* p.109, 111-112
Evans — *Thoughts I* p.27-28, 83
Flesch — *Unusual* p.80-81
Forbes — *Thoughts* p.46, 371, 452-453
Fuller — *Epigrams* p.110
Holmes — *I've* p.64-65
Lockridge — *World's* #5716
Montapert — *Distilled* p.138
Sheban — *Wisdom* no p.

EXCHANGE
Braude — *Speaker's* #470-471
Kin — *Dictionary* p.84
Prochnow — *Public* #2421

EXCISE
Woods — *Business* p.75-76

EXCITEMENT
See also **Action; Adventure; Emotion; Thrills**
Albert — *Stop* p.204-205
Curtis — *Practical* p.117
Edwards — *Useful* p.177
How To Live p.216-219
Prochnow — *Public* #604
Prochnow — *Speaker's* p.118
Speaker's Desk #749, 907, 1043

EXCLUSION
Peterson — *Art* p.83
Woods — *Religious* p.304

EXCOMMUNICATION
Seldes — *Great* p.331-332

EXCUSES
See also **Apology; Justification; Reason and reasoning**
Baillie — *Diary* #335
Braude — *Source* #80
Braude — *Speaker's* #472-478
Edwards — *Useful* p.177
Fuller — *Epigrams* p.110-111
Grizer — *Wit* p.35-36, 151-152
Henry — *5000* p.81
Hill — *Think* p.289-292
Holmes — *Design* p.64-65
Kin — *Dictionary* p.84
Liddle — *Thought I, II, III* p.17, 71
Maltz — *Creative* p.128-129
Mandel — *Stories* p.87-88
Montapert — *Distilled* p.138-139
Prochnow — *Public* #90, 815
Sheen — *Content.* p.102-103
Speaker's Desk See index p.299

EXECUTIONS
Fogg — *1000 See* index p.885
Harral — *Feature* p.146
Reader's — *20th* p.38-43
Unlimited Power p.56-60

EXECUTIVES
Edwards — *Useful* p.728
Forbes — *Thoughts* p.97, 289, 428, 431, 456; *See also* index p.548
Fuller — *Thesaurus* #2231-2235
Grizer — *Wit* p.152-153
Harral — *Feature* p.91-92
Kin — *Dictionary* p.31
Montapert — *Distilled* p.139-140
Prochnow — *Public* #159, 243, 307, 675, 1685
Prochnow — *Speaker's* p.118
Prochnow — *Success.* #194
Seldes — *Great* p.332

, Junior
Manchee — *Secret* p.215
, Qualifications for
Hubbard — *Scrap* p.143

EXERCISE
See also **Gymnastics; Work;** etc.
Baillie — *Diary* #244
Bradshaw — *Home.* p.12-22
Edwards — *Useful* p.177-178
Flesch — *Unusual* p.81
Flint — *Graham* p.64
Forbes — *Thoughts* p.103, 173, 359, 455, 457, 461
Grizer — *Wit* p.153-154
Keys Happiness p.60-64
Maltz — *Creative See* index p.224
Montapert — *Distilled* p.140
Prochnow — *Public* #932
Prochnow — *Success.* #708, 788, 1166
Reader's — *Getting* p.69-73
White — *Life* p.102, 142, 165

EXHIBITS
Harral — *Feature* p.148-149

EXILES
See also **Refugees**
Braude — *Stories* p.141
Flesch — *Unusual* p.81
Fogg — *1000 See* index p.885
Prochnow — *Success.* #1733
Sheban — *Wisdom* no p.

EXISTENCE. *See* **Life and living**

EXISTENTIALISM
Ginott — *Between* p.26-27
Ideas p.145-146
Montapert — *Distilled* p.141
Seldes — *Great* p.333
Woods — *Religious* p.306

"EXIT LINES"
Evans — *Thoughts I* p.196-197

EXITS
See also **Ends and endings**
Harnsberger — *Mark* p.109
Kin — *Dictionary* p.84
Prochnow — *Success.* #941

EXPANSION
Adams — *New* p.210

EXPECTATION
See also **Anticipation; Foresight and hindsight; Hope**
Book Proverbs p.109
Dirksen — *Quot.* #78, 2346
Edwards — *Useful* p.178
Flesch — *Unusual* p.81
Forbes — *Thoughts* p.148, 338, 476
Garland — *Subject* p.101
Grizer — *Wit* p.154
Henry — *5000* p.81
Hobe — *Tapestries* p.156
Kennedy — *Reader's* #311-312
Kin — *Dictionary* p.84
Kohn — *Pathways* p.155-158
Lockridge — *World's* #3438, 4420
Peterson — *Art* p.397
Prochnow — *Public* #804, 831
Prochnow — *Success.* #1734

EXPEDIENCY
See also **Compromise; Opportunity**
Braude — *Stories* p.141
Edwards — *Useful* p.178
Evans — *Unto* p.56, 58
Forbes — *Thoughts* p.112, 448
Humes — *Instant* p.316-323
Kin — *Dictionary* p.84
Seldes — *Great* p.333
Woods — *Religious* p.304-305

EXPENSE
See also **Cost; Extravagance**
Book Proverbs p.9
Edwards — *Useful* p.178
Flesch — *Unusual* p.81
Kohn — *Thoughts* p.35-38
Prochnow — *Public* #606, 1127
Prochnow — *Speaker's* p.118-119

EXPENSE ACCOUNTS
Grizer — *Wit* p.154
Prochnow — *Success.* #408
Speaker's Desk #77, 255, 983

EXPERIENCE
See also **Action; Age; Observation; Wisdom**
Adams — *New* p.80
Bach — *Make* p.28-36
Boas — *History* p.50-66
Book Proverbs p.111
Braude — *Source* #574-580
Braude — *Speaker's* #479-483
Braude — *Stories* p.141-143
Curtis — *Practical* p.46-47, 259, 403, 499
Dirksen — *Quot.* #39, 285, 296, 585, 890-891, 2000-2001, 2291, 2329
Droke — *Christian* p.172-175
Edwards — *Useful* p.178-180, 728
Evans — *Faith* p.101-102
Evans — *Quote* p.187-194
Evans — *This* p.3-4
Evans — *Thoughts I* p.31-35, 46-48, 79, 89
Evans — *Thoughts II (Open Door)* p.77-79, 207
Evans — *Thoughts III (Open Road)* p.18, 116, 120, 146
Evans — *Unto* p.49, 72, 84, 118-119
Flesch — *Unusual* p.82-83
Flint — *Graham* p.49
Forbes — *Thoughts See* index p.548-549
Fuller — *Epigrams* p.111-112
Ginott — *Between* p.49-53
Grizer — *Wit* p.154-158
Harnsberger — *Mark* p.110-112
Harral — *Feature* p.149
Henry — *5000* p.81
Holmes — *Design* p.22-25, 45, 47, 54, 63, 84-86, 95-97, 170-171
Hovey — *Treasury* p.171; *See also* index p.295-296
Hubbard — *Scrap* p.48
Johnson — *Bedside* p.137, 183, 250
Kennedy — *Reader's* #313-315

Kin — *Dictionary* p.84-85
Kohn — *Adventures* p.68-70
Liddle — *Thought V* p.14, 18, 27, 46
Lockridge — *World's See* index p.575
Lytle — *Leaves* p.60
Mandel — *Stories* p.88
Mandelbaum — *Choose* p.14-18
Modern Eloquence (14) p.331
Montapert — *Distilled* p.142
Nichols — *Third* p.235-236
Phillips — *Choice* p.170, 241, 272, 335
Prochnow — *Public See* index p.495
Prochnow — *Speaker's* p.119
Prochnow — *Success.* #735, 1043, 1267, 1277, 1735-1739
Reader's — *Getting* p.38, 60
Seldes — *Great* p.333-334
Speaker's Desk p.56-58; #14, 85, 103, 345, 387, 725
Wallis — *Treasure* p.234
Welk — *Guide.* p.84-86
White — *Job* p.33, 41, 45-47, 67
White — *Life* p.301-309
Woods — *Business.* p.76
Woods — *Religious* p.306-307

EXPERIMENT
See also **Science**
Braude — *Stories* p.143-144
Curtis — *Practical* p.218
Evans — *This* p.3-4
Flesch — *Unusual* p.83
Forbes — *Thoughts* p.248, 265, 355, 433
Fuller — *Thesaurus* #1136-1138
Kin — *Dictionary* p.85
Phillips — *Choice* p.239
Seldes — *Great* p.334
Speaker's Desk #931
Wallis — *Treasure* p.212
White — *Job* p.77-78, 83-84
Woods — *Business.* p.76-77

EXPERTS
Braude — *Stories* p.144
Grizer — *Wit* p.158
Harral — *Feature* p.149
Henry — *5000* p.81-82
Humes — *Instant* #36-38
Kin — *Dictionary* p.85
Liddle — *Thought I, II, III* p.180
Lockridge — *World's* #1851
Montapert — *Distilled* p.143
Prochnow — *Public* #4274
Prochnow — *Speaker's* p.120
Prochnow — *Success.* #239, 910
Woods — *Business.* p.77
Woods — *Wellsprings* p.52-53

EXPIATION. *See* **Retribution**

EXPLANATION
Braude — *Speaker's* #484-488
Braude — *Stories* p.144-145
Flesch — *Unusual* p.83
Fun Fare p.207-208
Prochnow — *Public* #1062
Prochnow — *Success.* #945, 1077
Speaker's Desk See index p.299

EXPLETIVES. *See* **Profanity**

EXPLOITATION
Seldes — *Great* p.334-335
Woods — *Religious* p.309

EXPLORERS AND EXPLORATION
See also **Discovery**
Applegarth — *Heir.* p.278
Evans — *Thoughts III (Open Road)* p.175
Fogg — *1000 See* index p.885
Fuller — *Thesaurus* #1141-1142
George — *Book* p.1, 118, 221, 253
Prochnow — *Public* #176, 1421
White — *Job* p.66-68

EXPLOSIONS AND EXPLOSIVES
Prochnow — *Public* #227
Prochnow — *Success.* #1059
Schermerhorn — *1500* p.147

EXPOSURE
Hulme — *Living* p.13-14
Lockridge — *World's* #228
Seldes — *Great* p.335

EXPRESSION
See also **Face; Language; Self-expression**
Forbes — *Thoughts* p.144, 252, 400, 491
Harnsberger — *Mark* p.112
Harral — *Feature* p.149-150
Kin — *Dictionary* p.85
Lytle — *Leaves* p. 40, 86
Prochnow — *Public* #1973
Reader's — *Getting* p.173

EXTERNALS
Woods — *Religious* p.309

EXTRAORDINARY
Lytle — *Leaves* p.115
Prochnow — *Public* #2325

EXTRAVAGANCE
Braude — *Stories* p.145

Edwards — *Useful* p.180, 503
Evans — *Thoughts II (Open Door)* p.118
Forbes — *Thoughts* p.74, 158
Fuller — *Epigrams* p.112
Fuller — *Thesaurus* #231-232
Grizer — *Wit* p.158-159
Hobe — *Tapestries* p.68
Hubbard — *Scrap* p.53
Liddle — *Thought I, II, III* p.69, 72, 163, 166
Lockridge — *World's* #12, 1804, 3651, 4362
Speaker's Desk #77, 255, 407, 504, 841

EXTREMES
See also **Excess; Extremism and extremists; Intemperance**
Edwards — *Useful* p.180-181
Evans — *Thoughts III (Open Road)* p.78
Evans — *Unto* p.61, 63
Flesch — *Unusual* p.83
Henry — *5000* p.82
Kin — *Dictionary* p.86
Pullar-Strecker — *Proverbs* #45-50

EXTREMISM AND EXTREMISTS
Dirksen — *Quot.* #1147
Flint — *Graham* p.49-50
Franke — *Buckley* p.82-85
Humes — *Instant* #324-329
Seldes — *Great* p.336

EXTREMITY
Woods — *Religious* p.309

EYEGLASSES
Kin — *Dictionary* p.106, 241
Menninger — *Blue.* p.214

EYES AND EYESIGHT
See also **Blind**
Applegarth — *Heir.* p.24, 51, 163, 193, 259, 286
Book Proverbs p.126
Du Noüy — *Human* p.4, 74, 97, 165
Edwards — *Useful* p.181-182
Flesch — *Unusual* p.83
Fuller — *Epigrams* p.112-113
Guideposts — *Faith* p.487-491
Harnsberger — *Mark* p.113
Henry — *5000* p.82
Hobe — *Tapestries* p.63
Keller — *Open* p.112
Kin — *Dictionary* p.86
Lockridge — *World's* #3018, 3257
Lytle — *Leaves* p.50
Mandel — *Stories* p.89
Montapert — *Distilled* p.143-144
New Joy p.118
New Topical p.83
Prochnow — *Public* #104, 1502, 2020-2021, 2023-2024, 2063, 2069, 2251, 2704, 3041
Sheban — *Wisdom* no p.
Wallis — *Treasure* p.25, 155, 168
Woods — *Religious* p.309

F

"FABLE AND FOIBLE"
Botkin — *Anecdotes* p.177-201

FABLES
See also **Mythology**
Alexander's Treasure. p.132
Asimov — *Treasury* #122
Botkin — *Anecdotes* p.xxvi, 178
Cerf — *Laugh* p.473-476
Edwards — *Useful* p.182
Flesch — *Unusual* p.83
Kronenberger — *Animal* p.66-70
Prochnow — *Success.* #1740

FABRICS
Harral — *Feature* p.150

FACE
See also **Ears; Eyes and eyesight;** etc.
Applegarth — *Heir.* p.163, 291
Auden — *Certain* p.165-166
Edwards — *Useful* p.103-104, 182-183
Esteve — *Experience* p.126-127
Flesch — *Unusual* p.83
Harnsberger — *Mark* p.114
Henry — *5000* p.83
Hubbard — *Scrap* p.117
Kin — *Dictionary* p.57, 87
Lockridge — *World's* #3224, 4604, 4618
Montapert — *Distilled* p.144-145
Peale — *Guideposts* p.118-121
Prochnow — *Public See* index p.495
Prochnow — *Success.* #1741
Sheban — *Wisdom* no p.
Wallis — *Words* p.14, 27
Walters — *How* p.125-127
Wilcox — *Heart* p.58-62
Words — *Inspir.* p.197-198

, *Expression of*
Adams — *New* p.84

, *Features of*
Safian — *Insults* p.77-83
Safian — *More* p.76-82

FACTORIES AND FACTORY WORKERS
Adams — *New* p.332
Guideposts — *Faith* p.318-322

FACTS
See also **Truth**
Braude — *Source* #581-582
Braude — *Speaker's* #725-728
Braude — *Stories* p.145
Dirksen — *Quot.* #397-398, 732, 968, 2002
Edwards — *Useful* p.183-184
Evans — *Unto* p.52, 114
Flesch — *Unusual* p.84
Forbes — *Thoughts* *See* index p.549
Fuller — *Epigrams* p.113
Grizer — *Wit* p.159-160
Harnsberger — *Mark* p.114-116, 202-203
Henry — *5000* p.83, 133-134
Hovey — *Treasury* p.171-172; #11, 27, 152, 422, 577, 860, 947-951, 1024, 1478, 1732
How To Live p.127
Humes — *Instant* p.38; #330-344
Johnson — *Bedside* p.249
Kennedy — *Reader's* #316-317
Kin — *Dictionary* p.87
Kohn — *Pathways* p.65-66
Liddle — *Thought I, II, III* p.19, 24, 127
Lockridge — *World's* #3543, 4604, 4618
Lytle — *Leaves* p.128
Montapert — *Distilled* p.145-146
Prochnow — *Public* #84, 116, 182, 200, 347, 448, 565, 979, 1476, 4089-4090
Prochnow — *Success.* #849, 948
Seldes — *Great* p.336-340
Speaker's Desk #76, 395, 695, 723, 896; p.58-59
Woods — *Religious* p.7, 309

, and faith
Kauffman — *For* p.120-122
, and inference
Hubbard — *Scrap* p.86
, Facing
Evans — *Faith* p.3-6, 114, 152, 226
Evans — *Thoughts I* p.81, 139, 188, 195, 205
Evans — *Thoughts II (Open Door)* p.12, 58
Evans — *Thoughts III (Open Road)* p.27, 35-38, 48-49, 60, 120, 197, 212
Flesch — *Unusual* p.84
Holmes — *Design* p.189-194
How To Live p.215
, False
Peterson — *Art* p.396
, Finding of
Woods — *Business.* p.77-78
, Interpretation of
Holmes — *Design* p.167-168, 177-178, 191-192
, Love of
Phillips — *Choice* p.49
, Personal
Kohn — *Pathways* p.66
, Scientific
Du Noüy — *Road* p.19-22, 25, 28-30
, versus truth
Curtis — *Golden* p.44

FACULTIES
See also **Senses**
Curtis — *Practical* p.113-116
Lytle — *Leaves* p.152

FACULTY. *See* **Professors; Teachers**

FAILINGS. *See* **Faults; Sin; Weakness**

FAILURE
See also **Defeat; Mistakes**
Alexander's Treasure. p.40
Blanton — *Faith* p.110-132
Braude — *Source* #583-594
Braude — *Speaker's* #61-62, 489-490
Braude — *Stories* p.145
Dirksen — *Quot.* #244, 345, 509, 892-894, 1682, 2003-2004
Edwards — *Useful* p.184, 728
Evans — *Faith* p.21, 129
Evans — *Quote* p.53-66
Evans — *Thoughts I* p.36, 117-118, 127-128
Evans — *Thoughts II (Open Door)* p.65, 73-74, 90, 148, 188-189, 198
Evans — *Thoughts III (Open Road)* p.15-21, 28, 31-32, 135, 171, 176-177, 200
Evans — *Thoughts IV* p.86, 199, 204
Evans — *Unto* p.33, 69, 116
Flesch — *Unusual* p.84
Forbes — *Thoughts* *See* index p.549
Fuller — *Epigrams* p.114
Garland — *Subject* p.103
Grizer — *Wit* p.160-162
Harnsberger — *Mark* p.116
Henry — *5000* p.83-84
Hill — *Think* p.136-142
Hovey — *Treasury* p.172; #15, 327, 350, 411, 460, 589, 611, 952-957, 1027, 1056, 1450, 1518, 1597
How To Live p.177-178, 314-318
Howell — *Better* p.67-68
Howell — *Lines* p.69-72

Hubbard — *Scrap* p.157
Kennedy — *Reader's* #318-320
Keys Happiness p.59, 240
Kin — *Dictionary* p.87
Kohn — *Adventures* p.97-99
Kohn — *Pathways* p.85-126
Liddle — *Thought I, II, III* p.100, 107, 168
Liddle — *Thought IV* p.20-22
Liddle — *Thought V* p.4, 9, 15, 19, 40-41
List — *Living* p.72-79
Lockridge — *World's* #3602, 3606
Lytle — *Leaves* p.16, 36, 53, 134
Maltz — *Creative* p.91-92, 100-102
Modern Eloquence (14) p.332
Montapert — *Distilled* p.146-147
Nichols — *New* p.43-44
Peale — *Courage* p.28
Peale — *Faith* p.109-134
Peale — *Guide* p.115-129
Price — *No* p.41-50
Prochnow — *Public* #428, 1897, 1941, 2280
Prochnow — *Success.* #1742-1745, 2364
Safian — *Insults* p.67-71
Safian — *More* p.67-71
Seldes — *Great* p.340
Sheen — *Content.* p.104-106, 149-151
Sheen — *Thoughts* p.30-31
Speaker's Desk #165, 327
Wallis — *Treasure* p.4
Watson — *Light* p.156-159
Woods — *Religious* p.309-310
Woods — *Wellsprings* p.57-68
Words Change p.26-29
, Art of
Peterson — *Twenty* p.22-23
, Confession of
Kahn — *Lessons* p.103-105
, Mechanism of
Maltz — *Creative* p.87-91

FAINTNESS
Prochnow — *Public* #2031
Speaker's Desk #1041

FAIRNESS
See also **Justice**
Book Proverbs p.142
Braude — *Source* #595
Forbes — *Thoughts* **p.56, 76, 111,** 229, 309, 453
Henry — *5000* p.84
How To Live p.70-71
Hubbard — *Scrap* p.107
Ideas p.146-147
Kin — *Dictionary* p.87-88
Welk — *Guide.* p.150-151

FAIRS
See also **Bazaars**
Harral — *Feature* p.150

FAIRY TALES
Botkin — *Anecdotes* p.241
Clark — *Windows* p.140
Goudge — *Comfort* p.345-352
Henry — *5000* p.84
Liddle — *Thought I, II, III* p.18
Peterson — *Art* p.233
Unlimited Power p.277-280

FAITH
See also **Belief; God; Jesus Christ; Religion;** etc.
Alexander's Treasure. p.92
Applegarth — *Heir.* p.117, 267, 288, 304-305
Bach — *Make* p.146-155, 182-194
Baillie — *Diary* #10
Bartlett — *Discovery* p.117-118, 127-157
Blanton — *Faith* p.204
Book Proverbs p.127
Braude — *Source* #596-602
Braude — *Speaker's* #491-492
Clark — *Windows* p.134
Curtis — *Daily* p.139-144
Curtis — *Human* p.150-156
Curtis — *Practical* p.109, 497, 511, 519
Detherage — *Sunrise* p.130, 167-172, 269
Dirksen — *Quot. See* index p.263
Droke — *Christian* p.176-182
Du Noüy — *Human* p.194-195, 256
Edwards — *Useful* p.184-187, 728
Emmons — *Mature* p.32, 39, 47, 76, 84-86, 131-149
Esteve — *Experience* p.157-159
Evans — *Faith* p.10, 20-22, 160, 187, 198, 202, 209-226
Evans — *Quote* p.125-139
Evans — *This* p.78-80
Evans — *Thoughts I* p.13-14, 44-45, 48, 78, 81, 107-110, 114, 120, 122, 128, 131, 140, 201, 205-206, 217
Evans — *Thoughts III (Open Road) See* index no p.
Evans — *Thoughts IV* p.83-84, 90, 167-169, 183-188
Evans — *Unto* p.16-17, 33, 38, 42-44, 56, 72, 87, 97, 113-114, 116, 119, 121
Felleman — *Poems* p.321-346
Flesch — *Unusual* p.84-85
Flint — *Graham* p.9, 14, 50
Forbes — *Thoughts See* index p.549

Fox — *Make* p.85, 204, 227
Fuller — *Epigrams* p.114-115
Garland — *Subject* p.103
Giniger — *Compact* p.91-148
Grizer — *Wit* p.163
Halverson — *Perspective* p.4, 38, 50, 55, 65, 101
Harnsberger — *Mark* p.116
Henry — *5000* p.84-85
Hobe — *Tapestries* p.45-55
Holmes — *I've* p.90-96
Hovey — *Treasury* p.172-177; *See also* index p.296
How To Live p.544-550, 568-572
Howell — *Better* p.69-72
Howell — *Lines* p.51-55
Hubbard — *Scrap* p.54, 61
Hulme — *Living* p.99-102
Humes — *Instant* p.46; #345-351
Hunter — *Gems* p.29-32
Irion — *Yes* p.83, 88-90
Johnson — *Bedside* p.84-85, 134, 167-170, 172-183, 209, 212-213, 322-333
Kahn — *Lessons* p.13-24
Keller — *Open* p.20-21, 38, 85-86, 107-108
Kennedy — *Fresh* p.191-193
Kennedy — *Reader's* #321-330
Keys Happiness p.163-168, 227-231, 241-243, 377-380, 556-575
Kin — *Dictionary* p.88
Knight's Illus. p.107-110
Knight's Treas. p.113-119
Kohn — *Adventures* p.57-78, 145-148
Kohn — *Best* p.138-140
Kohn — *Thoughts* p.22-27
Liddle — *Thought I, II, III See* index p.196
Liddle — *Thought IV* p.5, 7, 12, 25-26, 40-41
Liddle — *Thought V* p.12, 15, 19, 22
Lockridge — *World's* #1703, 1811, 2926, 2974, 4016, 4428, 4734, 4914, 5182, 5660
Lytle — *Leaves* p.5, 49, 57, 64, 83, 108, 112, 154-155, 180, 183
McCracken — *What* p.77-82
Manchee — *Secret* p.88-90
Mandel — *Stories* p.89-93
Mandelbaum — *Choose* p.16
Miller — *Harvest* p.73-80
Modern Eloquence (14) p.333-334
Montapert — *Distilled* p.147-148
More Words p.59, 61
Morris — *1000 See* index p.428-429
New Joy p.15
New Topical p.83-84
Nichols — *New* p.119-120, 167-168
Nichols — *Third* p.203-205
Nizer — *Thinking* p.40
Patterns For Living p.658-663
Peale — *Courage* p.61-78
Peale — *Faith* p.1-280
Peale — *Guideposts* p.111-129, 209-227
Petty — *Promises* p.67-78
Petty — *Wings* p.64-73
Phillips — *Choice* p.33, 36, 140, 164, 216
Porter — *Halo* p.3-13
Prochnow — *Public* #811, 1216, 1321, 2716, 2720, 2738-2739, 2742, 3042-3051
Prochnow — *Speaker's* p.120
Prochnow — *Success.* #764, 774, 1290, 1394, 1746-1748
Seldes — *Great* p.340-343
Sheban — *Content.* p.129-132
Sherman — *Your* p.68-73
Speaker's Desk p.59-61; #610
Strait — *Speaker's* p.62-68
Tanksley — *Friend* p.13, 26, 69
Voss — *Quotations* p.83-86
Wallis — *Treasure* p.48, 65, 69, 91-96, 113, 138, 173, 184, 211, 232, 234
Wallis — *Words* p.20, 43, 49, 55, 57, 68-72, 106, 117, 217
Watson — *Light* p.31-71
Webb — *Edge* p.59-63
White — *Job* p.101, 144, 146-147, 153, 156
White — *Life* p.208-220
Woods — *Inspir.* p.417-457
Woods — *Religious* p.310-316
Woods — *Wellsprings* p.73-74
Words Change p.31-33, 123-128
Words — *Inspir.* p.94, 179-180
Zobell — *Speaker's* p.50-52

, Active
Keller — *Open* p.117-118
, Affirmations of
Suter — *Prayers* #425-430
, Ages of
Adams — *New* p.19
, and daily life
Kauffman — *For* p.79-80
, and everyday work
Kauffman — *For* p.93-94
, and freedom
Kauffman — *For* p.99-100
, and patriotism
Kauffman — *For* p.154-155
, and prayer
Woods — *Religious* p.320
, and reason
Woods — *Religious* p.321-322
, Comfort of
Goudge — *Comfort* p.155-231

, *Definitions of*
Woods — *Religious* p.316-320
, *Directing youth in*
Guideposts — *Faith* p.173-209
, *for new life*
Guideposts — *Faith* p.75-125, 355-399, 449-496
, *Great dramas of*
Guideposts — *Faith* p.265-309
, *Healing power of*
Guideposts — *Faith* p.211-263
, *in repentance*
McDonagh — *Invit.* p.86-87
, *in space age*
Guideposts — *Faith* p.28
, *Inner struggle for*
Guideposts — *Faith* p.27-73
, *Living our*
Carruthers — *Sparks* p.137-166
, *of children*
Peale — *Guideposts* p.288-291
, *Origin of*
Woods — *Religious* p.320
, *Parents'*
Guideposts — *Faith* p.55-58
, *Power of*
Blanton — *Faith* p.17-38
Kennedy — *Fresh* p.69-70
, *Profession of*
Baillie — *Diary* #158
, *Quiet*
Guideposts — *Faith* p.311-353
, *to change world*
Guideposts — *Faith* p.401-447
, *to strengthen home*
Guideposts — *Faith* p.127-171
, *toward religion*
Hill — *Think* p.50-71
, *Triumphant*
Maxwell — *Courage* p.133-141
, *versus fear*
Holman — *Psych.* p.126-136

FAITHFULNESS. *See* **Loyalty**

FALL. *See* **Autumn**

"FALL, THE"
See also **Adam and Eve**
Woods — *Religious* p.322-323

"FALLEN ANGELS"
Safian — *Insults* p.74-76
Safian — *More* p.72-75

FALLIBILITY
Kin — *Dictionary* p.88

FALLING
Kin — *Dictionary* p.88
Prochnow — *Public* #2579, 2710

"FALLOUT SHELTERS"
Dirksen — *Quot.* #43

FALSEHOOD
See also **Dishonesty; Liars; Tall tales**
Book Proverbs p.53
Braude — *Source* #1004-1005
Dirksen — *Quot.* #159, 309, 400-401, 567, 731, 1317, 1726
Edwards — *Useful* p.187-188, 361-363
Esteve — *Experience* p.25-27
Evans — *Thoughts II (Open Door)* p.48-49
Evans — *Thoughts III (Open Road)* p.77
Evans — *Unto* p.45, 79
Flesch — *Unusual* p.158-159
Flint — *Graham* p.87-88
Forbes — *Thoughts* p.44, 91, 186, 233, 341, 371, 375, 393, 418, 438, 461, 467, 503
Fuller — *Epigrams* p.186-187
Grizer — *Wit* p.277-278
Harnsberger — *Mark* p.235-238
Henry — *5000* p.85, 165-166
Johnson — *Bedside* p.185, 255
Kin — *Dictionary* p.147-148, 154
Liddle — *Thought I, II, III* p.8, 12, 58, 86, 115, 126, 137, 166, 171
Liddle — *Thought IV* p.6, 8, 33, 44, 46
Liddle — *Thought V* p.9, 21, 41
Lockridge — *World's* #293, 1841, 2919, 5103; *See* index p.579
Lytle — *Leaves* p.176
Mandel — *Stories* p.93-94
Menninger — *Blue.* p.123-125
Myers — *Thunder* p.143-144
New Topical p.157
Prochnow — *Public* #865, 883, 2176, 2226, 2468, 3052-3057
Prochnow — *Speaker's* p.121
Prochnow — *Success.* #402, 615, 659, 2005, 2415
Seldes — *Great* p.605-609
Speaker's Desk #16, 57, 205, 457, 802, 1007, 1073
Woods — *Religious* p.324, 731
, *and statistics*
Ideas p.239-241

FAME
See also **Celebrities; Glory; Heroes and heroism; Honor; Reputation**
Applegarth — *Heir.* p.105

Book Proverbs p.114
Braude — *Source* #603-606
Braude — *Speaker's* #493-498
Braude — *Stories* p.146
Dirksen — *Quot.* #124, 154, 182, 247, 320, 805, 896, 2006-2008, 2053, 2313, 2339
Edwards — *Useful* p.188-190, 728
Flesch — *Unusual* p.86, 191
Fogg — *1000* #121, 628, 886
Forbes — *Thoughts* p.115, 127, 222, 308, 333, 345, 415, 452, 464
Fuller — *Epigrams* p.115-116
Garland — *Subject* p.104
Grizer — *Wit* p.164
Harnsberger — *Mark* p.116-117
Harral — *Feature* p.150
Henry — *5000* p.85-86
Johnson — *Bedside* p.91, 198, 248, 251
Kennedy — *Reader's* #231-232
Kin — *Dictionary* p.89, 177
Kohn — *Touch* p.168-169
Krishnamurti — *Think* p.46-47, 105-106
Liddle — *Thought I, II, III* p.8, 14, 26, 157, 162
Lindeman — *Emerson* p.147-148, 206
Lockridge — *World's* #1624, 2030, 3473, 3478, 3480, 3669, 4178, 5525
Lytle — *Leaves* p.25
Modern Eloquence (14) p.335
Montapert — *Distilled* p.148-149
Nichols — *Third* p.93-94, 187-188
Prochnow — *Public* #738, 1494, 2355, 3058-3062, 4091-4093
Prochnow — *Speaker's* p.122-123
Prochnow — *Success.* #1749-1751
Seldes — *Great* p.345-346
Sheban — *Wisdom* no p.
Speaker's Desk p.61-63; #127, 290
Voss — *Quotations* p.86-87
Woods — *Religious* p.324-325
Woods — *Wellsprings* p.12, 21-22
Words — *Inspir.* p.68

FAMILIARITY

See also **Acquaintance; Companionship; Friends and friendship; Knowledge**
Adams — *New* p.125
Dirksen — *Quot.* #754
Edwards — *Useful* p.190-191
Flesch — *Unusual* p.302
Fuller — *Thesaurus* #651-656
Harnsberger — *Mark* p.117
Henry — *5000* p.86
Hobe — *Tapestries* p.33
Kin — *Dictionary* p.89
Lockridge — *World's* #768, 2054
Peterson — *Art* p.331
Speaker's Desk #355, 809, 936

FAMILY

See also **Children; Home; Marriage; Parents and parenthood;** etc.
Applegarth — *Heir.* p.53, 133
Baillie — *Diary* #174
Barrows — *1000 See* index p.440
Braude — *Source* #607-610
Braude — *Stories* p.146-147
Curtis — *Daily* p.35-42
Daly — *Personality* p.104-110
Day — *Meditations* p.32-39
Droke — *Christian* p.182-185
Edwards — *Useful* p.140, 191
Evans — *Faith* p.3, 5, 14, 33-34, 38, 47-64, 73-76, 82, 184, 221-222
Evans — *Quote* p.9-28
Evans — *Thoughts I* p.18, 21-27, 56, 72, 87-89, 103-104, 118-119, 123-124, 139, 144, 183-186, 217-218, 220
Evans — *Thoughts II (Open Door)* p.21, 36, 39, 87-88, 95, 123, 169, 186-187
Evans — *Thoughts III (Open Road) See* index
Evans — *Thoughts IV* p.129, 203-204
Evans — *Unto* p.108, 139, 146-147
Felleman — *Poems* p.135-150
Flesch — *Unusual* p.86
Flint — *Graham* p.51
Forbes — *Thoughts* p.220, 242, 256, 265, 273, 291, 307, 374, 520
Fridy — *Meditat.* p.107
Fuller — *Epigrams* p.116-117
Fuller — *Thesaurus* p.162-171
Garland — *Subject* p.104-105
Guideposts — *Faith* p.143-146
Harral — *Feature* p.150-151
Henry — *5000* p.86
Hobe — *Tapestries* p.14, 166-171
Hovey — *Treasury* p.178-179; *See also* index p.296, 304
How To Live p.104-138
Johnson — *Bedside* p.119-120, 294-295, 303, 307
Kahn — *Lessons* p.167-198
Kin — *Dictionary* p.89
Kopplin — *Something* p.103-107
Liddle — *Thought I, II, III* p.17, 24, 28, 47, 86, 149, 151, 177
Liddle — *Thought IV* p.4, 7, 12, 21
Liddle — *Thought V* p.25
Lindbergh — *Unicorn* p.79-81

Lockridge — *World's* #3336, 3672, 4905, 5487
Mandel — *Stories* p.94
Mandelbaum — *Choose* p.59-63
Maurois — *Art* p.76-106
Menninger — *Blue.* p.59-60, 144, 193
Montapert — *Distilled* p.149
More Words p.63-64
Morris — *1000 See* index p.430
New Topical p.85-86
Peale — *Sin* p.130-156
Peterson — *Art* p.361
Prochnow — *Public* #648, 1006, 1042, 1048, 1526, 2634, 3063-3069, 4358
Prochnow — *Success.* #660, 1309, 1337, 1373, 1752
Reader's — *Getting* p.11-14
Schermerhorn — *1500* p.149
Seldes — *Great* p.346
Simpson — *Contemp.* p.237-248
Speaker's Desk #617
Strait — *Speaker's* p.69-71
Voss — *Quotations* p.87-89
Wallis — *Treasure* p.132, 134
Wallis — *Words* p.19, 109, 111-112, 114
Watson — *Light* p.239-258
Wheelis — *Moralist* p.102, 129
White — *Job* p.53-59
White — *Life* p.6-10
Woods — *Content.* p.139, 143, 146-147, 149, 155, 162
Woods — *Religious* p.325-326
Zobell — *Speaker's* p.53-54

, Acuteness in
Manchee — *Secret* p.232-237
, Blessing for trials in
Holmes — *I've* p.82
, Confusion in
Holmes — *I've* p.35-36
, Humor in
Copeland — *10,000* p.331-334
, Large
Peale — *Guideposts* p.295-298
, Meals of
Peterson — *Art* p.361
, Morale in
White — *Life* p.42-48
, Neglect of
Halverson — *Perspective* p.29
, Priorities of
Unlimited Power p.177-179
, Relationships in
How To Live p.123-127
Phillips — *Choice* p.45

FAMINE. *See* **Hunger**

FANATICISM
See also **Cults; Intolerance;** etc.
Braude — *Source* #611-612
Braude — *Stories* p.147
Dirksen — *Quot.* #324
Du Noüy — *Road* p.213-214
Edwards — *Useful* p.191-192, 728
Flesch — *Unusual* p.86-87
Grizer — *Wit* p.164
Henry — *5000* p.86
Hovey — *Treasury* p.179; #1010-1013
Kennedy — *Reader's* #333-334
Liddle — *Thought I, II, III* p.85, 184
Liddle — *Thought IV* p.45
Liddle — *Thought V* p.9
Lockridge — *World's* #1632, 3619, 3631, 3648, 5549
Prochnow — *Success.* #1753
Seldes — *Great* p.346-347
Woods — *Business.* p.78
Woods — *Religious* p.326

FANCY. *See* **Imagination**

FANS
Hadfield — *Delights* p.156

FANTASY. *See* **Dreams and dreaming; Fairy tales; Imagination**

FAR EAST. *See* **Orient**

FAREWELLS
See also **Death; Words, Dying**
Adams — *New* p.57
Alexander's Treasure. p.145
Auden — *Certain* p.106-107
Braude — *Source* #613-614, 1236
Braude — *Stories* p.98
Edwards — *Useful* p.192, 446-447
Flesch — *Unusual* p.148
Henry — *5000* p.87, 200
Humes — *Instant* #352, 353
Keller — *Open* p.125
Keys Happiness p.109-110
Kin — *Dictionary* p.108
Liddle — *Thought I, II, III* p.143
Lindeman — *Emerson* p.137-138
Lockridge — *World's* #4252
Mandel — *Stories* p.95
Menninger — *Blue.* p.179, 185, 204
Nichols — *Third* p.47-48
Prochnow — *Success.* #737, 812
Reader's — *Getting* p.28-30
Weisfeld — *Pulpit* p.36

FARMERS' ALMANACS. *See* **Almanacs**

FARMERS AND FARMING
See also **Agriculture; Country life**
Asimov — *Treasury* #440-443, 445, 538, 570, 590, 592
Botkin — *Anecdotes* See index p.198, 311
Botkin — *Treasury* p.169, 288-289, 597-604, 874-875
Braude — *Speaker's* #499-505
Cerf — *Laugh* p.155-159
Dirksen — *Quot.* #34, 1683
Fuller — *Epigrams* p.339
Fuller — *Thesaurus* #2311-2313
Hadfield — *Delights* p.210
Hobe — *Tapestries* p.114
Kin — *Dictionary* p.90
Kohn — *Touch* p.95-97, 173-176
Prochnow — *Public* #11, 25, 30, 54, 232, 363, 426, 871, 1107
Prochnow — *Success.* #428, 543, 909, 1754-1756
Sagendorph — *Old* p.255-256
Schermerhorn — *1500* p.150-152
Speaker's Desk See index p.299
Wallis — *Words* p.229, 235
Weisfeld — *Pulpit* p.12, 14, 16-17, 80-81, 83, 93, 129

, Colonial
Sagendorph — *Old* p.248-250

FASCINATION. *See* **Charm; Personality**

FASCISM
Curtis — *Practical* p.318, 354-355
Seldes — *Great* p.347-354

FASHION
See also **Appearance; Clothes; Customs; Vanity**
Braude — *Speaker's* #506-507
Edwards — *Useful* p.192-193
Evans — *Quote* p.215-222
Evans — *Thoughts IV* p.133
Flesch — *Unusual* p.87
Grizer — *Wit* p.165-166
Harnsberger — *Mark* p.119-120
Henry — *5000* p.87
Liddle — *Thought I, II, III* p.37, 173
Lockridge — *World's* #959, 1148, 1743, 2400, 3484, 4519
New Joy p.140
Prochnow — *Public* #527, 2708, 3072
Prochnow — *Speaker's* p.127
Prochnow — *Success.* #1757-1758
Simpson — *Contemp.* p.451-455

FASTIDIOUSNESS
See also **Cleanliness; Delicacy; Taste**
Edwards — *Useful* p.193
Lockridge — *World's* #2385

FASTING
Day — *Meditations* p.44
Flesch — *Unusual* p.87
New Topical p.86-87
Phillips — *Choice* p.271
Woods — *Religious* p.326-327

FAT. *See* **Overweight**

FATALISM
Flesch — *Unusual* p.87
Flint — *Graham* p.52
Kahn — *Lessons* p.52-53
Prochnow — *Public* #1690
Woods — *Religious* p.327

FATE
See also **Destiny; Fortune; Luck**
Braude — *Source* #617-618
Braude — *Stories* p.147
Curtis — *Practical* p.215-216
Edwards — *Useful* p.193-194
Flesch — *Unusual* p.87
Forbes — *Thoughts* p.65, 218, 340, 367, 392, 429, 438, 493
Fox — *Make* p.56-57
Fuller — *Epigrams* p.117-118
Grizer — *Wit* p.166
Henry — *5000* p.87-88
Hobe — *Tapestries* p.116
Hubbard — *Scrap* p.24, 76, 168
Kin — *Dictionary* p.90-91
Lockridge — *World's* #1291
Lytle — *Leaves* p.10
Seldes — *Great* p.384
Sheban — *Wisdom* no p.
Wallis — *Treasure* p.162.
Woods — *Religious* p.328

, and freedom
Adams — *New* p.184

, Coming of
Adams — *New* p.261

, Common
Dirksen — *Quot.* #2324

FATHER, HEAVENLY. *See* **God**

FATHERLESS
New Topical p.87

FATHERS
Applegarth — *Heir.* p.52, 54
Botkin — *Anecdotes* p.246, 249
Braude — *Source* #619-622
Braude — *Speaker's* #508-517
Dirksen — *Quot.* #137, 251, 811, 1272-1275, 1682, 1703, 2009, 2332
Evans — *Faith* p.61-64, 68
Evans — *Quote* p.9-28

Evans — *This* p.118-119
Evans — *Thoughts I* p.17, 44, 142
Evans — *Thoughts II (Open Door)* p.94-95, 114
Evans — *Thoughts III (Open Road)* p.20-21, 31, 157, 186, 209
Evans — *Thoughts IV* p.35, 40, 156-157
Evans — *Unto* p.109
Flesch — *Unusual* p.87-88
Flint — *Graham* p.52
Forbes — *Thoughts* p.183, 193, 217, 224, 311, 357, 403, 438, 474
Fuller — *Epigrams* p.118
Fuller — *Thesaurus* #986-990
Fun Fare p.180-182
Garland — *Subject* p.106
Goudge — *Comfort* p.147
Grizer — *Wit* p.167
Guideposts — *Faith* p.55-58, 95-99, 413-415
Harnsberger — *Mark* p.120-121
Harral — *Feature* p.153-154
Henry — *5000* p.88
Hobe — *Tapestries* p.85, 166-167, 170, 188
Hovey — *Treasury* p.179-180; *See also* index p.296
Kahn — *Lessons* p.194-197
Keys Happiness p.89, 136, 195, 208
Kin — *Dictionary* p.91, 186
Knight's Illus. p.113-115
Knight's Treas. p.123-126
Liddle — *Thought IV* p.23, 33
Lockridge — *World's* #713, 2587, 3841, 3867, 4097, 4717
Lytle — *Leaves* p.21, 88
Manchee — *Secret* p.234
Mandel — *Stories* p.95
Patterns For Living p.107-114, 165-169, 173-175
Peterson — *Art* p.98
Prochnow — *Public See* index p.495
Prochnow — *Speaker's* p.127-128
Prochnow — *Success.* #470, 921, 975, 1007, 1010, 1038, 1093, 1227, 1368, 1434, 1759-1762
Reader's — *Getting* p.55-56
Schermerhorn — *1500* p.152-155
Seaburg — *Great* p.208, 218, 228, 239, 262, 291, 323, 345, 353, 383
Seldes — *Great* p.354-355
Speaker's Desk #23, 69, 118, 191, 201, 275, 278, 301, 303, 313, 670, 848, 947, 1026, 1039, 1117
Wallis — *Treasure* p.130, 152
Wallis — *Words* p.106, 110-111, 113
Woods — *Religious* p.328
, Ten commandments for
Braude — *Source* #622

FATHER'S DAY
Braude — *Source* p.622
Hovey — *Treasury See* index p.304

FATHERS-IN-LAW
Asimov — *Treasury* #325

FATIGUE
Albert — *Stop* p.3-17; *See* index p.210
Alexander's Treasure. p.181
Auden — *Certain* p.166-167
Forbes — *Thoughts* p.250, 333, 452
Garland — *Subject* p.106
Holmes — *I've* p.65
How To Live p.73-77
Huxley — *You See* index p.285
Keys Happiness p.158-162
Montapert — *Distilled* p.150
Peale — *Stay* p.121-136
Prochnow — *Public* #1066
Prochnow — *Success.* #1039
Unlimited Power p.179

FAULTFINDING. *See* **Criticism**

FAULTS
See also **Defects**
Alexander's Treasure. p.253
Baillie — *Diary* #60, 108
Braude — *Stories* p.147-148
Dirksen — *Quot.* #313, 897-898 1919, 2010, 2034, 2249
Edwards — *Useful* p.194-195
Evans — *Quote* p.215-222
Evans — *This* p.66
Evans — *Thoughts I* p.93-94, 98-101, 162-163
Evans — *Thoughts II (Open Door)* p.25-26, 154, 169, 198
Evans — *Thoughts III (Open Road)* p.25, 65-66, 109, 167
Evans — *Thoughts IV* p.84, 207
Evans — *Unto* p.93
Flesch — *Unusual* p.88-89
Forbes — *Thoughts See* index p.549
Garland — *Subject* p.106-107
Grizer — *Wit* p.167-168
Harnsberger — *Mark* p.121
Henry — *5000* p.88-89
Hobe — *Tapestries* p.119
Holmes — *I've* p.9
Johnson — *Bedside* p.298

Liddle — *Thought I, II, III* p.40, 51, 57, 66, 73, 80, 82, 136, 145, 151, 153, 188
Liddle — *Thought IV* p.11, 24, 30, 40
Lockridge — *World's See* index p.575
Lytle — *Leaves* p.5, 73, 76
Mandel — *Stories* p.95
Montapert — *Distilled* p.150-151
Prochnow — *Public* #1357, 1512, 1695, 3073-3076, 4348
Prochnow — *Speaker's* p.128
Prochnow — *Success.* #386, 1763
Woods — *Religious* p.328-329
, Confessing
Dirksen — *Quot.* #85
, Daily
Baillie — *Diary* #313
, of others
Baillie — *Diary* #181
Kahn — *Lessons* p.108-109
Kennedy — *Fresh* p.112-114
, Sharing of
How To Live p.67

FAUST
Lockridge — *World's* #5635

FAVORITISM
Lockridge — *World's* #156, 2582
Prochnow — *Public* #1013

FAVORS
Flesch — *Unusual* p.89
Kin — *Dictionary* p.92
Lockridge — *World's* #3032, 3308, 3539, 4790
Montapert — *Distilled* p.151
Prochnow — *Public* #2560

FEAR
See also **Anxiety; Cowardice; Death, Fear of; Despair; Panic; Persecution; Superstition**
Adams — *New* p.89
Albert — *Stop* p.7-8, 58-59, 61, 115, 118, 156-157, 168
Alexander's Treasure. p.193, 200
Baillie — *Diary* #127
Bartlett — *Discovery* p.135-136
Blanton — *Faith* p.64-86
Book Proverbs p.109
Braude — *Source* #625-631
Braude — *Stories* p.148
Clark — *Windows* p.106
Curtis — *Daily* p.128
Curtis — *Human* p.42, 93, 154, 160
Curtis — *Practical* p.130-132, 541
Day — *Meditations* p.38-39
Detherage — *Sunrise* p.127-129
Dirksen — *Quot.* #43, 402, 587, 744, 2011-2012, 2294
Edwards — *Useful* p.195-196, 728
Emmons — *Mature* p.132
Evans — *Faith* p.5, 10, 67-68, 113-114
Evans — *Quote* p.153-162
Evans — *This* p.47-48
Evans — *Thoughts I* p.48, 55, 81, 130-134, 156, 195-196, 208
Evans — *Thoughts II (Open Door)* p.76, 149-150, 208
Evans — *Thoughts III (Open Road)* p.38, 191
Evans — *Thoughts IV* p.106, 169
Evans — *Unto* p.21, 36-40, 57, 97, 113, 118, 124
Flesch — *Unusual* p.7, 89, 250
Forbes — *Thoughts See* index p.84, 370, 549
Fox — *Make* p.3-4, 37, 58
Fuller — *Epigrams* p.118-119
Garland — *Subject* p.107
Grizer — *Wit* p.168-169
Guideposts — *Faith* p.72-73, 107-108
Harnsberger — *Mark* p.121-122, 136-137
Henry — *5000* p.89
Holmes — *Design* p.19-20, 34, 36-37, 50, 69, 106-107, 121, 229-230
Hovey — *Treasury* p.180-182; *See also* index p.296
Hubbard — *Scrap* p.24, 30, 59, 168
Huxley — *You See* index p.285
Johnson — *Bedside* p.31, 41, 82-83, 107, 195
Kennedy — *Fresh* p.88, 146-155
Kennedy — *Reader's* #335
Keys Happiness p.192-195, 213-217, 356-358
Kin — *Dictionary* p.8, 92
Knight's Illus. p.115
Krishnamurti — *Urgency* p.12-17
Liddle — *Thought I, II, III* p.11, 21, 39, 41, 66-67, 70, 73, 83, 96, 115, 118-119, 124-135, 142, 152, 155, 181, 186
Liddle — *Thought IV* p.10
Liebman — *Peace* p.81-104
Lockridge — *World's* p.1268, 1414, 1428, 1705, 1792, 2033-2034, 3723, 5652, 5851, 5865
Lytle — *Leaves* p.53, 55
Maltz — *Creative* p.125
Manchee — *Secret* p.73-97
Mandel — *Stories* p.95-97
Modern Eloquence (14) p.336
Montapert — *Distilled* p.152-153

Nichols — *Third* p.203-204
Peale — *Courage* p.94-112
Peale — *Faith* p.55-79
Peale — *Guide* p.130-146
Peale — *Guideposts* p.231-253
Prochnow — *Public* #140, 1032, 1393, 2055, 2483, 3077-3081, 4095-4098, 4326, 4406
Prochnow — *Speaker's* p.129
Prochnow — *Success.* #572
Reader's — *Getting* p.85-88
Seldes — *Great* p.355-360
Speaker's Desk p.63-65; *See* index p.299
Strait — *Speaker's* p.78
Unlimited Power p.43-47
Voss — *Quotations* p.89-91
Wallis — *Treasure* p.69, 94, 137, 146, 175, 225, 231
Woods — *Religious* p.329-332, 884

, and ethics
Sheen — *Way* p.136-138

, Battle
Peale — *Guideposts* p.236-238

, Conquest of
Clark — *Windows* p.120
Kohn — *Touch* p.185
Peale — *Courage* p.108-110
Peterson — *Twenty* p.12-13
Reader's — *20th* p.49-50
Sherman — *Your* p.74-89
Watson — *Light* p.73-131

, Death from
Peale — *Courage* p.105-108

, Freedom from
Price — *Wider* p.179-189

, Ghosts of
Hill — *Think* p.256-293

, in animals
Adams — *New* p.311

, in modern life
Adams — *New* p.330

, of freedom
Adams — *New* p.257

, of words
Adams — *New* p.255

, unholy
New Topical p.88

, versus faith
Holman — *Psych.* p.126-136

"FEARSOME CRITTERS"
See also **Animals, Mythical; Dragons; Snakes, Mythical;** etc.
Botkin — *Treasury* p.360, 638-650

FEASTS
See also **Dinners; Passover; Pentecost;** etc.
Edwards — *Useful* p.196
Garland — *Subject* p.107
Kin — *Dictionary* p.92

, Anniversary
New Topical p.90-91

, of Dedication
New Topical p.88

, of Jubilee
New Topical p.88

, of New Moon
New Topical p.88-89

, of Purim, or Lots
New Topical p.89

, of Sabbatical Years
New Topical p.89

, of Tabernacles
New Topical p.89-90

, of Trumpets
New Topical p.90

FEATHERS
Kin — *Dictionary* p.92

FEDERAL AGENCIES. *See* **Bureaucracy**

FEDERAL POWER. *See* **Government**

FEELINGS. *See* **Emotion; Heart; Sensibility; Sentiment**

FEET
Applegarth — *Heir.* p.166
Harral — *Feature* p.154
Kin — *Dictionary* p.93
Lytle — *Leaves* p.125
New Topical p.91
Prochnow — *Success.* #1071

FELLOWSHIP
See also **Brotherhood**
Adams — *New* p.393
Braude — *Speaker's* #63-76
Copeland — *10,000* p.994-996
Emmons — *Mature* p.22, 24
Flint — *Graham* p.53
Forbes — *Thoughts* p.203, 332, 500
Garland — *Subject* p.107-108
Hovey — *Treasury* #482, 497-498, 506, 600, 796, 813, 815, 1055, 1222, 1255, 1381, 1444, 1716, 1776
Hubbard — *Scrap* p.37
Kin — *Dictionary* p.93
Knight's Illus. p.116-117
Knight's Treas. p.126-127
Kohn — *Best* p.28-31
Lytle — *Leaves* p.122
More Words p.64-65
Nichols — *New* p.138-139
Phillips — *Choice* p.154, 213, 295, 298-299, 306, 352

Sheen — *Way* p.155-160
Voss — *Quotations* p.91-92
Wallis — *Words* p.29, 73-76
Woods — *Religious* p.332-334

FEMININITY. *See* **Women**

FENCES
Botkin — *Treasury* p.184, 625
Harral — *Feature* p.154
Kin — *Dictionary* p.93
Wallis — *Treasure* p.102, 220
Webb — *Edge* p.75

FENDERS
Prochnow — *Public* #189, 1510
Prochnow — *Success.* #476, 1057

FENS
Auden — *Certain* p.214-216

FEROCITY. *See* **Cruelty**

FERRYMEN
Botkin — *Anecdotes* p.192

FERTILITY
Sheban — *Wisdom* no p.

FERTILIZATION
Lytle — *Leaves* p.76

FERVOR. *See* **Enthusiasm**

FESTIVALS
Evans — *Unto* p.11
Prochnow — *Public* #986
, English
New Joy p.181

FETISHISM
Du Noüy — *Human* p.xii, 169-171, 179
Seldes — *Great* p.360

FEUDALISM
Seldes — *Great* p.360

FEUDS
Botkin — *Treasury* p.358, 891
Fogg — *1000* #246, 761, 898, 960, 1043, 1070, 1090

FEVER
Kin — *Dictionary* p.93

FICKLENESS
See also **Inconsistency; Indecision**
Edwards — *Useful* p.197,283
How To Live p.302
Kin — *Dictionary* p.93

Lockridge — *World's* #8, 188, 963, 1536, 5062

FICTION
Edwards — *Useful* p.197-198, 425-427
Flesch — *Unusual* p.191-192
Harnsberger — *Mark* p.333
, in logic and science
Curtis — *Practical* p.23-26

FIDDLERS. *See* **Violinists and violins**

FIDELITY. *See* **Constancy; Devotion; Faith; Loyalty; Trust**

FIELDS
Harral — *Feature* p.154
Hobe — *Tapestries* p.96
Lytle — *Leaves* p.110
Peale — *Courage* p.83

FIFTH AMENDMENT
Seldes — *Great* p.360

FIFTY (age)
Dirksen — *Quot.* #899
Flesch — *Unusual* p.90
How To Live p.507-509
Reader's — *20th* p.33-35

FIGHTING. *See* **Quarrels**

FIGS AND FIG TREES
Kin — *Dictionary* p.94
New Topical p.91-92

FIGURES, BODILY
Huxley — *You See* index p.285
Prochnow — *Public* #949
Safian — *Insults* p.84-90
Safian — *More* p.83-90

FIGURES, MATHEMATICAL
See also **Mathematics**
Kin — *Dictionary* p.94
Speaker's Desk #87, 652, 1091, 1099

FILIBUSTERS
Dirksen — *Quot.* #66

FINALISM
See also **Telefinalism**
Du Noüy — *Human* p.43-44, 52, 87, 217, 246-247
Du Noüy — *Road* p.146, 157, 179-193
Flint — *Graham* p.48
Peterson — *Art* p.160
Prochnow — *Success.* #926

FINANCE
See also **Money; Wealth**
Harral — *Feature* p.155

Lockridge — *World's* #716
Lytle — *Leaves* p.172
Sagendorph — *Old* p.199-206
, *and wealth*
Fuller — *Thesaurus* p.379-392
, *Goals of*
Albert — *Stop* p.182-183
, *Personal*
Keys Happiness p.73-75

FINCHES, PURPLE
Hobe — *Tapestries* p.26

FINDING. *See* **Discovery**

FINE ARTS
See also **Art and artists;** various subjects of fine arts
Adams — *New* p.158
Copeland — *World's See* index p.739
Harral — *Feature* p.155

FINGER BOWLS
Asimov — *Treasury* #344

FINGERPRINTS
Curtis — *Practical* p.217-218
Prochnow — *Public* #1345

FINGERS
Prochnow — *Public* #2077

FINISH. *See* **Ends and endings**

FINK, MIKE
Botkin — *Treasury* p.3, 6-7, 9, 30-50, 68, 597

FIRE
Applegarth — *Heir.* p.261
Asimov — *Treasury* #316
Evans — *This* p.140-141
Flesch — *Unusual* p.90
Forbes — *Thoughts* p.142, 171, 418, 455, 465, 474, 500
Fuller — *Epigrams* p.121
Harnsberger — *Mark* p.122-125
Henry — *5000* p.89-90
Kin — *Dictionary* p.94-95
Kohn — *Thoughts* p.111-112
Lytle — *Leaves* p.26, 185
New Topical p.92-93
Prochnow — *Public* #41, 477, 809, 1586, 2700
Prochnow — *Speaker's* p.129
Schermerhorn — *1500* p.156-157
Unlimited Power p.33-37
, *Fighting*
Asimov — *Treasury* #159
Harral — *Feature* p.155-157
Prochnow — *Speaker's* p.129-130
, *Forest*
Harral — *Feature* p.164
, *Open*
Peterson — *Art* p.201
, *Prevention of*
Harral — *Feature* p.157

FIRE STATIONS
Harral — *Feature* p.157

FIREFLIES
Kin — *Dictionary* p.94

FIREPLACES
Hobe — *Tapestries* p.33
Harral — *Feature* p.157
Lytle — *Leaves* p.7

FIRMAMENT. *See* **Sky**

FIRMNESS. *See* **Constancy; Decision; Purpose; Resolution**

FIRST
Clark — *Windows* p.138
Flesch — *Unusual* p.90
Grizer — *Wit* p.169-170
Kin — *Dictionary* p.95
Lytle — *Leaves* p.141
Montapert — *Distilled* p.155-156
Prochnow — *Public* #2646
Speaker's Desk #324, 1085

FIRST-BORN
New Topical p.93

"FIRST FRUITS"
New Topical p.93-94

FISH
See also names of fish
Applegarth — *Heir.* p.23, 207
Asimov — *Treasury* #238
Botkin — *Treasury* p.624, 647
Du Noüy — *Human* p.65, 72, 74-75, 83, 92
Flesch — *Unusual* p.90
Fuller — *Epigrams* p.121
Goudge — *Comfort* p.341-344, 367
Harnsberger — *Mark* p.125-126
Harral — *Feature* p.157-158
Henry — *5000* p.90
Kin — *Dictionary* p.95
New Topical p.94
Prochnow — *Public* #228, 275, 562, 1189
Prochnow — *Success.* #885, 1764
Weisfeld — *Pulpit* p.9
, *Group names of*
Kronenberger — *Animal* p.133

, *Mythical*
Botkin — *Treasury* p.583-585, 647-648

FISHERMEN AND FISHING
Asimov — *Treasury* #287
Baillie — *Diary* #155
Botkin — *Anecdotes* p.90, 99, 242, 266
Botkin — *Treasury* p.632-633, 639
Braude — *Speaker's* p.77-78; #518-531
Cerf — *Laugh* p.132-134
Copeland — *10,000* p.614-622
Dirksen — *Quot.* #900
Flesch — *Unusual* p.91
Fuller — *Thesaurus* #1846-1854
George — *Book* p.10, 124, 206, 325, 378, 403
Grizer — *Wit* p.170
Guideposts — *Faith* p.331-333
Harral — *Feature* p.158
Henry — *5000* p.90
Hobe — *Tapestries* p.59, 79
Irion — *Yes* p.90-92
Johnson — *Bedside* p.19-20, 263-270, 275-276
Kohn — *Pathways* p.101-103
Nichols — *Third* p.26-27
Peale — *Courage* p.24
Prochnow — *Public* #119, 349, 455, 491, 1416, 1437, 1514, 1694, 1756, 1971
Prochnow — *Speaker's* p.130-131
Prochnow — *Success.* #513, 706, 727, 1076, 1174, 1177, 1441, 1766
Schermerhorn — *1500* p.159-160
Seldes — *Great* p.362
Speaker's Desk #43, 282, 553, 590, 708, 753, 871
Wallis — *Treasure* p.193
Wallis — *Words* p.154
Woods — *Content.* p.76, 87, 110, 136
Woods — *Wellsprings* p.61
Words — *Inspir.* p.16-17

FISTS
Kin — *Dictionary* p.95

FITNESS. *See* **Physical fitness**

FLAG DAY
Hovey — *Treasury* #71, 679, 1046-1051

FLAGS
Harnsberger — *Mark* p.126
Harral — *Feature* p.158-159
Henry — *5000* p.91
Hovey — *Treasury* p.184-185; #71, 679, 1046-1051
Kin — *Dictionary* p.95
Prochnow — *Public* #3082, 4272
Seldes — *Great* p.362
Wallis — *Treasure* p.176

, *American*
Dirksen — *Quot.* #588
Grizer — *Wit* p.171
Liddle — *Thought I, II, III* p.127
Peterson — *Art* p.196

, *Tribute to*
Alexander's Treasure. p.111

"FLANDERS FIELDS"
New Joy p.208

"FLAT TIRES"
Safian — *Insults* p.91-94
Safian — *More* p.91-94

FLATTERY
See also **Compliments; Praise**
Alexander's Treasure. p.214
Book Proverbs p.53
Braude — *Source* #632-636
Braude — *Stories* p.148
Dirksen — *Quot.* #268, 1318-1320, 1995, 2013, 2312
Edwards — *Useful* p.198-200
Evans — *Thoughts I* p.97-98
Flesch — *Unusual* p.91
Forbes — *Thoughts* p.61, 103, 157, 413
Fuller — *Epigrams* p.121-122
Fuller — *Thesaurus* #236-237
Ginott — *Between* p.113-114
Henry — *5000* p.92
How To Live p.18-22
Kennedy — *Reader's* #336
Kin — *Dictionary* p.96
Liddle — *Thought I, II, III* p.9, 13, 94, 118, 154, 169
Liddle — *Thought IV* p.38-39, 46
Liddle — *Thought V* p.24, 41
Lockridge — *World's* p.575; #3769, 3803, 4000
Lytle — *Leaves* p.78
New Joy p.245
New Topical p.94
Prochnow — *Public* #51, 496, 658, 1478, 1503, 3083-3084
Reader's — *Getting* p.191-193
Prochnow — *Speaker's* p.132
Prochnow — *Success.* #328, 1767
Woods — *Religious* p.334
Words — *Inspir.* p.91

FLEAS
Flesch — *Unusual* p.91
Harnsberger — *Mark* p.126-128
Henry — *5000* p.92
Kin — *Dictionary* p.96

FLESH
See also **Skin**
Kin — *Dictionary* p.96
Prochnow — *Public* #2719
Woods — *Religious* p.334-335

FLEUR-DE-LIS
Applegarth — *Heir.* p.100

FLEXIBILITY
Evans — *Faith* p.139
Evans — *Thoughts II (Open Door)* p.53, 174-175
Evans — *Thoughts III (Open Road)* p.31, 199-200
How To Live p.283
Kin — *Dictionary* p.96
Kohn — *Through* p.63-66

FLIERS AND FLYING. *See* **Aviation**

FLIES
Flesch — *Unusual* p.91
Harnsberger — *Mark* p.128
Henry — *5000* p.95
Hubbard — *Scrap* p.146
Kin — *Dictionary* p.97

FLINT
Kin — *Dictionary* p.96

FLIRTATION
Braude — *Stories* p.148
Flesch — *Unusual* p.91
Fuller — *Thesaurus* #861-863
Henry — *5000* p.92
Lockridge — *World's* #2696, 5196

FLOOD
Botkin — *Anecdotes* p.83
Harral — *Feature* p.159
Prochnow — *Public* #39, 426, 531
, Biblical
Garland — *Subject* p.109-110
New Topical p.63-64
Prochnow — *Public* #2279

FLOOR SCRUBBING
Holmes — *I've* p.30-31

FLORIDA
Botkin — *Anecdotes* p.80, 190-192
Botkin — *Treasury See* index p.928

FLORISTS
Harral — *Feature* p.159
Manchee — *Secret* p.210

FLOUR
Botkin — *Anecdotes* p.59

FLOWERS
See also **Florists;** names of flowers
Alexander's Treasure. p.119, 152
Applegarth — *Heir.* p.99-105, 253, 306
Botkin — *Anecdotes* p.265
Braude — *Speaker's* #532-533
Dirksen — *Quot.* #35, 47, 91, 901-904, 1462
Edwards — *Useful* p.200-201
Fox — *Make* p.169
Goudge — *Comfort* p.56-60
Hadfield — *Love* p.99-103
Harnsberger — *Mark* p.128
Harral — *Feature* p.159
Henry — *5000* p.92-95
Hobe — *Tapestries* p.18, 24, 31, 61, 102, 107
Hubbard — *Scrap* p.45, 51, 65, 79, 100, 105, 113, 149
Kin — *Dictionary* p.96-97
Liddle — *Thought IV* p.7, 27
Lindbergh — *Unicorn* p.16-17
Lockridge — *World's* #3829
Lytle — *Leaves* p.32, 109
New Topical p.94-95
Peterson — *Art* p.208
Prochnow — *Public* #148, 1044, 2002, 3085
Prochnow — *Success.* #1768
Sheban — *Wisdom* no p.
Speaker's Desk #25, 39-40
Wallis — *Treasure* p.29, 66, 181, 183, 204
Wallis — *Words* p.57, 62, 174-176, 240
, Admiration of
Curtis — *Practical* p.200
, Buds of
Kohn — *Best* p.46-48
, Bulbs of
Fox — *Make* p.169
, White
Applegarth — *Heir.* p.261, 306

FLUCTUATION
Du Noüy — *Human* p.24, 42, 48-50, 78
Du Noüy — *Road* p.65, 83, 99, 112, 130, 147, 155, 179, 183

FLUX
Seldes — *Great* p.363

"FLYING DUTCHMAN"
Botkin — *Treasury* p.596, 741

FOES. *See* **Enemies**

FOG
Hobe — *Tapestries* p.115
Schermerhorn — *1500* p.163

FOIBLES
See also **Faults**
Dirksen — *Quot.* #905
Flesch — *Unusual* p.91
Hadfield — *Delights* p.98-99

FOLK ART
Botkin — *Anecdotes* p.xxvi-xxvii

FOLK SONGS
Harral — *Feature* p.159

FOLKLORE
See also **Fairy tales**
Botkin — *Anecdotes* p.xxiii, xxviii
Harral — *Feature* p.159-160
Hooker — *Index* p.134-143

FOLKWAYS
Botkin — *Anecdotes* p.xxvii

FOLLOWING
Flesch — *Unusual* p.91
Kin — *Dictionary* p.97
Montapert — *Distilled* p.156
Prochnow — *Public* #511, 1864, 2044, 2630

FOLLY. *See* **Fools and foolishness; Indiscretion; Rashness**

FOOD
See also **Diet; Dinners;** types of food; etc.
Asimov — *Treasury* #187-188
Bradshaw — *Home.* p.125-127
Braude — *Stories* p.148-149
Cowan — *Wit* p.128-133
Flesch — *Unusual* p.91-92
Fox — *Make* p.129
Fuller — *Epigrams* p.339-340
George — *Book See* index p.444
Harnsberger — *Mark* p.128-129
Harral — *Feature* p.160-164
Hovey — *Treasury* #232, 275, 366, 422, 462, 571, 597, 777-779, 815, 885, 951, 989, 1188, 1625, 1862
Hubbard — *Scrap* p.145
Johnson — *Bedside* p.197
Kennedy — *Reader's* #337
Kin — *Dictionary* p.97
Kronenberger — *Animal* p.74-89
Lockridge — *World's* #5206
Lytle — *Leaves* p.50
Prochnow — *Public* #50, 299, 434, 826, 862, 899, 910, 1808, 2735, 3087-3089
Prochnow — *Speaker's* p.132-133
Sagendorph — *Old* p.69-81
Seldes — *Great* p.363
Simpson — *Contemp.* p.456-459

, for family
White — *Life* p.73-85, 87-91
, in New Testament
Day — *Meditations* p.35-36
, in Old Testament
Day — *Meditations* p.34-35
, Jewish
Asimov — *Treasury* #348
, National
Lockridge — *World's* #2677
, Teenager complaints on
Ginott — *Between* p.50-52

FOOLS AND FOOLISHNESS
Botkin — *Anecdotes* p.27-36, 73-88, 90, 195
Botkin — *Treasury* p.409, 414, 430, 454-464
Braude — *Stories* p.149-150
Carruthers — *Sparks* p.127-128
Dirksen — *Quot. See* index p.263
Edwards — *Useful* p.201-202
Evans — *Unto* p.25, 27, 31, 50, 97
Flesch — *Unusual* p.92-93, 263
Fogg — *1000* #674
Forbes — *Thoughts See* index p.550
Fuller — *Epigrams* p.122-124
Grizer — *Wit* p.171-172
Halverson — *Perspective* p.32
Harnsberger — *Mark* p.129-130
Henry — *5000* p.96
Hobe — *Tapestries* p.136
Hubbard — *Scrap* p.166, 227
Kin — *Dictionary* p.74-75, 98, 234
Liddle — *Thought I, II, III* p.70, 144, 171, 176-177
Liddle — *Thought IV* p.5-6, 9, 13, 26
Liddle — *Thought V* p.5
Lockridge — *World's See* index p.575, #671
Montapert — *Distilled* p.157
New Topical p.95
Prochnow — *Public* #485, 2627, 2705; *See* index p.495
Prochnow — *Success.* #633, 657, 867, 1769-1774
Seldes — *Great* p.363, 546-547
Speaker's Desk #132; *See also* index p.300
Taylor — *With* p.108-111
Weisfeld — *Pulpit* p.3
Woods — *Religious* p.335
Woods — *Wellsprings* p.79-80

FOOTBALL
Cerf — *Laugh* p.134-136
Dirksen — *Quot.* #1686
Flesch — *Unusual* p.93
Fuller — *Thesaurus* #1856-1858
Harral — *Feature* p.164

Prochnow — *Public* #186, 774, 1027, 1088, 1121, 1237, 1649, 1697
Prochnow — *Speaker's* p.134-135
Prochnow — *Success.* #531, 871, 921
Schermerhorn — *1500* p.163-164
, *Coaches of*
Guideposts — *Faith* p.100-104
, *Players of*
Guideposts — *Faith* p.100-104
Peale — *Guideposts* p.161-164
Weisfeld — *Pulpit* p.131

FOOTNOTES
Flesch — *Unusual* p.93

FOOTPRINTS
Prochnow — *Public* #1432

FOPPERY. *See* **Fools and foolishness**

FORBEARANCE. *See* **Abstinence; Endurance; Patience; Tolerance**

FORBIDDEN
Harnsberger — *Mark* p.130-131
Lockridge — *World's* #5801
Prochnow — *Public* #2663
Sheban — *Wisdom* no p.

FORCE
See also **Energy; Oppression; Power; Strength; Violence;** etc.
Adams — *New* p.88
Curtis — *Practical* p.25
Dirksen — *Quot.* #589
Edwards — *Useful* p.202
Evans — *Unto* p.32, 65, 67, 70, 124-125
Flesch — *Unusual* p.93
Forbes — *Thoughts* p.8-9, 119, 136, 282, 291, 338, 382-383, 422, 428, 443, 465, 510
Henry — *5000* p.96-97
Hovey — *Treasury* p.185; #642, 1052-1053
Hulme — *Living* p.41-44, 130-132
Keller — *Open* p.108-109
Keller — *You* p.62-65
Kennedy — *Reader's* #338-339
Kin — *Dictionary* p.99
Lockridge — *World's* #3062, 4014
Lytle — *Leaves* p.165
Montapert — *Distilled* p.157-158
Prochnow — *Public* #2372
Seldes — *Great* p.364-367
Wheelis — *Moralist* p.45, 101-102
Woods — *Religious* p.335
, *and authority*
Wheelis — *Moralist* p.65-74
, *Creation of*
White — *Job* p.113-114
, *Great impelling*
Dirksen — *Quot.* #110
, *Invisible*
Kohn — *Thoughts* p.102-106
, *Opposing*
Evans — *This* p.61-62
, *Pull of*
Kohn — *Thoughts* p.163-166

FORDS
Botkin — *Anecdotes* p.48, 103
Schermerhorn — *1500* p.164-166

FORECASTING. *See* **Foresight and hindsight; Prophets and prophecy;** etc.

FOREFATHERS. *See* **Ancestry**

FOREHEAD
Prochnow — *Public* #2047

FOREIGN AID
Dirksen — *Quot.* #34, 97, 688, 734, 2374
Harral — *Feature* p.242
Kauffman — *For* p.24-25, 95-96
Woods — *Business.* p.79-80

FOREIGN GOVERNMENTS
Simpson — *'54* p.44, 157, 298

FOREIGN POLICY. *See* **International relations**

FOREIGN TRADE
Prochnow — *Success.* #201
Woods — *Business.* p.80-81

FOREKNOWLEDGE. *See* **Foresight and hindsight; Premonition; Prophets and prophecy**

FORESIGHT AND HINDSIGHT
See also **Anticipation; Caution; Prudence; Wisdom**
Book Proverbs p.116
Braude — *Source* #830
Edwards — *Useful* p.202-203
Evans — *Unto* p.7
Fox — *Make* p.19
Garland — *Subject* p.111-112
Henry — *5000* p.97
Kin — *Dictionary* p.99, 119
Liddle — *Thoughts V* p.12
Lytle — *Leaves* p.43
Montapert — *Distilled* p.158

Prochnow — *Speaker's* p.135
Speaker's Desk #336, 554, 605, 638, 902

FORESTS
See also **Fire, Forest**
Hobe — *Tapestries* p.58, 92
Lockridge — *World's* #5221
New Topical p.95

FORGETFULNESS
See also **Absent-mindedness; Amnesia; Neglect; Oblivion**
Alexander's Treasure. p.263
Braude — *Source* #637-638
Dirksen — *Quot.* #909-912, 1029
Edwards — *Useful* p.203
Emmons — *Mature* p.142, 147
Evans — *Quote* p.195-204
Evans — *Thoughts IV* p.173-174
Flesch — *Unusual* p.93-94
Fuller — *Epigrams* p.124-125
Garland — *Subject* p.112
Grizer — *Wit* p.172-173
Harnsberger — *Mark* p.131
Henry — *5000* p.97
Hovey — *Treasury* #1055
How To Live p.249
Keys Happiness p.511-513
Krishnamurti — *Think* p.161-162
Lockridge — *World's* #2253, 2260, 2324
Lytle — *Leaves* p.100-101, 143
Montapert — *Distilled* p.158-159
Prochnow — *Public* #43, 2315, 2513
Speaker's Desk #987, 1147
Woods — *Religious* p.336

FORGET-ME-NOTS
Baillie — *Diary* #75

FORGIVENESS
See also **Pardon; Reconciliation**
Alexander's Treasure. p.21, 264-265
Applegarth — *Heir.* p.45, 47
Auden — *Certain* p.167-168
Baillie — *Diary* #70, 176
Book Proverbs p.121
Braude — *Source* #639-648
Braude — *Speaker's* #534-535
Braude — *Stories* p.150-151
Clark — *Windows* p.68-69
Curtis — *Golden* p.168
Detherage — *Sunrise* p.67-68, 89, 172
Dirksen — *Quot.* #1323-1325, 1678, 2143
Droke — *Christian* p.185-186
Edwards — *Useful* p.203-204
Emmons — *Mature* p.96, 100
Esteve — *Experience* p.77-85
Evans — *Quote* p.195-204
Evans — *Thoughts I* p.69, 99, 140, 219
Evans — *Thoughts II (Open Door)* p.24, 44, 140, 185
Evans — *Thoughts III* p.19, 29, 31
Evans — *Thoughts IV* p.167-168, 203, 206
Evans — *Unto* p.133
Flesch — *Unusual* p.94
Flint — *Graham* p.53
Fox — *Make* p.28-29
Fuller — *Epigrams* p.125
Garland — *Subject* p.3, 112-113
Goudge — *Comfort* p.278-283
Grizer — *Wit* p.173
Guideposts — *Faith* p.70
Halverson — *Perspective* p.108
Henry — *5000* p.97-98
Hobe — *Tapestries* p.136-137
Holmes — *Design* p.225-226
Hovey — *Treasury* p.185-186; #337, 479, 491, 591, 726-727, 753, 1054-1056, 1274
How To Live p.469-473
Hulme — *Living* p.111-114
Johnson — *Bedside* p.9-10, 13, 165
Kennedy — *Reader's* #340-343
Kin — *Dictionary* p.99
Knight's Illus. p.122-125
Knight's Treas. p.131-135
Kohn — *Adventures* p.49-54
Liddle — *Thought I, II, III* p.12, 15, 86, 102, 143, 163
Liddle — *Thought IV* p.37
Lockridge — *World's* #340, 2253, 2637, 5091, 5643
Lytle — *Leaves* p.91, 133
Maltz — *Creative* p.146-147
Mandel — *Stories* p.97
Montapert — *Distilled* p.159-160
More Words p.1-2, 65-67
New Topical p.96
Peterson — *Art* p.311, 384
Phillips — *Choice* p.214, 364-365
Price — *Wider* p.217-226
Prochnow — *Public* #597, 2305, 3099-3101
Redhead — *Living* p.103-106
Sheen — *Thoughts* p.103-113
Sheen — *Way* p.122-124
Speaker's Desk #141
Strait — *Speaker's* p.79
Tanksley — *Friend* p.62
Voss — *Quotations* p.92-93
Wallis — *Treasure* p.79, 138, 170
Wallis — *Words* p.14
Watson — *Light* p.198-203
Woods — *Religious* p.336-338
Words — *Inspir.* p.116
Zobell — *Speaker's* p.54-56

"FORGOTTEN"
Dirksen — *Quot.* #912, 1150, 1687-1688
Prochnow — *Public* #225, 3102
Words — *Inspir.* p.65

FORM
Curtis — *Practical* p.429-431, 436-437
Edwards — *Useful* p.204-205
Ideas p.356-357
Prochnow — *Public* #1043
Woods — *Religious* p.338

FORMULAS
Flesch — *Unusual* p.94
Prochnow — *Public* #371

FORTITUDE. *See* **Courage; Endurance; Strength**

FORTS
See also names of forts
Kin — *Dictionary* p.99
Lindbergh — *Unicorn* p.15
Lytle — *Leaves* p.72
New Topical p.96

FORTUNE
See also **Chance; Destiny; Fate; Luck; Wealth**
Baillie — *Diary* #216
Copeland — *10,000* p.996
Dirksen — *Quot.* #205, 2105
Edwards — *Useful* p.205-206
Flesch — *Unusual* p.94
Fogg — *1000* #677, 687, 692, 947
Forbes — *Thoughts* p.152, 291, 356; *See also* index p.550
Fuller — *Epigrams* p.125-126, 340-341
Grizer — *Wit* p.173-174
Henry — *5000* p.98
Hobe — *Tapestries* p.133, 211
Johnson — *Bedside* p.136
Kin — *Dictionary* p.99-100
Lockridge — *World's See* index p.575
Lytle — *Leaves* p.25
Montapert — *Distilled* p.160-161
Prochnow — *Public* #820, 2049, 3103-3105, 4101-4102
Pullar-Strecker — *Proverbs* #31-38
Seldes — *Great* p.367
Woods — *Religious* p.339

FORTY (age)
Flesch — *Unusual* p.94
Forbes — *Thoughts* p.77, 398, 443, 498

FORTY-FIVE (age)
Flesoh — *Unusual* p.95
Words — *Inspir.* p.82

"FORTY-NINERS"
Botkin — *Treasury* p.282, 306, 309, 323, 379, 390, 491, 494, 861-865

FORTY-SIX (age)
Flesch — *Unusual* p.95

FOSSILS
Du Noüy — *Human* p.43-45, 57, 62-63, 66-68, 70-80
Du Noüy — *Road* p.161-162

FOUNDATIONS
See also **Beginners and beginnings**
Forbes — *Thoughts* p.280, 289, 433, 450, 487
Hobe — *Tapestries* p.35
Lytle — *Leaves* p.39
Mandel — *Stories* p.97
Montapert — *Distilled* p.161-162
New Topical p.96-97

"FOUNDING FATHERS"
See also **Pilgrims**
Seldes — *Great* p.367

FOUNTAINS
Goudge — *Comfort* p.35-37
Lytle — *Leaves* p.40
New Topical p.97
Prochnow — *Public* #2071

FOURTH OF JULY. *See* **Independence Day**

FOXES
Botkin — *Anecdotes* p.93, 184, 187
Botkin — *Treasury* p.26, 593, 653-655, 661, 669
Henry — *5000* p.98
Kin — *Dictionary* p.100
Lockridge — *World's* #5725
New Topical p.97
Prochnow — *Public* #1698

FRAGMENTS
Carruthers — *Sparks* p.135-136
Emmons — *Mature* p.71
Lytle — *Leaves* p.30, 175

FRAGRANCE. *See* **Perfume**

FRAILTIES. *See* **Faults; Weakness**

FRANCE
See also **French**
Cerf — *Laugh* p.424-425

Fuller — *Epigrams* p.126
Henry — *5000* p.99
Lockridge — *World's* #3159, 3888
Seldes — *Great* p.367
Simpson — *Contemp.* p.127-130
, *History—Revolution*
Fogg — *1000 See* index p.897
Seldes — *Great* p.840-841
Wheelis — *Moralist* p.74, 111

FRANCIS OF ASSISI, SAINT
Applegarth — *Heir.* p.35, 78
Baillie — *Diary* #274
Goudge — *Comfort* p.64-66, 177-178, 205-206, 225-226
Phillips — *Choice* p.41, 101, 188, 340, 367
Wallis — *Treasure* p.8, 238
Words — *Inspir.* p.31
, *Method*
Phillips — *Choice* p.205
, *Third order of*
Phillips — *Choice* p.368, 386-388

FRANKENSTEIN
Prochnow — *Public* #2398

FRANKLIN, BENJAMIN
Botkin — *Anecdotes* p.89, 179-180, 291, 299
Peterson — *Art* p.35

FRANKNESS
See also **Truth**
Braude — *Stories* p.151
Flint — *Graham* p.26
Fuller — *Epigrams* p.127
Fun Fare p.1-2, 178-180
Harnsberger — *Mark* p.132
Kin — *Dictionary* p.100
Mandel — *Stories* p.97
Nichols — *New* p.129-130, 195-196
Prochnow — *Public* #124, 496, 764, 1060, 1907, 2213, 3106-3107
Prochnow — *Speaker's* p.136
Speaker's Desk See index p.300

FRATERNITIES
See also **Brotherhood**
Flesch — *Unusual* p.95
Harral — *Feature* p.164
Nizer — *Thinking* p.206
Prochnow — *Public* #476
Schermerhorn — *1500* p.169-170

FRAUD
See also **Dishonesty**
Edwards — *Useful* p.206
Kin — *Dictionary* p.100
Menninger — *Blue.* p.125-126, 144-145
Prochnow — *Public* #1213
Seldes — *Great* p.367

FREAKS
Harral — *Feature* p.164-165

FRECKLES
Prochnow — *Public* #2254

FREE ENTERPRISE
See also **America, Way of life in; Capitalism**
Curtis — *Practical* p.315-321
Dirksen — *Quot.* #73, 561, 650, 700-701
Forbes — *Thoughts* p.20, 261, 366, 508, 512
Grizer — *Wit* p.176-177
Kauffman — *For* p.96-97
Myers — *Thunder* p.121-122
Prochnow — *Speaker's* p.138-140
Seldes — *Great* p.398-399
Wheelis — *Moralist* p.121
Woods — *Business.* p.81-85

FREE LOVE. *See* **Love, Free**

FREE SPEECH. *See* **Freedom, of speech**

FREETHINKERS. *See* **Freedom, of thought**

FREE TRADE. *See* **Trade, Free**

FREE VERSE. *See* **Poetry, Free verse in**

FREE WILL
Du Noüy — *Human* p.13, 40, 47-51, 104, 134, 147-148, 190, 197
Evans — *Unto* p.65-70, 73
Flesch — *Unusual* p.95
Flint — *Graham* p.53
Fox — *Make* p.56-57
Ideas p.156-157
Johnson — *Bedside* p.134, 201
Phillips — *Choice* p.39, 41
Seldes — *Great* p.406-407
Voss — *Quotations* p.94-95
White — *Job* p.66-68, 80-81, 95, 104, 164, 169, 181
Woods — *Religious* p.339-344

FREEDOM
See also **Academic freedom; Democracy; Heritage; Independence; Liberty; Patriotism; Republic**
Applegarth — *Heir.* p.222, 246
Baillie — *Diary* #59
Barker — *Treat* p.105-124

Bartlett — *Discovery* p.5-6
Braude — *Source* #649-659
Braude — *Speaker's* #536-537
Braude — *Stories* p.151-153
Curtis — *Human* p.183-200
Curtis — *Practical* p.25, 278-279, 292-293, 323-324, 541-542
Detherage — *Sunrise* p.62, 91-96, 162-163
Dirksen — *Quot. See* index p.263
Droke — *Christian* p.187-195
Edwards — *Useful* p.206-207, 728
Evans — *Faith* p.54, 127, 131-132, 135-136, 177-192
Evans — *This* p.134-135, 137-148
Evans — *Thoughts I* p.62, 113, 119, 143, 150, 153, 156
Evans — *Thoughts II (Open Door)* p.63-64, 68-70
Evans — *Thoughts III (Open Road)* p.80-81, 97, 131, 161, 163-172, 202
Evans — *Thoughts IV* p.147-150
Evans — *Unto* p.13-14, 33, 40, 53, 55-58, 71, 109, 126
Flesch — *Unusual* p.95-96
Flint — *Graham* p.53
Forbes — *Thoughts See* index p.550
Franke — *Buckley* p.92
Fuller — *Thesaurus* #2036-2042
Garland — *Subject* p.115
Grizer — *Wit* p.174-176
Halverson — *Perspective* p.64
Harnsberger — *Mark* p.132-133
Henry — *5000* p.99-100
Hill — *Think* p.147-154, 160-167
Hobe — *Tapestries* p.200
Hoffer — *Reflect.* p.35-36
Holmes — *Design* p.35-37, 39-49, 76-77
Hovey — *Treasury* p.186-190; *See* index p.296
Hubbard — *Scrap* p.32, 222
Humes — *Instant* #363-383
Johnson — *Bedside* p.1-2, 15, 90-91, 246, 258, 271
Kauffman — *For* p.97-98
Kennedy — *Fresh* p.6-8
Kennedy — *Reader's* #344-353
Kin — *Dictionary* p.100
Knight's Illus. p.125-127
Knight's Treas. p.135-137
Lair — *Baby* p.208-209
Liddle — *Thought I, II, III* p.7, 25, 31, 34, 44-45, 60, 70, 75, 83, 91, 108, 123, 140, 146, 157, 176, 185, 190
Liddle — *Thought IV* p.3, 9, 23, 26, 28, 31-32
Liddle — *Thought V* p.14, 21, 23, 25, 45
Lindbergh — *Unicorn* p.13-14
List — *Living* p.42-45
Lytle — *Leaves* p.55, 59
Mandel — *Stories* p.98
Mandelbaum — *Choose* p.21
Montapert — *Distilled* p.162-163
Morris — *1000* p.103, 131, 169, 200, 219, 258, 274, 281, 303, 322, 350
New Joy p.57
Nichols — *Third* p.249-250
Peale — *Guideposts* p.305-333
Peterson — *Art* p.218
Peterson — *New* p.16-17
Phillips — *Choice* p.59, 229, 318, 372
Price — *Wider* p.37-44, 47-52, 67-72, 75-81, 241-250
Prochnow — *Public* #1017, 1483, 1492, 2053, 2683, 3108-3109, 4319, 4379, 4408
Prochnow — *Speaker's* p.136-137
Prochnow — *Success. See* index p.491
Seldes — *Great* p.311-312, 367-385, 400-401
Sheban — *Wisdom* no p.
Sheen — *Thoughts* p.157-190
Speaker's Desk p.65-67; #100, 1099
Voss — *Quotations* p.95-97
Wallis — *Treasure* p.8, 47, 146, 174-178
Wallis — *Words* p.14
Wheelis — *Moralist See* index p.163
Woods — *Business.* p.85-88
Woods — *Content.* p.46
Woods — *Inspir.* p.124-165
Woods — *Religious* p.344-347, 543
Words — *Inspir.* p.126-127
Zobell — *Speaker's* p.57-60
, and faith
  Kauffman — *For* p.99-100
, and independence
  Sheen — *Content.* p.171-172
, and love
  Krishnamurti — *Think* p.23-31
, and politics
  Ideas p.151-153
, and security
  Adams — *New* p.256
, and silence
  Kauffman — *For* p.100-101
, Assumption of
  Hulme — *Living* p.63-65
, Dangers of
  Hubbard — *Scrap* p.58
, Four
  Dirksen — *Quot.* #402
, from want
  Curtis — *Practical* p.541, 549-551
  Dirksen — *Quot.* #402

, *Guardians of*
Hubbard — *Scrap* p.74
, *Limits of*
Ginott — *Between* p.137-150
, *Nature of*
Adams — *New* p.114
, *of man*
Adams — *New* p.112
, *of opinion*
Kauffman — *For* p.98
, *of press*
Dirksen — *Quot.* #408-409
Ideas p.153-154
Liddle — *Thought I, II, III* p.31, 97, 123, 165
Lockridge — *World's* #1966, 3570, 5796
Seldes — *Great* p.386-396
, *of speech*
Curtis — *Practical* p.293-295, 541
Dirksen — *Quot.* #402-403, 408, 410, 1824, 2362, 2367
Fogg — *1000* #538, 596, 624, 1076
Forbes — *Thoughts* p.152, 161, 201-202, 206, 208, 452
Grizer — *Wit* p.177
Hubbard — *Scrap* p.72
Ideas p.153-154
Kennedy — *Reader's* #336-357
Prochnow — *Success.* #466
Seldes — *Great* p.402-405
Woods — *Religious* p.353-354
Words — *Inspir.* p.175-176
, *of thought*
Hubbard — *Scrap* p.51, 223
Lockridge — *World's* #3861, 4197
Seldes — *Great* p.397-398, 405-406
Woods — *Religious* p.353-354
, *of travel*
Franke — *Buckley* p.92-93
, *Personal*
Peterson — *Art* p.123
, *Principles of*
Hubbard — *Scrap* p.204
, *Problem of*
Krishnamurti — *Think* p.16-22
, *Religious*
Hubbard — *Scrap* p.51, 186
Kennedy — *Reader's* #354-355
Peale — *Guideposts* p.326-328
Woods — *Religious* p.347-351
, *True*
Kauffman — *For* p.98-99
, *Varieties of*
Evans — *This* p.139-140
, *versus license*
Hunter — *Gems* p.32-33

FREEMASONS. *See* **Masonry**

FRENCH
Asimov — *Treasury* #214, 381, 406
Botkin — *Anecdotes* p.64, 136
Botkin — *Treasury* p.46
Flesch — *Unusual* p.96
Harnsberger — *Mark* p.134-135
Hovey — *Treasury* #157, 1278, 1301, 1762
Kin — *Dictionary* p.100
Lockridge — *World's* #1980, 3654, 4071-4072, 5015
Prochnow — *Public* #219
Schermerhorn — *1500* p.170-171
Speaker's Desk #337, 991
, *Humor of*
Copeland — *10,000* p.750-753

FRENCH-CANADIANS
Botkin — *Treasury* p.176

FRENCH LANGUAGE
Dirksen — *Quot.* #602
Flesch — *Unusual* p.96
Harnsberger — *Mark* p.133-134

FRENCH PROVERBS
Dirksen — *Quot. See* index p.264

FRESHMEN
Francis — *For* p.58-75

FRESHNESS
Prochnow — *Public* #288, 812, 848, 941, 2129, 2244

FRETFULNESS. *See* **Complaining; Discontent; Worry**

FREUD AND FREUDIANISM
Seldes — *Great* p.407
Woods — *Religious* p.354-355

FRICTION. *See* **Argument; Disagreement; Opposition;** etc.

FRIENDS AND FRIENDSHIP
See also **Brotherhood;** etc.
Alexander's Treasure. p.3, 8, 85, 126, 150, 208, 214-215, 218, 223, 342-343
Applegarth — *Heir.* p.74, 83, 105, 174, 249
Auden — *Certain* p.170
Baillie — *Diary* #299

Barrows — *1000 See* index p.439-440
Book Proverbs p.45
Braude — *Source* #83, 660-679
Braude — *Speaker's* #79-111, 538-542
Braude — *Stories* p.153-158
Copeland — *10,000* p.992-994
Curtis — *Practical* p.487-496
Detherage — *Sunrise* p.69-74
Dirksen — *Quot.* #110, 140, 184, 299, 307, 540, 875, 923-924, 1326, 2019, 2136, 2313
Droke — *Christian* p.195-201
Edwards — *Useful* p.207-210
Evans — *Quote* p.163-175
Evans — *Thoughts I* p.25-27, 70, 72, 80, 98-99, 107, 123, 218-220
Evans — *Thoughts II (Open Door)* p.49, 87-88, 94, 134-137, 186
Evans — *Thoughts III (Open Road)* p.16, 97, 100, 109, 157, 161, 181, 185
Evans — *Thoughts IV* p.207
Evans — *Unto* p.6, 27, 29, 62, 114-115
Felleman — *Poems* p.125-131
Flesch — *Unusual* p.96-97
Flint — *Graham* p.54
Fogg — *1000* #148, 312, 578, 677, 693, 873, 918, 1058
Forbes — *Thoughts* p.81, 95, 159, 346; *See* index p.550
Fox — *Make* p.148-149
Fuller — *Epigrams* p.127-131, 341-343
Fuller — *Thesaurus* #866-867
Garland — *Subject* p.115
Giniger — *Compact* p.270-271
Grizer — *Wit* p.177-183
Hadfield — *Love* p.40
Harnsberger — *Mark* p.135-136
Henry — *5000* p.101-102
Hobe — *Tapestries* p.22, 33-39, 67, 88, 158
Holmes — *Design* p.74-75, 80-81, 149
Holmes — *I've* p.99-100
Hovey — *Treasury* p.190-192; *See* index p.296
How To Live p.12-39
Howell — *Better* p.73-76
Howell — *Lines* p.25-32
Hubbard — *Scrap* p.14, 26, 29, 59, 75, 83, 108
Huxley — *You See* index p.285
Johnson — *Bedside* p.1-2, 4, 15, 62, 121, 152-162, 187, 201-202, 307
Keller — *Open* p.42, 87
Kennedy — *Reader's* #358-361
Keys Happiness p.4, 351-355
Kin — *Dictionary* p.100-102
Knight's Illus. p.127-128
Knight's Treas. p.137-138
Kopplin — *Something* p.3, 80-92
Lair — *Baby* p.23
Liddle — *Thought I, II, III See* index p.197
Liddle — *Thought IV* p.11, 13, 30, 32, 34
Liddle — *Thought V* p.4, 8, 12, 26, 45-46
Lockridge — *World's* #2342; *See* index p.576
Lytle — *Leaves* p.5, 25-26, 57, 76-80, 149
Maltz — *Creative* p.151-164
Mandel — *Stories* p.98-100
Mandelbaum — *Choose* p.31, 78-80
Menninger — *Blue.* p.60-61
Miller — *Harvest* p.29-34
Modern Eloquence (14) p.337-338
Montapert — *Distilled* p.163-165
Morris — *1000 See* index p.429
New Joy p.18, 33, 54-56, 136, 145-146, 248, 250
Nichols — *Third* p.86-87
Peale — *Courage* p.145
Peterson — *Art* p.319, 355
Phillips — *Choice* p.44, 58-59, 299, 347
Prochnow — *Public* #696, 1122, 1414, 1495, 2054, 2533, 2592, 2672, 3110-3116, 4103-4104
Prochnow — *Speaker's* p.140
Prochnow — *Success.* #432, 471, 974, 1433, 1778-1779
Pullar-Strecker — *Proverbs* #72-78
Seaburg — *Great* p.172, 187, 192, 203-204, 249, 251, 274, 321, 324, 326-327, 333, 341, 348, 353, 359, 368, 393
Seldes — *Great* p.407
Sheban — *Wisdom* no p.
Speaker's Desk p.67-70; #230, 288, 828, 984, 1029
Tanksley — *Friend* p.12
Voss — *Quotations* p.97-100
Wallis — *Treasure* p.97-102, 124, 141, 170
Welk — *Guide.* p.18-20
Woods — *Content.* p.171-172, 176, 178, 187, 202
Woods — *Inspir.* p.317-345
Woods — *Religious* p.355-356
Words — *Inspir.* p.11-13
Zobell — *Speaker's* p.60-63
, Art of
Maurois — *Art* p.107-135
Peterson — *Twenty* p.30-31
, "Fair-weather"
Safian — *Insults* p.72-73

, *How to win*
Reader's — *Getting* p.129-144
, *Mending*
Nichols — *New* p.127-128
, *Old*
Emmons — *Mature* p.148
, *Teenage*
Daly — *Personality* p.77-82

FRIGHT. *See* **Fear**

FRIVOLITY. *See* **Humor**

FROGS
Botkin — *Anecdotes* p.241, 273
Botkin — *Treasury* p.338, 494, 663
Flesch — *Unusual* p.97
Kin — *Dictionary* p.102
Kohn — *Through* p.49
Prochnow — *Public* #909, 1699
Wallis — *Words* p.49, 176

FRONTIERS
Applegarth — *Heir.* p.273
Botkin — *Treasury* p.3, 261, 272, 408, 491
Dirksen — *Quot.* #45, 1142
Forbes — *Thoughts* p.3, 31, 238, 363, 380, 505
Kronenberger — *Animal* p.89-91
Morris — *1000* p.2, 34-35, 188, 216, 238, 242, 304
Wallis — *Treasure* p.87
, *Life on*
New Joy p.86-87
, *New*
Words — *Inspir.* p.199-200

FROST, ROBERT
Nichols — *Third* p.147-148

FROST
Goudge — *Comfort* p.53-55

FRUGALITY. *See* **Economy; Thrift**

FRUIT
See also names of fruit
Harnsberger — *Mark* p.137-138
Harral — *Feature* p.165
Henry — *5000* p.102
Kin — *Dictionary* p.102
New Topical p.97-98
Prochnow — *Public* #2637
Prochnow — *Speaker's* p.140

FRUITFULNESS
Kohn — *Adventures* p.57-58
Lockridge — *World's* #3243

FRUSTRATION
See also **Defeat; "Little things"; Pressure**
Albert — *Stop* p.69, 144, 194
Braude — *Source* #678-679
Evans — *Faith* p.160, 217-218
Evans — *Thoughts IV* p.98-99, 167, 169, 196
Huxley — *You See* index p.285
Keller — *Open* p.30
Liddle — *Thought V* p.7
Maltz — *Creative* p.88, 124-136
Mandel — *Stories* p.100
Peale — *Stay* p.45-64
Speaker's Desk #25, 87, 248, 301, 349, 484, 486, 509, 527, 558, 597, 1000, 1112
Woods — *Religious* p.356
, *Dealing with*
Dirksen — *Quot.* #1143
, *Teenager*
Ginott — *Between* p.29-30

FUGITIVES
Prochnow — *Public* #1137

FULFILLMENT
See also **Achievement; Contentment**
Alexander's Treasure. p.59
Curtis — *Daily* p.16
Garland — *Subject* p.116
Mandel — *Stories* p.100
Mandelbaum — *Choose* p.113-116
Phillips — *Choice* p.95
Wallis — *Treasure* p.14
Woods — *Religious* p.356
, *Inspiration for*
Unlimited Power p.258-260
, *Joy of*
Hulme — *Living* p.137-139
, *of needs*
Sheen — *Content.* p.53-68
, *Prayer for*
Unlimited Power p.272

FULLNESS
Kin — *Dictionary* p.102
Prochnow — *Speaker's* p.141

FUN
See also **Pleasure**
Alexander's Treasure. p.272
Flesch — *Unusual* p.98
Harnsberger — *Mark* p.138
Kennedy — *Reader's* #362
Prochnow — *Public* #2306
Prochnow — *Success.* #925
Seldes — *Great* p.558
Speaker's Desk #54
Wallis — *Treasure* p.108

Woods — *Religious* p.535-536
Words — *Inspir.* p.163-166

FUNCTIONS AND FUNCTIONING
Prochnow — *Public* #754
White — *Job* p.37, 39-47, 71, 79, 84-85, 104, 108, 124, 175

FUND-RAISING
See also **Charity, Drives for**
Braude — *Source* #680
Harral — *Feature* p.165
Nizer — *Thinking* p.19

FUNDAMENTALS AND FUNDAMENTALISM
Braude — *Stories* p.200
Ideas p.157-158
Lytle — *Leaves* p.37, 61
Woods — *Religious* p.356-357

FUNERALS
Asimov — *Treasury* #93, 402, 532, 539, 541, 544
Botkin — *Anecdotes* p.7
Flesch — *Unusual* p.98
Fuller — *Thesaurus* #1776-1778
Fun Fare p.111
Harnsberger — *Mark* p.138-139
Harral — *Feature* p.165
Kennedy — *Reader's* #363-365
Lockridge — *World's* #473
Peale — *Guideposts* p.278-280
Peterson — *Art* p.351
Prochnow — *Public* #703
Schermerhorn — *1500* p.172-176
Speaker's Desk #71, 431, 481
Weisfeld — *Pulpit* p.8, 146, 177-182
Woods — *Religious* p.357
, Orations for
Copeland — *World's* p.3-8, 58-62, 263-265, 315-317, 324-326

FUR
Prochnow — *Speaker's* p.141

FURLOUGHS
Asimov — *Treasure* #640

FURNITURE
See also names of furniture
Applegarth — *Heir.* p.127
Braude — *Stories* p.158
Harral — *Feature* p.165-166
Lockridge — *World's* #4499
Prochnow — *Public* #171, 497

FUTILITY
Braude — *Stories* p.158
Kennedy — *Reader's* #366
Kohn — *Touch* p.125
Lytle — *Leaves* p.73, 116
Prochnow — *Public* #2056-2057
Speaker's Desk #237, 247, 488, 532, 700, 937, 1069, 1100, 1161
Woods — *Religious* p.357
Zobell — *Speaker's* p.63-64

FUTURE
See also **Destiny; Eternity; Heaven; Immortality; Tomorrow;** etc.
Adams — *New* p.209, 233-234, 265
Alexander's Treasure. p.318-319
Applegarth — *Heir.* p.66, 135, 167
Baillie — *Diary* #22
Bartlett — *Discovery* p.1-26
Braude — *Source* #681-685, 1241-1258
Braude — *Stories* p.158-159
Dirksen — *Quot. See* index p.264
Droke — *Christian* p.202-205
Edwards — *Useful* p.211-212
Evans — *This* p.116-117, 171-173, 180-181
Evans — *Thoughts I* p.47-48, 110-112, 120, 128-129, 133, 178-179
Evans — *Thoughts II (Open Door)* p.12-13, 16, 150, 208-209
Evans — *Thoughts III (Open Road)* p.38, 50-51, 119-121, 149, 151-152, 155-161, 165, 185
Evans — *Thoughts IV* p.90, 149-150
Evans — *Unto* p.16, 22-23, 40, 134, 140
Flesch — *Unusual* p.98
Flint — *Graham* p.54
Forbes — *Thoughts See* index p.550
Fox — *Make* p.114
Fuller — *Epigrams* p.131
Garland — *Subject* p.116-117
Grizer — *Wit* p.183-185, 338
Halverson — *Perspective* p.35
Henry — *5000* p.102-103
Hobe — *Tapestries* p.172
Holmes — *Design* p.121-128
Hovey — *Treasury* p.192; #5, 986, 1099-1101, 1247
How To Live p.567
Humes — *Instant* p.41; #384-389, 1248-1249
Kauffman — *For* p.101-102
Kin — *Dictionary* p.103
Kohn — *Adventures* p.145-158
Liddle — *Thought I, II, III* p.6, 21, 70, 73, 75, 84, 90, 103, 118, 156, 167, 172, 188
Liddle — *Thought V* p.3-4, 31, 39, 41

Lockridge — *World's* #850, 1105
Lytle — *Leaves* p.170
Montapert — *Distilled* p.165-166
Peterson — *Art* p.94
Prochnow — *Public* #197,1324, 1377, 1392, 3117-3118, 4284
Prochnow — *Success.* #180, 228, 525, 1396, 1780-1783, 2129-2130
Seldes — *Great* p.407-408
Sheen — *Thoughts* p.188-190
Wallis — *Treasure* p.137-138, 143, 187, 219
Wallis — *Words* p.50, 71, 105, 118, 153, 211, 214, 230
Watson — *Light* p.279-318
Woods — *Business.* p.88
Woods — *Religious* p.357-358
, Determined by ideas
Keller — *You* p.60-62
, Eye on the
Maxwell — *Courage* p.46-56
, Faith in
Peterson — *Art* p.29
, Fantasies of
Boas — *History* p.55-56
, Fear of
Kennedy — *Fresh* p.149-151
, Preparation for
Evans — *Faith* p.10, 29-30, 157-176
, Protection against
Kennedy — *Fresh* p.23-24

G

GABRIEL, ANGEL
Botkin — *Anecdotes* p.126, 170

GAD, TRIBE OF
New Topical p.98

GADGETS
Myers — *Thunder* p.32

"GAGS"
Botkin — *Treasury* p.176, 409, 461-464

GAIETY. *See* **Cheerfulness; Happiness; Joy; Laughter; Vivacity**

GAIN. *See* **Acquisition; Benefits** (personal) etc.

GALILEE
New Topical p.98-99
Wallis — *Words* p.55

GALILEO
Lockridge — *World's* #5162
Seldes — *Great* p.408

GALLANTRY
See also **Compliments; Courtesy; Respect**
Edwards — *Useful* p.212-213
Flesch — *Unusual* p.98
How To Live p.72
Kin — *Dictionary* p.104
List — *Living* p.55-58
Lockridge — *World's* #103, 526, 2412
Prochnow — *Public* #549
Prochnow — *Success.* #1130
Seldes — *Great* p.408
, French
Fun Fare p.7-9

GALLERY
Flesch — *Unusual* p.98-99

GAMBLERS AND GAMBLING
See also types of gambling
Albert — *Stop* p.171-172, 195
Asimov — *Treasure* #61, 87-88, 113
Book Proverbs p.101
Botkin — *Anecdotes* p.85, 266
Braude — *Speaker's* #543-544
Braude — *Stories* p.159
Cerf — *Laugh* p.188-191
Droke — *Christian* p.205-208
Edwards — *Useful* p.213-214, 658
Flesch — *Unusual* p.21, 99
Flint — *Graham* p.54
Fuller — *Epigrams* p.131-132
Fuller — *Thesaurus* #71-74
George — *Book* p.25, 150, 366
Grizer — *Wit* p.185-186
Henry — *5000* p.103-104
Hovey — *Treasury* #356
Johnson — *Bedside* p.64-75
Kin — *Dictionary* p.26, 104
Kronenberger — *Animal* p.91-92
Lockridge — *World's* #2616, 4181, 4844, 5779
Montapert — *Distilled* p.167
Prochnow — *Public* #1370
Seldes — *Great* p.408
Speaker's Desk p.70-71; #93, 380, 531, 658, 736, 886, 917, 1178
Woods — *Religious* p.358

Woods — *Wellsprings* p.20-21
, *Teenage*
Unlimited Power p.84-87

"GAMBLERS ANONYMOUS"
Kauffman — *For* p.102-104

"GAME, PLAYING THE". *See* **Sportsmanship**

"GAME OF LIFE." *See* **Life and living**

GAME WARDENS
Botkin — *Anecdotes* p.60

GAMES
See also **Recreation; Sports;** names of games
Flesch — *Unusual* p.99
Forbes — *Thoughts* p.60, 170, 334, 429, 433, 443, 446, 465, 502
Fun Fare p.150-151, 205
Harnsberger — *Mark* p.140
Harral — *Feature* p.166-167
Krishnamurti p.95-96
Lockridge — *World's* #1429, 4643
Prochnow — *Public* #188, 706, 1201, 1327, 1710
, *Early*
New Joy p.180
, *Name*
Peterson — *Art* p.294

GANGS
Guideposts — *Faith* p.198-201

GARAGES
Prochnow — *Public* #122

GARBAGE
Prochnow — *Public* #124, 841

GARDEN OF EDEN
Botkin — *Anecdotes* p.190
Harnsberger — *Mark* p.96
Wallis — *Words* p.55, 173

GARDENS AND GARDENING
Applegarth — *Heir.* p.189-190
Baillie — *Diary* #245
Braude — *Source* #686-689
Braude — *Stories* p.159
Cerf — *Laugh* p.159-162
Dirksen — *Quot.* #47, 199
Flesch — *Unusual* p.99
Fogg — *1000* #727
Hadfield — *Delights* p.159-161, 214-215
Henry — *5000* p.104
Hobe — *Tapestries* p.18, 57, 71, 91, 108
Holmes — *I've* p.118-119
Hovey — *Treasury* #91, 277, 713, 757, 1515
Hubbard — *Scrap* p.65
Kin — *Dictionary* p.104
Lytle — *Leaves* p.49
Manchee — *Secret* p.216-217
New Topical p.99
Peterson — *Art* p.169, 208, 251, 315
Prochnow — *Public* #138, 1071, 1410
Prochnow — *Speaker's* p.141
Prochnow — *Success.* #405
Wallis — *Treasure* p.184, 215, 238
Wallis — *Words* p.49, 52, 93, 143, 171, 173
Woods — *Content.* p.198-199, 203, 205

GARFISH
Botkin — *Anecdotes* p.99-100

GARMENTS. *See* **Clothes**

GARRULITY. *See* **Loquacity; Talk**

GASES
Du Noüy — *Road* p.66-69, 86, 88-89, 94-95, 183

GASOLINE AND GASOLINE STATIONS
Botkin — *Treasury* p.321, 596
Manchee — *Secret* p.228
Prochnow — *Public* #719, 746
Prochnow — *Success.* #938

GATES
Hobe — *Tapestries* p.49-50
Lytle — *Leaves* p.75, 111
New Topical p.100-101

GEESE
Botkin — *Treasury* p.669, 680, 907
Henry — *5000* p.110
Hobe — *Tapestries* p.100
Kin — *Dictionary* p.109
Peale — *Courage* p.146-147
Prochnow — *Public* p.110

GEHRIG, LOU
Reader's — *Getting* p.145-147

GEMS
See also **Jewels**
Edwards — *Useful* p.214
Harral — *Feature* p.167
Kin — *Dictionary* p.104
New Topical p.201

GENEALOGY
See also **Ancestry; Heritage;** etc.
Garland — *Subject* p.118
New Topical p.101
Zobell — *Speaker's* p.65-67

GENERALIZATION
See also **Principles; Reason and reasoning**
Braude — *Stories* p.159-160
Edwards — *Useful* p.728
Flesch — *Unusual* p.99
Seldes — *Great* p.408-409
Wheelis — *Moralist* p.99

GENERALS
Curtis — *Practical* p.106
Dirksen — *Quot.* #193
Kin — *Dictionary* p.104
Nichols — *Third* p.129-130
Peale — *Guideposts* p.310-312
Seldes — *Great* p.409

"GENERATION GAP"
Dirksen — *Quot.* #570
Franke — *Buckley* p.97
Grizer — *Wit* p.186
Kauffman — *For* p.199-200
Lair — *Baby* p.157-169

GENERATIONS
Flesch — *Unusual* p.99-100
Mandelbaum — *Choose* p.180-183
Seldes — *Great* p.409
Wheelis — *Moralist* p.30, 110

GENEROSITY
See also **Benevolence; Charity; Gifts and giving; Philanthropy**
Adams — *New* p.274
Book Proverbs p.127
Braude — *Source* #690-691, 1544-1547
Braude — *Stories* p.160
Dirksen — *Quot.* #325, 928
Edwards — *Useful* p.124-215
Evans — *Unto* p.89, 108
Flesch — *Unusual* p.100
Forbes — *Thoughts* p.94, 164, 175, 215, 372, 376, 378, 461, 490
Fuller — *Epigrams* p.133
Fuller — *Thesaurus* #241-248
Garland — *Subject* p.118
Hobe — *Tapestries* p.43-44
Kin — *Dictionary* p.105
Langdon — *Teach.* p.59-66
Liddle — *Thought I, II, III* p.14, 20, 23, 27, 37, 46, 62, 69, 104, 135
Liddle — *Thought IV* p.12, 31, 37, 44
Lockridge — *World's* #258, 1543, 3001, 4282, 4669
Montapert — *Distilled* p.168
Peale — *Guideposts* p.51-53
Prochnow — *Public* #128, 626, 734
Prochnow — *Speaker's* p.141-142
Speaker's Desk p.71-73; *See also* index p.300
Wallis — *Treasure* p.105, 108
Wallis — *Words* p.50
Weisfeld — *Pulpit* p.110-114
White — *Job* p.125-126, 130, 188
Wilcox — *Heart* p.85-87

GENESIS (Bible)
See also **Creation**
Guideposts — *Faith* p.444-447
Woods — *Religious* p.358-359

GENIES
Asimov — *Treasury* #372

GENIUS
See also **Ability; Mind; Originality; Talent;** etc.
Bach — *Make* p.39-40
Bartlett — *Discovery* p.43-44
Braude — *Source* #692-695
Braude — *Stories* p.160
Curtis — *Practical* p.421-429, 457
Dirksen — *Quot.* #261, 603, 814
Edwards — *Useful* p.215-216, 728
Evans — *Unto* p.143
Flesch — *Unusual* p.101-102
Fogg — *1000* #214, 261, 267, 725, 1095
Forbes — *Thoughts See* index p.551
Fuller — *Epigrams* p.133-134
Garland — *Subject* p.118-119
Grizer — *Wit* p.187
Harnsberger — *Mark* p.141-142
Henry — *5000* p.104
Hill — *Think* p.209-212, 219-220
Hovey — *Treasury* p.192; #27, 585, 876, 1102-1107, 1518, 1602
Hubbard — *Scrap* p.65, 71, 88, 208
Ideas p.159-160
Johnson — *Bedside* p.11, 248, 284
Kin — *Dictionary* p.105, 200
Liddle — *Thought I, II, III* p.59
Lockridge — *World's See* index p.576
Lytle — *Leaves* p.23, 116
Mandel — *Stories* p.100-101
Modern Eloquence p.339
Montapert — *Distilled* p.168-169
Peterson — *Art* p.278
Phillips — *Choice* p.92

Prochnow — *Public* #595, 867, 1471, 1700, 2059, 3119-3124
Prochnow — *Speaker's* p.142-143
Prochnow — *Success.* #206, 874, 1784-1790
Seldes — *Great* p.409-410
Speaker's Desk p.73-75
Voss — *Quotations* p.101-102
Wallis — *Words* p.145
Woods — *Religious* p.359

GENOCIDE
Seldes — *Great* p.410
Woods — *Religious* p.359-360

GENTILES
New Topical p.101
Seldes — *Great* p.410-411

GENTILITY
See also **Ancestry; Aristocracy; Breeding; Gentlemen;** etc.
Braude — *Stories* p.160
Dirksen — *Quot.* #189
Edwards — *Useful* p.216

GENTLEMEN
Applegarth — *Heir.* p.81
Braude — *Stories* p.160-161
Edwards — *Useful* p.216-217
Evans — *Thoughts I* p.66-68
Evans — *Thoughts III (Open Road)* p.90
Forbes — *Thoughts* p.5, 56, 62, 166, 170, 202, 308-309, 498
Fuller — *Thesaurus* #251-256
Grizer — *Wit* p.187-188
Halverson — *Perspective* p.80
Harnsberger — *Mark* p.142
Henry — *5000* p.105
Hobe — *Tapestries* p.174
Ideas p.160-162
Lockridge — *World's* #4603, 5003
Lytle — *Leaves* p.123
Montapert — *Distilled* p.169
New Joy p.16, 170
Prochnow — *Public* #375, 1316, 1701-1702, 3125-3127
Prochnow — *Speaker's* p.143
Prochnow — *Success.* #516, 563, 666, 1791-1792
Seldes — *Great* p.411-412
Wallis — *Treasure* p.45
Wallis — *Words* p.75, 150
Woods — *Wellsprings* p.47-48
, Characteristics of
Hubbard — *Scrap* p.36

GENTLENESS
See also **Compassion; Gentility; Humanity; Kindness; Mercy**
Edwards — *Useful* p.217
Flint — *Graham* p.54-55
Forbes — *Thoughts* p.336
Garland — *Subject* p.119
How To Live p.463-492
Johnson — *Bedside* p.4, 21, 77
Kin — *Dictionary* p.105
Lockridge — *World's* #505, 2810
Petty — *Wings* p.51-55
Price — *Wider* p.33
Prochnow — *Public* #537, 2266
Sheban — *Wisdom* no p.
Woods — *Religious* p.360
, Power of
Peterson — *Art* p.47

GEOGRAPHY
Applegarth — *Heir.* p.231
Prochnow — *Public* #88, 743

GEOLOGY
See also **Earth**
Edwards — *Useful* p.217-218
, and Scripture
Woods — *Religious* p.360
, Periods of
Du Noüy — *Human* p.55, 60, 62-69, 71-79, 98, 125, 170-171

GEOMETRY
Dirksen — *Quot.* #1987
Woods — *Religious* p.360

GEOPOLITICS
Seldes — *Great* p.412

GEORGIA
Botkin — *Anecdotes* p.10, 32, 38, 48, 96, 101, 211
Botkin — *Treasury* p.436, 439, 448, 450-451, 653, 661, 672

GERIATRICS
See also **Old age**
Keys Happiness p.392-396

GERMAN LANGUAGE
Flesch — *Unusual* p.102
Harnsberger — *Mark* p.142-149

GERMAN PROVERBS
Dirksen — *Quot. See* index p.264

GERMANS
Asimov — *Treasury* #405-406, 428, 431, 457
Copeland — *10,000* p.753-756
Harnsberger — *Mark* p.149-150
Lockridge — *World's* #3153-3154, 3161, 4045, 4047, 4049-4050, 4449, 4452
Schermerhorn — *1500* p.176-177

Seldes — *Great* p.412-414
Speaker's Desk #259, 452, 481, 689, 950, 1051, 1115, 1123, 1153

GERMANY
Henry — *5000* p.105
Hovey — *Treasury* #127, 151, 156, 374, 1595
Nizer — *Thinking* p.45, 97, 133-134, 172, 175, 214-216
Wheelis — *Moralist* p.71, 88-89, 95-96, 98, 100-101, 115, 145-146, 149
, Nazism in
Flint — *Graham* p.55
, West
Simpson — *Contemp.* p.130-133

GESTURES
Lockridge — *World's* #4445
Nizer — *Thinking* p.90, 129

GETHSEMANE
Hobe — *Tapestries* p.217
Wallis — *Words* p.55, 68

GETTING. *See* **Acquisition**

"GETTING AHEAD." *See* **Success**

"GETTING ALONG WITH OTHERS"
See also **Cooperation; Popularity**
Evans — *Quote* p.163-175
Keys Happiness p.72, 81-84
Menninger — *Blue.* p.35-41, 141-146
Peterson — *New* p.20-21
Sherman — *Your* p.132-137

"GETTING BY"
Evans — *Thoughts I* p.150-151

"GETTING UP." *See* **Awakening**

GETTYSBURG
Asimov — *Treasury* #149
Fogg — *1000* #232, 277, 416
Hubbard — *Scrap* p.88
Humes — *Instant* p.50
Reader's — *20th* p.71-75
Words — *Inspir.* p.144-145

GHANA
Simpson — *Contemp.* p.133

GHETTOS. *See* **Slums**

GHOST TOWNS
Harral — *Feature* p.168

GHOST-WRITING
Humes — *Instant* p.7, 12-19
Seldes — *Great* p.414

GHOSTS
Cerf — *Laugh* p.476-478
Flesch — *Unusual* p.103
Forbes — *Thoughts* p.409, 461, 498
George — *Book* p.18, 54, 365
Lockridge — *World's* #3658, 4077, 4367, 4409, 4803, 5677
Prochnow — *Public* #296, 942
Seldes — *Great* p.414

GIANTS
George — *Book* p.137, 303
Lockridge — *World's* #3662
Peterson — *Art* p.252
Prochnow — *Public* #2454
Sheban — *Wisdom* no p.

GIBEONITES
New Topical p.101-102

GIDDINESS. *See* **Fickleness**

GIFTS AND GIVING
See also **Benevolence; Charity; Generosity; Philanthropy**
Alexander's Treasure. p.215, 240
Applegarth — *Heir.* p.63, 174
Braude — *Source* #696-720
Braude — *Speaker's* #545-557
Braude — *Stories* p.161
Dirksen — *Quot.* #1013, 1251, 1327-1333, 1501, 2299
Droke — *Christian* p.209-214
Edwards — *Useful* p.217-218
Emmons — *Mature* p.22, 107-116, 158
Evans — *Unto* p.11, 16, 108, 113
Flesch — *Unusual* p.103, 225
Flint — *Graham* p.55, 132
Forbes — *Thoughts See* index p.551
Fox — *Make* p.10-11
Fuller — *Epigrams* p.135-136
Garland — *Subject* p.120
Grizer — *Wit* p.188-190
Halverson — *Perspective* p.85
Harral — *Feature* p.168-169
Henry — *5000* p.105
Hobe — *Tapestries* p.16, 40, 43-44, 63, 101, 127
Hovey — *Treasury* p.192-194; #1108-1120, 1415, 1435, 1779-1780; *See also* index p.296
How To Live p.23-26
Hubbard — *Scrap* p.202
Humes — *Instant* p.42-44, 1234-1235
Kauffman — *For* p.207

Kennedy — *Reader's* #367-370
Keys Happiness p.496-498
Kin — *Dictionary* p.106
Knight's Illus. p.128-131
Knight's Treas. p.139-143
Liddle — *Thought I, II, III* p.7, 12, 87, 110, 127, 139, 191
Liddle — *Thought IV* p.10-11, 13, 22, 36
Liddle — *Thought V* p.26, 38
Lockridge — *World's* #1623; *See* index p.576
Lytle — *Leaves* p.124, 130
Mandel — *Stories* p.53-54, 101-102, 234
Mandelbaum — *Choose* p.81-84
Montapert — *Distilled* p.170-171
New Joy p.177
New Topical p.201-202
Prochnow — *Public See* index p.497
Prochnow — *Speaker's* p.74, 143
Prochnow — *Success.* #1312, 1794-1795
Pullar-Strecker — *Proverbs* #186-195
Sheen — *Thoughts* p.121-123
Sheen — *Way* p.141-153
Voss — *Quotations* p.102-104
Wallis — *Treasure* p.83, 103-108, 173
Wallis — *Words* p.17, 35, 38, 160, 203-204, 222, 227
Welk — *Guide.* p.101-102
Woods — *Content.* p.43
Woods — *Religious* p.191, 360
Woods — *Wellsprings* p.15-16, 35-36
, Art of
Peterson — *Twenty* p.8-9
, Creative
Peterson — *Art* p.382
, Teenager
Daly — *Personality* p.68-73

GILA MONSTERS
Botkin — *Treasury* p.182

GIPSIES. *See* **Gypsies**

GIRAFFES
Applegarth — *Heir.* p.24
Prochnow — *Public* #750
Prochnow — *Success.* #725

GIRDLES
New Topical p.102-103

GIRL SCOUTS OF AMERICA
Harral — *Feature* p.169

GIRLS
Alexander's Treasure. p.33-34, 310
Cerf — *Laugh* p.101-104
Dirksen — *Quot.* #288-289
Edwards — *Useful* p.364
Harnsberger — *Mark* p.150-151
Harral — *Feature* p.169
Hobe — *Tapestries* p.178, 189
Liddle — *Thought I, II, III* p.53, 67
Lockridge — *World's* #904, 972, 2778, 2840, 3423, 4111, 4273, 5612
Prochnow — *Public* #798, 1564, 1744
Prochnow — *Success.* #618, 639, 679, 1037, 1176
Rogers — *Time* p.55-56
Sheban — *Wisdom* no p.
Wallis — *Treasure* p.53, 133
, Definition of
Braude — *Stories* p.423-424

GIVING. *See* **Gifts and giving**

GLACIERS
Harnsberger — *Mark* p.151-153
Peterson — *Art* p.244
Prochnow — *Public* #981

"GLAD HANDERS"
Harral — *Feature* p.169-170

GLADIATORS
Fogg — *1000* #31, 140

GLADNESS. *See* **Cheerfulness; Happiness; Joy**

GLAMOUR
Braude — *Stories* p.161
Evans — *This* p.4-5
Evans — *Unto* p.8, 27
Woods — *Religious* p.360

GLASS AND GLASS BLOWERS
Botkin — *Treasury* p.543
Harral — *Feature* p.170
Kin — *Dictionary* p.106

GLEE CLUBS
Peale — *Guideposts* p.76-79
Prochnow — *Public* #1256

GLITTER
Flesch — *Unusual* p.103
Prochnow — *Public* #2064

GLOOM. *See* **Grief; Pessimism and pessimists**

GLORY

See also **Distinction; Fame; Honor; Wonder**

Adams — *New* p.383
Baillie — *Diary* #171
Braude — *Stories* p.161
Dirksen — *Quot.* #1334, 2020
Edwards — *Useful* p.218-219
Evans — *Unto* p.134
Fogg — *1000* #283, 787, 976
Forbes — *Thoughts* p.106, 167, 186, 310, 489
Garland — *Subject* p.120-121
Henry — *5000* p.106
Hobe — *Tapestries* p.40
Kin — *Dictionary* p.106-107
Kohn — *Pathways* p.37-39
Liddle — *Thought I, II, III* p.135-136, 192
Lockridge — *World's See* index p.576
Lytle — *Leaves* p.147
McDonagh — *Invit.* p.114-120
New Topical p.103
Reader's — *Getting* p.112
Reader's — *20th* p.89
Seldes — *Great* p.414
Sheban — *Wisdom* no p.
Sheen — *Thoughts* p.14-15
Woods — *Religious* p.360

GLOSSOLALIA

Auden — *Certain* p.170-171

GLOVES

Kin — *Dictionary* p.107

GLOWWORMS

Hobe — *Tapestries* p.24
Kin — *Dictionary* p.107

GLUTTONY

See also **Eating; Feasts; Food; Intemperance; Overweight**

Book Proverbs p.106
Edwards — *Useful* p.219
Flint — *Graham* p.55-56
Kin — *Dictionary* p.107
Lockridge — *World's* #3865, 4194
McCracken — *What* p.39-44
New Topical p.104
Speaker's Desk #447, 464, 470, 703, 908, 949
Unlimited Power p.61-64
Woods — *Religious* p.362

GOALS

See also **Ambition; Aspiration; Desire; Ideals and idealism; Purpose**

Albert — *Stop* p.175-177; *See* index p.210
Alexander's Treasure. p.60
Applegarth — *Heir.* p.89, 296, 299
Braude — *Source* #721-725
Braude — *Stories* p.162
Casselberry — *How* p.41-45, 711-713
Curtis — *Daily* p.192-197
Dirksen — *Quot.* #324, 411, 781
Edwards — *Useful* p.17
Forbes — *Thoughts* p.75, 79, 253, 313, 321, 384, 412, 453
Fuller — *Epigrams* p.19-20
Garland — *Subject* p.11
Grizer — *Wit* p.35, 190-191
Guideposts — *Faith* p.337-340
Hobe — *Tapestries* p.118, 173
Hovey — *Treasury* p.194; *See also* index p.296
Jones — *If* p.55-64
Kahn — *Lessons* p.113-114
Kauffman — *For* p.104-105
Kohn — *Adventures* p.149-153
Kohn — *Touch* p.27-31
Lair — *Baby* p.101-112, 215, 227-228
Liddle — *Thought I, II, III* p.32-33, 35, 40-41, 56, 61, 68, 84, 88, 101, 126, 162, 178, 193
Liddle — *Thought IV* p.24-26, 30, 35, 45-46
Liddle — *Thought V* p.18-19, 21, 23, 35, 38, 45-46
Lockridge — *World's* #2468, 4595
Lytle — *Leaves* p.12, 37-38
Maltz — *Creative* p.27-29, 64-80, 217-218
Manchee — *Secret* p.140-141
Mandel — *Stories* p.6-7, 102-103
Menninger — *Blue.* p.68-75
Montapert — *Distilled* p.13-14, 171-173
New Joy p.200
Nichols — *New* p.3-23
Peale — *Courage* p.13-29
Peterson — *Art* p.128
Phillips — *Choice* p.102-103, 266
Prochnow — *Success.* #280
Sheen — *Way* p.105-114
Wallis — *Treasure* p.17, 207
Wallis — *Words* p.117, 122, 182, 236
Webb — *Edge* p.94-114
Welk — *Guide.* p.58-61
White — *Job* p.31-32, 90, 185-186
Woods — *Religious* p.13, 362
Word — *Inspir.* p.219-220
Zobell — *Speaker's* p.67-68

"GOAT-GETTERS"

Safian — *Insults* p.95-98
Safian — *More* p.95-99

GOATS

Auden — *Certain* p.171

Botkin — *Treasury* p.421, 453
Dirksen — *Quot.* #1568
Kin — *Dictionary* p.107
New Topical p.104

GOD
See also **Anthropomorphism; Anti-chance**
Alexander's Treasure. p.46, 57
Asimov — *Treasury See* index p.424
Auden — *Certain* p.172-176
Baillie — *Diary* #17, 33, 56, 78, 214-215, 364
Bartlett — *Discovery* p.145
Book Proverbs p.132
Clark — *Windows* p.30-31, 40, 90
Dirksen — *Quot. See* index p.264
Du Noüy — *Human* p.134-136, 148, 155-156, 167, 188-206
Du Noüy — *Road* p.159, 195, 221-222
Edwards — *Useful* p.219-221, 434
Evans — *Faith See* index no p.
Evans — *Quote* p.125-139
Evans — *This* p.104-105, 155-156, 189-190
Evans — *Thoughts See* index
Evans — *Thoughts II (Open Door) See* index no p.
Evans — *Thoughts III (Open Road) See* index no p.
Evans — *Thoughts IV See* index no p.
Evans — *Unto* p.7, 9, 12, 21, 32-33, 47-48, 56, 59, 80, 95-98, 116-117, 120, 123, 136, 142, 145-146
Flesch — *Unusual* p.64, 104-106, 196
Flint — *Graham* p.56-61, 101
Fogg — *1000 See* index p.887
Forbes — *Thoughts See* index p.551
Fox — *Make* p.32, 82-83, 135, 142-143, 148-151, 172-174, 178, 187-188, 217
Fridy — *Meditat.* p.13, 51-52, 87, 89
Fuller — *Epigrams* p.136-137
Garland — *Subject* p.62, 81-82, 121-122, 213
Giniger — *Compact* p.91-92, 149-165, 273-282
Hadfield — *Love* p.215
Halverson — *Perspective* p.9, 17, 47, 74-75, 99
Harnsberger — *Mark* p.153-156
Henry — *5000* p.106-108
Hobe — *Tapestries* p.16, 63, 67, 108, 134, 207
Holmes — *Design* p.12-13, 24, 29, 33-36, 43, 78, 172-173, 180
Holmes — *I've* p.116
Hovey — *Treasury* p.194-200; *See* index p.296-297
How To Live p.542-543
Howell — *Lines* p.120-122
Hubbard — *Scrap* p.120, 154, 202
Hulme — *Living* p.94-107
Ideas p.162-164
Johnson — *Bedside See* index p.363
Kahn — *Lessons* p.11-67
Kauffman — *For* p.135-136
Kennedy — *Fresh* p.8-11
Kennedy — *Reader's* #371-386
Kin — *Dictionary* p.108, 180
Knight's Treas. p.143-144
Kohn — *Pathways* p.185-189
Lair — *Baby* p.187-198
Liddle — *Thought I, II, III See* index p.197
Liddle — *Thought IV* p.5, 13, 18, 31, 34, 36-39, 43
Liddle — *Thought V* p.5, 7, 11, 13, 15, 23, 32, 34-35
Liebman — *Peace* p.145-175
Lockridge — *World's See* index p.576
Lytle — *Leaves* p.43, 57, 178
Mandel — *Stories* p.103-114
Montapert — *Distilled* p.174
More Words p.6-7, 68-70
Myers — *Thunder* p.35-37
New Joy p.125
New Topical p.104-105
Nichols — *Third* p.129-130
Patterns For Living p.699
Peterson — *Art* p.99, 342
Phillips — *Choice See* index p.426
Prochnow — *Public* #425, 1946, 2111, 2449, 2460, 2648, 2657, 3132-3141, 4108-4109
Prochnow — *Success.* #1361, 1796-1800
Seldes — *Great* p.293, 415, 429
Sheban — *Wisdom* no p.
Sheen — *Way* p.112-114
Speaker's Desk p.75-76; #53, 332, 392, 726
Strait — *Speaker's* p.80-84
Streiker — *Who* p.1-20
Tanksley — *Friend* p.25
Voss — *Quotations* p.72-73
Wallis — *Treasure See* index p.248
Wallis — *Words* p.29, 248
Watson — *Light* p.32-71
Wheelis — *Moralist* p.9, 32, 67, 111, 114, 140; *See* index p.163
White — *Job* p.79, 114, 154-161, 164, 172-173
White — *Life* p.201-207, 244-259
Woods — *Content. See* index p.380

Woods — *Religious* p.201-202, 245-246, 393, 496, 703
Zobell — *Speaker's* p.62
, *Acceptance by*
Redhead — *Living* p.87-95
, *Access to*
New Topical p.5
, *Acquaintance of*
Baillie — *Diary* #254
, *Aliveness of*
Kauffman — *For* p.105-107
, *and devil*
Flesch — *Unusual* p.105
, *and ego*
Sheen — *Lift* p.45-53
, *and freedom*
Woods — *Religious* p.351-353
, *and man*
Baillie — *Diary* #30
Braude — *Source* #726-733
Flesch — *Unusual* p.105-106
Kauffman — *For* p.108
Mandelbaum — *Choose* p.19-24
Montapert — *Distilled* p.175-176
Woods — *Religious* p.590-605
, *and world crisis*
Sheen — *Thoughts* p.183-184
, *Anger of*
New Topical p.15
Woods — *Religious* p.383-384
, *Approach to*
Baillie — *Diary* #256
, *as being*
Woods — *Religious* p.393-394
, *as shepherd*
Kohn — *Through* p.19-22
, *Attributes of*
Kohn — *Best* p.48-49
Woods — *Religious* p.371-372
, *Awareness of*
Kohn — *Touch* p.34-36
, *Belief in*
Ideas p.104-106
Phillips — *Choice* p.399
Seldes — *Great* p.257-258
Woods — *Religious* p.225
, *Bill of rights of*
Fox — *Make* p.150-151
, *Blasphemy against*
See also **Profanity**
Woods — *Religious* p.364-365
, *Call of*
New Topical p.36-37
, *Care of*
Emmons — *Mature* p.44, 74
Knight's Illus. p.29-31
Knight's Treas. p.20-23
, *Character of. See* **God, Attributes of**
, *Commandments of*
See also **Commandments, Ten**
Evans — *Thoughts IV See* index no p.
, *Comments on*
Woods — *Religious* p.388-393
, *Communion with*
Flint — *Graham* p.33
Knight's Illus. p.58-59
Knight's Treas. p.57-61
New Topical p.50-51
, *Concept of*
Kauffman — *For* p.106-107
, *Concern of*
Kohn — *Through* p.113-115
Unlimited Power p.158-209
, *Confusion about*
Price — *Wider* p.57-64
. *Considered as impersonal*
Woods — *Religious* p.365-367
, *Considered as personal*
Woods — *Religious* p.367-369
, *Constancy of*
Hunter — *Gems* p.33-34
, *Contemplation of*
Voss — *Quotations* p.104-106
, *Counsels and purposes of*
New Topical p.53-54
, *Courage from*
See also **Courage**
Maxwell — *Courage* p.27-88
Montapert — *Distilled* p.176-177
, *Death of. See* **Atheism; "God is dead" movement**
, *Dedication to*
Day — *Meditations* p.63-64
, *Definitions of. See* **God, Meaning of**
, *Delight in*
New Topical p.63
, *Denial of*
Liebman — *Peace* p.146-148
New Topical p.216-217
Woods — *Religious* p.20-21, 387-388
, *Devotion to*
Knight's Illus. p.197
New Topical p.68
, *Doctrines about*
New Topical p.303-306
, *Door to*
Baillie — *Diary* #79
Clark — *Windows* p.52, 114
Nichols — *New* p.50-52

, *Encounter with*
Sheen — *Content.* p.66-68
Suter — *Prayers* #173-206
, *Evidence of*
Flint — *Graham* p.49
Kohn — *Through* p.117-119
, *Existence of*
Woods — *Religious* p.372-374
, *Eyes of*
Baillie — *Diary* #199-200
Sheen — *Content.* p.182-184
, *Faithfulness of*
Knight's Illus. p.111
New Topical p.85
, *Fatherhood of*
Woods — *Inspir.* p.378-397
Woods — *Religious* p.369
, *Favor of*
New Topical p.87
, *Fear of*
New Topical p.87-88
, *Finding of*
Baillie — *Diary* #16, 272
Goudge — *Comfort* p.219-231
Woods — *Religious* p.369-371
, *Finger of*
Woods — *Wellsprings* p.75-76
, *Footprints of*
Clark — *Windows* p.18-19
, *Forgetting*
Knight's Illus. p.117-118
Knight's Treas. p.127-129
New Topical p.95-96
, *Forgiveness of*
Knight's Illus. p.119-122
Knight's Treas. p.129-131
, *Forsaking*
New Topical p.96, 217
, *Freedom of*
Price — *Wider* p.17-22
, *Fullness of*
Taylor — *With* p.61-65
, *Gifts of*
New Topical p.102
, *Glorification of*
Baillie — *Diary* #331
New Topical p.103
Woods — *Religious* p.388
, *Glory of*
Carruthers — *Sparks* p.125-126
Evans — *This* p.104-105
New Topical p.103-104
Woods — *Religious* p.361-362
, *Goodness of*
Baillie — *Diary* #332
Emmons — *Mature* p.73-78
New Topical p.105-106
Peterson — *Art* p.55, 336-337
Woods — *Religious* p.374-375
, *Government and*
Woods — *Religious* p.405-406
, *Grace of*
Baillie — *Diary* #198
Dirksen — *Quot.* #1226-1229
Ideas p.113-116
More Words p.75-77
Woods — *Wellsprings* p.72-73
, *Grandeur of*
Hadfield — *Delights* p.227
Kennedy — *Fresh* p.38-40
Knight's Illus. p.135-136
, *Gratitude from*
Unlimited Power p.210-255
, *Guidance of*
Hunter — *Gems* p.36-37
, *Help of*
Carruthers — *Sparks* p.39-40
Nichols — *New* p.174-175
Unlimited Power p.2-47
, *Infinity of*
White — *Job* p.159-161, 163-164
Woods — *Religious* p.375-376
, *Ingratitude to*
New Topical p.130
, *Intervention of*
Woods — *Religious* p.376-378
, *Judgment of*
More Words p.92-93
Porter — *Halo* p.128-131
Woods — *Religious* p.520-521
, *Justice of*
New Topical p.141
Phillips — *Choice* p.364
, *Kingdom of*
See also **Heaven**
Flint — *Graham* p.81
Fox — *Make* p.193
Hunter — *Gems* p.42-43
More Words p.95-97
Phillips — *Choice* p.xii, 104-106, 313, 391
Wallis — *Treasure* p.51, 151, 187
Wallis — *Words* p.29, 109, 113
Woods — *Religious* p.526-527
Words — *Change* p.125
, *Knowledge of*
Evans — *This* p.55, 104-105
Hobe — *Tapestries* p.95
Holmes — *Design* p.172-173
Montapert — *Distilled* p.176
Woods — *Religious* p.384-387

, Law of
See also **God, Commandments of**
Baillie — *Diary* #306
New Topical p.146
Phillips — *Choice* p.339
, Life with
Price — *Wider* p.25-34
, Light of
Baillie — *Diary* #225, 258
Clark — *Windows* p.152
Hobe — *Tapestries* p.18
Kohn — *Best* p.97
, Living
Baillie — *Diary* #148
, Love of
Baillie — *Diary* #207, 219, 328
Clark — *Windows* p.56-57
Flesch — *Unusual* p.157-158
Fox — *Make* p.38-39
Fridy — *Meditat.* p.68
Goudge — *Comfort* p.155-159
Halverson — *Perspective* p.20, 24
Hubbard — *Scrap* p.17, 30, 33
Hunter — *Gems* p.47
Knight's Illus. p.195-197
Knight's Treas. p.217-219
Maxwell — *Courage* p.91-101
Montapert — *Distilled* p.244
New Topical p.155-156
Sheen — *Light* p.198-213
Tanksley — *Friend* p.44
Taylor — *With* p.35-38
Voss — *Quotations* p.109-110
Woods — *Religious* p.10-11, 562-564, 567-570
Woods — *Wellsprings* p.75
, Meaning of
Flesch — *Unusual* p.104
Kopplin — *Something* p.157-178
Liebman — *Hope* p.132-133
Voss — *Quotations* p.106-108
, Mercy of
Baillie — *Diary* #131, 235
New Topical p.164-165
Sheen — *Content.* p.136-137
Words — *Inspir.* p.205-206
, Mission for
Woods — *Religious* p.637
, Modern idea of
Irion — *Yes* p.134-145
, Mystery of
Krishnamurti — *Urgency* p.8-11
Phillips — *Choice* p.38, 119, 408
, Nature of
Tanksley — *Friend* p.32
Voss — *Quotations* p.110-112
Woods — *Religious* p.378-380
, Need for
Clark — *Windows* p.62-63
Hunter — *Gems* p.58-59
New Topical p.129
, Obedience to
Guideposts — *Faith* p.428-434
New Topical p.180
, of Christians
Baillie — *Diary* #37
, One day with
Unlimited Power p.97-100
, Partnership with
Flint — *Graham* p.102
Kahn — *Lessons* p.30-35
Kennedy — *Fresh* p.41-50
, Peace of
See also **Peace, of mind**
Hunter — *Gems* p.76-77
Montapert — *Distilled* p.177-178
, Playing
Nichols — *New* p.134-135
, Power of
Clark — *Windows* p.104
Emmons — *Mature* p.79-83
Halverson — *Perspective* p.114
New Topical p.196
Woods — *Religious* p.380-382
, Presence of
Applegarth — *Heir.* p.13, 202
Baillie — *Diary* #302
Knight's Illus. p.252-254
Knight's Treas. p.292-298
Woods — *Religious* p.382-383
, Promises of
New Topical p.206-207
, Providence of
Baillie — *Diary* #295
Hobe — *Tapestries* p.16-17
Kennedy — *Fresh* p.29-30
Knight's Illus. p.260-262
Knight's Treas. p.302-307
New Topical p.212
, Reality of
Phillips — *Choice* p.400
, Reason and
Woods — *Religious* p.818-819
, Respect for
Flint — *Graham* p.119
, Responsibility of
Kohn — *Through* p.21-22
, Righteousness of
Baillie — *Diary* #89
New Topical p.118-119, 227

, *Sayings about*
Woods — *Religious* p.362-364
, *Seeking*
Krishnamurti — *Think* p.210-217
New Topical p.241-242
Voss — *Quotations* p.113-115
Woods — *Wellsprings* p.69-76
, *Sign of*
Baillie — *Diary* #350
, *Sociableness of*
Baillie — *Diary* #284
, *Song of*
Fox — *Make* p.105-106
, *Surrender to*
Guideposts — *Faith* p.140-142
, *Talking to*
Holmes — *I've* p.1-12
, *Thinking of*
Baillie — *Diary* #210, 268, 316
, *Trust in*
Humes — *Instant* #1224-1227
. *Tug of*
Kohn — *Best* p.51-53
, *Understanding*
Curtis — *Golden* p.14-23
, *Unity of*
New Topical p.283
, *Urge of*
Holmes — *Design* p.174-175
, *Victory of*
Maxwell — *Courage* p.209-217
, *Waiting upon*
New Topical p.289
, *Way to*
Sheban — *Wisdom* no p.
, *Will of*
See also **Consecration**
Baillie — *Diary* #14
Flesch — *Unusual* p.310-311
Halverson — *Perspective* p.77
Johnson — *Bedside* p.3, 213-214, 337
Knight's Illus. p.345-348
Knight's Treas. p.429-433
Kohn — *Best* p.114-116
Montapert — *Distilled* p.177
, *Wisdom of*
See also **God, Knowledge of**
New Topical p.297-298
Woods — *Religious* p.383
, *Word of*
Fox — *Make* p.86-87
Goudge — *Comfort* p.284-289
Hobe — *Tapestries* p.143, 210
Hovey — *Treasury* #6, 81, 136, 140, 154, 441, 449, 455, 477, 491, 499, 592, 1715
Kennedy — *Fresh* p.128-136
Wallis — *Words* p.33, 46
White — *Life* p.271-274
Woods — *Religious* p.1062-1063
, *Worship of*
Krishnamurti — *Think* p.132

"GOD IS DEAD" MOVEMENT
See also **Atheism**
Flint — *Graham* p.60
Sheen — *Content.* p.163-165
Strait — *Speaker's* p.85-87
Webb — *Edge* p.60-63
Wheelis — *Moralist* p.3-5, 21, 39-40

GODLESSNESS. *See* **Atheism**

GODLINESS
See also **God; Good; Holiness; Piety; Righteousness**
Evans — *Unto* p.66
Flint — *Graham* p.153
Hunter — *Gems* p.68-69
Woods — *Religious* p.395

GODPARENTS AND GODCHILDREN
Baillie — *Diary* #2
More Words p.70-71

GODS
See also **Idols and idolatry**
Flesch — *Unusual* p.106
Garland — *Subject* p.122
Henry — *5000* p.108
Seldes — *Great* p.429-431
, *Comic*
Botkin — *Treasury* p.175-178
, *False*
Evans — *Unto* p.94, 97
Flint — *Graham* p.11
Woods — *Religious* p.324
, *Ordaining of*
Adams — *New* p.232-233

GOETHE, JOHANN VON
Lockridge — *World's* #4147, 4224, 5492, 5507
Words — *Inspir.* p.13

"GOING STEADY"
Daly — *Personality* p.56-63
Flint — *Graham* p.156-157
Menninger — *Blue.* p.202-204
Sheen — *Content.* p.25-27

GOLD
Edwards — *Useful* p.221-222
Forbes — *Thoughts* p.39, 139, 190, 225, 241, 298, 340, 346, 454-455
Grizer — *Wit* p.192
Harral — *Feature* p.170
Henry — *5000* p.108
Hobe — *Tapestries* p.92
Kin — *Dictionary* p.108
Lockridge — *World's* #4250
Lytle — *Leaves* p.47, 150
Mandel — *Stories* p.114-115
Montapert — *Distilled* p.178
New Topical p.105
Prochnow — *Speaker's* p.143-145
Prochnow — *Success.* #1282
Seldes — *Great* p.431-432
Sheban — *Wisdom* no p.
Wallis — *Words* p.176
Woods — *Business.* p.89
Woods — *Religious* p.395
, *Standard of*
Dirksen — *Quot.* #645

"GOLD DIGGERS"
Braude — *Stories* p.162
Prochnow — *Public* #1703
Safian — *Insults* p.99-105
Safian — *More Insults* p.100-104

GOLDEN AGE
Applegarth — *Heir.* p.273
Dirksen — *Quot.* #230
Ideas p.164-165

GOLDEN MEAN
See also **Moderation**
Ideas p.165-166, 183
Seldes — *Great* p.422
Woods — *Content.* p.236

"GOLDEN RULE"
Alexander's Treasure. p.xxxi-1, 242-246, 338-341
Braude — *Source* #734-735
Braude — *Speaker's* #558-559
Curtis — *Daily* p.23
Curtis — *Golden* p.169-170
Dirksen — *Quot.* #933-934, 1222, 2081
Flesch — *Unusual* p.106
Forbes — *Thoughts* p.64, 95, 114, 125, 281, 396
Garland — *Subject* p.122
Henry — *5000* p.108-109
Hovey — *Treasury* p.200-201; #480, 825, 1163-1165
Hubbard — *Scrap* p.39
Kauffman — *For* p.207-208
Keys Happiness p.11-15
Knight's Illus. p.131-132
Lockridge — *World's* #2321, 5736
Manchee — *Secret* p.110-114
Mandel — *Stories* p.115
Menninger — *Blue.* p.102
Peale — *Guideposts* p.313-317
Prochnow — *Success.* #1801-1802
Seldes — *Great* p.432-434
Wallis — *Treasure* p.111, 132
Wallis — *Words* p.163
Watson — *Light* p.193-198
Woods — *Religious* p.395-396

GOLF
Asimov — *Treasury* #5, 8, 458-459, 469, 481, 490, 532, 563, 582
Braude — *Source* #736-742
Braude — *Speaker's* #560-573
Braude — *Stories* p.162-165
Cerf — *Laugh* p.137-141
Copeland — *10,000* p.603-610
Dirksen — *Quot.* #1698
Flesch — *Unusual* p.106
Flint — *Graham* p.21, 61
Fuller — *Thesaurus* #1861-1869
Grizer — *Wit* p.192
Harral — *Feature* p.170-171
Peale — *Guideposts* p.7-10
Prochnow — *Public* #674; *See* index p.497
Prochnow — *Speaker's* p.145-146
Prochnow — *Success.* #689, 811, 825, 872, 936, 1023, 1155, 1432, 1803
Schermerhorn — *1500* p.177-179
Speaker's Desk #27, 35, 125, 139, 190, 246, 583, 707, 935-936, 1036
Weisfeld — *Pulpit* p.17, 29, 91-92, 95-96

GOLGOTHA
Book Proverbs p.138
Wallis — *Words* p.58

GONDOLAS
Botkin — *Anecdotes* p.78

GOOD
See also **Brotherhood; "Golden Rule"; Kindness; Morality and morals; Virtues**
Applegarth — *Heir.* p.17, 78, 215, 243-244, 249
Asimov — *Treasury* #511
Bach — *Make* p.21-27
Baillie — *Diary* #223
Book Proverbs p.92, 94
Braude — *Source* #743-747
Braude — *Stories* p.165
Curtis — *Practical* p.47
Dirksen — *Quot. See* index p.264

Droke — *Christian* p.215-231
Edwards — *Useful* p.224-226
Evans — *Faith* p.16, 58, 65-68, 71-72, 79, 83-84, 90, 116, 164, 203-204
Evans — *Thoughts II (Open Door)* p.139-140
Evans — *Thoughts III (Open Road)* p.46-47, 109-110, 121, 202
Flesch — *Unusual* p.66, 106-107
Forbes — *Thoughts See* index p.351
Fox — *Make* p.78
Fuller — *Epigrams* p.137-138
Garland — *Subject* p.122-123
Guideposts — *Faith* p.198-201
Halversen — *Perspective* p.14, 91
Harnsberger — *Mark* p.156-157
Henry — *5000* p.109-110
Hobe — *Tapestries* p.62, 64-71, 110, 173
Holman — *Psych.* p.137-145
Holmes — *Design* p.22, 30, 32-34, 98, 117, 130, 206, 225-226
Hovey — *Treasury* p.201; *See* index p.297
How To Live p.36-39, 565
Johnson — *Bedside* p.1-2, 4, 6, 15, 21, 62, 90, 183, 212, 284, 299, 312, 333, 335
Keller — *Open* p.7, 77, 123-124
Kennedy — *Fresh* p.62-64
Kennedy — *Reader's* #387-395
Keys Happiness p.418-421
Kin — *Dictionary* p.108-109
Kohn — *Through* p.147-150
Lair — *Baby* p.119-121
Liddle — *Thought I, II, III See* index p.197
Liddle — *Thought IV* p.26, 28
Liddle — *Thought V* p.6-7, 26, 31, 41
Lockridge — *World's See* index p.576
Lytle — *Leaves* p.21, 41, 50, 57, 84, 121, 133, 141, 149, 159, 166, 169
Mandelbaum — *Choose* p.54, 180-183
Menninger — *Blue.* p.92
Montapert — *Distilled* p.114-115, 178-179
More Words p.72-73
New Joy p.25, 52
Peterson — *Art* p.122, 141, 190
Petty — *Promises* p.37-50
Petty — *Wings* p.56-63
Phillips — *Choice* p.21, 51, 83, 134, 158, 366
Price — *Wider* p.32
Prochnow — *Public* #2679, 2696, 2733, 2737
Prochnow — *Speaker's* p.146
Prochnow — *Success.* #1074, 1804
Seldes — *Great* p.434-435, 438
Sheban — *Wisdom* no p.
Sheen — *Thoughts* p.32-33, 59-60
Voss — *Quotations* p.115-117
Wallis — *Treasure* p.48, 109-114
Wallis — *Words* p.137, 230
Welk — *Guide.* p.81-83
Wheelis — *Moralist* p.18-19,37-54, 111
Woods — *Religious* p.396-399, 401-403
Words — *Inspir.* p.66
, Absolute
Du Noüy — *Human* p.130-131, 133, 225-226
, and evil
Adams — *New* p.384
Evans — *Unto* p.71, 84-85, 131
Flesch — *Unusual* p.107
Hubbard — *Scrap* p,86, 92
Kauffman — *For* p.108-109
Seldes — *Great* p.435-438
Woods — *Religious* p.399-401
, Desire for
Sheen — *Thoughts* p.61-63
, Discrimination against
Carruthers — *Sparks* p.67-68
, Impulse for
Baillie — *Diary* #305
, Inherent
Nichols — *New* p.136-137
, of all
Baillie — *Diary* #303
, Power of
Hubbard — *Scrap* p.118
Mandelbaum — *Choose* p.33-35
, Repayment with
Clark — *Windows* p.132
, Works of
Flesch — *Unusual* p.108
Mandel — *Stories* p.115-116
New Topical p.300-301
Prochnow — *Success.* #1806-1807

GOOD FRIDAY
Auden — *Certain* p.168-169
Flint — *Graham* p.62
Kohn — *Best* p.119-127

GOOD HUMOR. *See* **Cheerfulness; Humor**

GOOD NATURE. *See* **Cheerfulness; Kindness;** etc.

GOOD SENSE. *See* **Common sense; Sense**

GOOD TASTE. *See* **Choice; Discrimination; Values**

GOOD WILL
Copeland — *10,000* p.998-1000
Flesch — *Unusual* p.108
Forbes — *Thoughts See* index p.552
Garland — *Subject* p.123
Grizer — *Wit* p.193
Kahn — *Lessons* p.209-217
Peterson — *Art* p.62, 312
Seldes — *Great* p.438
Wallis — *Words* p.75, 82
Welk — *Guide.* p.39-41
Woods — *Religious* p.401

"GOODBYES." *See* **Farewells; Words, Dying**

GOODNESS. *See* **Good**

GOODS. *See* **Possessions**

GORDIAN KNOT
Prochnow — *Public* #2378

GORILLAS
Prochnow — *Success.* #1155

GOSPEL
See also **Bible; New Testament**
Edwards — *Useful* p.226
Flint — *Graham* p.10, 62-63, 136
Fridy — *Meditat.* p.23
Kennedy — *Reader's* #396-398
Knight's Illus. p.132-135
Knight's Treas. p.144-146
More Words p.73-75
New Topical p.106
Seldes — *Great* p.439
Strait — *Speaker's* p.88-89
Zobell — *Speaker's* p.69-71

GOSSIP
Adams — *New* p.262
Alexander's Treasure. p.135, 212, 328
Book Proverbs p.100
Braude — *Source* #748-756, 1644
Braude — *Speaker's* #574-579
Braude — *Stories* p.165-166
Dirksen — *Quot.* #237
Edwards — *Useful* p.38, 60, 226-227; 633
Emmons — *Mature* p.100
Evans — *Faith* p.14, 186
Evans — *Quote* p.187-194
Evans — *This* p.67, 157-158
Evans — *Thoughts II (Open Door)* p.134, 137-138, 154-155, 195
Evans — *Unto* p.28, 78
Flesch — *Unusual* p.108
Flint — *Graham* p.63
Fuller — *Epigrams* p.138-139
Fuller — *Thesaurus* #821-826
Grizer — *Wit* p.193
Guideposts — *Faith* p.58
Harnsberger — *Mark* p.157
Harral — *Feature* p.171
Henry — *5000* p.110-111
Keys Happiness p.76-80
Kin — *Dictionary* p.109, 159, 250
Liddle — *Thought I, II, III* p.60, 63, 89, 95-96, 121, 134, 155, 164
Lockridge — *World's* #141-142, 889, 1446, 2767, 2906
Lytle — *Leaves* p.23, 74-75
Mandel — *Stories* p.116-117
Menninger — *Blue.* p.143
Montapert — *Distilled* p.179
Myers — *Thunder* p.138-144
New Topical p.36
Prochnow — *Public* #503, 740, 1266, 1341, 2066, 2533, 3142-3144
Prochnow — *Speaker's* p.147
Prochnow — *Success.* #959, 964, 1190
Rogers — *Time* p.91-93
Safian — *Insults* p.106-109
Safian — *More* p.105-108
Sheen — *Way* p.156-157
Speaker's Desk #198, 355
Woods — *Religious* p.403-404
Woods — *Wellsprings* p.19-20
Words — *Inspir.* p.25

GOVERNMENT
See also **Americans and Americanism; Budgets, Governmental; Bureaucracy; Freedom; Law; Liberty; Patriotism; Politics and politicians; Rulers; Self-government; Statesmen and statesmanship**
Braude — *Source* #757-767
Braude — *Speaker's* p.148-154; #580-582
Braude — *Stories* p.166-170
Curtis — *Practical* p.343-347, 366-372, 377
Detherage — *Sunrise* p.94, 162, 166
Dirksen — *Quot.* #13, 29, 34, 54, 58, 68; *See* index p.264, 613
Droke — *Christian* p.232-237
Edwards — *Useful* p.227-230; 728
Esteve — *Experience* p.66-67, 112-113
Evans — *Quite* p.81-96
Evans — *This* p.133-134
Evans — *Unto* p.58, 60
Flesch — *Unusual* p.108-109
Fogg — *1000 See* index p.887

Forbes — *Thoughts See* index p.552
Franke — *Buckley* p.6-7
Fuller — *Epigrams* p.139-140
Grizer — *Wit* p.194-196
Harnsberger — *Mark* p.157-158
Harral — *Features* p.171-173
Henry — *5000* p.111-112
Hovey — *Treasury* #5, 58, 70, 537, 551, 768, 1327, 1347, 1349, 1562, 1585, 1588, 1598, 1636, 1756
Hubbard — *Scrap* p.179, 197, 204
Humes — *Instant* p.47; #390-404
Johnson — *Bedside* p.94, 125
Keller — *You* p.83-118
Kennedy — *Reader's* #399-401
Kin — *Dictionary* p.110
Liddle — *Thought III* p.31, 34, 47-48, 62, 78, 97, 113, 133, 141, 169, 184-185
Liddle — *Thought IV* p.6, 13
Lockridge — *World's See* index p.576
Montapert — *Distilled* p.179-180
Prochnow — *Public See* index p.497
Prochnow — *Success. See* index p.491
Seldes — *Great* p.439-457
Simpson — *Contemp.* p.1-9
Simpson — *'54* p.35, 149, 293
Speaker's Desk p.77-81; #50, 1006
Woods — *Business.* p.89-92
Woods — *Content.* p.110, 113
Woods — *Religious* p.404-405
Words — *Inspir.* p.138
Zobell — *Speaker's* p.71-74

, and religion
Woods — *Religious* p.404-409

, and rulers
Fuller — *Thesaurus* p.332-363

, Centralized
Woods — *Business.* p.93-95

, Crime in
Kauffman — *For* p.77-78

, Economic role in
Woods — *Business.* p.104-107

, Evils of
Dirksen — *Quot.* #614

, Intervention of
Woods — *Religious* p.409

, Officials of
Prochnow — *Success.* #24-46

, Ownership
Woods — *Business.* p.95-96

, Regulation
Woods — *Business.* p.96-104

, Spending
Woods — *Business.* p.107-111

GOVERNORS
Fuller — *Thesaurus* #1956
Sheban — *Wisdom* no p.

"GRAB BAGS"
Cerf — *Laugh* p.467-472

GRACE
See also **Charm; Delicacy;** etc.
Applegarth — *Heir.* p.44, 79, 131, 177
Baillie — *Diary* #122, 157, 171, 218, 220, 253
Curtis — *New* p.18-19
Edwards — *Useful* p.230-231
Flesch — *Unusual* p.109
Flint — *Graham* p.63
Forbes — *Thoughts* p.200, 297, 365-396, 473
Garland — *Subject* p.124-125
Guideposts — *Faith* p.51-54
Halverson — *Perspective* p.92
Henry — *5000* p.112
Hobe — *Tapestries* p.16, 113
Hovey — *Treasury* #491, 525, 586, 823, 1254, 1573, 1821
Johnson — *Bedside* p.2
Kin — *Dictionary* p.110
Knight's Treas. p.146-147
Liddle — *Thought I, II, III* p.16
Lockridge — *World's* #68, 632, 651, 679, 2560, 4189, 4258
Lytle — *Leaves* p.83
New Topical p.106-107
Nichols — *Third* p.74-75
Phillips — *Choice* p.35, 101, 107, 119, 139, 171, 226
Prochnow — *Public* #2068
Prochnow — *Success.* #1816-1817
Schermerhorn — *1500* p.180-181
Sheen — *Lift* p.116-127
Voss — *Quotations* p.117-118
Wallis — *Treasure* p.46, 65, 124, 225
Wallis — *Words* p.17, 49, 154
Welk — *Guide.* p.65-66
Woods — *Content.* p.27, 247
Woods — *Religious* p.409-413
Words Change p.41

, at meals
Unlimited Power p.223-226

, Christian
Suter — *Prayers* #207-277

, Definitions of
Woods — *Religious* p.413-414

, Divine. See **God, Grace of**

, Growth in
Baillie — *Diary* #308

GRACES
Flesch — *Unusual* p.109
Prochnow — *Success.* #1818

GRACIOUSNESS. *See* **Courtesy; Grace**

GRADES
Harral — *Feature* p.173
Prochnow — *Public* #110, 161, 208
Prochnow — *Success.* #996

GRADUALISM
Dirksen — *Quot.* #2029-2031
Flesch — *Unusual* p.109
Seldes — *Great* p.457

GRADUATION. *See* **Commencement**

GRAFT
Fogg — *1000* #76, 157, 736, 1013, 1070
Kin — *Dictionary* p.110

GRAIN
See also **Crops**
Kin — *Dictionary* p.110
Lockridge — *World's* #4952

GRAMMAR
See also **Language; Words**
Dirksen — *Quot.* #234
Flesch — *Unusual* p.109
Harnsberger — *Mark* p.159-162
Prochnow — *Public* #97, 304
Prochnow — *Speaker's* p.154
Prochnow — *Success.* #1367
Schermerhorn — *1500* p.181
Wallis — *Treasure* p.163
, "Split infinitive" in
Flesch — *Unusual* p.275

GRAND CANYON
Botkin — *Anecdotes* p.74, 106
Prochnow — *Success.* #955

GRANDCHILDREN
Braude — *Source* #768
Grizer — *Wit* p.196
Prochnow — *Public* #153, 506

GRANDPARENTS
Alexander's Treasure. p.299
Asimov — *Treasury* #117, 378, 501
Braude — *Source* #769-770
Harral — *Feature* p.173
Hobe — *Tapestries* p.171
Unlimited Power p.227-229

GRANT, ULYSSES S.
Harnsberger — *Mark* p.162-164

GRAPES AND GRAVEVINES
Applegarth — *Heir.* p.190
Kin — *Dictionary* p.110

GRASPING
Kin — *Dictionary* p.110

GRASS
Applegarth — *Heir.* p.192
Kin — *Dictionary* p.110
Mandelbaum — *Choose* p.15
New Topical p.107
Prochnow — *Public* #2040

"GRASS ROOTS"
Dirksen — *Quot.* #45

GRASSHOPPERS
Applegarth — *Heir.* p.198
Botkin — *Treasury* p.230, 282, 312, 427, 610

GRATITUDE
See also **Appreciation; Thankfulness; Thanksgiving**
Applegarth — *Heir.* p.80, 157
Baillie — *Diary* #124
Book Proverbs p.127
Braude — *Source* #771-777
Braude — *Speaker's* #583-586
Braude — *Stories* p.170
Clark — *Windows* p.176
Detherage — *Sunrise* p.122, 136, 163
Dirksen — *Quot.* #2, 149, 415
Droke — *Christian* p.237
Edwards — *Usefulness* p.231-232
Evans — *Faith* p.79-80
Evans — *Thoughts I* p.45, 50, 113-114, 129, 160
Evans — *Thoughts II (Open Door)* p.116-117, 126-127, 165, 167, 176-178, 180
Evans — *Thoughts III (Open Road)* p.161, 171, 175, 189-190, 196
Evans — *Thoughts IV* p.157-158, 199
Flesch — *Unusual* p.110
Fogg — *1000* #212, 624, 665, 780, 886, 1011
Forbes — *Thoughts* p.201, 205
Fuller — *Epigrams* p.140
Fuller — *Thesaurus* #261-268
Garland — *Subject* p.125
Grizer — *Wit* p.196-197
Guideposts — *Faith* p.363
Harnsberger — *Mark* p.164
Harral — *Feature* p.173
Henry — *5000* p.113
Hobe — *Tapestries* p.25-26
Hovey — *Treasury* p.201; #1172-1174, 1332
How To Live p.67, 479-483

Howell — *Better* p.77-80
Howell — *Lines* p.96
Hubbard — *Scrap* p.21, 23
Humes — *Instant* #405
Kennedy — *Reader's* #402-403
Kin — *Dictionary* p.111
Kohn — *Touch* p.65-69
Langdon — *Teach.* p.91-100
Liddle — *Thought I, II, III* p.9, 15, 17, 37, 54, 62, 89, 108, 189
Liddle — *Thought IV* p.9
Lockridge — *World's* #234-236, 238, 308-309, 463, 620, 3831, 3984, 4562
Lytle — *Leaves* p.34
Mandel — *Stories* p.117-119
Montapert — *Distilled* p.181
Morris — *1000* p.30, 93, 191, 204, 241, 380
Peterson — *Art* p.185, 375
Prochnow — *Public* #3156-3159
Prochnow — *Speaker's* p.155
Prochnow — *Success.* #1819-1820
Speaker's Desk p.81-82; *See* index p.300
Unlimited Power p.212-215, 240-243
Voss — *Quotations* p.118-119
Wallis — *Treasure* p.108, 131, 158, 213, 215-216, 228
Wallis — *Words* p.30, 49, 207-208
White — *Life* p.156
Woods — *Content.* p.55, 98, 234
Woods — *Religious* p.414
Woods — *Wellsprings* p.13-14, 17

GRAVES
See also **Cemeteries; Epitaphs; Monuments**
Dirksen — *Quot.* #459, 940-941, 1304, 1882, 1914, 2007, 2020
Edwards — *Useful* p.232
Harral — *Feature* p.174
Henry — *5000* p.113
Kin — *Dictionary* p.111
Woods — *Religious* p.414

GRAVITATION
Du Noüy — *Road* p.40, 48, 57, 70, 88, 95, 167
Forbes — *Thoughts* p.237, 280, 405, 510

GRAVITY
See also **Earnestness**
Curtis — *Practical* p.95
Edwards — *Useful* p.232-233
Flesch — *Unusual* p.259-260
Fuller — *Epigrams* p.141
Harnsberger — *Mark* p.428
Krishnamurti — *Think* p.97-98
Lockridge — *World's* #269, 3598
Phillips — *Choice* p.190
Prochnow — *Speaker's* p.155
Welk — *Guide.* p.78-80

GRAY, THOMAS
Flesch — *Unusual* p.110

GRAY (color)
Flesch — *Unusual* p.110

GRAZING
Prochnow — *Public* #320

GREAT BRITAIN
See also names of countries
Hubbard — *Scrap* p.193
Simpson — *Contemp.* p.133-144
, Parliament of
Flesch — *Unusual* p.203
Fuller — *Thesaurus* #1996-2000
Prochnow — *Success.* #1429
Seldes — *Great* p.713

GREAT PLAINS
Botkin — *Treasury* p.282. 319

GREATNESS
See also **Distinction; Fame; Glory; Heroes and heroism; Honor; Leaders and leadership**
Adams — *New* p.9, 26, 65, 379
Albert — *Stop* p.53-54
Applegarth — *Heir.* p.47, 73, 246, 293, 295
Bach — *Make* p.40-41
Braude — *Source* #778-794
Braude — *Stories* p.170-172
Detherage — *Sunrise* p.140, 163
Dirksen — *Quot. See* index p.264
Edwards — *Useful* p.233-236, 728
Esteve — *Experience* p.155
Evans — *Thoughts II (Open Door)* p.139-140
Evans — *Unto* p.114, 119
Flesch — *Unusual* p.110-111
Forbes — *Thoughts See* index p.552
Fuller — *Epigrams* p.141-142
Garland — *Subject* p.125-126
Grizer — *Wit* p.197-198
Halverson — *Perspective* p.3
Henry — *5000* p.113-114
Hovey — *Treasury* #6, 52, 61, 71, 97, 115, 342, 357, 531, 793, 1035, 1058, 1093, 1184, 1457, 1487, 1719
Hubbard — *Scrap* p.59, 94, 102, 155
Humes — *Instant* p.47-48; #406-418
Johnson — *Bedside* p.42, 194-195

Kennedy — *Reader's* #404-417
Kin — *Dictionary* p.111
Kohn — *Adventures* p.97-99
Kohn — *Pathways* p.33-36
Kohn — *Touch* p.7-8
Liddle — *Thought I, II, III* p.20, 23-24, 26, 56, 59, 64-65, 77, 114, 129, 187
Liddle — *Thought IV* p.3, 6, 15, 27, 29, 43
Liddle — *Thought V* p.28
Lockridge — *World's See* index p.576; #5709
Lytle — *Leaves* p.41, 63, 68, 76, 146, 173
Mandel — *Stories* p.119
Modern Eloquence (14) p.342-343
Montapert — *Distilled* p.181-183
New Joy p.234
Nichols — *Third* p.88
Peterson — *Art* p.32, 374
Prochnow — *Public* #1115, 1360, 1509, 1858, 2588, 3160-3170, 4420
Prochnow — *Success.* p.155-156; #763, 769, 780, 1822-1828
Seldes — *Great* p.457-459
Speaker's Desk p.82-85
Voss — *Quotations* p.120-121
Wallis — *Treasure* p.4, 84
Wallis — *Words* p.19
Woods — *Religious* p.414-415

GREECE
See also **Greek proverbs; Greeks; Mythology, Greek**
Henry — *5000* p.114
Hovey — *Treasury* #610, 930, 1072, 1458, 1716
Prochnow — *Success.* #762
Seldes — *Great* p.459
, Golden age of
Curtis — *Practical* p.291-292
, Seven sayings of
Book Proverbs p.137-138

GREED
See also **Avarice; Selfishness**
Book Proverbs p.106, 142
Bradshaw — *Home.* p.92-102
Braude — *Stories* p.172-173
Curtis — *Human* p.11, 41-42
Curtis — *Practical* p.130-132
Dirksen — *Quot.* #1344-1346
Droke — *Christian* p.238-239
Evans — *Unto* p.14
Flesch — *Unusual* p.111
Flint — *Graham* p.63
Forbes — *Thoughts* p.109, 133, 301, 367, 390, 392, 433, 451, 464
Fuller — *Epigrams* p.142-143
Fuller — *Thesaurus* #271-276
Garland — *Subject* p.126-127
Grizer — *Wit* p.198
Hovey — *Treasury* #1074
Johnson — *Bedside* p.255, 263, 280
Kennedy — *Reader's* #418-419
Kin — *Dictionary* p.111
Krishnamurti — *Think* p.174
Mandel — *Stories* p.119-121
Prochnow — *Public* #2189, 2369, 2402
Seldes — *Great* p.459
Speaker's Desk #100, 677
Woods — *Religious* p.415

GREEK PROVERBS
Dirksen — *Quot. See* index p.264

GREEKS
Curtis — *Practical* p.221-223
Lockridge — *World's* #3169, 4108-4110, 4537
Prochnow — *Success.* #1466

GREEN (color)
Flesch — *Unusual* p.111

"GREENHORNS"
Botkin — *Anecdotes* p.38
Botkin — *Treasury* p.360
Flesch — *Unusual* p.111

GREETING CARDS
Grizer — *Wit* p.198
Peale — *Guideposts* p.194-198
Peterson — *Art* p.381-382

GREETINGS
Lytle — *Leaves* p.80
Prochnow — *Public* #1523

GREGORIAN CHANT
Day — *Meditation* p.25

GREYBACKS
Botkin — *Treasury* p.648

GREYHOUNDS
Botkin — *Treasury* p.626
Kin — *Dictionary* p.111

GRIEF
See also **Despair; Tears; Unhappiness**
Alexander's Treasure. p.312
Applegarth — *Heir.* p.159
Asimov — *Treasury* #41
Blanton — *Faith* p.133-157
Braude — *Source* #1571-1574
Dirksen — *Quot.* #307, 327, 946, 1493, 1499, 1562, 1941, 2180-2183, 2271, 2388
Droke — *Christian* p.509

Edwards — *Useful* p.236, 564-565, 606-609, 733
Emmons — *Mature* p.134, 138-145
Evans — *Faith* p.17, 136, 201-202, 224
Evans — *Quote* p.141-152
Evans — *This* p.165-166, 193-194
Evans — *Thoughts I* p.21, 43, 102, 111, 117-118, 120, 128, 131, 139, 143, 185
Evans — *Thoughts II (Open Door)* p.15-16, 28, 68, 75, 163, 207, 209
Evans — *Thoughts III (Open Road)* p.35-41, 51, 67, 106, 111, 186, 199-200, 209
Evans — *Thoughts IV* p.89, 105-108, 135, 200
Evans — *Unto* p.3, 13, 23, 35, 116, 118, 145
Flesch — *Unusual* p.103, 111, 270
Flint — *Graham* p.138
Forbes — *Thoughts* p.68, 75, 104, 136, 183, 194, 231, 234, 241, 254, 273, 309, 319, 343, 357, 383, 409, 427, 462, 474, 488, 510
Fuller — *Epigrams* p.143-144, 369-370
Garland — *Subject* p.127, 200-201, 298-299
Goudge — *Comfort* p.252-267
Henry — *5000* p.114-115, 182-183, 262
Hobe — *Tapestries* p.45, 214-219, 225
Hovey — *Treasury* #74, 1034
How To Live p.510-522, 525-527
Hubbard — *Scrap* p.21, 46, 127
Huxley — *You See* index p.283
Johnson — *Bedside* p.24
Kahn — *Lessons* p.157-164
Keller — *Open* p.61, 89
Keys Happiness p.90-92, 476, 523-527
Kin — *Dictionary* p.106, 112, 169, 240, 279
Knight's Illus. p.310-314
Kohn — *Best* p.22-23
Kopplin — *Something* p.57-79
Krishnamurti — *Think* p.166
Lair — *Baby* p.125-131
Liddle — *Thought I, II, III* p.39, 109-110, 122, 138, 142
Liddle — *Thought IV* p.7, 40
Liddle — *Thought V* p.32, 42
Liebman — *Peace* p.105-133
Lockridge — *World's* #1276, 2093, 2295, 2320, 2325, 2503, 3448, 4316, 4666, 4885, 4913, 5005, 5212, 5700; *See also* index p.576
Lytle — *Leaves* p.13, 26-27, 30, 84, 154
Maltz — *Creative* p.171
Mandel — *Stories* p.239
Montapert — *Distilled* p.183-184, 311
Nichols — *Third* p.92
Peale — *Courage* p.229-230, 233-234
Peale — *Faith* p.135-162
Peale — *Guide* p.212-229
Peale — *Guideposts* p.231-253
Price — *No* p.51-66
Prochnow — *Public* #1884, 2070, 2132, 2563, 2585, 2596, 3171-3172, 3715-3722, 4221-4222
Prochnow — *Success.* #611, 2333
Reader's — *Getting* p.34
Reader's — *20th* p.10
Schermerhorn — *1500* p.253-254
Sheban — *Wisdom* no p.
Sheen — *Thoughts* p.124-125
Strait — *Speaker's* p.162-166
Suter — *Prayers* #463-475
Tanksley — *Friend* p.35
Voss — *Quotations* p.121-124
Wallis — *Treasure* p.138, 155, 226-227
Wallis — *Words* p.164
Walters — *How* p.76-80
Watson — *Light* p.120-127
White — *Life* p.154
Woods — *Content.* p.290-292, 308, 312
Woods — *Inspir.* p.346-377
Woods — *Religious* p.55, 360-361, 415-416, 658, 873, 948-949

GRIEVANCES. *See* **Complaining**

GRINDSTONES
Peterson — *Art* p.202

GRIT. *See* **Courage**

GROCERS
Copeland — *10,000* p.423-426
Manchee — *Secret* p.211

GROOMING. *See* **Neatness**

GROUCHINESS. *See* **Complaining**

GROUND HOGS. *See* **Woodchucks**

GROUPS
See also names and types of groups
Phillips — *Choice* p.284, 301, 308, 390
White — *Job* p.49-60, 138
Woods — *Religious* p.416

Words Change p.81-82
, *Action*
Jackson — *Coping* p.176-183
Wheelis — *Moralist* See index p.164
, *Relations of*
Menninger — *Blue.* p.106-113

GROVES
New Topical p.107

GROWLING. *See* **Complaining**

"GROWNUPS." *See* **Adults; Parents and parenthood;** etc.

GROWTH
See also **Advancement; Development; Height; Improvement; Progress**
Applegarth — *Heir.* p.230
Clark — *Windows* p.22-23
Curtis — *Human* p.115-134
Emmons — *Mature* p.88-94, 102, 129, 137
Flesch — *Unusual* p.112
Forbes — *Thoughts* See index p.552
Garland — *Subject* p.127-128
Halverson — *Perspective* p.66
Hobe — *Tapestries* p.14
Holman — *Psych.* p.30-41
Holmes — *Design* p.137-138, 169-170, 177
Hovey — *Treasury* #329, 333, 433, 510, 513, 1024, 1423, 1519, 1561, 1623, 1647, 1682, 1787, 1851
How To Live p.280-283
Kahn — *Lessons* p.84-95
Kauffman — *For* p.109-110
Knight's Illus. p.136-138
Knight's Treas. p.147-148
Kohn — *Adventures* p.100-103
Kohn — *Best* p.25-28
Kohn — *Through* p.37-39, 41-42
Lytle — *Leaves* p.10, 120, 135, 144
Mandel — *Stories* p.121
Menninger — *Blue.* p.7-8
Montapert — *Distilled* p.184-185
Nichols — *New* p.203-204
Nichols — *Third* p.20-41
Peterson — *Art* p.97
Phillips — *Choice* p.10, 55, 272
Prochnow — *Speaker's* p.156
Wallis — *Treasure* p.11, 162, 164
Wallis — *Words* p.3, 41, 89-94, 143
Welk — *Guide.* p.120-122
White — *Job* p.40, 159, 185-186
, *Beginning of*
Welk — *Guide.* p.29-31
, *Creative*
Maltz— *Creative* p.213-216
, *Daily*
Maltz — *Creative* p.202-203
, *Freedom for*
Peterson — *Art* p.123
, *Love needed for*
Hulme — *Living* p.115-118
, *National*
Dirksen — *Quot.* #34, 2370, 2379
, *Personal crises and*
Jackson — *Coping* p.201-208
, *Rate of*
Kohn — *Through* p.37-38
, *Teenager*
Ginott — *Between* p.213-241

GRUDGES
See also **Complaining; Discontent**
Kin — *Dictionary* p.112
Liddle — *Thought I, II, III* p.12
Peterson — *Art* p.176

GRUMBLING. *See* **Complaining; Discontent**

"GRUNDY, MRS."
Ideas p.184-185

GUARANTEES
Wallis — *Words* p.94

GUERILLAS
Seldes — *Great* p.459

GUESSING
Grizer — *Wit* p.199
Hobe — *Tapestries* p.148
Prochnow — *Public* #802, 1056

GUESTS
See also **Hospitality; Visitors and visiting**
Copeland — *10,000* p.1001
Dirksen — *Quot.* #2039
Edwards — *Useful* p.237
Flesch — *Unusual* p.112
Fuller — *Epigrams* p.144-145
Grizer — *Wit* p.199
How To Live p.429-431
Kin — *Dictionary* p.112
Prochnow — *Public* #212, 501
Prochnow — *Speaker's* p.157
Prochnow — *Success.* #1831-1832
Wallis — *Treasure* p.45, 100
Wallis — *Words* p.24, 45, 114
, *Rooms for*
Peterson — *Art* p.271
, *Teenager*
Daly — *Personality* p.87-91

GUIDANCE
See also **Advice; Counsel; God, Help of; Teachers**
Bartlett — *Discovery* p.151-152
Curtis — *Human* p.98-114
Edwards — *Useful* p.237, 492-493
Emmons — *Mature* p.77
Evans — *Thoughts IV* p.137, 199
Flesch — *Unusual* p.224
Garland — *Subject* p.128
Grizer — *Wit* p.199
Hobe — *Tapestries* p.45, 49, 176, 228
Knight's Illus. p.138-140
Knight's Treas. p.149-153
Lockridge — *World's* #44
Lytle — *Leaves* p.50, 104, 143
Mandel — *Stories* p.121
Prochnow — *Public* #1545, 4354
, Scientific
Albert — *Stop* p.179-180

"GUIDEPOSTS"
Guideposts — *Faith* p.3-27

GUIDES
Harnsberger — *Mark* p.165-166
Montapert — *Distilled* p.185-186
Prochnow — *Public* #116, 255, 347, 2650
Prochnow — *Success.* #1085
, Books as
Kronenberger — *Animal* p.94-96

GUILE. *See* **Cleverness; Cunning**

GUILT
See also **Conscience; Remorse; Sin**
Albert — *Stop See* index p.210
Blanton — *Faith* p.87-109
Book Proverbs p.121
Braude — *Speaker's* #587-588
Braude — *Stories* p.173
Edwards — *Useful* p.237-238
Esteve — *Experience* p.77-85
Evans — *Thoughts III (Open Road)* p.212
Evans — *Thoughts IV* p.14
Evans — *Unto* p.117
Flint — *Graham* p.63-64, 132
Fuller — *Epigrams* p.146-147
Garland — *Subject* p.128-129
Halverson — *Perspective* p.15
Henry — *5000* p.115
Johnson — *Bedside* p.107
Kennedy — *Reader's* #420-424
Kin — *Dictionary* p.113
Lockridge — *World's* #1990, 2041, 3700
Peale — *Faith* p.81-107
Prochnow — *Public* #762, 933
Prochnow — *Speaker's* p.157
Prochnow — *Success.* #1081, 1377
Seldes — *Great* p.459-460
Speaker's Desk #56, 200, 459, 469, 587, 1105, 1115
Wallis — *Words* p.14
Wheelis — *Moralist* p.96-97, 100
, Common
Phillips — *Choice* p.366
, False
Guideposts p.145-146
, or innocence
Peale — *Guideposts* p.329-333
, Praise and
Ginott — *Between* p.115-116

GULF STREAM
Wallis — *Treasure* p.168

GULLIBILITY
See also **Belief**
Kin — *Dictionary* p.113
Speaker's Desk #258, 294, 612-613, 637, 736, 772

GULLIVER'S TRAVELS
Flesch — *Unusual* p.112

GUNS
Dirksen — *Quot.* #34
Franke — *Buckley* p.110-111
Harnsberger — *Mark* p.166-167
Harral — *Feature* p.174
Prochnow — *Public* #337, 556, 638, 696, 756, 1510
Prochnow — *Success.* #919
, Shooting of
Kin — *Dictionary* p.232
Prochnow — *Public* #578, 583, 737

"GUSHERS." *See* **Flattery**

GYMNASTICS
See also **Exercise;** etc.
Edwards — *Useful* p.238
Prochnow — *Public* #1610
Schermerhorn — *1500* p.183

GYNECOLOGISTS
Asimov — *Treasury* #565-566

GYPSIES
Alexander's Treasure. p.130
Flesch — *Unusual* p.112

H

"HABEUS CORPUS"
Seldes — *Great* p.460

HABIMAH PLAYERS
Nizer — *Thinking* p.177-179

HABITS
See also **Fashion; Self-control; Tradition;** names of habits
Alexander's Treasure. p.127-129
Book Proverbs p.73
Braude — *Source* #795
Braude — *Speaker's* #589-593
Braude — *Stories* p.173
Casselberry — *How* p.87-107
Curtis — *Daily* p.186-191
Droke — *Christian* p.240-243
Edwards — *Useful* p.238-240
Evans — *Faith* p.1, 7-8, 56, 74, 95, 98, 105-108, 115-116, 126, 131-136, 154, 164-165, 204
Evans — *Quote* p.215-222
Evans — *Thoughts I* p.28, 68-69, 83, 144, 152-156
Evans — *Thoughts II (Open Door)* p.93-94, 96-97, 178
Evans — *Thoughts III (Open Road)* p.68, 76, 111, 151
Evans — *Thoughts IV* p.86, 111-115, 164, 189, 196
Evans — *Unto* p.121
Flesch — *Unusual* p.112
Forbes — *Thoughts See* index p.552
Fuller — *Epigrams* p.147-148
Fuller — *Thesaurus* #31-74
Grizer — *Wit* p.199-201
Harnsberger — *Mark* p.168-170
Harral — *Feature* p.174
Henry — *5000* p.115
Hobe — *Tapestries* p.40
Holman — *Psych.* p.65-76
Holmes — *Design* p.23-25
Hovey — *Treasury* p.201-202, #14, 43, 49, 468, 1175-1178, 1305, 1549, 1751, 1788
Hubbard — *Scrap* p.76, 167, 211, 214
Johnson — *Bedside* p.320
Keys Happiness p.333-336
Kin — *Dictionary* p.114
Kohn — *Pathways* p.95-99
Liddle — *Thought I, II, III* p.23, 57, 72, 99, 114, 136, 163
Liddle — *Thought V* p.15-16
List — *Living* p.80-86
Lockridge — *World's* #2067, 2333, 2602, 3083, 5750, 5786, 5804
Lytle — *Leaves* p.22, 81, 134, 137, 191
Maltz — *Creative* p.106-107, 113-116
Mandel — *Stories* p.121-122
Menninger — *Blue.* p.63-64
Modern Eloquence (14) p.344
Montapert — *Distilled* p.186-187
Peterson — *Art* p.186, 189
Prochnow — *Public* #10, 92, 1155, 1567, 3173-3174
Prochnow — *Speaker's* p.158
Reader's — *Getting* p.105-108
Seldes — *Great* p.460
Sheen — *Thoughts* p.43-56
Speaker's Desk #212, 331, 552, 638, 956; p.85
Wallis — *Treasure* p.45
Welk — *Guide.* p.109-111
Woods — *Wellsprings* p.31
, Bad
Bradshaw — *Home.* p.64-78
Sheen — *Way* p.176-178
, Breaking
Albert — *Stop* p.195
Baillie — *Diary* #18
, Conditioning and
Curtis — *Golden* p.72
, Good
Bradshaw — *Home.* p.75-78
Maxwell — *Courage* p.155-206
New Joy p.53
, Patterns of
Phillips — *Choice* p.273-274
, Sins as
Nichols — *Third* p.63-64

HAIR
Edwards — *Useful* p.240-241
Henry — *5000* p.115-116
Irion — *Yes* p.53-56
Kin — *Dictionary* p.114
Lockridge — *World's* #2748, 4171
Lytle — *Leaves* p.22, 178
New Topical p.108
Prochnow — *Public* #235, 317, 442, 546, 560, 694, 1840, 2633
Walters — *How* p.124-125
, Care of
Menninger — *Blue.* p.211-212, 219-220
, Cutting of
Dirksen — *Quot.* #1705
, Dryers of
Irion — *Yes* p.53-56
, Long
Kauffman — *For* p.246-247
, Styles of
Ginott — *Between* p.32-33
, Tonic for
Prochnow — *Public* #292

HALCYON DAYS. *See* **Calmness; Happiness; Peace**

HALF
Dirksen — *Quot.* #135
Kin — *Dictionary* p.114-115

HALLEY'S COMET
Harnsberger — *Mark* p.170

HALLOWEEN
Harral — *Feature* p.174

HAMBURGERS
Prochnow — *Public* #1706

HAMLET
Ideas p.186-187

HAMMERS
Wallis — *Treasure* p.80

HAMS
Prochnow — *Public* #202, 842, 889

HANDBOOKS
Lytle — *Leaves* p.45

HANDICAPPED
See also **Blind; Deaf;** etc.
Braude — *Speaker's* #594
Dirksen — *Quot.* #1403-1405
Droke — *Christian* p.243-247
Edwards — *Useful* p.122
Evans — *Thoughts I* p.121-122
Evans — *Thoughts II (Open Door)* p.11
Evans — *Thoughts III (Open Road)* p.157
Fox — *Make* p.6-7
Fridy — *Meditat.* p.13
Fuller — *Thesaurus* #701-707
Garland — *Subject* p.63, 70, 169
Guideposts — *Faith* p.89, 244-249
Harral — *Feature* p.174-175
Holman — *Psych.* p.25-26
How To Live p.380-381
Huxley — *You See* index p.288
Jackson — *Coping* p.136-143
Kauffman — *For* p.110
Kennedy — *Reader's* #425
Kin — *Dictionary* p.66, 115
Kohn — *Pathways* p.131-133
Kohn — *Through* p.26-28
Kohn — *Touch* p.55-56
Lockridge — *World's* #4334
Lytle — *Leaves* p.34
Mandel — *Stories* p.66, 122-123
Montapert — *Distilled* p.187
Peale — *Courage* p.208
Peale — *Guideposts* p.3-6, 7-14, 185-206
Price — *No* p.99-107
Reader's — *Getting* p.23-27, 96-100, 194-199
Unlimited Power p.121-126
Walters — *How* p.80-85
Watson — *Light* p.85-94, 153-156
Woods — *Religious* p.486
Woods — *Wellsprings* p.60

HANDICRAFTS. *See* **Crafts and craftsmen**

HANDLES
Flesch — *Unusual* p.113

"HANDOUTS"
Prochnow — *Success.* #599

HANDS
Alexander's Treasure. p.134, 153
Applegarth — *Heir.* p.69, 166, 245
Auden — *Certain* p.176
Edwards — *Useful* p.241
Garland — *Subject* p.129
Henry — *5000* p.116
Hovey — *Treasury* p.202-203; *See* index p.297
Keller — *Open* p.62, 88
Kin — *Dictionary* p.115
Lockridge — *World's* #4278
Lytle — *Leaves* p.123
New Topical p.108-109
Peterson — *Art* p.73, 240
Prochnow — *Public* #2075, 2456, 2612
Prochnow — *Success.* #1833
Sheban — *Wisdom* no p.
Wallis — *Treasure* p.8, 80, 107, 144, 157
Wallis — *Words* p.81, 160
, Care of
Menninger — *Blue.* p.214-215, 220
, Communication of
Kauffman — *For* p.110-111
, Healing of
Garland — *Subject* p.170
Guideposts — *Faith* p.395-399
, Holding
Guideposts — *Faith* p.412
, of the world
Keller — *Open* p.40-41
, Shaking of
Dirksen — *Quot.* #242
Harral — *Feature* p.175
Hubbard — *Scrap* p.144
Irion — *Yes* p.41-42

HANDWRITING
Braude — *Source* #796-797
Fuller — *Thesaurus* #731-733
Kennedy — *Reader's* #426

Prochnow — *Public* #827
, *Experts on*
Harral — *Feature* p.175

HANGINGS AND HANGMEN
Auden — *Certain* p.176-177
Botkin — *Anecdotes* p.212
Flesch — *Unusual* p.113
Fuller — *Epigrams* p.148
Fuller — *Thesaurus* #2566-2568
Henry — *5000* p.116
Kin — *Dictionary* p.115
Lockridge — *World's* #1452, 5888
Prochnow — *Success.* #1834-1835

HAPPENINGS. *See* **Events**

HAPPINESS.
See also **Contentment; Enjoyment; Joy; Pleasure**
Alexander's Treasure. p.1, 32, 197, 267, 270, 281-282
Applegarth — *Heir.* p.83-86, 88-92, 95, 129, 257
Bach — *Make* p.86-92
Baillie — *Diary* #48
Barker — *Treat* p.1-23
Bartlett — *Discovery* p.30-32, 39-40, 43, 138-139
Book Proverbs p.40
Braude — *Source* #798-812
Braude — *Speaker's* #112-116, 595-596
Braude — *Stories* p.174-176
Curtis — *Golden* p.109-117
Curtis — *Human* p.1-17
Curtis — *Practical* p.521
Detherage — *Sunrise* p.71, 84, 171
Dirksen — *Quot.* #326, 947, 976, 992, 1071, 1129, 1702, 2285
Droke — *Christian* p.247-255
Du Noüy — *Road* p.206-207, 215-217, 236-237
Edwards — *Useful* p.241-245, 728
Evans — *Faith* p.13, 18, 31-32, 41, 68, 139, 167, 198, 216
Evans — *Quote* p.141-152
Evans — *This* p.10-11, 49-50
Evans — *Thoughts I* See index no p.
Evans — *Thoughts II (Open Door)* See index no p.
Evans — *Thoughts III (Open Road)* See index no p.
Evans — *Thoughts IV* p.14, 19, 48, 53, 73-74, 95, 109, 124, 136-138, 145, 159
Evans — *Unto* p.3, 20, 56, 71, 114
Flesch — *Unusual* p.89, 113-115
Flint — *Graham* p.64, 104
Fogg — *1000* #450
Forbes — *Thoughts* See index p.552
Fuller — *Epigrams* p.148-150, 344
Garland — *Subject* p.129-130
Giniger — *Compact* p.199-202
Grizer — *Wit* p.201-207
Guideposts — *Faith* p.424-427
Harnsberger — *Mark* p.170-172
Harral — *Feature* p.175
Henry — *5000* p.116-117
Hobe — *Tapestries* p.16, 72-79, 123, 127
Holmes — *Design* p.35, 111, 209
Hovey — *Treasury* p.203-207; *See* index p.297
Howell — *Better* p.81-84
Howell — *Lines* p.85-86
Hubbard — *Scrap* p.16, 19, 21, 30, 36, 47, 70, 79, 83, 92, 98, 102, 106, 127, 198, 214, 227-228
Johnson — *Bedside* p.1, 61-62, 113, 117, 120, 123, 139, 213, 234, 244, 274
Kahn — *Lessons* p.167-168
Keller — *Open* p.15-16, 102-103, 107
Kennedy — *Reader's* #427-431
Keys Happiness p.11-15, 306, 396
Kin — *Dictionary* p.115-116
Kohn — *Adventures* p.108-112
Kohn — *Pathways* p.147-157
Kopplin — *Something* p.1-22
Krishnamurti — *Think* p.63-64, 69-70, 191
Krishnamurti — *Urgency* p.119-123
Liddle — *Thought I, II, III See* index p.196
Liddle — *Thought IV* p.8, 12-13, 15, 18, 21, 27, 30, 36-37, 39-40, 42-43
Liddle — *Thought V* p.9, 15-16, 20, 24, 29-30, 33, 36-37, 43
Lockridge — *World's See* index p.576
Lytle — *Leaves* p.5, 22-24, 81, 86, 151, 169
Maltz — *Creative* p.2, 20-21, 31-32, 41-45, 53-54
Mandel — *Stories* p.123-124
Miller — *Harvest* p.67-72
Modern Eloquence (14) p.345-346
Montapert — *Distilled* p.188-191
Morris — *1000 See* index p.430
Nichols — *Third* p.26-27
Peale — *Courage* p.177-204
Peale — *Guideposts* p.285-302
Peterson — *Art* p.135, 383

Prochnow — *Public* #1149, 1187, 1399, 1596, 1707, 2003, 2076, 2295, 2511, 3175-3179, 4112-4113
Prochnow — *Speaker's* p.158-159
Prochnow — *Success.* #1837-1839
Reader's — *Getting* p.183-185
Redhead — *Living* p.44-52
Sagendorph — *Old* p.43-46
Seldes — *Great* p.460-463
Sheban — *Wisdom* no p.
Sheen — *Thoughts* p.9-23
Sheen — *Way* p.13-50
Speaker's Desk p.85-88; #333, 580
Strait — *Speaker's* p.90-91
Voss — *Quotations* p.124-126
Wallis — *Treasure* p.11, 65, 112, 115-120, 157, 181, 216, 231, 237, 239
Wallis — *Words See* index p.248
Watson — *Light* p.1-30
Woods — *Content.* p.196, 274; *See* index p.380
Woods — *Religious* p.417-421
Words Change p.119-120
Words — *Inspir.* p.95, 215-216
, Achievement of
Phillips — *Choice* p.342
, and righeousness
Hunter — *Gems* p.92
, Art of
Maurois — *Art* p.292-323
Peterson — *Twenty* p.28-29
, as boomerang
Nichols — *New* p.29-30
, Contribution to
Peterson — *Art* p.45
, Doors to
Keller — *Open* p.11
, Duty of
Nichols — *New* p.27-28
, Formula for
Adams — *New* p.296
, Philosophy of
Wilcox — *Heart* p.30-32
, Pursuit of
Ideas p.187-188
Woods — *Business.* p.216-217
, Road to
Nichols — *New* p.25-39

"HAPPY MEDIUM." *See* **Moderation**

HARDSHIP
See also **Adversity; Difficulties; Poverty;** etc.
Edwards — *Useful* p.245
Evans — *Unto* p.82, 114
Fuller — *Epigrams* p.150-151
Harnsberger — *Mark* p.172
Hobe — *Tapestries* p.13
Hubbard — *Scrap* p.228
Kohn — *Pathways* p.127-145
Lytle — *Leaves* p.55
Montapert — *Distilled* p.191-192
Nichols — *New* p.55-56
Prochnow — *Public* #717, 2078-2079, 2110, 3180-3182
Prochnow — *Speaker's* p.159-160
Prochnow — *Success.* #730
Sheban — *Wisdom* no p.
Woods — *Religious* p.421

HARDWARE STORES
Guideposts — *Faith* p.95-99

HARES. *See* **Rabbits**

HARM. *See* **Injury**

HARMONY
See also **Music; Peace of mind**
Applegarth — *Heir.* p.184, 213, 269
Clark — *Windows* p.168
Dirksen — *Quot.* #891, 1348-1349
Forbes — *Thoughts* p.162, 229, 240, 321, 498, 502
Fox — *Make* p.79-80
Garland — *Subject* p.131
Hadfield — *Delights* p.55
Holmes — *Design* p.6, 54-55, 101, 122, 148-149, 152-153
Hubbard — *Scrap* p.182
Johnson — *Bedside* p.76
Lockridge — *World's* #5708
Peterson — *Art* p.204
Phillips — *Choice* p.395
Prochnow — *Public* #1470
Sheen — *Content.* p.137-140
Wallis — *Treasure* p.118
White — *Job See* index p.194
Woods — *Content.* p.110, 236, 260
Woods — *Religious* p.421-422

HARP-WEAVERS
Hobe — *Tapestries* p.168

HARTFORD, CONNECTICUT
Harnsberger — *Mark* p.172-174

HARTS
New Topical p.110

HARVARD UNIVERSITY
Botkin — *Anecdotes* p.18
Flint — *Graham* p.46
Franke — *Buckley* p.113-114
Prochnow — *Speaker's* p.160

HARVEST
Dirksen — *Quot.* #1350-1354
Evans — *Thoughts I* p.105-110, 113-114
Evans — *Unto* p.15, 23, 101

Garland — *Subject* p.131-132
Henry — *5000* p.117
Lockridge — *World's* #1463
Lytle — *Leaves* p.10
New Topical p.110
Prochnow — *Public* #2632
Woods — *Content.* p.93

"HARVEST HANDS"
Botkin — *Treasury* p.525

HASH
Prochnow — *Public* #1023

HASTE
See also **Punctuality**
Alexander's Treasure. p.12, 228, 333
Book Proverbs p.66
Braude — *Source* #813-814
Braude — *Stories* p.177
Curtis — *Human* p.10-11
Dirksen — *Quot.* #211
Edwards — *Useful* p.245-246
Evans — *This* p.50-51
Evans — *Unto* p.3, 20
Flesch — *Unusual* p.123, 271
Flint — *Graham* p.147
Forbes — *Thoughts* p.275, 455, 468
Fuller — *Epigrams* p.152
Grizer — *Wit* p.435-436
Harnsberger — *Mark* p.191, 453
Henry — *5000* p.117
Hobe — *Tapestries* p.25
Hoffer — *Reflect.* p.89
How To Live p.205-208
Humes — *Instant* #1093-1096
Johnson — *Bedside* p.125
Kin — *Dictionary* p.116, 124, 207
Kohn — *Best* p.60-61
Kohn — *Pathways* p.111-115
Liddle — *Thought V* p.8
Lockridge — *World's* #5083
Montapert — *Distilled* p.192, 204-205
Nizer — *Thinking* p.107
Peale — *Courage* p.81-82, 88
Peterson — *Art* p.349
Prochnow — *Public* #236, 600, 721, 987, 1309, 1780, 1792, 2556
Prochnow — *Speaker's* p.167-168, 292
Prochnow — *Success.* #594
Pullar-Strecker — *Proverbs* #150-157
Speaker's Desk #88-89, 155, 243, 309, 384, 398, 423, 472, 506, 565, 692, 1142
Weisfeld — *Pulpit* p.2-3
Woods — *Religious* p.957

HASTINGS, WARREN
Kronenberger — *Animal* p.70-72

HATCHETS
Prochnow — *Success.* #339

HATRED
See also **Enemies; Jealousy; Resentment; Revenge**
Albert — *Stop* p.87-88, 156-157, 168
Bartlett — *Discovery* p.85-86
Book Proverbs p.57
Braude — *Source* #815-817
Curtis — *Practical* p.148, 219
Dirksen — *Quot.* #416, 577, 1355-1357
Droke — *Christian* p.255-257
Edwards — *Useful* p.246-247, 395, 728
Esteve — *Experience* p.111-117
Evans — *Faith* p.79
Evans — *Thoughts I* p.73, 101-102
Evans — *Unto* p.14
Flesch — *Unusual* p.11, 115-116, 175
Forbes — *Thoughts* p.8, 15, 133, 149, 198, 240, 440
Fuller — *Epigrams* p.152-153, 210-211
Garland — *Subject* p.132
Ginott — *Between* p.216-217
Grizer — *Wit* p.207-208
Guideposts — *Faith* p.64
Harnsberger — *Mark* p.175
Henry — *5000* p.117
Holman — *Psych.* p.115-125
Holman — *Design* p.73-75, 142-143
Hovey — *Treasury See* index p.297
Hubbard — *Scrap* p.41
Kauffman — *For* p.111
Kennedy — *Fresh* p.87-88
Kennedy — *Reader's* #432
Kin — *Dictionary* p.116
Kohn — *Thoughts* p.141-144
Kohn — *Touch* p.134-139, 187-190
Krishnamurti — *Think* p.62-63
Liddle — *Thought I, II, III* p.27, 69-70, 136, 154
Liddle — *Thought IV* p.40, 45
Liddle — *Thought V* p.20
Liebman — *Peace* p.64-68
Lockridge — *World's* #348, 1119, 1808, 1986, 2331, 3166
Lytle — *Leaves* p.132
Mandel — *Stories* p.124-125
Menninger — *Blue.* p.42-45
Montapert — *Distilled* p.192-193
New Topical p.110-111
Nichols — *New* p.132-133

Patterns For Living p.511-518
Peale — *Courage* p.213
Prochnow — *Success.* #1358, 1841
Seldes — *Great* p.463-464
Sheban — *Wisdom* no p.
Woods — *Religious* p.422-423

HATS
Dirksen — *Quot.* #75, 132
Flesch — *Unusual* p.115
George — *Book* p.387
Harnsberger — *Mark* p.174-175
Kin — *Dictionary* p.39
Prochnow — *Public* #273, 658, 946, 1016, 1230
Prochnow — *Speaker's* p.212
Prochnow — *Success.* #319, 343, 967, 1034, 1840
, and milliners
Botkin — *Anecdotes* p.265
, Fur
Botkin — *Anecdotes* p.145

HAUGHTINESS. *See* **Pride**

HAUNTS
Botkin — *Anecdotes* p.217-218, 222

"HAVES AND HAVE NOTS"
Seldes — *Great* p.464

HAWKS
Botkin — *Treasury* p.672

HAY FEVER
Prochnow — *Public* #1245

HEAD
See also **Brains; Intelligence; Mind; Reason and reasoning; Understanding;** names of parts of head
Curtis — *Daily* p.72-75
Dirksen — *Quot.* #1706
Edwards — *Useful* p.247
Flesch — *Unusual* p.116
Grizer — *Wit* p.209
Henry — *5000* p.117-118
Kin — *Dictionary* p.116
Lockridge — *World's* #101, 105-106, 4657, 4684, 5274
Montapert — *Distilled* p.193
New Topical p.111-112
Prochnow — *Public* #732, 1015, 2039, 2080, 2248, 2629, 2700
Prochnow — *Success.* #1842-1843

HEADACHE
Harnsberger — *Mark* p.175
Harral — *Feature* p.175

HEALING
See also **Hands, Healing of; Medicine; Remedies**
Bach — *Make* p.175-178
Bartlett — *Discovery* p.141-142
Clark — *Windows* p.38
Flesch — *Unusual* p.116
Garland — *Subject* p.133, 140, 192-193
How To Live p.27-31
Kennedy — *Fresh* p.117-118
Kennedy — *Reader's* #433-435
Knight's Illus. p.140
Peale — *Guideposts* p.231-253
Peterson — *Art* p.174
Phillips — *Choice* p.29, 172, 308
Prochnow — *Public* #2667
Prochnow — *Success.* #1844
Unlimited Power p.139-143
Woods — *Content.* p.213
Woods — *Religious* p.423-424
, by prayer
Guideposts — *Faith* p.239-243
, for teenagers
Ginott — *Between* p.61-73
, in laughter
Clark — *Windows* p.136-137
, of symptoms
Fox — *Make* p.127
, Spiritual
Fox — *Make* p.126
Unlimited Power p.102-156

HEALTH
See also **Body; Diet; Exercise; Strength;** etc.
Albert — *Stop* p.9, 115-116
Applegarth — *Heir.* p.175
Book Proverbs p.40
Braude — *Speaker's* #117-125
Braude — *Stories* p.177
Casselberry — *How See* index p.202-203
Curtis — *Daily* p.78-85
Curtis — *Golden* p.118-127
Curtis — *Human* p.17-35
Dirksen — *Quot.* #41, 335
Droke — *Christian* p.257-261
Edwards — *Useful* p.247-249
Evans — *Faith* p.3, 18, 38, 74, 102, 106, 113, 141
Evans — *Quote* p.97-110
Evans — *Thoughts I* p.101, 165, 178
Evans — *Thoughts II (Open Door)* p.55, 58, 124, 176-180, 205
Evans — *Thoughts III (Open Road)* p.48, 50, 56, 75-77, 170
Evans — *Thoughts IV* p.14, 59, 109, 114, 193
Evans — *Unto* p.61-62

Flesch — *Unusual* p.116
Forbes — *Thoughts See* index p.553
Fuller — *Epigrams* p.153, 344-345
Fuller — *Thesaurus* #1711-1712
Grizer — *Wit* p.209-211
Harral — *Feature* p.176-182
Henry — *5000* p.118
Holmes — *Design* p.154-164; *See* index p.232
Hovey — *Treasury* #27, 74, 270, 287, 643, 681, 1112, 1181, 1187-1188, 1726, 1769, 1785, 1831
Hubbard — *Scrap* p.96, 220, 222
Johnson — *Bedside* p.278-284
Kennedy — *Reader's* #436-439
Keys Happiness p.285-288, 355, 368-373, 438-440, 485-487
Kin — *Dictionary* p.116-117
Liddle — *Thought I, II, III* p.10-11, 23, 38, 55, 76, 103, 139
Liddle — *Thought IV* p.9, 43
Lockridge — *World's* #1096, 5274
Lytle — *Leaves* p.20
Mandel — *Stories* p.125-127
Montapert — *Distilled* p.193-195
Peale — *Courage* p.78-94
Peale — *Stay* p.231-246
Prochnow — *Public* #710, 795, 1104, 3183-3185
Prochnow — *Speaker's* p.161
Sagendorph — *Old* p.60-68
Seldes — *Great* p.464
Sherman — *Your* p.58-63
Speaker's Desk p.83-93; #16, 72, 153, 158, 162, 277, 312, 940
Suter — *Prayers* #443-458
Wallis — *Words* p.20, 49, 71
Welk — *Guide.* p.115-117
White — *Life* p.67-72, 131-135
Woods — *Religious* p.424
Words — *Inspir.* p.50
, and religion
Holman — *Psych.* p.155-165
Sheen — *Content.* p.132-134
, Destruction of
Peale — *Guideposts* p.251-253
, Improvement of
Huxley — *You See* index p.285
, Inspector of
Botkin — *Anecdotes* p.77
, Investments in
Bradshaw — *Home.* p.48-54

HEARING
See also **Deaf; Ears; Listeners and listening**
Garland — *Subject* p.133
Henry — *5000* p.118
Kin — *Dictionary* p.117
Knight's Treas. p.153-154
Prochnow — *Public* #302, 911, 2660
Prochnow — *Speaker's* p.161-162

HEARSAY. *See* **Gossip; Rumor**

HEARSES
Kin — *Dictionary* p.117

HEART
See also **Emotion; Kindness; Love; Sensibility; Soul**
Applegarth — *Heir.* p.253
Baillie — *Diary* #149, 326
Braude — *Stories* p.178
Dirksen — *Quot.* #6, 760, 948-950, 1121, 1358-1360, 1635, 1992, 2057, 2262-2263, 2310, 2362
Edwards — *Useful* p.249-251
Evans — *Unto* p.36, 39, 135
Flesch — *Unusual* p.116
Flint — *Graham* p.64-65
Forbes — *Thoughts See* index p.653
Fuller — *Epigrams* p.345
Garland — *Subject* p.133
Harnsberger — *Mark* p.176
Henry — *5000* p.118-119
Hobe — *Tapestries* p.22, 86, 89, 124
Holman — *Psych.* p.42-53
Holmes — *Design* p.9, 106-107, 227-228
Hovey — *Treasury* p.208; *See* index p.297
Hubbard — *Scrap* p.41
Kennedy — *Reader's* #440-441
Keys Happiness p.65-67
Kin — *Dictionary* p.117
Kohn — *Thoughts* p.29-30
Liddle — *Thought I, II, III* p.26, 28, 37-38, 46-47, 70, 95, 128, 148, 160, 192-193
Liddle — *Thought IV* p.10, 18, 34, 43, 46
Lockridge — *World's* See Index p.576
Lytle — *Leaves* p.7, 54, 59, 88, 152, 156
Mandel — *Stories* p.127-128
Mandelbaum — *Choose* p.46-49
Montapert — *Distilled* p.195
New Topical p.112
Peterson — *Art* p.190
Phillips — *Choice* p.78, 97, 288
Prochnow — *Public* #1217, 2084, 2271, 2544, 2615, 2685, 3186, 4114-4115
Prochnow — *Success.* #1228, 1258, 1845-1846, 2048
Seldes — *Great* p.464-465

Sheen — *Thoughts* p.150-152
Tanksley — *Friend* p.11
Wallis — *Treasure* p.100, 120, 125, 138, 168, 234
Wallis — *Words* p.37-38, 50, 58, 75, 114, 121, 124, 159, 167, 204
Woods — *Content.* p.223-249
Woods — *Religious* p.424-425

, and mind
Krishnamurti — *Urgency* p.85-88
Taylor — *With* p.1-5

, Character of
New Topical p.112-113

, Cleansing of
Baillie — *Diary* #287

, Conquest of
Peterson — *Art* p.109

, Educated
Reader's — *Getting* p.162-164

, Empty
Baillie — *Diary* #164

, Heavy
See also **Grief;** etc.
Alexander's Treasure. p.261
Evans — *Thoughts I* p.44-46
Evans — *Unto* p.119

, Loss of
Words Change p.18-21

, Open to God
Baillie — *Diary* #111

, Physical aspects of
Fogg — *1000* #322, 920, 976
Lair — *Baby* p.11-12
New Joy p.139

, Purity of
Hunter — *Gems* p.85-86

HEAT
Du Noüy — *Road* p.66, 88, 95
Harnsberger — *Mark* p.176-177
Harral — *Feature* p.182
Mandel — *Stories* p.269
Prochnow — *Public* #851, 929, 2094, 2235

HEATHEN
Fox — *Make* p.67
More Words p.79
New Topical p.113

HEAVEN
See also **Eternity; Paradise**
Applegarth — *Heir.* p.167, 221, 272
Asimov — *Treasury* #462, 465, 480, 498, 510-511
Baillie — *Diary* #55, 153, 264
Book Proverbs p.120
Botkin — *Anecdotes* p.16, 22-23, 148, 169, 187, 192
Dirksen — *Quot.* #417, 1361
Droke — *Christian* p.262
Edwards — *Useful* p.251-253
Emmons — *Mature* p.134-135
Evans — *Thoughts IV* p.110, 184-185
Evans — *Unto* p.32, 47, 93, 135, 139, 141
Flesch — *Unusual* p.117, 199
Flint — *Graham* p.65-66, 81, 95
Forbes — *Thoughts* p.142, 148, 151, 202, 216, 320, 403, 432, 442, 466, 476, 479, 506
Fuller — *Epigrams* p.153-154
Garland — *Subject* p.134, 166
Goudge — *Comfort* p.293-313
Harnsberger — *Mark* p.177-178
Henry — *5000* p.119-120
Hobe — *Tapestries* p.55, 70
Holmes — *Design* p.99, 142
Hovey — *Treasury See* index p.297-298
Keller — *Open* p.57-59, 95
Kin — *Dictionary* p.117
Knight's Illus. p.141-146
Knight's Treas. p.154-158
Liddle — *Thought I, II, III* p.35, 68, 86, 95, 108, 122, 124, 142, 156, 192
Liddle — *Thought IV* p.43
Liddle — *Thought V* p.6, 15, 45
Lytle — *Leaves* p.94, 96
Mandel — *Stories* p.128-130
Montapert — *Distilled* p.195-196
More Words p.80-81
New Topical p.113-114
Phillips — *Choice* p.34-35
Prochnow — *Public* #834, 860, 1998, 2578, 3187-3190
Seldes — *Great* p.465
Sheban — *Wisdom* no p.
Speaker's Desk #23, 221, 252, 259, 366, 452, 513, 659, 857, 1112
Tanksley — *Friend* p.43
Wallis — *Treasure* p.17, 24, 83, 141-146, 179, 182, 184, 213
Wallis — *Words* p.19, 24, 56, 58, 95-102, 111, 114, 185, 203
Weisfeld — *Pulpit* p.6, 15-17, 178
Woods — *Religious* p.425-428, 527-528
Words Change p.84-87

, Judgment of
Baillie — *Diary* #276

, on earth
Baillie — *Diary* #359
Peterson — *Art* p.315

, Reality of
Maxwell — *Courage* p.244-251

, Reward of
Woods — *Wellsprings* p.81

, Within
Clark — *Windows* p.116

HEBREW PROVERBS
Dirksen — *Quot.* #1852, 1873, 2091, 2256, 2264; *See* index p.271

HEBREWS. *See* **Jews**

"HECKLING"
Humes — *Instant* p.56
Prochnow — *Public* #28
Prochnow — *Success.* #1167
Speaker's Desk #44, 55, 90, 802, 1102
, Handling of
Humes — *Instant* p.52-57

HEDGEHOGS
Kin — *Dictionary* p.118

HEDGES
Kin — *Dictionary* p.118
New Topical p.114

HEDGING
Dirksen — *Quot.* #119
Speaker's Desk #13, 322, 455, 469, 543, 614, 1071

HEDONISM
Menninger — *Blue.* p.78
Woods — *Religious* p.428

HEGELIANISM
Seldes — *Great* p.466
Woods — *Religious* p.428

HEIGHT
Fuller — *Thesaurus* #696
Kin — *Dictionary* p.118
Peterson — *Art* p.65, 226
Prochnow — *Public* #1927
Speaker's Desk #663

HEIRLOOMS
See also **Antiques**
Applegarth — *Heir.* p.107-113
Flesch — *Unusual* p.118
Prochnow — *Success.* #1849
Words — *Inspir.* p.183-184

HEIRS. *See* **Inheritance**

HELL
See also **Devil; Punishment**
Asimov — *Treasury* #428, 477, 491, 497, 503
Auden — *Certain* p.180-181
Book Proverbs p.120
Botkin — *Anecdotes* p.16, 132, 147, 187, 192, 198
Braude — *Source* #818-821
Dirksen — *Quot.* #417
Droke — *Christian* p.262
Edwards — *Useful* p.253
Flesch — *Unusual* p.117
Flint — *Graham* p.66-67
Fuller — *Epigrams* p.345
Garland — *Subject* p.135
Henry — *5000* p.120
Holmes — *Design* p.99, 142
Hovey — *Treasury* #55, 274, 455, 525, 589, 721, 753, 1154, 1359, 1695
Kennedy — *Reader's* #442-446
Kin — *Dictionary* p.118
Knight's Treas. p.158-159
Lockridge — *World's* #417, 5135, 5678
Lytle — *Leaves* p.57
Mandel — *Stories* p.130-131
New Topical p.115
Prochnow — *Success.* #1847
Seldes — *Great* p.466-467, 800
Sheban — *Wisdom* no p.
Speaker's Desk #252, 378, 483, 513, 579, 648, 664, 857, 1128, 1141, 1149, 1153
Wallis — *Treasure* p.188
Wallis — *Words* p.160
Woods — *Religious* p.428-432, 803-804

HELMETS
Prochnow — *Public* #907

HELP
See also **Charity; Self-help**
Applegarth — *Heir.* p.174, 244, 248
Baillie — *Diary* #247
Bartlett — *Discovery* p.93-109
Braude — *Source* #146-150, 822-825
Braude — *Speaker's* #597-599
Dirksen — *Quot.* #946, 1362
Edwards — *Useful* p.253-254
Flesch — *Unusual* p.117
Forbes — *Thoughts* p.3, 167, 207, 256, 309, 399, 409, 454, 461, 471
Fuller — *Epigrams* p.154
Fuller — *Thesaurus* #281
Garland — *Subject* p.135, 307-310
Guideposts — *Faith* p.403-407
Henry — *5000* p.120-121
Hovey — *Treasury* p.208; #8, 312, 809, 1236-1241, 1437
Humes — *Instant* p.45, 50-51; #42-44, 1268-1270

Johnson — *Bedside* p.307-308, 336
Keys Happiness p.196-200, 411, 523-527
Kin — *Dictionary* p.9, 16, 118
Liddle — *Thought I, II, III* p.28, 49, 55, 87, 123, 152, 184
Liddle — *Thought IV* p.23
Liddle — *Thought V* p.11, 16
Lockridge — *World's* #1519, 1697, 2250, 4009
Lytle — *Leaves* p.70, 78, 91, 118, 133, 153, 172
Maltz — *Creative* p.53-54
Mandel — *Stories* p.15, 131
Mandelbaum — *Choose* p.25-28, 53-57
Montapert — *Distilled* p.196-197
New Joy p.21
Peale — *Courage* p.204-218
Peale — *Guideposts* p.257-266
Peterson — *Art* p.216
Phillips — *Choice* p.183, 254
Prochnow — *Public* #817, 2432, 2506, 2661
Prochnow — *Speaker's* p.162
Prochnow — *Success.* #718, 856
Speaker's Desk See index p.300
Tanksley — *Friend* p.20
Wallis — *Treasure* p.79, 117, 121-126
Watson — *Light* p.11-15
, Community
Mandelbaum — *Choose* p.29-32
, in crises
Jackson — *Coping* p.152-159

HELPLESSNESS
Flesch — *Unusual* p.117
Kin — *Dictionary* p.118
Lytle — *Leaves* p.151
Prochnow — *Public* #2241

HENRY VIII
Flesch — *Unusual* p.117

"HENRY, JOHN"
Botkin — *Treasury* p.179, 230-240

"HEPCATS"
Prochnow — *Success.* #992

HERALDRY
Schermerhorn — *1500* p.80

HERBS
New Topical p.115

HERCULES
Prochnow — *Public* #2325, 2330, 2333

HERDS
Sheban — *Wisdom* no p.
, Human
Seldes — *Great* p.467-469

HEREDITY
Applegarth — *Heir.* p.110
Braude — *Stories* p.178-179
Dirksen — *Quot.* #775, 951, 1000
Du Noüy — *Human* p.103, 107, 122-123, 234-235
Flesch — *Unusual* p.117
Garland — *Subject* p.136
Henry — *5000* p.121
Hobe — *Tapestries* p.36
Holman — *Psych.* p.15-19
Hovey — *Treasury* p.208-210; #68, 71, 239, 478, 496, 1242-1248
Kennedy — *Reader's* #447
Kin — *Dictionary* p.119
Montapert — *Distilled* p.197
Wallis — *Words* p.106
Wilcox — *Heart* p.55-56

HERESY AND HERETICS
Carruthers — *Sparks* p.21-22
Curtis — *Practical* p.293
Flesch — *Unusual* p.117
Johnson — *Bedside* p.125
Kennedy — *Reader's* #448-449
Seldes — *Great* p.469-472
Woods — *Religious* p.432-435

HERITAGE
See also **America; Freedom; Liberty; Patriotism;** etc.
Applegarth — *Heir.* p.107, 111, 113, 245, 253
Dirksen — *Quot.* #42-43, 49-50
Evans — *Thoughts I* p.23, 34-35
Evans — *Thoughts II (Open Door)* p.83, 164-165
Evans — *Thoughts III (Open Road)* p.18, 161, 181
Evans — *Thoughts IV* p.146, 157
Evans — *Unto* p.56-58, 109
Flint — *Graham* p.12
Humes — *Instant* #419-434, 1189-1192
Lytle — *Leaves* p.71
Mandel — *Stories* p.131-132
Prochnow — *Public* #4365
Wallis — *Words* p.103-106
Woods — *Content.* p.32

HERMITS
See also **Solitude**
Evans — *Unto* p.118
Johnson — *Bedside* p.117
Kin — *Dictionary* p.119
Woods — *Content.* p.95

HEROD, KING
Fox — *Make* p.120

HEROES AND HEROISM
See also **Courage; Greatness; Leaders and leadership**
Applegarth — *Heir.* p.93, 251
Braude — *Source* #826-827
Edwards — *Useful* p.254-255
Evans — *Unto* p.27
Flesch — *Unusual* p.118
Fogg — *1000 See* index p.887
Forbes — *Thoughts* p.21, 110, 200, 203, 208-209, 377, 400, 449, 519
Fuller — *Epigrams* p.154-155; 345-346
Goudge — *Comfort* p.127-144
Harnsberger — *Mark* p.178
Harral — *Feature* p.182-183
Henry — *5000* p.121
Hovey — *Treasury* p.210; #52, 147, 666, 682, 879, 1244, 1249-1250, 1306, 1340, 1381, 1656
Johnson — *Bedside* p.107
Kauffman — *For* p.111-112
Kennedy — *Reader's* #450-453
Kin — *Dictionary* p.119
Liddle — *Thought IV* p.20, 38
Liddle — *Thought V* p.3
Liebman — *Peace* p.191-195
Lockridge — *World's* #25, 194, 746, 1615, 2994, 3381, 3550, 3832, 3865, 4722
Lytle — *Leaves* p.184
Modern Eloquence (14) p.347
Montapert — *Distilled* p.198
Nichols — *New* p.78-79
Peale — *Guideposts* p.161-164
Peterson — *Art* p.257
Prochnow — *Public* #1353, 1709
Prochnow — *Success.* #1848
Seldes — *Great* p.472-473
Sheen — *Thoughts* p.96-98
Speaker's Desk p.93-94, 96-98, #811
Taylor — *Within* p.112-113
Voss — *Quotations* p.126-127
Wallis — *Treasure* p.20, 70, 126
Wallis — *Words* p.19, 79
Woods — *Religious* p.435-436
, Decline of
Saturday — *Advent.* p.95-106
, Fictional
Kronenberger — *Animal* p.36-39
, Worship of
Day — *Meditations* p.44-45
Ideas p.188-190

HEROIN
Ginott — *Between* p.191-192, 199-202

HERRING
Botkin — *Anecdotes* p.258

HESITANCY
See also **Indecision**
Braude — *Source* #828-829
Flesch — *Unusual* p.18
Hubbard — *Scrap* p.149
Prochnow — *Public* #1534, 2206

HICCOUGHS
Prochnow — *Public* #152

HICKOCK, "WILD BILL"
Botkin — *Treasury* p.67-93

HIDING
Clark — *Windows* p.172
Kin — *Dictionary* p.119
Woods — *Religious* p.436

HIERARCHY
Wheelis — *Moralist* p.89-90, 93-105, 129-132, 150
Woods — *Religious* p.436

HIGH SCHOOLS
Ginott — *Between* p.145-149

"HIGHBROWS" AND "LOWBROWS"
Flesch — *Unusual* p.118
Ideas p.192-193
Liddle — *Thought I, II, III* p.116
Prochnow — *Success.* #1850
Safian — *More* p.130-132

HIGHWAYMEN
Botkin — *Anecdotes* p.144
Hobe — *Tapestries* p.128

HIGHWAYS
Fun Fare p.208-210
New Topical p.117
Prochnow — *Success.* #1354
, Construction of
Harral — *Feature* p.183

HIKING. *See* **Hitchhikers; Walking**

"HILLBILLIES"
Botkin — *Anecdotes* p.2, 14, 24, 29, 32, 83, 100, 247-251
Cerf — *Laugh* p.162-165
Prochnow — *Public* #279, 417
Speaker's Desk See index p.301

HILLS
See also **Mountains**
Botkin — *Treasury* p.320, 330, 429
Clark — *Windows* p.170

Lytle — *Leaves* p.37
, *Climbing of*
Woods — *Content.* p.62, 73, 195

HINDRANCES. *See* **Obstacles**

HINDUISM
See also **Krishna**
Phillips — *Choice* p.189
, *and Christianity*
Flint — *Graham* p.67-68

HINTS AND HINTING
Speaker's Desk #209, 331, 646, 995, 1046

"HIPPIES"
Asimov — *Treasury* #284-286
Franke — *Buckley* p.116
Grizer — *Wit* p.212
Prochnow — *Success.* #1091

HIPPOCRATIC OATH
Watson — *Light* p.181-182

HIPPOPOTAMUSES
Prochnow — *Public* #240

HIRING AND FIRING. *See* **Employment**

"HISSING" (of speakers)
Humes — *Instant* #419-434, 1189-1192

HISTORIANS
Curtis — *Practical* p.3, 124
Dirksen — *Quot.* #239
Flesch — *Unusual* p.118
Hubbard — *Scrap* p.48
Lockridge — *World's* #3836, 3839
Prochnow — *Public* #4337

HISTORICISM
Ideas p.193-195

HISTORY
See also **Biography**; names of countries, subdivision **History;** etc.
Adams — *New* p.180, 183
Applegarth — *Heir.* p.115-121
Braude — *Source* #831-834
Braude — *Stories* p.179-180
Cerf — *Laugh* p.1-9
Curtis — *Practical See* index p.121-193, 567
Dirksen — *Quot.* #77, 81, 197, 239, 340, 418, 640, 952-953, 1019, 1643, 1707
Edwards — *Useful* p.255-257
Evans — *This* p.127
Evans — *Thoughts III (Open Road)* p.175-176, 179, 185
Evans — *Unto* p.8, 33, 133
Flesch — *Unusual* p.118-119
Flint — *Graham* p.68
Forbes — *Thoughts See* index p.553
Fuller — *Epigrams* p.155
Grizer — *Wit* p.212-213
Harnsberger — *Mark* p.178-179
Harral — *Feature* p.183
Henry — *5000* p.121-122
Hoffer — *Reflect.* p.21-22, 69-70
Hooker — *Index* p.292-304
Hovey — *Treasury* p.210; *See* index p.297
Hubbard — *Scrap* p.146
Humes — *Instant* #435-455; p.32
Johnson — *Bedside* p.143, 194-195
Kennedy — *Reader's* #454-457
Kin — *Dictionary* p.119-120
Liddle — *Thought V* p.27, 31
Lockridge — *World's See* index p.577
Montapert — *Distilled* p.198-199
New Joy p.68-98
Nizer — *Thinking* p.167, 201
Prochnow — *Public* #147, 1128, 1536, 3191-3193, 4116, 4332
Prochnow — *Speaker's* p.162-163
Prochnow — *Success.* #218, 1184, 1851-1859
Seldes — *Great* p.473-479
Speaker's Desk #119, 275, 341, 397, 908, 969, 1177
Wallis — *Treasure* p.231
Wallis — *Words* p.24, 29-30, 57, 87, 105
Woods — *Religious* p.437-439
, *American. See* **U.S.-History**
, *Christian view of*
Hulme — *Living* p.102-103
, *Definitions of*
Flesch — *Unusual* p.118-119
, *Lessons of*
Bach — *Make* p.8-9
, *Meaning of*
Wheeler — *Moralist* p.68-69
, *Muse of*
Adams — *New* p.252
, *Pattern in*
Adams — *New* p.141
, *Political*
Auden — *Certain* p.182
, *Purpose of*
Nichols — *Third* p.235-236
, *Sense of*
Adams — *New* p.85
, *Study of*
Day — *Meditations* p.73

, Teaching of
Kauffman — *For* p.112-113
, Truth in
Adams — *New* p.224
, Writing of
Flesch — *Unusual* p.119-120
Prochnow — *Success.* #1860-1861

HITCHHIKERS
Lytle — *Leaves* p.115
Prochnow — *Public* #1184, 1711

HITLER, ADOLPH
Auden — *Certain* p.182-183
Seldes — *Great* p.479-480

HITTITES
New Topical p.117-118

HIVITES
New Topical p.118

HOARDING
See also **Greed; Misers**
Bartlett — *Discovery* p.36
Liddle — *Thought* p.26
Mandel — *Stories* p.132
Prochnow — *Speaker's* p.163

HOAXES
Botkin — *Treasury* p.361
Prochnow — *Public* #2442

HOBBIES
See also names of hobbies
Albert — *Stop* p.44, 49-50, 181-182
Braude — *Stories* p.180-181
Emmons — *Mature* p.88, 110
Grizer — *Wit* p.213
Harnsberger — *Mark* p.179
Harral — *Feature* p.183-186
List — *Living* p.66-71
Lockridge — *World's* #636, 2393, 5631
Menninger — *Blue.* p.34
Montapert — *Distilled* p.199-200
Prochnow — *Public* #1176
Wallis — *Treasure* p.117

"HOBBITS"
Kauffman — *For* p.135-136

HOBOES. *See* **Tramps**

HOGS
Botkin — *Anecdotes* p.3, 82, 90, 100-104, 196
Botkin — *Treasury* p.450, 570-571
Kin — *Dictionary* p.120, 249
New Topical p.261
Prochnow — *Public* #652
Schermerhorn — *1500* p.187

HOLES
Kin — *Dictionary* p.120
Prochnow — *Public* #2567

HOLIDAYS
See also names of holidays
Applegarth — *Heir.* p.149
Edwards — *Useful* p.257
Evans — *Quote* p.233-240
Evans — *Unto* p.11, 18
Flesch — *Unusual* p.120
Harral — *Feature* p.186-188
Howell — *Lines* p.111-114
Kin — *Dictionary* p.120
Lockridge — *World's* #4612
Prochnow — *Public* #336, 1539
Speaker's Desk #51
Strait — *Speaker's* p.168-169
Woods — *Content.* p.35, 61, 79, 160

HOLINESS
See also **Grace; Piety; Religion**
Applegarth — *Heir.* p.73, 212, 267, 302, 304
Book Proverbs p.40
Braude — *Source* #835-836
Dirksen — *Quot.* #2040
Edwards — *Useful* p.257-258
Esteve — *Experience* p.138-139, 151
Flesch — *Unusual* p.120
Garland — *Subject* p.136-137
Ideas p.346-347
Johnson — *Bedside* p.334-335
More Words p.78-79
New Topical p.118
Nichols — *Third* p.103-104
Phillips — *Choice* p.130, 225
Porter — *Halo* p.132-136
Wallis — *Treasure* p.111, 210
Wallis — *Words* p.23, 46, 55, 240
Woods — *Religious* p.214, 439-440, 883-884
, and truth
Curtis — *Practical* p.218

HOLLYWOOD, CALIFORNIA
See also **Actors and actresses; Motion pictures; Theater**
Botkin — *Anecdotes* p.264
Cerf — *Laugh* p.52-60
Copeland — *10,000* p.575-581
Edwards — *Useful* p.728
Fuller — *Thesaurus* #1446-1449
Fun Fare p.142-144, 232
Patterns For Living p.361-370
Prochnow — *Public* #1277

Prochnow — *Success.* #614
Simpson — *'54* p.50, 162, 303
Woods — *Religious* p.440

"HOLMES, SHERLOCK"
Auden — *Certain* p.183-184

HOLY DAYS AND HOLY WEEK
Day — *Meditations* p.62
Prochnow — *Success.* #1381
Suter — *Prayers* #400-403

HOLY GHOST. *See* **Holy Spirit (Holy Ghost)**

HOLY LAND. *See* **Palestine**

"HOLY OF HOLIES"
New Topical p.120-121

HOLY ORDERS. *See* **Ordination;** names of orders

HOLY ROMAN EMPIRE
See also **Rome and Romans**
Seldes — *Great* p.481

HOLY SPIRIT (Holy Ghost)
See also **God; Jesus Christ**
Flesch — *Unusual* p.120
Flint — *Graham* p.68-69
Garland — *Subject* p.137
Hobe — *Tapestries* p.110
Hovey — *Treasury* p.210-211; #6, 140, 477, 501, 521, 811, 958, 1151, 1253-1256, 1608, 1628, 1677, 1730
Kauffman — *For* p.113-114
Knight's Illus. p.147-150
Knight's Treas. p.159-162
More Words p.84-85
New Topical p.119
Seldes — *Great* p.480
Strait — *Speaker's* p.92-94
Wallis — *Words* p.33
Woods — *Religious* p.441-444
Zobell — *Speaker's* p.74-75
, Comfort of
Goudge — *Comfort* p.197-211
New Topical p.119
, Emblems of
New Topical p.78-79
, Gifts of
New Topical p.102, 169-170
, Indwelling of
New Topical p.130
, Inspiration of
New Topical p.131
, Offenses against
New Topical p.181
, Personality of
New Topical p.119
, Power of
New Topical p.196-197
, Sealing of
New Topical p.239
, Teaching of
New Topical p.120
, Titles and names of
New Topical p.272
, Witness of
New Topical p.298

HOME
See also **Children; Family; Houses; Parents and parenthood**
Alexander's Treasure. p.2, 16, 36-38, 313
Applegarth — *Heir.* p.117, 123-133, 291
Auden — *Certain* p.184-185
Bartlett — *Discovery* p.125-126
Book Proverbs p.80
Braude — *Source* #837-842
Braude — *Stories* p.181
Copeland — *10,000* p.283-334
Detherage — *Sunrise* p.38, 117-124, 162
Dirksen — *Quot.* #272, 355
Edwards — *Useful* p.258-260
Evans — *Faith* p.3, 27, 41, 48-64, 70, 73, 106, 184
Evans — *Quote* p.9-28
Evans — *This* p.7-8, 13-14
Evans — *Thoughts I* p.19, 103, 113, 145, 183, 218, 221
Evans — *Thoughts II (Open Door)* p.33-34, 44, 113-115, 119-120, 187-188
Evans — *Thoughts III (Open Road) See* index no p.
Evans — *Thoughts IV See* index no p.
Evans — *Unto* p.103, 106, 108
Felleman — *Poems* p.135-150
Flesch — *Unusual* p.120
Flint — *Graham* p.20, 69-70
Forbes — *Thoughts* p.45, 50, 70, 76, 124, 132, 176, 188, 209, 232, 321, 360, 411, 438, 474, 486
Fridy — *Meditat.* p.74, 109
Fuller — *Epigrams* p.155-156, 346
Garland — *Subject* p.137
Giniger — *Comfort* p.197-198
Goudge — *Comfort* p.353-359
Grizer — *Wit* p.213-214
Harnsberger — *Mark* p.179
Harral — *Feature* p.188-190
Henry — *5000* p.122-123
Hobe — *Tapestries* p.28, 89-90
Hovey — *Treasury* p.211-213; *See also* index p.297
How To Live p.115-118

Howell — *Better* p.85-90
Howell — *Lives* p.133-138
Hunter — *Gems* p.37-38
Johnson — *Bedside* p.294-316
Kennedy — *Reader's* #458-462
Keys Happiness p.271-273, 545-548
Kin — *Dictionary* p.120
Knight's Illus. p.150-156
Knight's Treas. p.163-168
Kohn — *Best* p.138, 145-146
Liddle — *Thought I, II, III* p.78, 91, 127, 173
Liddle — *Thought V* p.25, 30
Lockridge — *World's* #3644
Lytle — *Leaves* p.6, 21, 85, 166, 192
Mandel — *Stories* p.132-133
Mandelbaum — *Choose* p.69-72
Menninger — *Blue.* p.59-60
Modern Eloquence (14) p.348
Montapert — *Distilled* p.200
Patterns For Living p.39-50
Peterson — *Art* p.204, 217, 358
Phillips — *Choice* p.319
Prochnow — *Public* See index p.498
Prochnow — *Speaker's* p.164
Prochnow — *Success.* #174, 177, 878, 1000, 1106, 1374, 1862-1864
Speaker's Desk p.94-97; #866
Tanksley — *Friend* p.41, 57
Wallis — *Treasure* p.37, 75, 125, 127-134
Wallis — *Words* p.43, 49, 51, 76, 99, 101, 107-114, 127, 158, 236
Watson — *Light* p.252-258
Woods — *Content.* p.136, 139-165, 318
Woods — *Inspir.* p.241-283
Woods — *Religious* p.444

, and family
Barrows — *1000* See index p.440
Morris — *1000* See index p.430

, Beauty in
Curtis — *Daily* p.153-154

, Christian
Tanksley — *Friend* p.57

, Coming
Peterson — *Art* p.258

, Glory of
Woods — *Wellsprings* p.33

, God-centered
Peale — *Guideposts* p.285-302

, Going
Kohn — *Pathways* p.191-192

, Harmony in
Francis — *For* p.41-57

, Influence from
Keller — *You* p.211-243

, Life in
Fuller — *Thesaurus* p.171-174
Harral — *Feature* p.190-191

, Memories of
Words — *Inspir.* p.44

, Modern
White — *Life* p.19-25

, Privacy and sanctity of
Alexander's Treasure. p.119-122

HOME ECONOMICS
See also **Cooks and cookery;** etc.

HOME-TOWNS. *See* **Towns, Home**

HOMEMAKERS
Applegarth — *Heir.* p.256
Guideposts — *Faith* p.395-399
How To Live p.367-371
Kahn — *Lessons* p.193-194
Kin — *Dictionary* p.123
Manchee — *Secret* p.211-212
Prochnow — *Speaker's* p.166
Unlimited Power p.139-143, 222-223
Wallis — *Treasure* p.132-133

, Prayer for
Unlimited Power p.223

HOMER
Auden — *Certain* p.185-188
Flesch — *Unusual* p.120
Lockridge — *World's* #3584, 4414
Wallis — *Words* p.151

HOMESICKNESS
Clark — *Windows* p.16-17
Hobe — *Tapestries* p.114
Hubbard — *Scrap* p.31
Wallis — *Words* p.164, 236

HOMESTEADERS
Botkin — *Treasury* p.277, 290, 303, 314

HOMICIDE
See also **Murder**
McDonagh — *Invit.* p.144-154
New Topical p.121

HONESTY
See also **Integrity; Truth**
Book Proverbs p.107, 142
Braude — *Source* #843-844
Braude — *Stories* p.182
Dirksen — *Quot.* #3, 501, 1708-1709, 2036-2037, 2303

Droke — *Christian* p.263-268
Edwards — *Useful* p.260-261
Evans — *Quote* p.153-162
Evans — *Thoughts II (Open Door)* p.83-84, 88-90, 136-137
Evans — *Thoughts III (Open Road)* p.46-47, 60, 78, 151, 167, 176
Evans — *Thoughts IV* p.79-80, 95, 97, 133-134, 167, 193, 205
Evans — *Unto* p.89-90
Flesch — *Unusual* p.120
Flint — *Graham* p.71
Forbes — *Thoughts See* index p.553
Fuller — *Epigrams* p.156-157
Fuller — *Thesaurus* #286-294
Garland — *Subject* p.137-138
Grizer — *Wit* p.214-215
Harnsberger — *Mark* p.179-180
Henry — *5000* p.123
Hobe — *Tapestries* p.207
Hovey — *Treasury* #291, 309-310, 354, 773, 1017, 1036, 1308-1310, 1313, 1517, 1536, 1691
How To Live p.71-72
Hubbard — *Scrap* p.62, 82, 189
Johnson — *Bedside* p.5-11, 201
Kahn — *Lessons* p.201-208
Kennedy — *Reader's* #463-466
Kin — *Dictionary* p.120-121
Knight's Illus. p.156-159
Knight's Treas. p.168-172
Kopplin — *Something* p.113-114
Lair — *Baby* p.178-179
Langdon — *Teach.* p.19-25
Liddle — *Thought I, II, III* p.6, 22, 29, 32, 50-51, 128, 132, 141
Liddle — *Thought IV* p.31, 44
Lockridge — *World's* p.1099-1100, 2356, 2416
Lytle — *Leaves* p.74
Mandel — *Stories* p.133
Menninger — *Blue.* p.118-146
Montapert — *Distilled* p.200-201
Peale — *Sin* p.11-30
Prochnow — *Public See* index p.498
Prochnow — *Speaker's* p.164
Prochnow — *Success.* #612, 889, 1865
Sheen — *Content.* p.147-149
Speaker's Desk p.97-99; #70, 186, 376, 689, 754, 1125, 1154, 1173, 1178
Wheeler — *Moralist* p.34
Woods — *Religious* p.445
Zobell — *Speaker's* p.78

HONEY
Forbes — *Thoughts* p.96, 379, 455
Kin — *Dictionary* p.121
New Topical p.121
Words — *Inspir.* p.67

HONEYMOONS
See also **Bridegrooms; Brides; Marriage; Weddings**
Asimov — *Treasury* #596, 601, 629
Braude — *Speaker's* #600-603
Fuller — *Thesaurus* #896-898
How To Live p.63-65
Prochnow — *Public* #166
Prochnow — *Speaker's* p.164-165

HONOR
See also **Character; Fame; Ideals and idealism; Integrity; Tributes;** etc.
Braude — *Stories* p.182
Dirksen — *Quot.* #182, 216, 628, 954, 2038, 2121, 2363
Droke — *Christian* p.269
Edwards — *Useful* p.261-262
Evans — *This* p.30-31
Evans — *Thoughts III (Open Road)* p.101, 151, 170
Evans — *Unto* p.12, 52
Flesch — *Unusual* p.120
Fogg — *1000* #313, 322, 424, 497, 545, 916, 1026, 1068
Forbes — *Thoughts See* index p.553
Fuller — *Epigrams* p.157
Fuller — *Thesaurus* #296-298
Garland — *Subject* p.138
Harnsberger — *Mark* p.180
Henry — *5000* p.123
Hubbard — *Scrap* p.172
Johnson — *Bedside* p.3, 91
Kennedy — *Reader's* #468
Kin — *Dictionary* p.18, 121
Liddle — *Thought I, II, III* p.11-12, 34, 113, 148, 152, 160
Liddle — *Thought IV* p.10, 32
Liddle — *Thought V* p.9
Lockridge — *World's* #1099, 1100, 2356, 2416, 2562
Mandel — *Stories* p.133
Montapert — *Distilled* p.201
Nichols — *Third* p.61-62
Prochnow — *Public* #187, 256, 661, 1021, 2354-2355, 2464, 4119-4120
Prochnow — *Speaker's* p.165
Prochnow — *Success.* #182, 1254, 1866
Seldes — *Great* p.481
Sheban — *Wisdom* no p.
Sheen — *Thoughts* p.14-15
Speaker's Desk p.99-100; #290, 1050
Woods — *Religious* p.446

, National
Lockridge — *World's* #4756, 4787

, *Scythian*
Baillie — *Diary* #71
, *Sense of*
Alexander's Treasure. p.202-203
Auden — *Certain* p.188-189

HOOVER DAM
Prochnow — *Success.* #1146

HOPE
See also **Anticipation; Confidence; Encouragement; Faith; Trust**
Adams — *New* p.164
Alexander's Treasure. p.58
Applegarth — *Heir.* p.65
Baillie — *Diary* #18
Book Proverbs p.109
Braude — *Source* #845-847
Braude — *Stories* p.183
Detherage — *Sunrise* p.36, 170
Dirksen — *Quot.* #955-956, 1176, 1225, 2033, 2268
Droke — *Christian* p.269-270
Edwards — *Useful* p.262-264
Emmons — *Mature* p.141
Evans — *Thoughts III (Open Road)* p.35-41, 77, 86, 179, 200, 209
Evans — *Thoughts IV* p.84, 106, 169
Evans — *Unto* p.16, 119
Flesch — *Unusual* p.120-121
Forbes — *Thoughts* *See* index p.553
Fuller — *Epigrams* p.158
Garland — *Subject* p.138-139
Grizer — *Wit* p.215-217
Harnsberger — *Mark* p.180-181
Henry — *5000* p.123-124
Hobe — *Tapestries* p.49, 54, 64, 97, 226
Hovey — *Treasury* *See* index p.297
Howell — *Better* p.91-94
Howell — *Lives* p.56-57
Johnson — *Bedside* p.22-42, 254, 333-334
Kahn — *Lessons* p.109-112
Kauffman — *For* p.115-116
Kennedy — *Reader's* #467
Kin — *Dictionary* p.121-122
Knight's Illus. p.159-160
Liddle — *Thought I, II, III* p.10, 18, 21, 67, 70, 73, 78-79, 97-98, 112, 157, 186
Liddle — *Thought V* p.13, 27
Liebman — *Hope* p.13-47
Lockridge — *World's* #1622, 1705, 2047-2048, 3026, 3314, 3326, 4180, 4201
Lytle — *Leaves* p.15, 24-25, 30, 66, 71, 92-93, 102
McCracken — *What* p.83-88
McDonagh — *Invit.* p.87-88
Maltz — *Creative* p.54-56, 62-63
Manchee — *Secret* p.88-90
Mandel — *Stories* p.134-135
Montapert — *Distilled* p.201-202
Morris — *1000* *See* index p.430
New Joy p.256
New Topical p.121-122
Nichols — *Third* p.65, 92
Peale — *Courage* p.94-112
Porter — *Halo* p.14-23
Prochnow — *Public* #442, 2092-2093, 2103, 2591, 2716, 3200-3201, 4121-4122
Prochnow — *Speaker's* p.165-166
Prochnow — *Success.* #225, 1867-1868
Seldes — *Great* p.481
Sheban — *Wisdom* no p.
Sheen — *Thoughts* p.143-155
Sheen — *Way* p.191-192
Speaker's Desk #393, 451, 468, 494, 503, 515, 542, 988; p.100-101
Strait — *Speaker's* p.95-96
Tanksley — *Friend* p.16, 71
Voss — *Quotations* p.127-128
Wallis — *Treasure* p.12, 61, 135-138, 155, 228
Wallis — *Words* p.37, 43, 49, 115-118
Watson — *Light* p.279-318
Webb — *Edge* p.115-136
Woods — *Content.* p.226, 248-249, 277, 282, 286, 299, 336
Woods — *Inspir.* p.398-416
Woods — *Religious* p.446-448

HOPELESSNESS
See also **Despair**
Braude — *Source* #848-849
Flint — *Graham* p.71
Kohn — *Best* p.67-68
Prochnow — *Public* #977

HORACE
Lockridge — *World's* #3588

HORIZONS
See also **Future**
Adams — *New* p.266
Forbes — *Thoughts* p.1, 14, 178, 234, 238, 259, 505
Peterson — *Art* p.260
Wallis — *Words* p.102, 141

HORNS
Kin — *Dictionary* p.122
New Topical p.122
Prochnow — *Public* #678, 1821

HORSE RACING
Asimov — *Treasury* #87, 156
Braude — *Speaker's* #604-617
Copeland — *10,000* p.625-626
Dirksen — *Quot.* #1710
Fuller — *Thesaurus* #1871-1872
Grizer — *Wit* p.217

HORSE SENSE. *See* **Common sense**

HORSES
See also **Horse racing**
Applegarth — *Heir.* p.21
Asimov — *Treasury* #16, 176
Auden — *Certain* p.189-190
Botkin — *Anecdotes* p.4, 8, 83, 195, 269, 274
Botkin — *Treasury* p.119, 388, 455, 495, 671, 673, 763
Fuller — *Thesaurus* #2286-2288
Goudge — *Comfort* p.74-75
Harnsberger — *Mark* p.181-184
Harral — *Feature* p.191
Henry — *5000* p.124
Kin — *Dictionary* p.122
New Joy p.171, 197
New Topical p.122-123
Prochnow — *Public* #45, 328, 388, 553, 692, 968, 1866, 1922, 2391, 4306
Prochnow — *Speaker's* p.166
Prochnow — *Success.* #981, 1097
Schermerhorn — *1500* p.189-191
Weisfeld — *Pulpit* p.165, 174
, and colts
Kin — *Dictionary* p.50
Prochnow — *Public* #2222
, and mares
Kin — *Dictionary* p.156-157
, and mules
Speaker's Desk See index p.301
, traders of
Botkin — *Anecdotes* p.59, 113

HORSESHOES
Asimov — *Treasury* #80

HORTICULTURE. *See* **Gardens and gardening; Plants;** etc.

HOSPICES
Day — *Meditation* p.12-14, 17, 54

HOSPITALITY
See also **Guests; Hosts; Visitors and visiting;** etc.
Applegarth — *Heir.* p.249
Botkin — *Anecdotes* p.220, 223, 249
Dirksen — *Quot.* #2039
Edwards — *Useful* p.264
Fuller — *Thesaurus* #1006-1008
Garland — *Subject* p.139
Henry — *5000* p.124-125
Humes — *Instant* p.33; #16-24
Kin — *Dictionary* p.122
Kohn — *Best* p.100-103
Lockridge — *World's* #3091
New Topical p.123
Schermerhorn — *1500* p.191
Speaker's Desk #36, 161, 179, 242, 388, 589, 628, 776, 914
Wallis — *Words* p.76
Woods — *Content.* p.68, 171, 174
Woods — *Religious* p.449
, Mental
Adams — *New* p.44

HOSPITALS
Alexander's Treasure. p.160
Auden — *Certain* p.191-192
Botkin — *Anecdotes* p.242
Fuller — *Thesaurus* #1691
Harral — *Feature* p.191-193
Prochnow — *Public* #522, 716, 1065, 1529, 1714
, Children's
Guideposts — *Faith* p.405
, Jungle
Guideposts — *Faith* p.420-423
, Patients in
Flesch — *Unusual* p.204
Keys Happiness p.133-136
Prochnow — *Public* #168, 198, 2113, 2265
Pullar-Strecker — *Proverbs* #237-243

HOSTILITY
See also **Enemies; Hatred**
Albert — *Stop* p.82-83, 89-90
Holmes — *I've* p.9-10
Hulme — *Living* p.47-58
Liebman — *Peace* p.91-98
Menninger — *Blue.* p.41-46, 65-66

HOSTS
See also **Guests; Hospitality**
Auden — *Certain* p.192-193
Braude — *Source* #850-853
Braude — *Speaker's* #126-135
Copeland — *10,000* p.1001
Flesch — *Unusual* p.121
Kin — *Dictionary* p.122

HOTELS
See also **Hospices; Inns and innkeepers**
Asimov — *Treasury* #47
Botkin — *Anecdotes* p.85, 219, 237, 239, 245, 252, 275

Braude — *Speaker's* #618-625
Braude — *Stories* p.183-184
Copeland — *10,000* p.56-61
Fun Fare p.46
Harnsberger — *Mark* p.185
Harral — *Feature* p.193-194
Prochnow — *Public* #1, 63, 396, 613
Prochnow — *Speaker's* p.166
Prochnow — *Success.* #911, 1107
Schermerhorn — *1500* p.192-195
, and restaurants
Fuller — *Thesaurus* p.405-408
, Management of
Manchee — *Secret* p.212-213
Peale — *Guideposts* p.15-19

HOUDINI, HARRY
Putnam — *Art* p.297

HOURS
Forbes — *Thoughts* p.399, 458, 492
Kin — *Dictionary* p.122
Lytle — *Leaves* p.176

HOUSEHOLD HINTS
Sagendorph — *Old* p.100-109

HOUSES
See also **Builders and building; Home**
Applegarth — *Heir.* p.132-133
Bradshaw — *Home.* p.109-111
Flesch — *Unusual* p.68, 121
Grizer — *Wit* p.218
Harnsberger — *Mark* p.185-186
Harral — *Feature* p.194
Henry — *5000* p.125
Hobe — *Tapestries* p.31, 67-68, 89, 115, 166
Kin — *Dictionary* p.123
New Topical p.123-124
Prochnow — *Public* #42, 844, 2686
Prochnow — *Success.* #1698
Wallis — *Treasure* p.125, 130
Wallis — *Words* p.17, 26, 29, 76, 224
Woods — *Wellsprings* p.14-15

HOUSEWIVES. *See* **Homemakers**

HOUSEWORK
See also **Cleaning**; etc.
Guideposts — *Faith* p.143-146, 157-161, 339-340
Holmes — *I've* p.23-37
Kohn — *Touch* p.95-99
Lindbergh — *Gift* p.25-26
Peale — *Courage* p.172-173
Prochnow — *Public* #1599
Prochnow — *Success.* #1048
Rogers — *Time* p.43-50

"HOWLERS"
Botkin — *Treasury* p.485
Copeland — *10,000* p.847-850

HUDSON, HENRY
Wallis — *Words* p.118

HUGUENOTS
Fogg — *1000* #74, 552, 949

HUMAN BEINGS. *See* **Humanity; Man**

HUMAN DESTINY. *See* **Destiny**

HUMAN NATURE
See also **Character; Personality;** etc.
Adams — *New* p.67, 130, 246
Alexander's Treasure. p.4
Baillie — *Diary* #349
Bennett — *How* p.56-61
Botkin — *Anecdotes* p.204
Dirksen — *Quot.* #302, 957
Evans — *Unto* p.34, 47, 49, 61, 93
Flesch — *Unusual* p.121
Flint — *Graham* p.71
Forbes — *Thoughts* p.20, 22, 32, 34, 263, 284, 339, 410, 463
Fox — *Make* p.155-156
Fun Fare p.113-114
Grizer — *Wit* p.218
Halverson — *Perspective* p.12, 48, 73
Harnsberger — *Mark* p.186-187
Harral — *Feature* p.194-195
Hubbard — *Scrap* p.19
Johnson — *Bedside* p.133, 142-143, 184, 187, 197, 250-251, 320-323, 327
Kennedy — *Reader's* #476-481
Lockridge — *World's* #3634, 5028
Modern Eloquence (14) p.349-351
Montapert — *Distilled* p.202-203
Prochnow — *Public* #869, 1508, 1715
Wheeler — *Moralist* p.53-54
Woods — *Religious* p.449

HUMAN RELATIONS
Adams — *New* p.217
Braude — *Source* #854
Evans — *Unto* p.101
Harral — *Feature* p.195
Holmes — *Design* p.148-153
Keys Happiness p.277-280, 313-316, 344, 431-434
Maltz — *Creative* p.30
Montapert — *Distilled* p.273-274
Patterns For Living p.107-296

Peterson — *Art* p.188
Unlimited Power p.180-183
Welk — *Guide.* p.36-38, 172-176
Words Change p.72-75

HUMAN RIGHTS. *See* **Rights of man**

HUMANISTS
Auden — *Certain* p.193-195
Baillie — *Diary* #242
Gold — *Letters* p.127-137
Ideas p.196-198
Lockridge — *World's* #5110
Woods — *Religious* p.449-452

HUMANITARIANISM
Nizer — *Thinking* p.127-128
Woods — *Religious* p.452-453

HUMANITY
See also **Brotherhood; Life and living; Man (Mankind); Society**
Adams — *New* p.155
Applegarth — *Heir.* p.231, 304
Bartlett — *Discovery* p.81, 131-132
Dirksen — *Quot.* #1643, 1713
Edwards — *Useful* p.264-265
Evans — *This* p.21-22
Flesch — *Unusual* p.121-122
Fogg — *1000* #112, 237
Forbes — *Thoughts* p.553-554
Fox — *Make* p.114
Grizer — *Wit* p.218-219
Halverson — *Perspective* p.73
Harnsberger — *Mark* p.186-188
Henry — *5000* p.125-126
Hovey — *Treasury* *See* index p.297
How To Live p.563-572
Hubbard — *Scrap* p.14, 17, 24, 94, 99, 194, 208, 211
Humes — *Instant* p.49; #456-476
Kennedy — *Reader's* #469-475
Kin — *Dictionary* p.123
Krishnamurti — *Urgency* p.151-154
Liddle — *Thought I, II, III* p.23, 42, 55, 75, 90, 107, 175, 190
Liddle — *Thought IV* p.25, 33
Liddle — *Thought V* p.21
Maltz — *Creative* p.78-79
New Joy p.21
Peterson — *Art* p.257
Peterson — *New* p.32-33
Prochnow — *Public* #3202-3203, 4297
Prochnow — *Speaker's* p.167
Prochnow — *Success.* #1255, 1869
Seldes — *Great* p.481-488
Sheban — *Wisdom* no p.
Sheen — *Lift* p.168-183
Voss — *Quotations* p.128-130
Wallis — *Words* p.17, 26, 29, 76, 224
Wheeler — *Moralist* p.4
White — *Life* p.175-184
Woods — *Religious* p.453-454

HUMBLENESS. *See* **Humility; Meekness**

HUMBUG
See also **Deception; Fools and foolishness; Fraud**
Kin — *Dictionary* p.123
Seldes — *Great* p.489

HUMDRUM. *See* **Bores and boredom**

HUMILIATION
See also **Insult**
Braude — *Stories* p.184
Kennedy — *Reader's* #482
Lockridge — *World's* #1634

HUMILITY
See also **Meekness; Modesty**
Auden — *Certain* p.195
Baillie — *Diary* #29, 221
Book Proverbs p.126
Braude — *Source* #855-856
Braude — *Stories* p.184-185
Detherage — *Sunrise* p.149
Dirksen — *Quot.* #497, 629-630, 944, 948, 958-961, 1001, 1308, 1363-1367, 2040-2041
Edwards — *Useful* p.265-267
Emmons — *Mature* p.112
Evans — *Faith* p.89, 116, 173, 219
Evans — *Quote* p.153-162
Evans — *This* p.32, 130-131
Evans — *Thoughts II (Open Door)* p.47, 139
Evans — *Thoughts III (Open Road)* p.161, 177
Evans — *Thoughts IV* p.173-176, 197
Evans — *Unto* p.47, 50, 102, 113, 132
Flesch — *Unusual* p.122
Flint — *Graham* p.71
Fogg — *1000* #93, 128, 134, 271, 313, 345, 402, 449, 502, 651, 730, 866, 897, 972
Forbes — *Thoughts* p.62, 173, 245, 336, 339, 343, 352, 376, 424, 480, 503
Fridy — *Meditat.* p.59
Fuller — *Epigrams* p.159
Garland — *Subject* p.141
Goudge — *Comfort* p.207
Grizer — *Wit* p.219
Henry — *5000* p.126
Hobe — *Tapestries* p.15, 85
Hovey — *Treasury* #93, 1014, 1124, 1587, 1667-1678, 1714

How To Live p.270-274
Howell — *Lines* p.89-91
Hubbard — *Scrap* p.87
Johnson — *Bedside* p.4, 78, 321
Kahn — *Lessons* p.120-123
Kennedy — *Reader's* #483-490
Kin — *Dictionary* p.123
Knight's Illus. p.160-162
Knight's Treas. p.173-174
Kohn — *Pathways* p.52-53
Langdon — *Teach.* p.79-89
Liddle — *Thought I, II, III* p.18, 23, 35, 78, 108, 122, 173
Liddle — *Thought IV* p.6, 33, 36
Liddle — *Thought V* p.4, 13, 20, 30, 42-43, 45
Lockridge — *World's* #368, 1635, 2927, 3092, 3444, 4480, 5504, 5879
Lytle — *Leaves* p.16, 26, 192
Mandel — *Stories* p.135-138
Menninger — *Blue.* p.38
Montapert — *Distilled* p.203-204
New Topical p.125
Phillips — *Choice* p.54, 77, 90, 138-139, 146, 277
Prochnow — *Public* #2098, 2185, 2649, 3204-3205, 4123-4124, 4367
Prochnow — *Speaker's* p.167
Prochnow — *Success.* #1189, 1870-1871
Sheen — *Thoughts* p.115-128
Sheen — *Way* p.17-19
Speaker's Desk p.102-103
Voss — *Quotations* p.130-132
White — *Life* p.283-284, 307
Woods — *Religious* p.454-457
Woods — *Wellsprings* p.11, 15
Words — *Inspir.* p.39
Zobell — *Speaker's* p.78-81

, Prayer for
Unlimited Power p.74

, Self-confidence and
Albert — *Stop* p.53-54

HUMMINGBIRDS
Applegarth — *Heir.* p.37

HUMOR
See also **Jokes and joking; Laughter; Tricks and trickery;** types of humor and various subjects
Applegarth — *Heir.* p.86
Braude — *Source* #857-859
Curtis — *Practical* p.47, 74
Edwards — *Useful* p.267-268, 335, 728
Evans — *Quote* p.215-222
Evans — *Thoughts II (Open Door)* p.183
Evans — *Thoughts III (Open Road)* p.26, 78, 85-89
Evans — *Thoughts IV* p.126-130
Felleman — *Poems* p.150, 187-241
Flesch — *Unusual* p.10, 97-98, 122
Forbes — *Thoughts* p.21, 137, 271, 313, 472
Grizer — *Wit* p.219-222
Harnsberger — *Mark* p.188-191
Henry — *5000* p.126
Hovey — *Treasury* #1318, 1320
How To Live p.209-210
Hubbard — *Scrap* p.12, 21, 54, 63
Kennedy — *Reader's* #491-494
Kopplin — *Something* p.119-124
Liddle — *Thought I, II, III* p.20, 34, 78, 146, 148, 156
Liddle — *Thought IV* p.25, 41
Liddle — *Thought V* p.10
Lockridge — *World's* #46, 48, 303, 307, 439, 460, 3673, 3756, 4309, 5696, 5792
Mandel — *Stories* p.138
Montapert — *Distilled* p.204
Prochnow — *Public* #1716, 1879, 2165, 3206-3209, 4386
Prochnow — *Success.* #758, 843, 905, 1182, 1872-1873
Simpson — *Contemp.* p.259-287
Speaker's Desk #54, 102, 242, 352, 367, 757, 1038
Wallis — *Treasure* p.156-157
Wallis — *Words* p.17, 19, 71, 82, 143
Woods — *Religious* p.457

, American
Botkin — *Anecdotes* p.xxviii

, Dictionary of
Copeland — *10,000* p.765-774

, English
Copeland — *10,000* p.683-706

, Ethnic
See also **Jews, Humor of;** etc.
Asimov — *Treasury* p.211-310

, in speeches
Nizer — *Thinking* p.62, 76, 147-148

, Individual approach to
Fun Fare p.10-11, 62, 84, 159, 168, 207, 264, 283

, Lack of
Asimov — *Treasury* #176

, Minority
Botkin — *Anecdotes* p.38

, of Mark Twain
See also subjects indexed in Harnsberger
Peterson — *Art* p.225

, Sense of
Braude — *Source* #860-861
Dirksen — *Quot.* #2330
Forbes — *Thoughts* p.15, 156, 271, 313, 472
Kohn — *Touch* p.162-166

HUMORISTS
See also names of humorists
Cerf — *Laugh* p.27-31

HUNCHBACKS
Kin — *Dictionary* p.123

HUNGARIANS
Asimov — *Treasury* #454
Lockridge — *World's* #742
, Revolt of
Franke — *Buckley* p.120-121

HUNGER
See also **Appetite; Diet; Eating;** etc.
Dirksen — *Quot.* #631, 1156
Flesch — *Unusual* p.122-123
Forbes — *Thoughts* p.132, 165, 202
Fuller — *Epigrams* p.159-160
Garland — *Subject* p.105, 141-142
Grizer — *Wit* p.223
Harnsberger — *Mark* p.191
Henry — *5000* p.126-127
Hovey — *Treasury* p.213; #30, 356, 571, 591, 593, 597, 617, 815, 893, 1136, 1204, 1277-1279, 1848
Kin — *Dictionary* p.89, 124
Lockridge — *World's* #2997, 3885
Prochnow — *Public* #34, 80, 255, 501, 701, 1126, 1626, 2081, 2099-2100, 2882
Seldes — *Great* p.346, 489, 887
Sheban — *Wisdom* no p.
Woods — *Religious* p.457
, and education
Kauffman — *For* p.117-118
, and faith
Adams — *New* p.307
, and Gospel
Kauffman — *For* p.117
, Efforts to alleviate
Kauffman — *For* p.116-117
, Fighters of
Reader's — *20th* p.98-103

HUNTERS AND HUNTING
Asimov — *Treasury* #276, 411
Botkin — *Anecdotes* p.34, 90, 92-93, 96-97, 129, 171, 187
Botkin — *Treasury* p.7, 19, 25, 29, 273, 454, 508, 593, 604
Braude — *Speaker's* #626-627
Cerf — *Laugh* p.216-217
Copeland — *10,000* p.612-614
Fuller — *Thesaurus* #1876-1879
Harral — *Feature* p.195-196
Kin — *Dictionary* p.124
Kohn — *Thoughts* p.145-146
Krishnamurti — *Think* p.165-166
Lockridge — *World's* #2751, 4181
Prochnow — *Public* #202
Prochnow — *Speaker's* p.167
Prochnow — *Success.* #1012
Schermerhorn — *1500* p.46-47, 196-197
Speaker's Desk #288, 705, 814, 870, 1003

HURDY-GURDIES
Auden — *Certain* p.196-197

HURRICANES
Asimov — *Treasury* #371
Harral — *Feature* p.196
Unlimited Power p.6-9

HURRY. *See* **Haste**

HUSBANDS
See also **Marriage; Men; Wives**
Asimov — *Treasury* #545, 547, 557
Book Proverbs p.20
Braude — *Source* #862-864
Braude — *Speaker's* #136-137, 628-702
Dirksen — *Quot.* #165
Edwards — *Useful* p.729
Evans — *Thoughts III (Open Road)* p.17, 29, 137
Flesch — *Unusual* p.123
Flint — *Graham* p.44, 71-72
Fuller — *Epigrams* p.160-161
Fuller — *Thesaurus* #916-918
Fun Fare p.92-93
Garland — *Subject* p.142
George — *Book See* index p.444
Goudge — *Comfort* p.120-121
Guideposts — *Faith* p.152-156
Harral — *Feature* p.196
Henry — *5000* p.127
How To Live p.69-72, 92-95, 118
Huxley — *You See* index p.285
Kahn — *Lessons* p.185-191
Keys Happiness p.438-440, 477-479, 503-504, 551
Kin — *Dictionary* p.124
Liddle — *Thought I, II, III* p.27, 41, 51, 82, 123, 138
Liddle — *Thought* V p.6
Lockridge — *World's* #769, 772, 851, 879, 3819, 5157, 5245
Manchee — *Secret* p.232-233
New Joy p.186
New Topical p.125-126

Peale — *Courage* p.141-145
Prochnow — *Public See* index p.499
Prochnow — *Speaker's* p.168
Prochnow — *Success. See* index p.492
Reader's — *Getting* p.78-80
Safian — *More* p.109-117
Schermerhorn — *1500* p.197-199
Seaburg — *Great* p.174, 178, 182, 243, 276, 315, 327, 326, 339, 345, 407
Sheban — *Wisdom* no p.
Wallis — *Words* p.109
Weisfeld — *Pulpit* p.87-103
Woods — *Religious* p.457

, *"Bitter"*
Safian — *Insults* p.116-121
Safian — *More* p.113-117

, *"Henpecked"*
Asimov — *Treasury* #535-537, 552-554
Safian — *Insults* p.110-115
Safian — *More* p.109-113

, *Indifferent*
Holmes — *I've* p.47-48

, *Responsibilities of*
White — *Life* p.28-31, 44-48

HYDROGEN BOMB
Dirksen — *Quot.* #1715
Seldes — *Great* p.490

HYENAS
Botkin — *Anecdotes* p.270
Botkin — *Treasury* p.675

HYGIENE
See also **Health**
Auden — *Certain* p.197-198
Curtis — *Practical* p.74
Phillips — *Choice* p.171, 251

HYMNS
Applegarth — *Heir.* p.185, 187, 301
Garland — *Subject* p.143
Harnsberger — *Mark* p.191-192
Hovey — *Treasury* #30, 386, 498, 503, 593, 698, 1130
Kennedy — *Fresh* p.162-164
More Words p.20
Prochnow — *Public* #354
Wallis — *Words* p.44

, *Modern*
Kauffman — *For* p.202-204

HYPNOTISM
Albert — *Stop* p.21-22
Asimov — *Treasury* #42
Garland — *Subject* p.190
Prochnow — *Public* #958

HYPOCHONDRIACS
Albert — *Stop* p.110-111
Fuller — *Thesaurus* #1716-1720
Safian — *Insults* p.122-124
Safian — *More* p.118-120

HYPOCRISY
Book Proverbs p.57
Braude — *Source* #865-866
Braude — *Stories* p.185-186
Carruthers — *Sparks* p.23-24
Dirksen — *Quot.* #161, 1368-1373
Droke — *Christian* p.270-271
Edwards — *Useful* p.268-269
Evans — *This* p.67
Evans — *Thoughts II (Open Door)* p.43, 88
Flesch — *Unusual* p.123
Flint — *Graham* p.78, 86
Forbes — *Thoughts* p.148
Fuller — *Epigrams* p.161-162
Fuller — *Thesaurus* #301-303
Garland — *Subject* p.84-85, 143-144
Harnsberger — *Mark* p.192
Henry — *5000* p.127
Hobe — *Tapestries* p.204
Hovey — *Treasury* p.214; #1280-1283
Hubbard — *Scrap* p.164
Jackson — *Bedside* p.128, 340
Kahn — *Lessons* p.100-102
Kennedy — *Reader's* #495-496
Kin — *Dictionary* p.75, 124-125, 261
Knight's Illus. p.162
Knight's Treas. p.174-176
Liddle — *Thought IV* p.8
Lockridge — *World's See* index p.577
Montapert — *Distilled* p.205
New Topical p.126
Nichols — *Third* p.49-50
Prochnow — *Public* #2430
Prochnow — *Speaker's* p.168
Seldes — *Great* p.490
Tanksley — *Friend* p.19
Weisfeld — *Pulpit* p.1
Woods — *Religious* p.457-458

HYPOTHESIS. *See* **Theory**

I

"I." *See* **Self**

I.Q.
Ideas p.198-199

ICE AND ICE-STORMS
Harnsberger — *Mark* p.193
Kin — *Dictionary* p.126
Prochnow — *Success.* #980

ICE-SKATING
Guideposts — *Faith* p.384
Hadfield — *Delights* p.100
Woods — *Content.* p.69

ICEBERGS
Auden — *Certain* p.198-199

ICONOCLASTS
Seldes — *Great* p.490

IDAHO
Botkin — *Treasury* p.469, 603, 613, 622-623

IDEALS AND IDEALISM
See also **Aspiration; Character; Ethics; Honor; Integrity; Principles; Vision**
Adams — *New* p.71
Applegarth — *Heir.* p.137, 273
Bartlett — *Discovery* p.51-54
Braude — *Source* #874-877
Braude — *Stories* p.186
Curtis — *Practical* p.25, 101, 293-295, 522-527
Dirksen — *Quot.* #103, 632-633, 1171
Droke — *Christian* p.271-273
Edwards — *Useful* p.269-270, 729
Evans — *This* p.86
Evans — *Thoughts I* p.81-83
Evans — *Unto* p.13, 82-85, 123
Fogg — *1000* #87, 100, 235, 283, 309, 418, 530, 703, 851
Forbes — *Thoughts* p.21, 250, 318, 342; *See also* index p.554
Fuller — *Epigrams* p.162
Giniger — *Compact* p.167-170
Grizer — *Wit* p.225-226
Harnsberger — *Mark* p.195
Henry — *5000* p.124, 127-128
Hobe — *Tapestries* p.173-177
Holman — *Psych.* p.48-49
Hovey — *Treasury* p.214-215; *See* index p.297
Hubbard — *Scrap* p.17, 19, 22, 25, 27, 30, 62, 67, 94, 97, 172, 222
Humes — *Instant* #477-487
Hunter — *Gems* p.50-51
Keller — *Open* p.94
Kin — *Dictionary* p.126
Liddle — *Thought I, II, III* p.70, 93, 147
Liddle — *Thought V* p.5-6, 28, 40
Lockridge — *World's* #740, 750, 3427, 5771
Lytle — *Leaves* p.36, 38-39
Mandelbaum — *Choose* p.175-179
Modern Eloquence (14) p.352-353
Montapert — *Distilled* p.206-207
Nizer — *Thinking* p.206
Peterson — *Art* p.277, 322, 402
Prochnow — *Public* #1054, 2377
Prochnow — *Success.* #235, 298, 665, 1884-1885
Seldes — *Great* p.493
Speaker's Desk p.103-104
Voss — *Quotations* p.133-134
Wallis — *Treasure* p.7, 17, 19, 90, 211, 233
Wallis — *Words* p.119-124, 137
Woods — *Religious* p.458-460
, American
Words — *Inspir.* p.97
, and deeds
Kauffman — *For* p.119
, Creative
Peterson — *Art* p.328
, Role of
Phillips — *Choice* p.84

IDEAS AND IDEOLOGY
See also **Imagination; Inventors and inventions; Originality; Theory; Thought**
Adams — *New* p.103, 123
Applegarth — *Heir.* p.111, 138, 273
Braude — *Source* #867-873
Braude — *Stories* p.186
Curtis — *Golden* p.142-143
Curtis — *Human* p.6-7, 112-113
Curtis — *Practical* p.21, 29-32, 40, 61, 97, 323
Dirksen — *Quot.* #67, 419, 496, 907, 949, 962
Droke — *Christian* p.273-275
Du Noüy — *Human* p.9, 105, 124, 159-160, 191-193
Edwards — *Useful* p.270-271, 729
Esteve — *Experience* p.56-57
Flint — *Graham* p.72
Forbes — *Thoughts See* index p.554
Fuller — *Experience* p.162-163
Garland — *Subject* p.144-145
Grizer — *Wit* p.223-225
Harnsberger — *Mark* p.193-195
Henry — *5000* p.123-124, 128
Hoffer — *Reflect.* p.39-41
Holmes — *Design* p.20-23, 33-34, 53, 61, 63-64, 176, 180
Hovey — *Treasury* p.215; *See* index p.297
How To Live p.325-327
Hubbard — *Scrap* p.30, 224
Humes — *Instant* p.31; #488-497
Johnson — *Bedside* p.127, 190
Kennedy — *Reader's* #497-500
Keys Happiness p.310-312, 397-398

Kin — *Dictionary* p.126
Liddle — *Thought I, II, III* p.29, 87-88, 103, 146, 154, 179, 183
Liddle — *Thought IV* p.43
Lockridge — *World's See* index p.577
Mandel — *Stories* p.138-139
Montapert — *Distilled* p.205-206
Nizer — *Thinking* p.23, 31-33, 47, 167
Peterson — *Art* p.163, 328
Prochnow — *Public See* index p.499
Prochnow — *Speaker's* p.168-169
Prochnow — *Success.* #1252, 1280, 1303, 1877-1883, 2081
Reader's — *Getting* p.31-34
Seldes — *Great* p.490-493
Sheban — *Wisdom* no p.
Wallis — *Treasure* p.87-88, 231
Wallis — *Words* p.121, 167
White — *Job* p.114-116, 134
Woods — *Religious* p.460
Words — *Inspir.* p.203

, and social history
Boas — *History* p.71-89

, Change of
Boas — *History* p.44-70

, Complete
Adams — *New* p.152

, Crucial
Lair — *Baby* p.19

, Energy and
Albert — *Stop* p.205

, Fixed
Kin — *Dictionary* p.95

, History of
Boas — *History* p.3-23

, Life-changing
Bach — *Make* p.133-145

, Muddy
Kohn — *Through* p.31

, Personal factor of
Boas — *History* p.146-163

, Power of
Adams — *New* p.263

, Sources of new
Boas — *History* p.67-70

, Systems of
Boas — *History* p.90-116

IDENTIFICATION
Braude — *Speaker's* #703-711
Braude — *Stories* p.186-187
Grizer — *Wit* p.226
Holmes — *Design* p.182, 205-206, 215-216
Jones — *If* p.18-19
Prochnow — *Public* #523, 997
Wheeler — *Moralist* p.80, 82-83

IDENTITY
See also **Self**
Braude — *Speaker's* #712-713
Garland — *Subject* p.145
Grizer — *Wit* p.226-227
How To Live p.198
Prochnow — *Success.* #232
Woods — *Religious* p.460

, Discovering true
Webb — *Edge* p.21-23

, Mistaken
Harral — *Feature* p.223
Speaker's Desk See index p.302

, Personal
Phillips — *Choice* p.281

, Teenager
Ginott — *Between* p.27-46

IDIOTS
Harnsberger — *Mark* p.195
Henry — *5000* p.124, 128
Kin — *Dictionary* p.126
Prochnow — *Public* #37
Prochnow — *Success.* #1892
Seldes — *Great* p.493, 675

, Jokes about
Botkin — *Treasury* p.461

IDLENESS
See also **Ease; Inaction; Indolence; Laziness; Leisure; Rest; Unemployment**
Applegarth — *Heir.* p.148
Book Proverbs p.4
Braude — *Source* #878-881
Braude — *Stories* p.187
Dirksen — *Quot.* #231, 286, 1374-1379
Edwards — *Useful* p.271-273, 282
Evans — *Faith* p.26-27, 29, 210
Evans — *Quote* p.41-51
Evans — *Thoughts I* p.123, 134, 149, 210
Evans — *Thoughts II (Open Door)* p.123
Evans — *Thoughts III (Open Road)* p.131, 175, 200
Evans — *Unto* p.13, 49, 56, 83-84, 93, 101
Forbes — *Thoughts* p.49, 83, 111, 158, 190, 243, 347, 373, 376, 407, 427, 451, 511
Fuller — *Epigrams* p.163-164
Grizer — *Wit* p.227
Hadfield — *Delights* p.76
Henry — *5000* p.124-125, 128
Hubbard — *Scrap* p.36, 53, 198, 214-215
Keller — *You* p.229-231
Kin — *Dictionary* p.126-127
Liddle — *Thought I, II, III* p.159, 170
Liddle — *Thought IV* p.6, 13
Liddle — *Thought V* p.8, 35
Lytle — *Leaves* p.186

Mandel — *Stories* p.139
Montapert — *Distilled* p.207-208
New Topical p.126-127
Patterns For Living p.713-719
Prochnow — *Public* #2166, 2344
Prochnow — *Speaker's* p.169
Prochnow — *Success.* #1886
Safian — *Insults* p.125-128
Sheen — *Way* p.58-59
Speaker's Desk p.104-106
Woods — *Religious* p.460-461

IDOLS AND IDOLATRY
See also **Gods, False**
Curtis — *Practical* p.15
Garland — *Subject* p.145-146
Kin — *Dictionary* p.127
Krishnamurti — *Think* p.171-172
Lockridge — *World's* #5782
New Topical p.127-129
Seldes — *Great* p.493-495
Woods — *Religious* p.461-462

"IF." *See* **Possibilities**

IGNORANCE
See also **Fools and foolishness; Illiteracy; Innocence**
Asimov — *Treasury* #345, 360, 425
Book Proverbs p.116
Braude — *Stories* p.187
Dirksen — *Quot. See* index p.265
Edwards — *Useful* p.273-275, 729
Evans — *Faith* p.20-21, 135, 160, 173, 176, 179
Evans — *Quote* p.67-79
Evans — *This* p.129-130
Evans — *Thoughts III (Open Road)* p.148, 151
Evans — *Unto* p.41, 66-68, 143
Flesch — *Unusual* p.190-191, 300
Forbes — *Thoughts* p.29, 70, 78, 132, 169, 203, 219, 228, 272, 291, 316, 355-356, 358, 361, 363, 380, 429, 499
Fuller — *Epigrams* p.164-165
Garland — *Subject* p.146
Grizer — *Wit* p.228
Harnsberger — *Mark* p.195-197
Henry — *5000* p.125-128
Hoffer — *Reflect.* p.73-74
Hubbard — *Scrap* p.197, 227-228
Johnson — *Bedside* p.77, 113, 169, 302
Kennedy — *Reader's* #1076
Kin — *Dictionary* p.127-128
Kohn — *Best* p.51
Liddle — *Thought I, II, III* p.22, 35, 47, 78, 91, 134, 158, 162, 194
Lockridge — *World's See* index p.577
Lytle — *Leaves* p.112, 192
Mandelbaum — *Choose* p.137-151
Modern Eloquence (14) p.354
Montapert — *Distilled* p.208
Prochnow — *Public* #313, 563, 1910, 2016, 2167, 3212-3215, 4127-4129, 4368
Prochnow — *Speaker's* p.169-170
Prochnow — *Success.* #1065, 1198, 1887-1889
Seldes — *Great* p.495-496
Sheban — *Wisdom* no p.
Speaker's Desk p.106-108; *See* index p,301
Wallis — *Words* p.143
Wheeler — *Moralist* p.113
Woods — *Religious* p.462, 493

ILIAD
Lockridge — *World's* #3605

ILLEGITIMACY
Woods — *Religious* p.462

ILLINOIS
See also **Chicago, Ill.**
Botkin — *Anecdotes* p.18, 42, 50, 122, 157, 218-219, 225, 239
Botkin — *Treasury* p.67, 74, 277, 327, 329, 386, 418, 879n

ILLITERACY
See also **Ignorance**
Asimov — *Treasury* #83, 112
Prochnow — *Success.* #1296

ILLNESS
See also **Disease; Epidemics; Pain; Suffering**
Bach — *Make* p.174-176
Baillie — *Diary* #39, 101, 213
Casselberry — *How* p.119-120, 124-128, 131-133
Curtis — *Human* p.21-23, 25-29, 33-35
Dirksen — *Quot.* #2157-2159
Edwards — *Useful* p.275, 590
Evans — *Unto* p.28, 46
Flesch — *Unusual* p.262
Fuller — *Epigrams* p.260
Fuller — *Thesaurus* p.300-303
Guideposts — *Faith* p.331-333
Harnsberger — *Mark* p.197-198
Harral — *Feature* p.196
Henry — *5000* p.253
Huxley — *You See* index p.285-286
Irion — *Yes* p.109-112
Johnson — *Bedside* p.278, 284, 286-293
Kennedy — *Fresh* p.114-117
Kennedy — *Reader's* #1026
Keys Happiness p.37-40, 427-428
Kin — *Dictionary* p.128, 233-234
Krishnamurti — *Think* p.74-75

Lockridge — *World's* #285, 289, 2891, 3089, 4839
Montapert — *Distilled* p.208-209
New Topical p.249-250
Prochnow — *Public* #940, 1798, 4213-4215
Prochnow — *Speaker's* p.283
Prochnow — *Success.* #2303-2305
Reader's — *Getting* p.205-208, 222-225
Sheban — *Wisdom* no p.
Suter — *Prayers* #443-458
White — *Life* p.39-40, 131, 185-200
Woods — *Content.* p.55, 74, 307, 347
Woods — *Religious* p.929
, *Comfort and courage in*
Goudge — *Comfort* p.239-244
, *Crises of*
Jackson — *Coping* p.136-143
, *Fear of*
Hill — *Think* p.269-273
, *Prayer for*
Unlimited Power p.147
, *Symptoms of*
Adams — *New* p.146
Prochnow — *Public* #2252

ILLUMINATION
See also **Light; Understanding**
Curtis — *Practical* p.62-66
Phillips — *Choice* p.51, 107, 232
Woods — *Religious* p.462-463

ILLUSION
See also **Delusion**
Braude — *Source* #882-883
Curtis — *Practical* p.40
Forbes — *Thoughts* p.137, 236, 425
Fuller — *Epigrams* p.165
Garland — *Subject* p.146
Harnsberger — *Mark* p.198
Henry — *5000* p.127, 129
Hubbard — *Scrap* p.137
Liddle — *Thought I, II, III* p.178
Lockridge — *World's* #1090, 1253, 1757, 2363, 2402, 4349
Phillips — *Choice* p.51
Prochnow — *Success.* #1230
Sheban — *Wisdom* no p.
White — *Job* p.41-42, 85

ILLUSIVENESS
Prochnow — *Public* #2131

ILLUSTRATION. *See* **Example**

IMAGES
See also **Idols and idolatry; Self-image**
Curtis — *Practical* p.241
Phillips — *Choice See* index p.426
Woods — *Religious* p.463

IMAGINATION
See also **Daydreaming; Dreams and dreaming; Fairy tales; Ideas and ideology; Originality; Vision**
Albert — *Stop* p.105-106, 193-195
Applegarth — *Heir.* p.135-139
Asimov — *Treasury* #47
Auden — *Certain* p.200-201
Bartlett — *Discovery* p.107-109
Braude — *Source* #884-888
Braude — *Stories* p.187
Curtis — *Golden* p.100-103
Curtis — *Human* p.12
Curtis — *Practical* p.26, 421-429, 457
Du Noüy — *Road* p.59, 76-81, 160
Edwards — *Useful* p.192, 275-277
Esteve — *Experience* p.54-55
Flesch — *Unusual* p.160
Fogg — *1000* #34, 100, 121, 129, 292, 443, 653, 685, 738
Forbes — *Thoughts See* index p.554
Fuller — *Epigrams* p.165-166
Fuller — *Thesaurus* #306
Garland — *Subject* p.147
Grizer — *Wit* p.228-229
Hadfield — *Delights* p.192-193
Harnsberger — *Mark* p.198
Henry — *5000* p.127-129
Hovey — *Treasury* #699, 1814, 1831
How To Live p.304-307
Johnson — *Bedside* p.43, 45, 48, 63, 90, 122, 206, 235, 247, 254, 256, 313
Kennedy — *Reader's* #501
Keys Happiness p.68-72
Kin — *Dictionary* p.89-90
Kohn — *Touch* p.152-156
Liddle — *Thought I, II, III* p.162
Lockridge — *World's* #503, 1787, 2355, 3710, 3714, 3761, 4202, 4205, 4314, 5710, 5722, 5772
Lytle — *Leaves* p.146
Maltz — *Creative* p.199-200
Mandel — *Stories* p.140
Modern Eloquence (14) p.355-356
Montapert — *Distilled* p.209-210
Nichols — *New* p.108-110
Nizer — *Thinking* p.67, 131
Peterson — *New* p.40-41

Phillips — *Choice* p.266
Prochnow — *Public* #2381
Prochnow — *Speaker's* p.170-171
Prochnow — *Success.* #1890-1891
Rau — *Act* p.55-64
Sheban — *Wisdom* no p.
Speaker's Desk p.108-109
Wallis — *Treasure* p.29, 105
White — *Job* p.116, 119, 135, 144
Woods — *Content.* p.155, 228-229, 237, 244
Woods — *Religious* p.463
Words — *Inspir.* p.157-158
, and action
Wheelis — *Moralist* p.18
, Comfort in
Goudge — *Comfort* p.293-371
, Control of
Baillie — *Diary* #325
, Creative
Hill — *Think* p.205-207
, Power of
Jones — *If* p.116-123
, toward riches
Hill — *Think* p.100-113

IMBECILES. *See* **Idiots**

IMITATION
See also **Example; Plagiarism**
Braude — *Source* #889-893
Braude — *Stories* p.188
Edwards — *Useful* p.277
Evans — *Thoughts III (Open Road)* p.141
Evans — *Thoughts IV* p.156-157
Garland — *Subject* p.147-148
Henry — *5000* p.128-129
Johnson — *Bedside* p.13, 95
Kin — *Dictionary* p.128
Lytle — *Leaves* p.140
Mandel — *Stories* p.140-141
Prochnow — *Success.* #1295
Seldes — *Great* p.496
Sheban — *Wisdom* no p.
Speaker's Desk p.109-110, #63, 269

IMMATURITY
Evans — *Thoughts I* p.140-141
Kahn — *Lessons* p.177-184
Speaker's Desk #38

IMMEDIACY. *See* **Present**

IMMENSITY. *See* **Greatness**

IMMIGRANTS AND EMIGRANTS
See also **Pioneers**
Asimov — *Treasury* #373
Dirksen — *Quot.* #42, 50, 357, 519
Franke — *Buckley* p.122
Grizer — *Wit* p.229-230
Nizer — *Thinking* p.182
Peale — *Guideposts* p.257-259, 274-275
Prochnow — *Public* #1561

IMMORALITY
See also **Adultery; Vice**
Evans — *Thoughts I* p.28, 218
Evans — *Thoughts III (Open Road)* p.87, 111, 198-199, 205, 209-210
Evans — *Thoughts IV* p.94, 105, 123, 126, 128, 158
Flint — *Graham* p.72-74, 125
Guideposts — *Faith* p.450-496
Henry — *5000* p.128
Howell — *Better* p.95-106
Liebman — *Hope* p.101-118
Liebman — *Peace* p.26-29
Lockridge — *World's* #3898, 4534-4538, 5210, 5794
Words — *Religious* p.464

IMMORTALITY
See also **Eternity; Heaven; Soul**
Adams — *New* p.143, 239, 244
Applegarth — *Heir.* p.94, 266
Baillie — *Diary* #194
Braude — *Source* #894-895
Curtis — *Practical* p.25, 507, 510-519
Detherage — *Sunrise* p.156, 171
Dirksen — *Quot.* #965, 1162, 1383-1387, 1952, 2044-2046, 2309
Droke — *Christian* p.277
Du Noüy — *Human* p.128, 253-256
Edwards — *Useful* p.277-279
Emmons — *Mature* p.131-138
Evans — *Faith* p.13, 19-22, 25, 35, 59, 73-74, 134, 153, 193-206, 213, 225
Evans — *Quote* p.111-124
Evans — *This* p.59-60, 194-195
Evans — *Thoughts I* p.41-44, 49-51, 111-112, 211-212
Evans — *Thoughts IV* p.154-155, 158, 168-169, 176, 179-180, 184, 198
Evans — *Unto* p.4-5, 12-13, 121, 139-140, 142-147
Flint — *Graham* p.74-75
Forbes — *Thoughts* p.129, 283, 363, 412, 416, 448, 458
Garland — *Subject* p.149
Harnsberger — *Mark* p.198
Henry — *5000* p.128-130

Holmes — *Design* p.123-125
Hovey — *Treasury* p.215-216; #815, 1291-1298
How To Live p.531-537
Howell — *Lines* p.157-165
Hubbard — *Scrap* p.62, 88, 109, 136, 142, 149
Ideas p.7-9
Johnson — *Bedside* p.25, 32, 44, 79, 95, 339-340
Kahn — *Lessons* p.237-240
Kauffman — *For* p.119
Keller — *Open* p.14, 133, 138-140
Kennedy — *Reader's* #502-507
Kin — *Dictionary* p.8
Krishnamurti — *Think* p.73-74
Liebman — *Peace* p.134-144
Lockridge — *World's* #4434
Lytle — *Leaves* p.6, 92, opp. 104
Montapert — *Distilled* p.210-211
Morris — *1000 See* index p.431
New Topical p.151-152
Nichols — *Third* p.131-132
Peale — *Courage* p.189, 218-249
Peale — *Stay* p.284-300
Peterson — *Art* p.409
Prochnow — *Public* #2168, 3216, 3218, 4130-4131
Prochnow — *Speaker's* p.171
Prochnow — *Success.* #1893
Reader's — *Getting* p.116
Seldes — *Great* p.496-498
Sheban — *Wisdom* no p.
Voss — *Quotations* p.134-136
Wallis — *Treasure* p.139-146
Wallis — *Words* p.25, 92, 98-102
Woods — *Content.* p.34, 57, 269, 280, 284-285, 294, 327
Woods — *Inspir.* p.458-489
Woods — *Religious* p.464-474
, in nature
Guideposts — *Faith* p.477-478
, Proof of
Nichols — *New* p.180-181

IMMUNITY
Du Noüy — *Road* p.8, 163-167
Evans — *This* p.41-42

IMPAIRMENT (of mind and body)
See also **Alcoholism; Appetite; Drugs; Evil; Immorality; Vice;** etc.
Evans — *Thoughts IV* p.14, 28, 93-99, 113-114, 118, 124, 144-145, 189

IMPARTIALITY. *See* **Neutrality**

IMPATIENCE
See also **Haste; Restlessness**
Book Proverbs p.116
Braude — *Stories* p.188
Curtis — *Practical* p.94, 551
Day — *Meditations* p.37
Edwards — *Useful* p.279
Evans — *Thoughts I* p.71, 107-110, 128-129, 139-141, 160-164, 198-200, 210
Forbes — *Thoughts* p.518
Kin — *Dictionary* p.128
Lockridge — *World's* #1550
Lytle — *Leaves* p.169
Mandel — *Stories* p.141-142
Menninger — *Blue.* p.16-18
Peterson — *Art* p.289
Prochnow — *Public* #2089
Speaker's Desk #109

IMPERFECTIONS. *See* **Faults**

IMPERIALISM
Henry — *5000* p.130
Ideas p.201-203
Seldes — *Great* p.498
Woods — *Religious* p.474

IMPERISHABILITY
Henry — *5000* p.129

IMPERMANENCE
Dirksen — *Quot.* #368, 1392-1394, 1885
Sheban — *Wisdom* no p.

IMPERSONALITY
Henry — *5000* p.129
Prochnow — *Public* #2169

IMPERTINENCE. *See* **Arrogance; Insult; Rudeness**

IMPETUOSITY. *See* **Rashness**

IMPIETY
See also **Profanity**
Henry — *5000* p.129

IMPORTANCE
See also **Self-importance**
Adams — *New* p.92, 216
Braude — *Speaker's* #714-715
Dirksen — *Quot.* #127, 966-967
Evans — *Thoughts III (Open Road)* p.156-159, 178
Forbes — *Thoughts* p.226, 344
Garland — *Subject* p.150
Grizer — *Wit* p.230
Halverson — *Perspective* p.102
Henry — *5000* p.129
Hovey — *Treasury* p.46-47; #97, 158-160, 442, 1047, 1851, 1855
Kin — *Dictionary* p.128
Kohn — *Touch* p.37-38
Prochnow — *Success.* #1897-1898

Seldes — *Great* p.82
Woods — *Religious* p.78

IMPOSSIBILITY
Botkin — *Treasury* p.360
Braude — *Source* #896-899
Curtis — *Practical* p.109
Du Noüy — *Road* p.93, 116, 124
Edwards — *Useful* p.280
Forbes — *Thoughts* p.147, 307, 420, 436, 449, 508
Henry — *5000* p.129-131
Hovey — *Treasury* p.216-217; #968, 1002, 1299-1302
Kin — *Dictionary* p.128-129
Lytle — *Leaves* p.65, 166, 189
Montapert — *Distilled* p.211
Prochnow — *Public* #2317
Prochnow — *Speaker's* p.171-172
Prochnow — *Success.* #644, 1096
Speaker's Desk See index p.301
Tanksley — *Friend* p.78
Welk — *Guide.* p.165-166
, Belief in
Dirksen — *Quot.* #180
, Meaning of
Du Noüy — *Human* p.29-30

IMPOSTURE. *See* **Deception; Fraud**

IMPOTENCY
How To Live p.404-405
Lytle — *Leaves* p.175
, Spiritual
Maltz — *Creative* p.172

IMPRACTICABILITY
Speaker's Desk #272, 980

IMPRESSIONISM
Lockridge — *World's* #3688

IMPRESSIONS
See also **Appearances**
Edwards — *Useful* p.280
Evans — *Thoughts III (Open Road)* p.96
Evans — *Thoughts IV* p.118-119, 123
Harnsberger — *Mark* p.199
Liddle — *Thought I, II, III* p.44
Mandel — *Stories* p.142-143
Prochnow — *Public* #925
, First
Adams — *New* p.25
Nichols — *Third* p.40

IMPRESSIVENESS
Prochnow — *Public* #2170

IMPROVEMENT
See also **Progress; Self-improvement; Study**
Edwards — *Useful* p.280-281
Evans — *Thoughts I* p.102, 109, 162-165
Forbes — *Thoughts* p.65, 125, 168, 227, 233, 325, 359, 378, 384, 425, 443, 489
Garland — *Subject* p.150-151
Grizer — *Wit* p.231
Harral — *Feature* p.196
Henry — *5000* p.130-131
Kahn — *Lessons* p.13-15
Kin — *Dictionary* p.129
Lytle — *Leaves* p.65
Maltz — *Creative* p.205
Mandel — *Stories* p.144
Montapert — *Distilled* p.211-212
Prochnow — *Public* #1077
Prochnow — *Success.* #1899
Speaker's Desk p.192, 893, 1055, 1065
Tanksley — *Friend* p.36

IMPROVIDENCE
See also **Waste**
Edwards — *Useful* p.281
Humes — *Instant* p.37
Kin — *Dictionary* p.129

IMPRUDENCE. *See* **Indiscretion**

IMPULSE
See also **Desire; Instinct; Wishes**
Edwards — *Useful* p.281-282
Emmons — *Mature* p.121
Evans — *Unto* p.61
Harnsberger — *Mark* p.199
Keys Happiness p.289-293
Lockridge — *World's* #2622
Mandel — *Stories* p.144
Menninger — *Blue.* p.31

IMPUNITY
Lockridge — *World's* #533

IMPURITY
See also **Vulgarity**
Book Proverbs p.116
Edwards — *Useful* p.282
Flint — *Graham* p.75
Woods — *Religious* p.474

INABILITY
Edwards — *Useful* p.62
Flesch — *Unusual* p.29
Holmes — *Design* p.67-68
Lockridge — *World's* #1731
Montapert — *Distilled* p.50
Seldes — *Great* p.109-110

INACCESSIBILITY
Adams — *New* p.20
Henry — *5000* p.130

INACCURACY. *See* **Mistakes**

INACTION
See also **Idleness**
Braude — *Source* #900-901
Curtis — *Practical* p.37
Lockridge — *World's* #3735, 5809-5840
White — *Life* p.139-142
Woods — *Religious* p.474

INADEQUACY
See also **Inability**
Evans — *This* p.174-175
Kin — *Dictionary* p.129
Maltz — *Creative* p.131-132

INANITY. *See* **Bores and boredom**

INATTENTION. *See* **Neglect**

INCARNATION
Applegarth — *Heir.* p. 13, 28
Flint — *Graham* p.75-76
Kohn — *Thoughts* p.64-66
McDonagh — *Invit.* p.113-114
More Words p.86-88
Phillips — *Choice* p.410
Thurman — *Mood* p.109-118
Wallis — *Words* p.24, 30, 33-34, 57
Woods — *Religious* p.474-476

INCAS
Applegarth — *Heir.* p.104

INCENSE
New Topical p.129-130
Prochnow — *Public* #2573

INCENTIVES
See also **Ambition; Goals; Motivation and motives**
Curtis — *Practical* p.343-347
Dirksen — *Quot.* #634, 2371
Halverson — *Perspective* p.109
Woods — *Business.* p.113-114

INCLINATION. *See* **Desire; Impulse; Instinct; Wishes**

INCOME
See also **Wages;** etc.
Book Proverbs p.9
Dirksen — *Quot.* #162, 1018
Garland — *Subject* p.151-152
Grizer — *Wit* p.231-232
Harral — *Feature* p.196
Henry — *5000* p.130-131
Jones — *If* p.124-132
Kohn — *Thoughts* p.35-38
Lockridge — *World's* #5066
Montapert — *Distilled* p.212
Prochnow — *Public* #339, 360, 1521
Prochnow — *Success.* #565, 1902-1903

INCOME TAX
Braude — *Source* #902
Braude — *Speaker's* #716,724
Dirksen — *Quot.* #1719
Grizer — *Wit* p.232-233
Henry — *5000* p.131
Prochnow — *Public* #1297, 1312, 1533

INCOMPATIBILITY
Kin — *Dictionary* p.129

INCOMPETENCE. *See* **Inability; Inadequacy**

INCOMPLETENESS
Flesch — *Unusual* p.301
Kohn — *Thoughts* p.122-125
Lockridge — *World's* #3407
Nichols — *Third* p.123-124

INCOMPREHENSIBILITY
Henry — *5000* p.130
Prochnow — *Success.* #1904

INCONGRUITY
Speaker's Desk See index p.301

INCONSISTENCY
See also **Change; Fickleness; Indecision; Instability**
Baillie — *Diary* #74
Dirksen — *Quot.* #1926
Edwards — *Useful* p.282-283
Henry — *5000* p.131
Hubbard — *Scrap* p.200
Kin — *Dictionary* p.129
Lockridge — *World's* #1014
Mandel — *Stories* p.145
Speaker's Desk #153, 271

INCONVENIENCE
Henry — *5000* p.131
Lockridge — *World's* #253
Mandel — *Stories* p.145

INCORRUPTIBILITY
Henry — *5000* p.131-132

INCREDULITY
See also **Impossibility; Unbelief and unbelievers**
Edwards — *Useful* p.283
Fogg — *1000* #355
Henry — *5000* p.131-132

Lockridge — *World's* #3209
Seldes — *Great* p.498

INCUBATION
Curtis — *Practical* p.62-66
Prochnow — *Public* #319, 649

INDECISION
See also **Indifference**
Book Proverbs p.116
Braude — *Source* #903
Dirksen — *Quot.* #1395
Du Noüy — *Road* p.42, 157, 175-178, 183
Edwards — *Useful* p.283, 303
Evans — *Faith* p.139, 155-156, 169
Evans — *Thoughts I* p.118-119
Evans — *Thoughts IV* p.196
Forbes — *Thoughts* p.35, 106, 121, 126, 181, 203, 331
Fox — *Make* p.79-80
Grizer — *Wit* p.233
Henry — *5000* p.132, 136
Huxley — *You See* index p.286
Kennedy — *Fresh* p.90-92
Keys Happiness p.270
Kin — *Dictionary* p.129, 266
Kohn — *Best* p.119-121
Liddle — *Thought I, II, III* p.113
Liddle — *Thought IV* p.4-5, 29
Liebman — *Hope* p.72-100
Lytle — *Leaves* p.172
Mandel — *Stories* p.145-146
Montapert — *Distilled* p.212
Phillips — *Choice* p.21, 134
Price — *Wider* p.159-163
Prochnow — *Public* #1415
Speaker's Desk #466, 635, 680, 817, 876
Wheeler — *Moralist* p.9

INDEPENDENCE
See also **Freedom; Liberty; Self-reliance;** etc.
Curtis — *Practical* p.317
Edwards — *Useful* p.283-284
Emmons — *Mature* p.63, 67
Evans — *Faith* p.147
Evans — *Unto* p.83
Forbes — *Thoughts* p.176, 192, 213, 235, 348, 394, 397, 425, 468, 497, 517
Garland — *Subject* p.152-153
Grizer — *Wit* p.233
Halverson — *Perspective* p.22
Harnsberger — *Mark* p.199-200
Henry — *5000* p.131-132
Hubbard — *Scrap* p.29, 72, 102
Huxley — *You See* index p.286
Kin — *Dictionary* p.130
Liddle — *Thought I, II, III* p.60, 89
Liddle — *Thought IV* p.9
Liddle — *Thought V* p.45
Lockridge — *World's* #1062
Lytle — *Leaves* p.174
Montapert — *Distilled* p.212-213
Nichols — *New* p.193-194
Prochnow — *Public* #244, 4132
Seldes — *Great* p.499
Speaker's Desk p.110; #6
Woods — *Business.* p.114
Woods — *Content.* p.45, 109, 179, 230-232, 239, 278, 285, 295, 298, 314, 316, 346, 351
Woods — *Religious* p.477
, Creative
Adams — *New* p.407
, Declaration of. See **Declaration of Independence**

INDEPENDENCE DAY
Dirksen — *Quot.* #26, 2367
Evans — *Unto* p.12-13
Harnsberger — *Mark* p.131-132
Hovey — *Treasury* p.186, 303; #1057-1058, 1562; *See also* index p.303
Kohn — *Best* p.155-157
Prochnow — *Success.* #1215
Schermerhorn — *1500* p.168-169
Weisfeld — *Pulpit* p.138

INDETERMINACY. *See* **Indecision**

INDEXES
Braude — *Stories* p.188-189
Edwards — *Useful* p.284
Lytle — *Leaves* p.163

INDIA
See also **Indians, East**
Curtis — *Practical* p.375-376
Harnsberger — *Mark* p.200-201
Hovey — *Treasury* #344, 380, 580, 1224, 1278, 1720
Simpson — *Contemp.* p.144-145
, Soul of
Phillips — *Choice* p.372

INDIAN PROVERBS
Dirksen — *Quot.* #796
Prochnow — *Public* #299

INDIANA
Botkin — *Anecdotes* p.196, 224, 272
Botkin — *Treasury* p.119, 262, 270, 328, 417-418, 420, 469, 556, 562, 597, 791

INDIANS, EAST
Asimov — *Treasury* #319
Krishnamurti — *Think* p.84-85

INDIANS OF NORTH AMERICA
See also names of tribes
Asimov — *Treasury* #432-433

Botkin — *Anecdotes* p.37, 58, 169, 181, 223, 252, 264
Botkin — *Treasury* p.33, 36-43, 68, 151-152, 229, 265, 276, 415, 521, 562, 566, 624
Cerf — *Laugh* p.170-171
Grizer — *Wit* p.43
Harnsberger — *Mark* p.201-202
Harral — *Feature* p.197
Hubbard — *Scrap* p.95
Kohn — *Touch* p.62-63, 70, 75-78
Prochnow — *Public* #1135
Schermerhorn — *1500* p.201
, and textbooks
Kauffman — *For* p.25-26
, Signs of
New Joy p.162-163

INDIFFERENCE
See also **Neglect**
Baillie — *Diary* #283
Curtis — *Practical* p.55-56
Edwards — *Useful* p.284, 296
Evans — *Faith* p.7-8, 127, 143-144, 160, 166
Evans — *This* p.168-169
Evans — *Thoughts I* p.83-84, 114, 119, 129
Evans — *Thoughts III (Open Road)* p.126-129, 200
Evans — *Thoughts IV* p.127, 166, 177-178, 196, 206
Flint — *Graham* p.13-14, 76, 146
Forbes — *Thoughts* p.142, 175, 261
Fun Fare p.90-91
Garland — *Subject* p.16
Harral — *Feature* p.260
Henry — *5000* p.132
Hubbard — *Scrap* p.63, 67
Humes — *Instant* #90-96
Keller — *Open* p.24
Kennedy — *Reader's* #508-510
Kin — *Dictionary* p.130
Knight's Illus. p.210-214
Liddle — *Thought V* p.20, 26, 31
Lockridge — *World's* #47, 2261
Lytle — *Leaves* p.33
Prochnow — *Success.* #1905
Seldes — *Great* p.37-39
Sheen — *Content.* p.41-43
Strait — *Speaker's* p.15-19
Wheelis — *Moralist* p.32
Woods — *Religious* p.23, 477-478

INDIGENCE. *See* **Poverty**

INDIGESTION
Edwards — *Useful* p.285
Flesch — *Unusual* p.70
Henry — *5000* p.132

INDIGNATION. *See* **Anger**

INDIGNITY. *See* **Insult**

INDIRECTNESS
Lockridge — *World's* #4856

INDISCRETION
See also **Fools and foolishness; Mistakes; Rashness**
Book Proverbs p.53
Dirksen — *Quot.* #906, 963, 1321-1322, 1381, 2272
Droke — *Christian* p.185
Edwards — *Useful* p.201, 285
Evans — *This* p.14-15
Flesch — *Unusual* p.91
Forbes — *Thoughts* p.133, 158, 317, 328, 337, 367
Henry — *5000* p.95, 132
Kin — *Dictionary* p.97
Lockridge — *World's* #823; *See* index p.575
Lytle — *Leaves* p.119, 150
Montapert — *Distilled* p.156-157
Prochnow — *Public* #3286
Prochnow — *Success.* #1202
Sheban — *Wisdom* no p.
Woods — *Religious* p.335
, and wisdom
Hubbard — *Scrap* p.86

INDISPENSABILITY
Braude — *Source* #904-906
Braude — *Stories* p.189
Grizer — *Wit* p.233-234
Lindbergh — *Gift* p.47-48
Lockridge — *World's* #210
Lytle — *Leaves* p.78

INDIVIDUALS AND INDIVIDUALITY
See also **Character; Distinction; Eccentricity**
Adams — *New* p.316, 380
Applegarth — *Heir.* p.44, 256
Braude — *Source* #907
Braude — *Stories* p.189
Curtis — *Practical* p.542
Dirksen — *Quot.* #423, 637, 713, 2388
Du Noüy — *Human* p.61, 128-129, 152-153, 161-164, 177-178, 180-181, 187, 207, 235-236, 262-263, 268-269
Du Noüy — *Road See* index p.247
Edwards — *Useful* p.285-286, 729
Evans — *This* p.21-22, 25-26
Evans — *Unto* p.9, 58
Forbes — *Thoughts* p.66, 109, 127, 213, 342; *See also* index p.554
Garland — *Subject* p.153-154
Grizer — *Wit* p.234

Henry — *5000* p.132-133
Hobe — *Tapestries* p.117
Hoffer — *Reflect.* p.77-97
Hovey — *Treasury* #21, 70
Humes — *Instant* #498-507
Kennedy — *Reader's* #511-515
Keys Happiness p.340-344
Kin — *Dictionary* p.103
Kronenberger — *Animal* p.106-107
Liddle — *Thought I, II, III* p.37, 81, 106, 120, 142, 187
Lockridge — *World's* #4723
Lytle — *Leaves* p.115
Menninger — *Blue.* p.65
Montapert — *Distilled* p.213-214
Nichols — *New* p.86-87
Phillips — *Choice* p.32, 55, 67, 108, 231, 280, 283, 292, 334, 406
Prochnow — *Success.* #1907
Seldes — *Great* p.500-505
Speaker's Desk See index p.299
Wallis — *Treasure* p.119
Wallis — *Words* p.26, 153
Wheeler — *Moralist See* index p.164
Woods — *Business.* p.114-117
Woods — *Religious* p.479-482
Words Change p.80-81
Words — *Inspir.* p.115
, and community
Krishnamurti — *Urgency* p.138-139
, Cult of
Ideas p.203-204
, Responsibility of
Woods — *Religious* p.480-481
, Rugged
Dirksen — *Quot.* #713
, versus state
Ideas p.204-206

INDOCTRINATION
Woods — *Religious* p.482

INDOLENCE. *See* **Laziness**

INDULGENCE
See also **Alcoholism; Gluttony; Greed;** etc.
Edwards — *Useful* p.286
Evans — *Faith* p.33, 35, 49, 56, 98, 122, 131, 133, 135, 154, 215
Evans — *Unto* p.82
Forbes — *Thoughts* p.27, 192, 405
Kin — *Dictionary* p.185
Lockridge — *World's* #2346, 2623, 4355
Woods — *Religious* p.482

INDUSTRIAL REVOLUTION
Adams — *New* p.366

INDUSTRY
See also **Business; Commerce; Diligence; Labor; Work;** etc.
Braude — *Source* #910-911
Braude — *Stories* p.189
Curtis — *Practical See* index p.568
Dirksen — *Quot. See* index p.265
Edwards — *Useful* p.286-288
Evans — *Unto* p.95
Fogg — *1000 See* index p.888
Forbes — *Thoughts See* index p.554
Harral — *Feature* p.197
Henry — *5000* p.132-133
Hubbard — *Scrap* p.12, 123-124, 147
Kin — *Dictionary* p.130
Lockridge — *World's* #600, 1534
Lytle — *Leaves* p.27
Modern Eloquence (14) p.357
Montapert — *Distilled* p.214-215
New Topical p.130
Prochnow — *Public* #4133
Prochnow — *Success.* #118, 181, 270, 482, 748, 1335
Seldes — *Great* p.505-506
Speaker's Desk #187, 336, 942, 1065
Woods — *Business.* p.118-120
Woods — *Religious* p.482-483
, Bargaining in
Woods — *Business.* p.120-121
, Competence of
Woods — *Business.* p.117-118
, New
Woods — *Business.* p.159-160
, Relations with
Hovey — *Treasury See* index p.304

INEQUALITY
Adams — *New* p.414
Lockridge — *World's* #1617
New Joy p.66
Seldes — *Great* p.506-507

INEVITABILITY
Adams — *New* p.345
Braude — *Stories* p.189
Evans — *This* p.103-104
Henry — *5000* p.133

INEXHAUSTIBILITY
Lytle — *Leaves* p.45

INEXPERIENCE. *See* **Innocence**

INFALLIBILITY
Curtis — *Practical* p.284
Dirksen — *Quot.* #100
Seldes — *Great* p.507-508
Woods — *Religious* p.483-484

INFAMY. *See* **Depravity; Disgrace; Slander**

INFANCY. *See* **Babies; Birth**

INFANTILISM
Holman — *Psych.* p.30-32

INFERENCE
Curtis — *Practical* p.448-449

INFERIORITY
Braude — *Stories* p.189
Grizer — *Wit* p.235
Henry — *5000* p.133
How To Live p.238-245
Lockridge — *World's* #478
Mandel — *Stories* p.146
Phillips — *Choice* p.137
Seldes — *Great* p.508-509
Sherman — *You* p.123-129
Woods — *Religious* p.484

"INFERIORITY COMPLEX"
Holman — *Psych.* p.103-114
Ideas p.206-207
Lair — *Baby* p.146-147
Liebman — *Peace* p.46-53
Peale — *Guide* p.46-63

INFIDELITY
Dirksen — *Quot.* #1400-1402
Edwards — *Useful* p.288-290
Fuller — *Thesaurus* #901-904
Garland — *Subject* p.154
Keys Happiness p.237-240, 328-331
Lockridge — *World's* #86, 384, 2786
Woods — *Religious* p.485

INFIDELS. *See* **Atheism**

INFINITY
See also **Eternity**
Applegarth — *Heir.* p.197
Garland — *Subject* p.154-155
Henry — *5000* p.133
Hubbard — *Scrap* p.78, 110
Lockridge — *World's* #2909
Nichols — *Third* p.137-139
Sheban — *Wisdom* no p.
Woods — *Religious* p.485-486
, and God's power
Peterson — *Art* p.302

INFLATION
Braude — *Source* #912-913
Braude — *Stories* p.189
Dirksen — *Quot.* #34, 424, 1155
Grizer — *Wit* p.235-238
Humes — *Instant* #508-516
Kauffman — *For* p.120
Phillips — *Choice* p.166
Prochnow — *Speaker's* p.172-173
Prochnow — *Success.* #686, 1362, 1452
Seldes — *Great* p.510
Woods — *Business.* p.121-123

INFLECTION
Nizer — *Thinking* p.90

INFLEXIBILITY. *See* **Determination**

INFLUENCE
See also **Environment; Guidance; Power;** etc.
Bach — *Make* p.122-123
Baillie — *Diary* #95
Book Proverbs p.107
Carruthers — *Sparks* p.159-160
Detherage — *Sunrise* p.175, 177-178
Edwards — *Useful* p.290-291
Emmons — *Mature* p.36, 117-120, 128
Evans — *Faith* p.2, 61, 69-70, 107, 122, 145
Evans — *Thoughts I* p.134, 173, 199
Evans — *Thoughts II (Open Door)* p.26, 47, 94, 146, 168, 206
Evans — *Thoughts III (Open Road)* p.141-142
Evans — *Thoughts IV* p.76-77, 207
Evans — *Unto* p.66, 125
Forbes — *Thoughts* p.125-126, 159, 173, 189, 246, 344, 351, 357, 477
Garland — *Subject* p.155
Grizer — *Wit* p.238
Harnsberger — *Mark* p.202
Henry — *5000* p.132
Hill — *Think* p.281-283
Hovey — *Treasury* p.217; *See also* index p.297
Hubbard — *Scrap* p.23
Kennedy — *Reader's* #519-526
Knight's Treas. p.176-179
Kohn — *Best* p.147-149
Kohn — *Touch* p.126
Lockridge — *World's* #1507
Lytle — *Leaves* p.58, 117-118, 129, 131, 136
Mandel — *Stories* p.146-147
Montapert — *Distilled* p.215
Nizer — *Thinking* p.55

Peterson — *Art* p.287, 409
Phillips — *Choice* p.242, 366
Prochnow — *Public* #724, 1167, 1875, 2298
Reader's — *Getting* p.129-144
Sheen — *Content.* p.170-171
Wallis — *Treasure* p.147-152
Wallis — *Words* p.125-128
Welk — *Guide.* p.118-119
Woods — *Religious* p.159-160

, and character
Howell — *Lines* p.97-102

, Christian example of
Knight's Illus. p.162-164

, Others'
Lair — *Baby* p.212

INFORMATION. *See* **Facts; Knowledge**

"INFORMATION PLEASE"
Asimov — *Treasury* #242

INFORMERS
Kin — *Dictionary* p.131
Seldes — *Great* p.510-511
Woods — *Religious* p.486

INGENUITY
See also **Ability; Inventors and inventions; Originality; Resourcefulness**
Braude — *Stories* p.190-199
Cerf — *Laugh* p.393-396
Grizer — *Wit* p.238-239
Henry — *5000* p.134
Keys Happiness p.168
Mandel — *Stories* p.147-148
Prochnow — *Success.* #1908
Speaker's Desk See index p.301

INGRATIATION
Kin — *Dictionary* p.131

INGRATITUDE
Book Proverbs p.116
Dirksen — *Quot.* #425
Edwards — *Useful* p.291-293
Flint — *Graham* p.76
Fogg — *1000 See* index p.888
Forbes — *Thoughts* p.45, 445, 517
Fuller — *Thesaurus* #261-268
Henry — *5000* p.133
Kin — *Dictionary* p.131
Liddle — *Thought I, II, III* p.15, 106, 151, 168
Lockridge — *World's* #233, 237, 316, 1614, 2264, 3772, 5853
Lytle — *Leaves* p.26-27
Montapert — *Distilled* p.215-216
New Topical p.130
Speaker's Desk #123, 765, 1092
Woods — *Religious* p.486

INHERITANCE
See also **Ancestry; Eugenics; Wills and testaments**
Applegarth — *Heir.* p.109-110, 118, 162
Edwards — *Useful* p.293
Fuller — *Epigrams* p.166
Garland — *Subject* p.155-156
Grizer — *Wit* p.272
Harnsberger — *Mark* p.205
Henry — *5000* p.134
Ideas p.207-209
Keys Happiness p.136
Kin — *Dictionary* p.118, 131
Lockridge — *World's* #670, 739
Mandel — *Stories* p.159
More Words p.88-89
Nichols — *Third* p.208-224
Sheban — *Wisdom* no p.
Wallis — *Treasure* p.131
Woods — *Religious* p.486

INHUMANITY. *See* **Cruelty**

INIQUITY. *See* **Sin**

INITIATES AND INITIATIONS
Harral — *Feature* p.197-198
Henry — *5000* p.134

INITIATIVE. *See also* **Decision; Leaders and leadership; Originality**
Braude — *Source* #914-915
Braude — *Speaker's* #729
Braude — *Stories* p.199
Evans — *Unto* p.69
Forbes — *Thoughts* p.213, 221, 263, 389, 450, 466
Hobe — *Tapestries* p.201
Keller — *You* p.332-347, 359-374
Modern Eloquence (14) p.358
Montapert — *Distilled* p.216
Peale — *Guideposts* p.41-43
Prochnow — *Success.* #871
Woods — *Wellsprings* p.27-28

INJURY
See also **Accident**
Book Proverbs p.112
Edwards — *Useful* p.293
Fuller — *Epigrams* p.166-167
Fuller — *Thesaurus* #1741
Henry — *5000* p.133
Hovey — *Treasury* p.207; #1229-1232
Kin — *Dictionary* p.116, 131-132
Liddle — *Thought I, II, III* p.12, 25, 37, 113, 134, 156, 194
Lockridge — *World's* #15
Lytle — *Leaves* p.101
Montapert — *Distilled* p.216-217
Speaker's Desk #13
Woods — *Religious* p.421

INJUSTICE
See also **Oppression; Persecution; Tyrants and tyranny**
Adams — *New* p.269
Book Proverbs p.116
Dirksen — *Quot.* #1720, 2342
Edwards — *Useful* p.293-294
Evans — *Unto* p.120, 148
Flesch — *Unusual* p.283
Fogg — *1000* #266, 352, 394, 422, 596, 614, 662, 1028, 1059
Forbes — *Thoughts* p.388, 467, 506
Henry — *5000* p.133-134
Kin — *Dictionary* p.132, 187
Lockridge — *World's* #1486, 2395, 2610, 3636
New Topical p.130-131
Seldes — *Great* p.511-512
Speaker's Desk #625, 922, 1137
Webb — *Edge* p.60-61
Wheelis — *Moralist* p.49, 62-63
Woods — *Religious* p.486

INK
Edwards — *Useful* p.294
Henry — *5000* p.134
Prochnow — *Success.* #1909

INNOCENCE
See also **Ignorance; Purity; Virtues**
Adams — *New* p.369
Braude — *Stories* p.199
Dirksen — *Quot.* #971
Edwards — *Useful* p.294-295
Garland — *Subject* p.156-157
Hadfield — *Love* p.24
Henry — *5000* p.134
Hobe — *Tapestries* p.25
Hubbard — *Scrap* p.208
Kin — *Dictionary* p.131-132
Krishnamurti — *Think* p.86-92
Lockridge — *World's* #490, 656, 823, 2083, 2662, 3700
Mandel — *Stories* p.148
Prochnow — *Public* #2114
Speaker's Desk #203, 1119
Wallis — *Treasure* p.24
Woods — *Religious* p.486-487

INNOVATION
See also **Change; Discovery; Inventors and inventions; Novelty; Originality**
Braude — *Stories* p.199
Curtis — *Practical* p.377
Dirksen — *Quot.* #1721
Edwards — *Useful* p.295
Henry — *5000* p.134
Kin — *Dictionary* p.132

INNS AND INNKEEPERS
See also **Hotels**
Botkin — *Anecdotes* p.140, 142
Edwards — *Useful* p.295
Fuller — *Epigrams* p.167, 346
Fun Fare p.46-47
Henry — *5000* p.133-134

INQUIRY. *See* **Curiosity; Questions; Science; Study**

INQUISITION
Seldes — *Great* p.512
Wheelis — *Moralist* p.103, 139

INSANITY. *See* **Mental hospitals; Mental illness**

INSATIABILITY
Kin — *Dictionary* p.132

INSCRIPTIONS
Fogg — *1000 See* index p.888
Wallis — *Words* p.23, 49, 61-62, 91, 100, 128, 157

INSECTS
See also names of insects
Adams — *New* p.361
Applegarth — *Heir.* p.197
Botkin — *Treasury* p.423, 607, 648
Du Noüy — *Human* p.58, 67, 72, 74, 77-79, 97, 126, 155-158, 168
Du Noüy — *Road* p.41, 188, 201
George — *Book* p.126, 136, 148, 213, 232, 265, 360, 388
Goudge — *Comfort* p.66-70
Harral — *Feature* p.198
Henry — *5000* p.135
Kin — *Dictionary* p.34
New Topical p.131
, Group names of
Kronenberger — *Animal* p.133
, World of
Curtis — *Practical* p.273-274

INSECURITY
See also **Uncertainty**
Day — *Meditations* p.51
Flint — *Graham* p.22, 76, 154
Forbes — *Thoughts* p.153, 340, 361, 436, 466
Grizer — *Wit* p.240
Huxley — *You See* index p.286
Kin — *Dictionary* p.132
Maltz — *Creative* p.89
Phillips — *Choice* p.163
Prochnow — *Success.* #776, 1495

INSENSIBILITY. *See* **Indifference**

INSIGHT
See also **Intuition**
Applegarth — *Heir.* p.46
Garland — *Subject* p.157
Henry — *5000* p.135
How To Live p.436-440
Liddle — *Thought V* p.12
Lockridge — *World's* #1834
Lytle — *Leaves* p.14
Peale — *Courage* p.115-120
Phillips — *Choice* p.128, 168, 312, 316
Wheelis — *Moralist* p.27-28, 98

INSIGNIFICANCE
Evans — *Thoughts II (Open Door)* p.66-67
Evans — *Thoughts III (Open Road)* p.181
Kin — *Dictionary* p.132
Lytle — *Leaves* p.174
Nichols — *Third* p.45-46

INSINCERITY
See also **Deceit; Hypocrisy; Pretension; Treachery**
Book Proverbs p.116
Edwards — *Useful* p.296
Evans — *This* p.164-165
Evans — *Unto* p.88
Flint — *Graham* p.76
Harnsberger — *Mark* p.205
Henry — *5000* p.135
Phillips — *Choice* p.238
Prochnow — *Success.* #1467, 1911-1914

INSISTENCE. *See* **Perseverance**

INSOLENCE. *See* **Arrogance; Insult;** etc.

INSOLVENCY. *See* **Bankruptcy**

INSOMNIA
See also **Sleep**
Henry — *5000* p.135
Nichols — *New* p.228-230
Prochnow — *Public* #1255, 1401, 1463, 1720

INSPECTORS
Prochnow — *Public* #1963

INSPIRATION (general)
See also **Enthusiasm; God; Ideals and idealism; Influence; Jesus Christ; Religion;** etc.
Albert — *Stop* p.63-64
Barrows — *1000 See* index p.440-441
Bartlett — *Discovery* p.55-56
Braude — *Source* #916-917
Dirksen — *Quot.* #1722
Droke — *Christian* p.277
Edwards — *Useful* p.296
Evans — *Thoughts III (Open Road)* p.38, 180
Evans — *Unto* p.59
Felleman — *Poems* p.321-346
Fogg — *1000 See* index p.888
Forbes — *Thoughts* p.67, 107, 166, 199, 243, 328, 415
Fox — *Make* p.103-104
Garland — *Subject* p.157-158
Giniger — *Compact* p.74-75
Goudge — *Comfort* p.242-243
Harnsberger — *Mark* p.205
Henry — *5000* p.134
Hubbard — *Scrap* p.75, 87
Ideas p.209-211
Krishnamurti — *Think* p.113
Liddle — *Thought V* p.28
Lockridge — *World's* #702
Lytle — *Leaves* p.58, 167, 184
Mandel — *Stories* p.148-149
Miller — *Harvest* p.43-48
Peterson — *Art* p.44, 84, 291, 299, 339, 373
Prochnow — *Public* #1417
Prochnow — *Success.* #652
Voss — *Quotations* p.136-137
Wallis — *Treasure* p.12, 45, 149
Wallis — *Words* p.7, 129-132, 167
White — *Job* p.80-81, 117, 119, 124, 137, 166
Woods — *Religious* p.487-488
, Blackboard
Nichols — *Third* p.181-182
, Notebooks of
Peterson — *Art* p.70
, Source of
Holmes — *Design* p.94-95

INSTABILITY
See also **Change; Indecision; Mental illness**
Curtis — *Practical* p.378-379
Dirksen — *Quot.* #1406
Edwards — *Useful* p.296-297
Kin — *Dictionary* p.265
, Creative
Du Noüy — *Human* p.89-90

INSTALMENTS
Braude — *Source* #918-919
Braude — *Speaker's* #730-734
Braude — *Stories* p.199
Grizer — *Wit* p.240-241
Prochnow — *Public* #155, 497, 733, 803, 1273, 1298-1299, 1305, 1453
Prochnow — *Success.* #395

INSTINCT
See also **Impulse; Motivation and Motives**
Du Noüy — *Human* p.106-107, 157-159, 167-169, 177, 191

Edwards — *Useful* p.297
Forbes — *Thoughts* p.166, 275, 325, 426
Harnsberger — *Mark* p.205
Henry — *5000* p.135
Holman — *Psych.* p.54-64
Ideas p.211-212
Lockridge — *World's* #1542, 2782, 2872, 4642, 5191
Manchee — *Secret* p.100-101
Montapert — *Distilled* p.217-218
White — *Job* p.75-78, 80, 84, 166
Woods — *Religious* p.488
Words Change p.40
, Women's
Day — *Meditations* p.36-37

INSTITUTIONS
See also types of institutions
Braude — *Stories* p.200
Esteve — *Experience* p.61-69
Evans — *Thoughts I* p.145, 222
Forbes — *Thoughts* p.166, 342, 388, 410, 438, 473, 499, 504
Henry — *5000* p.135-136
Humes — *Instant* #517-520
Seldes — *Great* p.512-513
Wheelis — *Moralist* p.111
Woods — *Religious* p.488

INSTRUCTION. *See* **Education; Guidance; Teachers**

INSTRUMENTALISTS
Fuller — *Thesaurus* #1351-1363

INSTRUMENTS
Harral — *Feature* p.198

INSUBORDINATION. *See* **Disobedience**

INSUFFICIENCY. *See* **Inadequacy**

INSULARITY
Lockridge — *World's* #5762

INSULATION
Prochnow — *Public* #850

INSULT
See also **Arrogance; Ridicule;** etc.
Braude — *Stories* p.200
Edwards — *Useful* p.96-97, 280-281, 298
Flesch — *Unusual* p.47
Flint — *Graham* p.91
Forbes — *Thoughts* p.76, 158
Fuller — *Epigrams* p.58, 167-168
Grizer — *Wit* p.241-242
Henry — *5000* p.135
Kin — *Dictionary* p.55, 129, 133
Lockridge — *World's* #2433, 2658; *See also* index p.573
New Topical p.53
Nizer — *Thinking* p.70
Prochnow — *Public* #66, 757
Prochnow — *Speaker's* p.74, 173
Speaker's Desk #257, 413, 664, 798
, of teenagers
Ginott — *Between* p.80-81, 91-110

INSURANCE
Braude — *Source* #920
Braude — *Speaker's* #735-741
Cerf — *Laugh* p.396-399
Copeland — *10,000* p.439-441
Forbes — *Thoughts* p.165, 292, 485
Fuller — *Thesaurus* #2136-2140
Grizer — *Wit* p.242
Harnsberger — *Mark* p.206
Harral — *Feature* p.198-199
Prochnow — *Public* #41, 459, 764, 781, 1735
Prochnow — *Speaker's* p.174-175
Prochnow — *Success.* #1125
Schermerhorn — *1500* p.203-205
, Accident
Schermerhorn — *1500* p.2, 4
, Heavenly
Book Proverbs p.133
, Life
Braude — *Source* #921-925
, Salesmen of
Manchee — *Secret* p.213-214
Peale — *Guideposts* p.61-66

INTANGIBLES
See also **Character; Qualities;** etc.
Evans — *This* p.73-88
Peterson — *Art* p.66

INTEGRATION
See also **Races of man, Relations of**
Curtis — *Human* p.80-97
Flint — *Graham* p.76-77
Guideposts — *Faith* p.287-290
Krishnamurti — *Think* p.70, 104
Phillips — *Choice* p.42, 252, 311
Prochnow — *Success.* #584
, Spiritual
White — *Job* p.72, 78-81

INTEGRITY
See also **Character; Honesty; Honor;** etc.
Book Proverbs p.127
Braude — *Source* #926-930
Braude — *Speaker's* #742-745
Braude — *Stories* p.200
Detherage — *Sunrise* p.137-140
Dirksen — *Quot.* #1410-1411
Edwards — *Useful* p.298, 530-531
Evans — *Thoughts II (Open Door)* p.83-84, 88-89
Evans — *Thoughts III (Open Road)* p.101, 158, 161, 171, 175
Evans — *Thoughts IV* p.64-65
Evans — *Unto* p.12, 28, 36, 47, 52, 56, 83
Flint — *Graham* p.77
Forbes — *Thoughts* p.12, 51, 155, 220, 354, 447
Garland — *Subject* p.159
Halverson — *Perspective* p.102
Hobe — *Tapestries* p.41
Hovey — *Treasury* p.217-219; #279, 288, 853, 1307-1315, 1368, 1624
Johnson — *Bedside* p.201
Kennedy — *Reader's* #527-528
Kin — *Dictionary* p.133
Liddle — *Thought I, II, III* p.100
Lockridge — *World's* #1769
Mandel — *Stories* p.149-150
Menninger — *Blue.* p.38
Montapert — *Distilled* p.218
Nichols — *Third* p.59-60
Phillips — *Choice* p.334
Voss — *Quotations* p.138-139
Woods — *Religious* p.488-489

INTELLECT. *See* **Intelligence**

INTELLECTUALS
Dirksen — *Quot.* #432, 1723, 2365
Franke — *Buckley* p.125-126
Grizer — *Wit* p.243
Humes — *Instant* #521-529
Webb — *Edge* p.80-83
Woods — *Religious* p.490

INTELLIGENCE
See also **Common sense; Judgment; Knowledge; Mind; Reason and reasoning; Sense; Thought; Understanding; Wisdom**
Adams — *New* p.118, 267
Applegarth — *Heir.* p.136, 171
Bartlett — *Discovery* p.33-35
Braude — *Stories* p.200
Curtis — *Practical* p.77
Dirksen — *Quot.* #174, 205-206, 288, 846, 1121, 1984
Du Noüy — *Human See* index p.284
Du Noüy — *Road* p.53, 58, 75, 79, 112, 145, 189-190, 208, 237
Edwards — *Useful* p.298-300
Evans — *Unto* p.12, 21, 31, 45, 101, 114
Flint — *Graham* p.77
Forbes p.111, 120, 132, 228, 233, 344, 354, 388, 428, 433, 473; *See also* index p.555
Garland — *Subject* p.159-160
Grizer — *Wit* p.243
Harnsberger — *Mark* p.206-207
Harral — *Feature* p.199
Henry — *5000* p.135-136
Holman — *Psych.* p.54-65
Holmes — *Design* p.5-6, 11-12, 18, 21, 29, 31, 33-34, 43, 47-48, 50
Hovey — *Treasury* #5, 354, 873
How To Live p.100-103
Hubbard — *Scrap* p.215
Kennedy — *Reader's* #529-530
Kin — *Dictionary* p.133
Krishnamurti — *Think* p.19-20
Liddle — *Thought I, II, III* p.87, 119
Lockridge — *World's See* index p.577
Lytle — *Leaves* p.62
Menninger — *Blue.* p.8
Montapert — *Distilled* p.218-219
Nizer — *Thinking* p.82
Prochnow — *Public* #1556, 1594, 1802, 2172
Prochnow — *Speaker's* p.175
Prochnow — *Success.* #84, 770, 1308, 1915-1916
Seldes — *Great* p.513-516
Speaker's Desk p.110-112
White — *Job* p.80, 82, 89, 108, 114-120, 153, 166-167
Woods — *Religious* p.489-491
, Creative
White — *Job* p.133, 135-136, 144
, Development of
Krishnamurti — *Think* p.146-147
, of public
Nizer — *Thinking* p.70
, Tests of
Albert — *Stop* p.58
Henry — *5000* p.136
, versus wisdom
Kauffman — *For* p.230-231

INTEMPERANCE
See also **Alcoholism; Excess; Gluttony; Indulgence;** etc.
Edwards — *Useful* p.300-301
Henry — *5000* p.135
Kin — *Dictionary* p.133

Sagendorph — *Old* p.300-305
Speaker's Desk p.112-115
White — *Life* p.121-130

INTENTION. *See* **Goals; Motivation and motives; Purpose**

INTERCESSION
See also **Help; Prayer**
Applegarth — *Heir.* p.203-204, 208
Emmons — *Mature* p.41-42
Knight's Illus. p.165-166
Knight's Treas. p.179-181
Suter — *Prayers* #70-93

INTERDEPENDENCE
See also **Brotherhood; Family; Friends and friendship**; etc.
Dirksen — *Quot.* #453
Forbes — *Thoughts* p.250, 500
Grizer — *Wit* p.244
Kohn — *Adventures* p.42-45
Kohn — *Best* p.28-31
Kohn — *Touch* p.194-201
Mandel — *Stories* p.150-151
Phillips — *Choice* p.354-358
Wallis — *Words* p.79

INTEREST
See also **Attention; Lending and loans; Self-interest; Selfishness; Usury and usurers**
Bartlett — *Discovery* p.38-39
Edwards — *Useful* p.302
Evans — *Thoughts III (Open Road)* p.181
Forbes — *Thoughts See* index p.555
Harnsberger — *Mark* p.207-208
Henry — *5000* p.136-137
Kin — *Dictionary* p.133
Lockridge — *World's* #40, 67, 512, 1692, 1694, 2892, 3347, 4333
Montapert — *Distilled* p.220
Prochnow — *Public* #1913
Prochnow — *Success.* #1344, 1919-1921
Speaker's Desk #1037
Woods — *Business.* p.122-123
, *Conflict of*
Dirksen — *Quot.* #23
, *National*
Dirksen — *Quot.* #670
, *Prejudices of*
Dirksen — *Quot.* #478
, *Vested*
Seldes — *Great* p.517

INTERFERENCE
Braude — *Speaker's* #749
Braude — *Stories* p.200
Henry — *5000* p.127
Prochnow — *Success.* #1922
Woods — *Religious* p.491

INTERIOR DECORATION
Asimov — *Treasury* #389

INTERMARRIAGE
Asimov — *Treasury* #318
Keys Happiness p.422-425

INTERMITTENCY
Lindbergh — *Gift* p.109-110

INTERNAL REVENUE SERVICE
Prochnow — *Success.* #394, 418

INTERNATIONAL RELATIONS
Braude — *Source* #1848-1850
Copeland — *World's See* index p.736
Dirksen — *Quot.* #13, 34, 36, 264, 512, 590, 638, 1160, 1756
Droke — *Christian* p.278-282
Flesch — *Unusual* p.93
Franke — *Buckley* p.87-90
Fuller — *Thesaurus* #2016
Humes — *Instant* p.354-362; #530-542
Kauffman — *For* p.123-125
Prochnow — *Success.* #197, 267, 283, 978
Seldes — *Great* p.517-518
Voss — *Quotations* p.139-142
Woods — *Religious* p.491-492

INTERPRETATION
See also **Understanding**
Lytle — *Leaves* p.79
Mandel — *Stories* p.151
Woods — *Religious* p.492

INTERRUPTION
See also **Intermittency**
Henry — *5000* p.137
Hovey — *Treasury* p.219
Hulme — *Living* p.21
Kin — *Dictionary* p.133
Kohn — *Best* p.62-63
Phillips — *Choice* p.240
Prochnow — *Public* #61, 129, 2373
Prochnow — *Success.* #983, 1923

INTERVIEWS
Grizer — *Wit* p.244
Harnsberger — *Mark* p.208
Prochnow — *Success.* #1305

INTOLERANCE
See also **Bigotry; Dogmatism; Fanaticism; Persecution; Tyrants and tyranny**
Braude — *Source* #931-932

Edwards — *Useful* p.302
Flint — *Graham* p.77-78
Fogg — *1000 See* index p.888
Forbes — *Thoughts* p.109, 201, 234, 323, 353
Garland — *Subject* p.160
Halverson — *Perspective* p.116
Harnsberger — *Mark* p.209
Henry — *5000* p.135-137
Kennedy — *Reader's* #531-535
Kin — *Dictionary* p.133
Lockridge — *World's* #5526
Myers — *Thunder* p.38-50
Nizer — *Thinking* p.172
Prochnow — *Public* #2268
Seldes — *Great* p.518-519
Woods — *Religious* p.492

INTOXICATION. *See* **Alcoholism**

INTRIGUE. *See* **Conspiracy**

INTRODUCTIONS
Braude — *Speaker's* #750-751
Edwards — *Useful* p.493
Fuller — *Thesaurus* #786-791
Harnsberger — *Mark* p.370
Humes — *Instant* p.6-15, 20-25, 28-30
Lockridge — *World's* #1736
Nizer — *Thinking See* index p.233
Prochnow — *Public* #659
Prochnow — *Speaker's* p.176
Prochnow — *Success.* #5-23, 47-77, 89-90, 114-167
Schermerhorn — *1500* p.208-211
Speaker's Desk #32, 1115
Weisfeld — *Pulpit* p.138-143
, Formula
Nizer — *Thinking* p.43
, Public
Asimov — *Treasury* #291-292

INTUITION
See also **Insight**
Adams — *New* p.177
Braude — *Stories* p.201
Du Noüy — *Human* p.38, 135, 163, 233, 243
Evans — *Thoughts IV* p.38-39
Garland — *Subject* p.160-161
Johnson — *Bedside* p.213
Keys Happiness p.480-484
Manchee — *Secret* p.50-72
Montapert — *Distilled* p.220
Peterson — *Art* p.132
White — *Job* p.75, 80-82, 101, 120, 122, 130, 143, 166
Woods — *Religious* p.492-493
, Woman's
Manchee — *Secret* p.61-62

INVENTORS AND INVENTIONS
Braude — *Source* #933
Braude — *Speaker's* #752-755
Braude — *Stories* p.201
Du Noüy — *Human* p.xi, 137-139, 259-262
Edwards — *Useful* p.302
Forbes — *Thoughts* p.21, 42, 85, 119, 125, 140, 144, 233, 342, 434
Fuller — *Thesaurus* #1126-1131
Grizer — *Wit* p.244-246
Harnsberger — *Mark* p.209-210
Henry — *5000* p.136-138
Kin — *Dictionary* p.134
Lockridge — *World's* #298, 5720
Modern Eloquence (14) p.359
Montapert — *Distilled* p.220-221
Prochnow — *Public* #660, 1863, 1904, 1936
Speaker's Desk #57, 1055, 1101
, Method of
Curtis — *Practical* p.19-20

INVENTORY, PERSONAL. *See* **Self-inventory; Self-knowledge**

INVESTIGATION
See also **Study**
Kin — *Dictionary* p.134
Prochnow — *Public* #677
Seldes — *Great* p.519

INVESTMENT
Braude — *Source* #934
Grizer — *Wit* p.246
Halverson — *Perspective* p.40, 103
Mandel — *Stories* p.151-152
Montapert — *Distilled* p.221
Prochnow — *Speaker's* p.176
Woods — *Business.* p.123-126
, Foreign
Dirksen — *Quot.* #734, 1149

INVINCIBILITY
Halverson — *Perspective* p.60
Prochnow — *Public* #584
Wilcox — *Heart* p.57

INVISIBILITY
Halverson — *Perspective* p.86
Henry — *5000* p.138
Peterson — *Art* p.119
Prochnow — *Success.* #1924
, of world
Woods — *Religious* p.493

INVITATION
Kin — *Dictionary* p.134
Prochnow — *Public* #865
Wallis — *Words* p.43
, and challenge
Howell — *Lines* p.43-50

INVOICE
Prochnow — *Public* #608

INVOLVEMENT
Braude — *Source* #935
Flint — *Graham* p.78
Guideposts — *Faith* p.81-84
How To Live p.296-301
Humes — *Instant* #543-549

INVULNERABILITY. *See* **Invincibility**

IOWA
Botkin — *Treasury* p.52, 132, 303

IRELAND
See also **Irish**
Edwards — *Useful* p.729
Henry — *5000* p.136
Lockridge — *World's* #5161, 5166, 5173, 5204
Seldes — *Great* p.519-520

IRISH
Asimov — *Treasury* #414-415, 417-418
Botkin — *Anecdotes* p.8, 19, 38, 128
Cerf — *Laugh* p.426-430
Harnsberger — *Mark* p.210-212
Lockridge — *World's* #3614
Modern Eloquence (14) p.159-170
Schermerhorn — *1500* p.211-214
Weisfeld — *Pulpit* p.48, 114, 156, 174
, Bulls of
Asimov — *Treasury* #413-415
, Home rule of
Asimov — *Treasury* #7
, Humor of
Copeland — *10,000* p.727-750
Speaker's Desk See index p.301
, in Middle Ages
Kronenberger — *Animal* p.200-204
, Wishes of
Woods — *Content.* p.359

IRON
New Topical p.131-132

"IRON CURTAIN"
Dirksen — *Quot.* #629, 1735
Guideposts — *Faith* p.440-443
Ideas p.212-213
Peterson — *Art* p.155
Seldes — *Great* p.520

IRONING
Holmes — *I've* p.29-30
Irion — *Yes* p.28-30

IRONS
Kin — *Dictionary* p.134

IRONY
See also **Satire**
Edwards — *Useful* p.302-303
Grizer — *Wit* p.247
Henry — *5000* p.138
Prochnow — *Success.* #1925-1926
Seldes — *Great* p.520
, and pity
Henry — *5000* p.138
, Life's
Pullar-Strecker — *Proverbs* #1-4, 878

IRRATIONALITY
See also **Mental illness**
Henry — *5000* p.138
Prochnow — *Success.* #1927
Woods — *Religious* p.493

IRRELEVANCY
Henry — *5000* p.138

IRRESISTIBILITY
Clark — *Windows* p.50

IRRESOLUTION. *See* **Indecision**

IRRESPONSIBILITY
Prochnow — *Public* #2388

IRREVERENCE
See also **Atheism; Profanity;** etc.
Dirksen — *Quot.* #1412-1413

IRRITATIONS. *See* **Annoyances; Complaining; Frustration**

ISHMAELITES, THE
New Topical p.132

ISIS
Woods — *Religious* p.493

ISLAM
Woods — *Religious* p.493-494

ISLANDS AND ISLANDERS
Alexander's Treasure. p.217
Asimov — *Treasury* #89, 381
Keys Happiness p.232-236

Kin — *Dictionary* p.134
Lindbergh — *Gift* p.19-120
Lindbergh — *Unicorn* p.72-73
Sheban — *Wisdom* no p.

"ISMS"
See also names of "Isms," e.g. **Communism**
Liebman — *Hope* p.212
Seldes — *Great* p.521

ISOLATION. *See* **Loneliness; Solitude**

ISRAEL
Asimov — *Treasury* #333-337, 340
Cerf — *Laugh* p.430-433
Seldes — *Great* p.521
Simpson — *Contemp.* p.145-147
Voss — *Quotations* p.143-146
Woods — *Religious* p.494-496
, Armies of
New Topical p.18-19
, Journey through desert
New Topical p.64-66
, Strangers in
New Topical p.258-259
, Tribes of
New Topical p.277

ISSACHAR, TRIBE OF
New Topical p.132-134

ISSUES
See also **Argument; Conflict**
Kauffman — *For* p.45-46
Kin — *Dictionary* p.134

ITALIAN PROVERBS
Dirksen — *Quot. See* index p.265

ITALIANS
Asimov — *Treasury* #424-428
Peale — *Guideposts* p.51-53
Schermerhorn — *1500* p.214-216
Speaker's Desk #431, 463, 471, 1132, 1137, 1166

ITALY
Fuller — *Epigrams* p.168
Harnsberger — *Mark* p.213-214
Henry — *5000* p.136-138
Lockridge — *World's* #4757

"IVORY TOWERS"
Ideas p.214, 231
Seldes — *Great* p.521

IVY
Lytle — *Leaves* p.29

J

"JACK-OF-ALL-TRADES"
Speaker's Desk #890, 1049

JACKALS
Kin — *Dictionary* p.135

JACKANAPES
Prochnow — *Public* #2417

JACKDAWS
Auden — *Certain* p.204
Kin — *Dictionary* p.135

"JACKPOT"
Prochnow — *Public* #142

JACKSON, ANDREW
New Joy p.82-85

JAILS
See also **Prisons**
Fuller — *Thesaurus* #2561-2563
Harral — *Feature* p.199
Prochnow — *Public* #1017
, Songs of
Botkin — *Treasury* p.882-890

JAMES, HENRY
Adams — *New* p.35
Henry — *5000* p.138

JAMES, JESSE
Botkin — *Treasury* p.71-72

JAMES, WILLIAM
Applegarth — *Heir.* p.158

JANITORS
Prochnow — *Public* #1723

JANSENISM
Woods — *Religious* p.496

JAPAN
Hovey — *Treasury* #340, 731, 1239, 2198, 1595
Simpson — *Contemp.* p.148

JAPANESE
Botkin — *Anecdotes* p.163
How To Live p.173
Speaker's Desk #510

JAZZ
Edwards — *Useful* p.729
Nizer — *Thinking* p.25, 72, 83

JEALOUSY
See also **Covetousness; Envy; Rivalry; Suspicion**
Book Proverbs p.57
Braude — *Source* #936-938
Braude — *Speaker's* #756-759
Braude — *Stories* p.201
Edwards — *Useful* p.303-304
Evans — *Thoughts I* p.101
Evans — *Thoughts II (Open Door)* p.154
Flint — *Graham* p.78
Forbes — *Thoughts* p.332, 468, 501
Fuller — *Epigrams* p.169
Garland — *Subject* p.162
Henry — *5000* p.137
Hovey — *Treasury* #1029, 1056, 1515
Hubbard — *Scrap* p.75, 97
Kennedy — *Reader's* #538-539
Kin — *Dictionary* p.135
Krishnamurti — *Think* p.28-29
Lockridge — *World's* #29, 33, 334, 346, 384, 471, 530, 846, 2369, 5512, 5580, 5672
Lytle — *Leaves* p.27
Mandel — *Stories* p.152
Montapert — *Distilled* p.221-222
Myers — *Thunder* p.148-162
Prochnow — *Public* #2461
Speaker's Desk p.115-116; #336, 748
Woods — *Religious* p.496

JEFFERSON, THOMAS
Seldes — *Great* p.521-522

JEHOVAH. *See* **God**

JEOPARDY. *See* **Danger**

JEREMIAH
Henry — *5000* p.138

JERUSALEM
Fogg — *1000* #502, 547, 885, 1129
Wallis — *Words* p.55

JESUITS
Seldes — *Great* p.522-523

JESUS CHRIST
See also **Christianity; Communion; Cross; God; "Last Supper"; New Testament;** etc.
Asimov — *Treasury* #461-462
Baillie — *Diary* #23, 119, 156, 240
Curtis — *Practical* p.222
Detherage — *Sunrise* p.99-100, 127
Du Noüy — *Human* p.140, 174-175, 177, 180, 189, 245-255
Edwards — *Useful* p.77
Emmons — *Mature* p.18, 26-31
Evans — *Faith* p.16, 74, 77, 100, 164, 174, 197-198, 219-223
Evans — *Thoughts I* p.23, 50-51, 62, 71, 88, 111, 121, 197, 201
Evans — *Thoughts II (Open Door)* p.39, 46, 48, 94, 119-120, 146
Evans — *Thoughts III (Open Road) See* index, no p.
Evans — *Unto* p.11-12, 16-18, 31, 56, 67, 115, 141
Flesch — *Unusual* p.250
Flint — *Graham* p.23-25, 54, 78-79, 126
Forbes — *Thoughts* p.12, 14-15, 71, 78, 262, 356, 391, 456, 473, 475
Fox — *Make* p.68, 125
Fridy — *Meditat.* p.23-30, 68, 92, 94, 134
Garland — *Subject* p.42-43, 176, 184-185, 191, 284
Giniger — *Compact* p.93-127, 255-267
Halverson — *Perspective* p.48, 106
Henry — *5000* p.35-36
Hobe — *Tapestries* p.45, 51, 70-71, 109
Hovey — *Treasury* p.67-73; *See* index p.294, 297
Howell — *Lines* p.115-119
Hubbard — *Scrap* p.104, 156
Johnson — *Bedside See* index p.362
Kennedy — *Reader's* #540-553
Knight's Illus. p.166-172
Knight's Treas. p.181-186
Kohn — *Best* p.48-50
Montapert — *Distilled* p.59-60
More Words p.150
Peterson — *Art* p.400, 404
Phillips — *Choice* p.xii, 26, 35, 44-45, 64, 85, 95, 103, 125, 199, 259, 303, 313, 316, 408
Price — *No* p.123-144
Prochnow — *Public* #2629, 2717, 2731, 2866
Prochnow — *Success.* #1398
Seldes — *Great* p.523-528
Sheban — *Wisdom* no p.
Sheen — *Content.* p.161-162
Strait — *Speaker's* p.24-25
Tanksley — *Friend* p.24

Voss — *Quotations* p.146-150
Wallis — *Treasure See* index p.248
Wallis — *Words* p.4, 10, 21-30, 98-99, 102, 113, 127, 141-142, 154, 204, 227 et al.
Wheelis — *Moralist* p.8, 50, 52, 111, 146
Woods — *Religious* p.496-510, 626-627, 884

, Acceptance of
Knight's *Illus.* p.62-63
Tanksley — *Friend* p.66
, Appeal of
Kauffman — *For* p.46
, as carpenter
Guideposts — *Faith* p.380-384
, as child
Goudge — *Comfort* p.87
Hobe — *Tapestries* p.144
, as companion
Holmes — *I've* p.115
, as God
New Topical p.43-44
, as guest today
Guideposts — *Faith* p.491
, as head of Church
New Topical p.44
, as high priest
New Topical p.44
, as king
New Topical p.44-45
, as living person
Clark — *Windows* p.180
Guideposts — *Faith* p.462-466
, as mediator
New Topical p.45
, as Messiah
More Words p.24
, as physician
Bach — *Make* p.180-181
, as prophet
New Topical p.45
, as shepherd
Baillie — *Diary* #41
New Topical p.45
, Ascension of. See **Jesus Christ, Resurrection of**
, at the door
Sheen — *Content.* p.87-88
, Birth of
Asimov — *Treasury* #501
Baillie — *Diary* #121
Goudge — *Comfort* p.172-183
Keller — *Open* p.84
Lockridge — *World's* #352
, Character of
New Topical p.43
, Coronet of
Baillie — *Diary* #72
, Crucifixion of
See also **Calvary**
Asimov — *Treasury* #461, 466
Baillie — *Diary* #67
Fridy — *Meditat.* p.98
Hobe — *Tapestries* p.151-153
Hovey — *Treasury* p.142-143; #90, 347, 349, 441, 597, 728-732, 814, 915, 1064, 1334, 1365
Hulme — *Living* p.106-107
Kohn — *Best* p.121-123
More Words p.45
New Topical p.60-61
Phillips — *Choice* p.75
Woods — *Religious* p.506-507
, Definition of
Baillie — *Diary* #135
, Denial of
New Topical p.64, 111
, Dreams of
Guideposts — *Faith* p.57
, Entry into Jerusalem
Baillie — *Diary* #144
, Example of
New Topical p.82
, Excellency and glory of
New Topical p.82
, Fire of
Maxwell — *Courage* p.121-132
, Healing of
Guideposts — *Faith* p.120
, "Hippies" and
Kauffman — *For* p.125-126
, Human nature of
New Topical p.124-125
, Humility of
New Topical p.125
, Image of
Carruthers — *Sparks* p.131-132
Wallis — *Words* p.30, 41
, Imitation of
Baillie — *Diary* #42
, Law of
McDonagh — *Invit.* p.22-37
, Living with
Hulme — *Living* p.108-118
, Love for
Knight's Treas. p.211-212
New Topical p.155
, Love of
New Topical p.154-155
, Manger of
Hobe — *Tapestries* p.143, 152
Wallis — *Words* p.35
, Manhood of
Baillie — *Diary* #222

, Miracles of
New Topical p.168
, Mystical body of
Woods — *Religious* p.665-666
, Nature of
Guideposts — *Faith* p.385-389
, Object of
Baillie — *Living* #140
, Passion of
Baillie — *Diary* #338
More Words p.119-120
, Portrayals of
Guideposts — *Faith* p.354-363, 370-379, 390-394
, Power of
New Topical p.195-196
, Praise of
Goudge — *Comfort* p.160-171
, Prayer in name of
Baillie — *Diary* #21
Carruthers — *Sparks* p.115-116
, Preciousness of
New Topical p.201
, Prophecies about
New Topical p.207-208
, Realism of
Clark — *Windows* p.146
, Resurrection of
Evans — *Unto* p.12
Goudge — *Comfort* p.192-196
Lindbergh — *Unicorn* p.66-69
More Words p.10-11
New Topical p.20-21, 221-222
Woods — *Religious* p.507-508
, "Second coming of"
Flint — *Graham* p.127
Kauffman — *For* p.46-47
Knight's Illus. p.290-292
Knight's Treas. p.349-353
Maxwell — *Courage* p.233-243
More Words p.151
New Topical p.240-241
Woods — *Religious* p.903
Sermons of. See **"Sermon on the Mount"**
, Social reform of
Flint — *Graham* p.137
, Solitary life of
Peale — *Courage* p.66-67
, Teaching of
Curtis — *New* p.99-114
, Timeliness of
Carruthers — *Sparks* p.52-54
, Titles and names of
New Topical p.270-271
, Types of
New Topical p.280-281
, Understanding of
Clark — *Windows* p.148
Tanksley — *Friend* p.58
, Union with
New Topical p.283
, Vision of
Guideposts — *Faith* p.395-399
, Will and testament of
Words Change p.88-91
, Wit of
Guideposts — *Faith* p.365-369
, Witnesses to
Baillie — *Diary* #300
, Words of
Keller — *You* p.375-387

JEWELERS
Harral — *Feature* p.200
Manchee — *Secret* p.214

JEWELS
See also **Gems**
Applegarth — *Heir.* p.163, 274
Forbes — *Thoughts* p.138, 190, 341, 448, 480
Henry — *5000* p.138
Prochnow — *Public* #85, 352, 2342

JEWS
See also **Hebrew proverbs; Judaism; Zionism**
Asimov — *Treasury* #25, 39
Botkin — *Anecdotes* p.38-39, 41-42, 257-258, 261-266, 269
Curtis — *Practical* p.55, 133, 222-228
Edwards — *Useful* p.305
Fogg — *1000* #974, 1129, 1135
Guideposts — *Faith* p.134-138, 343
Harnsberger — *Mark* p.215-216
Henry — *5000* p.137-139
Hovey — *Treasury* #114, 335, 348, 398, 403, 610, 721, 725, 730, 749, 1124, 1150, 1416, 1657, 1752
Knight's Illus. p.172-174
Knight's Treas. p.186-188
Lockridge — *World's* #4489, 4524, 5099
Mandel — *Stories* p.152-153
New Topical p.134-136
Phillips — *Choice* p.11, 376
Prochnow — *Success.* #1928
Schermerhorn — *1500* p.216-221
Seldes — *Great* p.461-465, 528-532
Speaker's Desk See index p.301
Voss — *Quotations* p.150-152

Weisfeld — *Pulpit* p.38, 78
Woods — *Religious* p.510-514
, *Ambition of*
Asimov — *Treasury* #22, 352-353
, *Appearance of*
Asimov — *Treasury* #400-401
, *Diet of*
New Topical p.68
, *Education of*
Woods — *Religious* p.265
, *Girls*
Asimov — *Treasury* #318, 377
, *Humor of*
Asimov — *Treasury* p.211-278
Copeland — *10,000* p.669-683
, *in Germany*
Reader's — *20th* p.90-97
Wheelis — *Moralist* p.95, 115
, *Prophecy about*
Flint — *Graham* p.66
, *Religion of*
See also **Judaism**
Simpson — *Contemp.* p.213-214
, *Schools for*
Asimov — *Treasury* #323-324, 388

JOAN OF ARC
Fogg — *1000* #640, 841, 875, 917

JOB, BOOK OF
Asimov — *Treasury* #474
Baillie — *Diary* #362
Lockridge — *World's* #3605
Woods — *Religious* p.514

JOBS
See also **Labor; Wages; Work;** etc.
Albert — *Stop* p.44-46, 66-68
Dirksen — *Quot.* #2346
Evans — *Thoughts III (Open Road)* p.131-132
Forbes — *Thoughts* p.81, 121, 124, 139, 179, 182, 185, 205, 264, 277, 384, 453, 456
Grizer — *Wit* p.247-249
Harnsberger — *Mark* p.216
Harral — *Feature* p.200
Henry — *5000* p.139
Keys Happiness p.466-468
Montapert — *Distilled* p.222
Prochnow — *Public* #244, 805, 2422
Prochnow — *Success.* #977, 984, 1083, 1141, 1929
White — *Job* p.42-43, 75, 77-78, 84, 107
, *as training grounds*
Nichols — *Third* p.95-96
, *Right for*
Woods — *Business.* p.125
, *Satisfaction in*
Bartlett — *Discovery* p.55-71

JOHNSON, SAMUEL
Adams — *New* p.35
Baillie — *Diary* #146, 347
Reader's — *20th* p.12

"JOINERS"
Harral — *Feature* p.200

JOKES AND JOKING
See also **Comedy and comedians; Humor; Nonsense; Puns and punsters; Tricks and tricksters;** etc.
Book Proverbs p.130
Edwards — *Useful* p.304-305
Evans — *Thoughts III (Open Road)* p.85, 88
Evans — *Thoughts IV* p.126-127
Fogg — *1000* p.889
Fuller — *Epigrams* p.169-170
Grizer — *Wit* p.247, 249
Harnsberger — *Mark* p.216-217
Henry — *5000* p.137-139
Hovey — *Treasury* p.219-220; #1317-1320
Johnson — *Bedside* p.12, 20
Kin — *Dictionary* p.135-136
Liddle — *Thought IV* p.25
Lockridge — *World's* #1293, 1836, 4843, 5781
Nizer — *Thinking* p.80-81, 148
Prochnow — *Public* #327, 437, 473, 672, 1000, 2332
Prochnow — *Success.* #1930
Speaker's Desk #54, 57, 367, 402, 497, 596, 614, 661, 746, 757
Unlimited Power p.197-200
Woods — *Religious* p.496
, *Accents in*
Asimov — *Treasury* #10, 41, 309-313, 414, 429-430, 529
, *Apocryphal*
Asimov — *Treasury* #37
, *Arithmetical*
Botkin — *Treasury* p.375
, *Audience and*
Asimov — *Treasury* #5, 312
, *Books of*
Botkin — *Treasury* p.407
, *Categorization of*
Asimov — *Treasury* #3, 66

, *Children's*
Asimov — *Treasury* #244-246
, *Clichés and*
Asimov — *Treasury* #17
, *Culture and*
Asimov — *Treasury* #235, 294
, *Delayed laughter at*
Asimov — *Treasury* #67
, *Educational*
Asimov — *Treasury* #96
, *Elephant*
Asimov — *Treasury* p.57, 59
, *Emotional evaporation and*
Asimov — *Treasury* #77
, *Ethnic*
Asimov — *Treasury* #404-406, 436
, *Fables as*
Asimov — *Treasury* #122
, *Fantasy*
Asimov — *Treasury* #47
, *Flowery prose in*
Asimov — *Treasury* #1
, *Forgetfulness in*
Asimov — *Treasury* #557
, *Function of*
Asimov — *Treasury* #1, 321, 457, 466, 514, 557
, *Gestures and*
Asimov — *Treasury* #273
, *Hidden meanings of*
Asimov — *Treasury* p.30, 112
, *Humanity of*
Asimov — *Treasury* #4
, *Impossible*
Asimov — *Treasury* #47
, *Irrationality of*
Asimov — *Treasury* #81
, *Jewish*
See also **Jews, Humor of**
Asimov — *Treasury* #66
, *"Knock knock"*
Asimov — *Treasury* #253
, *Laughter at*
Asimov — *Treasury* #167
, *"Little moron"*
Asimov — *Treasury* #252
, *Logical fallacies and*
Asimov — *Treasury* #483-485
, *Long*
Asimov — *Treasury* #10, 397
, *Modifications of*
Asimov — *Treasury* #21, 35, 65, 74, 95-96, 149, 315, 399, 412, 448, 509, 588
, *Morals in*
Asimov — *Treasury* #142
, *Movies and*
Asimov — *Treasury* #8
, *Names in*
Asimov — *Treasury* #8, 20, 410
, *Old*
Asimov — *Treasury* #96, 283-284
, *Paradox in*
Asimov — *Treasury* #67
, *Point of view in*
Asimov — *Treasury* #1
, *Political cartoons and*
Asimov — *Treasury* #107
, *Practical*
Asimov — *Treasury* #306
Fuller — *Thesaurus* #431-437
Fun Fare p.35, 220
Kauffman — *For* p.211-212
, *Prejudices and*
Asimov — *Treasury* #40
, *Psychiatry and*
Asimov — *Treasury* #534
, *Punch lines in*
Asimov — *Treasury* #28, 91, 454, 582
, *"Put-downs" in*
Asimov — *Treasury* #161-162
, *Radio and*
Asimov — *Treasury* #20
, *Religion and*
Asimov — *Treasury* #457
, *Sessions of*
Asimov — *Treasury* #73-74
, *"Shaggy-dog"*
Asimov — *Treasury* #45-46
, *Sight gags and*
Asimov — *Treasury* #309
, *Similar*
Asimov — *Treasury* #29
, *Special knowledge and*
Asimov — *Treasury* #53, 135, 329
, *Stereotypes in*
Asimov — *Treasury* #8, 307
, *Subsidiary laughs in*
Asimov — *Treasury* #10, 582
, *Television and*
Asimov — *Treasury* #8
, *Translation of*
Asimov — *Treasury* #11, 17, 315
, *Tyranny and*
Asimov — *Treasury* #104 105
, *Variations of*
Asimov — *Treasury* #65, 75, 113, 459
, *Whimsy in*
Asimov — *Treasury* #63
, *Women and*
Asimov — *Treasury* #79, 512

, *Word–meaning changes and*
Asimov — *Treasury* #111
, *Written versus spoken*
Asimov — *Treasury* #55, 309

JONES, CASEY
Botkin — *Treasury* p.179, 241-246

JONSON, BEN
New Joy p.34-35

JORDAN RIVER
New Topical p.126-137

JOSEPH (Biblical)
Baillie — *Diary* #269

JOURNALISM AND JOURNALISTS
See also **Columnists; Newspapers**
Auden — *Certain* p.205-207
Botkin — *Anecdotes* p.216, 244
Braude — *Speaker's* #760, 767
Dirksen — *Quot.* #969
Edwards — *Useful* p.305-306
Grizer — *Wit* p.249-250
Henry — *5000* p.138
Hooker — *Index* p.1-8
Kennedy — *Reader's* #554-558
Lockridge — *World's* #951, 4413
Nizer — *Thinking* p.30, 82, 104
Prochnow — *Speaker's* p.177
Prochnow — *Success.* #1931-1932
Schermerhorn — *1500* p.221-222
Seldes — *Great* p.532-534
Sheban — *Wisdom* no p.

JOURNALS
See also **Diaries**
Applegarth — *Heir.* p.206
Harnsberger — *Mark* p.217-218
Keys Happiness p.408-411
Kronenberger — *Animal* p.108-119

JOURNEYS. *See* **Travel**

JOY
See also **Happiness; Laughter; Pleasure**
Alexander's Treasure. p.312, 314
Applegarth — *Heir.* p.83-91, 95, 176, 212
Clark — *Windows* p.34-35, 44-45
Detherage — *Sunrise* p.80, 128, 149-152
Dirksen — *Quot.* #1414-1417
Droke — *Christian* p.283
Edwards — *Useful* p.123, 214, 306-307
Emmons — *Mature* p.52, 94, 124-130
Evans — *Unto* p.23
Flesch — *Unusual* p.99, 171
Forbes — *Thoughts See* index p.555
Fox — *Make* p.182
Fuller — *Epigrams* p.346-347, 357
Garland — *Subject* p.70, 120, 163
Goudge — *Comfort* p.209
Grizer — *Wit* p.250
Harnsberger — *Mark* p.218
Henry — *5000* p.89, 139-140, 174-175
Hobe — *Tapestries* p.74, 123
Hovey — *Treasury* p.220; *See also* index p.298
How To Live p.209-210
Hubbard — *Scrap* p.17, 19, 21, 58, 91, 164
Johnson — *Bedside* p.1-2, 4, 15, 18, 20-21, 63
Keller — *Open* p.50, 135
Keys Happiness p.429-430
Kin — *Dictionary* p.67, 106, 136, 161
Knight's Illus. p.175-176
Knight's Treas. p.189-191
Langdon — *Teach.* p.111-116
Liddle — *Thought I, II, III* p.8, 33, 36, 38, 43, 81, 106
Liddle — *Thought V* p.24-25
Lockridge — *World's* #1276, 2087, 2295
Lytle — *Leaves* p.14, 26, 84, 116, 148
Maltz — *Creative* p.145-146
Mandelbaum — *Choose* p.14
Montapert — *Distilled* p.222-223
New Topical p.137-138
Peale — *Stay* p.172-192
Peterson — *Art* p.390
Petty — *Promises* p.18-24
Petty — *Wings* p.20-30
Price — *Wider* p.30
Prochnow — *Public* #2529, 2671, 4388, 4399
Prochnow — *Success.* #1764, 1934-1935
Sheban — *Wisdom* no p.
Sheen — *Content.* p.178-179, 285
Sheen — *Way* p.23-24, 42-44
Wallis — *Treasure* p.120, 153-158
Wallis — *Words* p.18-19, 133-138, 168, 185
Woods — *Content. See* index p.380
Woods — *Religious* p.225, 514-516
, *and fear*
Adams — *New* p.285
, *Difficulties versus*
Hulme — *Living* p.134-137
, *Everyday*
Barrows — *1000 See* index p.439

, *Prayer for*
Unlimited Power p.229

JUDAH, TRIBE OF
New Topical p.138

JUDAISM
Kennedy — *Reader's* #559
Voss — *Quotations* p.153-154
Woods — *Religious* p.516-518

JUDAS
Flint — *Graham* p.15, 40

JUDEA
Lockridge — *World's* #4041
Wallis — *Words* p.23
, *Modern*
New Topical p.138-139

JUDGES AND JUDGING
See also **Courts; Judgment; Justice; Jury; Law;** etc.
Adams — *New* p.74
Botkin — *Anecdotes* p.82, 165
Braude — *Source* #939-940
Braude — *Speaker's* #768-772
Braude — *Stories* p.221-222
Curtis — *Practical* p.411-415
Emmons — *Mature* p.98-99
Evans — *Faith* p.6, 14, 76, 110, 116, 212
Evans — *Thoughts I* p.46-48, 59, 90-91, 98-101, 124, 199
Evans — *Thoughts II (Open Door)* p.17, 26, 57, 133-134, 143-144, 153-154, 163-164
Evans — *Thoughts III (Open Road)* p.102, 160, 168
Evans — *Thoughts IV* p.106, 108, 110, 126, 136, 167
Fuller — *Thesaurus* #2486-2497
Grizer — *Wit* p.250
Henry — *5000* p.139
Kin — *Dictionary* p.136-137
Lockridge — *World's* #948
Montapert — *Distilled* p.223-224
More Words p.90, 92
Prochnow — *Public* #82, 216, 303, 463, 476, 513, 908, 2457, 2620, 2682
Prochnow — *Speaker's* p.177-178
Prochnow — *Success.* #1936
Seldes — *Great* p.534-536
Sheen — *Content.* p.156-158
Words — *Inspir.* p.155-156
, *Extraordinary*
New Topical p.139
, *Prayer of*
Braude — *Source* #940

JUDGMENT
See also **Decision; Intelligence; Opinion**
Braude — *Stories* p.201-202
Curtis — *Daily* p.12
Dirksen — *Quot.* #77, 115, 277, 426, 638, 640, 763, 1418-1422
Edwards — *Useful* p.307-309
Evans — *Quote* p.81-96
Evans — *Unto* p.19, 33, 48, 71, 121, 135
Flint — *Graham* p.79-80
Forbes — *Thoughts See* index p.555
Fox — *Make* p.66
Fuller — *Epigrams* p.170-171
Garland — *Subject* p.163-164
Grizer — *Wit* p.250-251
Halverson — *Perspective* p.11
Harnsberger — *Mark* p.219
Henry — *5000* p.139-140
Hobe — *Tapestries* p.198
Hovey — *Treasury* #1065, 1643
Johnson — *Bedside* p.125, 310, 313, 317-318
Kennedy — *Reader's* #560-564
Keys Happiness p.236
Kin — *Dictionary* p.137
Knight's Illus. p.177-178
Knight's Treas. p.191-194
Liddle — *Thought I, II, III* p.43, 105, 116, 122, 145, 151, 153
Liddle — *Thought IV* p.9, 17, 33, 37
Lockridge — *World's See* index p.578
Montapert — *Distilled* p.224-225
New Topical p.139-140
Nizer — *Thinking* p.115-116
Prochnow — *Public* #282, 1905, 2606
Prochnow — *Success.* #217, 1332, 1427
Reader's — *Getting* p.38
Sheban — *Wisdom* no p.
Speaker's Desk p.116-118
Voss — *Quotations* p.154-155
Wallis — *Words* p.17, 122
Woods — *Business.* p.126
Woods — *Religious* p.519-520
Woods — *Wellsprings* p.61-62
, *and freedom*
Adams — *New* p.270
. *and repression*
Phillips — *Choice* p.269
, *Criticism of*
Lytle — *Leaves* p.42
, *Group*
Adams — *New* p.368
, *Mass*
Nizer — *Thinking* p.115-116
, *Private*
Woods — *Religious* p.783
, *Public*
Curtis — *Practical* p.432-434

, *Quick*
Fuller — *Thesaurus* #471-492
Grizer — *Wit* p.379
Woods — *Wellsprings* p.49-50
, *Rash*
Sheen — *Thoughts* p.126-127
, *Revision of*
Adams — *New* p.76

JUDGMENT DAY
Asimov — *Treasury* #460
Curtis — *Practical* p.509-510
Hobe — *Tapestries* p.156
Maxwell — *Courage* p.113-120
New Topical p.140
Schermerhorn — *1500* p.222-223

JUJITSU
Prochnow — *Public* #181

JUMPING
Botkin — *Treasury* p.210, 616-617

JUNE
Alexander's Treasure. p.241
Evans — *This* p.16-17
Prochnow — *Public* #1725
Woods — *Content.* p.213
Words — *Inspir.* p.52

JUNGLE
Botkin — *Anecdotes* p.270
, *and community*
Wheelis — *Moralist* p.70-71, 85-92, 101

JUNKMEN AND JUNKYARDS
Kohn — *Best* p.69-71
Lytle — *Leaves* p.98

JURY
Dirksen — *Quot.* #338
Fuller — *Thesaurus* #2511-2517
Grizer — *Wit* p.251
Harnsberger — *Mark* p.219
Harral — *Feature* p.200-201
Henry — *5000* p.140
Hubbard — *Scrap* p.88
Kin — *Dictionary* p.137
Lockridge — *World's* #2965
Prochnow — *Public* #446, 472, 513, 697, 835, 1726
Prochnow — *Speaker's* p.178
Prochnow — *Success.* #1133, 1144, 1271
Schermerhorn — *1500* p.223
Seldes — *Great* p.536
, *Verdicts of*
Nizer — *Thinking* p.116

JUSTICE
See also **Courts; Judges and judging; Law; Punishment; Reward; Right**
Auden — *Certain* p.207-208
Book Proverbs p.127
Braude — *Speaker's* #773-774
Braude — *Stories* p.202-205
Curtis — *Practical* p.132-135, 412-413
Dirksen — *Quot. See* index p.265
Droke — *Christian* p.284-289
Edwards — *Useful* p.309-311
Evans — *Quote* p.81-96
Evans — *This* p.149-160
Evans — *Thoughts I* p.109-110, 122
Evans — *Thoughts IV* p.109
Evans — *Unto* p.23, 27, 116-117
Flint — *Graham* p.80, 93
Fogg — *1000* #152, 170, 334-335, 425-426, 872, 890, 899, 913, 1041, 1111
Forbes — *Thoughts See* index p.555-556
Fuller — *Epigrams* p.171-172
Fuller — *Thesaurus* #2601
Garland — *Subject* p.164
Grizer — *Wit* p.251-252
Henry — *5000* p.140-141
Hovey — *Treasury* p.220-221; #60, 62, 71, 115, 494, 610, 726, 1017, 1029, 1047-1048, 1051, 1274, 1323, 1329
Hubbard — *Scrap* p.14, 16, 47, 88-89, 126
Humes — *Instant* #550-568, 1257
Johnson — *Bedside* p.171, 196, 200
Kahn — *Lessons* p.218-224
Kauffman — *For* p.126-128
Kennedy — *Reader's* #565-568
Kin — *Dictionary* p.137-138
Knight's Illus. p.178-180
Knight's Treas. p.195
Liddle — *Thought I, II, III* p.9, 58, 113, 124, 134, 151
Liddle — *Thought IV* p.16
Liddle — *Thought V* p.3
Lockridge — *World's* #84, 369-370, 1068, 1137, 1153, 1683, 2610, 2893
Lytle — *Leaves* p.129
McCracken — *What* p.58-65
Mandel — *Stories* p.153-154
Mandelbaum — *Choose* p.126-130
Montapert — *Distilled* p.225-226
New Topical p.140-141
Porter — *Halo* p.56-68
Prochnow — *Public* #1297, 1552, 2444, 3288-3231, 4134-4135
Prochnow — *Speaker's* p.178-179

Prochnow — *Success.* #1937-1939
Seldes — *Great* p.536-539
Sheban — *Wisdom* no p.
Speaker's Desk p.118-120; #391, 493, 768, 817, 826, 917, 1058, 1078
Voss — *Quotations* p.156
Wheelis — *Moralist* p.12, 48-50, 70, 115, 120, 141, 143-144
Woods — *Business.* p.126
Woods — *Religious* p.521-523
, and charity
Kauffman — *For* p.128
, and crime
Kauffman — *For* p.73-77
, Distributive
Woods — *Religious* p.245

JUSTIFICATION
See also **Excuses; Reason and reasoning**
Braude — *Speaker's* #775-776
Dirksen — *Quot.* #1425
Henry — *5000* p.140
Woods — *Religious* p.523-524
, by faith
More Words p.93-94

JUVENILE DELINQUENCY
Braude — *Speaker's* #777
Braude — *Stories* p.89-96
Droke — *Christian* p.289-291
Flint — *Graham* p.22, 80
Grizer — *Wit* p.252
Harral — *Feature* p.201
Lair — *Baby* p.37
Nizer — *Thinking* p.211-213
Peale — *Guideposts* p.157-160, 165-173
Prochnow — *Success.* #389, 1395
Safian — *Insults* p.129-130
Safian — *More* p.121-122
Sheen — *Thoughts* p.93-95, 101-102

K

KANGAROOS
Prochnow — *Public* #1727
Schermerhorn — *1500* p.224

KANSAS
Botkin — *Anecdotes* p.20, 70, 90, 103
Botkin — *Treasury* p.61, 85; *See also* index p.929

"KATZENJAMMER KIDS"
Botkin — *Treasury* p.359

KEATS, JOHN
Wallis — *Words* p.180

KEELBOAT MEN
Botkin — *Treasury* p.3, 8, 31, 50, 53

"KEEP GOING." *See* **Endurance**

"KEEP UP WITH THE JONESES." *See* **Competition; Envy**

KELLER, HELEN
Harnsberger — *Mark* p.220
Holman — *Psych.* p.178
Reader's — *Getting* p.6, 165-169

KEMPIS, THOMAS À
Lockridge — *World's* #4557

KENITES, THE
New Topical p.141-142

KENTUCKY
Botkin — *Anecdotes* p.11, 13, 44, 80-81, 165-167, 197, 244-245; *See also* index p.314
Botkin — *Treasury See* index p.929

KENTUCKY DERBY
Botkin — *Anecdotes* p.274

KEYS
Braude — *Speaker's* #778
Kin — *Dictionary* p.139
Lytle — *Leaves* p.175
Peterson — *Art* p.207
Wallis — *Words* p.58, 98

KICKS
Prochnow — *Public* #823, 924, 1025, 1517
, Emotional
Sheen — *Content.* p.27-29

KIDNAPPING. *See* **Abduction**

"KIDS." *See* **Adolescence; Children; Youth**; etc.

KILLING
See also **Murder**
Dirksen — *Quot.* #429-430, 538, 623
Harnsberger — *Mark* p.220-221
Kin — *Dictionary* p.139

Prochnow — *Public* #2465
Seldes — *Great* p.539-540
Woods — *Religious* p.525-526

KILNS
Auden — *Certain* p.208-209

KIN. *See* **Family; Relatives**

KINDERGARTEN
Harral — *Feature* p.201

KINDNESS
See also **Good; Sympathy;** etc.
Alexander's Treasure. p.22-23
Applegarth — *Heir.* p.78-79, 81, 171
Bartlett — *Discovery* p.122
Book Proverbs p.127
Braude — *Source* #941-944
Braude — *Speaker's* #779
Braude — *Stories* p.205-206
Carruthers — *Sparks* p.33-34
Curtis — *Practical* p.278
Detherage — *Sunrise* p.65, 104, 158
Dirksen — *Quot.* #306, 973, 1426-1427
Droke — *Christian* p.291-293
Edwards — *Useful* p.311-313
Emmons — *Mature* p.95-101
Evans — *Thoughts II (Open Door)* p.84-85, 88-90, 119-120, 138, 153-158
Evans — *Thoughts III (Open Road)* p.19, 26-27, 30, 32, 49, 65, 70, 72, 85, 98-99, 118
Evans — *Thoughts IV* p.87, 104-105, 116, 167, 205, 208
Forbes — *Thoughts* p.81, 150, 177, 181, 235, 245, 293, 302, 355, 365-366, 455, 482, 517
Fuller — *Epigrams* p.172-173
Fuller — *Thesaurus* #311-316
Garland — *Subject* p.166
Goudge — *Comfort* p.211
Grizer — *Wit* p.253
Guideposts — *Faith* p.331-333
Harnsberger — *Mark* p.221
Henry — *5000* p.140-142
Hobe — *Tapestries* p.193-198
Holmes — *I've* p.67-68
Hovey — *Treasury* p.221; #1017, 1094, 1201, 1330-1332
How To Live p.36-39
Johnson — *Bedside* p.4, 86, 165, 195, 199, 307
Keller — *Open* p.28
Kennedy — *Reader's* #569-571
Keys Happiness p.65-67, 196-200
Kin — *Dictionary* p.139
Knight's Illus. p.180-182
Knight's Treas. p.196-201
Liddle — *Thought I, II, III* p.8, 18, 33, 37, 46, 51, 78, 81, 95, 129, 137
Liddle — *Thought IV* p.5, 9, 11, 16, 26, 28, 42, 151-152, 191
Liddle — *Thought V* p.16
Lockridge — *World's* #724, 1683, 2102, 2283, 2310-2311, 2330, 2396, 3386, 3733, 4842
Lytle — *Leaves* p.33, 177
Mandel — *Stories* p.155-156
Modern Eloquence (14) p.360
Montapert — *Distilled* p.226
Peale — *Guideposts* p.257-259
Peterson — *Art* p.141, 152
Petty — *Promises* p.51-60
Price — *Wider* p.31-32
Prochnow — *Public* #3232-3235
Prochnow — *Speaker's* p.179
Prochnow — *Success.* #1940-1942
Sheban — *Wisdom* no p.
Sheen — *Way* p.133-135
Speaker's Desk #93, 179, 187, 263, 401, 539, 589, 784, 1082; p.120-121
Voss — *Quotations* p.156-158
Wallis — *Treasure* p.26, 101, 112, 123-124, 151
Wallis — *Words* p.19, 75-76, 86, 159, 164
Woods — *Religious* p.528
Zobell — *Speaker's* p.68

KINESTHESIA
Phillips — *Choice* p.281

KINETIC THEORY
Du Noüy — *Road* p.66-68, 86, 95, 169, 183

KINGDOM
Lytle — *Leaves* p.119
Sheban — *Wisdom* no p.
, of heaven. See **Heaven**
, Within
Peterson — *Art* p.108

KINGS AND QUEENS
See also **Government; Power; Royalty; Rulers**
Applegarth — *Heir.* p.64, 74, 155, 178, 239, 274, 296
Edwards — *Useful* p.313
Fogg — *1000 See* index p.889
Fuller — *Epigrams* p.173-174
Fuller — *Thesaurus* p.347-353
Henry — *5000* p.141
Hobe — *Tapestries* p.162
Hovey — *Treasury* p.221-222; *See also* index p.298
Kin — *Dictionary* p.140, 207
Lockridge — *World's See* index p.578

New Topical p.142-144
Peterson — *Art* p.90
Prochnow — *Public* #2121
Prochnow — *Success.* #1943
Seldes — *Great* p.540-543
Woods — *Religious* p.528-529
, *"Divine right" of*
Ideas p.116-117
Woods — *Religious* p.246

KIPLING, RUDYARD
Harnsberger — *Mark* p.221-222

KISSING
Braude — *Speaker's* #138-147, 780-787
Braude — *Stories* p.206-207
Edwards — *Useful* p.313-314
Fuller — *Epigrams* p.175-176, 347-348
Hadfield — *Delights* p.154-155
Hadfield — *Love* p.121
Henry — *5000* p.141-143
Hobe — *Tapestries* p.119
Kin — *Dictionary* p.140
Liddle — *Thought I, II, III* p.123
Menninger — *Blue.* p.204
Prochnow — *Public* #379, 494, 1056, 1346
Schermerhorn — *1500* p.225

KITCHENS
Henry — *5000* p.141
Hobe — *Tapestries* p.14
Kin — *Dictionary* p.140
Prochnow — *Success.* #845

KITES
Keys Happiness p.389-391
Kin — *Dictionary* p.140

KITTENS. *See* **Cats, and kittens**

KNAVES AND KNAVERY. *See* **Mischief; Villainy; Wickedness**

KNEELING
Wallis — *Treasure* p.199

KNIGHTS
Harnsberger — *Mark* p.222
New Joy p.194

KNIGHTS OF COLUMBUS
Schermerhorn — *1500* p.227

KNIVES
Kin — *Dictionary* p.140

"KNOCK-KNOCKS"
Asimov — *Treasury* #253
Botkin — *Treasury* p.409, 474

KNOTS
Kin — *Dictionary* p.141

"KNOW-IT-ALLS"
Braude — *Source* #945

"KNOW-NOTHINGS." *See* **Fools and foolishness**

KNOWLEDGE
See also **Books and reading; Education; Learning; Self-knowledge; Thought; Wisdom;** etc.
Adams — *New* p.391
Albert — *Stop* p.56
Applegarth — *Heir.* p.174, 227, 296
Baillie — *Diary* #259
Book Proverbs p.124
Braude — *Source* #946-960
Braude — *Speaker's* #788-790
Braude — *Stories* p.207
Curtis — *Golden* p.141-142
Curtis — *Practical* p.3-4, 108, 136-139, 218, 220
Dirksen — *Quot. See* index p.265
Droke — *Christian* p.294-299
Du Noüy — *Road* p.76-77, 209
Edwards — *Useful* p.315-320, 729
Evans — *Faith* p.165
Evans — *Thoughts I* p.34, 107, 141, 151, 159-160, 169, 212
Evans — *Thoughts II (Open Door)* p.79
Evans — *Thoughts III (Open Road)* p.139-140, 147, 149-150, 205
Evans — *Thoughts IV* p.64-65, 175, 186
Evans — *Unto* p.7, 12, 84
Flint — *Graham* p.81
Fogg — *1000* #134, 326, 330, 420, 569, 616, 980
Forbes — *Thoughts See* index p.556
Fox — *Make* p.26
Fuller — *Epigrams* p.176-177
Fuller — *Thesaurus* p.183-200
Garland — *Subject* p.167
Grizer — *Wit* p.253-256
Harnsberger — *Mark* p.222-224
Henry — *5000* p.143-144
Hobe — *Tapestries* p.43, 199
Hovey — *Treasury* p.222; *See also* index p.298
Hubbard — *Scrap* p.12, 50, 79, 127
Humes — *Instant* #569-573
Johnson — *Bedside* p.12, 19, 77, 109, 111, 113, 127, 184, 232, 247-248, 250, 313-314
Keller — *Open* p.90
Kennedy — *Reader's* #572-573

Keys Happiness p.276
Kin — *Dictionary* p.141
Kohn — *Pathways* p.193-196
Krishnamurti — *Think* p.205-207
Liddle — *Thought I, II, III* p.10, 12, 22, 35, 38, 47, 50, 62, 88, 100, 129, 180, 187
Liddle — *Thought IV* p.21, 26, 32, 37, 42
Liddle — *Thought V* p.39-40
Lockridge — *World's See* index p.578
Lytle — *Leaves* p.28, 130, 172
Mandel — *Stories* p.156-157
Modern Eloquence (14) p.361-363
Montapert — *Distilled* p.226-228
New Joy p.43, 60
Nizer — *Thinking* p.80
Patterns For Living p.658-663
Peterson — *Art* p.308
Phillips — *Choice See* index p.427
Porter — *Halo* p.104-109
Prochnow — *Public* #2626; *See* index p.500
Prochnow — *Speaker's* p.179-180
Prochnow — *Success.* #561, 835, 877, 934, 1946-1953, 2091
Seldes — *Great* p.543-546
Sheban — *Wisdom* no p.
Sheen — *Thoughts* p.36-38
Speaker's Desk p.121-123; #308, 321, 822, 837
Voss — *Quotations* p.158-160
Wallis — *Treasure* p.93, 210, 231
Wallis — *Words* p.91, 146
Wheelis — *Moralist* p.4, 22-23, 33, 83, 113, 152-153
Woods — *Religious* p.529-532
, and God
Baillie — *Diary* #323
, and learning
Henry — *5000* p.144
, and tradition
Krishnamurti — *Think* p.142-150
, and wisdom
Henry — *5000* p.144
, Popular
Sheban — *Wisdom* no p.
, Sources of
Hill — *Think* p.86-87, 191-192
, Toward riches
Hill — *Think* p.82-99
, Use of
Holmes — *Design* p.179-188

KORAN
Fogg — *1000* #292
Woods — *Religious* p.532

KOREA AND KOREANS
Guideposts — *Faith* p.435-439
Hovey — *Treasury* #99, 243, 1239, 1459, 1486
Peale — *Guideposts* p.305-309

KRISHNA
Woods — *Religious* p.532-533

KU KLUX KLAN
Schermerhorn — *1500* p.225-227

L

LSD
Ginott — *Between* p.191, 192-194

LABELS
Evans — *Unto* p.32, 71-72

LABOR
See also **"Closed shop"; Labor unions; Work;** etc.
Applegarth — *Heir.* p.141-145, 298
Auden — *Certain* p.405-407
Braude — *Stories* p.208-209
Copeland — *World's* p.117-121, 208-211, 405-408, 416-417, 425-427, 481-482, 487-488
Curtis — *Practical* p.128, 316, 368
Dirksen — *Quot. See* index p.265
Edwards — *Useful* p.320-322
Evans — *Unto* p.15, 49, 83-84, 93, 101
Flesch — *Unusual* p.61
Forbes — *Thoughts See* index p.556
Fuller — *Epigrams* p.178
Grizer — *Wit* p.256-260
Harnsberger — *Mark* p.225
Harral — *Feature* p.201
Henry — *5000* p.144-146
Hovey — *Treasury* p.222-224; #1340-1348
Hubbard — *Scrap* p.27, 36, 46, 50, 58, 97, 159, 172, 222-223
Kin — *Dictionary* p.142
Liddle — *Thought I, II, III* p.81
Lockridge — *World's* #2056, 2757, 3472, 3692
Lytle — *Leaves* p.181
Montapert — *Distilled* p.228-229
Prochnow — *Public* #593, 1305, 2632, 2635, 2668, 3257-3258, 4140-4141

Prochnow — *Speaker's* p.180
Prochnow — *Success.* #269
Seldes — *Great* p.547-557
Speaker's Desk p.123-125
Tanksley — *Friend* p.61
Wallis — *Treasure* p.237-239
Woods — *Business.* p.126-128
Woods — *Religious* p.533

, and management
Keller — *You* p.119-143
, Groups of
Humes — *Instant* #1271-1273
, Manual
Day — *Meditations* p.76-77
, Monopoly of
Woods — *Business.* p.156-158
, Personal contact in
Reader's — *20th* p.8-10
, Problems of
Reader's — *20th* p.8-10
, Relations of
Droke — *Christian* p.300-303
Flint — *Graham* p.90-91
, Rights and duties of
Keller — *You* p.123-126
Woods — *Religious* p.533-534

LABOR DAY
Harral — *Feature* p.201-202
Hovey — *Treasury* *See* index p.304

LABOR UNIONS
Botkin — *Anecdotes* p.200, 280
Forbes — *Thoughts* p.268, 409, 411
Franke — *Buckley* p.159-162
Harnsberger — *Mark* p.491-492
Harral — *Feature* p.201, 309
Humes — *Instant* #25-26, 1198-1200, 1271-1273
Seldes — *Great* p.940-943
Woods — *Business.* p.257-263
Woods — *Religious* p.534-535
, Rules for
Wheelis — *Moralist* p.119

LACK. *See* **Deficiency**

LADDERS
Kin — *Dictionary* p.142

LADIES. *See* **Women**

"LAISSEZ-FAIRE"
Ideas p.231-233
Woods — *Business.* p.129-130
Woods — *Religious* p.535

LAKE MICHIGAN
Kohn — *Through* p.29-31

LAKES
Harnsberger — *Mark* p.225-226
Wallis — *Words* p.171

LAMBS. *See* **Sheep, and lambs**

"LAME DUCKS"
Prochnow — *Public* #1729
Prochnow — *Success.* #954

LAMENESS. *See* **Handicapped**

LAMPLIGHTERS
Wallis — *Treasure* p.147
Wallis — *Words* p.127
Woods — *Wellsprings* p.80-81

LAMPS
New Topical p.145
Wallis — *Treasure* p.169
Wallis — *Words* p.3, 29, 82, 128, 199, 230, 240

LAND. *See* **Earth**

LANDLORDS
Asimov — *Treasury* #186
Braude — *Speaker's* #791-798
Manchee — *Secret* p.215-216
Prochnow — *Public* #44, 713
Seldes — *Great* p.561

LANDSCAPE. *See* **Gardens and gardening**

LANGUAGE
See also **Accents; Linguists; Speech; Words**
Applegarth — *Heir.* p.110, 117, 182, 204
Auden — *Certain* p.92
Braude — *Source* #961
Braude — *Speaker's* #799-806
Curtis — *Practical* p.125, 432
Dirksen — *Quot.* #11, 153, 234, 646, 719, 879, 1017, 1124, 1643, 1728
Edwards — *Useful* p.322-324
Esteve — *Experience* p.53-59
Evans — *Unto* p.91, 96
Forbes — *Thoughts* p.204, 238, 496, 504
Fuller — *Thesaurus* #1231-1233
Harnsberger — *Mark* p.226-228
Harral — *Feature* p.202-203
Henry — *5000* p.146-147
Hoffer — *Reflect.* p.55-56
Kennedy — *Reader's* #574-582
Kin — *Dictionary* p.143
Liddle — *Thought I, II, III* p.24, 75, 100

Lockridge — *World's* #2057, 3982, 4074, 4120, 4139, 4220, 4492, 5291
Lytle — *Leaves* p.78
Mandel — *Stories* p.157
Montapert — *Distilled* p.229
New Topical p.145-146
Prochnow — *Public* #137, 492, 3259-3261, 4142
Prochnow — *Speaker's* p.181-184
Prochnow — *Success.* #1274, 1461
, Alphabets of
Flesch — *Unusual* p.8, 144-145
Prochnow — *Public* #915
, Bad
Asimov — *Treasury* #212
, Elasticity of
Nizer — *Thinking* p.53
, Paradox of
Adams — *New* p.292
, Universal
Ideas p.426-430
, Use and abuse of
Huxley — *You See* index p.286

LANTERNS
Wallis — *Treasure* p.157

LAOS
Guideposts — *Faith* p.424-427
Simpson — *Contemp.* p.148

LAO-TSE
Flesch — *Unusual* p.145

LARCHES
Auden — *Certain* p.218

LARKS
Applegarth — *Heir.* p.191
Henry — *5000* p.147

"LAST SUPPER"
Baillie — *Diary* #353

LAST WORDS. *See* **Words, Dying**

LATENESS
Evans — *Thoughts I* p.36-37, 46, 176
Fuller — *Thesaurus* #321-324
Grizer — *Wit* p.261-262
Kin — *Dictionary* p.143
Lytle — *Leaves* p.33, 173
Prochnow — *Public* #901, 1034, 1296
Speaker's Desk #614, 644, 1173

LATIMER, HUGH
Applegarth — *Heir.* p.72

LATIN
Asimov — *Treasury* #257
Flesch — *Unusual* p.145
Prochnow — *Success.* #1956

LATIN AMERICA
Prochnow — *Success.* #637
, Communism in
Flint — *Graham* p.81

LATIN PROVERBS
Dirksen — *Quot. See* index p.266

LATTER-DAY SAINTS
See also **Mormon, Book of**
Botkin — *Treasury* p.367, 567-568
Harnsberger — *Mark* p.294
Peale — *Guideposts* p.292-294
, Welfare program of
Hunter — *Gems* p.116-117

LAUGHTER
See also **Cheerfulness; Joy; Vivacity**
Alexander's Treasure. p.20
Applegarth — *Heir.* p.88-90, 175
Baillie — *Diary* #84
Braude — *Source* #962-964
Braude — *Stories* p.209
Curtis — *Practical* p.95
Dirksen — *Quot.* p.1888
Droke — *Christian* p.304
Edwards — *Useful* p.324-325; 394-395
Flesch — *Unusual* p.145-146, 175
Forbes — *Thoughts* p.11, 15, 115, 121, 156, 183, 210, 234, 298, 346, 385, 463, 480, 484, 509
Fuller — *Epigrams* p.178-179
Fun Fare p.18-19, 95, 163, 257
Grizer — *Wit* p.262
Harnsberger — *Mark* p.228-229
Henry — *5000* p.147-148
Hoffer — *Reflect.* p.14-15
Hubbard — *Scrap* p.21, 86, 110
Johnson — *Bedside* p.1, 13, 20
Kennedy — *Reader's* #583-586
Kin — *Dictionary* p.143-144, 163
Kopplin — *Something* p.5-6
Liddle — *Thought I, II, III* p.18, 20, 33, 36, 53, 73, 78, 104, 106-107, 157, 169, 191
Liddle — *Thought IV* p.3, 7-9, 18, 21, 40-41
Liddle — *Thought V* p.3, 24, 30, 45
Lockridge — *World's See* index p.578
Lytle — *Leaves* p.82-83
Montapert — *Distilled* p.230

Nizer — *Thinking* p.77
Peterson — *Art* p.134
Phillips — *Choice* p.138, 372
Prochnow — *Public* #1191, 1227, 1730, 2413, 3262-3265, 4143-4144
Prochnow — *Speaker's* p.184
Prochnow — *Success.* #1338, 1488, 1957-1959
Speaker's Desk #375, 395, 400, 479, 523, 541, 612, 731, 746, 859, 1140, 1166
Wallis — *Treasure* p.142
Wallis — *Words* p.17-18
Woods — *Content.* p.157, 170, 174, 189, 281, 291, 337
Woods — *Religious* p.537
Words — *Inspir.* p.159-160

, Art of
Peterson — *Twenty* p.16-17

, at yourself
Kohn — *Touch* p.162-166

, Healing in
Clark — *Windows* p.136-137

, Power of
Guideposts — *Faith* p.90-94
Peale — *Guideposts* p.231-235

LAUNDRY
Flesch — *Unusual* p.307
Fun Fare p.219-220
Harral — *Feature* p.203
Kin — *Dictionary* p.273
Prochnow — *Public* #38, 1301, 1408, 1731
Prochnow — *Speaker's* p.185

, Manager of
Manchee — *Secret* p.217-218

"LAVER OF BRASS"
New Topical p.146

LAW
See also **Common law; Courts; Judges; Justice; Lawyers; Punishment**; etc.
Book Proverbs p.89
Braude — *Source* #965-970
Braude — *Speaker's* #148-150
Braude — *Stories* p.209-225
Cerf — *Laugh* p.255-264
Curtis — *Practical* p.569; *See also* index p.405-407
Dirksen — *Quot. See* index p.266
Edwards — *Useful* p.325-329; 729
Evans — *Faith* p.19, 54-55, 71, 74, 78-79, 114, 132, 134, 147-148, 180-182
Evans — *Quote* p.81-96
Evans — *This* p.38-39
Evans — *Thoughts I* p.15, 151, 153-156
Evans — *Thoughts II (Open Door)* p.46, 84, 87-88, 189
Evans — *Thoughts III (Open Road)* p.21, 40, 68, 78-81, 108, 111, 121, 125, 165-171, 200-201
Evans — *Unto* p.14, 20, 31, 42, 55-56, 58, 60, 66, 133
Flesch — *Unusual* p.146-147
Flint — *Graham* p.81-82
Fogg — *1000 See* index p.890
Forbes — *Thoughts See* index p.556
Fuller — *Epigrams* p.179-180, 351-352
Fuller — *Thesaurus* #2596-2599
George — *Book See* index p.444
Grizer — *Wit* p.263-265
Halverson — *Perspective* p.119
Harnsberger — *Mark* p.222-231
Harral — *Feature* p.203-204
Henry — *5000* p.148-149
Holmes — *Design See* index p.233
Hooker — *Index* p.77-86
Hovey — *Treasury* p.224-225; *See* index p.298
Hubbard — *Scrap* p.14, 38, 42, 86, 128, 185
Humes — *Instant* #574-594, 1257
Kennedy — *Reader's* #587-590
Kin — *Dictionary* p.144
Knight's Illus. p.182-184
Knight's Treas. p.201-202
Liddle — *Thought I, II, III* p.124, 136, 164, 169, 194
Liddle — *Thought V* p.25
Lindeman — *Emerson* p.198
Lockridge — *World's* #752, 1139; *See also* index p.578
Lytle — *Leaves* p.75, 112
Modern Eloquence (14) p.41-57, 364-365
Montapert — *Distilled* p.230-231
More Words p.98-100
Prochnow — *Public* #1085, 1129, 1592, 1731, 1942, 3266-3269, 4145, 4315, 4341
Prochnow — *Speaker's* p.185
Prochnow — *Success.* #342, 458, 1960-1962
Pullar-Strecker — *Proverbs* #218-221
Seldes — *Great* p.561-573
Sheban — *Wisdom* no p.
Simpson — *Contemp.* p.51-56
Speaker's Desk See index p.302
Wheelis — *Moralist* p.69-70, 90-91, 95, 115, 121, 143-144
Woods — *Business.* p.131-132
Woods — *Religious* p.537-539

, and conscience
Kauffman — *For* p.129-130
, and justice
Fuller — *Thesaurus* p.441-466
, and lawsuits
Kin — *Dictionary* p.144
Reader's — *Getting* p.250
, and legal aid
Harral — *Feature* p.206
, Encounters with
Fun Fare p.54, 110, 191
, Enforcement of
Fuller — *Thesaurus* p.456-458
, Indictment in
Seldes — *Great* p.499
Sheban — *Wisdom* no p.
, "Loony"
Copeland — *10,000* p.178-181
, Natural
Flesch — *Unusual* p.185
Woods — *Religious* p.669-672
, of torts
Curtis — *Practical* p.400-402
, Respect for
Dirksen — *Quot.* #2366
, Rule of
Ideas p.234-236
, Study of
Nizer — *Thinking* p.82
, Verdicts of
Kin — *Dictionary* p.268
Prochnow — *Public* #303

LAWLESSNESS
See also **Crime and criminals**
Edwards — *Useful* p.340
Evans — *Thoughts IV* p.19, 25, 97-98, 118, 127, 133-139, 143-150, 158, 193
Evans — *Unto* p.32, 34, 58
Knight's Illus. p.184-186

LAWNS
Prochnow — *Public* #111
Prochnow — *Success.* #596, 1348

LAWYERS
See also **Courts; Judges; Law;** etc.
Asimov — *Treasury* #200-201, 210
Book Proverbs p.89
Botkin — *Anecdotes* p.xxvi, 10, 20, 45, 80, 82, 138, 157, 165, 186-187
Braude — *Speaker's* #807-815
Curtis — *Practical* p.408-411
Edwards — *Useful* p.329-330
Flesch — *Unusual* p.147
Fuller — *Epigrams* p.180-181
Fuller — *Thesaurus* p.451-456
Grizer — *Wit* p.265-267
Harral — *Feature* p.205
Henry — *5000* p.149
Hubbard — *Scrap* p.80
Humes — *Instant* p.23-24; #28-29
Kin — *Dictionary* p.144-145
Lockridge — *World's* #2933-2965, 3353, 4135, 4389, 4821, 4997, 5286
New Joy p.91, 188
Prochnow — *Public* #33, 411, 447, 543, 1302
Prochnow — *Speaker's* p.28-30, 185-186
Prochnow — *Success.* #191, 196, 532, 567, 1963-1964
Schermerhorn — *1500* p.229-232
Speaker's Desk #692; *See also* index p.302
Weisfeld — *Pulpit* p.141-142
, Fees of
Fuller — *Thesaurus* #2541-2545
, Humor of
Copeland — *10,000* p.459-484
, Skeptical
Unlimited Power p.79-83

LAXITY. *See* **Neglect**

LAYMEN
Hovey — *Treasury* #29, 440, 448, 469, 921
Lytle — *Leaves* p.126
More Words p.100-101
Strait — *Speaker's* p.97

LAZARUS
Baillie — *Diary* #54
Fridy — *Meditat.* p.26

LAZINESS
Baillie — *Diary* #50
Book Proverbs p.4
Braude — *Source* #908-909, 971-974
Braude — *Speaker's* #816
Braude — *Stories* p.225
Edwards — *Useful* p.286, 600
Evans — *Unto* p.15, 38, 56
Flesch — *Unusual* p.147, 267
Flint — *Graham* p.82-83, 136
Forbes — *Thoughts* p.86, 178, 208-209, 242, 259, 312, 336, 428, 443
Fuller — *Epigrams* p.181-182
Fuller — *Thesaurus* #326-327
Grizer — *Wit* p.267
Harnsberger — *Mark* p.231
Henry — *5000* p.133

Johnson — *Bedside* p.81, 198
Kennedy — *Reader's* #516-518
Kin — *Dictionary* p.130, 145
Krishnamurti — *Think* p.137-138
Lockridge — *World's* #17, 93, 172, 514, 695, 1533, 1763, 1814, 4196
McCracken — *What* p.28-33
Montapert — *Distilled* p.231
Nichols — *New* p.53-54
Nichols — *Third* p.121-122
Prochnow — *Public* #976, 1965, 2171, 2552
Prochnow — *Speaker's* p.186-187
Prochnow — *Success.* #667, 1965
Speaker's Desk See index p.302
Woods — *Content.* p.100, 115, 140, 209, 211, 341, 344, 347, 350-351

, Mental
Holmes — *Design* p.115-116

LEAD MINES
Auden — *Certain* p.219-225

LEADERS AND LEADERSHIP
See also **Executives; Greatness; Heroes and heroism**; etc.
Bartlett — *Discovery* p.142-143
Braude — *Source* #975-987
Braude — *Speaker's* #817-820
Braude — *Stories* p.226
Dirksen — *Quot.* #39, 63, 115, 2330
Droke — *Christian* p.305-309
Evans — *Faith* p.145-146
Evans — *This* p.121-135
Evans — *Thoughts III (Open Road)* p.150, 171
Evans — *Unto* p.56, 112, 114-115
Flesch — *Unusual* p.147
Forbes — *Thoughts* See index p.556
Franke — *Buckley* p.163
Fuller — *Thesaurus* #1401-1403
Grizer — *Wit* p.268-271
Halverson — *Perspective* p.2, 45
Harral — *Feature* p.205-206
Henry — *5000* p.149-150
Hill — *Think* p.118-125
Hovey — *Treasury* p.225-227; *See also* index p.298
Hubbard — *Scrap* p.27
Humes — *Instant* p.22; #595-615
Hunter — *Gems* p.43-44
Kennedy — *Reader's* #591-592
Liddle — *Thought I, II, III,* p.77, 125
Liddle — *Thought IV* p.30
Lytle — *Leaves* p.17, 62, 71, 86
Mandel — *Stories* p.157-158
Maurois—*Art* p.216-253
Modern Eloquence (14) p.366
Montapert — *Distilled* p.231-232
Nichols — *Third* p.240-241
Peterson — *Twenty* p.36-37
Prochnow — *Public* #1338, 2429
Prochnow — *Success.* #303, 1966-1967
Seldes — *Great* p.573-574
Woods — *Religious* p.539
Zobell — *Speaker's* p.81, 87

LEAGUE OF NATIONS
Copeland — *World's* p.365-372, 374-376, 448-450
Seldes — *Great* p.574

LEANING
Flesch — *Unusual* p.147
Kin — *Dictionary* p.145
Prochnow — *Success.* #1968

LEAP YEAR
Harral — *Feature* p.206

LEAR, EDWARD
, Limericks of
Copeland — *10,000* p.950-956

LEARNING
See also **Education; Knowledge; Scholars and scholarship; Self-improvement; Study; Teachers; Wisdom**; etc.
Book Proverbs p.124
Braude — *Source* #988-995
Detherage — *Sunrise* p.39-44
Dirksen — *Quot.* #141, 439, 983-987
Edwards — *Useful* p.330-333
Evans — *Faith* p.35, 96, 159-160
Evans — *Quot.* p.67-79
Evans — *Thoughts II (Open Door)* p.118, 128-129
Evans — *Thoughts III (Open Road)* p.139, 145, 149, 152, 155, 195-197, 199
Evans — *Thoughts IV* p.88, 109, 168-169, 175, 194
Evans — *Unto* p.7, 20, 31, 143
Flesch — *Unusual* p.147-148
Forbes — *Thoughts* See index p.556
Fuller — *Epigrams* p.182-184
Grizer — *Wit* p.271-272
Harnsberger — *Mark* p.232
Henry — *5000* p.150
Hovey — *Treasury* #361, 364, 586, 852, 863, 1263, 1337, 1356, 1561, 1643
How To Live p.179-182
Kin — *Dictionary* p.145-146
Krishnamurti — *Urgency* p.124-128

Kronenberger — *Animal* p.134-135
Liddle — *Thought I, II, III* p.5, 10, 20, 38, 52, 54, 59-60, 71, 74-75, 88, 120, 139-140, 168, 185
Liddle — *Thought IV* p.25, 32, 34, 46
Liddle — *Thought V* p.8, 17-18, 27-28, 35
Lockridge — *World's* #3393, 4348, 5688
Lytle — *Leaves* p.26-27, 160
Mandel — *Stories* p.159
Mandelbaum — *Choose* p.142-151
Montapert — *Distilled* p.232-233
New Joy p.26-27
Prochnow — *Public* #944, 982, 2730
Prochnow — *Success.* #680, 1223, 1406, 1417, 1969-1971
Seldes — *Great* p.574
Sheban — *Wisdom* no p.
Wallis — *Treasure* p.89
Wallis — *Words* p.139-146
Woods — *Religious* p.539-540
, and arts
Fuller — *Thesaurus* p.175-258
, Purpose of
Krishnamurti — *Think* p.159-166
, Teenager
Ginott — *Between* p.213

LEAVEN
Kin — *Dictionary* p.146
New Topical p.148
Prochnow — *Public* #2707

LEAVES
Applegarth — *Heir.* p.285-286
Irion — *Yes* p.62-63
Kin — *Dictionary* p.145
Lindbergh — *Unicorn* p.16-17
Lytle — *Leaves* p.74
Prochnow — *Public* #2586

LEBANON
New Topical p.148
Prochnow — *Success.* #762

LECTURES AND LECTURERS
Asimov — *Treasury* #124
Fuller — *Thesaurus* #1106-1111
Harnsberger — *Mark* p.232
Prochnow — *Public* #668, 1421
Schermerhorn — *1500* p.232
Walters — *How* p.167-188

LEE, ROBERT E.
Hubbard — *Scrap* p.132
New Joy p.212

Peterson — *Art* p.37
, Farewell to soldiers
Dirksen — *Quot.* #586

LEFT-HANDEDNESS
Harral — *Feature* p.206

"LEFT-OVERS"
Kohn — *Through* p.59-62
Prochnow — *Public* #826

LEGENDS. *See* **Mythology**

LEGISLATION
See also **Government; Law**
Forbes — *Thoughts* p.326, 414, 466, 498, 507
Prochnow — *Success.* #311
Seldes — *Great* p.575
, and taxes
Sagendorph — *Old* p.152-156
, Social
Nizer — *Thinking* p.102

LEGISLATURES. *See* **United States-Congress**

LEGS
Kin — *Dictionary* p.146

LEISURE
See also **Hobbies; Recreation; Rest;** etc.
Alexander's Treasure. p.102
Applegarth — *Heir.* p.147-151, 257
Bach — *Make* p.52-54
Braude — *Source* #996-999
Braude — *Stories* p.226
Dirksen — *Quot.* #52, 440
Edwards — *Useful* p.333, 729
Evans — *Faith* p.25, 33-38
Evans — *Thoughts II (Open Door)* p.165
Evans — *Thoughts III (Open Road)* p.55-61, 131
Evans — *Thoughts IV* p.54-56
Flesch — *Unusual* p.148-149
Forbes — *Thoughts* p.83, 120, 137, 247, 270, 386, 415, 426, 494, 517
Grizer — *Wit* p.272-274
Harnsberger — *Mark* p.232
Henry — *5000* p.150-151
Hovey — *Treasury* p.227; #1371-1377
Kin — *Dictionary* p.146
Liddle — *Thought I, II, III* p.171
Liddle — *Thought IV* p.19
Lockridge — *World's* #1430, 2404, 2492, 3147, 3460, 4237
Lytle — *Leaves* p.27
Mandel — *Stories* p.160-161

Montapert — *Distilled* p.233-234
Prochnow — *Public* #1199
Prochnow — *Speaker's* p.187-188
Prochnow — *Success.* #409, 1971
Seldes — *Great* p.575
Sheen — *Content.* p.110-112
Speaker's Desk p.125-126
Strait — *Speaker's* p.98-99
Wallis — *Words* p.50, 62, 128

LENDING AND LOANS
See also **Credit; Help; Usury and usurers**
Dirksen — *Quot.* #274, 793
Edwards — *Useful* p.333
Flesch — *Unusual* p.149
Fuller — *Thesaurus* #2161-2164
Henry — *5000* p.151
Kin — *Dictionary* p.146
Prochnow — *Public* #128, 516, 1033, 1525, 4146
Prochnow — *Speaker's* p.195
Prochnow — *Success.* #974, 978, 1127, 1972-1974

LENGTH
Flesch — *Unusual* p.155

LENINISM
Seldes — *Great* p.575-576

LENITY. *See* **Compassion; Mercy**

LENT
See also **Easter**
More Words p.101-102
Suter — *Prayers* #397-399

LEOPARDS
Kin — *Dictionary* p.146
New Topical p.148-194

LEPERS
Lytle — *Leaves* p.33
Peale — *Courage* p.135
Peale — *Guideposts* p.33-36

LEPRECHAUNS
Asimov — *Treasury* #578

LESSONS. *See* **Education; Learning; Schools; Study**

LETTERS AND LETTER WRITING
Adams — *New* p.58
Applegarth — *Heir.* p.153-159
Braude — *Source* #1000
Braude — *Stories* p.227
Cerf — *Laugh* p.196-201
Edwards — *Useful* p.334
Emmons — *Mature* p.119-120
Flesch — *Unusual* p.149
Fuller — *Epigrams* p.184
Fun Fare p.262
Grizer — *Wit* p.274
Harnsberger — *Mark* p.232-234
Harral — *Feature* p.206-207
Henry — *5000* p.151
Keller — *You* p.244-261
Keys Happiness p.205-208
Kin — *Dictionary* p.147
Kronenberger — *Animal* p.135-164
Lockridge — *World's* #2256, 2478, 5199
Lytle — *Leaves* p.50
Manchee — *Secret* p.33-34, 125-127
More Words p.57-58
Peterson — *Art* p.294, 319
Prochnow — *Public* #154, 670, 729, 959
Prochnow — *Success.* #1975
, Form
Dirksen — *Quot.* #1689
, Great
Adams — *New* p.251
, Teenage
Daly — *Personality* p.137-143
, "Unnecessary"
Unlimited Power p.240-243

LEVEL
Flesch — *Unusual* p.150
Kin — *Dictionary* p.147
Lytle — *Leaves* p.108
Montapert — *Distilled* p.234

LEVERS
Seldes — *Great* p.576

LEVI (Biblical)
Baillie — *Diary* #266

LEVIATHAN
Ideas p.236-237
New Topical p.149

LEVITES, THE
New Topical p.149-150

LEVITY. *See* **Humor; Jokes and joking**

LEWIS AND CLARK EXPEDITION
New Joy p.81, 155-158

LIARS
See also **Dishonesty; Falsehood; Tall tales**
Asimov — *Treasury* #43-44, 151, 414
Baillie — *Diary* #243

Botkin — *Anecdotes* p.89-109
Botkin — *Treasury* p.490-650
Dirksen — *Quot.* #331
Edwards — *Useful* p.335
Fuller — *Thesaurus* #331-336
Grizer — *Wit* p.274
Lockridge — *World's* #1667
Montapert — *Distilled* p.234
Prochnow — *Public* #357, 703, 788, 2404, 2439
Prochnow — *Speaker's* p.188-189
Safian — *Insults* p.131-132
Safian — *More* p.123-126
Schermerhorn — *1500* p.233-234
Sheban — *Wisdom* no p.
Woods — *Religious* p.540

, Bench for
Botkin — *Treasury* p.192, 554-555

, Club of
Botkin — *Treasury,* p.555-556

LIBEL
Kin — *Dictionary* p.147
Seldes — *Great* p.576

LIBERALISM AND LIBERALS
Braude — *Stories* p.227
Dirksen — *Quot.* #561, 650
Franke — *Buckley* p.166-173
Henry — *5000* p.151-152
Humes — *Instant* #616-620
Kin — *Dictionary* p.147
Prochnow — *Speaker's* p.189
Prochnow — *Success.* p.1977-1978
Seldes — *Great* p.576-580
Wheelis — *Moralist* p.117-118
Woods — *Business.* p.133-134
Woods — *Religious* p.540-543

LIBERALITY. *See* **Benevolence; Generosity**

LIBERTARIANS
Seldes — *Great* p.580

LIBERTY
See also **Civil rights; Democracy; Freedom; Heritage; Independence; Patriotism; Republic**
Bartlett — *Discovery* p.82-83, 128-129
Braude — *Source* #1001-1003
Curtis — *Practical* p.351-389; *See* index p.569
Dirksen — *Quot. See* index p.266
Du Noüy — *Human* p.87, 107, 109-119, 147-148, 178, 197, 226-227, 238
Edwards — *Useful* p.336-339, 729
Evans — *Quote* p.81-96
Evans — *This* p.134-135, 144-145
Evans — *Thoughts I* p.14, 62, 149, 155
Evans — *Thoughts II (Open Door)* p.63, 69-70
Evans — *Unto* p.32, 55-58
Flesch — *Unusual* p.150
Fogg — *1000 See* index p.890
Forbes — *Thoughts See* index p.556-557
Fuller — *Epigrams* p.184-185
Garland — *Subject* p.172
Grizer — *Wit* p.275-276
Halverson — *Perspective* p.115
Harnsberger — *Mark* p.234
Henry — *5000* p.152-153
Hovey — *Treasury* p.227-229; *See also* index p.298
How To Live p.162
Hubbard — *Scrap* p.43, 61, 78, 192, 203, 224
Humes — *Instant* p.46; #621-625
Hunter — *Gems* p.43-45
Ideas p.237-239
Keller — *Open* p.36
Kennedy — *Reader's* #593-594
Kin — *Dictionary* p.147
Liddle — *Thought I, II, III* p.7, 45, 58, 70, 83, 123, 141
Lytle — *Leaves* p.169
Modern Eloquence (14) p.367-368
Montapert — *Distilled* p.235
New Joy p.96
Nichols — *Third* p.207
Prochnow — *Public* #1604, 3270-3278, 4339, 4347, 4380
Prochnow — *Speaker's* p.189-190
Prochnow — *Success.* #734, 1979-1980
Seldes — *Great* p.580-604
Sheban — *Wisdom* no p.
Speaker's Desk p.126-127
Voss — *Quotations* p.160-162
Wallis — *Treasure* p.175
Wheelis — *Moralist* p.60
Woods — *Business.* p.134-139
Woods — *Religious* p.543

, and commitment
Baillie — *Diary* #257

, Christian
New Topical p.151

, Use of
Phillips — *Choice* p.39

"LIBERTY BELL"
Words — *Inspir.* p.123-125

LIBRARIANS
Alexander's Treasure. p.248-249
Braude — *Speaker's* #821-823
Keller — *You* p.176-180

LIBRARIES
See also **Books and reading; Knowledge; Librarians**
Alexander's Treasure. p.61
Applegarth — *Heir.* p.39-40
Dirksen — *Quot.* #2060
Edwards — *Useful* p.339-340
Fuller — *Thesaurus* #1226
Grizer — *Wit* p.276-277
Harnsberger — *Mark* p.234
Harral — *Feature* p.207-209
Keller — *You* p.171-181
Lockridge — *World's* #5640
Montapert — *Distilled* p.235-236
Prochnow — *Public* #297, 1482, 1734, 1777, 3279-3281, 4147, 4334
Prochnow — *Success.* #234, 242

LICE
Botkin — *Treasury* p.325, 524, 648
Kin — *Dictionary* p.152
Seldes — *Great* p.617-618

LICENSE
Dirksen — *Quot.* #442
Lockridge — *World's* #1761
Seldes — *Great* p.604-605

, versus freedom
Hunter — *Gems* p.32-33

LICENSE PLATES AND NUMBERS
Harral — *Feature* p.209
Prochnow — *Success.* #998

LICENTIOUSNESS. *See* **Lawlessness**

LIE DETECTORS
Prochnow — *Public* #1343

LIES. *See* **Dishonesty; Falsehood; Liars; Tall tales**

LIFE AND LIVING
See also **Action; Biography; Birth; Energy; Humanity; Man (mankind); Soul; Spirit; Vivacity**
Adams — *New* p.360
Albert — *Stop* p.10-14, 111
Alexander's Treasure. p.63, 338-341
Applegarth — *Heir.* p.40, 64, 88, 111, 161-169, 171, 173, 254
Baillie — *Diary* #357
Barker — *Treat* p.125-147
Braude — *Source* #1006-1034
Braude — *Speaker's* #151-164, 824-828
Braude — *Stories* p.14, 227-228
Curtis — *Daily* p.1-10
Curtis — *Practical* p.46-47, 234-235, 505
Detherage — *Sunrise* p.33-34, 87, 136, 144, 153, 178
Dirksen — *Quot. See* index p.266
Droke — *Christian* p.310-318
Du Noüy — *Road See* index p.248
Edwards — *Useful* p.340-346, 729
Esteve — *Experience* p.35-36, 48-51
Evans — *Quote* p.97-110
Evans — *This* p.184-186
Evans — *Thoughts III (Open Road) See* index, no p.
Evans — *Thoughts IV* p.159, 164-167, 170, 183, 188-189, 209
Evans — *Unto See* index p.158
Flesch — *Unusual* p.19, 150-152, 154
Flint — *Graham* p.83-84
Fogg — *1000* p.11, 29, 108, 152, 217, 359, 418, 550, 580, 630, 706, 828, 863, 975, 1005, 1072
Forbes — *Thoughts See* index p.557
Fox — *Make* p.72-73
Fridy — *Meditat.* p.66, 125
Fuller — *Epigrams* p.187-190, 352-353
Garland — *Subject* p.173
Giniger — *Compact* p.35-36
Grizer — *Wit* p.278-286, 288-290
Hadfield — *Delights* p.72-127
Halverson — *Perspective* p.58, 81, 105
Harnsberger — *Mark* p.238-239
Henry — *5000* p.153-156
Hobe — *Tapestries* p.11, 40, 73, 117, 172, 175
Holmes — *Design See* index p.233
Hovey — *Treasury* p.229-232; *See* index p.298
How To Live p.169-171
Howell — *Better* p.107-116
Howell — *Lines* p.7-16, 33-39
Hubbard — *Scrap* p.5, 12, 22, 37, 69, 78, 190, 215, 228
Humes — *Instant* #626-643
Johnson — *Bedside See* index p.364
Kauffman — *For* p.130-131
Kennedy — *Reader's* #595-607
Keys Happiness p.136, 556-575
Kin — *Dictionary* p.148, 150
Kopplin — *Something* p.142-156
Krishnamurti — *Think* p.191
Lair — *Baby* p.21-23
Liddle — *Thought I, II, III See* index p.198
Liddle — *Thought IV* p.3, 7, 13, 15, 19, 22, 29, 37, 39-40, 45-46

Liddle — *Thought V* p.5, 10, 13-14, 24-25, 27, 29, 34, 36, 39, 41, 44-45
Lockridge — *World's* #1094; *See also* index p.578
Lytle — *Leaves See* index p.197
Maltz — *Creative* p.2-3, 5, 20-21, 38-50, 98-100
Mandel — *Stories* p.161-163
Modern Eloquence (14) p.369-371
Montapert — *Distilled* p.140-141, 236, 241-243
New Joy p.38, 40-41, 234
Nichols — *Third* p.45-65
Patterns For Living p.38-39, 705-827
Peterson — *Art* p.38, 48, 118, 191, 266, 325, 362, 364, 369
Phillips — *Choice* p.102, 151, 161, 170, 390; *See also* index p.427
Prochnow — *Public* #284, 1002, 1050, 1103, 2512, 2577, 2594, 2674, 2698, 2703, 2727; *See also* index p.501
Prochnow — *Speaker's* p.190-194
Prochnow — *Success.* #399, 452, 558, 749, 1111, 1328, 1386, 1981-1985, 1999-2007
Pullar-Strecker — *Proverbs* #1-50
Reader's — *Getting* p.226-228
Reader's — *20th* p.5-7
Rogers — *Time* p.113-118
Seldes — *Great* p.332-333, 609-615
Sheban — *Wisdom* no p.
Speaker's Desk p.127-132
Strait — *Speaker's* p.100-109
Streiker — *Who* p.87-118, 189-216
Taylor — *With* p.119-121, 144-145
Voss — *Quotations* p.32-33, 162-166
Wallis — *Treasure* p.7, 18, 23, 25, 47, 90, 120, 138, 149, 151, 159-164, 226, 231
Wallis — *Words* p.3, 13, 19, 43, 45, 51, 66, 122, 137, 147-154
Woods — *Content.* p.21-57, 97, 112, 200, 234, 284, 286, 309, 313
Woods — *Religious* p.305-306, 543-549
Woods — *Wellsprings* p.23-42
Zobell — *Speaker's* p.87-92
, Absurdity of
Webb — *Edge* p.13-14
, Abundant
Hubbard — *Scrap* p.13
Hunter — *Gems* p.2-3
Kohn — *Adventures* p.93-95
Phillips — *Choice* p.67
, Active
Maltz — *Creative* p.145-146
, Aim of. See **Life and living, Purpose of**
, and art
Saturday — *Advent.* p.148-160
, and death
See also **Death**
Grizer — *Wit* p.287
Hubbard — *Scrap* p.43
Seldes — *Great* p.615
Woods — *Religious* p.548-549
, and love
Hubbard — *Scrap* p.173, 184, 201
, and moment
Adams — *New* p.324
, and sea
Adams — *New* p.157, 397
, and sorrow
Hubbard — *Scrap* p.193
, and thought
Hubbard — *Scrap* p.69
, and value
Wheelis — *Moralist* p.8
, Art of
Adams — *New* p.338
Alexander's Treasure. p.142
Flesch — *Unusual* p.13-14
How To Live p.224
Liebman — *Hope* p.182-239
Montapert — *Distilled* p.243
Nichols — *New* p.22-23
Peterson — *Art* p.330, 410
Peterson — *Twenty* p.38-39
, Artificial production of
Woods — *Religious* p.546
, as discipline
Adams — *New* p.264
, as drama
Hubbard — *Scrap* p.195
, as football
Welk — *Guide.* p.130-132
, as function
Adams — *New* p.87
, as inheritance
Hubbard — *Scrap* p.71
, as mirror
Hubbard — *Scrap* p.92
, as succession of events
Hubbard — *Scrap* p.53
, as tragedy
Hubbard — *Scrap* p.147
, Assignment of
Fox — *Make* p.170
, Beauty in
Curtis — *Daily* p.147
Hubbard — *Scrap* p.66
, Beginning of
See also **Birth**
Nichols — *New* p.5-6
Peterson — *Art* p.86
, Better
White — *Life* p.1-5

, Bridge of
Guideposts — *Faith* p.353
, Broken
Baillie — *Diary* #358
, Challenge of
Holmes — *Design* p.57-58
, Choosing
Mandelbaum — *Choose* p.3-49
, Climate of
Kohn — *Touch* p.11-17
, Consecrated
Hubbard — *Scrap* p.60, 87, 98
, Continuance of
Nichols — *New* p.161, 172-173
, Creative
Peterson — *Art* p.110, 362
, "Crossroads" in
Peale — *Guideposts* p.133-154
, Cycle of
Bartlett — *Discovery* p.92
, Daily routine of
Bach — *Make* p.93-105
Bennett — *How* p.21-41, 97-103
Clark — *Windows* p.62
Evans — *Unto* p.101, 121
Flesch — *Unusual* p.80
Irion — *Yes* p.51-53
Peterson — *Art* p.212
White — *Job* p.28-31
Words Change p.114-122
, Definition of
See also **Life and living, Meaning of; Life and living, Purpose of**
Montapert — *Distilled* p.236-237
, Depth of
Peterson — *Art* p.349
, Dignity of
Adams — *New* p.408
, Dimensions of
Kohn — *Best* p.50
Peterson — *Art* p.153
, Distractions of
Lindbergh — *Gift* p.29-30
, Double
Adams — *New* p.223
, Duty of
Hubbard — *Scrap* p.79
, End of
See also **Death; Words, Dying**
Hubbard — *Scrap* p.27
, Energy of
Krishnamurti — *Think* p.185-193
, Enjoyment of
How To Live p.172-173
Hubbard — *Scrap* p.46, 57, 66, 101, 135
, Expectancy of
Dirksen — *Quot.* #39, 2370
, Extension of
Reader's — *Getting* p.204
, Facing
See also **Life and living, New**
Maltz — *Creative* p.138-140
, Facts of
Words — *Inspir.* p.208
, Faith in
Kauffman — *For* p.79-80
, Fear of
Kennedy — *Fresh* p.151-154
, First
Du Noüy — *Human* p.34-36
, Fourth dimension of
Curtis — *New* p.85-98
, Full
Redhead — *Living* p.7-16
, Game of
Forbes — *Thoughts* p.11, 17, 45, 60, 107, 170, 433, 443, 446
Lair — *Baby* p.81-82, 107
Montapert — *Distilled* p.167-168
, Generous
Hubbard — *Scrap* p.218
, Gift of
Peterson — *Art* p.56
, Good
Bartlett — *Discovery* p.153-154
Montapert — *Distilled* p.238
Tanksley — *Friend* p.75
, Growth of
Hubbard — *Scrap* p.44
, Ideal
Hubbard — *Scrap* p.48
, Ideals of
Hubbard — *Scrap* p.72
, Imaginary
Adams — *New* p.5
, Incommunicables of
Adams — *New* p.100
, Influences of
Hubbard — *Scrap* p.67
, Interest in
Peale — *Stay* p.105-120
, Journey of
Hubbard — *Scrap* p.73
Montapert — *Distilled* p.328
, Ladder of
Hubbard — *Scrap* p.182
, Larger
Holmes — *Design* p.172-178
, Law of
Phillips — *Choice* p.9
, Length of
See also **Old age**
How To Live p.172-173
Kohn — *Thoughts* p.116-121

Montapert — *Distilled* p.237-238
Peterson — *Art* p.232
, *Levels of*
Wheelis — *Moralist* p.102-105
Words Change p.40-43
, *Looking at*
Kohn — *Pathways* p.45-83
, *Love of*
Hubbard — *Scrap* p.47, 181
Nichols — *Third* p.76-77
, *Meaning of*
See also **Life and living, Definition of; Life and living, Purpose of**
Adams — *New* p.174
Franke — *Buckley* p.190
Hubbard — *Scrap* p.68
Maltz — *Creative* p.8-9
Peterson — *Art* p.341
Phillips — *Choice* p.330
Wheelis — *Moralist* p.29-30, 39-41
Woods — *Religious* p.546-548
Words Change p.40-91
, *Meaningless*
Price — *Wider* p.205-214
, *Mistakes of*
Hubbard — *Scrap* p.57
, *Modern*
Adams — *New* p.179
Krishnamurti — *Urgency* p.18-26
Woods — *Religious* p.639
, *Multiple*
Peterson — *Art* p.356
, *Mystery of*
Hubbard — *Scrap* p.76
Kohn — *Pathways* p.177-196
Saturday — *Advent.* p.33-46
, *Natural*
New Topical p.152-153
, *New*
Flesch — *Unusual* p.95
Holmes — *Design* p.98-109, 195-203
Kohn — *Adventures* p.128
, *of dreams*
Adams — *New* p.412
, *of night*
Adams — *New* p.102
, *Paradoxical*
Baillie — *Diary* #116
, *Power of*
Adams — *New* p.286
Maltz — *Creative* p.22-37
, *Preparation for*
Hubbard — *Scrap* p.110
Kohn — *Thoughts* p.147-153
, *Principles of*
Montapert — *Distilled* p.239
Peale — *Guideposts* p.41-45
, *Priorities of*
Words Change p.80-83
, *Privileges of*
Hubbard — *Scrap* p.136
, *Process of*
Lair — *Baby* p.126
, *Prolonging of*
How To Live p.372-378
, *Propagation of*
Wheelis — *Moralist* p.155
, *Purpose of*
See also **Life and living, Definition of; Life and living, Meaning of**
Adams — *New* p.374
Curtis — *Human* p.15, 55-56, 58-59, 61, 63-64, 72-75, 172
Evans — *Thoughts IV* p.167, 173, 178, 189, 198
Hubbard — *Scrap* p.22, 30, 73, 84
Hunter — *Gems* p.86-87
Kennedy — *Fresh* p.180-183
Kennedy — *Reader's* #893-896
Montapert — *Distilled* p.238-240
Sheen — *Content.* p.93-95
Welk — *Guide.* p.42-45
Wilcox — *Heart* p.63-65
, *Real*
Krishnamurti — *Think* p.64
, *"Rearview"*
Evans — *Thoughts I* p.78-79
, *Retirement from*
See also **Retirement**
Maltz — *Creative* p.102-103
, *Reverence for*
Guideposts — *Faith* p.420-423
, *Reward of*
Montapert — *Distilled* p.240
Woods — *Content.* p.19-57
, *River of*
Hubbard — *Scrap* p.164
Krishnamurti — *Think* p.125-132
, *Roles in*
Peterson — *Art* p.236
, *Rules of*
Dirksen — *Quot.* #1057, 2320
Flesch — *Unusual* p.248-249
, *Sacredness of*
Hubbard — *Scrap* p.129
Hunter — *Gems* p.95
, *Sailors and*
Words — *Inspir.* p.87
, *Screen of*
Peterson — *Art* p.388

, *Seeing*
Patterns For Living p.3-11
, *Seriousness of*
Sherman — *Your* p.90-103
, *Shadows of*
Bradshaw — *Home.* p.103-111
, *Simple*
Adams — *New* p.79
Hobe — *Tapestries* p.114
, *Spiritual*
See also **Spirituality**
Hubbard — *Scrap* p.165, 171
New Topical p.152-153
, *Standards of*
Dirksen — *Quot.* #518, 771
, *Strong*
Hubbard — *Scrap* p.47
, *Struggle for*
Patterns For Living p.469-472
, *Successful*
Holmes — *Design* p.129-134
, *Thought of*
Hubbard — *Scrap* p.118
, *Time for*
Peterson — *New* p.28-29
, *to the point*
Adams — *New* p.2
, *Touched*
Peterson — *Art* p.279
, *Trials of*
Hubbard — *Scrap* p.68
, *Value of*
Baillie — *Diary* #85
Bartlett — *Discovery* p.45-46, 144-145
Jones — *If* p.150-155
Kopplin — *Something* p.108-118
Liebman — *Hope* p.240-250
, *Victory of*
Hubbard — *Scrap* p.111
, *Waste of*
Hubbard — *Scrap* p.72
, *Ways of*
Nichols — *New* p.217-232
Nichols — *Third* p.177-191
, *Weapons of*
Evans — *This* p.170-171
, *Wholeness of*
Adams — *New* p.98
Krishnamurti — *Think* p.45-50
, *with others*
Hobe — *Tapestries* p.35
Peterson — *Twenty* p.52-53
White — *Life* p.289-299
, *with world*
Nichols — *New* p.141, 160
, *Wonder of*
Kennedy — *Fresh* p.34-36
, *Zest of*
Alexander's Treasure. p.165
Woods — *Content.* p.19-57

LIFE EVERLASTING. *See* **Immortality**

LIFE INSURANCE. *See* **Insurance, Life**

LIFEGUARDS
Kin — *Dictionary* p.148
Prochnow — *Public* #374

LIFELESSNESS
Prochnow — *Public* #2178

LIGHT
See also **Dawn; Day; Knowledge; Sun; Understanding; Wisdom**
Applegarth — *Heir.* p.16, 166, 215
Dirksen — *Quot.* #997, 1437-1438
Du Noüy — *Road* p.31, 40, 43, 57, 58, 70
Edwards — *Useful* p.346-347
Flesch — *Unusual* p.152
Forbes — *Thoughts* p.209, 275, 304, 483, 520
Fuller — *Epigrams* p.190
Garland — *Subject* p.173-174, 256
Harnsberger — *Mark* p.240
Henry — *5000* p.156-157
Hovey — *Treasury* p.232-233; *See also* index p.298
Hubbard — *Scrap* p.68, 93
Keller — *Open* p.136
Keys Happiness p.209-212
Kin — *Dictionary* p.34, 148
Knight's Illus. p.187-188
Knight's Treas. p.202-205
Kohn — *Adventures* p.117-120
Lockridge — *World's* #2914, 2975, 2979, 3093-3094, 3560, 4166, 4520
Lytle — *Leaves* p.24, 108, 125
Mandel — *Stories* p.163-164
New Topical p.153
Peale — *Courage* p.70-71, 105, 227
Peterson — *Art* p.36, 298, 300, 336
Phillips — *Choice* p.92-93, 313
Prochnow — *Public* #2605-2606, 2681
Prochnow — *Success.* #1066
Seldes — *Great* p.616
Sheban — *Wisdom* no p.
Wallis — *Treasure* p.157, 168, 221
Wallis — *Words* p.3, 7, 13, 24, 33, 35, 62, 98, 102, 118, 153
Woods — *Religious* p.45, 550-553
Woods — *Wellsprings* p.33

, *Belief in*
Kohn — *Adventures* p.71-74
, *from sky*
Woods — *Wellsprings* p.73
, *Hiding our*
Carruthers — *Sparks* p.150-151
, *in ourselves*
Adams — *New* p.219
, *Refraction of*
Curtis — *Practical* p.245

LIGHTHOUSE KEEPERS
Lytle — *Leaves* p.54

LIGHTNING
Asimov — *Treasury* #469
Clark — *Windows* p.104-105
Harnsberger — *Mark* p.240-241
Kin — *Dictionary* p.149

LIGHTNING BUGS
Prochnow — *Success.* #1135

LIKING. *See* **Affection; Admiration; Esteem**

LILIES
Applegarth — *Heir.* p.103
Kin — *Dictionary* p.149
Prochnow — *Public* #2618

LILITH (Biblical)
Lockridge — *World's* #4104

LIMERICKS
Asimov — *Treasury* #439, 630-634
Cerf — *Laugh* p.319-324
Copeland — *10,000* p.939-956
Fun Fare p.165-166

LIMESTONE
Auden — *Certain* p.216-218

LIMITATIONS
Alexander's Treasure. p.303
Dirksen — *Quot.* #998
Emmons — *Mature* p.66
Evans — *Faith* p.20, 39
Evans — *Unto* p.116, 143
Flesch — *Unusual* p.152
Holmes — *Design* p.29-38, 44, 64-68, 191-192
Keller — *Open* p.134
Kin — *Dictionary* p.149
Kohn — *Pathways* p.19-23, 127-129, 137-139
Kohn — *Touch* p.51-56
Lytle — *Leaves* p.72
Prochnow — *Public* #2419
Prochnow — *Success.* #1988
Sheban — *Wisdom* no p.
Sheen — *Content.* p.53-54
Sheen — *Thoughts* p.81-83
Speaker's Desk #46
Woods — *Religious* p.553
, *and morality*
Wheelis — *Moralist* p.49, 52-54, 74

LINCOLN, ABRAHAM
Applegarth — *Heir.* p.67
Botkin — *Anecdotes See* index p.314
Botkin — *Treasury* p.6, 148, 256-261, 360, 406-407, 416
Copeland — *10,000* p.795-805
Curtis — *Practical* p.569
Evans — *This* p.130, 133-134
Evans — *Thoughts III (Open Road)* p.176, 197
Evans — *Thoughts IV* p.187-188
Henry — *5000* p.157-158
Holman — *Psych.* p.93-94
Hovey — *Treasury* #2, 68, 282, 587, 708, 1033, 1069, 1191, 1306, 1600
Hubbard — *Scrap* p.37, 45, 72, 134
Kohn — *Best* p.109-111
Kohn — *Touch* p.101-104
Liddle — *Thought I, II, III* p.18, 62, 109, 131
Modern Eloquence (14) p.67-82
New Joy p.86-92
Nichols — *Third* p.189-191
Peterson — *Art* p.63-64
Reader's — *20th* p.13, 71-75
Schermerhorn — *1500* p.234-235
Seldes — *Great* p.616
Wallis — *Treasure* p.3, 47, 114, 151, 171
Wallis — *Words* p.92
Woods — *Tapestries* p.22
Woods — *Wellsprings* p.26-27, 55-56
, *Disappointments of*
Manchee — *Secret* p.142-143
, *Letter from*
Hubbard — *Scrap* p.133

LINDBERGH, CHARLES
, *Famous flight of*
Fogg — *1000* #1000

LINE
Evans — *Thoughts I* p.59-60, 91, 117-118
Flesch — *Unusual* p.152-153
Prochnow — *Success.* #1990

LINEAGE. *See* **Ancestry; Genealogy; Heritage**

LINGERING. *See* **Delay**

LINGUISTS
Prochnow — *Public* #492

LIONS
Applegarth — *Heir.* p.25
Asimov — *Treasury* #277
Botkin — *Anecdotes* p.270
Henry — *5000* p.158
Kin — *Dictionary* p.149
New Topical p.153-154
Prochnow — *Public* #2565

LIONS CLUB
Harral — *Feature* p.209

LIPS. *See* **Mouth, Lips of**

LIQUOR
See also **Alcoholism**
Alexander's Treasure. p.180
Harnsberger — *Mark* p.241-243
White — *Life* p.113-120

LIQUOR DEALERS
Manchee — *Secret* p.218

LISTENERS AND LISTENING
See also **Hearing; Understanding**
Albert — *Stop* p.39, 41, 49
Baillie — *Diary* #44, 314
Braude — *Source* #1035-1038
Cerf — *Laugh* p.31-35
Dirksen — *Quot.* #148
Emmons — *Mature* p.9
Flesch — *Unusual* p.153
Fuller — *Epigrams* p.190-191
Grizer — *Wit* p.287-288
Henry — *5000* p.158
How To Live p.32-35, 265-266
Kauffman — *For* p.131-132
Keys Happiness p.347-350
Kin — *Dictionary* p.78, 149
Krishnamurti — *Think* p.32-37
Liddle — *Thought I, II, III* p.13, 19, 85, 121, 136, 153, 159
Maltz — *Creative* p.195-196
Mandel — *Stories* p.164-165
Menninger — *Blue.* p.196-198
Montapert — *Distilled* p.241
Peterson — *New* p.38-39
Prochnow — *Public* #830, 1342, 4404
Prochnow — *Success.* #673, 1991-1993
Unlimited Power p.235-239
Wallis — *Words* p.88
, Creative
Peterson — *Art* p.223

LITANY
Applegarth — *Heir.* p.253
More Words p.102-104

LITERALISM
Speaker's Desk See index p.302

LITERARY CRITICISM
Harnsberger — *Mark* p.243-245
Harral — *Feature* p.209
Simpson — *Contemp.* p.382-387

LITERATURE
See also **Books and reading**
Braude — *Speaker's* #826-827
Copeland — *10,000* p.49-53
Edwards — *Useful* p.347-348, 729-730
Flesch — *Unusual* p.153
Forbes — *Thoughts* p.137, 207, 209, 232, 289, 386, 399
Fuller — *Epigrams* p.191
Fuller — *Thesaurus* p.200-220
Harnsberger — *Mark* p.246
Harral — *Feature* p.209
Henry — *5000* p.158-159
Kennedy — *Reader's* #608-609
Kronenberger — *Animal* p.168-173
Liddle — *Thought I, II, III* p.16, 82, 102, 124, 143
Lockridge — *World's See* index p.578
Prochnow — *Public* #3310-3313, 4314, 4349
Prochnow — *Speaker's* p.194
Prochnow — *Success.* #1994-1996
Seldes — *Great* p.616-617
Wilcox — *Heart* p.40-41
Woods — *Religious* p.553-555
, Functions of
Hubbard — *Scrap* p.64, 81
, Hoaxes in
Harnsberger — *Mark* p.245-246
, Sacred
Phillips — *Choice* p.190, 383
, Taste in
Adams — *New* p.207
, Tendencies in
Speaker's Desk #124, 334, 577, 892

"LITTLE AUDREY" STORIES
Botkin — *Anecdotes* p.256
Botkin — *Treasury* p.359, 372

"LITTLE MORON" JOKES
Asimov — *Treasury* #252

"LITTLE SLAMS"
Prochnow — *Success.* #985

"LITTLE THINGS"
Adams — *New* p.26, 400

Alexander's Treasure. p.184, 188, 218, 255, 258, 295-296, 304
Applegarth — *Heir.* p.84
Braude — *Source* #1039-1046
Edwards — *Useful* p.348-349, 658-659
Evans — *Faith* p.36, 98-100, 115-116, 225-226
Evans — *Thoughts I* p.218-219
Evans — *Thoughts II (Open Door)* p.59-60, 66-67
Evans — *Thoughts III (Open Road)* p.110-111, 118, 198-199
Evans — *Thoughts IV* p.44-45, 164-165, 204-205
Flesch — *Unusual* p.294-295
Forbes — *Thoughts* p.78, 216, 462
Fuller — *Epigrams* p.283-284
Hadfield — *Love* p.21
Hovey — *Treasury* p.233; #530, 1158, 1425-1427, 1529
Kin — *Dictionary* p.258-259
Knight's Illus. p.209-210
Knight's Treas. p.367-370
Kohn — *Pathways* p.159-165
Kohn — *Touch* p.37-41
Liddle — *Thought I, II, III* p.10, 30, 35, 38, 51, 68, 70, 82, 96, 132, 149, 183
Lockridge — *World's* #42, 382, 515, 713, 1630
Lytle — *Leaves* p.6, 136, 175, 178
Manchee — *Secret* p.101-103
Mandel — *Stories* p.255-256
Nichols — *New* p.153-154
Nichols — *Third* p.76-77
Peale — *Courage* p.182
Peterson — *Art* p.31, 365
Prochnow — *Public* #2307, 3799-3804
Prochnow — *Success.* #1997-1998
Pullar-Strecker — *Proverbs* #19
Reader's — *Getting* p.77
Woods — *Wellsprings* p.63
, Historical
Curtis — *Practical* p.140-143
, Important
Wilcox — *Heart* p.72-73
, Magnitude of
Book Proverbs p.66
, Prayer for
Unlimited Power p.222, 243

"LITTLE WILLIES"
Copeland — *10,000* p.956-958

LITTLENESS
See also **Size**
Flesch — *Unusual* p.153-154
Halverson — *Perspective* p.102
Kin — *Dictionary* p.149-150, 259

Lockridge — *World's* #2903, 3067, 3569, 4523

LITURGY
Lockridge — *World's* #5286
More Words p.104-105
Woods — *Religious* p.555-557
, and Christian living
McDonagh — *Invit. p.96-108*
, Petition in
McDonagh — *Invit.* p.105-106
, Reform of
Auden — *Certain* p.225-226

LIVABILITY
Harral — *Feature* p.210

LIVELIHOOD. *See* **Jobs; Occupations; Professions; Wages;** etc.

LIVELINESS. *See* **Vivacity**

LIVING. *See* **Life and living**

LIZARDS
Du Noüy — *Human* p.68-69
Kin — *Dictionary* p.150

LOAFING. *See* **Ease; Laziness; Rest**

LOANS. *See* **Lending and loans**

LOATHING. *See* **Hatred**

LOBSTERS
Lockridge — *World's* #2678

"LOCAL COLOR"
See also names of places
Botkin — *Treasury* p.272, 491-492
Fun Fare p.214-216

LOCKS
Kin — *Dictionary* p.150
Peterson — *Art* p.297

LOCOMOTIVES
Applegarth — *Heir.* p.279

LOCUSTS
Fox — *Make* p.95-96
New Topical p.154
Sagendorph — *Old* p.285-287

LODGES
Harral — *Feature* p.210

LOGGING CAMPS
Botkin — *Anecdotes* p.280

LOGIC
See also **Reason and reasoning**
Auden — *Certain* p.226-228

Braude — *Speaker's* #830
Braude — *Stories* p.229
Curtis — *Practical* p.74, 391, 402
Dirksen — *Quot.* #999, 1800
Edwards — *Useful* p.349-350
Flesch — *Unusual* p.154-155
Forbes — *Thoughts* p.347, 509
Fuller — *Epigrams* p.191
Fun Fare p.264-265
Garland — *Subject* p.175
Ginott — *Between* p.55-56, 127-136
Harnsberger — *Mark* p.246-247
Henry — *5000* p.159
Johnson — *Bedside* p.141
Kin — *Dictionary* p.66, 150
Lockridge — *World's* #2484
Mandel — *Stories* p.165-166
Prochnow — *Public* #69, 275, 609, 900
Prochnow — *Speaker's* p.195
Speaker's Desk See index p.302

LOGICAL POSITIVISM. *See* **Positivism, Logical**

LOGOS
See also **God, Word of**
Woods — *Religious* p.557

LOITERING. *See* **Idleness;** etc.

LONDON
Flesch — *Unusual* p.155
Henry — *5000* p.159
Lockridge — *World's* #1977, 3158, 3160, 5149, 5200, 5491
Woods — *Content.* p.67, 122, 349

"LONE RANGER"
Asimov — *Treasury* #432
Prochnow — *Success.* #1158

LONELINESS
See also **Grief; Solitude;** etc.
Adams — *New* p.323
Auden — *Certain* p.347-348
Blanton — *Faith* p.158-181
Braude — *Source* #1049-1050
Dirksen — *Quot.* #447, 2311
Edwards — *Useful* p.730
Emmons — *Mature* p.17
Evans — *Faith* p.5-6, 60, 185, 221
Evans — *Thoughts I* p.21, 131-132, 221-222
Evans — *Thoughts III (Open Road)* p.15-17, 20, 22, 32, 122, 148, 185-186, 191
Evans — *Thoughts IV* p.78, 107, 155-156, 159, 177, 179-180
Evans — *Unto* p.3, 29, 36, 129
Flesch — *Unusual* p.155
Flint — *Graham* p.84-85
Forbes — *Thoughts* p.79, 391, 455
Garland — *Subject* p.176
Grizer — *Wit* p.290
Harnsberger — *Mark* p.247
Hobe — *Tapestries* p.27-32
Hovey — *Treasury* #74, 452, 506, 1094, 1228
Huxley — *You* p.286
Keller — *Open* p.33
Liddle — *Thought I, II, III* p.126, 140
Lockridge — *World's* #1279, 3845, 4462
Maltz — *Creative* p.89, 165-176
Mandel — *Stories* p.166
Montapert — *Distilled* p.243-244
Patterns For Living p.645-652
Peale — *Faith* p.163-189
Phillips — *Choice* p.277-278
Prochnow — *Public* #2183, 4405
Prochnow — *Success.* #1311
Seldes — *Great* p.617
Tanksley — *Friend* p.43
Taylor — *With* p.17
Wallis — *Treasure* p.102, 234
Woods — *Religious* p.557-558
, Freedom from
Price — *Wider* p.193-202

LONGEVITY. *See* **Old age**

LONGING
See also **Desire**
Lytle — *Leaves* p.108
Phillips — *Choice* p.208
Sheban — *Wisdom* no p.
Wallis — *Words* p.86

"LONG-WINDEDNESS"
Braude — *Speaker's* #831-836
Fuller — *Thesaurus* #341-363
Humes — *Instant* p.1-5

LOOKS. *See* **Appearance; Beauty; Fashion;** etc.

LOQUACITY
See also **Talk; Words;** etc.
Adams — *New* p.8
Baillie — *Diary* #311
Braude — *Source* #1648
Braude — *Speaker's* #1563-1565
Edwards — *Useful* p.350-351, 678
Kin — *Dictionary* p.151
Phillips — *Choice* p.240, 271
Prochnow — *Public* #663
Speaker's Desk #58, 73, 351

LORD. *See* **God; Jesus Christ**

LORD'S DAY. *See* **Sabbath**

LORD'S PRAYER. *See* **Prayer, Lord's**

LORD'S SUPPER. *See* **Communion**

LORDS AND LORDSHIPS
Flesch — *Unusual* p.155
Webb — *Edge* p.51-56

LOS ANGELES, CALIFORNIA
Asimov — *Treasury* #448

LOSING AND LOSSES
See also **Adversity; Misfortune; Waste**
Book Proverbs p.131
Dirksen — *Quot.* #2063-2064
Edwards — *Useful* p.351
Evans — *This* p.42-43
Flesch — *Unusual* p.155-156
Forbes — *Thoughts* p.384, 422, 444, 469, 493, 505
Garland — *Subject* p.177
Grizer — *Wit* p.290-291
Holmes — *I've* p.110
Kin — *Dictionary* p.151-152
Lockridge — *World's* #1429
Lytle — *Leaves* p.22, 178
Prochnow — *Public* #32, 4152-4153
Prochnow — *Success.* #365, 2002
Safian — *More* p.127-129
Tanksley — *Friend* p.64

"LOST"
Dirksen — *Quot.* #4
Grizer — *Wit* p.291
Guideposts — *Faith* p.291-295
Harnsberger — *Mark* p.247-248
Hovey — *Treasury* #439, 917, 1137, 1453, 1693, 1725
Irion — *Yes* p.7-9
Knight's Illus. p.190-195
Knight's Treas. p.208-211
Mandel — *Stories* p.166-167
Prochnow — *Public* #99, 381, 596, 625
Prochnow — *Success.* #794
Reader's — *Getting* p.199
Speaker's Desk #2, 246, 758, 1071, 1134

LOTS, BUILDING
Kohn — *Adventures* p.67

LOTTERY
Kin — *Dictionary* p.152
Prochnow — *Public* #1480
Prochnow — *Success.* #929

"LOTUS EATERS"
Prochnow — *Public* #2344

LOUDNESS. *See* **Noise**

LOUIS XIV
Flesch — *Unusual* p.156

LOUISIANA
Botkin — *Anecdotes* p.46, 50, 70, 244-245
Botkin — *Treasury* p.3, 674-676, 678-689, 805, 908

LOUISIANA-FRENCH
Botkin — *Treasury* p.674-676, 678

"LOUISIANA PURCHASE"
Braude — *Stories* p.168-169

LOURDES
Guideposts — *Faith* p.31-32
Phillips — *Choice* p.172

LOVE
See also **Affection; Courtship; Desire; Marriage; Romance; Self-love;** etc.
Albert — *Stop* p.150-151, 153
Alexander's Treasure. p.26-27, 66-71, 140-141
Applegarth — *Heir.* p.77, 142, 171-179, 298
Baillie — *Diary* #99, 361
Barker — *Treat* p.47-66
Barrows — *1000* p.441-442
Bartlett — *Discovery* p.156-157
Blanton — *Faith* p.182-203
Book Proverbs p.29
Braude — *Source* #1051-1064
Braude — *Speaker's* #837
Clark — *Windows* p.76
Copeland — *10,000* p.197-226, 990-992
Curtis — *Daily* p.133-138
Curtis — *Golden* p.111-114, 136-137, 169, 171
Curtis — *Human* p.135-149
Curtis — *Practical* p.114, 148, 487-496
Detherage — *Sunrise* p.71-72, 74-82, 119, 121, 130, 147, 183, 186
Dirksen — *Quot.* #160, 194, 1439-1441, 1487, 2297
Droke — *Christian* p.318-322
Edwards — *Useful* p.351-359, 730
Emmons — *Mature* p.102-106
Esteve — *Experience* p.119-123
Evans — *Faith* p.43-44, 79
Evans — *Quote* p.177-186
Evans — *Thoughts I* p.24-25, 73, 101-102, 111, 113, 123-124, 143, 201
Evans — *Thoughts II (Open Door)* p.21-25, 43-46, 105-110, 113-115, 138, 169-170, 187

Evans — *Thoughts III (Open Road)* p.15, 20-23, 49, 69, 77, 98, 141, 156
Evans — *Thoughts IV* p.41, 116-117, 155
Evans — *Unto* p.36, 117
Felleman — *Poems* p.93-122
Flesch — *Unusual* p.156-158
Flint — *Graham* p.85-87
Fogg — *1000* #696, 717
Forbes — *Thoughts See* index p.557
Fox — *Make* p.37
Fridy — *Meditat.* p.95
Fuller — *Epigrams* p.192-199, 353-355
Fuller — *Thesaurus* p.148-152
Garland — *Subject* p.177-178
Giniger — *Compact* p.204-267
Ginott — *Between* p.215-216
Gold — *Letters* p.3-14
Grizer — *Wit* p.291-292
Guideposts — *Faith* p.64, 70-72, 184, 403-407
Hadfield — *Delights* p.128
Harnsberger — *Mark* p.248-249
Henry — *5000* p.159-164
Hobe — *Tapestries* p.33, 35-36, 67, 87, 101, 106, 119-135, 154, 166
Holmes — *Design See* index p.233
Holmes — *I've* p.42-43
Hovey — *Treasury* p.233-236; *See also* index p.298
How To Live p.27-31, 40-42, 53-56, 73-77, 387-390
Howell — *Better* p.117-124
Howell — *Lines* p.17-24
Hubbard — *Scrap* p.8, 109, 126, 128, 140, 147, 158, 190, 204, 223
Hunter — *Gems* p.45-46
Johnson — *Bedside* p.4, 21, 148-166, 202, 206, 225-226, 232, 298, 303
Kahn — *Lessons* p.56-61, 170-176
Kennedy — *Reader's* #610-619
Keys Happiness p.11-15, 174-183, 196-200, 277-280, 288, 304-306, 446-448, 477-479, 484
Kin — *Dictionary* p.152-153
Knight's Illus. p.197-199
Knight's Treas. p.213-216
Kopplin — *Something* p.93-102
Lair — *Baby* p.22, 26-28, 41-56, 171-186
Langdon — *Teach.* p.101-110
Liddle — *Thought I, II, III See* index p.198
Liddle — *Thought IV* p.11-12, 18, 22-23, 27, 37-38, 41, 45
Liddle — *Thought V* p.8, 10-11, 31, 33, 37, 44, 46
Liebman — *Peace* p.38-80
Lindbergh — *Unicorn* p.9-18
Lockridge — *World's See* index p.578-579
Lytle — *Leaves* p.34, 77, 80, 84, 102, 125, 154, 164
McCracken — *What* p.89-94
Maltz — *Creative* p.60-62
Mandel — *Stories* p.167-171
Mandelbaum — *Choose* p.42-45
Menninger — *Blue.* p.46-49
Miller — *Harvest* p.23-28
Modern Eloquence (14) p.121-131, 372-373
More Words p.105-106, 108
Morris — *1000 See* index p.431
Myers — *Thunder* p.164-176
New Joy p.65, 102, 105, 113, 144, 206
Nichols — *New* p.131
Nichols — *Third* p.68-87
Patterns For Living p.114-126, 126-132
Peale — *Courage* p.129-159
Peale — *Faith* p.191-217
Peterson — *Art* p.187, 305, 311, 324-325, 360
Peterson — *New* p.60-61
Petty — *Promises* p.9-17
Petty — *Wings* p.9-19
Phillips — *Choice See* index p.427
Price — *Wider* p.29-30
Prochnow — *Public See* index p.502
Prochnow — *Speaker's* p.196-199
Prochnow — *Success.* #212
Schermerhorn — *1500* p.237-239
Seldes — *Great* p.618-620
Sheen — *Thoughts* p.25-41
Sheen — *Way* p.45-47, 61-82
Simpson — *Contemp.* p.227-236
Speaker's Desk p.132-137; #174, 191, 350, 522, 614, 761, 829
Strait — *Speaker's* p.110-115
Streiker — *Who* p.147-187
Tanksley — *Friend* p.17, 59
Unlimited Power p.367
Voss — *Quotations* p.166-170
Wallis — *Treasure* p.31, 41-42, 75, 96, 101, 106, 112, 130, 138, 146, 165-170, 222
Wallis — *Words* p.28-30, 37, 43, 49, 62, 82, 86, 117, 138, 144, 155-160, 167
Watson — *Light* p.239-258
Woods — *Content.* p.121-136, 146-147
Woods — *Inspir.* p.241-283
Woods — *Religious* p.558-571
Words — *Inspir.* p.43, 63-64, 204
Zobell — *Speaker's* p.92-93
, and beauty
Hubbard — *Scrap* p.55-56

, *and death*
Hubbard — *Scrap* p.204
, *and friendship*
Flesch — *Unusual* p.157
Prochnow — *Success.* #2003-2004
, *and fulfillment*
Taylor — *With* p.93-97
, *and growth*
Adams — *New* p.341
, *and hate*
Adams — *New* p.333
Braude — *Stories* p.229-233
Flesch — *Unusual* p.158
Holman — *Psych.* p.115-125
, *and kindness*
Mandel — *Stories* p.171-172
, *and knowledge*
Adams — *New* p.326
, *and marriage*
See also **Marriage**
Cowan — *Wit* p.80-92
, *and peace*
Hunter — *Gems* p.48-49
, *and regret*
Adams — *New* p.115
, *and separation*
Taylor — *With* p.8-11
, *and sex*
Day — *Meditations* p.37
Ginott — *Between* p.175-176
Krishnamurti — *Urgency* p.73-76
, *and skill*
Hubbard — *Scrap* p.79
, *and transcendence*
Wheelis — *Moralist* p.29
, *Art of*
Maurois — *Art* p.1-36
, *as a bridge*
Adams — *New* p.349-350
, *as a river*
Hubbard — *Scrap* p.52
, *as unity*
Clark — *Windows* p.112
, *Beginning of*
Nichols — *Third* p.68
, *Blindness of*
Baillie — *Diary* #179
, *Christian*
Kohn — *Adventures* p.46-49
, *Compared to justice*
Wheelis — *Moralist* p.48-50
, *Consciousness of*
Hubbard — *Scrap* p.66
, *Curve of*
Sheen — *Content.* p.29-32
, *Definitions of*
Nizer — *Thinking* p.198-199
, *Eternal*
Keller — *Open* p.126
, *Exclusive*
Adams — *New* p.273
, *Experience of*
Sheen — *Content.* p.21-23
, *Failure to*
Peterson — *Art* p.104
, *False*
Woods — *Religious* p.324
, *Fear of losing*
Hill — *Think* p.273-274
, *Field of*
Hubbard — *Scrap* p.69
, *First*
Hadfield — *Love* p.51, 55
Sheban — *Wisdom* no p.
, *Free*
Lockridge — *World's* #3651, 4197
Seldes — *Great* p.399-400
, *God's. See* **God, Love of**
, *Great*
Guideposts — *Faith* p.326-330
, *Healing of*
Peale — *Guideposts* p.243-244
, *in practice*
Kauffman — *For* p.132-134
, *in wartime*
Kauffman — *For* p.134-135
, *Intensity of*
Montapert — *Distilled* p.244-245
, *is relatedness*
Liebman — *Hope* p.119-133
, *Joy of*
Keller — *Open* p.35
, *Lack of*
Lair — *Baby* p.33
, *Language of*
Hubbard — *Scrap* p.38
, *Mature*
See also **Love, Middle-aged**
Ginott — *Between* p.175-176
Nichols — *Third* p.71
, *Medicine for*
Hadfield — *Delights* p.141
, *Mental*
Lair — *Baby* p.180-181
, *Middle-aged*
Adams — *New* p.56
, *Misuse of word*
Webb — *Edge* p.63
, *Mystery of*
Hubbard — *Scrap* p.76
, *Nature of*
Hadfield — *Delights* p.140
Hubbard — *Scrap* p.80, 95
, *of country. See* **Patriotism**
, *of fellow man. See* **Brotherhood**
, *of material things*
Hubbard — *Scraps* p.57
, *of nature. See* **Nature**
, *of world*
Nichols — *Third* p.72-73

, *Perfect*
Hubbard — *Scrap* p.100
, *Personal*
Day — *Meditations* p.78
, *Philosophy of*
Hubbard — *Scrap* p.64
Taylor — *With* p.90-92
, *Platonic*
Ideas p.295-296
Taylor — *With* p.85-87
, *Poetry of*
Adams — *New* p.385
, *Possessive*
List — *Living* p.50-54
, *Power of*
Clark — *Windows* p.44
Holmes — *Design* p.73-74, 141-147
Wheelis — *Moralist* p.139-140
, *Qualities of*
Hubbard — *Scrap* p.55, 71
, *Received as children*
Lair — *Baby* p.28-29
, *Religious*
See also **God**
Goudge — *Comfort* p. 201-204
, *Returned for evil*
Hubbard — *Scrap* p.108
, *Romantic*
See also **Romance**
Auden — *Certain* p.228-237
Ginott — *Between* p.147-148, 167, 175
Ideas p.342-344
Montapert — *Distilled* p.245
, *Seductive*
Taylor — *With* p.73-75
, *Simplicity of*
Krishnamurti — *Think* p.167-175
, *Surrogate of*
Taylor — *With* p.134-135
, *Talk of*
Lair — *Baby* p.184
, *Teenage*
Daly — *Personality* p.43-46
, *Tests of*
Francis — *For* p.159-178
Hubbard — *Scrap* p.101
, *True*
Day — *Meditations* p.61-62
Sheen — *Content.* p.23-25
Taylor — *With* p.79
Webb — *Edge* p.63-66
, *Twelfth century*
Kronenberger — *Animal* p.192-193
, *Varieties of*
Saturday — *Advent.* p.206-218
, *Way of*
Clark — *Windows* p.126
, *Wife's*
Guideposts — *Faith* p.326-330
, *Young*
Guideposts — *Faith* p.205-206

"LOVED ONES"
Evans — *Faith* p.33-34, 54, 74, 184, 195-196, 198, 224
Evans — *Thoughts I* p.26, 43, 67, 112, 120, 129, 132, 160, 177-178, 183-184, 217
Evans — *Thoughts II (Open Door)* p.105, 110, 164
Evans — *Thoughts III (Open Road)* See index no p.
Evans — *Thoughts IV* p.157-159, 167-169, 177, 179-180, 183-184, 193, 197-198, 205, 207, 209-210

LOVELESSNESS
Phillips — *Choice* p.122

LOVELINESS. *See* **Beauty; Charm;** etc.

LOVERS
See also **Love**
Flesch — *Unusual* p.158
Goudge — *Comfort* p.111-123
Woods — *Content.* p.121-126, 129-136, 142

LOWLINESS. *See* **Humility**

"LOWBROW." *See* **"Highbrows" and "lowbrows"**

LOYALTY
Book Proverbs p.107
Braude — *Source* #1065-1066
Braude — *Stories* p.233
Dirksen — *Quot.* #659
Droke — *Christian* p.323-324
Emmons — *Mature* p.20
Evans — *Faith* p.82, 100
Evans — *Thoughts II (Open Door)* p.34-35, 44, 87-90, 113, 169; *See also* index no p.
Evans — *Thoughts III (Open Road)* p.15, 59, 65, 68, 121, 169-171
Evans — *Thoughts IV* p.46, 70
Evans — *Unto* p.21, 84
Flesch — *Unusual* p.85
Forbes — *Thoughts* p.176-177, 288, 318, 348, 406, 410, 431
Fridy — *Meditat.* p.78
Garland — *Subject* p.178
Halverson — *Perspective* p.18
Harnsberger — *Mark* p.249-250

Hovey — *Treasury* #565, 1060, 1093
How To Live p.71
Hubbard — *Scrap* p.64
Ideas p.242-244
Johnson — *Bedside* p.4, 109, 171, 322
Kennedy — *Reader's* #620-624
Kin — *Dictionary* p.153
Knight's Illus. p.111-113
Knight's Treas. p.119-123
Liddle — *Thought V* p.26
Lockridge — *World's* #406, 1230, 3927, 2396
Lytle — *Leaves* p.72, 139, 145
Manchee — *Secret* p.132-133
Menninger — *Blue.* p.142
Montapert — *Distilled* p.245-246
New Topical p.84-85
Phillips — *Choice* p.85
Price — *Wider* p.32-33
Prochnow — *Public* #2350, 2359
Prochnow — *Speaker's* p.121, 199-200
Seldes — *Great* p.620-621
Speaker's Desk #94, 110, 288, 353, 984
Wallis — *Treasure* p.47
Wallis — *Words* p.106
Woods — *Religious* p.14-15, 572
Woods — *Wellsprings* p.74
Words — *Inspir.* p.169-170

LOYOLA, SAINT IGNATIUS OF
Applegarth — *Heir.* p.68

LUCK
See also **Destiny; Fate; Fortune; Gamblers and gambling;** etc.
Braude — *Source* #1067-1069
Braude — *Speaker's* #186-189, 838-840
Braude — *Stories* p.233-235
Dirksen — *Quot.* #16, 157, 174, 541, 1741
Edwards — *Useful* p.359-360
Flesch — *Unusual* p.158
Forbes — *Thoughts* p.6, 19, 72, 123, 171, 177, 289, 303, 313, 316, 334, 465, 473, 509
Fuller — *Epigrams* p.199
Grizer — *Wit* p.292-293
Harnsberger — *Mark* p.250-251
Harral — *Feature* p.210
Henry — *5000* p.164-165
Hubbard — *Scrap* p.133
Kauffman — *For* p.135-136
Kin — *Dictionary* p.153-154
Liddle — *Thought I, II, III* p.6, 10, 33, 36, 55, 64, 123, 137, 166, 171
Lockridge — *World's* #59, 168
Lytle — *Leaves* p.113, 115, 169
Maltz — *Creative* p.72-73
Manchee — *Secret* p.165-188
Modern Eloquence (14) p.374
Nichols — *New* p.88-89
Prochnow — *Speaker's* p.200
Speaker's Desk p.137-138; #185, 474, 701, 942, 1123, 1131
Wallis — *Words* p.181
, Bad
Dirksen — *Quot.* #157, 1741
Hill — *Think* p.53-54
Kin — *Dictionary* p.128
Prochnow — *Public* #4240
, Good
Fuller — *Epigrams* p.343
Prochnow — *Success.* #1120

LULLABIES
Henry — *5000*
Prochnow — *Public* #643

LUMBERING AND LUMBERMEN
See also **Bunyan, Paul**
Botkin — *Treasury* p.51, 524, 623, 843-851
Schermerhorn — *1500* p.239-240

LUNCHES
Flesch — *Unusual* p.158
Hadfield — *Delights* p.61
Prochnow — *Success.* #137, 969

LUSITANIA SINKING
Fogg — *1000* #1071

LUST
See also **Covetousness; Desire; Passion**
Dirksen — *Quot.* #1442-1444
Edwards — *Useful* p.360
McCracken — *What* p.45-49
Seldes — *Great* p.621
Sheban — *Wisdom* no p.
Woods — *Religious* p.572-574

LUTHER, MARTIN
Baillie — *Diary* #185
Kennedy — *Reader's* #625
Lockridge — *World's* #4045
Seldes — *Great* p.621
Woods — *Religious* p.574

LUXURY
See also **Elegance; Extravagance**
Dirksen — *Quot.* #449-450
Edwards — *Useful* p.360-361
Flesch — *Unusual* p.158
Grizer — *Wit* p.293
Hoffer — *Reflect.* p.20
Kin — *Dictionary* p.154

Kohn — *Pathways* p.59-63
Krishnamurti — *Think* p.67-68, 182-183
Liddle — *Thought I, II, III* p.104, 122
Lockridge — *World's* #3207, 5138
Lytle — *Leaves* p.42
Prochnow — *Public* #1451, 1737, 2331, 3334-3337
Seldes — *Great* p.621-622
Woods — *Religious* p.574

LYING. *See* **Dishonesty; Falsehood; Liars**

LYNCHING
Botkin — *Anecdotes* p.171
Seldes — *Great* p.622
Woods — *Religious* p.574-575

M

M.I.T.
Asimov — *Treasury* #248, 268, 270

McCANLESS MASSACRE
Botkin — *Treasury* p.69, 79, 83

McCARTHYISM
Franke — *Buckley* p.186-188
Ideas p.248-250

MacCOOL, FINN
Botkin — *Treasury* p.176

MACEDONIAN EMPIRE
New Topical p.157-158

MACHIAVELLI, NICCOLO
Flesch — *Unusual* p.160
Seldes — *Great* p.622

MACHINES AND MACHINERY
See also **Mechanics and mechanization;** types of machines
Auden — *Certain* p.237-238
Evans — *Faith* p.159
Evans — *Thoughts III (Open Road)* p.155-156, 188, 198
Flesch — *Unusual* p.160
Forbes — *Thoughts* p.85, 140, 212, 438, 501
Fuller — *Thesaurus* #2271-2272
Grizer — *Wit* p.293-294
Harral — *Feature* p.210
Henry — *5000* p.166
Keller — *Open* p.83
Lockridge — *World's* #4285
Peterson — *Art* p.220
Seldes — *Great* p.622
Woods — *Business.* p.140-142
Woods — *Religious* p.575
Words — *Inspir.* p.221-222
, Tyranny of
Ideas p.244-246

MACROSCOPIC SCIENCE
Du Noüy — *Road* p.41, 108, 148-149, 153, 155, 170-172

MADNESS. *See* **Mental illness**

MADONNAS
See also **Mary, Virgin**
Irion — *Yes* p.49-51
Thurman — *Mood* p.13-16

MAGARAC, JOE
Botkin — *Treasury* p.179, 246-254

MAGAZINES
Botkin — *Anecdotes* p.63
Cerf — *Laugh* p.293-295
Farral — *Feature* p.210-211
Fuller — *Thesaurus* #1251-1252
Prochnow — *Public* #403, 780, 1281
Prochnow — *Speaker's* p.200-201
Seldes — *Great* p.622

MAGI
Hobe — *Tapestries* p.146
Wallis — *Words* p.36

MAGIC AND MAGICIANS
See also **Alchemy; Miracles**
Asimov — *Treasury* #11
Esteve — *Experience* p.125-129
Garland — *Subject* p.179
Harral — *Feature* p.210
Kennedy — *Fresh* p.110-112
Peale — *Guideposts* p.97-100
Prochnow — *Public* #921, 1004
Wallis — *Treasure* p.105

MAGISTRATES
Lockridge — *World's* #618
New Topical p.158

MAGNA CARTA
Curtis — *Practical* p.24
Seldes — *Great* p.622-623

MAGNANIMITY
See also **Benevolence; Generosity; Kindness; Mercy**
Edwards — *Useful* p.363-364

Fogg — *1000* #42, 112, 167, 407, 412, 446, 500, 507, 810, 885, 986, 1129
Forbes — *Thoughts* p.377, 437
Johnson — *Bedside* p.328-329
Lockridge — *World's* #260, 296

MAGNETISM
Edwards — *Useful* p.364
Forbes — *Thoughts* p.36, 80, 450
Garland — *Subject* p.179

MAHOMET. *See* **Mohammedanism**

MAIDS
Fuller — *Epigrams* p.200
Fun Fare p.42-44
Prochnow — *Public* #196, 479, 740, 841
Prochnow — *Success.* #1101
Schermerhorn — *1500* p.241-242

MAIL
Grizer — *Wit* p.294
Harral — *Feature* p.211
Prochnow — *Public* #1554
Prochnow — *Success.* #326

MAINE
Botkin — *Anecdotes* p.6-7, 20, 33, 56-57, 92, 114, 206-207, 250
Botkin — *Treasury* p.308, 361, 392, 770, 825n
Kin — *Dictionary* p.155

MAJESTY. *See* **Dignity; Kings and queens; Royalty**

MAJORITY
See also **Democracy; Government; Politics; Republic; Votes and voting**
Dirksen — *Quot.* #451, 660, 667, 832, 2147
Edwards — *Useful* p.364
Evans — *Unto* p.84, 135
Flesch — *Unusual* p.160
Forbes — *Thoughts* p.127, 161, 174, 184, 201, 509
Harnsberger — *Mark* p.252
Henry — *5000* p.166
Kauffman — *For* p.136-138
Kin — *Dictionary* p.155
Menninger — *Blue.* p.111-112
Prochnow — *Public* #3338-3341
Seldes — *Great* p.623-627

"MAKE-BELIEVE." *See* **Fairy tales; Imagination**

MAKE-UP
See also **Cosmetics**
Kin — *Dictionary* p.155
Menninger — *Blue.* p.208-211

MAKING. *See* **Accomplishment**

MALADJUSTMENT
Evans — *Unto* p.61
Kohn — *Touch* p.46-50

MALE CHAUVINISM
Asimov — *Treasury* #79, 511

MALICE
See also **Anger; Hatred; Resentment; Revenge;** etc.
Book Proverbs p.57
Braude — *Stories* p.235
Edwards — *Useful* p.364-365
Fun Fare p.29
Grizer — *Wit* p.294
Harnsberger — *Mark* p.252-253
Johnson — *Bedside* p.236-244
Kin — *Dictionary* p.155, 242
Lockridge — *World's* #508, 3065, 3309, 3315, 3383
New Topical p.158
Pullar-Strecker — *Proverbs* #58-66
Seldes — *Great* p.627
Woods — *Religious* p.575

MALTHUS, THOMAS ROBERT
Flesch — *Unusual* p.160

MAMMALS
Du Noüy — *Human* p.66, 74-77, 93, 94-95, 170-171

MAMMON
Flesch — *Unusual* p.160
Henry — *5000* p.166
Seldes — *Great* p.627
Woods — *Religious* p.575-576

MAN (Mankind)
See also **Civilization; Humanity; Men**
Adams — *New* p.113
Applegarth — *Heir.* p.21, 161-162, 165-166
Auden — *Certain* p.243-247
Bartlett — *Discovery* p.6-7, 23-24
Book Proverbs p.142
Braude — *Source* #1070-1082
Braude — *Speaker's* #841-845
Braude — *Stories* p.235-237
Curtis — *Practical* p.1-120; *See also* index p.570
Detherage — *Sunrise* p.48, 103, 105, 139, 169, 185-186
Dirksen — *Quot.* #7, 385; *See also* index p.266

Droke — *Christian* p.325-331
Du Noüy — *Road See* index p.248
Edwards — *Useful* p.365-368, 730
Esteve — *Experience* p.1-3
Evans — *This* p.11-12, 23-25
Evans — *Thoughts IV* p.173-174, 185-186
Evans — *Unto* p.9, 18, 22-23, 30, 42, 47, 51, 65-66, 93-94, 96-97, 105, 112-113, 147
Flesch — *Unusual* p.160-162
Flint — *Graham* p.88-90
Fogg — *1000* #482, 674
Forbes — *Thoughts* p.141, 198, 283, 301, 316, 379, 400, 463, 519; *See also* index p.558
Fuller — *Epigrams* p.200-292, 355
Fun Fare p.270-272
Garland — *Subject* p.181-182
Grizer — *Wit* p.295-296
Hadfield — *Delights* p.132-133
Harnsberger — *Mark* p.253-256
Henry — *5000* p.166-169
Hobe — *Tapestries* p.42, 85, 135
Hoffer — *Reflect.* p.3-25
Hovey — *Treasury* p.236-237; #31, 36, 127, 1449-1456
How To Live p.563-565
Howell — *Better* p.125-130
Hubbard — *Scrap* p.11-12, 14, 24, 26, 191
Johnson — *Bedside* p.45-47, 76, 86, 111-112, 127, 136-137, 141-142, 187, 194-196, 213, 231, 250, 277-278, 326-327, 334
Kauffman — *For* p.139-141
Kennedy — *Reader's* #626-645
Kin — *Dictionary* p.156
Kohn — *Best* p.49-50
Liddle — *Thought IV* p.7, 14, 20, 39
Liddle — *Thought V* p.16, 22, 28, 31, 42-43
Lockridge — *World's See* index p.579; #5521
Lytle — *Leaves* p.19, 29, 56-57, 77, 117, 125, 153, 170, 178, 185-186
Mandel — *Stories* p.172-174
Montapert — *Distilled* p.246-248
New Topical p.158-160
Patterns For Living p.472-496, 501-511
Phillips — *Choice* p.68, 78, 122, 230, 313, 341, 352, 364
Prochnow — *Public* #3342-3374; *See* index p.502
Prochnow — *Speaker's* p.201
Prochnow — *Success. See* index p.495
Pullar-Strecker — *Proverbs* #51-71
Seldes — *Great* p.627-642
Sheban — *Wisdom* no p.
Sheen — *Thoughts* p.171-190
Sheen — *Way* p.161-192
Simpson — *Contemp.* p.203-288
Speaker's Desk p.138-140
Strait — *Speaker's* p.116-119
Voss — *Quotations* p.170-175
Wallis — *Treasure* p.163-164, 232
Wallis — *Words* p.4, 44, 123-124, 149, 153-154, 233
Wheelis — *Moralist* p.23, 30, 42-43, 79-82, 110-112, 114-116
Woods — *Religious* p.576-605
Woods — *Wellsprings* p.1-82
Zobell — *Speaker's* p.93-95
, and child
Lindbergh — *Unicorn* p.9
, and flight
Adams — *New* p.12
, and God. See **God, and Man**
, and himself
Flesch — *Unusual* p.161-162
, and his senses
Adams — *New* p.170
, and nature
Adams — *New* p.218, 290
Dirksen — *Quot.* #1163
Hubbard — *Scrap* p.53
Sheban — *Wisdom* no p.
Wheelis — *Moralist* p.42-43
Woods — *Religious* p.678-679
, and space
Kauffman — *For* p.204-205
, and the brutes
Adams — *New* p.90
, and truth
Dirksen — *Quot.* #2320
, and war
Hubbard — *Scrap* p.12
, and woman
Hubbard — *Scrap* p.67, 118, 225
, as animal
Adams — *New* p.312
, as book
Hubbard — *Scrap* p.126
, as writer
Hubbard — *Scrap* p.205
, Attributes of
Montapert — *Distilled* p.247
, Average
Forbes — *Thoughts* p.74, 122, 235, 290, 306, 380, 426, 496, 510
, Cause of
Hubbard — *Scrap* p.145
, Coming of age of
Kauffman — *For* p.138-139
, Confidence in
Hubbard — *Scrap* p.61
, Declaration of rights of
Fogg — *1000* #328

, Defined and interpreted
Woods — *Religious* p.578-583
, Destiny and goal of
Woods — *Religious* p.583-585
, Destruction of
Maxwell — *Courage* p.1-8
, Dialectical
Woods — *Religious* p.241
, Difference of
Adams — *New* p.83
, Disintegration of
Adams — *New* p.396
, Doctrines concerning
New Topical p.306
, Duty of
Hubbard — *Scrap* p.29
, Emancipation of
Keller — *Open* p.104
, Fall of
New Topical p.85
, Forgotten
Woods — *Business.* p.81
, Future of
Adams — *New* p.196-197
, Good
Hubbard — *Scrap* p.26, 118
, Government's duty to
Hubbard — *Scrap* p.55
, Haters of
Lockridge — *World's* #5565
, Heritage of
Adams — *New* p.121
, Honest
Hubbard — *Scrap* p.31
, House of
Esteve — *Experience* p.5-9
, Humanist view of
Wheeler — *Moralist* p.80-81
, Ignorance of
Hubbard — *Scrap* p.61
, in image of God
Nizer — *Thinking* p.45
, Individual
Montapert — *Distilled* p.247
, Influence of
Hubbard — *Scrap* p.126
, Kinship with Divine
Hubbard — *Scrap* p.167
, Life of
Hubbard — *Scrap* p.156
, Measure of a
Hubbard — *Scrap* p.16
, Modern
Adams — *New* p.211, 221
Liebman — *Hope* p.72-100
Saturday — *Advent.* p.3-16
Woods — *Religious* p.589-590
, Nakedness of
Adams — *New* p.299-300
, Potential of
Woods — *Religious* p.585-586
, Power of
Hubbard — *Scrap* p.94
, Progress of
Hubbard — *Scrap* p.29
, Purpose of
Dirksen — *Quot.* #2384
, Study of
Montapert — *Distilled* p.248-249
, Uncommon
Nichols — *New* p.16-17
Words — *Inspir.* p.211-212
, Universal
Kronenberger — *Animal* p.314-315
, Wickedness of
Woods — *Religious* p.587-589
, with hoe
Hubbard — *Scrap* p.174
, Wonder of
Kennedy — *Fresh* p.36-38
, Work of
Krishnamurti — *Think* p.131-132
, Worship of
Lockridge — *World's* #3622
, Worth of
Hubbard — *Scrap* p.137

MANAGEMENT
See also **Executives; Leaders and leadership; Labor relations; Personnel**
Dirksen — *Quot.* #311, 859, 2315
Flesch — *Unusual* p.162-163
Forbes — *Thoughts* p.106, 195, 264, 284, 290, 318, 328, 336, 356, 372, 462, 470, 512
Grizer — *Wit* p.296-297
Harral — *Feature* p.211-212
Montapert — *Distilled* p.249
Prochnow — *Speaker's* p.201
Prochnow — *Success.* #602
Woods — *Business.* p.142-147

MANASSEH, TRIBE OF
New Topical p.160

MANHOOD. *See* **Man; Men**

MANIFESTATIONS
White — *Job* p.120, 134, 137-139, 175-176

MANKIND. *See* **Man (Mankind)**

MANLINESS. *See* **Courage; Men**

MANNA
New Topical p.160-161

MANNERS. *See* **Behavior; Conduct; Courtesy; Customs; Etiquette; Refinement**

MANSIONS
Evans — *Unto* p.141
Harral — *Feature* p.212
Lytle — *Leaves* p.99

MANUFACTURING
Fuller — *Thesaurus* #2261
Harral — *Feature* p.212
Seldes — *Great* p.642-643

MAORIS
Weisfeld — *Pulpit* p.31

MAPS
Applegarth — *Heir.* p.274-275
Harral — *Feature* p.212
Lytle — *Leaves* p.88
Prochnow — *Public* #4389

MARCHES
Kin — *Dictionary* p.156
Lytle — *Leaves* p.118
, Camp
Fuller — *Thesaurus* #2456

MARCUS AURELIUS
Flesch — *Unusual* p.163

"MARGINS"
Evans — *Thoughts I* p.117-118
Kohn — *Adventures* p.79-83

MARIE ANTOINETTE
Flesch — *Unusual* p.163
Kronenberger — *Animal* p.72-73

MARIJUANA
Ginott — *Between* p.165, 191-198

MARINES
Cerf — *Laugh* p.334-335
Harral — *Feature* p.212

MARKETS AND MARKETING
Dirksen — *Quot.* #526
Forbes — *Thoughts* p.73, 103, 348, 434
Holmes — *I've* p.34-35
Kin — *Dictionary* p.157
Seldes — *Great* p.643
Woods — *Religious* p.605-606

MARKSMANSHIP
See also **Guns**
Botkin — *Treasury* p.7-8, 49, 69, 82, 85, 195, 557, 617-619, 621, 627
Harral — *Feature* p.212

MARNE, BATTLE OF
Asimov — *Treasury* #154

MARRIAGE
See also **Children; Divorce; Family; Fathers; Husbands; Love; Mothers; Parents and parenthood; Weddings; Wives**
Asimov — *Treasury* #325, 345-367, 553-555, 637
Auden — *Certain* p.248-256
Blanton — *Faith* p.182-203
Book Proverbs p.20
Braude — *Source* #1084-1099, 1100-1102
Braude — *Speaker's* #194-199, 846-884
Cerf — *Laugh* p.110-120
Copeland — *10,000* p.226-277, 990-992
Dirksen — *Quot.* #178, 228, 267, 303, 1005, 1447-1450, 2071-2075, 2253
Droke — *Christian* p.331-344
Edwards — *Useful* p.373-378, 730
Evans — *Faith* p.43-48
Evans — *Quote* p.9-28
Evans — *Thoughts I* p.18, 60, 70, 72, 91-93, 138-139, 184-186
Evans — *Thoughts II (Open Door)* p.21-24, 43, 59, 166, 168-170, 183
Evans — *Thoughts III (Open Road)* p.17, 24-32, 50, 79, 97, 100, 107, 125
Evans — *Thoughts IV* p.43-50, 73-74, 105, 126, 157, 193, 205
Flesch — *Unusual* p.163-165
Flint — *Graham* p.70, 78, 87, 91-92
Fogg — *1000* #34, 49, 101, 530, 573, 831, 1006, 1113
Fuller — *Epigrams* p.203-208, 356
Fuller — *Thesaurus* p.152-162
Fun Fare p.20, 92, 162, 250, 252, 267
Garland — *Subject* p.183-184
Gold — *Letters* p.73-81
Grizer — *Wit* p.298-299
Hadfield — *Delights* p.172
Hadfield — *Love* p.137-140, 142-145
Harnsberger — *Mark* p.256-257
Harral — *Feature* p.213
Henry — *5000* p.170-171
Hobe — *Tapestries* p.39, 126
Holmes — *I've* p.39-51
Hovey — *Treasury* #38, 141, 581, 1267, 1622
How To Live p.44-52, 57-62, 66-72, 387-390
Hubbard — *Scrap* p.62, 102
Johnson — *Bedside* p.294-295, 299, 301, 303-307

Kahn — *Lessons* p.185-191
Kauffman — *For* p.141-142
Kennedy — *Reader's* #646-652
Keys Happiness p.119-123, 191, 237-240, 260, 304-306, 407, 422-425, 446-448, 477-479, 484, 507-510, 527, 541-544, 555
Kin — *Dictionary* p.157, 275
Liddle — *Thought I, II, III See* index p.198
Liddle — *Thought IV* p.4, 17, 25, 27, 34, 41
Liddle — *Thought V* p.6, 20-21, 30
Lockridge — *World's See* index p.579
Lytle — *Leaves* p.24-25
Mandel — *Stories* p.174-176
Mandelbaum — *Choose* p.59-63
Montapert — *Distilled* p.250
Modern Eloquence (14) p.121-131, 375-376
New Topical p.161-162
Patterns For Living p.142-145
Peale — *Faith* p.191-217
Peale — *Guideposts* p.285-287
Peale — *Sin* p.103-129
Peterson — *New* p.44-45
Prochnow — *Public* #489, 509, 769, 923, 927, 1042; *See also* index p.502
Prochnow — *Speaker's* p.202-208
Prochnow — *Success.* #159, 478, 869, 928, 968, 1128, 2024, 2031
Pullar-Strecker — *Proverbs* #79-93
Reader's — *Getting* p.10
Rogers — *Time* p.23-29
Sagendorph — *Old* p.94-100
Schermerhorn — *1500* p.122-124, 242-243
Seaburg — *Great* p.87-158
Seldes — *Great* p.643-644
Sheban — *Wisdom* no p.
Speaker's Desk p.142-149; *See also* index p.302
Tanksley — *Friend* p.46
Voss — *Quotations* p.175-177
Wallis — *Treasure* p.132
Wallis — *Words* p.157-159
Weisfeld — *Pulpit* p.41, 87-103
White — *Life* p.11-18
Woods — *Religious* p.606-612, 620
Words Change p.118

, and divorce
Braude — *Stories* p.239-255
Strait — *Speaker's* p.120-123

, Appreciation in
Peale — *Courage* p.142

, Argument in
Guideposts — *Faith* p.167-171

, Art of
Maurois — *Art* p.37-75

, Brokers of
Asimov — *Treasury* #370, 380

, Counseling for
How To Live p.78-84

, Crises of
Jackson — *Coping* p.120-127

, Early
Kahn — *Lessons* p.176-184
Sheen — *Content.* p.25-27

, Ecumenical context of Christian
McDonagh — *Invit.* p.109-120

, for eternity
Hunter — *Gems* p.49-50

, Gallantry in
Peale — *Courage* p.143-144

, Happiness in
Bartlett — *Discovery* p.123-125
Peale — *Guide* p.186-211

, Joy of
Holmes — *I've* p.49-50

, Love in
Liebman — *Hope* p.142-181

, Meaning of
Kohn — *Best* p.166-170

, Mixed
Guideposts — *Faith* p.134-138

, Money in
Guideposts — *Faith* p.162-166

, "Past tense"
Safian — *Insults* p.136-139

, Perspective in
Kohn — *Touch* p.132

, Politeness in
Peale — *Courage* p.142-143

, "Present tense"
Safian — *Insults* p.133-135

, Principles of
Kahn — *Lessons* p.168-170

, Proposals of
Asimov — *Treasury* #556

, Psalm for
Holmes — *I've* p.50

, Quarrels in
Reader's — *Getting* p.178

, Re-
Keys Happiness p.503-504

, Relationships in
Lindbergh — *Gift* p.65-76, 79

, Sex in
Guideposts — *Faith* p.147-151
Reader's — *Getting* p.158-161

, Silences in
Kohn — *Best* p.170

, Temple (L.D.S.)
Hunter — *Gems* p.104-105
, Trivialities in
Hill — *Think* p.222-223

MARS
Curtis — *Practical* p.54

MARTHA (Biblical)
Woods — *Religious* p.612

MARTHA'S VINEYARD, MASS.
Botkin — *Anecdotes* p.93, 114, 236

MARTIAL LAW
Seldes — *Great* p.644

MARTIANS
Asimov — *Treasury* #596-597
Cerf — *Laugh* p.478-480

MARTIN-TOLLIVER FEUD
Botkin — *Treasury* p.891

MARTYRS AND MARTYRDOM
See also **Heroes and heroism; Sacrifice; Saints and sainthood**
Applegarth — *Heir.* p.72, 207, 214, 236, 262
Braude — *Source* #1103
Day — *Meditations* p.77
Dirksen — *Quot.* #393
Edwards — *Useful* p.379
Fogg — *1000 See* index p.891
Fuller — *Epigrams* p.208
Garland — *Subject* p.184
Harnsberger — *Mark* p.257-258
Henry — *5000* p.170
Hovey — *Treasury* p.237; #712, 731, 829, 1457-1460
Hubbard — *Scrap* p.177
Johnson — *Bedside* p.89
Kin — *Dictionary* p.158
Liddle — *Thought I, II, III* p.25, 114
Lockridge — *World's* #761, 914, 2394
Lytle — *Leaves* p.65
New Topical p.162
Seldes — *Great* p.644-645
Sherman — *Your* p.114-119
Woods — *Religious* p.612-613

MARVELS. *See* **Wonder**

MARXISM
See also **Communism**
Seldes — *Great* p.645-647
Woods — *Religious* p.613-614

MARY, VIRGIN
Ideas p.199-201; 436-437
Woods — *Religious* p.33, 463-464, 614-617, 1034

MARY MAGDALENE
Fridy — *Meditat.* p.97

MARYLAND
Botkin — *Anecdotes* p.19, 76, 140, 144
Botkin — *Treasury* p.330, 680-681, 722

MASCOTS
Harral — *Feature* p.213-214

MASKS
Flesch — *Unusual* p.165
Holman — *Psych.* p.146-154
Lockridge — *World's* #1714
Peterson — *Art* p.344, 396
Phillips — *Choice* p.73
Sheen — *Content.* p.89-91
Woods — *Religious* p.617

MASONRY
Nizer — *Thinking* p.205-206
Seldes — *Great* p.401

MASQUERADES
Asimov — *Treasury* #355

MASS (religious)
Day — *Meditations* p.9
Seldes — *Great* p.647
Woods — *Religious* p.617-619

"MASS-MAN"
Sheen — *Way* p.164-166

MASS PRODUCTION. *See* **Production, Mass**

MASSACHUSETTS. *See also* **Boston;** etc.
Botkin — *Anecdotes* p.58, 75, 144, 209; *See also* index p.315
Botkin — *Treasury* p.457, 460, 506, 731, 742, 771-773, 806-807, 829

MASSES
See also **Mobs; People**
Dirksen — *Quot.* #455, 683, 1743
Harnsberger — *Mark* p.258
Seldes — *Great* p.648-650

MASTER. *See* **Jesus Christ**

MASTERPIECES
See also **Art; Painters and paintings**
Dirksen — *Quot.* #245

Flesch — *Unusual* p.165
Hobe — *Tapestries* p.35, 62
Lytle — *Leaves* p.12
Prochnow — *Success.* #2032

MASTERS AND MASTERY
See also **Despotism; Kings and queens; Power; Rulers; Slavery; Tyrants and tyranny**
Edwards — *Useful* p.379-380
Forbes — *Thoughts See* index p.558
Kin — *Dictionary* p.158
Lockridge — *World's* #1659
New Topical p.162
Peterson — *Art* p.106
Prochnow — *Public* #3378-3379
Seldes — *Great* p.650-651
Wheelis — *Moralist* p.51-52, 58-59, 74, 142-143

MASTERS, OLD. *See* **Painters and paintings**

MASTERSON, BAT
Botkin — *Treasury* p.68

MATERIAL THINGS
See also **Substance**
Evans — *Unto* p.51, 71
Seldes — *Great* p.651

MATERIALISM
Dirksen — *Quot.* #2993
Du Noüy — *Human* p.xiii-xvi, 9, 13, 40, 42, 47-51, 134, 153
Du Noüy — *Road* p.32, 143, 152, 191, 191n, 192, 223, 239
Flint — *Graham* p.92-93
Forbes — *Thoughts* p.236, 342
Garland — *Subject* p.185
Humes — *Instant* p.644-648
Ideas p.246-248
Kennedy — *Reader's* #653-655
Lair — *Baby* p.149
Lockridge — *World's* #5483
Mandel — *Stories* p.176
Montapert — *Distilled* p.250-251
Seldes — *Great* p.651
Wheelis — *Moralist* p.154
White — *Job* p.152-153
Woods — *Business.* p.147
Woods — *Religious* p.619

MATERNITY. *See* **Mothers**

MATHEMATICIANS
Asimov — *Treasury* #138, 144-145
Fuller — *Thesaurus* #1146-1154
George — *Book* p.111, 135, 291, 364, 403

MATHEMATICS
See also **Statistics**
Applegarth — *Heir.* p.46, 56
Asimov — *Treasury* #142, 455-456
Braude — *Speaker's* #36-43
Curtis — *Practical* p.23, 56, 221
Dirksen — *Quot.* #506
Du Noüy — *Road* p.28, 35, 38, 47-48, 52, 58, 119
Edwards — *Useful* p.380
Flesch — *Unusual* p.166
Forbes — *Thoughts* p.357, 371
Harral — *Feature* p.214
Kennedy — *Reader's* #656
Kin — *Dictionary* p.6
Prochnow — *Public* #89, 329, 516, 1037
Prochnow — *Speaker's* p.209

MATRIMONY. *See* **Marriage; Weddings**

MATTER
See also **Mind, and matter**
Du Noüy — *Human* p.11, 16, 19, 21, 36, 41
Du Noüy — *Road* p.39-40, 56, 59, 65-66, 86, 229
Garland — *Subject* p.185-186
Woods — *Religious* p.620-621
, and spirit
Woods — *Religious* p.621
, Mystery of
Saturday — *Advent.* p.57-68

MATURITY
See also **Adults; Age; Middle-aged; Old age**
Braude — *Source* #1104-1106
Detherage — *Sunrise* p.153-158
Dirksen — *Quot.* #1278
Evans — *Thoughts II (Open Door)* p.26-27, 39
Forbes — *Thoughts* p.238, 284
Garland — *Subject* p.186-187
Grizer — *Wit* p.299-300
Halverson — *Perspective* p.36
Holman — *Psych.* p.33-41
Hovey — *Treasury* p.237-238; #649, 1441, 1461-1468, 1531, 1732, 1751, 1875
Kauffman — *For* p.142
Kennedy — *Reader's* #657-661
Kin — *Dictionary* p.158
Mandel — *Stories* p.177-178
Menninger — *Blue.* p.5-49
Montapert — *Distilled* p.251-252
Nichols — *New* p.48-49
Peterson — *New* p.46-47
Phillips — *Choice* p.140
Voss — *Quotations* p.178-179

Wallis — *Treasure* p.45
Welk — *Guide.* p.21-23
Woods — *Religious* p.621

, *Attainment of*
Liebman — *Hope* p.211-239

, *Emotional*
Liebman — *Hope* p.240-250
Patterns For Living p.142-145

, *Spiritual*
Kohn — *Best* p.72-73

MAXIMS. *See* **Proverbs; Quotations**

MAY (month)
Hadfield — *Delights* p.78
Kin — *Dictionary* p.158
Kohn — *Best* p.145-146
New Joy p.229
Peterson — *Art* p.149

MAY DAY
Day — *Meditations* p.75-76
New Joy p.181

MAYFLOWER
Harral — *Feature* p.214
Hovey — *Treasury* #68, 1058

MAYORS
Fuller — *Thesaurus* #1961
Harral — *Feature* p.214
Prochnow — *Public* #175

, *Standards of*
Nizer — *Thinking* p.44

MEALS
See also **Eating;** names of meals; etc.
Applegarth — *Heir.* p.126
Flesch — *Unusual* p.166
Hadfield — *Delights* p.60-67
Harral — *Feature* p.214
Prochnow — *Public* #209
Wallis — *Treasure* p.134
Woods — *Religious* p.621

"MEANIES"
Safian — *Insults* p.140-142
Safian — *More* p.133-134

MEANING
Curtis — *Human* p.167-182
Flesch — *Unusual* p.166-167
Peterson — *Art* p.341
Prochnow — *Public* #837, 887, 953, 1945

, *Mastery of*
Curtis — *Practical* p.29-32

MEANINGLESSNESS
Flesch — *Unusual* p.167
Webb — *Edge* p.129-136

MEANNESS
See also **Cruelty; Malice; Unkindness**
Botkin — Treasury p.409, 466-468
Braude — *Speaker's* #885
Edwards — *Useful* p.381
Flesch — *Unusual* p.62, 166
Kin — *Dictionary* p.158

MEANS
See also **Expediency; Method; Money; Property; Wealth**
Edwards — *Useful* p.381
Flesch — *Unusual* p.167
Kin — *Dictionary* p.158-159
Lockridge — *World's* #255, 4237
Seldes — *Great* p.651
Wheelis — *Moralist* p.10, 34-35, 71, 141
Woods — *Religious* p.621

MEASLES
Prochnow — *Success.* #1015

MEASUREMENT
Forbes — *Thoughts* p.225, 384, 401, 486, 502
Harnsberger — *Mark* p.259
Kin — *Dictionary* p.159, 182
Kohn — *Through* p.53-57
Lytle — *Leaves* p.86, 99, 129, 176
New Topical p.162-163

MEAT
Kin — *Dictionary* p.159
Prochnow — *Public* #291, 541
Prochnow — *Speaker's* p.210

, *Offerings of (Biblical)*
New Topical p.163

MECHANICAL ARTS
Du Noüy p.137-139, 259-262

MECHANICS AND MECHANIZATION
See also **Machines and machinery**
Curtis — *Practical* p.240, 335-337
Dirksen — *Quot.* #2370
Flesch — *Unusual* p.167
Phillips — *Choice* p.120
Prochnow — *Public* #189
Prochnow — *Success.* #1057
Woods — *Religious* p.621

MEDALS
Dirksen — *Quot.* #1745
Kin — *Dictionary* p.159

MEDDLING. *See* **Gossip**

MEDIA
See also **Newspapers; Television;** etc.
Seldes — *Great* p.652

MEDICINE
See also **Drugs; Health; Illness; Physicians;** etc.
Applegarth — *Heir.* p.185, 196, 302
Auden — *Certain* p.256-257
Bartlett — *Discovery* p.17-18, 141-142
Curtis — *Practical* p.221, 251-253, 259-270
Edwards — *Useful* p.381-382
Flesch — *Unusual* p.167-168
Forbes — *Thoughts* p.88, 98, 132, 414, 423, 479
Fuller — *Epigrams* p.208-209
Fuller — *Thesaurus* #1726-1731
Garland — *Subject* p.187-188
Harnsberger — *Mark* p.259-261
Harral — *Feature* p.214-216
Henry — *5000* p.172
Hobe — *Tapestries* p.79
Humes — *Instant* #649-651
Kin — *Dictionary* p.159
Kronenberger — *Animal* p.190-191
Modern Eloquence (14) p.377
Phillips — *Choice* p.252
Prochnow — *Public* #3383-3384
Prochnow — *Speaker's* p.210-211
Prochnow — *Success.* #291, 704, 2034-2035
Seldes — *Great* p.652
Simpson — *Contemp.* p.177-181
Simpson — *'54* p.53, 164, 306
Wallis — *Treasure* p.211
Wallis — *Words* p.18
Watson — *Light* p.180-182
, and health
Fuller — *Thesaurus* p.295-312
, and prayer
Holmes — *Design* p.158-159
, Associations of
Humes — *Instant* #27, 1218
, Preventive
Peterson — *Art* p.205
, Science of
Braude — *Speaker's* #886-889
Hooker — *Index* p.202-214

MEDIEVALISM. *See* **Middle Ages**

MEDIOCRITY
See also **Bores and boredom; Monotony; Standardization**
Adams — *New* p.55
Braude — *Source* #1107-1108
Dirksen — *Quot.* #664, 1811
Edwards — *Useful* p.382
Evans — *Thoughts II (Open Door)* p.139-140
Evans — *Thoughts III (Open Road)* p.147-149
Flesch — *Unusual* p.168
Forbes — *Thoughts* p.27, 191, 290, 310, 317, 355, 457
Hubbard — *Scrap* p.104
Humes — *Instant* #652-653
Liddle — *Thought I, II, III* p.117
Lockridge — *World's See* index p.579
Prochnow — *Public* #3385-3387
Seldes — *Great* p.652-653
Woods — *Religious* p.621-622

MEDITATION
See also **Prayer; Self-analysis; Thought;** etc.
Baillie — *Diary* #20, 246
Braude — *Source* #1109-1110
Curtis — *Human* p.8, 127-130, 192
Curtis — *New* p.59-71
Dirksen — *Quot.* #1006, 1451
Edwards — *Useful* p.382-383, 555
Flesch — *Unusual* p.168
Forbes — *Thoughts* p.100, 198-199, 205, 332, 427, 450
Garland — *Subject* p.188
Hobe — *Tapestries* p.142
Johnson — *Bedside* p.20, 272, 275
Kennedy — *Reader's* #662
Keys Happiness p.359-360
Liddle — *Thought I, II, III* p.170
Lockridge — *World's* #1559, 2077
Montapert — *Distilled* p.252
Nichols — *New* p.169-171
Nichols — *Third* p.147-148, 151
Peterson — *Art* p.327
Phillips — *Choice See* index p.427
Prochnow — *Public* #3388-3389
Prochnow — *Speaker's* p.211
Sheen — *Lift* p.140-156
Sheen — *Way* p.139-140
Woods — *Content.* p.271
Woods — *Religious* p.622
, and energy
Krishnamurti — *Urgency* p.140-146
, Breathing in
Phillips — *Choice* p.194
, Confessional
Phillips — *Choice* p.268
, Discursive
Phillips — *Choice* p.173, 198-236
, Morning
Clark — *Windows* p.20-21

, Practical
Day — *Meditations* p.6
, Room for
Peterson — *Art* p.156
, Secret of
Sheen — *Content.* p.114-117
, Strength from
Maxwell — *Courage* p.155-165

MEDO-PERSIAN KINGDOM
New Topical p.163-164

MEEKNESS
See also **Humility; Modesty**
Albert — *Stop* p.124-125
Braude — *Source* #1111
Dirksen — *Quot.* #1452-1454
Edwards — *Useful* p.139, 383
Flesch — *Unusual* p.168
Garland — *Subject* p.188
Guideposts — *Faith* p.259-263
Harnsberger — *Mark* p.476
Johnson — *Bedside* p.206-207, 211
Keys Happiness p.356-358
Kin — *Dictionary* p.160, 252, 256
Kohn — *Pathways* p.121-122, 147-149
Lockridge — *World's* #12, 172, 506, 2323, 2349
Mandelbaum — *Choose* p.171-174
New Topical p.164
Petty — *Wings* p.74-80
Phillips — *Choice* p.79
Prochnow — *Public* #1819, 2597
Woods — *Religious* p.622-623

MEETINGS
See also **Conventions (meetings)**
Dirksen — *Quot.* p.408
Edwards — *Useful* p.383-384
Kin — *Dictionary* p.16
Woods — *Religious* p.623
, Conducting
Prochnow — *Success.* #2

MELANCHOLY. *See* **Depression; Grief; Unhappiness**

MELCHIZEDEK (Biblical)
Garland — *Subject* p.188

MELODRAMA. *See* **Drama; Theater**

MELODY. *See* **Music**

MELONS
Kin — *Dictionary* p.160

"MELTING-POT"
Seldes — *Great* p.653

MEMOIRS. *See* **Autobiography**

MEMORIAL DAY
Braude — *Source* #1112-1113
Evans — *Thoughts IV* p.154-155
Evans — *Unto* p.13
Hovey — *Treasury See* index p.303
Kohn — *Best* p.150-152
Kohn — *Touch* p.113
Sagendorph — *Old* p.42

MEMORIALS
See also **Monuments**
Dirksen — *Quot.* #86
Emmons — *Mature* p.144-145
Humes — *Instant* #654-661
Kin — *Dictionary* p.160
Reader's — *20th* p.32
Seaburg — *Great* p.417-423
Speaker's Desk #338, 435, 481, 485
, Speeches for
Copeland — *World's* p.91-97, 144-145, 263-265, 269-270, 299-301, 325-326, 346-350

MEMORY (faculty) AND MEMORIES
Adams — *New* p.139
Alexander's Treasure. p.263-264
Applegarth — *Heir.* p.65, 108, 296
Auden — *Certain* p.257-258
Baillie — *Diary* #178
Boas — *History* p.52-55
Braude — *Source* #1114-1116
Braude — *Stories* p.256-257
Curtis — *Practical* p.136
Dirksen — *Quot.* p.89, 254, 277, 305, 331, 665, 776, 1007
Du Noüy — *Human* p.103, 105-107, 212
Edwards — *Useful* p.384-386, 543, 730
Emmons — *Mature* p.56-57, 156
Evans — *Thoughts I* p.32, 43, 50, 217, 219-222
Evans — *Thoughts II (Open Door)* p.38, 53, 77, 93, 113-115
Evans — *Thoughts III (Open Road)* p.21, 205-206
Evans — *Thoughts IV* p.118-119, 150-155, 205
Evans — *Unto* p.4, 6-7, 9, 17, 22, 70, 110
Flesch — *Unusual* p.169, 242
Forbes — *Thoughts* p.128, 154, 192, 299, 354, 366
Fuller — *Epigrams* p.209, 356-357
Fuller — *Thesaurus* #371-375
Garland — *Subject* p.267
Grizer — *Wit* p.300
Guideposts — *Faith* p.239-243

Harnsberger — *Mark* p.261-263
Harral — *Feature* p.216, 287-288
Henry — *5000* p.173-174
Hobe — *Tapestries* p.21-22, 61, 179
Holmes — *Design* p.45, 114, 213-214
Hovey — *Treasury* #38, 48, 359, 481-482, 488, 721, 897, 1160, 1209, 1526, 1662
How To Live p.183-185
Howell — *Better* p.131-134
Howell — *Lines* p.149-152
Hubbard — *Scrap* p.78
Humes — *Instant* #905-907
Johnson — *Bedside* p.206, 249, 254
Kennedy — *Reader's* #663-665
Keys Happiness p.209-212, 511-513
Kin — *Dictionary* p.160
Kohn — *Best* p.150-152
Kohn — *Pathways* p.171-175
Kohn — *Touch* p.110-113
Liddle — *Thought I, II, III* p.13, 23, 95, 109, 112, 153, 157
Liddle — *Thought IV* p.19
Liddle — *Thought V* p.12, 17
Lockridge — *World's* #3706; *See also* index p.579
Lytle — *Leaves* p.6, 20, 91, 100-101, 103, 155, 163, 167-168
Mandel — *Stories* p.178
Modern Eloquence (14) p.378
New Joy p.116-117
Nizer — *Thinking* p.32
Peterson — *Art* p.206
Peterson — *New* p.52-53
Phillips — *Choice* p.177-178, 241
Prochnow — *Public* #552, 768, 778, 824, 928, 1049, 1851, 2387, 2569
Prochnow — *Speaker's* p.211-212
Prochnow — *Success.* #253, 407, 688, 782, 2036-2038, 2239
Reader's — *Getting* p.144
Speaker's Desk p.149-150; #46, 813, 1016, 1062
Wallis — *Treasure* p.23, 61, 75, 226
Wallis — *Words* p.49, 93, 109, 159, 161-164
Woods — *Wellsprings* p.79
Words — *Inspir.* p.183-184
Zobell — *Speaker's* p.95-100

, Aids to
Auden — *Certain* p.263-264

, Immortality of
Peterson — *Art* p.46

, Improvement of
Huxley — *You See* index p.286

, Subconscious
Curtis — *Golden* p.85-87

, Systems of
Weisfeld — *Pulpit* p.128

MEN

See also **Brothers; Fathers; Husbands; Male chauvinism; Man (mankind); Sons**
Alexander's Treasure. p.94
Braude — *Speaker's* #190-193
Copeland — *10,000* p.983-984
Cowan — *Wit* p.105-118
Edwards — *Useful* p.386-387
Flesch — *Unusual* p.169
Forbes — *Thoughts See* index p.558
Fun Fare p.42, 94, 175-176, 180, 184, 270, 296
Halverson — *Perspective* p.43
Harral — *Feature* p.216-217
How To Live p.88-89
Hubbard — *Scrap* p.66, 77, 98
Keys Happiness p.283-284, 502
Kin — *Dictionary* p.160
Liddle — *Thought I, II, III* p.14, 27, 48, 78, 84, 150
Montapert — *Distilled* p.253
New Joy p.43, 102
Speaker's Desk #633
Words — *Inspir.* p.69, 84-85

, American
Words — *Inspir.* p.128

, and sex
How To Live p.400-403

, and women
Adams — *New* p.282
Flesch — *Unusual* p.169-170

, Equality of
Fogg — *1000* #328

, Forgotten
Baillie — *Diary* #64

, Great
Kohn — *Adventures* p.31-34
Kronenberger — *Animal* p.73

, Learned
Fuller — *Thesaurus* #1081-1095

, Nature of
Phillips — *Choice* p.118, 132

, Power of
How To Live p.96-99

, World of
Evans — *This* p.57-58

MENDACITY. *See* **Falsehood**

MENDING
Kin — *Dictionary* p.160, 214
Prochnow — *Public* #439, 882

MENTAL HEALTH
Bradshaw — *Home.* p.1-11
Halverson — *Perspective* p.6
Lair — *Baby* p.147

Montapert — *Distilled* p.254
White — *Life* p.147-160

MENTAL HOSPITALS
Prochnow — *Public* #971
Schermerhorn — *1500* p.25
Weisfeld — *Pulpit* p.141

MENTAL ILLNESS
Asimov — *Treasury* #53-55
Auden — *Certain* p.238-242
Copeland — *10,000* p.120-123
Dirksen — *Quot.* #282
Edwards — *Useful* p.295-296, 363
Flesch — *Unusual* p.160
Guideposts — *Faith* p.185-187
Harnsberger — *Mark* p.203-205, 252
Henry — *5000* p.134
Johnson — *Bedside* p.122
Keys Happiness p.227-231
Kin — *Dictionary* p.154-155
Lockridge — *World's* #320, 439, 642, 5165
Sheban — *Wisdom* no p.
Speaker's Desk #326-327, 739, 854, 893, 927, 1022, 1145
Woods — *Religious* p.623
, and the Church
Words Change p.102-105

MENTAL RETARDATION. *See* **Children, Retarded**

MENTAL TELEPATHY (E.S.P.)
Harnsberger — *Mark* p.264

MENUS
Harral — *Feature* p.218
Prochnow — *Public* #24, 300, 585

MERCENARY
Speaker's Desk #684, 687, 879

MERCHANTS AND MERCHANDISING
Dirksen — *Quot.* #1910
Forbes — *Thoughts* p.104, 224, 490
Fox — *Make* p.112-113
Harral — *Feature* p.218
Kin — *Dictionary* p.160
Prochnow — *Public* #56
Seldes — *Great* p.653
Sheban — *Wisdom* no p.

"MERCHANTS OF DEATH"
Seldes — *Great* p.653-654

MERCURY
Prochnow — *Public* #2302

MERCY
See also **Kindness; Sympathy; Tolerance**; etc.
Alexander's Treasure. p.159
Applegarth — *Heir.* p.203
Braude — *Source* #1117-1118
Clark — *Windows* p.130
Day — *Meditations* p.54-58
Dirksen — *Quot.* #1008-1009, 1308, 2076
Droke — *Christian* p.345
Edwards — *Useful* p.333-334, 387-388
Evans — *Faith* p.77-78
Evans — *This* p.149-160
Evans — *Unto* p.117
Flesch — *Unusual* p.170
Flint — *Graham* p.93
Fox — *Make* p.216
Fuller — *Epigrams* p.210
Garland — *Subject* p.189-190
Guideposts — *Faith* p.244-249
Henry — *5000* p.174
Hobe — *Tapestries* p.197
Hovey — *Treasury* #31, 492, 676, 1274, 1507
Hubbard — *Scrap* p.89
Johnson — *Bedside* p.224-225
Kennedy — *Reader's* #666
Kin —*Dictionary* p.160-161
Kohn — *Through* p.147-150
Liddle — *Thought I, II, III* p.137, 172
Lockridge — *World's* #1433, 5869
New Topical p.164
Prochnow — *Public* #578, 2153, 2356, 2461, 2497, 2599, 2676, 3396-3398
Prochnow — *Success.* #2045
Sheban — *Wisdom* no p.
Sheen — *Way* p.182-184
Speaker's Desk #93, 381, 944; p.150-151
Woods — *Religious* p.623-626

MERCY SEAT
New Topical p.165

MERIT
See also **Excellence; Good; Perfection**
Book Proverbs p.111, 114
Edwards — *Useful* p.388, 719
Flesch — *Unusual* p.171
Forbes — *Thoughts* p.72, 88, 145, 216, 267, 312, 353, 385, 392, 418, 496, 509
Fox — *Make* p.157
Garland — *Subject* p.343-344
Harnsberger — *Mark* p.264
Henry — *5000* p.174, 320
Kin — *Dictionary* p.67, 161, 283
Liddle — *Thought I, II, III* p.44

Lockridge — *World's* #51, 156, 168-169, 302, 404, 462, 481, 1512, 2508, 2557, 3403, 3568, 4317
Lytle — *Leaves* p.6, 10-11, 187
Mandel — *Stories* p.178, 280-281
Montapert — *Distilled* p.341
Prochnow — *Public* #2668
Sheban — *Wisdom* no p.
Tanksley — *Friend* p.55-56
Woods — *Religious* p.626, 1080
Words — *Inspir.* p.31

"MERMAID, THE LITTLE"
Lindbergh — *Unicorn* p.11-12

MERRIMENT. *See* **Happiness; Joy; Laughter**

MERRY-GO-ROUND
Prochnow — *Public* #542

MESMERISM. *See* **Hypnotism**

MESSAGES AND MESSENGERS
Humes — *Instant* p.43; #1244-1245
Kin — *Dictionary* p.161
Lytle — *Leaves* p.20, 127
Prochnow — *Public* #4366
Wallis — *Words* p.88

MESSIAH. *See* **Jesus Christ**

META-CONSCIOUSNESS
Wheelis — *Moralist* p.107-121

METALS AND METALLURGY
See also names of metals
Hooker — *Index* p.159-170
New Topical p.165

METAMORPHOSIS
Kin — *Dictionary* p.161

METAPHORS
Boas — *History* p.24-43
Dirksen — *Quot.* #67, 347

METAPHYSICS
Edwards — *Useful* p.388-389
Flesch — *Unusual* p.171
Fox — *Make* p.36, 116-117, 228-229
Garland — *Subject* p.191-192
Hooker — *Index* p.9-16
Liebman — *Peace* p.102-104
Lockridge — *World's* #3745
Seldes — *Great* p.654
Woods — *Religious* p.627-628

METER READERS
Harral — *Feature* p.218

METHOD
Edwards — *Useful* p.389
Forbes — *Thoughts See* index p.558
Franke — *Buckley* p.191-192
Kin — *Dictionary* p.161
Lytle — *Leaves* p.183
Prochnow — *Public* #3399-3400
, *"in their madness"*
Speaker's Desk See index p.302

MIAMI, FLORIDA
Botkin — *Anecdotes* p.80, 192
Prochnow — *Success.* #719

MICE
Alexander's Treasure. p.326
Applegarth — *Heir.* p.19
Asimov — *Treasury* #52, 62
Botkin — *Anecdotes* p.268, 271
Harnsberger — *Mark* p.304-306
Henry — *5000* p.183
Kin — *Dictionary* p.169
Prochnow — *Public* #59
Wallis — *Words* p.35

MICHELANGELO BUONARROTI
Peterson — *Art* p.68

MICHIGAN
Botkin — *Anecdotes* p.49, 251, 263, 843
Botkin — *Treasury* p.206, 611, 845n

MICROBES
Applegarth — *Heir.* p.167
Du Noüy — *Road* p.79, 126, 137, 179-180
Harnsberger — *Mark* p.265
Seldes — *Great* p.654

MICROCOSM
Boas — *History* p.212-238

MICRONS
Du Noüy — *Road* p.121-122

MICROPHONE-FRIGHT
Nizer — *Thinking* p.93

MICROSCOPES
Prochnow — *Public* #1742

MIDDLE-AGED
Baillie — *Diary* #82
Dirksen — *Quot.* #125, 349, 762, 1010
Flesch — *Unusual* p.171-172
Grizer — *Wit* p.301
How To Live p.507-509
Keys Happiness p.33-36

Lindbergh — *Gift* p.83-88
Prochnow — *Speaker's* p.212
Prochnow — *Success.* #604, 2046-2047
Sheen — *Content.* p.43-45
Wallis — *Treasure* p.12, 14
Wilcox — *Heart* p.14-16
, Crises of
Jackson — *Coping* p.128-135
, Prayer for
Rogers — *Time* p.75-77
Unlimited Power p.250

MIDDLE AGES
Curtis — *Practical* p.47, 133, 137
Flesch — *Unusual* p.172
Johnson — *Bedside* p.87
Kronenberger — *Animal* p.189-206
Wheelis — *Moralist* p.9, 22, 32

MIDDLE CLASS
See also **Bourgeoisie**
Prochnow — *Public* #984, 2445
Seldes — *Great* p.654-655
, English
Auden — *Certain* p.258-259

MIDDLE EAST
Sheban — *Wisdom* no p.

MIDIANITES
New Topical p.165

MIDNIGHT
Edwards — *Useful* p.389-390
Henry — *5000* p.175

MIGHT. *See* **Power; Strength**

MILAN CATHEDRAL
Applegarth — *Heir.* p.217

MILITARY SERVICE
See also **Armed forces; War;** etc.
Braude — *Stories* p.257-259
Cerf — *Laugh* p.325-335
Fun Fare p.194-197
Hovey — *Treasury* #24, 352, 374, 420, 563, 699, 1255, 1259, 1290, 1334, 1715, 1804
Kennedy — *Reader's* #670
Seaburg — *Great See* index p.461-462
Seldes — *Great* p.655-656
Walters — *How* p.54-56
Woods — *Religious* p.629
, Discipline of
Fuller — *Thesaurus* #2441-2442
, Industrial complex of
Humes — *Instant* p.37
, Officers of
Asimov — *Treasury* #18, 32-34, 220, 250, 271, 280
Copeland — *World's See* index p.737
Fuller — *Thesaurus* #2406-2427
Hubbard — *Scrap* p.47
, Regulations of
Fuller — *Thesaurus* #2446

MILK
Botkin — *Anecdotes* p.77
Dirksen — *Quot.* #666
Flesch — *Unusual* p.172
Harral — *Feature* p.218
Kin — *Dictionary* p.161-162
New Topical p.165-166
Prochnow — *Public* #226, 424, 881, 886, 1139
Prochnow — *Speaker's* p.212

MILLENIUM
Woods — *Religious* p.629

MILLIONAIRES
See also **Wealth**
Flesch — *Unusual* p.172
Grizer — *Wit* p.301-302
Peterson — *Art* p.390
Prochnow — *Public* #221
Schermerhorn — *1500* p.245-246
Walters — *How* p.23-28

MILLS AND MILLERS
Botkin — *Anecdotes* p.59
Hobe — *Tapestries* p.12
Kin — *Dictionary* p.162
New Topical p.166
Welk — *Guide.* p.18-20

MILTON, JOHN
Flesch — *Unusual* p.172
Wallis — *Words* p.180

MIND
See also **Brain; Consciousness; Genius; Intelligence; Mental; Peace, of mind; Reason and reasoning; Sense; Soul; Subconscious; Thought; Understanding;** etc.
Auden — *Certain* p.259-262
Baillie — *Diary* #281
Braude — *Stories* p.259
Curtis — *Daily* p.62-68
Curtis — *Golden* p.67-70
Curtis — *Practical* p.211, 382-383, 533-534
Dirksen — *Quot.* #168; *See also* index p.266
Droke — *Christian* p.346-348

Du Noüy — *Human* p.12-13, 134-141, 236-237
Edward — *Useful* p.390-393, 730
Evans — *Thoughts III (Open Road)* p.198
Evans — *Thoughts IV* p.96, 118, 123-124, 126, 189
Flesch — *Unusual* p.172-174
Flint — *Graham* p.93-94
Forbes — *Thoughts See* index p.558-559
Garland — *Subject* p.193-194
Grizer — *Wit* p.302-304
Harnsberger — *Mark* p.266-269
Henry — *5000* p.175
Holmes — *Design See* index p.233-234
Hovey — *Treasury* p.238; *See also* index p.299
How To Live p.186-189
Hubbard — *Scrap* p.25, 128, 177
Johnson — *Bedside* p.63, 109, 127-128, 133, 248-249, 258, 309
Keys Happiness p.274-276, 368-373, 427-428, 499-502
Kin — *Dictionary* p.162
Krishnamurti — *Think* p.172-175, 202-209
Liddle — *Thought I, II, III* p.50, 54, 61, 70, 88, 93, 95, 124, 140, 145, 174
Liddle — *Thought IV* p.3, 20, 29
Liddle — *Thought V* p.25, 42
Lockridge — *World's See* index p.579
Lytle — *Leaves* p.18, 178
Mandel — *Stories* p.178-179
Montapert — *Distilled* p.254-255
New Joy p.244
Nizer — *Thinking* p.81-82
Peale — *Faith* p.27-54
Peterson — *Art* p.69, 77
Phillips — *Choice* p.54, 97, 126, 164, 196-197
Prochnow — *Public* #1095, 1265, 1440, 1754, 1968, 2255, 2694
Prochnow — *Success.* #894, 943, 952, 1261, 1478, 2048
Seldes — *Great* p.656-658
Sherman — *Your* p.52-59
Speaker's Desk #61, 66, 413, 776, 779; p.151-155
Wallis — *Treasure* p.168, 283
Wallis — *Words* p.50, 121, 142-143, 234
Watson — *Light* p.19-23
White — *Job* p.78, 80-82, 167
Woods — *Religious p.629-632*

, and body
Flesch — *Unusual* p.173-174
Montapert — *Distilled* p.255-256
Reader's — *Getting* p.170-173

, and enrichment
Keller — *Open* p.93

, and God
Woods — *Religious* p.631-632

, and heart
Adams — *New* p.168
Flesch — *Unusual* p.174
Krishnamurti — *Urgency* p.85-88
Taylor — *With* p.1-5

, and matter
Flesch — *Unusual* p.174
Fogg — *1000* #643
Hubbard — *Scrap* p.180

, and religion
Taylor — *With* p.76

, Attentive
Krishnamurti — *Think* p.133-141

, Attitude of
Holmes — *Design* p.40-41
Montapert — *Distilled* p.253-254
Peterson — *Art* p.71

, Change of
Braude — *Source* #1119-1120
Harral — *Feature* p.218

, Closed
Peterson — *Art* p.230

, Control of
Bennett — *How* p.62-68
Hill — *Think* p.287-289

, Crude
Krishnamurti — *Think* p.20-21

, Cultivated
Adams — *New* p.70

, Energies of
Blanton — *Faith* p.39-63

, Exercise for
Peterson — *Art* p.337

, Fatigue of
Speaker's Desk #583, 585

, Focused
Peterson — *Art* p.265

, Growth of
Holmes — *Design* p.165-171

, Health of
Peale — *Courage* p.78-94

, Independent
Adams — *New* p.43

, Individual
Curtis — *Golden* p.91-105

, Infinite
Peterson — *Art* p.229

, Inhospitable
Adams — *New* p.315

, Insulation with
Kohn — *Adventures* p.17-19

, Laws of
Fox — *Make* p.21-29

, *Laziness of*
Holmes — *Design* p.115-116
, *Nature of*
Sheen — *Content.* p.69-91
, *Open*
See also **Tolerance**
Adams — *New* p.104
Kauffman — *For* p.151-152
Krishnamurti — *Think* p.65-70
Peterson — *Art* p.243
Reader's — *Getting* p.186-187
, *Organization of*
Nizer — *Thinking* p.32-33
, *Pictures of*
Peterson — *Art* p.388
Sherman — *Your* p.45-52
, *Poise of*
Albert — *Stop* p.31-33, 65-66
How To Live p.190-194
, *Power of*
Adams — *New* p.101
Book Proverbs p.124
Hill — *Think* p.190-199
, *Presence of*
Braude — *Speaker's* #890-901
, *Prisons of*
Peterson — *Art* p.91
, *Progress of*
Adams — *New* p.45
, *Relaxation of*
Albert — *Stop* p.71-75
, *Renewal of*
Krishnamurti — *Think* p.117-124
, *Shallow*
Woods — *Religious* p.631
, *Stimulation of*
Vogue — *Arts* p.41-52
, *Treasure of*
Peterson — *Art* p.340
, *Universal*
Curtis — *Golden* p.91-105
, *Universe of*
Saturday — *Advent.* p.275-285
, *X-Ray*
Peterson — *Art* p.85

"MIND-WAKERS"
Humes — *Instant* p.35-41, 51-1185

MINIMUM
Mandelbaum — *Choice* p.198-201

MINISTERS AND MINISTRY. *See* **Clergymen**

MINK
Prochnow — *Public* #921, 1097
Prochnow — *Success.* #913

MINNESOTA
Asimov — *Treasury* #449
Botkin — *Anecdotes* p.122
Botkin — *Treasury* p.177n, 320-346

MINORCA
Asimov — *Treasury* #155

MINORITIES
See also **Democracy; Races of man, Relations of**
Braude — *Source* #1121-1122
Dirksen — *Quot.* #21, 72, 667, 1011, 1687
Edwards — *Useful* p.393-394
Evans — *Unto* p.84
Forbes — *Thoughts* p.161, 174, 201, 449, 509
Hoffer — *Reflect.* p.29-30
Kauffman — *For* p.136-138
Kin — *Dictionary* p.163
Liddle — *Thought I, II, III* p.144
Seldes — *Great* p.658-660
Wallis — *Treasure* p.48
Woods — *Business.* p.149
Woods — *Religious* p.633
, *Opinions of*
Menninger — *Blue.* p.111-112
, *Power of*
Flint — *Graham* p.94
, *Rights of*
Woods — *Business.* p.150

MINOTAUR
Prochnow — *Public* #2338

MINSTRELS
Harnsberger — *Mark* p.269-272

MINT
Harral — *Feature* p.220

MINUTES
Adams — *New* p.162, 187
Applegarth — *Heir.* p.64-65, 69, 261
Flesch — *Unusual* p.174, 176
Kin — *Dictionary* p.163
Lytle — *Leaves* p.171, 176
Nichols — *New* p.67-68
Peterson — *Art* p.128
Woods — *Religious* p.633, 640

MIRABEAU, COMTE DE
Adams — *New* p.39

MIRACLES
See also **Mystics and mysticism; Mystery; Wonder**
Adams — *New* p.134
Applegarth — *Heir.* p.191, 193, 199, 201, 212, 284

Braude — *Speaker's* #902
Curtis — *Practical* p.509
Edwards — *Useful* p.394
Evans — *Thoughts IV* p.180, 186
Flesch — *Unusual* p.174-175
Forbes — *Thoughts* p.192, 236-238, 322
Fuller — *Thesaurus* #1616-1619
Harnsberger — *Mark* p.272-274
Hobe — *Tapestries* p.24
Kennedy — *Reader's* #683-684
Kin — *Dictionary* p.163
Knight's Illus. p.200-201
Kohn — *Adventures* p121-124
Lockridge — *World's* #1404
Lytle — *Leaves* p.133, 193
Mandel — *Stories* p.179
New Topical p.167-168
Peale — *Courage* p.163-164
Peale — *Guideposts* p.251-253
Peterson — *Art* p.54
Prochnow — *Success.* #622, 1005, 2049
Seldes — *Great* p.660-662
Wallis — *Treasure* p.24, 32, 69
Wallis — *Words* p.35, 85, 157, 160, 173, 240
Woods — *Religious* p.633-637
Woods — *Wellsprings* p.53-54
Words — *Inspir.* p.14-15, 24-25
Zobell — *Speaker's* p.100-104

, and natural law
Ideas p.250-252

, Little
Day — *Meditations* p.18

, through evil agents
New Topical p.168

, through God's servants
See also **Jesus Christ, Miracles of**
New Topical p.168-169

MIRE. *See* **Mud**

MIRRORS
Applegarth — *Heir.* p.49
Baillie — *Diary* #312
Flesch — *Unusual* p.175
Fuller — *Epigrams* p.210
Holman — *Psych.* p.146-154
Kin — *Dictionary* p.151, 163
Lytle — *Leaves* p.40, 73
Prochnow — *Success.* #503, 1070
Wallis — *Treasure* p.107, 150

MIRTH. *See* **Cheerfulness; Jokes and joking; Joy; Laughter**; etc.

MISBEHAVIORAL SCIENCES
Saturday — *Advent.* p.17-32

MISCEGENATION
Woods — *Religious* p.637

MISCHIEF
See also **Evil; Injury; Malice**; etc.
Edwards — *Useful* p.395
Henry — *5000* p.176
Kin — *Dictionary* p.163
Krishnamurti — *Think* p.123, 145-146

MISCONDUCT. *See* **Sin**

MISERS
See also **Greed**
Braude — *Stories* p.259
Edwards — *Useful* p.395-396
Forbes — *Thoughts* p.140, 244, 379
Grizer — *Wit* p.304
Kin — *Dictionary* p.164
Lockridge — *World's* #1520, 2341, 4194, 4986
Mandel — *Stories* p.179
Prochnow — *Public* #1363, 1914, 3401-3402
Prochnow — *Speaker's* p.214
Prochnow — *Success.* #569

MISERY
See also **Grief; Illness; Unhappiness**; etc.
Asimov — *Treasury* #125, 311, 341-342
Dirksen — *Quot.* #1012, 1931
Edwards — *Useful* p.396-397
Evans — *Unto* p.96
Flesch — *Unusual* p.175
Flint — *Graham* p.94
Forbes — *Thoughts* p.165, 419, 482
Garland — *Subject* p.81, 194-195
Harnsberger — *Mark* p.274-275
Henry — *5000* p.176
Hubbard — *Scrap* p.25
Johnson — *Bedside* p.112, 139
Kin — *Dictionary* p.164
Liddle — *Thought I, II, III* p.8, 53, 104
Liddle — *Thought IV* p.29
Lockridge — *World's* #899, 1450, 2427, 2597, 2828, 5869
Prochnow — *Public* #1467
Woods — *Religious* p.637

MISFITS
Unlimited Power p.188-191

MISFORTUNE
See also **Adversity; Defeat; Disaster; Failure; Luck, Bad**
Alexander's Treasure. p.28
Braude — *Source* #1123-1125
Braude — *Stories* p.259
Dirksen — *Quot.* #254, 1747, 1931, 2078–2079
Edwards — *Useful* p.397-398

Evans — *Thoughts I* p.80-81, 121-122
Flesch — *Unusual* p.175
Fogg — *1000* #331, 363, 622, 642, 665
Forbes — *Thoughts* p.164, 325, 343, 363, 372, 400-401, 452, 459
Garland — *Subject* p.195
Grizer — *Wit* p.304-305
Harnsberger — *Mark* p.275
Henry — *5000* p.176
Kin — *Dictionary* p.164-165
Liddle — *Thought I, II, III* p.54-55, 89, 111, 137, 182-183
Liddle — *Thought IV* p.18, 34
Lockridge — *World's See* index p.579
Lytle — *Leaves* p.17
Montapert — *Distilled* p.256
Prochnow — *Public* #898, 3403-3404, 4160-4161
Prochnow — *Success.* #2050-2052
Speaker's Desk p.155-156
Wallis — *Treasure* p.157
Woods — *Content.* p.314
Woods — *Religious* p.637

MISGIVING. *See* **Doubt**

MISOGYNY
See also **Male chauvinism**
Kin — *Dictionary* p.165

MISREPRESENTATION. *See* **Fraud**

"MISS AMERICA"
Peale — *Guideposts* p.299-302

MISSILES
Kohn — *Adventures* p.31-34

MISSIONARIES
Droke — *Christian* p.349
Edwards — *Useful* p.730
Flesch — *Unusual* p.175
Fuller — *Thesaurus* #1521
Guideposts — *Faith* p.440-443
Harnsberger — *Mark* p.275-277
Harral — *Feature* p.223
Johnson — *Bedside* p.214-215
Kennedy — *Reader's* p.685-690
New Topical p.170
Wallis — *Words* p.221-224
Weisfeld — *Pulpit* p.4, 125-126, 138, 155, 158
Woods — *Religious* p.637-639
Woods — *Wellsprings* p.71
Zobell — *Speaker's* p.104-107
, as ministers
New Topical p.171
, L.D.S.
Hunter — *Gems* p.51-57
, Spirit of
Wheelis — *Moralist* p.44

MISSIONS
Flint — *Graham* p.9-10, 94
Hovey — *Treasury* p.238-239; *See also* index p.299, 303
Kauffman — *For* p.50-52
Knight's Illus. p.201-205
Knight's Treas. p.219-226
More Words p.111-112

MISSISSIPPI
Botkin — *Anecdotes* p.13, 24, 82, 169
Botkin — *Treasury* p.428, 476, 571, 696

MISSISSIPPI RIVER
Botkin — *Anecdotes* p.70
Botkin — *Treasury See* index p.930
Harnsberger — *Mark* p.278-280

MISSOURI
Botkin — *Anecdotes* p.2, 16, 24, 98-99, 101, 189, 215
Botkin — *Treasury See* index p.930
Harnsberger — *Mark* p.280-281

MISTAKES
See also **"Boners"**
Asimov — *Treasury* #483-485
Baillie — *Diary* #105
Braude — *Source* #1126-1135
Braude — *Speaker's* #903-909
Braude — *Stories* p.260-262
Carruthers — *Sparks* p.29-31
Curtis — *Practical* p.38, 55
Dirksen — *Quot.* #392, 887, 1106, 1139, 1726, 2080, 2282
Edwards — *Useful* p.167-168, 398-399
Emmons — *Mature* p.147
Evans — *Faith* p.3-4, 64, 85, 88, 93-94, 101-102, 147
Evans — *Thoughts I See* index no p.
Evans — *Thoughts II (Open Door)* p.16, 37, 77-78, 133-134, 163, 184
Evans — *Thoughts III (Open Road)* p.18-19, 67, 121, 129-130, 161, 176, 195, 212
Evans — *Thoughts IV* p.145, 194-195
Evans — *Unto* p.6-7, 33-35, 63-64, 66, 69, 77, 84, 97, 105, 133
Flesch — *Unusual* p.22, 79, 85, 176

Forbes — *Thoughts* p.44, 232, 250, 311, 467; *See also* index p.559
Fox — *Make* p.95-96
Fuller — *Epigrams* p.108, 210
Grizer — *Wit* p.56-57, 150, 305-307
Guideposts — *Faith* p.207-209
Henry — *5000* p.78, 130
Hobe — *Tapestries* p.14
Holmes — *I've* p.8
Hovey — *Treasury* #25, 165, 167-169, 330, 669, 911-913, 1467, 1518
How To Live p.318, 432-434
Johnson — *Bedside* p.89
Kauffman — *For* p.142-143
Kennedy — *Reader's* #304
Keys Happiness p.178
Kin — *Dictionary* p.82, 165
Kohn — *Pathways* p.106
Krishnamurti — *Think* p.190-191
Liddle — *Thought I, II, III* p.15, 35, 42, 60, 77-78, 132, 158, 167-168, 184-186, 188
Lockridge — *World's* #1637, 1755, 3311, 4427, 4510, 3541, 3563, 3651, 4006
Lytle — *Leaves* p.142
Mandel — *Stories* p.179
Mandelbaum — *Choose* p.261-283
Modern Eloquence (14) p.379
Montapert — *Distilled* p.133-134, 256-257
Nichols — *New* p.69-70
Nizer — *Thinking* p.115
Peale — *Courage* p.37-38
Peterson — *Art* p.288
Phillips — *Choice* p.145
Prochnow — *Public* #201, 677, 1007, 1497, 1520, 1683, 1830, 2379, 2658, 3020-3021, 3405-3409, 4078-4079
Prochnow — *Speaker's* p.41, 115-116, 214
Prochnow — *Success.* #967, 1270, 1364, 1372, 1380, 1901, 2053, 2414
Seldes — *Great* p.662; #326-327
Speaker's Desk #92, 249, 363, 379, 1009; *See* index p.299
White — *Job* p.43-44, 65-67, 77, 83, 95, 97
Woods — *Religious* p.282-283; p.639
Words — *Inspir.* p.151-152

, Learning from
Peale — *Stay* p.137-156

, Quoted
Flesch — *Unusual* p.175
Kronenberger — *Animal* p.206-211

, Repentance for
Evans — *Faith See* index p.239-240

, Typographical
Prochnow — *Public* #201, 512, 525, 1830
Schermerhorn — *1500* p.379-380

MISTRESSES
Cowan — *Wit* p.93-104
Kin — *Dictionary* p.165
Lockridge — *World's* #4888

MISUNDERSTANDING
See also **Disagreement**
Alexander's Treasure. p.106, 316
Braude — *Stories* p.262-264
Dirksen — *Quot.* #363
Evans — *Thoughts I* p.46-47, 55-59, 87-89, 93-94, 98, 186-187
Evans — *Thoughts III (Open Road)* p.29-30, 97, 195
Evans — *Thoughts IV* p.106, 197, 208-214
Flesch — *Unusual* p.176
Flint — *Graham* p.94
Kin — *Dictionary* p.165
Kohn — *Pathways* p.105-106
Prochnow — *Public* #302
Speaker's Desk See index p.302

MISUSE
Krishnamurti — *Think* p.192-193
Mandel — *Stories* p.180

MIXTURE
Kin — *Dictionary* p.165
Prochnow — *Public* #2443

MOABITES
New Topical p.171-172

MOB
See also **Panic; Rebellion;** etc.
Dirksen — *Quot.* #456-457, 626, 2115, 2117
Edwards — *Useful* p.399-400
Franke — *Buckley* p.193
Grizer — *Wit* p.307-308
Henry — *5000* p.176-177
Kin — *Dictionary* p.165, 254
Prochnow — *Public* #3410-3412
Seldes — *Great* p.663
Sheban — *Wisdom* no p.

MOCKINGBIRDS
Hubbard — *Scrap* p.16

"MOCK-ORAL YARNS"
Botkin — *Treasury* p.490-491

MOCKERY *See* **Ridicule**

MODEL TRAINS
Harral — *Feature* p.224

MODELS
Harral — *Feature* p.223-224
Lockridge — *World's* #3848
Lytle — *Leaves* p.90, 156
Woods — *Religious* p.639

MODERATION
See also **Abstinence; Conservation; Self-control; Temperance**
Alexander's Treasure. p.133
Book Proverbs p.106
Braude — *Source* #1136-1138
Curtis — *Practical* p.414-415
Dirksen — *Quot.* #1147, 1748, 2081
Edwards — *Useful* p.400-401
Evans — *Faith* p.36, 109-112, 118
Evans — *Thoughts I* p.27-28
Evans — *Thoughts II (Open Door)* p.57-58, 64
Evans — *Thoughts IV* p.114-115
Evans — *Unto* p.61-64
Flesch — *Unusual* p.176
Forbes — *Thoughts* p.75, 94, 102, 130, 272, 466
Franke — *Buckley* p.193
Garland — *Subject* p.196-197
Henry — *5000* p.177
Hubbard — *Scrap* p.22, 57
Kin — *Dictionary* p.166
Liddle — *Thought I, II, III* p.23, 143
Lockridge — *World's* #957, 1768
Lytle — *Leaves* p.43
Menninger — *Blue.* p.80
Modern Eloquence (14) p.380
Montapert — *Distilled* p.257
Peterson — *Art* p.394
Prochnow — *Public* #3413-3414
Prochnow — *Success.* #1306, 2054
Seldes — *Great* p.663-664
Speaker's Desk #371, 513, 897
Woods — *Content.* p.39, 305, 344
Woods — *Religious* p.639

"MODERN AGE"
Braude — *Source* #1139-1140
Braude — *Speaker's* #910-916
Curtis — *Now* p.5-16
Droke — *Christian* p.349-351
Flint — *Graham* p.94
Franke — *Buckley* p.193-195
Grizer — *Wit* p.308-309
How To Live p.558-562
Sheban — *Wisdom* no p.
Wheelis — *Moralist* p.7, 9, 22, 32, 84, 114, 126, 131

MODERN ART. *See* **Art and artists, Modern**

MODERNITY
See also **Present; Progress**
Curtis — *Practical* p.435, 483
Edwards — *Useful* p.730
Harvey — *Treasury* p.129-130; #657-661, 934
Prochnow — *Public* #1081
Wallis — *Words* p.42, 67, 105
Woods — *Religious* p.639-640

MODESTY
See also **Bashfulness; Decency; Delicacy; Humility; Meekness; Refinement**
Asimov — *Treasury* #326, 580-581, 585, 639
Braude — *Source* #1141
Braude — *Speaker's* #917-918
Braude — *Stories* p.264-265
Dirksen — *Quot.* #1631
Edwards — *Useful* p.401-403
Evans — *Thoughts II (Open Door)* p.88-89
Evans — *Thoughts IV* p.133
Flesch — *Unusual* p.176
Fogg — *1000* #304, 638, 695, 699, 985
Forbes — *Thoughts* p.62, 233, 268, 355, 450, 465
Fuller — *Epigrams* p.211-212
Fuller — *Thesaurus* #376-390
Harnsberger — *Mark* p.281-282
Henry — *5000* p.177
How To Live p.274
Hubbard — *Scrap* p.225
Kin — *Dictionary* p.166-167
Liddle — *Thought I, II, III* p.81
Liddle — *Thought V* p.43
Lockridge — *World's* p.2498, 4769; *See also* index p.579
Menninger — *Blue.* p.38
Nichols — *New* p.102-103
Nizer — *Thinking* p.66
Prochnow — *Public* #2018, 3415-3417
Prochnow — *Success.* #1302
Sheban — *Wisdom* no p.
Speaker's Desk p.156-157; #24, 722, 1044
Woods — *Religious* p.640

MOHAMMEDANISM
See also **Koran**
Adams — *New* p.37
Curtis — *Practical* p.223-228
Hill — *Think* p.187-189
Hubbard — *Scrap* p.170
Krishnamurti — *Think* p.147-148
Prochnow — *Success.* #1563, 1805
Seldes — *Great* p.664
Woods — *Religious* p.640

MOHAWK INDIANS
Botkin — *Anecdotes* p.58

MOLECULES
Du Noüy — *Human* p.16, 18, 21-25, 33-34, 46, 58-59, 248
Du Noüy — *Road See* index p.249

MOMENTS. *See* **Minutes**

MONARCHIES AND MONARCHS
See also **Kings and queens; Rulers**
Dirksen — *Quot.* #1038, 2027
Harnsberger — *Mark* p.282-283
Lockridge — *World's* #5776
Seldes — *Great* p.664
Woods — *Religious* p.640

MONASTICISM AND MONKS
Flesch — *Unusual* p.178
Kin — *Dictionary* p.168
Seldes — *Great* p.671
Woods — *Religious* p.641

MONDAY
Kin — *Dictionary* p.167

MONEY
See also **Dollars; Gold; Wealth;** etc.
Alexander's Treasure. p.231-235
Applegarth — *Heir.* p.49
Auden — *Certain* p.265-267
Braude — *Source* #1142-1150
Braude — *Speaker's* #919-922
Braude — *Stories* p.265
Casselberry — *How* p.179-195
Curtis — *Daily* p.100-106
Curtis — *Practical* p.313, 317-318, 348-349
Detherage — *Sunrise* p.93, 178
Dirksen — *Quot.* #332, 1013, 1345, 1748, 1817, 2082-2085, 2302
Edwards — *Useful* p.403-404, 730
Esteve — *Experience* p.123
Evans — *Faith* p.29, 32, 75-76
Evans — *Quote* p.223-232
Evans — *Thoughts IV* p.73-74, 128, 165, 205
Flesch — *Unusual* p.176-178
Flint — *Graham* p.94-95
Forbes — *Thoughts See* index p.559
Fridy — *Meditat.* p.113-114
Fuller — *Epigrams* p.212-214, 358
Garland — *Subject* p.197
Grizer — *Wit* p.310-315
Halverson — *Perspective* p.28
Harnsberger — *Mark* p.284-287
Harral — *Feature* p.224
Henry — *5000* p.177-178
Holmes — *I've* p.5-6
Hovey — *Treasury* p.239-240; *See also* index p.299
Hubbard — *Scrap* p.53, 96, 106, 117, 133, 142, 202, 214, 225
Jones — *If* p.75-85
Kennedy — *Reader's* #691-698
Kin — *Dictionary* p.41, 167
Lair — *Baby* p.144
Liddle — *Thought I, II, III See* index p.198
Liddle — *Thought IV* p.22, 37, 43, 46
Lockridge — *World's See* index p.579
Lytle — *Leaves* p.147-148
Mandel — *Stories* p.180-183
Mandelbaum — *Choose* p.17
Modern Eloquence (14) p.381
Montapert — *Distilled* p.258
Myers — *Thunder* p.123, 158-159
New Joy p.57
New Topical p.172
Peale — *Courage* p.211-212
Peterson — *Art* p.49
Prochnow — *Public* p.503; #898, 1668
Prochnow — *Speaker's* p.215-217
Prochnow — *Success. See* index p.495
Seldes — *Great* p.664-670
Sheban — *Wisdom* no p.
Speaker's Desk p.157-164
Wallis — *Words* p.203-204
Watson — *Light* p.15-18
Woods — *Business.* p.150-152
Woods — *Content.* p.47, 66, 185, 208
Woods — *Religious* p.641-643
Zobell — *Speaker's* p.107, 151-153
, and ethics
Kauffman — *For* p.144-145
, and marriage
Holmes — *I've* p.43-44
, as a god
Myers — *Thunder* p.30-31
, Collection of
Speaker's Desk #924, 1094, 1105
, "Grabbers" of
Prochnow — *Public* #1367
, Interest rates for
Kauffman — *For* p.143-144
, International
Dirksen — *Quot.* #34
, Lenders of
See also **Lending and loans; Money, Interest rates for**
Lockridge — *World's* #734
, Love of
Baillie — *Diary* #324
Hunter — *Gems* p.47-48

, Nickels as
Peale — *Guideposts* p.41-45
, Standard of
Adams — *New* p.318
, Use of
Montapert — *Distilled* p.258

MONGOOSES
Asimov — *Treasury* #258
Kin — *Dictionary* p.168

MONISM
Seldes — *Great* p.670-671
Taylor — *With* p.39-43

MONKEYS
Botkin — *Treasury* p.657, 675
Fun Fare p.105
Kin — *Dictionary* p.168
Lockridge — *World's* #4413
Prochnow — *Public* #74

MONOGAMY
Lockridge — *World's* #4095
Seldes — *Great* p.671

MONOGRAMS
Wallis — *Words* p.35

MONOLOGS
Prochnow — *Public* #1745
Prochnow — *Success.* #1032

MONOMANIA
Edwards — *Useful* p.404-405

MONOPOLY
Flesch — *Unusual* p.178
Seldes — *Great* p.671-672
Woods — *Business.* p.153-156
Woods — *Religious* p.643

MONOTHEISM
Boas — *History* p.187-211
Woods — *Religious* p.643

MONOTONY
See also **Bores and boredom; Routine**
Edwards — *Useful* p.51, 145, 730
Evans — *Thoughts IV* p.17, 198
Evans — *Unto* p.119
Flesch — *Unusual* p.178
Fuller — *Thesaurus* #186-195
Harnsberger — *Mark* p.287-289
Johnson — *Bedside* p.199
Kin — *Dictionary* p.28
Krishnamurti — *Think* p.122
Prochnow — *Public* #2155, 4390

MONROE DOCTRINE
Ideas p.253-255

MONSTERS
Prochnow — *Public* #2398

MONTAIGNE, MICHEL DE
Flesch — *Unusual* p.178
Reader's — *20th* p.13

MONTANA
Botkin — *Anecdotes* p.231
Botkin — *Treasury* p.9, 47, 325, 364, 366, 564, 851

MONTHS
Henry — *5000* p.178-179
New Topical p.172

MONUMENTS
See also **Epitaphs; Statues**
Braude — *Source* #1151-1153
Braude — *Stories* p.265
Dirksen — *Quot.* #182, 458, 2086-2087
Edwards — *Useful* p.405
Fogg — *1000 See* index p.892
Fuller — *Epigrams* p.214-215
Harral — *Feature* p.224, 301
Henry — *5000* p.179-180
Kin — *Dictionary* p.168
Prochnow — *Public* #3427-3428

MOOD
See also **Depression; Discouragement; Temper**
Evans — *Thoughts III (Open Road)* p.29, 36-39, 48, 66-67
Evans — *Thoughts IV* p.86, 199
Harnsberger — *Mark* p.290
Kohn — *Touch* p.12-17
Lockridge — *World's* #1828
Nizer — *Thinking* p.121
Words Change p.26-29

MOON
Curtis — *Practical* p.211
Flesch — *Unusual* p.178
Goudge — *Comfort* p.23, 25, 31-34
Hadfield — *Delights* p.45, 241
Harnsberger — *Mark* p.290
Henry — *5000* p.180
Kin — *Dictionary* p.168
New Joy p.220, 224
New Topical p.172-173
Prochnow — *Public* #967, 4343
Prochnow — *Success.* #1025
, and moonlight
Hobe — *Tapestries* p.113
, flights and walk
Dirksen — *Quot.* #55, 1165, 1167
Guideposts — *Faith* p.444-447
Peterson — *Art* p.234

MOOSE
Asimov — *Treasury* #411

MORALE
Evans — *Thoughts III (Open Road)* p.197
Mandel — *Stories* p.183
Seldes — *Great* p.675
, National
Dirksen — *Quot.* #1171

MORALISM AND MORALISTS
Adams — *New* p.159
Johnson — *Bedside* p.212
Lockridge — *World's* #1131
Phillips — *Choice* p.72
Woods — *Religious* p.649

MORALITY AND MORALS
See also **Conduct; Decency; Good; Honesty; Right; Values; Virtues**
Book Proverbs p.132
Curtis — *Practical* p.551-552
Droke — *Christian* p.351-352
Du Noüy — *Human* p.129-134, 140, 142, 153-154, 191-195, 209-212, 214-217, 249-251, 270-273
Edwards — *Useful* p.405-407, 730
Evans — *Faith* p.73, 79-80, 154, 163-164
Evans — *This* p.53-71, 145-146
Evans — *Thoughts III (Open Road)* p.47, 80, 89, 128-129, 145, 156, 158, 171
Evans — *Thoughts IV* p.88, 94, 98, 123-124, 127-128, 133-134, 138, 149
Flesch — *Unusual* p.179
Flint — *Graham* p.95-97
Forbes — *Thoughts* p.10, 359, 369, 413, 420, 425, 444, 459, 511
Fuller — *Epigrams* p.215-216
Garland — *Subject* p.198
Grizer — *Wit* p.316
Harnsberger — *Mark* p.290-294
Harral — *Feature* p.224-225
Henry — *5000* p.180-181
Hobe — *Tapestries* p.42
Hovey — *Treasury* p.240-241; *See also* index p.299
Hubbard — *Scrap* p.126, 200, 214
Ideas p.340-342
Johnson — *Bedside* p.83, 90, 116, 335
Kauffman — *For* p.146-147
Keller — *You* p.62-65
Kennedy — *Fresh* p.3-6
Kennedy — *Reader's* #703-707
Krishnamurti — *Urgency* p.47-49
Liddle — *Thought I, II, III* p.59, 103, 125, 146
Liddle — *Thought IV* p.17, 38, 42
Liddle — *Thought V* p.15, 34, 38
Liebman — *Hope* p.101-118
Lockridge — *World's* #1031, 2424, 3788, 4092, 4094, 4115, 4353, 5794
Lytle — *Leaves* p.165
Montapert — *Distilled* p.259
Nizer — *Thinking* p.191
Seldes — *Great* p.672-675
Sheen — *Content.* p.48-49
Sheen — *Way* p.170-172
Speaker's Desk #72, 139, 164-166, 906
Strait — *Speaker's* p.124-128
Wallis — *Treasure* p.25, 113-114
Wallis — *Words* p.14, 132
Wheelis — *Moralist See* index p.166
Woods — *Religious* p.643, 647-656
Words — *Inspir.* p.149-150
, and economics
Woods — *Religious* p.652
, and freedom
Woods — *Religious* p.653
, and God
Woods — *Religious* p.653-654
, and goodness
Wheelis — *Moralist* p.37-54
, and inhumanity
Kauffman — *For* p.122-123
, and religion
Woods — *Religious* p.654-655
, and state
Woods — *Religious* p.655
, Antithesis of
Wheelis — *Moralist* p.25-36
, Apathy of
Keys Happiness p.252-253
, Atmosphere of
Woods — *Religious* p.643
, Beauty of
Woods — *Religious* p.643
, Code of
See also **Commandments, Ten**
Woods — *Religious* p.644
, Crisis of
Myers — *Thunder* p.11-23
Peale — *Sin* p.1-10
, Definition of
Curtis — *Practical* p.97, 104
, Dignity of
Woods — *Religious* p.644
, Disorder of
Woods — *Religious* p.644

, *Doubt of*
Webb — *Edge* p.78-80
, *Education of*
Woods — *Religious* p.644
, *Evil of*
Woods — *Religious* p.644
, *Excellence of*
Woods — *Religious* p.644
, *Force of*
Evans — *This* p.27-28
Kennedy — *Reader's* #699-702
Woods — *Religious* p.645
, *Freedom of*
Kahn — *Lessons* p.48-55
, *Guidelines of*
Kauffman — *For* p.145-146
, *Heroism of*
Woods — *Religious* p.645
, *Instinct of*
Woods — *Religious* p.645
, *Law of*
Hunter — *Gems* p.58
Sheen — *Way* p.28-30
Woods — *Religious* p.645-646
, *Obligation of*
Woods — *Religious* p.646
, *Order of*
Wheelis — *Moralist* p.57-58, 61-62, 77, 102, 105, 128
Woods — *Religious* p.646-647
, *Paralysis of*
Woods — *Religious* p.647
, *"Pearls" of*
Baillie — *Diary* #229
, *Philosophy of*
Woods — *Religious* p.647
, *Positive*
Woods — *Religious* p.652
, *Principles of*
Dirksen — *Quot.* #59, 1062
, *Problems of*
Myers — *Thunder* p.14-16
, *Progress of*
Flint — *Graham* p.96
Wheelis — *Moralist* p.125-128
Woods — *Religious* p.647
, *Question of*
Dirksen — *Quot.* #112
, *Standards of*
Woods — *Religious* p.647-648
, *Support of*
Prochnow — *Success.* #1170
, *Theology of*
McDonagh — *Invit.* p.vii-ix, 16-21, 183-200
Woods — *Religious* p.648
, *Today's*
Myers — *Thunder* p.11-23, 40-41
, *Truth of*
Woods — *Religious* p.648

MORMON, BOOK OF
Zobell — *Speaker's* p.21-24

MORMONS. *See* **Latter-Day Saints; Priests and priesthood, Mormon**

MORNING
See also **Dawn; Day; Sunrise**
Alexander's Treasure. p.210
Auden — *Certain* p.98-99
Detherage — *Sunrise* p.29-30
Edwards — *Useful* p.407-408
Flesch — *Unusual* p.179
Forbes — *Thoughts* p.194, 274, 398
Hadfield — *Delights* p.13-32
Henry — *5000* p.181
Hobe — *Tapestries* p.12, 98, 106, 111, 117, 193
Hubbard — *Scrap* p.73
Johnson — *Bedside* p.58
Lockridge — *World's* #4521
Lytle — *Leaves* p.172
Montapert — *Distilled* p.259-260
New Topical p.173
Prochnow — *Public* #1, 3429-3430
Prochnow — *Success.* #1289
Wallis — *Words* p.211-212
, *Influences of*
Wilcox — *Heart* p.28-29

MORONS. *See* **Idiots**

MOROSENESS. *See* **Depression; Pessimism and pessimists;** etc.

MORTALITY. *See* **Death; Humanity; Man (mankind)**

MORTALS
Garland — *Subject* p.198-199

MORTARBOARD
Prochnow — *Public* #669

MORTGAGES
Prochnow — *Public* #42, 220
Prochnow — *Speaker's* p.217-218
Woods — *Religious* p.656

MORTICIANS
Asimov — *Treasury* #306
Botkin — *Anecdotes* p.260
Flesch — *Unusual* p.179-180
George — *Book* p.380
Harnsberger — *Mark* p.491

MOSES
Asimov — *Treasury* #458-459, 486-487
Kin — *Dictionary* p.169
Lockridge — *World's* #3782, 4040
Prochnow — *Public* #963
Woods — *Religious* p.656
, Law of
See also **Commandments, Ten**
New Topical p.147-148

MOSES, ANNA MARY ROBERTSON ("Grandma")
Kohn — *Touch* p.167-169

MOSLEMS. *See* **Mohammedanism**

MOSQUITOES
Botkin — *Treasury* p.205, 600, 608-609, 646
Harnsberger — *Mark* p.295-296
Prochnow — *Public* #1069
Prochnow — *Success.* #1151
Schermerhorn — *1500* p.251-252

MOSS
Kin — *Dictionary* p.169

MOTELS
Harral — *Feature* p.225
Prochnow — *Success.* #481
Unlimited Power p.192-196

MOTHERS
See also **Children; Family; Parents and parenthood;** etc.
Alexander's Treasure. p.239, 285
Applegarth — *Heir.* p.52-54, 57-58, 131, 227, 230, 293, 298-299
Asimov — *Treasury* #116, 347, 387, 393, 638
Braude — *Sources* #1154-1159
Braude — *Speaker's* #200-203, 923
Braude — *Stories* p.265-266
Detherage — *Sunrise* p.27-28, 119-124
Dirksen — *Quot.* #50, 64, 1015, 1272, 2088-2091, 2128, 2361
Droke — *Christian* p.352-353
Edmunds — *Useful* p.409-411
Evans — *Faith* p.57-60
Evans — *Quote* p.9-28
Evans — *This* p.117-118
Evans — *Thoughts I* p.18, 137-138, 219
Evans — *Thoughts II (Open Door)* p.22-23, 33-37, 94-95, 105-106, 114-115
Evans — *Thoughts III (Open Road)* p.20-21, 31, 157
Evans — *Thoughts IV* p.35, 153-154
Evans — *Unto* p.12, 106, 146
Flesch — *Unusual* p.180
Flint — *Graham* p.97
Fuller — *Epigrams* p.216, 358
Fuller — *Thesaurus* #991-993
Garland — *Subject* p.199
Goudge — *Comfort* p.146
Grizer — *Wit* p.316
Guideposts — *Faith* p.157-161
Henry — *5000* p.181-182
Hobe — *Tapestries* p.90, 166-169
Hovey — *Treasury* p.241-243; *See* index p.299
Hubbard — *Scrap* p.205
Kennedy — *Reader's* #708-709
Keys Happiness p.471
Kin — *Dictionary* p.169
Knight's Illus. p.205-208
Knight's Treas. p.226-234
Liddle — *Thought I, II, III* p.8, 69, 85, 91, 97, 112, 138, 155, 162
Liddle — *Thought IV* p.27
Liddle — *Thought V* p.27
Lockridge — *World's* #5612
Lytle — *Leaves* p.88, 90-91
Manchee — *Secret* p.234-235
Mandel — *Stories* p.183-184
Peale — *Courage* p.234-236, 240
Peale — *Guideposts* p.76-79
Peterson — *Art* p.159
Prochnow — *Public See* index p.503
Prochnow — *Speaker's* p.218
Prochnow — *Success.* #1002, 1007, 1079, 1087, 1275
Reader's — *20th* p.85-89
Schermerhorn — *1500* p.252
Seaburg — *Great* p.210, 213, 244, 250, 273, 280, 287, 295-296, 320, 322, 330, 357, 394
Seldes — *Great* p.675
Sheban — *Wisdom* no p.
Sheen — *Way* p.86-88
Speaker's Desk #87, 93, 277, 554, 628, 657, 720, 815, 921, 996, 1066, 1146-1147
Wallis — *Treasure* p.51, 127, 132-134
Wallis — *Words* p.106, 109-114, 127
White — *Life* p.26-32
Woods — *Content.* p.143-144
Woods — *Religious* p.619-620, 656-657
Words — *Inspir.* p.193
Zobell — *Speaker's* p.109-110
, Homes for
Harral — *Feature* p.214

, Jewish
Asimov — *Treasury* #317, 319
, Love of
Krishnamurti — *Think* p.61-62
, Prayer for
Kohn — *Best* p.143-145
Peale — *Courage* p.52

MOTHER'S DAY
Braude — *Source* #1160-1162
Emmons — *Mature* p.156
Evans — *Unto* p.11-12, 108
Fun Fare p.138-140
Harral — *Feature* p.225
Hovey — *Treasury See* index p.304
Kahn — *Lessons* p.192-193
Keys Happiness p.31-32, 110
Kohn — *Best* p.141-149

MOTHERS-IN-LAW
Asimov — *Treasury* #525-529, 541-542
Braude — *Speaker's* #204-205, 924-931
Braude — *Stories* p.266
Copeland — *10,000* p.277-279
Fuller — *Thesaurus* #936-937
Kin — *Dictionary* p.169
Prochnow — *Public* #21
Prochnow — *Success.* #972
Reader's — *Getting* p.64-68
Schermerhorn — *1500* p.252-253
Woods — *Religious* p.657

MOTHS
New Topical p.173
Prochnow — *Public* #256

MOTION PICTURES
Asimov — *Treasury* #8-9, 49
Grizer — *Wit* p.316-317
Harral — *Feature* p.154-155, 225-227
Lockridge — *World's* #3786
Prochnow — *Public* #421, 1051, 1257, 1425
Prochnow — *Speaker's* p.218
Prochnow — *Success.* #215, 451, 997, 1015
Seldes — *Great* p.675-676
Simpson — *Contemp.* p.407-413
Woods — *Religious* p.657-658
, as art
Nizer — *Thinking* p.124
, as entertainment
Nizer — *Thinking* p.124
, Engineers of
Nizer — *Thinking* p.192
, Industry of
Nizer — *Thinking* p.124, 185
, Moral standards of
Nizer — *Thinking* p.191-192
, Producers of
Guideposts — *Faith* p.477-478
, Propaganda of
Nizer — *Thinking* p.192
, Theater–managers of
Manchee — *Secret* p.219-220
, Value of
Nizer — *Thinking* p.124

MOTIVATION AND MOTIVES
See also **Ambition; Goals; Incentives; Purpose**
Braude — *Source* #1163-1164
Braude — *Speaker's* #932
Curtis — *Practical* p.101, 347
Dirksen — *Quot.* #1016
Edwards — *Useful* p.411-412
Evans — *Thoughts II (Open Door)* p.133-138
Evans — *Unto* p.88-90, 117
Flesch — *Unusual* p.180
Forbes — *Thoughts* p.25, 59, 89, 424, 437
Garland — *Subject* p.199-200
Grizer — *Wit* p.316
How To Live p.268-269
Lair — *Baby* p.209-210
Lockridge — *World's* #1799
Lytle — *Leaves* p.120
Montapert — *Distilled* p.260
Peale — *Courage* p.17-19
Peterson — *Art* p.327
Prochnow — *Success.* #1232, 2064
Seldes — *Great* p.676
, Power of
Bartlett — *Discovery* p.134-135
, Teenager
Ginott — *Between* p.116-118

MOTORISTS. *See* **Drivers and driving**

MOTTOES
See also **Slogans**
Botkin — *Treasury* p.410
Fogg — *1000 See* index p.892-893
Harnsberger — *Mark* p.297-298
Lytle — *Leaves* p.89
Wallis — *Words* p.114, 229
, Grecian
New Joy p.245

MOUNT EVEREST
Wallis — *Words* p.76, 213, 218

MOUNT SINAI
Lockridge — *World's* #5000

MOUNTAIN CLIMBING
Adams — *New* p.226
Baillie — *Diary* #107
Bartlett — *Discovery* p.96-97
Kahn — *Lessons* p.90-93
Peterson — *Art* p.227, 318, 376

MOUNTAIN LIONS
Botkin — *Treasury* p.182

MOUNTAINS
See also names of mountains
Adams — *New* p.405
Applegarth — *Heir.* p.73, 217, 273
Botkin — *Anecdotes* p.11, 97, 117, 220
Clark — *Windows* p.134
Dirksen — *Quot.* #2092
Flesch — *Unusual* p.180
Fox — *Make* p.221-222
Harnsberger — *Mark* p.298-304
Henry — *5000* p.182
Hovey — *Treasury* #88, 99, 151, 277, 294, 339, 1659, 1816
Hubbard — *Scrap* p.63
Kin — *Dictionary* p.169
Lincoln — *Unicorn* p.28-29
New Topical p.115-116, 173-174
Nichols — *Third* p.111-112
Peale — *Courage* p.216-217
Peterson — *Art* p.23, 228
Prochnow — *Public* #1541
Prochnow — *Success.* #2065
Wallis — *Treasure* p.29
Wallis — *Words* p.121, 174, 179
Woods — *Content.* p.212, 218, 265
Woods — *Religious* p.658

MOURNING. *See* **Grief**

MOUSETRAPS
Henry — *5000* p.183
Prochnow — *Public* #1573

MOUTH
Henry — *5000* p.183
Kin — *Dictionary* p.170
Prochnow — *Public* #2638
, Lips of
Kin — *Dictionary* p.149

MOVEMENT
Flesch — *Unusual* p.180
Harnsberger — *Mark* p.306-307
Kin — *Dictionary* p.170
Phillips — *Choice* p.280, 316
Prochnow — *Public* #1987, 2186

MOVING PICTURES. *See* **Motion pictures**

MOZART, WOLFGANG
Flesch — *Unusual* p.180

MUD
Flesch — *Unusual* p.180
Kin — *Dictionary* p.163, 170

"MUDDLEHEADS"
Flesch — *Unusual* p.181
Safian — *More* p.135-136

MUFFLERS
Prochnow — *Public* #132

MUIR, JOHN
Kohn — *Touch* p.157-160

"MULE SKINNERS"
Botkin — *Anecdotes* p.274

MULES
Botkin — *Anecdotes* p.84, 183, 199, 274
Botkin — *Treasury* p.596, 671
Harnsberger — *Mark* p.307-308
Kin — *Dictionary* p.170
New Topical p.174
Prochnow — *Public* #11, 823
Schermerhorn — *1500* p.255

MULTIPLICITY
Lindbergh — *Gift* p.26-27

MULTITUDE
See also **Crowd; Mob; People**
Baillie — *Diary* #315
Flesch — *Unusual* p.181
Kin — *Dictionary* p.170
Prochnow — *Public* #2521
Prochnow — *Success.* #2066

MUNICIPAL GOVERNMENT
See also **Cities**
Harral — *Feature* p.227

MUNIFICENCE. *See* **Generosity**

MURDER
See also **Assassination; Killing**
Asimov — *Treasury* #530
Edwards — *Useful* p.412
Flesch — *Unusual* p.181
Fuller — *Thesaurus* #2576
Henry — *5000* p.183
Kin — *Dictionary* p.170
Lockridge — *World's* #954, 4207, 4426, 4541
More Words p.113-114
Myers — *Thunder* p.94-106
New Topical p.174-175
Prochnow — *Public* #2086
Seaburg — *Great* p.180, 241-242, 247, 288-289, 291, 359-360, 362

Seldes — *Great* p.676
Wheelis — *Moralist* p.45-46, 58, 62-63, 129, 154
Woods — *Religious* p.659

MURMURING. *See* **Complaining; Discontent; Resentment**

MUSCLES
Forbes — *Thoughts* p.302, 386, 461, 484
Prochnow — *Public* #2161

MUSES
Curtis — *Practical* p.520

MUSEUMS
Asimov — *Treasury* #90
Harral — *Feature* p.228
Prochnow — *Public* #672
Prochnow — *Success.* #998

MUSHROOMS
Sagendorph — *Old* p.295-300

MUSIC
See also types of music
Adams — *New* p.247
Alexander's Treasure. p.59, 335
Applegarth — *Heir.* p.37, 181-187
Asimov — *Treasury* #376
Bartlett — *Discovery* p.59, 105-106
Braude — *Source* #1165-1168
Braude — *Speaker's* #206-208, 933-941
Braude — *Stories* p.267
Copeland — *10,000* p.43-48
Curtis — *Practical* p.457-467
Dirksen — *Quot.* #128-129, 322, 460, 2093-2094
Edwards — *Useful* p.413-415
Emmons — *Mature* p.9, 72
Flesch — *Unusual* p.181-182
Fogg — *1000* #20, 26, 78, 94, 130, 139, 188, 229, 261, 653, 711, 790, 840, 1069, 1125, 1134
Forbes — *Thoughts* p.111, 142, 197, 207, 238, 271
Fuller — *Epigrams* p.216-217
Fuller — *Thesaurus* p.229-244
Fun Fare p.153-155
Garland — *Subject* p.202
Goudge — *Comfort* p.333-334
Grizer — *Wit* p.317
Hadfield — *Delights* p.52-59, 162-163, 206, 230-231
Hadfield — *Love* p.128-131
Harnsberger — *Mark* p.308-315
Harral — *Feature* p.128, 228-232
Henry — *5000* p.184-185
Hobe — *Tapestries* p.96, 126
Hooker — *Index* p.276-282
Hovey — *Treasury See* index p.299
How To Live p.348-350
Howell — *Better* p.135-140
Howell — *Lines* p.106
Hubbard — *Scrap* p.37, 52, 69-71, 86, 117, 151
Johnson — *Bedside* p.18, 23, 45, 47, 135, 255, 270
Kahn — *Lessons* p.79-81
Kennedy — *Reader's* #710-715
Kin — *Dictionary* p.170-171
Kronenberger — *Animal* p.211-217
Liddle — *Thought I, II, III* p.13
Lindeman — *Emerson* p.147
Lockridge — *World's See* index p.579
Lytle — *Leaves* p.79, 117, 124, 128
Miller — *Harvest* p.17-22
Montapert — *Distilled* p.260
New Topical p.176
Patterns For Living p.370-373
Peterson — *Art* p.194
Phillips — *Choice* p.276, 279, 282, 288
Prochnow — *Public* #994, 1589, 1854, 1869, 3438-3439, 4166
Prochnow — *Speaker's* p.218-219
Prochnow — *Success.* #842, 864, 950, 2067-2070
Reader's — *Getting* p.200-204
Schermerhorn — *1500* p.255-256
Seldes — *Great* p.676
Sheban — *Wisdom* no p.
Simpson — *Contemp.* p.428-438
Simpson — *'54* p.55, 171, 209
Speaker's Desk p.166-170; #46, 542, 651, 704, 878, 925, 933, 952, 973, 999, 1078, 1107
Wallis — *Treasure* p.20, 29-30, 194
Wallis — *Words* p.165-168
White — *Job* p.100-101, 134-136
Woods — *Content.* p.172, 180, 186, 256-260
Woods — *Religious* p.623, 659-661

, Appreciation of
How To Live p.448-452

, Chamber
Auden — *Certain* p.58

, Church
Baillie — *Diary* #285

, Conductors of
Peale — *Guideposts* p.57-60

, Dissonant
Nizer — *Thinking* p.74

, Familiar
Adams — *New* p.370

, German
Nizer — *Thinking* p.175-176

, *Lessons in*
Ginott — *Between* p.58-59, 71-73
, *Modern*
Prochnow — *Music* #65, 533
, *Perfection in*
Peale — *Guideposts* p.57-60
, *Pleasures of*
Saturday — *Advent.* p.190-205

MUSICIANS
See also **Composers; Singers;** etc.
Asimov — *Treasury* #118, 224-225, 279
Cerf — *Laugh* p.264-271
Fun Fare p.205
How To Live p.344-347

MUSLIMS. *See* **Mohammedanism**

MUSSOLINI, BENITO
Seldes — *Great* p.677

MUSTACHES
Asimov — *Treasury* #172
Prochnow — *Public* #2257

MUTABILITY. *See* **Fickleness; Indecision; Uncertainty**

MUTATION
Du Noüy — *Human* p.83-84, 86, 88, 123, 217-218

MUTES
Prochnow — *Public* #2162-2163

MUTINY. *See* **Rebellion**

MYSTERY
See also **Miracles; Suspense;** etc.
Adams — *New* p.245
Applegarth — *Heir.* p.137, 259-260, 266, 268
Braude — *Stories* p.267
Edwards — *Useful* p.415-416
Flesch — *Unusual* p.183
Flint — *Graham* p.97
Garland — *Subject* p.202
Harnsberger — *Mark* p.315
Henry — *5000* p.185
Hobe — *Tapestries* p.61
Hubbard — *Scrap* p.15
Lytle — *Leaves* p.108
Prochnow — *Public* #1746
Seldes — *Great* p.677
Sheen — *Content.* p.69-71
Voss — *Quotations* p.179-182
Wallis — *Treasure* p.24, 210
Wallis — *Words* p.65, 86, 97, 146
Woods — *Religious* p.662-665
, *Novels of*
Nichols — *Third* p.119-120
, *of universe*
Alexander's Treasure. p.75
, *Religious*
Woods — *Religious* p.661-662

MYSTICS AND MYSTICISM
Curtis — *Practical* p.247
Du Noüy — *Road* p.205-207, 224, 233-234
Flesch — *Unusual* p.183
Goudge — *Comfort* p.223-225
Guideposts — *Faith* p.395-399
Ideas p.257-259
Irion — *Yes* p.21-24
Johnson — *Bedside* p.132
Lockridge — *World's* #3544, 3646
Lytle — *Leaves* p.6, 104
Seldes — *Great* p.677
Taylor — *With* p.70-72
Woods — *Religious* p.664-667
, *Definition of*
Phillips — *Choice* p.168

MYTHOLOGY
Dirksen — *Quot.* #309
Edwards — *Useful* p.17-18, 416
Flesch — *Unusual* p.183
Johnson — *Bedside* p.87-89
Phillips — *Choice* p.33, 33n, 76, 116
Seldes — *Great* p.677-678
Woods — *Religious* p.667-668
, *Biological function of*
Curtis — *Practical* p.503-504
, *Greek*
Evans — *This* p.46-47

N

NAGGING. *See* **Criticism**

NAILS
Baillie — *Diary* #7
Kin — *Dictionary* p.172

NAIVETÉ
See also **Innocence**
Kin — *Dictionary* p.172
Mandel — *Stories* p.184-185
Prochnow — *Public* #1747

NAKEDNESS. *See* **Nudity**

NAMES
See also **Nicknames; Reputation**
Braude — *Source* #1169-1170
Braude — *Speaker's* #942-950
Braude — *Stories* p.267-268
Dirksen — *Quot.* #203, 2095
Edwards — *Useful* p.416-417
Evans — *Unto* p.28, 32, 71

Flesch — *Unusual* p.183-184
Forbes — *Thoughts* p.19, 49, 190, 197, 311, 458
Fuller — *Thesaurus* #831-838; p.145-146
Fun Fare p.193-194
Harnsberger — *Mark* p.316-317
Harral — *Feature* p.232-233
Henry — *5000* p.185-186
Hovey — *Treasury* #318, 357, 365-366, 380, 455, 499, 610, 710, 773, 837, 1087, 1300, 1310, 1751
Kohn — *Adventures* p.64-67
Kronenberger — *Animal* p.217-222
Lockridge — *World's* #95, 843, 2491, 2495, 2991, 3327, 3548, 4233
Mandel — *Stories* p.185
More Words p.115-116
New Joy p.172-173
Peterson — *Art* p.294
Prochnow — *Public* See index p.504
Prochnow — *Speaker's* p.220
Prochnow — *Success.* #868, 1376, 1492
Schermerhorn — *1500* p.158-159
Seldes — *Great* p.678
Speaker's Desk #547, 735, 901, 957, 1031, 1090
, *Bible*
Schermerhorn — *1500* p. 46
, *Dropping*
Humes — *Instant* p.20-26
, *Pronunciation of English*
Kronenberger — *Animal* p.243-244
, *Proper*
Auden — *Certain* p.267-276

NAPHTALI, TRIBE OF
New Topical p.176-177

NAPOLEON BONAPARTE
Auden — *Certain* p.276-277
Flesch — *Unusual* p.184
Hubbard — *Scrap* p.130, 137, 158, 206, 228
Lockridge — *World's* #4047
Seldes — *Great* p.678

NAPS. *See* **Sleep**

NARCISSISM
Auden — *Certain* p.278
Maltz — *Creative* p.17
Phillips — *Choice* p.127

NARCOTICS. *See* **Drugs;** names of drugs

NARROW-MINDEDNESS
Asimov — *Treasury* #445-446
Flint — *Graham* p.98
Forbes — *Thoughts* p.44, 109, 163
Kin — *Dictionary* p.172

NATIONAL DEBT
Dirksen — *Quot.* #13, 28, 34, 48, 58, 80, 87, 118, 1148-1150, 2367, 2380
Seldes — *Great* p.680
Woods — *Business.* p.210-213

NATIONAL DECAY
Dirksen — *Quot.* #461

NATIONAL DEFENSE
Dirksen — *Quot.* #571, 1665, 1749, 2290
Wheelis — *Moralist* p.119-120

NATIONAL HONOR
Woods — *Religious* p.668

NATIONAL STRENGTH
Dirksen — *Quot.* #700, 2367

NATIONAL UNITY
Dirksen — *Quot.* #653, 735, 2356

NATIONALISM
Dirksen — *Quot.* #569
Nichols — *Third* p.239-241

NATIONALIZATION
Woods — *Business.* p.158-159

NATIONS
Adams — *New* p.137, 181
Book Proverbs p.142
Braude — *Source* #1171
Copeland — *10,000* p.641-764
Curtis — *Practical* p.3
Dirksen — *Quot.* See index p.267
Edwards — *Useful* p.417
Flesch — *Unusual* p.184-185
Flint — *Graham* p.98-99
Forbes — *Thoughts* p.19, 105, 148, 177, 188, 242, 261, 293, 321, 347, 363, 377, 406, 411, 438, 442, 479, 504, 517
Fun Fare p.7, 69, 77, 229, 304
Harnsberger — *Mark* p.318
Henry — *5000* p.186
Hovey — *Treasury* See index p.299
Lockridge — *World's* #2583, 2586, 3672, 4441, 4528, 4736, 5113
Prochnow — *Public* #1131, 2102, 2527, 2583, 2588, 3440-3453
Prochnow — *Success.* #332, 468, 578, 787, 1381, 1456, 2073-2075
Seldes — *Great* p.678-680
Simpson — *Contemp.* p.1-50

Speaker's Desk #337
Wallis — *Treasure* p.171-178
Wallis — *Words* p.191, 233
Wheelis — *Moralist* p.46-48, 54, 91, 95, 98, 100-101, 105, 129-131, 139
Woods — *Religious* p.668-669
, and doctrines
Sheen — *Content.* p.163-186
, Beauty in
Curtis — *Daily* p.155
, Dangers of
Dirksen — *Quot.* #61, 567
, Duties to
Nichols — *Third* p.245-246
, Fate of
Adams — *New* p.47
, Great
Adams — *New* p.398
, Harmony of
Keller — *Open* p.78-79
, Internal enemies in
Adams — *New* p.95
, Self-determination of
Dirksen — *Quot.* #2364
, Small
Adams — *New* p.69
, Underdeveloped
Dirksen — *Quot.* #689, 734, 2220, 2372, 2375-2376, 2389

NATIVES
Fun Fare p.229-231

NATIVITY OF CHRIST. *See* **Jesus Christ, Birth of**

NATURAL RESOURCES
Dirksen — *Quot.* #1655
Seldes — *Great* p.680

NATURAL SELECTION
See also **Choice**
Du Noüy — *Human* p.83-84, 86, 88, 123, 218, 226-227
Seldes — *Great* p.680-681
Woods — *Religious* p.673

NATURALISM
Woods — *Religious* p.673-674

NATURALISTS
Curtis — *Practical* p.207-210
George — *Book* p.34, 136, 192, 420
How to Live p.544-550
Reader's — *Getting* p.101-104

NATURALNESS
Flesch — *Unusual* p.185
Price — *Wider* p.151-156
Webb — *Edge* p.34-56
, and supernatural
Woods — *Religious* p.669

NATURE
See also various subjects of nature
Adams — *New* p.406
Alexander's Treasure. p.3-4, 9, 12-13, 51, 57, 176, 344
Applegarth — *Heir.* p.78, 150, 154, 181-182, 189-199, 268
Asimov — *Treasury* #442
Auden — *Certain* p.278-283
Baillie — *Diary* #27, 339
Barrows — *1000* p.442-444
Bartlett — *Discovery* p.99-100
Botkin — *Treasury* p.278-279, 290-303
Braude — *Source* #1172-1174
Curtis — *Human* p.54, 68-69, 145
Curtis — *Practical* p.14-20, 51-52, 108, 117-118, 195-211, 242, 264
Dirksen — *Quot.* #158-160, 573, 1163, 2096-2098, 2284
Droke — *Christian* p.354-356
Edwards — *Useful* p.417-420
Evans — *Unto* p.42
Felleman — *Poems* p.349-368
Flesch — *Unusual* p.185-186, 251
Fogg — *1000* #797
Forbes — *Thoughts See* index p.560
Fox — *Make* p.31, 50
Fuller — *Epigrams* p.217-218
Garland — *Subject* p.203
Goudge — *Comfort* p.56-70, 81-83
Grizer — *Wit* p.317
Harnsberger — *Mark* p.319-320, 425
Harral — *Feature* p.233
Henry — *5000* p.186-187
Hobe — *Tapestries* p.26, 91-105
Hoffer — *Reflect.* p.3-16, 24
Holmes — *Design* p.4, 22, 34, 71, 101
Hovey — *Treasury* #6, 10-11, 25-26, 32-33, 41-42, 47, 86, 100, 243, 643-649, 1415, 1500-1503, 1515; *See also* index p.299
Howell — *Better* p.141-148
Hubbard — *Scrap* p.13, 25, 28
Ideas p.259-260
Johnson — *Bedside See* index p.365
Kennedy — *Reader's* #716-720
Keys Happiness p.527
Kin — *Dictionary* p.172
Knight's Illus. p.208-209
Knight's Treas. p.235-237
Kopplin — *Something* p.11-22
Liddle — *Thought I, II, III* p.79, 98, 103, 108, 110-111, 142, 174, 180, 183, 191
Liddle — *Thought IV* p.9
Liddle — *Thought V* p.21

Lindeman — *Emerson* p.11-23, 146
Lockridge — *World's See* index p.580
Lytle — *Leaves* p.6, 25, 109, 193
Modern Eloquence (14) p.382-384
Montapert — *Distilled* p.260-261
Nichols — *Third* p.113-114
Patterns for Living p.3-106
Peterson — *Art* p.118, 267-268
Phillips — *Choice,* p.4, 10, 30, 39, 288-289
Prochnow — *Public* #695, 1143, 2390, 4167-4168
Prochnow — *Success.* #606, 2076
Reader's — *Getting* p.169, 225
Seldes — *Great* p.681-682
Sheban — *Wisdom* no p.
Speaker's Desk #21, 39, 86, 93, 211, 843; p. 170-172
Voss — *Quotations* p.182-184
Wallis — *Treasure* p.29-32, 74, 94, 106, 145, 179-184, 193, 225
Wallis — *Words* p.29-30, 169-176, 186, 239-240
White — *Life* p.201-207
Woods — *Content.* p.21, 24, 27, 41, 80, 87, 98, 103, 106, 193-221, 301, 343
Woods — *Inspir.* p.284-316
Woods — *Religious* p.674-679
Words — *Inspir.* p.29, 46

, *and art*
Hubbard — *Scrap* p.41, 205
, *and God*
Woods — *Religious* p.675-678
, *and humanity*
Bradshaw — *Home.* p.100-102
, *and mind*
Woods — *Religious* p.679
, *and society*
Hubbard — *Scrap* p.63
, *and warfare*
Adams — *New* p.279
, *Appreciation of*
How to Live p.173
, *Army of*
Hubbard — *Scrap* p.172
, *as force*
Wheelis — *Moralist* p.92, 153
, *as retreat*
Nichols — *Third* p.112
, *Beauty in*
Curtis — *Daily* p.149-150
Hobe — *Tapestries* p.102
Hubbard — *Scrap* p.52, 66, 96
, *Color in*
Adams — *New* p.261
, *Drama of*
Hubbard — *Scrap* p.32
, *God of*
Hubbard — *Scrap* p.43
Tanksley — *Friend* p.32
, *Heart of*
Baillie — *Diary* #86
, *Humanized*
Ideas p.288-289
, *Imagination and*
Hubbard — *Scrap* p.25
, *Joys of*
Hubbard — *Scrap* p.64
, *Law of*
Hubbard — *Scrap* p.15-16, 201
, *Love of*
Morris — *1000 See* index p.432
Nichols — *Third* p.112
, *Luxuries of*
Kohn — *Pathways* p.61-62
, *Motherhood of*
Hubbard — *Scrap* p.71
, *Possessing of*
Adams — *New* p.362
, *Precepts of*
Hubbard — *Scrap* p.64
, *Protest of*
Adams — *New* p.14
, *Remedies of*
Adams — *New* p.1
, *Rhythm in*
Adams — *New* p.258
Albert — *Stop* p.10-14
, *Secrecy of*
Adams — *New* p.259
, *Soul of*
Hubbard — *Scrap* p.65
, *Sounds of*
Sheban — *Wisdom* no p.
, *Study of*
Unlimited Power p.11-14
, *Waste in*
Adams — *New* p.99
, *Wonder of*
How to Live p.110-114
Hubbard — *Scrap* p.154
, *Worship of*
Lockridge — *World's* #3622

NAVAJO INDIANS
Botkin — *Anecdotes* p.173

NAVIGATION
See also **Boats; Ships**
Henry — *5000* p.188
Kin — *Dictionary* p.172
Kronenberger — *Animal* p.7-10

NAVY
See also **Sailors**
Applegarth — *Heir.* p.108
Botkin — *Anecdotes* p.277
Cerf — *Laugh* p.332-334

Fuller — *Epigrams* p.358-359
Henry — *5000* p.188
Prochnow — *Public* #441
Schermerhorn — *1500* p.257-258

NAZARETH
Wallis — *Words* p.55

NAZARITES
New Topical p.177

NAZIS
Asimov — *Treasury* #105-107, 284, 322
Fridy — *Meditat.* p.54
Seldes — *Great* p.682

NEATNESS
Daly — *Personality* p.127-131
Forbes — *Thoughts* p.178, 392
Kin — *Dictionary* p.173
Menninger — *Blue.* p.205-221
Prochnow — *Speaker's* p.221
Prochnow — *Success.* #518
Speaker's Desk #591, 1066

NEBRASKA
Botkin — *Anecdotes* p.171
Botkin — *Treasury See* index p.930
, *"Kinkaiders" of*
Botkin — *Treasury* p.303

NECESSITY
See also **Essentials; Obligations**
Book Proverbs p.115
Dirksen — *Quot.* #1691
Edwards — *Useful* p.420-421
Flesch — *Unusual* p.182, 186
Forbes — *Thoughts* p.144, 198, 225, 377, 387, 430
Fuller — *Epigrams* p.218-219
Grizer — *Wit* p.318
Harnsberger — *Mark* p.320
Henry — *5000* p.188
Hubbard — *Scrap* p.110
Kin — *Dictionary* p.171, 173
Lockridge — *World's* #1639-1640, 3019, 3207, 3403, 4336, 5278
Montapert — *Distilled* p.261
Prochnow — *Public* #3458-3459, 4169
Prochnow — *Success.* #2077-2080
Seldes — *Great* p.682-683
Speaker's Desk p.172-174; #62, 249, 344, 500, 655
Woods — *Religious* p.679-681
, *Living above*
Kohn — *Pathways* p.59-63

NECK
Kin — *Dictionary* p.173

NECKTIES
Prochnow — *Public* #4330
Prochnow — *Success.* #354

NEED
See also **Necessity**
Book Proverbs p.115
Forbes — *Thoughts* p.260, 405
Garland — *Subject* p.204
Grizer — *Wit* p.318
Guideposts — *Faith* p.403-407
Hovey — *Treasury* #22, 39
Keys Happiness p.411
Kohn — *Thoughts* p.137-140
Krishnamurti — *Think* p.174
Mandelbaum — *Choose* p.31
Montapert — *Distilled* p.262
Prochnow — *Public* #1438
Prochnow — *Success.* #1247
Seldes — *Great* p.683
Wallis — *Treasure* p.121
Woods — *Religious* p.681
, *for others*
Lair — *Baby* p.175-176, 223
, *Fulfillment of*
Sheen — *Content.* p.53-68

NEEDLES
Baillie — *Diary* #46
Flesch — *Unusual* p.186
Kin — *Dictionary* p.173

NEEDY. *See* **Charity; Poverty**

NEGATIVISM
Albert — *Stop* p.6-7, 27-28, 153-154, 156-160, 191-193, 196-198
Evans — *Unto* p.38, 70
Fox — *Make* p.120, 219-220
Franke — *Buckley* p.202
Holmes — *Design* p.20-23, 33, 36, 57-58, 102, 132, 158
Hovey — *Treasury* #1504-1510; p.243-244
Maltz — *Creative* p.81-95
Montapert — *Distilled* p.262-263
Woods — *Religious* p.681
, *and memory*
Holmes — *Design* p.213-214
, *Influences of*
Holmes — *Design* p.40-41

NEGLECT
See also **Delay; Forgetfulness; Indifference**
Book Proverbs p.130
Braude — *Source* #1175, 1548-1549

Braude — *Stories* p.269
Edwards — *Useful* p.421
Evans — *Unto* p.105
Flint — *Graham* p.99
Henry — *5000* p.130
Kin — *Dictionary* p.173
Knight's Illus. p.210-214
Knight's Treas. p.238
Liddle — *Thought I, II, III* p.98
Lytle — *Leaves* p.85
Mandel — *Stories* p.185-186
Prochnow — *Public* #2105, 2734

NEGOTIATION
See also **Compromise**
Grizer — *Wit* p.318
Lockridge — *World's* #289

NEGROES
Applegarth — *Heir.* p.56-58, 145, 184, 228, 291, 298
Asimov — *Treasury* #4, 115, 434-437
Auden — *Certain* p.39-42
Botkin — *Treasury* p.428-429, 465; See also index p.930
Copeland — *10,000* p.641-669
Dirksen — *Quot.* #671
Flesch — *Unusual* p.186-187
Franke — *Buckley* p.202-204
Guideposts — *Faith* p.51-52, 77-80, 202-204, 313-317
Harnsberger — *Mark* p.321-322
Henry — *5000* p.188-189
Hovey — *Treasury* #21, 75, 244, 454, 1029, 1665
Hubbard — *Scrap* p.182
Humes — *Instant* #662-673
Kauffman — *For* p.32-34
Modern Eloquence (14) p.179-194
Patterns for Living p.679-689
Peale — *Guideposts* p.269-273, 295-298
Schermerhorn — *1500* p.258-262
Seldes — *Great* p.683-685
Speaker's Desk See index p.303
Walters — *How* p.17-18
Woods — *Religious* p.681-682
, *Audiences of*
Humes — *Instant* #1246-1247
, *Boys*
Goudge — *Comfort* p.88
, *Folklore of*
Nizer — *Thinking* p.101
, *Proverbs of*
Dirksen — *Quot.* #1966

NEIGHBORS
Applegarth — *Heir.* p.208
Asimov — *Treasury* #379
Auden — *Certain* p.283-285
Bach — *Make* p.68-69
Bartlett — *Discovery* p.72-92
Braude — *Speaker's* #951-953
Braude — *Stories* p.269
Dirksen — *Quot.* #540, 672, 933-934, 1222, 2081
Evans — *Unto* p.30, 49-50
Flesch — *Unusual* p.187
Forbes — *Thoughts* p.23, 251, 281, 338, 371-372, 377, 389, 415, 433, 454
Fuller — *Epigrams* p.219
Garland — *Subject* p.205
Grizer — *Wit* p.319
Henry — *5000* p.189
Hobe — *Tapestries* p.134
Holmes — *I've* p.102
Hovey — *Treasury* p.244; #22, 264, 321, 506, 735, 870, 1084, 1097, 1434, 1440, 1511-1517, 1732
Kahn — *Lessons* p.201-224
Kennedy — *Reader's* #721
Keys Happiness p.548
Kin — *Dictionary* p.174
Liddle — *Thought I, II, III* p.14, 25, 49, 51, 105, 139, 166, 194
Lockridge — *World's* #4970
Lytle — *Leaves* p.89, 117
Mandelbaum — *Choose* p.73-77
Myers — *Thunder* p.145-147, 156-157
Prochnow — *Public* #1522, 2548
Prochnow — *Speaker's* p.221
Prochnow — *Success.* #222, 702, 722
Seldes — *Great* p.685
Sheban — *Wisdom* no p.
Sheen — *Content.* p.141-162
Unlimited Power p.160-163
Wallis — *Treasure* p.80, 99, 102, 119, 176, 212
Wallis — *Words* p.10, 13-14, 76, 79, 82, 203, 233
Wheelis — *Moralist* p.43, 90-91, 129
Woods — *Religious* p.682-684

NEO-ORTHODOXY
Woods — *Religious* p.684

NEO-PLATONISM
Hubbard — *Scrap* p.222

NERO
Flesch — *Unusual* p.187

NERVE. *See* **Boldness; Courage**

NERVES AND NERVOUSNESS
See also **Neuroses and neurotics**
Casselberry — *How* p.62-64, 77-78
Du Noüy — *Road* p.34, 53-55, 57-58, 191-192

Grizer — *Wit* p.319
Huxley — *You See* index p.286
Keys Happiness p.201-204
Kin — *Dictionary* p.174
Manchee — *Secret* p.75-76
Montapert — *Distilled* p.263
Prochnow — *Public* #261, 326
Prochnow — *Speaker's* p.221-222
Speaker's Desk #788
Walters — *How* p.119-121

NESTORIANISM
Woods — *Religious* p.684

NETHERLANDS, THE
Simpson — *Contemp.* p.148

NETHINIM
New Topical p.177

NETS
Kin — *Dictionary* p.174
Prochnow — *Public* #2516

NETTLE
Kin — *Dictionary* p.174

NEUROLOGISTS
Asimov — *Treasury* #124

NEUROSES AND NEUROTICS
Curtis — *Practical* p.7-9
Flesch — *Unusual* p.187
Ideas p.260-262
Liebman — *Peace* p.84-91
Seldes — *Great* p.685-686
Sheen — *Content.* p.99-102
Sherman — *Your* p.83-89
Woods — *Religious* p.684-685
, *and breakdowns*
Halverson — *Perspective* p.49
How to Live p.351-356
, *Debt to*
Adams — *New* p.178
, *Development of*
Phillips — *Choice* p.115

NEUTRALITY
See also **Broad-mindedness; Indecision; Indifference; Tolerance; Unconcern**
Baillie — *Diary* #255
Braude — *Speaker's* #954
Curtis — *Practical* p.125
Dirksen — *Quot.* #1388-1389
Edwards — *Useful* p.421
Evans — *Thoughts I* p.83-84
Garland — *Subject* p.205-206
Henry — *5000* p.129, 189
Kennedy — *Reader's* #722
Kin — *Dictionary* p.174
Lockridge — *World's* #1797
Prochnow — *Success.* #1896
Seldes — *Great* p.686

NEVADA
Botkin — *Anecdotes* p.198
Botkin — *Treasury* p.67, 556, 611

"NEW BIRTH"
Flint — *Graham* p.99
New Topical p.177-178

"NEW DEAL"
Botkin — *Anecdotes* p.163
Dirksen — *Quot.* #13, 118, 685
Seldes — *Great* p.686

NEW ENGLAND
See also names of states
Botkin — *Anecdotes* p.19, 134, 205
Botkin — *Treasury See* index p.930
Harnsberger — *Mark* p.322
Prochnow — *Public* #4280, 4300

NEW HAMPSHIRE
Botkin — *Anecdotes* p.6, 114, 211, 284
Botkin — *Treasury* p.421

NEW JERSEY
Asimov — *Treasury* #203
Botkin — *Anecdotes* p.163, 238
Botkin — *Treasury* p.596, 599, 708, 887

NEW MEXICO
Botkin — *Anecdotes* p.86-87, 125, 173, 189
Botkin — *Treasury* p.69-70, 93, 104, 131, 180, 183, 277, 312, 396, 571, 716

"NEW MORALITY" MOVEMENT
Flint — *Graham* p.99-100

NEW ORLEANS, LOUISIANA
Botkin — *Anecdotes* p.70, 244
Botkin — *Treasury* p. 3, 9, 52-53, 57, 124, 262, 597, 605, 674, 678
Guideposts — *Faith* p.287-290

NEW TESTAMENT
Hobe — *Tapestries* p.51
Kennedy — *Reader's* #723-728
Seldes — *Great* p.697
Wallis — *Words* p.4, 10, 223
Woods — *Religious* p.685-690

"NEW WORLD ORDER"
Bartlett — *Discovery* p.2-4

NEW YEAR
Alexander's Treasure. p.92
Botkin — *Anecdotes* p.45
Braude — *Source* #1178-1184
Braude — *Speaker's* #209-211
Droke — *Christian* p.357-360
Emmons — *Mature* p.154
Evans — *Faith* p.101-102
Evans — *This* p.182-183
Evans — *Unto* p.18-19, 21-22
Fridy — *Meditat.* p.87
Fuller — *Epigrams* p.359
Harral — *Feature* p.235
Hobe — *Tapestries* p.116, 172
Hovey — *Treasury* #337, 1518-1527; p.245-246; *See also* index p.304
Hubbard — *Scrap* p.73
Knight's Treas. p.238-240
Kohn — *Best* p.104-108
Liddle — *Thought I, II, III* p.90, 118, 184, 193
Liddle — *Thought V* p.17, 43
Peterson — *Art* p.19, 23-24
Prochnow — *Success.* #1473
Strait — *Speaker's* p.169
Suter — *Prayers* #394-396
Thurman — *Mood* p.110-127
Wallis — *Treasure* p.137, 228
Woods — *Content.* p.182

NEW YORK
Botkin — *Anecdotes* p.9, 39, 41, 58-61, 77, 90, 92, 116, 134, 155, 212, 241, 250, 262, 264-265
Botkin — *Treasury* p.459, 740
Flesch — *Unusual* p.188
Grizer — *Wit* p.320
Harnsberger — *Mark* p.323
Schermerhorn — *1500* p.263-264
Sheban — *Wisdom* no p.

NEW YORK CITY
Botkin — *Anecdotes See* index p.316
Botkin — *Treasury* p.768, 796, 805
Franke — *Buckley* p.207-216
Harnsberger — *Mark* p.323
Henry — *5000* p.190
Simpson — *Contemp.* p.103-109
, *Broadway*
Copeland — *10,000* p.258, 567-575
, *East side*
Botkin — *Anecdotes* p.257-258, 266
, *Fifth Ave.*
Botkin — *Anecdotes* p.263
, *Madison Ave.*
Simpson — *Contemp.* p.81-86
, *Manhattan*
Guideposts — *Faith* p.350-353
Woods — *Content.* p.63
, *Seventh Ave.*
Botkin — *Anecdotes* p.261
, *Waldorf Astoria Hotel*
Botkin — *Anecdotes* p.168

NEW YORK PUBLIC LIBRARY
Botkin — *Anecdotes* p.263

"NEWCOMERS"
Botkin — *Anecdotes* p.27-36

NEWLYWEDS
See also **Bridegrooms; Brides; Honeymoons**
How to Live p.387-390
Lockridge — *World's* #2085
Prochnow — *Public* #204

NEWNESS
See also **Novelty**
Braude — *Source* #1176-1177
Flesch — *Unusual* p.187-188
Henry — *5000* p.189-190
Lockridge — *World's* #4509
Montapert — *Distilled* p.263-264
Prochnow — *Public* #2631

NEWS
See also **Facts;** various media of the news
Edwards — *Useful* p.421-422
Evans — *Unto* p.27, 36
Flesch — *Unusual* p.188
Fuller — *Epigrams* p.219-220
Harral — *Feature* p.233
Henry — *5000* p.190
Kin — *Dictionary* p.175
Prochnow — *Public* #1359
Prochnow — *Success.* #672
Seldes — *Great* p.686-688
, *Commentators of*
Braude — *Stories* p.69
, *Services of*
Harral — *Feature* p.235

NEWSPAPERS
See also **Columnists; Journalism and journalists; News;** etc.
Braude — *Speaker's* #223-224
Cerf — *Laugh* p.295-301
Dirksen — *Quot.* #462-463, 696-698, 1017, 1735, 1780
Edwards — *Useful* p.422-423, 496-497
Flesch — *Unusual* p.188-189, 225
Fuller — *Epigrams* p.359
Fuller — *Thesaurus* #1236-1248
Fun Fare p.37, 82-84, 173, 202, 204, 241
Grizer — *Wit* p.320-321
Harnsberger — *Mark* p.324-326, 372-373

Harral — *Feature* p.234
Henry — *5000* p.191, 218
Kronenberger — *Animal* p.242-243
Lockridge — *World's* #4057
New Joy p.45
Prochnow — *Public* *See* index p.504
Prochnow — *Speaker's* p.222, 240-241
Prochnow — *Success.* #265, 465, 710, 2082-2083, 2182-2184
Schermerhorn — *1500* p.262-263
Seldes — *Great* p.688-697, 762-772
Simpson — *Contemp.* p.388-399
Simpson — *'54* p.78, 227, 340
Woods — *Religious* p.776

, *Carriers of*
Harral — *Feature* p.233-235
Prochnow — *Public* #686
, *Country*
Schermerhorn — *1500* p.93-95
, *Errors in*
Copeland — *10,000* p.817-841
, *Feature stories in*
Harral — *Feature* p.220-223
, *Headlines in*
Evans — *Unto* p.28, 36, 38

NIAGARA FALLS, NEW YORK
Flesch — *Unusual* p.189
Harnsberger — *Mark* p.326-327
Schermerhorn — *1500* p.264

NICHOLAS, SAINT. *See* **Santa Claus**

NICKNAMES
Edwards — *Useful* p.423
Harral — *Feature* p.235
Kin — *Dictionary* p.175
Safian — *Insults* p.213-220
Safian — *More* p.184-188
, *Fear of*
Carruthers — *Sparks* p.143-145
, *Railroad*
Botkin — *Treasury* p.488
, *State*
Botkin — *Treasury* p.317-318

NIETZSCHE, FRIEDRICH
Lockridge — *World's* #4125-4126

NIGHT
See also **Evening; Midnight; Moon; Stars; Sunset; Twilight**
Auden — *Certain* p.101
Detherage — *Sunrise* p.179-180
Dirksen — *Quot.* #798
Edwards — *Useful* p.423-424
Evans — *Thoughts I* p.23-24, 123, 131-132
Evans — *Unto* p.36, 39
Flesch — *Unusual* p.189
Garland — *Subject* p.207
Goudge — *Comfort* p.26-28
Harnsberger — *Mark* p.328
Henry — *5000* p.191-192
Hobe — *Tapestries* p.26, 50, 54, 112-113, 127, 164
Hubbard — *Scrap* p.39, 148
Irion — *Yes* p.131-133
Kin — *Dictionary* p.175
New Topical p.178
Prochnow — *Public* #2580, 2684, 2702, 3461-3468
Wallis — *Treasure* p.168
Woods — *Content.* p.195-196, 208, 218-219, 266, 318, 353-356, 358
, *and day*
Adams — *New* p.291

NIGHTCLUBS
Cerf — *Laugh* p.61-64
Prochnow — *Public* #174

NIGHTINGALES
Applegarth — *Heir.* p.37
Henry — *5000* p.192
Hobe — *Tapestries* p.24
Sheban — *Wisdom* no p.

NIHILISM
Ideas p.262-279
Seldes — *Great* p.697
Wheelis — *Moralist* p.1-23, 115
Woods — *Religious* p.690

NILE RIVER
New Topical p.178-179

NINETEENTH CENTURY
Woods — *Religious* p.690-691

NINEVEH
New Topical p.179

NIRVANA
Phillips — *Choice* p.103n.
Woods — *Religious* p.691-692

NO'S. *See* **Refusal**

NOAH (Biblical)
Harnsberger — *Mark* p.328-329

NOBEL PRIZE WINNERS
Dirksen — *Quot.* #673

NOBILITY
See also **Aristocracy; Dignity; Distinction; Greatness; Rank; Rulers; Titles**
Dirksen — *Quot.* #103

Edwards — *Useful* p.424-425
Fogg — *1000* #202
Forbes — *Thoughts* p.7, 18, 34, 45, 110, 130, 141, 168, 189, 356
Harnsberger — *Mark* p.329-330
Henry — *5000* p.192
Howell — *Lines* p.87-88
Hubbard — *Scrap* p.224
Kin — *Dictionary* p.176
Lockridge — *World's* #876, 1150, 2272
Lytle — *Leaves* p.139
Morris — *1000 See* index p.432-433
Peale — *Courage* p.19
Peterson — *Art* p.122
Prochnow — *Public* #3469-3473
Wallis — *Words* p.128
Woods — *Religious* p.692

"NOBODY"
Keys Happiness p.258-260

NOISE
Dirksen — *Quot.* #1739
Edwards — *Useful* p.425
Evans — *This* p.96-97
Flesch — *Unusual* p.189
Fogg — *1000* #213, 1084
Forbes — *Thoughts* p.132, 163, 324, 480
Fuller — *Epigrams* p.220
Grizer — *Wit* p.321
Harnsberger — *Mark* p.350-351
Kennedy — *Reader's* #729-730
Kin — *Dictionary* p.176
Prochnow — *Public* #130, 700, 711
Prochnow — *Success.* #949, 2085
Seldes — *Great* p.697
, *Age of*
Adams — *New* p.329

NONCOMBATANTS
Kin — *Dictionary* p.176
Woods — *Religious* p.692

NONCONFORMITY
See also **Independence**
Braude — *Source* #1185-1187
Flint — *Graham* p.100
Hoffer — *Reflect.* p.33
How to Live p.285
Lair — *Baby* p.29
Seldes — *Great* p.697-699
Vogue — *Arts* p.171-178
Voss — *Quotations* p.184-186
Woods — *Religious* p.692

NONESSENTIALS
Wallis — *Treasure* p.231

NONEXISTENCE
Woods — *Religious* p.692-692

NONPARTISANSHIP
Dirksen — *Quot.* #15, 24

NONRESISTANCE
Flesch — *Unusual* p.190
Fox — *Make* p.108-109
Kennedy — *Reader's* #731
Lockridge — *World's* #5741, 5809-5840
Seldes — *Great* p.699
Woods — *Religious* p.693
, *Law of*
Baillie — *Diary* #28

NONSENSE
See also **Humor; Jokes and joking**
Botkin — *Anecdotes* p.256
Dirksen — *Quot.* #128, 1752
Edwards — *Useful* p.425
Felleman — *Poems* p.187-241
Flesch — *Unusual* p.189-190
Fuller — *Epigrams* p.220
Henry — *5000* p.193
Kin — *Dictionary* p.176
Liddle — *Thought I, II, III* p.52
Nichols — *New* p.35-36
Prochnow — *Public* #514, 2328, 3474
Prochnow — *Success.* #2086-2088

NONSENSE VERSE
Copeland — *10,000* p.915-926
New Joy p.110-111

NONVIOLENCE. *See* **Nonresistance**

NOON
Detherage — *Sunrise* p.83-84

NORDICS
Seldes — *Great* p.699-702

NORMALITY
Edwards — *Useful* p.730
Flesch — *Unusual* p.190
Hovey — *Treasury* p.246; #1528-1531
Lytle — *Leaves* p.9
Seldes — *Great* p.700
Sheen — *Way* p.173-175

NORTH CAROLINA
Botkin — *Anecdotes* p. 10, 32, 95, 146-147, 152, 164, 242
Botkin — *Treasury* p.232, 316, 424, 581, 593, 601-602, 725, 812, 897-901

NORTH DAKOTA
Botkin — *Anecdotes* p.25, 172
Peale — *Guideposts* p.321-325

NORTH POLE
See also **Arctic**
Reader's — *20th* p.18-24

NORWAY
Hovey — *Treasury* #1153

NOSES
Henry — *5000* p.193
Kin — *Dictionary* p.176

NOSTALGIA
Maltz — *Creative* p.172-173

NOTHING AND NOTHINGNESS
Asimov — *Treasury* #493
Auden — *Certain* p.288-290
Baillie — *Diary* #81
Dirksen — *Quot. See* index p.267
Evans — *Thoughts III (Open Road)* p.60
Flesch — *Unusual* p.191
Garland — *Subject* p.207-208
Henry — *5000* p.193
Hovey — *Treasury* p.246-247; #13, 24, 107, 121, 249, 933, 1039, 1150, 1254, 1333, 1366, 1415, 1532-1534
Kin — *Dictionary* p.176-177
Prochnow — *Public* #2389
Prochnow — *Success.* #2093
Seldes — *Great* p.700
Sheen — *Way* p.33-35
Taylor — *With* p.46-54
, in ourselves
Baillie — *Diary* #227
, of life
Dirksen — *Quot.* #484

NOTIONS
Flesch — *Unusual* p.191
Kohn — *Adventures* p.84-89

NOTORIETY. *See* **Fame; Reputation; Scandal**

NOUNS
Asimov — *Treasury* #635-636
Prochnow — *Public* #308

NOVA SCOTIA
Botkin — *Treasury* p.624

NOVELISTS
Lockridge — *World's* #703, 915, 949, 961, 969
Patterns for Living p.329-334

NOVELS. *See* **Fiction**

NOVELTY
See also **Newness; Originality; Variety**
Edwards — *Useful* p.427-428
Harnsberger — *Mark* p.333
Hubbard — *Scrap* p.32
Kin — *Dictionary* p.177
Lockridge — *World's* #377, 451, 2067, 2602

NOVEMBER
Alexander's Treasure. p.51
Hubbard — *Scrap* p.141

NOW. *See* **Present; Today**

NUCLEAR POWER AND WARFARE
Forbes — *Thoughts* p.504
Franke — *Buckley* p.219-222
Harral — *Feature* p.78
Hovey — *Treasury See* index p.304
Woods — *Religious* p.694-697
, and the Bible
Kauffman — *For* p.149-150

NUDITY
Kin — *Dictionary* p.172
Lockridge — *World's* #5667
Safian — *Insults* p.143-144
Safian — *More* p.137-138
Woods — *Religious* p.697

NUMBERS
See also **Mathematics**
Auden — *Certain* p.286-291
Du Noüy — *Road* p.10, 69, 75, 85, 101, 104, 111, 120-121, 179
Harral — *Feature* p.235
Kin — *Dictionary* p.177
Prochnow — *Public* #2633
Prochnow — *Success.* #1477

NUMISMATICS
Harral — *Feature* p.125, 235-236
Schermerhorn — *1500* p.80-81

NUNS
Asimov — *Treasury* #476, 500
Baillie — *Diary* #154

NURSERY RHYMES
See also **Counting Rhymes**
Kronenberger — *Animal* p.222-225

NURSES AND NURSING
Applegarth — *Heir.* p.189, 241
Harral — *Feature* p.236
Hovey — *Treasury* #27, 423
Kin — *Dictionary* p.177
Lockridge — *World's* #3846

Prochnow — *Public* #168
Prochnow — *Success.* #899
, *History of*
Nizer — *Thinking* p.199-204
, *Home*
White — *Life* p.143-146

NUTHATCHES
Kohn — *Pathways* p.177-180

NUTS AND NUTTING
Prochnow — *Public* #327, 582
Woods — *Content.* p.28-29

O

OAK TREES
See also **Acorns**
New Topical p.179

OATHS
See also **Loyalty; Profanity; Promise; Vows**
Book Proverbs p.103
Edwards — *Useful* p.428
Flesch — *Unusual* p.192
Fuller — *Epigrams* p.220-221
Henry — *5000* p.193
Keller — *You* p.103
Kin — *Dictionary* p.178
New Topical p.179-180
Seldes — *Great* p.700
Woods — *Religious* p.697

OATS
Kin — *Dictionary* p.178

OBEDIENCE
See also **Duty; Humility**
Applegarth — *Heir.* p.296
Baillie — *Diary* #351
Curtis — *Practical* p.322
Detherage — *Sunrise* p.87, 89
Dirksen — *Quot.* #477, 1463-1466, 2099-2101
Droke — *Christian* p.360-361
Edwards — *Useful* p.428-429, 620
Evans — *This* p.114, 126
Evans — *Thoughts III (Open Road)* p.171
Evans — *Unto* p.12, 14, 52, 68, 102, 133, 134
Flesch — *Unusual* p.192, 278
Flint — *Graham* p.22, 100
Forbes — *Thoughts* p.389, 392, 485, 495
Garland — *Subject* p.208
Grizer — *Wit* p.321
Henry — *5000* p.193-194
Hovey — *Treasury* p.247; #1353, 1535-1538, 1678
Hubbard — *Scrap* p.60
Hunter — *Gems* p.60-64
Johnson — *Bedside* p.246
Kennedy — *Reader's* #732
Kin — *Dictionary* p.178, 245, 284
Knight's Illus. p.214-219
Knight's Treas. p.240-243
Kohn — *Touch* p.86-89, 90-94
Liddle — *Thought I, II, III* p.8, 74
Liddle — *Thought V* p.15
Lytle — *Leaves* p.118, 155, 190
More Words p.117
Phillips — *Choice* p.88, 125
Prochnow — *Public* #807, 2726, 3475-3479
Prochnow — *Speaker's* p.223
Prochnow — *Success.* #1055, 2094, 2355
Seldes — *Great* p.700
Sheban — *Wisdom* no p.
Sheen — *Content.* p.36-38
Speaker's Desk #244
White — *Life* p.133-134
Woods — *Religious* p.697-699, 965-966
, *Joy from*
Maxwell — *Courage* p.177-185
, *Literal*
Speaker's Desk See index p.302

OBESITY. *See* **Overweight**

OBJECTION. *See* **Opposition**

OBJECTIVES
See also **Aims; Goals**
Dirksen — *Quot.* #107
Du Noüy — *Road* p.26-27
Evans — *Thoughts I* p.130-131
Forbes — *Thoughts* p.87, 313, 415
Kin — *Dictionary* p.178
Liddle — *Thought I, II, III* p.32-33, 41
Liddle — *Thought IV* p.35
Mandel — *Stories* p.186
Prochnow — *Public* #995
Welk — *Guide.* p.52-54, 112-114, 169-171

OBJECTIVITY
Humes — *Instant* #36-38
Kennedy — *Reader's* #733

OBLIGATIONS
See also **Debt; Duty; Responsibility**
Curtis — *Practical* p.397
Dirksen — *Quot.* #481, 1021

Edwards — *Useful* p.429
Evans — *Faith* p.12, 76, 168
Evans — *Thoughts I* p.37, 59-60, 90, 119, 129
Evans — *Thoughts II (Open Door)* p.11-12, 208
Evans — *Thoughts III (Open Road)* p.166, 212
Evans — *Thoughts IV* p.89
Evans — *Unto* p.9, 109
Flesch — *Unusual* p.192-193
Forbes — *Thoughts* p.56, 154, 201, 226, 235, 259, 264, 273, 374, 415, 440, 485
Garland — *Subject* p.208-209
Harnsberger — *Mark* p.334
Lockridge — *World's* #327, 5147
Speaker's Desk p.174
Woods — *Religious* p.699

OBLIVION
See also **Death; Nothing and nothingness; Obscurity**
Curtis — *Practical* p.532-533
Edwards — *Useful* p.429
Lockridge — *World's* #881, 1416
Woods — *Religious* p.699

OBSCENITY
See also **Impurity; Pornography**
Evans — *Faith* p.69-70
Humes — *Instant* p.54-55
Seldes — *Great* p.700-702
Woods — *Religious* p.699-700

OBSCURITY
See also **Concealment; Oblivion; Secrecy**
Asimov — *Treasury* #229
Edwards — *Useful* p.429-430
Flesch — *Unusual* p.193
Forbes — *Thoughts* p.254, 271, 312, 337
Harnsberger — *Mark* p.334
Henry — *5000* p.194
Lockridge — *World's* #1471
Lytle — *Leaves* p.114
, and the famous
Adams — *New* p.203

OBSERVATION
See also **Attention**
Braude — *Stories* p.269-270
Du Noüy — *Road* p.30-32, 111
Edwards — *Useful* p.430, 457
Flesch — *Unusual* p.193
Forbes — *Thoughts* p.200, 215, 263, 280, 332, 341
Grizer — *Wit* p.321-322
Krishnamurti — *Urgency* p.77-81
Lockridge — *World's* #5714, 5718
Lytle — *Leaves* p.189
Mandel — *Stories* p.186
Montapert — *Distilled* p.264-265
Patterns for Living p.3-11
Phillips — *Choice* p.120, 188
Prochnow — *Public* #359
Rau — *Act* p.9-17

OBSESSION
Mandel — *Stories* p.187

OBSOLESCENCE
Woods — *Business.* p.160

OBSTACLES
See also **Adversity; Difficulties; Handicapped;** etc.
Braude — *Source* #1188-1189
Braude — *Stories* p.270
Droke — *Christian* p.361-364
Forbes — *Thoughts* p.38, 75, 360, 365, 425, 518
Garland — *Subject* p.209
Grizer — *Wit* p.322
Hobe — *Tapestries* p.183-184
Hovey — *Treasury* p.247; #99, 1345, 1539-1540, 1663
Hubbard — *Scrap* p.132
Krishnamurti — *Think* p.91-92
Liddle — *Thought V* p.11, 38
Prochnow — *Public* #574, 2416
Speaker's Desk #27, 178, 210, 651, 766, 1172
Wallis — *Words* p.72
Wilcox — *Heart* p.17-19

OBSTINACY
See also **Determination; Independence; Rebellion; Self-will**
Book Proverbs p.102
Edwards — *Useful* p.430-431, 460-461
Evans — *Faith* p.148
Evans — *Thoughts II (Open Door)* p.38
Flesch — *Unusual* p.276
Forbes — *Thoughts* p.92, 280, 498
Fuller — *Epigrams* p.221
Fuller — *Thesaurus* #571-572
Grizer — *Wit* p.439
Henry — *5000* p.194
Kin — *Dictionary* p.178-179, 190
Lockridge — *World's* #276, 380, 3076, 3230, 3856, 4387, 5724
Lytle — *Leaves* p.176
Prochnow — *Public* #287, 955, 2106
Prochnow — *Speaker's* p.295
Prochnow — *Success.* #2349
Speaker's Desk p.174-175, 343, 376, 1015

Woods — *Religious* p.700
, *and loneliness*
Maltz — *Creative* p.169

OBVIOUS
Curtis — *Practical* p.38
Dirksen — *Quot.* #1022
Flesch — *Unusual* p.193
Kin — *Dictionary* p.179
Mandel — *Stories* p.187-188
Prochnow — *Success.* #2096

OCCULT POWER
White — *Job* p.179-182

OCCUPATIONS
See also **Business; Employment; Professions; Trade;** etc.
Book Proverbs p.129
Droke — *Christian* p.583
Edwards — *Useful* p.431-432
Forbes — *Thoughts* p.162, 176, 251, 286, 320, 511
Grizer — *Wit* p.486
Harnsberger — *Mark* p.334-335
Harral — *Feature* p.237-239
Henry — *5000* p.194-195
Hovey — *Treasury* p.283-285; #291, 864, 1834-1839
Howell — *Lines* p.107-110
Humes — *Instant* #1121-1133
Keys Happiness p.374-376, 441-445
Liddle — *Thought I, II, III* p.55, 147
Lockridge — *World's* #1843
Mandel — *Stories* p.188
Montapert — *Distilled* p.265
New Topical p.20
Tanksley — *Friend* p.40
Wallis — *Words* p.228
Woods — *Religious* p.1039-1040
, *Unusual*
Harral — *Feature* p.315-316

OCEAN
See also **Sea**
Dirksen — *Quot.* #2151-2152
Henry — *5000* p.195
Hobe — *Tapestries* p.95
Prochnow — *Public* #736, 852

OCTOBER
Hadfield — *Delights* p.182

OCTOGENARIANS
Harral — *Feature* p.239-240

OCULISTS
Prochnow — *Public* #1752

ODDNESS. *See* **Eccentricity**

ODDS. *See* **Chance; Gamblers and gambling; Luck**

ODOR
See also **Perfume**
Flesch — *Unusual* p.267-268, 274
Fuller — *Epigrams* p.264
Hadfield — *Delights* p.68
Harnsberger — *Mark* p.442-443
Harral — *Feature* p.240
Kin — *Dictionary* p.244

ODYSSEY
Lockridge — *World's* #3605
Prochnow — *Public* #2283

OEDIPUS COMPLEX
Asimov — *Treasury* #116

OFFENSE
See also **Injury; Injustice; Insult;** etc.
Book Proverbs p.112
Edwards — *Useful* p.432-433
Flesch — *Unusual* p.194
Garland — *Subject* p.210
Kennedy — *Reader's* #735
Kin — *Dictionary* p.179
New Topical p.180-181
Prochnow — *Public* #2662
Prochnow — *Success.* #2099

OFFERINGS AND OFFERS
Kennedy — *Reader's* #734
Kin — *Dictionary* p.179
New Topical p.181-182
Prochnow — *Public* #437, 906, 1040

OFFICE BOYS
Copeland — *10,000* p.418-421
Prochnow — *Public* #159, 500, 739

OFFICE SEEKERS
See also **Politics and politicians**
Fuller — *Thesaurus* #1966-1970 #1966-1970

OFFICERS. *See* **Military service, Officers of**

OFFICES
See also **Authority; Business; Officials and officeholding; Politics and politicians; Position; Power; Trust**
Edwards — *Useful* p.433
Flesch — *Unusual* p.194
Forbes — *Thoughts* p.395, 432, 439, 512
George — *Book* p.66, 225, 306
Henry — *5000* p.195-196
Kin — *Dictionary* p.179
Lockridge — *World's* #2563

Prochnow — *Success.* #977, 2100-2101
Woods — *Religious* p.701

OFFICIALS AND OFFICEHOLDING
Braude — *Speaker's* #1135-1136
Dirksen — *Quot. See* index p.267
Evans — *Unto* p.56
Flesch — *Unusual* p.194
Fuller — *Thesaurus* #1926
Humes — *Instant* #824-829
Kin — *Dictionary* p.179
Nizer — *Thinking* p.55, 139-140
Sheen — *Thoughts* p.90-92
, Duty of
Fogg — *1000* #210, 226, 1136
, Rewards of
Humes — *Instant* #1263-1264
, Rules of
Dirksen — *Quot.* #2320

OHIO
Botkin — *Anecdotes* p.145
Botkin — *Treasury* p.47, 123, 262, 269, 398, 420, 459, 596

OHIO RIVER
Botkin — *Anecdotes* p.112
Botkin — *Treasury* p.8, 56, 262, 597, 606
Guideposts — *Faith* p.360-363

OIL AND OIL FIELDS
Botkin — *Anecdotes* p.103, 132, 230, 273-275
Botkin — *Treasury* p.176, 538
Harral — *Feature* p.240-241
New Topical p.182

OKINAWA
Guideposts — *Faith* p.326-330

OKLAHOMA
Botkin — *Anecdotes* p.29, 103, 169
Botkin — *Treasury See* index p.930

OLD AGE
Applegarth — *Heir.* p.65, 169, 186
Asimov — *Treasury* #99, 102, 175, 201, 274, 567
Baillie — *Diary* #40, 288
Barrows — *1000 See* index p.446
Bartlett — *Discovery* p.48, 84-85
Botkin — *Anecdotes* p.12
Braude — *Source* #1190-1194
Braude — *Speaker's* #212-214, 955-957
Braude — *Stories* p.270
Carruthers — *Spark* p.103-105
Cerf — *Laugh* p.372-375
Dirksen — *Quot.* #1025
Edwards — *Useful* p.433-434
Emmons — *Mature* p.88-91, 93
Evans — *Thoughts I* p.38, 219-222
Evans — *Thoughts II (Open Door)* p.53-55, 77-78, 203-207
Evans — *Thoughts IV* p.18-19, 53-60
Flesch — *Unusual* p.111-112, 194-196
Flint — *Graham* p.10
Fogg — *1000* #1037, 1106
Forbes — *Thoughts* p.11, 34, 36, 39, 55, 61, 77, 109, 207, 253, 298, 301, 344, 352, 457
Fuller — *Thesaurus* #1781-1782
Fun Fare p.233-235
Garland — *Subject* p.176
Goudge — *Comfort* p.245-251
Grizer — *Wit* p.290, 323
Halverson — *Perspective* p.110
Harral — *Feature* p.241
Hoffer — *Reflect.* p.92
Holmes — *I've* p.103
How To Live p.493-509
Howell — *Lines* p.153-156
Hubbard — *Scrap* p.50, 77
Johnson — *Bedside* p.277, 338-356
Kauffman — *For* p.150-151
Keys Happiness p.81-84, 392-396, 514-517, 537-540
Kin — *Dictionary* p.151, 180
Knight's Illus. p.219-222
Knight's Treas. p.243-245
Lindeman — *Emerson* p.144
Montapert — *Distilled* p.265-266
Morris — *1000* p.50, 178, 218-219, 250, 281, 302, 313, 323
New Joy p.84, 114-126
Peterson — *Art* p.126, 224
Price — *No* p.87-97
Prochnow — *Public* #410, 2631, 4170
Prochnow — *Success.* #670, 1829-1830, 2104-2107, 2470
Reader's — *Getting* p.57-60, 185
Seaburg — *Great* p.218, 220, 224, 234, 239, 243, 248, 253, 273, 283, 320, 330, 378, 393
Seldes — *Great* p.617
Sheban — *Wisdom* no p.
Sheen — *Content.* p.46-48
Speaker's Desk #127, 873, 886
Tanksley — *Friend* p.45
Wallis — *Words* p.93-94, 138, 163, 230
Walters — *How* p.69-74
Watson — *Light* p.259-277
Woods — *Content.* p.319-338
Woods — *Religious* p.701
Words Change p.34-37

Words — *Inspir.* p.33, 49
, *Art of*
Maurois — *Art* p.254-291
, *Creative*
Maltz — *Creative* p.177-189
, *Dignity of*
Maltz — *Creative* p.182-183
, *Emancipation of*
Words Change p.36
, *Fear of*
Hill — *Think* p.274-276
Hubbard — *Scrap* p.47
Sherman — *Your* p.94-99
, *Perspective in*
Words Change p.36-37
, *Prayer for*
Alexander's Treasure. p.103, 216, 329
Guideposts — *Faith* p.373

"OLD FOGIES"
Safian — *Insults* p.145-147

"OLD HUNDREDTH"
Applegarth — *Heir.* p.185, 187

OLD TESTAMENT
Flesch — *Unusual* p.196
Wallis — *Words* p.7
Woods — *Religious* p.701

OLD THINGS
See also **Age; Antiques**
Alexander's Treasure. p.87-88

"OLIVE BRANCH." *See* **Forgiveness**

OLIVE TREES
New Topical p.182-183

OM (sacred symbol)
Woods — *Religious* p.703

OMEGA
Prochnow — *Public* #2281, 2748

OMENS
See also **Superstition**
Flesch — *Unusual* p.196
Fogg — *1000* #13, 61, 224, 489, 617, 710, 755, 910
Kin — *Dictionary* p.180
Woods — *Religious* p.703

OMISSION
Applegarth — *Heir.* p.255

OMNIPRESENCE. *See* **God**

ONE (age)
Woods — *Content.* p.27
Words — *Inspir.* p.98

"ONE WORLD"
Mandelbaum — *Choose* p.85-89
Woods — *Religious* p.703

ONENESS
Flesch — *Unusual* p.196
Garland — *Subject* p.214
Hobe — *Tapestries* p.126
Sheban — *Wisdom* no p.
Woods — *Religious* p.703
, *with infinite life*
Peterson — *Art* p.302

ONE-SIDEDNESS. *See* **Prejudice**

ONIONS
Guideposts — *Faith* p.337-340
Kin — *Dictionary* p.180

OPENINGS. *See* **Speeches and speaking, Openings of**

OPENMINDEDNESS. *See* **Broadmindedness; Tolerance**

OPERA
Asimov — *Treasury* #376
Flesch — *Unusual* p.196-197
Harnsberger — *Mark* p.335-338
Harral — *Feature* p.241
Prochnow — *Public* #1527
, *and concerts*
Fuller — *Thesaurus* #1341-1371
, *Singers of*
Guideposts — *Faith* p.428-434
, *Traditions of*
Nizer — *Thinking* p.75

OPERATIONS
Flesch — *Unusual* p.197
Lockridge — *World's* #5086
Prochnow — *Public* #1656
, *Recovery from*
Holmes — *I've* p.59-60

OPINION
See also **Belief; Ideas and ideology; Impressions; Judgment; Public opinion; Theory**
Braude — *Source* #1196-1197
Braude — *Stories* p.270
Curtis — *Golden* p.143
Curtis — *Practical* p.72, 432-433
Dirksen — *Quot.* #464-465, 2103-2105, 2330
Edwards — *Useful* p.434-437
Evans — *Unto* p.77, 85
Flesch — *Unusual* p.197
Forbes — *Thoughts* See index p.560

Fuller — *Epigrams* p.221-222
Garland — *Subject* p.214
Grizer — *Wit* p.324-326
Harnsberger — *Mark* p.338-340
Henry — *5000* p.196
Hill — *Think* p.158-159
Hovey — *Treasury* p.248; #1541-1544
Hubbard — *Scrap* p.126
Kennedy — *Reader's* #738-739
Kin — *Dictionary* p.180-181
Krishnamurti — *Think* p.81-82
Kronenberger — *Animal* p.225-226
Liddle — *Thought I, II, III* p.19, 23, 30, 33, 42, 56, 60, 69-80, 88, 100, 129, 148, 157
Liddle — *Thought IV* p.29-30, 34
Liddle — *Thought V* p.34
Lockridge — *World's See* index p.580
Lytle — *Leaves* p.67
Montapert — *Distilled* p.266-267
Price — *Wider* p.143-147
Prochnow — *Public* #419, 422, 718, 741, 793, 853, 1091, 2479, 3484-3489
Prochnow — *Speaker's* p.223
Seldes — *Great* p.702-708
Speaker's Desk p.175-178; #113, 118, 584, 673, 713, 771, 1011, 1035
Woods — *Religious* p.704-705

, Imposed
Adams — *New* p.50

, Propagating
Adams — *New* p.106

OPOSSUMS
Botkin — *Treasury* p.427, 437, 452

OPPORTUNISM
Dirksen — *Quot.* #424
Prochnow — *Success.* #663
Wheelis — *Moralist* p.90

OPPORTUNITY
See also **Chance; Circumstances; Fortune; Time**
Applegarth — *Heir.* p.64, 121
Book Proverbs p.130
Braude — *Source* #1198-1202
Braude — *Speaker's* #958-961
Braude — *Stories* p.271-272
Casselberry — *How* p.170-176
Detherage — *Sunrise* p.54, 109, 111, 113-114, 183
Dirksen — *Quot.* #1, 42, 232, 481, 520, 552, 1027, 1076, 1467-1470, 2305, 2325, 2346
Droke — *Christian* p.364-371
Edwards — *Useful* p.437-439
Emmons — *Mature* p.107, 143
Evans — *Faith* p.7, 9, 15, 19, 95, 116, 159
Evans — *Quote* p.53-66
Evans — *Thoughts I* p.110-112, 129, 154
Evans — *Thoughts II (Open Door)* p.71, 127, 204, 208
Evans — *Thoughts III (Open Road)* p.51, 125, 131, 140, 142, 147, 150, 177, 181, 195
Evans — *Thoughts IV* p.65-66, 166
Flesch — *Unusual* p.198
Fogg — *1000* #343
Forbes — *Thoughts See* index p.560-561
Fox — *Make* p.167-168
Fuller — *Epigrams* p.223
Garland — *Subject* p.215
Grizer — *Wit* p.327-331
Harral — *Feature* p.241
Henry — *5000* p.196-197
Hill — *Think* p.153-154
Hobe — *Tapestries* p.64
Hovey — *Treasury* p.248; #14, 69, 88-89, 678, 801, 877, 1190, 1545-1548, 1684
Howell — *Better* p.149-154
Howell — *Lines* p.40-42
Hubbard — *Scrap* p.225
Kin — *Dictionary* p.181
Knight's Treas. p.246
Liddle — *Thought I, II, III* p.21, 30, 56, 65, 89, 124
Liddle — *Thought IV* p.6, 13
Liddle — *Thought V* p.7, 18, 23, 27, 37
Lockridge — *World's* #355, 479, 4249
Lytle — *Leaves* p.6, 34, 52, 113, 173
Mandel — *Stories* p.188-190
Modern Eloquence (14) p.385-386
Montapert — *Distilled* p.267
Peale — *Guideposts* p.80-84
Prochnow — *Public* #766, 1575, 1755, 1923, 2107, 3490-3492
Prochnow — *Success.* #357, 381, 511, 570, 1092, 1188, 1220, 2108-2109
Sheban — *Wisdom* no p.
Speaker's Desk p.178-179; #234, 249, 283, 382, 528, 637, 700
Streiker — *Who* p.119-146
Tanksley — *Friend* p.77
Wallis — *Treasure* p.185-188
Wallis — *Words* p.212
Woods — *Business.* p.160-162
Woods — *Content.* p.26, 38, 51-52
Woods — *Wellsprings* p.66-67
Words — *Inspir.* p.77

, versus obedience
Kauffman — *For* p.154-155

OPPOSITES
Flesch — *Unusual* p.198
Kohn — *Thoughts* p.80-81

OPPOSITION
See also **Argument; Controversy;** etc.
Bartlett — *Discovery* p.119-121
Book Proverbs p.80
Braude — *Source* #1203
Edwards — *Useful* p.439-440
Evans — *Thoughts IV* p.87
Flesch — *Unusual* p.48
Forbes — *Thoughts* p.82, 316, 488
Garland — *Subject* p.215-216
Kin — *Dictionary* p.178

OPPRESSION
See also **Cruelty; Dictatorship; Tyrants and tyranny**
Braude — *Source* #1204
Edwards — *Useful* p.440
Flint — *Graham* p.101
Forbes — *Thoughts* p.15, 231, 425, 502, 506, 508
Garland — *Subject* p.216-217
Johnson — *Bedside* p.32-38
Liddle — *Thought I, II, III* p.50
Maltz — *Creative* p.132-133
Seldes — *Great* p.708-709
Sheban — *Wisdom* no p.
Woods — *Religious* p.705
, Reduction of
Mandelbaum — *Choose* p.167-183

OPTICIANS
Manchee — *Secret* p.220-221

OPTIMISM
See also **Cheerfulness**
Alexander's Treasure. p.224
Braude — *Source* #1205-1212
Braude — *Speaker's* #962
Braude — *Stories* p.272-274
Dirksen — *Quot.* #165
Droke — *Christian* p.371-374
Flesch — *Unusual* p.198
Fogg — *1000* #17, 429, 559, 619, 693, 929, 1113
Forbes — *Thoughts* p.76, 94, 118, 225, 234, 238, 374, 430
Fuller — *Epigrams* p.223-224
Garland — *Subject* p.217
Grizer — *Wit* p.331-333
Harnsberger — *Mark* p.340
Henry — *5000* p.197
Hovey — *Treasury* #1251, 1549-1551, 1810; p.248
How To Live p.568-592
Keller — *Open* p.50
Kennedy — *Reader's* #740
Keys Happiness p.131-132
Kin — *Dictionary* p.181
Kohn — *Adventures* p.71-74
Liddle — *Thought I, II, III* p.31, 98, 186, 191
Lockridge — *World's* #5592
Lytle — *Leaves* p.113
Mandel — *Stories* p.190-191
Modern Eloquence (14) p.231-237, 387-388
Montapert — *Distilled* p.267-268
Peale — *Sin* p.153-156
Peterson — *Art* p.183, 273
Prochnow — *Public* #235, 440, 1284, 1335, 1434, 1464, 1756-1760
Prochnow — *Speaker's* p.223
Prochnow — *Success.* #514, 547, 551, 613, 707, 1327
Safian — *Insults* p.148-149
Seldes — *Great* p.709
Speaker's Desk #52, 107, 247, 251, 321, 432, 460, 647, 676, 876, 943, 1109
Unlimited Power p.227-229
Wallis — *Treasure* p.185
Wallis — *Words* p.20
Wilcox — *Heart* p.42-45
Woods — *Religious* p.705-706
Words — *Inspir.* p.110

OPTIMIST CLUB
Harral — *Feature* p.241
Prochnow — *Success.* #1150

ORACLES
Prochnow — *Public* #2298

ORANGES
Kin — *Dictionary* p.181

ORATORIOS
Flesch — *Unusual* p.198

ORATORS AND ORATORY
See also **Eloquence**
Botkin — *Anecdotes* p.165
Dirksen — *Quot.* #2106-2107
Edwards — *Useful* p.440-441, 731
Evans — *This* p.147
Evans — *Unto* p.37, 78
Fogg — *1000 See* index p.893-894
Henry — *5000* p.197-198
Hubbard — *Scrap* p.6, 13, 22, 87, 195
Kin — *Dictionary* p.181-182
Lindeman — *Emerson* p.146
Lockridge — *World's* #9
Lytle — *Leaves* p.157, 161, 163

Nizer — *Thinking* p.70, 90, 129
Prochnow — *Public* #3493, 4378
Schermerhorn — *1500* p.268-270
Woods — *Religious* p.706

ORCHARDS
See also **Trees;** names of trees and fruits
Sagendorph — *Old* p.120-126

ORCHESTRAS
Harral — *Feature* p.241-242
Peale — *Guideposts* p.76-79

ORDER. *See* **Organization**

ORDINATION
Hovey — *Treasury* #108
Woods — *Religious* p.706-707

OREGON
Botkin — *Anecdotes* p.108, 200, 232
Botkin — *Treasury* p.205, 277, 284, 301, 520

ORGAN
Wallis — *Words* p.168

ORGANIZATION
See also **Discipline; Efficiency; Government; Law; Neatness;** etc.
Braude — *Speaker's* #1420
Braude — *Stories* p.274, 371-372
Curtis — *Human* p.51-66
Dirksen — *Quot.* #2355, 2381
Du Noüy — *Road* p.59, 68, 74-75, 107
Edwards — *Useful* p.441-442
Evans — *Thoughts IV* p.138, 183, 198
Flesch — *Unusual* p.198, 282-283
Forbes — *Thoughts* p.122-123, 155, 173, 180, 250, 263, 384, 394, 408, 415, 443, 476, 483
Harnsberger — *Mark* p.341
Henry — *5000* p.198
Holmes — *I've* p.25
Hovey — *Treasury* p.248-249; #33, 70, 458, 466, 487, 500, 587, 709, 1358, 1552-1556, 1560, 1627, 1718, 1779
Hubbard — *Scrap* p.169
Humes — *Instant* #675-681
Keller — *Open* p.73-74
Kin — *Dictionary* p.182
Kohn — *Pathways* p.91-94
Krishnamurti — *Urgency* p.70-72, 135-137
Liddle — *Thought I, II, III* p.51, 133
Lockridge —*World's* #4809
Modern Eloquence (14) p.389
Prochnow — *Public* #135, 434, 1005, 1857
Prochnow — *Success.* #804
Seldes — *Great* p.709
Wheelis — *Moralist* p.70, 72, 89-90
Woods — *Religious* p.706
, and change
Adams — *New* p.23

ORGANIZATIONS
See also **Clubs; Groups;** names of organizations
Boas — *History* p.71-74
Esteve — *Experience* p.6-7
Harral — *Feature* p.242
Lockridge — *World's* #4615
Peterson — *Art* p.307
Wheelis — *Moralist* p.129-132

ORIENT
See also names of countries
Cerf — *Laugh* p.450-452
Harnsberger — *Mark* p.341
Sheban — *Wisdom* no p.

ORIGINALITY
See also **Distinction; Individuals and individuality; Inventors and invention**
Braude — *Stories* p.278
Edwards — *Useful* p.442-443
Evans — *Unto* p.30
Flesch — *Unusual* p.188, 199
Forbes — *Thoughts* p.99, 119, 504
Fuller — *Epigrams* p.225
Grizer — *Wit* p.334
Harnsberger — *Mark* p.341
Henry — *5000* p.198
Hobe — *Tapestries* p.201
Hubbard — *Scrap* p.145
Kennedy — *Reader's* #741-742
Lockridge — *World's* #632, 2867, 2931
Lytle — *Leaves* p.116
Montapert — *Distilled* p.268
Speaker's Desk p.179-180; #253, 699, 754

ORNAMENT
See also **Art**
Edwards — *Useful* p.443
Hooker — *Index* p.265-270
Lytle — *Leaves* p.163
Prochnow — *Public* #2058

ORPHANS
Kin — *Dictionary* p.182
Prochnow — *Speaker's* p.224
Unlimited Power p.281-285

ORTHODOXY
Flesch — *Unusual* p.199

Hubbard — *Scrap* p.59
Lockridge — *World's* #3638
Seldes — *Great* p.709-710
Woods — *Religious* p.710-711

OSTENTATION. *See* **Ceremony; Pretension**

OSTEOPATHY
Harnsberger — *Mark* p.341-342

OSTRICHES
Baillie — *Diary* #209
Kin — *Dictionary* p.182
New Topical p.183
Prochnow — *Public* #456

OTHERS. *See* **People**

OTTERS
Goudge — *Comfort* p.75-76

OURSELVES. *See* **Self**

OUTDOOR LIFE
See also **Nature;** etc.
Harral — *Feature* p.242
White — *Life* p.161-166
, and people
Seaburg — *Great See* index p.462

"OUTWITTED"
Lytle — *Leaves* p.125
Speaker's Desk See index p.303

OVERCONFIDENCE
Evans — *Unto* p.35
Lytle — *Leaves* p.169

OVERFLOW
White — *Job* p.34-36, 105, 142

OVERSIGHT
Alexander's Treasure. p.89-90
Flesch — *Unusual* p.200
Mandel — *Stories* p.191
Peterson — *Art* p.130

OVERWEIGHT
See also **Diet**
Asimov — *Treasury* #261
Braude — *Speaker's* #963-973
Fuller — *Thesaurus* #681-690
Huxley — *You See* index p.286-287
Keys Happiness p.485-487
Kin — *Dictionary* p.90
Lockridge — *World's* #3413
Prochnow — *Public* #791, 1181, 1751, 2042
Schermerhorn — *1500* p.266
White — *Life* p.82-84
Woods — *Religious* p.334

OVERWORK
Albert — *Stop* p.5-6, 110
Kin — *Dictionary* p.183
Manchee — *Secret* p.156-158
Prochnow — *Public* #1761

OWLS
Botkin — *Anecdotes* p.182
Kin — *Dictionary* p.183
Kohn — *Pathways* p.123-126
Lockridge — *World's* #5222
New Topical p.183
, Barn
Auden — *Certain* p.294-296
, Hoot
Botkin — *Treasury* p.673

OWNERSHIP
Kennedy — *Reader's* #743-744
Lytle — *Leaves* p.151
Prochnow — *Public* #4398
Woods — *Business.* p.162-163
Woods — *Religious* p.711

OXEN
Applegarth — *Heir.* p.21
Botkin — *Treasury* p.424, 632
New Topical p.183-184
Prochnow — *Public* #2572

OXFORD
Woods — *Content.* p.65

OYSTERS
Asimov — *Treasury* #332
Botkin — *Anecdotes* p.4, 179
Harnsberger — *Mark* p.342-343
Henry — *5000* p.198
Kin — *Dictionary* p.183
Prochnow — *Public* #288
Wallis — *Treasure* p.225

OZARKS
Botkin — *Anecdotes* p.2, 97, 247-251
Botkin — *Treasury* p.429, 503, 555, 692

P

P.T.A.
Harral — *Feature* p.260
Hovey — *Treasury See* index p.303-304

PACE
Evans — *Thoughts II (Open Door)* p.174-175, 198

Evans — *Thoughts III (Open Road)* p.115
Keys Happiness p.533-536
, Change of
Nichols — *Third* p.97-98

PACIFISM
See also **Peace**
Flesch — *Unusual* p.200
Flint — *Graham* p.101
Franke — *Buckley* p.225
Kennedy — *Reader's* #745-746
Prochnow — *Success.* #2118
Seldes — *Great* p.710-711
Sheban — *Wisdom* no p.
Woods — *Religious* p.711-713
, and Christian
Day — *Meditations* p.42

"PACK RATS"
Botkin — *Anecdotes* p.90

PACKAGING
Fox — *Make* p.112-113

PAGANS AND PAGANISM
Kin — *Dictionary* p.184
Seldes — *Great* p.711
Woods — *Religious* p.713
, Gods of
Fuller — *Thesaurus* #1661

PAGEANTS
Harral — *Feature* p.242
, Children's
Guideposts — *Faith* p.341-343

PAIN
See also **Illness; Suffering;** etc.
Curtis — *Practical* p.262
Dirksen — *Quot.* #909, 2108-2109, 2113
Edwards — *Useful* p.444
Flesch — *Unusual* p.201
Forbes — *Thoughts* p.20, 145, 243, 310, 453
Fuller — *Epigrams* p.225
Garland — *Subject* p.219
Harnsberger — *Mark* p.344
Henry — *5000* p.198-199
Hobe — *Tapestries* p.123
Huxley — *You See* index p.287
Johnson — *Bedside* p.83, 96, 190, 281, 285
Kennedy — *Reader's* #747
Kin — *Dictionary* p.184
Liddle — *Thought V* p.24, 34
Lockridge — *World's* #2650
Montapert — *Distilled* p.269
New Joy p.104
Peale — *Stay* p.264-283
Prochnow — *Public* #1223, 2009, 2109, 3924
Prochnow — *Speaker's* p.224
Prochnow — *Success.* #2119
Seldes — *Great* p.711
Sheban — *Wisdom* no p.
Sheen — *Thoughts* p.124-125
Speaker's Desk p.180-181; #868
Tanksley — *Friend* p.27
Wallis — *Words* p.167
Watson — *Light* p.95-99
White — *Job* p.37-38
Woods — *Religious* p.713-714
, Avoidance of
Menninger — *Blue.* p.79-80
, Paradoxes of
Taylor — *With* p.99-105
, Prayer to help
Unlimited Power p.126

PAINTERS AND PAINTING
Applegarth — *Heir.* p.28-29, 31
Asimov — *Treasury* #213
Curtis — *Practical* p.432, 438-439, 445-455
Edwards — *Useful* p.444-445
Flesch — *Unusual* p.201
Fogg — *1000* #100, 267, 544, 615, 840, 1121
Fuller — *Thesaurus* #1261-1293
Guideposts — *Faith* p.357-363, 374-379, 390-394
Harnsberger — *Mark* p.344-347
Harral — *Feature* p.243
Henry — *5000* p.199
Hooker — *Index* p.265-270
How To Live p.332-337
Hubbard — *Scrap* p.26
Keys Happiness p.457-461
Kin — *Dictionary* p.184
Kronenberger — *Animal* p.226-230
Lockridge — *World's* #2281, 4916-4947
Mandel — *Stories* p.191
Nizer — *Thinking* p.73
Patterns For Living p.373-377
Peterson — *Art* p.260, 377
Phillips — *Choice* p.267-268
Prochnow — *Speaker's* p.224
Prochnow — *Success.* #2120
Reader's — *Getting* p.246-250
Woods — *Content.* p.260-261
Zobell — *Speaker's* p.89-92
, House
Asimov — *Treasury* #612
Prochnow — *Public* #431
, "Old masters of"
Harnsberger — *Mark* p.258-259

PAKISTAN
Simpson — *Contemp.* p.149

PALACES
Flesch — *Unusual* p.202
Kin — *Dictionary* p.184
Prochnow — *Success.* #2121

PALEONTOLOGY
Du Noüy — *Human* p.66-69

PALESTINE
Harnsberger — *Mark* p.347-348
New Topical p.120

PALM SUNDAY
Fridy — *Meditat.* p.92

PALMISTRY
Harral — *Feature* p.243
Prochnow — *Public* #224

PALMS
Lytle — *Leaves* p.24
New Topical p.185

PAMPERING. *See* **Indulgence**

PAMPHLETS
Flesch — *Unusual* p.202
Prochnow — *Success.* #2122

PAN
Prochnow — *Public* #2390

PANACEA. *See* **Remedies**

PANDEMONIUM. *See* **Confusion; Noise**

PANDORA
Prochnow — *Public* #2318

PANIC
See also **Depression; Fear; Mob**
Edwards — *Useful* p.445
Lockridge — *World's* #713
Prochnow — *Public* #1518

PANTHEISM
Ideas p.284-286
Lockridge — *World's* #5231
Woods — *Religious* p.714-715

PANTOMIME
Nizer — *Thinking* p.101

PAPACY. *See* **Popes**

PAPER
Lockridge — *World's* #5604
Prochnow — *Public* #1188

PARABLES
See also **Fables**
Asimov — *Treasury* #403
Garland — *Subject* p.220
Johnson — *Bedside* p.144, 323
Lytle — *Leaves* p.132
More Words p.118-119
New Topical p.185
Phillips — *Choice* p.42, 50, 93, 99, 220, 391
Prochnow — *Public* #1013
Woods — *Religious* p.715

PARACHUTES
Prochnow — *Public* #544, 579, 821

PARADISE
See also **Arcadia (Paradise); Eternity; Heaven; Immortality;** etc.
Auden — *Certain* p.296-298
Baillie — *Diary* #104
Edwards — *Useful* p.445
Garland — *Subject* p.220
Henry — *5000* p.199
Kin — *Dictionary* p.185
Lockridge — *World's* #2722
Lytle — *Leaves* p.73-74
Mandel — *Stories* p.191-192
Prochnow — *Public* #2312, 2394
Wallis — *Words* p.98
Woods — *Religious* p.715
, Search for
Hoffer — *Reflect.* p.71

PARADOX
Adams — *New* p.334, 373
Asimov — *Treasury* #67; p.68-123
Day — *Meditations* p.74
Flesch — *Unusual* p.202
Hobe — *Tapestries* p.44
Kin — *Dictionary* p.185
Lockridge — *World's* #892, 5022
Phillips — *Choice See* index p.427
Wallis — *Treasure* p.105
Woods — *Religious* p.715

PARAKEETS
Asimov — *Treasury* #64

"PARASITES"
Braude — *Stories* p.278
Seldes — *Great* p.712
Welk — *Guide.* p.123-126

PARATROOPERS
Asimov — *Treasury* #30

PARDON
See also **Compassion; Forgiveness; Mercy**
Edwards — *Useful* p.85, 445
Garland — *Subject* p.220
Henry — *5000* p.199-200
Kin — *Dictionary* p.185
Lockridge — *World's* #16-17, 314, 1435, 2260, 5871
New Topical p.185-186

PARENTS AND PARENTHOOD
See also **Children; Family; Fathers; Mothers**
Adams — *New* p.377
Braude — *Source* #1216-1235
Braude — *Speaker's* #974-989
Braude — *Stories* p.279-280
Detherage — *Sunrise* p.41, 121
Dirksen — *Quot.* #137, 250-251, 1471-1476, 2110-2111
Edwards — *Useful* p.444-446
Esteve — *Experience* p.21
Evans — *Faith* p.6, 27, 31, 39-40, 46, 49-57, 80, 168, 174
Evans — *This* p.109-119
Evans — *Thoughts I See* index, no p.
Evans — *Thoughts II (Open Door)* p.31-32, 36, 94-95, 98, 116, 128-129, 156-159, 163-164
Evans — *Thoughts III (Open Road)* p.18-21, 31, 68-69, 91, 137, 139, 141-142, 161, 170, 178, 181, 188
Evans — *Thoughts IV* p.34-36, 40, 77-78, 119, 144, 159-160
Evans — *Unto* p.77, 106, 147
Flesch — *Unusual* p.202-203
Flint — *Graham* p.22-23, 101, 103
Forbes — *Thoughts* p.47, 82, 209, 328, 360, 409, 417, 453, 459
Fun Fare p.116, 138, 180, 224, 290, 298
Garland — *Subject* p.220-221
Gold — *Letters* p.109-111
Grizer — *Wit* p.335-336
Henry — *5000* p.200
Holmes — *I've* p.71-86
Hovey — *Treasury* p.249-250; *See also* index p.299
How To Live p.104-138
Hubbard — *Scrap* p.26
Hunter — *Gems* p.37-38
Johnson — *Bedside* p.119-120, 298-301, 303-304, 313
Kahn — *Lessons* p.192-198
Kennedy — *Reader's* #748
Keys Happiness p.20, 50, 294-297, 552-555
Kin — *Dictionary* p.185
Lair — *Baby* p.26-33, 116
Liddle — *Thought I, II, III* p.17, 47, 166, 178, 192
Liddle — *Thought IV* p.19
Liddle — *Thought V* p.15, 22
Lockridge — *World's* #868, 935, 4335
Mandel — *Stories* p.192-194
Mandelbaum — *Choose* p.64-68
Myers — *Thunder* p.79-93
New Topical p.186-187
Patterns For Living p.157-165
Peale — *Courage* p.131-134
Peterson — *Art* p.217
Peterson — *New* p.48-49
Prochnow — *Public* #1504, 1538, 1545, 4171
Prochnow — *Speaker's* p.225
Prochnow — *Success.* #2123-2126
Pullar-Strecker — *Proverbs* #94-102
Reader's — *Getting* p.150-153, 226-228
Sheen — *Way* p.89-91
Tanksley — *Friend* p.33
Wallis — *Treasure* p.51, 90, 129, 131, 181
White — *Life* p.7-8, 13, 26-32, 42-48, 49-50
Woods — *Religious* p.716
, and children
Speaker's Desk See index p.303
, and teenagers
Ginott — *Between See* index p.253
, Duty to
Krishnamurti — *Think* p.115
, Guidance of
Hunter — *Gems* p.66-67
, Guidelines for
Ginott — *Between See* index p.251
, Obligations of
Du Noüy — *Human* p.209-212
, Prayer for
Peterson — *Art* p.334
, Responsibility of
Hunter — *Gems* p.64-68
Knight's Illus. p.222-224
Knight's Treas. p.246-249

PARIS, FRANCE
Botkin — *Anecdotes* p.159, 215, 275
Hubbard — *Scrap* p.173
Lockridge — *World's* #1154, 3148, 3150-3151, 3155, 3162, 3164, 3708, 3781, 4050, 4944
Reader's — *20th* p.25-27

PARISHES AND PARISHIONERS
Kin — *Dictionary* p.185

Weisfeld — *Pulpit* p.91-103
Words — *Change* p.106-109

PARKING
Asimov — *Treasury* #123
Grizer — *Wit* p.336
Harral — *Feature* p.243
Prochnow — *Public* #60, 728, 1762
, Meters for
Harral — *Feature* p.243
Prochnow — *Success.* #907

PARKS
Harral — *Feature* p.243
Kohn — *Best* p.69-71
, Benches for
Peale — *Guideposts* p.174-178
, National
Kauffman — *For* p.164-165

PAROCHIAL SCHOOLS. *See* **Education, Parochial**

PARODIES
See also **Satire**
Copeland — *10,000* p.926-939

PARROTS
Asimov — *Treasury* #67, 396, 600
Botkin — *Anecdotes* p.243
Fuller — *Thesaurus* #2291-2293
Prochnow — *Public* #404
Prochnow — *Success.* #987, 1013
Schermerhorn — *1500* p.274, 276
Speaker's Desk #507, 653, 1000
Weisfeld — *Pulpit* p.98, 110

PARSONAGES
Weisfeld — *Pulpit* p.144-151

PARSONS. *See* **Clergymen**

PARTIALITY. *See* **Injustice**

PARTICIPATION
Evans — *Thoughts II (Open Door)* p.56-57

PARTICLES
Du Noüy — *Road See* index p.250
Lytle — *Leaves* p.108

PARTIES
Asimov — *Treasury* #168-170, 188
Daly — *Personality* p.83-87
Edwards — *Useful* p.447-448
Flesch — *Unusual* p.203
Fuller — *Thesaurus* #741-746
Harral — *Feature* p.243-244
Henry — *5000* p.200
Prochnow — *Public* #43, 130, 749, 904, 1194
Prochnow — *Success.* #1078, 2127
Seldes — *Great* p.713-714
Walters — *How* p.147-165

"PARTY CHATTER"
Fun Fare p.210, 267

PARTING. *See* **Farewells**

PARTNERS
See also **Marriage; Partnership**
Asimov — *Treasury* #360-361, 395
Clark — *Windows* p.114

PARTNERSHIP
Braude — *Speaker's* #990-991
Fuller — *Thesaurus* #2241-2242
Grizer — *Wit* p.337
Halverson — *Perspective* p.99
Mandel — *Stories* p.194
Wallis — *Treasure* p.42, 66

PARTRIDGES
Applegarth — *Heir.* p.36
Kin — *Dictionary* p.186

PASCAL, BLAISE
Du Noüy — *Road* p.40, 195, 197, 221-224, 222n, 229
Lockridge — *World's* #1668

PASSION
See also **Anger; Desire; Jesus Christ, Passion of**
Book Proverbs p.112
Edwards — *Useful* p.448-451
Evans — *Unto* p.61
Flesch — *Unusual* p.203
Fuller — *Epigrams* p.225-226
Henry — *5000* p.201
Kin — *Dictionary* p.186
Krishnamurti — *Urgency* p.132-134
Lockridge — *World's See* index p.580
Lytle — *Leaves* p.188
Montapert — *Distilled* p.269
Seldes — *Great* p.715
Speaker's Desk p.181-182
Woods — *Religious* p.716-717

PASSIVES
Humes — *Instant* p.15-16

PASSOVER
Garland — *Subject* p.222-223
Guideposts — *Faith* p.188-191
New Topical p.90

Strait — *Speaker's* p.169
, and exodus
McDonagh — *Invit.* p.98-101

PASSPORTS
Kin — *Dictionary* p.186
Prochnow — *Public* #813

PAST
See also **Antiquity; Old age; Time; Yesterday**
Adams — *New* p.131, 209
Applegarth — *Heir.* p.66, 107, 110, 113, 120
Bach — *Make* p.30
Braude — *Source* #1237-1258
Braude — *Stories* p.280
Carruthers — *Sparks* p.27-28
Curtis — *Practical* p.136, 395
Dirksen — *Quot.* #752, 1029-1030, 1857, 2112
Edwards — *Useful* p.451-452
Evans — *Thoughts I* p.47, 78-79, 127-128, 176-177, 179
Evans — *Thoughts III (Open Road)* p.201
Evans — *Thoughts IV* p.168, 198-200
Evans — *Unto* p.6, 8-9, 19, 22-23, 31, 35, 50, 64
Flesch — *Unusual* p.203
Forbes — *Thoughts* p.1, 69, 76, 151, 178, 180, 183, 220, 349, 365, 368
Fox — *Make* p.101-102
Grizer — *Wit* p.337-338
Harnsberger — *Mark* p.349
Henry — *5000* p.201
Hobe — *Tapestries* p.172
How To Live p.282-283
Kauffman — *For* p.154
Kennedy — *Fresh* p.147-149
Kin — *Dictionary* p.36
Lair — *Baby* p.31-32
Liddle — *Thought I, II, III* p.84-90, 103, 115, 163, 188
Liddle — *Thought V* p.3
Lindeman — *Emerson* p.145
Lockridge — *World's* #850, 1105, 2370, 4222, 4409, 4640, 5163
Montapert — *Distilled* p.269-270
Peterson — *Art* p.46, 94
Prochnow — *Success.* #2128-2130
Seldes — *Great* p.715
Sheen — *Lift* p.191-197
Wallis — *Treasure* p.219, 222, 233, 238
Wallis — *Words* p.50, 94, 105-106, 118, 211
Watson — *Light* p.74-78
Wilcox — *Heart* p.5-7
, and future
Flesch — *Unusual* p.204
Sheban — *Wisdom* no p.
, Elusive
Adams — *New* p.86
, Influence of
Holmes — *Design* p.112-113
, Lessons from
Evans — *Faith* p.8-10, 21, 214
Saturday — *Advent.* p.69-80

PASTEUR, LOUIS
Webb — *Edge* p.29-30

PASTORS. *See* **Clergymen**

PASTURES
Kin — *Dictionary* p.186

PATCHES
Kin — *Dictionary* p.186

PATENTS
Harral — *Feature* p.244
Woods — *Business.* p.163-164

PATERNALISM
See also **Fathers**
Dirksen — *Quot.* #34, 73, 650, 674

PATHOLOGISTS
Curtis — *Practical* p.54

PATHS
Lytle — *Leaves* p.125
Prochnow — *Success.* #650
Woods — *Religious* p.718-719

PATIENCE
See also **Endurance; Perseverance; Resignation; Waiting**
Alexander's Treasure. p.333
Applegarth — *Heir.* p.295, 306
Book Proverbs p.68, 110
Braude — *Source* #1259-1265
Braude — *Speaker's* #992-994
Braude — *Stories* p.280-281
Dirksen — *Quot.* #211-212, 264, 466, 759, 1477-1480, 1595
Edwards — *Useful* p.202, 452-454
Emmons — *Mature* p.65, 68
Evans — *Faith* p.6, 10, 14, 32-33
Evans — *Quote* p.153-162
Evans — *Thoughts II (Open Door)* p.59-60
Evans — *Thoughts III (Open Road) See* index no p.

Evans — *Thoughts IV* p.19, 106, 108, 167, 200-201
Flesch — *Unusual* p.204
Fogg — *1000* #280, 358, 725
Forbes — *Thoughts See* index p.561
Fuller — *Epigrams* p.226
Fuller — *Thesaurus* #391
Garland — *Subject* p.223-224
Goudge — *Comfort* p.208
Grizer — *Wit* p.338-339
Henry — *5000* p.201-202
Hobe — *Tapestries* p.87
Holmes — *I've* p.57-59
Hovey — *Treasury* #979, 1017
Howell — *Lines* p.92-93
Hubbard — *Scrap* p.126
Johnson — *Bedside* p.86, 134
Kennedy — *Reader's* #749
Kin — *Dictionary* p.98, 187
Knight's Treas. p.249-252
Langdon — *Teach.* p.67-77
Liddle — *Thought I, II, III* p.7, 16-17, 29, 40, 63, 72, 101, 135, 182
Liddle — *Thought V* p.9
Lockridge — *World's* #1451, 1465, 1642, 1793, 5703, 5887
Lytle — *Leaves* p.12, 73, 87, 126, 137, 187
Mandel — *Stories* p.195-197
Montapert — *Distilled* p.270
New Joy p.46
New Topical p.187
Nichols — *New* p.111-113
Nichols — *Third* p.201-203
Petty — *Promises* p.30-36
Price — *Wider* p.31
Prochnow — *Public* #119, 1853, 2433, 4172-4173
Prochnow — *Success.* #1051, 2131-2133
Sherman — *Your* p.148-152
Speaker's Desk p.182-183; #76, 343, 373, 389, 393, 396, 501, 515, 540, 972
Voss — *Quotations* p.186-188
Wallis — *Treasure* p.46, 194, 203, 226
Wallis — *Words* p.49, 110, 117
Watson — *Light* p.79-82
Woods — *Content.* p.300, 302, 310, 358
Woods — *Religious* p.719
Words Change p.33
Words — *Inspir.* p.185-186

PATIENTS. *See* **Hospitals, Patients in; Physicians, and patients**

PATRIARCHY
New Topical p.187-188
Prochnow — *Public* #2429

PATRIOTISM
See also **Americans and Americanism; Freedom; Heroes and heroism; Liberty; War; etc.**
Braude — *Source* #1266-1268
Braude — *Speaker's* #215-219, 995
Braude — *Stories* p.282
Copeland — *10,000* p.996-998
Detherage — *Sunrise* p.159-166
Dirksen — *Quot.* #34, 564-565, 675, 1755, 2307, 2316, 2357
Droke — *Christian* p.374-377
Edwards — *Useful* p.454-455, 731
Evans — *This* p.142-143, 147-148
Evans — *Thoughts II (Open Door)* p. 70
Evans — *Unto* p.15, 58, 115
Felleman — *Poems* p.153-183
Flesch — *Unusual* p.204-205
Flint — *Graham* p.103
Fogg — *1000 See* index p.894
Forbes — *Thoughts* p.58, 228, 276
Fuller — *Epigrams* p.227-228
Fuller — *Thesaurus* #396-407
Garland — *Subject* p.224
Grizer — *Wit* p.339
Harnsberger — *Mark* p.349-351
Henry — *5000* p.202-203
Hobe — *Tapestries* p.141, 200-201
Hovey — *Treasury* p.250; #290, 1562-1563
Howell — *Better* p.155-160
Howell — *Lines* p.143-148
Hubbard — *Scrap* p.64, 74
Humes — *Instant* #682-692
Kennedy — *Reader's* #750-753
Kin — *Dictionary* p.187
Knight's Illus. p.225-233
Knight's Treas. p.252-258
Liddle — *Thought IV* p.15, 43, 45
Lockridge — *World's* #2060
Miller — *Harvest* p.81-87
Modern Eloquence (14) p.390-391
Morris — *1000 See* index p.431
Prochnow — *Public* #938, 1926, 2336, 2688, 4362
Prochnow — *Success.* #185, 223
Seldes — *Great* p.236-239, 715-718
Sheban — *Wisdom* no p.
Speaker's Desk p.183-184; #378, 1030, 1079, 1182
Strait — *Speaker's* p.168-169
Voss — *Quotations* p.188-190
Wheelis — *Moralist* p.104
White — *Job* p.59-60
Woods — *Inspir.* p.124-165
Woods — *Religious* p.719-720

, *and faith*
Kauffman — *For* p.154-155
, *and peace*
Barrows — *1000 See* index p.444
, *Higher*
Suter — *Prayers* #36-69
, *Instant*
Kauffman — *For* p.155-156
, *Prayer of*
Words — *Inspir.* p.117
, *Speeches of*
Copeland — *World's See* index p.735-736

PATRON SAINTS. *See* **Saints and sainthood;** names of saints

PATRONS AND PATRONAGE
Curtis — *Practical* p.439
Hubbard — *Scrap* p.212
Kin — *Dictionary* p.187

"PATTER"
Fun Fare p.106, 247

PATTERNS
Evans — *This* p.87-88
Evans — *Thoughts III (Open Road)* p.179-180, 208

PAUL, SAINT
Baillie — *Diary* #32
Flesch — *Unusual* p.250
Fridy — *Meditat.* p.13, 68, 102
Keller — *You* p.41-44

PAUPERISM. *See* **Poverty**

PAUSE
Flesch — *Unusual* p.205
Harnsberger — *Mark* p.351-352
How To Live p.205-208
Wallis — *Treasure* p.194

PAWNSHOPS
Alexander's Treasure. p.47
Harral — *Feature* p.244
Prochnow — *Speaker's* p.225
Prochnow — *Success.* #726

PAYMENT
See also **Salaries; Wages;** etc.
Prochnow — *Speaker's* p.225-226
Welk — *Guide.* p.62-64

PEACE
See also **Quiet; Rest**
Applegarth — *Heir.* p.119, 184, 277, 294
Baillie — *Diary* #291
Barrows — *1000 See* index **p.444**
Bartlett — *Discovery* p.154-156
Braude — *Source* #1269-1272
Braude — *Speaker's* #220
Copeland — *World's* p.185-187, 206, 351-353, 360-365, 391-393, 525-529, 558-567
Curtis — *Human* p.183-200
Curtis — *Practical* p.351-389
Detherage — *Sunrise* p.34, 106
Dirksen — *Quot. See* index p.267; p.1040, 1103
Droke — *Christian* p.377-388
Du Noüy — *Human* p.140, 218-219, 267-272
Edwards — *Useful* p.455, 721
Evans — *Quote* p.141-152
Evans — *Thoughts I* p.27, 43, 81, 91, 123, 131, 196
Evans — *Thoughts II (Open Door)* p.65, 73, 75, 89, 153, 188-189, 199, 208
Evans — *Thoughts III (Open Road)* p.35-36, 40, 47, 49, 55-56, 81, 111, 130, 165, 170, 209, 211
Evans — *Unto* p.7, 16-17, 20, 36, 50, 84, 95, 102-103, 113, 124-127
Flesch — *Unusual* p.205, 293
Flint — *Graham* p.103
Fogg — *1000* #303, 423, 565, 577, 815, 896, 969, 1130, 1137
Forbes — *Thoughts See* index p.561
Franke — *Buckley* p.227-229
Fuller — *Epigrams* p.228
Garland — *Subject* p.224
Giniger — *Compact* p.278
Goudge — *Comfort* p.208
Grizer — *Wit* p.339-340
Guideposts — *Faith* p.32-33, 408-412
Hadfield — *Delights* p.225
Harnsberger — *Mark* p.352-353
Henry — *5000* p.203-204
Hobe — *Tapestries* p.52, 138-142
Hovey — *Treasury* p.250-251; *See also* index p.299, 304
How To Live p.215
Hubbard — *Scrap* p.68, 96
Humes — *Instant* #693-707
Hunter — *Gems* p.69-72
Johnson — *Bedside* p.61-83, 294, 336-337, 356
Kauffman — *For* p.156-160
Kennedy — *Reader's* #754-756
Kin — *Dictionary* p.187-188
Knight's Illus. p.233
Liddle — *Thought I, II, III* p.7, 13, 58, 62, 65, 78, 108, 168, 185
Liddle — *Thought IV* p.17-18, 32
Liddle — *Thought V* p.26, 29, 38
Lockridge — *World's* #1616, 1762, 1854, 1856, 2783, 3808, 3851

Lytle — *Leaves* p.85, 121, 130, 142
Mandel — *Stories* p.197
Mandelbaum — *Choose* p.90-94
Montapert — *Distilled* p.271
New Joy p.44
New Topical p.188
Peale — *Courage* p.209
Peterson — *Art* p.170, 174, 399
Peterson — *New* p.22-23
Petty — *Promises* p.25-29
Petty — *Wings* p.31-37
Price — *Wider* p.30-31
Prochnow — *Public* #1174, 1540, 2295, 2305, 2587, 2665, 2698, 2728, 4174
Prochnow — *Success.* #268, 295, 431, 464, 1437, 2134-2137
Seldes — *Great* p.718-721
Sheban — *Wisdom* no p.
Sheen — *Content.* p.175-186
Sheen — *Way* p.25-27
Speaker's Desk p.184-189; #53, 298
Tanksley — *Friend* p.21
Voss — *Quotations* p.190-192
Wallis — *Treasure* p.65, 96, 118, 131, 189-194, 239
Wallis — *Words* p.33, 36, 49-52, 88, 135
Watson — *Light* p.302-311
Woods — *Content.* p.349; *See also* index p.381
Woods — *Religious* p.720-722, 998

, and defense
Kauffman — *For* p.82-83

, and joy
Adams — *New* p.206

, and love
Hunter — *Gems* p.48-49

, and peacemakers
Hobe — *Tapestries* p.141
Hunter — *Gems* p.77-78
Knight's Treas. p.259-261
Prochnow — *Public* #2601

, Attaining
Adams — *New* p.268

, Community
Mandelbaum — *Choose* p.126-130

, Dynamic
Peterson — *Art* p.165

, of mind
See also **Conscience**
Albert — *Stop* p.152-169
Baillie — *Diary* #355
Carruthers — *Sparks* p.80-81
Clark — *Windows* p.46
Evans — *Faith* p.84, 88, 116, 128, 152, 154, 185-186, 218-220
Evans — *This* p.51
Evans — *Thoughts IV* p.17, 93, 95, 97, 99, 125, 138, 167-168
Flesch — *Unusual* p.205-206
Forbes — *Thoughts* p.92-93, 382, 417
Fox — *Make* p.74
Giniger — *Compact* p.189-190
Guideposts — *Faith* p.424-427
How To Live p.246-279
Howell — *Lines* p.79-84
Hubbard — *Scrap* p.164
Johnson — *Bedside* p.61-83
Kennedy — *Fresh* p.71-79
Keys Happiness p.146-148, 261-270
Kohn — *Best* p.33-35
Liebman — *Peace* p.3-22, 119-133
Lindbergh — *Gift* p.23-24
List — *Living* p.22-28
Montapert — *Distilled* p.271-272
New Topical p.189
Nichols — *New* p.20-21
Nichols — *Third* p.159-160
Peale — *Stay* p.212-230
Peterson — *Art* p.27, 78, 359
Phillips — *Choice* p.xvi, 54, 126, 163, 340, 342
Sheen — *Way* p.115-140
Suter — *Prayers* #351-365
Voss — *Quotations* p.192-194
Watson — *Light* p.213-238
Welk — *Guide.* p.98-100
Woods — *Religious* p.722-723
Words — *Change* p.88-91

, Offerings of
New Topical p.188-189

, World
Suter — *Prayers* #1-35

PEACE CORPS
Franke — *Buckley* p.54, 227-229

PEACOCKS
Irion — *Yes* p.106-109

PEANUTS
Applegarth — *Heir.* p.145

PEARL HARBOR
Asimov — *Treasury* #12
New Joy p.174

PEARLS
Kin — *Dictionary* p.188

Prochnow — *Public* #2640
Wallis — *Treasure* p.225

"PECOS BILL"
Botkin — *Treasury* p.175, 180-185

"PECOS PETE"
Botkin — *Treasury* p.594

PECULIARITY. *See* **Eccentricity**

PEDANTRY
See also **Teachers**
Asimov — *Treasury* #258-259
Curtis — *Practical* p.419-420
Edwards — *Useful* p.455-456
Flesch — *Unusual* p.206
Lockridge — *World's* #2483, 5687

PEDESTRIANS
Flesch — *Unusual* p.206
Grizer — *Wit* p.340-341
Hubbard — *Scrap* p.65
Lockridge — *World's* #2749
Prochnow — *Public* #114, 264, 644, 1169, 1252, 1763
Prochnow — *Success.* #669, 1140
Speaker's Desk #65, 85, 213, 328, 981

PEDIGREE. *See* **Ancestry**

"PEEVES." *See* **Complaining**

PEGASUS
Prochnow — *Public* #2308

PENALTY. *See* **Punishment**

PENANCE. *See* **Penitence; Repentance; Retribution**

PENCILS
Harral — *Feature* p.244

PENELOPE
Prochnow — *Public* #2350

PENETRATION
Lockridge — *World's* #402, 450

PENITENCE
See also **Repentance; Retribution**
Day — *Meditations* p.43-44
Fogg — *1000* #74, 294, 359, 994
Kin — *Dictionary* p.188
Lockridge — *World's* #2638, 5599
More Words p.120-121
Woods — *Religious* p.723

, and charity
McDonagh — *Invit.* p.79-95

PENN, WILLIAM
Applegarth — *Heir.* p.119

PENNIES
Harral — *Feature* p.244-245
Prochnow — *Success.* #544

PENNSYLVANIA
Botkin — *Anecdotes* p.20, 42, 116, 138, 180
Botkin — *Treasury* p.33, 226, 248, 262, 269, 690, 750, 864-873
, Settlement of
Irion — *Yes* p.76-79

PENNSYLVANIA-DUTCH
Botkin — *Anecdotes* p.78, 134
Botkin — *Treasury* p.807

PENS
Edwards — *Useful* p.456-457
Fuller — *Epigrams* p.229
Henry — *5000* p.204
Kin — *Dictionary* p.188
Lockridge — *World's* #2540
Prochnow — *Public* #258, 550
Prochnow — *Success.* #999

PENSIONS AND PENSIONERS
Asimov — *Treasury* #81
Flesch — *Unusual* p.206
Prochnow — *Success.* #900
Woods — *Business.* p.164-165

PENTECOST
Hovey — *Treasury See* index p.303
More Words p.121-123
New Topical p.89
Suter — *Prayers* #422-424
Woods — *Religious* p.723-724
Words Change p.106-109

PENURY. *See* **Poverty**

PEOPLE
See also **Humanity; Man (Mankind); Society**
Baillie — *Diary* #238
Boas — *History* p.167-186
Bradshaw — *Home.* p.112-121
Braude — *Stories* p.283
Curtis — *Daily* p.20-26
Dirksen — *Quot. See* index p.267
Edwards — *Useful* p.457, 477
Evans — *Unto* p.9, 20, 50, 65-66
Flesch — *Unusual* p.199-200, 206-207
Flint — *Graham* p.103-104

Fogg — *1000* #629, 671, 702, 818, 992, 1055
Forbes — *Thoughts* p.126, 196, 268, 397, 473, 491, 506; *See also* index p.561
Fuller — *Epigrams* p.229
Grizer — *Wit* p.341-342
Harnsberger — *Mark* p.353-354
Henry — *5000* p.204-205
Hovey — *Treasury* #34, 79, 89, 490, 621, 1189
Huxley — *You See* index p.287; *See* appendix p.279-282
Kin — *Dictionary* p.188-189
Lockridge — *World's* #4620
Lytle — *Leaves* p.6, 117
Mandel — *Stories* p.197-198
Modern Eloquence (14) p.392-393
Montapert — *Distilled* p.272
Nichols — *New* p.123-124
Peterson — *Art* p.170, 275
Prochnow — *Public See* index p.505
Prochnow — *Success.* #358, 371, 400, 492, 494-495, 533, 539, 559, 576, 690, 1379, 2110-2114
Seldes — *Great* p.721-728
Wallis — *Words* p.19, 75-76
Woods — *Content.* p.169-189
Woods — *Religious* p.711, 724

, Beauty in
Curtis — *Daily* p.150-151

, Comfort in
Goudge — *Comfort* p.87-151

, Enjoyment of
Maltz — *Creative* p.30-31

, Exceptional
Seaburg — *Great See* index p.461

, Group names of
Kronenberger — *Animal* p.133

, Knowing
Hulme — *Living* p.3-6

, Living with
Nichols — *New* p.121-139

, Meaning of
Boas — *History* p.37-39

, Meeting
Keller — *Open* p.72

, Opinion of
Adams — *New* p.348

, Protection from
Hulme — *Living* p.35-46

, Two kinds of
Nichols — *Third* p.233-234

, Voice of
Seldes — *Great* p.952

, Will of
Ideas p.459-461

PEP. *See* **Energy; Enthusiasm**

PEPYS, SAMUEL
Reader's — *20th* p.12

PERCEPTION. *See* **Appreciation; Judgment; Understanding**

PERDITION. *See* **Hell**

"PERFECT PAIRS"
Safian — *More* p.139-140

PERFECTION
See also **Excellence; Ideals**
Albert — *Stop* p.108-110, 124, 139-140
Braude — *Source* #1273-1275
Braude — *Speaker's* #996-997
Braude — *Stories* p.283
Clark — *Windows* p.178
Dirksen — *Quot.* #1486-1487
Edwards — *Useful* p.457-458
Evans — *Thoughts II (Open Door)* p.198
Evans — *Thoughts III (Open Road)* p.25-26, 31, 65-66, 196
Flesch — *Unusual* p.207
Forbes — *Thoughts See* index p.562
Fridy — *Meditat.* p.49
Garland — *Subject* p.225
Grizer — *Wit* p.342
Guideposts — *Faith* p.37
Harnsberger — *Mark* p.354-355
Henry — *5000* p.205
Hobe — *Tapestries* p.62
Hoffer — *Reflect.* p.3-4
Hovey — *Treasury* p.251; #1572-1573
Kin — *Dictionary* p.189
Kohn — *Touch* p.70-74
Krishnamurti — *Think* p.130
Liddle — *Thought I, II, III* p.181, 183
Liddle — *Thought V* p.12
Lockridge — *World's* #2470, 2642, 2667, 3471, 5082
Lytle — *Leaves* p.79, 178
Mandel — *Stories* p.198
New Topical p.189
Peterson — *Art* p.30
Phillips — *Choice* p.120, 188
Prochnow — *Public* #37, 276, 1764, 3510-3514
Prochnow — *Speaker's* p.226-227
Speaker's Desk p.189
Wallis — *Treasure* p.48, 170, 216
Wallis — *Words* p.122
Woods — *Religious* p.724-726
Woods — *Wellsprings* p.13

, Aim for
Adams — *New* p.96
Nichols — *New* p.71-73

, *Moral*
Hubbard — *Scrap* p.118
, *New*
Adams — *New* p.124

PERFIDY. *See* **Treachery**

PERFORMANCE
Braude — *Source* #1276-1277
Dirksen — *Quot.* #172
Evans — *This* p.68
Evans — *Thoughts I* p.119, 215-216
Evans — *Thoughts IV* p.134-135
Garland — *Subject* p.225-226
Lockridge — *World's* #39
Lytle — *Leaves* p.188
Woods — *Religious* p.726

PERFUME
Applegarth — *Heir.* p.201, 268, 282
Fun Fare p.94
Lytle — *Leaves* p.83

PERIL. *See* **Danger**

PERIODS (time)
Boas — *History* p.117-145
Flesch — *Unusual* p.207

PERIPATETICS
Prochnow — *Public* #2425

PERISHABILITY
Kin — *Dictionary* p.189

PERJURY. *See* **Falsehood**

PERMANENCE
Braude — *Source* #294
Evans — *Unto* p.121, 140, 142
Kin — *Dictionary* p.189
Prochnow — *Public* #2659

PERMISSION
Kin — *Dictionary* p.146-147

PERMISSIVENESS
Flint — *Graham* p.102
Lair — *Baby* p.162
Wheelis — *Moralist* p.112

PERMUTATIONS
Du Noüy — *Road* p.90-94

PERPETUAL MOTION
Lockridge — *World's* #5211

PERPETUITY
Sheban — *Wisdom* no p.

PERPLEXITY
Applegarth — *Heir.* p.201
Flesch — *Unusual* p.207-208
Prochnow — *Success.* #2138-2139
Sheban — *Wisdom* no p.

PERSECUTION
See also **Oppression**
Dirksen — *Quot.* #1454, 1488-1490, 1587
Edwards — *Useful* p.458-459
Evans — *This* p.102-103
Flesch — *Unusual* p.208
Forbes — *Thoughts* p.323, 390, 466
Garland — *Subject* p.226
Henry — *5000* p.205
Kin — *Dictionary* p.189
Knight's Illus. p.234
Knight's Treas. p.261-262
Lockridge — *World's* #4977
New Topical p.189-190
Prochnow — *Public* #2602
Prochnow — *Success.* #2140
Seldes — *Great* p.728-729
Sheban — *Wisdom* no p.
Woods — *Religious* p.726-728
, *Christian*
Nizer — *Thinking* p.128
, *Jewish*
Nizer — *Thinking* p.128, 183, 194
, *Protestant*
Nizer — *Thinking* p.128

PERSEVERANCE
See also **Diligence; Effort; Industry**
Alexander's Treasure. p.5, 78, 139
Book Proverbs p.74
Braude — *Source* #1278-1284, 1591-1592, 1685
Braude — *Speaker's* #998-999
Braude — *Stories* p.283-285
Dirksen — *Quot.* #224, 270
Droke — *Christian* p.388-390
Edwards — *Useful* p.459-460
Evans — *Thoughts IV* p.86
Flesch — *Unusual* p.208
Forbes — *Thoughts* p.54, 159, 192, 213, 217, 273, 346, 360, 365, 390, 405, 450, 453, 519
Fuller — *Epigrams* p.230
Garland — *Subject* p.157, 226-227
Grizer — *Wit* p.342-345
Harnsberger — *Mark* p.355
Henry — *5000* p.205
Hobe — *Tapestries* p.13-15, 183
Holmes — *I've* p.53-69
Hovey — *Treasury* #16, 18
Humes — *Instant* #708-710

Johnson — *Bedside* p.114
Kennedy — *Reader's* #757-762
Kin — *Dictionary* p.189
Knight's Illus. p.235-236
Kohn — *Thoughts* p.52-55
Kohn — *Through* p.79-84
Krishnamurti — *Think* p.196-197
Liddle — *Thought I, II, III* p.99, 102, 119, 125, 132, 146, 153
Liddle — *Thought IV* p.8, 23, 25, 27-28
Liddle — *Thought V* p.34
Lockridge — *World's* #185, 2414, 4090, 4109
Lytle — *Leaves* p.6, 57, 134, 145
Manchee — *Secret* p.141-145
Mandel — *Stories* p.198-200
Modern Eloquence (14) p.394
Montapert — *Distilled* p.272-273
New Joy p.62, 252
New Topical p.190
Peale — *Courage* p.24, 31-32
Phillips — *Choice* p.247
Prochnow — *Public* #287, 618, 3515-3518
Prochnow — *Speaker's* p.227
Prochnow — *Success.* #2141
Reader's — *Getting* p.1-6
Speaker's Desk p.189-191; #111, 191, 350, 363, 734, 880, 1158
Voss — *Quotations* p.194-195
Watson — *Light* p.138-141
Woods — *Religious* p.728

, and success
Kauffman — *For* p.160-161
, toward wealth
Hill — *Think* p.170-189

PERSIAN PROVERBS
Dirksen — *Quot.* #612

PERSIAN RUGS
Fox — *Make* p.115

PERSISTENCE. *See* **Perseverance**

"PERSONAL GLIMPSES"
Fun Fare p.45-46, 59, 72, 96, 161, 174, 235, 292-293

PERSONALITY
See also **Character; Individuals and individuality**
Applegarth — *Heir.* p.256, 304
Braude — *Stories* p.285
Curtis — *Human* p.137-140
Curtis — *Practical* p.324
Dirksen — *Quot.* #1758
Du Noüy — *Human* p.104, 133-134, 243
Du Noüy — *Road* p.75-76, 150-151, 197
Evans — *This* p.27, 41-42
Flint — *Graham* p.104
Forbes — *Thoughts* p.33, 40, 55, 118, 176, 240, 246, 291, 298, 320, 346, 409
Garland — *Subject* p.227
Grizer — *Wit* p.345
Harral — *Feature* p.245
Hovey — *Treasury* #123, 296-297, 355, 878, 910, 1727, 1751
How To Live p.195-198
Hubbard — *Scrap* p.42
Ideas p.289-290
Johnson — *Bedside* p.197, 250
Kennedy — *Reader's* #763-774
Keys Happiness p.258-260, 556-575
Kin — *Dictionary* p.189
Liddle — *Thought IV* p.22
Lockridge — *World's* #2364
Lytle — *Leaves* p.10, 116
Menninger — *Blue.* p.8, 25-26, 50-67, 162-165
Modern Eloquence (14) p.395
Montapert — *Distilled* p.273
Nizer — *Thinking* p.104-106, 124-125, 131-132, 138
Peterson — *Art* p.79, 222
Phillips — *Choice* See index p.427-428
Prochnow — *Public* #783, 864, 4302
Reader's — *Getting* p.7-10
Simpson — *'54* p.58, 175, 311
Wallis — *Treasure* p.20, 117, 132, 145
Wallis — *Words* p.62, 75, 79, 93, 144, 153
Watson — *Light* p.185-212
White — *Job* p.152-153, 171-172
Woods — *Religious* p.728-730

, and God
Curtis — *Daily* p.166-172
, Dependence on love
Holmes — *Design* p.140-150
, Development and crises of
Jackson — *Coping* p.80-87
, Dual
Nizer — *Thinking* p.124-125
, Integrated
Holman — *Psych.* p.60-61
, Magnetic
Hill — *Think* p.214-216
, Teenage
Daly — *Personality* p.159-163
, Wholeness of
Peterson — *Art* p.309

PERSONNEL
See also **Employees; Employers, Executives; Management**
Forbes — *Thoughts* p.158, 176, 227, 236, 286, 512
Fuller — *Thesaurus* #2246-2249

Keys Happiness p.72
Prochnow — *Speaker's* p.228

PERSPECTIVE
Adams — *New* p.4
Dirksen — *Quot.* #77
Evans — *Unto* p.6-8, 113
Grizer — *Wit* p.345
Halverson — *Perspective* p.1, 104
Kin — *Dictionary* p.189
Kohn — *Touch* p.130-133
Liebman — *Hope* p.134-141
Lytle — *Leaves* p.6, 20, 139
Mandel — *Stories* p.201
Peterson — *New* p.30-31
Prochnow — *Success.* #220
Voss — *Quotations* p.196-198
Woods — *Religious* p.730
Woods — *Wellsprings* p.38

PERSPIRATION
Fox — *Make* p.103-104
Prochnow — *Public* #1765

PERSUASION
See also **Argument**
Dirksen — *Quot.* #6, 2345
Forbes — *Thoughts* p.212, 288, 299, 327, 339, 379, 481
Fuller — *Epigrams* p.230-231
Garland — *Subject* p.227
Grizer — *Wit* p.346
Montapert — *Distilled* p.274
Speaker's Desk #112, 1135
Vogue — *Arts* p.181-190

PERTINACITY. *See* **Obstinacy**

PERU
Applegarth — *Heir.* p.104
, Jungle of
Unlimited Power p.75-78

PERVERSENESS. *See* **Disobedience; Obstinacy; Rebellion; Self-will**

PESSIMISM AND PESSIMISTS
See also **Cynics and cynicism; Depression**
Alexander's Treasure. p.224
Braude — *Source* #1208-1212
Braude — *Stories* p.285-286
Dirksen — *Quot.* #1032, 1491-1494
Edwards — *Useful* p.408-409, 731
Evans — *Thoughts II (Open Door)* p.75
Flesch — *Unusual* p.208
Forbes — *Thoughts* p.94, 118, 234, 385, 409
Fuller — *Epigrams* p.231
Fuller — *Thesaurus* #411
Grizer — *Wit* p.346
Harnsberger — *Mark* p.355-356
Henry — *5000* p.205-206
How To Live p.568-572
Keller — *Open* p.66
Kennedy — *Reader's* #775-776
Kin — *Dictionary* p.190
Kohn — *Adventures* p.71-74
Liddle — *Thought I, II, III* p.31, 154
Lockridge — *World's* #1104, 3774, 5593
Lytle — *Leaves* p.139
Modern Eloquence (14) p.231-237
Peterson — *Art* p.273
Prochnow — *Public* #440, 565, 1284, 1335, 1464, 1766-1767
Prochnow — *Speaker's* p.228
Prochnow — *Success.* #450, 724, 1383
Safian — *Insults* p.150-151
Speaker's Desk #14, 271, 296, 649, 866
Wallis — *Treasure* p.185
Woods — *Religious* p.731
, Today's
Liebman — *Hope* p.13-47

PESTILENCE. *See* **Disease; Epidemics**

PETER, SAINT
Botkin — *Anecdotes* p.16, 23, 39, 44, 148, 169, 187-189
Fridy — *Meditat.* p.29
Woods — *Religious* p.731

PETRIFIED FOREST
Botkin — *Treasury* p.557, 560, 595

PETS
See also **Cats; Dogs;** etc.
Harral — *Feature* p.246-247

PETTINESS
See also **Meanness**
Braude — *Stories* p.286
Evans — *Unto* p.8
Lockridge — *World's* #312

"PETTING"
Daly — *Personality* p.64-67
Flint — *Graham* p.157
Speaker's Desk #106, 335

PH.D.'S
Asimov — *Treasury* #128, 131, 470

PHARISEES, THE
New Topical p.190-191
Sheen — *Thoughts* p.111-113
Woods — *Religious* p.731-732

PHARMACISTS
Harral — *Feature* p.248

PHILADELPHIA, PENNSYLVANIA
Asimov — *Treasury* #27, 610
Botkin — *Anecdotes* p.41, 116, 138, 140

PHILANTHROPY AND PHILANTHROPISTS
See also **Charity**
Dirksen — *Quot.* #2119-2120
Edwards — *Useful* p.461
Flesch — *Unusual* p.208
Flint — *Graham* p.104
Henry — *5000* p.206
Johnson — *Bedside* p.191
Lockridge — *World's* #3676, 4833
Phillips — *Choice* p.378
Prochnow — *Public* #4177-4178

PHILIPPINES
Hovey — *Treasury* #731
Simpson — *Contemp.* p.149

PHILISTINES
Flesch — *Unusual* p.208
Ideas p.290-292
New Topical p.191-192
Woods — *Religious* p.732

PHILOSOPHERS
Asimov — *Treasury* #82, 142-143
Curtis — *Practical* p.3, 5, 364-365, 389
Dirksen — *Quot.* #305
Flesch — *Unusual* p.208-209
Forbes — *Thoughts* p.301, 426, 443
George — *Book* p.58, 67, 92, 110, 118, 127, 142, 266, 272, 305, 350, 356
Lockridge — *World's* #1813, 2728, 2784, 4116, 4559, 4959
Manchee — *Secret* p.55-57
Prochnow — *Public* #4395
Prochnow — *Success.* #732, 2142-2143
Wallis — *Treasure* p.231
Wallis — *Words* p.172
Woods — *Religious* p.732-733
, "Cracker-box"
Botkin — *Treasury* p.6, 272, 323, 358, 408
, German
Nizer — *Thinking* p.174
, Young
Nichols — *New* p.210-213

PHILOSOPHER'S STONE
Ideas p.292-293

PHILOSOPHY
See also **Belief; Ideas and ideology; Philosophers; Reason and reasoning; Theory; Thought**
Adams — *New* p.110
Asimov — *Treasury* #134, 327-328
Bartlett — *Discovery* p.27-28
Braude — *Stories* p.287
Curtis — *Practical* p.52-53, 73-74, 101, 140, 363-364
Dirksen — *Quot.* #352
Edwards — *Useful* p.461-463, 731
Evans — *Unto* p.120
Flesch — *Unusual* p.209-210
Flint — *Graham* p.104-105
Fogg — *1000 See* index p.895
Forbes — *Thoughts* p.122, 133, 169, 182, 189-190, 229, 244, 309, 344, 385, 449, 461
Fuller — *Epigrams* p.231-232
Garland — *Subject* p.228
Grizer — *Wit* p.346-347
Harnsberger — *Mark* p.356
Henry — *5000* p.206-207
Hobe — *Tapestries* p.174
Hooker — *Index* p.9-16
Hubbard — *Scrap* p.10, 99, 161
Johnson — *Bedside* p.192, 212
Kennedy — *Reader's* #777-782
Kin — *Dictionary* p.190
Lockridge — *World's* #23, 55, 1820, 2608, 2729, 3209, 3666, 4115, 4117-4118, 4122, 4517, 5691
Montapert — *Distilled* p.274-275
Prochnow — *Public* #884, 3519-3526
Prochnow — *Success.* #2144-2145
Sagendorph — *Old* p.48-59
Seldes — *Great* p.729-732
Sheban — *Wisdom* no p.
Simpson — *Contemp.* p.288-338
Taylor — *With* p.106-107
Wallis — *Words* p.236
Woods — *Religious* p.733-735
, Active
Maltz — *Creative* p.34-36
, and science
Du Noüy — *Human* p.19-20
, of life
Adams — *New* p.343
Alexander's Treasure. p.100, 239
Baillie — *Diary* #248
Kauffman — *For* p.161-162
List — *Living* p.94-96
Menninger — *Blue.* p.68-117
, Walking
Peterson — *Art* p.261

PHOTOGRAPHY AND PHOTOGRAPHERS
Braude — *Speaker's* #1000-1001

Braude — *Stories* p.287
Flesch — *Unusual* p.210
Harnsberger — *Mark* p.356
Harral — *Feature* p.248-250
Hooker — *Index* p.271-275
Irion — *Yes* p.57-60
Lockridge — *World's* #2281
Manchee — *Secret* p.221-222
Prochnow — *Public* #761, 1278, 1379
Prochnow — *Speaker's* p.54

PHOTONS
Du Noüy — *Road* p.53, 143, 148, 176, 230

PHYSICAL CHARACTERISTICS
Fuller — *Thesaurus* p.113-130
Maltz — *Creative* p.16-18
Peale — *Sin* p.157-177
Rau — *Act* p.28-37
Speaker's Desk #161, 1155
, Perfection of
Holmes — *Design* p.220-221

PHYSICAL FITNESS
See also **Athletics;** etc.
Asimov — *Treasury* #593
Forbes — *Thoughts* p.271, 297, 463
Grizer — *Wit* p.170
Keys Happiness p.60-64
Prochnow — *Public* #725, 2041
Reader's — *Getting* p.69-73

PHYSICAL WORLD. *See* **Nature;** etc.

PHYSICIANS
See also **Hospitals; Medicine;** etc.
Asimov — *Treasury* #23-24, 40, 102-103, 127, 129, 256
Baillie — *Diary* #279
Braude — *Speaker's* #31-34
Braude — *Stories* p.118-123
Cerf — *Laugh* p.245-255
Copeland — *10,000* p.484-499
Curtis — *Practical* p.251-253, 264-270
Dirksen — *Quot.* #865-866, 1975-1976
Flesch — *Unusual* p.64, 210-211
Fogg — *1000* #66, 90, 254, 633, 942
Fuller — *Epigrams* p.90-92
Fuller — *Thesaurus* p.295-299
Fun Fare p.86, 107, 252-255
Garland — *Subject* p.228-229
George — *Book See* index p.444
Grizer — *Wit* p.125-126
Guideposts — *Faith* p.424-427
Harnsberger — *Mark* p.83-84
Harral — *Feature* p.250-251
Henry — *5000* p.172
How To Live p.372-378
Humes — *Instant* #27, 1218
Kennedy — *Reader's* #273
Kin — *Dictionary* p.71-72, 190
Lockridge — *World's* #4135, 4389, 5025, 5488
Manchee — *Secret* p.208
Mandel — *Stories* p.74-75
New Joy p.168-170, 253-255
Nizer — *Thinking* p.134-135
Prochnow — *Public* #2667; *See also* index p.493
Prochnow — *Speaker's* p.97-100
Prochnow — *Success.* #417, 420, 440, 537, 641, 658, 850, 924, 1139, 2146-2148
Pullar-Strecker — *Proverbs* #237-243
Reader's — *20th* p.28-32, 57-61
Schermerhorn — *1500* p.116-121
Sheban — *Wisdom* no p.
Weisfeld — *Pulpit* p.3, 31, 100, 129-130
Woods — *Religious* p.736
, and cures
Lockridge — *World's* #3028-3052
, and patients
Braude — *Speaker's* #323-366
Modern Eloquence (14) p.59-65
Speaker s Desk See index p.298
, as judges
Reader's — *Getting* p.96-100
, Fees of
Fuller — *Thesaurus* #1681
, Women as
Unlimited Power p.281-285

PHYSICS AND PHYSICISTS
Asimov — *Treasury* #144, 205, 244, 467
Garland — *Subject* p.229
Hooker — *Index* p.152-158

PHYSIOCRATS
Curtis — *Practical* p.325

PHYSIOGNOMY
See also **Face**
Edwards — *Useful* p.463-464
George — *Book* p.267
Kin — *Dictionary* p.190

PHYSIOLOGY AND PHYSIOLOGISTS
Curtis — *Practical* p.54, 72
Prochnow — *Public* #77

PIANO AND PIANISTS
Asimov — *Treasury* #578

Hubbard — *Scrap* p.226
Prochnow — *Public* #100, 113, 199, 829, 1007, 1908
Prochnow — *Success.* #1044
Unlimited Power p.230-234
Wallis — *Words* p.168

PICKETING
Day — *Meditations* p.27, 57-58
Prochnow — *Public* #1401
Woods — *Business.* p.165-166

PICKLES
Prochnow — *Success.* #880, 948

PICKPOCKETS
Prochnow — *Public* #1768

PICNICS
Hadfield — *Delights* p.95
Harral — *Feature* p.251
Prochnow — *Speaker's* p.228
Prochnow — *Success.* #936
Woods — *Content.* p.150, 186

PICTURES
See also **Art and artists; Painters and paintings;** etc.
Flesch — *Unusual* p.211
Goudge — *Comfort* p.335-336
Hubbard — *Scrap* p.101
Ideas p.432-434
Kin — *Dictionary* p.190
Lytle — *Leaves* p.42
Prochnow — *Public* #647, 1924
Prochnow — *Success.* #2149

"PIE IN THE SKY"
Seldes — *Great* p.732

PIETY
See also **Devotion; Good; Holiness; Religion; Reverence**
Applegarth — *Heir.* p.177
Asimov — *Treasury* #329
Dirksen — *Quot.* #1495-1497
Edwards — *Useful* p.464
Flesch — *Unusual* p.211
Henry — *5000* p.207
Kin — *Dictionary* p.190
Lair — *Baby* p.189-192
Lockridge — *World's* #2918, 4283, 4968, 5235
Menninger — *Blue.* p.92
New Joy p.59
Porter — *Halo* p.119-127
Woods — *Religious* p.736-737
, Mercenary
Baillie — *Diary* #3

PIKE'S PEAK
Botkin — *Treasury* p.184, 213, 309-310

PILATE
Wallis — *Words* p.56

PILGRIMAGES
Applegarth — *Heir.* p.272, 276
Baillie — *Diary* #344
Hobe — *Tapestries* p.68
Sheban — *Wisdom* no p.
Wallis — *Treasure* p.25, 161-162

PILGRIMS
Evans — *Unto* p.15, 52
Garland — *Subject* p.230
Harnsberger — *Mark* p.357
Hobe — *Tapestries* p.214
Hovey — *Treasury* #68, 1809
Kohn — *Best* p.79-82
Kohn — *Touch* p.62-63, 65-69
Wallis — *Treasure* p.174-175
Woods — *Content.* p.188
Woods — *Religious* p.737
, and strangers
New Topical p.192-193

PILLARS
New Topical p.193

PILLOWS
Kin — *Dictionary* p.191
Prochnow — *Public* #156

PILLS. *See* **Medicine**

PILOTS. *See* **Aviation; Boats**

PINNACLE GROUSE
Botkin — *Treasury* p.646

PIONEERS. *See also* **Immigrants and emigrants; Pilgrims;** etc.
Applegarth — *Heir.* p.273
Bartlett — *Discovery* p.70
Curtis — *Practical* p.542
Dirksen — *Quot.* #2370, 2379
Evans — *Faith* p.21, 187
Evans — *This* p.97, 145-146
Evans — *Thoughts III (Open Road)* p.175
Evans — *Unto* p.52, 82
Flesch — *Unusual* p.211
Forbes — *Thoughts* p.363, 488
Garland — *Subject* p.230-231
Irion — *Yes* p.76-79
Kin — *Dictionary* p.191
Peale — *Guideposts* p.321-325
Prochnow — *Public* #345
Prochnow — *Success.* #2150
Wallis — *Words* p.106
Zobell — *Speaker's* p.110-114
, Folk tales of
Botkin — *Treasury* p.412

PIPELINES
Harral — *Feature* p.251-252

PIPERS
Kin — *Dictionary* p.191

PIPES
Flesch — *Unusual* p.211
Hadfield — *Delights* p.71

PIRATES
Flesch — *Unusual* p.211

PISTOLS. *See* **Guns**

PITTSBURGH, PENNSYLVANIA
Botkin — *Anecdotes* p.42
Botkin — *Treasury* p.8, 33, 53, 57, 248

PITY
See also **Mercy; Self-pity; Sympathy; Understanding**
Adams — *New* p.372
Edwards — *Useful* p.464-465
Flesch — *Unusual* p.211
Forbes — *Thoughts* p.137, 141, 307, 407, 498
Fuller — *Epigrams* p.232
Garland — *Subject* p.231
Henry — *5000* p.207-208
Johnson — *Bedside* p.186
Kin — *Dictionary* p.191
Lockridge — *World's* #275, 669, 3477, 3701, 3992, 5227, 5795
Prochnow — *Public* #1130, 2112, 2537, 3527, 4328
Prochnow — *Success.* #2151-2152
Woods — *Religious* p.737-738

PLACE NAMES
Irion — *Yes* p.76-79

PLACES
Edwards — *Useful* p.465
Flesch — *Unusual* p.211-212
Guideposts — *Faith* p.259-263
Hobe — *Tapestries* p.78
Kin — *Dictionary* p.191
Lockridge — *World's* #3391, 3659, 3660
Prochnow — *Success.* #773
Woods — *Content.* p.61-88

PLAGIARISM
Braude — *Speaker's* #1002
Edwards — *Useful* p.465-466
Fogg — *1000* #321, 1088
Harnsberger — *Mark* p.358
Henry — *5000* p.208
Lockridge — *World's* #1129, 2487
Prochnow — *Public* #1114
Prochnow — *Speaker's* p.229

PLAGUE
Kin — *Dictionary* p.191
New Topical p.193

PLAINNESS
Flesch — *Unusual* p.212
Lockridge — *World's* #1746-1747
Lytle — *Leaves* p.159

PLAINS
Botkin — *Treasury* p.228, 319, 332

PLANETARIUMS
Prochnow — *Success.* #1025

PLANETS
Curtis — *Practical* p.54, 245
Goudge — *Comfort* p.23
Prochnow — *Success.* #1004

PLANS AND PLANNING
See also **Method; Purpose**
Albert — *Stop* p.11-12, 19-20, 23-24, 203, 206-207
Baillie — *Diary* #186
Braude — *Source* #1285-1287
Evans — *Thoughts I* p.80-81, 120, 131
Evans — *Thoughts III (Open Road)* p.185, 209
Evans — *Unto* p.118
Flesch — *Unusual* p.251
Forbes — *Thoughts* p.50, 112, 152, 337, 351, 365, 379, 420, 478, 513
Grizer — *Wit* p.347
Hill — *Think* p.114-155
Humes — *Instant* #39-41, 711-723, 1254-1255
Ideas p.293-294
Liddle — *Thought I, II, III* p.47, 51, 112, 132, 176
Lockridge — *World's* #1523, 3532
Lytle — *Leaves* p.186
Mandel — *Stories* p.201-202
Montapert — *Distilled* p.275
Peterson — *Art* p.171
Prochnow — *Public* #2437
Prochnow — *Speaker's* p.229-230
Prochnow — *Success.* #793
Wallis — *Treasure* p.84, 163, 222
Woods — *Business.* p.166-176
Woods — *Content.* p.229

PLANTATIONS
Botkin — *Anecdotes* p.46, 193

PLANTS
See also **Gardens and gardening**
Applegarth — ***Heir.* p.261**

Auden — *Certain* p.301-303
Harral — *Feature* p.252
Hubbard — *Scrap* p.25
Peterson — *Art* p.290
, *Talking to*
Peterson — *Art* p.124

PLATITUDES. *See* **Proverbs; Quotations**

PLATO
Asimov — *Treasury* #142
Flesch — *Unusual* p.212
Lockridge — *World's* #3579, 3582

PLAY
See also **Recreation;** etc.
Applegarth — *Heir.* p.147, 151
Auden — *Certain* p.405-407
Curtis — *Daily* p.107-112
Curtis — *Practical* p.77
Flesch — *Unusual* p.212
Forbes — *Thoughts* p.45, 136, 419, 506, 509
Grizer — *Wit* p.347-348
Hubbard — *Scrap* p.38, 47, 127
Kin — *Dictionary* p.192
Modern Eloquence p.396
Peterson — *Art* p.199
Prochnow — *Public* #4416
Wallis — *Words* p.111

PLAY RHYMES
See also **"Rope-skipping" rhymes**
Botkin — *Treasury* p.768-803

"PLAYBOYS"
Safian — *Insults* p.152-160
Safian — *More* p.141-148

"PLAYGIRLS"
Safian — *Insults* p.161-167
Safian — *More* p.149-155

PLAYS AND PLAY PRODUCTION. *See* **Drama; Theater**

PLAYWRIGHTS AND PLAYWRITING
Flesch — *Unusual* p.212
Fuller — *Thesaurus* #1376-1385

PLEADING
Lockridge — *World's* #2618
Prochnow — *Public* #2115

PLEASANTNESS
See also **Charm; Cheerfulness**
Edwards — *Useful* p.466-467
Flesch — *Unusual* p.212-213
Grizer — *Wit* p.348
Hulme — *Living* p.125-130
Kin — *Dictionary* p.192
Lockridge — *World's* #536, 2096
Lytle — *Leaves* p.126, 149
Peterson — *Art* p.133, 136
Prochnow — *Public* #1474
Speaker's Desk #179, 713, 925, 1049, 1107
Woods — *Wellsprings* p.25-26

PLEASURE
See also **Amusements; Enjoyment; Happiness; Joy**
Applegarth — *Heir.* p.87
Auden — *Certain* p.303-304
Baillie — *Diary* #234
Book Proverbs p.77
Braude — *Source* #1288-1289
Braude — *Stories* p.287
Curtis — *Practical* p.6-7, 512
Dirksen — *Quot.* #1498-1499, 2121
Edwards — *Useful* p.467-470
Evans — *Thoughts III (Open Road)* p.55-56
Evans — *Unto* p.71
Flesch — *Unusual* p.213-214
Flint — *Graham* p.105
Fogg — *1000* #2, 217, 828, 965, 1060
Forbes — *Thoughts* See index p.562
Fuller — *Epigrams* p.232-233
Garland — *Subject* p.233
Grizer — *Wit* p.348
Harnsberger — *Mark* p.359-360
Henry — *5000* p.208
Hubbard — *Scrap* p.16, 37
Johnson — *Bedside* p.21, 41, 77, 83, 112-113, 116, 142, 190, 234, 341
Kin — *Dictionary* p.192
Liddle — *Thought I, II, III* p.8, 23-24, 27, 30, 58, 91, 100, 106, 116, 189, 194
Liddle — *Thought V* p.42, 46
Lockridge — *World's* See index p.581
Lytle — *Leaves* p.12
Maltz — *Creative* p.96-109
Mandel — *Stories* p.202
Menninger — *Blue.* p.78
Montapert — *Distilled* p.275-276
New Joy p.20, 177, 199
Peale — *Courage* p.200-201
Prochnow — *Public* #3528-3531, 4179
Prochnow — *Success.* #2153-2157
Reader's — *Getting* p.77
Sheen — *Lift* p.39-44
Sheen — *Thoughts* p.34-35
Sheen — *Way* p.48-50

Speaker's Desk p.104, 152, 191-193
Wallis — *Treasure* p.226
Wallis — *Words* p.121, 172, 204
Woods — *Content.* #43, 115, 117, 229-230, 245, 301
Woods — *Religious* p.738-740
Woods — *Wellsprings* p.22
Words — *Inspir.* p.57
, Enduring
Kohn — *Pathways* p.167-175
, Importance of
Kauffman — *For* p.162-163
, Perennial
Kohn — *Pathways* p.167-170
, Sharing of
Peterson — *Art* p.134

PLEDGES
Harnsberger — *Mark* p.360
Hovey — *Treasury* #1779-1780
Kennedy — *Reader's* #783
, of allegiance
Dirksen — *Quot.* #99, 521, 769

PLENTY. *See* **Abundance**

PLIABILITY. *See* **Adjustment**

PLINY
Lockridge — *World's* #3589

PLOWS AND PLOWING
Adams — *New* p.142
Kin — *Dictionary* p.192
New Topical p.193-194

PLUCK. *See* **Courage**

PLUMBERS AND PLUMBING
Flesch — *Unusual* p.214
Harnsberger — *Mark* p.360
Harral — *Feature* p.252
Manchee — *Secret* p.222
Prochnow — *Public* #452, 568

PLURALISM
Woods — *Religious* p.40-742

PLUTARCH
Lockridge — *World's* #3580

PLUTOCRACY
Seldes — *Great* p.733

PLYMOUTH COLONY
See also **Pilgrims**
Kohn — *Touch* p.65-69

PLYMOUTH ROCK
Hovey — *Treasury* #1058

POCKETS
Flesch — *Unusual* p.214
Kin — *Dictionary* p.192
Prochnow — *Success.* #1002

POETRY
See also **Ballads**
Applegarth — *Heir.* p.28-31, 154
Braude — *Source* #1290-1291
Braude — *Stories* p.287
Copeland — *10,000* p.881-905
Curtis — *Practical* p.124, 140, 469-474
Day — *Meditations* p.8-9
Edwards — *Useful* p.470-472
Flesch — *Unusual* p.215-216
Fogg — *1000* #544, 615
Fuller — *Epigrams* p.236-238
Harnsberger — *Mark* p.361
Harral — *Feature* p.252-253
Henry — *5000* p.209-210
Hobe — *Tapestries* p.59
Howell — *Better* p.161-164
Hubbard — *Scrap* p.26, 52, 74, 76, 94, 125, 207
Johnson — *Bedside* p.45-47, 254
Kennedy — *Reader's* #784-788
Lockridge — *World's* #2672, 2730, 4058, 4068, 4365, 4491, 4498, 4690, 4729, 5080
Lytle — *Leaves* p.30, 143, 159
Mandelbaum — *Choose* p.16
Patterns For Living p.340-348
Prochnow — *Public* #348, 726, 897, 2308, 3532-3534
Prochnow — *Speaker's* p.230
Prochnow — *Success.* #2159
Saturday — *Advent.* p.107-120
Sheban — *Wisdom* no p.
Wallis — *Treasure* p.30
Wallis — *Words* p.132, 142, 164, 174
Woods — *Content.* p.254
Woods — *Religious* p.742-743
, Anglo–Saxon
Auden — *Certain* p.22-25
, Beauty in
Words — *Inspir.* p.201-202
, Comic
Asimov — *Treasury* #268-269
Cerf — *Laugh* p.409-414
Copeland — *10,000* p.905-913
Fun Fare p.20, 157, 165, 246, 290
Goudge — *Comfort* p.360-371
, Comic chains of
Copeland — *10,000* p.913-915
, English
Auden — *Certain* p.373-376

, *Free verse in*
Ideas p.154-156
, *Horses in*
Adams — *New* p.238
, *Light*
Prochnow — *Public* #1605
Prochnow — *Speaker's* p.316
, *Modern*
Sheban — *Wisdom* no p.

POETS
Asimov — *Treasury* #162
Braude — *Source* #1290-1291
Curtis — *Practical* p.4-5, 52, 429, 445, 449-450
Flesch — *Unusual* p.214-215
George — *Book See* index p.444
Goudge — *Comfort* p.323-335
Hadfield — *Delights* p.208-209
Henry — *5000* p.209
Kin — *Dictionary* p.192
Lockridge — *World's* #691, 1750, 1815, 2718, 3556, 4070, 4552, 5008, 5289
Patterns For Living p.335-339
Peale — *Guideposts* p.126-129
Prochnow — *Success.* #736, 1450, 2158
Schermerhorn — *1500* p.280
Sheban — *Wisdom* no p.
Simpson — *Contemp.* p.368-377
Wallis — *Treasure* p.152
Woods — *Religious* p.742

POINT OF VIEW. *See* **Opinion; Views**

POISE
Braude — *Stories* p.292
Evans — *Unto* p.85
Forbes — *Thoughts* p.46, 81, 180, 322, 352, 452, 478
Nizer — *Thinking* p.35, 95
Speaker's Desk #21-22, 35, 134, 214, 262, 487, 573, 621, 626, 631, 743, 946, 977
Wallis — *Treasure* p.193

POISON AND POISONING
Henry — *5000* p.210
Kin — *Dictionary* p.193
Lockridge — *World's* #4206
Prochnow — *Public* #260
Seldes — *Great* p.733

"POISON-PENS"
Kin — *Dictionary* p.193

POKER
Asimov — *Treasury* #88
Schermerhorn — *1500* p.281
Speaker's Desk #27

"POKER FACE"
Maltz — *Creative* p.154-155

POLAND AND POLISH
Asimov — *Treasury* #423-426
Kin — *Dictionary* p.193
Nichols — *Third* p.213-214
Prochnow — *Success.* #264

POLARIZATION
Sheen — *Content.* p.19-21

POLE VAULTERS
Peale — *Guideposts* p.169-173

POLICE
Braude — *Speaker's* #1024-1029
Copeland — *10,000* p.113-119
Franke — *Buckley* p.232-233
Fuller — *Thesaurus* #2551-2552
Grizer — *Wit* p.349
Harnsberger — *Mark* p.362
Harral — *Feature* p.253-255
Prochnow — *Public* #29, 45, 115, 668, 690, 705, 991, 1978
Prochnow — *Success.* #528, 979, 1114

"POLICE STATE"
Ideas p.296-298

POLICY. *See* **Purpose; Tact**

POLITENESS. *See* **Courtesy**

POLITICAL PARTIES
See also names of parties
Dirksen — *Quot.* #21, 57, 59, 1028, 1759
Fogg — *1000* #201, 241, 406
Fuller — *Thesaurus* #1906-1907
Nizer — *Thinking* p.52, 140
, *Conventions of*
Franke — *Buckley* p.57-58, 234-235
, *Leaders of*
Dirksen — *Quot.* #76

POLITICAL SCIENCE
Fun Fare p.249-250
Hooker — *Index* p.54-64

POLITICAL SLOGANS
Fogg — *1000* #54, 67, 403-404, 837, 907, 921, 1010

POLITICS AND POLITICIANS
See also **Democracy; Government; Statesmen and statesmanship**
Adams — *New* p.136, 215, 308, 325
Alexander's Treasure. p.94

Asimov — *Treasury* #105, 181, 183-185
Botkin — *Anecdotes* p.134-135, 157-176
Braude — *Source* #1296-1315
Braude — *Speaker's* #221, 1032-1047
Braude — *Stories* p.292-299
Cerf — *Laugh* p.10-16
Copeland — *10,000* p.518-532
Cowan — *Wit* p.119-127
Curtis — *Practical* p.3, 355-364, 366-368
Dirksen — *Quot.* #15, 119, 190, 240, 342, 469, 686-687, 917, 1033-1035, 1081, 1630, 1760-1762, 1802, 2122-2123
Droke — *Christian* p.391-398
Edwards — *Useful* p.475-477, 731
Evans — *Unto* p.47, 56, 78
Flesch — *Unusual* p.216
Flint — *Graham* p.105-106
Forbes — *Thoughts* p.65, 107, 126, 202, 299, 358, 433, 448, 499
Franke — *Buckley* p.7-8, 234-238
Fuller — *Epigrams* p.233-235
Fuller — *Thesaurus* p.332-347
Garland — *Subject* p.234-235
George — *Book* p.10, 43, 175, 178, 306, 357, 384
Gold — *Letters* p.89-99
Grizer — *Wit* p.349-352
Harnsberger — *Mark* p.363-366
Harral — *Feature* p.255
Henry — *5000* p.210-211
Hovey — *Treasury* p.251-253; *See also* index p.299
Hubbard — *Scrap* p.202
Humes — *Instant* #724-747
Ideas p.299-300
Johnson — *Bedside* p.125
Kennedy — *Reader's* #789-796
Kin — *Dictionary* p.193
Liddle — *Thought I, II, III* p.31, 43, 78, 92, 100, 103, 125, 189
Liddle — *Thought V* p.22, 32, 37-38, 44
Lockridge — *World's* #4209, 4979, 5014, 5780; *See also* index p.581
Modern Eloquence (14) p.21-39
Nizer — *Thinking* p.52
Prochnow — *Public* #281, 372, 1551, 3537-3542, 4371; *See also* index p.506
Prochnow — *Speaker's* p.231-234
Prochnow — *Success.* #172, 287, 296, 473, 530, 538, 545, 564, 575, 591, 954, 989, 1001, 1244
Safian — *Insults* p.168-170
Safian — *More* p.156-157
Schermerhorn — *1500* p.282-284
Seldes — *Great* p.733-738
Simpson — *Contemp.* p.34-50
Speaker's Desk p.193-198; *See also* index p.303
Wallis — *Treasure* p.69
Walters — *How* p.44-51
Weisfeld — *Pulpit* p.127
Woods — *Business.* p.176-177
Woods — *Religious* p.743-744
, and morality
Peale — *Sin* p.178-197
, and principles
Kauffman — *For* p.163
, and violence
Wheelis — *Moralist* p.34-35
, Campaigns of
Prochnow — *Public* #551, 708, 1082, 1340, 1429
, Clubs of
See also **Political parties**
Nizer — *Thinking* p.54
, Extremism of
Strait — *Speaker's* p.129
, Life of
Fridy — *Meditat.* p.75
, Organization of
Woods — *Religious* p.743
, "Plums of"
Prochnow — *Public* #1770
, Power of
Wheelis — *Moralist* p.68-69, 115, 121, 129
Woods — *Religious* p.743
, Promises of
Dirksen — *Quot.* #4, 61
, Speeches of
Botkin — *Anecdotes* p.158
Copeland — *World's See* index p.734-735
Nizer — *Thinking* p.70
, Storytellers of
Botkin — *Anecdotes* p.158

POLLUTION
Dirksen — *Quot.* #1163, 1171
Esteve — *Experience* p.116, 147
Humes — *Instant* #1222-1223; p.40
Kauffman — *For* p.163-164
Kin — *Dictionary* p.193

POLYGAMY
Fuller — *Thesaurus* #941-943

POMEGRANATE TREES
New Topical p.194

POMPOSITY
Fuller — *Thesaurus* #421-427
Humes — *Instant* p.27-28

"PONY EXPRESS"
Peale — *Guideposts* p.225-227

POOLS AND PONDS
New Topical p.194

POOR. *See* **Poverty**

POPCORN
Botkin — *Treasury* p.228, 628

POPE, ALEXANDER
Flesch — *Unusual* p.217

POPES
Asimov — *Treasury* #39, 368, 419, 479
Botkin — *Anecdotes* p.186, 262
Fuller — *Thesaurus* #1501-1504
Seldes — *Great* p.711-712, 739-742
Weisfeld — *Pulpit* p.20, 31
Woods — *Religious* p.745-746
, Infallibility of
Ideas p.286-288

POPPY, CALIFORNIA
Hubbard — *Scrap* p.13

POPULARITY
See also **Charm**
Braude — *Source* #1316-1318
Braude — *Stories* p.299
Dirksen — *Quot.* #1763
Edwards — *Useful* p.477-478
Evans — *Thoughts I* p.197
Evans — *Thoughts II (Open Door)* p.73, 146-147
Evans — *Thoughts III (Open Road)* p.109, 121
Evans — *Thoughts IV* p.27-28, 103
Evans — *Unto* p.77, 83, 90
Flesch — *Unusual* p.218
Garland — *Subject* p.235
Henry — *5000* p.212
Kin — *Dictionary* p.194
Liddle — *Thought I, II, III* p.130, 151
Liddle — *Thought V* p.22
Lockridge — *World's* #2750, 5807
Prochnow — *Public* #698
Prochnow — *Speaker's* p.234
Speaker's Desk p.198-199
Woods — *Religious* p.746
, Secret of
Manchee — *Secret* p.189-195

POPULATION
Dirksen — *Quot.* #689-691
Grizer — *Wit* p.352
Harral — *Feature* p.255
Humes — *Instant* p.40-41; #748-750
Lockridge — *World's* #2741
Prochnow — *Success.* #281, 607, 1444
Seldes — *Great* p.742
, Control of
Boas — *History* p.83-85
, Explosion of
Woods — *Religious* p.746
, Increase in
Nizer — *Thinking* p.182

PORCHES
Hobe — *Tapestries* p.89

PORNOGRAPHY
, Moral degradation of
Flint — *Graham* p.21, 106

PORTERS
Guideposts — *Faith* p.313-317

PORTRAITS
Kronenberger — *Animal* p.236-239
Prochnow — *Success.* #790

PORTS
Kin — *Dictionary* p.194
Lockridge — *World's* #2668, 2741

POSING. *See* **Pretension**

POSITION
Edwards — *Useful* p.478
Montapert — *Distilled* p.276-277
Prochnow — *Public* #706
Sheban — *Wisdom* no p.

"POSITIVE THINKING." *See* **Confidence; Self-confidence; Thought**

POSITIVENESS. *See* **Certainty; Decision; Determination; Dogmatism; Resolution**

POSITIVISM, LOGICAL
Ideas p.241-242

POSSESSIONS
See also **Money; Property; Wealth**
Alexander's Treasure. p.113
Applegarth — *Heir.* p.215
Braude — *Source* #1319-1320
Curtis — *Daily* p.93-99
Curtis — *Practical* p.432
Detherage — *Sunrise* p.67, 176
Dirksen — *Quot.* #1502-1503
Edwards — *Useful* p.478-479
Emmons — *Mature* p.12-13, 152
Evans — *This* p.140-141
Evans — *Thoughts III (Open Road)* p.209-210

Evans — *Thoughts IV* p.79-80
Evans — *Unto* p.15, 51, 93, 103, 120
Flesch — *Unusual* p.218
Flint — *Graham* p.149
Forbes — *Thoughts* p.22, 175, 403, 440
Fox — *Make* p.123-124
Grizer — *Wit* p.353
Halverson — *Perspective* p.51, 59, 81
Harnsberger — *Mark* p.366
Henry — *5000* p.212
Hobe — *Tapestries* p.68
Kin — *Dictionary* p.109, 194
Liddle — *Thought I, II, III* p.135, 145
Liddle — *Thought IV* p.23, 46
Lindbergh — *Gift* p.31-34
Lockridge — *World's* #1623-2337
Lytle — *Leaves* p.6, 31, 147
Mandelbaum — *Choose* p.3-4, 16-17
Montapert — *Distilled* p.277
Nichols — *Third* p.47-48
Phillips — *Choice* p.58, 61
Pullar-Strecker — *Proverbs* #186-217
Seldes — *Great* p.438, 742-743
Wallis — *Treasure* p.173
White — *Job* p.178-179
Woods — *Content.* p.37, 49, 91, 109, 155, 178, 293, 300, 302
Woods — *Religious* p.747

POSSESSIVENESS
Huxley — *You See* index p.287
Sheban — *Wisdom* no p.
, Social
Phillips — *Choice* p.56

POSSIBILITIES
See also **Potentialities**
Applegarth — *Heir.* p.137
Evans — *Thoughts III (Open Road)* p.50-51, 126, 139, 148, 157, 196, 209
Flesch — *Unusual* p.218
Forbes — *Thoughts* p.298, 339, 491
Garland — *Subject* p.56, 236-237
Holmes — *Design* p.60-70
Kin — *Dictionary* p.127
Kohn — *Touch* p.124-125
Peterson — *Art* p.322
Wallis — *Treasure* p.69
Wallis — *Words* p.117,180
Woods — *Religious* p.747

POSTAL SERVICE
Applegarth — *Heir.* p.74, 153
Fun Fare p.175
Harral — *Feature* p.255-257
Reader's — *20th* p.24
Schermerhorn — *1500* p.285
Wallis — *Words* p.76

POSTERITY
See also **Children; Future**
Braude — *Stories* p.299
Curtis — *Practical* p.536
Edwards — *Useful* p.479
Forbes — *Thoughts* p.8, 224, 323, 327
Henry — *5000* p.213
Lockridge — *World's* #3739, 4005, 5097
Nizer — *Thinking* p.87
Prochnow — *Public* #1339
Prochnow — *Success.* #1400
, Preparing for
Humes — *Instant* p.49-50; #1228-1231

POSTPONEMENT
See also **Delay**
Evans — *Thoughts I* p.83, 144, 166, 175, 206-207
Kin — *Dictionary* p.194
Nichols — *New* p.84-85
Prochnow — *Public* #1067, 1162
Wallis — *Words* p.50

POSTURE
Bradshaw — *Home.* p.55-62
Menninger — *Blue.* p.218
, Improvement of
Huxley — *You See* index p.287
, Self-confidence and
Albert — *Stop* p.61-62

POTATOES
Botkin — *Treasury* p.187, 597-598, 603
Holmes — *I've* p.27
Kin — *Dictionary* p.194
, and bugs
Botkin — *Treasury* p.282

POTENTIALITIES
See also **Possibilities**
Curtis — *Golden* p.58-62, 148, 187-206
Evans — *Thoughts III (Open Road)* p.148, 178
Kohn — *Touch* p.123-126
Liddle — *Thought V* p.11-12
Montapert — *Distilled* p.277-278
Peterson — *Art* p.60, 153
Reader's — *20th* p.14-16
, Unrealized
Holmes — *Design* p.12-13
Phillips — *Choice* p.66

, Wealth of
Maltz — *Creative* p.216

POTTERY
Henry — *5000* p.213

POVERTY
See also **Adversity; Depression; Hardship**
Baillie — *Diary* #337
Book Proverbs p.9, 115
Braude — *Source* #1321-1324
Braude — *Stories* p.299-300
Day — *Meditations* p.11-12, 25-26, 33, 48-52
Dirksen — *Quot. See* index p.268
Droke — *Christian* p.398-400
Edwards — *Useful* p.479-482
Evans — *Unto* p.50, 82, 101-103
Flesch — *Unusual* p.216-219
Flint — *Graham* p.107
Forbes — *Thoughts See* index p.562
Franke — *Buckley* p.239-240
Fuller — *Epigrams* p.238-239
Fuller — *Thesaurus* #2201-2211
Garland — *Subject* p.235, 237
Grizer — *Wit* p.353-354, 487
Harnsberger — *Mark* p.307, 501
Henry — *5000* p.213-214
Hovey — *Treasury* #146, 356-357, 382, 631, 1088, 1514
Hubbard — *Scrap* p.9, 14, 29, 31, 43, 68, 75, 107, 144, 225
Hudson — *5000* p.297
Humes — *Instant* #751-768
Johnson — *Bedside* p.120, 129, 189, 310
Kauffman — *For* p.164-169
Kennedy — *Reader's* #797-802
Kin — *Dictionary* p.188, 195-196, 272
Kronenberger — *Animal* p.239-240
Liddle — *Thought I, II, III* p.46-47, 52, 78, 86, 92, 98, 163, 175, 194
Liddle — *Thought V* p.18, 35, 44
Lockridge — *World's* #158, 1441, 1517, 2549, 2585, 4059, 4659, 4849, 5117, 5121
Lytle — *Leaves* p.47, 151, 181, 192
Modern Eloquence (14) p.397
Montapert — *Distilled* p.276
New Joy p.251
New Topical p.194-195
Prochnow — *Public See* index p.506
Prochnow — *Speaker's* p.234-235
Prochnow — *Success.* #493, 581, 890, 920, 1100, 2160-2165, 2251-2254, 2432
Pullar-Strecker — *Proverbs* #205-217
Reader's — *20th* p.62-64
Seldes — *Great* p.738-739, 743-745
Sheban — *Wisdom* no p.
Speaker's Desk p.199-201; #571, 621, 721
Strait — *Speaker's* p.130-132
Woods — *Business.* p.181-182
Woods — *Religious* p.744-745, 747-748

, Advantages of
Nizer — *Thinking* p.142

, and crime
Kauffman — *For* p.75-76

, and the Church
Flint — *Graham* p.106

, Fear of
Hill — *Think* p.259-266

, Hatred for
Krishnamurti — *Think* p.103

, Programs for
Dirksen — *Quot.* #13, 33-34, 79, 706

, Reduction of
Mandelbaum — *Choose* p.153-166

POWER
See also **Authority; Force; God, Power of; Holy Spirit (Holy Ghost); Influence; Position; Strength**
Adams — *New* p.13, 46, 78
Bartlett — *Discovery* p.87, 139-141
Braude — *Source* #1325-1329
Curtis — *Golden* p.64-75
Detherage — *Sunrise* p.59-60
Dirksen — *Quot. See* index p.268
Droke — *Christian* p.400-403
Edwards — *Useful* p.482-483
Evans — *Unto* p.7, 14, 71
Flesch — *Unusual* p.219
Flint — *Graham* p.24, 107
Forbes — *Thoughts See* index p.562-563
Fuller — *Epigrams* p.239
Garland — *Subject* p.192-193, 237
Giniger — *Compact* p.128-146
Grizer — *Wit* p.354-355
Harnsberger — *Mark* p.367
Harral — *Feature* p.257
Henry — *5000* p.214
Hobe — *Tapestries* p.42, 184
Hovey — *Treasury* p.253-254; *See* index p.299
Humes — *Instant* #769-778
Johnson — *Bedside* p.22, 246, 250
Jones — *If* p.106-115

Kennedy — *Reader's* #803-809
Keys Happiness p.111-113
Kin — *Dictionary* p.161, 196
Knight's Illus. p.236-237
Knight's Treas. p.262-265
Krishnamurti — *Think* p.105
Kronenberger — *Animal* p.240-242
Liddle — *Thought I, II, III* p.29, 109
Liddle — *Thought IV* p.41
Lockridge — *World's* #31, 895, 3019, 4012, 4254, 4761
Lytle — *Leaves* p.53, 69, 164, 167
Mandelbaum — *Choose* p.16
Peale — *Guide* p.1-22, 147-165
Peterson — *New* p.42-43
Phillips — *Choice* p.365, 382, 396
Prochnow — *Public* #2477, 3503, 3549-3551, 3749
Prochnow — *Speaker's* p.235-236
Prochnow — *Success.* #1234, 2166-2169
Seldes — *Great* p.655, 745-757
Sheen — *Way* p.109-111
Speaker's Desk p.201-203
Wheelis — *Moralist* p.80, 116, 120-121, 126, 139-140
Woods — *Business.* p.177-181
Woods — *Content.* p.36
Woods — *Religious* p.629, 748-749
, *Absolute*
Ideas p.300-302
, *Balance of*
Forbes — *Thoughts* p.428
Ideas p.47-49
, *Control of*
Halverson — *Perspective* p.56
, *Craving for*
Adams — *New* p.328
Dirksen — *Quot.* #448, 2127
, *Creative*
Curtis — *Practical* p.457
Peterson — *Art* p.162
, *Hidden*
Nichols — *Third* p.34-35
, *of individual*
Mandelbaum — *Choose* p. 95-98
, *of mankind*
Webb — *Edge* p.58-59
, *Personal*
Keller — *You* p.195-210
, *Physical*
Casselberry — *How* p.141-167
, *Problem of*
Adams — *New* p.327
, *Quiet*
Peterson — *Art* p.61
, *Sphere of*
Baillie — *Diary* #26
, *Subconscious*
Alexander's Treasure. p.158
, *Transforming*
Fridy — *Meditat.* p.128
, *Use of*
Curtis — *Golden* p.51-61

PRACTICALITY
Flesch — *Unusual* p.219
Kennedy — *Reader's* #810-812
Kin — *Dictionary* p.196
Lockridge — *World's* #3762
Montapert — *Distilled* p.278
Prochnow — *Success.* #1408
Woods — *Wellsprings* p.18

PRACTICE
See also **Experience**
Evans — *Thoughts I* p.107, 153
Evans — *Thoughts II (Open Door)* p.56-57
Forbes — *Thoughts* p.329-330, 356, 370, 472
Fox — *Make* p.25
Garland — *Subject* p.237-238
Hovey — *Treasury* #16, 80
How To Live p.453-457
Kin — *Dictionary* p.196
Mandel — *Stories* p.203
Speaker's Desk #103
Woods — *Religious* p.749-750

PRAGMATISM
Ideas p.302-304
Kin — *Dictionary* p.196
Seldes — *Great* p.757
Woods — *Religious* p.750

PRAIRIE CHICKENS
Botkin — *Anecdotes* p.150

PRAISE
See also **Applause; Appreciation; Compliments; Encouragement; Flattery; Self-praise**
Alexander's Treasure. p.229
Applegarth — *Heir.* p.91, 113, 183, 199, 301
Book Proverbs p.114
Botkin — *Anecdotes* p.16, 28, 90
Botkin — *Treasury* p.276-317, 318, 492
Braude — *Source* #1330-1334
Braude — *Speaker's* #222
Braude — *Stories* p.300-301
Dirksen — *Quot.* #1040, 1507-1509
Droke — *Christian* p.403-405
Edwards — *Useful* p.483-485
Flesch — *Unusual* p.219-220
Forbes — *Thoughts* p.157, 160, 468; *See also* index p.563
Fuller — *Epigrams* p.239-240
Garland — *Subject* p.238

George — *Book* p.17, 44, 64, 415
Grizer — *Wit* p.355-356
Harnsberger — *Mark* p.307
Henry — *5000* p.214-215
Hobe — *Tapestries* p.26, 106
Hovey — *Treasury* #1766
How To Live p.425-428
Johnson — *Bedside* p.123, 250-251
Keys Happiness p.51-52, 188-191
Kin — *Dictionary* p.51, 196
Liddle — *Thought I, II, III* p.69, 117, 130-131, 138, 143, 151, 153, 159, 161, 192-193
Liddle — *Thought IV* p.40-41, 45
Lockridge — *World's* #66, 98, 146-153, 284, 291, 313, 366, 457, 1511, 1625, 1673, 1752, 3234, 4627
Lytle — *Leaves* p.28, 31
Mandel — *Stories* p.204
Montapert — *Distilled* p.278-279
New Topical p.197-198
Prochnow — *Public* #1900, 2653, 2729, 3552-3556, 4188
Prochnow — *Speaker's* p.236-237
Prochnow — *Success.* #1415, 2170
Reader's — *Getting* p.182
Seldes — *Great* p.757-758
Sheban — *Wisdom* no p.
Speaker's Desk p.203
Suter — *Prayers* #278-316
Vogue — *Arts* p.155-161
Wallis — *Treasure* p.80, 183
Wallis — *Words* p.183-186
Woods — *Religious* p.750-751
Words — *Inspir.* p.223-224
, *Epithets of*
Auden — *Certain* p.304-306
, *for teenagers*
Ginott — *Between* p.111-124

PRANKS. *See* **Tricks and trickery**

PRAYER
See also **Devotion; God; Worship**
Adams — *New* p.93
Alexander's Treasure. p.176, 193
Applegarth — *Heir.* p.175, 201-209, 296
Asimov — *Treasury* #474, 488
Auden — *Certain* p.307
Baillie — *Diary* #128
Book Proverbs p.132
Botkin — *Anecdotes* p.194
Braude — *Source* #1335-1346
Braude — *Speaker's* #1048-1058
Braude — *Stories* p.301-303
Carruthers — *Sparks* p.107-120
Curtis — *Daily* p.205-213
Curtis — *New* p.45-57
Detherage — *Sunrise* p.34, 36, 68, 100, 166, 169
Dirksen — *Quot.* #85, 415, 1021, 1041-1044, 1510-1520, 1684, 2131-2133, 2350
Droke — *Christian* p.406-419
Edwards — *Useful* p.485-490
Emmons — *Mature* p.32-47
Evans — *Faith* p.6, 22, 51, 58, 116, 184
Evans — *Quite* p.125-139
Evans — *This* p.83-85
Evans — *Thoughts I* p.78, 93, 120-121, 140, 162, 199, 202
Evans — *Thoughts II (Open Door)* p.47
Evans — *Thoughts III (Open Road)* p.36-37, 47, 145, 161, 179, 185-187, 208
Evans — *Thoughts IV* p.27, 34, 99-100, 186-188
Evans — *Unto* p.62, 68, 115, 119, 121, 128-130
Flesch — *Unusual* p.220-222
Flint — *Graham* p.107-109
Forbes — *Thoughts* p.9-10, 52, 166, 194, 198, 200, 214, 270, 293, 388, 409, 456, 472, 502
Fox — *Make* p.1-2, 111, 118-119, 136, 141, 144, 158-159, 162, 164, 179-180, 195, 197, 202, 208, 215, 225-226
Fridy — *Meditat.* p.33-36, 38, 40-41
Fuller — *Epigrams* p.240
Fuller — *Thesaurus* #1606-1612
Garland — *Subject* p.238-239
George — *Book* p.285, 331, 368
Giniger — *Compact* p.149-165
Grizer — *Wit* p.356
Guideposts — *Faith* p.65-68, 267-270
Halverson — *Perspective* p.33, 52-53
Harnsberger — *Mark* p.367-369
Henry — *5000* p.215-216
Hobe — *Tapestries See* index p.254
Holmes — *Design See* index p.234
Hovey — *Treasury* p.254-258; *See* index p.299
How To Live p.551-557
Hubbard — *Scrap* p.27
Hunter — *Gems* p.78-80
Johnson — *Bedside* p.24, 36, 57, 78-81, 91, 144, 167, 188, 196, 209-233, 294, 303, 319, 325
Kahn — *Lessons* p.36-47
Kauffman — *For* p.169-178
Kennedy — *Reader's* #813-822
Keys Happiness p.97-99, 111-113, 139-141, 301-303, 322-327
Kin — *Dictionary* p.196-197

Knight's Illus. p.237-243
Knight's Treas. p.266-277
Liddle — *Thought I, II, III See* index p.199
Liddle — *Thought IV* p.7, 37
Liddle — *Thought V* p.5, 27, 30
Lockridge — *World's* #82, 2360, 3111, 4377
Lytle — *Leaves* p.6, 28, 30, 57, 104-105, opp. 136, 152, 160, 168, 190
Mandel — *Stories* p.204-209
Montapert — *Distilled* p.279
More Words p.123-125
New Topical p.198-199
Nichols — *New* p.182-183
Peale — *Faith* p.265-280
Peale — *Guideposts* p.87-107
Peterson — *Art* p.59, 72, 78
Phillips — *Choice See* index p.428
Prochnow — *Public* #140, 358, 735, 836, 911, 1052, 1444, 2664, 3557-3565, 4140, 4189-4192
Prochnow — *Speaker's* p.237-239
Prochnow — *Success.* #548, 833, 920, 1498, 2171-2175
Reader's — *Getting* p.121
Rogers — *Time* p.57-62
Sagendorph — *Old* p.42-43
Schermerhorn — *1500* p.286-288
Seaburg — *Great* p.260-261, 313, 332-333, 337-338, 350-351, 395, 400, 405
Seldes — *Great* p.758
Sheban — *Wisdom* no p.
Sheen — *Lift* p.140-156
Speaker's Desk #10, 50, 81, 148, 318, 332, 542, 610, 815, 827, 880, 902, 1010, 1068
Strait — *Speaker's* p.133-138
Voss — *Quotations* p.198-201
Wallis — *Treasure* p.59-60, 69, 195-204, 213, 225, 239
Wallis — *Words* p.29, 46, 61-62, 157, 180, 187-194, 230
Watson — *Light* p.62-68
Weisfeld — *Pulpit* p.76-86
White — *Job* p.169-175
Woods — *Content.* p.234, 246, 265, 273-276, 280, 283, 301, 325, 342, 352
Woods — *Religious* p.751-766
Words Change p.46
Zobell — *Speaker's* p.114-115

, Actor's
Hubbard — *Scrap* p.15

, and freedom
Kauffman — *For* p.178

, Answers to
Guideposts — *Faith* p.243, 291-300
New Topical p.199-200
Words Change p.22-25

, as a collect
More Words p.31-32

, as a direction
Unlimited Power p.93-96

, as energy
Peale — *Guide* p.94-114

, as force
Clark — *Windows* p.96

, as thought
Peterson — *Art* p.121

, Children's
Guideposts — *Faith* p.171
Reader's — *Getting* p.89-91

, Comfort of
Goudge — *Comfort* p.284-289

, Creative
Unlimited Power p.206-209

, Daily
Suter — *Prayers* #366-379

, Defined and explained
Woods — *Religious* p.755-759

, Deprecating
Book Proverbs p.105

, Difficulties in
Phillips — *Choice* p.242, 245

, Distraction in
Baillie — *Diary* #5

, Effectiveness of
Carruthers — *Sparks* p.118-120
Tanksley — *Friend* p.65
Woods — *Religious* p.760-761

, Evening
Hubbard — *Scrap* p.43

, Family
Curtis — *Daily* p.38-40
Nichols — *New* p.184-185
Redhead — *Living* p.134-142

, Favorite
Dirksen — *Quot.* #1684

, Fellowship of
Guideposts — *Faith* p.313-317

, Fool's
Hubbard — *Scrap* p.85

, for birth of child
Kohn — *Best* p.165

, for middle-aged
Rogers — *Time* p.75-77

, for others
Baillie — *Diary* #273, 294
New Topical p.200

, Healing of
Guideposts — *Faith* p.213-217

, in crises
Peale — *Guideposts* p.87-90, 93-100

, in shorthand
Peale — *Guideposts* p.101-103
, in war
Fogg — *1000* #14, 186, 390
Guideposts — *Faith* p.232
Peale — *Guideposts* p.310-312
, Learning of
Carruthers — *Sparks* p.113-115
Day — *Meditations* p.21-22
, Life of
Suter — *Prayers* #317-328
, Living
Clark — *Windows* p.28-29
, Lord's
Applegarth — *Heir.* p.205
Flesch — *Unusual* p.155
Rogers — *Time* p.63-73
Wallis — *Treasure* p.203
Wallis — *Words* p.191
Woods — *Religious* p.558
, Man's
Braude — *Stories* p.353
, Meetings of
Peale — *Guideposts* p.147-150
, Methods and time of
Woods — *Religious* p.762-766
, Morning
Kohn — *Adventures* p.127-128
Nichols — *New* p.185
Woods — *Content.* p.99, 265
, Mother's. See **Mothers, Prayer for**
, National
Nichols — *Third* p.242
, Nature of
Auden — *Certain* p.306
, Necessity of
Woods — *Religious* p.761-762
, of relinquishment
Guideposts — *Faith* p.218-222
, on radio
Peale — *Guideposts* p.104-107
, Optimist's
Hubbard — *Scrap* p.35, 211
, Parents'
Peterson — *Art* p.334
, Perfect
Nichols — *New* p.186-187
, Place of
Clark — *Windows* p.110
, Power of
Peale — *Courage* p.41-61
Reader's — *20th* p.104-106
White — *Life* p.167-174
, Practical
Nichols — *New* p.186
, Private
New Topical p.200
, Public
New Topical p.200
, Questions about
Carruthers — *Sparks* p.116-118
, School
Dirksen — *Quot.* #98-99
Franke — *Buckley* p.242-243
, Social and family
New Topical p.201
, Thankful
Nichols — *New* p.185
, Unanswered
Carruthers — *Sparks* p.111-112
Unlimited Power p.173-176
, Universal
Nichols — *Third* p.223
, Unselfish
Clark — *Windows* p.118
, Value of
Albert — *Stop* p.74-75, 94, 178-179
Carruthers — *Sparks* p.109-110
, West Point cadet's
Guideposts — *Faith* p.115

PREACHERS AND PREACHING. *See* **Clergymen; Missionaries**

PRECAUTION
Braude — *Speaker's* #1066-1070
Braude — *Stories* p.303
Speaker's Desk See index p.304

PRECEDENT. *See* **Customs; Tradition**

PRECEPTS. *See* **Advice; Principles**

PRECIPICES
Auden — *Certain* p.218-219

PRECISION
Du Noüy — *Road* p.65-66
Grizer — *Wit* p.356
Prochnow — *Public* #2120
Woods — *Religious* p.782

PRECOCITY
Kin — *Dictionary* p.197
Prochnow — *Public* #1772

PREDESTINATION
See also **Fatalism; Fate**
Harnsberger — *Mark* p.370
Ideas p.304-305
Woods — *Religious* p.772-773

PREDICTABILITY
Hoffer — *Reflect.* p.67-68

PREDICTION. *See* **Prophets and prophecy**

PREFACE. *See* **Introductions**

PREHISTORIC AGE
Flesch — *Unusual* p.224
Ideas p.391-393

PREJUDICE
See also **Discrimination; Intolerance**
Adams — *New* p.27
Alexander's Treasure. p.62
Applegarth — *Heir.* p.47, 271
Bartlett — *Discovery* p.76-77
Braude — *Source* #1353-1354
Braude — *Speaker's* #1073
Curtis — *Practical* p.124-125
Dirksen — *Quot.* #478, 497, 501, 2134, 2215
Droke — *Christian* p.426-432
Edwards — *Useful* p.493-495
Evans — *Faith* p.142
Evans — *Thoughts I* p.99-101
Evans — *Thoughts III (Open Road)* p.151, 166
Flesch — *Unusual* p.224
Flint — *Graham* p.110
Forbes — *Thoughts See* index p.563
Fuller — *Epigrams* p.242
Fuller — *Thesaurus* #441-452
Garland — *Subject* p.240
Harnsberger — *Mark* p.370-371
Henry — *5000* p.217
Hobe — *Tapestries* p.88
Hovey — *Treasury* p.258-259; #443, 1504, 1631-1639
Humes — *Instant* #779-790
Johnson — *Bedside* p.125, 172
Kahn — *Lessons* p.211-215
Kennedy — *Reader's* #837-840
Kin — *Dictionary* p.198
Knight's Illus. p.251-252
Liddle — *Thought I, II, III* p.23, 54, 61, 120, 158, 167, 181
Liddle — *Thought IV* p.10, 29, 35
Liddle — *Thought V* p.45
Lindeman — *Emerson* p.212-213
Lockridge — *World's* #626, 3467-3468
Lytle — *Leaves* p.63
Montapert — *Distilled* p.279-280
Nizer — *Thinking* p.20, 34
Prochnow — *Public* #1459, 1754, 3566-3573, 4193
Prochnow — *Speaker's* p.240
Prochnow — *Success.* #249, 750, 2178
Seldes — *Great* p.758-759
Speaker's Desk #341; p.205-206, 274
Voss — *Quotations* p.202-203
Wallis — *Treasure* p.42
Wallis — *Words* p.13, 26
Woods — *Religious* p.773-774

PREMIUMS
Harral — *Feature* p.257

PREMONITION
Asimov — *Treasury* #15
Evans — *Thoughts II (Open Door)* p.208-209
Fogg — *1000* #16, 71, 274, 336, 470, 510, 554, 639, 646, 693, 1017
Grizer — *Wit* p.356-357
Harral — *Feature* p.257
Lindbergh — *Unicorn* p.77
Lockridge — *World's* #4646
Manchee — *Secret* p.51-55
Unlimited Power p.38-42
Woods — *Religious* p.335-336

PREOCCUPATION. *See* **Absent-mindedness**

PREPARATION
See also **Education; Learning; Schools** etc.
Evans — *This* p.8-9
Evans — *Thoughts I* p.160, 177, 215-216
Evans — *Thoughts II (Open Door)* p.12-13, 59-60, 68, 97, 123, 148, 173-174
Evans — *Thoughts III (Open Road) See* index no p.
Evans — *Thoughts IV* p.13, 17, 19, 63-70, 166, 169
Flint — *Graham* p.110
Garland — *Subject* p.241
Grizer — *Wit* p.357
Hovey — *Treasury* #16, 422
Kennedy — *Reader's* #841-843
Kohn — *Thoughts* p.39-42
Lytle — *Leaves* p.156-157, 188, 190-191
Mandel — *Stories* p.210-212
Modern Eloquence (14) p.398
Montapert — *Distilled* p.280
Wallis — *Words* p.141, 224
Wilcox — *Heart* p.46-48
Zobell — *Speaker's* p.115

PREPAREDNESS
Braude — *Speaker's* #1074-1077
Grizer — *Wit* p.357-358
Halverson — *Perspective* p.8
Henry — *5000* p.217-218
Mandel — *Stories* p.212-213
Prochnow — *Public* #536, 985, 2559

PREREQUISITES
Speaker's Desk #645, 696, 997

PRESBYTERIANS
Botkin — *Anecdotes* p.122
Botkin — *Treasury* p.424-425
Harnsberger — *Mark* p.371-372
Peale — *Guideposts* p.142-146
Weisfeld — *Pulpit* p.9, 11

PRESCRIPTIONS
Grizer — *Wit* p.358-359
Harral — *Feature* p.257

PRESENCE
Hobe — *Tapestries* p.136
Hovey — *Treasury* p.36-37; *See also* p.293
Lindbergh — *Unicorn* p.27
Lytle — *Leaves* p.190

PRESENT
See also **Today**
Adams — *New* p.209
Braude — *Source* #1241-1258
Braude — *Stories* p.304-305
Edwards — *Useful* p.495-496
Evans — *Thoughts I* p.128-129, 183
Evans — *Unto* p.4, 9-10
Flesch — *Unusual* p.225
Forbes — *Thoughts* p.1, 151, 208, 220, 240, 284, 365, 429, 448, 459, 476, 509
Fox — *Make* p.45-46
Grizer — *Wit* p.338, 359-360
Henry — *5000* p.128
Hobe — *Tapestries* p.11-12
Hubbard — *Scrap* p.58
Kin — *Dictionary* p.198
Liddle — *Thought I, II, III* p.33
Liddle — *Thought IV* p.32, 38
Lindbergh — *Gift* p.125-128
Lockridge — *World's* #850, 3437
Lytle — *Leaves* p.89, 171-172
Nichols — *New* p.208-209
Peterson — *Art* p.28
Prochnow — *Public* #610, 1018, 2706
Prochnow — *Success.* #2179
Sheen — *Lift* p.157-167
Wallis — *Words* p.50, 94, 105, 211, 214
Woods — *Religious* p.775
, Living in
Curtis — *Practical* p.94
Nichols — *New* p.143-144
Vogue — *Arts* p.73-80

PRESENTATION
See also **Introductions**
Humes — *Instant* #39-41; p.31

PRESENTIMENT. *See* **Premonition**

PRESERVATION
See also **Self-preservation**
Prochnow — *Public* #953

PRESIDENTS
Braude — *Stories* p.167-168
Cerf — *Laugh* p.16-25
Dirksen — *Quot.* #20, 113-114, 203, 351, 553, 692-695, 1661, 1663, 1761-1781, 1793, 1832
Franke — *Buckley* p.243
Fuller — *Thesaurus* #1931-1940
Grizer — *Wit* p.360-361
Harral — *Feature* p.258
Henry — *5000* p.218
Kin — *Dictionary* p.198
Prochnow — *Public* #1313
Prochnow — *Success.* #308
Seldes — *Great* p.759-762
Simpson — *Contemp.* p.10-33
Simpson — *'54* p.66, 199, 318
Woods — *Religious* p.776
, Cabinet of
Dirksen — *Quot.* #1792
, Quotations on America by
New Joy p.70-74

PRESSURE
See also **Frustration; Tension; Worry**
Albert — *Stop* p.12-14, 64-66, 89
Casselberry — *How* p.134-136, 157-158, 171, 175-176
Evans — *Faith* p.5-6, 10, 12-13, 89, 122, 133, 149-150, 171, 186
Evans — *Thoughts I* p.140-141, 198-199, 209-210
Evans — *Thoughts II (Open Door)* p.15, 59-60, 67, 183
Evans — *Thoughts III (Open Road)* p.86, 119, 149
Evans — *Thoughts IV* p.106
Forbes — *Thoughts* p.130, 198, 292, 384, 394
How To Live p.190-194
Ideas p.385-386
Kauffman — *For* p.208-209
Peale — *Sin* p.176-177
Peale — *Stay* p.157-171
Peterson — *Art* p.113
Seldes — *Great* p.772-773
Unlimited Power p.88-92
, Prayer for
Unlimited Power p.5

"PRESSURE-COOKER" HUMOR
Botkin — *Anecdotes* p.38

PRESUMPTION
Kin — *Dictionary* p.199

Lockridge — *World's* #3066, 3403
New Topical p.202

PRETENSION
See also **Hypocrisy; Insincerity;** etc.
Braude — *Stories* p.305
Curtis — *Practical* p.97
Dirksen — *Quot.* #152
Edwards — *Useful* p.9-10, 138, 497-498
Evans — *Faith* p.45-46, 50, 126, 143
Evans — *Thoughts I* p.87-88
Evans — *Unto* p.87
Flesch — *Unusual* p.6-7, 225
Forbes — *Thoughts* p.329
Grizer — *Wit* p.361-362
Harnsberger — *Mark* p.430
Henry — *5000* p.5
Jones — *If* p.19-23
Kin — *Dictionary* p.199
Lockridge — *World's* #127-128, 137, 211, 300, 1734, 1970, 1981, 2049, 2504, 2506, 2569, 3454, 3861
Lytle — *Leaves* p.61
Mandel — *Stories* p.213
Peterson — *Art* p.344
Prochnow — *Public* #2391
Woods — *Religious* p.776

PRETEXT
Kin — *Dictionary* p.199

PREVENTION
Edwards — *Useful* p.498
Garland — *Subject* p.241-242
Kin — *Dictionary* p.199
Mandelbaum — *Choose* p.207-213

PRICE
Alexander's Treasure. p.219-220
Flesch — *Unusual* p.225
Fuller — *Epigrams* p.242-243
Fuller — *Thesaurus* #2086
Grizer — *Wit* p.362-364
Prochnow — *Public* #1598, 2490
Prochnow — *Speaker's* p.241
Prochnow — *Success.* #310, 828, 903, 918, 2185
Welk — *Guide.* p.93-94
Woods — *Business.* p.182-191

PRIDE
Asimov — *Treasury* #413
Book Proverbs p.57
Braude — *Source* #1355-1358
Braude — *Speaker's* #1078-1079
Braude — *Stories* p.305
Dirksen — *Quot.* #699, 774, 1039, 1165, 1521-1524
Edwards — *Useful* p.498-501, 731
Evans — *Quote* p.153-162
Evans — *Thoughts I* p.53, 57, 83
Evans — *Thoughts II (Open Door)* p.38
Evans — *Thoughts IV* p.50, 209
Evans — *Unto* p.102
Flesch — *Unusual* p.226
Flint — *Graham* p.110-111
Fogg — *1000* #50, 79, 243, 477, 555, 558, 947, 1056
Forbes — *Thoughts See* index p.563
Fridy — *Meditat.* p.61
Fuller — *Epigrams* p.243
Fuller — *Thesaurus* #456-457
Garland — *Subject* p.242
Grizer — *Wit* p.364-365
Harnsberger — *Mark* p.373
Henry — *5000* p.219
Hobe — *Tapestries* p.190-192
Hovey — *Treasury* #55
Johnson — *Bedside* p.76-77, 318, 320
Kennedy — *Reader's* #844-858
Keys Happiness p.493-495
Kin — *Dictionary* p.65, 199, 202
Knight's Illus. p.255-256
Knight's Treas. p.298-299
Krishnamurti — *Think* p.49, 156-157
Liddle — *Thought I, II, III* p.172
Liddle — *Thought IV* p.22
Liddle — *Thought V* p.4, 12
Lockridge — *World's See* index p.581
Lytle — *Leaves* p.28-29, 71, 149
McCracken — *What* p.11-16
Mandel — *Stories* p.213-214
Montapert — *Distilled* p.280-281
New Topical p.202-203
Phillips — *Choice* p.79, 146
Prochnow — *Public* #133, 2412, 2530, 3574-3577
Prochnow — *Speaker's* p.241
Prochnow — *Success.* #929, 2186
Seldes — *Great* p.773
Speaker's Desk p.206-208
Voss — *Quotations* p.204-205
White — *Job* p.187-189
Woods — *Religious* p.776-778
Woods — *Wellsprings* p.14

, False
Sherman — *Your* p.109-114
Speaker's Desk #113

, Local
Fun Fare p.38, 52, 133, 188

, National
Hubbard — *Scrap* p.27, 45

PRIESTS AND PRIESTHOOD
Asimov — *Treasury* #228, 416, 469, 499, 505-507, 618

Botkin — *Anecdotes* p.125, 243
Du Noüy — *Road* p.195, 202-211, 217
Flesch — *Unusual* p.226
Fuller — *Thesaurus* #1481-1483
Harnsberger — *Mark* p.373-374
Hunter — *Gems* p.82-83
Lockridge — *World's* #618, 749, 3676, 4389, 5011
More Words p.125-126
New Topical p.203-204
Schermerhorn — *1500* p.289-290
Seldes — *Great* p.773-776
Sheban — *Wisdom* no p.
Weisfeld — *Pulpit* p.1, 115-119, 126
Woods — *Religious* p.778-782

, High
New Topical p.116-117

, Mormon
Zobell — *Speaker's* p.116

PRIMNESS. *See* **Precision**

PRINCES
Hobe — *Tapestries* p.220
Kin — *Dictionary* p.199
Lockridge — *World's See* index p.581
Seldes — *Great* p.777

PRINCIPLES
See also **Duty; Ideals and idealism; Morality and morals; Values; Vision**
Braude — *Source* #1359-1361
Braude — *Stories* p.305
Edwards — *Useful* p.501-502
Evans — *Faith* p.71, 98, 131-132, 140, 145, 148, 156, 165, 180, 188
Evans — *Quote* p.177-186
Evans — *Thoughts I* p.27, 35, 62, 78, 83-84, 90-91, 98, 144, 160-162, 197
Evans — *Thoughts II (Open Door)* p.22-23, 53, 73-74, 146-147, 174-175, 188-189
Evans — *Thoughts III (Open Road) See* index no p.
Evans — *Thoughts IV* p.94, 133, 177, 198
Evans — *Unto* p.13, 47, 55, 82-83, 85, 134, 144
Flesch — *Unusual* p.226
Fogg — *1000* #256, 571, 1047, 1097
Forbes — *Thoughts See* index p.563
Fox — *Make* p.214
Garland — *Subject* p.243
Grizer — *Wit* p.366
Harnsberger — *Mark* p.374-375
Henry — *5000* p.219
Humes — *Instant* #791-793
Kennedy — *Reader's* #859-861
Kin — *Dictionary* p.200
Liddle — *Thought I, II, III* p.5, 44, 65, 101, 106, 192
Liddle — *Thought IV* p.16, 22, 36
Lockridge — *World's* #1082, 1827, 3738, 5611
Modern Eloquence (14) p.399-400
Montapert — *Distilled* p.281
Prochnow — *Public* #679, 3578-3579
Prochnow — *Success.* #2187
Seldes — *Great* p.777-778
Wheelis — *Moralist* p.73-74
Woods — *Religious* p.782-783

PRINTERS AND PRINTING
Braude — *Stories* p.305-306
Flesch — *Unusual* p.226
Harnsberger — *Mark* p.375-380
Harral — *Feature* p.258
Hubbard — *Scrap* p.27, 58, 60, 92
Kin — *Dictionary* p.200
Knight's Illus. p.256-259
Lockridge — *World's* #4948
Seldes — *Great* p.779

PRISONERS
Auden — *Certain* p.46-51
Copeland — *10,000* p.113-119
George — *Book* p.13. 17, 109, 238, 295, 367, 373, 407
Guideposts — *Faith* p.55-58
Peale — *Guideposts* p.20-23, 263-266
Prochnow — *Public* #33, 254, 481, 777, 2591
Prochnow — *Success.* #1377
Weisfeld — *Pulpit* p.10-11

, -of-war
Fuller — *Thesaurus* #2366
Guideposts — *Faith* p.343
Unlimited Power p.230-234

, Prayer for
Goudge — *Comfort* p.142-143

, Reform and rehabilitation of
Nizer — *Thinking* p.118
Peale — *Guideposts* p.263-266

, Solitary confinement of
Day — *Meditations* p.8

PRISONS
See also **Jails**
Asimov — *Treasury* #114
Botkin — *Anecdotes* p.94
Flesch — *Unusual* p.226
Harral — *Feature* p.258-259
Henry — *5000* p.219-220
Hovey — *Treasury* #69, 122, 601
Hubbard — *Scrap* p.224

Lockridge — *World's* #5729, 5751, 5759
Mandel — *Stories* p.143
New Topical p.204-205
Prochnow — *Public* #480, 682
Prochnow — *Success.* #2188
Schermerhorn — *1500* p.291-292
Seldes — *Great* p.779-780
Woods — *Religious* p.231
, and society
Kauffman — *For* p.178-179
, Chapels in
Peale — *Guideposts* p.263-266
, Poetry in
Hadfield — *Delights* p.97
, Wardens of
Nizer — *Thinking* p.118
Prochnow — *Public* #1773

PRIVACY
Evans — *Faith* p.183-186
Franke — *Buckley* p.244-245
How To Live p.421-424
Lytle — *Leaves* p.153
Seldes — *Great* p.780
, Teenager
Ginott — *Between* p.39-41

PRIVATE ENTERPRISE. *See* **Free enterprise**

PRIVATE PROPERTY
Dirksen — *Quot.* #561
Kauffman — *For* p.65-66
Wheelis — *Moralist* p.118, 153-154

PRIVILEGE
Evans — *Thoughts I* p.118-119
Grizer — *Wit* p.366
Harnsberger — *Mark* p.380
Ideas p.336-338
Seldes — *Great* p.780-781
Woods — *Religious* p.783-784
, Special
Dirksen — *Quot.* #2346

PRIZE FIGHTING
See also **Boxing**
Botkin — *Anecdotes* p.80
Fuller — *Thesaurus* #1886-1887
Woods — *Religious* p.784

PRIZES
Kin — *Dictionary* p.200
Prochnow — *Speaker's* p.242

PROBABILITIES
See also **Possibilities; Potentialities**
Applegarth — *Heir.* p.139
Asimov — *Treasury* #94
Du Noüy — *Road See* index p.251
Flesch — *Unusual* p.227
Kin — *Dictionary* p.200
Lockridge — *World's* #3854
Prochnow — *Success.* #2189

PROBATION
Garland — *Subject* p.244

PROBLEMS
See also **Difficulties; Disappointment; Discouragement; Worry;** etc.
Albert — *Stop* p.160-161, 166-168
Braude — *Source* #1362-1368
Braude — *Speaker's* #311-313
Braude — *Stories* p.106
Carruthers — *Sparks* p.93-96
Curtis — *Daily* p.127-132
Curtis — *Golden* p.156-158
Curtis — *Human* p.2-3, 154-158, 160-163
Dirksen — *Quot.* #1970
Evans — *Thoughts I* p.17, 78, 120-122, 133, 166, 208
Evans — *Thoughts II (Open Door)* p.11, 15, 21, 27, 53, 75, 207, 209
Evans — *Thoughts III (Open Road) See* index no p.
Evans — *Thoughts IV* p.27, 83, 89, 106, 206
Evans — *Unto* p.109
Flesch — *Unusual* p.227
Forbes — *Thoughts See* index p.563
Fox — *Make* p.167-171, 175-176, 211
Grizer — *Wit* p.366-367
Holmes — *I've* p.105-106
Hovey — *Treasury* p.259-260; *See* index p.299
How To Live p.199-204
Humes — *Instant* p.38; #794-817, 1201-1202
Kahn — *Lessons* p.141-156
Lair — *Baby* p.133-142
Liddle — *Thought I, II, III* p.30
Liddle — *Thought V* p.13, 18, 21, 38
Montapert — *Blue.* p.24-27
Montapert — *Distilled* p.281-282
Nichols — *Third* p.30-33
Peale — *Courage* p.26-27
Phillips — *Choice* p.207, 369
Prochnow — *Public* #9, 234, 354, 859, 1329, 2415
Prochnow — *Speaker's* p.95
Speaker's Desk #268, 461, 917, 1144, 1162
Wallis — *Treasure* p.225, 227
Wallis — *Words* p.118
Welk — *Guide.* p.106-108

, *Small*
Peterson — *Art* p.131
, *Solution of*
Evans — *Faith* p.3-7, 17, 21, 51, 60, 95, 115, 128, 148, 223
Garland — *Subject* p.244-245
How To Live p.444-447
Kauffman — *For* p.179-180
Keller — *You* p.21-37
Mandelbaum — *Choose* p.187-228
Montapert — *Distilled* p.282

PROCESSES
Braude — *Speaker's* #1465-1469
Flesch — *Unusual* p.227
Phillips — *Choice* p.102, 171, 402

PROCRASTINATION
See also **Delay; Postponement**
Alexander's Treasure. p.10, 284
Bach — *Make* p.35-36
Book Proverbs p.63
Braude — *Source* #1369-1372
Braude — *Stories* p.306
Casselberry — *How* p.102-105
Dirksen — *Quot.* #1942
Edwards — *Useful* p.502-503
Emmons — *Mature* p.123
Evans — *Thoughts I* p.37, 83
Fuller — *Thesaurus* #461
Grizer — *Wit* p.367-368
Harnsberger — *Mark* p.380
Henry — *5000* p.220
Hubbard — *Scrap* p.25
Johnson — *Bedside* p.246, 251
Keys Happiness p.149-152
Kin — *Dictionary* p.200
Knight's Treas. p.300-302
Liddle — *Thought V* p.8
Mandel — *Stories* p.213
Montapert — *Distilled* p.283
New Topical p.206
Woods — *Religious* p.784

PRODIGALS AND "PRODIGAL SON"
Botkin — *Anecdotes* p.112
Flesch — *Unusual* p.119, 227
Fridy — *Meditation* p.43
Kin — *Dictionary* p.200
Prochnow — *Success.* #2190
Sheen — *Content.* p.124-127

PRODUCTION AND PRODUCTIVITY
Dirksen — *Quot.* #2370
Forbes — *Thoughts* p.105, 134, 215, 240, 255, 326, 393, 410, 463, 467, 493
Fuller — *Thesaurus* #1391-1397
Grizer — *Wit* p.368
Prochnow — *Speaker's* p.242
Seldes — *Great* p.781
Woods — *Business.* p.191, 195
, *and incentives*
Dirksen — *Quot.* #2371
, *Forgotten man and*
Dirksen — *Quot.* #1150
, *Joy of*
Maltz — *Creative* p.23-25
, *Mass*
Curtis — *Practical* p.318-319, 537
Dirksen — *Quot.* #2387
Forbes — *Thoughts* p.105, 493
Prochnow — *Speaker's* p.209
Woods — *Business.* p.192-193
, *Means of*
Seldes — *Great* p.651-652

PROFANITY
Asimov — *Treasury* #383
Braude — *Speaker's* #1080-1081
Droke — *Christian* p.433
Edwards — *Useful* p.113, 503-504
Evans — *Faith* p.70
Evans — *This* p.155-156
Evans — *Thoughts III (Open Road)* p.88-92, 95, 172
Evans — *Unto* p.96
Flesch — *Unusual* p.55, 227
Flint — *Graham* p.111
Fuller — *Thesaurus* #66-68
Guideposts — *Faith* p.318-322
Harnsberger — *Mark* p.380-382
Henry — *5000* p.220
Hunter — *Gems* p.83-84
Kennedy — *Reader's* #75, 862-868
Kin — *Dictionary* p.28, 62
Kohn — *Best* p.67-68
Lockridge — *World's* #3200
Lytle — *Leaves* p.161
Myers — *Thunder* p.51-64
New Topical p.29-30, 260-261
Prochnow — *Public* #1774, 2462
Schermerhorn — *1500* p.292-293
Seldes — *Great* p.85
Speaker's Desk #9, 139, 356, 516, 930, 1000
Weisfeld — *Pulpit* p.11-12, 32-33, 77, 81-82, 132
Woods — *Religious* p.83, 210-211

PROFESSIONS
Braude — *Stories* p.306-307
Copeland — *10,000* p.459-565
Flesch — *Unusual* p.227
Prochnow — *Public* #410
Prochnow — *Speaker's* p.243

PROFESSIONALS
Flesch — *Unusual* p.227
Prochnow — *Success.* #2191

, Dangers of
Curtis — *Practical* p.334-335
, Fees of
Braude — *Speaker's* #1082-1107

PROFESSORS
Asimov — *Treasury* #19, 124, 136-137, 144, 146, 257
Fuller — *Thesaurus* #1026-1032
Fun Fare p.12-13
Manchee — *Secret* p.205-206
Prochnow — *Public* #18, 61, 592, 990, 1516, 4349
Prochnow — *Speaker's* p.243
Speaker's Desk See index p.304

PROFIT
See also **Business; Money;** etc.
Baillie — *Diary* #143
Dirksen — *Quot.* #705
Forbes — *Thoughts* p.16, 36, 59, 98, 284, 328, 349, 369, 384, 391, 404, 431, 469
Garland — *Subject* p.245-246
Grizer — *Wit* p.368-369
Kin — *Dictionary* p.104, 201
Modern Eloquence (14) p.401
Montapert — *Distilled* p.283
Prochnow — *Public* #1098
Prochnow — *Success.* #766, 867
Seldes — *Great* p.781-782
Woods — *Business.* p.195-200
Woods — *Religious* p.784-785
, Motive of
Dirksen — *Quot.* #701, 2371
Words Change p.116
, Sharing of
Woods — *Business.* p.200

PROGRESS
See also **Achievement;** etc.
Adams — *New* p.188
Bartlett — *Discovery* p.56-57
Braude — *Source* #1373-1382
Braude — *Speaker's* #1108
Braude — *Stories* p.307-308
Dirksen — *Quot.* #34, 542, 716, 802, 1045-1046, 1144, 2370, 2383
Droke — *Christian* p.434-441
Du Noüy — *Human* p.117, 146-147, 152-153, 160-161, 214, 219-220, 262-265
Edwards — *Useful* p.504-506, 731
Evans — *This* p.11-12
Evans — *Thoughts I* p.164-165
Evans — *Unto* p.21, 23, 114, 144, 146
Flesch — *Unusual* p.227-228
Forbes — *Thoughts See* index p.563
Garland — *Subject* p.246
Grizer — *Wit* p.369-372
Halverson — *Perspective* p.71
Harnsberger — *Mark* p.382-383
Harral — *Feature* p.259
Henry — *5000* p.220-221
Hovey — *Treasury* p.260; #448, 629, 876, 950, 1521, 1643-1645, 1789
Hubbard — *Scrap* p.29, 65, 184, 218
Humes — *Instant* #818-823
Ideas p.306-307
Kennedy — *Reader's* #869-877
Keys Happiness p.118
Kin — *Dictionary* p.201
Kohn — *Through* p.75-78
Krishnamurti — *Think* p.162-163
Liddle — *Thought I, II, III* p.21, 81, 87-88, 94, 118
Liddle — *Thought V* p.18
Lockridge — *World's See* index p.581
Lytle — *Leaves* p.144, 146, 173, 190
Mandel — *Stories* p.214
Modern Eloquence (14) p.402-404
Montapert — *Distilled* p.283-284
Peterson — *New* p.34-35
Phillips — *Choice* p.100-144
Prochnow — *Public* #230, 1918, 1937, 3580-3581, 4325, 4362
Prochnow — *Speaker's* p.244-246
Prochnow — *Success.* #199, 210, 250, 363, 636, 678, 731, 819, 1036, 1185, 2192-2194
Seldes — *Great* p.782-784
Sheban — *Wisdom* no p.
Sheen — *Way* p.162-163
Speaker's Desk p.208-210
Wheelis — *Moralist* p.123-132
Woods — *Business.* p.201-202
Woods — *Religious* p.785-787
, and liberty
Adams — *New* p.51
, and work
Hunter — *Gems* p.118-119

PROHIBITION
Fuller — *Epigrams* p.243-244
Harnsberger — *Mark* p.383
Modern Eloquence (14) p.151-157

PROJECTION
Menninger — *Blue.* p.28-29
Phillips — *Choice* p.74, 96, 107, 228

PROJECTS
Humes — *Instant* #39-41, 1193-1195, 1254-1255
Lindbergh — *Gift* p.56

PROLETARIAT
Curtis — *Practical* p.282-288
Ideas p.307-309
Lockridge — *World's See* index p.581
Seldes — *Great* p.784-785
Woods — *Business.* p.203

PROMISE
Book Proverbs p.81
Braude — *Source* #1383-1386
Braude — *Stories* p.309
Dirksen — *Quot.* #1781
Edwards — *Useful* p.506-507
Emmons — *Mature* p.23, 86
Evans — *This* p.188-195
Evans — *Thoughts III (Open Road)* p.26-27
Flesch — *Unusual* p.228
Forbes — *Thoughts* p.84, 233, 307, 386, 421, 440, 508
Garland — *Subject* p.246-247
Grizer — *Wit* p.372-373
Halverson — *Perspective* p.80
Harnsberger — *Mark* p.383
Henry — *5000* p.221
Hobe — *Tapestries* p.110, 161, 227
Kin — *Dictionary* p.201
Kohn — *Thoughts* p.134-136
Liddle — *Thought I, II, III* p.103, 130, 147
Lockridge — *World's* #37, 3250
Montapert — *Distilled* p.284-285
Petty — *Promises* p.79-86
Prochnow — *Public* #3582-3583
Prochnow — *Success.* #2195
Wallis — *Treasure* p.191
Woods — *Religious* p.787

PROMOTERS
Dirksen — *Quot.* #179

PROMOTION
Braude — *Source* #1387-1390
Flesch — *Unusual* p.228
Garland — *Subject* p.247-248
Grizer — *Wit* p.373
Keys Happiness p.431-434
Prochnow — *Speaker's* p.246

PROMPTNESS. *See* **Punctuality**

PROOF
Braude — *Speaker's* #1109-1112
Evans — *Unto* p.45, 72
Flesch — *Unusual* p.228
Fuller — *Epigrams* p.244
Henry — *5000* p.221-222
Kin — *Dictionary* p.203
Prochnow — *Public* #31, 950
Speaker's Desk #162, 174, 204, 206, 350, 356, 422, 557, 679, 728, 834, 886
Woods — *Religious* p.787

PROOFREADING
Harral — *Feature* p.259
Peale — *Guideposts* p.46-50

PROPAGANDA
Evans — *Unto* p.37, 78-79, 89
Grizer — *Wit* p.373
Hovey — *Treasury* p.260-261; #1646-1648
Ideas p.309-310, 327
Kennedy — *Reader's* #878
Seldes — *Great* p.785-786
, Definition of
Wheelis — *Moralist* p.145

PROPERTY
See also **Possessions;** types of property
Curtis — *Practical* p.128, 288-289
Dirksen — *Quot.* #451, 702, 705
Edwards — *Useful* p.507
Evans — *Thoughts IV* p.79
Evans — *Unto* p.60
Flesch — *Unusual* p.229
Forbes — *Thoughts* p.141, 150, 268, 315, 324, 326, 368, 417, 422
Fuller — *Epigrams* p.244-245
Fuller — *Thesaurus* p.403-405
Garland — *Subject* p.248
Grizer — *Wit* p.373-374
Henry — *5000* p.222
Kennedy — *Reader's* #879-881
Kin — *Dictionary* p.201
Lockridge — *World's* #5496
Nizer — *Thinking* p.172
Prochnow — *Public* #3584-3586
Prochnow — *Speaker's* p.247
Seldes — *Great* p.786-793
Woods — *Business.* p.203-207
Woods — *Religious* p.787-788
, Rights of
Franke — *Buckley* p.246

PROPHETS AND PROPHECY
Asimov — *Treasury* #489
Braude — *Stories* p.309
Clark — *Windows* p.174
Dirksen — *Quot.* #393, 1782
Evans — *Unto* p.50, 96, 115, 136
Flesch — *Unusual* p.229
Flint — *Graham* p.66, 111
Fogg — *1000 See* index p.896
Fuller — *Epigrams* p.245
Garland — *Subject* p.248-249
Grizer — *Wit* p.374
Harnsberger — *Mark* p.383-384
Harral — *Feature* p.257
Henry — *5000* p.222-223
Hoffer — *Reflect.* p.65-75

Hovey — *Treasury* #81, 681, 686, 931, 1349, 1434, 1865
Kennedy — *Reader's* #882-885
Kin — *Dictionary* p.202
Knight's Illus. p.259-260
Lockridge — *World's* #2736, 3620, 4183
More Words p.126-128
Prochnow — *Public* #305, 2290
Prochnow — *Success.* #2196-2197
Seldes — *Great* p.793
Sheban — *Wisdom* no p.
Wallis — *Words* p.34, 57, 61
Woods — *Religious* p.788-790
, Biblical
Flint — *Graham* p.17-18
New Topical p.70, 208-210
, False
New Topical p.210-211
Woods — *Religious* p.324

PROPORTION
Harnsberger — *Mark* p.384
Keller — *Open* p.73-74
Kin — *Dictionary* p.202
Mandel — *Stories* p.214
, Sense of
Kohn — *Touch* p.130-132, 187-190
Kopplin — *Something* p.125-133

PROPOSALS
Curtis — *Practical* p.3-4, 72
Humes — *Instant* #39-41, 45, 1193-1195, 1254-1255
Prochnow — *Public* #326, 340, 348, 373, 470, 483, 552, 748, 917, 1053

PROPRIETY
Lockridge — *World's* #472, 5598

PROSE
Auden — *Certain* p.308-312
Flesch — *Unusual* p.229
Prochnow — *Public* #1456
, Poetic
Harnsberger — *Mark* p.361

PROSELYTISM
Lockridge — *World's* #4767
New Topical p.211

PROSODY
Curtis — *Practical* p.438

PROSPECTS
Lytle — *Leaves* p.145
Prochnow — *Public* #411

PROSPERITY
See also **Success; Wealth**
Copeland — *10,000* p.996
Curtis — *Daily* p.102-104, 106, 173-179
Curtis — *Human* p.35-50
Dirksen — *Quot.* #23, 61, 387, 567, 703, 1985, 2135-2137
Edwards — *Useful* p.507-509, 731
Evans — *Unto* p.46, 50, 102, 104
Flesch — *Unusual* p.229
Flint — *Graham* p.112
Forbes — *Thoughts See* index p.563
Fuller — *Epigrams* p.359-360
Garland — *Subject* p.249
Grizer — *Wit* p.374-375
Harnsberger — *Mark* p.384-385
Johnson — *Bedside* p.117, 191, 232
Kin — *Dictionary* p.202
Liddle — *Thought I, II, III* p.18, 46, 48, 61, 135
Lockridge — *World's* #1408, 1481, 3775, 4028, 5223
Lytle — *Leaves* p.151
Modern Eloquence (14) p.406
Prochnow — *Public* #820, 1285, 1318, 1775, 2458-2459, 3587-3590, 4194-4196
Prochnow — *Success.* #424, 590, 854, 1264, 2198
Seldes — *Great* p.793-794
Speaker's Desk p.211-213
Wallis — *Treasure* p.66, 226
Woods — *Business.* p.208-209
Woods — *Religious* p.790
, and adversity
Hubbard — *Scrap* p.98
, Material
Nichols — *Third* p.245-246

PROSTITUTION
Hubbard — *Scrap* p.12
Lockridge — *World's* #699, 745
Seldes — *Great* p.794

PROTECTION
Curtis — *Human* p.98-114
Evans — *Unto* p.37, 121
Garland — *Subject* p.249-250
Kin — *Dictionary* p.202
Lytle — *Leaves* p.54, 191
New Topical p.211-212
Prochnow — *Success.* #1263
Speaker's Desk #994

PROTECTIONISM VS. FREE TRADE
Dirksen — *Quot.* #1172

PROTEIN MOLECULES
Du Noüy — *Road* p.41n, 50, 103, 113, 123, 126-133, 145

PROTEST
Kauffman — *For* p.180-181
Seldes — *Great* p.794

PROTESTANTISM
See also names of Protestant churches
Auden — *Certain* p.313-314
Baillie — *Diary* #241
Edwards — *Useful* p.509
Flesch — *Unusual* p.229
Redhead — *Living* p.116-124
Seldes — *Great* p.794-795
Weisfeld — *Pulpit* p.115-119, 154, 174
Woods — *Religious* p.791-792
Words — *Change* p.114-128

PROTONS
Du Noüy — *Human* p.19, 21-22, 46, 188
Du Noüy — *Road* p.41, 51, 108, 147, 192, 230

PROVERBS
See also under specific nationalities, various subjects
Botkin — *Anecdotes* p.xxiii, 178
Braude — *Stories* p.256
Dirksen — *Quot.* #1838-2273
Edwards — *Useful* p.26-27, 509-511
Flesch — *Unusual* p.166
Fogg — *1000 See* index p.896
Forbes — *Thoughts* p.137, 144, 204, 263
Harral — *Feature* p.260
Hubbard — *Scrap* p.225
Keys Happiness p.30
Liddle — *Thought I, II, III* p.10, 39-40, 58, 66, 73, 87, 94, 96-97, 132-133, 162, 166-167
Liddle — *Thought IV* p.5, 10, 14, 16, 23, 28-29, 36
Liddle — *Thought V* p.3-4, 8-9, 15, 20, 23, 26, 42, 44
Lockridge — *World's* #1285
Montapert — *Distilled* p.252
New Joy p.229
Prochnow — *Public* #402, 1776, 3380-3382
Words — *Inspir.* p.74-75
, Children's
Peterson — *Art* p.284

PROVIDENCE
See also **Economy; Foresight and hindsight; God; Prudence;** etc.
Applegarth — *Heir.* p.20
Book Proverbs p.82
Curtis — *Practical* p.170, 499-500
Dirksen — *Quot.* #1525
Edwards — *Useful* p.511-512
Flesch — *Unusual* p.229
Flint — *Graham* p.112
Halverson — *Perspective* p.42
Harnsberger — *Mark* p.385-387
Henry — *5000* p.229
Hobe — *Tapestries* p.43
Hubbard — *Scrap* p.7, 215
Kin — *Dictionary* p.202-203
Liddle — *Thought I, II, III* p.8
Liddle — *Thought IV* p.5
Lytle — *Leaves* p.114, 166
Prochnow — *Speaker's* p.247-248
Seldes — *Great* p.795
Woods — *Religious* p.792-794

PROVINCETOWN, MASSACHUSETTS
Botkin — *Anecdotes* p.74
Botkin — *Treasury* p.192, 635

PROVINCIALISM
Botkin — *Anecdotes* p.16

PROVISION
Kin — *Dictionary* p.203
Lytle — *Leaves* p.154

PROWESS. *See* **Ability**

PRUDENCE
See also **Common sense; Discretion; Expediency; Foresight and hindsight; Thrift; Wisdom**
Dirksen — *Quot.* #1381, 1526-1527, 2138
Edwards — *Useful* p.512-513
Flesch — *Unusual* p.229
Forbes — *Thoughts* p.69, 111, 164, 186, 206, 269, 292, 318, 328, 395, 436, 473, 485
Garland — *Subject* p.250
Henry — *5000* p.229
Johnson — *Bedside* p.280
Kin — *Dictionary* p.47, 203
Lockridge — *World's* #66, 190, 1072, 4601
Lytle — *Leaves* p.57
New Topical p.212-213
Porter — *Halo* p.47-55
Prochnow — *Public* #3591-3602, 4197
Woods — *Content.* p.245
Woods — *Religious* p.794

PRUDERY. *See* **Modesty**

PRUNING
Kohn — *Through* p.135-136

PSALMS
Johnson — *Bedside* p.327-328
Lytle — *Leaves* p.48
Prochnow — *Public* #458
Woods — *Religious* p.794-795

, *91st*
Guideposts — *Faith* p.98
, *139th*
Peterson — *Art* p.129

PSEUDOPSYCHOLOGY
Hooker — *Index* p.17-36

PSEUDOSTATEMENTS
Curtis — *Practical* p.45-46

PSYCHE
Woods — *Religious* p.795

PSYCHIATRY AND PSYCHIATRISTS
See also **Psychoanalysis**
Albert — *Stop* p.145, 157
Asimov — *Treasury* #13, 76-77, 256, 387, 564-565, 567-568
Braude — *Speaker's* #1113-1132
Braude — *Stories* p.309-310
Flint — *Graham* p.112
Fuller — *Thesaurus* #1686-1687
Garland — *Subject* p.251
Gold — *Letters* p.85-86
Grizer — *Wit* p.375-376
Guideposts — *Faith* p.259-263
Harral — *Feature* p.260
Liebman — *Peace* p.183-191, 199-203
Prochnow — *Public* #795
Prochnow — *Success.* #125, 1069, 1081
Simpson — *Contemp.* p.181-187
Woods — *Religious* p.795-797
, *and religion*
Bach — *Make* p.178-179

PSYCHIC PHENOMENA
Woods — *Religious* p.797-798

PSYCHOANALYSIS
Cerf — *Laugh* p.271-273
Curtis — *Practical* p.8
Edwards — *Useful* p.731
Flesch — *Unusual* p.230
Liebman — *Peace* p.29-34
Phillips — *Choice See* index p.428; p.250, 252, 263-264
Seldes — *Great* p.795
Sheen — *Way* p.128-130
Woods — *Religious* p.798-801

PSYCHOLOGY AND PSYCHOLOGISTS
Asimov — *Treasury* #192
Braude — *Speaker's* #1133-1134
Braude — *Stories* p.311
Curtis — *Practical* p.38-39
Du Noüy — *Human* p.9-10, 15, 17-18, 191-193, 208-209
Flesch — *Unusual* p.230
Flint — *Graham* p.112
Fox — *Make* p.212-213
Garland — *Subject* p.251-252
Hooker — *Index* p.17-36
Kennedy — *Reader's* #886-888
Keys Happiness p.358
Mandel — *Stories* p.214-215
Montapert — *Distilled* p.285
Phillips — *Choice* p.3, 249, 252, 254, 264
Prochnow — *Public* #1559
Prochnow — *Speaker's* p.249
Prochnow — *Success.* #1079
Seldes — *Great* p.795-796
Simpson — *Contemp.* p.181-187
Wheelis — *Moralist* p.7-8, 40-41
Woods — *Religious* p.731, 800-801
, *and religion*
Liebman — *Peace* p.176-203
, *Child*
Speaker's Desk #112, 201, 298, 769
, *Growth in*
Menninger — *Blue.* p.7
, *Reverse*
Ginott — *Between* p.43-44

PSYCHOSOMATIC MEDICINE
Holmes — *Design* p.75, 145, 154-155, 161
Reader's — *Getting* p.170-173

PUBLIC
See also **People; Society**
Edwards — *Useful* p.513-514
Flesch — *Unusual* p.230
Fogg — *1000* #619-620, 686, 702
Harnsberger — *Mark* p.387
Henry — *5000* p.230
Hovey — *Treasury* #37
Kin — *Dictionary* p.203
Lockridge — *World's* #3489
Seldes — *Great* p.796
, *Intelligence of*
Nizer — *Thinking* p.70

PUBLIC ADMINISTRATION
Grizer — *Wit* p.376-377
Hooker — *Index* p.87-98

PUBLIC OFFICE. *See* **Officials and officeholding**

PUBLIC OPINION
Adams — *New* p.306
Braude — *Source* #1391
Dirksen — *Quot.* #464-465, 643, 704, 748, 1047, 2358
Evans — *This* p.125-126
Evans — *Unto* p.77
Flesch — *Unusual* p.230
Fogg — *1000* #334

Forbes — *Thoughts* p.62, 148, 164, 468, 482
Grizer — *Wit* p.326-327
Harnsberger — *Mark* p.387-388
Humes — *Instant* #830-835
Ideas p.328-329
Johnson — *Bedside* p.125
Lockridge — *World's* #1070
New Joy p.66
Seldes — *Great* p.797-799
, *Court of*
Peale — *Guideposts* p.329-333

PUBLIC OWNERSHIP
Seldes — *Great* p.799

PUBLIC RELATIONS
See also **Publicity**
Fuller — *Thesaurus* #2111-2112
Prochnow — *Success.* #301
Seldes — *Great* p.799

PUBLIC SCHOOLS. *See* **Education; Schools**

PUBLIC SPEAKING. *See* **Speeches and speakers**

PUBLIC UTILITIES
Prochnow — *Speaker's* p.251

PUBLIC WELFARE
Dirksen — *Quot.* #1175
Evans — *Unto* p.29
Forbes — *Thoughts* p.242, 263, 267, 451, 471
Franke — *Buckley* p.320-321
Humes — *Instant* #1148
Johnson — *Bedside* p.198
Kauffman — *For* p.229-230
Seldes — *Great* p.977-978
Woods — *Religious* p.802

PUBLICANS, THE
New Topical p.213

PUBLICITY
See also **Advertising; Public relations**
Dirksen — *Quot.* #1783
Edwards — *Useful* p.731
Evans — *Unto* p.27, 78, 89-90
Hovey — *Treasury* p.261; #1649-1652
Hubbard — *Scrap* p.64
Nizer — *Thinking* p.193
Seldes — *Great* p.796-797
Speaker's Desk #855
Woods — *Business.* p.213-214

PUBLISHERS AND PUBLISHING
Braude — *Stories* p.323
George — *Book* p.8, 20, 292
Harnsberger — *Mark* p.388
Prochnow — *Public* #759
Seldes — *Great* p.799-800

PUERTO RICANS
Asimov — *Treasury* #466

PULLMANS
Braude — *Stories* p.323-324
Schermerhorn — *1500* p.296

PUMPKINS
Botkin — *Treasury* p.600-601
Kin — *Dictionary* p.204

"PUNCH LINES"
Asimov — *Treasury* #367
Fun Fare p.155

PUNCTUALITY
See also **Haste**
Braude — *Source* #1401-1403
Braude — *Stories* p.324-325
Edwards — *Useful* p.137-138, 507, 514
Flesch — *Unusual* p.230
Forbes — *Thoughts* p.209, 269, 393, 450, 490
Grizer — *Wit* p.377
Henry — *5000* p.221, 230
Kin — *Dictionary* p.201, 204
Liddle — *Thought I, II, III* p.11, 36, 66, 73, 125
Lockridge — *World's* #997
Lytle — *Leaves* p.131, 171, 173-174
Modern Eloquence (14) p.405
Prochnow — *Public* #965, 1290, 2124
Prochnow — *Speaker's* p.252
Prochnow — *Success.* #2200-2201

PUNCTUATION
Auden — *Certain* p.202-203
Fun Fare p.118
Prochnow — *Public* #248, 1953
Prochnow — *Speaker's* p.253
Schermerhorn — *1500* p.297

PUNISHMENT
See also **Capital punishment; Crime and criminals; Discipline; Justice; Law;** etc.
Braude — *Speaker's* #1164-1165
Edwards — *Useful* p.514-515
Evans — *Thoughts I* p.102, 108
Evans — *Thoughts III (Open Road)* p.66-67
Evans — *Thoughts IV* p.95, 97
Evans — *Unto* p.39, 117
Flesch — *Unusual* p.230-231

Forbes — *Thoughts* p.332, 407, 422, 496
Fuller — *Epigrams* p.245-246
Garland — *Subject* p.253
Grizer — *Wit* p.377
Harnsberger — *Mark* p.388-390
Henry — *5000* p.230-231
Hubbard — *Scrap* p.68, 111
Johnson — *Bedside* p.83
Kennedy — *Reader's* #889-891
Kin — *Dictionary* p.188, 204
Lair — *Baby* p.120-121
Lockridge — *World's* #5870
New Topical p.213-214
Prochnow — *Public* #517, 2353, 2472
Prochnow — *Speaker's* p.253-254
Seldes — *Great* p.800
Woods — *Religious* p.802-803

PUNS AND PUNSTERS
Asimov — *Treasury* #228, 240, 242-243, 250-251
Botkin — *Anecdotes* p.xxv
Cerf — *Laugh* p.303-311
Copeland — *10,000* p.850-869
Flesch — *Unusual* p.230
Fun Fare p.73, 308-309
Harnsberger — *Mark* p.390-391
Henry — *5000* p.230
Lockridge — *World's* #1184, 2670
Prochnow — *Speaker's* p.251-252
, Bilingual
Asimov — *Treasury* #625

PUPILS. *See* **Students**

PUPPETS
Irion — *Yes* p.67-68

PURCHASING POWER
Woods — *Business.* p.214-215

PURGATION
Phillips — *Choice* p.34, 42-64, 196, 244

PURGATORY. *See* **Hell**

PURGING
Applegarth — *Heir.* p.47
Lytle — *Leaves* p.122

PURIFICATION
See also **Baptism**
Lockridge — *World's* #3598
New Topical p.214-215

PURITANS AND PURITANISM
Auden — *Certain* p.313-314
Curtis — *Practical* p.317
Dirksen — *Quot.* #2344
Flesch — *Unusual* p.231
Hovey — *Treasury* #1285
Ideas p.330-331
Prochnow — *Success.* #2202
Seldes — *Great* p.800-801
Woods — *Religious* p.804-805
, Beliefs of
Keller — *You* p.28-29
, Humor of
Botkin — *Anecdotes* p.xxv

PURITY
See also **Chastity; Innocence; Perfection; Virtues**
Applegarth — *Heir.* p.255
Edwards — *Useful* p.515
Flesch — *Unusual* p.231
Forbes — *Thoughts* p.9, 143, 209, 478, 484
Garland — *Subject* p.253-254
Henry — *5000* p.231
Kennedy — *Reader's* #892
Kin — *Dictionary* p.204-205
Prochnow — *Public* #2486, 2600
Prochnow — *Speaker's* p.254
Woods — *Religious* p.805-806

PURPOSE
See also **Goals; Motivation and motives;** etc.
Braude — *Speaker's* #746-748
Curtis — *Daily* p.130
Curtis — *Human* p.167-182
Curtis — *Practical* p.101
Detherage — *Sunrise* p.67, 89, 115
Edwards — *Useful* p.301-302, 472-473, 515-516
Evans — *Faith* p.65-68, 81, 155
Evans — *This* p.132
Evans — *Thoughts I* p.120, 123-124
Evans — *Thoughts III (Open Road)* p.201; *See also* index no p.
Evans — *Unto* p.22, 48
Flesch — *Unusual* p.231
Flint — *Graham* p.113
Forbes — *Thoughts* p.80, 152, 278, 384, 519; *See also* index p.564
Fuller — *Epigrams* p.246
Garland — *Subject* p.254
Grizer — *Wit* p.377
Henry — *5000* p.136, 210
Hobe — *Tapestries* p.116-118
Holman — *Psych.* p.54-64
Hovey — *Treasury* p.261-262; *See also* index p.300
How To Live p.563-572
Humes — *Instant* #836-854
Keller — *You* p.38-59
Kin — *Dictionary* p.193, 205

Liddle — *Thought I, II, III* p.32-33, 150
Liddle — *Thought IV* p.29
Liddle — *Thought V* p.7
List — *Living* p.87-93
Lockridge — *World's* #1006, 1732, 1799, 1855, 1859, 3906
Lytle — *Leaves* p.134
Mandel — *Stories* p.215-216
Montapert — *Distilled* p.219-220, 286
Prochnow — *Public* #385, 3593
Prochnow — *Success.* #815, 1195, 1476, 1917-1918
Seldes — *Great* p.733
Speaker's Desk #252, 416, 438, 1084
Voss — *Quotations* p.205-208
Wallis — *Treasure* p.25, 70, 73, 155, 161, 212, 228
Wallis — *Words* p.122, 213
Watson — *Light* p.32-36
Welk — *Guide.* p.133-136
White — *Job* p.62, 64, 66, 76-77, 88, 101, 121-122, 139-140, 143
Woods — *Religious* p.806
, and pleasure
Hadfield — *Delights* p.77
, Consistent
Adams — *New* p.185
, Controlling
Kohn — *Touch* p.183-186
, of birth
Keller — *Open* p.121
, Singleness of
Braude — *Source* #1404
, Tenacity of
Book Proverbs p.74

PURSUIT
Edwards — *Useful* p.516
Flesch — *Unusual* p.231
Lytle — *Leaves* p.37
Prochnow — *Success.* #2203
Woods — *Religious* p.806

"PUSH"
See also **Ambition**
Peterson — *Art* p.31, 297
, and "pull"
Weisfeld — *Pulpit* p.27-28

PUSSY WILLOWS
Kohn — *Best* p.46-48

"PUT-DOWNS" (humor)
Asimov — *Treasury* p.124-158

PYRAMIDS
Flesch — *Unusual* p.231
Kin — *Dictionary* p.205
, men like
New Joy p.20

PYTHAGORAS
Lockridge — *World's* #4035

Q

QUACKERY
See also **Fraud;** etc.
Edwards — *Useful* p.516
Henry — *5000* p.231
Kin — *Dictionary* p.206

QUAKERS
Botkin — *Anecdotes* p.41, 64, 116-117, 138, 152, 180-181, 215
Fun Fare p.100-101
George — *Book* p.294, 423
Seldes — *Great* p.801
Speaker's Desk #501, 651
Woods — *Religious* p.806
, Rules of
Nichols — *New* p.217-218

QUALIFICATIONS
Braude — *Speaker's* #1166-1167
Hill — *Think* p.127-129
Lytle — *Leaves* p.63
Montapert — *Distilled* p.286-287
Speaker's Desk #116, 1182

QUALITIES
See also **Character;** names of qualities
Braude — *Source* #1405-1408
Edwards — *Useful* p.516-517
Evans — *Unto* p.3
Flesch — *Unusual* p.231
Forbes — *Thoughts* p.168, 175, 178, 219, 221, 239
Kin — *Dictionary* p.206
Lytle — *Leaves* p.116
New Joy p.28
Prochnow — *Success.* #2205
Woods — *Religious* p.806
, Enduring
Reader's — *20th* p.48-51

QUALITY
See also **Excellence**
Bartlett — *Discovery* p.33
Curtis — *Practical* p.51-52
Forbes — *Thoughts* p.2, 177, 190, 281, 333, 381, 513

Garland — *Subject* p.254-255
Grizer — *Wit* p.378
Henry — *5000* p.231
Kohn — *Thoughts* p.76-79
Lindeman — *Emerson* p.199
Montapert — *Distilled* p.287
Prochnow — *Public* #1969
, *versus quantity*
Adams — *New* p.133

QUANTITY
Garland — *Subject* p.255
Prochnow — *Public* #749

QUANTUM MECHANICS
Du Noüy — *Road* p.27, 52, 70, 86, 108, 229

QUARRELS
See also **Argument; Conflict; Hatred; Temper;** etc.
Book Proverbs p.112
Braude — *Source* #1409
Braude — *Stories* p.325
Dirksen — *Quot.* #187, 195, 699, 1184
Edwards — *Useful* p.517
Evans — *Thoughts I* p.21, 46-47, 55-59, 87-88, 103-104, 139
Evans — *Thoughts III (Open Road)* p.97, 211
Evans — *Thoughts IV* p.43, 49-50, 203-204, 210
Flesch — *Unusual* p.90, 231-232
Forbes — *Thoughts* p.50, 87, 175, 319, 321, 403, 412, 455, 490, 508
Fuller — *Epigrams* p.120-121, 247-248
Fuller — *Thesaurus* #466
Grizer — *Wit* p.378
Harral — *Feature* p.261
Henry — *5000* p.232
Hovey — *Treasury* p.183; #1035, 1039-1041, 1161, 1386, 1662, 1712
How To Live p.85-87
Huxley — *You See* index p.287
Johnson — *Bedside* p.302
Kin — *Dictionary* p.94, 206
Krishnamurti — *Think* p.28, 191-192
Lockridge — *World's* #523, 1426, 2881, 3657
Montapert — *Distilled* p.154-155
New Joy p.16
Peale — *Courage* p.23
Prochnow — *Public* #423, 912, 937, 1657, 2738, 4099-4100, 4198
Prochnow — *Speaker's* p.254
Prochnow — *Success.* #1040
Seldes — *Great* p.360-362
Speaker's Desk #11, 18, 53, 95, 188, 194, 259, 293, 385, 437, 451, 1046
Walters — *How* p.89-96
Woods — *Religious* p.334, 807
, *Marital*
Holmes — *I've* p.46-47

QUEENS AND KINGS. *See* **Kings and queens**

QUEST. *See* **Search**

QUESTIONNAIRES
Prochnow — *Public* #518

QUESTIONS
See also **Curiosity;** etc.
Applegarth — *Heir.* p.263
Carruthers — *Sparks* p.35-72
Dirksen — *Quot.* #1022, 1048-1049, 2014, 2139
Edwards — *Useful* p.32, 295, 517
Flesch — *Unusual* p.14, 232
Flint — *Graham* p.76
Harral — *Feature* p.261
Henry — *5000* p.232
Hovey — *Treasury* p.262; *See also* index p.300
Humes — *Instant* #855
Keys Happiness p.385-388
Kin — *Dictionary* p.15, 207
Krishnamurti — *Think* p.149-150
Lockridge — *World's* #826
Lytle — *Leaves* p.32, 153
Montapert — *Distilled* p.24, 287-288
Nichols — *Third* p.28-29
Peterson — *Art* p.341
Prochnow — *Public* #134, 264, 445, 635, 930, 935, 1111, 1925, 2621
Prochnow — *Success.* #2206-2207
Seldes — *Great* p.801
Wallis — *Treasure* p.210, 232
Wallis — *Words* p.93, 146
, *Answers to*
Braude — *Source* #1410-1412
, *Anticipation of*
Manchee — *Secret* p.79-81
, *Difficult*
Speaker's Desk See index p.304
, *Meaningless*
Curtis — *Practical* p.43-45

"QUIBBLES"
Botkin — *Anecdotes* p.xxv

"QUICKIES"
Cerf — *Laugh* p.35-39

QUICKSAND
Kin — *Dictionary* p.207

QUIET. *See* **Peace; Silence;** etc.

QUIETISM
Ideas p.331-333
Wheelis — *Moralist* p.19

QUILTS
Harral — *Feature* p.261-262

QUITTERS AND QUITTING
Carruthers — *Sparks* p.141-143
Evans — *Thoughts III (Open Road)* p.145
Halverson — *Perspective* p.54
Kauffman — *For* p.181
Kennedy — *Fresh* p.167-176
Kin — *Dictionary* p.208
Prochnow — *Public* #469

QUOTATIONS
See also **Proverbs; Sayings**
Braude — *Source* #1413-1414
Cerf — *Laugh* p.459-465
Curtis — *Practical* p.23
Edwards — *Useful* p.380-381, 518-520, 661
Flesch — *Unusual* p.4, 11, 212, 232-233, 295
Fun Fare p.64-65, 155, 289
Harnsberger — *Mark* p.259
Keys Happiness p.30
Kin — *Dictionary* p.191, 225
Lockridge — *World's* #1991, 5499, 5510, 5603, 5614, 5630
Lytle — *Leaves* p.100, 113, 165
Montapert — *Distilled* p.19-20
Nichols — *Third* p.182-183
Prochnow — *Public* #382, 580, 3594-3597
Prochnow — *Success.* #1251, 2033
Seldes — *Great* p.733
Woods — *Religious* p.738
, and "cross-quotemanship"
Humes — *Instant* p.36-37
, as "contemporary antiquities"
Humes — *Instant* p.39-40
, as paragraph starters
Humes — *Instant* p.37-39
, Curious
Kronenberger — *Animal* p.48-56
, Favorite
Peterson — *Art* p.373
, of Benjamin Franklin
New Joy p.79
, Use of in speeches
Nizer — *Thinking* p.80, 210

R

RABBIS
Asimov — *Treasury See* index p.428
Fuller — *Thesaurus* #1486-1488
Kin — *Dictionary* p.209
Peale — *Guideposts* p.278-280
Weisfeld — *Pulpit See index* under Rabbis

RABBITS
Auden — *Certain* p.177-180
Irion — *Yes* p.100-104
Kin — *Dictionary* p.116
Kohn — *Pathways* p.147-149
Prochnow — *Public* #1231, 1493, 1778, 2174, 3688
, "Brer" stories of
Botkin — *Treasury* p.358, 408, 653-669, 674, 720

"RABBLE-ROUSING"
Kin — *Dictionary* p.209

RABELAIS, FRANÇOIS
Lockridge — *World's* #2480

RACCOONS
Botkin — *Treasury* p.15, 19, 25, 663

RACES AND RACING
Dirksen — *Quot.* #761, 1583, 1710
Harnsberger — *Mark* p.392-393
Peterson — *Art* p.157
Prochnow — *Public* #296, 825

RACES OF MAN
Copeland — *10,000* p.641-764
Flint — *Graham* p.113-114
Henry — *5000* p.232
Hovey — *Treasury* p.263-264; #94, 249, 264, 355, 373, 493, 508, 708, 1206, 1276, 1633, 1661-1666, 1839
Lockridge — *World's* #2777
Prochnow — *Speaker's* p.255
Seldes — *Great* p.801-804
Wallis — *Treasure* p.161-162
Woods — *Religious* p.807
, Brain and
Du Noüy — *Human* p.142-143

, *Colored*
Bartlett — *Discovery* p.88-90
, *Concept of*
Curtis — *Practical* p.149-156
, *Relations of*
See also **Civil rights; Equality; Prejudice**
Asimov — *Treasury* #115, 435-436
Braude — *Source* #1415-1422
Dirksen — *Quot.* #34, 761
Droke — *Christian* p.441-444
Flint — *Graham* p.87, 114
Garland — *Subject* p.94
Guideposts — *Faith* p.287-290
Hovey — *Treasury See* index p.304
Ideas p.49-51, 190-192
Kauffman — *For* p.181-182
Kennedy — *Reader's* #901-908
Knight's Illus. p.262-266
Lockridge — *World's* #5272
Myers — *Thunder* p.103
Peterson — *Art* p.39
Rogers — *Time* p.85-90
Strait — *Speaker's* p.139-145
Voss — *Quotations* p.208-209
Woods — *Religious* p.807-813

RACINE, WISCONSIN
Lockridge — *World's* #1600, 1655, 1668, 2482

RADIANCE. *See* **Light**

RADICALS AND RADICALISM
Bartlett — *Discovery* p.25-26
Dirksen — *Quot.* #560, 1785
Flesch — *Unusual* p.233
Harnsberger — *Instant* #856-862
Lockridge — *World's* #4609
Prochnow — *Public* #1292
Seldes — *Great* p.804-805
Woods — *Religious* p.813

RADIO
Asimov — *Treasury* #20, 295, 432
Fun Fare p.123-124, 199, 231, 287
Harral — *Feature* p.262-263
Prochnow — *Public* #199, 948
Prochnow — *Speaker's* p.255-256
Prochnow — *Success.* #421, 1094
Simpson — *Contemp.* p.400-406
Simpson — *'54* p.81, 231, 345
, *Announcers of*
Unlimited Power p.131-134
, *Broadcasting*
Prochnow — *Success.* #444, 447
, *Gags of*
Copeland — *10,000* p.584-603
, *Prediction of*
Fogg — *1000* #1096
, *Singers on*
Unlimited Power p.244-246

RAFTSMEN
Botkin — *Treasury* p.50, 837-843

RAGE. *See* **Anger**

"RAGS TO RICHES"
Cerf — *Laugh* p.177-191

RAILLERY. *See* **Humor; Sarcasm;** etc.

RAILROADS
See also **Trains**
Botkin — *Anecdotes* p.11, 42, 66, 70, 231
Botkin — *Treasury* p.488, 520, 629
Copeland — *10,000* p.94-99
Fun Fare p.309-313
Harnsberger — *Mark* p.393-394
Harral — *Feature* p.264-265
Hubbard — *Scrap* p.70
Prochnow — *Speaker's* p.256-257
Prochnow — *Success.* #122, 133, 274, 745
Schermerhorn — *1500* p.302-304
, *Elevated*
Asimov — *Treasury* #229
, *Engineers of*
Peale — *Guideposts* p.313-317
, *"Rawhide"*
Botkin — *Treasury* p.520
, *Stations of*
Guideposts — *Faith* p.313-317

RAIN
See also **Storms;** types of storms
Alexander's Treasure. p.199, 216, 236
Asimov — *Treasury* #236
Auden — *Certain* p.398
Edwards — *Useful* p.521
Flesch — *Unusual* p.233
Goudge — *Comfort* p.30-32
Henry — *5000* p.232-233
Hobe — *Tapestries* p.56
Hubbard — *Scrap* p.113
Kin — *Dictionary* p.209
Kohn — *Pathways* p.55-58
New Joy p.204-205
New Topical p.215-216

Peale — *Courage* p.126, 182-183
Prochnow — *Public* #39, 145, 174, 355, 1408, 2258
Prochnow — *Speaker's* p.257
Prochnow — *Success.* #1078, 1112, 2209-2210
Wallis — *Treasure* p.181, 227
Weisfeld — *Pulpit* p.77, 80-81

RAINBOWS
Curtis — *Practical* p.199
Edwards — *Useful* p.521
Flesch — *Unusual* p.233
Goudge — *Comfort* p.32-34
Henry — *5000* p.233
Johnson — *Bedside* p.44
Keller — *Open* p.101
Wallis — *Words* p.97
White — *Job* p.86-87
Woods — Wellsprings p.39-40

RAINCOATS
Prochnow — *Public* #194

RAISES. *See* **Wages, Raises in**

RANCHERS AND RANCHING
Botkin — *Anecdotes* p.35, 85, 199
Prochnow — *Success.* #1044

RANCOR. *See* **Resentment**

RANK
See also **Ancestry; Distinction; Nobility; Position;** etc.
Edwards — *Useful* p.521-522, 614-615
Fuller — *Epigrams* p.248
Kin — *Dictionary* p.209
Lockridge — *World's* #4363

RASHNESS
See also **Haste; Impulse**
Baillie — *Diary* #80
Book Proverbs p.102
Edwards — *Useful* p.522, 529-530
Kennedy — *Reader's* #87
Kin — *Dictionary* p.210
Lockridge — *World's* #3823
Prochnow — *Public* #194, 1780-1782
Sheen — *Thoughts* p.126-127
Woods — *Religious* p.813

"RAT RACE"
Kauffman — *For* p.208-209

RATIONALISM
Adams — *New* p.202
Evans — *Thoughts III (Open Road)* p.201
Holmes — *Design* p.99-100
Menninger — *Blue.* p.27-28
Seldes — *Great* p.805
Wheelis — *Moralist* p.29
Woods — *Religious* p.813-814
, Definition of
Curtis — *Practical* p.55

RATIONING
Asimov — *Treasury* #282
Fuller — *Thesaurus* #2356-2358

RATS
Harral — *Feature* p.265
Kin — *Dictionary* p.210

RATTLESNAKES
Botkin — *Anecdotes* p.74, 226
Botkin — *Treasury* p.175-176, 182, 268, 379, 565, 622

RAVENS
Kin — *Dictionary* p.210
New Topical p.216

RAYON
Asimov — *Treasury* #542

REACHING
How To Live p.12-39, 266-268
Kin — *Dictionary* p.210
Nichols — *New* p.197-198
Peterson — *Art* p.73

REACTION
Forbes — *Thoughts* p.16, 211, 268
Halverson — *Perspective* p.57
Kennedy — *Reader's* #909

REACTIONARIES
Dirksen — *Quot.* #560
Humes — *Instant* #863-869
Lockridge — *World's* #2791
Seldes — *Great* p.805-806

READERS
Harnsberger — *Mark* p.394-397

READINESS
Book Proverbs p.130
Garland — *Subject* p.257-258

READING. *See* **Books and reading; Learning; Study**

REAL ESTATE
Braude — *Speaker's* #1169-1170
Copeland — *10,000* p.437-439
Fuller — *Thesaurus* #2141-2142
Harral — *Feature* p.267
Prochnow — *Speaker's* p.257
Prochnow — *Success.* #419
Schermerhorn — *1500* p.305-307

, Agents for
Manchee — *Secret* p.223-224
Weisfeld — *Pulpit* p.88

REALISM
Edwards — *Useful* p.731
Flesch — *Unusual* p.235
Humes — *Instant* #870-875
Kennedy — *Reader's* #916-917
Kin — *Dictionary* p.210
Lockridge — *World's* #966, 3621
Speaker's Desk #271, 354, 548
, Highest
Dirksen — *Quot.* #627

REALITY
See also **Facts; Truth**
Curtis — *Practical* p.7-9, 11, 21, 35-37
Dirksen — *Quot.* #1787
Du Noüy — *Road* p.39-40, 52, 55, 70-71
Esteve — *Experience* p.97-101
Evans — *Thoughts III (Open Road)* p.116
Evans — *Unto* p.8, 21, 63, 107, 118
Flesch — *Unusual* p.235
Forbes — *Thoughts* p.25, 289, 329, 428, 461
Garland — *Subject* p.258
Grizer — *Wit* p.381
Halverson — *Perspective* p.62
Holmes — *Design* p.11-14, 29, 40-41, 55, 78, 87, 91, 109, 115, 123-125, 180
Hovey — *Treasury* #1038
How To Live p.303-434
Johnson — *Bedside* p.41, 127, 137, 139
Kennedy — *Fresh* p.137-145
Kohn — *Best* p.106-108
Lockridge — *World's* #2969
Lytle — *Leaves* p.11, 110
Mandel — *Stories* p.216
Montapert — *Distilled* p.289
Phillips — *Choice See* index p.428
Prochnow — *Success.* #827
Wallis — *Words* p.143
Webb — *Edge* p.22-28
White — *Job* p.39-41, 45, 109
Woods — *Religious* p.814-817
Woods — *Wellsprings* p.30
, Dealing with
Menninger — *Blue.* p.13-20
, Escape from
Flint — *Graham* p.115
, Facing
Maltz — *Creative* p.138-140
, Ideal and
Curtis — *Practical* p.522-527
, Observing
Adams — *New* p.62
, Presence of
Woods — *Religious* p.814
, Sensitivity to
Krishnamurti — *Think* p.151-158
, Ultimate
Kauffman — *For* p.217-218

REALIZATION
Fox — *Make* p.131
Kauffman — *For* p.182-183
Woods — *Religious* p.817

REAPERS AND REAPING
Book Proverbs p.123
Hobe — *Tapestries* p.80
Kin — *Dictionary* p.210
Lockridge — *World's* #5256
New Topical p.216
Prochnow — *Public* #2589, 2654, 2721-2722

REASON AND REASONING
See also **Common sense; Intelligence; Judgment; Logic, Thought; Wisdom;** etc.
Alexander's Treasure. p.192
Curtis — *Practical* p.4, 103, 124-125, 275
Dirksen — *Quot.* #479, 538, 1051, 2345, 2362
Edwards — *Useful* p.527-529, 731
Flesch — *Unusual* p.235-236
Forbes — *Thoughts See* index p.564
Fuller — *Epigrams* p.248-249
Garland — *Subject* p.259-260
Grizer — *Wit* p.381-382
Harnsberger — *Mark* p.397
Henry — *5000* p.233-234
Hovey — *Treasury* #11, 76, 1646
Hubbard — *Scrap* p.42, 75, 97, 123
Humes — *Instant* #876-879
Kin — *Dictionary* p.210-211
Liddle — *Thought I, II, III* p.126, 149, 158
Liddle — *Thought IV* p.10, 29
Liddle — *Thought V* p.17
Lockridge — *World's See* index p.582
Lytle — *Leaves* p.24, 30, 65, 102, 108
Montapert — *Distilled* p.289-290
Prochnow — *Public* #98, 196, 395, 691, 737, 892, 923, 3607-3615
Prochnow — *Speaker's* p.257
Prochnow — *Success.* #2216-2219
Seldes — *Great* p.806-808
Sheban — *Wisdom* no p.

Speaker's Desk p.213-214; #286, 288, 379, 422, 477, 602, 643, 863, 1077, 1144, 1146, 1165
Wheelis — *Moralist* p.7, 22, 32, 84, 114-116
Woods — *Religious* p.817-820
, and faith. See **Faith, and reason**
, and religion
Holman — *Psych.* p.166-178
Woods — *Religious* p.819-820
, Mechanisms of
Du Noüy — *Human* p.5-6, 12, 232

REASSURANCE. *See* **Encouragement**

REBELLION
See also **Discontent; Disobedience**
Edwards — *Useful* p.529
Evans — *Thoughts IV* p.144
Fogg — *1000* #407, 414, 419, 556, 668, 813, 890, 911, 934, 990, 1100, 1105, 1112, 1798
Garland — *Subject* p.69
Henry — *5000* p.234
Huxley — *You See* index p.287
Kennedy — *Reader's* #918-920
Seldes — *Great* p.808-811
Sheban — *Wisdom* no p.
Wheelis — *Moralist* p.51-52, 55-63, 142-143
Woods — *Religious* p.820-821
, of teenagers
Ginott — *Between* p.21-46

REBIRTH. *See* **Reincarnation**

REBUKE. *See* **Criticism**

RECEIVING
Flesch — *Unusual* p.236
Johnson — *Bedside* p.201
Kin — *Dictionary* p.211
Peterson — *Art* p.178
Prochnow — *Public* #2678, 2692

RECEPTIVITY
Garland — *Subject* p.260-261
Lockridge — *World's* #4581
, Psychic
White — *Job* p.120
, Spiritual
White — *Job* p.118-121, 174-175, 186

RECESSION. *See* **Depression, Business**

RECHABITES
New Topical p.217

RECIPES
Lytle — *Leaves* p.146, 166
Prochnow — *Public* #438, 714
Wallis — *Words* p.35, 49, 146

RECIPROCITY
Kin — *Dictionary* p.211
Mandel — *Stories* p.216
Weisfeld — *Pulpit* p.132

RECKLESSNESS. *See* **Boldness; Carelessness; Rashness;** etc.

RECOGNITION
Braude — *Speaker's* #1171-1172
Flesch — *Unusual* p.236
Ginott — *Between* p.49-59
Grizer — *Wit* p.382
Harnsberger — *Mark* p.398
Kin — *Dictionary* p.211
Mandel — *Stories* p.216

RECOLLECTION. *See* **Memory (faculty) and Memories**

RECOMMENDATION
Flesch — *Unusual* p.236
Prochnow — *Public* #683

RECOMPENSE. *See* **Compensation**

RECONCILIATION
See also **Forgiveness**
Evans — *Thoughts I* p.43, 81, 122
Evans — *Thoughts III (Open Road)* p.96-98
Garland — *Subject* p.261
Hovey — *Treasury* #39, 81, 115, 334, 721, 726, 753, 1709
Kin — *Dictionary* p.211
Lockridge — *World's* #85
More Words p.129-130
Prochnow — *Public* #637
Woods — *Religious* p.821
, and the Church
Kauffman — *For* p.183

RECORD
Dirksen — *Quot.* #2352
Evans — *Thoughts I* p.11-12, 90
Evans — *Thoughts III (Open Road)* p.151-152, 160, 201, 211
Evans — *Thoughts IV* p.33, 67-68, 119, 187
Harral — *Feature* p.267
Prochnow — *Success.* #1349

RECREATION
See also **Amusements; Hobbies; Leisure; Sports;** types of recreation
Braude — *Source* #1435-1440
Droke — *Christian* p.444-446

Edwards — *Useful* p.530
Forbes — *Thoughts* p.12, 16, 100, 115, 317
Fuller — *Thesaurus* p.313-331
Harral — *Feature* p.267-268
Hooker — *Index* p.283-291
Lockridge — *World's* #4485
, *Need for*
Albert — *Stop* p.47-48

RED CROSS
Harral — *Feature* p.268-269

"RED HERRINGS"
Prochnow — *Public* #2373

REDEEMER. *See* **Jesus Christ**

REDEMPTION
See also **Christianity; Forgiveness; Salvation**; etc.
Dirksen — *Quot.* #1528-1530
Edwards — *Useful* p.531
Flint — *Graham* p.115-116
Garland — *Subject* p.261-262
Halverson — *Perspective* p.55, 83
Hovey — *Treasury* #90, 451, 491, 504, 525, 582, 629, 719, 721, 1440, 1451
Johnson — *Bedside* p.319
Kauffman — *For* p.49-50
More Words p.131, 133
New Topical p.217-218
Woods — *Religious* p.821-822
, *Doctrines about*
New Topical p.307-319

REDUCING
See also **Diet; Overweight**
Prochnow — *Public* #932, 1784
Prochnow — *Success.* #1352
Schermerhorn — *1500* p.15

REFERENCE
Prochnow — *Public* #508, 839
Prochnow — *Speaker's* p.257

REFINEMENT
See also **Breeding; Delicacy; Etiquette; Taste**
Edwards — *Useful* p.531-532
Flesch — *Unusual* p.236
Harnsberger — *Mark* p.398
Lockridge — *World's* #131, 2258

REFLECTION
See also **Contemplation; Meditation; Self-analysis; Thought**
Adams — *New* p.147
Bennett — *How* p.69-75
Book Proverbs p.116
Braude — *Source* #1485-1487
Detherage — *Sunrise* p.181-186
Dirksen — *Quot.* #280
Edwards — *Useful* p.532, 553
Evans — *Unto* p.19
Felleman — *Poems* p.291-317
Flesch — *Unusual* p.237
Forbes — *Thoughts* p.286, 413, 422, 482
Garland — *Subject* p.262
Harnsberger — *Mark* p.398
Kin — *Dictionary* p.212
Lockridge — *World's* #4303
Lytle — *Leaves* p.59, 105
Montapert — *Distilled* p.290-291
Prochnow — *Speaker's* p.258
Speaker's Desk #37
Woods — *Religious* p.822

REFLEXES
Du Noüy — *Human* p.122, 131, 212-213
Kin — *Dictionary* p.212
, *Conditioned*
Du Noüy — *Human* p.122-123, 131, 212-213

REFORM AND REFORMERS
See also **Improvement; Progress; Repentance**
Braude — *Stories* p.325-326
Curtis — *Practical* p.378-379
Dirksen — *Quot.* #362, 1052, 1166, 2141
Droke — *Christian* p.446-448
Edwards — *Useful* p.532-533, 731
Evans — *Thoughts III (Open Road)* p.26
Flesch — *Unusual* p.237
Forbes — *Thoughts* p.23, 32, 148, 230, 389, 410, 512
Fuller — *Epigrams* p.249
Harnsberger — *Mark* p.398-400
Henry — *5000* p.235
Humes — *Instant* p.29-30; #880-899, 1258-1259
Kennedy — *Reader's* #921-923
Kin — *Dictionary* p.212
Liddle — *Thought I, II, III* p.5, 175
Lockridge — *World's* #937, 3718, 3768
Peterson — *Art* p.100
Prochnow — *Public* #769, 1291, 1785
Prochnow — *Speaker's* p.258
Prochnow — *Success.* #1211, 2220, 2225
Seldes — *Great* p.811-813
Speaker's Desk p.214-218
Woods — *Business* p.216-217
Woods — *Religious* p.822-825
, *Schools for*
Guideposts — *Faith* p.38-40

, *Social (1841)*
Lindeman — *Emerson* p.23-38

REFORMATION, THE
Fogg — *1000* #105, 165, 333, 408, 444, 532, 541, 874, 882
Phillips — *Choice* p.120n, 153, 242
Seldes — *Great* p.813
Woods — *Religious* p.823-824
, *Vocabulary of*
Auden — *Certain* p.314-315

REFRIGERATORS
Holmes — *I've* p.33-34
Prochnow — *Public* #840

REFUGEES
Fuller — *Thesaurus* #2361
Nizer — *Thinking* p.166, 168, 181-183
, *Industries of*
Nizer — *Thinking* p.182

REFUSAL
Alexander's Treasure. p.72
Braude — *Source* #1441-1442
Dirksen — *Quot.* #1018
Flesch — *Unusual* p.189, 238
Guideposts — *Faith* p.143-146
Humes — *Instant* #298-303
Keys Happiness p.435
Kin — *Dictionary* p.175, 212
Lockridge — *World's* #231, 2406
More Words p.133-135
Peale — *Sin* p.42-44
Prochnow — *Public* #1786, 2367, 2510
Prochnow — *Success.* #2084, 2226
Reader's — *Getting* p.250
Woods — *Religious* p.826

REGARD. *See* **Admiration; Esteem; Respect;** etc.

REGENERATION
Flint — *Graham* p.116
Garland — *Subject* p.263-264
Keller — *Open* p.24
Kohn — *Through* p.33-35
White — *Job* p.86-88
, *Environmental and spiritual*
Sheen — *Thoughts* p.52-54

REGIMENTATION. *See* **Regulations**

REGRET
See also **Conscience; Grief; Repentance; Self-blame**
Albert — *Stop* p.68-69, 88-89, 102-104
Braude — *Stories* p.326
Edwards — *Useful* p.732
Evans — *Faith* p.64, 88, 102, 112, 123-124, 149
Evans — *This* p.143-144
Evans — *Thoughts I* p.55-56, 79-80, 127-130, 140
Evans — *Thoughts III (Open Road)* p.195
Evans — *Thoughts IV* p.85, 191, 199, 206
Evans — *Unto* p.72, 105, 131
Flesch — *Unusual* p.238
Fogg — *1000* #159, 235, 529, 539, 644, 658, 957
Forbes — *Thoughts* p.71, 243, 429, 468
Garland — *Subject* p.264
How To Live p.275-279
Johnson — *Bedside* p.19
Kin — *Dictionary* p.212
Lockridge — *World's* #1442, 2591, 2600
Lytle — *Leaves* p.123
Prochnow — *Public* #2321
Sheban — *Wisdom* no p.
Speaker's Desk #908
Wallis — *Treasure* p.19, 124, 156

REGULATIONS
See also **Order**
Dirksen — *Quot.* #705
Evans — *Unto* p.58, 66
Flesch — *Unusual* p.238
Forbes — *Thoughts* p.174, 483, 508
Prochnow — *Success.* #2227-2229

REHABILITATION
Huxley — *You See* index p.287

REINCARNATION
Bach — *Make* p.199-201
Phillips — *Choice* p.38, 47, 94-98, 127, 258
Prochnow — *Public* #1023
Woods — *Religious* p.825-826

"REJECTION SLIPS"
Fun Fare p.283

"REJOINDERS"
See also **Answers**
Humes — *Instant* p.52
Speaker's Desk See index p.304

REJUVENATION
Speaker's Desk #602, 941

RELATIONSHIPS
Adams — *New* p.378

Forbes — *Thoughts* p.75, 218, 250, 265, 284, 308, 347, 364, 448, 469-470, 472, 479, 482, 510
Krishnamurti — *Urgency* p.27-33
Lindbergh — *Gift* p.64-76
Menninger — *Blue.* p.35-36, 98-106
Phillips — *Choice See* index p.428
Pullar-Strecker — *Proverbs* #72-102
Watson — *Light* p.185-212
Welk — *Guide.* p.147-149
White — *Job* p.49-50
, Personal
Curtis — *Golden* p.164-173
Huxley — *You See* appendix p.279-282

RELATIVES
See also **Family;** names of relatives
Braude — *Speaker's* #1173-1174
Braude — *Stories* p.326-327
Flesch — *Unusual* p.238
Henry — *5000* p.235
Hubbard — *Scrap* p.19
Kin — *Dictionary* p.212-213
Lockridge — *World's* #1806
Prochnow — *Success.* #555, 2230
Sheban — *Wisdom* no p.
Wallis — *Treasure* p.25, 41

RELATIVITY
Botkin — *Anecdotes* p.185
Curtis — *Practical* p.236-238
Grizer — *Wit* p.382-383
Liddle — *Thought I, II, III* p.62
Woods — *Religious* p.826
, of time
Du Noüy — *Human* p.199-200
, Theory of
Asimov — *Treasury* #135
Saturday — *Advent.* p.219-236

RELAXATION
See also **Recreation; Rest; Sports;** etc.
Albert — *Stop* p.66, 71-76, 125-127, 157
Casselberry — *How* p.96, 144, 171, 175-176
Curtis — *Practical* p.64-67, 81
Evans — *Faith* p.26, 35-36, 145, 149-150
Evans — *Thoughts III (Open Road)* p.55
Flesch — *Unusual* p.238-239
Forbes — *Thoughts* p.128, 130, 232
Fox — *Make* p.5, 23
Fuller — *Thesaurus* #1786
Grizer — *Wit* p.383
Halverson — *Perspective* p.49
How To Live p.212-215
Hubbard — *Scrap* p.196
Huxley — *You See* index p.287
Johnson — *Bedside* p.61, 256, 258-276, 282
Keys Happiness p.123, 142-145
Liddle — *Thought IV* p.6, 10, 17
Montapert — *Distilled* p.291
Peterson — *Art* p.43
Prochnow — *Speaker's* p.259
Sherman — *Your* p.36-39
, Art of
Peterson — *Twenty* p.34-35
, Mental
Keys Happiness p.499-502

RELIABILITY. *See* **Dependability; Integrity; Self-reliance**

RELICS
Woods — *Religious* p.826

RELIEF
See also **Public Welfare**
Botkin — *Anecdotes* p.5, 246
Peale — *Guideposts* p.51-53
Prochnow — *Public* #792
Woods — *Business.* p.217-218

RELIGION
See also **Belief; Catholicism; Christianity; Church; Creeds, Denominations; Faith; God; Holiness; Jesus Christ; Jews; Protestantism; Worship;** etc.
Alexander's Treasure. p.131
Applegarth — *Heir.* p.12-13, 27, 86, 93, 149, 206, 260-261, 296
Asimov — *Treasury* p.311-344
Baillie — *Diary* #220
Barrows — *1000 See* index p.444-445
Bartlett — *Discovery* p.134-135
Book Proverbs p.132-135
Botkin — *Anecdotes* p.111-132
Braude — *Source* #1443-1468
Braude — *Speaker's* #1175-1179
Braude — *Stories* p.327-331
Cerf — *Laugh* p.231-239
Curtis — *Daily* p.198-204
Curtis — *Practical* p.73, 316-317, 500-504, 520, 541
Detherage — *Sunrise* p.43, 68, 97-100, 170, 199
Dirksen — *Quot.* #98-99, 186, 237, 384, 399, 486, 612, 707-708, 816, 1021, 1788-1789, 2357

Droke — *Christian* p.449-468
Du Noüy — *Human See* index p.287
Edwards — *Useful* p.534-543, 732
Evans — *Faith* p.46
Evans — *This* p.158-160
Evans — *Unto* p.32, 120, 123
Flesch — *Unusual* p.239-242
Flint — *Graham* p.46, 70, 116-118
Fogg — *1000* p.836, 874, 1118
Forbes — *Thoughts See* index p.565
Francis — *Buckley* p.254-255
Fuller — *Epigrams* p.250-251
Garland — *Subject* p.266-267
Harnsberger — *Mark* p.400-402
Harral — *Feature* p.269
Henry — *5000* p.236
Holmes — *Design* p.165-166, 172-173, 196
Hooker — *Index* p.37-45
Hovey — *Treasury* p.264; *See* index p.300
Hubbard — *Scrap* p.13, 15, 30, 32, 41, 47, 51, 104, 149, 208, 227
Humes — *Instant* #899-904
Huxley — *You See* index p.287
Johnson — *Bedside* p.12, 16-18, 34-39, 52-53, 168-188, 192-194, 211, 213-214, 232, 249, 319, 335
Kahn — *Lessons* p.25-29
Kauffman — *For* p.184-186
Kennedy — *Reader's* #924-941
Keys Happiness p.97-99, 103-106, 422-425, 575
Kin — *Dictionary* p.213
Krishnamurti — *Think* p.35-37, 151-158
Lair — *Baby* p.189
Liddle — *Thought I, II, III See* index p.199
Liddle — *Thought IV* p.42, 44
Liddle — *Thought V* p.14, 21, 24, 35
Lockridge — *World's See* index p.582
Lytle — *Leaves* p.68, 73, 88, 108
Mandel — *Stories* p.217-220
Mandelbaum — *Choose* p.22-23
Modern Eloquence (14) p.407-408
Montapert — *Distilled* p.291-293
More Words p.135-136
Nizer — *Thinking* p.87, 125-126, 204, 206, 209
Patterns For Living p.620-704
Phillips — *Choice* p.81, 307, 355; *See also* index p.428
Prochnow — *Public* #1562, 2309, 3615, 3641
Prochnow — *Speaker's* p.260-262
Prochnow — *Success.* #155, 2231-2237
Reader's — *Getting* p.125-128, 183-185
Sagendorph — *Old* p.40-42
Schermerhorn — *1500* p.309
Seldes — *Great* p.813-830
Sheban — *Wisdom* no p.
Sheen — *Thoughts* p.171-190
Simpson — *Contemp.* p.203-207
Simpson — *'54* p.83, 235, 348
Speaker's Desk p.218-224; #133, 221, 492, 519, 869, 978, 997, 1144
Tanksley — *Friend* p.63
Voss — *Quotations* p.210-212
Wallis — *Treasure* p.87, 131, 191, 205-212
Wallis — *Words* p.49, 62, 71, 86, 132, 240
Weisfeld — *Pulpit* p.29
White — *Job* p.149-156, 177
Woods — *Religious* p.826-847
Zobell — *Speaker's* p.116-117

, and art
Baillie — *Diary* #271
, and biology
Fogg — *1000* #550
, and health
Holman — *Psych.* p.155-165
, and love
Liebman — *Peace* p.78-80
, and magic
Adams — *New* p.281
, and mind
Taylor — *With* p.76
, and morals
Fuller — *Thesaurus* p.259-294
, and philosophy
Copeland — *World's See* index p.738
, and psychology
Liebman — *Peace* p.176-203
, and science
Baillie — *Diary* #228
Irion — *Yes* p.134-145
, Anglican
Simpson — *Contemp.* p.207-212
, as an ambulance
Sheen — *Thoughts* p.175-176
, Beginning of
Taylor — *With* p.67-69
, beyond reason
Holman — *Psych.* p.166-178
, Center of
Baillie — *Diary* #251
, Comparative
Woods — *Religious* p.169-170
, Conflict of
Woods — *Religious* p.847-848

, *Convictions of*
Flint — *Graham* p.118
, *Criticism of*
Carruthers — *Sparks* p.48-49
Ideas p.334-335
Woods — *Religious* p.832-834
, *Crutch or Cross of*
Sheen — *Thoughts* p.119-120
, *Decline of*
Woods — *Religious* p.839-840
, *Definitions of*
Flesch — *Unusual* p.239
Woods — *Religious* p.834-839
, *Depth of*
Kohn — *Through* p.55-57
, *Devoutness in*
Fuller — *Thesaurus* #1601-1602
Taylor — *With* p.113-115
, *Education for*
Flint — *Graham* p.104-105, 118
How To Live p.128-132
Wallis — *Treasure* p.89
Woods — *Religious* p.267-268
, *Enjoyment of*
Carruthers — *Sparks* p.87-89
, *Everyday*
White — *Life* p.275-288
, *Examples of*
Baillie — *Diary* #224
, *Experience of*
Peale — *Guideposts* p.20-21
Woods — *Religious* p.307-309
, *Faith in*
See also **Faith**
Keys Happiness p.412-417
, *False*
Carruthers — *Sparks* p.19-20
Woods — *Religious* p.324
, *Formalism*
Edwards — *Useful* p.204
, *Freedom of*
Dirksen — *Quot.* #402, 412, 708, 915
McDonagh — *Invit.* p.168-182
Voss — *Quotations* p.212-214
, *Groups in*
Humes — *Instant* #30-31, 1203-1204
, *Help of*
Albert — *Stop* p.140-142, 200
, *Honesty in*
Kauffman — *For* p.114-115
, *in schools*
Flint — *Graham* p.126
, *in subconscious*
Sheen — *Content.* p.84-86
, *Irreligious*
Streiker — *Who* p.21-54
, *Leaders of*
Phillips — *Choice* p.183-189
Sheban — *Wisdom* no p.
, *Liberalism of*
Braude — *Stories* p.327
Woods — *Religious* p.541-542
, *Life in*
Krishnamurti — *Urgency* p.38-42
, *Lost dimension in*
Saturday — *Advent.* p.47-56
, *National*
Woods — *Religious* p.843-844
, *Natural*
Woods — *Religious* p.844
, *Nature and function of*
Woods — *Religious* p.840-843
, *Necessity of*
Woods — *Religious* p.844-845
, *New*
Woods — *Religious* p.685
, *New look in*
Kauffman — *For* p.147-149
, *Orders in*
Woods — *Religious* p.848
, *Organized*
Flint — *Graham* p.101
Woods — *Religious* p.845
, *Personal*
Reader's — *20th* p.50-51
, *Petitions in*
Baillie — *Diary* #230
, *Popularity of*
Sheen — *Thoughts* p.173-174
, *Pseudo-*
Woods — *Religious* p.795
, *Return to*
Keller — *Open* p.38
, *Revealed*
Woods — *Religious* p.845-846
, *Revival of*
Carruthers — *Sparks* p.163-164
, *Service in*
Kauffman — *For* p.185-186
, *Sharing*
Peale — *Guideposts* p.217-220
, *State*
Woods — *Religious* p.846-847
, *Talk about*
Baillie — *Diary* #345
, *Test for office in*
Woods — *Religious* p.848

, *Traditions in*
Dirksen — *Quot.* #99
, *True*
Baillie — *Diary* #348
, *Truths in*
Peale — *Guideposts* p.179-182
, *United*
Words Change p.128
, *Wars of*
Flint — *Graham* p.118
, *World*
Bach — *Make* p.156-169
Flint — *Graham* p.153

RELINQUISHMENT
Guideposts — *Faith* p.218-222

REMARKS
Harnsberger — *Mark* p.403
Kin — *Dictionary* p.213
Prochnow — *Public* #1043, 1047
Prochnow — *Success.* #806, 914

REMEDIES
See also **Cure; Healing**
Braude — *Stories* p.278
Flesch — *Unusual* p.242
Garland — *Subject* p.267
Kin — *Dictionary* p.213
Lytle — *Leaves* p.43, 111
Prochnow — *Success.* #2238
Speaker's Desk #172, 423, 1043
, *Simple*
White — *Life* p.136-142

REMEMBRANCE. *See* **Memory (faculty) and memories; Reminders**

REMINDERS
Kin — *Dictionary* p.213
Prochnow — *Public* #407

REMISSION
Dirksen — *Quot.* #1531-1532

REMORSE. *See* **Conscience; Grief; Regret; Repentance; Self-blame**

RENAISSANCE
Auden — *Certain* p.315-317
Kronenberger — *Animal* p.73-74
Lockridge — *World's* #5129

RENDEZVOUS
Lytle — *Leaves* p.146

RENEWAL
Applegarth — *Heir.* p.167
Humes — *Instant* #908-915
Lytle — *Leaves* p.16, 99, 114
Peterson — *New* p.36-37
Wallis — *Treasure* p.198
Woods — *Religious* p.848

RENOWN. *See* **Fame**

RENT
Prochnow — *Success.* #441, 817
Seldes — *Great* p.830

RENUNCIATION
See also **Abstinence**
Garland — *Subject* p.268
Hubbard — *Scrap* p.16
Lockridge — *World's* #3385
Phillips — *Choice* p.44, 49, 52, 54, 63
Woods — *Religious* p.848-849

REPAIR. *See* **Mending**

REPARATION. *See* **Retribution**

REPARTEE
See also **Conversation; Humor; Talk; Wit**; etc.
Botkin — *Anecdotes* p.xxv
Edwards — *Useful* p.544
Flesch — *Unusual* p.242
Lockridge — *World's* #3206, 3603
Nizer — *Thinking* p.111
Prochnow — *Public* #486
Prochnow — *Speaker's* p.262
Prochnow — *Success.* #2240

REPENTANCE
See also **Grief; Guilt; Regret; Retribution**; etc.
Applegarth — *Heir.* p.302
Baillie — *Diary* #109, 321
Book Proverbs p.121
Detherage — *Sunrise* p.48
Dirksen — *Quot.* #1053, 1533-1541
Edwards — *Useful* p.543-546, 732
Evans — *Faith* p.8-10, 19, 74, 85-103, 115-116, 126, 223-226
Evans — *Quote* p.195-204
Evans — *This* p.44-45, 66-67
Evans — *Thoughts I See* index, no p.
Evans — *Thoughts II (Open Door) See* index, no p.
Evans — *Thoughts III (Open Road)* p.38, 108, 155, 195-196, 209
Evans — *Thoughts IV* p.94, 99, 159, 167-168, 188, 194-195
Evans — *Unto* p.13, 39, 110, 131, 132-133
Flesch — *Unusual* p.242-243
Flint — *Graham* p.118-119
Fogg — *1000* #1, 13, 43, 74, 124, 462, 637, 756, 994

Fox — *Make* p.69-70
Fuller — *Epigrams* p.251-252
Garland — *Subject* p.267-269
Goudge — *Comfort* p.278-283
Harnsberger — *Mark* p.403
Henry — *5000* p.237
Hovey — *Treasury* p.265; #1678-1730
Hunter — *Gems* p.87-88
Johnson — *Bedside* p.232, 333
Kennedy — *Reader's* #942-944
Kin — *Dictionary* p.214
Knight's Treas. p.307-310
Liddle — *Thought I, II, III* p.32, 41, 74, 150, 175
Liddle — *Thought V* p.32
Lockridge — *World's* #3056, 4647
McDonagh — *Invit.* p.80-81, 86-87
Mandel — *Stories* p.220
New Topical p.218-219
Prochnow — *Public* #432, 4201
Sheban — *Wisdom* no p.
Sheen — *Lift* p.191-197
Speaker's Desk p.224
Strait — *Speaker's* p.146
Tanksley — *Friend* p.37
Woods — *Religious* p.191, 848-850
Zobell — *Speaker's* p.117-121

REPETITION
See also **Routine**
Applegarth — *Heir.* p.255
Bartlett — *Discovery* p.64
Braude — *Stories* p.331
Evans — *Unto* p.33, 68, 77
Flesch — *Unusual* p.236, 242
Grizer — *Wit* p.383
Jones — *If* p.163-169
Kin — *Dictionary* p.82, 214
Kohn — *Through* p.49-52
Lockridge — *World's* #4481
Prochnow — *Public* #1000, 1925, 2613
Reader's — *Getting* p.144

REPHAIM (Giants)
New Topical p.219

REPLENISHMENT. *See* **Regeneration**

REPLIES. *See* **Answers**

REPORT CARDS
Prochnow — *Public* #278
Prochnow — *Success.* #1116

REPORTERS AND REPORTING
Copeland — *10,000* p.53-56
Dirksen — *Quot.* #151
Schermerhorn — *1500* p.309-310

REPOSE. *See* **Peace; Rest; Sleep**

REPRESENTATION, PROPORTIONAL
Ideas p.327-328

REPRESENTATIVES
Lytle — *Leaves* p.130

REPRESSION
See also **Self-control**
Humes — *Instant* #916-921
Ideas p.335-336
Liebman — *Peace* p.26-29
Woods — *Religious* p.850-851

REPRISAL. *See* **Revenge**

REPROACH. *See* **Criticism**

REPRODUCTION
See also **Birth**
Woods — *Religious* p.851

REPROOF. *See* **Criticism**

REPTILES
See also **Snakes**; types of reptiles
Du Noüy — *Human* p.67, 69, 73-76, 170-171
New Topical p.220

REPUBLIC
See also **Democracy; Freedom; Government; Liberty; States**
Curtis — *Practical* p.351
Dirksen — *Quot.* #34, 45, 49, 1038, 2027
Edwards — *Useful* p.547
Forbes — *Thoughts* p.176, 379, 476
Harnsberger — *Mark* p.403
Henry — *5000* p.237
Hubbard — *Scrap* p.87
Lockridge — *World's* #3171, 3176, 3616
Seldes — *Great* p.830-831
, Founders of
Dirksen — *Quot.* #2369

REPUBLICAN PARTY
Botkin — *Anecdotes* p.44, 167
Hovey — *Treasury* #278, 551, 1057
Prochnow — *Success.* #120-121, 143, 147, 205, 240, 254, 306
Seldes — *Great* p.831

REPUTATION
See also **Fame**
Book Proverbs p.114
Braude — *Source* #1469-1472
Braude — *Speaker's* #1180-1182

Braude — *Stories* p.331-332
Dirksen — *Quot.* #200, 413
Edwards — *Useful* p.547-549
Evans — *Faith* p.156
Evans — *This* p.131-133, 167
Evans — *Thoughts I* p.66-69
Evans — *Thoughts II (Open Door)* p.129-130
Evans — *Thoughts IV* p.29-30, 117
Evans — *Unto* p.28, 90
Flesch — *Unusual* p.243
Forbes — *Thoughts* p.19, 49, 64, 127, 190, 196-197, 304, 311, 323, 334, 458, 467-468
Fuller — *Epigrams* p.252-253
Fuller — *Thesaurus* #76-78
Garland — *Subject* p.269-270
Grizer — *Wit* p.384
Harnsberger — *Mark* p.403-404
Henry — *5000* p.237-238
Hobe — *Tapestries* p.40-41
Hovey — *Treasury* #23
Kin — *Dictionary* p.214-215
Kopplin — *Something* p.110-113
Liddle — *Thought I, II, III* p.20, 71, 105-106, 109, 128, 191
Lockridge — *World's* #207, 1631, 1753, 3100, 3231
Mandel — *Stories* p.220
Montapert — *Distilled* p.293
New Joy p.54
Sheen — *Thoughts* p.14-15
Speaker's Desk p.224-225
Wallis — *Treasure* p.45
Woods — *Religious* p.851

REQUIEM
Hobe — *Tapestries* p.158

RESCUE
Adams — *New* p.148
Guideposts — *Faith* p.277-281
Prochnow — *Public* #441

RESEARCH
See also **Knowledge; Science**
Droke — *Christian* p.469-470
Evans — *Unto* p.114
Forbes — *Thoughts* p.226, 292, 460, 489, 504
Nizer — *Thinking* p.28-29, 142, 169
Prochnow — *Success.* #86, 1390
Woods — *Business.* p.218-220
Woods — *Religious* p.851
, Basic
Saturday — *Advent.* p.135-147
, Historical
Curtis — *Practical* p.132
, Personal
Peterson — *Art* p.127

RESENTMENT
See also **Anger; Discontent; Hatred; Jealousy; Rebellion**
Albert — *Stop* p.122-123, 165, 167
Edwards — *Useful* p.412-413, 549
Emmons — *Mature* p.97
Evans — *Thoughts III (Open Road)* p.111
Evans — *Unto* p.34, 50
Forbes — *Thoughts* p.327, 472
Garland — *Subject* p.270-271
Grizer — *Wit* p.384
Huxley — *You See* index p.287
Johnson — *Bedside* p.162
Maltz — *Creative* p.90
New Topical p.175-176
Prochnow — *Public* #2160
Prochnow — *Success.* #515

RESERVE
See also **Concealment; Dignity; Modesty; Secrecy; Silence**
Baillie — *Diary* #333
Edwards — *Useful* p.549
Keys Happiness p.313-316
Kin — *Dictionary* p.215
Kohn — *Best* p.41-43
Lockridge — *World's* #2407
Peterson — *Art* p.338

RESIGNATION
See also **Acceptance; Patience; Stoicism**
Dirksen — *Quot.* #1542
Edwards — *Useful* p.549-550
Evans — *Unto* p.116, 118
Flesch — *Unusual* p.243
Fogg — *1000 See* index p.896
Fuller — *Epigrams* p.253
Henry — *5000* p.238
Hubbard — *Scrap* p.49, 108
Keys Happiness p.107-108
Kin — *Dictionary* p.215
Lockridge — *World's* #5605
Maltz — *Creative* p.129-130
New Topical p.220
Woods — *Content.* p.293
Woods — *Religious* p.851-852

RESILIENCY
See also **Endurance; Flexibility**
Peterson — *Art* p.92, 95
Wallis — *Treasure* p.14

RESISTANCE
See also **Rebellion**
Forbes — *Thoughts* p.15, 140, 360
Garland — *Subject* p.271
Lockridge — *World's* #4625
Lytle — *Leaves* p.55
Peterson — *Art* p.87
Phillips — *Choice* p.67, 254-255, 257

Seldes — *Great* p.831
White — *Job* p.61, 71-72, 103, 107, 123, 137

RESOLUTION
See also **Constancy; Decision; Perseverance; Purpose**
Alexander's Treasure. p.207
Applegarth — *Heir.* p.64
Baillie — *Diary* #193
Dirksen — *Quot.* #1543
Edwards — *Useful* p.198, 550-551
Evans — *Faith* p.7-8, 40, 91, 101-102, 155, 223-226
Evans — *Thoughts III (Open Road)* p.118-119
Evans — *Thoughts IV* p.165, 197-198
Evans — *Unto* p.22
Flesch — *Unusual* p.243
Forbes — *Thoughts See* index p.565
Henry — *5000* p.90, 238
Hubbard — *Scrap* p.123, 133
Humes — *Instant* #922-927
Kin — *Dictionary* p.94, 216
Liddle — *Thought I, II, III* p.59, 130, 189, 193
Lockridge — *World's* #871, 917, 1004, 1965, 2381, 3823
Lytle — *Leaves* p.181
Mandel — *Stories* p.220
Montapert — *Distilled* p.155, 293-294
Nichols — *New* p.187
Prochnow — *Public* #265
Prochnow — *Speaker's* p.262
Pullar-Strecker — *Proverbs* #126-141

RESORTS
Asimov — *Treasury* #349-350, 368, 375
Prochnow — *Public* #1385, 1815, 1832-1833

RESOURCEFULNESS
See also **Ingenuity**
Braude — *Source* #1473-1476
Braude — *Speaker's* #1183-1207
Evans — *Thoughts IV* p.135
Evans — *Unto* p.84
Hovey — *Treasury* #5, 8, 335
Manchee — *Secret* p.22-49
Mandel — *Stories* p.220-221
Speaker's Desk #24, 368, 377, 385, 404, 409, 529, 675, 941-942, 1081

RESOURCES
See also **Natural resources**
Detherage — *Sunrise* p.173-178
Dirksen — *Quot.* #579, 1149, 1655
Emmons — *Mature* p.81
Forbes — *Thoughts* p.151, 160, 335, 366, 506
Hobe — *Tapestries* p.24
Lytle — *Leaves* p.16, 114
Prochnow — *Speaker's* p.263

RESPECT
See also **Honor; Self-respect**
Braude — *Speaker's* #302-303
Braude — *Stories* p.332
Dirksen — *Quot.* #111
Edwards — *Useful* p.122
Evans — *Thoughts II (Open Door)* p.44, 170
Evans — *Thoughts III (Open Road)* p.16, 21, 26, 30, 32, 49, 69, 71, 78-81, 125, 149
Evans — *Unto* p.57
Flesch — *Unusual* p.243
Forbes — *Thoughts* p.158, 212, 406
Grizer — *Wit* p.385
Harnsberger — *Mark* p.404
Kennedy — *Reader's* #945-946
Kin — *Dictionary* p.216
Liddle — *Thought I, II, III* p.55, 100
Lockridge — *World's* #362, 2011, 4653
Mandel — *Stories* p.222
Prochnow — *Public* #694
Speaker's Desk #3, 95, 241
Woods — *Religious* p.852
, and love
Krishnamurti — *Think* p.57

RESPECTABILITY
Dirksen — *Quot.* #2142
Flesch — *Unusual* p.243
Kennedy — *Reader's* #947-948
Lockridge — *World's* #701, 4857
Prochnow — *Success.* #2243
Woods — *Religious* p.852

RESPONSE
See also **Answers**
Humes — *Instant* #938-942
Kohn — *Adventures* p.113-117
Prochnow — *Public* #96
, Illustrations for
Prochnow — *Success.* #168-277
, of teenagers
Ginott — *Between* p.21-46

RESPONSIBILITY
See also **Duty; Integrity; Obligations**
Braude — *Stories* p.332

Carruthers — *Sparks* p.139-141
Curtis — *Daily* p.113-118
Detherage — *Sunrise* p.61, 156, 178
Dirksen — *Quot.* #43, 481, 650, 709-710, 1544-1545, 1792-1794, 2367, 2381
Droke — *Christian* p.471-474
Edwards — *Useful* p.551
Evans — *Faith* p.21, 27, 49-54, 80, 117, 133, 165, 168, 177-192
Evans — *This* p.129-130
Evans — *Thoughts I* p.23, 89, 134, 142-145, 154, 160, 188-189, 209
Evans — *Thoughts II (Open Door)* p.26, 205
Evans — *Thoughts III (Open Road)* p.17-19, 68-69, 106, 128, 141, 150, 152, 168-169, 177, 201
Evans — *Thoughts IV* p.24-25, 148
Evans — *Unto* p.5, 69, 73, 87, 94, 112
Flesch — *Unusual* p.243
Forbes — *Thoughts* *See* index p.565
Garland — *Subject* p.272-273
Grizer — *Wit* p.385-387
Halverson — *Perspective* p.112
Hovey — *Treasury* p.265-266; *See also* index p.300
Hubbard — *Scrap* p.70
Humes — *Instant* p.17, 46, 928-937, 1208-1209
Johnson — *Bedside* p.109
Kennedy — *Reader's* #949-964
Knight's Illus. p.9
Lair — *Baby* p.122
Langdon — *Teach.* p.47-57
Liddle — *Thought I, II, III* p.61, 156, 187
Liddle — *Thought V* p.20, 37
Mandel — *Stories* p.221-222
Menninger — *Blue.* p.38
Montapert — *Distilled* p.294
Phillips — *Choice* p.69, 80, 270, 363
Prochnow — *Public* #794, 1857, 2453, 4333
Prochnow — *Speaker's* p.263-264
Prochnow — *Success.* #200, 299, 768, 1283, 2244
Sheen — *Content.* p.50-52
Speaker's Desk #686, 995, 1044
Voss — *Quotations* p.214-216
Wallis — *Treasure* p.118, 212
Wallis — *Words* p.87, 153, 233
Wheelis — *Moralist* p.41, 46, 95-96, 100
Woods — *Religious* p.853

, in business
Kauffman — *For* p.188-189
, Local
Woods — *Business.* p.139-140
, of Christians
Kauffman — *For* p.186-188
, Personal
Kennedy — *Fresh* p.182-184
, Rebellion from
Flint — *Graham* p.119
, Scientific
Du Noüy — *Road* p.22, 71-72, 220, 224-226
, Shifting
Carruthers — *Sparks* p.148-149
, Social
Keller — *You* p.195-210
, Teenager
Ginott — *Between* p.149-150, 167
, Welcome of
Price — *Wider* p.167-175

REST
See also **Peace; Quiet; Relaxation; Sleep**
Albert — *Stop* p.11-12, 15, 47-48, 110, 126-127
Alexander's Treasure. p.248
Baillie — *Diary* #267
Book Proverbs p.110
Edwards — *Useful* p.546, 551-552
Evans — *This* p.51
Flesch — *Unusual* p.243
Forbes — *Thoughts* p.100, 279, 322, 400, 403, 409
Henry — *5000* p.237-239
Hobe — *Tapestries* p.81-84, 216, 218
Johnson — *Bedside* p.194, 279, 281, 283, 308, 339-340
Kin — *Dictionary* p.216
Knight's Treas. p.310-312
Kohn — *Thoughts* p.97-98
Lockridge — *World's* #2878, 3464, 4311
Lytle — *Leaves* p.18, 60, 153
Montapert — *Distilled* p.294
Peterson — *Art* p.76
Prochnow — *Public* #120, 1403, 2463, 2502
Prochnow — *Success.* #796, 2245
Sheen — *Way* p.55-57, 139-140
Wallis — *Treasure* p.189, 194
Wallis — *Words* p.43, 61
Woods — *Content.* p.346, 350-351, 353
Woods — *Religious* p.850, 853

RESTAURANTS
Asimov — *Treasury* #344

Braude — *Speaker's* #1208-1213
Cerf — *Laugh* p.201-207
Copeland — *10,000* p.61-72
Harral — *Feature* p.106, 269-270
Prochnow — *Public* #12, 24, 269, 300, 1253, 1362
Prochnow — *Speaker's* p.265
Prochnow — *Success.* #1024, 1121
Schermerhorn — *1500* p.310-312
, Business of
Unlimited Power p.273-276
, Managers of
Manchee — *Secret* p.224

RESTITUTION
See also **Compensation**
Knight's Treas. p.312-313
Woods — *Religious* p.853

RESTLESSNESS
See also **Discontent**
Baillie — *Diary* #309
Dirksen — *Quot.* #575
Edwards — *Useful* p.552
Evans — *Thoughts III (Open Road)* p.13, 59, 115-117
Evans — *Thoughts IV* p.55, 137, 166
Huxley — *You See* index p.288
Prochnow — *Public* #2149
Woods — *Religious* p.853

RESTORATION
Garland — *Subject* p.273
Lytle — *Leaves* p.89, 193

RESTRAINT
See also **Moderation**
Curtis — *Practical* p.415
Evans — *Thoughts III (Open Road)* p.168
Evans — *Thoughts IV* p.95, 99
Evans — *Unto* p.53, 61-62
Fuller — *Thesaurus* #1641-1642
Kin — *Dictionary* p.216
Lockridge — *World's* #3652
Sheen — *Thoughts* p.64-66
Wheelis — *Moralist* p.45-46, 48

RESTRICTIONS. *See* **Restraint**

RESULTS
Curtis — *Practical* p.94
Evans — *Faith* p.53, 71-72, 79, 108, 114, 117-118, 131, 153, 161
Evans — *Thoughts I* p.54-55, 60, 200
Evans — *Thoughts III (Open Road)* p.21, 47, 49-51, 81, 107-108, 159, 165, 201
Evans — *Thoughts IV* p.94, 99, 110, 134, 145
Evans — *Unto* p.33-35, 39, 50, 55, 62, 65-70, 72, 80, 102, 108, 117, 123, 125, 131, 133, 136, 141
Flesch — *Unusual* p.243-244
Henry — *5000* p.239
Hobe — *Tapestries* p.82
Kin — *Dictionary* p.54-55, 216
Liddle — *Thought I, II, III* p.35, 43
Lockridge — *World's* #3431, 3902
Montapert — *Distilled* p.295
Prochnow — *Public* #943, 1646
Prochnow — *Success.* #2246
Seldes — *Great* p.217
Wheelis — *Moralist* p.34-35, 39, 73
Woods — *Religious* p.853

RÉSUMÉS. *See* **Qualifications**

RESURRECTION
See also **Eternity; Heaven; Immortality; Jesus Christ, Resurrection of**
Baillie — *Diary* #76
Dirksen — *Quot.* #47, 86, 1054, 1566
Edwards — *Useful* p.552
Emmons — *Mature* p.136, 155
Evans — *Faith* p.193-206
Evans — *Thoughts I* p.41, 49-51
Evans — *Thoughts II (Open Door)* p.108-110
Evans — *Thoughts III (Open Road)* p.190, 205, 210
Evans — *Thoughts IV* p.177
Flesch — *Unusual* p.244
Flint — *Graham* p.119-120
Fridy — *Meditat.* p.26, 97
Garland — *Subject* p.274
Halverson — *Perspective* p.82
Henry — *5000* p.239
Hobe — *Tapestries* p.60, 151, 156
Hovey — *Treasury* #347, 749, 811, 813-814, 816, 821-822, 825, 1657
Hulme — *Living* p.106-107
Johnson — *Bedside* p.339
Kauffman — *For* p.191-192
Knight's Illus. p.266-271
Knight's Treas. p.313-319
Liddle — *Thought I, II, III* p.10
Lytle — *Leaves* p.95, 194
More Words p.137-138
Prochnow — *Speaker's* p.266
Seldes — *Great* p.831-832
Wallis — *Treasure* p.144
Wallis — *Words* p.65-68, 99-100
Webb — *Edge* p.137-142

RETAILING
Grizer — *Wit* p.387-389

RETALIATION. *See* **Revenge**

RETARDATION. *See* **Children, Retarded**

RETICENCE. *See* **Reserve**

RETIREMENT
Braude — *Source* #1477-1480
Braude — *Speaker's* #1214-1219
Dirksen — *Quot.* #2314
Edwards — *Useful* p.552-553
Evans — *Thoughts I* p.177, 209-210
Grizer — *Wit* p.390-391
Humes — *Instant* #943-944
Maltz — *Creative* p.102-103
Montapert — *Distilled* p.295
Peterson — *Art* p.123
Prochnow — *Public* #262
Prochnow — *Success.* #785
Reader's — *Getting* p.219-221
Woods — *Religious* p.854

RETRACTION
See also **Apology**
Braude — *Source* #1481-1482
Mandel — *Stories* p.222-223

RETREAT
Bartlett — *Discovery* p.38
Braude — *Stories* p.333
Evans — *This* p.39-41
How To Live p.250-254
Maltz — *Creative* p.126-127
Phillips — *Choice* p.303-304
, Catholic
Porter — *Halo* p.vii-ix, 2
, Houses for
Day — *Meditations* p.62

RETRIBUTION
See also **Judgment; Justice; Punishment**
Braude — *Stories* p.333
Dirksen — *Quot.* #1546-1547
Edwards — *Useful* p.553
Evans — *Unto* p.135
Henry — *5000* p.240
Kin — *Dictionary* p.216-217
Sheen — *Lift* p.191-197

RETROGRESSION
Braude — *Source* #1483-1484

RETROSPECTION. *See* **Memory (faculty) and memories; Reflection**

RETURN
Adams — *New* p.119
Kin — *Dictionary* p.217
Lindbergh — *Unicorn* p.83-85
Prochnow — *Public* #2073

REUNION
Woods — *Religious* p.854

REUNION, TRIBE OF
New Topical p.222

REVELATION
See also **Bible; God, Word of**; etc.
Flesch — *Unusual* p.244
Forbes — *Thoughts* p.137, 142, 323
Garland — *Subject* p.275
Henry — *5000* p.240
Hobe — *Tapestries* p.68
Hunter — *Green* p.89-90
Kin — *Dictionary* p.217
Liebman — *Peace* p.165-171
More Words p.138-139
Wallis — *Treasure* p.25
Wallis — *Words* p.61, 203
Woods — *Content.* p.33, 45, 70, 106, 132, 204, 209, 235-236, 240, 245, 280
Woods — *Religious* p.855-860
, and reason
Woods — *Religious* p.858-860

REVENGE
See also **Punishment**
Auden — *Certain* p.318
Book Proverbs p.112
Braude — *Source* #1488-1491, 1729-1730
Braude — *Speaker's* #1220-1223, 1488-1507
Braude — *Stories* p.333
Dirksen — *Quot.* #714, 1678, 2143-2144
Droke — *Christian* p.474-475
Edwards — *Useful* p.553-554, 677-678
Flesch — *Unusual* p.244, 303
Fogg — *1000* #393, 968
Forbes — *Thoughts* p.240, 326, 458
Fox — *Make* p.71
Fuller — *Epigrams* p.253-254
Fun Fare p.29, 136, 272
Grizer — *Wit* p.389, 392, 468
Henry — *5000* p.239-240
Johnson — *Bedside* p.13
Kin — *Dictionary* p.17, 214, 216-218, 267
Krishnamurti — *Think* p.130-131
Liddle — *Thought I, II, III* p.12, 14, 16, 25, 37, 56, 126, 137, 152
Liddle — *Thought IV* p.31
Lockridge — *World's* #28-29, 3139, 4987
Lytle — *Leaves* p.74
Mandel — *Stories* p.267
Montapert — *Distilled* p.295-296

New Topical p.222
Prochnow — *Public* #1787, 2471, 2608, 2699, 3822-3823, 4202-4203
Prochnow — *Success.* #2421
Speaker's Desk p.225; #10, 132, 194, 305, 418, 815, 843, 857, 1155
Woods — *Content.* p.295
Woods — *Religious* p.860, 1032

REVERE, PAUL
New Joy p.75

REVERENCE
See also **Devotion; Honor; Religion; Worship**
Applegarth — *Heir.* p.173, 308
Dirksen — *Quot.* #1548-1552
Edwards — *Useful* p.554-555
Evans — *Faith* p.50-51, 167-168, 225
Evans — *This* p.130-131
Evans — *Unto* p.8, 56
Harnsberger — *Mark* p.404-405
Hunter — *Gems* p.91
Kennedy — *Reader's* #965-966
Kin — *Dictionary* p.218
Knight's Treas. p.319-321
Lytle — *Leaves* p.23, 67, 70
Peale — *Guideposts* p.179-182
Seldes — *Great* p.832
Speaker's Desk #3, 999
Voss — *Quotations* p.216-219
Wallis — *Treasure* p.25, 57, 60, 129, 193
Woods — *Religious* p.860-861

REVERIE. *See* **Daydreaming; Imagination; Meditation**

"REVERSE ENGLISH"
Braude — *Speaker's* #1224-1229

REVERSES. *See* **Failure; Misfortune; Trouble**; etc.

REVIVALS
See also **Evangelism**
Botkin — *Anecdotes* p.32, 113
Flint — *Graham* p.120-121
Fuller — *Thesaurus* #1576-1578
Kennedy — *Reader's* #967
Knight's Illus. p.271-272
Knight's Treas. p.321-323
Nichols — *Third* p.227-228
Woods — *Religious* p.861

REVOLT
Krishnamurti — *Think* p.12-13, 78-85, 138-193, 140-141
Prochnow — *Success.* #566
, *Teenager*
Flint — *Graham* p.157

REVOLUTION
See also **Violence; War**
Asimov — *Treasury* #111
Dirksen — *Quot.* #2145, 2386
Edwards — *Useful* p.555-556
Esteve — *Experience* p.87-95
Flesch — *Unusual* p.244-245
Forbes — *Thoughts* p.9, 119, 150, 158, 174, 436, 488
Fuller — *Epigrams* p.254
Fuller — *Thesaurus* #2061-2064
Garland — *Subject* p.276
Grizer — *Wit* p.392-393
Henry — *5000* p.240-241
Hoffer — *Reflect.* p.45-46
Humes — *Instant* #945-956
Kauffman — *For* p.192-193
Kennedy — *Reader's* #968-971
Kin — *Dictionary* p.218
Lockridge — *World's See* index p.582
Prochnow — *Public* #3651-3653
Prochnow — *Success.* #2247-2250
Seldes — *Great* p.832-840
Sheen — *Way* p.39-41, 188-190
Speaker's Desk p.225-226
Tanksley — *Friend* p.68
Wheelis — *Moralist* p.111, 149
Woods — *Business.* p.221-222
, *Moral*
Flint — *Graham* p.121

REWARD
See also **Compensation; Gifts and giving**
Baillie — *Diary* #330
Dirksen — *Quot.* #1553-1558
Droke — *Christian* p.475
Edwards — *Useful* p.556
Evans — *Unto* p.62, 68, 94, 136
Forbes — *Thoughts* p.148-149, 160, 287, 332, 338, 345, 359, 397, 437, 442-443, 473
Garland — *Subject* p.276-277
Grizer — *Wit* p.393-394
Kahn — *Lessons* p.62-67
Kin — *Dictionary* p.218
Knight's Illus. p.272-274
Knight's Treas. p.324-326
Lair — *Baby* p.82
Liddle — *Thought I, II, III* p.34, 65, 91, 113, 131
Lockridge — *World's* #1478, 5172, 5255
Lytle — *Leaves* p.121
Mandel — *Stories* p.223-224
Modern Eloquence (14) p.409
Montapert — *Distilled* p.296

Prochnow — *Public* #1039, 2274, 2603, 3654-3656
Prochnow — *Speaker's* p.266
Speaker's Desk #20, 169
Woods — *Religious* p.861-862

RHEIMS CATHEDRAL
Applegarth — *Heir.* p.100

RHETORIC
See also **Eloquence; Orators and oratory; Speech**
Curtis — *Practical* p.438
Edwards — *Useful* p.556-557
Flesch — *Unusual* p.245
Woods — *Religious* p.862

RHEUMATISM
Flesch — *Unusual* p.245
Prochnow — *Public* #389
Prochnow — *Speaker's* p.266

RHINOCEROS
Applegarth — *Heir.* p.24

RHODE ISLAND
Botkin — *Anecdotes* p.76

RHODORA
Hobe — *Tapestries* p.61

RHYTHM
See also **Music; Poetry**
Applegarth — *Heir.* p.184, 268
Watson — *Light* p.34
White — *Job* p.46, 69, 85, 88-92
, and atmosphere
Rau — *Act* p.65-73
, with universe
Clark — *Windows* p.70

RICE
Prochnow — *Public* #321

RICH. *See* **Wealth**

RICHELIEU, DUC DE
Lockridge — *World's* #3782, 4209-4210

RICKENBACKER, EDDIE
Guideposts — *Faith* p.267-270

RIDDLES
Botkin — *Treasury* p.360, 777
Cerf — *Laugh* p.313-317
Flesch — *Unusual* p.246
Prochnow — *Public* #290

RIDERS AND RIDING
Kin — *Dictionary* p.219
Prochnow — *Public* #692, 968
Prochnow — *Success.* #981

RIDICULE
See also **Sarcasm; Satire**
Botkin — *Treasury* p.780
Dirksen — *Quot.* #1055
Edwards — *Useful* p.304, 560-561, 601
Flesch — *Unusual* p.246
Forbes — *Thoughts* p.17, 34, 158
Harnsberger — *Mark* p.407
Henry — *5000* p.242, 258
Johnson — *Bedside* p.318
Kin — *Dictionary* p.219, 239
Lair — *Baby* p.160
Lockridge — *World's* #336, 640, 2327, 2488, 3553, 5800
New Topical p.236

RIFLES
Botkin — *Treasury* p.14, 44
Kin — *Dictionary* p.219

RIGHT
See also **Honesty; Integrity; Justice; Morality and morals; Righteousness**
Adams — *New* p.222
Dirksen — *Quot.* #711, 2147, 2364
Edwards — *Useful* p.561
Evans — *This* p.101-102
Evans — *Thoughts III (Open Road)* p.47, 107-108, 121-122, 171
Flesch — *Unusual* p.246-247
Forbes — *Thoughts* p.31, 35, 106, 111, 115, 127, 146, 181, 260; *See also* index p.565
Grizer — *Wit* p.394-395
Harnsberger — *Mark* p.407-408
Henry — *5000* p.242
Hobe — *Tapestries* p.50
Hovey — *Treasury* p.266; #62, 98, 119, 127, 677, 881, 1060, 1071, 1537, 1666, 1687-1689, 1771
Kin — *Dictionary* p.219
Liddle — *Thought I, II, III* p.11, 34-35, 41, 43, 46-47, 83, 98, 109, 122, 156, 176, 178
Lockridge — *World's* #1701
Lytle — *Leaves* p.127
Montapert — *Distilled* p.297-298
More Words p.139-141
Nichols — *Third* p.38-39
Prochnow — *Public* #1313, 1607, 3667, 3668
Prochnow — *Speaker's* p.266-267
Prochnow — *Success.* #1163, 1276, 2258
Wallis — *Treasure* p.111
Wheelis — *Moralist* p.67, 116
Woods — *Religious* p.864-865

, *Action for*
Curtis — *Human* p.66-79
Humes — *Instant* #1213-1217
, *and left*
Flesch — *Unusual* p.247
, *and wrong*
Flesch — *Unusual* p.247
Hubbard — *Scrap* p.95
Kauffman — *For* p.193
Seldes — *Great* p.849
Wheelis — *Moralist* p.28, 95, 115
Woods — *Religious* p.865
, *Prevailing*
Maxwell — *Courage* p.218-224

RIGHTEOUSNESS
See also **Self-righteousness; Virtues**
Baillie — *Diary* #63
Braude — *Stories* p.333
Curtis — *Practical* p.88, 112, 1168
Dirksen — *Quot.* #712, 1168, 1289, 1431, 1495
Evans — *Unto* p.50, 65
Flint — *Graham* p.121
Forbes — *Thoughts* p.37, 165, 189, 321, 424
Garland — *Subject* p.277-278
Halverson — *Perspective* p.23
Henry — *5000* p.242
Lytle — *Leaves* p.9, 61
Mandelbaum — *Choose* p.42-45
New Topical p.225-226
Prochnow — *Public* #2496-2497, 2505, 2527, 2531, 2555, 2598
Prochnow — *Speaker's* p.267
Woods — *Religious* p.865-866
Zobell — *Speaker's* p.121-122
, *and happiness*
Hunter — *Gems* p.92
, *Imputed*
New Topical p.226-227

RIGHTS OF MAN
See also **Bill of Rights; Equality; Freedom; Liberty**
Dirksen — *Quot.* #611
Evans — *Thoughts IV* p.150
Evans — *Unto* p.32, 56
Forbes — *Thoughts* p.110, 150, 246, 259, 391, 451, 492, 495, 505, 509
Garland — *Subject* p.278
Henry — *5000* p.242-243
Ideas p.237-239, 338-340
Mandelbaum — *Choose* p.101, 105-108, 117-120, 130
Prochnow — *Success.* #853
Seldes — *Great* p.846-849
Welk — *Guide.* p.162-164
Wheelis — *Moralist* p.52, 118-119
Woods — *Business.* p.222-223
Woods — *Religious* p.866-867

RIGIDITY
Price — *Wider* p.133-139
Woods — *Religious* p.867

RILEY, JAMES WHITCOMB
Botkin — *Treasury* p.408, 500-501

RINGS
New Topical p.227

RIO GRANDE RIVER
Botkin — *Treasury* p.181, 281

RISING, EARLY
Baillie — *Diary* #68
Dirksen — *Quot.* #870
Flesch — *Unusual* p.247
Liddle — *Thought I, II, III* p.11, 86
New Joy p.142

RISK
See also **Danger**
Flesch — *Unusual* p.247
Grizer — *Wit* p.395
Hovey — *Treasury* #446
Kennedy — *Reader's* #972
Kin — *Dictionary* p.220
Liddle — *Thought I, II, III* p.113
Mandel — *Stories* p.224
Montapert — *Distilled* p.298
Prochnow — *Public* #2319
Prochnow — *Success.* #2261
Woods — *Religious* p.867
, *Calculated*
Adams — *New* p.322

RITES AND RITUAL. *See* **Ceremony; Religion**

RIVALRY
See also **Envy; Jealousy; Opposition**
Edwards — *Useful* p.159, 561
Flesch — *Unusual* p.247
Kin — *Dictionary* p.80, 220
Woods — *Religious* p.868-869

RIVERMEN SONGS
Botkin — *Treasury* p.829

RIVERS
See also names of rivers
Adams — *New* p.298
Botkin — *Anecdotes* p.67-68, 70, 112, 195, 227
Goudge — *Comfort* p.35-36
Harnsberger — *Mark* p.408-411
Kin — *Dictionary* p.220
New Topical p.227-228

Prochnow — *Public* #2562
Wallis — *Words* p.153
, and men
Adams — *New* p.75
, Muddy
Kohn — *Through* p.31

ROADS
See also **Highways**
Auden — *Certain* p.319-327
Evans — *Thoughts III (Open Road) See* index, no p.
Flesch — *Unusual* p.248
Forbes — *Thoughts* p.163, 294, 323, 332, 410, 426, 509, 518
Harnsberger — *Mark* p.411
Hovey — *Treasury* #31, 142, 221, 356, 423, 1039, 1066, 1244, 1255, 1309, 1796
Kin — *Dictionary* p.220
Lindbergh — *Unicorn* p.44
Peterson — *Art* p.335
Wallis — *Treasure* p.188, 207
Wallis — *Words* p.10, 94

"ROARERS"
See also **Tall tales**
Botkin — *Treasury* p.3-4, 51, 272, 493

ROBBERS AND ROBBERY. *See* **Burglars and burglary; Thieves and thievery**

ROBESPIERRE, MAXIMILIEN DE
Lockridge — *World's* #3782

ROBINS
Applegarth — *Heir.* p.34
Hobe — *Tapestries* p.60
Irion — *Yes* p.72-75
Kohn — *Thoughts* p.154-155
Wallis — *Treasure* p.100, 138

ROCKEFELLER CREED
Braude — *Stories* p.88

ROCKETS
Prochnow — *Success.* #1025

ROCKS
Kin — *Dictionary* p.220
New Topical p.228-229
Prochnow — *Public* #981
, Building on
Peale — *Guideposts* p.274-277

ROCKY MOUNTAINS
Botkin — *Treasury* p.9, 227-228, 284, 307, 469, 594

RODEOS
See also **Cowboys**
Botkin — *Anecdotes* p.35
Harral — *Feature* p.270

ROGERS, WILL
Botkin — *Anecdotes* p.2
Peterson — *Art* p.352

ROGUES AND ROGUERY
See also **Crimes and criminals;** etc.
Dirksen — *Quot.* #1892
Edwards — *Useful* p.561
Flesch — *Unusual* p.248
Kin — *Dictionary* p.209, 220-221
Woods — *Religious* p.869
, Cheerful
Botkin — *Anecdotes* p.54

ROMAN CATHOLIC CHURCH. *See* **Catholicism**

ROMANCE
See also **Love;** etc.
Braude — *Source* #1492-1495
Braude — *Speaker's* #225-232, 1230-1293
Cerf — *Laugh* p.104-110
Edwards — *Useful* p.561-562
Evans — *This* p.12-13
Flint — *Graham* p.121-122
Fogg — *1000 See* index p.897
Fuller — *Epigrams* p.254-255
Harnsberger — *Mark* p.412
How To Live p.53-56
Hubbard — *Scrap* p.14, 54
Kahn — *Lessons* p.171-176
Keys Happiness p.477-479
Lockridge — *World's* #1019, 3987
New Joy p.149
Prochnow — *Public* #286, 321, 335, 1045
Speaker's Desk p.226-227
Woods — *Religious* p.869

ROMANS 8:28
Knight's Illus. p.278-279
Knight's Treas. p.332-334

ROMANTICISM
See also **Classicism**
Curtis — *Practical* p.442-443
Johnson — *Bedside* p.191

ROME AND ROMANS
Botkin — *Anecdotes* p.186, 262
Curtis — *Practical* p.222-223
Henry — *5000* p.243
Hovey — *Treasury* #335, 348, 403, 812, 821, 840, 857, 1334, 1458

Hubbard — *Scrap* p.71
Kronenberger — *Animal* p.15-17
Lockridge — *World's* #4106-4107
New Topical p.229-230
Seldes — *Great* p.849-851
, Compared to America
Flint — *Graham* p.91, 122
, Emperors of
Asimov — *Treasury* #473
, Law of
Curtis — *Practical* p.24
, Sack of
Baillie — *Diary* #170

ROOFS
Prochnow — *Public* #355

"ROOKIES"
Prochnow — *Success.* #1060

ROOKS
Kin — *Dictionary* p.221

ROOMMATES
Kin — *Dictionary* p.221

ROOMS
Curtis — *Practical* p.83

ROOSEVELT, THEODORE
Harnsberger — *Mark* p.412-413
Seldes — *Great* p.851

ROOSTERS
Botkin — *Anecdotes* p.95
Prochnow — *Public* #25

ROOTS
Kohn — *Best* p.19-22, 44-46
, Strength of
Kohn — *Adventures* p.103-108

ROPE
Kohn — *Touch* p.42-45

"ROPE CHOKERS"
Botkin — *Anecdotes* p.275

"ROPE-SKIPPING" RHYMES
Botkin — *Treasury* p.791

ROSARY
Lytle — *Leaves* p.17
Woods — *Religious* p.869

ROSES
Applegarth — *Heir.* p.99-100, 190, 212
Hadfield — *Love* p.98, 104-105, 110-111
Hobe — *Tapestries* p.24, 82
Lytle — *Leaves* p.33, 100, 104, 109
Nichols — *Third* p.193
Wallis — *Treasure* p.32, 94, 149, 168, 181
Wallis — *Words* p.85, 97, 203
, Thorns of
Peterson — *Art* p.193
, Yellow
Peterson — *Art* p.198

ROSETTA STONE
Prochnow — *Public* #2408

ROTATION
Lindeman — *Emerson* p.200

ROUGE
Kin — *Dictionary* p.221

"ROUGH AND READY"
Fuller — *Thesaurus* #496-507

"ROUGHING IT"
Prochnow — *Public* #1472, 1790

"ROUNDUPS." *See* **Rodeos**

ROUNDNESS
Kin — *Dictionary* p.221
Prochnow — *Public* #2407

ROUSSEAU, JEAN JACQUES
Flesch — *Unusual* p.248
Lockridge — *World's* #3593

ROUTINE
See also **Monotony**
Evans — *Faith* p.11-12, 25-27, 149, 225
Evans — *Thoughts I* p.155, 183, 211
Evans — *Thoughts II (Open Door)* p.78-79, 143-144
Evans — *Thoughts III (Open Road)* p.57-59, 116-117, 131, 156
Evans — *Thoughts IV* p.16, 56, 165, 198
Flesch — *Unusual* p.248
Forbes — *Thoughts* p.67, 431
Kennedy — *Fresh* p.81-83
Kennedy — *Reader's* #973-974
Prochnow — *Speaker's* p.268
Speaker's Desk #383, 552, 638, 725
, Perils of
Fridy — *Meditat.* p.122

ROVERS. *See* **Wandering and wanderers**

ROWING
Kin — *Dictionary* p.221
, *on Thames river*
Baillie — *Diary* #96

"ROYAL PREROGATIVE"
Ideas p.344-346

ROYALTY
See also **Kings and queens; Rulers**
Auden — *Certain* p.327-330
George — *Book See* index p.445
Harnsberger — *Mark* p.413-416
Henry — *5000* p.243-244
Kronenberger — *Animal* p.246-247
Lockridge — *World's* #3758
Simpson — *'54* p.86, 243, 355
Walters — *How* p.39-43
Wilcox — *Heart* p.49-54
Woods — *Religious* p.869

RUBBER
Fox — *Make* p.47-48

RUBBISH
Kin — *Dictionary* p.221

RUBENS, PETER PAUL
Lockridge — *World's* #4944

RUDENESS
See also **Arrogance; Insult**
Applegarth — *Heir.* p.79
Flesch — *Unusual* p.248
Fuller — *Thesaurus* #511-524
Kin — *Dictionary* p.221
Peterson — *Art* p.355
Prochnow — *Success.* #2262-2263
Speaker's Desk #134, 297, 395
, *"Squelching" of*
Humes — *Instant* p.57

RUGGEDNESS
Prochnow — *Public* #4359

RUIN
Dirksen — *Quot.* #546, 1056
Edwards — *Useful* p.562
Henry — *5000* p.244
Kin — *Dictionary* p.221-222
Lockridge — *World's* #4506, 4854
Peterson — *Art* p.69
Prochnow — *Public* #1036, 1958, 2130
Woods — *Religious* p.107, 870

RULERS
See also **Kings and queens; Royalty**
Flesch — *Unusual* p.248
Fogg — *1000 See* index p.897
Seldes — *Great* p.851
Sheban — *Wisdom* no p.
Woods — *Religious* p.870

RULES
See also **Principles; Standards**
Flesch — *Unusual* p.248
Forbes — *Thoughts See* index p.565
Harnsberger — *Mark* p.417
Kin — *Dictionary* p.222
Lockridge — *World's* #4580
Lytle — *Leaves* p.164
Montapert — *Distilled* p.299
Prochnow — *Public* #1380, 2532, 2695
Prochnow — *Speaker's* p.268
Prochnow — *Success.* #2264-2265
Wheelis — *Moralist* p.28-29, 49, 61, 68, 100, 109, 118-121
Woods — *Religious* p.870
, *Breaking of*
Nichols — *Third* p.99-100
, *Eternal*
Dirksen — *Quot.* #2355

RUMBA
Prochnow — *Success.* #1104

RUMMAGE SALES
Prochnow — *Success.* #1457

RUMOR
See also **Gossip; Reputation; Scandal; Slander**
Braude — *Source* #1496-1497
Braude — *Speaker's* #1294-1295
Braude — *Stories* p.333
Edwards — *Useful* p.562
Evans — *Unto* p.44, 90
Harnsberger — *Mark* p.417
Henry — *5000* p.244
Kin — *Dictionary* p.117
Lockridge — *World's* #621
Prochnow — *Public* #2652
Prochnow — *Success.* #351

"RUNNING AWAY"
See also **Escape**
Evans — *Thoughts I* p.195-196
Evans — *Thoughts III (Open Road)* p.115, 118-119, 207
Flesch — *Unusual* p.249
Fox — *Make* p.107

RURAL LIFE. *See* **Country life**

RUSH. *See* **Haste**

RUSSIA AND RUSSIANS
Cerf — *Laugh* p.433-437

Flesch — *Unusual* p.249
Flint — *Graham* p.122
Grizer — *Wit* p.395-396
Guideposts — *Faith* p.428-434
Harnsberger — *Mark* p.418
Hovey — *Treasury* #92, 156, 256, 972, 1124, 1278, 1595, 1825
Lockridge — *World's* #2767, 4815
Prochnow — *Success.* #854, 866, 875, 1500
Seldes — *Great* p.851
Simpson — *Contemp.* p.149-155
Woods — *Content.* p.68
Woods — *Religious* p.956
, Army life in
Asimov — *Treasury* #589

RUSSIAN PROVERBS
Dirksen — *Quot.* #845, 1940, 2085, 2109, 2245-2246

RUST
Kin — *Dictionary* p.222

RUSTICITY. *See* **Country life**

RUTH, BABE
Kohn — *Touch* p.170-171
Peterson — *Art* p.61

RUTHLESSNESS. *See* **Cruelty**

RUTLEDGE, ANN
Peterson — *Art* p.25

"RUTS"
Bartlett — *Discovery* p.66-67
Flesch — *Unusual* p.249
Prochnow — *Success.* #372
, Avoidance of
Holmes — *Design* p.114-115

S

SABBATH
See also **Rest**
Applegarth — *Heir.* p.307
Carruthers — *Sparks* p.155-156
Dirksen — *Quot.* #1233, 1549
Droke — *Christian* p.476-478
Edwards — *Useful* p.562-564
Emmons — *Mature* p.20
Evans — *Unto* p.48, 131
Flesch — *Unusual* p.280
Garland — *Subject* #3624, 6162, 6188, 6820
Harnsberger — *Mark* p.419-420, 459
Henry — *5000* p.244-245
Hovey — *Success* p.274-275; *See* index p.301
Hunter — *Gems* p.92-95
Kenneth — *Reader's* #975-976
Kin — *Dictionary* p.223
Knight's Illus. p.188-190
Knight's Treas. p.205-206
Liddle — *Thought I, II, III* p.20, 44, 64, 74, 86, 187
Liddle — *Thought IV* p.13
Liddle — *Thought V* p.7
Lytle — *Leaves* p.29
Mandel — *Stories* p.224
More Words p.142-143, 159-160
Myers — *Thunder* p.65-78
New Topical p.230-231
Prochnow — *Public* #117, 2463, 3669-3671
Prochnow — *Speaker's* p.268
Sagendorph — *Old* p.262-263
Taylor — *With* p.88-89
Wallis — *Treasure* p.62, 133, 184
Woods — *Content.* p.141, 345
Woods — *Religious* p.870-871, 970-971
Zobell — *Speaker's* p.122-123

SABLES
Kin — *Dictionary* p.223

SACKCLOTH
New Topical p.231

SACRAMENT
Flint — *Graham* p.123
Hobe — *Tapestries* p.63
More Words p.143, 145
Wallis — *Treasure* p.134
Wallis — *Words* p.157
Woods — *Religious* p.84, 871-872

SACREDNESS
Hovey — *Treasury* p.266; #355, 401, 1690-1691
Lockridge — *World's* #942
Woods — *Religious* p.872

SACRIFICE
See also **Martyrs and martyrdom; Saints and sainthood; Self-sacrifice**
Adams — *New* p.375
Applegarth — *Heir.* p.88, 168, 244
Dirksen — *Quot.* #23-34, 1058, 1559-1561, 2378
Fogg — *1000 See* index p.897

Forbes — *Thoughts* p.11, 17, 19, 110, 112, 141, 166, 235, 288, 327, 418, 440, 447
Fuller — *Epigrams* p.255
Garland — *Subject* p.281
Grizer — *Wit* p.396
Harnsberger — *Mark* p.420
Henry — *5000* p.245
Hobe — *Tapestries* p.36, 152
Hovey — *Treasury* #20, 29, 39, 78, 592, 678, 713, 727, 753, 814, 1062, 1067, 1815
Humes — *Instant* #957-960
Kauffman — *For* p.194
Kennedy — *Reader's* #977
Knight's Illus. p.279-280
Knight's Treas. p.334-338
Kohn — *Touch* p.18-22
Lockridge — *World's* #2279, 2319, 2334, 5109, 5207
Lytle — *Leaves* p.120, 130
Mandel — *Stories* p.225
More Words p.145-147
New Topical p.35-36, 57, 231-232
Phillips — *Choice* p.63, 271, 393
Sheen — *Way* p.179-181
Wallis — *Treasure* p.70
Wallis — *Words* p.56, 58, 65
White — *Job* p.32-33, 36-37, 95
White — *Life* p.280
Woods — *Religious* p.872-873

"SAD SACKS"
Safian — *Insults* p.171-173

SADDLES
Kin — *Dictionary* p.223
, Empty
Dirksen — *Quot.* #51

SADNESS. *See* **Grief**

SAFARIS
Asimov — *Treasury* #384

SAFEGUARDS. *See* **Safety**

SAFETY
Braude — *Speaker's* #1296-1297
Dirksen — *Quot.* #567
Droke — *Christian* p.478-483
Evans — *Faith* p.54, 128, 149, 153, 155, 161
Evans — *Thoughts I* p.12, 22-27, 90-91, 117-118, 142-143, 190-191, 197, 200
Evans — *Thoughts III (Open Road)* p.19, 160, 166
Evans — *Thoughts IV* p.26-27, 35, 104, 124-125, 133-134, 143, 145, 149, 154, 158
Evans — *Unto* p.37, 60
Flesch — *Unusual* p.249
Forbes — *Thoughts* p.119, 163, 187, 436, 489, 495
Fuller — *Epigrams* p.255-256
Garland — *Subject* p.281-282
Harral — *Feature* p.270-272
Henry — *5000* p.245
Kin — *Dictionary* p.223
Lytle — *Leaves* p.62, 103, 180
Prochnow — *Public* #311, 913, 2304, 2521
Prochnow — *Success.* #1137
Schermerhorn — *1500* p.315, 317
Speaker's Desk p.227-229; #254, 421, 446, 561, 679, 755, 767, 911, 1068
Woods — *Religious* p.873-874
, and liberty
Dirksen — *Quot.* #753
, Automobile
Flint — *Graham* p.15
, Prayer for
Unlimited Power p.27
, Women's rules for
Unlimited Power p.32

SAGACITY. *See* **Cleverness; Knowledge; Wisdom**

SAILING
Adams — *New* p.175
Dirksen — *Quot.* #300
Kahn — *Lessons* p.99-100
Kin — *Dictionary* p.223
Lytle — *Leaves* p.134

SAILORS
Botkin — *Anecdotes* p.180, 207
Botkin — *Treasury* p.178, 185, 192, 388, 596, 630, 829-851
Copeland — *10,000* p.103-113
Fuller — *Epigrams* p.256
Fuller — *Thesaurus* #2430-2437
George — *Book See* index p.444
Henry — *5000* p.245
Kronenberger — *Animal* p.264-266
Peale — *Guideposts* p.213-216
Prochnow — *Public* #462
Prochnow — *Speaker's* p.285-286
Prochnow — *Success.* #995
Speaker's Desk #68, 234, 255, 529, 581
Weisfeld — *Pulpit* p.81-82, 98

SAINT LOUIS, MISSOURI
Botkin — *Anecdotes* p.25, 215, 267
Botkin — *Treasury* p.43, 57, 123, 597, 606

SAINT PATRICK'S DAY
Words — *Inspir.* p.66

SAINT VALENTINE'S DAY. *See* **Valentines**

SAINTS AND SAINTHOOD
See also **Good; Holiness; Martyrs and martyrdom; Piety; Purity;** names of saints
Applegarth — *Heir.* p.81, 144, 211-215, 248
Auden — *Certain* p.331
Braude — *Source* #1498
Dirksen — *Quot.* #2148
Droke — *Christian* p.484
Edwards — *Useful* p.565
Flesch — *Unusual* p.249-250
Flint — *Graham* p.125
Fuller — *Epigrams* p.256
George — *Book* p.24, 51, 187, 324. 329, 408
Goudge — *Comfort* p.124-127
Harnsberger — *Mark* p.420
Kennedy — *Reader's* #978-979
Kin — *Dictionary* p.224
Lockridge — *World's* #877, 1187, 5008, 5529
Lytle — *Leaves* p.57, 101
Mandel — *Stories* p.226
More Words p.147-150
New Topical p.235-236
Seldes — *Great* p.852
Voss — *Quotations* p.219-220
Wallis — *Treasure* p.109, 113, 126, 156, 192
Wallis — *Words* p.19, 62, 87, 128
Woods — *Religious* p.874-877, 883
, Afflicted
New Topical p.6-7
, and sinners
Woods — *Religious* p.877
, Character of
New Topical p.39
, Communion of
New Topical p.50
, Comparison to
New Topical p.232
, Death of
New Topical p.61
, Happiness of
New Topical p.109
, Patron
Flesch — *Unusual* p.205
, Privileges of
New Topical p.205-206
, Reward of
New Topical p.223-224
, Titles and names of
New Topical p.273
, Warfare of
New Topical p.291

SALARIES
See also **Wages**
Applegarth — *Heir.* p.143
Braude — *Speaker's* #1298-1300
Fuller — *Thesaurus* #2251-2254
Prochnow — *Public* #5, 605, 939, 952, 1364, 1636, 1793
Prochnow — *Success.* #1334

SALESMEN AND SALESMANSHIP
See also **Advertising; Business; Commerce; Customers; Trade;** etc.
Botkin — *Treasury* p.358
Braude — *Source* #1499-1501
Braude — *Speaker's* #1301-1331
Braude — *Stories* p.333-336
Cerf — *Laugh* p.399-401
Copeland — *10,000* p.444-447
Edwards — *Useful* p.732
Flesch — *Unusual* p.258
Forbes — *Thoughts* p.13, 185, 204, 210, 219, 256, 297, 303, 306, 374, 397
Fox — *Make* p.89-90
Fuller — *Thesaurus* #2091-2097
Grizer — *Wit* p.396-405, 415-416
Harral — *Feature* p.272-273
Keys Happiness p.310-312
Kin — *Dictionary* p.230
Manchee — *Secret* p.219, 225-226
Modern Eloquence (14) p.410-411
Montapert — *Distilled* p.299-300
New Joy p.137
Prochnow — *Public* #68, 93, 123, 157, 280, 539, 550, 574, 650, 681, 725, 1005
Prochnow — *Speaker's* p.279
Prochnow — *Success.* #803, 2295
Prochnow — *Teacher's* p.269-272
Pullar-Strecker — *Proverbs* #196-199
Schermerhorn — *1500* p.317-320
Speaker's Desk See index p.304
, and sex
Hill — *Think* p.214-216
, Art of
Peterson — *Twenty* p.26-27
, Resistance to
Woods — *Business.* p.223
, Traveling
Botkin — *Anecdotes* p.2, 56, 81, 158, 234, 237-239

SALMON
Lockridge — *World's* #2678

SALOONS
See **Bars; Cocktails and cocktail parties; Taverns**

SALT
Halverson — *Perspective* p.94

Hovey — *Treasury* #68, 444, 643-644
New Topical p.232-233
Prochnow — *Public* #712, 2604

SALUTES AND SALUTATIONS
Asimov — *Treasury* #273
Dirksen — *Quot.* #1799
Kin — *Dictionary* p.224
New Topical p.233
Prochnow — *Public* #127, 298
, *Tibetan*
Peterson — *Art* p.89

SALVATION
See also **Conversion; Forgiveness; Redemption; Sin**
Baillie — *Diary* #91
Curtis — *Practical* p.77
Dirksen — *Quot.* #1563-1566
Flesch — *Unusual* p.250
Flint — *Graham* p.123-125
Forbes — *Thoughts* p.8, 71, 356, 500
Fox — *Make* p.62-63, 121-122
Garland — *Subject* p.282
Halverson — *Perspective* p.44
Hobe — *Tapestries* p.139, 217
Hovey — *Treasury* p.266-267; *See also* index p.300
Johnson — *Bedside* p.324
Kennedy — *Reader's* #980-984
Kin — *Dictionary* p.224
Knight's Illus. p.280-289
Knight's Treas. p.338-349
Kohn — *Touch* p.199-201
McDonagh — *Invit.* p.80-82
New Topical p.233-234
Prochnow — *Public* #834
Prochnow — *Success.* #1272
Seldes — *Great* p.852
Speaker's Desk #156
Strait — *Speaker's* p.147-148
Wallis — *Treasure* p.169
Wallis — *Words* p.224
Weisfeld — *Pulpit* p.15
Woods — *Religious* p.877-883

SALVATION ARMY
Harral — *Feature* p.274
Peale — *Courage* p.135

SAMARIA AND SAMARITANS
Hovey — *Treasury* #31
Kin — *Dictionary* p.224
New Topical p.234-235

SAMPLES
Evans — *Thoughts I* p.27-28, 31, 91
Grizer — *Wit* p.406
Kin — *Dictionary* p.224

SAN ANTONIO, TEXAS
Botkin — *Anecdotes* p.16, 227
Botkin — *Treasury* p.146, 158, 169, 354

SAN FRANCISCO, CALIFORNIA
Asimov — *Treasury* #448
Botkin — *Anecdotes* p.17, 157
Botkin — *Treasury* p.125, 228-229, 281
Kronenberger — *Animal* p.10-13

SANCTIFICATION
Baillie — *Diary* #102

SANCTUARIES
Applegarth — *Heir.* p.217-225
Halverson — *Perspective* p.111
How To Live p.246-249, 254
Kohn — *Through* p.47-48

SAND
Forbes — *Thoughts* p.54, 203, 214, 250

SANDWICHES
Prochnow — *Public* #12, 587, 889-926

SANITATION. *See* **Cleanliness**

SANITY
See also **Judgment**
Flesch — *Unusual* p.250
Forbes — *Thoughts* p.119, 369, 406, 443
Kin — *Dictionary* p.224
Lockridge — *World's* #3610
Prochnow — *Public* #1061
Sheban — *Wisdom* no p.

SANTA CLAUS
Alexander's Treasure. p.47
Asimov — *Treasury* #628
Giniger — *Compact* p.147-148
Grizer — *Wit* p.406
Harnsberger — *Mark* p.421-423
Irion — *Yes* p.10-13
Lytle — *Leaves* p.87
Peterson — *Art* p.401
Prochnow — *Speaker's* p.273
Prochnow — *Success.* #356
Schermerhorn — *1500* p.320-322
, *"Virginia's letter" to*
Alexander's Treasure. p.149-150

SAPPHO
Lockridge — *World's* #4776

SARCASM
See also **Irony; Ridicule; Satire**
Braude — *Speaker's* #1332-1338

Braude — *Stories* p.337-338
Edwards — *Useful* p.520-521, 565
Evans — *Thoughts I* p.72, 92, 185
Evans — *Thoughts II (Open Door)* p.85, 154-155, 183
Ginott — *Between* p.80-81
Kin — *Dictionary* p.224
Lockridge — *World's* #3191
Prochnow — *Public* #503
Speaker's Desk #39, 77, 239, 329, 373, 611, 904, 1096, 1116

SARDINES
Asimov — *Treasury* #275

SARONGS
Flesch — *Unusual* p.250

SATAN. *See* **Devil**

SATIETY
Edwards — *Useful* p.565-566
Lockridge — *World's* #1427

SATIRE
See also **Criticism; Irony; Ridicule; Sarcasm**
Edwards — *Useful* p.566-567, 732
Fogg — *1000 See* index p.898
Harnsberger — *Mark* p.424
Henry — *5000* p.245-246
Lockridge — *World's* #4991

SATISFACTION
See also **Contentment; Self-satisfaction**
Braude — *Stories* p.338
Dirksen — *Quot.* #205
Flesch — *Unusual* p.250
Flint — *Graham* p.26, 84
Forbes — *Thoughts* p.12, 108, 169, 340, 460, 479
Garland — *Subject* p.283
Grizer — *Wit* p.406-407
Henry — *5000* p.246
Krishnamurti — *Think* p.29-30
Lockridge — *World's* #2090, 3403
Lytle — *Leaves* p.181, 186
Montapert — *Distilled* p.300
New Joy p.52
Prochnow — *Public* #839, 1027, 1311
Prochnow — *Success.* #1410
Speaker's Desk #144, 225, 303, 371, 374, 631, 662, 986, 1155
Wallis — *Treasure* p.15
Wallis — *Words* p.51, 86, 229

SATURATION
Kohn — *Through* p.145-146

SATURDAY
Kin — *Dictionary* p.225

SAUNAS
New Joy p.189-192

SAVAGES AND SAVAGERY
Adams — *New* p.135
Harnsberger — *Mark* p.424-425
Ideas p.280-282

SAVING. *See* **Economy; Thrift**

SAVIOUR. *See* **Jesus Christ**

SAWMILLS
Botkin — *Anecdotes* p.98
Prochnow — *Public* #922

SAXOPHONES
Prochnow — *Public* #756, 1595

SAYINGS. *See* **Proverbs; Quotations;** names of nationalities

"SCABS"
Kin — *Dictionary* p.225
Seldes — *Great* p.852-853

SCANDAL
See also **Disgrace; Reputation; Shame; Slander**
Dirksen — *Quot.* #2150
Edwards — *Useful* p.567-568
Flesch — *Unusual* p.250
Henry — *5000* p.246
Kin — *Dictionary* p.225-226
Lockridge — *World's* #889, 970, 1020, 1422, 5859
Prochnow — *Public* #1242, 2134, 4209
Woods — *Religious* p.884

"SCAPEGOATS"
Botkin — *Anecdotes* p.38
Huxley — *You See* index p.288
New Topical p.236

SCARECROWS
Reader's — *20th* p.50-51

SCARS
Hobe — *Tapestries* p.218

"SCAVENGER HUNTS"
Day — *Meditations* p.16-17

SCENERY. *See* **Nature**

SCEPTICISM. *See* **Skepticism**

SCHEDULES
Baillie — *Diary* #205
Halverson — *Perspective* p.46
Prochnow — *Success.* #1, 2

SCHEMES. *See* **Plans and planning**

SCHISMS
Woods — *Religious* p.884-885

SCHOLARS AND SCHOLARSHIP
See also **Learning**
Applegarth — *Heir.* p.227
Evans — *Unto* p.114
Flesch — *Unusual* p.309
Humes — *Instant* #961-963
Kin — *Dictionary* p.226
Lindeman — *Emerson* p.103-119
Lockridge — *World's* #1600
Prochnow — *Speaker's* p.273
Prochnow — *Success.* #809
Suter — *Prayers* #141-147
Woods — *Religious* p.885

SCHOOLS
See also **Education; Students; Teachers; Universities and colleges**
Applegarth — *Heir.* p.227-231
Botkin — *Anecdotes* p.61, 123, 144
Braude — *Speaker's* #1339-1340
Copeland — *10,000* p.334-353
Dirksen — *Quot.* #301, 356, 482, 1145
Evans — *Thoughts I* p.36-38, 143-145, 150-151, 153, 172-176, 207
Evans — *Thoughts IV* p.63-70
Evans — *Unto* p.106-107
Flesch — *Unusual* p.251
Forbes — *Thoughts* p.33, 70, 360, 434, 496
Fuller — *Thesaurus* p.179-183; #1051-1053
Harnsberger — *Mark* p.425
Harral — *Feature* p.274-282
Hobe — *Tapestries* p.14, 23
Hovey — *Treasury* p.267; *See also* index p.300
Lytle — *Leaves* p.143
Modern Eloquence (14) p.111-120
New Joy p.119
Prochnow — *Public* #27, 265, 336, 499, 528, 684, 1090, 2128
Prochnow — *Speaker's* p.274-276
Prochnow — *Success.* #638, 932, 951, 1142, 1321
Schermerhorn — *1500* p.322-325
Seldes — *Great* p.853-854
, African
Guideposts — *Faith* p.416-419
, Homework
Ginott — *Between* p.71, 82, 232-234
Prochnow — *Success.* #931, 1072
, Social life in
Ginott — *Between* p.143-145

SCHWEITZER, ALBERT
Applegarth — *Heir.* p.56, 173
Guideposts — *Faith* p.420-423
Kohn — *Touch* p.149-151
Wallis — *Treasure* p.149
Wallis — *Words* p.168, 235

SCIENCE
See also **Discovery; Inventors and inventions; Research; Scientists;** names of sciences
Alexander's Treasure. p.75
Applegarth — *Heir.* p.154, 193
Auden — *Certain* p.332-336
Bartlett — *Discovery* p.10-12, 50-51
Braude — *Source* #1502-1504
Braude — *Speaker's* #1341-1342
Braude — *Stories* p.339
Curtis — *Practical See* index p.573
Droke — *Christian* p.485-490
Du Noüy — *Human See* index p.287
Edwards — *Useful* p.569-571, 732
Evans — *Unto* p.20, 45, 114
Flesch — *Unusual* p.251-253
Fogg — *Unusual* #134, 144, 264, 466, 471, 628, 638, 694, 739, 1000
Forbes — *Thoughts See* index p.566
Fuller — *Epigrams* p.256-257
Garland — *Subject* p.284-285
Harral — *Feature* p.282-283
Henry — *5000* p.246-247
Hovey — *Treasury* p.267-268; #91, 1700-1703
Hubbard — *Scrap* p.69, 75, 215, 225
Humes — *Instant* #964-976, 1260-1262
Hunter — *Gems* p.97-98
Johnson — *Bedside* p.211, 280
Keller — *Open* p.98-99
Kennedy — *Fresh* p.53
Kennedy — *Reader's* #985-995
Kin — *Dictionary* p.226
Liddle — *Thought V* p.5, 13-14, 32
Lockridge — *World's* #3677, 3893, 4454, 4488, 4506, 4805, 5284, 5511, 5597
Lytle — *Leaves* p.58

Montapert — *Distilled* p.301-302
New Topical p.236
Patterns For Living p.469-619
Peale — *Courage* p.65-66
Phillips — *Choice* p.11-12, 86, 117, 401
Prochnow — *Public* #420, 530, 3672-3673
Prochnow — *Speaker's* p.276-277
Prochnow — *Success.* #805, 1249
Seldes — *Great* p.854-857
Sheban — *Wisdom* no p.
Simpson — *Contemp.* p.188-195
Speaker's Desk p.229-233
Wallis — *Words* p.4, 71, 118
Wheelis — *Moralist* p.9, 22, 126, 132, 152
Woods — *Religious* p.885-903
Words — *Inspir.* p.189-190
, and art. See **Art, and science**
, and creation
Woods — *Religious* p.891-892
, and God
See also **Religion, and science**
Adams — *New* p.131
Alexander's Treasure. p.288-292
Baillie — *Diary* #228
Braude — *Source* #1505
Du Noüy — *Human* p.xiii-xiv, xvi-xvii, 112-119, 132-133, 182, 184-185, 224-225, 242-243
Flesch — *Unusual* p.252-253
Flint — *Graham* p.126-127
Holmes — *Design* p.165
How To Live p.543, 548, 550
Kohn — *Pathways* p.51
Peale — *Guideposts* p.326-328
Webb — *Edge* p.87
Woods — *Religious* p.892-903
, and invention
Copeland — *World's* p.429-431, 627-631, 655-656, 683-688
, and law
Holmes — *Design* p.32-33, 64, 71, 103, 107, 113, 167
, and religion. See **Religion, and science; Science, and God**
, and truth
Kauffman — *For* p.195
, as religion
Ideas p.349-350
Woods — *Religious* p.890-891
, Claims of
Baillie — *Diary* #183
, Discovery of
Adams — *New* p.237
, German
Nizer — *Thinking* p.174-175
, Humility of
Curtis — *Practical* p.93-94, 216-217
, Laws of
Du Noüy — *Human* *See* index p.284
, Method of
Ideas p.350-352
Wheelis — *Moralist* p.9, 32
, Passion in
Curtis — *Practical* p.94
, Patience in
Curtis — *Practical* p.93

SCIENCE OF MIND
Curtis — *Golden* p.3-211
Holmes — *Design* p.195

SCIENTISTS
Adams — *New* p.335
Asimov — *Treasury* #80, 82
Flesch — *Unusual* p.253
Forbes — *Thoughts* p.105, 291, 345, 505
Fuller — *Thesaurus* #1116-1122
Prochnow — *Success.* #2266
Woods — *Religious* p.903
, and religion
Du Noüy — *Human* p.132-133, 182, 242-243
, and thinkers
Seaburg — *Great* p.168, 217, 228, 238, 240, 242, 250, 253, 277

SCISSORS
Prochnow — *Public* #1794

SCOFFING. *See* **Ridicule**

SCOLDING. *See* **Criticism**

SCORPIONS
New Topical p.236-237

SCOTLAND
Henry — *5000* p.247
Wallis — *Words* p.164
, Church in
Weisfeld — *Pulpit* p.166, 169
, Clans of
Asimov — *Treasury* #413

SCOTSMEN
Asimov — *Treasury* #407-413
Cerf — *Laugh* p.437-439
Curtis — *Practical* p.55
Flesch — *Unusual* p.253

Modern Eloquence (14) p.213-216
Prochnow — *Public* #1795
Prochnow — *Speaker's* p.277
Prochnow — *Success.* #2267
Schermerhorn — *1500* p.325-332
Weisfeld — *Pulpit* p.11, 97
, *Stories of*
Copeland — *10,000* p.706-727
Fun Fare p.77
Speaker's Desk See index p.304

SCOTT, SIR WALTER
Flesch — *Unusual* p.253
Wallis — *Words* p.82

SCOUTS AND SCOUTMASTERS. *See* **Boy Scouts of America; Girl Scouts of America**

"SCREWBALLS"
Dirksen — *Quot.* #170
Safian — *Insults* p.174-176
Safian — *More* p.158-159

SCRIBES. *See* **Writers**

SCRIPTURES
See also **Bible; New Testament; Old Testament; Psalms**; etc.
Applegarth — *Heir.* p.233-241
Baillie — *Diary* #342
Flint — *Graham* p.127
Henry — *5000* p.247
Hubbard — *Scrap* p.108, 208
Kauffman — *For* p.195-196
Kin — *Dictionary* p.226
Lytle — *Leaves* p.45, 51
New Topical p.237-238
Seldes — *Great* p.857
Woods — *Religious* p.903
, *and propaganda*
Kauffman — *For* p.196

SCRUPLES. *See* **Conscience; Honesty; Integrity**

SCULPTURE AND SCULPTORS
Applegarth — *Heir.* p.28, 31
Curtis — *Practical* p.450-451
Dirksen — *Quot.* #1059
Flesch — *Unusual* p.201, 253-254
Fogg — *1000* #27, 32, 89, 445, 615, 623
Fuller — *Thesaurus* #1296-1297
George — *Book* p.1, 103, 192, 223, 228
Harral — *Feature* p.283
Henry — *5000* p.247
Hooker — *Index* p.261-264
Hubbard — *Scrap* p.26
Lytle — *Leaves* p.12, 62
Nizer — *Thinking* p.74
Peale — *Courage* p.49-50
Peterson — *Art* p.41, 78
Prochnow — *Success.* #2268
Woods — *Wellsprings* p.63

SEA
See also **Lakes; Ocean;** etc.
Applegarth — *Heir.* p.189, 207
Barrows — *1000* See index p.443-444
Dirksen — *Quot.* #2151-2152
Edwards — *Useful* p.571-572
Flesch — *Unusual* p.254
Forbes — *Thoughts* p.185, 334, 430
Fun Fare p.34-35, 200-202
Garland — *Subject* p.285
Goudge — *Comfort* p.337-341
Harnsberger — *Mark* p.426-427
Harral — *Feature* p.283
Henry — *5000* p.247-248
Hobe — *Tapestries* p.215
Hubbard — *Scrap* p.98, 107, 147
Kin — *Dictionary* p.227
Lindbergh — *Gift* p.19-120
Lockridge — *World's* #1232-1236, 1251, 4037, 5462-5479
New Topical p.238-239
Prochnow — *Public* #2087, 2562
, *Accidents of*
Unlimited Power p.20-23
, *Chime of*
Hadfield — *Delights* p.56
, *Power of*
Clark — *Windows* p.154-155
, *Voices of*
Adams — *New* p.287
, *Voyages on*
Cerf — *Laugh* p.441-442
Woods — *Content.* p.66, 72, 80, 83, 87

SEA GULLS
Adams — *New* p.304
Applegarth — *Heir.* p.21
Esteve — *Experience* p.5

SEALS
Harral — *Feature* p.284
New Topical p.239-240

SEARCH
Applegarth — *Heir.* p.201
Flesch — *Unusual* p.255-256
Goudge — *Comfort* p.212-218
Grizer — *Wit* p.379
Guideposts — *Faith* p.291-295
Kin — *Dictionary* p.227-228
Krishnamurti — *Urgency* p.67-69

Lytle — *Leaves* p.81, 104, 108, 156
Mandel — *Stories* p.226-227
Peterson — *Art* p.132, 343
Prochnow — *Public* #652, 2420, 2621, 2677
Prochnow — *Speaker's* p.277
Prochnow — *Success.* #819, 2273-2275
Taylor — *With* p.108-115
Wallis — *Words* p.50, 88, 91, 118, 132, 141, 145-146, 171, 203
, for Best
Peterson — *Art* p.320

SEARCHLIGHTS
Wallis — *Words* p.55

SEASHORE. *See* **Beaches**

SEASICKNESS
Asimov — *Treasury* #92
Prochnow — *Public* #1221, 1949
Prochnow — *Speaker's* p.277
Schermerhorn — *1500* p.332-333
Speaker's Desk #845, 1076

SEASONS
See also names of seasons
Alexander's Treasure. p.24, 240
Auden — *Certain* p.337-342
Braude — *Source* #1506-1507
Dirksen — *Quot.* #86, 88-89, 308, 1079, 1084
Evans — *Quote* p.233-240
Evans — *Unto* p.11, 19, 22, 43, 59
Felleman — *Poems* p.371-392
Goudge — *Comfort* p.40-57
Henry — *5000* p.248
Hobe — *Tapestries* p.56-61
Kin — *Dictionary* p.227
New Joy p.161
Prochnow — *Public* #245
Sagendorph — *Old* p.27-37
Woods — *Content.* p.100

SEATS
Prochnow — *Public* #105, 885

SEATTLE, WASHINGTON
Schermerhorn — *1500* p.52

SECLUSION. *See* **Solitude**

SECONDHAND
Kin — *Dictionary* p.227
Woods — *Wellsprings* p.36-37

"SECONDS"
Evans — *Thoughts III (Open Road)* p.95-96
Lockridge — *World's* #1544

SECRECY
See also **Concealment; Mystery; Silence**
Book Proverbs p.131
Braude — *Source* #1508-1509
Braude — *Speaker's* #1343-1344
Braude — *Stories* p.339
Clark — *Windows* p.54
Dirksen — *Quot.* #141, 1060
Edwards — *Useful* p.572-573, 732
Evans — *Thoughts III (Open Road)* p.25
Flesch — *Unusual* p.254
Forbes — *Thoughts* p.203, 422, 454
Fuller — *Epigrams* p.257-258
Grizer — *Wit* p.407-408
Harral — *Feature* p.284
Henry — *5000* p.248
Hobe — *Tapestries* p.110
How To Live p.421-424
Huxley — *You See* index p.288
Kin — *Dictionary* p.227
Lockridge — *World's* #90, 841, 2298, 2989, 3704
Lytle — *Leaves* p.83-84
Mandel — *Stories* p.227
Prochnow — *Public* #2388, 3674-3675, 4210
Prochnow — *Success.* #2269-2270
Sheban — *Wisdom* no p.
Speaker's Desk #146, 434, 499, 721, 803, 1119-1120, 1178
Wallis — *Worth* p.62
, Value of
Nizer — *Thinking* p.54

SECRETARIES
See also **Stenographers**
Braude — *Speaker's* #1345-1346
Manchee — *Secret* p.227
Prochnow — *Public* #730, 1645
Prochnow — *Success.* #1182
, Dedication of
Welk — *Guide.* p.159-161

SECTIONALISM
Botkin — *Anecdotes* p.16

SECTS
See also **Creeds**
Edwards — *Useful* p.573-574
Flesch — *Unusual* p.254
Seldes — *Great* p.857-858
Woods — *Religious* p.903-904

SECULARISM
Kennedy — *Reader's* #996-1001
Woods — *Religious* p.904-908

SECURITY
See also **Confidence; Safety**
Applegarth — *Heir.* p.271

Braude — *Source* #1510-1512
Curtis — *Practical* p.351-389
Dirksen — *Quot.* #2346, 2367
Droke — *Christian* p.490-491
Evans — *Unto* p.35, 37, 40, 103
Flint — *Graham* p.127-128
Forbes — *Thoughts* See index p.566
Garland — *Subject* p.286-287
Grizer — *Wit* p.409
Halverson — *Perspective* p.90
Holmes — *Design* p.51, 54, 105-106, 210
Johnson — *Bedside* p.111, 124, 142
Keller — *Open* p.17-18
Kennedy — *Reader's* #1002-1004
Keys Happiness p.441-448
Kin — *Dictionary* p.227
Kohn — *Best* p.32-35
Kohn — *Touch* p.202-205
Liddle — *Thought I, II, III* p.30, 62, 123
Lindbergh — *Unicorn* p.36-37
Maltz — *Creative* p.10-21
Montapert — *Distilled* p.302
More Words p.152
Phillips — *Choice* p.163, 374
Prochnow — *Speaker's* p.278
Prochnow — *Success.* #169, 740, 1411, 2271
Seldes — *Great* p.858
Wallis — *Words* p.118
Woods — *Business.* p.224-228
Woods — *Religious* p.908-909

, False
Evans — *This* p.47-48

, Inner
Holmes — *Design* p.105-106

, National
Dirksen — *Quot.* #714

, Physical
Kennedy — *Fresh* p.24-26

, Sense of
Menninger — *Blue.* p.19-20

SEDITION
See also **Treason**
Kin — *Dictionary* p.228
Seldes — *Great* p.858
Woods — *Religious* p.909

SEEDS
Applegarth — *Heir.* p.104, 190, 264
Evans — *Thoughts I* p.105-110
Kin — *Dictionary* p.228
New Topical p.241
Sheban — *Wisdom* no p.

, Garden
Alexander's Treasure. p.211

, Invisible
Adams — *New* p.409

, Vitality of
Sagendorph — *Old* p.287-290

SEEING. *See* **Eyes; Sight**

SEEKING. *See* **Search**

SEEMING. *See* **Appearance**

SEGREGATION
Prochnow — *Success.* #252
Seldes — *Great* p.858-859
Sheban — *Wisdom* no p.

SELECTION. *See* **Choice**

SELF
Bach — *Make* p.46-47
Baillie — *Diary* #211
Bartlett — *Discovery* p.27-54
Boas — *History* p.146-163
Book Proverbs p.103
Braude — *Stories* p.339
Curtis — *Daily* p.12-19
Curtis — *New* p.73-83
Detherage — *Sunrise* p.23, 48-50
Dirksen — *Quot.* #2299
Flesch — *Unusual* p.200, 256
Forbes — *Thoughts* p.233, 332, 354, 380, 392, 402-403, 408, 428-429, 436, 448, 453, 495, 497, 504, 506, 512
Fox — *Make* p.60-61
Francis — *For* p.11-25
Garland — *Subject* p.288-289
Hadfield — *Delights* p.121
Harnsberger — *Mark* p.427
Henry — *5000* p.123
Holman — *Psych.* p.14-29
Hovey — *Treasury* p.268-270; #55, 358, 1704-1714
Hulme — *Living* p.1-21
Kahn — *Lessons* p.69-164
Keys Happiness p.258-260, 496-498
Kin — *Dictionary* p.134, 182, 284-285
Kohn — *Pathways* p.15-44
Lytle — *Leaves* p.102
Maltz — *Creative* p.169-170
Mandelbaum — *Choose* p.231-257
Montapert — *Distilled* p.31, 217, 268, 302-303, 343-344
Nichols — *New* p.5-139
Peale — *Sin* p.100-102
Peterson — *Art* p.106, 127, 231, 263, 292
Peterson — *Twenty* p.14-15
Phillips — *Choice* p.30, 44, 96, 131, 146, 174, 177-180, 185, 208, 292; *See also* index p.429

Prochnow — *Public* #933, 1861, 2279
Prochnow — *Success.* #1206, 2016-2021, 2115-2117, 2276
Rau — *Act* p.86-97
Reader's — *20th* p.14-16
Sheban — *Wisdom* no p.
Sheen — *Content.* p.89-91
Sheen — *Lift* p.128-139
Sherman — *Your* p.29-42
Streiker — *Who* p.55-85
Taylor — *With* p.55-60
Walters — *How* p.111-127
Webb — *Edge* p.13-15, 23-26
Welk — *Guide.* p.55-57
White — *Job* p.33-34
Woods — *Content. See* index p.380
Woods — *Religious* p.909-910
Woods — *Wellsprings* p.9

, *-abandonment. See* **Self-sacrifice**

, *-abasement. See* **Self-criticism**

, *-acceptance*
Fridy — *Meditat.* p.49
Lair — *Baby* p.57-70
Liebman — *Peace* p.53-56
Maltz — *Creative* p.77-78
Phillips — *Choice* p.38, 80-82
Vogue — *Arts* p.55-62

, *-accusation. See* **Self-blame**

, *-admiration. See* **Self-esteem; Self-praise**

, *-analysis*
See also **Meditation; Reflection; Self-knowledge**
Albert — *Stop* p.164-165
Braude — *Source* #1513-1517
Braude — *Stories* p.340
Edwards — *Useful* p.578-579
Evans — *Thoughts I* p.11-12, 219
Flint — *Graham* p.78
Forbes — *Thoughts* p.66, 162, 172, 205, 389, 485
Grizer — *Wit* p.409, 412
Hubbard — *Scrap* p.119, 127
Liddle — *Thought V* p.41
Lockridge — *World's* #3537
Mandelbaum — *Choose* p.137-141
Mandel — *Stories* p.228
Montapert — *Distilled* p.305-306
New Topical p.243
Phillips — *Choice* p.183-207, 334
Sheen — *Content.* p.93-119
Suter — *Prayers* #329-350
Wallis — *Words* p.51, 91
Wheelis — *Moralist* p.41

, *Questions for*
Hill — *Think* p.144-146, 283-287

, *-apology. See* **Self-defense**

, *-appraisal. See* **Self-analysis**

, *-appreciation. See* **Self-esteem**

, *-approbation. See* **Self-praise**

, *-approval. See* **Self-praise**

, *-assertion. See* **Self-confidence**

, *-assurance. See* **Self-confidence**

, *-balance. See* **Self-control**

, *-blame*
Baillie — *Diary* #163
Braude — *Speaker's* #1349-1350
Braude — *Stories* p.340-341
Dirksen — *Quot.* #318
Evans — *Unto* p.39
Fox — *Make* p.183-184
Garland — *Subject* p.289
Holmes — *Design* p.104-105
Hulme — *Living* p.23-29
Johnson — *Bedside* p.191
Keys Happiness p.462-465
Kin — *Dictionary* p.228
Peterson — *Art* p.332

, *-centeredness. See* **Self-importance**

, *-change. See* **Self-improvement**

, *-conceit. See* **Self-praise**

, *-concept. See* **Self-knowledge**

, *-condemnation. See* **Self-blame**

, *-confidence*
See also **Courage**
Albert — *Stop* p.52-62, 198
Braude — *Source* #1518-1522
Braude — *Speaker's* #1351-1354
Flesch — *Unusual* p.258
Forbes — *Thoughts* p.108, 117, 301, 314, 373, 443, 471, 495
Grizer — *Wit* p.410
Hill — *Think* p.56-58
Hubbard — *Scrap* p.150
Jones — *If* p.65-74
Keys Happiness p.227-231
Kin — *Dictionary* p.228
Liddle — *Thought I, II, III* p.11, 24, 64, 107-108, 119, 182
Liddle — *Thought IV* p.5, 24, 34, 39
Liddle — *Thought V* p.26, 36
Lockridge — *World's* #2558
Maltz — *Creative* p.19-20, 77
Montapert — *Distilled* p.304
Nizer — *Thinking* p.152
Peale — *Stay* p.247-263
Peterson — *Art* p.105, 366
Prochnow — *Public* #1796

Prochnow — *Success.* #149, 173, 212
Sherman — *Your* p.144
Speaker's Desk #61, 228, 240, 251, 339, 573, 668-669, 837
Wheelis — *Moralist* p.102-104
, and humility
Albert — *Stop* p.53-54
, -conflict. See **Self-blame**
, -conquest. See **Self-control**
, -consciousness
See also **Bashfulness**
Baillie — *Diary* #151, 250
Curtis — *Golden* p.57
Flesch — *Unusual* p.256
Johnson — *Bedside* p.196, 250
Kennedy — *Reader's* #1005
Keys Happiness p.356-358
Phillips — *Choice* p.6, 16, 210
Wheelis — *Moralist* p.31
, -contempt. See **Self-criticism**
, -contribution. See **Self-sacrifice**
, -control
See also **Abstinence; Discretion; Habit; Prudence; Temperance**
Bartlett — *Discovery* p.110-126
Braude — *Source* #1523-1525, 1540-1541
Braude — *Stories* p.344-345
Dirksen — *Quot.* #1062
Edwards — *Useful* p.575-576
Evans — *Faith* p.8, 19, 28, 53-56, 119-125, 131-136, 139, 159, 179-182
Evans — *Quote* p.205-214
Evans — *Thoughts I* p.70-71, 83, 91, 103, 141, 156
Evans — *Thoughts II (Open Door)* p.45-47, 169
Evans — *Thoughts III (Open Road)* p.50, 67, 72, 100, 165
Evans — *Thoughts IV* p.76-77, 114, 124, 199
Evans — *Unto* p.123
Flesch — *Unusual* p.256-258
Flint — *Graham* p.128-130
Forbes — *Thoughts* p.14, 25, 51, 65, 86-87, 124, 146, 151, 170, 195, 258, 285, 291, 312, 322, 335, 338, 392, 469
Fox — *Make* p.12-13
Grizer — *Wit* p.410-412
Halverson — *Perspective* p.16
Hubbard — *Scrap* p.36, 54, 99, 167, 318, 226
Huxley — *You See* index p.288
Johnson — *Bedside* p.246
Kahn — *Lessons* p.96-105
Kin — *Dictionary* p.183, 228
Knight's Illus. p.292-293
Knight's Treas. p.353-354
Kohn — *Touch* p.179-182
Krishnamurti — *Think* p.100-106
Lockridge — *World's* #1507, 4624
Lytle — *Leaves* p.128
Maltz — *Creative* p.197-199
Mandel — *Stories* p.227-228
Montapert — *Distilled* p.304-305
Nichols — *New* p.159-160
Peale — *Sin* p.70-102, 198-207
Price — *Wider* p.33-34
Prochnow — *Public* #2416, 3676-3678
Prochnow — *Success.* #2277, 2290
Reader's — *Getting* p.61-63
Sheen — *Lift* p.83-91
Sheen — *Thoughts* p.108-110
Sheen — *Way* p.131-132
Speaker's Desk p.233
Unlimited Power p.261-263
Voss — *Quotations* p.220-222
Wallis — *Words* p.72, 177-182
Watson — *Light* p.161-183
White — *Life* p.40-41
Wilcox — *Heart* p.69-71
Woods — *Religious* p.910-912, 974
, -criticism
Blanton — *Faith* p.110-132
Carruthers — *Sparks* p.157-158
Dirksen — *Quot.* #173
Evans — *This* p.32
Hulme — *Living* p.9-11
Kin — *Dictionary* p.229
Lair — *Baby* p.25-39
Liebman — *Peace* p.46-53
Maltz — *Creative* p.17
Peale — *Faith* p.109-134
Phillips — *Choice* p.126
Woods — *Religious* p.910
, -cure
Kin — *Dictionary* p.228-229
Maltz — *Creative* p.193-195
, -deception
Edwards — *Useful* p.576-577
Evans — *Unto* p.91
Flint — *Graham* p.130
Johnson — *Bedside* p.252
Lockridge — *World's* #117, 122, 144, 277-279, 1790, 4051
New Topical p.242

Phillips — *Choice* p.65-66, 137, 146
Woods — *Religious* p.910-911

, *-dedication. See* **Self-sacrifice**

, *-defense*
Hulme — *Living* p.32-34
Keys Happiness p.462-465
Kin — *Dictionary* p.228-229
Phillips — *Choice* p.127
Woods — *Religious* p.911

, *-delusion. See* **Self-deception**

, *-denial*
See also **Abstinence; Asceticism; Moderation; Sacrifice; Temperance**
Edwards — *Useful* p.577-578
Flesch — *Unusual* p.256
Flint — *Graham* p.128
Forbes — *Thoughts* p.54, 200, 289, 326, 392, 407
Fuller — *Epigrams* p.258
Lockridge — *World's* #2279
Lytle — *Leaves* p.126
New Topical p.242-243
Peale — *Sin* p.193-197
Phillips — *Choice* p.23, 29, 82, 189
Prochnow — *Success.* #2278
White — *Job* p.27
Woods — *Religious* p.911

, *-dependence. See* **Self-reliance**

, *-deprecation. See* **Self-criticism**

, *-destruction*
See also **Suicide**
Baillie — *Diary* #139
Braude — *Stories* p.341
Mandel — *Stories* p.229
Peterson — *Art* p.100
White — *Job* p.117-118, 123, 127, 129, 131, 134-135, 139, 141, 145

, *-determination. See* **Self-will**

, *-development. See* **Self-improvement**

, *-direction. See* **Self-improvement**

, *-discipline. See* **Self-control**

, *-discovery*
Adams — *New* p.411
Baillie — *Diary* #233
Clark — *Windows* p.64
Curtis — *Daily* p.180-185
Forbes — *Thoughts* p.142, 206, 265
Fridy — *Meditat.* p.43
Holmes — *Design* p.71-81
Lair — *Baby* p.143-150
Liebman — *Peace* p.56-58
Lytle — *Leaves* p.76
Maltz — *Creative* p.17, 140-145
Peterson — *Art* p.343

, *-dispraise. See* **Self-blame**

, *-education. See* **Self-improvement**

, *-emergence. See* **Self-knowledge**

, *-esteem*
See also **Egoism and egotists; Self-praise**
Braude — *Stories* p.341-342
Curtis — *Daily* p.148-149
Detherage — *Sunrise* p.45-50
Flesch — *Unusual* p.256
Johnson — *Bedside* p.188
Lockridge — *World's* #1633, 1796, 1847, 2080, 3088, 2932, 4825
Mandelbaum — *Choose* p.215-219, 242-244
Nichols — *Third* p.78-80
Phillips — *Choice* p.126
Prochnow — *Speaker's* p.278
Prochnow — *Success.* #2279

, *-examination. See* **Self-analysis**

, *-expression*
Curtis — *Daily* p.180-185
How To Live p.291
Kohn — *Best* p.64-66
Krishnamurti — *Think* p.156
Krishnamurti — *Urgency* p.129-131
Lair — *Baby* p.113-123
Sheban — *Wisdom* no p.
Woods — *Content.* p.25

, *-forgetfulness. See* **Unselfishness**

, *-fulfillment. See* **Self-expression**

, *-giving. See* **Unselfishness**

, *-government*
Dirksen — *Quot.* #621
Johnson — *Bedside* p.200, 299-300
Seldes — *Great* p.859

, *-hate. See* **Self-blame; Self-criticism**

, *-help*
See also **Self-improvement**
Dirksen — *Quot.* #1169, 2392
Flesch — *Unusual* p.257
Mandel — *Stories* p.228-229
Modern Eloquence (14) p.412-414
Woods — *Religious* p.912

, *-honesty. See* **Self-knowledge**

, *-image*
Dirksen — *Quot.* #280
Hulme — *Living* p.44-46
Maltz — *Creative* p.127-128; *See also* index p.225
, *teenager*
Ginott — *Between* p.81-84, 121-124

, *-importance*
Adams — *New* p.59
Braude — *Source* #1526-1530
Braude — *Speaker's* #1355
Braude — *Stories* p.345-346

Curtis — *Human* p.11
Flesch — *Unusual* p.257
Flint — *Graham* p.128
Grizer — *Wit* p.409-410
Holmes — *Design* p.37-38
Lockridge — *World's* #3239
Prochnow — *Success.* #2280
Reader's — *Getting* p.229-245
Reader's — *20th* p.49
Woods — *Wellsprings* p.59

, *-improvement*
See also **Education; Improvement; Progress; Reform and reformers; Study**
Applegarth — *Heir.* p.73
Edwards — *Useful* p.579-580
Flesch — *Unusual* p.257
Forbes — *Thoughts* p.271, 343, 359, 378
Grizer — *Wit* p.413
How To Live p.174-178
Keller — *Open* p.65
Liebman — *Peace* p.41-46
Mandel — *Stories* p.230
Montapert — *Distilled* p.305-306
Peterson — *New* p.8-9
Phillips — *Choice* p.168, 183; *See* index p.429
Prochnow — *Success.* #808

, *-incrimination. See* **Self-blame**

, *-indulgence. See* **Self-interest**

, *-interest*
Adams — *New* p.82
Braude — *Source* #1531-1532
Curtis — *Practical* p.547-549
Evans — *Unto* p.29, 47
Flesch — *Unusual* p.257
Forbes — *Thoughts* p.64, 79, 83, 133, 139, 197, 344, 370
Hubbard — *Scrap* p.83
Keller — *You* p.45-49
Kohn — *Best* p.72-73
Lockridge — *World's* #1507, 1791, 1845, 3399
Prochnow — *Success.* #2281
Seldes — *Great* p.859-860
Wheelis — *Moralist* p.44
White — *Job* p.84
Woods — *Religious* p.912

, *-inventory*
See also **Self-knowledge**
Curtis — *Daily* p.14-15
Halverson — *Perspective* p.117
List — *Living* p.7-12

, *-justification. See* **Self-defense**

, *-knowledge*
See also **Intelligence; Knowledge; Self-analysis; Understanding; Wisdom**
Adams — *New* p.21
Bach — *Make* p.39-40
Bradshaw — *Home.* p.9-11
Braude — *Source* #1536-1537
Clark — *Windows* p.160
Curtis — *Golden* p.3-13, 185
Dirksen — *Quot.* #433-434, 974, 1063, 2345
Edwards — *Useful* p.582-583
Esteve — *Experience* p.33-34
Flint — *Graham* p.130
Forbes — *Thoughts* p.152, 188, 205, 231, 247, 285, 293, 348, 422
Henry — *5000* p.141-143, 249
Holmes — *Design* p.89
How To Live p.174-178, 421-424
Hubbard — *Scrap* p.224
Johnson — *Bedside* p.76, 95
Keller — *Open* p.47
Keys Happiness p.21-24
Kin — *Dictionary* p.229
Krishnamurti — *Think* p.42-43, 111-112
Krishnamurti — *Urgency* p.64-65
Lockridge — *World's* #2247-2249, 2910, 5596
McDonagh — *Invit.* p.177-178
Menninger — *Blue.* p.9-10, 62
Montapert — *Distilled* p.303, 306
Nichols — *New* p.7-9
Phillips — *Choice* p.68, 80, 82, 109; *See also* index p.429
Prochnow — *Success.* #1944-1945, 2283
Sheban — *Wisdom* no p.
Sheen — *Lift* p.55-62
Voss — *Quotations* p.226-228
Webb — *Edge* p.16-21
White — *Job* p.67-69
Woods — *Religious* p.912-913
Woods — *Wellspring* p.18-19

, *-love*
See also **Conceit; Egoism and egotists; Self-esteem; Self-praise; Selfishness; Snobs and snobbery; Vanity**
Adams — *New* p.7
Baillie — *Diary* #356
Braude — *Speaker's* #1358
Dirksen — *Quot.* #227, 861
Edwards — *Useful* p.583-584
Flesch — *Unusual* p.257
Flint — *Graham* p.129
Franke — *Buckley* p.270-271

Henry — *5000* p.249
Liebman — *Peace* p.38-58
Lockridge — *World's See* index p.582
Maltz — *Creative* p.17
Phillips — *Choice See* index p.429
Prochnow — *Public* #4211-4212
Prochnow — *Success.* #2284-2286
Taylor — *With* p.31-34
Woods — *Religious* p.914-915
, *-loyalty. See* **Self-confidence**
, *-made*
Dirksen — *Quot.* #145
Evans — *This* p.32
Evans — *Unto* p.30
Grizer — *Wit* p.414
Harnsberger — *Mark* p.427
Henry — *5000* p.249-250
Lockridge — *World's* #3221
Lytle — *Leaves* p.115
Prochnow — *Public* #81, 1366, 1797
Prochnow — *Success.* #1062
, *-management. See* **Self-control**
, *-mastery. See* **Self-control**
, *-observation. See* **Self-knowledge**
, *-pity*
Flint — *Graham* p.130
Holmes — *I've* p.57
Kennedy — *Fresh* p.112-114
Lair — *Baby* p.39
Lockridge — *World's* #2359
Peale — *Guideposts* p.243-244
Sheen — *Content.* p.79-81
Sherman — *Your* p.104-119
White — *Life* p.283
Woods — *Religious* p.915
, *teenager*
Ginott — *Between* p.67-68
, *-possession. See* **Self-control**
, *-praise*
See also **Conceit; Egotism; Self-esteem**
Albert — *Stop* p.59
Braude — *Stories* p.340, 345
Carruthers — *Sparks* p.157-158
Dirksen — *Quot.* #147, 173, 354, 1064, 1247-1248, 2129-2130
Edwards — *Useful* p.574-575, 584
Henry — *5000* p.250
Kin — *Dictionary* p.229
Nichols — *New* p.10-11
Phillips — *Choice* p.130
Prochnow — *Speaker's* p.279
Prochnow — *Success.* #2287-2288
Woods — *Religious* p.586-587, 915
, *-preservation*
Johnson — *Bedside* p.110
Kin — *Dictionary* p.229
Lytle — *Leaves* p.123
Phillips — *Choice* p.80, 161
Seldes — *Great* p.860
Sheen — *Way* p.112-114
Woods — *Religious* p.915
, *-realization. See* **Self-knowledge**
, *-recognition. See* **Self-knowledge**
, *-regard. See* **Self-esteem; Self-praise**
, *-rejection. See* **Self-denial**
, *-reliance*
See also **Confidence; Independence; Responsibility**
Bach — *Make* p.34-35
Edwards — *Useful* p.584-585; 732
Evans — *Thoughts I* p.142-143, 190
Evans — *Unto* p.84, 109, 114, 128
Flesch — *Unusual* p.257
Forbes — *Thoughts* p.38, 58, 62, 102, 205, 213, 257, 316, 338, 363, 499
Grizer — *Wit* p.415
Henry — *5000* p.250
Hobe — *Tapestries* p.13
Kin — *Dictionary* p.229-230
Liddle — *Thought V* p.11, 19, 34
Lindeman — *Emerson* p.53-73
Lytle — *Leaves* p.85, 144
Montapert — *Distilled* p.307-308
Prochnow — *Success.* #2289
Seldes — *Great* p.860
Speaker's Desk #667, 680, 684, 818, 842-843, 884
Wallis — *Words* p.82
Woods — *Business.* p.223-224
Woods — *Religious* p.915
, *-renewal*
Adams — *New* p.199
Flesch — *Unusual* p.257
Peterson — *Art* p.133
White — *Job* p.86-88
, *-reproach. See* **Self-blame**
, *-respect*
See also **Dignity; Pride; Self-acceptance; Self-esteem**
Applegarth — *Heir.* p.48
Braude — *Source* #1538-1539
Edwards — *Useful* p.585-586
Evans — *Faith* p.73-74, 91, 125-126, 129-130, 136
Evans — *Thoughts II (Open Door)* p.159-160

Evans — *Thoughts III (Open Road)* p.69, 79, 102, 110, 149
Evans — *Thoughts IV* p.95, 97, 124-125, 148
Flesch — *Unusual* p.257
Flint — *Graham* p.130
Forbes — *Thoughts* p.56, 147, 158, 171, 343, 447, 492, 502
Huxley — *You See* index p.288
Kin — *Dictionary* p.230
Kohn — *Touch* p.119-122
Liddle — *Thought V* p.29, 36, 42
List — *Living* p.34-41
Lockridge — *World's* #2774
Nichols — *Third* p.63-64
Phillips — *Choice* p.53
Voss — *Quotations* p.229-230
Woods — *Religious* p.915
, Loss of
Hulme — *Living* p.68-71
, -restraint. See **Self-control**
, -revelation. See **Self-knowledge**
, -righteousness
See also **Righteousness**
Dirksen — *Quot.* #1572-1576
Edwards — *Useful* p.586
Evans — *Unto* p.64
Flint — *Graham* p.111
Garland — *Subject* p.289
Guideposts — *Faith* p.139-142
Kauffman — *For* p.197
New Topical p.243
Woods — *Religious* p.915-916
, -rule. See **Self-control; Will**
, -sacrifice
Baillie — *Diary* #132
Flesch — *Unusual* p.258
Flint — *Graham* p.130
Forbes — *Thoughts* p.118, 166, 346, 404, 474
Harnsberger — *Mark* p.421
Henry — *5000* p.250
Hubbard — *Scrap* p.29
Lockridge — *World's* #5623, 5745
Peterson — *Art* p.354
Phillips — *Choice* p.127
Prochnow — *Success.* #2291-2292
Sheen — *Content.* p.32-34
Woods — *Religious* p.916
, -satisfaction. See **Self-confidence; Self-praise**
, -scrutiny. See **Self-analysis**
, -searching. See **Self-analysis; Self-discovery**
, -sharing. See **Unselfishness**
, -sufficiency
See also **Self-righteousness**
Evans — *Unto* p.30, 35
Flint — *Graham* p.130
Forbes — *Thoughts* p.291, 293, 471
Kennedy — *Fresh* p.64-67, 100-102
, -suggestion
See also **Autosuggestion**
Albert — *Stop* p.21
, -surrender
Flesch — *Unusual* p.258
, Prayer for
Unlimited Power p.55
, -understanding. See **Self-knowledge**
, -will
See also **Disobedience; Obstinacy; Will**
Edwards — *Useful* p.586
List — *Living* p.29-33
New Topical p.243-244
Phillips — *Choice* p.22
Woods — *Religious* p.916-917
, -withdrawal
Hulme — *Living* p.36-38

SELFISHNESS
See also **Covetousness; Greed; Misers**
Albert — *Stop* p.168, 188-189
Alexander's Treasure. p.148
Braude — *Speaker's* #1356-1357
Braude — *Source* #1533-1535
Braude — *Stories* p.343
Detherage — *Sunrise* p.54, 62, 71, 144
Dirksen — *Quot.* #150, 1065, 1571
Droke — *Christian* p.493-494
Edwards — *Useful* p.580-582
Evans — *Faith* p.79
Evans — *Unto* p.14, 123
Flesch — *Unusual* p.258
Flint — *Graham* p.129
Forbes — *Thoughts See* index p.567
Fuller — *Epigrams* p.258-259
Grizer — *Wit* p.414
Harnsberger — *Mark* p.427-428
Henry — *5000* p.248-249
Hovey — *Treasury* #732, 1034, 1066
Hubbard — *Scrap* p.25, 63
Huxley — *You See* index p.288
Johnson — *Bedside* p.7
Keller — *Open* p.100
Keller — *You* p.55-58
Kennedy — *Reader's* #1006
Kin — *Dictionary* p.229, 263
Knight's Illus. p.273-295
Knight's Treas. p.355-356

Krishnamurti — *Think* p.198-200
Liddle — *Thought I, II, III* p.20, 104, 151, 162, 189
Liddle — *Thought V* p.16
Lockridge — *World's* #1535, 2279, 2296, 2392, 3479, 5178
Mandel — *Stories* p.230-231
New Topical p.243
Phillips — *Choice* p.87
Prochnow — *Speaker's* p.278-279
Prochnow — *Success.* #2282, 2293-2294
Seldes — *Great* p.859
Speaker's Desk p.233-234; #259, 456, 1086
Voss — *Quotations* p.223-224
Wheelis — *Moralist* p.44
Woods — *Religious* p.912

SELFLESSNESS. *See* **Generosity; Unselfishness**

SELLING. *See* **Salesmen and salesmanship**

SEMANTICS
See also **Language**
Prochnow — *Speaker's* p.279-280
Seldes — *Great* p.860

SEMINARIES
Woods — *Religious* p.917

SENATE AND SENATORS—U.S.
Dirksen — *Quot. See* index p.269
Grizer — *Wit* p.416
Prochnow — *Public* #760
Prochnow — *Success.* #812
Seldes — *Great* p.860

SENSE
See also **Common sense; Judgment; Wisdom;** etc.
Book Proverbs p.100
Dirksen — *Quot.* #312, 1797
Edwards — *Useful* p.586-587
Flesch — *Unusual* p.259
Forbes — *Thoughts* p.124, 146, 237, 276, 303
Kin — *Dictionary* p.230
Lockridge — *World's* #1852, 4590
Montapert — *Distilled* p.308
Prochnow — *Public* #78, 1493
Prochnow — *Success.* #2296

SENSE OF HUMOR. *See* **Humor, Sense of**

SENSIBILITY
Edwards — *Useful* p.587
Flesch — *Unusual* p.259
Lockridge — *World's* #4579, 4590
Porter — *Halo* p.78-89
Prochnow — *Public* #1053, 1574

SENSITIVITY
Edwards — *Useful* p.587
Evans — *Thoughts I* p.56-57, 87-88, 141, 186-188
Kin — *Dictionary* p.230
Krishnamurti — *Think* p.178-180
Phillips — *Choice* p.360-363
Unlimited Power p.120

SENSUALITY
Adams — *New* p.339
Book Proverbs p.116
Edwards — *Useful* p.587-588, 687
Kin — *Dictionary* p.230, 271
Lockridge — *World's* #2901, 4579, 5697
Woods — *Religious* p.917-918

SENTENCES
Flesch — *Unusual* p.259
Prochnow — *Public* #651
Prochnow — *Success.* #2298-2299
, Long
Humes — *Instant* p.15, 17, 19

SENTIMENT
Copeland — *10,000* p.998-1000
Curtis — *Practical* p.74
Edwards — *Useful* p.588
Flesch — *Unusual* p.259
Forbes — *Thoughts* p.80, 127, 206, 310, 473
How To Live p.463-468
Hubbard — *Scrap* p.38, 57, 77
Ideas p.352-355
Lockridge — *World's* #267, 3470
Prochnow — *Public* #2424
Prochnow — *Speaker's* p.280
Woods — *Religious* p.918
, and opinion
Adams — *New* p.17
, Purge of
Curtis — *Practical* p.41

SENTINELS
Schermerhorn — *1500* p.335-336

"SEPARATED BRETHREN"
Woods — *Religious* p.918

SEPARATION
Evans — *Thoughts III (Open Road)* p.16-17, 28-30, 206
Hubbard — *Scrap* p.21
More Words p.152-154
Woods — *Religious* p.918
, and loneliness
Maltz — *Creative* p.174-175
, and love
Taylor — *With* p.8-11

"SEPHIROT TREE"
Boas — *History* p.227-228, 230

SEPTEMBER
New Joy p.222

SEPULCHERS
Kin — *Dictionary* p.230
Prochnow — *Public* #2651

SEQUOIA TREES
Bartlett — *Discovery* p.102-103

SERENDIPITY
Peterson — *Art* p.251

SERENITY
See also **Contentment; Peace, of mind**
Baillie — *Diary* #260
Emmons — *Mature* p.16
Evans — *Thoughts III (Open Road)* p.115
Forbes — *Thoughts* p.347, 401, 437
Giniger — *Compact* p.171-203
Harnsberger — *Mark* p.428
Kennedy — *Reader's* #1007-1014
Keys Happiness p.123
Liddle — *Thought V* p.22, 32
Lockridge — *World's* #1513
Lytle — *Leaves* p.20
Nichols — *New* p.100-101
Prochnow — *Public* #2136
Wallis — *Words* p.51
Woods — *Content.* p.287-318; *See also* index p.381
Woods — *Inspir.* p.417-457
Woods — *Religious* p.918-919

SERIOUSNESS. *See* **Gravity**

"SERMON ON THE MOUNT"
Applegarth — *Heir.* p.84
Keys Happiness p.11-15, 358
Wallis — *Treasure* p.74, 211
Wallis — *Words* p.233
Woods — *Religious* p.919

SERMONS
Asimov — *Treasury* #260, 304, 460
Baillie — *Diary* #360
Botkin — *Treasury* p.422-425, 427
Flesch — *Unusual* p.260
Fogg — *1000* #60, 93, 190, 279, 444, 504, 629
Forbes — *Thoughts* p.100, 272, 299
Fuller — *Thesaurus* #1541-1559
Harnsberger — *Mark* p.428-429
Hobe — *Tapestries* p.64
Hovey — *Treasury* #75, 115, 133, 154, 480, 522, 540, 1043, 1153, 1183, 1279, 1311, 1583, 1775, 1859
Johnson — *Bedside* p.127-128
Kennedy — *Reader's* #1015-1019
Kin — *Dictionary* p.231
Liddle — *Thought IV* p.19
Lockridge — *World's* #2932
Lytle — *Leaves* p.9, 159-160, 162
Prochnow — *Speaker's* p.280-281
Prochnow — *Success.* #1245, 1293
Tanksley — *Friend* p.67
Wallis — *Treasure* p.8, 184
Wallis — *Words* p.42, 128
Weisfeld — *Pulpit* p.2, 5-6, 49-64, 171
Woods — *Content.* p.49, 175, 265
Woods — *Religious* p.919-920
, Excerpts from
Prochnow — *Success.* #728-842
, Greatest
See also **"Sermon on the Mount"**
Price — *Wider* p.121-128
, Length of
Weisfeld — *Pulpit* p.20, 23, 33-34
, Preparation of
Weisfeld — *Pulpit* p.36-37

SERPENTS
See also **Snakes**
Auden — *Certain* p.342-343
Garland — *Subject* p.291
New Topical p.244
, and doves
Adams — *New* p.276
, Sea
Botkin — *Treasury* p.361

SERVANTS AND SERVITUDE
See also **Maids**
Copeland — *10,000* p.361-372
Dirksen — *Quot.* #650
Edwards — *Useful* p.588-589
Forbes — *Thoughts* p.88, 198, 225, 493
Fuller — *Epigrams* p.259
Fuller — *Thesaurus* #2276-2283
Garland — *Subject* p.291
Grizer — *Wit* p.416
Kin — *Dictionary* p.156, 231
Kronenberger — *Animal* p.254
Lockridge — *World's* #2426
New Topical p.244-246
Prochnow — *Public* #58, 101, 1868, 2016-2017, 2363, 2653, 2677

Prochnow — *Speaker's* p.282
Woods — *Religious* p.920-921

SERVICE
See also **Duty; Help**
Alexander's Treasure. p.254-255
Applegarth — *Heir.* p.124, 243-251, 299, 304
Braude — *Source* #1542-1543
Braude — *Stories* p.346
Curtis — *Practical* p.106, 349-350
Dirksen — *Quot.* #126, 2154
Droke — *Christian* p.494-503
Emmons — *Mature* p.19, 43, 104-105, 113, 130
Esteve — *Experience* p.11
Evans — *Faith* p.26, 33, 35, 39, 40, 62, 223
Evans — *Thoughts II (Open Door)* p.143-145
Evans — *Thoughts III (Open Road)* p.16, 19-21, 32, 55-56, 59, 155, 161, 175-176, 178, 190
Evans — *Thoughts IV* p.16, 78
Flesch — *Unusual* p.260
Fogg — *1000* #440, 548, 575, 598
Forbes — *Thoughts See* index p.567
Garland — *Subject* p.291-292
Grizer — *Wit* p.416-417
Guideposts — *Faith* p.424-427
Harral — *Feature* p.284
Henry — *5000* p.281
Hovey — *Treasury* p.270-271; #33, 307, 501, 796, 1418, 1537, 1715-1722, 1825
Hubbard — *Scrap* p.20, 29, 59, 79, 89, 227
Humes — *Instant* #977-989
Kennedy — *Reader's* #1020-1025
Knight's Illus. p.295-298
Knight's Treas. p.357-359
Lockridge — *World's* #1097, 1700, 2548, 5277
Lytle — *Leaves* p.10, 121, 137, 151
Mandel — *Stories* p.232-233
Modern Eloquence (14) p.415
Montapert — *Distilled* p.308-309
New Joy p.138
Peterson — *Art* p.296
Prochnow — *Public* #58, 251, 361, 634, 653, 746, 951, 1597
Prochnow — *Speaker's* p.282
Prochnow — *Success.* #1246
Speaker's Desk #28, 329, 1116
Strait — *Speaker's* p.149-154
Wallis — *Treasure* p.8, 107, 123-124
Wallis — *Words* p.17, 43, 91, 195-200, 224
White — *Job* p.51, 96-97
White — *Life* p.236-243
Woods — *Religious* p.920

SERVICE STATIONS. *See* **Gasoline and gasoline stations**

SERVICEMEN. *See* **Armed forces; Marines; Sailors; Soldiers**

SETTLEMENTS
See also **Pioneers**
Mandel — *Stories* p.233-234
Prochnow — *Public* #82

SEVEN DEADLY SINS. *See* **Sin, Seven deadly**

SEVEN YEARS' WAR
Asimov — *Treasury* #155

SEVENTY (age)
Flesch — *Unusual* p.260
Peale — *Courage* p.165
Prochnow — *Success.* #2300

SEVENTY-FIVE (age)
Flesch — *Unusual* p.260

SEVERITY
Kennedy — *Reader's* #889
Lockridge — *World's* #1726, 1803, 2623

SEWING MACHINES
Harral — *Feature* p.284

SEX
Albert — *Stop* p.68-69, 148-151
Braude — *Speaker's* #1359-1360
Droke — *Christian* p.503
Flesch — *Unusual* p.260
Flint — *Graham* p.32, 130-132
Fuller — *Epigrams* p.259
Gold — *Letters* p.47-54
Harnsberger — *Mark* p.429-430
How To Live p.56, 383-409
Keys Happiness p.33-36
Lair — *Baby* p.85-99
Lockridge — *World's* #4423
Peale — *Sin* p.45-70
Seldes — *Great* p.860-861
Sheban — *Wisdom* no p.
Speaker's Desk #89, 149
Strait — *Speaker's* p.155-156
Woods — *Religious* p.921-928
, Adjustment in
Keys Happiness p.304-306
, and love
Sheen — *Content.* p.34-36
, appeal in
Huxley — *You See* index p.288
, as God
Myers — *Thunder* p.31-32

, Attraction in
Woods — *Religious* p.923
, Education in
Ginott — *Between* p.163-165
How To Live p.119-122
Kauffman — *For* p.197-198
Woods — *Religious* p.922-923
, Energy in
Hill — *Think* p.210-213
, Guidance in
Harral — *Feature* p.284
, Immorality in
Myers — *Thunder* p.107-118
, Knowledge of
How To Live p.406-409
, Mystery of
Sheen — *Content.* p.55-57
, Problems of
Kauffman — *For* p.198
, Relationships of
How To Live p.49-52, 73-77
Reader's — *Getting* p.158-161
, Revolution of
Franke — *Buckley* p.271
How To Live p.153-154, 383-385
Lair — *Baby* p.90
Sheen — *Thoughts* p.39-41
Woods — *Religious* p.774-775
, Teenager
Ginott — *Between* See index p.254

SEXES
See also **Men; Women**
Edwards — *Useful* p.589
Menninger — *Blue.* p.40-41, 58-59
Prochnow — *Success.* #2039-2044
Speaker's Desk p.234-236
, Battle of
How To Live p.85-103
, Superiority of
Hubbard — *Scrap* p.94

SHADOWS
Adams — *New* p.11, 260
Henry — *5000* p.251
Hobe — *Tapestries* p.51, 214, 216
Kin — *Dictionary* p.231
Kohn — *Thoughts* p.160-162
Krishnamurti — *Think* p.76-77
Lytle — *Leaves* p.107
Phillips — *Choice* See index p.429
Prochnow — *Public* #2481
Sheban — *Wisdom* no p.
Wallis — *Words* p.23
Woods — *Religious* p.928
, and light
Hubbard — *Scrap* p.68

"SHAGGY DOG" STORIES
Asimov — *Treasury* #45-46; p.49-67
Botkin — *Anecdotes* p.90, 178, 204, 256
Fun Fare p.21, 237, 285-286

SHAKERS, RECIPES OF
Sagendorph — *Old* p.253-255

SHAKESPEARE, WILLIAM
Flesch — *Unusual* p.260-261
Harral — *Feature* p.285
Henry — *5000* p.251
Lockridge — *World's* #3577, 5159, 5492
Wallis — *Words* p.8, 20, 25
, Quotations of
Peterson — *Art* p.330
, Religion in
Baillie — *Diary* #296

SHALLOWNESS
Evans — *This* p.47
Kohn — *Best* p.37-40
Prochnow — *Public* #2083

SHAME
Flesch — *Unusual* p.261
Forbes — *Thoughts* p.175, 497
Henry — *5000* p.251-252
Hovey — *Treasury* p.271; #716, 1723-1724
Kin — *Dictionary* p.231
Liddle — *Thought I, II, III* p.135
Lockridge — *World's* #178, 229, 434, 471, 4025, 4804, 5073, 5749
Woods — *Religious* p.928-929

"SHANGRI-LAS." *See* **Utopias**

SHARECROPPERS
Botkin — *Anecdotes* p.46

SHARING. *See* **Charity; Generosity; Gifts and giving; Help;** etc.

SHARKS
Kin — *Dictionary* p.231

"SHARPIES"
Safian — *Insults* p.177-178

SHAVING
Kin — *Dictionary* p.231
Menninger — *Blue.* p.219
Prochnow — *Public* #744
Prochnow — *Success.* #485

SHAW, GEORGE BERNARD
Flesch — *Unusual* p.261

SHEEP
See also **Shepherds**
Asimov — *Treasury* #70
Botkin — *Anecdotes* p.89
Henry — *5000* p.252
Kin — *Dictionary* p.231
Kohn — *Through* p.21
New Topical p.246-247
Prochnow — *Public* #511
Prochnow — *Success.* #1323
, and ewes
Kin — *Dictionary* p.83
Prochnow — *Public* #365
, and lambs
Applegarth — *Heir.* p.20
Henry — *5000* p.146
Hobe — *Tapestries* p.70
Kin — *Dictionary* p.142-143
New Topical p.144-145
Prochnow — *Public* #569
, and rams
Kin — *Dictionary* p.209
, and sheepmen
Botkin — *Treasury* p.364-366

SHELLEY, PERCY BYSSHE
Hubbard — *Scrap* p.128, 148

SHELLS
Esteve — *Experience* p.108-109, 128, 137-138
Lindbergh — *Gift* p.19-120
Lindbergh — *Unicorn* p.82
Prochnow — *Public* #102

SHEPHERDS
Baillie — *Diary* #363
Hobe — *Tapestries* p.69, 144, 228
Hovey — *Treasury* #385, 398-400, 406, 423, 445, 480, 753, 1160, 1182, 1333, 1725
Kin — *Dictionary* p.232
Lytle — *Leaves* p.44, 46
New Topical p.247-248
Sheban — *Wisdom* no p.
, Responsibilities of
Unlimited Power p.19-22

SHERIFFS
Harral — *Feature* p.285
Prochnow — *Public* #777
Weisfeld — *Pulpit* p.128

SHIELDS
New Topical p.248

SHILOH, BATTLE OF
Botkin — *Anecdotes* p.167

SHIPS
See also **Boats**
Adams — *New* p.61, 336
Alexander's Treasure. p.91, 95, 122
Applegarth — *Heir.* p.21, 108, 283
Asimov — *Treasury* #265, 301, 354, 373
Copeland — *10,000* p.100-103
Forbes — *Thoughts* p.110, 195, 322, 400, 426, 441, 478, 506
Garland — *Subject* p.293
Goudge — *Comfort* p.337-341
Harnsberger — *Mark* p.430-434
Henry — *5000* p.252
Kin — *Dictionary* p.232
Lockridge — *World's* #1254-1255, 1274, 2046
New Topical p.248-249
Peterson — *Art* p.306, 377
Prochnow — *Public* #2509
Wallis — *Words* p.228
Woods — *Wellsprings* p.81-82

SHIPWRECKS
Asimov — *Treasury* #11, 583
Kin — *Dictionary* p.232
Prochnow — *Public* #386, 2348

SHIRKING. *See* **Neglect**

SHIRTS
Kin — *Dictionary* p.232
Prochnow — *Public* #38
, Enchanted
Hobe — *Tapestries* p.77

SHOCK
Curtis — *Practical* p.6-7
Lockridge — *World's* #1548

SHOEMAKERS
Henry — *5000* p.253
Keys Happiness p.493-495
Kin — *Dictionary* p.50, 232

SHOES
Flesch — *Unusual* p.266-267
Harral — *Feature* p.285
Kin — *Dictionary* p.232
New Topical p.249
Prochnow — *Public* #163, 4323
Prochnow — *Success.* #2325
Wallis — *Treasure* p.48

SHOOTING. *See* **Guns**

SHOPLIFTING
Grizer — *Wit* p.417
Guideposts — *Faith* p.192-194

SHOPPING
Grizer — *Wit* p.417-418
Kin — *Dictionary* p.233
Prochnow — *Public* #455, 1144

, *Window*
Harral — *Feature* p.323

SHOPS AND SHOPKEEPERS
See also **Clerks**
Botkin — *Anecdotes* p.2-3, 9, 41, 81, 125, 185, 198
Copeland — *10,000* p.426-437
Fuller — *Thesaurus* #2071-2072
Kin — *Dictionary* p.233
Seldes — *Great* p.862

SHORTAGES
Kohn — *Best* p.41-43

SHORT CUTS
Adams — *New* p.342
Evans — *Faith* p.166
Evans — *This* p.8-9
Evans — *Thoughts I* p.150-151, 160
Evans — *Thoughts IV* p.33
Halverson — *Perspective* p.27
Kauffman — *For* p.199

SHORTNESS
Flesch — *Unusual* p.261
Fuller — *Thesaurus* #691-695
Kin — *Dictionary* p.233
Prochnow — *Public* #2210
Prochnow — *Success.* #2301-2302

SHORTSIGHTEDNESS
See also **Foresight and hindsight**
Evans — *Thoughts III (Open Road)* p.75
Woods — *Wellsprings* p.11

SHOW AND SHOWMANSHIP
Book Proverbs p.126
Flesch — *Unusual* p.261-262
Edwards — *Useful* p.732
Lockridge — *World's* #4134
Nizer — *Thinking* p.139
Safian — *Insults* p.179-181
Safian — *More* p.160-162
Speaker's Desk #308

SHOW BUSINESS. *See* **Actors and actresses; Television; Theater;** etc.

SHOWBREAD
New Topical p.248

SHREWDNESS. *See* **Cleverness**

SHREWS
Kin — *Dictionary* p.233

SHRINES
Peale — *Guideposts* p.37-40

SHRUBBERY
Harral — *Feature* p.286

SHYNESS
See also **Meekness**
Asimov — *Treasury* #134, 638
Daly — *Personality* p.1-7
Krishnamurti — *Think* p.30-31, 54
Menninger — *Blue.* p.55-56
Speaker's Desk #309, 488

"SICK, SICK" STORIES
Botkin — *Anecdotes* p.256

SICKNESS. *See* **Illness**

"SIDEWALK" RHYMES
Botkin — *Treasury* p.796-803

SIDONIANS
New Topical p.250-251

SIEGES
New Topical p.251-252

SIGHS
Prochnow — *Public* #2144-2145

SIGHT
See also **Eyes and eyesight**
Flesch — *Unusual* p.155, 255
How To Live p.164-168
Kin — *Dictionary* p.228, 234
Kohn — *Thoughts* p.87-90
Montapert — *Distilled* p.333
Prochnow — *Public* #791, 1233
Prochnow — *Success.* #2272
Sheban — *Wisdom* no p.
Wallis — *Words* p.72, 234
, *Gift of*
Alexander's Treasure. p.9
, *Restoration of*
Unlimited Power p.127-130
, *through heart*
Kohn — *Adventures* p.11-13

SIGHTSEEING
Lockridge — *World's* #2702

SIGNALS
Prochnow — *Public* #338

"SIGN-OFFS"
Cerf — *Laugh* p.487-493

SIGNS
Baillie — *Diary* #125
Braude — *Stories* p.346
Fun Fare p.13, 144
Garland — *Subject* p.293-294
Grizer — *Wit* p.418-429
Harral — *Feature* p.286
Prochnow — *Public* #752

Prochnow — *Success.* #938, 1146
Schermerhorn — *1500* p.338-340
Wallis — *Words* p.58

, and signposts
Kin — *Dictionary* p.234

, Humorous
Copeland — *Errors* p.841-842

, Painters of
Botkin — *Treasury* p.546

, Seeking for
Zobell — *Speaker's* p.125-127

SILENCE
See also **Concealment; Peace; Secrecy**
Alexander's Treasure. p.81, 96
Applegarth — *Heir.* p.256-257, 269
Baillie — *Diary* #133
Book Proverbs p.35
Braude — *Source* #1550-1551, 1635
Braude — *Speaker's* #1362-1363
Braude — *Stories* p.346-347
Clark — *Windows* p.26-27, 46, 100
Curtis — *New* p.69-71
Dirksen — *Quot.* #124, 183, 246, 484, 1066, 2015, 2160-2165, 2252
Edwards — *Useful* p.517-518, 590-592
Emmons — *Mature* p.15-16
Evans — *Thoughts I* p.24, 56, 71-73, 87
Flesch — *Unusual* p.232, 262, 274
Flint — *Graham* p.132
Forbes — *Thoughts* p.9, 50, 106, 130, 143, 205, 279, 309, 359, 362, 437, 468
Fuller — *Epigrams* p.260-261
Garland — *Subject* p.255
Grizer — *Wit* p.429
Harnsberger — *Mark* p.434
Henry — *5000* p.253-254
Hobe — *Tapestries* p.31, 52, 83, 107, 110
Hovey — *Treasury* p.262-263; #43, 75, 122, 595, 600, 639, 963, 1658-1660, 1659
Hubbard — *Scrap* p.78, 224, 227
Johnson — *Bedside* p.273
Kennedy — *Reader's* #897-900
Kin — *Dictionary* p.207, 224, 249
Kohn — *Adventures* p.25-28, 43-45
Krishnamurti — *Think* p.172-173
Liddle — *Thought I, II, III See* index p,199
Liddle — *Thought IV* p.9, 12-13, 26, 32
Liddle — *Thought V* p.10, 28-29
Lockridge — *World's* #81, 178, 1447, 1466, 2063, 3417, 3603, 5884, 5904
Lytle — *Leaves* p.46
Mandel — *Stories* p.234-235
Montgomery — *Distilled* p.288, 309
New Joy p.18
Nichols — *Third* p.152-154
Peale — *Courage* p.35-36, 91-94
Phillips — *Choice* p.158, 162
Prochnow — *Public* #143, 165, 1152, 1235, 1799, 1908, 1964, 2187-2188, 2564, 3679-3684, 4394
Prochnow — *Speaker's* p.255, 283-284
Prochnow — *Success.* #913, 1107, 1268, 2208, 2306-2312
Pullar-Strecker — *Proverbs* #167-181
Schermerhorn — *1500* p.299
Seldes — *Great* p.862
Sheban — *Wisdom* no p.
Speaker's Desk p.236-238; #224, 351, 434, 507
Unlimited Power p.235-239
Wallis — *Treasure* p.100, 168
Wallis — *Words* p.50-51, 61, 86, 88, 186
Watson — *Light* p.32-34
Woods — *Religious* p.929-930, 965

, Power in
Clark — *Windows* p.78

, Time for
Sheen — *Content.* p.112-114

SILK
Kin — *Dictionary* p.224

SILVER
Kin — *Dictionary* p.234-235
New Topical p.252

, Free
Seldes — *Great* p.401

"SILVER RULE"
Menninger — *Blue.* p.102-103

SIMEON, TRIBE OF
New Topical p.252

SIMILARITY
Kin — *Dictionary* p.235

SIMILES
Harnsberger — *Mark* p.435-438
Prochnow — *Public* #1501

SIMPLETONS. *See* **Fools and foolishness**

SIMPLICITY
See also **Brevity; Innocence; Sincerity**
Alexander's Treasure. p.65, 134, 226-227, 341
Applegarth — *Heir.* p.253-257
Braude — *Stories* p.347
Curtis — *Practical* p.49, 51
Dirksen — *Quot.* #975, 1067, 2327
Edwards — *Useful* p.592-593
Esteve — *Experience* p.29-39
Evans — *Faith* p.38
Flesch — *Unusual* p.263
Forbes — *Thoughts* p.54, 210, 329, 362, 437, 450
Fox — *Make* p.206
Garland — *Subject* p.294
Henry — *5000* p.254
Hubbard — *Scrap* p.215
Hunter — *Gems* p.100
Johnson — *Bedside* p.257
Kennedy — *Reader's* #1027-1033
Kohn — *Pathways* p.117-119
Liddle — *Thought I, II, III* p.65, 157
Liddle — *Thought IV* p.41
Lindbergh — *Gift* p.24-26, 35
Lockridge — *World's* #3642
Montapert — *Distilled* p.309
New Topical p.253
Nizer — *Thinking* p.89
Peterson — *Art* p.24, 390
Peterson — *New* p.50-51
Phillips — *Choice* p.16, 148, 175, 178, 346
Prochnow — *Public* #1911, 3685-3688
Prochnow — *Success.* #2313-2316
Speaker's Desk p.238
Wallis — *Treasure* p.31, 133
Wallis — *Words* p.52, 135
Watson — *Light* p.231-238
White — *Job* p.72, 151-156
Woods — *Content.* p.89, 117, 141, 154
Woods — *Religious* p.930

"SIMUL" PRINCIPLE
Hulme — *Living* p.104-106

SIN
See also **Crime and criminals; Depravity; Evil; Guilt; Immorality; Vice; Wickedness**; etc.
Applegarth — *Heir.* p.46-47, 87, 172, 213, 220, 224
Auden — *Certain* p.343-345
Baillie — *Diary* #106, 195
Braude — *Source* #1552-1553
Dirksen — *Quot.* #1577-1579, 2166-2169, 2277
Droke — *Christian* p.504-508
Edwards — *Useful* p.593-595
Evans — *Faith* p.67-72, 79, 90, 92
Evans — *Thought I* p.110-111
Evans — *Unto* p.34, 39-40, 61, 85, 102
Flesch — *Unusual* p.264-265, 293
Flint — *Graham* p.21, 24-25, 64-65, 75-76, 85, 90, 129, 132-135, 139, 144-145
Forbes — *Thoughts* p.192, 209, 324, 463, 467, 472, 475
Fuller — *Epigrams* p.261-262
Fuller — *Thesaurus* #1646-1647
Garland — *Subject* p.294-295
Guideposts — *Faith* p.47-50
Halverson — *Perspective* p.14, 34
Harnsberger — *Mark* p.439-440
Henry — *5000* p.254-255
Hovey — *Treasury* p.271; *See also* index p.300
Hubbard — *Scrap* p.36
Johnson — *Bedside* p.186-187, 319-326, 329-330, 333, 338-340
Kennedy — *Reader's* #1034-1040
Kin — *Dictionary* p.235
Knight's Illus. p.299-306
Knight's Treas. p.359-364
Kronenberger — *Animal* p.261-262
Liddle — *Thought I, II, III* p.61, 100, 128, 151, 189
Lockridge — *World's* #877, 1289, 1421, 2638, 3418, 3768
Lytle — *Leaves* p.11, 19, 76, 120, 175
McDonagh — *Invit.* p.80-82
Mandel — *Stories* p.235
More Words p.154-155, 164-165
New Topical p.253-254, 276-277
Peale — *Sin* p.70-102
Prochnow — *Public* #277, 2524, 2676, 2744, 3689-3696, 4216-4218
Prochnow — *Success.* #2317-2319
Rogers — *Time* p.101-105
Seldes — *Great* p.862-863
Sheban — *Wisdom* no p.
Speaker's Desk p.239-242; #531
Strait — *Speaker's* p.157-161
Wallis — *Words* p.41, 56
Woods — *Religious* p.930-939
Words — *Inspir.* p.192
Zobell — *Speaker's* p.128-130

, Consequences of
Woods — *Religious* p.936-937

, Definitions of
Woods — *Religious* p.934-936

, Doctrines concerning
New Topical p.306-307

, Memories of
Baillie — *Diary* #189
, National
New Topical p.255-256
, Offering for
New Topical p.255
, Original
Baillie — *Diary* #12
Ideas p.282-284
Wheelis — *Moralist* p.111
Woods — *Religious* p.707-710
, Prevalence of
Woods — *Religious* p.937
, Seven deadly
Ideas p.355-356
McCracken — *What* p.9-49
, Unforgivable
Fox — *Make* p.177

SINCERITY
See also **Truth**
Alexander's Treasure. p.337
Braude — *Source* #1554-1556
Braude — *Stories* p.348
Droke — *Christian* p.506
Edwards — *Useful* p.595-596, 732
Evans — *Faith* p.65, 80-84, 93, 125-126, 129-130
Evans — *Thoughts II (Open Door)* p.85-90, 136-137, 158
Evans — *Thoughts III (Open Road)* p.102, 158
Evans — *Thoughts IV* p.174-175, 209-210
Evans — *Unto* p.51, 87-88
Flesch — *Unusual* p.264
Flint — *Graham* p.135
Forbes — *Thoughts* p.36, 155, 180, 191, 195, 220, 318, 346, 351, 359, 437
Fuller — *Epigrams* p.262-263
Garland — *Subject* p.295-296
Henry — *5000* p.255
Hobe — *Tapestries* p.41
Hubbard — *Scrap* p.22
Johnson — *Bedside* p.3, 5, 76, 128, 171
Kennedy — *Reader's* #1041
Kin — *Dictionary* p.235
Knight's Illus. p.306-309
Liddle — *Thought I, II, III* p.46, 141, 148, 157
Liddle — *Thought IV* p.23
Lockridge — *World's* #63, 326, 861, 910, 1226, 4113, 5740
Mandel — *Stories* p.236-238
Menninger — *Blue.* p.38
Modern Eloquence (14) p.416
New Topical p.254-255
Peterson — *Art* p.344
Prochnow — *Public* #3697-3698
Prochnow — *Success.* #1009
Sheban — *Wisdom* no p.
Speaker's Desk p.242; #256, 485
Woods — *Religious* p.937-938

SINGERS
See also **Opera, Singers of**
Asimov — *Treasury* #230-231
Fuller — *Thesaurus* #1366-1368
Guideposts — *Faith* p.121-125
Lockridge — *World's* #4018
Peale — *Guideposts* p.269-273, 281-282
Prochnow — *Speaker's* p.284
, Negro
Guideposts — *Faith* p.51-54

SINGING
See also **Songs**
Guideposts — *Faith* p.89, 323-325
Harnsberger — *Mark* p.438-439
How To Live p.338-340
Hubbard — *Scrap* p.68
Kin — *Dictionary* p.235
Knight's Treas. p.364-367
Kohn — *Adventures* p.76-78
Kohn — *Pathways* p.153-154
Peterson — *Art* p.138
Prochnow — *Public* #261, 392, 570, 671, 1171, 1279, 2357
Tanksley — *Friend* p.31
Wallis — *Treasure* p.156

SINGING GAMES
See also **Counting rhymes**
Botkin — *Treasury* p.803-813

SINGLE-MINDEDNESS
Braude — *Source* #1557
Forbes — *Thoughts* p.289
Phillips — *Choice* p.225

SINGULARITY
Edwards — *Useful* p.596
Flesch — *Unusual* p.264
Prochnow — *Public* #765

SIRENS
Prochnow — *Public* #2357

SISTERS
Guideposts — *Faith* p.483-486
Hobe — *Tapestries* p.84
Menninger — *Blue.* p.66
Prochnow — *Public* #142

SITTING
Hadfield — *Delights* p.89
Kin — *Dictionary* p.235

"SIX NATIONS"
Botkin — *Anecdotes* p.76

SIXTH SENSE
Flint — *Graham* p.135-136

, toward riches
Hill — *Think* p.246-255

SIXTY (age)
Flesch — *Unusual* p.265
Forbes — *Thoughts* p.128, 398, 486, 498
Prochnow — *Success.* #2320-2321

SIXTY-FIVE (age)
Maltz — *Creative* p.177-189

SIZE
Dirksen — *Quot.* #715
Esteve — *Experience* p.155
Flesch — *Unusual* p.145
Harnsberger — *Mark* p.440
Kin — *Dictionary* p.236
Kohn — *Thoughts* p.76-79
Lytle — *Leaves* p.177
Mandel — *Stories* p.238
Prochnow — *Public* #590, 789, 816
Prochnow — *Speaker's* p.184
Prochnow — *Success.* #1955
, Small
Flesch — *Unusual* p.267
Kin — *Dictionary* p.238
Lytle — *Leaves* p.139
Prochnow — *Success.* #2326-2327

SKATING
Harnsberger — *Mark* p.440
Prochnow — *Public* #529

SKEPTICISM
See also **Doubt; Unbelief and unbelievers**
Curtis — *Practical* p.39
Edwards — *Useful* p.568-569, 732-733
Evans — *Thoughts II (Open Door)* p.74
Evans — *Unto* p.41, 43
Flesch — *Unusual* p.265
Fogg — *1000* #47, 326, 471, 486, 608, 750, 811, 868, 961
Forbes — *Thoughts* p.218, 269
Grizer — *Wit* p.430
Henry — *5000* p.255
Ideas p.347-349
Johnson — *Bedside* p.31, 284
Kin — *Dictionary* p.226, 236
Lockridge — *World's* #4160
Menninger — *Blue.* p.82-83
Prochnow — *Success.* #2322-2323
Seldes — *Great* p.863-864
Speaker's Desk #58, 83, 366, 414, 555, 825, 978, 1063
Vogue — *Arts* p.13-23
Woods — *Religious* p.939
Woods — *Wellsprings* p.55

SKILL
See also **Ability**
Braude — *Source* #1558
Curtis — *Practical* p.335-337
Forbes — *Thoughts* p.1, 135, 333, 365, 431
Garland — *Subject* p.296
Hobe — *Tapestries* p.13, 15
Kennedy — *Reader's* #1042
Kin — *Dictionary* p.236
Prochnow — *Public* #2275

SKIN
Huxley — *You See* index p.284
Kin — *Dictionary* p.236
Lytle — *Leaves* p.40
Menninger — *Blue.* p.206-209, 218
Prochnow — *Public* #667, 754
, Care of
Bradshaw — *Home.* p.31-38
Menninger — *Blue.* p.208-209, 218
, Dark
Krishnamurti — *Think* p.183-184

SKUNKS
Kin — *Dictionary* p.236
Speaker's Desk #90, 1123

SKY
Flesch — *Unusual* p.265
Garland — *Subject* p.108
Hadfield — *Delights* p.43
Henry — *5000* p.255-256
Hobe — *Tapestries* p.102
Kin — *Dictionary* p.236
Kohn — *Adventures* p.137-139
Lindbergh — *Unicorn* p.61-73
Nichols — *New* p.151-152
Prochnow — *Success.* #2324
Wallis — *Words* p.98, 131
, Night
See also **Stars**
Irion — *Yes* p.131-133

SKYLARKS
Applegarth — *Heir.* p.36-37

SKYSCRAPERS
Asimov — *Treasury* #266
Irion — *Yes* p.123-125
Schermerhorn — *1500* p.341

SLANDER
See also **Gossip; Reputation; Rumor; Scandal**
Adams — *New* p.10
Book Proverbs p.78

Braude — *Stories* p.348
Dirksen — *Quot.* #567, 1580, 1879, 1972, 2170-2171
Edwards — *Useful* p.60-61, 596-598
Forbes — *Thoughts* p.401, 437, 462
Harnsberger — *Mark* p.440-441
Henry — *5000* p.27, 256
Hobe — *Tapestries* p.40
Johnson — *Bedside* p.185
Kennedy — *Reader's* #1043
Kin — *Dictionary* p.39, 236-237
Liddle — *Thought I, II, III* p.60-63, 69, 89, 95-96, 101, 121, 126, 134, 148, 155
Lockridge — *World's* #2263, 3806
Lytle — *Leaves* p.74
New Topical p.256
Prochnow — *Public* #3699-3701
Seldes — *Great* p.107-108
Woods — *Religious* p.98

SLANG
Botkin — *Treasury* p.470-475
Edwards — *Useful* p.733
Speaker's Desk #91, 125, 424, 921, 962
, English school
Kronenberger — *Animal* p.65-66
, Seventeenth century
Kronenberger — *Animal* p.262-263
, Tramp and underworld
Kronenberger — *Animal* p.14-15
, Victorian
Kronenberger — *Animal* p.92-93

SLAVES AND SLAVERY
Curtis — *Practical* p.278
Dirksen — *Quot.* #394, 618, 765, 775, 1000, 1691
Edwards — *Useful* p.598-599
Esteve — *Experience* p.11-17
Evans — *Thoughts I* p.155-156
Evans — *Unto* p.55
Fogg — *1000 See* index p.898
Forbes — *Thoughts* p.15, 56, 98, 131, 161, 225, 363, 378, 382, 386, 389, 438, 517
Fuller — *Epigrams* p.263
Garland — *Subject* p.296
Harnsberger — *Mark* p.441
Henry — *5000* p.256-257
Kennedy — *Reader's* #1044-1045
Kin — *Dictionary* p.237
Lockridge — *World's* #1071, 1143, 1483, 1565, 3211, 3487, 5489
Mandel — *Stories* p.238-239
Seldes — *Great* p.864-872
Sheban — *Wisdom* no p.
Wheelis — *Moralist* p.51-52, 58-59, 74, 142-143
Woods — *Religious* p.940
, Agricultural
Hubbard — *Scrap* p.199
, and civilization
Hubbard — *Scrap* p.48
, and rebellion
Wheelis — *Moralist* p.55-63
, Industrial
Hubbard — *Scrap* p.18

SLAVS
Botkin — *Treasury* p.246, 865

SLEEP
Albert — *Stop* p.64-76
Alexander's Treasure. p.155, 237, 278, 330
Baillie — *Diary* #319
Curtis — *Daily* p.159-165
Dirksen — *Quot.* #1377, 2172-2175
Edwards — *Useful* p.599-600
Evans — *Thoughts I* p.38, 94, 125, 131-132, 160, 209
Flesch — *Unusual* p.67, 184, 265-266
Fox — *Make* p.98
Fuller — *Epigrams* p.263-264, 360
Fuller — *Thesaurus* #26-27
Garland — *Subject* p.296-297
Goudge — *Comfort* p.328
Hadfield — *Delights* p.228-243
Hadfield — *Love* p.172
Harnsberger — *Mark* p.441-442
Harral — *Feature* p.286
Henry — *5000* p.257
Hubbard — *Scrap* p.42, 86, 100, 155, 227
Johnson — *Bedside* p.279, 282
Kennedy — *Reader's* #1046
Keys Happiness p.45-50
Kin — *Dictionary* p.237-238
Kohn — *Touch* p.177
Lockridge — *World's* #2301, 3199, 4442, 4555
Lytle — *Leaves* p.171
Montapert — *Distilled* p.309-310
New Joy p.147
Phillips — *Choice* p.211
Prochnow — *Public* #22, 218, 356, 364, 474, 720, 810, 901, 922, 1200, 1426, 1947, 1997, 2441, 2545, 3702-3703
Prochnow — *Speaker's* p.284-385
Prochnow — *Success.* #1148, 1193, 2071-2072
Reader's — *Getting* p.188-190

Sheban — *Wisdom* no p.
Unlimited Power p.177-179
Wallis — *Treasure* p.194
Wallis — *Words* p.99, 101
Woods — *Content.* p.242-243, 353-359
Woods — *Religious* p.940
, *Improvement of*
Huxley — *You See* index p.288
, *in church*
Words Change p.98-101
, *Walking in*
George — *Book* p.236, 238
Schermerhorn — *1500* p.344

SLIDE RULES
Asimov — *Treasury* #147

"SLIPS"
See also **"Boners"; Mistakes**
Flesch — *Unusual* p.266
Fun Fare p.3, 89, 187-188
Kin — *Dictionary* p.238
Speaker's Desk #32, 71, 82, 221, 225, 277, 316, 342, 463, 534, 624, 752, 865, 988

SLOGANS
See also **Battles, Slogans; Political slogans**
Harral — *Feature* p.287
Prochnow — *Public* #4292
Seldes — *Great* p.872-873

SLOTH. *See* **Laziness;** etc.

"SLOWING DOWN"
Nichols — *New* p.145-146
Peale — *Courage* p.81-82
Peterson — *Art* p.303, 407

SLOWNESS
Harnsberger — *Mark* p.442
Kin — *Dictionary* p.238
Prochnow — *Public* #412, 535, 2741
Prochnow — *Success.* #1329

SLUMS
Reader's — *Getting* p.209-212
Woods — *Religious* p.360
, *Landlords of*
Day — *Meditations* p.52

SMARTNESS. *See* **Cleverness; Common sense; Intelligence**

SMELLS. *See* **Odor; Perfume**

SMILES
See also **Cheerfulness; Happiness; Laughter;** etc.
Adams — *New* p.192
Applegarth — *Heir.* p.81
Braude — *Stories* p.348
Edwards — *Useful* p.600-601
Flesch — *Unusual* p.267
Forbes — *Thoughts* p.117, 158, 212, 235, 471, 477, 480
Fox — *Make* p.20
Grizer — *Wit* p.430-431
Harnsberger — *Mark* p.443-444
Harral — *Feature* p.287
Henry — *5000* p.258
Hobe — *Tapestries* p.62
Kin — *Dictionary* p.238
Montapert — *Distilled* p.310
New Joy p.128-129
Peterson — *Art* p.92
Prochnow — *Public* #1957, 2301, 4369
Prochnow — *Success.* #940
Wallis — *Treasure* p.119, 151, 157
Wallis — *Words* p.17-18
Welk — *Guide.* p.156-158

SMITH, JOSEPH
Hunter — *Gems* p.38-41

SMOKE SCREEN
See also **Concealment**
Evans — *This* p.164-165

SMOKING
Asimov — *Treasury* p.90, 167, 282-283
Braude — *Source* #1559-1564
Braude — *Speaker's* #1364-1366
Braude — *Stories* p.349
Casselberry — *How* p.119-120
Dirksen — *Quot.* #1786
Flesch — *Unusual* p.267
Flint — *Graham* p.136
Fuller — *Thesaurus* #61-65
Fun Fare p.248
Harnsberger — *Mark* p.444-445
Harral — *Feature* p.287
Krishnamurti — *Think* p.96-97, 165
Prochnow — *Public* #10
Prochnow — *Success.* #2089
Reader's — *Getting* p.154-157
, *Teenage*
Daly — *Personality* p.111-115
, *to stop*
Flesch — *Unusual* p.190
Keys Happiness p.124-130

SMOOTHNESS
Dirksen — *Quot.* #139

SMUGNESS. *See* **Complacency; Self-righteousness**

SNAILS
Alexander's Treasure. p.198

SNAKES
See also **Rattlesnakes; Serpents**
Botkin — *Anecdotes* p.226, 270
Botkin — *Treasury* p.582-583, 592, 594, 625, 647
George — *Book* p.398
Harnsberger — *Mark* p.445
Kin — *Dictionary* p.238, 270
Prochnow — *Public* #2088
, *Bites of*
Asimov — *Treasury* #417
, *Mythical*
Botkin — *Treasury* p.582-584, 592, 647

SNEERING. *See* **Ridicule; Sarcasm**

SNEEZES
Flesch — *Unusual* p.267
Kin — *Dictionary* p.239

"SNIPE HUNTS"
Botkin — *Treasury* p.359, 383

SNOBS AND SNOBBERY
See also **Arrogance; Conceit;** etc.
Braude — *Stories* p.72
Curtis — *Practical* p.433-434
Edwards — *Useful* p.601
Evans — *Unto* p.88
Flesch — *Unusual* p.149-150, 267-268
Fuller — *Epigrams* p.264
Fuller — *Thesaurus* #546-551
Harnsberger — *Mark* p.446
Hubbard — *Scrap* p.83
Keys Happiness p.313-316
Lockridge — *World's* #1983, 4887
Prochnow — *Public* #133, 1581
Prochnow — *Success.* #1976, 2328
Reader's — *Getting* p.19-22
Safian — *Insults* p.182-185
Safian — *More* p.163-164
Seldes — *Great* p.873

SNORING
Flesch — *Unusual* p.268
Harnsberger — *Mark* p.446-447
Prochnow — *Public* #1803, 1980

SNOW AND SNOWSTORMS
Flesch — *Unusual* p.268
Goudge — *Comfort* p.38-39
Henry — *5000* p.258
Hobe — *Tapestries* p.58
Kin — *Dictionary* p.239
Kohn — *Adventures* p.76-78
Kohn — *Through* p.73-74
New Joy p.221
Prochnow — *Public* #1996, 2004
Prochnow — *Success.* #1110
Sagendorph — *Old* p.271-274
Wallis — *Treasure* p.182, 234
, *Blue*
Botkin — *Treasury* p.212
, *Snowflakes of*
Applegarth — *Heir.* p.110, 192
Kohn — *Pathways* p.61-62, 133
Peterson — *Art* p.57
Prochnow — *Public* #4356

SNUFF
Asimov — *Treasury* #304

SOAP
Harnsberger — *Mark* p.448-449
Weisfeld — *Pulpit* p.172

"SOAP OPERAS"
Auden — *Certain* p.293-294

SOBRIETY
See also **Abstinence; Moderation; Self-control; Temperance**
Edwards — *Useful* p.601
New Topical p.256-257
Sheban — *Wisdom* no p.
Woods — *Religious* p.940

SOCIAL BREEDING. *See* **Breeding; Etiquette; Eugenics**

SOCIAL CONTRACT
Ideas p.358, 375

SOCIAL CREDIT
Ideas p.375-376

SOCIAL DEMOCRATS
Seldes — *Great* p.875

SOCIAL ETHICS
Woods — *Religious* p.941

SOCIAL FAITH
Woods — *Religious* p.942

SOCIAL GOSPEL
Woods — *Religious* p.942

SOCIAL ORDER
See also **Society**
Baillie — *Diary* #282
Dirksen — *Quot.* #503, 716
Evans — *Unto* p.7
Flesch — *Unusual* p.268

Flint — *Graham* p.136-137
Hovey — *Treasury* #29, 31, 437, 497, 522, 526
Kauffman — *For* p.200
Lockridge — *World's* #4093
Phillips — *Choice* p.320, 407
Seldes — *Great* p.873-875
Wheelis — *Moralist* p.46, 117-118
Woods — *Religious* p.940-943

, Atheism in
See also **Atheism**
Woods — *Religious* p.941
, Christian
Baillie — *Diary* #307
, Discontent in
Adams — *New* p.140
, Legislation for
Dirksen — *Quot.* #13
Nizer — *Thinking* p.102
, Morality in
Wheelis — *Moralist* p.105
, Reform of
Braude — *Stories* p.349

SOCIAL SECURITY ACT
Woods — *Business.* p.235-238

SOCIAL WORK
See also **Public welfare**
Hooker — *Index* p.99-109
Keller — *You* p.182-194
Kennedy — *Reader's* #1052
Krishnamurti — *Think* p.212-213
Lockridge — *World's* #3612
Woods — *Religious* p.943

, Creed of
Braude — *Stories* p.87

SOCIALISM
Braude — *Source* #1565-1567
Dirksen — *Quot.* #61, 650, 2368
Flesch — *Unusual* p.268
Franke — *Buckley* p.272-273
Fuller — *Thesaurus* #2056-2057
Grizer — *Wit* p.431
Henry — *5000* p.258-259
Hovey — *Treasury* #926
Kennedy — *Reader's* #1047-1051
Lockridge — *World's* #5007
Prochnow — *Public* #1805
Prochnow — *Speaker's* p.285
Prochnow — *Success.* #1315, 2329-2330
Seldes — *Great* p.875-881
Weisfeld — *Pulpit* p.9
Wheelis — *Moralist* p.117, 120
Woods — *Business.* p.231-233
Woods — *Religious* p.943-944

SOCIETIES. *See* **Clubs; Organizations;** names of societies

SOCIETY
See also **Humanity; Man (mankind); People; Social order**
Albert — *Stop* p.20, 60, 201
Baillie — *Diary* #112
Braude — *Stories* p.349
Curtis — *Practical* *See* index p.574
Detherage — *Sunrise* p.71, 73, 101-106, 124
Dirksen — *Quot.* #34, 1068, 1091, 1141, 2176-2177, 2274
Edwards — *Useful* p.601-604
Flint — *Graham* p.137-138
Forbes — *Thoughts* *See* index p.568
Franke — *Buckley* p.273
Fuller — *Epigrams* p.265
Fuller — *Thesaurus* #130-145, 796-797
Fun Fare p.210-212
Grizer — *Wit* p.431-432
Harnsberger — *Mark* p.449
Henry p.259
Hubbard — *Scrap* p.30, 63, 176, 187
Humes — *Instant* #45-50, 1236-1239; p.40
Johnson — *Bedside* p.61-62, 86, 118, 201, 271
Kauffman — *For* p.201-202
Liddle — *Thought V* p.20, 25, 36
Lockridge — *World's* *See* index p.583
Lytle — *Leaves* p.9
Mandelbaum — *Choose* p.31
Phillips — *Choice* p.22, 303, 389-390
Prochnow — *Public* #3704-3707
Prochnow — *Speaker's* p.285
Prochnow — *Success.* #1235
Seldes — *Great* p.881-883
Sheban — *Wisdom* no p.
Speaker's Desk p.242-244; #134, 136, 904
Wheelis — *Moralist* p.92, 111-113
Woods — *Religious* p.944-945

, and religion
Woods — *Religious* p.945
, "Climbing" in
Prochnow — *Success.* #2260
, Destiny of a sane
Keller — *Open* p.31
, Free
Adams — *New* p.314
, Ills of
Dirksen — *Quot.* #34
Esteve — *Experience* p.122-123
Keller — *You* p.191-193

, *Immoral*
See also **Immorality**
Myers — *Thunder* p.11-23
, *New*
Krishnamurti — *Think* p.140-141
, *Teenage*
Ginott — *Between* p.137-150

SOCIOLOGY
Franke — *Buckley* p.273
Hooker — *Index* p.46-53
Johnson — *Bedside* p.143
Woods — *Religious* p.945-946

SOCKS
Irion — *Yes* p.69-72

SOCRATES
Asimov — *Treasury* #143
Flesch — *Unusual* p.268
Kohn — *Touch* p.24-25
Lockridge — *World's* #1798, 4075
Reader's — *20th* p.11
Wallis — *Words* p.20, 29
, *Method of*
Ideas p.376-378

SOFTNESS
Kin — *Dictionary* p.239
Kohn — *Thoughts* p.167-169
Prochnow — *Public* #2123, 2192-2194

SOIL
See also **Earth**
Hovey — *Treasury* #643-644, 648, 869, 871
, *and plants*
Sagendorph — *Old* p.110-120
, *Fertile*
Botkin — *Treasury* p.597-604
, *Parable of*
Fridy — *Meditat.* p.117

SOLACE. *See* **Consolation; Sympathy**

SOLDIERS
See also **Armed forces; War**
Copeland — *10,000* p.103-113
Dirksen — *Quot.* #360, 624, 2332, 2334
Edwards — *Useful* p.604
Flesch — *Unusual* p.268
Fuller — *Epigrams* p.266
Fuller — *Thesaurus* #2430-2437
George — *Book See* index p.444
Goudge — *Comfort* p.137-139
Guideposts — *Faith* p.90-94
Henry — *5000* p.259-260
Hobe — *Tapestries* p.154, 162, 213
Humes — *Instant* #990-994
Keys Happiness p.213-217
Kin — *Dictionary* p.239
Kronenberger — *Animal* p.264-266
Lockridge — *World's* #2477
Lytle — *Leaves* p.119
Modern Eloquence (14) p.83-100
New Joy p.174
Prochnow — *Public* #298, 534, 744, 963, 1801, 2628
Prochnow — *Speaker's* p.285-286
Prochnow — *Success.* #2331
Seldes — *Great* p.953-973
Woods — *Religious* p.946
Zobell — *Speaker's* p.123-125
, *Prayer by*
Unlimited Power p.47
, *Uniforms of*
Harral — *Feature* p.284

SOLEMNITY
See also **Gravity**
Dirksen — *Quot.* #1070
Flesch — *Unusual* p.268-269
Woods — *Religious* p.946

SOLIDARITY
See also **Unity**
Adams — *New* p.72
Curtis — *Practical* p.546-547
Flesch — *Unusual* p.269

SOLITUDE
See also **Loneliness; Quiet; Rest; Silence**
Alexander's Treasure. p.274-275
Applegarth — *Heir.* p.203, 259
Auden — *Certain* p.347-348
Baillie — *Diary* #262, 315
Bartlett — *Discovery* p.93, 98, 102-103
Book Proverbs p.125
Braude — *Source* #1568-1570
Braude — *Stories* p.349-350
Detherage — *Sunrise* p.43, 145-148
Dirksen — *Quot.* #406, 484, 764, 803, 1071-1075, 1849-1850, 1904, 1982, 2176, 2178-2179, 2298
Droke — *Christian* p.508
Edwards — *Useful* p.604-606
Emmons — *Mature* p.17, 35
Esteve — *Experience* p.131-135
Evans — *Thoughts I* p.67, 88, 141-143, 186, 189-191, 217-218
Evans — *Thoughts IV* p.23-24, 118, 177
Evans — *Unto* p.64
Flesch — *Unusual* p.8, 269
Forbes — *Thoughts* p.68, 130, 205, 325, 391, 406, 493
Fuller — *Epigrams* p.266-267

Guideposts — *Faith* p.121-125, 487-491
Hadfield — *Delights* p.90, 94, 121
Henry — *5000* p.260-261
Hobe — *Tapestries* p.27, 31, 72, 117, 139
Holmes — *Design* p.144-145, 177
Hovey — *Treasury* p.26-27; #42-50, 506, 675, 832, 1128, 1161, 1538
Hubbard — *Scrap* p.29, 63, 87, 222
Johnson — *Bedside* p.61, 117-118, 201, 271-273, 316
Keller — *Open* p.51
Kennedy — *Reader's* #536-537, 1053-1056
Keys Happiness p.545-548
Kin — *Dictionary* p.239
Krishnamurti — *Think* p.176-184
Lair — *Baby* p.214
Liddle — *Thought I, II, III* p.25, 46, 77, 79, 168, 174
Liddle — *IV* p.26
Lindbergh — *Gift* p.41-43, 48, 56-59
Lockridge — *World's* #1118, 1189-1224, 2100, 2422, 3003, 3136
Montapert — *Distilled* p.310-311
Nichols — *New* p.155-156
Nichols — *Third* p.224
Peterson — *Art* p.162
Phillips — *Choice* p.115, 120, 165, 168
Prochnow — *Public* #2450, 3708-3714, 4219-4220, 4409
Prochnow — *Speaker's* p.20
Prochnow — *Success.* #1459, 1533, 2332
Seldes — *Great* p.884
Sheban — *Wisdom* no p.
Voss — *Quotations* p.231-232
Watson — *Light* p.32-36
Woods — *Content.* p.95, 115, 140, 202, 234, 244, 341-359
Woods — *Religious* p.15, 494, 903, 946-947
Words — *Inspir.* p.181-182

SOLOMON
Lockridge — *World's* #4800
Prochnow — *Public* #146, 656, 1301, 2618
, *Wisdom of*
Adams — *New* p.243

SOLUTION
Flesch — *Unusual* p.269
Humes — *Instant* p.45; #995-1000, 1254-1255
Prochnow — *Public* #2378
Wallis — *Words* p.118

SOLVENCY
Evans — *Thoughts II (Open Door)* p.58
Flesch — *Unusual* p.269
Lockridge — *World's* #5065

SOMNAMBULISM. *See* **Sleep, Walking in**

SONGS
See also types of songs
Auden — *Certain* p.348-354
Fuller — *Epigrams* p.360
Garland — *Subject* p.298-299
Henry — *5000* p.261-262
Hobe — *Tapestries* p.22, 111-112, 114, 198
Kin — *Dictionary* p.240
Lytle — *Leaves* p.99, 105
New Joy p.59
Prochnow — *Public* #205, 533, 698
Sheban — *Wisdom* no p.
Wallis — *Treasure* p.101, 157-158
Wallis — *Words* p.167
Woods — *Content.* p.172, 180, 186
Woods — *Religious* p.947-948
, *Drinking*
Auden — *Certain* p.129-130
, *Hard-time*
Botkin — *Treasury* p.283
, *Popular*
Kauffman — *For* p.237
, *War*
Guideposts — *Faith* p.472-476
, *Writers of*
Guideposts — *Faith* p.472-476

SONS
Alexander's Treasure. p.285
Applegarth — *Heir.* p.57-58
Dirksen — *Quot.* #2335
Evans — *Thoughts I* p.17-18, 142
Goudge — *Comfort* p.93-95, 147
Hobe — *Tapestries* p.85, 167, 170, 188
Holmes — *I've* p.73-75
Irion — *Yes* p.49-51, 67-69
Kin — *Dictionary* p.239
Kopplin — *Something See* Preface
Lytle — *Leaves* p.90
Manchee — *Secret* p.235-236
Prochnow — *Public* #87, 223, 768, 1028, 2520, 2526, 2740
Prochnow — *Success.* #1004
Woods — *Religious* p.947
, *Honor of*
Liebman — *Hope* p.160-181

SOPHISTICATION
Braude — *Source* #1845-1847
Dirksen — *Quot.* #1618-1619
Evans — *Unto* p.48, 88
Flesch — *Unusual* p.270
Flint — *Graham* p.153
Knight's Illus. p.351-352
Knight's Treas. p.442-444
Prochnow — *Public* #1806
Woods — *Religious* p.1076

SOPHISTRY
See also **Argument**
Edwards — *Useful* p.606
Evans — *Unto* p.102
Lockridge — *World's* #1676, 1710

SOPHOCLES
Lockridge — *World's* #3584

SORCERERS. *See* **Witches and witchcraft**

SORROW. *See* **Grief**; etc.

SOUL
See also **Animism; Conscience; Immortality; Spirit**
Alexander's Treasure. p.163
Applegarth — *Heir.* p.166, 212, 306
Baillie — *Diary* #290
Braude — *Source* #1575-1576
Curtis — *Practical* p.25
Droke — *Christian* p.510-511
Edwards — *Useful* p.609-610
Evans — *Unto* p.9, 13, 84, 122, 140-141
Flesch — *Unusual* p.270
Flint — *Graham* p.138
Fogg — *1000* #106, 342, 486, 621, 1083, 1095
Forbes — *Thoughts See* index p.568
Fuller — *Epigrams* p.267-268
Garland — *Subject* p.299
Goudge — *Comfort* p.214-216
Harnsberger — *Mark* p.450-451
Henry — *5000* p.262-263
Hobe — *Tapestries* p.62, 85, 107, 119
Hovey — *Treasury See* index p.300
How To Live p.208
Hubbard — *Scrap* p.19, 66, 124
Johnson — *Bedside* p.42, 44, 63, 90, 95, 134, 165, 184, 226, 246, 248, 258, 272, 328, 335, 337-339
Keys Happiness p.364
Kin — *Dictionary* p.240
Kohn — *Adventures* p.21-23, 117-120
Kohn — *Thoughts* p.130-133
Kohn — *Touch* p.127-129, 191-193
Krishnamurti — *Think* p.43-44
Liddle — *Thought I, II, III* p.37, 47, 49, 52, 54, 68, 137, 139, 149, 151, 176
Liddle — *Thought IV* p.33
Liddle — *Thought V* p.12
Lockridge — *World's See* index p.583
Lytle — *Leaves* p.96, 119, 154
Montapert — *Distilled* p.311-312
More Words p.155-156
New Joy p.219
Nichols — *Third* p.140-160
Peale — *Courage* p.158-159, 172-173
Phillips — *Choice* p.26, 36, 97, 161, 187, 329, 356
Prochnow — *Public* #2261, 2643, 3723-3729
Prochnow — *Success.* #2334-2335
Pullar-Strecker — *Proverbs* #247-251
Reader's — *Getting* p.109-112
Seldes — *Great* p.884-885
Sheban — *Wisdom* no p.
Sheen — *Way* p.167-169
Taylor — *With* p.122-133
Voss — *Quotations* p.232-233
Wallis — *Treasure* p.74, 83, 93, 95
Wallis — *Words* p.4, 52, 62, 151
Woods — *Content.* p.50, 57, 136, 231, 235, 242, 248, 269, 280, 285
Woods — *Religious* p.949-956
Words — *Inspir.* p.111, 147
, and God
Woods — *Religious* p.954-956
, Definitions of
Woods — *Religious* p.953-954
, Healing of
White — *Life* p.221-235
, Salvation of
Wheelis — *Moralist* p.35
, -shakers
Humes — *Instant* p.42-51; #1186-1287
, Transmigration of
Ideas p.397-399
, Welfare of
Mandelbaum — *Choose* p.30
, -winning
Knight's Illus. p.314-321
Knight's Treas. p.376-387

SOUND
See also **Music; Noise; Voice**
Flesch — *Unusual* p.270
Garland — *Subject* p.299

Harnsberger — *Mark* p.451
Harral — *Feature* p.287
Henry — *5000* p.263
Prochnow — *Public* #274, 1112, 1807, 2150
Wallis — *Words* p.151

SOUP
Cerf — *Laugh* p.401-403
Prochnow — *Public* #222

SOURCES
Braude — *Stories* p.350
Kin — *Dictionary* p.240
White — *Job* p.114, 169-170, 174
Woods — *Religious* p.956

SOUTH, THE
See also **Dixie;** names of states
Botkin — *Anecdotes* p.20-24, 163-169
Fun Fare p.133-135

SOUTH AMERICA
Flint — *Graham* p.40
Fun Fare p.69-70

SOUTH CAROLINA
Botkin — *Anecdotes* p.21, 43, 47-48, 120, 165, 243
Botkin — *Treasury* p.665-667, 670-672, 727, 905, 911

SOUTH DAKOTA
Botkin — *Anecdotes* p.35
Botkin — *Treasury* p.86, 119, 154, 277, 527

SOVEREIGNTY
See also **Government; Kings and queens; Rulers**
Kin — *Dictionary* p.240
Seldes — *Great* p.885
Words — *Inspir.* p.217-218

SOVIET UNION. *See* **Russia**

SOWING AND REAPING
Book Proverbs p.123
Evans — *Thoughts I* p.107-110, 154
Evans — *Thoughts III (Open Road)* p.201-202
Forbes — *Thoughts* p.366, 472, 475
Fox — *Make* p.47-48
Hobe — *Tapestries* p.117
Knight's Treas. p.387-389
Lockridge — *World's* #5256, 5899
Lytle — *Leaves* p.39
Prochnow — *Public* #2589, 2654, 2721, 2745

SPACE
Hovey — *Treasury* #42, 1731-1737; p.272-273
Howell — *Better* p.173-178
Lindbergh — *Unicorn* p.61
Lockridge — *World's* #2973
Lytle — *Leaves* p.171
, -age
Nichols — *Third* p.125-139
Prochnow — *Success.* #756, 857, 916, 1405
, and man
Kauffman — *For* p.204-205
, Beauty in
Lindbergh — *Gift* p.114-116
, Exploration of
Dirksen — *Quot.* #55, 1142, 1165, 1167
Kauffman — *For* p.205-207
, Flight in
Asimov — *Treasury* #161
Woods — *Religious* p.956
, Outer
Braude — *Source* #1215
Braude — *Speaker's* #1367-1371
Hovey — *Treasury* p.304
, Small
Peterson — *Art* p.385
, Time and
Clark — *Windows* p.124

SPAGHETTI
Prochnow — *Public* #1808

SPAIN AND SPANIARDS
Lockridge — *World's* #3939
Seldes — *Great* p.885-886
Woods — *Content.* p.63

SPANISH PROVERBS
Dirksen — *Quot.* #431, 1901, 1912-1913, 2012, 2017, 2037, 2110, 2175

SPARROWS
Applegarth — *Heir.* p.33-34
Asimov — *Treasury* #65-66
Auden — *Certain* p.355-356
Curtis — *Practical* p.110
Wallis — *Treasure* p.138, 161
Woods — *Wellsprings* p.38-39

SPARTANS
Asimov — *Treasury* #194-198

SPEARS
New Topical p.257
Prochnow — *Public* #2574

SPECIALIZATION
Braude — *Source* #1577

Braude — *Stories* p.350
Curtis — *Practical* p.334-335
Edwards — *Useful* p.610
Flesch — *Unusual* p.271
Humes — *Instant* #1001-1004
Speaker's Desk #239, 725
, *Self-confidence and*
Albert — *Stop* p.55-56

SPECIFICATIONS
Grizer — *Wit* p.432-433
Humes — *Instant* p.7-9, 14

SPECTATORS
See also **Audience**
Flesch — *Unusual* p.271
Prochnow — *Success.* #2337-2338

SPECULATION
See also **Gamblers and gambling; Imagination; Philosophy, Thought;** etc.
Edwards — *Useful* p.610-611, 733
Flesch — *Unusual* p.271
Grizer — *Wit* p.433-434
Harnsberger — *Mark* p.452
Kin — *Dictionary* p.241
Lytle — *Leaves* p.108
Prochnow — *Speaker's* p.287
Woods — *Business.* p.238-239

SPEECH
See also **Accents; Conversation; Talk; Words;** etc.
Alexander's Treasure. p.77, 195-197
Book Proverbs p.35
Braude — *Stories* p.350-351
Dirksen — *Quot.* #1077, 1799, 2164, 2184-2188
Du Noüy — *Human* p.104-105, 107, 122
Edwards — *Useful* p.611-612
Evans — *Quote* p.187-194
Evans — *Thoughts II (Open Door)* p.153-158
Flesch — *Unusual* p.271
Harnsberger — *Mark* p.452-453
Henry — *5000* p.263-265
Hobe — *Tapestries* p.174
Hubbard — *Scrap* p.6, 8, 21, 51
Kin — *Dictionary* p.241-242
Liddle — *Thought I, II, III* p.10, 26, 45, 132-133
Liddle — *Thought IV* p.5, 15
Liddle — *Thought V* p.29
Lockridge — *World's* #1288, 1595, 1840
Lytle — *Leaves* p.6, 27, 157
Mandel — *Stories* p.240
Prochnow — *Public See* index p.511
Prochnow — *Success.* #179, 190, 506, 1214, 1299, 1307, 2339-2340
Pullar-Strecker — *Proverbs* #167-185
Seldes — *Great* p.886
Woods — *Religious* p.957
Zobell — *Speaker's* p.130-132
, *Esophageal*
Guideposts — *Faith* p.225-227
, *Freedom of. See* **Freedom of speech**
, *Vernacular*
Fun Fare p.177-178

SPEECHES AND SPEAKERS
Albert — *Stop* p.60
Asimov — *Treasury* #289-292
Botkin — *Anecdotes* p.xxv, 112, 158
Braude — *Source* #1392-1400, 1578-1580
Braude — *Speaker's* #1137-1163
Braude — *Stories* p.311-323
Dirksen — *Quot.* #5, 31, 95, 101-102, 107, 238, 718-720, 1784, 1799-1804, 1874
Flesch — *Unusual* p.270
Flint — *Graham* p.138
Forbes — *Thoughts See* index p.568
Fuller — *Epigrams* p.268-270, 361
Fuller — *Thesaurus* #756-782
Grizer — *Wit* p.434-435
Harral — *Feature* p.260-261, 288
Holmes — *I've* p.60
Keller — *You* p.348-358
Kennedy — *Reader's* #1057-1066
Kin — *Dictionary* p.241
Kronenberger — *Animal* p.272
Lockridge — *World's* #5026
Mandel — *Stories* p.239-240
Modern Eloquence (14) p.217-229
Montapert — *Distilled* p.285-286, 312
Nizer — *Thinking* p.20, 22, 24-29, 94, 129, 237-238
Prochnow — *Public* #75; *See also* index p.507
Prochnow — *Speaker's* p.249-251, 287-291
Prochnow — *Success.* #78, 135, 258, 540, 585, 605, 754, 2336
Safian — *Insults* p.186-188
Speaker's Desk #206, 252, 272, 300, 597, 699, 778, 780, 788, 861, 1102, 1173
, *After-dinner*
Copeland — *World's See* index p.739-740
Dirksen — *Quot.* #720
Nizer — *Thinking* p.20

, *Anxiety in*
Nizer — *Thinking* p.24
, *Art of*
Nizer — *Thinking* p.21
, *Before thinking*
Curtis — *Practical* p.71-72
, *Beginnings. See* **Speeches and speakers, Openings of**
, *Bombast in*
Nizer — *Thinking* p.30, 169
, *Choosing*
Prochnow — *Success.* #1
, *Climax of*
Nizer — *Thinking* p.41
, *Closings of*
Prochnow — *Success.* #278-303, 1506
Speaker's Desk #63, 699, 742, 787, 789, 989, 1028
, *Commemorative*
Humes — *Instant* #1240-1243
, *Commencement. See* **Commencement**
, *Conduct of*
Baillie — *Diary* #118
, *Confidence in*
Nizer — *Thinking* p.33, 93
, *Controlled*
Sheen — *Thoughts* p.134-136
, *Delivery of*
Prochnow — *Success.* #83, 87
, *Devices to curtail*
Nizer — *Thinking* p.20
, *Documentation of*
Nizer — *Thinking* p.30
, *Dramatic effects*
Nizer — *Thinking* p.90, 100
, *Dullness of*
Nizer — *Thinking* p.152
, *E.A.S.E. formula for*
Humes — *Instant* p.3-19, 48
, *Electrifying*
Humes — *Instant* p.8-9, 14-15
, *Emotion in*
Nizer — *Thinking* p.93, 187
, *Emphasis in*
Nizer — *Thinking* p.70
, *Endings for. See* **Soul-shakers; Speeches and speakers, Closings of**
, *Excerpts from*
Prochnow — *Success.* #728-842
, *Experience in*
Nizer — *Thinking* p.117
, *Experiments of*
Nizer — *Thinking* p.34
, *Extemporaneous*
Nizer — *Thinking* p.232
, *Facts in*
Nizer — *Thinking* p.30, 82
, *Fears of*
Nizer — *Thinking* p.93
, *Formula for*
Nizer — *Thinking* p.22-24, 40-41, 63, 69, 168, 177
, *Generalities in*
Nizer — *Thinking* p.29
, *Grammar of*
Humes — *Instant* p.15-19
Nizer — *Thinking* p.25
, *Humorous*
Copeland — *World's See* index p.739
, *Illustrations for*
Prochnow — *Success.* #80
, *Introductory*
See also **Introductions**
Nizer — *Thinking* p.50-51
, *Momentum in*
Nizer — *Thinking* p.145, 149
, *Nervousness in*
Nizer — *Thinking* p.65
, *Notes for*
Nizer — *Thinking* p.33
, *Openings of*
Humes — *Instant* p.27-34, 46-51
Nizer — *Thinking* p.145-148
Prochnow — *Success.* #78-113
Seaburg — *Great See* index p.462
Speaker's Desk #55, 443, 734, 778, 951
, *Organizing of*
Prochnow — *Success.* #78-113
, *Originality of*
Nizer — *Thinking* p.148, 151
, *Outlines for*
Prochnow — *Success.* #79
, *Personal*
Copeland — *World's* p.315, 377, 705-706, 708-709
, *Persuasion of*
Nizer — *Thinking* p.24, 30, 63, 139, 169, 184
, *Plot of*
Nizer — *Thinking* p.33
, *Poetry of*
Nizer — *Thinking* p.184
, *Preparation of*
Nizer — *Thinking* p.26, 29-33, 69-70, 169
, *Rhythm in*
Nizer — *Thinking* p.24-26, 28, 102-103, 121, 142, 173
, *Silence of*
Nizer — *Thinking* p.26
, *Simplicity of*
Humes — *Instant* p.17-19
, *Style of*
Dirksen — *Quot.* #1799

, *Subjects of*
Humes — *Instant* p.3-4, 33-34
, *Timing of*
Prochnow — *Success.* #82
, *Tips for*
See also **Speeches and speakers, Formula for**
Walters — *How* p.182-188
, *Vituperation of*
Kin — *Dictionary* p.271
, *Vividness of*
Nizer — *Thinking* p.169
Speaker's Desk See index p.306

SPEECHOGRAPH
Nizer — *Thinking* p.27-29, 33, 70, 83, 142, 147, 173, 184

SPEED
See also **Haste**
Du Noüy — *Road* p.39, 70, 133-134
Prochnow — *Public* #1834, 2741
Prochnow — *Success.* #982

"SPELLBINDERS"
Botkin — *Anecdotes* p.157-176

SPELLING
Asimov — *Treasury* #558
Braude — *Speaker's* #1372-1377
Braude — *Stories* p.351
Flesch — *Unusual* p.271-272
Harnsberger — *Mark* p.453-454
Prochnow — *Public* #27, 36, 195, 400, 827, 893, 960, 998
Prochnow — *Speaker's* p.292
Prochnow — *Success.* #1016, 1029, 1089, 1161

SPENDING AND SPENDERS
See also **Extravagance**
Braude — *Source* #1581-1582
Dirksen — *Quot.* #1805
Flesch — *Unusual* p.272
Forbes — *Thoughts* p.72, 211, 240, 246, 296, 335, 362, 442, 469, 477
Grizer — *Wit* p.436
Harral — *Feature* p.288
Humes — *Instant* #1005-1008
Kin — *Dictionary* p.242
Lytle — *Leaves* p.78, 174
Montapert — *Distilled* p.312
Prochnow — *Public* #2374
Prochnow — *Speaker's* p.292
Prochnow — *Success.* #587, 810

SPHINX
Harnsberger — *Mark* p.454-455

"SPICED TONGUE"
Fun Fare p.33, 78-79, 106, 177, 213

SPIDERS
Adams — *New* p.151
Alexander's Treasure. p.78
Applegarth — *Heir.* p.20-21, 25
Auden — *Certain* p.356-357
Baillie — *Diary* #120
Harral — *Feature* p.288
Hobe — *Tapestries* p.95
Irion — *Yes* p.112-115
Wallis — *Treasure* p.19

SPIES
Asimov — *Treasury* #4
Fogg — *1000* #57, 236, 365, 370, 630, 778
Kin — *Dictionary* p.242

SPINACH
Prochnow — *Public* #397, 788
Prochnow — *Success.* #477

SPINOZA, BARUCH
Flesch — *Unusual* p.272
Lockridge — *World's* #2733

SPINSTERS
Braude — *Speaker's* #1378-1379
Braude — *Stories* p.270
Copeland — *10,000* p.281-282
Fuller — *Thesaurus* #871-873
Lockridge — *World's* #674, 2716, 5171
Prochnow — *Success.* #564
Schermerhorn — *1500* p.345-346

SPIRES
Wallis — *Words* p.41, 44, 118

SPIRIT
See also **Emotion; Enthusiasm; God; Holy Spirit (Holy Ghost); Ideals and idealism; Religion; Soul; Spirituality; Zeal**
Dirksen — *Quot.* #485, 760, 1078, 1581
Droke — *Christian* p.511-512
Edwards — *Useful* p.612
Evans — *Unto* p.84, 141
Flesch — *Unusual* p.272-273
Flint — *Graham* p.19, 139
Forbes — *Thoughts See* index p.568
Garland — *Subject* p.301
Harnsberger — *Mark* p.455
Henry — *5000* p.265
Hobe — *Tapestries* p.53
Hovey — *Treasury* p.273; *See also* index p.300

How To Live p.538-562
Keys Happiness p.107-108
Liddle — *Thought I, II, III* p.103, 149, 187, 193
Lockridge — *World's* #3536
Lytle — *Leaves* p.23, 48
Montapert — *Distilled* p.312-313
Peterson — *Art* p.80
Phillips — *Choice* p.96, 132, 210, 251, 396, 401
Prochnow — *Public* #2564, 2595
Prochnow — *Success.* #2341
Sagendorph — *Old* p.39
Seldes — *Great* p.886-887
Sheban — *Wisdom* no p.
Woods — *Content.* p.214, 227, 231, 234, 265-286, 305
Woods — *Religious* p.957-959

, Affinity of
Sheban — *Wisdom* no p.
, Aloofness of
Peterson — *Art* p.338
, Awakening of
Flint — *Graham* p.139
Sheban — *Wisdom* no p.
, Beauty of
Peale — *Guideposts* p.299-302
, Birth of
Keller — *Open* p.55-56
, Blindness of
Woods — *Reilgious* p.960
, Bondage of
New Topical p.31
, Conflict of
Woods — *Religious* p.960
, Consciousness of
Curtis — *New* p.22-26
, Development of
Taylor — *With* p.6-7
, Disease of
Flint — *Graham* p.139
, Dryness of
Baillie — *Diary* #346
, Economics of
Halverson — *Perspective* p.5
, Equilibrium of
Baillie — *Diary* #145
, Essence of
Peterson — *Art* p.93
, Experience of
Baillie — *Diary* #261
Johnson — *Bedside* p.109
, Eyesight of
Price — *Wider* p.97-105
, Fidelity of
Adams — *New* p.91
, Formation of
Woods — *Religious* p.961
, Growth of
Adams — *New* p.401
Fox — *Make* p.36
Kohn — *Through* p.38-39
, Happiness of
Hadfield — *Delights* p.81
, Health of
Kohn — *Adventures* p.79-83
, Holy. See **Holy Spirit**
, Human
Woods — *Religious* p.959-960
, Illness of
Unlimited Power p.112-117
, Illumination of
Flint — *Graham* p.139
, Impotence of
Maltz — *Creative* p.172
, Inheritance of
Sheen — *Content.* p.173-174
, Inventory of
Peterson — *Art* p.20
, Knowledge of
Baillie — *Diary* #24
, Lethargy of
Woods — *Religious* p.961
, Life of
Curtis — *New* p.33-34
Flint — *Graham* p.139-140
Fox — *Make* p.223-224
Hubbard — *Scrap* p.37
Woods — *Religious* p.961
, Lifting of
Peterson — *Art* p.34
, Necessity of
Flint — *Graham* p.140
, of '76 and '77
Nizer — *Thinking* p.170-174
, of the age
Ideas p.379-381
, Poverty of
Dirksen — *Quot.* #2391
Kohn — *Touch* p.160-161
, Power of
Johnson — *Bedside* p.130, 167, 317
Keller — *Open* p.45
Peterson — *Art* p.54
, Progress of
Woods — *Religious* p.961
, Qualities of
Peterson — *Art* p.310
, Resources of
Day — *Meditations* p.42
Kohn — *Touch* p.144-147
, Struggle of
Woods — *Religious* p.962
, Suicide of
Maltz — *Creative* p.12-14, 179-180
, Techniques of
Peale — *Guideposts* p.57-84
, Transactions of
Baillie — *Diary* #8
, Unseen world of
Bartlett — *Discovery* p.152-153

, *Vertigo of*
Flint — *Graham* p.147-148
, *Vision of*
Flint — *Graham* p.140
, *Warfare of*
Flint — *Graham* p.149
, *World of*
Woods — *Religious* p.962
, *Youthful*
See also **Youth**
Maltz — *Creative* p.32-33
Peterson — *Art* p.269

SPIRITUALISM
Bach — *Make* p.197-198
Flesch — *Unusual* p.275
George — *Book* p.374
Speaker's Desk #784
Woods — *Religious* p.962

SPIRITUALITY
Applegarth — *Heir.* p.259-269
Fox — *Make* p.202
Garland — *Subject* p.301
Holmes — *Design* p.204-210; *See also* index p.235
Lair — *Baby* p.187-198
Liddle — *Thought V* p.19, 43
Sheban — *Wisdom* no p.
Woods — *Religious* p.960-962
Zobell — *Speaker's* p.132-133
, *Highest*
Day — *Meditations* p.38

SPITE. *See* **Malice**

SPONTANEITY
Curtis — *Practical* p.101
Nizer — *Thinking* p.151

"SPOONERISMS"
Asimov — *Treasury* #232, 234

SPOONS
Kin — *Dictionary* p.242

SPORTS
See also **Athletics; Recreation;** names of sports
Braude — *Speaker's* #1380-1390
Copeland — *10,000* p.625-639
Dirksen — *Quot.* #886
Flesch — *Unusual* p.275
Fuller — *Epigrams* p.270
Fuller — *Thesaurus* p.317-331
Fun Fare p.151-153
Harral — *Feature* p.288-291
Henry — *5000* p.265
Hovey — *Treasury* #16, 469, 1506, 1612
Kennedy — *Reader's* #1067-1068
Kronenberger — *Animal* p.273-282
Prochnow — *Public* #1481
Prochnow — *Success.* #2342
Simpson — *Contemp.* p.460-467
Simpson — *'54* p.90, 247, 358
, *as character builder*
Ideas p.381-382
Reader's — *Getting* p.128
, *Fanaticism for*
Gold — *Letters* p.69-70
, *"Good"*
See also **Sportsmanship**
Daly — *Personality* p.13-17
, *in newspapers*
Peterson — *Art* p.120
, *Parents' fear of*
Ginott — *Between* p.236-237
, *Spectator*
Fun Fare p.36, 93, 151

SPORTSMANSHIP
Braude — *Stories* p.352-353
Evans — *Thoughts IV* p.27-28, 103
Wallis — *Treasure* p.132

SPOTS
Kin — *Dictionary* p.242
Kohn — *Thoughts* p.113-115

SPRING
See also **Flowers; Nature;** etc.
Adams — *New* p.169, 359
Applegarth — *Heir.* p.62, 94, 189
Curtis — *Practical* p.195
Dirksen — *Quot.* #47, 86, 106, 1080
Edwards — *Useful* p.612
Goudge — *Comfort* p.41-43, 362-363
Hadfield — *Love* p.17-81
Henry — *5000* p.266
Hobe — *Tapestries* p.60
Kahn — *Lessons* p.77-79
Kohn — *Best* p.36-53
Kohn — *Pathways* p.191-192
Kohn — *Thoughts* p.15-55
Kohn — *Touch* p.106-107
Liddle — *Thoughts I, II, III* p.110, 142
Patterns For Living p.18-21
Peterson — *Art* p.103, 117, 149, 161
Prochnow — *Public* #3739-3740
Prochnow — *Success.* #2343
Sagendorph — *Old* p.27-30
Sheban — *Wisdom* no p.
Wallis — *Treasure* p.184
Wallis — *Words* p.172, 175, 182
Woods — *Content.* p.211-212, 226

SPRINGS (water)
Adams — *New* p.171
Kohn — *Best* p.58-59

SPURGEON
Prochnow — *Public* #3754

SPURS
Kin — *Dictionary* p.242

"SQUARE DEAL." *See* **Fairness**

"SQUELCHES"
Fun Fare p.136-137
Humes — *Instant* p.56
Safian — *Insults* p.221-224
Safian — *More Insults* p.189-192
Speaker's Desk See index p.305

SQUIRRELS
Botkin — *Anecdotes* p.129
Botkin — *Treasury* p.17, 605
Prochnow — *Public* #2180
Weisfeld — *Pulpit* p.113

STABILITY
See also **Character**
Braude — *Stories* p.353-354
Day — *Meditations* p.76
Forbes — *Thoughts* p.258, 389
How To Live p.379-382
Kin — *Dictionary* p.243
, Internal
Holmes — *Design* p.54
, Physical
Holmes — *Design* p.156-157

STAGE. *See* **Actors and actresses; Theater**

STAGE DRIVERS
Botkin — *Anecdotes* p.144, 198-199

"STAGE INTERLUDES"
Fun Fare p.16, 72, 103-105, 293

STAGNATION
Forbes — *Thoughts* p.117-138, 143

STAIRS
Prochnow — *Public* #1550

STAMINA. *See* **Endurance; Strength**

STAMMERING. *See* **Stuttering**

STAMP ACT
Botkin — *Anecdotes* p.136

STAMPS
Flesch — *Unusual* p.273
Prochnow — *Success.* #2344

STANDARD OF LIVING
Curtis — *New* p.17-32
Dirksen — *Quot.* #518, 771, 2346, 2386
Forbes — *Thoughts* p.32, 41, 122, 153, 168, 178, 298, 326, 403, 479
Ideas p.382-383
Prochnow — *Success.* #1103
Seldes — *Great* p.887
Woods — *Business.* p.139

STANDARDIZATION
See also **Efficiency; Method**
Dirksen — *Quot.* #2387
Edwards — *Useful* p.733

STANDARDS
See also **Character; Morality and morals; Principles;** etc.
Dirksen — *Quot.* #1695, 2391
Evans — *Faith* p.12, 49, 71, 127-128, 137-156
Evans — *This* p.56-57, 59-60
Evans — *Thoughts I* p.161
Evans — *Thoughts II (Open Door)* p.65, 168, 189
Evans — *Thoughts III (Open Road)* p.27, 46-47, 139, 156, 158, 177, 207
Evans — *Thoughts IV* p.95, 104, 127-128, 136-137, 143-144
Evans — *Unto* p.17, 66, 72, 85
Forbes — *Thoughts* p.29, 64, 109, 159, 179, 189, 215, 315, 407, 445, 483
Garland — *Subject* p.301-302
Harnsberger — *Mark* p.455
Lytle — *Leaves* p.9, 187
Peale — *Sin* p.31-44
Speaker's Desk #277
, Double
Woods — *Religious* p.253
, Loss of
Sheen — *Thoughts* p.84-86
, Single
Evans — *Unto* p.85
, Teenager
Ginott — *Between* p.149-150, 167

"STAR-SPANGLED BANNER"
Fogg — *1000* #1134

STARS
See also **Planets; Sky, Night**
Applegarth — *Heir.* p.198, 213, 230, 259
Bartlett — *Discovery* p.51-54, 96
Dirksen — *Quot.* #2189-2191
Du Noüy — *Human* p.32n, 34, 55
Edwards — *Useful* p.612-613
Fogg — *1000* #288

Forbes — *Thoughts* p.136, 142, 163, 171, 174, 202, 317, 359, 382, 405, 476, 499
Goudge — *Comfort* p.21, 26
Hadfield — *Delights* p.37
Henry — *5000* p.266-267
Hobe — *Tapestries* p.102, 111, 143, 161, 170
Hubbard — *Scrap* p.23, 25-26, 32, 203
Kin — *Dictionary* p.243
Kohn — *Adventures* p.140-144
Lockridge — *World's* #1261-1284
Lytle — *Leaves* p.69
New Topical p.257-258
Nichols — *Third* p.137-139
Peterson — *Art* p.241
Prochnow — *Public* #2474
Wallis — *Treasure* p.17, 19-20, 25, 29, 51, 138, 183, 210
Wallis — *Words* p.33, 35, 44, 85, 131, 175
Woods — *Content.* p.208, 218, 333
Woods — *Religious* p.962
Words — *Inspir.* p.60-61
, Christmas
Peterson — *Art* p.395
, Light of
Kohn — *Pathways* p.41-44
, Names of
Auden — *Certain* p.273-276

STARVATION. *See* **Hunger**

STATEMENTS
Edwards — *Useful* p.32-33
Flesch — *Unusual* p.303
Kin — *Dictionary* p.16

STATES
See also names of states
Curtis — *Practical* p.128
Edwards — *Useful* p.613
Flesch — *Unusual* p.273
Forbes — *Thoughts See* index p.569
Henry — *5000* p.267-268
Lockridge — *World's* #3175, 3264-3298, 3637, 5119
Prochnow — *Success.* #129
Seldes — *Great* p.887-893
Wheelis — *Moralist* p.34-35, 47-48, 80, 97-98, 105, 115, 118-121
Woods — *Business.* p.240-241
Woods — *Religious* p.962-964
, Corporative
Ideas p.98-99
, Functions of
Du Noüy — *Human* p.268-269
, Monopolies of
Woods — *Religious* p.964
, Rights of
Woods — *Business.* p.241-242
, Slang for
Botkin — *Treasury* p.327

STATESMEN AND STATESMANSHIP
See also **Government; Politics and politicians**
Curtis — *Practical* p.358-359, 365
Dirksen — *Quot.* #39, 190, 361, 486, 1081, 2280, 2317, 2329
Edwards — *Useful* p.613-614
Flesch — *Unusual* p.273-274
Forbes — *Thoughts* p.150, 278, 358, 448, 480
George — *Book* p.43, 56, 70, 75-76, 89, 120, 147, 288, 300, 357, 366, 376, 386
Harnsberger — *Mark* p.456
Henry — *5000* p.268
Humes — *Instant* #1009-1021
Johnson — *Bedside* p.85
Kennedy — *Reader's* #1069
Liddle — *Thought I, II, III* p.43, 92
Lockridge — *World's* #4979
Lytle — *Leaves* p.57
Nizer — *Thinking* p.139
Prochnow — *Public* #1454
Prochnow — *Speaker's* p.293-294
Prochnow — *Success.* #1253, 2345
Seldes — *Great* p.893

STATION. *See* **Rank**

STATISM
Franke — *Buckley* p.281
Woods — *Business.* p.242-243
Woods — *Religious* p.964

STATISTICIANS
Prochnow — *Public* #1809, 2043

STATISTICS
See also **Facts**
Braude — *Source* #1583-1585
Braude — *Speaker's* #1391-1392
Dirksen — *Quot.* #32-33, 96
Du Noüy — *Human* p.20-26
Edwards — *Useful* p.733
Evans — *This* p.25-26
Fuller — *Thesaurus* #2221-2222
Grizer — *Wit* p.436-437
Ideas p.239-241
Kin — *Dictionary* p.243
Kohn — *Touch* p.156
Liddle — *Thought I, II, III* p.31, 43
Nizer — *Thinking* p.102, 139, 184
Prochnow — *Public* #18, 69, 200, 1547
Prochnow — *Speaker's* p.294

Prochnow — *Success.* #1317
Wallis — *Words* p.7

STATUE OF LIBERTY
Applegarth — *Heir.* p.118
, Inscription on
Words — *Inspir.* p.139

STATUES
See also **Monuments**
Liddle — *Thought I, II, III* p.34
Prochnow — *Public* #2202

STATURE
See also **Height**
Braude — *Stories* #1586
Dirksen — *Quot.* #1808
Flesch — *Unusual* p.274
Grizer — *Wit* p.437
Kin — *Dictionary* p.243

STATUS
See also **Rank**
Braude — *Source* #1587-1588
Mandel — *Stories* p.240
, Symbols of
Myers — *Thunder* p.32

"STATUS QUO"
Braude — *Source* #1589-1590
Braude — *Speaker's* #1393-1394
Braude — *Stories* p.354
Myers — *Thunder* p.33
Seldes — *Great* p.893

STEADFASTNESS
See also **Constancy; Loyalty**
Book Proverbs p.74
Emmons — *Mature* p.84-86
Forbes — *Thoughts* p.243, 254
Garland — *Subject.* p.302
Johnson — *Bedside* p.201
Lytle — *Leaves* p.131
New Joy p.175
New Topical p.258, 283-284
Nichols — *Third* p.25
Prochnow — *Public* #2220
, Prayer for
Unlimited Power p.172

STEALING. *See* **Burglars and burglary**

STEAM POWER
White — *Job* p.183-194, 186

STEAMBOATS
Botkin — *Anecdotes* p.67, 70
Botkin — *Treasury* p.597

"STEEL RULE"
Menninger — *Blue.* p.104

STENOGRAPHERS
See also **Secretaries**
Braude — *Speaker's* #1395-1398
Braude — *Stories* p.355
Copeland — *10,000* p.416-418
Prochnow — *Public* #131, 210, 248, 412, 612, 880
Prochnow — *Speaker's* p.295

STEPMOTHERS
Flint — *Graham* p.140
Kin — *Dictionary* p.243

STEPS
Dirksen — *Quot.* #784, 1809
Evans — *Thoughts I* p.28, 46, 152-153
Flesch — *Unusual* p.274
Forbes — *Thoughts* p.179, 193, 264, 418
Kin — *Dictionary* p.243
Prochnow — *Public* #996

STEREOTYPES
Asimov — *Treasury See* index p.429-430
Peale — *Sin* p.127-129
Prochnow — *Public* #2446

STERILITY
Lockridge — *World's* #4443

STERILIZATION
Woods — *Religious* p.964

STERNNESS. *See* **Decision; Discipline; Purpose; Resolution**

STEVENSON, ROBERT LOUIS
Kohn — *Touch* p.170

STEWARDS AND STEWARDESSES
Manchee — *Secret* p.197-198
More Words p.158-159
Unlimited Power p.177-179

STEWARDSHIP
Applegarth — *Heir.* p.179
Carruthers — *Sparks* p.152-154
Edwards — *Useful* p.615
Flint — *Graham* p.141
Fridy — *Meditat.* p.112
Hovey — *Treasury* p.273; #341, 487, 608, 644, 647-649, 752, 1740-1743
Kauffman — *For* p.207-208
Lytle — *Leaves* p.140
Strait — *Speaker's* p.170
Wallis — *Words* p.201-204
Words Change p.94-97

"STICK-TO-IT-TIVENESS." *See* **Endurance; Patience; Persistence**

STILLNESS. *See* **Silence**

STIMULANTS
See also names of stimulants
White — *Life* p.103-111

STIMULI
Adams — *New* p.18

STINGINESS
See also **Misers**
Asimov — *Treasury* #295, 408-409, 441
Fuller — *Thesaurus* #556-566
Kin — *Dictionary* p.244
Prochnow — *Public* #1409
Schermerhorn — *1500* p.372-373
Speaker's Desk See index p.305

STOCK MARKET
See also **Investment**
Braude — *Speaker's* #1399-1401
Fuller — *Thesaurus* #2146-2147
Grizer — *Wit* p.437-438
Keys Happiness p.367
Prochnow — *Public* #1455
Prochnow — *Success.* #668

STOCKBROKERS
Copeland — *10,000* p.443-444
Manchee — *Secret* p.228-229

STOICISM
See also **Endurance; Resignation**
Edwards — *Useful* p.615
Flesch — *Unusual* p.274
Hubbard — *Scrap* p.161
Menninger — *Blue.* p.81-82
Speaker's Desk #143, 500, 588, 661

STOMACH
Dirksen — *Quot.* #2193-2194
Flesch — *Unusual* p.274
Hubbard — *Scrap* p.200
Kin — *Dictionary* p.244

STONE AGE
Bartlett — *Discovery* p.4

STONECUTTERS
Hadfield — *Love* p.197
Peterson — *Art* p.84

STONES
Kohn — *Best* p.40
Lindbergh — *Unicorn* p.16-17, 42-43
Prochnow — *Public* #2510, 2622

"STOOL PIGEONS"
Fuller — *Thesaurus* #2591-2592

STOPS AND STOPPING
Flesch — *Unusual* p.274
Prochnow — *Success.* #2346-2347
Speaker's Desk #34, 242

STORES AND STOREKEEPERS. *See* **Shops and shopkeepers**

STORIES AND STORYTELLING
Botkin — *Anecdotes* p.xxvi-xxvii, 112, 158
Braude — *Speaker's* #1402-1403
Edwards — *Useful* p.615
Flesch — *Unusual* p.275
Harnsberger — *Mark* p.317-318
Henry — *5000* p.269, 277
Humes — *Instant* p.29-32
Lytle — *Leaves* p.163
Prochnow — *Public* #323
Prochnow — *Success.* #1324, 2348

"STORMALONG, OLD"
Botkin — *Treasury* p.178, 185-192, 834

STORMS
See also types of storms
Auden — *Certain* p.401-404
Curtis — *Practical* p.197-198
Harnsberger — *Mark* p.457
Henry — *5000* p.268-269
Kin — *Dictionary* p.245
Kohn — *Pathways* p.141-142
Kohn — *Through* p.85-88
Prochnow — *Public* #642, 2383
Prochnow — *Success.* #1160
Woods — *Wellsprings* p.29-30

STOWE, HARRIET BEECHER
Applegarth — *Heir.* p.155

"STRAIGHT MEN"
Asimov — *Treasury* #72

STRANGENESS
Evans — *This* p.5-8

STRANGERS
Applegarth — *Heir.* p.249
Evans — *This* p.124-125
Fox — *Make* p.67
Henry — *5000* p.269-270
Hobe — *Tapestries* p.181-198
Prochnow — *Public* #556, 936, 992, 2522, 2656
Wallis — *Words* p.14, 29, 81, 199
, and Pilgrims
Baillie — *Diary* #182

STRATEGY
Evans — *This* p.95-96

Flesch — *Unusual* p.275-276
Fun Fare p.79, 91
Halverson — *Perspective* p.21
Henry — *5000* p.270
Kin — *Dictionary* p.245
Prochnow — *Public* #115, 547

STRAW
Kin — *Dictionary* p.245

STRAWBERRIES
Prochnow — *Public* #627
, Boxes for
Clark — *Windows* p.72

STREAMS
Hobe — *Tapestries* p.92
Kohn — *Adventures* p.133-136
Lytle — *Leaves* p.51

STREETCARS
Botkin — *Anecdotes* p.30

STREETS
Irion — *Yes* p.127-131
, -Corner-speakers on
Botkin — *Anecdotes* p.xxv, 280
, Scenes on
Fun Fare p.9, 30, 54, 87, 145-147, 208, 244-246

STRENGTH
See also **Courage; Endurance; Energy; Force; Health; Power**
Albert — *Stop* p.57-58, 83-85
Alexander's Treasure. p.266
Detherage — *Sunrise* p.20, 33, 104, 152, 178
Dirksen — *Quot.* #721, 1582-1585, 1810, 2179, 2195
Droke — *Christian* p.512-513
Edwards — *Useful* p.615
Evans — *Thoughts III (Open Road)* p.191, 197, 202
Flint — *Graham* p.25
Forbes — *Thoughts* See index p.569
Garland — *Subject* p.304
Henry — *5000* p.270
Hobe — *Tapestries* p.116, 197
How To Live p.109
Johnson — *Bedside* p.278, 332
Keys Happiness p.341-344, 488-492
Kin — *Dictionary* p.245
Liddle — *Thought I, II, III* p.7, 20, 32, 43, 61, 85, 118, 128, 182
Liddle — *Thought IV* p.5, 28, 31, 38, 42
Liddle — *Thought V* p.12, 24-25
Lindbergh — *Gift* p.57-58
Lytle — *Leaves* p.17, 66, 189
Maltz — *Creative* p.58-60
Montapert — *Distilled* p.313
Nichols — *Third* p.153-154
Peale — *Courage* p.69
Peale — *Guideposts* p.122-125
Phillips — *Choice* p.87
Prochnow — *Public* #641, 2284, 2366, 2475, 2546, 2731
Prochnow — *Speaker's* p.295
Sheban — *Wisdom* no p.
Sheen — *Content.* p.154-156
Wallis — *Treasure* p.84, 187
Wallis — *Words* p.49
Wallis — *Religious* p.965
Words — *Inspir.* p.185-186
, for today
Maxwell — *Courage* p.75-88
, Inner
How To Live p.230-233
, of heart
Johnson — *Bedside* p.63
, Prayer for
Unlimited Power p.9

STRESS. *See* **Frustration; Pressure; Tension; Worry**

STRETCHING
Evans — *Thoughts III (Open Road)* p.178, 187

STRICTNESS. *See* **Discipline**

STRIFE
See also **Quarrels; Struggle;** etc.
Braude — *Stories* p.355-356
Dirksen — *Quot.* #567, 1252, 1293
Evans — *Unto* p.125
Hubbard — *Scrap* p.128, 215
Mandel — *Stories* p.240-242
New Topical p.259
Prochnow — *Public* #2553

STRIKES
Day — *Meditations* p.26
Grizer — *Wit* p.438-439
Hubbard — *Scrap* p.18
Seldes — *Great* p.893-895
Woods — *Business.* p.243-246

STROKES
Kin — *Dictionary* p.245
Lytle — *Leaves* p.138
Prochnow — *Public* #664

STRUGGLE
See also **Battles; Conflict; Discouragement; Strife;** etc.
Detherage — *Sunrise* p.44, 47, 60
Dirksen — *Quot.* #724, 2365
Evans — *Thoughts IV* p.105-106

Forbes — *Thoughts* p.164, 254, 344, 415-416, 419, 450, 491, 518
Garland — *Subject* p.305
Hobe — *Tapestries* p.154
Howell — *Better* p.179-184
Howell — *Lines* p.60-64
Lytle — *Leaves* p.138
Mandel — *Stories* p.242-243
Montapert — *Distilled* p.314
Prochnow — *Public* #489, 2204
Prochnow — *Success.* #350, 1243
Seldes — *Great* p.895-896
, for existence
Seldes — *Great* p.896
White — *Job* p.61-65

STUBBORNNESS. *See* **Obstinacy**

STUDENTS
See also **Scholars and scholarship**
Applegarth — *Heir.* p.158
Cerf — *Laugh* p.365-372
Curtis — *Practical* p.1
Dirksen — *Quot.* #276, 319, 1141, 2390
Evans — *Thoughts III (Open Road)* p.147, 157
Evans — *Thoughts IV* p.129
Fuller — *Thesaurus* #1036, 1061-1066
Grizer — *Wit* p.439
Keller — *You* p.279-301
Lytle — *Leaves* p.172
Mandelbaum — *Choose* p.27
Prochnow — *Public* #94, 109-110, 169, 684; *See also* index p.511
Prochnow — *Success.* #791, 906, 947, 989, 996
Wallis — *Treasure* p.90
, Duty of
Krishnamurti — *Think* p.56-57
, Good
Daly — *Personality* p.92-98
, Middle-aged
Kronenberger — *Animal* p.194-196
, Movement of
Keller — *You* p.77-82

STUDY
See also **Books and reading; Education; Knowledge; Learning; Scholars and scholarship; Self-improvement**
Applegarth — *Heir.* p.167
Edwards — *Useful* p.616-617
Evans — *Thoughts I* p.36, 174-175
Flesch — *Unusual* p.276
Forbes — *Thoughts* See index p.569
Garland — *Subject* p.305-306
Henry — *5000* p.270
Kin — *Dictionary* p.245
Krishnamurti — *Think* p.139-140
Lockridge — *World's* #3848
Lytle — *Leaves* p.47, 60, 62, 112, 172
Modern Eloquence (14) p.417
Montapert — *Distilled* p.314-315
Prochnow — *Public* #443, 453, 671, 2570
Speaker's Desk p.244
Wallis — *Treasure* p.14, 167, 181-182, 231, 233
Wallis — *Words* p.141

STUPIDITY
See also **Fools and foolishness;** etc.
Asimov — *Treasury* #287
Braude — *Stories* p.356
Curtis — *Practical* p.40, 75
Dirksen — *Quot.* #489, 683, 1082, 2196-2197
Evans — *Unto* p.66
Flesch — *Unusual* p.276
Forbes — *Thoughts* p.406, 451, 498
Fuller — *Epigrams* p.270-271
Fuller — *Thesaurus* #576-583
Harnsberger — *Mark* p.458-459
Henry — *5000* p.271
Kin — *Dictionary* p.245
Lockridge — *World's* #1009, 1448, 2547, 2585, 3010, 5194
Prochnow — *Public* #1198, 1388, 1431, 1471, 1758
Prochnow — *Speaker's* p.296
Prochnow — *Success.* #504, 517, 1167, 2351-2352
Seldes — *Great* p.896

STUTTERING
Asimov — *Treasury* #118-119, 281, 357
Fuller — *Thesaurus* #711-713
Nizer — *Thinking* p.94
Schermerhorn — *1500* p.351-352
Speaker's Desk #272, 348, 558, 786

STYLE
See also **Eloquence; Fashion; Originality; Speech; Writing and writers**
Curtis — *Practical* p.429-431, 442
Dirksen — *Quot.* #2327
Edwards — *Useful* p.617-619
Flesch — *Unusual* p.276-277
Henry — *5000* p.271
Hubbard — *Scrap* p.81

Lockridge — *World's* #3115, 4726, 5280
Lytle — *Leaves* p.27
Prochnow — *Success.* #2353-2354

SUBCONSCIOUS
Albert — *Stop* p.172-173, 175-177, 179, 187, 203-204
Curtis — *Golden* p.69-70, 135-136
Flesch — *Unusual* p.300
Garland — *Subject* p.323
How To Live p.225-229, 461-462
Ideas p.404-406
Keys Happiness p.499-502
Montapert — *Distilled* p.315
Peterson — *Art* p.295
Phillips — *Choice See* index p.430
Rau — *Act* p.134-141
Woods — *Religious* p.1013-1014
, Activity of
Fox — *Make* p.24
, Religion in
Sheen — *Content.* p.84-88
, toward riches
Hill — *Think* p.226-235

SUBLIMATION
Holman — *Psych.* p.52-53
Menninger — *Blue.* p.41-42, 44-45

SUBLIMITY
See also **Beauty; Holiness; Perfection**
Edwards — *Useful* p.619-620
Lockridge — *World's* #3412
Woods — *Content.* p.251-262
Woods — *Religious* p.965

SUBMARINES
Asimov — *Treasury* #275, 429
Prochnow — *Public* #462

SUBMISSION. *See* **Humility; Meekness; Obedience; Resignation**

SUBORDINATION
Flesch — *Unusual* p.278
Lockridge — *World's* #3885

SUBSIDIES
Woods — *Business.* p.246-247

SUBSTANCE
See also **Material things**
Adams — *New* p.376
Curtis — *Practical* p.51, 436-437
Flesch — *Unusual* p.287
Forbes — *Thoughts* p.7, 47, 136, 153, 167, 196, 198, 202, 211, 416
Harnsberger — *Mark* p.473
Lockridge — *World's* #2064, 4620
Seldes — *Great* p.908
Sheban — *Wisdom* no p.
, Importance of
Nizer — *Thinking* p.29

SUBSTITUTION
Albert — *Stop* p.118-119, 127-128
Braude — *Source* #1593
Fox — *Make* p.21-22
Kohn — *Best* p.106-108
Prochnow — *Public* #986
Wallis — *Words* p.199

SUBTLETY
Braude — *Stories* p.357-359
Edwards — *Useful* p.620
Flesch — *Unusual* p.278
Prochnow — *Public* #79

SUBTRACTION
Prochnow — *Public* #1037

SUBURBIA
Botkin — *Anecdotes* p.265
Grizer — *Wit* p.440
Keys Happiness p.472-476
Lockridge — *World's* #4621
Woods — *Religious* p.966-967

SUBVERSIVENESS
Keller — *You* p.104-106
Seldes — *Great* p.896

SUBWAYS
Asimov — *Treasury* #399, 615
Guideposts — *Faith* p.81-84
Prochnow — *Public* #1368

SUCCESS
See also **Fame; Position; Power; Prosperity; Victory; Wealth**
Albert — *Stop* p.20-23, 42-43, 182-183
Applegarth — *Heir.* p.85, 120, 142, 246
Barker — *Treat* p.87-104
Bartlett — *Discovery* p.47-48
Blanton — *Faith* p.110-132
Braude — *Source* #1594-1620
Braude — *Speaker's* #1404-1411
Braude — *Stories* p.359-370
Carruthers — *Sparks* p.63-64
Curtis — *Golden* p.153-154, 161-163
Curtis — *Human* p.35-50
Curtis — *Practical* p.106-107, 347-348
Detherage — *Sunrise* p.87, 131-134
Dirksen — *Quot.* #201, 345, 490, 509, 968, 1170, 1811, 2198-2199
Droke — *Christian* p.514-523

Edwards — *Useful* p.620-622, 733
Evans — *Faith* p.4, 18, 21, 40, 96, 150, 162, 167-168, 170, 187
Evans — *Quote* p.53-66
Evans — *Thoughts I* p.117-118
Evans — *Thoughts II (Open Door)* p.53, 73-77, 90, 188-189, 209
Evans — *Thoughts III (Open Road)* p.21, 60, 71-72, 139, 146, 171, 176-177, 181, 197
Evans — *Unto* p.33-34, 92, 95
Flesch — *Unusual* p.278-279
Fogg — *1000* #280, 347, 445, 580, 638, 749
Forbes — *Thoughts* See index p.569
Fuller — *Epigrams* p.271-272
Garland — *Subject* p.307
Grizer — *Wit* p.440-450
Halverson — *Perspective* p.29, 69
Harnsberger — *Mark* p.459
Henry — *5000* p.271-272
Hobe — *Tapestries* p.14-15, 105, 213
Holmes — *Design* p.129-131, 133-134, 210, 228
Hovey — *Treasury* p.273-274; *See* index p.300
How To Live p.304-307
Howell — *Lines* p.65-68
Hubbard — *Scrap* p.13, 16, 40, 56, 71, 78, 95, 102, 133, 136, 169
Johnson — *Bedside* p.61, 234
Jones — *If* p.34-44, 86-95
Kauffman — *For* p.209-210
Kennedy — *Reader's* #1070-1075
Kin — *Dictionary* p.245-246
Kohn — *Pathways* p.85-126
Liddle — *Thought I, II, III See* index p.199
Liddle — *Thought IV* p.13, 15, 17, 20-21, 28
Liddle — *Thought V* p.9, 13, 16, 19-20, 32
Lockridge — *World's* #980, 1779, 2547, 3196, 4015, 4148, 4238, 4408, 5248
Lytle — *Leaves* p.6, 10, 20, 128, 166
Maltz — *Creative* p.51-80, 100-102
Mandel — *Stories* p.243-244
Modern Eloquence (14) p.418-419
Montapert — *Distilled* p.315
New Joy p.53
Peale — *Courage* p.13-17, 21
Peale — *Faith* p.109-134
Peale — *Guide* p.80-93
Peterson — *Art* p.164, 186, 324, 354
Prochnow — *Public See* index p.512; #991, 1812-1813
Prochnow — *Speaker's* p.296-297
Prochnow — *Success.* #2364; *See also* p.244-248
Reader's — *Getting* p.39-54; 116
Seldes — *Great* p.896-897
Sheen — *Content.* p.149-151
Sheen — *Thoughts* p.30-31
Sherman — *Your* p.153-158
Speaker's Desk #83, 91, 185-186, 272, 290, 325, 444, 619, 705, 931, 1109, 1138, 1171; *See also* p.244-248
Tanksley — *Friend* p.41
Wallis — *Treasure* p.1, 3-4, 20, 66, 157, 237
Wallis — *Words* p.230
Watson — *Light* p.133-134
Welk — *Guide.* p.15-17
Woods — *Business.* p.248-250
Woods — *Content.* p.30, 56, 302, 329
Woods — *Religious* p.967
Words — *Inspir.* p.36-38
Zobell — *Speaker's* p.134-135
, and anxiety
Hubbard — *Scrap* p.87
, and caution
Hubbard — *Scrap* p.54
, and failure
Flesch — *Unusual* p.279
Hubbard — *Scrap* p.173, 223
Montapert — *Distilled* p.316-317
, and mental attitude
Hubbard — *Scrap* p.20
, and merit
Hubbard — *Scrap* p.91
, and persistence
Kauffman — *For* p.160-161
, and work
Hubbard — *Scrap* p.61
, Art of
Nichols — *Third* p.105-106
Peterson — *Twenty* p.42-43
, Business
Hubbard — *Scrap* p.61
, Cheerfulness and
Hubbard — *Scrap* p.29
, Conditions of
Hubbard — *Scrap* p.70
, Definition of
Montapert — *Distilled* p.316
Nichols — *Third* p.88-108
Welk — *Guide.* p.141-143
, Essentials of
Hubbard — *Scrap* p.58
, Goals of
Maltz — *Creative* p.64-80
, Perils of
Hubbard — *Scrap* p.69
, Praying for
Unlimited Power p.184-187

, Price of
Sheen — *Thoughts* p.67-68
, Qualities for
Montapert — *Distilled* p.317
, Rules for
Montapert — *Distilled* p.317-318
, Secret of
Bach — *Make* p.56-57
Hubbard — *Scrap* p.69
, Stressing
Humes — *Instant* #1256
, Ten commandments of
Braude — *Stories* p.364, 366
, True
Redhead — *Living* p.61-69
, Ways to
Nichols — *New* p.62-89
, Will for
Welk — *Guide.* p.95-97

SUCCESSION, ORDER OF
Du Noüy — *Human* p.8, 15, 20, 198, 202

"SUCKERS"
Kin — *Dictionary* p.246
Prochnow — *Public* #1320
Prochnow — *Success.* #1236
Seldes — *Great* p.897

SUFFERING
See also **Adversity; Grief; Illness; Pain**
Braude — *Source* #1621
Braude — *Stories* p.370
Dirksen — *Quot.* #1586-1587
Edwards — *Useful* p.622-623
Flesch — *Unusual* p.279-280
Flint — *Graham* p.141
Forbes — *Thoughts* p.19, 57, 116, 194, 259, 353, 387, 439, 449, 484, 488
Fridy — *Meditat.* p.54-55
Garland — *Subject* p.307-308
Grizer — *Wit* p.450-451
Halverson — *Perspective* p.113
Henry — *5000* p.272-273
Hovey — *Treasury* #365, 593
Hubbard — *Scrap* p.169
Kahn — *Lessons* p.157-164
Kauffman — *For* p.210-211
Keller — *Open* p.34
Kennedy — *Reader's* #1076-1082
Krishnamurti — *Urgency* p.82-84
Lockridge — *World's* #773, 2270, 3411, 3799
Lytle — *Leaves* p.13
Mandelbaum — *Choose* p.26
Montapert — *Distilled* p.318
Phillips — *Choice* p.67, 71, 135-144
Prochnow — *Public* #960
Prochnow — *Success.* #2365
Voss — *Quotations* p.234-235
Wallis — *Treasure* p.118, 228
Wallis — *Words* p.58, 71
White — *Job* p.37-38, 85, 110-111
Woods — *Content.* p.303, 307
Woods — *Religious* p.967-970
, Chastening of
Knight's Treas. p.370-376
, Christ's words on
Keller — *You* p.382-385
, Immunity to
Nizer — *Thinking* p.134
, Long
Petty — *Wings* p.38-50
, of the good
Carruthers — *Sparks* p.41-42
, Sharing of
Price — *No* p.67-77
, Value of
Woods — *Religious* p.969-970

SUFFICIENCY
See also **Self-sufficiency**
Flesch — *Unusual* p.77
Kin — *Dictionary* p.81
Prochnow — *Public* #974
Prochnow — *Success.* #1722

SUGAR
Kin — *Dictionary* p.246
Prochnow — *Success.* #437

SUGGESTION
See also **Association; Autosuggestion**
Braude — *Speaker's* #1412-1414
Garland — *Subject* p.308
Lockridge — *World's* #4435
Prochnow — *Speaker's* p.297-298
Reader's — *Getting* p.27
, Mass
Curtis — *Practical* p.537

SUICIDE
See also **Self-destruction**
Asimov — *Treasury* #342
Braude — *Source* #1622
Edwards — *Useful* p.623
Evans — *Faith* p.4, 22
Evans — *Thoughts III (Open Road)* p.57
Evans — *Unto* p.4
Flesch — *Unusual* p.280
Flint — *Graham* p.141
Henry — *5000* p.273
Kin — *Dictionary* p.247
Krishnamurti — *Urgency* p.50-59
Lair — *Baby* p.200-202
Lockridge — *World's* #754, 4551, 4593, 5637, 5746
Prochnow — *Public* #2409

Seaburg — *Great* p.181, 184-185, 197, 230, 241-242, 247, 252, 256, 261, 291
Seldes — *Great* p.897-898
Woods — *Religious* p.970-971
, among youth
Lair — *Baby* p.33-34
, by hara-kiri
Prochnow — *Public* #2409
, prevented by God
Unlimited Power p.70-74

SUITABILITY
Evans — *Thoughts II (Open Door)* p.16-17, 56
Kin — *Dictionary* p.13, 92, 247
Speaker's Desk See index p.299
Weisfeld — *Pulpit* p.1-18
Wheelis — *Moralist* p.109

SULKING
Baillie — *Diary* #162
Prochnow — *Public* #2277

SULLIVAN, ANNE (Anne Sullivan Macy)
Reader's — *20th* p.52-56

SUMER AND SUMERIANS
Curtis — *Practical* p.220
Wheelis — *Moralist* p.79, 131

SUMMER
Auden — *Certain* p.338-339
Dirksen — *Quot.* #1084
Goudge — *Comfort* p.43-47
Hadfield — *Love* p.83-179
Henry — *5000* p.273
Hobe — *Tapestries* p.56, 146
Hubbard — *Scrap* p.8, 67
Irion — *Yes* p.3-7
Kin — *Dictionary* p.247
Kohn — *Best* p.54-73
Kohn — *Thoughts* p.57-98
Liddle — *Thought I, II, III* p.97
New Topical p.259
Patterns For Living p.21-26
Peterson — *Art* p.249
Prochnow — *Public* #851, 868, 1815
Sagendorph — *Old* p.27-32
Words — *Inspir.* p.73

SUN
See also **Dawn; Day; Light; Sunrise; Sunset**
Adams — *New* p.289, 402
Applegarth — *Heir.* p.101
Clark — *Windows* p.74
Edwards — *Useful* p.623-624
Flesch — *Unusual* p.280
Forbes — *Thoughts* p.99, 102, 478, 509, 518
Fuller — *Epigrams* p.272
Goudge — *Comfort* p.23-24
Hadfield — *Delights* p.44
Henry — *5000* p.273-274
Johnson — *Bedside* p.130-131, 136-137, 140, 145-147, 197, 210
Kin — *Dictionary* p.247
Lockridge — *World's* #4502
New Topical p.259-260
Prochnow — *Public* #2127, 2724
Prochnow — *Success.* #2366
Wallis — *Treasure* p.183
, Age of
Du Noüy — *Human* p.32n, 55
Nichols — *New* p.59-60

SUNDAY, BILLY
Weisfeld — *Pulpit* p.36-37

SUNDAY. *See* **Sabbath**

SUNDAY SCHOOLS
Applegarth — *Heir.* p.57
Braude — *Source* #1623
Copeland — *10,000* p.353-360
Flesch — *Unusual* p.280
Flint — *Graham* p.142
Fuller — *Thesaurus* #1571
Prochnow — *Public* p.346, 370, 457, 1052
Prochnow — *Speaker's* p.298
Prochnow — *Success.* #844, 1051
Schermerhorn — *1500* p.357-359
Unlimited Power p.188-191
Weisfeld — *Pulpit* p.49-64
Woods — *Religious* p.972
, Teachers of
Flint — *Graham* p.142

SUNDIALS
Applegarth — *Heir.* p.62-63
Hobe — *Tapestries* p.123
Wallis — *Words* p.18, 157
, Mottoes for
Henry — *5000* p.274

SUNLIGHT. *See* **Light; Sun**

SUNRISE
See also **Dawn; Light; Morning; Sun**
Edwards — *Useful* p.624
Henry — *5000* p.274
Hobe — *Tapestries* p.17, 111
Wallis — *Words* p.25

SUNSET
See also **Evening; Sun; Twilight**
Edwards — *Useful* p.624
Hadfield — *Delights* p.235
Henry — *5000* p.274
Hobe — *Tapestries* p.17, 102, 112

Irion — *Yes* p.127-131
Kahn — *Lessons* p.158
Lockridge — *World's* #697, 5665
Wallis — *Treasure* p.193
Woods — *Content.* p.218, 226, 333

SUNSHINE
Alexander's Treasure. p.73
Kohn — *Best* p.55-57
Lytle — *Leaves* p.52, 83, 112, 127
Peterson — *Art* p.254
Wallis — *Treasure* p.31, 157

SUPERCILIOUSNESS. *See* **Arrogance**

SUPERFICIALITY
See also **Appearance**
Flesch — *Unusual* p.280
Flint — *Graham* p.142
Kohn — *Touch* p.144-147
Mandel — *Stories* p.244

SUPERFLUITY
See also **Extravagance; Luxury**
Edwards — *Useful* p.624-625
Flesch — *Unusual* p.281
Forbes — *Thoughts* p.178, 196, 328, 337
Kin — *Dictionary* p.247
Lockridge — *World's* #5681
Lytle — *Leaves* p.100
Seldes — *Great* p.901

SUPERIORITY
See also **Excellence; Perfection**
Adams — *New* p.27, 272
Dirksen — *Quot.* #140, 166, 184, 1085-1086
Evans — *This* p.97-98
Flesch — *Unusual* p.281
Forbes — *Thoughts* p.295, 364, 420, 424
Fun Fare p.188-189
Garland — *Subject* p.310
Grizer — *Wit* p.451
Harnsberger — *Mark* p.460
Henry — *5000* p.274-275
Lockridge — *World's* #1579, 2075, 3549
Prochnow — *Public* #2289
Prochnow — *Success.* #2367
Seldes — *Great* p.898

SUPERLATIVES
Braude — *Stories* p.370
Curtis — *Practical* p.499
Woods — *Religious* p.972

SUPERMARKETS. *See* **Markets and marketing**

"SUPERMEN"
Ideas p.386-387
Lockridge — *World's* #625
Seldes — *Great* p.898
Woods — *Religious* p.972

SUPERNATURAL
See also **Ghosts**
Flesch — *Unusual* p.281
Lockridge — *World's* #5481
Seldes — *Great* p.899
Woods — *Religious* p.972-973

SUPERSTITION
See also **Belief; Fear; Ignorance**
Asimov — *Treasury* #14
Braude — *Source* #1624-1625
Curtis — *Practical* p.17
Du Noüy — *Human* p.165-175
Edwards — *Useful* p.625-626
Flesch — *Unusual* p.281
Forbes — *Thoughts* p.111, 203, 391
Fuller — *Thesaurus* #1631-1636
Garland — *Subject* p.308-309
Grizer — *Wit* p.451-452
Harnsberger — *Mark* p.459
Henry — *5000* p.275
Hubbard — *Scrap* p.34, 67, 181
Hunter — *Gems* p.101-102
Ideas p.387-389
Johnson — *Bedside* p.125
Liddle — *Thought I, II, III p.120*
Lockridge — *World's* #1706
Nizer — *Thinking* p.179
Seldes — *Great* p.899-900
Speaker's Desk p.431
Woods — *Religious* p.973-974
, versus luck
Manchee — *Secret* p.168-170

SUPERVISION
Forbes — *Thoughts* p.26, 113, 142
Kin — *Dictionary* p.247

SUPPERS. *See* **Dinners**

SUPPLICATION. *See* **Prayer**

SUPPLY AND DEMAND
Prochnow — *Success.* #834
Woods — *Business.* p.247-248

SUPPORT. *See* **Encouragement; Help**

SUPRACONSCIOUSNESS
White — *Job* p.81-82

SUPREMACY. *See* **Superiority**

SUPREME COURT
Seldes — *Great* p.900-901
Woods — *Religious* p.974

, *Justices of*
Reader's — *Getting* p.185

SURENESS. *See* **Certainty**

SURFEIT. *See* **Satiety; Superfluity**

SURFING
Asimov — *Treasury* #235

SURGEONS AND SURGERY
Curtis — *Practical* p.45
Kin — *Dictionary* p.248
Prochnow — *Public* #1422
Woods — *Religious* p.974

SURPLUS. *See* **Satiety; Superfluity**

SURPRISE
See also **Wonder**
Applegarth — *Heir.* p.177
Braude — *Stories* p.370-371
Flesch — *Unusual* p.282
Harnsberger — *Mark* p.7
Kin — *Dictionary* p.248
Peterson — *Art* p.102
Prochnow — *Public* #258, 1057, 2318
Prochnow — *Success.* #950
Speaker's Desk #165, 205, 215, 313, 373, 727, 1181
Wallis — *Treasure* p.155, 161

SURRENDER
Curtis — *New* p.21-22
Flint — *Graham* p.142
Lockridge — *World's* #2830
Lytle — *Leaves* p.155

SURVEYS
See also **Statistics**
Grizer — *Wit* p.452
Prochnow — *Public* #1160

SURVIVAL
Adams — *New* p.236
Braude — *Source* #1626-1627
Evans — *Thoughts IV* p.149
Forbes — *Thoughts* p.23, 166, 168, 235, 447
Lockridge — *World's* #849
Nichols — *Third* p.145-146
Seldes — *Great* p.901-902
Woods — *Religious* p.974

SUSCEPTIBILITY
Hill — *Think* p.281-282

SUSPENSE
See also **Anticipation; Expectation; Mystery; Uncertainty**
Edwards — *Useful* p.626
Lockridge — *World's* #3449
Prochnow — *Public* #340, 544, 2382
, *in speeches*
Nizer — *Thinking* p.23

SUSPICION
See also **Doubt; Fear; Uncertainty**
Baillie — *Diary* #208
Book Proverbs p.57
Braude — *Source* #1628-1630
Braude — *Speaker's* #1415-1419
Dirksen — *Quot.* #216, 729, 1812
Edwards — *Useful* p.139, 626-627
Evans — *Unto* p.38
Flesch — *Unusual* p.63, 282
Forbes — *Thoughts* p.243, 252, 279, 355, 364, 501
Grizer — *Wit* p.452-453
Henry — *5000* p.64, 275
Kennedy — *Reader's* #1083-1086
Kin — *Dictionary* p.248
Lockridge — *World's* #87, 89, 325, 391, 535, 1073
Lytle — *Leaves* p.75
Prochnow — *Success.* #2368
Speaker's Desk #235, 407, 449, 452, 454
Woods — *Religious* p.975

SWALLOWS
Applegarth — *Heir.* p.78
Auden — *Certain* p.359
, *First*
Adams — *New* p.358

SWANS
Henry — *5000* p.276
Kin — *Dictionary* p.248
Prochnow — *Public* #2280

SWEARING. *See* **Oaths; Profanity**

SWEDENBORG, EMANUEL
Guideposts — *Faith* p.35

SWEDISH
Botkin — *Anecdotes* p.280
Copeland — *10,000* p.756-758
Schermerhorn — *1500* p.359-360
Speaker's Desk #413, 478, 518, 559, 597, 705, 1003, 1187

SWEET PEAS
Applegarth — *Heir.* p.102

SWEETNESS
Henry — *5000* p.276
Kin — *Dictionary* p.249
Woods — *Religious* p.975

SWIFTNESS. *See* **Speed**

SWIMMING
Fuller — *Thesaurus* #1891-1893
Holmes — *I've* p.119-120
Kin — *Dictionary* p.249
Prochnow — *Public* #374, 459, 536
Prochnow — *Success.* #930, 1129
Schermerhorn — *1500* p.360-361
Woods — *Content.* p.71, 170

SWINDLERS
Fuller — *Thesaurus* #2121-2132
Prochnow — *Public* #449
Prochnow — *Success.* #1058
Safian — *Insults* p.31-37

SWINE. *See* **Hogs**

"SWINGS AND ROUNDABOUTS"
Pullar-Strecker — *Proverbs* #39-44

SWISS
Lockridge — *World's* #3156-3157

"SWORD OF DAMOCLES"
Maxwell — *Courage* p.1-8
Woods — *Wellsprings* p.31-32

SWORDFISH
Botkin — *Treasury* p.196

SWORDS
New Topical p.261
Prochnow — *Public* #2364, 2574
Seldes — *Great* p.902
Sheban — *Wisdom* no p.

SYLLOGISM
Curtis — *Practical* p.13

SYMBOLS AND SYMBOLISM
See also **Signs**
Adams — *New* p.235
Applegarth — *Heir.* p.100, 107
Garland — *Subject* p.311
Hovey — *Treasury* #72, 144, 392, 402, 590, 600, 716-717, 719, 776, 796, 811, 982, 985, 1038, 1047, 1416
Lytle — *Leaves* p.107
More Words p.160-162
Phillips — *Choice See* index p.429
Wallis — *Words* p.17, 41
White — *Job* p.40, 42
Woods — *Religious* p.975-976

, of astronauts' faith
Guideposts — *Faith* p.110-115

, Religious
Guideposts — *Faith* p.110-115

SYMPATHY
See also **Comfort; Compassion; Consolation; Pity; Sensibility; Understanding**
Alexander's Treasure. p.262
Applegarth — *Heir.* p.127, 251
Braude — *Source* #1631-1634
Braude — *Stories* p.371
Curtis — *Practical* p.417-443
Droke — *Christian* p.523-524
Edwards — *Useful* p.627-629
Flesch — *Unusual* p.282
Forbes — *Thoughts* p.3, 5, 218, 227, 357, 367, 382, 404, 502, 513, 515, 517
Grizer — *Wit* p.453
Henry — *5000* p.276
Hobe — *Tapestries* p.158
Hovey — *Treasury* p.304; #9, 405
How To Live p.484-488
Howell — *Better* p.165-172
Howell — *Lines* p.94-95
Hubbard — *Scrap* p.41, 204
Johnson — *Bedside* p.19, 163, 252
Kennedy — *Reader's* #1087-1088
Keys Happiness p.337-340
Kohn — *Touch* p.148-151
Liddle — *Thought I, II, III* p.54
Liddle — *Thought V* p.34
Lockridge — *World's* #2255, 4587, 5642
Lytle — *Leaves* p.56, 93-94, 112
Maltz — *Creative* p.52-53
Morris — *1000* p.30, 100, 179, 186, 200, 204, 232, 240, 250, 287, 302, 312, 340
Prochnow — *Public* #1406
Prochnow — *Success.* #1260, 2369-2370
Sheban — *Wisdom* no p.
Sheen — *Content.* p.143-145
Speaker's Desk See index p.305
Wallis — *Treasure* p.42
Wallis — *Words* p.75, 179
Wilcox — *Heart* p.79-81
Woods — *Religious* p.976
Woods — *Wellsprings* p.47

, Letters of
How To Live p.523-524

SYMPTOMS. *See* **Illness, Symptoms of**

SYNAGOGUES
See also **Temples**
Asimov — *Treasury* #67, 330, 332, 381
New Topical p.261-262
Woods — *Religious* p.976

SYNCRETISM
Hovey — *Treasury* #144, 344, 699-700, 1668

SYNDICALISM
Seldes — *Great* p.902
Woods — *Business.* p.250

SYNONYMS
Prochnow — *Public* #195, 1059, 1816

SYRIA
New Topical p.262-263

T

TABERNACLES
See also **Temples**
Lytle — *Leaves* p.50
New Topical p.263-264

"TABLES TURNED"
Asimov — *Treasury* p.180-210
Braude — *Speaker's* #1421-1422

TABOOS
Seldes — *Great* p.902-903

TACITURNITY. *See* **Silence**

TACT
See also **Discretion; Judgment; Sensibility;** etc.
Alexander's Treasure. p.250
Asimov — *Treasury* #598
Book Proverbs p.100
Braude — *Source* #1636-1643
Braude — *Speaker's* #1423-1428
Edwards — *Useful* p.629
Fuller — *Thesaurus* #586-591
Fun Fare p.191
Grizer — *Wit* p.453-454
Henry — *5000* p.276-277
Kin — *Dictionary* p.249
Liddle — *Thought IV* p.12
Liddle — *Thought V* p.10
Lockridge — *World's* #2358, 2390, 3386, 4718, 5228
Manchee — *Secret* p.114-117
Mandel — *Stories* p.245
Nizer — *Thinking* p.118-119
Prochnow — *Public* #573, 748, 1159, 1164, 1206, 1436, 1859, 3745-3747
Prochnow — *Speaker's* p.298-300
Schermerhorn — *1500* p.362-363
Speaker's Desk See index p.305

"TACTLESS BOORS"
Safian — *Insults* p.189-191

TAFT, WILLIAM HOWARD
Kohn — *Touch* p.163-165

TAILORS AND TAILORING
Asimov — *Treasury* #392
Kin — *Dictionary* p.249
Lockridge — *World's* #4135, 4794
Manchee — *Secret* p.229-230
Prochnow — *Public* #806, 882

TALENT
See also **Cleverness; Genius;** etc.
Braude — *Source* #1645-1647
Dirksen — *Quot.* #154, 803, 1588, 1811
Edwards — *Useful* p.629-630
Evans — *Faith* p.29, 39-40, 95, 164, 171-172, 175, 188
Evans — *Thoughts I* p.110, 133, 149, 208-209
Evans — *Thoughts III (Open Road)* p.61, 70, 110, 146-149, 158, 178, 181
Evans — *Thoughts IV* p.103-104, 116
Flesch — *Unusual* p.283
Forbes — *Thoughts See* index p.570
Fuller — *Epigrams* p.273
Garland — *Subject* p.311-312
Halverson — *Perspective* p.37
Harnsberger — *Mark* p.461
Henry — *5000* p.277
Hovey — *Treasury* #29, 88
Johnson — *Bedside* p.198
Keys Happiness p.223-226
Lockridge — *World's See* index p.583
Lytle — *Leaves* p.55, 114
Mandel — *Stories* p.245
Montapert — *Distilled* p.318-319
New Joy p.176
Peterson — *Art* p.307
Prochnow — *Public* #414, 1159, 1164, 2207
Redhead — *Living* p.96-101
Sherman — *Your* p.138-152
Vogue — *Arts* p.131-138

, Development of
Welk — *Guide.* p.87-89
, Parable of
Fridy — *Meditat.* p.78
, Praise for
Guideposts — *Faith* p.478

TALISMANS
Lytle — *Leaves* p.77
Nichols — *Third* p.192-207

TALK
See also **Communication; Conversation; Eloquence; Loquacity; Oratory; Speeches and speakers**
Applegarth — *Heir.* p.71, 73
Braude — *Source* #1649
Dirksen — *Quot.* #1088-1089, 1096, 2200-2201
Edwards — *Useful* p.630-632, 733
Flesch — *Unusual* p.283
Forbes — *Thoughts* p.52, 127, 133, 149, 167, 198, 223, 241, 313, 355, 415, 459-460, 483
Fuller — *Thesaurus* #806-818
Grizer — *Wit* p.455
Harnsberger — *Mark* p.461-466
Henry — *5000* p.277-278
Holmes — *I've* p.101
Kin — *Dictionary* p.45, 250
Liddle — *Thought I, II, III* p.89, 121, 134, 138, 145, 153, 156, 168, 177
Liddle — *Thought IV* p.13, 20
Liddle — *Thought V* p.17, 29, 35
Lockridge — *World's* See index p.583
Mandel — *Stories* p.246
Prochnow — *Public* #629, 836, 1845, 4228
Prochnow — *Success.* #645, 1068, 2371
Sheban — *Wisdom* no p.
Woods — *Religious* p.976

, Small
Evans — *Unto* p.62

"TALL TALES"
Botkin — *Anecdotes* p.74, 89-109, 256
Botkin — *Treasury* p.465, 491, 554
Cerf — *Laugh* p.483-487
Copeland — *10,000* p.629-639
Harral — *Feature* p.291
Speaker's Desk #7, 43, 126, 216, 384, 398, 460, 476, 576, 714, 1142

TALLNESS. *See* **Height**

TANGANYIKA, AFRICA
Simpson — *Contemp.* p.155

TANGIBLES. *See* **Material things; Possessions**

TAOISM
Flesch — *Unusual* p.283
Woods — *Content.* p.98
Woods — *Religious* p.976-977

TARDINESS. *See* **Delay**

TASKS
See also **Duty; Work**
Dirksen — *Quot.* #725
Forbes — *Thoughts* p.157, 199, 250, 264, 289, 423, 444, 456
Lytle — *Leaves* p.135, 138, 179-180
Wallis — *Treasure* p.73, 187, 232, 237-238, 240
Wallis — *Words* p.228

, Common
Alexander's Treasure. p.65

TASTE
See also **Appreciation; Choice; Discernment; Judgment; Values;** etc.
Edwards — *Useful* p.632-633, 733
Flesch — *Unusual* p.283-284
Forbes — *Thoughts* p.144, 233, 519
Fuller — *Epigrams* p.273-274
Garland — *Subject* p.312
Henry — *5000* p.278
Ideas p.389-391
Kin — *Dictionary* p.251
Lockridge — *World's* #1552, 1598, 4373, 5705
Lytle — *Leaves* p.51, 123
Prochnow — *Public* #466
Prochnow — *Speaker's* p.300

, Public
Adams — *New* p.24

TATTOOING
Flesch — *Unusual* p.284
Prochnow — *Public* #2, 498

TAVERNS
See also **Bars**
Botkin — *Anecdotes* p.xxviii, 8, 28, 71, 140, 142, 187, 237-238, 240
Hadfield — *Delights* p.96
Lockridge — *World's* #2053

TAXES
Braude — *Source* #1650-1657
Braude — *Speaker's* #1432-1434
Braude — *Stories* p.372-373
Dirksen — *Quot.* #13, 491-492, 1091, 1658, 1719, 1813-1814
Edwards — *Useful* p.633
Flesch — *Unusual* p.284
Fogg — *1000* #714, 637, 714, 872

Fuller — *Epigrams* p.274
Fuller — *Thesaurus* #2191-2194
Grizer — *Wit* p.455-457
Harnsberger — *Mark* p.467
Harral — *Feature* p.291-292
Henry — *5000* p.278
Hovey — *Treasury* p.275; #149, 310, 1755-1756
Humes — *Instant* #1022-1024
Kennedy — *Reader's* #1089
Kin — *Dictionary* p.251
Liddle — *Thought I, II, III* p.103, 127, 165
Lockridge — *World's* #5020
Prochnow — *Public See* index p.512
Prochnow — *Speaker's* p.300-301
Prochnow — *Success. See* index p.500
Seldes — *Great* p.903-905
Woods — *Business.* p.250-255
Woods — *Wellsprings* p.41-42
, and taxpayers
Prochnow — *Public* #1427, 1818
Prochnow — *Success.* #330, 341, 413, 457, 541, 628-630, 635, 692
, Collectors of
Dirksen — *Quot.* #1815
, Reform of
Franke — *Buckley* p.289-290

TAXIS AND TAXI DRIVERS
Asimov — *Treasury* #192-193, 520
Botkin — *Anecdotes* p.263
Fun Fare p.30-32
Guideposts — *Faith* p.334-336
Peale — *Guideposts* p.30-32
Prochnow — *Public* #312, 1374
Prochnow — *Speaker's* p.301
Prochnow — *Success.* #1053
Schermerhorn — *1500* p.363-364

TEA
Kin — *Dictionary* p.251
Krishnamurti — *Think* p.123-124
Patterns For Living p.50-53
Prochnow — *Public* #524, 891
, Taxation of
New Joy p.76-77

TEACHERS
See also **Education; Knowledge; Learning; Professors; Schools;** etc.
Applegarth — *Heir.* p.15, 56, 227-229, 231
Asimov — *Treasury* #620
Braude — *Source* #1658-1671
Braude — *Speaker's* #1435-1464
Copeland — *10,000* p.334-353
Dirksen — *Quot.* #726, 1092, 1408, 1672, 2275, 2361
Droke — *Christian* p.525-528
Du Noüy — *Human* p.208, 212-213, 218
Edwards — *Useful* p.297-298, 633-635
Evans — *Faith* p.40, 49-57, 145, 168, 173-174
Evans — *Quote* p.67-79
Evans — *This* p.116-117
Evans — *Thoughts I* p.33, 89, 97, 109, 144-145, 171-176, 185, 201-202
Evans — *Thoughts II (Open Door)* p.36, 46, 95, 98, 125, 127-129, 139-140
Evans — *Thoughts III (Open Road)* p.19, 21-22, 58, 68-69, 137-139, 141, 157, 161, 178, 187
Evans — *Thoughts IV* p.63-70, 123, 129, 137
Evans — *Unto* p.18, 107
Flesch — *Unusual* p.251, 284-285
Forbes — *Thoughts* p.35, 81, 131, 145, 238, 260, 391, 452
Fuller — *Epigrams* p.274-275
Fuller — *Thesaurus* #1056-1057
Garland — *Subject* p.312
George — *Book* p.197, 217, 423
Grizer — *Wit* p.241, 457
Guideposts — *Faith* p.116-120
Harnsberger — *Mark* p.467-468
Harral — *Feature* p.292-293
Henry — *5000* p.278-279
Hobe — *Tapestries* p.14
Hovey — *Treasury* p.275; *See also* index p.301
Humes — *Instant* #1025-1029
Hunter — *Gems* p.102-104
Kennedy — *Reader's* #1090-1095
Kin — *Dictionary* p.251
Lair — *Baby* p.16-17, 20-22, 203-216
Liddle — *Thought I, II, III* p.11, 75, 93, 131, 134, 144, 147, 165
Liddle — *Thought IV* p.3, 21, 33
Liddle — *Thought V* p.6, 9, 14, 16, 28
Lockridge — *World's* #3840, 4369, 4421
Lytle — *Leaves* p.9, 60, 63, 74, 110, 112, 116
Manchee — *Secret* p.226-227
Mandel — *Stories* p.246-247
Montapert — *Distilled* p.218, 319
Peterson — *Art* p.284, 304
Prochnow — *Public* #13, 71, 109, 135, 143, 169, 632, 835, 962, 1846, 4282
Prochnow — *Speaker's* p.301-302
Prochnow — *Success.* #273, 922, 1037, 1099, 2373

Seaburg — *Great* p.205, 228, 238, 240, 277, 353, 356, 391
Seldes — *Great* p.905-906
Sheban — *Wisdom* no p.
Wallis — *Treasure* p.87-90
Wallis — *Words* p.27, 141-145
Woods — *Religious* p.977
, Home
Zobell — *Speaker's* p.75-77
, Inspiration of
Unlimited Power p.258-260

TEAMWORK
Braude — *Source* #1672
Kin — *Dictionary* p.251
Prochnow — *Success.* #1350
Wallis — *Words* p.76

TEARS
See also **Grief**
Braude — *Source* #1673-1676
Dirksen — *Quot.* #2202-2203
Edwards — *Useful* p.635-636
Forbes — *Thoughts* p.11, 234, 252, 273, 279, 385, 416, 449
Fuller — *Epigrams* p.275
Hadfield — *Love* p.120
Henry — *5000* p.279-280
Hubbard — *Scrap* p.143, 183
Johnson — *Bedside* p.24
Kin — *Dictionary* p.61, 251-252
Lockridge — *World's* #398, 845, 2198, 5878
Lytle — *Leaves* p.16, 27, 29
Prochnow — *Public* #144, 384, 1397, 2190
Prochnow — *Speaker's* p.303
Sheban — *Wisdom* no p.
Wallis — *Treasure* p.191, 226-227
Wallis — *Words* p.99
Woods — *Religious* p.977-978, 1053

TEASING
Krishnamurti — *Think* p.131

TECHNOCRACY
Braude — *Source* #1677
Edwards — *Useful* p.733

TECHNOLOGY
See also **Science**
Forbes — *Thoughts* p.183, 238, 298
Humes — *Instant* #1030-1043
Wheelis — *Moralist* p.7, 22, 73, 96, 126, 132, 149-150
Woods — *Business.* p.256
Woods — *Religious* p.978

TEENAGERS
See also various subjects, subdivision **Teenager**
Braude — *Source* #1678
Dirksen — *Quot.* #230
Flint — *Graham* p.142-143
Fun Fare p.119-120
Harral — *Feature* p.293
Prochnow — *Success.* #541, 738, 1000, 1116, 1356, 1414, 1439
Sheen — *Way* p.97-104
Walters — *How* p.59-66
, Autonomy of
Ginott — *Between* p.20, 33, 145-149, 235-236
, Code for
How To Live p.144-147
, Personal test for
Francis — *For* p.113-131
, Work of
How To Live p.148-152

TEETH
Harnsberger — *Mark* p.468-469
Kin — *Dictionary* p.252
Menninger — *Blue.* p.215, 220
Prochnow — *Public* #376, 416, 572, 727, 2323
Sheban — *Wisdom* no p.
, Decay of
Keys Happiness p.255-257

TEETOTALISM
See also **Abstinence**
Flesch — *Unusual* p.285
Kin — *Dictionary* p.252

TELEFINALISM
Du Noüy — *Human See* index p.288

TELEGRAMS
Asimov — *Treasury* #246, 341
Fun Fare p.66-67
Harral — *Feature* p.293

TELEGRAPHY
Botkin — *Anecdotes* p.76

TELEPATHY
Grizer — *Wit* p.457
Hill — *Think* p.241-244

TELEPHONE
Asimov — *Treasury* #68
Flesch — *Unusual* p.285
Fun Fare p.126-130
Grizer — *Wit* p.457-458
Harnsberger — *Mark* p.469-470
Harral — *Feature* p.137, 293-296
Keys Happiness p.285-288
Menninger — *Blue.* p.187-191
New Joy p.201-203
Prochnow — *Public* #48, 84, 101, 182, 591, 830, 1376

Prochnow — *Speaker's* p.303
Prochnow — *Success.* #131, 983, 1014, 1091, 1339, 2374
Walters — *How* p.96-97

, *Books for*
New *Joy* p.172-173
, *Booths for*
Prochnow — *Public* #622
, *Teenager technique*
Daly — *Personality* p.131-136

TELEVISION
Asimov — *Treasury* #8
Braude — *Source* #1679
Braude — *Speaker's* #1470-1471
Braude — *Stories* p.373
Franke — *Buckley* p.291-292
Grizer — *Wit* p.458-459
Harral — *Feature* p.296-297
Prochnow — *Public* #1558
Prochnow — *Speaker's* p.304
Prochnow — *Success.* #227, 489, 865, 917, 925, 1018, 1041, 1119, 1122, 1132
Simpson — *Contemp.* p.400-406
Simpson — *'54* p.81, 231, 345

, *and radio*
Cerf — *Laugh* p.65-74

TEMPER
See also **Anger, Emotion; Passion, Rashness**; etc.
Albert — *Stop* p.82, 94
Book Proverbs p.81
Braude — *Source* #1680-1682
Edwards — *Useful* p.636-637, 733
Evans — *Thoughts III (Open Road)* p.29-30, 66, 71, 111
Evans — *Thoughts IV* p.107-108
Forbes — *Thoughts* p.17, 49, 95, 126, 191, 349, 367, 452, 472, 512
Fuller — *Thesaurus* #596-598
Grizer — *Wit* p.459
Guideposts — *Faith* p.239-243
Harnsberger — *Mark* p.470
Hovey — *Treasury* #75, 80, 535, 713, 1444
Johnson — *Bedside* p.6, 8, 13
Kin — *Dictionary* p.252
Liddle — *Thought I, II, III* p.7, 30, 85
Liddle — *Thought IV* p.36
Lockridge — *World's* #3475
Lytle — *Leaves* p.118, 123
Modern Eloquence (14) p.420
Montapert — *Distilled* p.319
Prochnow — *Speaker's* p.304

TEMPERAMENT
Curtis — *Practical* p.435, 463-465
Edwards — *Useful* p.733
Ginott — *Between* p.42-73
Harnsberger — *Mark* p.470-471
Lindeman — *Emerson* p.178
Lockridge — *World's* #229, 3611, 4260

TEMPERANCE
See also **Abstinence; Balance; Moderation; Teetotalism**
Asimov — *Treasury* #130
Dirksen — *Quot.* #2124
Edwards — *Useful* p.637-639, 733
Evans — *Faith* p.33, 112, 180
Evans — *Thoughts IV* p.114-115, 148
Flesch — *Unusual* p.285
Forbes — *Thoughts* p.171, 178, 453
Fuller — *Epigrams* p.275-276
Garland — *Subject* p.312-313
Henry — *5000* p.280
Hovey — *Treasury* #327, 560, 571, 1693
Kennedy — *Reader's* #1096-1099
Kin — *Dictionary* p.252
Knight's Treas. p.390-402
Lockridge — *World's* #3693
Lytle — *Leaves* p.141
McCracken — *What* p.64-70
Petty — *Wings* p.81-89
Sheen — *Content.* p.59-61
Strait — *Speaker's* p.171
Woods — *Religious* p.978

TEMPERATURE
Asimov — *Treasury* #391
Prochnow — *Public* #1260

TEMPLES
See also **Synagogues**
Alexander's Treasure. p.15
Applegarth — *Heir.* p.163, 220, 234, 282
Lytle — *Leaves* p.41
, *First*
New Topical p.264-265
, *Second*
New Topical p.265-266
, *Work of*
Hunter — *Gems* p.105

TEMPO. *See* **Pace**

TEMPORAL THINGS
Woods — *Religious* p.978-979

TEMPTATION
See also **Desire; Habits; Sin**; etc.
Baillie — *Diary* #123, 301

Book Proverbs p.111
Braude — *Source* #1683-1684
Braude — *Speaker's* #1472-1474
Braude — *Stories* p.373-374
Carruthers — *Sparks* p.99-101
Dirksen — *Quot.* #1236, 1589
Droke — *Christian* p.529-531
Edwards — *Useful* p.639-641, 733
Evans — *Faith* p.91-92, 97-98, 101-102, 115-116, 123-124, 134, 142, 155, 212
Evans — *Quote* p.194-204
Evans — *Thoughts I* p.91, 197
Evans — *Thoughts II (Open Door)* p.47-48, 93-97
Evans — *Thoughts III (Open Road)* p.21, 106
Evans — *Thoughts IV* p.28, 86, 106, 135, 200, 206
Evans — *Unto* p.114
Flesch — *Unusual* p.285-286
Flint — *Graham* p.68-69, 143-144
Forbes — *Thoughts* p.88, 254, 270, 300, 324, 360, 458, 472
Fox — *Make* p.198-200
Fuller — *Epigrams* p.276-277
Garland — *Subject* p.313-314
Grizer — *Wit* p.460
Halverson — *Perspective* p.13
Henry — *5000* p.280
Hovey — *Treasury* p.275-276; #288, 503, 1161, 1680, 1760-1765, 1780
Johnson — *Bedside* p.91, 187, 321-322, 331
Kin — *Dictionary* p.252-253
Knight's Treas. p.402-403
Liddle — *Thought I, II, III* p.163, 171, 189
Lockridge — *World's* #860, 4175
Lytle — *Leaves* p.28-29, 75, 144, 164
Mandel — *Stories* p.247-248
More Words p.163-164
New Topical p.266-267
Prochnow — *Public* #390, 3751-3754
Prochnow — *Success.* #381, 384
Seldes — *Great* p.906
Speaker's Desk #939, 1023, 1164
Strait — *Speaker's* p.172
Woods — *Religious* p.979-981
Zobell — *Speaker's* p.135-137

TEN COMMANDMENTS. *See* **Commandments, Ten**

TENACITY. *See* **Perseverance**

"TENDERFEET"
Botkin — *Anecdotes* p.35, 74
Botkin — *Treasury* p.360, 379, 391

TENDERNESS
See also **Kindness; Sensitivity; Sympathy; Understanding;** etc.
Braude — *Source* #1687-1688
Edwards — *Useful* p.641
Forbes — *Thoughts* p.169, 269, 323, 412
How To Live p.69
Prochnow — *Public* #2208
Wallis — *Words* p.82
, and power
Sheen — *Content.* p.184-186

TENNESSEE
Botkin — *Anecdotes* p.11, 23, 32, 34, 81, 145, 244
Botkin — *Treasury* *See* index p.932

TENNIS
Bennett — *How* p.49-55
Peale — *Guideposts* p.93-96

TENNYSON, ALFRED LORD
Adams — *New* p.40
Flesch — *Unusual* p.286

TENSION
See also **Frustration; Pressure; Worry**
Albert — *Stop* p.68-69, 89, 97-113, 125, 156-157
Braude — *Source* #1689
Evans — *Thoughts III (Open Road)* p.29-30, 86
Forbes — *Thoughts* p.177, 238, 292
How To Live p.190-194, 211-215
Huxley — *You See* index p.288
Keys Happiness p.285-288
Kohn — *Best* p.33-35
Mandel — *Stories* p.248
Montapert — *Distilled* p.319-320
Peale — *Stay* p.157-171
Peterson — *Art* p.168, 172
Rau — *Act* p.38-43
, Handling
Menninger — *Blue.* p.24-32
, Reducing
Carruthers — *Sparks* p.101-103

TENTS
New Topical p.267
Prochnow — *Public* #2046

TERROR
See also **Fear; Superstition**
Adams — *New* p.230
Flesch — *Unusual* p.286
Kin — *Dictionary* p.253
Prochnow — *Public* #2209
Prochnow — *Success.* #219

Seldes — *Great* p.906-907
Woods — *Religious* p.981

TESTIMONIALS
Braude — *Source* #1690
Harral — *Feature* p.297

TESTIMONY
Knight's Illus. p.322-327
Lockridge — *World's* #2031
Wallis — *Words* p.25
Zobell — *Speaker's* p.138-140

TESTS AND TESTING
Evans — *Thoughts III (Open Road)* p.40
Hobe — *Tapestries* p.40
Kin — *Dictionary* p.253
Lytle — *Leaves* p.14, 42, 63, 130, 162, 191
Mandel — *Stories* p.248-249
Zobell — *Speaker's* p.141

TEXAS AND TEXANS
See also **Alamo, The**
Asimov — *Treasury* #444, 447
Botkin — *Anecdotes* p.71, 81, 170-171, 193, 227, 251-252; *See also* index p.319
Botkin — *Treasury* p.114-118, 121, 131, 134, 141, 158, 351, 507, 758; *See also* index p.932
Braude — *Source* #1691-1693
Cerf — *Laugh* p.171-175
Flesch — *Unusual* p.286
Prochnow — *Public* #145
Prochnow — *Success.* #851, 1110, 1130
Words — *Inspir.* p.72-73

THANKFULNESS
See also **Gratitude; Thanksgiving**
Alexander's Treasure. p.105, 253, 314
Baillie — *Diary* #44
Dirksen — *Quot.* #1093
Edwards — *Useful* p.641-642
Emmons — *Mature* p.13, 52-60, 72, 157
Fuller — *Epigrams* p.361-362
Halverson — *Perspective* p.67
Henry — *5000* p.280-281
Johnson — *Bedside* p.189-208, 211, 231
Kin — *Dictionary* p.253
Kohn — *Best* p.82-84
Lytle — *Leaves* p.34
Peale — *Courage* p.159-177
Peterson — *Art* p.374-375
Prochnow — *Public* #154, 1060, 1759
Speaker's Desk #107, 183, 621, 631, 650, 659, 776, 1161
Unlimited Power p.221-222
, Prayer of
Unlimited Power p.246

THANKSGIVING
Alexander's Treasure. p.6, 19
Applegarth — *Heir.* p.194-195, 204
Braude — *Source* #1694-1699
Carruthers — *Sparks* p.129-130
Dirksen — *Quot.* #727, 1094-1095, 1592-1594
Droke — *Christian* p.531-533
Emmons — *Mature* p.157
Evans — *Faith* p.79-80
Evans — *Thoughts I* p.113-114
Evans — *Thoughts IV* p.157-158
Evans — *Unto* p.15, 108-109, 119
Garland — *Subject* p.315
Halverson — *Perspective* p.97
Harnsberger — *Mark* p.471-472
Harral — *Feature* p.298
Henry — *5000* p.281
Hobe — *Tapestries* p.25-26
Hovey — *Treasury* p.276; *See also* index p.304
Hubbard — *Scrap* p.23
Kennedy — *Reader's* #1100-1102
Knight's Illus. p.327-328
Knight's Treas. p.404-406
Kohn — *Best* p.77-85
Kohn — *Touch* p.61-69
Liddle — *Thought I, II, III* p.86, 170
New Topical p.267-268
Peale — *Courage* p.168-169
Peterson — *Art* p.366
Prochnow — *Success.* #820
Schermerhorn — *1500* p.368
Strait — *Speaker's* p.173-174
Suter — *Prayers* #278-316
Unlimited Power p.251-255
Wallis — *Treasure* p.14, 204, 213-216
Wallis — *Words* p.76, 185-186, 205-208
Welk — *Guide.* p.127-129
Woods — *Content.* p.55, 98, 103, 105, 188, 265, 289, 299, 302
Woods — *Religious* p.981
, Art of
Peterson — *Twenty* p.44-45
, in liturgy
McDonagh — *Invit.* p.106-108
, Prayer for
Kohn — *Thoughts* p.126-127
Nichols — *Third* p.220-221
Unlimited Power p.215
, to God
Goudge — *Comfort* p.355-356
Kauffman — *For* p.211
Keller — *Open* p.69

THEATER
See also **Actors and actresses; Drama; Motion pictures;** etc.
Asimov — *Treasury* #203, 317, 560
Botkin — *Anecdotes* p.257-258
Cerf — *Laugh* p.74-81
Dirksen — *Quot.* #118, 147, 155
Edwards — *Useful* p.642-643
Fogg — *1000* #91, 95, 98, 209, 227, 305, 670, 693, 708, 711, 765, 798, 1088
Fuller — *Epigrams* p.277, 362
Harral — *Feature* p.298-299
Kronenberger — *Animal* p.282-290
Lockridge — *World's* #940, 3679-3690, 5385-5386, 5388, 5763
Nizer — *Thinking* p.93, 100-101, 139, 179-180
Prochnow — *Public* #53, 885, 1378
Prochnow — *Speaker's* p.304-305
Prochnow — *Success.* #963, 1117, 1218
Schermerhorn — *1500* p.348-351, 370
Simpson — *Contemp.* p.414-427
Simpson — *'54* p.94, 250, 361
, and film
Fuller — *Thesaurus* p.244-258
, and social questions
Hubbard — *Scrap* p.42
, Gags of
Copeland — *10,000* p.584-603
, Idols of
Curtis — *Practical* p.16
, Traditions of
Hubbard — *Scrap* p.9

THEISM
Seldes — *Great* p.907
Woods — *Religious* p.981-982

THEOCRACY
New Topical p.268-269
Woods — *Religious* p.982

THEOLOGY AND THEOLOGIANS
See also **Bible; Christianity; Clergymen; Doctrine; Religion;** etc.
Curtis — *Practical* p.3, 97, 503-505
Edwards — *Useful* p.643
Flesch — *Unusual* p.286
Flint — *Graham* p.61, 144
Hovey — *Treasury* #272, 274, 698, 712, 826, 1045, 1432, 1588, 1668
Hubbard — *Scrap* p.41, 218
Kennedy — *Reader's* #1103-1108
Lockridge — *World's* #4569-4575
Woods — *Religious* p.982-987
, New
Flint — *Graham* p.100

THEORY
See also **Ideas and ideology; Political science; Thought;** etc.
Braude — *Stories* p.374
Curtis — *Practical* p.23-26, 47
Du Noüy — *Road* p.59, 77-81, 87
Edwards — *Useful* p.643
Evans — *This* p.97-98
Flesch — *Unusual* p.286-287
Forbes — *Thoughts* p.70, 397, 410, 485
Harnsberger — *Mark* p.472-473
Lytle — *Leaves* p.188
Mandel — *Stories* p.249
Seldes — *Great* p.908

THERAPY
See also **Help;** etc.
Mandel — *Stories* p.249

THERMODYNAMICS
Curtis — *Practical* p.236-240

THIEVES AND THIEVERY
See also **Burglars and burglary**
Asimov — *Treasury* #295
Dirksen — *Quot.* #9
Flesch — *Unusual* p.287
Harnsberger — *Mark* p.412
Harral — *Feature* p.299
Henry — *5000* p.281-282
Johnson — *Bedside* p.186
Kin — *Dictionary* p.220, 253
Lockridge — *World's* #2620, 4992, 5129
New Topical p.268
Prochnow — *Public* #233, 690, 711, 760, 947, 1009, 2423
Seldes — *Great* p.849, 908
Woods — *Religious* p.981

THINKERS AND THINKING. *See* **Thought**

THIRST
Book Proverbs p.50
Garland — *Subject* p.316
Kin — *Dictionary* p.254
Lockridge — *World's* #4828
Sheban — *Wisdom* no p.

THIRTY (age)
Patterns For Living p.756-768

THIRTY-NINE (age)
Flesch — *Unusual* p.289

THOMISM
Woods — *Religious* p.987

THOREAU, HENRY DAVID — *WALDEN*
Hobe — *Tapestries* p.91
Peterson — *Art* p.140

THORNS
Forbes — *Thoughts* p.304, 310, 403
Kin — *Dictionary* p.254
Prochnow — *Public* #2719

THOUGHT
See also **Ideas; Knowledge; Mind; Wisdom;** etc.
Adams — *New* p.128
Albert — *Stop* p.8, 24-29, 33-34, 111-113
Alexander's Treasure. p.55, 102, 225
Bach — *Make* p.33-34
Bartlett — *Discovery* p.46
Book Proverbs p.88, 104
Braude — *Source* #1700-1704, 1706-1707
Braude — *Speaker's* #1475-1477
Braude — *Stories* p.374
Curtis — *Golden* p.140-141
Curtis — *Human* p.12
Curtis — *Practical* p.4-6, 11, 13, 26, 29-32, 40, 43-45, 51, 59, 61-67, 69, 71-72, 130-132, 337, 374-376, 503
Dirksen — *Quot.* #494-495, 1012, 1096-1098, 2204-2205, 2292, 2344
Droke — *Christian* p.533-541
Du Noüy — *Human* p.xv, 5, 12-25, 45, 140, 232
Edwards — *Useful* p.643-647, 733
Evans — *This* p.85-86
Evans — *Thoughts IV* p.119, 123-124, 163
Evans — *Unto* p.52, 63, 70, 86, 91
Flesch — *Unusual* p.287-290
Forbes — *Thoughts See* index p.570
Fox — *Make* p.27, 88, 129, 230-231
Fuller — *Epigrams* p.277-279
Garland — *Subject* p.315-316
Grizer — *Wit* p.460-464
Harnsberger — *Mark* p.473-475
Henry — *5000* p.282-283
Hill — *Think* p.16-31
Hobe — *Tapestries* p.64
Holmes — *Design* p.15-28; *See also* index p.235
Hovey — *Treasury* #42-43, 46, 49, 1102, 1504
How To Live p.199-204
Hubbard — *Scrap* p.23, 118, 147, 190, 194, 227
Keller — *Open* p.44
Kennedy — *Reader's* #1109-1116
Kin — *Dictionary* p.253
Liddle — *Thought I, II, III* p.7, 13-14, 50, 54, 57, 69, 108, 114-115, 121, 129, 132, 135, 138, 152, 155, 164-165, 177, 181, 183, 189
Liddle — *Thought IV* p.2, 6, 16-18, 20-21, 28, 34, 36, 39, 46
Liddle — *Thought V* p.2, 9, 15, 19, 29, 34, 45
Lockridge — *World's See* index p.584
Lytle — *Leaves* p.12, 14, 58, 65, 74, 102, 109, 116, 159, 166
Mandel — *Stories* p.250
Modern Eloquence (14) p.421
Montapert — *Distilled* p.320-323
Nichols — *Third* p.34-35
Nizer — *Thinking* p.47, 92, 167-168
Peterson — *Art* p.41, 179
Phillips — *Choice* p.124, 164, 166
Prochnow — *Public See* index p.513
Prochnow — *Speaker's* p.305
Prochnow — *Success.* #1455, 2375, 2380
Seldes — *Great* p.908-911
Speaker's Desk #150, 166, 248-251, 284, 426, 895
Wallis — *Treasure* p.90, 142, 183, 210, 227
Wallis — *Words* p.142-143, 163, 168
Woods — *Religious* p.987-989
Words — *Inspir.* p.173-174

, and action
Flesch — *Unusual* p.289-290
Flint — *Graham* p.144

, Art of
Maurois — *Art* p.136-173
Peterson — *Twenty* p.20-21

, as prisms
Taylor — *With* p.12

, "Big"
Holmes — *Design* p.82-88

, Change of
Peale — *Guide* p.230-248

, Character from
Hunter — *Gems* p.7-8

, Courageous
Peterson — *Art* p.111

, Daily
Bradshaw — *Home.* p.122-132

, Ending
Krishnamurti — *Urgency* p.147-150

, *for happiness*
Kopplin — *Something* p.7-10
, *Force of*
Wilcox — *Heart* p.20-22
, *New*
Curtis — *Practical* p.62-66
Holmes — *Design* p.3-14
, *Orderly*
Krishnamurti — *Think* p.58-64
, *Patterns of*
Holmes — *Design* p.19, 22-26, 32, 40, 46-47, 115, 129, 220
, *"Positive thinking"*
See also works of Norman Vincent Peale
Albert — *Stop* p.8, 11-12, 24-29, 59-60, 191, 195-196
Flint — *Graham* p.107
Holmes — *Design* p.30, 39-41, 57, 131-132
Montapert — *Distilled* p.323
Tanksley — *Friend* p.73
, *Power of*
Peterson — *Art* p.75, 77
, *Purity of*
Book Proverbs p.88
Hunter — *Gems* p.108
, *Stimulation of*
New Joy p.32
, *Time for*
Bradshaw — *Home.* p.118-119
, *Universal*
Du Noüy — *Human* p.220-222, 258, 261, 267-268

THOUGHTFULNESS
Braude — *Stories* p.374
Manchee — *Secret* p.98-123
Mandel — *Stories* p.250
Prochnow — *Public* #194

THOUGHTLESSNESS
Kauffman — *For* p.211-212
Manchee — *Secret* p.132-133

THREATS
Edwards — *Useful* p.647
Kin — *Dictionary* p.254
Speaker's Desk #310, 364, 567, 1094, 1160
Streiker — *Who* p.119-146

"THREE AGES SYSTEM"
Ideas p.391-393

THRESHING
New Topical p.269

THRIFT
See also **Economy**
Braude — *Source* #1708-1711
Braude — *Stories* p.374-376
Dirksen — *Quot.* #293, 873, 1013, 1671, 1829, 2149, 2378
Edwards — *Useful* p.210-211, 733
Evans — *Unto* p.49
Flesch — *Unusual* p.98
Forbes — *Thoughts See* index p.570
Fun Fare p.77, 147-148
Grizer — *Wit* p.407, 464-465
Henry — *5000* p.283
Hubbard — *Scrap* p.82, 176
Johnson — *Bedside* p.262
Kin — *Dictionary* p.102, 225, 254
Liddle — *Thought I, II, III* p.7, 72, 84, 112
Liddle — *Thought IV* p.4, 30
Lockridge — *World's* #842, 1505, 1772, 4724
Lytle — *Leaves* p.148, 170
Modern Eloquence (14) p.422
Montapert — *Distilled* p.301
Peterson — *Art* p.224
Prochnow — *Public* #45, 475, 662, 1110, 1881, 1912, 1939, 4208
Prochnow — *Speaker's* p.305-306
Prochnow — *Success.* #329, 483, 586, 712, 858
Schermerhorn — *1500* p.370-371
Woods — *Business.* p.88

THRILLS
See also **Excitement**
Evans — *Faith* p.111, 123
Evans — *Thoughts III (Open Road)* p.115-117
Evans — *Thoughts IV* p.85
Prochnow — *Public* #1550

THRONES
Flesch — *Unusual* p.290
Lockridge — *World's* #3915
Maxwell — *Courage* p.35-45

THRUSHES
Applegarth — *Heir.* p.35
Kin — *Dictionary* p.254

THUCYDIDES
Lockridge — *World's* #3582

THUNDER
Botkin — *Treasury* p.28-29
Henry — *5000* p.283
Kin — *Dictionary* p.255
Prochnow — *Success.* #1219

TICKETS AND TICKET OFFICES
Flesch — *Unusual* p.290
Harral — *Feature* p.299

TIDES AND TIDAL WAVES
Alexander's Treasure. p.7
Asimov — *Treasury* #278
Fox — *Make* p.33-34, 53-54
Kin — *Dictionary* p.255
Prochnow — *Public* #967
Woods — *Wellsprings* p.67-68

"TIES, BINDING"
Kohn — *Best* p.28-31

TIES, MEN'S
Harral — *Feature* p.217

TIGERS
Applegarth — *Heir.* p.25
Asimov — *Treasury* #69
Goudge — *Comfort* p.71-72
Hubbard — *Scrap* p.139
Kin — *Dictionary* p.255
Prochnow — *Success.* #461

"TIGHTWADS"
See also **Misers**
Safian — *Insults* p.192-197
Safian — *More* p.165-167

TIME
See also **Age; Hours; Minutes; Past; Present; Today; Tomorrow; Yesterday;** etc.
Albert — *Stop* p.23-24
Alexander's Treasure p.316
Applegarth — *Heir.* p.61, 64, 67-69, 148
Auden — *Certain* p.359-363
Baillie — *Diary* #64
Book Proverbs p.134
Bradshaw — *Home.* p.105-107, 127-132
Braude — *Source* #1712-1722
Braude — *Stories* p.376-377
Casselberry — *How* p.169-178
Curtis — *Daily* p.86-92
Curtis — *Practical* p.531, 533, 556
Detherage — *Sunrise* p.13-14, 16, 20, 35, 37, 42, 51-56, 84, 122, 186
Dirksen — *Quot.* #497, 1099-1101, 1692, 2206-2210, 2218
Droke — *Christian* p.541-548
Du Noüy — *Human* p.8-9, 188, 198-200, 208-209, 212-213, 235, 260-261, 265-266, 275-276
Edwards — *Useful* p.647-651
Evans — *Faith* p.29, 136, 209-218, 225-226
Evans — *Quote* p.97-110
Evans — *This* p.179-182
Evans — *Thoughts I* p.22, 44, 78, 108-110, 127-128, 133, 215-216
Evans — *Thoughts II (Open Door)* p.14, 16, 66-67, 103-110, 123-124
Evans — *Thoughts III (Open Road)* p.35-36, 58, 67, 105, 116, 145-146, 181, 196, 211
Evans — *Thoughts IV* p.53-54, 86, 161-170, 196, 209
Evans — *Unto* p.3, 19, 21-23, 43, 77
Flesch — *Unusual* p.290-291
Fogg — *1000* #43, 80
Forbes — *Thoughts See* index p.570
Fuller — *Epigrams* p.279-281, 362-363
Fun Fare p.55
Garland — *Subject* p.316-317
Grizer — *Wit* p.465-467
Hadfield — *Love* p.220
Harnsberger — *Mark* p.475-476
Harral — *Feature* p.300
Hobe — *Tapestries* p.12, 218
Hovey — *Treasury* p.277; #20, 29, 38, 119, 523, 941, 1178, 1770-1774
Hubbard — *Scrap* p.11, 22, 40, 62, 82, 94, 101, 198, 204
Hudson — *5000* p.283-285
Humes — *Instant* p.11; #1044-1054
Johnson — *Bedside* p.24
Kahn — *Lessons* p.220-240
Keller — *Open* p.132
Kennedy — *Reader's* #1117-1122
Keys Happiness p.345-347, 470-471
Kin — *Dictionary* p.75, 255-256
Knight's Illus. p.329-331
Knight's Treas. p.407-409
Kohn — *Best* p.104-105
Kohn — *Pathways* p.181-184
Liddle — *Thought I, II, III See* index p.200
Liddle — *Thought IV* p.5-6, 12, 18, 22, 24-25, 32, 45-46
Liddle — *Thought V* p.8, 21, 24, 27, 29, 44
Lindbergh — *Gift* p.116
Lindbergh — *Unicorn* p.77-86
Lockridge — *World's See* index p.584
Lytle — *Leaves* p.19, 21, 27, 31, 170, 172-174
Mandel — *Stories* p.250-251
Modern Eloquence (14) p.423-424
Montapert — *Distilled* p.323-324
New Joy p.24, 37, 57, 120-121
New Topical p.269-270
Peale — *Courage* p.21-22
Peterson — *Art* p.81, 147, 213, 247, 281, 313, 321, 379

Prochnow — *Public See* index p.513
Prochnow — *Speaker's* p.306-307
Prochnow — *Success.* #617, 642, 1149, 1288, 2381-2390
Seldes — *Great* p.911
Sheban — *Wisdom* no p.
Speaker's Desk p.251-254; #348, 605, 782, 832, 1110
Wallis — *Treasure* p.13, 31, 95, 220
Wallis — *Words* p.117, 212-214
Watson — *Light* p.142-147
Woods — *Religious* p.989-991
Woods — *Wellsprings* p.82
Words Change p.117
, and space
Clark — *Windows* p.124
Flesch — *Unusual* p.291
, and timelessness
Evans — *This* p.49-50
, and you
Grizer — *Wit* p.468
, Anxiety of
Sheen — *Content.* p.39-41
, Balancing of
Vogue — *Arts* p.111-117
, Beginning of
Saturday — *Advent.* p.161-174
, Borrowing of
Grizer — *Wit* p.468
Peale — *Guideposts* p.260-262
, Daily
Peale — *Courage* p.22
, Enjoyment of
See also **Enjoyment**
Maltz — *Creative* p.25-26
, Expenditure of. See **Time, Use of; Time, Waste of**
, Keeping of
See also **Clocks and watches**
Harral — *Feature* p.300
, Measurement of
Holmes — *Design* p.7-8
, Passage of
Adams — *New* p.212
Evans — *This* p.190-191
, Saving of
Braude — *Source* #1723
Braude — *Speaker's* #1478-1479
, Shortness of
New Day p.16
, Use of
Bennett — *How* p.42-48
Words Change p.64-67
, Value of
Kopplin — *Something* p.134-141
Montapert — *Distilled* p.324-325
, Waste of
Braude — *Source* #1724
Woods — *Wellsprings* p.37-38

TIMETABLES
Harral — *Feature* p.301

TIMING
Braude — *Source* #1725-1726
Flesch — *Unusual* p.291
Halverson — *Perspective* p.19
How To Live p.328-331
Mandel — *Stories* p.252
Montgomery — *Distilled* p.325
, Teenager
Daly — *Personality* p.73-77

TINFOIL
Flesch — *Unusual* p.291

TIPS AND TIPPING
Asimov — *Treasury* #416
Braude — *Source* #1727-1728
Braude — *Speaker's* #1480-1487
Guideposts — *Faith* p.334-336
Harral — *Feature* p.301
Mandel — *Stories* p.252
Prochnow — *Public* #55, 314
Prochnow — *Speaker's* p.308
Prochnow — *Success.* #915, 1085
Schermerhorn — *1500* p.373-374

"TIPTOE" LIVING
Kohn — *Pathways* p.155-157

TIREDNESS. *See* **Fatigue**

"TIT FOR TAT." *See* **Revenge**

TITHING
Flint — *Graham* p.144
Hovey — *Treasury* p.277-278; #1029, 1775-1780
Hunter — *Gems* p.108-112
Knight's Illus. p.331-333
Knight's Treas. p.409-410
New Topical p.270
Words Change p.96-97

TITLES
See also **Aristocracy; Books and reading, Titles of; Kings and queens; Royalty**
Edwards — *Useful* p.651-652
Evans — *Unto* p.71
Harnsberger — *Mark* p.476
Liddle — *Thought I, II, III* p.113
Lockridge — *World's* #5784

TOASTMASTERS
Fun Fare p.1-2, 178

Nizer — *Thinking* p.53, 59, 67, 110, 145
Prochnow — *Speaker's* p.308-309
Prochnow — *Success.* #717, 1052
Schermerhorn — *1500* p.374
, *Responsibilities of*
Prochnow — *Success.* #1-4

TOASTS
See also subjects to be toasted
Braude — *Source* #1731-1736
Braude — *Speaker's* #309-338
Braude — *Stories* p.377-379
Copeland — *10,000* p.983-1007
Fuller — *Epigrams* p.325-327
Hudson — *5000* p.285-286
Humes — *Instant* p.47-48
Prochnow — *Public* #96, 367, 1447, 1539, 1631, 1885
Prochnow — *Speaker's* p.309
Prochnow — *Success.* #2391
, *Ceremonial*
Humes — *Instant* p.47-48
, *Drinking*
Braude — *Speaker's* #35-55
Fuller — *Epigrams* p.335-339
, *General*
Copeland — *10,000* p.1001-1005
, *Stories about*
Copeland — *10,000* p.1005-1007
, *Wedding*
Nizer — *Thinking* p.197

TOBACCO
See also **Cigarettes; Cigars; Smoking**
Bradshaw — *Home.* p.79-91
Flesch — *Unusual* p.291-292
Fuller — *Epigrams* p.63, 281
Hudson — *5000* p.286
Prochnow — *Public* #1708
Prochnow — *Speaker's* p.309
Seldes — *Great* p.911-912
, *and courtesy*
Kauffman — *For* p.72-73
, *Chewing of*
Botkin — *Anecdotes* p.95
, *Effects of*
White — *Life* p.104-106

TODAY
See also **Present**
Alexander's Treasure. p.10, 56, 72, 80, 187-188, 210, 239, 257, 319
Applegarth — *Heir.* p.66, 250
Bach — *Make* p.30-31
Barker — *Treat* p.67-86
Bartlett — *Discovery* p.44-45, 66
Book Proverbs p.61
Bradshaw — *Home.* p.94-100
Carruthers — *Sparks* p.15-17, 133-135
Curtis — *Daily* p.43-48
Evans — *Thoughts I* p.129-130, 164, 176, 206-207
Evans — *Thoughts IV* p.11, 135, 164-166, 209
Flesch — *Unusual* p.192, 292
Forbes — *Thoughts See* index p.571
Fox — *Make* p.75-76, 160-161
Grizer — *Wit* p.469-470
Hobe — *Tapestries* p.11-12, 111
Holmes — *Design* p.110-120
How To Live p.255-258
Hubbard — *Scrap* p.48, 124
Hudson — *5000* p.286
Keys Happiness p.16-20, 306
Kin — *Dictionary* p.256
Kohn — *Touch* p.72, 167-172
List — *Living* p.17-21
Lockridge — *World's* #751, 854, 869, 908, 992, 1001, 1424, 1711, 2983, 3571, 4019, 4050, 4357, 4494, 5061, 5108, 5208, 5853, 5861
Lytle — *Leaves* p.6, 170
Mandel — *Stories* p.252-253
Mandelbaum — *Choose* p.231-233, 254-257
Montapert — *Distilled* p.264, 325
New Joy p.24, 39
Nichols — *New* p.157-158, 224-225
Nichols — *Third* p.149-150, 161-175, 199-200
Peale — *Courage* p.125-128, 140
Peterson — *Art* p.88, 107, 168, 195, 239, 270, 316, 337
Prochnow — *Success.* #2392
Pullar-Strecker — *Proverbs* #16-18, 142-149
Speaker's Desk #663, 670, 727, 866, 890, 929, 948, 1041, 1157
Vogue — *Arts* p.83-90
Wallis — *Treasure* p.217-222
Wallis — *Words* p.209-214
Watson — *Light* p.23-30, 214-219
Welk — *Guide.* p.32-35
Woods — *Content.* p.35
Woods — *Religious* p.694
Zobell — *Speaker's* p.141-144
, *Prayer for*
Holmes — *I've* p.69

"TOGETHERNESS"
Holmes — *I've* p.106
Lytle — *Leaves* p.111, 122, 167
Mandel — *Stories* p.253

TOIL. *See* **Labor; Work**

TOLERANCE
See also **Broad-mindedness**
Boas — *History* p.81-84
Braude — *Source* #1737-1739
Braude — *Stories* p.379
Carruthers — *Sparks* p.65-66, 90-91
Curtis — *Practical* p.508
Dirksen — *Quot.* #1102, 1422, 1595-1597
Droke — *Christian* p.549-553
Edwards — *Useful* p.652
Emmons — *Mature* p.98, 101
Evans — *Faith* p.45, 109, 111, 137, 141-142, 190
Evans — *This* p.68-71
Evans — *Thoughts I* p.61-62
Evans — *Thoughts III (Open Road)* p.158
Evans — *Thoughts IV* p.148
Evans — *Unto* p.16, 42, 57
Flesch — *Unusual* p.292
Flint — *Graham* p.98, 144-145
Fogg — *1000* #104, 109, 153, 412, 753, 810-811, 836, 885, 947, 986, 1076, 1118
Forbes — *Thoughts* p.70, 121, 123, 155, 160-161, 177, 197, 234, 247, 313, 342, 346, 360, 452, 462
Fuller — *Epigrams* p.282
Fuller — *Thesaurus* #601-603
Grizer — *Wit* p.470
Harnsberger — *Mark* p.477
Hovey — *Treasury* p.278; *See also* index p.301
Hudson — *5000* p.287
Johnson — *Bedside* p.199, 301
Keller — *Open* p.19
Kennedy — *Reader's* #1123-1127
Kin — *Dictionary* p.256
Kohn — *Pathways* p.52-53
Liddle — *Thought I, II, III* p.22, 74, 102, 105
Liddle — *Thought IV* p.9, 40
Liddle — *Thought V* p.33, 42
Liebman — *Peace* p.73
Lytle — *Leaves* p.75
Mandel — *Stories* p.253-254
Montapert — *Distilled* p.326
Myers — *Thunder* p.42-45
Prochnow — *Public* #3789-3791, 4278
Prochnow — *Success.* #1050, 1394, 1484, 2393-2395
Seldes — *Great* p.912
Speaker's Desk #287
Woods — *Religious* p.991-994
Woods — *Wellsprings* p.51
Words — *Inspir.* p.18

TOMORROW
See also **Future**
Alexander's Treasure. p.257, 284
Applegarth — *Heir.* p.61, 63, 66, 171
Baillie — *Diary* #239
Book Proverbs p.61
Braude — *Source* #1740-1741
Dirksen — *Quot.* #2211, 2301
Evans — *This* p.177-186
Evans — *Thoughts I* p.112, 129-130, 164, 206-207
Flesch — *Unusual* p.292-293
Forbes — *Thoughts See* index p.571
Grizer — *Wit* p.470-471
Hobe — *Tapestries* p.11-12
Hudson — *5000* p.287
Kauffman — *For* p.212-214
Keller — *Open* p.127
Kin — *Dictionary* p.256
Lockridge — *World's* #4019, 5108
Lytle — *Leaves* p.171
Maltz — *Creative* p.128-129
Nichols — *Third* p.235-236
Peterson — *Art* p.372
Prochnow — *Public* #1445, 2554
Prochnow — *Success.* #380, 382, 550, 2396-2397
Wallis — *Treasure* p.138, 217, 220, 222
Wallis — *Words* p.3, 72, 117, 229

TONGUE
See also **Gossip; Language; Slander; Speech**
Book Proverbs p.35
Edwards — *Useful* p.652-653
Forbes — *Thoughts* p.49, 90, 194, 323, 383, 483
Fuller — *Epigrams* p.282
Hudson — *5000* p.287
Kin — *Dictionary* p.256-257
Knight's Illus. p.333-336
Knight's Treas. p.410-415
Lockridge — *World's* #2540
Lytle — *Leaves* p.56, 160, 162
Mandel — *Stories* p.254-255
Montapert — *Distilled* p.326
Peterson — *Art* p.89
Prochnow — *Public* #1150, 1217, 1229
, "Slips" of
See also **"Boners"**
Alexander's Treasure. p.42
Asimov — *Treasury* #299

"TONGUE TWISTERS"
Botkin — *Treasury* p.774

TONIC
Evans — *Thoughts I* p.205

TOOLS
Forbes — *Thoughts* p.2, 42, 85, 247, 282, 338, 355, 507

Lockridge — *World's* #2494
Prochnow — *Public* #452
Wallis — *Treasure* p.237-238

TORAH
Woods — *Religious* p.994

TORCHES
Kin — *Dictionary* p.257
Lytle — *Leaves* p.117
Sheban — *Wisdom* no p.
Wallis — *Treasure* p.136

TORTOISES
Auden — *Certain* p.363-365

TOTALITARIANISM. *See* **Despotism; Dictatorship; Tyrants and tyranny**

TOUCH
Garland — *Subject* p.318
Lair — *Baby* p.151-156
Lytle — *Leaves* p.34
, Sense of
Keller — *Open* p.25

TOUGHNESS
See also **Ruggedness**
Kin — *Dictionary* p.257
Prochnow — *Public* #541, 931
Speaker's Desk #349, 370, 481, 571, 621, 867

TOURISTS
See also **Travel**
Botkin — *Treasury* p.377
Fun Fare p.69, 229, 274-276
Harral — *Feature* p.301
Prochnow — *Public* #107, 289, 293, 464, 743, 938, 993, 1822, 1929
Prochnow — *Speaker's* p.310
Prochnow — *Success.* #992, 1237
Reader's — *Getting* p.35-38
Speaker's Desk #21, 691, 977

TOURNAMENTS
Prochnow — *Public* #633

TOWELS
Irion — *Yes* p.18-21
Prochnow — *Public* #186, 702, 1705

TOWERS
Kin — *Dictionary* p.257
New Topical p.274

TOWNS
See also **Cities**
Dirksen — *Quot.* #204, 2927, 2295
Flesch — *Unusual* p.293
Harral — *Feature* p.302
Hobe — *Tapestries* p.21
Kin — *Dictionary* p.269
Lockridge — *World's* #3693
, and country
Flesch — *Unusual* p.293
, Country
Schermerhorn — *1500* p.95-96
, Home
Keys Happiness p.449-453
, Small
Dirksen — *Quot.* #2295
Lair — *Baby* p.163-164
Prochnow — *Public* #1800

TOYS
Harral — *Feature* p.302
Lockridge — *World's* #3835, 4989
Prochnow — *Public* #52, 337
Prochnow — *Speaker's* p.310

TRACKS
Kohn — *Best* p.147-149

TRACTORS
Patterns For Living p.30-33

TRACTS, PRINTED
Knight's Treas. p.415-418

TRADE
See also **Commerce**
Edwards — *Useful* p.653-654
Flesch — *Unusual* p.293
Forbes — *Thoughts* p.194, 335, 359, 391, 482, 494
Grizer — *Wit* p.471
Kennedy — *Reader's* #1128
Kin — *Dictionary* p.257
Lockridge — *World's* #1695, 1733, 2834-2865, 4840, 5027
Lytle — *Leaves* p.40
Nichols — *Third* p.101-102
Prochnow — *Public* #217
Prochnow — *Success.* #1055
Seldes — *Great* p.912-913
Woods — *Religious* p.995
, Free
Dirksen — *Quot.* #1172
Franke — *Buckley* p.91-92
, World
Prochnow — *Success.* #744, 1259

TRADE UNIONS. *See* **Labor unions**

TRADERS
Woods — *Religious* p.995

TRADITION
See also **Customs**
Auden — *Certain* p.366
Braude — *Source* #1351-1352
Dirksen — *Quot.* #72, 84, 121
Du Noüy — *Human* p.120-124, 137-138, 174, 177, 186, 211, 218
Edwards — *Useful* p.654
Flint — *Graham* p.145
Garland — *Subject* **p.318**
Ideas p.394-397
Keller — *Open* p.76
Kennedy — *Reader's* #1129-1132
Keys Happiness p.493-495
Kin — *Dictionary* p.257
Krishnamurti — *Urgency* p.108-111
Lockridge — *World's* #1702
Prochnow — *Public* #1823, 3792-3793
Prochnow — *Speaker's* p.310
Seldes — *Great* p.913
Speaker's Desk p.254-255
Woods — *Religious* p.995-997
, and freedom
Wheelis — *Moralist* p.91-92

TRAFFIC
See also **Automobiles**
Braude — *Stories* p.379-392
Grizer — *Wit* p.471-473
Harral — *Feature* p.303-304
Prochnow — *Public* #716, 1407, 1412
Prochnow — *Speaker's* p.310
Prochnow — *Success.* #415, 720, 1485
, Automobile
Braude — *Source* #1742-1749
Braude — *Speaker's* #1508-1527
, Policemen for
Prochnow — *Public* #1014, 1491, 1824
, Lights for
Prochnow — *Public* #569, 980

TRAGEDY
See also **Adversity; Disaster; Theater**
Applegarth — *Heir.* p.49, 255
Edwards — *Useful* p.654
Evans — *This* p.33
Kennedy — *Reader's* #1133-1135
Prochnow — *Public* #1825-1827, 3791-3796
Prochnow — *Success.* #632, 1265
Woods — *Religious* p.997-998

TRAINING. *See* **Education**

TRAINS
See also Pullmans; Railroads
Asimov — *Treasury* #31, 298
Botkin — *Treasury* p.453-454, 714
Clark — *Windows* p.102
Fuller — *Thesaurus* #1801-1802
Prochnow — *Public* #160, 290, 346, 554, 893, 988, 2541
Prochnow — *Success.* #1102
Schermerhorn — *1500* p.375-376
, Missing of
Baillie — *Diary* #43
, Porters of
Fuller — *Thesaurus* #1806

TRAITORS
See also **Treason**
Fogg — *1000* #365, 630, 964
Lockridge — *World's* #3897, 5850
Seldes — *Great* p.913-914

TRAITS. *See* **Character**

TRAMPS
Botkin — *Treasury* p.882-887
Copeland — *10,000* p.133-140
Forbes — *Thoughts* p.295, 416, 428
Guideposts — *Faith* p.344-349
Harral — *Feature* p.186
Keys Happiness p.403-407
Prochnow — *Success.* #587
Schermerhorn — *1500* p.376-378
, Songs of
Kronenberger — *Animal* p.300-304

TRANQUILITY. *See* **Peace**

TRANQUILIZERS
Albert — *Stop* p.97-99
Prochnow — *Success.* #859

TRANSCENDENCE
Lytle — *Leaves* p.72, 110
Woods — *Religious* p.998

TRANSFIGURATION
Curtis — *New* p.65-66
Woods — *Religious* p.999

TRANSFORMATION
Curtis — *New* p.64
Du Noüy — *Human* p.90-99
Hadfield — *Delights* p.186-187
Kin — *Dictionary* p.258
Tanksley — *Friend* p.80

TRANSGRESSION. *See* **Sin**

TRANSIENCY
Halverson — *Perspective* p.68
Lytle — *Leaves* p.15

TRANSITION
Flesch — *Unusual* p.293
Lytle — *Leaves* p.98
Woods — *Religious* p.999

TRANSLATIONS AND TRANSLATORS
Auden — *Certain* p.366-368
Braude — *Speaker's* #1528
Braude — *Stories* p.392
Curtis — *Practical* p.475–479
Flesch — *Unusual* p.293
Harnsberger — *Mark* p.478
Lockridge — *World's* #2487
Wallis — *Words* p.10

TRANSMUTATION
Curtis — *New* p.64-65
Ideas p.399-400
Seldes — *Great* p.914
Woods — *Religious* p.999

TRANSPORTATION
See also types of transportation
Fun Fare p.87-88
Harral — *Feature* p.304-307
Kronenberger — *Animal* p.304-305
Prochnow — *Speaker's* p.311
Prochnow — *Success.* #1382

TRAVEL
See also **Adventure; Experience; Tourists**
Adams — *New* p.416
Applegarth — *Heir.* p.11, 166, 271-279
Asimov — *Treasury* #350
Braude — *Source* #1750-1752
Braude — *Speaker's* #1529-1548
Braude — *Stories* p.392
Cerf — *Laugh* p.439-458
Curtis — *Practical* p.91-93
Dirksen — *Quot.* #431, 602, 1104, 2212-2215
Edwards — *Useful* p.654-655
Evans — *Thoughts I* p.93, 111-112, 122, 176-179
Flesch — *Unusual* p.1, 293-294
Forbes — *Thoughts* p.65, 232, 294, 332, 487
Fuller — *Epigrams* p.283
Fuller — *Thesaurus* p.313-317
Fun Fare p.9-10, 14-15, 30, 87, 120, 168-172, 208, 309
Gold — *Letters* p.33-43
Grizer — *Wit* p.473-474
Harnsberger — *Mark* p.1, 478-482
Harral — *Feature* p.307-308
Henry — *5000* p.139
Hubbard — *Scrap* p.89
Hudson — *5000* p.288
Kennedy — *Reader's* #1136-1138
Keys Happiness p.114-118
Kin — *Dictionary* p.258
Kronenberger — *Animal* p.305-314
Liddle — *Thought I, II, III* p.173, 186
Lockridge — *World's* #3655, 5285, 5702
Lytle — *Leaves* p.119
Modern Eloquence (14) p.171-177
Montapert — *Distilled* p.326-327
New Topical p.274-275
Prochnow — *Public* #151, 345, 417, 1050, 1308, 3797-3798, 4233-4235
Prochnow — *Speaker's* p.311-312
Prochnow — *Success.* #1933, 2398-2400
Reader's — *Getting* p.35-38
Simpson — *Contemp.* p.196-202
Wallis — *Treasure* p.138, 143-144, 161, 231
Wallis — *Words* p.35-36, 51, 76, 94, 111, 113, 132
Woods — *Content.* p.63-64, 67, 72, 74-75, 80-83

, Agents for
Manchee — *Secret* p.230-231
, Art of
Peterson — *Twenty* p.10-11
, Guideposts for
Bradshaw — *Home.* p.107-109
, Hints for
Daly — *Personality* p.147-153
Reader's — *Getting* p.36
, Hurried
Adams — *New* p.208
, Tales of
Botkin — *Anecdotes* p.90
, Tours
Harral — *Feature* p.302

TREACHERY
See also **Conspiracy; Traitors; Treason**
Book Proverbs p.53
Edwards — *Useful* p.655-656
Harnsberger — *Mark* p.482
Hudson — *5000* p.288
Johnson — *Bedside* p.119
Kin — *Dictionary* p.258
List — *Living* p.46-49
Lockridge — *World's* #744, 4838

TREASON
See also **Rebellion; Revolution**
Dirksen — *Quot.* #728

Edwards — *Useful* p.656
Fogg — *1000* #124, 320, 334, 382, 563, 756, 848
Fuller — *Epigrams* p.283
Ideas p.400-401
Kin — *Dictionary* p.258
Seldes — *Great* p.914-915
Woods — *Religious* p.999

TREASURES
See also **Beauty**
Alexander's Treasure. p.100,118
Bradshaw — *Home.* p.119-121
Emmons — *Mature* p.48-51, 148, 150
Forbes — *Thoughts* p.60, 101, 182, 470
Fox — *Make* p.86-87
Lytle — *Leaves* p.147, 149, 168
Prochnow — *Public* #2615
Sheban — *Wisdom* no p.
Wallis — *Words* p.106, 164, 204
Woods — *Wellsprings* p.17
, *Eternal*
Hunter — *Gems* p.112-113
, *Life's*
Tanksley — *Friend* p.48
Words — *Inspir.* p.41
, *Mental*
Peterson — *Art* p.340

TREATIES
Dirksen — *Quot.* #115-117
Lockridge — *World's* #1853, 2769, 3870
Seldes — *Great* p.10-12

TREATMENT
Barker — *Treat* p.148-152
Curtis — *Golden* p.174-186
Fox — *Make* p.137-138, 185-186, 191-192
Garland — *Subject* p.320

TREES
See also **Flowers; Forests; Leaves; Nature; Woods**
Alexander's Treasure. p.123
Applegarth — *Heir.* p.281-289
Baillie — *Diary* #137
Braude — *Stories* p.355-356
Clark — *Windows* p.150-151
Edwards — *Useful* p.656
Flesch — *Unusual* p.294
Forbes — *Thoughts* p.117, 266, 284, 345, 451
Fuller — *Epigrams* p.283
Garland — *Subject* p.320-321
Harnsberger — *Mark* p.482-483
Harral — *Feature* p.308-309
Hobe — *Tapestries* p.60-61, 95-97
Holmes — *I've* p.11-12
Hubbard — *Scrap* p.68, 116, 167
Hulme — *5000* p.288-289
Irion — *Yes* p.123-125
Lindbergh — *Unicorn* p.18, 62-64, 86
New Topical p.275-276
Prochnow — *Public* #207, 566, 796, 871, 970, 985, 2593, 2637, 4287
Wallis — *Treasure* p.31, 105, 113, 150, 225
Wallis — *Words* p.3, 55, 94, 98, 117, 167, 171, 174, 199
Woods — *Content.* p.206
, *Evergreen*
Kohn — *Pathways* p.127-129
, *Winter*
Irion — *Yes* p.119-121

TRESPASSES. *See* **Sin**

TRIALS
Edwards — *Useful* p.656-658
Flesch — *Unusual* p.294, 298-299
Fogg — *1000 See* index p.900
Forbes — *Thoughts* p.38, 41, 343, 400, 424
Holmes — *I've* p.11
Howell — *Lives* p.60-64
Hubbard — *Scrap* p.45
Hudson — *5000* p.289
Humes — *Instant* #1055-1057
Kin — *Dictionary* p.258, 261
Liddle — *Thought I, II, III* p.19, 67, 172
Liddle — *Thought IV* p.5, 23, 38-40
Liddle — *Thought V* p.3-4, 14, 22, 28, 30, 32, 35
Lytle — *Leaves* p.17, 30, 41
Montapert — *Distilled* p.327
Prochnow — *Success.* #761, 2401-2402
Speaker's Desk p.255-257
Taylor — *With* p.84
Woods — *Religious* p.999-1000
Words — *Inspir.* p.86

TRIBUTES
Lytle — *Leaves* p.80
New Topical p.277-278
Prochnow — *Speaker's* p.312-313
Reader's — *Getting* p.81-84

TRICKS AND TRICKERY
See also **Jokes and joking**
Botkin — *Anecdotes* p.3-4, 9, 53-72, 90, 207, 237
Botkin — *Treasury* p.175, 358, 360
Kin — *Dictionary* p.258
Prochnow — *Public* #295, 2352

TRIFLES. *See* **"Little things"**

TRINITY
See also **Holy Spirit (Holy Ghost)**
Flint — *Graham* p.145
Garland — *Subject* p.321
McDonagh — *Invit.* p.96-97
More Words p.166-167
New Topical p.278
Seldes — *Great* p.915
Woods — *Religious* p.1000-1002

TRIPLETS
Asimov — *Treasury* #616

TRIUMPH. *See* **Victory**

TRIVIA. *See* **"Little things"**

"TROJAN HORSE"
Seldes — *Great* p.915-916

TROJAN WAR
Flesch — *Unusual* p.295

TROMBONES
Prochnow — *Public* #295
Prochnow — *Success.* #1115

TROTSKYISM
Ideas p.401-403

TROUBLE
See also **Adversity; Discouragement; Problems; Trials; Worry;** etc.
Applegarth — *Heir.* p.83-84, 201, 296
Baillie — *Diary* #192
Braude — *Source* #1753-1755
Dirksen — *Quot.* #798, 1105, 1258, 1597
Droke — *Christian* p.553-555
Edwards — *Useful* p.659-661
Evans — *Thoughts I* p.24, 93, 117, 127-128, 130-133, 208
Evans — *Thoughts III (Open Road)* p.199-200
Evans — *Thoughts IV* p.206
Evans — *Unto* p.29, 47, 116, 121, 145
Flesch — *Unusual* p.295
Forbes — *Thoughts* p.68, 98, 273, 331, 400, 450; *See also* index p.571
Fox — *Make* p.92
Fuller — *Epigrams* p.284
Grizer — *Wit* p.474-476
Halverson — *Perspective* p.31, 66
Harnsberger — *Mark* p.483
Hobe — *Tapestries* p.219, 225
Holmes — *Design* p.66-67, 106-107
Hovey — *Treasury* p.278-279; *See also* index p.301
Hubbard — *Scrap* p.222
Hudson — *5000* p.290
Kahn — *Lessons* p.144-148
Kennedy — *Reader's* #1139
Keys Happiness p.254
Kin — *Dictionary* p.40, 183, 259
Kohn — *Adventures* p.136
Kohn — *Best* p.40
Liddle — *Thought I, II, III See* index p.200
Lytle — *Leaves* p.13-14, 23, 25, 120
Mandel — *Stories* p.29, 256-257
Montapert — *Distilled* p.327-328
Nichols — *New* p.41-62
Peale — *Courage* p.29-40
Prochnow — *Public See* index p.513
Prochnow — *Success.* #507, 956, 1148-1149, 1462, 2403
Wallis — *Treasure* p.187, 223-228
Wallis — *Words* p.179
Woods — *Religious* p.1002
Woods — *Wellsprings* p.27
Words Change p.68-71
Zobell — *Speaker's* p.144-145
, and hope
Kauffman — *For* p.214-215
, Borrowing
Botkin — *Treasury* p.459-460
, Handling
Carruthers — *Sparks* p.97-98
, Helpful
Kohn — *Through* p.135-136
, Keeping out of
Manchee — *Secret* p.81-85
, Makers of
Hoffer — *Reflect.* p.27-46
, Release of
Peale — *Guide* p.23-45
, Time of
Seldes — *Great* p.916

TROUT
Botkin — *Treasury* p.624
Kin — *Dictionary* p.259

TRUANCY
Speaker's Desk #118, 779

TRUCKS AND TRUCKING
Harral — *Feature* p.309
Prochnow — *Success.* #119

TRUMPETS AND TRUMPET PLAYERS
Guideposts — *Faith* p.207-209
New Topical p.278
Nichols — *Third* p.213-214
Wallis — *Words* p.38

TRUMPS
Prochnow — *Public* #987

TRUST
See also **Belief; Confidence; Faith; Responsibility**
Alexander's Treasure. p.185-186
Bach — *Make* p.149-154
Braude — *Source* #1756
Clark — *Windows* p.42-43
Dirksen — *Quot.* #729, 1816, 2360
Droke — *Christian* p.556-557
Edward — *Useful* p.661-662
Emmons — *Trust* p.73-78
Evans — *Quote* p.163-175
Evans — *Thoughts I* p.11-12, 24-27, 78
Evans — *Thoughts III (Open Road)* p.19, 126
Evans — *Thoughts IV* p.79, 134
Evans — *Unto* p.15, 38, 47, 94, 117
Flesch — *Unusual* p.295-296
Fogg — *Unusual* #666
Forbes — *Thoughts* p.12, 93, 142, 224-225, 267, 343, 381, 437, 441, 453, 461, 468, 484, 500
Fuller — *Epigrams* p.285
Garland — *Subject* p.322
Grizer — *Wit* p.476-477
Hobe — *Tapestries* p.46, 50
Hovey — *Treasury* #544-545, 1021, 1159, 1182
Hudson — *5000* p.290
Irion — *Yes* p.47-48
Johnson — *Bedside* p.127, 187
Keller — *Open* p.43
Kennedy — *Reader's* #1140-1141
Keys Happiness p.510
Kin — *Dictionary* p.259-260
Knight's Illus. p.336-338
Knight's Treas. p.418-420
Lair — *Baby* p.113-123
Liddle — *Thought I, II, III* p.35, 44, 64, 82, 99, 107, 113, 126, 182, 185
Liddle — *Thought IV* p.5
Liddle — *Thought V* p.12, 26
Lytle — *Leaves* p.69
Mandel — *Stories* p.257-258
Montapert — *Distilled* p.328
New Joy p.167
New Topical p.278-279
Peale — *Guideposts* p.165-168
Peterson — *Art* p.333
Prochnow — *Public* #380, 449
Prochnow — *Success.* #2405
Seldes — *Great* p.916
Speaker's Desk p.257-258
Wallis — *Treasure* p.90, 94-95, 101, 209, 212, 220, 223
Wallis — *Words* p.215-218
Woods — *Religious* p.1002-1003

TRUTH
See also **Accuracy; Facts; Honesty; Integrity**
Alexander's Treasure. p.279
Applegarth — *Heir.* p.72, 296
Baillie — *Diary* #141, 167, 216, 318
Bartlett — *Discovery* p.15-16, 150
Book Proverbs p.88, 138
Braude — *Source* #1757-1767
Braude — *Speaker's* #1549-1550
Braude — *Stories* p.392-395
Clark — *Windows* p.58, 84
Curtis — *Human* p.60, 141, 183-199
Curtis — *New* p.20-21, 99-100, 104, 129-130
Curtis — *Practical* p.3, 35, 37-40, 45-46, 218, 222, 262-264
Detherage — *Sunrise* p.55, 62, 95, 103, 163, 175
Dirksen — *Quot.* *See* index p.270
Droke — *Christian* p.558-562
Edwards — *Useful* p.62, 662-667, 733-734
Evans — *Faith* p.16, 71-72, 81, 131
Evans — *Quote* p.177-186
Evans — *This* p.89-107
Evans — *Thoughts I* p.110, 123, 155, 171, 202
Evans — *Thoughts II (Open Door)* p.43-45, 48-50, 158
Evans — *Unto* p.12, 21, 23, 41-42, 55, 57, 61, 63, 72, 77-81, 84, 90, 113, 135, 144
Flesch — *Unusual* p.29, 285, 295-298, 303
Flint — *Graham* p.145-146
Fogg — *1000* #456, 666, 810
Forbes — *Thoughts* p.144, 191, 214, 301, 368, 410, 485-486; *See also* index p.571
Fox — *Make* p.17-18, 178, 181, 185-186, 209-210, 216
Franke — *Buckley* p.294-295
Fuller — *Epigrams* p.286-288
Garland — *Subject* p.322-323
Grizer — *Wit* p.477-479
Halverson — *Perspective* p.72
Harnsberger — *Mark* p.484-487
Hobe — *Tapestries* p.62, 126, 202-207
Hovey — *Treasury* p.279; *See also* index p.301
Hubbard — *Scrap* p.25, 47, 53, 86, 94, 156, 165, 168, 187, 195-196, 200, 223-225
Hudson — *5000* p.290-292
Humes — *Instant* #1058-1075
Kennedy — *Reader's* #1142-1151
Johnson — *Bedside* p.4-5, 90-91, 140, 142, 152, 184-185, 199, 248, 235, 250
Kin — *Dictionary* p.39, 260, 268

Kopplin — *Something* p.117-118
Krishnamurti — *Think* p.129-130
Langdon — *Teach.* p.27-33
Liddle — *Thought I, II, III See* index p.200
Liddle — *Thought IV* p.18-19, 22, 28-30, 35, 45
Liddle — *Thought V* p.8-9, 11, 22, 42
Lockridge — *World's* #1626, 3317, 4344, 5723; *See also* index p.584
Lytle — *Leaves* p.19, 58-59, 108, 128, 141
Mandel — *Stories* p.258
Menninger — *Blue.* p.92
Miller — *Harvest* p.59-66
Modern Eloquence (14) p.425-426
Montapert — *Distilled* p.329
Myers — *Thunder* p.134-147
New Joy p.29, 63, 242
New Topical p.279-280
Nichols — *Third* p.197-198
Nizer — *Thinking* p.190, 192
Phillips — *Choice* p.12, 48-49, 70, 131
Prochnow — *Public* #394, 4008; *See also* index p.513
Prochnow — *Speaker's* p.313-314
Prochnow — *Success.* #189, 366, 560, 567, 753, 1474, 2404, 2406-2415
Seldes — *Great* p.916-936
Sheban — *Wisdom* no p.
Speaker's Desk p.258-262; *See also* index p.305
Voss — *Quotations* p.235-238
Wallis — *Treasure* p.29, 65, 73, 93, 96, 155, 209
Wallis — *Words* p.86, 137, 145-146
Wheelis — *Moralist* p.9, 12, 14, 32, 34
White — *Life* p.260-266
Woods — *Content.* p.234, 243, 277, 281
Woods — *Religious* p.223-240, 1002-1011, 1032
Words — *Inspir.* p.23
, Achieving
  Adams — *New* p.68
, and business
  Kauffman — *For* p.214-215
, and error
  Flesch — *Unusual* p.297
, and falseness
  See also **Truth, and lying**
  Seldes — *Great* p.916
, and fiction
  Flesch — *Unusual* p.297
, and love
  Baillie — *Diary* #317
, and lying
  Flesch — *Unusual* p.297-298
, and reality
  Adams — *New* p.173
, and religion
  Woods — *Religious* p.1009-1010
, and science
  Kauffman — *For* p.195
, and trust
  Kauffman — *For* p.215-216
, Appearance of
  Sheen — *Content.* p.127-129
, Certainty of
  Adams — *New* p.186
, Conflict of
  Woods — *Religious* p.1010-1011
, Definitions of
  Woods — *Religious* p.1007-1009
, in daily life
  Krishnamurti — *Think* p.54-55
, Merciless
  Book Proverbs p.138
, of being
  Fox — *Make* p.85, 91
, Power of
  Adams — *New* p.52
, Quest of
  Baillie — *Diary* #343
, Seeing
  Adams — *New* p.3
, to yourself
  Mandelbaum — *Choose* p.239-241
, Undisputed
  Adams — *New* p.54

TUBAS
  Prochnow — *Success.* #1075

TUBERS. *See* **Bulbs**

TUBS
  Kin — *Dictionary* p.261

TULIPS
  Peterson — *Art* p.161

TUNA
  Botkin — *Treasury* p.196

TUNNELS
  Flesch — *Unusual* p.299
  Peale — *Guideposts* p.274-277
  Redhead — *Living* p.34-41

TURKEY AND TURKS
  Curtis — *Practical* p.141
  Lockridge — *World's* #2787
  Simpson — *Contemp.* p.155

TURKEYS (fowl)
Botkin — *Treasury* p.674

TURKISH PROVERBS
Dirksen — *Quot.* #2138

"TURNABOUT"
Braude — *Speaker's* #1551-1552
Braude — *Stories* p.395-397
Speaker's Desk See index p.305

TURNING
Kin — *Dictionary* p.261
Prochnow — *Public* #1025, 2214, 2609

TURNIPS
Botkin — *Treasury* p.602-603

TWAIN, MARK. *See* **Clemens, Samuel L.** (and references to Harnsberger — *Mark*)

TWENTIETH CENTURY
Woods — *Religious* p.1011

TWENTY-ONE (age)
Peterson — *Art* p.42
Words Change p.122

TWENTY-SEVEN (age)
Flesch — *Unusual* p.299

TWILIGHT
See also **Evening; Sunset**
Alexander's Treasure. p.43, 212
Edwards — *Useful* p.667-668
Felleman — *Poems* p.395-406
Hudson — *5000* p.292
Kohn — *Through* p.97-99
Prochnow — *Success.* #2416

TWINS
Grizer — *Wit* p.479
Lytle — *Leaves* p.127
Prochnow — *Public* #535
Schermerhorn — *1500* p.378-379

TWO
Flesch — *Unusual* p.299
Kin — *Dictionary* p.261
Lytle — *Leaves* p.123

TWO-FACED. *See* **Hypocrisy**

TYPE AND TYPESETTERS
Botkin — *Treasury* p.550
New Joy p.118

TYPEWRITERS
Prochnow — *Public* #400

"TYPICAL"
Braude — *Stories* p.397
Prochnow — *Public* #1012
Prochnow — *Success.* #1109

TYRANTS AND TYRANNY
See also **Dictatorship; Oppression**
Auden — *Certain* p.369-371
Braude — *Source* #1769-1771
Braude — *Stories* p.397
Dirksen — *Quot.* #373, 438, 1108-1109, 1691, 1813, 1820, 2219, 2336
Edwards — *Useful* p.668
Evans — *Unto* p.17
Fogg — *1000* #364, 623, 774, 1105, 1113
Forbes — *Thoughts* p.15, 58, 67, 118, 202, 212, 225, 231, 316, 368, 390, 405
Hubbard — *Scrap* p.181
Hudson — *5000* p.292
Kennedy — *Reader's* #1152-1154
Kin — *Dictionary* p.261
Liddle — *Thoughts V* p.23, 31
Lockridge — *World's* #2732, 2739, 2911, 2919, 3417, 3425
Prochnow — *Success.* #2417
Seldes — *Great* p.936-938
Woods — *Religious* p.1011
, in Middle Ages
Kronenberger — *Animal* p.198-200

TYRE
New Topical p.281-282

U

UGANDA, AFRICA
Guideposts — *Faith* p.416-419

UGLINESS
Hudson — *5000* p.292-293
Kin — *Dictionary* p.262
Krishnamurti — *Think* p.49-50
Lockridge — *World's* #822, 824, 2604, 2653, 3210, 5006
Speaker's Desk #141, 323
White — *Job* p.143-145

ULCERS
Kin — *Dictionary* p.261

ULTIMATUM
See also **Decision; Determination**
Prochnow — *Public* #797

UMBRELLAS
Asimov — *Treasury* #77
Flesch — *Unusual* p.299
Irion — *Yes* p.104-106
Kin — *Dictionary* p.262
Prochnow — *Public* #318

"UN-ALTAR-ABLE BEAUS"
Safian — *Insults* p.198-200

UN-AMERICANISM
See also **Subversiveness**
Seldes — *Great* p.939

UNAWARENESS
See also **Ignorance; Unconcern**
Sheban — *Wisdom* no p.

UNBELIEF AND UNBELIEVERS
See also **Agnosticism; Atheism; "God is dead" movement; Skepticism;** etc.
Book Proverbs p.121
Carruthers — *Sparks* p.146-147
Dirksen — *Quot.* #1598-1600
Edwards — *Useful* p.668-669
Evans — *Unto* p.41-43
Flesch — *Unusual* p.299
Halverson — *Perspective* p.30
Lockridge — *World's* #1837
Lytle — *Leaves* p.69
New Topical p.282
Speaker's Desk #205, 215, 366, 953, 1125
Wallis — *Words* p.4, 68
Woods — *Religious* p.1011-1013
, Absurdity of
Webb — *Edge* p.74-93
, Types of
Liebman — *Peace* p.148-153

UNCERTAINTY
See also **Doubt; Indecision**
Asimov — *Treasury* #399
Dirksen — *Quot.* #1087
Edwards — *Useful* p.415, **669-670**
Evans — *Faith* p.3-4, 21, 155, 169-170, 201-202
Evans — *Thoughts I* p.12-14, **45**, 101, 112, 128-133, 159-160
Evans — *Thoughts II (Open Door)* p.53, 123-124
Evans — *Thoughts III (Open Road)* p.51, 126, 159
Evans — *Thoughts IV* **p.136**
Evans — *Unto* p.37
Flesch — *Unusual* p.183, 299
Forbes — *Thoughts* p.148, 467, 500
Kin — *Dictionary* p.171, 262
Kohn — *Adventures* p.84-89
Lockridge — *World's* #96
Maltz — *Creative* p.10-11, 89-90
Mandel — *Stories* p.259
New Joy p.227
Prochnow — *Public* #1870
Woods — *Religious* p.1013

"UNCLE REMUS" TALES
Botkin — *Treasury* p.436, 652-653, 661

"UNCLE SAM"
Botkin — *Treasury* p.278, 286, 358
Words — *Inspir.* p.134

UNCONCERN
Curtis — *New* p.66
Du Noüy — *Human* p.251-252
Edwards — *Useful* p.137
Flesch — *Unusual* p.59
Flint — *Graham* p.146
Krishnamurti — *Think* p.213-214
Phillips — *Choice* p.40, 44, 50, 160
Sheen — *Way* p.31-32
Woods — *Religious* p.234-235

UNCONSCIOUS MIND. *See* **Subconscious**

UNCONVENTIONALITY
Woods — *Religious* p.1014

"UNDERDOG"
Ideas p.406, 423-424

UNDERPRIVILEGED. *See* **Poverty**

UNDERSTANDING
See also **Help; Kindness; Sympathy;** etc.
Baillie — *Diary* #134, 292
Bartlett — *Discovery* p.27-28
Braude — *Source* #1772-1776
Braude — *Speaker's* **#1553-1554**
Braude — *Stories* p.398-399
Curtis — *Golden* p.147-149
Curtis — *Practical* p.3, 16-19
Detherage — *Sunrise* p.42-44, **71**, 141-144, 169
Dirksen — *Quot.* #83, 978, 1195, 1409, 1821
Droke — *Christian* p.563-566
Du Noüy — *Road* p.68-70
Edwards — *Useful* p.670
Evans — *Faith* p.16
Evans — *Quote* p.163-175
Evans — *This* p.31-32, 75-77
Evans — *Thoughts I* p.25, 46-49, 81, 107-108, 122

Evans — *Thoughts II (Open Door)* p.183-184
Evans — *Thoughts III (Open Road)* p.15-19, 29-30, 48, 65-67, 98, 110, 196
Evans — *Thoughts IV* p.167, 206, 209, 213-214
Evans — *Unto* p.8, 41
Flesch — *Unusual* p.45, 191, 300
Flint — *Graham* p.146
Forbes — *Thoughts* See index p.571
Fridy — *Meditat.* p.60
Fuller — *Epigrams* p.288
Garland — *Subject* p.324
Grizer — *Wit* p.479-480
Hadfield — *Delights* p.219-227
Harnsberger — *Mark* p.491
Hobe — *Tapestries* p.15, 39, 87
Hovey — *Treasury* p.279-280; *See also* index p.301
How To Live p.70, 489-492
Kauffman — *For* p.218-219
Kennedy — *Reader's* #1155-1156
Keys Happiness p.251, 476
Kin — *Dictionary* p.263
Kohn — *Pathways* p.49-53
Lockridge — *World's* See index p.584
Maltz — *Creative* p.76
Mandel — *Stories* p.259-260
Mandelbaum — *Choose* p.117-120
Montapert — *Distilled* p.329-330
Nichols — *New* p.114-115
Peterson — *Art* p.215
Porter — *Halo* p.99-103
Prochnow — *Public* #2728, 4317
Prochnow — *Success.* #245, 383, 647, 934, 958, 1406
Rau — *Act* p.74-85
Seldes — *Great* p.939-940
Sheen — *Content.* p.159-161
Speaker's Desk #324, 949; p.262
Wallis — *Treasure* p.79, 101, 124, 183, 227
Wallis — *Words* p.75, 179, 198
Wheelis — *Moralist* p.83, 114-115
Woods — *Religious* p.1014
Zobell — *Speaker's* p.145-148
, Delayed
Adams — *New* p.182
, Need of
Sherman — *Your* p.130-137

UNDERSTATEMENT
Botkin — *Anecdotes* p.90
Prochnow — *Public* #1168

UNDERTAKERS. *See* **Morticians**

UNEMPLOYMENT
Braude — *Source* #1777
Curtis — *Practical* p.327, 344
Kauffman — *For* p.220-221
Kin — *Dictionary* p.263
Prochnow — *Success.* #361
Woods — *Business.* p.256-257

UNESSENTIALS. *See* **"Little things"**

UNEXPECTEDNESS
See also **Surprise**
Evans — *Unto* p.118
Flesch — *Unusual* p.300-301
Fox — *Make* p.217
Manchee — *Secret* p.154-156
Pullar-Strecker — *Proverbs* #11

UNFAIRNESS. *See* **Injustice**

UNFAITHFULNESS
See also **Treachery**
Flint — *Graham* p.146
Kin — *Dictionary* p.264
Lockridge — *World's* #3927

UNFINISHED. *See* **Incompleteness**

UNFOLDMENT
Curtis — *Human* p.115-134

UNGAINLINESS. *See* **Awkwardness**

UNHAPPINESS
See also **Discontent; Grief; Misfortune;** etc.
Auden — *Certain* p.3-4, 104-105
Baillie — *Diary* #110
Braude — *Source* #1778
Edwards — *Useful* p.384, 670-671
Evans — *Thoughts II (Open Door)* p.65
Evans — *Thoughts IV* p.98-99
Flesch — *Unusual* p.168, 301
Flint — *Graham* p.70
Fogg — *1000* #261, 339, 558, 729, 737, 931
Forbes — *Thoughts* p.167, 234, 329, 388, 517
Fuller — *Thesaurus* #366-368
Grizer — *Wit* p.480
Henry — *5000* p.172-173
How To Live p.356
Lockridge — *World's* #2278, 2350, 3405
Montapert — *Distilled* p.330
Peale — *Guide* p.166-185
Prochnow — *Public* #849, 2199
Prochnow — *Success.* p.2092
Woods — *Religious* p.623, 1014

UNICORNS
Fox — *Make* p.99-100
Lindbergh — *Unicorn* p.49-57
New Topical p.282-283

UNIFORMITY
See also **Standardization**
Adams — *New* p.275
, Impossibility of
Book Proverbs p.124

UNIFORMS
Harral — *Feature* p.309

UNIMPORTANCE. *See* **Insignificance**

"UNIMPRESSED"
Speaker's Desk See index p.306

UNION. *See* **Unity**

UNIONS. *See* **Labor unions**

UNIQUENESS
See also **Individuals and individuality**
Keys Happiness p.258-260
Kohn — *Pathways* p.41-44
Lair — *Baby* p.36
Mandelbaum — *Choose* p.235-238

UNITARIANS
Seldes — *Great* p.944
Woods — *Religious* p.1014-1015

UNITED NATIONS
Franke — *Buckley* p.300-302
Giniger — *Compact* p.268-269
Grizer — *Wit* p.481
Hovey — *Treasury* #1327, 1609
Ideas p.424-426
Prochnow — *Success.* #243
Seldes — *Great* p.944
Simpson — *Contemp.* p.110-122
Simpson — *'54* p.99, 254, 366
, Building of
Guideposts — *Faith* p.350-353
Peale — *Guideposts* p.274-275
, International relations in
Droke — *Christian* p.566-567
, Location of
Guideposts — *Faith* p.351-352

UNITED STATES
See also **America;** names of states
Forbes — *Thoughts* p.106, 113, 129, 177, 226, 278, 297, 376, 396
Fuller — *Thesaurus* #2031-2032
Hovey — *Treasury See* index p.301
Prochnow — *Speaker's* p.314-315
, as leader
Dirksen — *Quot.* #34, 36, 2372, 2381
, Congress
See also **Congressmen; Senate and senators-U.S.**
Botkin — *Treasury* p.4, 26-27, 276-277, 283-285, 320, 342, 408
Copeland — *World's* p.735
Curtis — *Practical* p.302, 306
Dirksen — *Quot.* #110; *See also* index p.261
Flesch — *Unusual* p.46
Franke — *Buckley* p.44
Fuller — *Thesaurus* #1941-1948
Henry — *5000* p.45
Lockridge — *World's* #5791
Prochnow — *Public* #358
Prochnow — *Speaker's* p.73
Prochnow — *Success.* #775, 1401, 1638
Schermerhorn — *1500* p.89-90
Seldes — *Great* p.211-213
, Constitution. See **Constitution—U.S.**
, Department of State
Prochnow — *Success.* #824
, Government
See also **Government; U.S., Congress**
Woods — *Business.* p.111-113
, History
Dirksen — *Quot.* #26, 34, 522, 2365
, French and Indian War
Botkin — *Anecdotes* p.135
, Revolution
Botkin — *Anecdotes* p.58, 138
Curtis — *Practical* p.275
Fogg — *1000 See* index p.897
, War of 1812
Botkin — *Anecdotes* p.145
, Civil War
Botkin — *Anecdotes* p.21-22, 78, 101, 147-148, 159, 167
Botkin — *Treasury* p.71-74, 571
Fogg — *1000 See* index p.881
Fuller — *Thesaurus* #2326-2329
Prochnow — *Success.* #114-115, 119, 133, 729
, World War I
Asimov — *Treasury* #154
Baillie — *Diary* #34
Botkin — *Anecdotes* p.11

Copeland — *World's See* index p.737
Curtis — *Practical* p.190-193
Fogg — *1000* p.901
, *World War II*
Asimov — *Treasury* #369
Botkin — *Anecdotes* p.14, 32, 163, 277-279
Copeland — *World's See* index p.737
Wheelis — *Moralist* p.12, 69, 91
, *President*
Humes — *Instant* p.46-47

UNITY
Dirksen — *Quot.* p.653, 715, 2356
Edwards — *Useful* p.671
Flint — *Graham* p.146-147
Forbes — *Thoughts* p.3, 6, 18, 30, 57, 141, 173, 222, 238, 261, 405, 495
Grizer — *Wit* p.481
Hobe — *Tapestries* p.27, 85, 88
Hudson — *5000* p.293
Humes — *Instant* #1076-1078
Hunter — *Gems* p.113-114
Kennedy — *Reader's* #1157-1159
Kin — *Dictionary* p.264
Knight's Illus. p.338-339
Lytle — *Leaves* p.27
Mandel — *Stories* p.260
New Joy p.84-85
Phillips — *Choice* p.5, 163
Prochnow — *Public* #2512
Seldes — *Great* p.946
Wallis — *Treasure* p.60-61
Woods — *Business.* p.263
Woods — *Religious* p.172, 1015-1022
, *of body, mind, and spirit*
Holmes — *Design* p.42-43, 72-73
, *of mankind*
Woods — *Religious* p.1022-1023
, *True*
Woods — *Wellsprings* p.48-49

UNIVERSAL LANGUAGE. *See* **Language, Universal**

UNIVERSALITY
Applegarth — *Heir.* p.177
Flesch — *Unusual* p.301
Kin — *Dictionary* p.264
Lytle — *Leaves* p.188
Woods — *Religious* p.1023

UNIVERSE
See also **Creation; Earth; God; Infinity; Planets;** etc.
Baillie — *Diary* #130
Bartlett — *Discovery* p.106-107
Dirksen — *Quot.* #386, 779, 2046
Du Noüy — *Human* p.3-6, 9, 14-16, 38, 41-42, 45, 160, 189
Du Noüy — *Road See* index p.254
Esteve — *Experience* p.151-155
Flesch — *Unusual* p.301
Forbes — *Thoughts* p.55, 81, 146, 181, 420, 438, 499-500, 519
Garland — *Subject* p.325-326
Harnsberger — *Mark* p.492
Hobe — *Tapestries* p.64
Holmes — *Design See* index p.236
Ideas p.147-148
Kennedy — *Reader's* #1160-1164
Kin — *Dictionary* p.264
Kohn — *Adventures* p.125-126
Kohn — *Best* p.17-19
Lockridge — *World's* #2967, 2971, 3109, 3797, 4807
New Joy p.247
Woods — *Religious* p.1023-1028
, *and God*
Nichols — *Third* p.155-156
Woods — *Religious* p.1026-1028
, *Beauty in*
Curtis — *Daily* p.148
, *Rhythm of*
Curtis — *Practical* p.148
, *Understanding of*
Curtis — *Golden* p.24-35
, *Unified*
Kohn — *Adventures* p.42-45
, *Wonders of*
Keller — *Open* p.70

UNIVERSITIES AND COLLEGES
See also names of universities and colleges
Botkin — *Anecdotes* p.130, 170
Braude — *Source* #370-373
Braude — *Speaker's* #229-236
Braude — *Stories* p.66-69
Copeland — *World's* p.573-576, 592-595, 604-606, 673-675, 702-707
Dirksen — *Quot.* #241, 260, 276, 1141
Flesch — *Unusual* p.301
Forbes — *Thoughts* p.359
Franke — *Buckley* p.36-38
Fuller — *Thesaurus* p.175-179
Grizer — *Wit* p.481
Harral — *Feature* p.126, 309-315
Hovey — *Treasury* p.112-113, 280-281; #21, 38, 237, 309-310, 353, 372, 567-570, 710, 843, 853, 1096, 1308, 1456-1457, 1636, 1759, 1802-1803

Humes — *Instant* #1079-1092
Kennedy — *Reader's* #165-168
Modern Eloquence (14) p.111-120
Montapert — *Distilled* p.66
Prochnow — *Public* #249, 387, 944, 1192, 1476, 1481, 1647, 1938, 4239, 4420
Prochnow — *Speaker's* p.67-68, 315
Prochnow — *Success.* #234, 321, 752-753, 863, 984, 1046, 1435, 1476
Schermerhorn — *1500* p.81-84
Seldes — *Great* p.187
Sheen — *Thoughts* p.139-141
Wallis — *Words* p.145
Weisfeld — *Pulpit* p.110-133
Woods — *Content.* p.177
Woods — *Religious* p.1028
, Alumni of
Franke — *Buckley* p.5
Prochnow — *Success.* #595
, and democracy
Hubbard — *Scrap* p.21
, and coeds
Prochnow — *Public* #270, 387, 930, 1274
, and curriculum
Nizer — *Thinking* p.81-82
, and deans
Asimov — *Treasury* #407
, Militancy in
Guideposts — *Faith* p.188-191

UNKINDNESS
See also **Cruelty; Injury; Insult;** etc.
Book Proverbs p.116
Edwards — *Useful* p.671
Lytle — *Leaves* p.32

UNKNOWN
Adams — *New* p.348-349
Dirksen — *Quot.* #1111
Flesch — *Unusual* p.301-302
Guideposts — *Faith* p.479-482
Kohn — *Pathways* p.193-196
Lytle — *Leaves* p.105
Mandel — *Stories* p.260-261
Prochnow — *Success.* #1458, 2418
Sheban — *Wisdom* no p.
Woods — *Religious* p.1028
Speaker's Desk #983

UNPOPULARITY
Kohn — *Touch* p.100-105

UNPREDICTABILITY
Flesch — *Unusual* p.302

UNPREPAREDNESS
Speaker's Desk #1

"UNPROVABLE"
Adams — *New* p.172

UNREALISM
Menninger — *Blue.* p.16

UNREASONABILITY
Flesch — *Unusual* p.302

UNREST
See also **Discontent; Restlessness**
Flesch — *Unusual* p.302
Flint — *Graham* p.147
Kin — *Dictionary* p.264
Peterson — *Art* p.210

UNRIGHTEOUSNESS
Woods — *Religious* p.1028

UNSCRUPULOUSNESS
Prochnow — *Public* #2435

UNSEEN. *See* **Unknown**

UNSELFISHNESS
See also **Generosity; Gifts and giving**
Baillie — *Diary* #237
Braude — *Stories* p.343-344
Dirksen — *Quot.* #1601-1602
Forbes — *Thoughts* p.9, 170, 359, 486
Garland — *Subject* p.327
Kahn — *Lessons* p.201-206
Keller — *You* p.51, 55-58
Keys Happiness p.100-102
Knight's Illus. p.293-295
Liddle — *Thought I, II, III* p.62-63
Lytle — *Leaves* p.117
Mandel — *Stories* p.231-232
Mandelbaum — *Choose* p.250-253
Menninger — *Blue.* p.32-35, 39
Peterson — *Art* p.158
Price — *Wider* p.229-237
Prochnow — *Public* #406
Voss — *Quotations* p.225-226
Wallis — *Treasure* p.108
Wallis — *Words* p.204
Watson — *Light* p.223-225
Welk — *Guide.* p.152-153
Wheelis — *Moralist* p.47
Woods — *Religious* p.912-914
Words — *Inspir.* p.80-81

UNSETTLED. *See* **Discontent; Restlessness; Unrest**

UNTALENTED
Hoffer — *Reflect.* p.30-31, 49-50, 63

UNTOUCHABILITY
Evans — *This* p.41-42

UPRIGHTNESS. *See* **Honesty; Honor; Steadfastness**

"UPS AND DOWNS"
Fun Fare p.197
Holman — *Psych.* p.88-102
Reader's — *Getting* p.117-121

"UPSTARTS"
Kronenberger — *Animal* p.315-317

"UPWARD"
Lytle — *Leaves* p.37, 39, 184

URBAN AFFAIRS. *See* **Cities**

URGENCY. *See* **Haste**

URIM AND THUMMIN
New Topical p.234

USE
Flesch — *Unusual* p.302
Kin — *Dictionary* p.265
Lytle — *Leaves* p.115, 190
Mandel — *Stories* p.261
Sheen — *Thoughts* p.99-100

USEFULNESS
See also **Help; Merit;** etc.
Applegarth — *Heir.* p.141-142
Edwards — *Useful* p.671-673
Evans — *Unto* p.13, 115
Flesch — *Unusual* p.302
Forbes — *Thoughts* p.9, 47, 164, 169-170, 190, 368, 393, 463, 486
Grizer — *Wit* p.481-482
Liddle — *Thought I, II, III* p.62, 73, 79, 145, 160
Lytle — *Leaves* p.148
Mandel — *Stories* p.261-262
Menninger — *Blue.* p.92
Montapert — *Distilled* p.330-331
Prochnow — *Success.* #1250
Speaker's Desk p.262-263
Tanksley — *Friend* p.64
Wallis — *Words* p.51
Woods — *Religious* p.1029

USELESSNESS
Flesch — *Unusual* p.302-303
Lockridge — *World's* #3561
Woods — *Religious* p.1028

USHERS
Harral — *Feature* p.316
Prochnow — *Public* #4, 105
Prochnow — *Success.* #896

USURY AND USURERS
Edwards — *Useful* p.673
Lockridge — *World's* #4190
New Topical p.284
Seldes — *Great* p.946
Woods — *Religious* p.1028-1029

UTAH
Botkin — *Anecdotes* p.174

UTE INDIANS
Botkin — *Anecdotes* p.174

UTILITARIANISM. *See* **Usefulness**

UTOPIAS
Bach — *Make* p.106-117
Curtis — *Practical* p.273-274
Forbes — *Thoughts* p.255, 463, 505
Ideas p.430-432
Keys Happiness p.232-236
Lockridge — *World's* #900
Lytle — *Leaves* p.39
Prochnow — *Public* #1390, 2377
Seldes — *Great* p.946
Woods — *Religious* p.1029

V

"V.I.P.'s"
Walters — *How* p.39-58

VACATIONS
See also **Travel**
Applegarth — *Heir.* p.150
Braude — *Source* #1779-1781
Braude — *Speaker's* #1555-1560
Cerf — *Laugh* p.218-223
Grizer — *Wit* p.482-483
Harral — *Feature* p.316-317
Peterson — *Art* p.202
Prochnow — *Public* See index p.514
Prochnow — *Success.* #313, 376, 693, 721, 939, 997, 1225
Wallis — *Words* p.174
Woods — *Content.* p.65
, Daily
Peterson — *Art* p.255
, Memories from
Peterson — *Art* p.206

, *Need for*
Sheen — *Thoughts* p.47-48

VACILLATION. *See* **Indecision**

VACUUM CLEANERS
Prochnow — *Public* #206, 655

VAGABONDS. *See* **Wandering and wanderers**

VAGRANTS
See also **Tramps**
Edwards — *Useful* p.673
Kin — *Dictionary* p.266
Lytle — *Leaves* p.76
Prochnow — *Public* #2221

VAGUENESS. *See* **Indecision; Weakness**

VALENTINES
Edwards — *Useful* p.673
Hadfield — *Love* p.56-57
Harral — *Feature* p.317
Words — *Inspir.* p.54

VALETS (15th century)
Kronenberger — *Animal* p.193-194

VALLEYS
Clark — *Windows* p.48-49
New Topical p.285-286

VALOR. *See* **Chivalry; Courage; Heroes and heroism**

VALUES
See also **Ideals and idealism**
Bartlett — *Discovery* p.147-148
Braude — *Source* #1782-1783
Braude — *Speaker's* #1561-1562
Droke — *Christian* p.568-575
Emmons — *Mature* p.12-14, 146, 151, 153, 158
Evans — *Quote* p.177-186
Evans — *Unto* p.6, 15, 18, 37-38, 71, 84, 115, 121
Forbes — *Thoughts* p.241, 322, 354, 376, 397, 404, 442, 464, 467, 469, 514, 517
Fuller — *Epigrams* p.289
Garland — *Subject* p.328-329
Grizer — *Wit* p.483-484
Harnsberger — *Mark* p.493-494
Hovey — *Treasury See* index p.301
Humes — *Instant* #1097
Johnson — *Bedside* p.313
Kin — *Dictionary* p.267
Lair — *Baby* p.94-95
Lockridge — *World's* #256, 381, 404, 415, 538, 944, 990, 1510, 2018, 2430
Lytle — *Leaves* p.82, 104
Mandel — *Stories* p.262-266
Montapert — *Distilled* p.331
Peterson — *Art* p.357
Phillips — *Choice* p.292, 405
Seldes — *Great* p.946-947
Sheen — *Way* p.106-108
Speaker's Desk #524, 538; *See also* index p.306
Strait — *Speaker's* p.175-178
Wheelis — *Moralist* p.8, 10, 29-30
Woods — *Business.* p.263-264
Woods — *Religious* p.1029-1031
Zobell — *Speaker's* p.148-153
, *American*
Dirksen — *Quot.* #510, 625
, *Confusion in*
Adams — *New* p.317
, *Face*
Evans — *Unto* p.90
, *False estimates of*
Dirksen — *Quot.* #2304
, *Relative*
Nichols — *Third* p.45-46
, *Spiritual*
Woods — *Religious* p.1030-1031
, *Teenager*
Ginott — *Between* p.150, 152-176, 212, 231

VAMPIRES
Botkin — *Treasury* p.688

VANDALISM
Woods — *Religious* p.1031

VANITY
See also **Boasting; Conceit**
Adams — *New* p.153
Braude — *Source* #1784
Braude — *Stories* p.399
Dirksen — *Quot.* #7491, 2339
Edwards — *Useful* p.673-677
Evans — *Unto* p.25, 31, 50, 89
Flesch — *Unusual* p.303
Fogg — *1000 See* index p.900
Forbes — *Thoughts* p.21, 162, 201, 347
Fuller — *Epigrams* p.289-290
Fuller — *Thesaurus* #606-628
Garland — *Subject* p.329
Grizer — *Wit* p.484
Harnsberger — *Mark* p.494
Hudson — *5000* p.293-294
Kennedy — *Reader's* #1165-1166
Kin — *Dictionary* p.266-267
Lockridge — *World's See* index p.584
New Topical p.286

Prochnow — *Public* #1196, 2515-2516, 3818-3821, 4273
Prochnow — *Speaker's* p.315
Prochnow — *Success.* #2420
Reader's — *20th* p.84
Speaker's Desk p.263-265; #97, 230, 245, 251, 253, 283, 521, 547, 567, 586, 668, 691, 719, 963
Weisfeld — *Pulpit* p.24-25, 34-35
Wheelis — *Moralist* p.14
Woods — *Content.* p.36
Woods — *Religious* p.1031-1032

VARIETY
Albert — *Stop* p.66-68
Bartlett — *Discovery* p.31-32, 82-83
Braude — *Stories* p.399
Edwards — *Useful* p.677
Harnsberger — *Mark* p.494-495
Hudson — *5000* p.294
Kin — *Dictionary* p.267
Liddle — *Thought I, II, III* p.140, 154
Lockridge — *World's* #3601
Prochnow — *Public* #4288
Prochnow — *Success.* #412, 1319
Wallis — *Treasure* p.79, 149, 174, 222
Wallis — *Words* p.81

VEGETABLES
Botkin — *Anecdotes* p.90
Hadfield — *Delights* p.126
Kin — *Dictionary* p.267

VEGETARIANISM
See also **Diet**
Edwards — *Useful* p.734
Flesch — *Unusual* p.303
Ideas p.434-436
Weisfeld — *Pulpit* p.29-30

VEGETATION
Du Noüy — *Human* p.63-66, 77-78

VEILS
New Topical p.284-285

VENDING MACHINES
Harral — *Feature* p.317

VENERATION. *See* **Reverence; Worship**

VENGEANCE. *See* **Revenge**

VENTRILOQUISM
Botkin — *Anecdotes* p.247, 355, 269
Harral — *Feature* p.317

VENUS (goddess)
Curtis — *Practical* p.493

VENUS (planet)
Curtis — *Practical* p.220

VERACITY. *See* **Honesty; Truth**

VERBOSITY. *See* **Loquacity; Talk**

VERBS
Lytle — *Leaves* p.145
Wallis — *Words* p.72

VERITY. *See* **Truth**

VERMONT
Botkin — *Anecdotes* p.4-5, 33-34, 55, 92, 138-139, 153, 190, 203, 211
Botkin — *Treasury* p.825-828
Seldes — *Great* p.947

VERSATILITY
Curtis — *Practical* p.81
Fogg — *1000* #11, 291, 440, 445, 508, 526
Lytle — *Leaves* p.142
Prochnow — *Speaker's* p.315

VESPERS
Baillie — *Diary* #4
Lytle — *Leaves* p.96

VETERANS
Harral — *Feature* p.317-318
, Disabled
Guideposts — *Faith* p.239-240
Peale — *Guideposts* p.185-189

VETERANS DAY
Braude — *Source* #134-135
Evans — *Unto* p.14

VETERINARIANS
Harral — *Feature* p.318
Prochnow — *Public* #940

VEXATION. *See* **Anger**

VIBRATIONS
Peterson — *Art* p.143
White — *Job* p.90, 101, 136, 191

VICE
See also **Sin; Wickedness;** etc.
Bartlett — *Discovery* p.136-137
Book Proverbs p.132
Dirksen — *Quot.* #2223
Edwards — *Useful* p.678-681

Evans — *Thoughts III (Open Road)* p.76, 89
Evans — *Unto* p.32, 63
Flesch — *Unusual* p.303-304
Forbes — *Thoughts* p.243, 361, 373, 430, 496, 512
Fuller — *Epigrams* p.290-291
Harnsberger — *Mark* p.495
Hudson — *5000* p.294
Johnson — *Bedside* p.77, 95, 279-280, 322
Kin — *Dictionary* p.268
Liddle — *Thought I, II, III* p.140, 154
Lockridge — *World's See* index p.584
Prochnow — *Public* #2225, 4241-4242
Seldes — *Great* p.947-948
Speaker's Desk p.265-267
Woods — *Religious* p.1032

VICE-PRESIDENTS
Dirksen — *Quot.* #59, 109, 1825
Prochnow — *Public* #1835-1836
Prochnow — *Speaker's* p.316
Seldes — *Great* p.948

VICISSITUDES. *See* **Adversity; Trouble**; etc.

VICTORY
See also **Conquerors and conquest; Success**
Adams — *New* p.389
Dirksen — *Quot.* #504, 511, 805, 837, 1112-1113, 1643, 1826, 2224-2225, 2326
Edwards — *Useful* p.681
Evans — *This* p.151-152
Flesch — *Unusual* p.304
Flint — *Graham* p.148
Forbes — *Thoughts* p.139, 178, 450, 474, 482, 508; *See also* index p.572
Fox — *Make* p.194
Hobe — *Tapestries* p.138
Hovey — *Treasury* #16, 75, 281, 610, 933, 972, 1042, 1518; *See also* index p.301
Hudson — *5000* p.294-295
Hulme — *Living* p.146-158
Kennedy — *Reader's* #1167-1171
Kin — *Dictionary* p.268-269
Knight's Illus. p.340-341
Knight's Treas. p.422-423
Lytle — *Leaves* p.38
Maltz — *Creative* p.200-201
Mandel — *Stories* p.267-268
Montapert — *Distilled* p.331-332, 337
Prochnow — *Public* #103, 708, 2322
Prochnow — *Success.* #2422-2424
Seldes — *Great* p.948-949
Wallis — *Words* p.58, 182
Woods — *Religious* p.1033
, Technique for
Peale — *Guideposts* p.7-10

VIENNA
Asimov — *Treasury* #457

VIETNAM WAR
Dirksen — *Quot.* #34
Franke — *Buckley* p.304-312
Kauffman — *For* p.250-252
Simpson — *Contemp.* p.155-156

VIEWS
Adams — *New* p.107
Braude — *Source* #1292-1295
Braude — *Speaker's* #1003-1023
Braude — *Stories* p.287-292
Grizer — *Wit* p.484-485
Lytle — *Leaves* p.9, 139, 148, 151
Mandel — *Stories* p.202-203, 268
Prochnow — *Public* #589

VIGILANCE
See also **Alertness; Attention; Caution; Watchmen**; etc.
Baillie — *Diary* #161
Braude — *Source* #1785
Dirksen — *Quot.* #1603-1605, 2058
Edwards — *Useful* p.681, 692
Evans — *Unto* p.58
Kin — *Dictionary* p.269, 273
New Topical p.291-292
Woods — *Religious* p.1033

VIGOR. *See* **Energy; Strength; Vivacity**; etc.

VILLAGES. *See* **Towns**

VILLAINY. *See* **Wickedness**

VINDICTIVENESS. *See* **Malice; Revenge**

VINEGAR
Kin — *Dictionary* p.269

VINES AND VINEYARDS
Clark — *Windows* p.129
New Topical p.286-288

VIOLENCE
See also **Combat; Revolution; War**
Edwards — *Useful* p.682
Evans — *Unto* p.28
Forbes — *Thoughts* p.8-9, 105, 141, 212, 304, 365

Grizer — *Wit* p.485
Holmes — *I've* p.66-67
Humes — *Instant* #1098-1109
Huxley — *You See* index p.288
Kauffman — *For* p.221-223
Kin — *Dictionary* p.269
Lair — *Baby* p.38
Lockridge — *World's* #388, 395, 1581, 4372
Prochnow — *Public* #2360
Seldes — *Great* p.949-950
Wheelis — *Moralist* p.34-35, 115, 141, 147
Woods — *Religious* p.1033-1034

VIOLETS
Applegarth — *Heir.* p.102
Kohn — *Touch* p.140-141

VIOLINISTS AND VIOLINS
Botkin — *Anecdotes* p.227
Botkin — *Treasury* p.321, 346, 727, 803
Flesch — *Unusual* p.89
Kin — *Dictionary* p.93
Peale — *Guideposts* p.67-70
Prochnow — *Speaker's* p.316
Unlimited Power p.286-289

VIPERS. *See* **Serpents; Snakes**

VIRGIL
Lockridge — *World's* #4411

VIRGIN MARY. *See* **Mary, Virgin**

VIRGINIA
Botkin — *Anecdotes* p.16, 24, 31, 50, 64, 117, 141, 200, 220, 227, 302
Botkin — *Treasury* p.157-158, 560, 821n, 881, 890, 905

VIRGINIA REEL
Botkin — *Treasury* p.809

VIRTUES
See also **Character; Chastity; Excellence; Good; Integrity; Merit; Morality and morals; Purity**
Adams — *New* p.410
Applegarth — *Heir.* p.44
Bartlett — *Discovery* p.136-137
Book Proverbs p.132
Braude — *Source* #1786-1787
Braude — *Stories* p.400
Detherage — *Sunrise* p.35, 128, 189
Dirksen — *Quot.* #159, 224-225, 313, 422, 898, 1053, 1114, 2355
Droke — *Christian* p.575-576
Edwards — *Useful* p.682-686, 734
Evans — *Quote* p.177-186
Evans — *Thoughts I* p.27
Evans — *Thoughts III (Open Road)* p.80, 108, 130, 202
Evans — *Thoughts IV* p.94, 104, 124
Evans — *Unto* p.32, 51, 63, 70, 85
Flesch — *Unusual* p.304-305
Fogg — *1000* #555, 666, 766, 817, 872, 1047, 1095, 1130
Forbes — *Thoughts See* index p.572
Fuller — *Epigrams* p.292-294
Garland — *Subject* p.321
Grizer — *Wit* p.485-486
Harnsberger — *Mark* p.495-496
Hobe — *Tapestries* p.169
Hovey — *Treasury* p.281; #646, 676, 873, 992, 1174, 1177, 1321
Hudson — *5000* p.295-296
Johnson — *Bedside* p.76, 91, 128, 198, 247, 250-251, 279, 302, 322, 330
Kennedy — *Reader's* #1172-1173
Kin — *Dictionary* p.270
Liddle — *Thought I, II, III* p.6, 14, 18, 23, 35, 40, 46, 50, 120, 160
Liddle — *Thought IV* p.11, 15-16
Liddle — *Thought V* p.32, 34, 43
Lockridge — *World's See* index p.584
Lytle — *Leaves* p.29-30, 43, 140
Menninger — *Blue.* p.84
Montapert — *Distilled* p.332
Nichols — *New* p.91-120
Peterson — *Art* p.35
Prochnow — *Public* #2227, 2523, 2729, 3824-3829, 4243-4244
Prochnow — *Speaker's* p.316-317
Seldes — *Great* p.950-951
Speaker's Desk p.267-269
Voss — *Quotations* p.238-239
Wallis — *Treasure* p.130, 203
Wheelis — *Moralist* p.33-34, 74
Woods — *Religious* p.1035-1038

, Precepts of
Words — *Inspir.* p.32
, Seven cardinal
McCracken — *What* p.51-94

VISION
See also **Eyes and eyesight; Ideals and idealism; Imagination;** etc.
Bartlett — *Discovery* p.55
Braude — *Stories* p.400-401
Clark — *Windows* p.36-37
Detherage — *Sunrise* p.20, 37, 47, 90
Droke — *Christian* p.477-583
Forbes — *Thoughts* p.14, 44, 109, 134, 147, 174, 204, 228, 398, 411, 420, 487
Fox — *Make* p.196

Giniger — *Compact* p.166-170
Grizer — *Wit* p.486
Guideposts — *Faith* p.478-482
Harral — *Feature* p.318-319
Hobe — *Tapestries* p.67
Hovey — *Treasury* p.281-283; #88, 490, 989, 1049, 1154, 1808-1833
Hudson — *5000* p.296
Humes — *Instant* #1110-1120
Kin — *Dictionary* p.270
Knight's Illus. p.341-343
Knight's Treas. p.423-427
Lockridge — *World's* #1141
Lytle — *Leaves* p.36
Modern Eloquence (14) p.427
Montapert — *Distilled* p.332-333
New Topical p.288
Prochnow — *Speaker's* p.317
Prochnow — *Success.* #2425-2426
Unlimited Power p.112-117, 139-143
Voss — *Quotations* p.240-241
Wallis — *Words* p.26, 61-62, 72, 124, 131
Woods — *Content. See* index p.381
Woods — *Religious* p.45, 1038-1039

VISITORS AND VISITING
See also **Guests; Hospitality**
Edwards — *Useful* p.686
Hobe — *Tapestries* p.36
Keys Happiness p.251
Kin — *Dictionary* p.270
Mandel — *Stories* p.268-269
Prochnow — *Public* #6
Prochnow — *Success.* #1256

VITAMINS
Flesch — *Unusual* p.305

VIVACITY
See also **Action; Cheerfulness; Energy; Enthusiasm**; etc.
Curtis — *Practical* p.240-241
Edwards — *Useful* p.686
Ideas p.437-438, 455
Kin — *Dictionary* p.271
Kohn — *Thoughts* p.91-96
Lockridge — *World's* #3471
Lytle — *Leaves* p.186
Maltz — *Creative* p.45-47
Mandel — *Stories* p.7
Unlimited Power p.153-156

VIVISECTION
Curtis — *Practical* p.72

VOCABULARY
See also **Words**
Braude — *Speaker's* #1566-1567
Flesch — *Unusual* p.306
Harnsberger — *Mark* p.496-497
Harral — *Feature* p.319
Keller — *Open* p.81
Montapert — *Distilled* p.333
Prochnow — *Public* #1375, 1929
Prochnow — *Success.* #2427

VOCATIONS. *See* **Occupations; Professions**

VOICE
See also **Singing; Sound; Speech**
Adams — *New* p.415
Alexander's Treasure. p.84
Applegarth — *Heir.* p.175
Evans — *This* p.96-97, 123-124
Garland — *Subject* p.332
Hadfield — *Delights* p.50
Harnsberger — *Mark* p.497-498
Hovey — *Treasury* #75, 300, 355, 366, 385, 424, 641, 823, 870, 1140, 1230, 1360, 1683
Hudson — *5000* p.296
Keys Happiness p.169-171
Kin — *Dictionary* p.271
Montapert — *Distilled* p.334
Nizer — *Thinking* p.90, 129, 132
Prochnow — *Public* #718, 2157, 2340, 2342, 2456, 2480, 3830
Prochnow — *Success.* #352, 403, 2428-2431
Rau — *Act* p.109-115
Wallis — *Words* p.30, 224
, *"Cartoon"*
Unlimited Power p.144-147
, *Lack of*
Lytle — *Leaves* p.142, 157
Peale — *Guideposts* p.203-206

"VOICE OF AMERICA"
Peale — *Guideposts* p.305-309

VOLCANOES
Harnsberger — *Mark* p.498

VOLITION. *See* **Will**

VOLTAIRE, FRANÇOIS
Adams — *New* p.41
Seldes — *Great* p.951

VOODOO
Bach — *Make* p.3-6

VOTES AND VOTING
See also **Elections; Politics and politicians**
Braude — *Source* #1788-1790
Dirksen — *Quot.* #56, 1666, 1674, 1827, 2367
Flesch — *Unusual* p.74

Franke — *Buckley* p.314
Guideposts — *Faith* p.334-336
Harnsberger — *Mark* p.498-499
Harral — *Feature* p.319
Kin — *Dictionary* p.271
Liddle — *Thought I, II, III* p.25
Prochnow — *Public* #1205
Prochnow — *Success.* #971, 1156
Seldes — *Great* p.68, 951-952
Woods — *Religious* p.1040

VOWELS
New Joy p.221

VOWS
See also **Oaths; Promise; Weddings**
Edwards — *Useful* p.687
Flesch — *Unusual* p.306
Kin — *Dictionary* p.271
Lockridge — *World's* #2066
New Topical p.288-289
Woods — *Religious* p.1040

VOYAGERS AND VOYAGES
Auden — *Certain* p.376-382
Evans — *Thoughts I* p.130-131
Wallis — *Treasure* p.161-162

VULGARITY
See also **Profanity**
Edwards — *Useful* p.687
Evans — *Faith* p.69-70
Fuller — *Epigrams* p.294-295
Kin — *Dictionary* p.271-272
Lockridge — *World's* #925, 1709, 5799
Woods — *Religious* p.1040

VULNERABILITY
See also **Susceptibility**
Braude — *Source* #1791
Prochnow — *Public* #2276

W

W.C.T.U.
Harral — *Feature* p.319

WAFFLES
Prochnow — *Public* #685

WAGERS. *See* **Gamblers and gambling**

WAGES
See also **Salaries**
Braude — *Speaker's* #1568-1570
Flesch — *Unusual* p.205, 306
Forbes p.211, 214, 246, 335, 362-363, 381, 389, 394, 442, 473, 477, 487
Grizer — *Wit* p.486-487
Harnsberger — *Mark* p.500
Hudson — *5000* p.296-297
Kin — *Dictionary* p.187
Lytle — *Leaves* p.168, 186
Montapert — *Distilled* p.270-271
New Joy p.88-89
Prochnow — *Public* #752, 939, 1156, 1244, 1358, 2666
Prochnow — *Speaker's* p.318
Prochnow — *Success.* #312, 882
Seldes — *Great* p.952-953
Woods — *Business.* p.264-268
Woods — *Religious* p.1040-1041
, Raises in
Grizer — *Wit* p.379
Prochnow — *Public* #952
Prochnow — *Success.* #923

WAGON INSCRIPTIONS
Botkin — *Treasury* p.282

WAITERS AND WAITRESSES
See also **Restaurants**
Fuller — *Thesaurus* #2306-2308
Harral — *Feature* p.319
Prochnow — *Public See* index p.514
Prochnow — *Success.* #915, 1121

WAITING
See also **Delay; Patience**
Adams — *New* p.213
Alexander's Treasure. p.1, 333
Edwards — *Useful* p.688
Emmons — *Mature* p.37
Evans — *Thoughts I* p.13, 17-18, 81-82, 108-110
Flesch — *Unusual* p.306
Forbes — *Thoughts* p.98, 388, 397, 416
Halverson — *Perspective* p.21
Kennedy — *Reader's* #1174
Kin — *Dictionary* p.272
Kohn — *Touch* p.173-178
Lytle — *Leaves* p.47, 67
Wallis — *Words* p.182
, Power of
Kohn — *Thoughts* p.107-110
Kohn — *Touch* p.106-109

WALES. *See* **Welsh**

WALKING
Applegarth — *Heir.* p.278
Clark — *Windows* p.122-123
Dirksen — *Quot.* #135, 1115
Edwards — *Useful* p.688
Flesch — *Unusual* p.306
Garland — *Subject* p.333
Guideposts — *Faith* p.180-184
Hadfield — *Delights* p.94
Hobe — *Tapestries* p.109
Kin — *Dictionary* p.272
Kohn — *Best* p.13-16
Liddle — *Thought I, II, III* p.55
Lockridge — *World's* #624
Lytle — *Leaves* p.42
Peterson — *Art* p.211
Peterson — *New* p.24-25
Prochnow — *Public* #95, 1003, 1269, 2133, 2230, 2425, 3875
Prochnow — *Success.* #1431
Reader's — *Getting* p.122-124
Unlimited Power p.268-272
Woods — *Content.* p.62, 65, 67, 187, 201, 210, 226

, in woods
Peterson — *Art* p.192
, Joys of
Hubbard — *Scrap* p.65

WALL STREET
Botkin — *Anecdotes* p.54, 62
Cerf — *Laugh* p.403-408
Grizer — *Wit* p.487
Seldes — *Great* p.953

WALLACE, WILLIAM A. ("Big-foot")
Botkin — *Treasury* p.133, 157-174, 323, 560

WALLS
Kennedy — *Fresh* p.80-88
Kin — *Dictionary* p.272
New Topical p.289-290
Wallis — *Treasure* p.102
Wallis — *Words* p.150

, Stone
Botkin — *Anecdotes* p.6
, Writing on
Maxwell — *Courage* p.15-23

WANDERING AND WANDERERS
See also **Travel**
Alexander's Treasure. p.104
Bartlett — *Discovery* p.61
Evans — *Unto* p.52
Lockridge — *World's* #4848
Lytle — *Leaves* p.172
New Joy p.207
Prochnow — *Public* #2232, 2233
Woods — *Content.* p.64, 66, 81, 175, 178, 185

WANTS. *See* **Adversity; Desire; Necessity; Wishes**

WAR
See also **Armed forces; Cold war; Soldiers; Violence; U.S.-History** (names of wars)
Auden — *Certain* p.382-394
Braude — *Source* #1792-1798
Dirksen — *Quot. See* index p.271
Droke — *Christian* p.584-594
Edwards — *Useful* p.689-692, 734
Evans — *Unto* p.14, 36, 123, 125
Felleman — *Poems* p.153-183
Flesch — *Unusual* p.306-307
Flint — *Graham* p.37, 148
Fogg — *1000 See* index p.901
Forbes — *Thoughts See* index p.592
Franke — *Buckley* p.316
Fuller — *Epigrams* p.295-296
Fuller — *Thesaurus* p.410-440
Fun Fare p.194
Grizer — *Wit* p.488
Harnsberger — *Mark* p.501-505
Harral — *Feature* p.319-320
Hobe — *Tapestries* p.141
Hovey — *Treasury See* index p.301
Hubbard — *Scrap* p.12, 14, 128, 135, 142, 178, 218
Hudson — *5000* p.297-300
Humes — *Instant* #1134-1147
Kauffman — *For* p.223-229
Kennedy — *Reader's* #1175-1184
Kin — *Dictionary* p.273
Knight's Illus. p.343-345
Knight's Treas. p.428-429
Liddle — *Thought I, II, III* p.13, 48, 57, 120, 168, 184-185
Liddle — *Thought V* p.8, 38
Lockridge — *World's* #2773; *See also* index p.584
Maltz — *Creative* p.14-17
Modern Eloquence (14) p.83-100
Montapert — *Distilled* p.335
Myers — *Thunder* p.101-102
New Topical p.290
Prochnow — *Public See* index p.514
Prochnow — *Speaker's* p.318-319
Prochnow — *Success.* #340, 671, 1200, 2433-2443
Schermerhorn — *1500* p.384-386
Seldes — *Great* p.953-973
Sheban — *Wisdom* no p.
Sheen — *Content.* p.95-97
Speaker's Desk p.269-273; #664, 712
Strait — *Speaker's* p.179-180
Voss — *Quotations* p.241-243
Wheelis — *Moralist* p.103-104, 120

Woods — *Religious* p.161, 1041-1050
, *and church*
Kauffman — *For* p.227-229
, *and divorce*
Hunter — *Gems* p.114-115
, *and peace*
Adams — *New* p.403
Braude — *Stories* p.401-403
Day — *Meditations* p.42-45
Grizer — *Wit* p.488
, *and progress*
Hubbard — *Scrap* p.180
, *Art of*
Fogg — *1000* See index p.901
, *Beginning of*
Saturday — *Advent.* p.175-189
, *Causes of*
Hubbard — *Scrap* p.82
, *Civilians in*
Fuller — *Thesaurus* #2331-2346
, *Condemnation of*
Woods — *Religious* p.1043-1047
, *Declaration against*
Peterson — *Art* p.392
, *Defense of*
Woods — *Religious* p.1047-1048
, *Destruction of*
Peterson — *Art* p.384
, *Effect of*
Adams — *New* p.182
, *Evils of*
Hubbard — *Scrap* p.45
, *Foolishness of*
Hubbard — *Scrap* p.33
, *Foxholes of*
Guideposts — *Faith* p.435-439
, *Hatred of*
Hubbard — *Scrap* p.41
, *Illusions of*
Hubbard — *Scrap* p.9
, *Just*
Woods — *Religious* p.1048-1049
, *Logic of*
Hubbard — *Scrap* p.35
, *Losses of*
Hunter — *Gems* p.115-116
, *Opposition to*
Day — *Meditations* p.42-43
, *Preparedness for*
Fogg — *1000* #376, 577, 632, 685, 969, 1110
, *Sons in*
Holmes — *I've* p.80-82
, *Spirit in*
Webb — *Edge* p.68-70
, *Strategy of*
Fuller — *Thesaurus* #2386-2393
, *Total*
Ideas p.393-395
, *Unjust*
Woods — *Religious* p.1049-1050
, *Vulgarity of*
Hubbard — *Scrap* p.44
, *Waste of*
Hubbard — *Scrap* p.37, 46
, *Women and*
Hubbard — *Scrap* p.31

WARNING. *See* **Advice**

WARRIORS
Kin — *Dictionary* p.273
Nizer — *Thinking* p.127-128

WASHING. *See* **Laundry**

WASHINGTON, GEORGE
Botkin — *Anecdotes* p.138, 140, 153, 178
Botkin — *Treasury* p.255, 256-258, 285
Evans — *This* p.130
Evans — *Thoughts III (Open Road)* p.171-172
Harnsberger — *Mark* p.506-507
Hubbard — *Scrap* p.21, 74, 178, 190, 199
Kohn — *Best* p.112-113
Liddle — *Thought I, II, III* p.185, 187
Peterson — *Art* p.74
Wallis — *Treasure* p.178
Weisfeld — *Pulpit* p.160
Words — *Inspir.* p.118-121, 129
, *Benediction of*
New Joy p.68-69

WASHINGTON, D.C.
Asimov — *Treasury* #221
Botkin — *Anecdotes* See index p.320
Botkin — *Treasury* p.768, 777
Fun Fare p.67-69

WASTE
Baillie — *Diary* #184
Book Proverbs p.12
Braude — *Stories* p.403
Edwards — *Useful* p.692
Evans — *Thoughts III (Open Road)* p.136, 139, 145, 150, 199
Flesch — *Unusual* p.307
Forbes — *Thoughts* p.118, 189, 243, 399, 463, 469, 482
Grizer — *Wit* p.489

Humes — *Instant* #1222-1223; p.40
Kin — *Dictionary* p.273
Lockridge — *World's* #4506
Lytle — *Leaves* p.175
Modern Eloquence (14) p.428
Prochnow — *Public* #1537, 2674
Prochnow — *Success.* #646
Zobell — *Speaker's* p.150-151
, and renewal
Adams — *New* p.161
, Government
Dirksen — *Quot.* #33
, Nothing is
Nichols — *New* p.37-39
, of life
Kohn — *Touch* p.73-74

WATCHES. *See* **Clocks and watches**

WATCHFULNESS. *See* **Vigilance**

WATCHMEN
Lytle — *Leaves* p.85, 90
Prochnow — *Public* #2580

WATER
Adams — *New* p.364
Auden — *Certain* p.395-397
Baillie — *Diary* #114
Du Noüy — *Road* p.49, 52, 89, 132-133, 152
Fuller — *Epigrams* p.363
Garland — *Subject* p.334-335
Hadfield — *Delights* p.87, 103
Harnsberger — *Mark* p.508-511
Harral — *Feature* p.320
Kin — *Dictionary* p.273
Lockridge — *World's* #5219
New Topical p.292-293
Prochnow — *Public* #384, 1397, 2500, 2568, 2571
Prochnow — *Speaker's* p.319
Wallis — *Treasure* p.187

WATER BEETLES
Guideposts — *Faith* p.477-478

WATER LILIES
Kohn — *Pathways* p.131-133

WATERLOO
Flesch — *Unusual* p.307-308
Fogg — *1000* #12, 116, 136, 458, 512, 814, 985
Hubbard — *Scrap* p.151

WATERMELONS
Botkin — *Treasury* p.173, 513
Prochnow — *Public* #123
Wallis — *Words* p.86

WATT, JAMES
Applegarth — *Heir.* p.56

WAVE MECHANICS
Du Noüy — *Road* p.32, 83, 108, 110, 153, 168

WAVE-OFFERING
New Topical p.293

WAVERING. *See* **Doubt**

WAVES
Lindbergh — *Unicorn* p.78
Peterson — *Art* p.291
White — *Job* p.88-91

WAVES OF PROBABILITY
Du Noüy — *Road* p.55, 141, 181, 230, 235

WAX
Kin — *Dictionary* p.273

WAY
See also **Method**
Evans — *Thoughts III (Open Road)* p.175-176
Forbes — *Thoughts* p.124, 179, 190, 439, 475, 487, 494
Hobe — *Tapestries* p.45, 67
Hovey — *Treasury* #355, 525, 1149, 1255, 1312, 1366, 1431, 1487, 1796, 1820
Kin — *Dictionary* p.273
Lytle — *Leaves* p.70, 73, 138, 150
Phillips — *Choice See* index p.430
Woods — *Religious* p.1050
, of life
Menninger — *Blue.* p.76-86

WAYFARERS. *See* **Wandering and wanderers**

WEAKNESS
Albert — *Stop* p.57-58
Bach — *Make* p.12-20
Book Proverbs p.116
Braude — *Source* #1799-1801
Braude — *Stories* p.403
Edwards — *Useful* p.184, 692-693
Evans — *Faith* p.7-8, 97, 132, 201
Evans — *Unto* p.25, 31, 69, 93
Flesch — *Unusual* p.308
Forbes — *Thoughts* p.22, 43, 96, 122, 183, 226, 319, 330, 332, 337, 343, 400, 447, 484, 486
Fuller — *Epigrams* p.296-297
Grizer — *Wit* p.489

Harnsberger — *Mark* p.512
Henry — *5000* p.98-99
Kennedy — *Fresh* p.59-60
Kin — *Dictionary* p.274
Liddle — *Thought I, II, III* p.7, 42
Lockridge — *World's See* index p.585
Montapert — *Distilled* p.335-336
Nichols — *New* p.205-207
Prochnow — *Public* #524, 1439, 1553, 1564
Seldes — *Great* p.973
Sheban — *Wisdom* no p.
Sheen — *Content.* p.154-156
Speaker's Desk p.273-274
Wallis — *Treasure* p.84

WEALTH
See also **Money; Possessions; Property;** etc.
Alexander's Treasure. p.223
Applegarth — *Heir.* p.263
Asimov — *Treasury* #375
Barker — *Treat* p.24-46
Book Proverbs p.9
Braude — *Source* #1802-1811
Braude — *Speaker's* #233-235
Braude — *Stories* p.404-405
Curtis — *Golden* p.128-138
Dirksen — *Quot.* #196, 249, 505, 1120, 1175, 1201, 1609-1613, 1709, 1829-1830, 2146, 2234, 2283
Droke — *Christian* p.595-599
Edwards — *Useful* p.557-560, 693-697
Emmons — *Mature* p.12, 149-153
Evans — *Unto* p.7, 49, 101, 103
Flesch — *Unusual* p.246-308
Flint — *Graham* p.121, 149
Forbes — *Thoughts See* index p.523, 565
Fuller — *Epigrams* p.297-299
Fuller — *Thesaurus* #2181-2187
Garland — *Subject* p.277, 335
Grizer — *Wit* p.489-492
Guideposts — *Faith* p.162-166
Halverson — *Perspective* p.59
Harnsberger — *Mark* p.405-406
Henry — *5000* p.241
Hobe — *Tapestries* p.17, 98
Hovey — *Treasury* #71, 679, 982, 1046, 1071, 1210, 1216, 1457, 1752, 1825
Hubbard — *Scrap* p.14, 17, 96
Hudson — *5000* p.301, 302
Johnson — *Bedside* p.128, 190, 262-263, 278, 280, 282, 309-310
Kin — *Dictionary* p.218-219, 274
Knight's Illus. p.274-277
Knight's Treas. p.326-331
Krishnamurti — *Think* p.77, 156-157
Liddle — *Thought I, II, III* p.11, 27, 37, 45-47, 69, 72, 76, 90, 92, 100-111, 119, 159-160
Liddle — *Thought IV* p.6, 13, 22, 35, 40, 43-44, 46
Lockridge — *World's* #1631, 1783, 2289, 3289, 3567; *See also* index p.582
Lytle — *Leaves* p.29-30, 57, 127, 149, 151
Mandel — *Stories* p.269-271
Mandelbaum — *Choose* p.3-4
Montapert — *Distilled* p.296-297, 336
New Joy p.159
New Topical p.224-225
Peterson — *Art* p.158
Prochnow — *Public See* index p.508
Prochnow — *Speaker's* p.266, 320-321
Prochnow — *Success.* #2255-2257; 2444-2445
Pullar-Strecker — *Proverbs* #205-217
Seldes — *Great* p.841-843, 973-977
Sheban — *Wisdom* no p.
Sheen — *Thoughts* p.11-13
Sheen — *Way* p.109-111
Speaker's Desk p.274-277; #290, 950, 1171
Voss — *Quotations* p.244-245
Wallis — *Words* p.49, 52, 172
Woods — *Business.* p.268-270
Woods — *Content.* p.38, 54, 66, 91-92, 110, 155, 178, 300, 308-309
Woods — *Inspir.* p.84-123
Woods — *Religious* p.863-864, 1050-1053
Woods — *Wellsprings* p.29, 41

, and poverty
Flesch — *Unusual* p.245-246
Seldes — *Great* p.843-846

, Concentration of
Woods — *Business.* p.43-45

, Disadvantages of
Nizer — *Thinking* p.140-141

, for old age
Peterson — *Art* p.224

, Redistribution of
Woods — *Business.* p.270-271

, True
Kohn — *Touch* p.157-161

WEAPONS
See also **Guns**
Kin — *Dictionary* p.274
Prochnow — *Public* #34

WEARINESS
Garland — *Subject* p.336
Prochnow — *Public* #2722-2723

WEATHER
See also types of weather and storms
Alexander's Treasure. p.24
Auden — *Certain* p.398-404
Botkin — *Treasury* p.227, 279, 287-289, 303-308, 319, 332-335, 337-346, 414
Braude — *Source* #1812-1813
Flesch — *Unusual* p.308
Forbes — *Thoughts* p.13, 185, 500
Fuller — *Epigrams* p.299-300
Harnsberger — *Mark* p.52, 513-515
Harral — *Feature* p.320-322
Henry — *5000* p.302
Keys Happiness p.84, 365-367
Kin — *Dictionary* p.49
Kohn — *Adventures* p.28-30
Kohn — *Thoughts* p.130-133
Kohn — *Touch* p.11-17
New Joy p.160
Prochnow — *Public* #112, 507, 852, 888, 1485
Prochnow — *Speaker's* p.321-322
Prochnow — *Success.* #866, 1010, 1496
Sagendorph — *Old* p.13-26
Speaker's Desk #52, 318, 460, 710, 758, 1005
, Reporting of
Sagendorph — *Old* p.274-276
, Stormy
Kohn — *Best* p.119-120

WEBSTER, DANIEL
Adams — *New* p.42
Botkin — *Anecdotes* p.143-145

WEDDINGS
See also **Bridegrooms; Brides; Marriage**
Applegarth — *Heir.* p.293
Asimov — *Treasury* #385
Botkin — *Anecdotes* p.251
Flesch — *Unusual* p.308
Fuller — *Thesaurus* #891-892
Harral — *Feature* p.322-323
Kohn — *Best* p.166-170
Prochnow — *Public* #144, 234, 372, 838, 900, 1276, 1530
Prochnow — *Speaker's* p.322
Wallis — *Treasure* p.169
Weisfeld — *Pulpit* p.41-48
, Anniversaries of
Kohn — *Best* p.166-170
Woods — *Content.* p.135
, Golden
Asimov — *Treasury* #622
, Silver
Weisfeld — *Pulpit* p.43
, Gowns for
Lockridge — *World's* #4841
, Receptions for
Fun Fare p.267-268

WEEDS
Applegarth — *Heir.* p.101
Kahn — *Lessons* p.87-88
Kin — *Dictionary* p.275
Lytle — *Leaves* p.150-151, 180
Nichols — *New* p.125-126
Prochnow — *Public* #111

WEEKS
Harral — *Feature* p.323
New Topical p.293

WEEPING. *See* **Tears**

WEIGHT
Harral — *Feature* p.323
New Topical p.293-294
Prochnow — *Public* #770, 802, 914, 920, 949, 1021, 1732, 1903
Prochnow — *Success.* #1080
, Machines for
Botkin — *Anecdotes* p.264
, Reduction of
See also **Diet; Overweight**
Keys Happiness p.485-487

WELCOME
See also **Hospitality**
Edwards — *Useful* p.697
Fuller — *Epigrams* p.364
Henry — *5000* p.302
Hovey — *Treasury* #50, 1844-1845; p.285
Kin — *Dictionary* p.275
Lockridge — *World's* #1409-1410, 5847
Prochnow — *Public* #2032

WELFARE STATE
See also **Public welfare**
Dirksen — *Quot.* #13
Ideas p.455-457
Woods — *Business.* p.272-276
Woods — *Religious* p.1053-1054

WELL-DOING. *See* **Benevolence; Good; Kindness; Philanthropy**

WELLS
New Topical p.294
Peterson — *Art* p.342

WELSH
Botkin — *Treasury* p.771

WENCESLAS, KING
Hobe — *Tapestries* p.44

WESLEY, JOHN
Baillie — *Diary* #73
Weisfeld — *Pulpit* p.160

WEST
See also names of states, characters
Copeland — *10,000* p.171-178
Fun Fare p.38-40
Henry — *5000* p.302-303

WEST POINT
Fun Fare p.227

WEST VIRGINIA
Botkin — *Treasury* p.177, 179, 230, 330, 679

WESTMINSTER BRIDGE
Hobe — *Tapestries* p.101

"WET BLANKETS"
Safian — *More* p.168-170
Speaker's Desk See index p.306

WHALES AND WHALING
Applegarth — *Heir.* p.20
Botkin — *Anecdotes* p.75, 89, 203, 209
Botkin — *Treasury* p.186, 194, 199, 506, 633, 636, 829, 832

WHEAT
Botkin — *Treasury* p.176, 292, 525

WHEELS
Kin — *Dictionary* p.276
Prochnow — *Public* #644-645

WHETSTONES
Botkin — *Treasury* p.394
Kin — *Dictionary* p.276

WHIMS. *See* **Fickleness**

WHIMSEY
Asimov — *Treasury* #63
Felleman — *Poems* p.187-241

WHINING. *See* **Complaints**

WHIPS
Kin — *Dictionary* p.276
Prochnow — *Public* #2097

WHIRLWIND
New Topical p.294-295

WHISKERS. *See* **Beards**

WHISKY
Botkin — *Treasury* p.505, 526, 528, 530, 855, 884
Prochnow — *Public* #710

WHISPERING
See also **Gossip**
Evans — *Unto* p.28, 37, 78
Kin — *Dictionary* p.276
Prochnow — *Public* #798

WHIST
Prochnow — *Public* #1935

WHISTLES
Kin — *Dictionary* p.276
Prochnow — *Public* #603, 809

WHITE HOUSE
Botkin — *Anecdotes* p.149

WHITE MOUNTAINS
Botkin — *Treasury* p.621

WHITEWASHING
Botkin — *Treasury* p.402

WHITMAN, WALT
Irion — *Yes* p.42-46
New Joy p.51

WHITSUNDAY. *See* **Pentecost**

"WHIZZERS"
Botkin — *Treasury* p.390-391

WHOLENESS
Braude — *Source* #1814-1815
Clark — *Windows* p.92
Holmes — *Design* p.39-40, 230
Kin — *Dictionary* p.276
Peterson — *Art* p.309
, Seeing the
Krishnamurti — *Urgency* p.43-46
, Sense of
Baillie — *Diary* #61

WHOLESALE
Prochnow — *Speaker's* p.322

"WHOPPER WIT"
See also **Tall tales**
Botkin — *Anecdotes* p.89-109

"WHY." *See* **Questions**

WICKEDNESS
See also **Corruption; Cruelty; Sin;** etc.
Baillie — *Diary* #173
Book Proverbs p.116

Edwards — *Useful* p.314-315, 697-698
Evans — *Faith* p.67-72, 79, 90, 92
Evans — *Unto* p.56, 66, 71
Flesch — *Unusual* p.304, 309
Fox — *Make* p.64-65
Fuller — *Epigrams* p.300-301
Henry — *5000* p.303
Kin — *Dictionary* p.140, 277
Lockridge — *World's* #2640
New Topical p.9-10, 294-295
Prochnow — *Public* #2555
Woods — *Religious* p.1054

, Character of
New Topical p.39-40

, Death of
New Topical p.61

, Happiness of
New Topical p.109-110

, Titles and names of
New Topical p.273-274

"WIDE OPEN SPACES"
Ideas p.457-459

WIDOWHOOD
Asimov — *Treasury* #532, 540-541, 544
Flesch — *Unusual* p.309
Fuller — *Epigrams* p.301
Garland — *Subject* p.337-338
How To Live p.515-516
Keys Happiness p.244-247
Kin — *Dictionary* p.277
Lockridge — *World's* #2645, 2681, 3938, 3943-3960, 3962, 3966-3970, 3972-3976, 5629
New Topical p.295-296
Prochnow — *Public* #2664
Prochnow — *Success.* #2447
Schermerhorn — *1500* p.389
Woods — *Wellsprings* p.63-64

, Grass
Book Proverbs p.23

WIENERS
Guideposts — *Faith* p.434

WIGS
Asimov — *Treasury* #104

"WILD OATS"
Prochnow — *Public* #956

WILDCATS
Prochnow — *Public* #357
Speaker's Desk p.7, 912

WILDERNESS
Kennedy — *Fresh* p.121-124

WILDLIFE
See also **Animals;** names of animals; etc.
Peterson — *Art* p.145

WILL
See also **Decision; Determination; Free will; God, Will of; Purpose; Resolution; Self-will**
Baillie — *Diary* #94
Bartlett — *Discovery* p.110-111
Braude — *Source* #1818
Curtis — *Human* p.12
Curtis — *Practical* p.116, 507
Edwards — *Useful* p.700-701, 734
Flesch — *Unusual* p.310-311
Forbes — *Thoughts See* index p.573
Fox — *Make* p.49
Fuller — *Thesaurus* #631
Grizer — *Wit* p.492
Henry — *5000* p.304
Hobe — *Tapestries* p.17, 88, 117
Hovey — *Treasury* #1387, 1604
Hubbard — *Scrap* p.75, 164
Johnson — *Bedside* p.249-250
Kin — *Dictionary* p.277
Kohn — *Best* p.114-116
Liddle — *Thought IV* p.28
Liddle — *Thought V* p.35
Lockridge — *World's* #31, 254, 1699
Lytle — *Leaves* p.75, 135, 137, 144, 156
Maltz — *Creative* p.106-107
Mandel — *Stories* p.271
Modern Eloquence (14) p.429
Montapert — *Distilled* p.336-337
Peterson — *Art* p.238
Prochnow — *Public* #2746, 3851-3855
Prochnow — *Success.* #1082
Seldes — *Great* p.978, 979
Sheen — *Thoughts* p.57-68
Woods — *Content.* p.31
Woods — *Religious* p.1054-1057

WILLOW TREES
Adams — *New* p.294
Applegarth — *Heir.* p.286

WILLS AND TESTAMENTS
See also **Death; Inheritance**
Braude — *Source* #191-192, 1816-1817
Braude — *Stories* p.38-39
Edwards — *Useful* p.701-702
Flesch — *Unusual* p.145
Fuller — *Thesaurus* #2606-2607
Sheban — *Wisdom* no p.

WILSON, WOODROW
Weisfeld — *Pulpit* p.16

WIND
See also **Clouds; Rain;** etc.
Adams — *New* p.363
Botkin — *Anecdotes* p.90
Botkin — *Treasury* p.280, 512, 611, 614
Curtis — *Practical* p.198
Edwards — *Useful* p.702
Flesch — *Unusual* p.311
Garland — *Subject* p.339
Henry — *5000* p.304-305
Hobe — *Tapestries* p.46, 219
Holmes — *I've* p.120-121
Hubbard — *Scrap* p.103
Kohn — *Through* p.73-74
New Topical p.296
Peterson — *Art* p.166
Prochnow — *Public* #3856-3857
Prochnow — *Success.* #1159, 2450
Wallis — *Words* p.138
Woods — *Content.* p.212, 217
Woods — *Wellsprings* p.40-41
, East
Botkin — *Anecdotes* p.19

WINDMILLS
Botkin — *Anecdotes* p.104, 165
Prochnow — *Public* #2381

WINDOWS
Alexander's Treasure. p.91
Applegarth — *Heir.* p.308
Lytle — *Leaves* p.158
Peterson — *Art* p.272
Prochnow — *Success.* #1073
Wallis — *Treasure* p.45, 47, 74
Wallis — *Words* p.131, 240
, Church
Reader's — *Getting* p.225
, Golden
Peterson — *Art* p.357
, Lighted
Peterson — *Art* p.298
, Rose
Peale — *Courage* p.38
, Stained-glass
Peterson — *Art* p.36
Woods — *Wellsprings* p.60-61

"WIND-UP" STORIES. *See* **Speeches and speaking, Closing of**

WINE
Curtis — *Practical* p.520
Edwards — *Useful* p.702-703
Flesch — *Unusual* p.311
Fuller — *Epigrams* p.303-304, 364-367
Henry — *5000* p.305
Kin — *Dictionary* p.278
Lockridge — *World's* #1968, 2668-2669, 2671-2672, 4605
New Topical p.296-297
Prochnow — *Public* #2538
Prochnow — *Success.* #2451
Woods — *Religious* p.1057

WINGS
Kin — *Dictionary* p.278
Sheban — *Wisdom* no p.
Wallis — *Treasure* p.18
Wallis — *Words* p.71, 175, 179, 218

WINKING
Flesch — *Unusual* p.311
Kin — *Dictionary* p.278

WINNING. *See* **Success; Victory**

WINTER
See also **Ice and ice-storms; Snow**
Alexander's Treasure. p.41, 175
Auden — *Certain* p.341-342
Dirksen — *Quot.* #308
Goudge — *Comfort* p.52, 55
Hadfield — *Love* p.218-241
Henry — *5000* p.306
Hobe — *Tapestries* p.58-59, 217
Kin — *Dictionary* p.278
Kohn — *Best* p.24-35
Kohn — *Thoughts* p.129-171
Lindbergh — *Unicorn* p.62-65
New Topical p.297
Patterns For Living p.14-18
Peterson — *Art* p.67
Prochnow — *Public* #1838, 4360
Sagendorph — *Old* p.35-37
Woods — *Content.* p.201, 219
Words — *Inspir.* p.55
, of 1784
Auden — *Certain* p.400-401

WISCONSIN
Botkin — *Anecdotes* p.50, 164
Botkin — *Treasury* p.177, 849

WISDOM
See also **Brain; Intelligence; Judgment; Knowledge; Sense;** etc.
Alexander's Treasure. p.30, 211
Applegarth — *Heir.* p.51, 267
Baillie — *Diary* #278
Barrows — *1000* p.445-446
Bartlett — *Discovery* p.128-129
Book Proverbs p.82
Braude — *Source* #1819-1822
Braude — *Stories* p.406
Curtis — *Golden* p.139-150
Curtis — *Practical* p.88-89, 389

Detherage — *Sunrise* p.42, 187-190
Dirksen — *Quot. See* index p.271
Edwards — *Useful* p.703-705, 734
Evans — *Unto* p.8, 25, 31, 48, 110
Flesch — *Unusual* p.311-312
Fogg — *1000* #173, 272, 385
Forbes — *Thoughts See* index p.573
Fuller — *Epigrams* p.304-306
Garland — *Subject* p.340
Grizer — *Wit* p.493-495
Harnsberger — *Mark* p.515
Henry — *5000* p.306-307
Hobe — *Tapestries* p.42, 84, 199
Hovey — *Treasury* #5, 330, 510, 536, 742, 761, 952, 1349, 1518, 1637, 1803, 1807
How To Live p.435-562
Hubbard — *Scrap* p.68, 72, 74, 129, 225, 228
Huxley — *You See* index p.289
Johnson — *Bedside* p.21, 25, 96, 212-213, 252, 254, 282, 302, 304, 356
Kahn — *Lessons* p.71-76
Kennedy — *Reader's* #1185-1186
Kin — *Dictionary* p.278-279
Kohn — *Pathways* p.123-126
Liddle — *Thought I, II, III See* index p.200
Liddle — *Thought IV* p.6, 10, 12-14, 19, 31-32
Liddle — *Thought V* p.6, 21, 32, 34, 39-41
Lockridge — *World's* p.585
Lytle — *Leaves* p.62, 74, 133
McCracken — *What* p.53-57
Mandel — *Stories* p.272-274
Mandelbaum — *Choose* p.7-13
Modern Eloquence (14) p.430-431
Montapert — *Distilled* p.337-338
Morris — *1000 See* index p.433-434
New Joy p.34-35
Peterson — *Art* p.130, 286
Petty — *Promises* p.61-66
Phillips — *Choice* p.344
Porter — *Halo* p.93-98
Prochnow — *Public See* index p.515
Prochnow — *Success.* #579, 877, 1217, 1389, 1480, 2452-2455
Reader's — *Getting* p.60
Seldes — *Great* p.979
Sheban — *Wisdom* no p.
Simpson — *Contemp.* p.288-338
Speaker's Desk p.277-279; #267, 320, 837, 873
Voss — *Quotations* p.245-247
Wallis — *Treasure* p.93, 139, 229-234
Wallis — *Words* p.19-20, 106, 143
Welk — *Guide.* p.75-77
Wilcox — *Heart* p.66-68
Woods — *Content.* p.232, 279
Woods — *Religious* p.1057-1059
Zobell — *Speaker's* p.154-155

, Ancient
Holmes — *Design* p.74-75
, and folly
Flesch — *Unusual* p.311
, and ignorance
Flesch — *Unusual* p.311
, and learning
Flesch — *Unusual* p.311-312
, Beyond
Adams — *New* p.386
, Growth of
Adams — *New* p.53
, Path to
Adams — *New* p.165
, Prayer for
Unlimited Power p.60
, versus intelligence
Kauffman — *For* p.230-231
, Words of
Hunter — *Gems* p.117-118
Zobell — *Speaker's* p.155-157

"WISE MEN"
Applegarth — *Heir.* p.55
Forbes — *Thoughts* p.131, 133, 196, 248, 285, 296, 370, 383, 404, 438, 505
Grizer — *Wit* p.495-496
Kohn — *Best* p.94
Kohn — *Touch* p.29-31
Wallis — *Words* p.36

"WISECRACKS"
Botkin — *Treasury* p.429, 478
Copeland — *10,000* p.779-795
Speaker's Desk See index p.306

WISHBONES
Prochnow — *Public* #397

WISHES
See also **Ambition; Aspiration; Desire; Hope**
Alexander's Treasure p.48, 227
Book Proverbs p.3
Braude — *Source* #1823-1824
Edwards — *Useful* p.688-689, 705-706, 720
Evans — *This* p.99-100
Evans — *Thoughts III (Open Road)* p.139
Flesch — *Unusual* p.312
Francis — *For* p.179-191
Henry — *5000* p.307
Hovey — *Treasury* p.285; #28, 34, 52, 1399, 1840-1843

Ideas p.461
Johnson — *Bedside* p.234-255
Lockridge — *World's* #494, 3325, 3451, 4016, 4832, 4837
Mandel — *Stories* p.272
Menninger — *Blue.* p.14
Montapert — *Distilled* p.334-335
Nichols — *Third* p.185-186
Prochnow — *Public* #158, 241, 916, 1195, 1383, 1498, 1577, 3831
Speaker's Desk #194, 503, 688
Wallis — *Words* p.71, 86, 152

WIT
See also **Humor; Jokes and joking; Puns and punsters; Satire;** etc.
Book Proverbs p.100
Botkin — *Treasury* p.499
Braude — *Source* #1825-1826
Braude — *Stories* p.406-407
Copeland — *10,000* p.776-779
Dirksen — *Quot.* #439, 794, 2243-2244
Edwards — *Useful* p.706-707
Flesch — *Unusual* p.312-313
Forbes — *Thoughts* p.131, 187, 299, 314
Fuller — *Epigrams* p.306-307
Gold — *Letters* p.29-30
Grizer — *Wit* p.496
Harnsberger — *Mark* p.516
Henry — *5000* p.308
Hubbard — *Scrap* p.126, 218
Kin — *Dictionary* p.279
Liddle — *Thought I, II, III* p.27, 74, 145
Lockridge — *World's See* index p.585
Nizer — *Thinking* p.76, 147-148
Prochnow — *Public* #1888, 1924, 3877-3879, 4257-4258
Speaker's Desk p.279-282; #125, 237, 402

WITCHES AND WITCHCRAFT
Botkin — *Anecdotes* p.207
Du Noüy — *Human* p.127-129
George — *Book* p.411
Johnson — *Bedside* p.54-55
Prochnow — *Public* #206
Seldes — *Great* p.979-980
Wheelis — *Moralist* p.136-137
Woods — *Religious* p.1059
, Hunting
Menninger — *Blue.* p.29

WITHDRAWAL
Edwards — *Useful* p.129
Hulme — *Living* p.123-125
Kin — *Dictionary* p.68
White — *Job* p.109-111

"WITHERING"
Kohn — *Best* p.44-46

WITNESSES
See also **Evidence; Testimony**
Dirksen — *Quot.* #12, 16, 1317
Flint — *Graham* p.149
Fuller — *Thesaurus* #2501-2506
Hovey — *Treasury* #527, 569, 640, 813, 821, 916-917, 1269, 1474, 1485
Kauffman — *For* p.231-232
Kennedy — *Reader's* #1187
Kin — *Dictionary* p.279
Knight's Treas. p.433-437
Lytle — *Leaves* p.66, 83
More Words p.168-169
Prochnow — *Public* #484
Wallis — *Words* p.219-224
Woods — *Religious* p.1059

"WIT'S END"
Botkin — *Anecdotes* p.204, 255-280

WIVES
Alexander's Treasure. p.35, 309
Applegarth — *Heir.* p.292-295, 299
Asimov — *Treasury See* index p.431
Book Proverbs p.20
Braude — *Source* #862-864
Braude — *Speaker's* #136-137, 236-241, 628-702
Dirksen — *Quot.* #2235-2237
Edwards — *Useful* p.698-700
Evans — *Thoughts III (Open Road)* p.17, 29, 91, 137
Flesch — *Unusual* p.309-310
Fuller — *Epigrams* p.301-303
Fuller — *Thesaurus* #921-933
Fun Fare p.92-93
Garland — *Subject* p.338
Goudge — *Comfort* p.120-121
Guideposts — *Faith* p.328-330
Henry — *5000* p.303-304
How To Live p.66-68
Huxley — *You See* index p.288-289
Kahn — *Lessons* p.185-191
Kin — *Dictionary* p.277
Lockridge — *World's See* index p.585
Manchee — *Secret* p.233
New Topical p.298-299
Peterson — *Art* p.137, 367
Prochnow — *Public See* index p.515
Prochnow — *Speaker's* p.322
Prochnow — *Success.* #360, 502, 523, 765, 846, 893, 988, 1011, 1034, 2448-2449
Safian — *Insults* p.201-210

Safian — *More* p.171-181
Schermerhorn — *1500* p.390-393
Seaburg — *Great See* index p.462
Wallis — *Words* p.109-110, 118
Weisfeld — *Pulpit* p.87-103
Woods — *Religious* p.457, 1054

, Christian
Rogers — *Time* p.31-34

, Jewish
Asimov — *Treasury* #516-520, 522

, of V.I.P.'s
Walters — *How* p.56-58

, Suggestions to
Flint — *Graham* p.149-150

WIZARDS
Prochnow — *Public* #1317, 1363

"WOBBLIES"
Botkin — *Treasury* p.524

WOE. *See* **Grief**

WOLVES
Botkin — *Anecdotes* p.92
Botkin — *Treasury* p.24, 622, 665-666
Dirksen — *Quot.* #2245, 2246
Fun Fare p.296-297
Hubbard — *Scrap* p.94
New Topical p.299

WOMEN
See also **Daughters; Mothers; Wives;** etc.
Alexander's Treasure. p.17, 35, 63
Applegarth — *Heir.* p.80, 227, 291-299
Book Proverbs p.23
Braude — *Source* #1074-1082, 1827-1829
Braude — *Speaker's* #242-262, 842-845, 1582-1585
Braude — *Stories* p.408-416
Copeland — *10,000* p.187-197, 984-989
Cowan — *Wit* p.1-176
Curtis — *Practical* p.494-496
Dirksen — *Quot. See* index p.271
Edwards — *Useful* p.707-713, 734
Evans — *Faith* p.57-58, 67
Evans — *This* p.57-58
Flesch — *Unusual* p.144, 313-314
Flint — *Graham* p.150
Fogg — *1000 See* index p.901
Fuller — *Epigrams* p.307-312, 348-351
Fuller — *Thesaurus* p.147; #841-843
Fun Fare p.5-6, 17, 48, 138, 162, 167-168, 276-279
Garland — *Subject* p.341
Grizer — *Wit* p.496-497
Hadfield — *Delights* p.131
Harnsberger — *Mark* p.516-518
Harral — *Feature* p.324-328
Henry — *5000* p.308-311
Hobe — *Tapestries* p.169
Humes — *Instant* #32-34, 1149-1159, 1278
Kennedy — *Reader's* #1188-1193
Keys Happiness p.281-282, 502
Kin — *Dictionary* p.93, 142, 279-280
Liddle — *Thought I, II, III See* index p.200
Liddle — *Thought IV* p.4, 18, 27, 37, 41, 45
Liddle — *Thought V* p.16, 21-22, 46
Lindbergh — *Gift* p.27-28
Lockridge — *World's See* index p.585
Modern Eloquence (14) p.432-435
Montapert — *Distilled* p.338
New Topical p.299-300
Nizer — *Thinking* p.40-41, 67, 214-215
Phillips — *Choice See* index p.430
Prochnow — *Public See* index p.515
Prochnow — *Speaker's* p.323-325
Prochnow — *Success. See* index p.502
Rogers — *Time* p.13-22
Sagendorph — *Old* p.94-100
Schermerhorn — *1500* p.394-395
Seldes — *Great* p.557-558, 980-981
Sheban — *Wisdom* no p.
Speaker's Desk p.282-287, #149, 768
Voss — *Quotations* p.247-249
Wallis — *Treasure* p.132-133
Weisfeld — *Pulpit* p.16-17
Woods — *Religious* p.1059
Words — *Inspir.* p.122

, Age of
Adams — *New* p.284-285

, American
Dirksen — *Quot.* #75
Patterns For Living p.132-141

, and love
Unlimited Power p.70-74

, and men
See also **Men, and women**
Hubbard — *Scrap* p.204

, and realism
Adams — *New* p.205

, and sex
How To Live p.396-399

, *and war*
Hubbard — *Scrap* p.31
, *as humans*
Adams — *New* p.319
, *as policewomen*
Harral — *Feature* p.328
, *as shopkeepers*
Manchee — *Secret* p.231-232
, *as stereotypes*
Asimov — *Treasury* #79
, *Clubs for*
Dirksen — *Quot.* #353
, *Coming of age*
Lindbergh — *Gift* p.95-96
, *Complicated life of*
Lindbergh — *Gift* p.25-26
, *Creativity of*
Adams — *New* p.395
, *Giving of*
Lindbergh — *Gift* p.46-47
, *Greatest*
Peterson — *Art* p.137
, *Heart of*
Hubbard — *Scrap* p.81
Sheban — *Wisdom* no p.
, *Liberation of. See* **Women, Rights of**
, *Middle-aged*
Reader's — *Getting* p.179-182
, *Modern*
Sheban — *Wisdom* no p.
, *Nature of*
Phillips — *Choice* p.117, 120, 132-133
, *Opportunity for*
Wilcox — *Heart* p.88-90
, *Perfect*
Weisfeld — *Pulpit* p.24
, *Power of*
Hill — *Think* p.223-224
How To Live p.99
Keller — *You* p.214-215
, *Precepts of*
Words — *Inspir.* p.42
, *Rights of*
Asimov — *Treasury* #86, 463, 512-513
Bartlett — *Discovery* p.84-85
Seldes — *Great* p.981-983
, *Role of*
Dirksen — *Quot.* #1795
, *Search for God by*
Unlimited Power p.50-55
, *Self-deception of*
Hubbard — *Scrap* p.73
, *Speeches on*
Copeland — *World's* p.3-34, 196-198, 207-208, 321-322, 639-641, 643-646, 651-655, 671-672
, *Suffrage for*
Fuller — *Thesaurus* #2051-2052
, *Tribute to*
Hubbard — *Scrap* p.69, 214
, *Weariness of*
Baillie — *Diary* #160
, *Will of*
New Joy p.19
, *Worries of*
Peale — *Courage* p.85-86

WONDER
See also **Admiration; Curiosity; Miracles; Mystery**
Applegarth — *Heir.* p.296, 306
Edwards — *Useful* p.713
Flesch — *Unusual* p.15, 314
Harnsberger — *Mark* p.518-519
Henry — *5000* p.311
How To Live p.110-114
Hubbard — *Scrap* p.73
Irion — *Yes* p.117
Kennedy — *Fresh* p.31-40
Kin — *Dictionary* p.280
Kohn — *Adventures* p.17-19
Lockridge — *World's* #409, 3678
Lytle — *Leaves* p.106, 111
Nichols — *Third* p.115-116
Prochnow — *Public* #360
Prochnow — *Success.* #324
Voss — *Quotations* p.250-251
Wallis — *Treasure* p.21, 24, 51, 125, 210, 232
Wallis — *Words* p.86, 145, 154, 175, 207
Woods — *Religious* p.1061-1062
, *Faculty of*
Adams — *New* p.313
Johnson — *Bedside* p.213, 247-248

WOODCHUCKS
Botkin — *Anecdotes* p.62, 143

WOODPECKERS
Botkin — *Anecdotes* p.81
Prochnow — *Success.* #901
Wallis — *Treasure* p.4

WOODS
Alexander's Treasure. p.236
Hadfield — *Delights* p.90
Hobe — *Tapestries* p.58, 95
Kin — *Dictionary* p.281
Kohn — *Thoughts* p.111-112
Prochnow — *Success.* #901
Sagendorph — *Old* p.88-94

"WOOLGATHERERS"
Safian — *Insults* p.211-212

WOOLWORTH'S
Irion — *Yes* p.42-46

WORD OF GOD. *See* **God, Word of**

WORDS
See also **Language; Loquacity; Names; Slang; Speech; Talk; Writers and writing;** types of words
Adams — *New* p.104
Albert — *Stop* p.31-33
Alexander's Treasure. p.77, 90, 189, 231, 276-277
Applegarth — *Heir.* p.39, 71, 73, 117, 157
Book Proverbs p.104
Botkin — *Treasury* p.274-275
Braude — *Source* #1830-1837
Braude — *Stories* p.416
Cerf — *Laugh* p.225-229
Dirksen — *Quot.* #110, 506, 1067, 1124-1125
Edwards — *Useful* p.713-715, 734
Evans — *This* p.4-5, 100-102
Evans — *Unto* p.77-78
Flesch — *Unusual* p.314-315
Forbes — *Thoughts See* index p.573
Fox — *Make* p.142-143
Fuller — *Epigrams* p.312-313
Grizer — *Wit* p.497-498
Harnsberger — *Mark* p.519-522
Harral — *Feature* p.328
Henry — *5000* p.313-315
Hobe — *Tapestries* p.197
Hoffer — *Reflect.* p.40-43
Hovey — *Treasury* p.283; *See also* index p.301
Kennedy — *Reader's* #1194
Keys Happiness p.344, 502
Kin — *Dictionary* p.281
Kohn — *Touch* p.57-59
Kronenberger — *Animal* p.3-5
Lair — *Baby* p.16
Liddle — *Thought I, II, III See* index p.200
Liddle — *Thought IV* p.4, 15, 19, 28
Liddle — *Thought V* p.10, 17, 23, 26, 35-36, 39
Lockridge — *World's* #1298-1300, 1418, 1748, 2064, 2472, 2568, 2913, 2922, 4464
Lytle — *Leaves* p.30, 157-158, 162-163, 191
Mandel — *Stories* p.275-276
Montapert — *Distilled* p.338-339
New Joy p.62
Nizer — *Thinking* p.53
Peterson — *Art* p.33, 54-55, 83, 89
Prochnow — *Public See* index p.515
Prochnow — *Speaker's* p.325
Prochnow — *Success.* #1378, 2462-2463
Seldes — *Great* p.983-985
Sheban — *Wisdom* no p.
Woods — *Business.* p.72-73
Woods — *Religious* p.1063-1064
Words — *Inspir.* p.28

, and ideas
Adams — *New* p.394

, and money
Adams — *New* p.303

, and phrases
Kronenberger — *Animal* p.230-231
Prochnow — *Public* #1026

, as character basis
Nichols — *New* p.221-223

, Beauty of
Adams — *New* p.302

, Big
Humes — *Instant* p.15-17
Schermerhorn — *1500* p.47
Speaker's Desk #32, 82, 147, 225, 360, 484, 491, 585, 751, 763, 785

, Coined
Schermerhorn — *1500* p.81

, Dying
Auden — *Certain* p.404-405
Fogg — *1000 See* index p.890
Montapert — *Distilled* p.229-230

, Facetious
Botkin — *Treasury* p.273-274

, Famous men's
New Joy p.94-95

, Four-letter
Peterson — *Art* p.345

, Great
See also **Epigrams; Proverbs; Quotations**
Peterson — *Art* p.125, 317

, Hard
Book Proverbs p.12

, Healing
Peterson — *Art* p.125

, Important
New Joy p.240

, Influence of
Saturday — *Advent.* p.237-251
Words Change p.60-63

, Inspirational
Peterson — *Art* p.339

, Key
Nichols — *New* p.33-34

, "of difference"
Fun Fare p.132

, Old-fashioned
Sheen — *Thoughts* p.137-138

, *Origin of*
Braude — *Stories* p.275-278
, *Phonetics of*
Schermerhorn — *1500* p.130
, *Play on*
Asimov — *Treasury* #228, 231, 235
, *Plurals of*
Prochnow — *Public* #765
, *Power of*
Adams — *New* p.320
Keller — *You* p.144-170
Kennedy — *Fresh* p.51
, *Pronunciation of*
Kin — *Dictionary* p.201
, *Right*
Adams — *New* p.117
, *Spreading*
Humes — *Instant* p.43; #1244-1245
, *Stories of*
Humes — *Instant* p.39
, *to live by*
Nichols — *New* p.235-236
Peterson — *Art* p.345
, *Today's*
Adams — *New* p.388
, *Unfamiliar*
Fun Fare p.42
, *Vitality of*
Adams — *New* p.301

WORDSWORTH, WILLIAM
Flesch — *Unusual* p.315-316

WORK
See also **Deeds; Labor; Occupations; Tasks;** etc.
Alexander's Treasure. p.262-272
Applegarth — *Heir.* p.29, 44, 112, 141-143, 148, 151, 178, 243
Auden — *Certain* p.405-407
Bach — *Make* p.42-45
Braude — *Source* #1838-1844
Braude — *Stories* p.416-417
Curtis — *Daily* p.27-34
Curtis — *Practical* p.106-108
Detherage — *Sunrise* p.47, 107-116
Droke — *Christian* p.600-606
Edwards — *Useful* p.715-716, 734
Emmons — *Mature* p.122
Evans — *Faith* p.9, 22-32, 37, 40, 187-188
Evans — *Quote* p.41-51
Evans — *Thoughts I See* index, no p.
Evans — *Thoughts II (Open Door)* p.13-14, 85-88, 107-108, 131-132, 144-145, 149-152, 165, 173, 206-207
Evans — *Thoughts III (Open Road)* p.37, 55, 61, 65, 108, 119, 131-132, 149-152, 155, 181-182
Evans — *Thoughts IV* p.13, 54-60, 69, 77-78, 87, 104
Evans — *Unto* p.64, 69, 87, 93, 101, 118, 143
Flesch — *Unusual* p.316-317
Forbes — *Thoughts See* index p.573
Fuller — *Epigrams* p.313-316, 367
Goudge — *Comfort* p.334-335
Grizer — *Wit* p.498-504
Harnsberger — *Mark* p.522-524
Harral — *Feature* p.328-329
Henry — *5000* p.315-317
Hobe — *Tapestries* p.80-82
Hovey — *Treasury* p.285-286; *See also* index p.301
Hubbard — *Scrap* p.20, 28, 37, 44, 68, 110, 210
Johnson — *Bedside* p.12, 44, 234, 245
Kennedy — *Reader's* #1195-1203
Keys Happiness p.466-469
Kin — *Dictionary* p.281-282
Knight's Illus. p.348-351
Knight's Treas. p.437-442
Kohn — *Touch* p.127-129
Liddle — *Thought I, II, III See* index p.200
Liddle — *Thought IV* p.6, 12, 17, 27, 42
Liddle — *Thought V* p.12, 16, 25, 35, 43, 46
Lockridge — *World's* #863, 976, 1444, 2494, 4337-4338, 4476, 4483, 5880
Lytle — *Leaves* p.6, 33, opp.168, 179
Mandel — *Stories* p.276-277
Mandelbaum — *Choose* p.17
Modern Eloquence (14) p.436-437
Montapert — *Distilled* p.339-340
Morris — *1000* p.434-435
Nichols — *New* p.76-77
Nichols — *Third* p.229-230
Phillips — *Choice* p.310, 318-320
Prochnow — *Public See* index p.515
Prochnow — *Speaker's* p.325-327
Prochnow — *Success. See* index p.502
Sheen — *Way* p.51-59
Speaker's Desk p.287-291; *See also* index p.306
Tanksley — *Friend* p.50
Voss — *Quotations* p.251-252
Wallis — *Treasure* p.13, 20, 59, 69, 74-75, 141-142, 235-240
Wallis — *Words* p.225-230, 235
Watson — *Light* p.3-7, 134-137

Welk — *Guide.* p.26-28
Woods — *Business.* p.276-278
Woods — *Content. See* index p.381
Woods — *Inspir.* p.84-123
Woods — *Religious* p.1064
Zobell — *Speaker's* p.157-158
, and amusement
Hubbard — *Scrap* p.31
, and play
Hubbard — *Scrap* p.38
, and prayer
Kauffman — *For* p.231-232
, and progress
Hunter — *Gems* p.118-119
, and success
Hubbard — *Scrap* p.61
, and workers
Book Proverbs p.85
Copeland — *10,000* p.447-449
Forbes — *Thoughts* p.53, 169, 262, 327, 380, 410, 422, 432, 446, 449, 453, 460-461, 511, 513
Grizer — *Wit* p.504-505
Harral — *Feature* p.329
Montapert — *Distilled* p.113
Seaburg — *Great* p.228, 266-267, 325, 359, 364
Seldes — *Great* p.985-989
, and workmanship
Hubbard — *Scrap* p.30
Keys Happiness p.493-495
, Art of
Maurois — *Art* p.174-215
Peterson — *Twenty* p.50-51
, as mission of mankind
Hubbard — *Scrap* p.74
, Conditions of
Fuller — *Thesaurus* #2256
, Creative
Hubbard — *Scrap* p.123
, Discipline of
Bartlett — *Discovery* p.57-58
, Drudgery of
Hubbard — *Scrap* p.9
, Energy and
Hubbard — *Scrap* p.47
, Freedom to
Bach — *Make* p.44-45
, Habit of
Day — *Meditations* p.34
, Inspiring
Humes — *Instant* #1186-1188
, Joys of
Hubbard — *Scrap* p.58, 62, 72
, Keys to happiness in
Kopplin — *Something* p.6-7
, Love of
Hubbard — *Scrap* p.156
, Necessity of
Hubbard — *Scrap* p.59
, World's
Hubbard — *Scrap* p.27

WORKS, GOOD
See also **Good**
Dirksen — *Quot.* #458, 1316, 1616-1617
Lindeman — *Emerson* p.119-132
Mandel — *Stories* p.277-278
Woods — *Religious* p.1066-1067

WORLD
See also **Earth; Humanity; Life; Man (mankind); Nature; Society**
Applegarth — *Heir.* p.86, 94, 159, 193, 272-273, 282
Book Proverbs p.3
Braude — *Source* #1851-1852
Braude — *Speaker's* #263-267
Curtis — *Daily* p.49-55
Curtis — *Practical* p.74, 535-536, 542-546, 552-553
Dirksen — *Quot. See* index p.271
Edwards — *Useful* p.716-718
Flesch — *Unusual* p.317-319
Flint — *Graham* p.150-152
Forbes — *Thoughts* p.149, 194, 199, 262, 398, 407, 432, 440, 444, 500
Fuller — *Epigrams* p.315-316, 367
Grizer — *Wit* p.505
Henry — *5000* p.317-319
Hobe — *Tapestries* p.97
Hovey — *Treasury See* index p.301
Irion — *Yes* p.34-38
Johnson — *Bedside* p.45, 132-133, 258
Kin — *Dictionary* p.282
Lockridge — *World's See* index p.585
Modern Eloquence (14) p.438
Montapert — *Distilled* p.340-341
Phillips — *Choice* p.125, 128, 228, 311
Prochnow — *Public* #1326, 1593, 2240, 2643, 2708, 2746, 3905-3906, 4350
Prochnow — *Speaker's* p.327-328
Prochnow — *Success.* #746, 2466-2468
Seldes — *Great* p.989-991
Simpson — *Contemp.* p.110-202
Wallis — *Treasure* p.8, 24, 29, 131, 139, 158, 181
Wallis — *Words* p.20, 61, 88, 97
Woods — *Content.* p.21, 32, 34, 39, 41, 43, 46, 48, 52, 65
Woods — *Religious* p.1067-1076

, *and Christianity*
Woods — *Religious* p.1071-1072
, *and church*
Woods — *Religious* p.1072-1073
, *and God*
Johnson — *Bedside* p.135-136
Woods — *Religious* p.1073-1075
, *and man*
Woods — *Religious* p.1075-1076
, *Beauty and wonder of*
See also **Beauty; Wonder**
Hubbard — *Scrap* p.66, 189
, *Community of*
Baillie — *Diary* #212
, *Condemnation of*
Woods — *Religious* p.1069-1070
, *End of*
Auden — *Certain* p.409-418
Sheen — *Content.* p.134-135
, *Horizons of*
Bartlett — *Discovery* p.2-3, 19-20
Wallis — *Words* p.231-236
, *Illness of. See* **World, Problems of**
, *Knowledge of*
Bach — *Make* p.63-73
, *Leadership of*
Flint — *Graham* p.152-153
, *Modern*
Lockridge — *World's* #3613
, *One*
Kennedy — *Fresh* p.187-189
, *Order of*
Hovey — *Treasury See* p.304
, *Personal*
Peterson — *Art* p.408
, *Praise of*
Woods — *Religious* p.1070-1071
, *Prayer for*
Unlimited Power p.169-172
, *Problems of*
Humes — *Instant* #1250-1253
Keller — *Open* p.67
Mandelbaum — *Choose* p.133-135
Myers — *Thunder* p.11-23
Nizer — *Thinking* p.188-191
, *Purpose of*
Nichols — *Third* p.170-171
, *Roundness of*
Peterson — *Art* p.245
, *Understanding of*
Curtis — *Golden* p.36-47
, *Unrest of*
See also **World, Problems of**
Keys Happiness p.241-243
Tanksley — *Friend* p.39

"WORLD NEIGHBORS" ORGANIZATION
Guideposts — *Faith* p.438-439

WORLD WARS. *See* **U.S., History** (names of wars)

WORLDLINESS. *See* **Sophistication**

WORMS
Asimov — *Treasury* #57
Flesch — *Unusual* p.319
Kin — *Dictionary* p.282

WORRY
See also **Anxiety; Fear; Trouble; Uncertainty**; etc.
Adams — *New* p.150
Albert — *Stop See* index p.212
Alexander's Treasure. p.301
Blanton — *Faith* p.64-86
Braude — *Source* #1853-1859
Braude — *Stories* p.417
Detherage — *Sunrise* p.68, 93
Droke — *Christian* p.607-613
Edwards — *Useful* p.734
Emmons — *Mature* p.80
Evans — *Faith* p.5, 9-10
Evans — *Thoughts I* p.13, 23, 131-133, 144, 205-210
Evans — *Thoughts II (Open Door)* p.11-13, 149-150
Evans — *Thoughts III (Open Road)* p.38-39, 48
Evans — *Thoughts IV* p.89
Flesch — *Unusual* p.96, 319
Flint — *Graham* p.153
Forbes — *Thoughts* p.42, 117, 125, 146, 206, 340, 344, 431, 461, 477, 479, 518
Fuller — *Epigrams* p.316-317, 368
Fuller — *Thesaurus* #636
Giniger — *Compact* p.152-157
Grizer — *Wit* p.506-507
Harnsberger — *Mark* p.424
Harral — *Feature* p.329
Hill — *Think* p.278-280
Hobe — *Tapestries* p.32, 227
Holman — *Psych.* p.77-87
Hovey — *Treasury* p.286-288; #393, 1855-1863
Hubbard — *Scrap* p.21, 137
Johnson — *Bedside* p.198
Kennedy — *Reader's* #1204
Keys Happiness p.85-89, 254
Kin — *Dictionary* p.283
Knight's Illus. p.352-353
Knight's Treas. p.445-447

Kopplin — *Something* p.52-56
Krishnamurti — *Think* p.109-110
Liddle — *Thought I, II, III See* index p.200
Liddle — *Thought IV* p.10, 39
Maltz — *Creative* p.4-5, 52, 178
Mandel — *Stories* p.278-280
Modern Eloquence (14) p.439
Montapert — *Distilled* p.341-342
Nichols — *New* p.57-58
Nichols — *Third* p.218-219
Peale — *Faith* p.55-79
Peale — *Guideposts* p.231-253
Peale — *Stay* p.65-85
Peterson — *Art* p.58
Prochnow — *Public* #977, 1238, 1434
Prochnow — *Speaker's* p.328
Prochnow — *Success.* #445, 588-589, 1487
Schermerhorn — *1500* p.395-396
Seldes — *Great* p.991
Sherman — *Your* p.81-83
Speaker's Desk #759, 910, 1175
Voss — *Quotations* p.253
Wallis — *Treasure* p.138, 226-228, 232, 240
Woods — *Religious* p.1076
Woods — *Wellsprings* p.16-17

WORSHIP
See also **Christianity; Church; God; Religion; Reverence;** etc.
Applegarth — *Heir.* p.11-17, 20, 168, 223, 301-308
Book Proverbs p.132
Braude — *Source* #30, 1860–1861
Clark — *Windows* p.24-25
Dirksen — *Quot.* #1620-1623
Edwards — *Useful* p.718-719
Emmons — *Mature* p.18-25, 30-31, 43, 55, 59
Flesch — *Unusual* p.319-320
Forbes — *Thoughts* p.12, 62, 181, 407
Fox — *Make* p.194
Harnsberger — *Mark* p.525
Henry — *5000* p.319-320
Hobe — *Tapestries* p.106-110
Hovey — *Treasury* p.288; *See also* index p.302
Howell — *Better* p.185-190
Johnson — *Bedside* p.213
Kauffman — *For* p.233-234
Kennedy — *Reader's* #1205-1214
Knight's Illus. p.353-354
Knight's Treas. p.447-448
Liddle — *Thought I, II, III* p.46, 76, 100, 144, 166, 169, 192
Lockridge — *World's* #1018
Lytle — *Leaves* p.56, 187
More Words p.170-172
Peterson — *New* p.12-13
Phillips — *Choice See* index p.430
Seldes — *Great* p.991
Sheban — *Wisdom* no p.
Strait — *Speaker's* p.181-183
Tanksley — *Friend* p.61
Voss — *Quotations* p.254-255
Wallis — *Treasure* p.62, 75, 134, 175, 215
Wallis — *Words* p.112, 237-240
Woods — *Religious* p.8, 1076-1080
, Community of
Adams — *New* p.73
, in liturgy
McDonagh — *Invit.* p.103-105
, Levels of
Clark — *Windows* p.32-33
, Spirit of
Baillie — *Diary* #354
, Uplift from
Maxwell — *Courage* p.186-197

WORTHLESSNESS
Hoffer — *Reflect.* p.83
Speaker's Desk #272, 681, 1169

WOUNDS
Day — *Meditations* p.63
Henry — *5000* p.320
Kin — *Dictionary* p.283
Prochnow — *Public* #2592

WRATH. *See* **Anger**

WRINKLES
Dirksen — *Quot.* #760
Forbes — *Thoughts* p.117, 217, 495
Kin — *Dictionary* p.283
Prochnow — *Public* #2029

WRITERS AND WRITING
See also **Books and reading; Literature; Words;** etc.
Alexander's Treasure. p.205
Auden — *Certain* p.418-425
Braude — *Source* #162-167
Braude — *Speaker's* #97-102
Braude — *Stories* p.417
Curtis — *Practical* p.4-5
Dirksen — *Quot.* #154, 2262-2264, 2311
Edwards — *Useful* p.35-36, 719
Flesch — *Unusual* p.320-322
Fogg — *1000 See* index p.878
Fuller — *Epigrams* p.317-321
Fun Fare p.6, 61, 262
Harnsberger — *Mark* p.525-528
Harral — *Feature* p.330-331
Henry — *5000* p.13-14, 320-321

Keller — *You* p.144-170
Kennedy — *Reader's* #1215-1225
Kin — *Dictionary* p.283
Kronenberger — *Animal* p.318-325
Lockridge — *World's See* index p.585
Lytle — *Leaves* p.108
Mandel — *Stories* p.281
New Topical p.237
Nizer — *Thinking* p.104, 174
Patterns For Living p.436-445
Peterson — *Art* p.67, 146
Phillips — *Choice* p.283, 286-287
Prochnow — *Public See* index p.515
Prochnow — *Success.* #600, 1001, 1127, 1438, 1562-1563, 2469
Safian — *More* p.182-183
Seldes — *Great* p.991-992
Sheban — *Wisdom* no p.
Woods — *Content.* p.45, 285

, Art of
Hubbard — *Scrap* p.165
, Conversational style of
Adams — *New* p.280
, Duty of
Adams — *New* p.351
, Freedom of
Adams — *New* p.201
, Honesty of
Adams — *New* p.357
, Pessimism of
Flint — *Graham* p.153-154
, Style of
Dirksen — *Quot.* #257, 1083

WRONG
See also **Dishonesty; Evil; Sin; Wickedness;** types of wrong
Adams — *New* p.277
Book Proverbs p.121
Edwards — *Useful* p.720
Evans — *This* p.101-102
Evans — *Thoughts III (Open Road)* p.47, 107-108, 121-122
Flesch — *Unusual* p.322
Forbes — *Thoughts* p.146, 175, 220, 231, 370, 455, 472, 505, 507-508, 510
Harnsberger — *Mark* p.528
Henry — *5000* p.321
Hovey — *Treasury* #60, 127, 522, 583, 624, 681, 695, 729, 795, 934; p.288-289
Kennedy — *Fresh* p.129-133
Kin — *Dictionary* p.283-284
Liddle — *Thought* p.34, 43, 61, 122, 145
Lockridge — *World's* #1701, 2916
Montapert — *Distilled* p.342
Prochnow — *Public* #818, 859, 1119, 3914
Prochnow — *Success.* #843, 1163, 1322
Seldes — *Great* p.992

WYOMING
Botkin — *Anecdotes* p.171, 175
Botkin — *Treasury* p.192, 611

X

X-RAY
Applegarth — *Heir.* p.166
Flesch — *Unusual* p.322
Harral — *Feature* p.331
Prochnow — *Public* #1051

XENOPHON
Lockridge — *World's* #3582

Y

Y.M.C.A.
Harral — *Feature* p.331

YALE UNIVERSITY
Weisfeld — *Pulpit* p.13

"YANG AND YIN"
Curtis — *Practical* p.148-149

"YANKEE PEDDLERS"
Botkin — *Anecdotes* p.234
Botkin — *Treasury* p.292-358, 361, 389

YANKEES
Botkin — *Anecdotes* p.16, 68, 70, 95, 180
Botkin — *Treasury* p.20, 272, 361, 385, 392, 407, 492, 499
Speaker's Desk #206, 294, 341, 365, 392, 398, 424, 790, 1151, 1155

YARN
Botkin — *Anecdotes* p.90
Botkin — *Treasury* p.490, 594

YAWNING
Prochnow — *Public* #2242

YEARNING. *See* **Aspiration; Desire; Hope; Longing; Wishes;** etc.

YEARS
See also **New Year;** various ages
Applegarth — *Heir.* p.69
Dirksen — *Quot.* #2265
Evans — *Unto* p.6, 18-23
Forbes — *Thoughts* p.344, 397
Hovey — *Treasury* #38, 41, 335, 371, 389, 658, 926, 1241
Kin — *Dictionary* p.284
Lytle — *Leaves* p.145
Montapert — *Distilled* p.342-343
New Topical p.301
, Passing of
Sheen — *Content.* p.39-52

YELLOWSTONE NATIONAL PARK
Botkin — *Anecdotes* p.172
Botkin — *Treasury* p.47

"YES." *See* **Acceptance**

YESTERDAY
See also **Memory (faculty) and memories; Past**
Applegarth — *Heir.* p.66-67
Book Proverbs p.61
Dirksen — *Quot.* #2266-2267
Evans — *Unto* p.142
Flesch — *Unusual* p.322
Forbes — *Thoughts* p.56, 59, 175, 218, 237, 273, 298, 398, 514
Grizer — *Wit* p.323
Harral — *Feature* p.299
Hobe — *Tapestries* p.11, 21-23
Kin — *Dictionary* p.284
New Joy p.120-121
Wallis — *Treasure* p.137, 188, 217, 220

YODELING
Harnsberger — *Mark* p.529

YOGA
Woods — *Religious* p.1080

YOKES
Lytle — *Leaves* p.13

YOM KIPPUR
Asimov — *Treasury* #329, 332, 478

YOUTH
See also **Adolescence; Children; Teenagers;** etc.
Adams — *New* p.166
Applegarth — *Heir.* p.72, 274
Braude — *Source* #1862-1866
Braude — *Speaker's* #268-272, 1586-1587
Braude — *Stories* p.417-424
Detherage — *Sunrise* p.30, 33, 35-36, 176
Dirksen — *Quot. See* index p.271
Edwards — *Useful* p.720-723, 734
Evans — *Faith See* index p.241-242
Evans — *Quote* p.29-40
Evans — *This* p.3-17
Evans — *Thoughts I See* index no p.
Evans — *Thoughts II (Open Door) See* index no p.
Evans — *Thoughts III (Open Road) See* index no p.
Evans — *Thoughts IV* p.15, 23-27, 55, 63-70, 116, 125, 138
Evans — *Unto* p.105, 107, 109-110
Flesch — *Unusual* p.322-323
Flint — *Graham* p.35, 46, 61, 154, 157
Forbes — *Thoughts See* index p.574
Fuller — *Epigrams* p.321
Grizer — *Wit* p.507-509
Hadfield — *Love* p.38-39
Harnsberger — *Mark* p.529-530
Harral — *Feature* p.331-335
Henry — *5000* p.321-323
Hobe — *Tapestries* p.188-189, 194
Hovey — *Treasury* p.289; *See also* index p.302-303
Howell — *Better* p.191-194
Howell — *Lines* p.139-142
Hubbard — *Scrap* p.80, 92, 98
Humes — *Instant* p.30, 36; #35, 1160-1182, 1279-1282
Keller — *Open* p.92
Kennedy — *Reader's* #1226
Keys Happiness p.119-123, 222, 274-276
Kin — *Dictionary* p.284-286
Knight's Illus. p.354-359
Knight's Treas. p.449-451
Lair — *Baby* p.157-169
Liddle — *Thought I, II, III* p.38, 41, 53, 60, 124, 148, 154, 165, 184
Liddle — *Thought IV* p.6, 16, 18, 33
Liddle — *Thought V* p.27, 29
Lockridge — *World's See* index p.585
Lytle — *Leaves* p.21
Mandel — *Stories* p.282
Modern Eloquence (14) p.440
Montapert — *Distilled* p.344
New Joy p.154, 159

Nichols — *New* p.178-179, 226-227
Nizer — *Thinking* p.114
Patterns For Living p.756-768
Peale — *Courage* p.131-132
Peterson — *Art* p.26, 164, 283, 301, 368, 391
Price — *No* p.79-86
Prochnow — *Public* #1068, 1134, 1428, 1883, 1932, 2338, 2569, 2773, 2950, 3302, 3336, 3621, 3915-3919, 3967, 4267-4268
Prochnow — *Speaker's* p.328
Prochnow — *Success.* #207, 333, 387, 625, 682, 728, 800, 895, 1233, 1366, 1399, 2470-2471
Reader's — *Getting* p.215-218
Seaburg — *Great* p.180, 184, 189, 192, 195, 205, 251, 261-262, 348, 359, 365, 370, 372, 374, 407
Seldes — *Great* p.993
Sheban — *Wisdom* no p.
Sheen — *Content.* p.19-38
Sheen — *Thoughts* p.96-98
Sheen — *Way* p.93-104
Speaker's Desk #78
Strait — *Speaker's* p.184-186
Voss — *Quotations* p.255-258
Wallis — *Treasure* p.11-14, 24
Wallis — *Words* p.68, 92, 106, 122, 128
Walters — *How* p.59-68
White — *Life* p.7, 50-51
Woods — *Content.* p.77, 121-123, 294, 336
Woods — *Religious* p.1081
Zobell — *Speaker's* p.158-160

, Admonition to
Hunter — *Gems* p.5
, Alienation of
Kauffman — *For* p.18
, and Bible
Kauffman — *For* p.32
, and Christ
Kauffman — *For* p.237
, and Church
Kauffman — *For* p.237-238
, and communication
Kauffman — *For* p.238-239
, and discrimination
Kauffman — *For* p.239-240
, and fun
Kauffman — *For* p.240-242
, and future
Kauffman — *For* p.242-246
, and long hair
Kauffman — *For* p.246-247
, and manifestoes
Kauffman — *For* p.247-248
, and old age
Barrows — *1000 See* index p.446
Braude — *Source* #1867-1868
Droke — *Christian* p.613-619
Flesch — *Universal* p.323
Hubbard — *Scrap* p.50, 112, 165, 196
Morris — *1000* p.50, 178, 218-219, 250, 281, 302, 313, 323
Sheban — *Wisdom* no p.
, and reform
Hubbard — *Scrap* p.181
, and rules
Kauffman — *For* p.248-249
, and sex
Kauffman — *For* p.249-250
, and war
Kauffman — *For* p.250-252
, Art of
Peterson — *Twenty* p.48-49
, Challenge of
Peale — *Guideposts* p.157-182
, Consistence with
Kauffman — *For* p.234-236
, Crises of
Jackson — *Coping* p.113-119
, Discipline of
Kauffman — *For* p.236
, Humor of
Copeland — *10,000* p.391-405
, Magic of
Adams — *New* p.371
, Perpetual
Peterson — *Art* p.269
, Point of view of
Braude — *Stories* p.288
, Rebellion of
How To Live p.118
, Understanding
Adams — *New* p.365
Kauffman — *For* p.219-220
, Values of
How To Live p.160-162

YUKON
Henry — *5000* p.323

Z

"ZANIES"
Fuller — *Thesaurus* #641-643
Fun Fare p.21-22

ZEAL
See also **Enthusiasm**
Baillie — *Diary* #117, 157

Braude — *Source* #1869-1870
Dirksen — *Quot.* #441, 1624-1625, 2272-2273
Droke — *Christian* p.620
Edwards — *Useful* p.723-724
Flesch — *Unusual* p.70
Flint — *Graham* p.158
Forbes — *Thoughts* p.153, 202, 214, 495
Garland — *Subject* p.345-346
Henry — *5000* p.323
Hovey — *Treasury* #303, 499, 700, 1012, 1667, 1803
Humes — *Instant* #1183-1885
Kin — *Dictionary* p.286
Lockridge — *World's* #2913, 2530, 3453
Lytle — *Leaves* p.182
Maltz — *Creative* p.201-202
Manchee — *Secret* p.139-164
Montapert — *Distilled* p.344-345
New Topical p.301
Prochnow — *Public* #2243, 4269-4270
Prochnow — *Speaker's* p.328
Sheen — *Life* p.184-190
Weisfeld — *Pulpit* p.26
Woods — *Content.* p.19-57
Woods — *Religious* p.1081-1082

ZEBRAS
Prochnow — *Public* #997

ZEBULUN, TRIBE OF
New Topical p.301

ZIONISM
See also **Jews**
Hunter — *Gems* p.119-120
Nizer — *Thinking* p.88
Woods — *Religious* p.1082

ZODIAC
Prochnow — *Public* #353

ZOOLOGY
Hooker — *Index* p.194-201

ZOOS
Asimov — *Treasury* #277
Flesch — *Unusual* p.324
Harral — *Feature* p.335
Prochnow — *Public* #59, 294, 325, 468

ZULUS, AFRICAN
Lair — *Baby* p.26-27, 31, 34, 38-39